COUNTRIES AT
THE CROSSROADS

COUNTRIES AT THE CROSSROADS

An Analysis of Democratic Governance

Jake Dizard
Christopher Walker
Sarah Cook
EDITORS

FREEDOM HOUSE
NEW YORK • WASHINGTON, D.C.

ROWMAN & LITTLEFIELD PUBLISHERS, INC.
LANHAM • BOULDER • NEW YORK • TORONTO • PLYMOUTH, UK

Published by Rowman & Littlefield Publishers, Inc.
A wholly owned subsidiary of The Rowman & Littlefield Publishing Group, Inc.
4501 Forbes Boulevard, Suite 200, Lanham, Maryland 20706
www.rowmanlittlefield.com

Estover Road, Plymouth PL6 7PY, United Kingdom

Copyright © 2010 by Freedom House

All rights reserved. No part of this book may be reproduced in any form or by any electronic or mechanical means, including information storage and retrieval systems, without written permission from the publisher, except by a reviewer who may quote passages in a review.

British Library Cataloguing in Publication Information Available

Library of Congress Cataloging-in-Publication Data

Countries at the crossroads : an analysis of democratic governance / Jake Dizard, Christopher Walker, Sarah Cook, editors. — 2010 ed.
   p. cm.
   Includes bibliographical references.
   ISBN 978-1-4422-0547-5 (cloth : alk. paper) — ISBN 978-1-4422-0548-2 (pbk. : alk. paper) — ISBN 978-1-4422-0549-9 (electronic)
  1. Democracy—Case studies. 2. Representative government and representation—Case studies. I. Dizard, Jake. II. Walker, Christopher, 1964– III. Cook, Sarah, 1979–
JC423.C7196 2010
321.8—dc22

                                                   2010018174

∞™ The paper used in this publication meets the minimum requirements of American National Standard for Information Sciences—Permanence of Paper for Printed Library Materials, ANSI/NISO Z39.48-1992.

Printed in the United States of America

CONTENTS

Countries at the Crossroads 2007–2010 Country List vii
Acknowledgments ix
Expert Advisory Committee xi
The Vulnerable Middle 1
   Jake Dizard and Christopher Walker
Comparative Country Scores .15
Introduction to Country Reports 19
Country Reports
   Argentina 21
   Bahrain 39
   Brazil 59
   Cambodia 81
   Cote d'Ivoire 103
   Democratic Republic of Congo 125
   East Timor 149
   El Salvador 173
   Ghana 191
   Guatemala 211
   Haiti 233
   Honduras 251
   Indonesia 273
   Jordan 297
   Kenya 319
   Lebanon 341
   Liberia 361

Malawi 381

Malaysia 401

Mexico 421

Nepal 445

Nicaragua 467

Nigeria 487

Saudi Arabia 507

Sierra Leone 525

South Africa 543

Sri Lanka 563

Tanzania 585

Uganda 607

Vietnam 625

Yemen 649

Zimbabwe 669

Analysis Methodology 687

Methodology Questions 691

Freedom House Board of Trustees 697

About Freedom House 699

COUNTRIES AT THE CROSSROADS
2007 – 2010

2007 COUNTRIES	2010 COUNTRIES
Algeria	Argentina
Angola	Bahrain
Bangladesh	Brazil
Bhutan	Cambodia
Bolivia	Cote d'Ivoire
Burkina Faso	Democratic Republic of Congo
China	East Timor
Colombia	El Salvador
Ecuador	Ghana
Egypt	Guatemala
Eritrea	Haiti
Ethiopia	Honduras
Honduras	Indonesia
Iran	Jordan
Laos	Kenya
Libya	Lebanon
Mauritania	Liberia
Mozambique	Malawi
Paraguay	Malaysia
Peru	Mexico
Philippines	Nepal
Russia	Nicaragua
Rwanda	Nigeria
Swaziland	Saudi Arabia
Syria	Sierra Leone
Tajikistan	South Africa
Thailand	Sri Lanka
Tunisia	Tanzania
Turkey	Uganda
Zambia	Vietnam
	Yemen
	Zimbabwe

ACKNOWLEDGMENTS

Countries at the Crossroads is the product of the collective contributions of numerous Freedom House staff members and consultants. This study was also made possible by the generous support of the United States Agency for International Development.

Country report authors made an outstanding contribution to this effort, working to produce 32 clear, informed analyses of a highly diverse group of countries. The report authors are: Osita Afoaku, Michael Buehler, William Case, D. Elwood Dunn, David R. Dye, Daniel P. Erikson, Martha Farmelo, David Fleischer, Martin Gainsborough, Francisco González, E. Gyimah-Boadi, Bruce Heilman, David Holiday, Anita Isaacs, Gregory D. Johnsen, Nelson Kasfir, Thomas R. Lansner, Fred H. Lawson, A. Carl LeVan, Robert B. Lloyd, Russell E. Lucas, Duncan McCargo, Robert Oberst, Manuel Orozco, Lok Raj Baral, William Reno, Mark Y. Rosenberg, Rebecca Rouse, Oussama Safa, Dennis Shoesmith, Patrick Ukata, and Peter VonDoepp.

A group of distinguished regional experts served on the advisory committee, providing valuable input on the narratives and scores. They are: Joel Barkan, Chris Fomunyoh, Anthony Gambino, Jeffrey Herbst, Toby Jones, Josh Kurlantzick, Marc Lynch, Robert Maguire, Maria Victoria Murillo, Eric Olson, Amit Pandya, Anthony Pereira, Michael Shifter, Rotimi Suberu, Bridget Welsh, and Mona Yacoubian.

The *Countries at the Crossroads* methodology was originally developed with the expert contribution of a group of senior advisers, including Larry Diamond, Hoover Institution; Paul Martin, Columbia University; Rick Messick, World Bank; Ted Piccone, Brookings Institution; Louise Shelley, George Mason University; Jay Verkuilen, City University of New York; and Ruth Wedgwood, Johns Hopkins University.

Freedom House staff devoted extensive time and energy to launch this edition. Jake Dizard was the managing editor of the study. Christopher Walker, director of studies, and Thomas O. Melia, deputy executive director of Freedom House, provided overall guidance and support for the project, in addition to serving on the survey's internal review committee. Asia research analyst and assistant editor Sarah Cook supplied important research, editorial, and administrative support, as did staff members Tyler Roylance, Joanna Perry, Eliza Young, and Kelly Tek and interns Raymond Lu, Greta Sommers, Susanna McCarthy, Jennifer Lam, Jennifer Brandt, and Joshua Siegel. Editorial assistants Caitlin Fogarty and Sara Rhodin provided indispensable research and editorial assistance. Colleagues in the Washington, D.C. and other Freedom House offices supplied important feedback on the reports. Ida Walker and Lynne Glasner were the proofreaders, and Beverly Butterfield designed and typeset the volume.

EXPERT ADVISORY COMMITTEE

JOEL BARKAN
Senior Associate, Center for Strategic & International Studies, Professor Emeritus of Political Science, University of Iowa

CHRIS FOMUNYOH
Senior Associate, National Democratic Institute

ANTHONY GAMBINO
Independent consultant, Washington D.C.

JEFFREY HERBST
Provost, Miami University (Ohio)

TOBY JONES
Assistant Professor of History, Rutgers University

JOSH KURLANTZICK
Fellow for Southeast Asia, Council on Foreign Relations

MARC LYNCH
Associate Professor of Political Science and International Affairs, George Washington University

ROBERT MAGUIRE
Associate Professor of International Affairs, Trinity Washington University

MARIA VICTORIA MURILLO
Associate Professor of Political Science, Columbia University

ERIC OLSON
Senior Advisor, Mexico Institute, Woodrow Wilson International Center for Scholars

AMIT PANDYA
Senior Associate, Henry L. Stimson Center

ANTHONY PEREIRA
Professor of Political Science, Tulane University

MICHAEL SHIFTER
President, Inter-American Dialogue

ROTIMI SUBERU
Professor of Politics and International Relations, Bennington College

BRIDGET WELSH
Associate Professor in Political Science, Singapore Management University

MONA YACOUBIAN
Special Advisor, Muslim World Initiative, United States Institute of Peace

COUNTRIES AT THE CROSSROADS 2010

THE VULNERABLE MIDDLE

Jake Dizard and Christopher Walker

INTRODUCTION

At a time when democracy has undergone a worrisome global deterioration, a strategically important subset of partially democratic, developing states have been dealt an especially hard blow. These countries, whose institutions remain fragile, occupy the world's political and economic "middle ground." Because they have been viewed as the most promising candidates for accession to the ranks of consolidated democracies, the challenges they currently face raise serious questions about the prospects for deepening democratic roots and expanding effective governance around the world.

Countries at the Crossroads, Freedom House's comprehensive assessment of democratic governance, examines just such a selection of middle-performing states. The analysis of the 32 countries in this *Crossroads* edition provides a clear diagnosis of the factors that separate stronger performers from those that continue to stagnate or backslide in ways that threaten essential rights and freedoms.

While the 2010 edition offers some grounds for optimism, there is considerably more evidence to suggest that many middle-performing states are heading in the wrong direction on fundamental aspects of democratic governance. Of the 21 states with previous *Crossroads* data, declines exceeded improvements in both number and degree.

A regionally diverse set of states including Cambodia, Honduras, Kenya, Nicaragua, Sri Lanka, Uganda, and Yemen heads the list of countries where deterioration is evident. In these and other cases, the survey findings reveal particular pressures on what democracy scholars call "coordination goods"—institutions that are critical for sharing information, enabling political organization, and establishing transparent and accountable governance systems. The media freedom subcategory registered the sharpest fall among the countries with previous data, and various impediments have also affected civic engagement and freedom of association, pointing to a pattern of government behavior that limits the space for citizens to influence public policy.

In the broader global context, a number of factors have combined to obstruct the deepening of democracy in middle-performing countries. The

---

Jake Dizard is managing editor of *Countries at the Crossroads* and **Christopher Walker** is director of studies at Freedom House.

global economic crisis, the persistent fragility of state institutions, the power of armed nonstate actors, and various forms of domestic political upheaval contribute to an inhospitable landscape for democratic consolidation. There is, moreover, an emerging contestation of the very concept of democratic governance, stimulated by China's model of selective economic liberalism and political authoritarianism. Beijing's growing engagement in the developing world and its often opaque financial assistance represent a new countervailing influence on aspirations to democratic governance in Africa, Asia, the Middle East, and Latin America.

The Democracy Recession's Impact on the "Middle Class" of States

The effects of the worldwide erosion of democracy on the states in the "grey zone," as scholar Thomas Carothers describes them, are clear. *Freedom in the World*, Freedom House's annual analysis of political rights and civil liberties, examines all of the world's 194 countries. Among the middle-performing, Partly Free states, which possess some but not all of the safeguards and guarantees of fully institutionalized democratic systems, there has been a demonstrable step backward over the past five years. In that time, a total of 57 countries within this category experienced declines, while only 38 improved.

The decline in performance among the Partly Free countries was both broad and deep. A review of the more detailed scoring data for the countries assessed by *Freedom in the World* during this period reveals a total of 254 points in negative score changes, compared with 152 points in score improvements. The declines occurred across all of the institutions examined in *Freedom in the World*'s seven subcategories.

While *Freedom in the World* offers a broad, global view of democratic development, *Countries at the Crossroads* applies a sharper analytical lens, focusing on the condition and degree of democratic governance in selected emerging states. A total of 75 separate indicators are assessed in the *Crossroads* methodology.

> Because partially democratic states have been viewed as the most promising candidates for accession to the ranks of consolidated democracies, the challenges they currently face raise serious questions about the prospects for deepening democratic roots and expanding effective governance around the world.

The states in the middle ground of governance, representing the lion's share of countries examined in *Crossroads*, exhibit highly varied forms of government. They include multiparty systems with levels of political competition that generally meet the criteria of consolidated democracy; nascent democracies established in the wake of armed conflict; dominant-party states in which multiparty systems exist on paper but genuine electoral competition is suppressed; and those on the authoritarian end of the governance spectrum.

For this *Crossroads* cycle, 11 states were added to broaden the range of case studies with respect to political form, geographical location, and income level. The new countries include the strongest performers in this edition: Argentina, Brazil, Mexico, and Ghana. The first three also have the highest income levels in this year's country set, aside from the oil-rich kingdoms of Bahrain and Saudi Arabia. At the other end of the income scale, *Crossroads* has added states such as Liberia and the Democratic Republic of Congo; the latter and Saudi Arabia are two of the weakest performers on democratic governance in this year's edition. The diversity of the new *Crossroads* country set offers a richer comparative view of the challenges and opportunities facing these governments.

OTHER NOTABLE FINDINGS

The declines in the media freedom and civic engagement subcategories represent the most troubling signs of deterioration among the countries with previous data. This analysis also found noteworthy movement in several other areas, whether positive, negative, or an ambiguous mixture of the two.

- **Property Rights Erode:** Several countries, including Bahrain, Sri Lanka, East Timor, Kenya, Uganda, Cambodia, and Vietnam, experienced declines in the protection of property rights. Land grabs occurred in a number of cases, typically within a context of rising land values and poor titling and registration systems. In Vietnam, for example, rapid economic growth has encouraged the abuse of land-use rights certificates and created increasing conflict between victims of expropriation and the government, which is perceived to favor private developers.

- **Due Process and Prosecutorial Independence Suffer:** In a total of 16 countries, ongoing problems surrounding citizen interaction with the justice system resulted in declines in the subcategory that examines the degree to which public officials are prosecuted for abuse of power, whether prosecutors are independent of political control, and whether citizens' due process rights are respected. A number of factors contributed to the declines. In abuse-prone environments such as Zimbabwe and Sri Lanka, the scores worsened as a result of severe due process violations. In countries that previously performed well in this area, like South Africa, Malaysia, and Nicaragua, political pressure on prosecutors increased. Even in relatively reform-oriented states, a scarcity of resources often limits the degree of improvement on these issues.

- **Headway on Anticorruption Standards:** One of the bright spots in this year's analysis was the improvement by a number of countries in the sphere of establishing and depoliticizing anticorruption norms and standards. East Timor, Tanzania, and Indonesia were among the countries to improve. East Timor's ombudsman launched several investigations into allegations against high-ranking officials, including the prime minister and justice minister. In Tanzania, the primary anticorruption bureau was given increased powers to conduct investigations and take action against corrupt officials. And in Indonesia, a set of agencies has prosecuted public officials for abuse of power, while the news media continue to vigorously report on allegations of corruption.

- **Post-Conflict Progress:** In post-conflict states such as Sierra Leone, East Timor, and Liberia, civilian control has been achieved with the help of the United Nations, and efforts to solidify and expand democratically accountable institutions have made gains. Nevertheless, issues such as ethnic divisions and patronage-based political cultures loom as potential sources of instability.

- **Law versus Implementation:** The legal framework for democratic governance continues to improve. In some cases, this is a reflection of genuine reformist impulses on the part of the political leadership. In others, it results from a desire to appease international donors who insist on identifiable achievements in exchange for funds. The trend toward strong legislation is welcome, but in many states examined by *Crossroads*, the gulf between laws and implementation is vast. In countries where the will to reform appears sincere, scarcity of resources is often a primary obstacle, as is a lack of institutional capacity to manage implementation even when financing is available. In many other states—especially those where power is highly concentrated—a lack of political will on the part of the executive is the central problem. When it comes to rule of law and anticorruption efforts, leaders may understandably fear that the strengthening of institutions will be a threat to their power, perhaps even leading to their arrest. Implementation also encounters resistance from other stakeholders who benefit from the status quo. Corrupt judges, for instance, may cite the theoretically legitimate principle of judicial autonomy to inhibit reform plans. Moreover, threatened groups can point to reasonable concerns that the goal of "reform" is merely to replace one set of elites with another. These conflicting interests among powerful actors often result in institutional clashes, disrupting the process of moving from legislation to action.

The number of countries with a negative trajectory or substandard performance overall presents a special challenge to policymakers, including those at the World Bank and the Millennium Challenge Corporation, who have sought to create inducements for developing countries to improve democratic accountability. Advocates of good governance should be particularly concerned that a number of states have undergone declines despite receiving substantial attention from the international policy and donor communities. In these cases, the regression signals a weakening of hard-won institutional reforms, as well as a shrinking of space for citizens to play a meaningful role in their own governance.

It is important to note that "middle ground" countries are not the only ones having difficulty achieving deeper reforms. Over the past several years, obstacles to improved democratic governance have been rising in mature and developing systems alike. Trust in key institutions in the United States and European Union countries has plummeted. Established democracies are dealing with vexing problems related to fiscal management, social welfare, and the quality of government more generally. The economic crisis is forcing officials and policymakers to choose from a menu of unpalatable options, stirring doubts in the minds of citizens about the governability of their countries. But the more resilient institutions of mature democracies provide a greater margin for error, and the primacy of citizens' voices in reform discussions is generally assured. By contrast, the hurdles and risks faced by developing countries are far more daunting.

The number of countries with a negative trajectory or substandard performance overall presents a special challenge to policymakers, including those at the World Bank and the Millennium Challenge Corporation, who have sought to create inducements for developing countries to improve democratic accountability.

The headwinds of the current environment have underscored the reality that enacting meaningful, durable reforms is an exceedingly difficult business even under the best of circumstances. Indeed, it is often easier to fail than to succeed in the democratic reform enterprise. Haiti is a vivid example of this harsh reality. The slow but noteworthy progress that the country achieved in the latest *Crossroads* cycle may well have been crushed in a moment, quite literally, by the devastating earthquake of January 2010.

FREE EXPRESSION AND ASSOCIATION UNDER DURESS

Scholars and policymakers have long understood that independent news media and a vigorous civil society play an important role in reducing corruption, improving governmental responsiveness, and achieving generally better development outcomes. The World Bank, the Organization for Economic Cooperation and Development, and the United Nations, among other multilateral institutions, emphasize that open expression and free association are critical factors in encouraging governmental transparency and accountability. The ongoing weaknesses and new declines identified in these areas by *Countries at the Crossroads 2010* are therefore all the more disconcerting.

The states examined here confront a variety of serious governance challenges, and growing pressure on free expression and association can short-circuit broader reform ambitions. Muzzling media and sidelining independent civil society actors reduces the monitoring of state institutions and hampers the formulation and dissemination of alternative policy options. In the absence of these corrective mechanisms, government performance can quickly degrade.

The tools used by the authorities to hinder the news media are diverse, ranging from the misuse of ambiguously worded laws and politicized regulatory bodies to outright violence against journalists.

In Nicaragua, the government of President Daniel Ortega has adopted an antagonistic attitude toward the news media, retreating from a period in which the country's press was relatively free, albeit concentrated in the hands of a small number of owners. The government's tactics include granting access to government events only to "friendly" journalists and channeling lucrative government advertising away from outlets that are perceived as critical of the authorities. Physical harassment of journalists by government supporters has increased, including the destruction of reporters' equipment and broadcast facilities. The threat of legal and administrative action against critical news outlets has also risen. A slander conviction and the withdrawal of a radio license were among the steps taken to generate a chilling effect during the survey period.

Sri Lanka, which has historically enjoyed at least some media freedom, has suffered as a result of its political upheaval. A dramatic increase in violence against journalists has been noted, with the perpetrators enjoying impunity. Over 30 journalists have been killed since 2004, and many others have fled the country. The fear created by this violence has caused some critical outlets to soften their tone or close down altogether. Moreover, restrictions on reporting in war zones and various legal actions have resulted in a distinctly less hospitable environment for open and independent journalism.

Bahrain's government, for its part, employs administrative and legal controls to curb free expression. The state monopolizes the broadcast media and enforces laws that restrict coverage by private print outlets. Unlike in Nicaragua and Sri Lanka, but much like many of its Middle Eastern peers, the government in Bahrain aggressively curtails internet freedom, applying sophisticated filtering systems and occasionally detaining bloggers to deter others who might push the boundaries of free expression.

Pressure on the nongovernmental organizations (NGOs) that make up a core component of civil society resulted in declines in a number of countries. In Cambodia, where the NGO community is large relative to the country's size, government hostility is intensifying. Prime Minister Hun Sen made his views clear in a September 2008 speech, stating that "Cambodia has been heaven for NGOs for too long…they insult the government just to ensure their financial survival." He similarly impugned the UN special representative and threatened to expel certain NGOs from the country. One activist was forced to flee abroad and was subsequently convicted in absentia on "disinformation" charges.

FOUR TIERS OF PERFORMANCE

The 32 countries examined in this edition of *Crossroads* can be loosely organized into four tiers based on the overall quality of their democratic governance.

I. Established Democracies: Argentina, Brazil, Ghana, Indonesia, Mexico, and South Africa

In these countries, the strength of institutions and the public voice are firmly established. Some have made remarkable progress from extremely precarious starting points. Each faces a diverse range of challenges, and long-term stability will require further reform, but their political systems are generally able to self-correct.

II. Fragile Progress: East Timor, El Salvador, Guatemala, Haiti, Lebanon, Liberia, Malawi, Nepal, Sierra Leone, and Tanzania

This tier encompasses states that have made progress in some areas of democratic governance but nevertheless remain fragile, due to either the immaturity of institutions or a history of internal conflict. A number of states in which the United Nations had an extended post-conflict presence, including East Timor, Liberia, and Sierra Leone, have made notable gains. This suggests a salutary impact from the international operations that deserves closer examination.

III. Faltering Reform: Cambodia, Honduras, Jordan, Kenya, Malaysia, Nicaragua, Nigeria, Sri Lanka, and Uganda

States in this tier have previously exhibited some reformist impulses but are now backsliding due to political crisis or a concentration of power. In Cambodia, Nicaragua, Sri Lanka, and Uganda, the authorities have tended toward consolidation and even monopolization of power. Reform ambitions in Jordan, Malaysia, and Nigeria have stagnated. In Kenya and Honduras, severe political turmoil in recent years has raised doubts about these countries' prospects for improved governance.

IV. Power Concentrators: Bahrain, Cote d'Ivoire, Democratic Republic of Congo, Saudi Arabia, Vietnam, Yemen, and Zimbabwe

In these states, undemocratic governance predominates and prospects for democratic gains are dim. Bahrain, Saudi Arabia, Vietnam, Yemen, and Zimbabwe have little or no history of political freedom. The ruling powers there actively deny space for alternative political viewpoints. The other two countries, Cote d'Ivoire and the Democratic Republic of Congo, confront unresolved internal conflicts that have understandably distracted from democratic reform. However, leaders in these countries have also used instability to justify delaying changes that might constrain their authority or result in their removal from power.

Honduras, a country in which violence by nonstate actors is among the most pressing problems, generally provides significant space for civil society, even if NGOs' influence on the policy making process is limited. However, there are signs that extralegal intimidation of activists is being perpetrated not just by criminal and other nonstate groups, but by state security forces. In 2008, two plainclothes policemen were discovered with a "blacklist" of 135 activists, one of whom had been killed earlier in the year and was labeled "deceased."

In Uganda, NGOs initially flourished after President Yoweri Museveni took power nearly a quarter-century ago. Today, the government regards groups that address political issues as possible threats, and has applied legal tools to limit their influence. For instance, it requires all NGOs to gain approval—which is not always given—from an NGO Registration Board that includes representatives of security agencies. In 2006, the government tightened supervision by requiring the annual renewal of NGO registrations. Civic groups have also found themselves increasingly locked out of policy discussions due to stricter party discipline in the parliament.

One common factor in nearly all cases of pressure on coordination goods is the role of the national leadership in setting a harmful tone. Harsh rhetoric aimed at the media or NGOs carries the most weight when uttered by presidents or ministers, and laws clamping down on free expression and association tend to be initiated by the executive branch.

Long-Term Leaders

Free expression and association have come under particular stress in a group of eight countries examined in this cycle of *Crossroads*: Bahrain, Cambodia, Jordan, Saudi Arabia, Uganda, Vietnam, Yemen, and Zimbabwe. These states have sidestepped an elemental aspect of democratic governance: the rotation of power. Their political systems are not open to the rise and fall of competing political parties and groupings, and no interchange of government and opposition has occurred in at least the past 10 years. Instead, power is retained indefinitely by an individual or through the managed transfer of power within families or party hierarchies.

An examination of *Crossroads* scores reveals a significant difference between these eight states and the rest of the country set with respect to the Accountability and Public Voice category. The long-term leader states receive an average score of 2.13 on this topic, 47 percent lower than the average of 4.02 for countries where power rotations have occurred. Within the category, the most notable disparity is in the area of Civic Engagement and Civic Monitoring, where the long-term leader group scores an average of 2.50, more than 2 points lower than the other countries, which average 4.79. Similarly, in the Media Independence and Freedom of Expression subcategory, the average score of the long-term leader countries is less than half that of their more dynamic counterparts. And in the Civil Liberties category, the collective average of 2.22 for the class of eight contrasts sharply with the average of 4.40 for the other 24 countries.

The issues covered by these scores—civic engagement, free expression, and free association—are aligned precisely with the coordination goods that can convert diffuse political sentiments into organized political movements. The small ruling elites in long-term leader countries, who are determined to retain power, clearly have a narrow interest in preventing such movements. However, the suppression of public checks on government behavior gives rise to rampant corruption, and the associated politicization and dysfunction of what should be independent "referee" institutions—the judiciary, electoral commissions, prosecutorial services, and ombudsman agencies, among others—leads to routine injustice. The rulers may keep their grip on the state, but their governments' ability to implement effective policies in critical spheres like education, health, employment, and public infrastructure is seriously undermined, and the increasingly frustrated public is left with no legal means of airing or addressing their grievances.

REGIONAL DEVELOPMENTS

Africa

The 2010 edition of *Crossroads* features 12 states from sub-Saharan Africa, making it the survey's largest region. West and Central Africa are represented by six states, including the strongest performer in this edition, Ghana, where the smooth transfer of power following an extremely close presidential election in 2008 symbolized the country's democratic progress. Two other countries in this subregion, Liberia and Sierra Leone, showed promising signs but remained constrained by overwhelming poverty and persistent corruption. Nigeria, by far the most populous country in this group, was mostly stagnant at a low level of performance, having held elections in 2007 that were sharply criticized by international observers.

Eastern and southern Africa present a mixed picture. Kenya, roiled since late 2007 by enormous political volatility, demonstrates the potential consequences of misgovernment. Rather than undertaking deep reforms, Kenyan elites treated policy making as a zero-sum game in which the politicization of ethnicity was viewed as a legitimate tool. The spark of a controversial election ignited open ethnic violence, causing turmoil that is reflected across a wide range of *Crossroads* categories. Uganda also slipped, particularly in the area of Accountability and Public Voice. President Yoweri Museveni's administration applied a range of measures to limit political pluralism, undercutting the presidential campaign of opposition candidate Kizza Besigye and moving to curb the independence and effectiveness of Ugandan civil society. Zimbabwe, where the regime headed by President Robert Mugabe continued to place its own survival above the welfare of Zimbabwean citizens, remains one of the poorest performers in the survey. South Africa, although it is still one of the better performers, continued to wrestle with critical rule of law issues and stagnated in its *Crossroads* scores. Tanzania, meanwhile, experienced notable gains across a range of categories, as the parliament stepped up its oversight role and anticorruption efforts began to acquire more coherence.

Latin America

The Latin American countries examined in the survey can be organized into two groups. One consists of Argentina, Brazil, and Mexico, each of which was analyzed for the first time and ranks among the edition's better performers. Nonetheless, each also confronts governance problems that cut to the core of the citizen-state relationship. In Argentina, a multiyear executive effort to accrue greater political power has resulted in heightened tensions with the news media and other institutions. Brazil faces the challenge of reforming a byzantine political power structure that hinders the fight against corruption within the national parliament and state governments. Governance in Mexico and Brazil is also being tested by the growing power of organized criminals. In both countries, ineffective policing and justice systems have increased the pressure to militarize the fight against crime, leading to human rights violations. Crime-induced institutional corrosion is especially threatening in Mexico, where the transition to plural democracy occurred only in 2000 and the balance of power between different institutions and political forces remains unsettled.

In many states examined by Crossroads, the gulf between laws and implementation is vast. Where the will to reform appears sincere, scarcity of resources is a primary obstacle. Where power is highly concentrated, leaders may fear that the strengthening of institutions will be a threat to their power.

The second group consists of the Central American states, whose fragile economies and institutions are buffeted by tumultuous politics and virulent organized crime. Nicaragua suffered one of the survey's most precipitous declines, as President Daniel Ortega sought to concentrate power within the executive branch and his Sandinista political party. Ortega entered office already possessing significant influence over other branches by virtue of earlier political pacts, and he worked to limit free expression and association as his party expanded its power through widely denounced local elections in 2008. Honduras was scored prior to the June 2009 coup, but it nonetheless regressed due to executive mismanagement and power concentration as well as widespread corruption and an inability to combat crime. Guatemala and El Salvador performed better, but they too faced major challenges from criminal groups. Despite a political will to reform and the establishment of a UN-sponsored commission to fight crime and impunity, Guatemalan institutions appeared enormously vulnerable to criminal influence. In El Salvador, a hard-line antigang policy continued to yield more questions about rights abuses than sustainable gains against crime.

Asia

The selection of Asian countries features a relatively stable democracy in Indonesia; authoritarian "power concentrators" in Vietnam and Cambodia; fragile new democracies in East Timor and Nepal; and semiauthoritarian, ethnically based governments in Malaysia and Sri Lanka. This diversity of these regimes was reflected in their scoring performance. Among the countries analyzed, scores in the Accountability and Public Voice category improved overall, largely due to gains in the electoral processes of East Timor, Indonesia, Malaysia, and Nepal. Performance within the Rule of Law category slipped in five of the seven countries due to poor protection of property rights and problems with the justice system, as well as weaknesses in democratic civilian control over security forces.

In terms of country trends, Sri Lanka and Cambodia experienced the largest declines. In both countries, perceived successes—military in Sri Lanka and economic in Cambodia—emboldened leaders to push for further concentration of power. In Sri Lanka, President Mahinda Rajapaksa's political project has undermined previously functioning institutions, while in Cambodia the already limited space for political dissent has continued to narrow under Prime Minister Hun Sen. In Vietnam, which like China is carefully watched as a key experiment in "authoritarian capitalism," the ruling Communist Party mounted a harsh crackdown on a nascent civic movement pushing for democratic reforms. Nepal, while remaining highly fragile, achieved notable gains in most categories as a repressive monarchy gave way to the beginnings of a constitutional republic. East Timor's scores likewise rose, as competitive politics and civic participation improved along with several Civil Liberties subcategories. Indonesia, a complex mosaic both socially and in terms of institutional strength, continued to make incremental progress, especially with respect to electoral process, civilian control of the military, and anticorruption standards.

Middle East

Five countries from this region were examined in the current edition of *Crossroads*. One was fractious, conflict-plagued Yemen, where the authorities used arbitrary and abusive methods to counteract civil unrest even as President Ali Abdullah Saleh's determination to retain power hardened. Jordan, where reform efforts have apparently stagnated, registered a slight decline in this year's analysis based on setbacks related to the electoral framework and civil society activity.

In Bahrain, where a Sunni minority rules over a Shiite majority, heightened tensions led to declines in citizen protection from state terror, freedom of association, and religious freedom, among other topics.

Two states that were included in the country set for the first time, Lebanon and Saudi Arabia, occupied the upper and lower bounds of regional performance, respectively. Lebanon's unique political system allows participation by a variety of faiths and ethnicities, but its rigidity limits the prospects for progress in critical areas, including judicial reform and anticorruption efforts. Saudi Arabia, while demonstrating a faint, incipient reform impulse, remains a religion-based autocracy in which citizen rights are tightly circumscribed in nearly all areas.

Opacity within narrow elite classes is common to the region as a whole, leading to particularly low scores for the anticorruption environment. Minority rights, women's rights, and accountable government are among the subcategories in which Middle Eastern states consistently lag behind those in other regions. Indeed, property rights and freedom of religion are the only subcategories in which the regional average score rises to a mediocre 3.0.

CONCLUSION

As Amartya Sen once noted, "a country does not have to be deemed fit for democracy; rather, it has to become fit through democracy." This observation is relevant to the full constellation of political systems examined in *Countries at the Crossroads*. Even for the best performers in the analysis, it is critical to safeguard and encourage the institutions on which democratic governance thrives. However, for systems with underdeveloped democratic institutions—the middle performers that form the core of the *Crossroads* survey—the challenge is more profound, and Sen's comment is especially apt. Unless they build democratically accountable governing mechanisms, it will be all but impossible for countries like Nigeria, Vietnam, and Yemen to break cycles of poverty while improving basic human rights.

The status of democratic governance in each state is the product of a complex interplay of historical, economic, and other factors. Moreover, some states with broadly similar starting points now find themselves in vastly different circumstances. The difficulty of explaining a particular country's successes or failures makes it all the more important to compare its performance with those of its regional and global peers.

The ultimate outcome of the story told by this analysis remains unclear, but it will have far-reaching implications for both the citizens of the countries examined and the larger aspirations of global democracy. If the middle-performing countries slip away from the path of democratic development, their numerous governance deficiencies will remain unresolved, exposing citizens in these countries to further limitations on basic freedoms. A shrinking pool of democracies also would have negative implications beyond any single country's borders. It would shape, for instance, the treatment of human rights issues in international bodies, including the United Nations. Alternatively, should these countries make their way into the ranks of consolidated democracies, they could tip the global balance and reinvigorate democratic governance as the most sustainable path to a more just and prosperous future.

COMPARATIVE COUNTRY SCORES: ACCOUNTABILITY AND PUBLIC VOICE

Country	Electoral Laws and Elections	Effective and Accountable Government	Civic Engagement	Media Independence	Category Average
Argentina	5.00	4.25	6.00	4.29	4.88
Bahrain	2.00	2.50	2.00	2.14	2.16
Brazil	5.25	4.25	6.00	4.14	4.91
Cambodia	2.75	2.25	3.33	3.00	2.83
Congo-DRC	1.75	1.00	1.67	1.71	1.53
Cote d'Ivoire	1.50	2.00	3.33	2.71	2.39
East Timor	4.25	4.25	5.00	3.71	4.30
El Salvador	4.00	2.50	5.33	4.14	3.99
Ghana	5.50	4.75	5.67	5.43	5.34
Guatemala	4.25	3.00	6.00	4.29	4.38
Haiti	2.75	2.50	3.67	4.29	3.30
Honduras	4.00	2.50	3.67	4.00	3.54
Indonesia	5.00	3.75	5.67	4.57	4.75
Jordan	2.75	2.25	3.00	2.29	2.57
Kenya	3.50	4.00	6.00	4.29	4.45
Lebanon	3.50	2.25	5.00	4.57	3.83
Liberia	4.75	3.75	5.00	4.29	4.45
Malawi	4.25	4.50	5.00	4.14	4.47
Malaysia	3.25	3.25	3.67	2.43	3.15
Mexico	5.50	4.25	5.67	4.57	5.00
Nepal	4.25	3.50	4.00	3.29	3.76
Nicaragua	3.25	2.00	4.00	4.00	3.31
Nigeria	2.00	2.75	4.67	3.86	3.32
Saudi Arabia	0.00	1.25	1.00	0.43	0.67
Sierra Leone	5.25	4.25	5.67	4.43	4.90
South Africa	4.25	4.75	6.00	4.57	4.89
Sri Lanka	4.50	3.50	3.33	2.86	3.55
Tanzania	3.25	4.25	5.00	3.86	4.09
Uganda	2.50	3.75	4.33	3.43	3.50
Vietnam	1.00	2.25	1.67	1.00	1.48
Yemen	2.75	1.75	3.67	1.71	2.47
Zimbabwe	1.75	2.00	1.00	0.57	1.33

COMPARATIVE COUNTRY SCORES: CIVIL LIBERTIES

Country	Protection from State Abuse	Gender Equity	Minority Rights	Freedom of Belief	Freedom of Association	Category Average
Argentina	3.88	4.67	3.75	6.00	5.25	**4.71**
Bahrain	3.13	3.00	2.50	3.67	3.25	**3.11**
Brazil	3.50	4.33	4.25	6.67	5.50	**4.85**
Cambodia	1.63	3.67	3.00	4.33	2.75	**3.08**
Congo-DRC	1.13	1.33	1.00	4.67	1.75	**1.98**
Cote d'Ivoire	1.88	2.67	3.00	4.00	2.75	**2.86**
East Timor	3.88	4.67	4.50	6.67	5.00	**4.94**
El Salvador	2.88	3.33	3.00	6.67	4.50	**4.08**
Ghana	4.00	5.00	5.25	6.67	5.75	**5.33**
Guatemala	1.88	3.67	3.50	5.33	3.00	**3.48**
Haiti	2.50	3.67	3.00	6.67	4.00	**3.97**
Honduras	2.38	3.33	2.75	6.00	3.75	**3.64**
Indonesia	3.13	3.00	2.75	4.00	5.00	**3.58**
Jordan	2.88	2.67	3.25	4.00	2.75	**3.11**
Kenya	2.88	3.67	3.50	6.67	4.75	**4.29**
Lebanon	2.63	4.00	3.50	4.33	5.50	**3.99**
Liberia	3.13	4.00	4.00	5.00	4.75	**4.18**
Malawi	3.25	3.67	4.75	5.33	4.50	**4.30**
Malaysia	2.50	3.67	1.75	3.00	3.50	**2.88**
Mexico	3.00	4.00	4.25	6.33	5.00	**4.52**
Nepal	2.38	3.67	4.00	4.67	3.75	**3.69**
Nicaragua	3.63	3.00	2.25	6.67	3.75	**3.86**
Nigeria	1.50	2.00	3.00	5.33	5.00	**3.37**
Saudi Arabia	1.00	0.33	1.00	0.00	0.00	**0.47**
Sierra Leone	3.50	3.33	3.50	5.67	5.50	**4.30**
South Africa	3.50	4.33	4.75	7.00	5.75	**5.07**
Sri Lanka	2.75	4.67	2.50	5.00	4.25	**3.83**
Tanzania	3.25	4.33	4.50	5.33	3.25	**4.13**
Uganda	2.75	3.00	4.00	5.33	3.75	**3.77**
Vietnam	2.38	4.67	3.75	3.00	1.75	**3.11**
Yemen	1.63	1.67	3.00	3.67	2.50	**2.49**
Zimbabwe	0.88	2.67	2.50	4.00	1.00	**2.21**

COMPARATIVE COUNTRY SCORES: RULE OF LAW

Country	Independent Judiciary	Civil/Criminal Proceedings	Security Force Accountability	Protection of Property Rights	Category Average
Argentina	3.60	4.20	4.25	4.67	**4.18**
Bahrain	3.00	3.80	2.25	3.67	**3.18**
Brazil	5.00	3.40	3.50	4.33	**4.06**
Cambodia	1.20	2.00	1.75	2.67	**1.90**
Congo-DRC	1.00	1.60	1.00	1.00	**1.15**
Cote d'Ivoire	2.20	2.40	2.50	2.67	**2.44**
East Timor	3.40	3.40	3.50	4.00	**3.58**
El Salvador	3.20	3.20	3.75	4.00	**3.54**
Ghana	4.80	4.00	4.75	5.00	**4.64**
Guatemala	3.60	3.20	3.25	3.00	**3.26**
Haiti	2.40	2.20	3.25	2.67	**2.63**
Honduras	3.00	3.00	3.00	3.67	**3.17**
Indonesia	2.80	2.60	3.25	3.33	**3.00**
Jordan	3.00	2.60	2.25	4.33	**3.05**
Kenya	3.60	3.00	3.00	4.00	**3.40**
Lebanon	3.40	3.00	2.75	5.00	**3.54**
Liberia	2.80	2.40	4.25	4.00	**3.36**
Malawi	3.80	3.80	4.25	4.67	**4.13**
Malaysia	3.00	4.20	3.50	4.67	**3.84**
Mexico	4.00	3.40	4.00	4.33	**3.93**
Nepal	3.00	2.40	2.00	4.00	**2.85**
Nicaragua	2.20	4.00	3.50	4.00	**3.43**
Nigeria	3.40	2.60	3.00	3.00	**3.00**
Saudi Arabia	1.40	1.40	0.75	2.33	**1.47**
Sierra Leone	3.80	2.80	4.25	5.00	**3.96**
South Africa	4.60	4.00	4.50	4.00	**4.28**
Sri Lanka	3.00	3.20	2.50	3.33	**3.01**
Tanzania	3.40	3.40	4.25	3.67	**3.68**
Uganda	4.20	3.80	2.25	3.33	**3.40**
Vietnam	2.00	2.40	1.75	3.33	**2.37**
Yemen	2.80	2.20	2.00	3.00	**2.50**
Zimbabwe	1.20	2.20	0.50	0.33	**1.06**

COMPARATIVE COUNTRY SCORES: ANTICORRUPTION AND TRANSPARENCY

Country	Anticorruption Environment	Anticorruption Systems	Anticorruption Norms and Standards	Governmental Transparency	Category Average
Argentina	3.75	3.25	4.25	3.00	3.56
Bahrain	2.75	2.00	2.25	2.50	2.38
Brazil	3.00	3.00	4.50	4.00	3.63
Cambodia	2.25	2.00	2.00	2.50	2.19
Congo-DRC	0.50	0.75	1.00	2.00	1.06
Cote d'Ivoire	2.00	1.75	2.00	2.33	2.02
East Timor	2.75	3.00	3.00	3.17	2.98
El Salvador	3.00	2.75	3.25	3.17	3.04
Ghana	4.00	4.00	4.25	3.17	3.85
Guatemala	3.25	2.75	3.00	4.33	3.33
Haiti	1.75	1.75	2.50	2.17	2.04
Honduras	3.00	3.00	3.00	2.83	2.96
Indonesia	2.50	2.25	4.00	2.83	2.90
Jordan	2.00	2.75	2.50	2.67	2.48
Kenya	2.75	2.50	3.50	3.50	3.06
Lebanon	1.75	2.50	3.00	3.17	2.60
Liberia	2.00	2.50	3.25	3.50	2.81
Malawi	3.25	3.50	3.50	3.50	3.44
Malaysia	3.25	3.25	2.25	3.00	2.94
Mexico	3.25	3.75	3.75	4.67	3.85
Nepal	3.50	2.50	3.00	3.50	3.13
Nicaragua	3.75	2.75	3.00	3.33	3.21
Nigeria	2.00	2.75	2.75	2.33	2.46
Saudi Arabia	1.50	1.50	1.25	1.00	1.31
Sierra Leone	2.75	3.50	3.75	3.17	3.29
South Africa	3.50	4.00	3.75	4.33	3.90
Sri Lanka	3.25	3.00	3.25	3.50	3.25
Tanzania	3.25	3.00	3.25	3.67	3.29
Uganda	3.25	3.75	3.50	3.83	3.58
Vietnam	2.50	2.25	2.75	2.67	2.54
Yemen	1.25	2.75	1.75	1.83	1.90
Zimbabwe	1.00	1.00	1.00	1.17	1.04

INTRODUCTION TO COUNTRY REPORTS

The *Countries at the Crossroads 2010* survey contains reports on 32 countries. Each report begins with a section containing basic political and economic data arranged in the following categories: capital, population, and gross national income (GNI) per capita. In addition, numerical ratings are provided for Accountability and Public Voice, Civil Liberties, Rule of Law, and Anticorruption and Transparency.

The capital was obtained from the CIA *World Factbook 2010*. Population data were obtained from the Population Reference Bureau's *2009 World Population Data Sheet*. Data on GNI per capita are based on the purchasing power parity method and were obtained from the 2008 World Bank World Development Indicators database, except for Bahrain and Zimbabwe, where the GNI data are based on the Atlas method and were obtained from the 2007 World Bank World Development Indicators database (www.worldbank.org).

The Accountability and Public Voice, Civil Liberties, Rule of Law, and Anticorruption and Transparency categories contain numerical ratings between 0 and 7 for each country, with 0 representing the weakest performance and 7 representing the strongest performance. For a full description of the methods used to determine the survey's ratings, please see the chapter on Survey Methodology.

Following the political and economic data, each country report is divided into five parts: an introduction, and analyses of Accountability and Public Voice, Civil Liberties, Rule of Law, and Anticorruption and Transparency. The introduction provides a brief historical background and a description of major events. The Accountability and Public Voice, Civil Liberties, Rule of Law, and Anticorruption and Transparency sections summarize each government's degree of respect for the rights and liberties covered in the *Countries at the Crossroads* survey. The Anticorruption and Transparency section is followed by a set of recommendations highlighting the specific areas of most immediate concern for the government to address.

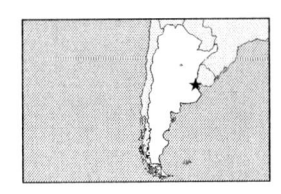

ARGENTINA

CAPITAL: Buenos Aires
POPULATION: 40.3 million
GNI PER CAPITA (PPP): $14,020

SCORES	2006	2010
ACCOUNTABILITY AND PUBLIC VOICE:	N/A	4.88
CIVIL LIBERTIES:	N/A	4.71
RULE OF LAW:	N/A	4.18
ANTICORRUPTION AND TRANSPARENCY:	N/A	3.56

(scores are based on a scale of 0 to 7, with 0 representing weakest and 7 representing strongest performance)

Martha Farmelo

INTRODUCTION

Argentina, though rich in natural resources, has historically been unable to sustain economic prosperity or political and social stability. Its political development in the 20th century was marked by numerous dictatorships and the populism of President Juan Perón and his wife, Eva, who promoted the interests of the working classes while courting both right- and left-wing factions. Today, Peronist parties continue to dominate Argentine politics, and opposition at the national level is fragmented.

Argentina most recently returned to civilian rule in 1983, after a seven-year military dictatorship that resulted in the death or disappearance of some 30,000 people. The presidency of Raúl Alfonsín (1983–89) of the Radical party featured a truth commission, the trials and convictions of military junta members, and later, hyperinflation and economic chaos.

During the 1990s, Peronist president Carlos Menem radically restructured the economy, pegging the peso to the U.S. dollar, scaling up the public debt, dismantling part of the social welfare state, undoing Peronist labor protections, and privatizing state assets on a massive scale. His presidency was fraught with allegations of corruption; he protected himself by increasing the number of Supreme Court judges from five to nine and stacking the court with loyalists.

During and after his tenure, the country's already feeble political institutions were almost completely discredited. In addition, the economy entered a devastating four-year recession in 1998. In December 2001, a government

---

Martha Farmelo is a freelance analyst based in Argentina. She was formerly the director of institutional development at the Buenos Aires–based Association for Civil Rights, where she launched the programs on freedom of expression and access to public information.

freeze on bank accounts mobilized the usually quiescent middle class. Massive pot-banging protests throughout the country precipitated the resignation of President Fernando de la Rúa of the centrist Alianza coalition. The crisis is remembered for its succession of five presidents in less than two weeks, but Argentines adhered to their constitution during the tumult. The slogan "out with all of them"—all politicians and Supreme Court justices—persisted as both a demand and defining point of political debate.

By 2002, over 50 percent of Argentines were poor, up from 25 percent just four years earlier, and 45 percent of the adult population was either unemployed or underemployed. In the wake of the devaluation of the peso and the default on public debt (except that held by multilateral lenders), the economy continued to spiral downward.

In May 2003, Argentines elected Néstor Kirchner, the little-known Peronist governor of Santa Cruz, as their president with the weakest mandate in Argentine history. He oversaw an economic recovery that was bolstered by high international soy prices and increased demand for Argentine exports. He paid off debt to the International Monetary Fund (IMF) early, a move that some considered a populist and ill-advised use of reserves, given the country's levels of poverty and indigence. And several of his other measures—such as a reform of the national Council of Magistrates, institutionalization of executive authority to reassign budget items with no congressional oversight, and excessive use of "necessity and urgency" decrees (NUDs)—deepened the already heavily "presidentialist" political system.

Kirchner sought to make justice for the victims of the last dictatorship the hallmark of his presidency. Several cases were reopened in 2003 after Congress annulled laws that had granted immunity to members of the military who were not in command positions and put a time limit on prosecutions. Kirchner also democratized the previously closed-door selection of Supreme Court justices, establishing a process that allows organizations and individuals to opine about candidates. Early on, he decreed full and timely access to public information held by the national executive branch. Yet his wife, then senator Cristina Fernández de Kirchner, helped scuttle a comprehensive access to information bill that had broad support among politicians and civil society but expired in November 2005.

Fernández won the presidency in October 2007 with 45 percent of the vote, and her party achieved a stronger majority in both the Chamber of Deputies and the Senate. Her campaign was helped by the economic recovery and the lack of a united opposition. However, she was seen as her husband's chosen successor (the party violated its own nomination procedures by failing to hold a primary election) and has been criticized for her husband's continued involvement in day-to-day decisions. Fernández's campaign promises were vague, and she has not introduced any substantive changes to her husband's cabinet or policies.

ACCOUNTABILITY AND PUBLIC VOICE 4.88
FREE AND FAIR ELECTORAL LAWS AND ELECTIONS	5.00
EFFECTIVE AND ACCOUNTABLE GOVERNMENT	4.25
CIVIC ENGAGEMENT AND CIVIC MONITORING	6.00
MEDIA INDEPENDENCE AND FREEDOM OF EXPRESSION	4.29

Argentina is a federal system composed of 23 provinces and a federal district for the capital, each with its own executive, judicial, and legislative bodies. Presidents can serve up to two four-year terms. Suffrage is universal and obligatory, yet turnout in the 2007 presidential election was only 73 percent, down from 85 percent in 1983.[1] National elections in recent years have been generally considered free and fair. The right to organize political parties is respected, and people's political choices are basically free from domination by powerful groups. However, candidates linked to the incumbent administration enjoy special campaigning opportunities financed with public funds. During the 2007 presidential race, Fernández received airtime on state-owned Channel 7, while opposition candidates drew virtually no coverage.[2] Despite restrictions on public advertising during electoral campaigns, Néstor Kirchner dedicated substantial funds to advertisements promoting his image while his wife ran for president.[3]

Argentina has a bicameral National Congress. Members of the Chamber of Deputies are elected through an open-list, proportional-representation system, with a minimum of five representatives per province. Under a 1994 constitutional reform, three senators represent each of the 23 provinces and the city of Buenos Aires, with two from the party that comes in first place and one from the second-ranked party.

Peronists are the strongest political force in the country. Though once unified under the Justicialist Party (PJ), they now belong to a variety of groups, including the president's Front for Victory coalition, which includes the PJ. The Radical party, once a solid opposition force, has remained quite weak after many years of decline, especially during the 2001 political crisis. Party ideology is often vague, and the main political forces each have left- and right-wing factions. Some Peronists operate in the opposition, while some non-Peronists have allied themselves with the government. In general, opposition forces on both the left and the right remain divided.

Fernández came to power with ample control over the Congress: her coalition held 40 of 72 Senate seats and 125 of 254 seats in the lower house, and she had additional support from other pro-Kirchner forces. However, growing fragmentation among the Peronists has made it more difficult for Fernández to exercise partisan control.

In March 2009, Congress approved Fernández's initiative to move legislative elections up from October to June of that year, apparently motivated by defections from the pro-Kirchner bloc. Néstor Kirchner promoted the congressional candidacies of a key governor and several mayors who stated from the outset that they would not leave their current posts if elected. The elections proved a major defeat for the Kirchners. Different Peronist factions ran different slates, and when the new Congress convenes in December 2009, the government will no longer hold a majority in either chamber.[4] Néstor Kirchner won a seat in the lower house for the province of Buenos Aires, but his list came in behind that of a conservative alliance including dissident Peronists.

Provincial governors have significant influence over the nomination of congressional candidates, and the electoral system effectively asks citizens to vote for parties—or perhaps for the figure heading a given candidate list—rather than for individuals. As a result, lawmakers tend to be more loyal to their parties than to their constituents.

Argentina has comprehensive federal campaign finance laws, including some public funding for parties, restrictions on anonymous donations, and strict oversight rules. However, the conventional wisdom is that legitimate contributions are complemented by illegal revenues. Parties often submit timely income and spending reports that are available online, but verification and analysis are deficient. The federal electoral court responsible for investigating irregularities is considered ineffective, in part because of excessive delays in its probes. In addition, widespread clientelism by political parties, sometimes involving national government officials, reduces the opportunity for the effective rotation of power. During the last elections, Social Development Minister Alicia Kirchner (Néstor Kirchner's sister) personally distributed refrigerators, mattresses, and subsidies to low-income families. Beneficiaries of government unemployment aid and related subsidies complain that disbursals are tainted by partisan favoritism, and that they are sometimes forced to participate in political events under threat of losing their benefits.[5]

Several measures enacted under Kirchner and Fernández deepened already serious weaknesses in Argentina's system of checks and balances. Congress is seen as a rubber-stamp body and is largely ineffective in providing oversight of the executive branch. The director of the National Audit Agency, a congressional body that audits the executive, is appointed by the opposition party with the largest congressional representation, though four of its seven auditors represent the governing party. In early 2009, a proposal to shift control of the agency's external communications from the director to the auditors (that is, from the opposition to the governing party) was defeated, and the agency began opening its audit sessions to the public.

In a continuation of measures first passed under President Menem as a special tool for dealing with the financial crisis, each year Congress passes a measure authorizing the president's chief of staff to reallocate spending without congressional approval or oversight. A lawsuit brought in 2006 by an Argentine civil rights organization to challenge the constitutionality of the measure is pending before the Supreme Court.

As of April 2009, Fernandez had issued five NUDs. By contrast, her husband issued a total of 235 during his presidency, in what was widely considered an abuse of his authority.[6] However, the decrees appeared to improperly usurp congressional power. One NUD announced in March 2009 diverted funds from the tariff on soy exports into an emergency fund for provincial governments, prompting accusations that the president was buying governors' loyalty.[7] Another increased the national budget by 36 billion pesos (US$10 billion) in light of increased revenues, again bypassing Congress's budgetary authority.[8] In 2006, after a 12-year delay, Congress passed a law creating a bicameral oversight committee. However, the measure failed to establish a time limit for congressional approval or rejection of NUDs, which are considered valid until Congress acts. Furthermore, 10 of the 14 committee members are allies of the current administration. The panel has ratified every NUD issued since its creation.

The consistent use since June 2006 of recorded, roll-call voting (rather than the raising of hands or oral voting) in the Chamber of Deputies represents a positive development. The Chamber generally publishes results online within 48 hours. The Senate, which has used roll-call voting since 2004, releases results only in response to formal requests, generally by specialized nongovernmental organizations (NGOs).

Roll-call voting was key to resolving the Fernández administration's biggest political conflict to date. Beginning in March 2008, farmers protesting a decree that greatly increased the tax on soy exports disrupted the transport of foodstuffs throughout the country. In July, after months of conflict and complaints that the president had usurped Congress's role in establishing tax policy, Fernández submitted the measure to Congress for approval. The ensuing legislative debate and voting were televised, and several legislators broke party discipline in favor of their constituents' interests. The president's bill was ultimately defeated in a dramatic tie-breaking vote by the vice president, and the whole process left the legislature with renewed credibility and activism. During the same period, the legislatures of the provinces of Mendoza and Tierra del Fuego and the city of Buenos Aires adopted roll-call voting, joining Tucumán, the only other province with such a system.

Current NGOs have built on the history of brave human rights groups formed during the last dictatorship. NGOs play a prominent role in monitoring and influencing government policy on a variety of issues. They are generally free from legal impediments and political pressure from the state, as are their donors. NGOs are occasionally invited to testify or comment on pending legislation. However, the absence of a legislative agenda and scant information regarding committee meetings makes it difficult to influence pending bills.

By law, civil-service positions are awarded through merit-based competition, though noncompetitive employment contracts, often funded by multilateral donors, are used to bypass that system. The Argentine civil service is considered relatively professional.

Government interference with the press is largely indirect, unlike past regimes' overt censorship, media closures, and attacks on journalists. Néstor Kirchner never held a press conference during his presidency, and rarely made contact with the media. Both he and his wife have characterized critical media as political opponents, sometimes publicly criticizing specific journalists and outlets. Executive officials call journalists to complain about critical coverage, and block access to official sources and events as punishment.

Defamation of public officials remains a criminal offense. In May 2008, the Inter-American Court of Human Rights ordered the government to modify its defamation laws, and several bills to decriminalize defamation are pending before Congress. Journalists are sometimes investigated and forced to defend themselves against such charges, though they are rarely jailed. In August 2009, the operations director of the national intelligence service filed a defamation suit against the director and president of *La Nación*, a prominent daily newspaper.

Government intimidation and physical violence against journalists continues to occur in some provinces. The national government generally refrains from traditional censorship and direct subsidies to the media. However, it regularly makes generous advertising allocations to favored outlets and withholds such contracts in order to punish critical coverage. Direct payments to journalists by the national and local governments are sometimes used to facilitate positive reporting. Government advertising manipulation is most marked at the local level, where media are more dependent on such revenue.

Two legal rulings in recent years restricted advertising abuses. In September 2007, the Supreme Court ruled that the government of Neuquén province violated the free speech rights of the *Río Negro* newspaper by withdrawing advertising in retaliation for critical coverage and ordered the province to present a plan for reversing such practices. In February 2009, a federal court ruled that the government of Néstor Kirchner discriminated against the publishing company Perfil by denying advertising as punishment for its editorial line, and ordered the government to advertise in Perfil publications.

After a 2005 reform made nonprofit organizations eligible for broadcasting licenses, the government allocated some licenses in limited areas. In March 2009, the president took out advertisements to announce a draft reform of the broadcasting law—a remnant of the last dictatorship—and plans for public debates before the bill's submission to Congress.

Freedom of cultural expression and academic freedom are generally unrestricted. The state does not hinder access to the internet, and the number of households with an internet connection rose 18 percent during 2008, to 3.43 million residential connections.[9]

CIVIL LIBERTIES 4.71

PROTECTION FROM STATE TERROR, UNJUSTIFIED IMPRISONMENT, AND TORTURE	3.88
GENDER EQUITY	4.67
RIGHTS OF ETHNIC, RELIGIOUS, AND OTHER DISTINCT GROUPS	3.75
FREEDOM OF CONSCIENCE AND BELIEF	6.00
FREEDOM OF ASSOCIATION AND ASSEMBLY	5.25

Argentina has made great strides since 1983 in assuring respect for civil liberties, but it still has many deficits to overcome. Arbitrary arrests continue to occur, especially of low-income and other marginalized persons, and excessive violence and torture by security forces remains a serious problem. Causes include low salaries and lack of interrogation skills, and the government has yet to reform police regulations dating from the last dictatorship. Punishment for such abuses is more common than several years ago, though few cases are denounced and even fewer end in conviction. Most statements are taken by judges or prosecutors, which helps prevent the practice of coercing confessions.

Prison conditions are deplorable. Endemic torture, violence, overcrowding, and disregard for health and safety seriously threaten the lives of inmates. Immigrant prisoners, who make up 21 percent of the federal prison population, are especially vulnerable, in part because they usually lack adequate legal representation.[10] Foreign detainees made 38 percent of the complaints received by the prison ombudsman in 2007.[11] Approximately 60 percent of the country's detainees are awaiting trial or the outcome of their trial, and the rate is as high as 80 percent in the province of Buenos Aires.[12] Judges jail those charged with crimes almost automatically. The federal and provincial governments establish their own time limits for pretrial detention; the maximum is generally two years with the possibility of a one-year extension, but the limits are often disregarded.

The government has taken some steps to comply with a May 2005 Supreme Court ruling that recognized the massive violation of the rights of prisoners in the province of Buenos Aires, who represent roughly half of the country's inmates. A partial reform of the criminal code in 2007 resulted in a decrease in the prison population, but since then, new measures including stricter rules on prisoner releases have begun to raise the overall number of inmates again.[13] The lack of official information on the number of detainees, their legal status, and basic conditions of detention is a serious impediment to wise policy making. In addition, while Argentina was one of the first countries to ratify the UN Optional Protocol for the Prevention of Torture (OPCAT), debates on monitoring and jurisdiction have stalled passage of a federal law on implementation.

Argentina is a source, transit, and destination country for adults and children trafficked for sexual exploitation and forced labor. Argentina has made significant yet insufficient efforts to combat trafficking, including the 2008 passage of its first federal legislation and the creation of national programs on the issue.

In November 2007, crime was considered the top issue for the incoming president to address.[14] There is a public perception that crime is on the rise, though annual statistics for 2005–2007 showed a slight overall decline.[15] The sense of insecurity is heightened by police corruption and reports that officials sometimes collude with criminals to secure temporary releases that are used to commit crimes. The 2008 murders of three Argentines who were allegedly involved in ephedrine trafficking exposed the activities of Mexican cartels in Argentina. The cartels' presence was denied by the government but reported in detail by the press.

Citizens whose rights are violated by the state can contact the national or local ombudsman, or take their cases to court with a public or private lawyer. In practice, however, access to these options is limited, especially for low-income and other socially marginalized people. The government has no clear policy for addressing this problem, leaving the task largely to NGOs. The national ombudsman has a low profile and plays a limited role in assuring citizens' right to petition. Most cases brought to the courts suffer from the broader problems in the functioning of the judicial system, described below.

Argentina has traditionally enjoyed a less "machista" culture than other countries in the region, and many women occupy significant positions in the public and private sectors. Two Supreme Court justices and the ministers of defense, social development, health, and production are women. A 30 percent electoral quota law was passed in 1991, and a 2000 ruling established that for every three candidates on the list, at least one must be a woman. Today, 40 percent of members of Congress are women, many of whom head important committees.[16] In the last presidential election, both the winner and the runner-up were women. However, Fernández and a significant number of female legislators and ministers at the national and provincial levels are relatives of politicians.

The Convention on the Elimination of All Forms of Discrimination against Women (CEDAW) was incorporated into Argentine law with constitutional status in 1994. Some additional statutes favor women's rights, including a law addressing reproductive health. In March 2009, Congress passed a law aimed at eliminating all forms of violence and discrimination against women, which now requires regulations and implementation. In practice, compliance with CEDAW is generally deficient. Women face discrimination in the workplace and hold a disproportionately high number of low-paying jobs. The wage gap between men and women has worsened in recent years; as of early 2008, women earned 29 percent less than men for equal work.[17] Relatively generous maternity-leave policies (typically three months with pay) are a double-edged sword, as employers may prefer to hire men to ensure continuous service.

Judicial and police responses to domestic violence are grossly inadequate. Access to therapeutic abortions in the limited cases permitted by law is often obstructed by doctors, who seek unnecessary judicial authorizations or otherwise fail to provide timely procedures due to fear of prosecution or personal objections.

Although the government carries out some programs to promote gender equality, it does not produce information on violations of women's rights and rarely punishes those responsible. To date there is no concerted, comprehensive policy approach to gender equality. The National Council of Women has a low profile, and its budget decreased by 80 percent over the last several years.[18]

A government study released in November 2008 found that 30 percent of people in Argentina had experienced discrimination, and that 50 percent had witnessed an act of discrimination. Low-income residents are seen as the most common victims.[19] Lack of awareness and acknowledgment of racism complicates efforts to combat discrimination. A national antidiscrimination institute under the Ministry of Justice is charged with investigating violations of a 1988 law that prohibits discrimination based on race, religion, nationality, ideology, political opinion, sex, economic position, social class, or physical characteristics. It carries out educational programs to promote pluralism and combat discriminatory attitudes.

Argentina hosts significant numbers of immigrants, many of them from Paraguay and Bolivia. A 2004 law codifies nearly all provisions of the UN International Convention on the Protection of the Rights of All Migrant Workers and Members of Their Families—including the right to a two-year work permit for registered migrant workers. The government conducted a campaign in 2006 to register tens of thousands of domestic workers, many of whom are immigrant women, and provide them the benefits and protections guaranteed by law. However, authorities have yet to regulate or implement the 2004 law, and there is no comprehensive policy to combat discrimination or enforce immigrants' rights.

Argentina's indigenous peoples, who constitute 3 to 5 percent of the population, live largely in conditions of extreme poverty and social exclusion. The constitution recognizes the identities and rights of indigenous peoples (including the right to bilingual education), and Argentina is a signatory to International Labor Organization (ILO) Convention 169, on the rights of indigenous groups. Although the government implements some programs, including education for indigenous leaders on their legal rights, it largely ignores the plight of indigenous peoples. Violent evictions of native communities in areas such as the far northwestern provinces have occurred despite a 2006 law imposing a four-year suspension on all such expulsions where indigenous claims to ancestral lands are pending. Judges tend to have little knowledge of indigenous peoples' rights.

Argentina's legal framework respects most provisions of the UN Convention on the Rights of Persons with Disabilities, which the country ratified in 2008.

The Committee on Disability in the lower house of Congress summoned several civil society organizations to assist in a review of existing laws and guide reforms to bring Argentina into full compliance with the convention. However, implementation of statutes on issues such as transportation, education, health, and employment is extremely poor, due largely to ignorance of the issues and lack of political will.

Freedom of religion is guaranteed in the constitution and generally respected in practice. Interference in religious observance is rare, and the state is not involved in the internal affairs of any faith. However, the state openly favors Roman Catholicism. Although a 1994 constitutional reform abolished Catholicism as the official religion, the government supports Catholic institutions with special tax benefits and subsidies, pays the salaries of certain members of the Catholic hierarchy, and tolerates Catholic symbols such as crucifixes in numerous government spaces, including courtrooms. There have been several reports in recent years of anti-Semitic acts, including vandalism in Jewish cemeteries and a violent May 2009 attack on a street celebration organized by the city of Buenos Aires and the Israeli embassy to mark the anniversary of Israel's founding. Efforts to identify and convict the material and intellectual authors of the 1994 bombing of a Jewish community center in Buenos Aires, which left 86 dead and 300 injured, have been grossly inadequate.

The government generally recognizes freedom of association and assembly. In November 2006, the Supreme Court ruled that the government must give legal status to the Association for Transvestite and Transsexual Identity, overturning a lower court finding that the group failed to contribute to the "common good."[20] The country's powerful trade union movement has long been dominated by the Peronist General Labor Confederation (CGT). The Argentine Workers' Central (CTA) was founded in 1992 as a nonpartisan labor federation that would oppose then president Menem's structural adjustment policies. The CTA has been unable to obtain full legal standing due to a rule allowing only one union per sector, despite ILO support for its petition.

Argentines have a robust tradition of social protest, and the blocking of streets and highways is a common (and controversial) tactic. Unlike their predecessors, Kirchner and Fernández have refrained from using force to break up demonstrations. However, serious government violence has occurred in some provinces. In July 2008, a court in Neuquén province gave a life sentence to the police officer responsible for killing a schoolteacher during a 2007 union protest. In contrast, in December 2008, a former member of Kirchner's government received a suspended sentence and retained his driver's license after being convicted of running over 40 protesters with his vehicle in Santa Cruz province. While there have been few new cases of legal charges against protesters, thousands of people still face long-standing charges for participating in social protests, with some cases dating to the 1990s.[21]

RULE OF LAW 4.18
INDEPENDENT JUDICIARY 3.60
PRIMACY OF RULE OF LAW IN CIVIL AND CRIMINAL MATTERS 4.20
ACCOUNTABILITY OF SECURITY FORCES AND MILITARY
 TO CIVILIAN AUTHORITIES 4.25
PROTECTION OF PROPERTY RIGHTS 4.67

Argentina's judicial system is divided into federal and provincial court systems, each consisting of a supreme court, appellate courts, and district courts. In general, judicial and law enforcement institutions continue to be highly politicized and suffer from extremely low public confidence. Negative perceptions are fueled by inordinate delays and general inefficiency.

The national Supreme Court is a notable exception. Its justices, including four nominated by Néstor Kirchner and confirmed by the Senate, have taken important steps to improve the court's transparency and legitimacy. Building on earlier progress, such as the introduction of timely publication of dockets and sentences, the court in 2006 launched online announcements of broader opportunities to submit *amicus curiae* briefs (previously restricted to those invited by one of the parties involved). It also established rules and procedures for holding public hearings and began to implement them in November 2007.

During much of 2006, the Supreme Court's functioning was impeded by the failure of the executive branch to name justices to fill two empty positions. The court consequently needed a majority of five members out of seven to rule, leaving it effectively paralyzed. The executive branch ultimately announced its decision to refrain from appointing additional justices and bring the number of justices back down to the pre-Menem level of five through attrition. This move echoed civil society proposals designed to address the relative difficulty of reaching consensus among nine judges and to avoid a court in which the vast majority of justices were appointed by a single president.

The Supreme Court is relatively independent from political pressures, as evidenced by its increasing willingness to issue rulings that require the executive to address major policy challenges and ensure the protection of human rights, as opposed to addressing a plaintiff's narrow complaint. For example, in 2008, the Supreme Court ordered the national government, the province of Buenos Aires, and the city of Buenos Aires to carry out the long-awaited cleanup of the Riachuelo-Matanza River, which separates the city and the province. It also ordered fines for delays by the relevant intergovernmental body, headed by the national secretary of the environment.[22]

There has been little change in the lower federal courts, which are plagued by corporatist attitudes and minimal transparency. Appointments of federal judges are subject to major delays, leading to an excess of unfilled positions. Concern about lax procedures for the appointment of temporary judges led the Supreme Court to require that the process involve the same bodies responsible for appointing permanent judges: the Council of Magistrates, which proposes three candidates for a position; the executive branch, which selects one of those candidates; and the Senate, which confirms the nominee. Reforms made by the Supreme Court have not been considered by the court just below it, the Cámara de Casación Penal, or Penal Cassation Chamber, which filters all appeals from the federal criminal system to the Supreme Court. This court is considered to be one of the least transparent, and its judges are among the most resistant to change. It does not always respect the legal precedents set by the Supreme Court, although it is constitutionally required to do so. Nor does it maintain consistency in its own interpretation of criminal law. Indeed, the chamber was accused of deliberately stalling or otherwise interfering with key cases related to the crimes of the dictatorship. Courts in the provinces also suffer from weak transparency and political interference, especially from the provincial executive branches.

Furthermore, in contrast to his improvements in the selection of Supreme Court justices, Kirchner promoted and signed 2006 legislation that threatens judicial independence by restructuring the Council of Magistrates, which oversees the appointment, promotion, and dismissal of judges. The new law eliminated minority party representation and reduced the numbers of judges, lawyers, and academics on the panel, increasing the influence of the governing party and altering the balance between political and professional opinion called for in the constitution. The Supreme Court is considering a constitutional challenge to the law brought by the Buenos Aires Bar Association. The Council of Magistrates continued to wield discretion in the selection and removal of judges, a highly politicized process that lends itself to the appointment of judges with poor qualifications or little political independence. Judges have at times been investigated after making controversial rulings, fueling the general fear among judges of personal and political repercussions for their decisions. Judges receive academic and technical training but not specialized training to carry out justice in a fair and unbiased manner. Unlike judges, prosecutors are for the most part considered independent of political control.

Criminal defendants are presumed innocent until proven guilty, and the constitution provides for the right to a fair and timely public trial. However, in practice defendants often wait years for their trials to begin and end. Contributing factors include outdated and inefficient judicial infrastructure and procedures, inadequate human resources and experience, a culture of slow proceedings, and the absence of accountability for delays.

The public defender system is critical for meeting defendants' need for legal counsel. Experts estimate that as many as 90 percent of detainees are represented by public defenders.[23] However, a lack of resources for the service leads to deficiencies such as infrequent lawyer-defendant contact and inadequate follow-up on cases. Argentina currently has no coherent policy for addressing these deficits at the federal or provincial levels. The 1994 constitution calls for trial by jury, but implementing legislation has yet to be passed. Compliance with judicial decisions occurs as a general rule, though less often in complex cases involving rulings against the state, especially when they imply major changes in public policy. Low-income and other marginalized persons generally lack access to public attorneys to bring their concerns before the authorities in both civil and criminal matters.

Civilian control over the military has been consolidated, and security forces do not unduly interfere in the political process. In recent years Argentina has taken a series of measures to prosecute former military and police personnel accused of grave human rights violations during the last military dictatorship. The executive branch actively encourages such prosecutions.

In June 2005, the Supreme Court struck down the "impunity laws" that had limited prosecution of the perpetrators of state terrorism, contributing to the opening of new cases. In July 2007, the court also annulled the pardons for accused and convicted human rights abusers issued by Menem in 1989–90. More than 500 people currently face charges for these crimes, the vast majority of whom are in pretrial detention, and 44 police and military officials have been convicted for crimes such as torture, disappearances, and extrajudicial execution, with many receiving lengthy or life sentences.[24] In October 2007, Catholic priest Christian von Wernich received a life sentence for his participation in homicide, torture, and illegal detentions while serving as police chaplain in the province of Buenos Aires.

Despite these advances, the majority of such abuse cases move very slowly, which has provoked significant public debate. Attorneys involved in human rights trials have received multiple threats, and the security of witnesses is a grave concern. In September 2006, Jorge Julio López, a torture victim who testified in one of the cases, disappeared the day before he was to attend a final trial session and remains missing. In December 2006, Luis Gerez was abducted for 48 hours and tortured after publicly accusing former police chief Luis Patti of participating in torture during the dictatorship. Patti, a former mayor in the province of Buenos Aires, was elected to the Chamber of Deputies in October 2006. Congress blocked him from taking his seat based on information linking him to crimes against humanity, although he had not been convicted in court. The Supreme Court ruled in Patti's favor, but because he was detained on charges of human rights violations, he never occupied his seat. Sitting legislators have immunity from prosecution.

In August 2008 Congress annulled the Code of Military Justice and created a new process for trying military officials in federal civilian courts. Lack of political will results in relatively few sanctions for members of the security forces involved in abusing power for personal gain, a relatively common practice.

The World Bank Doing Business 2009 report rated Argentina 113 of 181 countries for doing business overall, and 45 of 181 on contract enforcement.[25] Property rights are guaranteed by law, though problems in the judicial system sometimes compromise contract enforcement. The state generally protects citizens from the unjust confiscation of their property. In a glaring exception, an inadequate legal framework and conflicting jurisprudence on government confiscation of bank savings in 2001 and 2002 remain unresolved, leaving open the possibility that such measures—typical in Argentina during extreme economic crises—could again be implemented.

ANTICORRUPTION AND TRANSPARENCY 3.56
ENVIRONMENT TO PROTECT AGAINST CORRUPTION	3.75
PROCEDURES AND SYSTEMS TO ENFORCE ANTICORRUPTION LAWS	3.25
EXISTENCE OF ANTICORRUPTION NORMS, STANDARDS, AND PROTECTIONS	4.25
GOVERNMENTAL TRANSPARENCY	3.00

For the average citizen, bureaucratic red tape can be time consuming but has a limited effect on opportunities for petty corruption. Still, corruption—both petty and serious, mostly involving the executive branch—constitutes a structural problem in Argentina, and only a handful of politicians have ever been convicted. Allegations of major corruption generally receive significant attention from the news media, including high-level scandals involving the current government. Néstor Kirchner and Planning Minister Julio de Vido are under investigation for "illicit enrichment." In June 2007, Economy Minister Felisa Miceli resigned after failing to account for more than US$60,000 in dollars and pesos found in her office bathroom. In August 2007, customs officers discovered US$800,000 in cash in a suitcase carried by Venezuelan American businessman Guido Antonini Wilson, who was traveling on a plane chartered by Argentina's state oil company. This event spurred the resignation of Claudio Uberti, head of the agency in charge of privatized highway concessions, who was also on the plane. Antonini stated that the suitcase contained Venezuelan government funds destined for Fernández's presidential campaign. U.S. courts have given prison sentences to two Venezuelans involved in the case, which is still under investigation in Argentina.

The 1999 Public Ethics Law requires asset declarations for members of all three branches of government. The federal anticorruption office has a complete database of executive declarations, which are made available on request. As of March 2009, Media Secretary Enrique Albistur was under investigation for conflict of interest related to state advertising contracts he allegedly awarded to firms linked to himself and family members, which is prohibited by law. It is difficult to obtain asset declarations for members of Congress, even when requested by specialized NGOs. In 2007, the Supreme Court made its own asset declarations public for the first time, after arguing for years that it was exempt from the 1999 law. Only some lower federal judges have followed suit, and questions have been raised regarding the accuracy of their statements. There is no control for conflicts of interest involving judges.

Argentine law includes criminal penalties for official corruption, but these are not implemented effectively, due primarily to lack of political will. Victims of corruption generally assume that they have few mechanisms to pursue their rights, in part because cases usually take more than a decade to be resolved and only a handful have resulted in convictions.

The several agencies tasked with investigating corruption generally suffer from a lack of independence from the executive branch. Most cases fall under the purview of federal courts in the capital, which are known for their vulnerability to political influence. As a result, while some cases are investigated, they consistently stall and are often closed before actual trial or conviction. The situation is worse in the provinces, where the independence of executive agencies and the justice system is seriously compromised.

Created in 1999, the federal Anti-Corruption Office has two directors tasked with prevention and investigation, respectively. However, it cannot prosecute cases, and while the directors have generally had excellent personal reputations, they report to the justice minister, weakening the agency's independence and effectiveness.

A special prosecutor's office for administrative matters forms part of the Public Ministry, which, in turn, reports to the president. In March 2009, special prosecutor Manuel Garrido resigned, alleging that Prosecutor General Esteban Righi had signed a 2008 resolution that reduced his functions and limited his role in denouncing corruption cases. The special prosecutor had initiated criminal investigations of senior government officials, including the secretaries of media and transportation.

Argentina has no adequate law to protect whistleblowers, and anticorruption activists and investigators do not feel secure when reporting cases of bribery and corruption. The top regulators of privatized public services are generally allies of the current administration, making the agencies ineffective. Argentina has some public enterprises that had previously been privatized (such as mail service, water works, and the national airlines), and they are widely believed to be tainted by corruption. The national tax administrator implements a sophisticated internal audit system to ensure the accountability of tax collection. Corruption is not common in the education system.

Kirchner's decree establishing public access to executive branch information is still in effect, but like scattered provincial and municipal statutes, it is underutilized. While the national government has freedom of information officers in each ministry, journalists, NGOs, and university students report that responses to formal requests are often slow, incomplete, or nonexistent. The government never actively publicized the right to access information.

Given Fernández's role in scuttling the access to information bill in 2005, and her hold over Congress since then, no similar bill has received serious consideration. Many NGOs fear that a bad public information bill—for example, one that establishes the same requirements for private businesses as for public institutions, which Fernández has supported—would be worse than no bill at all.

Even when access is provided, government data are often unreliable, incomplete, or out of date, leading to calls for a legal framework to govern its production. In early 2007 the national statistics agency (INDEC) modified the consumer price index so as to underreport inflation. This in turn lowered the official rates of poverty and indigence and made comparisons with past inflation rates impossible. In May 2008, a federal judge ordered INDEC to provide clear and complete information regarding the methodological changes after the agency failed to comply with a freedom of information request by a civil rights NGO, and the government lost an appeal of the ruling. The scandal destroyed INDEC's credibility. The government also canceled publication of widely used data on production and sales in the agricultural sector, such as the amounts of grains produced; that information was considered politically sensitive in light of the conflict over the tax on soy exports.

The 2008 Open Budget Index ranked Argentina 25 out of 85 countries evaluated. The government provides some information at the beginning of the budget year. However, it is extremely difficult to obtain data regarding expenditures during and at the end of the budget cycle[26]—a situation that is greatly aggravated by the executive's authority to reallocate budget items at will, as mentioned above.

Argentina's legal framework for government contracting is outdated and deficient, opening the door to numerous allegations of contracting-related corruption. Sole-source contracting is used disproportionately, due to the slowness of competitive bidding and lack of ministerial planning, which leads to unreasonably short time frames for nonurgent procurement. An online information system launched in December 2005 improved access to information for providers of goods and services. Public works are contracted separately by the Planning Ministry, and various irregularities occur in both sole-source and competitive processes.

RECOMMENDATIONS

- The national and provincial governments should enact comprehensive access to information laws that apply to all three branches of government, are based on principles of maximum disclosure, and include provisions regarding the production and proper archiving of information.
- Measures should be taken to ensure compliance with existing limits on pretrial detention, and Congress and provincial legislatures should pass laws that restrict the use of pretrial detention, making it an exception rather than the rule. The national government should enact legislation to implement the UN Optional Protocol for the Prevention of Torture (OPCAT).
- Congress should pass and implement a law that assures the full independence of the various oversight bodies, including the National Audit Agency, the executive auditor (Sindicatura General de la Nación), and the

Anti-Corruption Office; modifies the process for the designation of their heads; and expands their purview and functions.
- Congress should enact legislation that modifies the composition and functioning of the Council of Magistrates to ensure its independence from executive control, and the council itself should reform the procedures for selection and removal of federal judges so as to end the excessive delays in their appointment.
- The government should design and implement a policy to provide proper access to public attorneys for low-income and other marginalized persons, allowing them to defend their rights in both civil and criminal matters.

NOTES

For URLs and endnote hyperlinks, please visit the *Countries at the Crossroads* homepage at http://freedomhouse.org/template.cfm?page=139&edition=8.

[1] Jorge Lanata, "Democracia de Baja Intensidad" [Low-Intensity Democracy], *Crítica de la Argentina*, April 5, 2009, 6.
[2] Committee to Protect Journalists (CPJ), "Argentina," in *Attacks on the Press in 2007* (New York: CPJ, 2008).
[3] Open Society Institute, *The Price of Silence: The Growing Threat of Soft Censorship in Latin America* (New York: Open Society Institute, 2008), 14.
[4] "La Matemática Parlamentaria" [Parliamentary Math], *Crítica de la Argentina*, June 30, 2009, 10.
[5] C. Gruenberg and V. Pereyra Iraola, *El Clientelismo en la Gestión de Programas Sociales contra la Pobreza* [Clientelism in the Management of Social Antipoverty Programs] (Buenos Aires: Center for the Implementation of Public Policies for Equity and Growth, January 2009), 6.
[6] "CFK: The Most Democratic President Since Alfonsín?" *Argentine Post*, March 22, 2009.
[7] "Argentina Sends 30 Pct Soy Tax Income to Provinces," ABC News, March 19, 2009.
[8] See tracking of the number and content of NUDs by the Association for Civil Rights at http://adclegislativo.digbang.com/verdecretosporano.php?iddocumento=2008&idpresidencia=13.
[9] "El Acceso a Internet Creció 18,5% en el Ultimo Año" [Access to the Internet Increased 18.5% in the Last Year], Infobae.com, March 16, 2009.
[10] Data from the Federal Prison Service, "Internos Extranjeros en el Ambito del Servicio Penitenciario Federal."
[11] Ministry of Justice, Security, and Human Rights, *Prison Ombudsman Annual Report* (Buenos Aires: Ministry of Justice, Security, and Human Rights, 2007), 51.
[12] Center for Legal and Social Studies, *Human Rights in Argentina: 2008 Report* (Buenos Aires: Center for Legal and Social Studies, 2008), 153–154.
[13] Interview with Alvaro Herrero, Executive Director, Association for Civil Rights, Buenos Aires, March 26, 2009.
[14] Data from the Centro de Estudios de Opinión Pública [Center for Public Opinion Studies], cited in *Human Rights in Argentina: 2008 Report*, 95.
[15] Data from the Ministry of Justice, Security, and Human Rights website, http://www2.jus.gov.ar/politicacriminal/TotalPais2007_evol.pdf (accessed April 6, 2009).

[16] Fundación Directorio Legislativo, *Informe No. 1, Congreso de la Nación: Las Legisladoras, Su Influencia y Participación dentro de las Cámaras 2000–2008* [Report No. 1, National Congress: Female Legislators, Their Influence and Participation in Both Chambers 2000–2008] (Buenos Aires: Fundación Directorio Legislativo, September 2008), 2, 9.

[17] International Trade Union Confederation, *Gender (In)equality in the Labour Market: An Overview of Global Trends and Developments* (Brussels: International Trade Union Confederation, March 2009), 17.

[18] S. Cesilini, M. Butinof, and H. Farfan, *Argentina: Perfil de Género de País* [Argentina: Country Gender Profile] (Buenos Aires: International Cooperation Agency of Japan, December 2007), 57.

[19] National Institute Against Xenophobia, Discrimination and Racism (INADI), "Map of Discrimination in Argentina," November 2008.

[20] Interview with Mariela Belski, Director of Social Rights Program, Association for Civil Rights, Buenos Aires, April 16, 2009.

[21] Interview with Gastón Chillier, Executive Director, Center for Legal and Social Studies, Buenos Aires, March 10, 2009.

[22] Center for Legal and Social Studies, *Human Rights in Argentina: 2008 Report*, 153–154.

[23] Center for Legal and Social Studies, *Human Rights in Argentina: 2007 Report* (Buenos Aires: Center for Legal and Social Studies, 2007), 149.

[24] Center for Legal and Social Studies, weblog on prosecutions for state terrorism crimes, accessed March 13, 2009.

[25] World Bank, "Argentina," in *Doing Business 2009: Comparing Regulation in 181 Economies* (Washington, D.C.: World Bank, 2009).

[26] Open Budget Initiative, "Argentina," in *Open Budget Index 2008* (Washington, D.C.: Center on Budget and Policy Priorities, 2008).

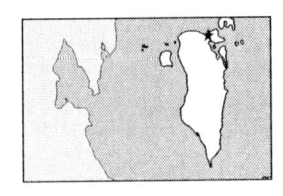

BAHRAIN

CAPITAL: Manama
POPULATION: 1.2 million
GNI PER CAPITA (ATLAS): $19,350

SCORES	2006	2010
ACCOUNTABILITY AND PUBLIC VOICE:	2.44	2.16
CIVIL LIBERTIES:	3.64	3.11
RULE OF LAW:	3.67	3.18
ANTICORRUPTION AND TRANSPARENCY:	2.08	2.38

(scores are based on a scale of 0 to 7, with 0 representing weakest and 7 representing strongest performance)

Fred H. Lawson

INTRODUCTION

Prospects for political liberalization in Bahrain, which had brightened after influential organizations critical of the country's autocratic system of government decided to participate in the 2006 parliamentary elections, have dimmed in subsequent years. Elected members of parliament (MPs) find their attempts to shape public policy consistently blocked either by the Council of Ministers or by pro-regime MPs. Demands to reform the electoral process to reduce discrimination against the Shiite majority by the ruling Sunni elite have been ignored. Freedoms of association and of the press have deteriorated. Violent confrontations between security forces and opposition groups have increased in frequency, while reliable reports of mistreatment and torture of political activists in custody have resurfaced. Efforts to reduce corruption in public and private enterprises look promising, but deeply entrenched practices keep the country's physical and financial assets in the hands of powerful elites and the ruling family.

Sheikh Hamad bin Isa al-Khalifa, who succeeded his father as ruler in March 1999, ended a large popular uprising that took place from 1994 to 1999 by announcing plans for a comprehensive reform program, including restoration of the constitution and the National Assembly (al-Majlis al-Watani). After winning overwhelming support for the program in a February 2001 referendum, however, the government took steps that restricted democratic participation in

---

Fred H. Lawson is Professor of Government at Mills College and Visiting Senior Fellow at the Georgetown University School of Foreign Service in Qatar. He is author of *Bahrain: The Modernization of Autocracy* (Boulder, Colo.: Westview Press, 1989) and "Repertoires of Contention in Contemporary Bahrain," in Quintan Wiktorowicz, ed., *Islamic Activism* (Bloomington: Indiana University Press, 2003).

governance. These included amending the constitution to give the appointed upper house equal legislative powers as the elected lower house, denying MPs the right to introduce bills, revising the Press and Publications Law to be more restrictive, and promulgating a decree conferring full immunity on officials suspected of human rights violations committed prior to 2002.

Liberal and radical critics of the regime were caught off guard by such measures, as well as by the ruler's decision to declare the country a monarchy and himself king. To protest the changes, four major political societies boycotted the October 2002 parliamentary elections.[1] These were the predominantly Shiite Islamic National Accord Society (al-Wefaq) and Islamic Action Society (al-Amal al-Islami), the liberal nationalist National Democratic Action Society (al-Wa'd), and the nominally socialist Progressive National Bloc (al-Tajammu' al-Qawmi al-Taqaddumi). Two influential Sunni societies, the Islamic Platform (al-Minbar al-Islami) and Purity (al-Asalah), joined the leftist Progressive Platform (al-Minbar al-Taqaddumi) in contesting the elections and ended up in command of the parliament. The most significant debates in the National Assembly during its initial four-year term pitted the former Muslim Brothers of the Islamic Platform against the more radical (Salafi Sunni) representatives of Purity; neither opposed the government on any fundamental issue.

ACCOUNTABILITY AND PUBLIC VOICE   2.16

FREE AND FAIR ELECTORAL LAWS AND ELECTIONS	2.00
EFFECTIVE AND ACCOUNTABLE GOVERNMENT	2.50
CIVIC ENGAGEMENT AND CIVIC MONITORING	2.00
MEDIA INDEPENDENCE AND FREEDOM OF EXPRESSION	2.14

Bahrain's head of state is nominated and confirmed by the ruling family, the al-Khalifa, with no input from the general population. The country has a long tradition of primogeniture, whereby the ruler's oldest son is expected to accede to power upon his father's death. Thus Sheikh Hamad was immediately endorsed as ruler (emir) upon his father's death, and then named his own son, Sheikh Salman, as crown prince. On February 15, 2002, the emir declared the country to be a hereditary monarchy and assumed the title of king. According to an amended constitution issued the same day, King Hamad appoints the prime minister and other ministers; all judges, governors, and ambassadors; members of the Consultative Council (Majlis al-Shura); and commanders of the armed forces. The king is also empowered to dissolve the National Assembly, draft amendments to the constitution, and issue decrees that enjoy the force of law until they are ratified by the legislature.

The king and royal family's position is similarly dominant in practice. Since independence in 1971, the most powerful state agencies, such as the Ministry of the Interior and the Ministry of Justice and Islamic Affairs, have consistently been headed by members of the ruling family. The number of al-Khalifa ministers in the cabinet is presently greater than at any time since 1926.[2] King Hamad displays a marked propensity to dispense personal favors and benefits to mollify his critics and opponents. Bahraini activist Abdulhadi Khalaf observes that the ruler "remains the only one who possesses the right to set the parameters of the political process, and to chart its path, pace, and scope. The King has remained adamant that he alone should determine which social groups and political networks should have the right to express their opinions on public affairs."[3]

It remains illegal to form or belong to any political party. Licensed political societies have taken on some of the functions of political parties, particularly in mobilizing popular support behind candidates for election to the Chamber of Representatives (Majlis al-Nuwwab) and brokering coalitions among representatives during parliamentary debates. Nevertheless, MPs have no formal allegiance to such societies and are not subject to the kind of discipline that might be exercised by actual party organizations. Under the terms of the 2005 law that governs political societies, the Ministry of Justice and Islamic Affairs can petition the High Civil Court to disband any such society.

In the summer of 2006, al-Wefaq announced that it would end its boycott of the parliamentary system and put forward candidates in the upcoming elections for the National Assembly. A majority of al-Wa'd members immediately endorsed such an approach. Preparations for the 2006 parliamentary elections were shaken in late September by the release of a dossier of documents indicating that state officials had engaged in a concerted effort to rig the voting and stir up tensions between the Shiite and Sunni communities. The file, which had been compiled by a former adviser to the Ministry for Cabinet Affairs, was submitted to the king, the crown prince, and several Western embassies.[4]

Overall direction of the campaign was attributed to a senior member of the ruling family, who at the time was acting as both head of the primary intelligence-gathering agency and the commission charged with supervising the elections. The report alleged that the national intelligence agency, the Central Informatics Organization, had disbursed some US$6 million to fund anti-Shiite articles in the local press, organize counterdemonstrations to public protests orchestrated by al-Wefaq, and spread rumors about leaders of the opposition by means of mobile telephone text messages. The al-Khalifa sheikh who was named in the dossier responded that these activities were not illegal and that the motivation behind the allegations was to "weaken national unity."[5] The High Criminal Court immediately issued an injunction that prohibited any discussion of the matter in the local press, while the report's author was labeled a British spy, deported, and sentenced in absentia to four years in prison.[6] The entire episode has come to be known as Bandargate, after the name of the individual who compiled the file, Salah al-Bandar.

Although opposition parties participated in the 2006 elections, the polls were ultimately marred by greater government interference and irregularities than the 2002 contest. The campaigning period was blemished by sectarian tensions, hatemongering, and harassment of female candidates.[7] Shortly before the voting, Prime Minister Khalifa bin Salman al-Khalifa issued a decree that banned strikes and other forms of public activism in the vicinity of the country's military and civil defense bases, airports, harbors, hospitals, pharmacies, telecommunications facilities, electrical stations, waterworks, educational institutions, bakeries, and oil and gas installations.[8] There were also reliable reports of vote buying, intimidation of candidates, destruction of campaign offices, and instances of "electioneering in places of worship."[9] Although local observers reported relatively few problems on election day, the government reportedly ordered soldiers to vote for progovernment candidates and sent 8,000 government-loyal "floaters" to vote in districts with close races.[10] In addition, large numbers of dual Saudi/Bahraini nationals cast ballots at the Saudi border voting station.[11] Gerrymandered voting districts and the granting of citizenship to Jordanian, Yemeni, Iraqi, Syrian, and Saudi expatriates by the government prior to the polls, apparently with a view toward manipulating electoral outcomes in favor of the Sunni minority, further undermined the fairness of the vote.

The predominantly Shiite al-Wefaq emerged with 17 of the 40 seats in the Chamber of Representatives. The Islamic Platform and Purity won seven and five seats, respectively. Nine Sunni Islamist independents emerged victorious as well.[12] Islamic parties received strong support overall, winning 30 out of 40 seats, while liberals gained 10.[13] Some 72 percent of eligible voters cast ballots in the initial round, and 69 percent participated in run-offs, substantial increases compared to four years earlier.[14] None of the other societies that had boycotted the 2002 elections, including al-Wa'd, captured a single seat in the Chamber. King Hamad responded to the dominance of Islamist representatives in the lower house by appointing a majority of secularists to the upper Consultative Council.[15] Ten women were appointed to the upper house, an increase from the four who had served in the 2002 Council.

Although parliament has no power to draft legislation, since the 2006 elections members of the Chamber of Representatives have sought to exercise greater oversight over the executive, particular with regards to state expenditures. On several occasions, the Chamber has set up special commissions to investigate allegations of mismanagement.[16] Parliamentarians have also called for ministers to come before the Chamber to answer questions concerning alleged misuse of public funds.[17] While such actions have generated greater public awareness of alleged corruption and applied political pressure on the government, the lack of more robust formal parliamentary powers limits their ultimate effectiveness in enhancing government accountability. Indeed, the king and Council of Ministers continue to propose and promulgate important legislation despite the expressed opposition of the parliament. For instance, the Chamber of Representatives was unable to block passage of a 2006 draft law to combat terrorism, although members strenuously objected to the bill when it was first introduced.[18]

The government's dominance over policy making is buttressed by sharp divisions in the lower house between pro-regime representatives and critics of the status quo. In one instance, the Chamber voted in May 2005 to quash a motion put forward by Shiite representatives to challenge the decree granting immunity for pre-2002 abuses before the Constitutional Court.[19] Efforts by al-Wefaq and independent representatives to question the minister of state for cabinet affairs and the minister of agriculture and municipalities have consistently been blocked by representatives of Islamic Platform and Purity.[20]

Over time, al-Wefaq and its allies have become increasingly frustrated by their inability to significantly influence policy making. The society's representatives have therefore adopted protest tactics, such as exiting chamber sessions in the hope that the resulting lack of a quorum might derail proceedings. Walking out has also been used to express general displeasure with government policies. In May 2008, for example, leaving was used to express incredulity over newly published census figures that indicated the total number of Bahraini citizens had swelled some 42 percent, a number that implicitly acknowledged the scale of Sunni naturalization used by the authorities as a means of offsetting the Shiite majority.[21]

Within Bahrain's civil service, middle- and lower-level administrators, both citizens and expatriates, are comprised largely of well-trained professionals whose expertise and sense of public duty place the country near the top of international rankings related to administrative corruption and overall ease of doing business.[22] High-ranking bureaucrats, however, frequently defer to the wishes of the political elite.

Outside parliament, public criticism of government policy is largely channeled through organized political societies, which must be licensed by the Ministry of Justice and Islamic Affairs under the 2005 Political Societies Law. License approval is conditioned on not receiving funding from foreign sources and having all members be 21 years of age or older. Only after it became clear that the authorities intended to declare illegal any association that did not agree to conform to the new regulations, on the grounds that refusing to register was tantamount to challenging the 2002 constitution, did al-Wefaq, the Islamic Action Society, and the National Democratic Action Society register with the ministry.[23] More radical members of al-Wefaq, who insisted that the society should refuse on principle to abide by the new regulations, formed a breakaway society under the name the Movement for Liberties and Democracy, or Truth (al-Haqq) in 2005.[24]

While nongovernmental organizations (NGOs) voice criticisms of state policy, they have faced increasing official harassment as the government has backtracked from the openness permitted in 2002 and 2003. The 1989 Societies Law prohibits any organization from operating without official permission. In 2007, the Ministry of Social Development drafted a new NGO law that contains some improvements over the current law but still falls short of international standards; it has yet to be submitted to parliament.[25] In 2004, the government dissolved the Bahrain Center for Human Rights (BCHR), which had gained prominence for issuing a stream of reports that highlighted widespread poverty and discrimination against members of the Shiite community. Efforts to reconstitute the organization under a different name have been restricted as the government has not granted a 2005 request to formally register it;[26] the organization continues to operate informally and publish reports. International efforts to advance human rights have also come under pressure. In May 2006, the authorities ordered the closure of the local office of the U.S.-based National Democratic Institute. In November 2008, the interior minister warned that in the future, Article 134 of the Criminal Code, which makes it illegal to "participate in meetings abroad or with international bodies to discuss the internal affairs of the Kingdom," would be more strictly enforced. The announcement was made after several Bahraini activists spoke to the U.S. Congressional Caucus on Religious Freedom and Human Rights.

Despite constitutional guarantees for freedom of expression, press freedom remains significantly restricted in practice. The government maintains a monopoly on all broadcast media outlets. Six privately owned newspapers, four in Arabic and two in English, publish daily, and some are critical of the government. Sawt al-Ghad, the country's first private radio station, which was launched in 2005, was shut down by the authorities in 2006. Though privately owned, print media remain constrained by the 2002 Press and Publications Law, under which journalists can be imprisoned for up to five years or face heavy fines for criticizing Islam or the king, publishing information that threatens state security, or encouraging sectarianism. In a positive development, the Ministry of Information introduced a revised Press and Publications Law in May 2008 that would substantially reduce the penalties for printing objectionable material and limit the government's power to impose sanctions. The ministry also hinted that it might permit private television and radio stations to operate, though they would first be required to obtain a license.[27] The Consultative Council quickly passed the revised law, but it has yet to pass the lower house, where it faces opposition from conservative Sunni Islamists.

In the meantime, journalists critical of the government continue to face charges under provisions of the penal code and 2006 antiterrorism law.[28] Journalists who cover contentious issues such as protests, government scandals, corruption, and human rights are subject to arrest and prosecution. In recent years, the total number of cases brought against journalists has increased. According to the Bahrain Journalists Association, 27 cases of alleged defamation were brought against journalists in 2006 and 32 in 2007. The government has been especially aggressive in its campaign against those writing about the 2006 Bandargate scandal.[29] Physical assaults against journalists have also occurred on occasion.

Bahrain has one of the highest internet penetration rates in the Middle East, reaching nearly 35 percent in mid-2009. In recent years, the country's blogosphere has become popular as an arena for political and social discussion, eluding restrictions on print media.[30] Partly in response, the government imposes restrictions on the flow of information online. All websites are required to register with the Ministry of Information, and site administrators face the same libel laws as print journalists and are held jointly responsible for content posted on their websites or related chat rooms. In recent years, several dozen websites featuring content critical of the government have been blocked by the authorities. Many Bahrainis reportedly used proxy servers, however, to circumvent such censorship. In January 2009, the government further tightened restrictions, issuing decrees that reportedly led to pervasive filtering of content.[31] The Ministry of Information monitors websites, particularly content related to relations between Shiites and Sunnis.[32] The government has detained several bloggers in recent years, though none has as yet been sentenced to prison.[33]

CIVIL LIBERTIES 3.11

PROTECTION FROM STATE TERROR, UNJUSTIFIED IMPRISONMENT, AND TORTURE	3.13
GENDER EQUITY	3.00
RIGHTS OF ETHNIC, RELIGIOUS, AND OTHER DISTINCT GROUPS	2.50
FREEDOM OF CONSCIENCE AND BELIEF	3.67
FREEDOM OF ASSOCIATION AND ASSEMBLY	3.25

The 2002 constitution prohibits long-term detention without trial and protects citizens from torture. It bars the use of information obtained through torture in judicial proceedings. Nevertheless, in recent years, the authorities have increasingly disregarded such protections as torture and arbitrary detention of political activists have increased.

Individual activists have faced increased harassment, including arrest, in recent years. In February 2007, security forces raided the residences of the former head of the BCHR, Abd al-Hadi al-Khawaja and the leader of al-Haqq, Hasan Mushaima, and took the two men into custody along with a third outspoken critic of the regime. The three were charged with "advocating a change of the government system in illegal ways" and "using indecent language to describe the regime." All three were released after two days in detention following large-scale popular protests on their behalf.[34] Increasingly active women's rights NGOs have also been subject to harassment. In 2005, the government brought criminal charges against Ghada Yusuf Jamsheer, president of several women's rights groups, for defaming the Islamic judiciary.[35] Although the charges were dropped in 2006, the government subsequently placed her under surveillance.[36]

More broadly, beginning in late 2005 the government initiated a violent crackdown on Shiite and opposition activists. In September 2006, the Special Security Forces (SSF) raided a seminar organized by al-Haqq and used tear gas and rubber bullets against participants.[37] Security forces arrested five Shiite protesters for involvement in a series of December 2007 protests in which demonstrators and security forces clashed violently. While some were immediately released, 15 were kept in detention, placed in solitary confinement, and allegedly tortured during interrogation.[38] In July 2008, five of the detainees were sentenced to five to seven years in prison on charges of stealing a weapon and burning a police vehicle, six were sentenced to one year and subsequently granted a pardon by the king, and four were cleared of all charges. Large-scale protests continued to erupt throughout 2008 and 2009, with some turning violent.[39]

Reflecting an apparent increase in the use of physical violence by security forces, credible allegations have repeatedly surfaced in recent years of protesters being tortured in police custody, including being subjected to electrical shocks and beatings during interrogation.[40] In April 2008, a doctors' report submitted to the High Criminal Court confirmed cases of abuse.[41] In addition to opposition activists, human rights defenders—including those affiliated with the Bahrain Human Rights Society, which generally enjoys fairly close ties with the government—have increasingly also been victims of abuse following peaceful demonstrations and advocacy efforts.[42] There have been no significant efforts on the part of the government to thoroughly investigate and punish those responsible for abuses, a fact condemned by the UN Human Rights Council during its 2008 Universal Periodic Review of Bahrain.[43]

According to the U.S. State Department, prisons generally met international human rights standards, though this was difficult to confirm as the International Committee of the Red Cross had not visited such facilities since 2000.[44] Nevertheless, while few reports of routine mistreatment of prisoners came to light between 2004 and 2007, some of the above-mentioned cases of alleged torture took place at prison facilities.

Bahrain's long tradition of petitioning the ruler to express public grievances has diminished in recent years, as such criticisms are expressed more frequently in speeches before the National Assembly or popular demonstrations. No significant petitions were submitted to the Royal Court between 2007 and 2009.[45]

The incidence of criminal violence and overall street crime remains low in Bahrain.[46] In August 2006, the king promulgated a new antiterrorism statute, the Protecting Society from Terrorist Acts Law. The statute permits the security services to hold anyone suspected of engaging in terrorism for up to 90 days without judicial review. The law's definition of "terrorist activity" remains vague, however, listing actions such as behavior that might "damage national unity" as punishable and allowing the death penalty to be imposed for actions that "disrupt provisions of the Constitution or laws, or prevent state enterprises or public authorities from exercising their duties."[47] Since its passage, the law has been applied against nonviolent critics of the government. In January 2009, three men, including the leader of al-Haqq, were arrested and threatened with charges of inciting terrorism, which could have carried a life sentence, though they were ultimately released through royal pardon three months later.[48]

The government has taken important steps in recent years to combat human trafficking, though reports persist of forced transportation and exploitation of household staff, construction laborers, and sex workers.[49] In January 2008, the government enacted comprehensive legislation that prohibits all forms of human trafficking and carries punishments ranging from substantial fines to lengthy prison terms. The judicial system subsequently handed down its first trafficking conviction in December 2008.[50]

The 2002 constitution states that "people are equal in human dignity, and citizens are equal before the law.... There shall be no discrimination among them on the basis of sex, origin, language, religion or creed." Nevertheless, legal protection for women's rights remains ambiguous. While Article 5 of the constitution guarantees full equality between men and women, the same article also notes that gender equality is bounded by "the provisions of Islamic canon law (Sharia)." Similarly, while Bahrain has adhered to the Convention on the Elimination of All Forms of Discrimination against Women (CEDAW), it has also stipulated that the treaty's implementation must conform to the tenets of Islamic law and that traditional restrictions on the movements of female family members be retained.

Eighteen women stood as candidates in the 2006 Chamber of Representatives elections. Only one woman, a progovernment candidate who ran unopposed, won a seat.[51] Women remain underrepresented in government positions, political parties, and the judicial system. Outside parliament, women have become increasingly organized and active in recent years. An informal group that calls itself the Women's Petition Committee has played a leading role in orchestrating public protests against the resurgence of Islamic law in family matters.[52] Discrimination against women persists in the workplace and legal system. The penal code does not specifically address violence against women. Incidents of violence often go unpunished, in part due to the fact that women rarely report such crimes, though the Batelco Care Center for Family Violence, which offers assistance to victims of domestic abuse, has reported an increased willingness to report mistreatment. While rape is punishable by life in prison and honor killings are banned, marital rape is not a crime under Bahraini law.[53]

Women are subject to discrimination in family matters such as divorce, child custody, and inheritance due to the absence of a codified family law and the handling of such matters in Sharia courts.[54] Attempts by the government to draw up a unified civil code to govern family affairs have generated concerted opposition from both Shiite and Sunni community leaders. As occurred in 2005,[55] a draft family law introduced to the National Assembly in December 2008 drew serious objections from the Shiite Islamic Council of Scholars, whose members demanded that any code regulating family matters be authorized by the highest authorities in the Shiite world, including Grand Ayatollah Ali Sistani in Iraq.[56] In May 2009 parliament passed a version of the law that will apply only to Sunnis.

The 2002 constitution stipulates that citizens enjoy protection against discrimination on the basis of religion. Nevertheless, members of the country's main religious group—Arabic speakers who follow the Shiite branch of the Islamic faith and who make up between one-half and two-thirds of the native-born population—face discrimination from Sunnis in general and the ruling family in particular. This also has socioeconomic implications: the poorest neighborhoods of Manama and the most dilapidated villages in the surrounding countryside are invariably inhabited by Shiites.

According to a report issued in February 2009 by the BCHR, Shiite citizens occupy no more than 13 percent of senior posts in the state bureaucracy, with those positions housed primarily in agencies responsible for social services.[57] Shiite citizens are largely excluded from the higher ranks of many key state agencies and ministries, although they are represented in the diplomatic corps and Constitutional Court. There are widespread reports that the Bahraini government denies citizenship to Shiites who meet legal requirements in order to maintain and enhance Sunni dominance in the country, while actively granting citizenship to non-Shiite foreigners in order to affect the electoral balance.[58]

Islam is the state religion and the government exerts direct control over religious practice. The government funds and monitors official religious institutions such as mosques, community centers, and courts, and has established a body to oversee clerical appointments.[59] The government has also sought to increase control over religious education. In January 2007, the Ministry of Justice and Islamic Affairs ordered all Islamic schools to obtain licenses and submit their curriculums to a state-affiliated Higher Council for Islamic Affairs for approval.[60] In 2007, the Ministry of Education announced it would develop a new mandatory religious education curriculum for all public schools that would focus on Islamic jurisprudence and de-emphasize radicalism.[61]

Although the government had previously been tolerant of Shiite religious freedom and expression, in recent years Shiite practices have drawn heightened state scrutiny. In January 2009, the Ministry of Justice and Islamic Affairs issued new regulations prohibiting preachers from making "any mention of people, institutions, or countries by their names or characteristics" during their weekly sermons.[62] The new regulations have been enforced against Shiite preachers and places of worship. In one incident following their promulgation, the Ministry of Justice and Islamic Affairs banned Friday evening prayers at the al-Sadiq mosque in Manama after security forces shut down a service led by al-Haqq activist Sheikh Abdul-Haidi al-Mokhodhur in late January 2009. SSF forces later attacked Shiites praying outside the mosque. By contrast, the BCHR has alleged government neglect in response to reports that some Sunni preachers, including MP Jassim al-Saeedi, emphasize sectarian hatred during their sermons.[63]

As popular unrest escalated in the spring of 2008, state officials intervened more directly in Sunni religious affairs as well. In June 2008, a prominent Sunni preacher, who also served as an independent Islamist MP, was removed from his post and transferred to a mosque in a predominantly Sunni district after appearing to criticize a highly respected Shiite scholar during a sermon.[64] Six months later, the Ministry of Justice and Islamic Affairs revoked his right to preach at any mosque.[65] The country's tiny Jewish and Christian communities are largely permitted to worship freely.

Members of foreign national communities are not subject to significant economic discrimination, although few of the hundreds of thousands of Indians, Pakistanis, Bangladeshis, Filipinos, and Palestinians who reside in the country have been granted citizenship. Most expatriates who have become citizens possess only third-class citizenship, which entitles them to bring cases before the courts but not to vote or run for elective office. After a Bangladeshi national was convicted of murdering his Bahraini supervisor in May 2008, the Ministry of the Interior announced plans to terminate the work permits of thousands of Bangladeshis.[66] The government lifted a brief ban on permits for unskilled Bangladeshis by July, however, while conditioning the suspension on adherence to the law.[67]

Bahrain's 2002 constitution guarantees "the freedom to form associations and unions . . . for lawful objectives and by peaceful means," with the Trade Unions Law of the same year providing additional legal structure. In October 2006, King Hamad further augmented labor rights by banning the dismissal of employees for engaging in trade union activities. Nevertheless, all trade unions are required to join the General Federation of Bahrain Trade Unions (GFBTU), which has reported that the Bahraini government has repeatedly refused to register a set of six unions, while prohibiting strikes within a broad swath of sectors defined as "essential services."[68]

The organizers of any public meeting must notify the head of public security three days in advance, so the official can determine whether a police presence will be necessary. Throughout 2007 and 2008, Bahraini officials repeatedly invoked this law to ban meetings and order the dispersal of unauthorized gatherings, significantly restricting freedom of assembly. The increased frequency of popular protests since the summer of 2006 has been accompanied by a return to violent suppression tactics on the part of the police and security services. Riot police have used tear gas, truncheons, and rubber bullets to break up demonstrations in districts around the capital, the most violent of which occurred in December 2007. In March 2009, the police and security services fired live ammunition into a group of protesters.[69]

RULE OF LAW 3.18

INDEPENDENT JUDICIARY	3.00
PRIMACY OF RULE OF LAW IN CIVIL AND CRIMINAL MATTERS	3.80
ACCOUNTABILITY OF SECURITY FORCES AND MILITARY TO CIVILIAN AUTHORITIES	2.25
PROTECTION OF PROPERTY RIGHTS	3.67

Extensive political, juridical, and economic prerogatives remain firmly in the hands of senior members of the ruling family. Members of the al-Khalifa are virtually exempt from civil and criminal law, although they answer to a family council headed by senior sheikhs. The king, acting in his capacity as head of the Higher Judicial Council, which oversees the judiciary, is involved in the appointment of all judges. Periodic royal pardons, including ones for imprisoned political opponents and activists, serve to undermine the independence and authority of the courts, reinforcing perceptions that political favors rather than legal principles underpin the criminal justice system.

Civil courts exercise jurisdiction over cases that involve civil, criminal, or commercial statutes. Islamic (Sharia) courts, divided into Sunni and Shiite branches, are responsible for adjudicating matters of personal status or inheritance. A Constitutional Court, consisting of a presiding judge and six associate judges, all appointed by the king, was created in 2002 with the authority to determine the constitutionality of laws and administrative regulations. In recent years, the courts have on occasion ruled against the government. In May 2006, a court forced the king's cousin to take down an illegally constructed wall.[70] In March 2007, the Constitutional Court issued a landmark decision in which it found unconstitutional a 1970 decree that permitted the state to appropriate private land for development projects. The government complied with the decision, placing certain projects on hold as the cabinet and parliament discussed new legislation to replace the overturned decree.[71] Nevertheless, these cases are largely the exception, and the judiciary's ability to rule against government officials and members of the royal family for more serious abuses of power remains severely restricted. As such, public officials are rarely prosecuted for wrongdoing. Decree 56 of 2002 continues to provide government officials immunity from investigation and prosecution for pre-2002 human rights abuses.[72]

The Bahraini justice system suffers from lengthy court delays due to understaffing, outdated procedures, and chronic lack of funding. In July 2009, the government established a committee headed by Deputy Prime Minister Jawad al-Arrayed to oversee judicial reforms aimed at improving efficiency. The committee will reportedly oversee the creation of specialized courts to help reduce a large case backlog. New education programs are also planned to train prosecutors and judges and adequately prepare them for appointments within the new courts.[73] Some local experts suggested, however, that reform should focus on the system's primary bottleneck, the five Execution Courts that must review and implement verdicts.[74]

Legal protection surrounding trial procedures has improved since a 2002 constitutional amendment that guarantees defendants the presumption of innocence until guilt is proven. Police are required to obtain a warrant prior to arrest, and detainees must be presented before the Office of the Public Prosecutor within 48 hours of being taken into custody. This right has generally been respected in practice, though disregarded in the cases of some political detainees. Detainees have the right to consult with an attorney and to be appointed government-provided counsel if unable to pay. Defendants are ensured an open trial in which they can present evidence and witnesses in their defense. Nevertheless, in practice, defendants are often detained for extended periods of time and denied family visits or access to counsel, particularly in the early stages of detention.

Members of the ruling family dominate the highest ranks of the military, while mid-level and junior officer posts are mostly occupied by expatriates, who remain in the country at the sole discretion of the government. Conventional police units are complemented by an extensive internal security apparatus. Although subject to civilian control, in recent years the political role of the security forces in repressing demonstrators at the government's behest has increased. Although the Ministry of the Interior and Bahrain Defense Forces employ their own police and military tribunals to dispense justice internally, there have been no reports of members of the police or security services being punished for inflicting harm on protesters or detainees.

The constitution protects private property and requires fair compensation in cases of expropriation for the public good. In practice, property rights continue to be susceptible to contravention by the al-Khalifa. Influential members of the ruling family routinely requisition tracts of productive agricultural land for commercial development. In recent years, influential sheikhs have also confiscated shoreline properties along the northern coast and attached them to lands reclaimed from the sea at public expense in order to yield valuable parcels of real estate. Such projects infringe not only on private property but also on lands that have long been considered community property by local residents.[75] After the authorities sold the island of Fasht al-Jarim to a consortium of foreign developers in the spring of 2007, representatives of al-Wefaq attempted to bring the sale up for debate in the National Assembly, but the speaker of the Chamber of Representatives ruled that debate on the issue should be postponed.[76]

ANTICORRUPTION AND TRANSPARENCY 2.38

ENVIRONMENT TO PROTECT AGAINST CORRUPTION	2.75
PROCEDURES AND SYSTEMS TO ENFORCE ANTICORRUPTION LAWS	2.00
EXISTENCE OF ANTICORRUPTION NORMS, STANDARDS, AND PROTECTIONS	2.25
GOVERNMENTAL TRANSPARENCY	2.50

In recent years—and especially since the 2006 elections—parliament and civil society groups have played an increasingly important oversight role in demanding greater transparency from the government. Together with official pronouncements condemning corruption and a small number of prosecutions of low-level officials, a degree of deterrence has been established at the lower ranks of the bureaucracy, reducing petty corruption. Few changes have been made, however, that tackle the structural aspects of the system that encourage corruption, and the high-level use of public funds for private benefit continues to occur with impunity.

It is hard to distinguish between the perquisites of office and corrupt administrative practices in Bahrain. High-ranking officials enjoy magnificent houses, servants, and expensive automobiles. Despite a growing private sector, state-run enterprises still make up a large proportion of the economy. Oil revenues flow directly into the central treasury, obviating the need for taxes to fund state agencies, and comprising an estimated 70 percent of government revenue. Bahrain ranked 43rd out of 180 countries on Transparency International's 2008 Corruption Perceptions Index.

In recent years, the government has taken some steps to counter corrupt practices in state-owned enterprises, including efforts to eliminate questionable business practices at Aluminum Bahrain and Bahrain Telecommunications. During 2008, inquiries were made into the operation of several key public enterprises at the instigation of the Economic Development Board (EDB), which is chaired by the crown prince. The investigation uncovered massive payments by the state-affiliated Arab Shipbuilding and Repair Yard to senior foreign executives.[77] Also at the urging of the EDB, in January 2008 the son of the long-serving prime minister was removed as head of the company operating the country's international airport; he nonetheless retained the post of head of the Department of Civil Aviation.[78] Despite such efforts, the Financial Audit Bureau's (FAB) 2008 report on the activities of state-owned enterprises found that 232 million dinars (US$615 million) in oil revenue was unaccounted for in 2008.[79]

Officials in Bahrain are not required to disclose their financial assets. Cabinet ministers are required to stop business activities within six months of taking up their official positions, but enforcement is sporadic. Bahrain continues to lack both comprehensive anticorruption laws and an independent anticorruption agency. The 2001 National Action Charter envisaged the creation of "an office for financial control and an office for administrative control," which would be charged with overseeing increased transparency among state institutions. These two agencies have yet to be established, and mention of them was omitted from the 2002 constitution. However, a 2002 decree created the FAB, which is charged with overseeing state revenues and expenditures.[80] Though primarily accountable to the king, the quality of the FAB's annual reports has gradually improved since it began functioning in 2004. Although it is not authorized to review the expenditures of the royal family or the ministries of defense or interior, it has exposed instances of missing government funds, including in the oil sector.

Official commitment to combating corruption remains ambiguous. Although the crown prince in September 2007 announced the beginning of a campaign to eradicate official corruption and the prosecution of corrupt high officials, cases that have been prosecuted to date primarily involve junior-level employees rather than top officials.

Media outlets, blogs, and civil society groups (such as the Bahrain Transparency Society) have become more aggressive in airing information about alleged corruption. Nonetheless, public discussion of corruption by members of the ruling family remains taboo. In May 2009, a reporter for *Al-Wasat* newspaper was brought before the Office of the Public Prosecutor on charges of defaming the Civil Service Bureau in an article that detailed alleged irregularities in overtime payments for senior executives in the public sector.[81] Corruption is not prevalent within public educational institutions.

Under pressure from MPs, the government has become somewhat more transparent about its expenditures in recent years, but much opacity remains. Freedom of information legislation is not in place. Nonetheless, ministries are required to publish certain information related to their work and have generally cooperated with the FAB in producing accounts.

The government is required to submit its annual budget to the National Assembly for approval, though monitoring of expenditures is carried out by the FAB. The Chamber of Representatives has been more aggressive in reviewing proposed budgets, though these efforts have sometimes met with resistance from the government. In May 2007, several MPs put forward changes to the state budgeting process that would have enhanced transparency. When the proposal came to the floor for a vote, however, progovernment representatives absented themselves, leaving the body without a quorum.[82]

Procurement of government contracts has reportedly become more transparent, though the process remains closely linked to the government. In 2003, the government created, by royal decree, a tender board that meets weekly to screen all proposed projects. A cabinet minister appointed by the king heads the board; until mid-2009, the minister of oil and gas affairs held the position.

RECOMMENDATIONS

- Reintroduce the revised Press and Publications Law to the National Assembly, and press government allies in the Chamber of Representatives to support the proposed revisions.
- Follow standard procedures in granting citizenship to all persons, and end discrimination in favor of select individuals who hold positions in the military and security forces.
- Take firm steps to stop the use of violence in response to public protests, including rationalization of the protest permitting process and prosecution of state agents responsible for abuses.
- Abandon newly imposed restrictions on religious schools and Friday sermons, and adopt less coercive means, such as permanent dialogue councils comprised of religious leaders, to dampen sectarian conflict.
- Initiate a campaign to persuade progovernment members of both houses of the National Assembly of the virtues of implementing a civil family code that protects the rights of women in accordance with the 2002 Constitution.

- Publicly endorse the mission and activities of the Bahrain Transparency Society, and order all state officials and managers of public sector enterprises to comply with requests for information made by the Society.

NOTES

For URLs and endnote hyperlinks, please visit the *Countries at the Crossroads* homepage at http://freedomhouse.org/template.cfm?page=139&edition=8.

[1] Katja Niethammer, "Opposition Groups in Bahrain," in *Political Participation in the Middle East*, ed. Ellen Lust-Okar and Saloua Zerhouni (Boulder, Colo.: Lynne Rienner Press, 2008), 147.
[2] Abdulhadi Khalaf, "The Outcome of a Ten-Year Process of Political Reform in Bahrain," Arab Reform Brief No. 24, (Washington, D.C.: Carnegie Endowment for International Peace, December 2008), 6.
[3] Ibid.
[4] Hassan M. Fattah, "Report Cites Bid by Sunnis in Bahrain to Rig Elections," *International Herald Tribune*, October 2, 2006, 2.
[5] Ibid.
[6] "Bahraini Shiites Demand Investigation," *Daily Star* (Beirut), October 5, 2006; Clare Dunkley, "Clean Break, Dirty Tricks," *Middle East Economic Digest*, November 17–23, 2006.
[7] Jim Krane, "Bahrain Polls Crowded in Tense Elections, *Washington Post*, November 25, 2006.
[8] Habib Toumi, "Unions Hit Out at Ban on Strikes at 'Vital Facilities'," *Gulf News*, November 22, 2006.
[9] Dunkley, "Clean Break, Dirty Tricks"
[10] Sofie Bille and Elena Moroni, *Report on Elections in the Arab World 2006—A Human Rights Evaluation* (Amman, Jordan: Amman Center for Human Rights Studies, May 2, 2007).
[11] Krane, "Bahrain Polls Crowded in Tense Elections."
[12] F. Gregory Gause, "Bahrain Parliamentary Election Results," *International Journal of Middle East Studies* 39 (May 2007): 170–71; Habib Toumi, "Islamists Consolidate Bahrain Poll Sweep," *Gulf News*, December 4, 2006.
[13] Inter-Parliamentary Union, "Bahrain Majlis Al-Nuwab," Inter-Parliamentary Union home page.
[14] Habib Toumi, "Bahrain Opposition Storm to Poll Victory," *Gulf News*, November 27, 2006.
[15] Habib Toumi, "Bahrain King Appoints Liberal Upper Council to Offset Islamists," *Gulf News*, December 7, 2006.
[16] Habib Toumi, "Bahraini Panel Insists on Full Property Disclosure," *Gulf News*, January 15, 2008.
[17] Ibid.
[18] Mohammed Almezel, "MPs Shoot Down Anti-Terror Law," *Gulf News*, April 18, 2005.
[19] Mohammed Almezel, "Bahraini Parliament Upholds Amnesty Law," *Gulf News*, May 18, 2005.
[20] "Bahrain's al-Wifaq Loses Vote," *Bahrain Tribune*, April 9, 2008.
[21] "Bahrain Shia MPs Walk Out over Population Row," Reuters, May 14, 2008.
[22] Transparency International, *2008 Corruption Perceptions Index* (Berlin: Transparency International, September 22, 2008); World Bank, "Bahrain," in *Doing Business 2009:*

Comparing Regulation in 181 Economies (Washington, D.C.: World Bank, 2009).
23   Niethammer, "Opposition Groups," 152.
24   *Gulf States Newsletter*, September 2, 2005.
25   Human Rights Watch, "Bahrain," in *World Report 2009* (New York: Human Rights Watch, 2009).
26   Ibid.
27   "New Bahrain Press Law Ends Jail for Most Offences," Reuters, May 6, 2008; Habib Toumi, "Bahrain Moves to Scrap Jail Terms for Journalists," *Gulf News*, May 6, 2008.
28   International Federation of Journalists, *Breaking the Chains: Press Freedom Report 2009* (Brussels: International Federation of Journalists, 2009).
29   Article 19, "Bahrain: Article 19 Supports Collective Appeal for Stronger Protection of Freedom of Expression in Bahrain," press release, November 7, 2007; International Press Institute (IPI), "Bahrain," in *World Press Freedom Review* (Vienna: IPI, May 8, 2008).
30   "Bahrain: Where Bloggers Are Potent Troublemakers," *Los Angeles Times*, August 25, 2008.
31   Alexandra Sandels, "Bahrain Hit by Mass Web Censorship Campaign," Menassat, February 2, 2009.
32   Habib Toumi, "Bahrain Takes Tough Measures to Tackle Growing Violence," *Gulf News*, April 14, 2008.
33   "Bahrain: Blogger in Jail for Four Months," Reuters, March 29, 2008.
34   Mazen Mahdi, "Activists' Arrest Sparks Violent Protests in Bahrain," *Arab News*, February 3, 2007; Habib Toumi, "Tension Prevails a Day after Police Clash with Protesters," *Gulf News*, February 4, 2007.
35   Human Rights Watch, "Bahrain: Courts Try to Silence Women's Rights Activist," press release, June 2, 2005.
36   International Freedom of Expression Exchange (IFEX), "Women's Rights Activist Gahda Jamsheer Threatened, Media Ban Continues, Her Home Reportedly Put under Surveillance by State Security Agents," news release, February 6, 2009.
37   Toby Jones, "Bahrain: Must Be Election Season," Qahwa Sada Blog, October 12, 2006.
38   Amnesty International, "Bahrain," in *Amnesty International Annual Report 2008* (London: Amnesty International, 2009).
39   Ibid.
40   Ibid.
41   Bahrain Center for Human Rights, (BCHR), "Court-Appointed Medical Examiners Confirm Torture," news release, April 2008.
42   Front Line Defenders, "Bahrain: Deteriorating Situation for Human Rights Defenders," press release, March 2, 2009.
43   Islamic Human Rights Commission, *Bahrain: Submission to the UN Universal Periodic Review* (London: Islamic Human Rights Commission, March 10, 2008).
44   Bureau of Democracy, Human Rights, and Labor, "Bahrain," in *2008 Country Reports on Human Rights Practices* (Washington, D.C.: U.S. Department of State, February 25, 2009).
45   Bahrain Ministry of Foreign Affairs, *Draft Action Plan to Implement Bahrain's Pledges, Voluntary Commitments and UPR Outcomes* (Manama: Bahrain Ministry of Foreign Affairs, March 28, 2008).
46   Overseas Security Advisory Council, "Bahrain," in *2009 Crime and Safety Report* (Washington, D.C.: Overseas Security Advisory Council, March 2, 2009).
47   Edward Burke, "Bahrain: Reaching a Threshold," Working Paper 61 (Madrid: Fundación para las Relaciones Internacionales y el Diálogo Exterior [FRIDE], June 2008), 20.
48   *Gulf States Newsletter*, February 2, 2009; "22 Activists Speak for 1st Time at Bahrain

Trial," *Kuwait Times*, March 26, 2009; *Gulf States Newsletter*, April 20, 2009.
[49] Bureau of Democracy, Human Rights, and Labor, "Bahrain," in *2008 Country Reports on Human Rights Practices*.
[50] Office to Monitor and Combat Trafficking in Persons, "Bahrain," in *Trafficking in Persons Report 2008* (Washington, D.C: U.S. Department of State, 2008).
[51] Burke, *Bahrain*, 6.
[52] Ibid., 22.
[53] Freedom House, "Bahrain," in *Women's Rights in the Middle East and North Africa, Gulf Edition 2009* (New York: Freedom House, February 11, 2009).
[54] Ibid.
[55] Sandy Russell Jones, "The Battle over Family Law in Bahrain," *Middle East Report*, no. 242 (Spring 2007): 33.
[56] "Bahrain Shiite Clergy Feud with Parliament over Family Law," Associated Press, January 3, 2009.
[57] Women Living under Muslim Laws, "Bahrain: Discrimination and Sectarian Oppression on the Rise," news release, February 27, 2009.
[58] "Q&A: Bahrain Election," British Broadcasting Corporation, November 23, 2006.
[59] International Coalition for Religious Freedom, "Bahrain," in *Religious Freedom World Report* (Washington, D.C.: International Coalition for Religious Freedom, 2008).
[60] Habib Toumi, "Clergy Up in Arms over Religious School Decision," *Gulf News*, January 16, 2007.
[61] Bureau of Democracy, Human Rights, and Labor, "Bahrain," in *International Religious Freedom Report 2009* (Washington, D.C.: U.S. Department of State, October 26, 2009).
[62] "Shiite Scholars Prohibit Commitment to Religious Preaching Restraints," *al-Arabiyya*, February 10, 2009; Habib Toumi, "Row of Fatwa on Sermons in Bahrain," *Gulf News*, February 11, 2009.
[63] BCHR, "Bahrain: An Oppressive Campaign against Shia," news release, January 15, 2009.
[64] Salman al-Dawasari, "Bahrain: Salafi Sheikh Suspended from Preaching Following Angry March," *Al-Sharq al-Awsat*, June 21, 2008.
[65] Habib Toumi, "Controversial Friday Sermon Preacher in Bahrain Suspended," *Gulf News*, January 5, 2009.
[66] "Labour Row," *Economist*, June 23, 2008.
[67] "Bahrain Lifts Ban on Work Permits," *Bangladesh News*, July 25, 2008.
[68] Human Rights Watch, "Bahrain."
[69] "Police 'Use Guns' at Bahrain Protests," British Broadcasting Corporation, April 3, 2009; Digby Lidstone, "A Kingdom That Burns by Night," *Financial Times*, April 8, 2009.
[70] Democracy Coalition Project, *Bahrain* (Washington, D.C.: Democratic Coalition Project, 2006).
[71] "Bahrain: Land Law Delays," Zawya, April 11, 2008.
[72] Human Rights Watch, "Bahrain."
[73] "Judicial Reforms to Clear Backlog," *Gulf Daily News*, July 25, 2009.
[74] Ibid.
[75] "Fishermen to Continue Reclamation Protests," *Gulf Daily News*, July 14, 2008.
[76] *Gulf States Newsletter*, June 8, 2007.
[77] *Gulf States Newsletter*, July 28, 2008.
[78] Simeon Kerr, "Bahrain Crown Prince Cuts Lines of Patronage," *Financial Times*, February 24, 2008.
[79] Bureau of Democracy, Human Rights, and Labor, "Bahrain," in *2008 Country Reports on*

Human Rights Practices.

[80] Carnegie Endowment for International Peace and FRIDE, "Bahrain," in *Arab Political Systems: Baseline Information and Reforms* (Washington, D.C./Madrid: Carnegie Endowment for International Peace and FRIDE, March 6, 2008).

[81] Bahrain Center for Human Rights and IFEX, "Journalist Summoned for Allegedly Defaming Civil Service Bureau," news release, May 8, 2009.

[82] "Clean Up Act!" bahrainit.tv, May 3, 2006; *Gulf States Newsletter*, June 3, 2007.

BRAZIL

CAPITAL: Brasilia
POPULATION: 191.5 million
GNI PER CAPITA (PPP): $10,070

SCORES	2006	2010
ACCOUNTABILITY AND PUBLIC VOICE:	N/A	4.91
CIVIL LIBERTIES:	N/A	4.85
RULE OF LAW:	N/A	4.06
ANTICORRUPTION AND TRANSPARENCY:	N/A	3.63

(scores are based on a scale of 0 to 7, with 0 representing weakest and 7 representing strongest performance)

David Fleischer

INTRODUCTION

Brazil has been an independent nation since 1822, and a republic governed by a federalist constitution since 1889. Starting in 1930, Getúlio Vargas led a period of considerable autocratic modernization and incipient industrialization. Vargas was toppled by the military in December 1945, and the 1946 constitution installed a democratic regime. Vargas returned by direct election as president in 1950, but his populist regime ended in August 1954 when he committed suicide rather than again be removed by the military. In 1955, Juscelino Kubitschek was elected president, promising "50 years of progress in 5," with a new intense phase of import-substitution-industrialization and the construction of the new inland capital Brasília.

The 1960s and 1970s were characterized by intense rural-urban migration. In March 1964 the military removed President João Goulart and proceeded to rule Brazil until March 1985. Unlike other military regimes in South America, Brazil held congressional elections every four years and political parties were allowed to operate, though with severe restrictions. After a prolonged 10-year "political transition," democracy finally returned when, in January 1985, the Electoral College chose Brazilian Democratic Movement Party (PMDB) member Tancredo Neves as president. Neves died before taking office and Vice President José Sarney completed the five-year mandate. During this period,

---

David Fleischer is emeritus professor of Political Science at the University of Brasília and a founding member of Transparency Brazil. He received his Ph.D. from the University of Florida (1972) and was visiting professor at the UFMG (1969–1971) and The George Washington University (1997). He served in the Peace Corps in Minas Gerais, Brazil (1962–1964).

a new constitution was approved in 1988, but rampant inflation inhibited development. On November 15, 1989, the first direct elections for president since 1960 were held and Fernando Collor de Mello of the Party of National Reconstruction (PRN) narrowly defeated the Workers' Party (PT) candidate. However, Collor was impeached by the National Congress in December 1992 following a corruption scandal.

In October 2002, PT candidate Luiz Ignácio "Lula" da Silva was elected president following the eight-year presidency of Fernando Henrique Cardoso of the Brazilian Social Democracy Party (PSDB). This marked a new phase of maturity for the Brazilian political system: peaceful alternation in power between the two main political parties. Lula, a poor migrant from the northeast and former labor union leader, had lost the 1994 and 1998 elections to the renowned sociologist, former senator, and finance minister Cardoso.[1]

Lula rose to power as head of the metalworkers' labor union in São Paulo in the late 1970s and in 1980 helped found the leftist PT, which favored a large state role in the economy, redistribution of wealth, and nationalist policies. After the 1994 election, the PT became less radical and concentrated on electing more officials and eventually achieving the presidency.[2] Meanwhile, during the Cardoso presidency, nationalist elements of the constitution were altered to permit privatization of many state enterprises, and other market-friendly measures were adopted. However, both foreign debt and unemployment soared, especially after a currency devaluation in 1999. In the 2002 campaign, the PT assumed a more market-friendly posture, and Lula defeated PSDB candidate José Serra in a runoff with 62.5 percent of the vote.

As president, Lula shocked orthodox PT militants by maintaining austere orthodox macroeconomic policies. This belt tightening helped the economy expand by 5.2 percent in 2004. The government suffered a major debacle in 2005 with the *mensalão* scandal, a scheme involving monthly payments to various parties and their deputies in return for progovernment votes. Although Lula was not personally implicated, the scandal hurt his approval ratings, which sank to 28 percent in December 2005. However, fears regarding reelection prospects diminished in early 2006 as Lula's standing began to improve in the polls.[3] When balloting was held in October 2006, Lula fell just short in the first round but topped PSDB candidate Geraldo Alckmin in the runoff with 60.8 percent.

Growth continued at higher than 5 percent in 2007 and 2008. Despite a subsequent sharp slowdown caused by the global financial crisis, as of mid-2009 Lula's popularity remains high, aided by sustained economic growth that has considerably improved both Brazilian self-confidence and the nation's international standing. Over the past seven years, the country has experienced considerable upward social mobility, and extreme poverty declined from 17.3 percent of the population in 2001 to 10.2 percent in 2007.[4] Perhaps no policy has been more successful than the conditional cash transfer program known as *bolsa família* (family stipend), which provides US$50 per month for low-income families who keep children vaccinated and in school. By the 2006 elections, this program reached some 11 million families—and importantly, some 40 million voters in an electorate of 125.8 million.[5]

Despite this progress, Brazil has some persistent social and governance problems. As a coalition-based presidential system, maintaining the government support base requires significant bargaining, which encourages corruption, a vice also present in many other governance realms. Violence by organized criminals is a major problem in large cities and provokes severe police abuses. The 27 state governors possess a level of autonomy sometimes not matched by accountability. Land reform remains a difficult question, with actors from giant agribusinesses to landless peasants seeking new territory along an enormous and ambiguously titled frontier. Moreover, Brazil still has one of the most unequal income distributions in the world, as well as notable racial disparities. Nonetheless, a combination of structural and policy shifts have left the country in a position to confront these issues. As Brazil's international prominence rises, success or failure to achieve sustainable social and economic progress will be on display for the world to see.

ACCOUNTABILITY AND PUBLIC VOICE 4.91

FREE AND FAIR ELECTORAL LAWS AND ELECTIONS	5.25
EFFECTIVE AND ACCOUNTABLE GOVERNMENT	4.25
CIVIC ENGAGEMENT AND CIVIC MONITORING	6.00
MEDIA INDEPENDENCE AND FREEDOM OF EXPRESSION	4.14

Brazil has a generally free and fair election system. Voters go to the polls every two years, alternating between municipal and general elections. Voting is obligatory for most Brazilians. In the October 2008 municipal elections, the electorate numbered 130,469,549 eligible voters,[6] and turnout was 85.46 percent. Balloting is overseen by a national election governance body, the National Election Court (TSE), with regional election courts (TREs) in each state and election judges and registry offices at the municipal level.[7] The TSE, which commands high respect from both the population and elites, has seven judges with two-year mandates on rotation from the Supreme Court (STF), the top federal appeals court (STJ), and the Brazilian Bar Association (OAB).

Occasionally, the TSE engages in what some observers consider the judicialization of politics, determining election norms that should be the prerogative of Congress. For example, in response to a rash of party switching in 2002–2003 and 2006–2007 that facilitated President Lula's efforts to construct a coalition in Congress, in 2007 the TSE decided that the mandate of those elected belongs to the party that elected them and not the individual officeholder. Hence, elected officeholders who switch parties could lose their mandates under some circumstances. Candidates for president, governor, and mayor must receive an absolute majority of the valid vote or face a second-round runoff election three weeks later.

In spite of Lula's 2006 reelection, the PT dropped to 83 deputies (from 91 in 2002) and 11 senators (versus 14 in 2002). The Lula bloc in the Chamber of Deputies was similar at 321, while the opposition declined from 170 to 153. In the Senate, the Lula bloc declined from 48 to 44, while the opposition increased 2 seats to 34. The campaign was considered free and fair.[8] Since the mid-1990s, four parties—the PMDB, PT, PSDB and the Liberal Front Party (PFL), which in 2007 changed its name to the Democrats (DEM)—have held the largest blocs in Congress. In the 2008 municipal elections, the PT and PMDB secured gains, while the two major opposition parties, the PSDB and PFL/DEM, suffered declines.[9] This result was typical of gains accrued by the parties in power at the federal level.[10]

Each state elects three senators by simple majority to eight-year terms in alternation. In 2009, 11 parties are represented in the Senate. The Chamber of Deputies has 513 deputies, with a minimum of 8 from small states and a maximum of 70 for the state of São Paulo. This produces skewed regional representation; very small states such as Amapá and Roraima, proportionate to their populations, should have only one deputy, whereas Brazil's largest state should have a 120-deputy delegation. The election of state and federal deputies uses an open-list proportional representation system. Because there is no minimum required percentage, in 2006, 21 parties elected at least one deputy. This system produces some unexpected results. In some states, a candidate with 200,000 votes is not elected, but in other states a candidate with 500 votes is elected.

Election finance comes from several sources, including a party fund and seven weeks of free television and radio time distributed by the TSE, proportionate to each party's votes received in the last election. Contributions from individuals and firms are capped by law, but perhaps 80 percent of campaign finance comes from off-the-books (*caixa dois*) contributions not officially reported to the TSE. The TREs often unquestioningly accept suspiciously low spending declarations from candidates without investigation. The election courts lack sufficient material and human resources to monitor contributions, which are often decisive in elections and bring great influence to private sector groups. Congress, with its own vested interests in mind, has never approved stronger laws to this effect. Another indirect form of financing comes from "cultural contributions" made by public and private companies to nongovernmental organizations (NGOs) and organizations linked to certain parties and candidates—which then expect budget allocations back to the donors.

Citizens who have been convicted in court are allowed to run for office in Brazil until their last appeal has been exhausted. Thus, many become candidates in hopes of gaining parliamentary immunity. Politicians are judged exclusively at the Supreme Court. In 2008, 40 percent of Brazil's 513 federal deputies had cases pending with the courts.[11] This hurts Congress's credibility and makes it more difficult to fulfill its role of checking the executive. Cases most frequently involve tax evasion but also include money laundering, fraud, corruption, and even murder.

Election courts are empowered to remove from office officials who violate laws prohibiting the "abuse of private and public economic power." Two of the 27 governors elected in 2006 were removed in early 2009 after defeated candidates brought cases alleging vote buying and illegal use of state governments' human and material resources.

Brazil's system of checks and balances is patterned roughly on the U.S. model. The president has line item veto power and Congress hardly ever overrides his vetoes. Very few of the president's 25,000 political appointments must be confirmed by the Senate. To a large extent, the president dominates the congressional agenda via party coalitions whose cohesion is maintained through the distribution of key appointments and budget appropriations to parties and individual legislators.[12] The STF on occasion rules that decisions by Congress and the executive are unconstitutional, and both other branches abide by these high court decisions.

The civil service is recruited by competitive public exams and has career and promotion plans detailed by law. In spite of a large number of political appointees, Brazil is considered to have a high-quality, well-trained permanent bureaucracy. Once a public servant's status becomes permanent, it is very difficult to effect removal or dismissal except via complicated administrative procedures. However, the large number of confidence appointees means that bureaucrats are subject to political pressures. For example, in 2009, the first woman to head the Federal Tax Service (SRF), Lina Maria Vieira, was summarily dismissed by the finance minister because she had implemented a broad anti-tax evasion policy against large firms and banks, including firms controlled by the family of powerful Senator José Sarney.[13] In addition, nepotism remains a problem; when the STF in August 2008 issued an edict prohibiting nepotism in hiring, the resulting revelations of the extent of such hires caused a scandal that lasted into August 2009.[14]

Brazil has a very large and well-developed civil society. Civic groups and NGOs are allowed to testify and comment on pending legislation, and their efforts receive considerable coverage in the media. However, the influence or impact of these efforts is spotty. On certain issues, such as environmental protection, press coverage has some impact. International NGOs such as the World Wildlife Foundation and Greenpeace are very active in Brazil. Civic groups are also active in the annual budget process but have little impact on the joint budget committee. At the municipal level, NGOs and civic groups exercise more influence, especially in the south and southeast regions. Good governance groups have an increasingly vocal presence in Brazil.

In general, NGOs are free from government pressure, although they must file with the SRF every year to maintain their nonprofit status. In 2009, the PSDB and DEM installed a parliamentary commission of inquiry (CPI) to investigate the activities of and federal funding for NGOs and civil society public interest organizations (OSCIPs) during Lula's first term. Since 2001, Senator Mozarildo Cavalcanti (PTB-Roraima) has been denouncing NGOs, especially transnational groups, that he deems "enemies of the Amazon region" and pressuring for their exclusion by the federal government.[15] NGO activists are subject to threats and intimidation, and many have been killed because of their militancy, especially in land tenure conflicts. Notable examples are Chico Mendes, the leader of rubber tappers in the state of Acre, murdered in December 1988, and Dorothy Stang, an American nun murdered in Anapu, Pará in February 2005. Attempts to convict Vitalmiro Bastos de Moura (the farmer who allegedly ordered Stang's murder) have not been successful, illustrating the difficulties in achieving justice in such cases.

Although the Lula government is frequently dissatisfied with media coverage, it strongly supports constitutional and legal protections for freedom of expression and media freedom. Brazil still has some laws and decrees left over from the military regime, including, until recently, a draconian 1967 press law that limited journalism work to those with a BA degree in social communications. The law also contained articles that inhibited freedom of expression by the press and journalists, with fines and prison terms for defamation, libel, and slander. In February 2008, STF minister Carlos Ayres de Britto issued a temporary injunction suspending a large portion of the law, and in April 2009 the full court abolished it entirely.[16] Before the press law was overturned, criminal prosecutions for libel and defamation were common.

Civil defamation complaints are also often filed by aggrieved subjects of media reports. One of Brazil's major press freedom issues is that courts frequently impose censorship on media outlets in such cases. A notable incident of prior newspaper censorship occurred in July 2009, after federal police indicted Fernando Sarney, the son of Senate president José Sarney, on various corruption-related charges. On July 30, Federal District Supreme Court president Dácio Vieira (a friend of the Sarney family) issued an injunction imposing prior censorship on any reporting of Fernando's indictment in *O Estado de São Paulo*, one of Brazil's major daily newspapers.[17]

Intimidation and attacks against journalists remain a problem as well, especially for reporters investigating crime and corruption in rural areas. The most notorious episode was the murder of TV Globo journalist Tim Lopes in June 2002 while he was investigating the use of child prostitutes by drug traffickers in Rio de Janeiro.[18] In 2008 two journalists were held and tortured by a Rio militia. A 2009 Committee to Protect Journalists report warned of continued impunity in five of the eight cases of dead journalists over the previous decade.[19]

Brazil's presidency has an annual budget allocation of around US$600 million for official publicity that is used by state agencies to promote their activities and achievements. In 2008, this propaganda machine reached 4,417 media outlets. Such revenue is hotly sought after by the Brazilian media as an important contribution to their bottom lines. This mechanism is also practiced by state and larger city governments.[20] To a certain extent this advertising influences media policies and opinions. State governors, especially, exercise control over local newspapers through advertising.

Media ownership is highly concentrated, especially in the broadcast sector, and owners use their outlets to further personal interests. Many important politicians own media outlets in their home states, which are used to further their political and economic interests and attack their enemies. In August 2009, federal police and prosecutors indicted leaders of the Universal Church of the Kingdom of God (IURD) for illegally siphoning off contributions to finance the church-owned media empire, Record TV and radio network, which is in fierce competition with the dominant Globo TV and media network.[21] Following the indictment, both networks used considerable portions of their evening news programs to attack each other.

The federal government owns the Brazilian Communication Firm, which operates a news agency, plus official television and radio stations. However, the audience ratings for TV Brasil are extremely low, as are those of other federal and state broadcast channels. The federal government still maintains a one-hour obligatory radio network program carried by all radio stations called the Voice of Brazil, broadcast every weeknight. Access to the internet suffers few restrictions, although some limitations were imposed on campaigning via social networking sites during the 2008 municipal elections.[22]

CIVIL LIBERTIES 4.85

PROTECTION FROM STATE TERROR, UNJUSTIFIED IMPRISONMENT, AND TORTURE	3.50
GENDER EQUITY	4.33
RIGHTS OF ETHNIC, RELIGIOUS, AND OTHER DISTINCT GROUPS	4.25
FREEDOM OF CONSCIENCE AND BELIEF	6.67
FREEDOM OF ASSOCIATION AND ASSEMBLY	5.50

Although both the Cardoso and Lula governments made advances on human rights, certain sensitive cases from the military regime (1964–1985) have yet to be revealed. In 1996, it was estimated that there were 358 deaths during this period, including 138 disappearances.[23] As part of the final stage of transition from the military regime, Congress granted a general amnesty to both sides: military personnel and the regime's civilian defenders, as well as opponents who attacked the government through armed guerrilla actions.[24] In August 2001, an Amnesty Commission was installed at the Ministry of Justice to examine requests for amnesty and compensation for those who suffered persecution during the period. By 2007, 29,079 cases had been analyzed, with another 28,558 on the agenda. President Lula, his chief of staff Dilma Rousseff, and former chief of staff José Dirceu were among those who received amnesty and monetary compensation.[25] Generally, public opinion favors the truth, amnesty, and compensation process, but only the most notorious cases get media coverage.

It was assumed by most that the 1979 amnesty precluded any trials of military personnel involved in the torture, persecution, and killing of antimilitary activists. However, civil suits have been filed against some known torturers. In the case filed in 2007 against former army colonel Carlos Alberto Brilhante Ustra, the government assumed his defense in a São Paulo court.[26] As of mid-2009, there is a movement to alter the amnesty law to allow prosecution of those accused of perpetrating torture during the military era.

Abuses including torture and even death at the hands of state agents remain one of Brazil's most pressing human rights issues, although the victims are no longer political. Confronted with well-armed, lethal urban gangs, the police have been accused of seeking to cut corners in ways that lead to rights violations. In Rio de Janeiro, for example, 1,330 deaths at the hands of police were registered in 2007 and another 1,137 in 2008.[27] Although these police killings were recorded as "acts of resistance," the UN Special Rapporteur for Extrajudicial Killings has reported that a significant portion appeared to have been executions.[28] Nor is the human dignity of prison inmates well respected. State and federal prisons are overcrowded and most prisoners lack legal assistance. Violence and sexual abuse are common. Trials are slow, and prisoners often remain incarcerated after their sentence has expired for lack of an adequate control system. In addition, leaders of Brazil's numerous large organized crime organizations, such as the First Capital Command (PCC) in São Paulo and the Red Command (CV) in Rio de Janeiro, maintain command from behind prison walls via cell phones and visits by couriers. After these privileges were rescinded in 2006, the PCC organized an "uprising" in the city of São Paulo, with scores of attacks on police barracks and outposts that left at least 150 people dead.

These issues are both caused by and symptoms of crime, which remains one of Brazil's major social maladies. The number of homicides in Brazil reached a peak of 51,043 in 2003 before steadily declining to 42,179 in 2008. However, a study compiled by the Brazilian Forum for Public Security contrasted a decrease in homicides in larger cities with an increase in smaller interior cities. The most significant reduction was in the state of São Paulo, where killings decreased 7.8 percent between 2007 and 2008.[29] Adolescents are particularly at risk. A recent study of 267 cities found a national homicide rate of 200 per 100,000 for youths between 12 and 18.[30] Other crimes, including kidnapping and armed robbery, also present major challenges to authorities in many cities. Indeed, the prevalence of such crime and the impunity for most criminals is one reason the public has not demanded more drastic action to decrease the volume of police abuses.

In 2007, the Lula government created the National Program of Public Security with Citizenship (Pronasci) within the Ministry of Justice to initiate social programs, train police officers, and offer special stipends for police operating in dangerous areas. Police in São Paulo affirm that the decrease in the homicide rates is due to improved management and higher imprisonment rates. Others feel that the reduction in conflicts between rival organized crime groups explain the lower violence, because the PCC has consolidated its control in the state.

When abuses by state-level civil and military police occur, citizens have the right to seek justice and file a complaint or criminal suit, usually through a public defender, but a police inquest might also be installed. Occasionally, the police involved are demoted, expelled from the force, or imprisoned, but such cases are rare due to numerous problems ranging from lack of cooperation within the police to poor coordination among the various agencies involved in investigations.[31] Unlike most Latin American countries, Brazil has no independent national human rights ombudsman. In April 1997, the Cardoso government created, within the Ministry of Justice, the National Secretariat for Human Rights, renamed the Special Secretariat for Human Rights (SEDH) in 2003. This unit monitors human rights issues and coordinates policy across branches of government, focusing on vulnerable sectors of society. In addition, a majority of states in Brazil now have police ombudsmen located in state capitals. However, the ombudsmen do not have independent investigative capacity and turn over complaints to the internal affairs divisions of state police forces or state prosecutors.[32] In practice, the poor have much less access to receive redress, especially in rural areas.

Successive Brazilian governments have generally refrained from using state power to persecute political opponents. There are exceptions at the state and local levels, where opposition newspapers are harassed, or firms owned by opposition leaders are subjected to strict tax audits. Arbitrary arrests of political and economic opponents also occur mostly at the state and local level, but judges usually are quick to grant habeas corpus requests by defense lawyers or public defenders. This depends on the economic status of the person who has been arrested.

More frequent are arbitrary arrests of those suspected of regular criminal offenses. It is common for persons accused of crimes to be imprisoned for long periods without trial, especially in the case of the poor. The justice system is severely overloaded; absent legal assistance, the poor languish in prison until their case comes to trial. Between July 2008 and July 2009, a National Council of Justice (CNJ) task force reviewed 28,052 cases in 13 states and freed 4,781 prisoners held without trial for extended periods, including 310 minors.[33] The task force plans to complete its survey in the remaining 14 states and elaborate new guidelines and rules to ameliorate these problems.

Over the last 10 years, the federal police has conducted investigations of international human trafficking, including women destined for prostitution in Europe, the kidnapping of children for "placement" with families overseas, and the illegal extraction of organs for transplant. Similar trafficking cases also occur internally.[34] In addition, Labor Ministry investigators frequently discover and sometimes prosecute cases of semi-slave labor in rural areas, as well as the exploitation of illegal immigrants in urban areas.[35]

Brazilian law ensures that both men and women are entitled to all civil and political rights, and the state has taken some steps to ensure effective protections for women. In 1985, President Sarney created the National Council for

Women's Rights (CNDM). The Special Secretariat for Women's Policies (SPM) was established by Lula on his first day in office in January 2003. In August 2006, Congress passed the Maria da Penha Law, which criminalized domestic violence in accordance with Article 226 of the constitution.[36] Over the past three years, this law has slowly been enforced in most states to reduce what remain high levels of domestic abuse. By 2008, states and cities had established 386 special police precincts to deal with cases involving women.[37] These precincts are staffed by female police officers, as women seeking to enforce their rights had been frequently ridiculed and humiliated by male police officers.

Brazil features a 30 percent quota for women candidates on the open lists for deputy. However, because 98 percent of the electorate votes for an individual rather than the party list, just 45 women—9 percent of the total—were elected as federal deputies in 2006, and 11 of 81 senators.[38] Women have gained access to the judiciary with appointments to the superior courts. Ellen Gracie Northfleet, appointed to the STF in 2000, served as STF president in 2006–2008.

Protection against gender discrimination in private sector employment is more difficult. According to the 2007 National Survey Sample of Housing Units (PNAD), the average salary for women was 33.9 percent lower than the average for men.[39] In spite of the data for the private sector routinely collected by government agencies, no efforts have been made to correct this situation. Some firms require younger women to present a doctor's certificate that they have had their fallopian tubes tied, thus guaranteeing that they will not take a six-month maternity leave with pay, as required by labor legislation.

Brazilians consider their nation to be a "racial democracy," and many observers believe that this myth long prevented Brazil from undertaking an honest reckoning with the realities of racism. There are many laws that prohibit racial discrimination, but much informal discrimination still exists. The 2006 PNAD described the racial composition of Brazil's population as 49.9 percent white, 6.9 percent black, and 42.6 percent pardo, or mixed race, with most of the rest Asian/Indian.[40] A 1995 poll found that 89 percent of the sample agreed that "whites discriminate against blacks in Brazil"; the response was almost the same (91 percent) in 2008.[41] Brazil's indigenous population is very small—734,000 in the 2000 census—but indigenous populations occupy significant territory and are involved in sensitive legal issues (see Rule of Law).[42]

Brazil has many antidiscrimination laws and policies. In 2003, Lula created a special cabinet-level position for the promotion of racial equality. Many universities integrate affirmative action criteria in their entrance exams that favor Afro-Brazilians, members of indigenous groups, and the poor. However, this practice has not been confirmed by law, and various groups have challenged these "racial quotas" in federal courts; they may soon be tested at the STF.[43]

In the public sector, quotas have been implemented in some ministries. The Ministry of Justice, for example, has a 20 percent quota for Afro-Brazilians, but in reality these measures have not been very effective. In the private sector, there is considerable disguised discrimination in hiring and salary levels. A Ministry of Planning report in 2008 revealed that white men make nearly twice the monthly income of Afro men and nearly three times that of Afro women, a pay gap that stands when adjusted for equal work and similar qualifications.[44] The state has legislation banning such discriminatory practices, but in practice these customs are entrenched.

Although Brazil has traditionally been more tightly linked to the Catholic Church than any other religion, there are no restrictions on the practice of religion, and the government does not take religion into account when making political appointments. The Vatican is seeking to establish a new agreement with Brazil to guarantee religious instruction in all public schools and gain new tax exemptions. The Catholic Church also has radio stations, but only one cable TV station. There are a few Roman Catholic priests in Congress, but the Church places restrictions on their candidacies.

Evangelical Christian churches have expanded in Brazil since 1960, and 43 evangelical deputies and senators were elected in 2006, down from 60 in the 2002 balloting. The practices of some evangelical churches, which are not hierarchical like the Catholic Church, have come under scrutiny. As noted previously, the practices of the large and influential IURD have led to criminal indictments.

The state guarantees the freedom of association and the right of assembly. The only restriction on public assembly is the need to request a parade permit in advance of marches along public thoroughfares; these permits are sometimes denied. Protests are common in urban areas, and public demonstrations occasionally become tense, especially when a countergroup is present. At times these protests become violent and the destruction of property and looting of stores ensues, at which point the police intervene.

Labor unions remain strong in Brazil, especially for industrial workers, whose strikes can bring entire sectors to a standstill. The Lula government is protective of labor unions and sensitive to their demands. Nonetheless, trade unions are not fully free and independent in Brazil insofar as a specific category of workers can be represented by only one union in each municipality. Pressure to break this singular representation rule faces resistance from labor unions. All public and private employees have one day's salary deducted each year as their obligatory "labor contribution." Union organizers are subject to violence in rural areas.

RULE OF LAW   4.06

INDEPENDENT JUDICIARY	5.00
PRIMACY OF RULE OF LAW IN CIVIL AND CRIMINAL MATTERS	3.40
ACCOUNTABILITY OF SECURITY FORCES AND MILITARY TO CIVILIAN AUTHORITIES	3.50
PROTECTION OF PROPERTY RIGHTS	4.33

The Brazilian judiciary is considered generally independent and impartial, at least at the federal level. First-level federal judges, who are well trained, are recruited by competitive public exams that are free of political interference. Appointments to the federal regional courts, the STJ, and the Supreme Court are by presidential nomination, subject to confirmation by the Senate.

However, the justice system still faces serious problems, particularly on the state level. As of August 2009, the CNJ was investigating the possible removal of 107 federal and state judges for corruption.[45] After some 15 years of deliberation, under pressure from the executive branch and despite strong opposition from the judiciary, Congress finally approved a judicial reform package in 2004. This reform established the CNJ and an equivalent body for public prosecutors.[46] Since 2005, the CNJ has been reviewing and analyzing the administration of justice in federal and state courts and has suspended some judges. Most observers suggest that the CNJ has performed well so far but faces many long-term challenges.

Presidential appointments to the higher federal courts are never rejected by the Senate. Since 2003, for example, Lula has appointed 7 of the 11 members of the Supreme Court. Nonetheless, the STF has maintained proper distance and independence from government pressures. STF sessions are broadcast live on cable television, so the public occasionally witnesses some lively verbal exchanges among judges. One such spat occurred in April 2009, when STF president Gilmar Mendes was accused by Judge Joaquim Barbosa—the first Afro-Brazilian appointed to the high court—of destroying Brazilian justice.[47] This transparency in STF deliberations has increased public awareness of judicial operations and procedures, including conflicts between judges.

The executive and legislative branches generally comply with judicial decisions. Members of Congress complain about intervention by the judiciary to "impose" rules, but this occurs in the absence of adequate legislation by Congress itself. Opposition parties in Congress frequently contest procedural decisions by the ruling bloc via a Direct Action for Unconstitutionality (ADIn) at the Supreme Court, which is an important tool for combating abusive actions by the government coalition. Other plaintiffs, including professional associations such as the OAB and state agencies such as the Public Ministry, also make effective use of ADIns.[48]

Under Brazil's legal system, accused criminals are presumed innocent until proven guilty—all the way until the final appeal has been exhausted. This system permits literally hundreds of appeals and other legal maneuvers that competent and high-priced lawyers can string out for years. If the accused is a first-time defendant, the judge will often grant release during the appeal process, although in practice this generally applies only to those of high socioeconomic status. Generally, citizens receive a fair and public hearing, but it is rarely timely. All defendants have the right to independent counsel, but the poor must depend on public defenders, of which there is a shortage in almost all states. In general, federal prosecutors are independent of political manipulation, but this is not always the case at the state level.

The case of Banco Opportunity CEO Daniel Dantas exemplifies the gap in justice between rich and poor Brazilians. In July 2008, a federal judge in São Paulo twice ordered his arrest by the federal police, who had been investigating his illegal activities for several months. His lawyers quickly bypassed two layers of federal courts and went straight to Supreme Court president Mendes, who granted habeas corpus after each arrest.[49] Most jurists considered Mendes' actions—which are not characteristic of the behavior of high court judges—very irregular.

High government officials and ruling party politicians accused of crimes were rarely prosecuted in the past because of parliamentary immunity for deputies and senators, as well as the fact that they can only be judged by the Supreme Court. This situation changed dramatically after the mensalão case in 2005. In 2007, Federal Chief Prosecutor Antônio Fernando Souza filed a brief at the STF accusing 40 people of involvement in the scandal. To great surprise, the STF accepted all 40 cases and determined that federal courts would hear each case and take testimony from witnesses. One of the cases accepted was that of the formerly all-powerful presidential chief of staff, José Dirceu, who was forced to resign and was expelled from the Chamber of Deputies in December 2005.[50]

The Brazilian Armed Forces are under civilian control and since the installation of the 1988 constitution the military has refrained from intervention in politics, though it retains strong influence. For example, only in 1999 was President Cardoso able to install a Ministry of Defense and relegate the three former armed forces ministries to command status. The military very rarely becomes involved in domestic security operations, except when convoked specifically by state governors to supplement local police activities. In 2004, the government created the National Public Security Force (FNSP) coordinated by the National Secretariat for Public Security (SENASP) under the Ministry of Justice. This force is recruited among the best qualified state-level military policemen and trained to be a highly mobile group ready for specific local interventions. Usually, these actions are to combat drug traffickers. The FNSP has been used in four states: Espírito Santo, Mato Grosso do Sul, Rio de Janeiro, and Goiás. The FNSP receives specific training in human rights and crisis management. Its limited operations since 2005 have been praised for efficiency and respect of citizens' rights, especially during the Pan American Games in Rio in 2007.[51]

However, control and accountability of regular state-level civil and military police are very problematic. In many states, these police forces become involved in local politics. Acting as a corporate segment of the electorate, the police are often able to elect retired officers to state legislatures, who then act as a powerful lobby in support of police units. In some states, public prosecutors and the federal police have also discovered corruption schemes aimed at the enrichment of senior police officers, usually through over-invoicing service and procurement contracts. When discovered, these cases are subject to internal police inquests as well as indictments by public prosecutors.

Worse yet is the involvement of state police with organized crime in large cities such as Rio de Janeiro. There, police have created local private militias that expel criminals from neighborhoods and subsequently extort and harass residents, while imposing exclusive distribution of services such as cooking gas and cable television. According to a study by the Public Policy and Human Rights research unit at the Federal University of Rio de Janeiro, in May 2009 such militias were operating in 171 communities. On July 28, 2009, public prosecutors in Rio de Janeiro requested that the judiciary freeze the assets of city council member Cristiano Girão, who was arrested for links with the community militia during the 2008 municipal election campaign.[52] A former civil police chief in Rio de Janeiro, Alvaro Lins, was elected state deputy in 2006 but was expelled and arrested in August 2008 after investigations revealed that he oversaw a broad corruption scheme.[53] It is also common for off-duty military and civil police to have a second job with a private security company; this is prohibited by law but tolerated by state authorities.

The state gives all citizens the right to own property. Restrictions on foreign land ownership are a sensitive subject. Foreign investors now own 34,591 farms covering 4,038,000 hectares, and the National Land Reform Institute (INCRA) has requested that Congress restrict land ownership by foreigners in the Amazon.[54] The 1988 constitution and relevant legislation guarantee property rights and contracts, but enforcing contracts can be difficult and time consuming, and there are typically multiple layers of conflicting deeds for farmland registered at local notary's offices. Conflicts involving squatters' rights often explode into violence.

The Landless Workers Movement (MST) is one of the largest and best articulated civic groups in Brazil. The country began experiencing severe land tenure conflicts in the early 1960s, but the issue was muffled during most of the military regime. In 1984, the MST was born as a Marxist-inspired social movement favoring massive land expropriations and distribution to landless peasants. The MST is not registered as a formal organization in Brazil in order to avoid legal action by its adversaries; rather, it uses front organizations to receive donations from the private sector, the Brazilian government, and foreign entities. Thus, when laws are broken, police and prosecutors indict MST leaders individually. The MST's central strategy involves invading and occupying land it deems unproductive in order to force the federal government to accelerate expropriations and distribution. Although the MST leadership has never publicly adopted a strategy of violence, fighting frequently erupts during their actions. State courts usually decree evictions of MST land evasions rather quickly, but governors are often reluctant to issue eviction orders to state police units. Although the group previously received support from the PT and some sectors of the Church, relations with the PT cooled after Lula became president in 2003. Between 2000 and 2007, the MST affirms that it led 2,190 invasions, with 450,000 families either settled or awaiting settlement.[55]

Although there are provisions for the land rights of indigenous populations, these often conflict with infrastructure projects. In addition, Indian tribes are divided into two groups–those who are adequately "civilized" (and thus emancipated) and others that remain under the tutelage of the National Indian Foundation (FUNAI). Many Indian groups prefer to not be declared civilized, but some tribes take advantage of this new status to allow resource extraction in their forest areas, often for meager financial return.

One major battle occurred after the Collor government initiated studies for the demarcation of the massive Raposa Serra do Sol Indian reservation in the state of Roraima. While demarcation was effected by presidential decree in 2005, it was challenged by the governor of Roraima at the Supreme Court. Finally, in a 10-to-1 decision on March 19, 2009, the STF decided in favor of continuous demarcation of 12 million hectares. This meant that all non-Indians (mostly rice growers and three small towns) lost their property rights, and the area was exclusively reserved for 18,000 Indians, with financial compensation for the former owners. The STF stipulated a number of rules to reconcile native and government control, but the decision will serve as a benchmark for the other 22 pending cases involving the demarcation of Indian reservations.[56] More generally, the state at times expropriates private property for use in infrastructure projects, with compensation arbitrated by the courts.

ANTICORRUPTION AND TRANSPARENCY   3.63

ENVIRONMENT TO PROTECT AGAINST CORRUPTION	3.00
PROCEDURES AND SYSTEMS TO ENFORCE ANTICORRUPTION LAWS	3.00
EXISTENCE OF ANTICORRUPTION NORMS, STANDARDS, AND PROTECTIONS	4.50
GOVERNMENTAL TRANSPARENCY	4.00

Corruption is a very serious problem in Brazil. In the most comprehensive available analysis, Getúlio Vargas Foundation economist Marcos Gonçalves Silva estimated that the direct and indirect impacts of corruption cost Brazil's economy some US$5 billion per year (0.5 percent of GDP), roughly half the US$10 billion in public investments earmarked in the 2006 budget.[57] In 2008, Transparency International's Corruption Perceptions Index ranked Brazil 80th out of 180 nations with a score of 3.5.[58] During the Lula period, Brazil's numerical score has declined from 3.9 to 3.5, dropping especially sharply in 2006, when its score of 3.3 reflected the effects of the mensalão scandal.

The government has excessive regulations, requirements, and controls that provide opportunities for corruption. Bureaucratic procedures at the local level are frequently used by officials to solicit bribes and kickbacks from citizens.

In 1987, the government created the Integrated System of Financial Administration (SIAFI), which registers all expenditures by federal government units, online, every day. Only those with a special password and training may operate the system, but for journalists, congressional staff, and watchdog NGOs with access, SIAFI is a very powerful tool. However, federal bureaucrats often divide expenditures into several slices issued on different days within various layers of the bureaucracy, which makes deciphering and monitoring certain expenditures more difficult. Since its inception, SIAFI has developed techniques that make detection of such manipulation much easier. Indeed, the Office of the Comptroller General (CGU) uses the database to monitor suspected corruption cases.

The state still plays a large role in Brazil's economy: in 2008, it was estimated that the government had a 40 percent participation in Brazil's GDP.[59] Privatizations have improved since the 1990s, when such processes were often fraught with corruption and manipulation involving government agents, exemplified in the July 1998 auction of giant state telecommunications firm Telebrás. A substantial portion of current state ownership is related to Petrobras, the national oil company that is one of the largest state enterprises in the world and therefore a target of rent seekers. With the discovery of giant new reserves that place Brazil among the world's oil heavyweights, Petrobras is set to expand considerably over the next decade.[60] In mid-2009, the Senate installed a CPI to investigate "philanthropic" donations made by the firm to NGOs and cultural entities linked to the PT and allied parties. The CPI will also question the mechanism whereby Petrobras and the National Petroleum Regulatory Agency (ANP) distribute royalties to municipalities adjacent to petroleum fields, amid allegations that towns governed by PT mayors received upward adjustments of these royalties prior to the 2008 municipal elections. In addition, opposition parties suspect that Petrobras pressured its suppliers to make campaign contributions to the PT and allied parties.[61]

In spite of laws and regulations to the contrary, most Brazilian politicians use public funds for their private benefit.[62] One recent example occurred in Congress, where deputies and senators receive four round-trip air tickets per month to visit their home states on weekends. Many instead used the equivalent mileage for tickets for family and friends. In July 2009, the Chamber of Deputies initiated 44 investigations regarding the "sale" of these tickets.[63]

Some of the most dramatic cases of private appropriation of public resources involve powerful regional kingpins who are elected to Congress and thus gain political immunity. Perhaps the most prominent recent example involves the three-time president of the Senate and former national president, José Sarney. According to *Veja* magazine, when first elected Senate president in 1995, he installed a "staff mafia" that has done his bidding ever since.[64] Sarney and other senators allegedly used secret administrative acts (never published in the daily record) to hire and fire relatives, cronies, and friends.[65] Sarney also used his influence in several cabinet ministries and federal agencies to ensure financial gain for his family's businesses (commanded by his son, Fernando Sarney). His daughter, Roseana Sarney, is the governor of their home state of Maranhão, and his son José Sarney Filho represents the state as a federal deputy.

Asset declarations are required from all senior officials in the three branches of government. Candidates for deputy and senator must file declarations with the election courts. All such statements are open to public and media scrutiny, and the press often questions seeming omissions of assets.

Since 2003, Lula has unchained the federal police and prosecutors, which were restrained under the Cardoso government, to actively investigate corruption in Brazil. Armed with federal court orders to search and seize, tap telephones, requisition call records, and gain access to income tax returns and bank transactions, many corruption schemes involving politicians and their allies have been uncovered. However, most politicians are protected by the STF trial privilege. The mensalão case—brought before the High Court by a federal prosecutor general appointed by President Lula—remains the most prominent exception to such impunity.[66] As of September 2009, no final verdicts have been rendered.

The government's external control units, which include the CGU and the Congress-linked Federal Accounts Court (TCU), discover many violations of anticorruption laws and request indictments with federal prosecutors, but often to no avail. The TCU is composed of nine judges, who serve until the mandatory retirement age of 70; one-third are chosen by the president, with Senate confirmation, one-third by the Senate, and one-third by the Chamber of Deputies. The politicians chosen usually have been recently defeated at the polls and are expected to cover for their respective parties and groups in TCU deliberations. On July 27, 2009, STF president Gilmar Mendes harshly derided the TCU's ineffectiveness at revealing the wave of corruption, much of it nepotism related, sweeping Congress.[67] This spate of scandals—especially in the Senate—was revealed in the press shortly after José Sarney was elected Senate president in February 2009 and Senator Renan Calheiros, himself a longtime target of corruption allegations, became the PMDB floor leader.

The transparency of tax collections has similarly come under question in relation to the scandal in which the SRF head Vieira was dismissed on attempting to collect back taxes from large evaders (see Accountability and Public Voice). After a series of personnel shifts and investigations, the episode resulted in the resignation of some 60 technicians in the SRF, including 12 top administrators who complained about political interference.[68]

In June 2009, 43 federal employees accused of corruption were dismissed, bringing the total to 2,179 since 2003, according to data from the CGU.[69] The Brazilian media gives broad and accurate coverage of corruption at the federal level, but less for smaller states and municipalities, as local media outlets are often owned or controlled by politicians. In general, at the national level, whistleblowers, anticorruption activists, journalists, and government investigators feel secure in reporting cases of corruption and bribery, although there is no specific federal law protecting them. However, at the state and municipal levels this is not always the case. Educational institutions are generally free of corruption and graft regarding admission and grades.

Citizens' legal right to petition government agencies for information is guaranteed in Article 5 of the 1988 constitution, as regulated by law.[70] However, Brazil does not have a comprehensive freedom of information law, although such a proposal is under deliberation in Congress. Most government agencies maintain transparency websites that reveal information the agency deems appropriate, but "sensitive" information is not easily available. As seen previously, many agencies disguise their expenditures in the SIAFI system. In practice, the most powerful instrument to obtain government information is via a formal request by a deputy or senator.

Brazil's annual budget process has several stages, culminating in a detailed budget proposal submitted on August 1 for approval before the holiday recess in December. The elaboration of the budget proposal in Congress is done by the Joint Budget Committee (CMO), composed of 31 deputies and 11 senators and subject to complete rotation of the hotly disputed spots each year. Although the CMO does hold some public hearings, input from organized civic groups is very limited.[71] However, a participatory budget mechanism that incorporates demands from neighborhood associations is sometimes used at the municipal level. This system was famously installed by the local PT government in Porto Alegre, Rio Grande do Sul during four successive administrations (1989–2004).[72] Participatory budgeting is used by other city governments, though many use it for political cooptation.

The only detailed source of expenditures by the federal government is via SIAFI. The Senate and Chamber of Deputies have oversight committees that are supposed to monitor budget implementation. This is difficult because the executive branch—in the name of "austerity"—frequently freezes expenditures in specific areas, only to liberate spending later if tax collections permit the availability of funds. Although this manipulation is related to achieving the primary surplus target, it is one of the mechanisms used by the president to maintain cohesion in his congressional coalition.[73]

Brazil's procurement procedures are quite complicated, even when these are transferred to online competitive bidding; frequently the result is overpriced goods and services.[74] Despite the detailed rules, the press frequently carries stories about biased bidding procedures that favor specific suppliers, usually enabled via collusion among bidders to divide up the spoils. In mid-2006, the federal police revealed the so-called "bloodsucker" scandal, in which over-invoiced ambulances were acquired for distribution to local governments, with intermediation by federal deputies. Of the 69 deputies involved who sought reelection that year, only five were reelected.[75] The levels of corruption in the area of foreign assistance are low, as both foreign donors and the Foreign Affairs Ministry have quite efficient control and monitoring procedures.

RECOMMENDATIONS

- Proportional elections should be changed from open list to closed list format in order to strengthen political parties and downgrade with the importance of high name recognition and unlimited financial resources.
- Election laws should be changed to prohibit candidates with criminal records from running for office.
- Merit-based civil service requirements should be extended, with the number of political appointments made by the president, governors, and mayors reduced.
- Congress should pass affirmative action legislation that implements quotas for university admissions based on the racial and class origin of applicants.
- Government should increase the repression of private militias in urban neighborhoods and strengthen mechanisms to ensure that civil and military police who participate in such groups are expelled.
- The government should finalize and implement the demarcation of the remaining 22 Indian reserves.
- The use of state enterprises to finance political campaigns should be prohibited, with strict accountability imposed in the Regional Election Courts.
- The use of political criteria to select TCU judges should be abolished and only technical criteria used.

NOTES

For URLs and endnote hyperlinks, please visit the *Countries at the Crossroads* homepage at http://freedomhouse.org/template.cfm?page=139&edition=8.

[1] David Fleischer, "Brazil: From Military Regime to a Workers' Party Government," in *Latin America: Its Promise and Its Presence*, ed. J. K. Black (Boulder, Colo.: Westview Press, 2005), 470–500.
[2] David Samuels, "From Socialism to Social Democracy: Party Organization and the Transformation of the Workers' Party in Brazil," *Comparative Political Studies* 37, no. 9 (2004): 999–1024.
[3] For details from these Datafolha polls.
[4] Flávio Tayra, "Mobilidade Social e Crise Global," *Revista SuperHiper*, March 2009.
[5] Wendy Hunter and Timothy Power, "Rewarding Lula: Executive Power, Social Power, and the Brazilian Elections in 2006," *Latin American Politics and Society* 49, no. 1 (2007): 1–30.
[6] The Federal District does not have municipal elections.
[7] For an overview of Brazil's election governance system, see David Fleischer and Leonardo Barreto, "El Impacto de la Justicia Electoral sobre el Sistema Político Brasileño," *América Latina Hoy*, no. 51 (2009): 117–138.
[8] David Fleischer, "Political Outlook in Brazil in the Wake of Municipal Elections: 2009–2010" (paper presented at "Political Outlook in Brazil after 2008," The Woodrow Wilson International Center for Scholars, Washington, D.C., November 10, 2008).
[9] Ibid.

[10] David Fleischer, "As Eleições Municipais no Brasil: Uma Análise Comparativa (1982–2002)," *Opinião Pública* [Campinas] 8, no. 1 (2002): 80–105.
[11] David Fleischer, *Brazil Focus Weekly Report: 19-25 April 2008*, April 2008.
[12] Sérgio Abranches, "O Presidencialismo de Coalizão: O Dilema Institucional Brasileiro," *Dados* 31, no. 1 (1988): 5–33.
[13] Elio Gaspari, "O Que Significa 'Controlar' a Receita?" *Folha de São Paulo*, July 15, 2009.
[14] Felipe Recondo, "Governo Vai Rastrear Parentes," *O Estado de São Paulo*, July 23, 2009.
[15] Andréa de Lima, "Senado Abre CPI para Investigate Atuação de ONGs," *Folha de São Paulo*, February 24, 2001.
[16] Eva Menezes, "Justiça Brasileira Revoga a Lei de Imprensa," Journalism nas Américas Blog, University of Texas at Austin's Knight Center for Journalism in the Americas, May 1, 2009.
[17] Felipe Recondo, "Justiça Censura Estado e Proíbe Informações sobre Sarney," *O Estado de São Paulo*, July 31, 2009.
[18] Cristina Guimarães, "Caso Tim Lopes Mobiliza Todo o País," TimLopes.com.
[19] Committee to Protect Journalists (CPJ), *Getting Away With Murder 2009* (New York: CPJ, March 23, 2009).
[20] Fernando de Barros e Silva, "Bolsa-Mídia de Lula," *Folha de São Paulo*, June 1, 2009.
[21] "Juiz Acata Denúncia contra Líder da Universal," *Folha de São Paulo*, August 11, 2009.
[22] Freedom House, "Brazil," in *Freedom on the Net: A Global Assessment of Internet and Digital Media* (Washington, D.C.: Freedom House, 2009).
[23] Janaina de Almedia Teles, Suzana K. Lisbao, and Maria Amelia Teles, *Dossiê Ditatura: Mortos e Desaparecidos Políticos no Brasil (1964–1985)* (São Paulo: Imprensa Oficial do Estado de Sao Paulo, 2009).
[24] Law No. 6,683, August 28, 1979.
[25] Felipe Seligman and Valdo Cruz, "Comissão de Anistia Declara Lamarca Coronel do Exército," *Folha de São Paulo*, June 14, 2007.
[26] Maurício Thuswohl, "AGU Assume Defesa do Ex-Coronel Ustra," *Carta Maior*, October 10, 2008.
[27] Secretaria de Segurança, *Balanco das Incidencias Criminais e Administrativas no Estado do Rio de Janeiro* (Rio de Janeiro: Governo de Rio de Janeiro, 2008), 23.
[28] Philip Alston, *Report of the Special Rapporteur on Extrajudicial, Summary, or Arbitrary Executions* (Geneva: UN Human Rights Council, August 29, 2008).
[29] Forum Brasileiro de Segurança Pública (FBSP), *Anuário do Forum Brasileiro de Segurança Pública 2008* (São Paulo: FBSP, 2009).
[30] Demétrio Weber, "Violência Matará 33 Mil Adolescentes até 2012," *O Globo*, July 22, 2009.
[31] Alston, *Report of the Special Rapporteur on Extrajudicial, Summary, or Arbitrary Executions*, 12, 32–36, 40–42.
[32] Bruno Konder Comparato, "As Ouvidorias de Polícia no Brasil: Controle e Participação" (PhD diss., Universidade de São Paulo, 2005).
[33] "Mutirão do CNJ Liberta 4,7 Mil em um Ano," BOL Notícias, August 15, 2009.
[34] For information on human trafficking in Brazil, see www.projeto fabrica.com.br/i-migrantes/trafico_sh.htm.
[35] Leonardo Sakamoto, ed., *Trabalho Escravo no Brasil do Século XXI* (Brasília: Organização Internacional do Trabalho, 2005); José de Souza Martins, "A Irredutível Economia da Escravidão," *O Estado de São Paulo*, July 26, 2009.
[36] United Nations Development Fund for Women (UNIFEM), "Brazil Enacts Law on Violence against Women," news release, August 9, 2006; *Constitution of the Federal Republic of Brazil*, Art. 226.

37. Renato Sérgio de Lima, "Mapeamento das Delegacias de Mulher no Brasil," FBSP, November 24, 2008.
38. Sylvio Costa and Antônio Augusto de Queiroz, ed., *O Que Esperar do Novo Congresso: Perfil e Agenda da Legislatura 2007–2011* (Brasília: Congresso em Foco and Departamento Intersindical de Assessoria Parlamentar, 2007), 41.
39. Cléia Paixão, "Mulheres Lançam Campanha Nacional por Igualdade de Salários e Oportunidades," Estado de Alagoas Secretaria de Mulher, Cidadania e Direitos Humanos, news release, 2008.
40. Instituto de Pesquisa Economica Aplicada (IPEA), *Desigualdades Raciais, Racismo e Políticas Públicas: 120 Anos após a Abolição* (Brasília: IPEA, May 13, 2008).
41. Datafolha Opinião Pública, "Preconceito Admitido por Brasileiros Diminui," November 27, 2008; The opposite view is that these "affirmative action" initiatives might lead to "reverse discrimination." See Diogo Schelp, "Queremos Dividir o Brasil Como na Foto?" *Revista Veja*, no. 2128 (September 2, 2009) and Demétrio Magnoli, *Uma Gota de Sangue: História do Pensamento Racial* (São Paulo: Contexto, 2009).
42. Instituto Socio-Ambiental, "ISA Lanca Livro de Referencia para a Questão Indígena no Brasil," news release, October 24, 2006.
43. Roldao Arruda, "DEM Tenta Impedir Matrícula de Cotistas," *O Estado de São Paulo*, July 22, 2009.
44. Luana Pinheiro and Vera Soares, *Brasil: Retrato das Desigualdades - Gênero, Raça* (Brasilia/New York: IPEA and UNIFEM, 2008), 32.
45. Felipe Seligman, "CNJ Investiga Pelo Menos 107 Magistrados," *Folha de São Paulo*, August 4, 2009.
46. Pedro Lenza, "Reforma do Judiciário. Emenda Constitucional Nº 45/2004–Ezquematização das Principais Novidades," *Jus Navigandi* 9, no. 618 (March 18, 2005).
47. Mariângela Gallucci, "Joaquim Barbosa Bate-Boca com Mendes no STF," *O Estado de São Paulo*, April 22, 2009.
48. Matthew M. Taylor, "Citizens against the State: The Riddle of High Impact, Low Functionality Courts in Brazil," *Revista de Economia Política* 25, no. 4 (October/December 2005).
49. "Preso de Novo, Daniel Dantas Volta à Carceragem da PF," VoteBrasil, July 10, 2008.
50. Valdo Cruz, "STF Transforma José Dirceu em Réu do Mensalão," *Folha de São Paulo*, August 31, 2007.
51. Guilherme Fister, "Segurança sem Perder a Ternura," *Zero Hora*, January 20, 2006.
52. Dimmi Amora, "Vereador Girão Seria Miliciano; MP Pede Bloqueio de Bens e Cassação de Vereador Acusado de Ser Miliciano," *O Globo*, July 29, 2009.
53. Luisa Belchior, "Com Placar Apertado, Alerj Aprova Cassação de Álvaro Lins," *Folha de São Paulo*, August 13, 2008.
54. "Estrangeiros Compram Mais Imoveis Rurais," *Zero Hora*, February 24, 2009.
55. For a recent analysis of the MST's finances and strategy, see Policarpo Junior and Sofia Krause, "Por dentro do Cofre do MST," *Revista Veja*, no. 2128 (September 2, 2009), 64–72.
56. Claudia Andrade, "Por 10 a 1, Supremo Mantém Demarcação Contínua da Reserva Raposa/Serra do Sol," UOL Notícias, March 19, 2009.
57. Florência Costa, "Corrupção Mata," *IstoÉ*, October 3, 2009.
58. Transparency International, *2008 Corruption Perceptions Index* (Berlin: Transparency International, September 22, 2008).
59. Roberto Blum, "Brasil: De Que Esquerda Estamos Fallando," *Correio Internacional*, September 16, 2008.

60. Kelly Lima, "Brasil Pode Ter 8ª Maior Reserva de Petróleo do Mundo," PortalExame, November 8, 2007.
61. Cristiane Jungblut and Isabel Braga, "CPI Investigará Repasses da Petrobrás," *O Globo*, May 25, 2009; Cirilo Junior, "PF Investiga Suposto Desvio de Royalties da Petrobrás; ANP não ê Indício de Irregularidade," *Folha de São Paulo*, July 4, 2009.
62. Marita Boos, "A Mistura do Público com o Privado Deveria Dar Cadeira," *O Globo*, July 24, 2009.
63. "Relatorio Revela Comercio de Passagens na Camara," DiviNews, September 10, 2009.
64. Reinaldo Azevedo, "Sarney e Cúpula do Senado na Festa da Família Agaciel," *Veja*, June 11, 2009.
65. It was revealed that some 633 "secret acts" were issued since 1996. See Claudia Andrade, "Senado Vai Investigar Novos Atos Secretos," UOL Notícias, August 13, 2009.
66. Rosanne D'Agostino, "Supremo Luta contra o Tempo para Julgar Mensalão," UOL Notícias, February 20, 2009.
67. "Gilmar Mendes Diz que TCU 'Falha' No Congresso," *Folha de São Paulo*, July 28, 2009.
68. Kennedy Alencar, Leandra Peres, and Valdo Cruz, "Lula Repreende Mantega e Exige 'Retomada' da Receita," *Folha de São Paulo*, August 27, 2009.
69. Marcelo de Moraes, "Expulsão de Servidores Corruptos Bate Recorde," *O Estado de São Paulo*, July 28, 2009.
70. Marco Aurélio Ventura Peixoto, "Habeas Data: A Polêmica Garantia Constitucional de Conhecimento e Retificação de Informações Pessoais em Poder do Estado," *Jus Navigandi* 6, no. 52 (November 2001).
71. Instituto de Estudos Socioeconômicos, "Nota Técnica 110: Reforma Orçamentária: Proposta Tímida," June 14, 2006.
72. Rebecca Neaera Abers, *Inventing Local Democracy: Grassroots Politics in Brazil* (Boulder, Colo.: Lynne Rienner, 2000).
73. Lee J. Alston et al., *Political Institutions, Policymaking Processes and Policy Outcomes in Brazil* (Washington, D.C.: Inter-American Development Bank, March 2006); Octávio Amorim Neto and Fabiano Santos, "The Executive Connection: Patronage and Party Discipline in Brazil," *Party Politics* 7, no. 2 (2001).
74. Juliana Simão. "Licitação Online: Governo Federal Muda Lei e Cria Portal B2B para Fazer Compras na Internet," *IstoÉ Dinheiro*, July 27, 2009.
75. Costa and de Queiroz, *O Que Esperar do Novo Congresso- Perfil e Agenda da Legislatura 2007/2011*, 15.

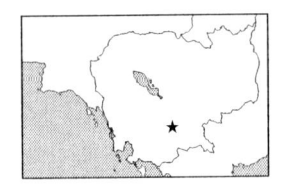

CAMBODIA

CAPITAL: Phnom Penh
POPULATION: 14.8 million
GNI PER CAPITA (PPP): $1,820

SCORES	2006	2010
ACCOUNTABILITY AND PUBLIC VOICE:	3.23	2.83
CIVIL LIBERTIES:	3.36	3.08
RULE OF LAW:	2.04	1.90
ANTICORRUPTION AND TRANSPARENCY:	2.54	2.19

(scores are based on a scale of 0 to 7, with 0 representing weakest and 7 representing strongest performance)

Duncan McCargo

INTRODUCTION

Cambodia has come a long way since the 1975–79 Khmer Rouge period during which an estimated 1.5 million Cambodians out of a population of 7 million were killed in one of the 20th century's most appalling genocides. The Khmer Rouge were toppled by a Vietnamese invasion, which ushered in a period of civil conflict. In 1992–93, peace agreements were implemented under the auspices of United Nations Transitional Authority in Cambodia (UNTAC), an early peacekeeping and post-conflict reconstruction mission.

The logistically smooth 2008 general elections, widely hailed as the country's freest and least violent polls to date, were a sideshow that should not divert attention from the main act: Prime Minister Hun Sen and the Cambodian People's Party (CPP) have been gradually but inexorably tightening their grip on power and resources. Indeed, authoritarianism has become normalized in Cambodia.

The CPP entered the 2008 elections as the only significant competitor, a very different situation from the 1993 elections, in which the winner was the royalist FUNCINPEC party. At that time, Hun Sen became the "second" prime minister in a two-headed administration, subsequently seizing power in 1997 to ensure his supremacy in the 1998 elections. Following the 2003 polls, there was a genuine struggle between the CPP and its major rivals, which briefly formed an "Alliance of Democrats." Hun Sen was unable to form a new government for the better part of a year. By 2008, however, both the pragmatic royalist FUNCINPEC and the populist, nationalist, and staunchly anti-Hun Sen Sam

---

Duncan McCargo is Professor of Southeast Asian politics at the University of Leeds. He was a Leverhulme Trust fellow in Phnom Penh, 2004–05.

Rainsy Party (SRP) were marginalized well before the election, undermined by state harassment and politically-inspired court cases.

Cambodia's fourth general elections therefore marked the culmination of a long process by which the CPP has outfoxed the competition and secured considerable electoral support. This time, the ruling party won 58 percent of the popular vote and nearly three-fourths of National Assembly seats. A border dispute with Thailand over the Preah Vihear temple in mid-2008 gave Hun Sen a useful opportunity for nationalistic grandstanding just prior to the elections. The dispute turned violent in both October 2008 and April 2009, resulting in the deaths of several Thai and two Cambodian soldiers. In addition to suppressing dissent, populist demagoguery has been central to the CPP's electoral success.

In recent years, Cambodia has become considerably more stable. Viewed from the vantage point of Phnom Penh, life is more orderly, politics is more predictable, the economy has grown remarkably (10.8 percent in 2006, 10.2 percent in 2007, and an estimated 6 percent in 2008),[1] and crime has declined. Although people in more remote rural areas remain overwhelmingly poor and powerless, the CPP is as popular as ever in the settled rice-growing villages of the central plains, a result of economic growth and government patronage programs.[2] Though lacking a formal organizational structure similar to the Vietnamese Communist Party, the CPP and Hun Sen have established a formidable informal network of supporters throughout the country, using district working groups to reach from the center to commune chiefs who work closely with loyal, male heads of household in every village. District working parties are now very influential and consult closely with commune councils, giving a more bottom-up aspect to the party, but the CPP is still heavily reliant on personal relationships rather than institutionalized positions, and the relationship between higher and lower levels is consultative and patronizing rather than responsive.

Cambodia is currently staging the Khmer Rouge Tribunal, a hybrid local-international court intended to bring former leaders of the murderous regime to justice. (See box on page 94.) The tribunal has received global media attention amid talk of an end to the culture of impunity. But while five elderly figures from the 1970s face charges relating to genocide, in 2009 Hun Sen's CPP is getting away with a disturbing range of political abuses. Cambodia's elite is quietly enriching itself, grabbing huge tranches of land across the country. Community leaders, labor activists, and critical journalists who challenge the CPP face threats, intimidation, and sometimes violence.

Despite concerted attempts at donor coordination, the Hun Sen government has consistently outmaneuvered international donors and thwarted efforts to impose governance-related conditions. International aid and assistance accounts for more than 50 percent of the Cambodian government's annual budget. Every year, donors issue ritual protestations concerning the government's appalling record on tackling corruption and then proceed to provide even more aid than has been requested: in 2006, US$513 million was requested and US$713 million granted; in 2007, US$689 million requested and US$790 million granted.[3] Over US$1 billion in aid was pledged in 2008. In return, donors eventually receive new laws, new policies, and promises of implementation. Meanwhile, the CPP is consolidating its authoritarianism, while average Cambodians remain stripped of a sense of citizenship and participation in the governing of their country.[4] The growing role of China as a major aid donor, pledging some US$600 million in assistance, has further undermined attempts to press for greater democratic governance and transparency, as Hun Sen has used China's competing contributions as a bargaining card.

ACCOUNTABILITY AND PUBLIC VOICE 2.83

FREE AND FAIR ELECTORAL LAWS AND ELECTIONS	2.75
EFFECTIVE AND ACCOUNTABLE GOVERNMENT	2.25
CIVIC ENGAGEMENT AND CIVIC MONITORING	3.33
MEDIA INDEPENDENCE AND FREEDOM OF EXPRESSION	3.00

Cambodia is a constitutional monarchy. Under the constitution, "Cambodian people are masters of their own country. All powers belong to the people." In practice, although elections have been held regularly since 1993, political choices are largely dominated by the CPP and an informal power network centered on Prime Minister Hun Sen. Current king Norodom Sihamoni is mostly a symbolic figure and plays a relatively minor role in national politics compared to his father, King Norodom Sihanouk, who abdicated the throne in 2004 due to health problems.

The country has a bicameral parliament, consisting of a Senate and National Assembly (NA). The NA's 123 members are elected by popular vote to five-year terms. The government, consisting of the prime minister and a council of ministers, is chosen and approved by a two-thirds vote in the NA.

In all general elections held since 1993, multiple parties have contested the polls, the secret ballot has been applied, and thousands of international observers have been present. Although the technical aspects of elections have improved over time, the integrity of the process has been undermined in a number of ways. Opposition parties and their leaders have faced legal and other forms of harassment, while political violence has often increased in periods surrounding elections. The National Election Commission (NEC) has repeatedly taken actions perceived as favoring the CPP, while failing to meet legal obligations to punish political intimidation and other violations of electoral laws.[5]

In July 2008, Cambodia held its fourth general elections. The regional Asian Network for Free Elections (ANFREL) found that although some aspects of the election process had improved compared to previous polls—including a reduction in violence—the process as a whole could not be regarded as fair.[6] According to the Committee for Free and Fair Elections in Cambodia (COMFREL), the polls remained characterized by the presence of partisan election officials, coercion, disparities in media access, inadequate responses to election violations, and voters being turned away from polling stations. The opposition SRP and Human Rights Party rejected the results, charging that they had been "manipulated and rigged by the ruling CPP" with the collusion of the National Election Committee (NEC).[7]

The NEC's performance during the 2008 election process raised concerns about partisanship. This included a decision to allow commune election commissions, many of them aligned with the CPP, to tally polling results, a measure condemned by COMFREL as illegal and likely to lead to controversy. More serious were reliable reports that the NEC deleted 585,723 names from voter lists during a 2007 revision and fraudulently issued copies of a form that allowed people not on the rolls to vote.[8]

While opposition parties are permitted in Cambodia and enjoy considerable public support, the CPP is both popular and extremely dominant. There exists no real prospect that power will rotate in the near future. All 24 provincial governors are loyal to or supportive of the ruling coalition, as are 98 percent of Commune Council chiefs, who are charged with voter registration. As a result, campaigning for opposition parties is difficult in many rural areas considered CPP strongholds.

The 2008 elections saw the virtual demise of FUNCINPEC, one of the two main opposition parties, reinforcing the CPP's dominance. The CPP won 58 percent of the popular vote and 90 out of 123 NA seats. While the SRP gained 26 seats (up from 24 in 2003), the implosion of FUNCINPEC left non-CPP parties extremely marginalized.[9] The SRP remains a primarily urban party that has been unable to garner significant rural support. It was also weakened when several high-profile figures defected to the CPP prior to the elections in return for lucrative advisory posts or following intimidation.

A number of factors contributed to FUNCINPEC's deterioration. Former leader Prince Norodom Ranarridh was forced out of the party elite in October 2006 as a result of internal divisions exploited by Hun Sen. He subsequently faced court cases on charges of adultery and corruption, leading him to temporarily flee the country. Meanwhile, the party's long-standing collaboration with the CPP undermined its credibility in the eyes of the electorate as a viable alternative.

The ability of the CPP to retain its power has been made easier in part by legal changes made in 2006. Constitutional amendments permit a party with an absolute majority of parliamentary seats to form a government, whereas previously a two-thirds majority was required. The adjustments were made following the 2003 elections, when there were unsuccessful attempts to form an alternative administration by an anti-CPP coalition.

Effective regulation of campaign financing is absent, further contributing to CPP dominance of the political arena. There are no legal limits or disclosure requirements on donations to political parties. This has enabled the CPP to develop a system of patronage whereby donations from business tycoons help fund development projects in rural areas, thereby boosting the party's popularity.

The 61-member Senate held its first elections in January 2006. Only commune councillors and members of the NA were eligible to vote, however. In practice, the Senate performs a largely ceremonial function, with seats serving as a reward for loyal and wealthy supporters of the regime.

The NA does not effectively exercise scrutiny or oversight over the activities of the executive.[10] The ability of opposition members of parliament (MPs) to challenge the government is limited as parliamentary procedures organize MPs into groups, meaning that outspoken parliamentarians have their opportunities to speak strictly rationed. The courts are subordinated to the power of the executive branch.

Appointment, promotion, and dismissal of civil servants are neither merit based nor transparent. In addition to positions being granted as a way to distribute patronage, some senior posts are reportedly awarded to the highest bidder. Global Witness describes the method of securing senior positions in the Forest Administration as a "job auction," with posts in the provinces sold for between US$2,000 and US$30,000.[11]

Cambodia's community of nongovernmental organizations (NGOs) is large relative to the country's size. By law, civic associations are supposed to register with the Ministry of Interior, but in practice unregistered community-based and informal organizations operate freely. Approximately 200 international NGOs, 400 local NGOs, and nearly 600 registered associations operate, covering a variety of social issues including health, poverty reduction, and education. NGOs working on such issues enjoy greater freedom and ability to influence government policy compared to the relatively small number of human rights–oriented organizations. Nonetheless, although civic groups are occasionally involved in policy debates and the drafting of legislation, new legislation is rarely enforced even when passed and ultimately has little impact on addressing social problems.

Numerous local NGOs receive foreign funding without reporting any government restrictions on grants or donations. Nonetheless, the government has interfered in some foreign-funded programs, as well as issued statements raising concerns that NGO activity in the country may face greater obstacles in the future. In May 2007, 12 trainee lawyers working as interns at human rights and other NGOs in a program supported by the United States Agency for International Development (USAID) were forced to resign from their internships by the president of the progovernment bar association.[12] In September 2008, Hun Sen declared in a radio speech that "Cambodia has been heaven for NGOs for too long ... the NGOs are out of control ... they insult the government just to ensure their financial survival."[13] As of mid-2009, an NGO law was being drafted. Although its text has yet to be made public, some activists fear the new bill might be used to curtail their freedom to organize.

Adding to such concerns was the July 2009 conviction in abstentia of Moeung Sonn, president of the Khmer Civilisation Foundation, to a two-year jail term on charges of "disinformation" over comments he made suggesting lights installed at the ancient temple complex of Angkor Wat could cause damage to the site. Sonn fled to France in May after the initial charges were filed, thereby avoiding imprisonment.[14]

In recent years the government has become increasingly intolerant of those who voice concerns about its human rights record. In 2007, Prime Minister Hun Sen described anyone expressing support for the latest human rights report by United Nations Special Representative Yash Gai as "the vilest person," and made a formal complaint about Gai to the UN secretary-general. Also that year, the information minister threatened to expel the Open Society Institute from the country over criticisms of alleged mismanagement at the Khmer Rouge Tribunal.[15]

Cambodia's print media are accessible to all major parties and present a diversity of viewpoints as well as criticism of the government, though they reach less than 10 percent of the population. By contrast, most broadcast media is closely linked to the ruling party, and outlets carry little critical news. A majority of 141 Cambodian media workers—mostly from print media—interviewed in 2007 described media freedom as "somewhat free" (73) or "very free" (21); 26 said "controlled," and only 10 "strictly controlled."[16]

Freedom of expression is enshrined in the Cambodian constitution. However, articles of the 1995 Press Law contradict and undermine such guarantees by prohibiting the publication of material deemed prejudicial to "national security and political stability." The government has also relied on provisions from the 1992 UNTAC Criminal Code covering libel and criminal defamation, disinformation, and incitement to curb critical coverage by the print media. Prominent politicians, including governors and a deputy prime minister, as well as powerful businesspeople with close ties to the CPP, make extensive use of defamation laws to file cases against print media for critical reporting. Since 2006, defamation is no longer a criminal offense; nonetheless, individuals unable to pay fines in civil cases may still face imprisonment. The offense of "spreading disinformation" continues to carry a jail sentence of up to three years and was used in 2008 to charge a prominent opposition newspaper editor. Hun Sen himself brought a defamation action against popular opposition MP Mu Sochua, who was promptly stripped of her parliamentary immunity and then convicted by a Phnom Penh court in August 2009.[17]

Although murders and physical assaults on journalists have declined in recent years, nine local journalists have been killed since 1994. There have been no convictions of those responsible. Shortly before the July 2008 elections, outspoken opposition journalist Khim Sambo and his son were murdered; the attack appears to have been carried out by contract killers confident they would not be arrested, suggesting they had high-level state connections.[18]

In a 2007 survey of 150 journalists conducted by the Cambodian League for the Promotion and Defense of Human Rights (LICADHO), 54 percent of interviewees reported being threatened with physical harm or legal action.[19] There is little evidence of state action to curtail or investigate such threats. On the contrary, high-ranking officials have themselves threatened journalists. In 2007, Prime Minister Hun Sen made a personal verbal attack on Radio Free Asia reporter Um Sarim, causing him to flee the country for several weeks.

The government seeks to maximize its influence over media content either via direct censorship or more informal measures, such as ensuring that most media ownership rests in the hands of figures closely aligned with the CPP. There is evidence of direct government involvement in censoring the state-owned television station TVK.[20] Other stations typically have informal "protocols" not to report on certain issues or feature particular prominent figures known to be critical of the government. In an incident of explicit government interference in media coverage, Minister of Information Khieu Kanharith ordered newspapers in 2007 to limit reporting about a critical report by Global Witness on illegal logging. The minister's instructions had no legal basis.

The director of one of Cambodia's leading private television stations has refused to reveal who owns the Apsara Media Group, rumored to be leading members of the ruling CPP. Hun Mana, daughter of Prime Minister Hun Sen, runs another leading TV station, Bayon TV.[21] The three leading newspapers—*Raemei Kampuchea*, *Koh Santepheap Daily*, and *Kampuchea Thmei Daily*—are all progovernment; many other newspaper owners have close ties to the CPP. The English-language newspapers *Cambodia Daily* and *Phnom Penh Post* carry more critical reporting than the Khmer-language press, and some stories that first appear in English find their way into vernacular newspaper reporting. Additional critical reporting can be found on radio, notably the Beehive Radio station, which also rebroadcasts Voice of America and Radio Free Asia. The authorities have repeatedly denied licenses to other independent radio outlets, such as a proposed Voice of Democracy station backed by the Cambodian Center for Human Rights. Critical radio stations may be subject to arbitrary suspension or even permanent closure, as happened in two cases during the run-up to the 2008 general elections.[22]

The government uses the media it controls, such as TVK, largely to provide official points of view and propagandize on behalf of the CPP. Positive images of CPP leaders inspecting rural projects or providing assistance to the poor are staple news items. This style of television news is emulated by private, state-licensed stations. Bribery of reporters is widespread; a survey showed that 25 percent of journalists knew of cases where bribes were paid for favorable coverage, while 34 percent were aware of bribes being paid to prevent stories appearing.[23] There is no evidence that the state restricts internet access, which remains largely the preserve of a small urban elite. If passed, however, a proposed bill would extend some existing restrictions on broadcast media to audiovisual online content.

CIVIL LIBERTIES 3.08

PROTECTION FROM STATE TERROR, UNJUSTIFIED IMPRISONMENT, AND TORTURE	1.63
GENDER EQUITY	3.67
RIGHTS OF ETHNIC, RELIGIOUS, AND OTHER DISTINCT GROUPS	3.00
FREEDOM OF CONSCIENCE AND BELIEF	4.33
FREEDOM OF ASSOCIATION AND ASSEMBLY	2.75

The Cambodian constitution codifies an impressive set of human rights, including those in the UN Charter and Universal Declaration of Human Rights. Cambodia ratified the United Nations Convention against Torture in 1992 and its adjoining optional protocol in 2007. In practice, however, there is little protection from abuse by either state or nonstate actors due to shortcomings in the court system and a prevailing culture of impunity.

Police routinely torture detainees during the initial stages of investigation in order to force confessions, according to reports from local NGOs and Human Rights Watch. Cases of arbitrary arrest and detention continue to be reported, with the Cambodian Human Rights and Development Association (ADHOC) investigating 85 such cases in 2008.[24] Large numbers of sex workers, homeless individuals, beggars, and drug addicts are reported to be held in government-run "social rehabilitation centers" following detention in police roundups; NGOs have documented cases of detainees beaten to death or raped. Following the exposure of the facilities in June and September 2008, some detainees were released.

Prison conditions are poor and, due to overcrowding, appear to be worsening.[25] Inmates often lack access to fresh water and basic medical facilities, while some have reported being subject to torture. "Welcome beatings" for new prisoners by guards and trusted inmates (known as cell leaders) are common. In some prisons, guards have delegated many of their duties to cell leaders, while others demand bribes in exchange for allowing relatives to visit inmates.[26]

Prior to 2007, pretrial detention was limited to six months, though the authorities frequently flouted the requirement. During the summer of 2007, a new criminal procedure code came into force and was hailed by some observers as an important step forward. However, under the new code, pretrial detention for felonies is permissible for up to 18 months. More broadly, an analysis of the code by LICADHO questioned the degree to which it was an improvement, finding the amendments introduced to be either neutral or negative in outcome.

Political opponents and other peaceful activists are regularly subjected to attack, and extrajudicial killings by security forces continue. In 2008, ADHOC investigated 40 instances of murder committed by the security forces or government officials; six of the victims were political activists.[27] Human rights defenders involved in land disputes are also regularly targeted with violence and threats. Impunity remains the norm in such cases.

Abuses by nonstate actors, such as illegal land seizures by wealthy individuals, remain widespread. The state takes little action to protect citizens or punish perpetrators in such cases. Partly reflecting the ineffectiveness of the court system, mob killings and vigilantism have also emerged as a serious problem, leading to 17 deaths in 2006. Such incidents have since declined, although the authorities have taken little action to investigate previous killings or arrest perpetrators. Guns, including AK-47 assault rifles, are readily available and widely used by criminals and gangs. Rival youth gangs regularly fight turf battles on the streets of the capital Phnom Penh. In March 2009, the Cambodian government reported that crime had fallen by 20 percent in 2008, but these statistics have been disputed by NGOs.[28]

Cambodia has three existing human rights bodies, while the establishment of a new National Human Rights Commission was announced in 2006. The independence and impartiality of the existing committees remains questionable, however, as they are under the authority of the National Assembly, the Senate and the government, all of which are dominated by the CPP. As of mid-2009, the new body had yet to be established as the government repeatedly postponed passage of a law outlining its mandate and authority.[29] In practice, most investigatory and advocacy work on human rights issues is done by NGOs, notably ADHOC, the Cambodian Center for Human Rights, and LICADHO.

The state generally addresses issues related to women and minorities in response to international pressure from donors and NGOs. Women's issues are given a weak voice through the Ministry of Women's and Veterans' Affairs. Cambodia ratified the Convention on the Elimination of Discrimination against Women (CEDAW) in 1992, but has not passed other antidiscrimination legislation. Several more recent laws, including the 2005 Law on the Prevention of Domestic Violence and the Protection of Victims, contain provisions that contravene CEDAW principles.

A 2007 study by an NGO coalition found Cambodia's laws to be, "severely lacking in protective measures and guarantees of equality for women in Cambodia"; existing legislation was found to contain discriminatory or inadequate provisions, including those related to marriage, domestic violence, and rape.[30] As with many Cambodian laws, legislation protecting women and punishing offenders is inadequately enforced, reportedly contributing to an increase in violence against women and child rape: 20 to 25 percent of Cambodian women are estimated to have been victims of domestic violence.[31] In some cases, police have reportedly released offenders in exchange for bribes.[32] Women remain significantly disadvantaged economically and socially, lagging behind males in access to education and health care. There is no evidence of significant government efforts to prevent gender discrimination in employment.

Trafficking of women and girls, both within the country and from outside, primarily for work in the sex trade, remains a serious problem. A new Law on the Suppression of Human Trafficking and Sexual Exploitation was adopted in 2008 but has yet to be effectively enforced. Despite the new legislation,

ADHOC reported a 38 percent increase in trafficking cases in 2008.[33] According to another report, law enforcement agencies have potentially distorted anti-trafficking statistics by conflating measures taken against ordinary sex workers with attempts to "rescue" trafficking victims.[34]

Most Cambodians would identify themselves as ethnically "Khmer," though the country is home to several minority groups, including populations of both immigrant and transgenerational Chinese, Vietnamese, Thai, various "hill tribes," and Cham Muslims. No specific legislation outlaws discrimination based on ethnicity or religion, and government policies are characterized by ambiguity and confusion. For example, Cham Muslims, who number approximately 300,000, are not classed by the government as a minority, although many do not speak Khmer as a first language.[35] Public discussion of the Vietnamese and Chinese minorities is politically sensitive and problems facing these communities receive little government attention.

The rights of non-Khmer ethnic minorities, who constitute 10 percent of the population, are inadequately protected. They suffer from discrimination related to citizenship, residency, electoral participation, access to education and health care, and control over natural resources. Ethnic minority languages have also come under threat from government assimilation policies, including decentralization reforms that restrict non-Khmer speakers from representing their communities in local state institutions.[36] The government has recently prepared new sub-decrees ostensibly aimed at assisting indigenous populations, especially those in the highland regions, where an estimated 220,000 people reside. These have proven controversial, however. Although they potentially offer indigenous communities collective land titles, NGOs have criticized the decrees as providing insufficient guarantees to enforce such titles. In practice, indigenous groups continue to suffer from extensive land grabbing and occupy a marginalized place in Cambodian society.

Cambodia has a significant disabled population, including some 40,000 amputees injured by landmines. A Law on the Protection and Promotion of the Rights of Persons with Disabilities was approved by the Council of Ministers in February 2008, but has yet to be ratified by the NA.

Buddhism is the state religion and the constitution provides for religious freedom. Most Cambodians are Theravada Buddhists, and citizens are generally able to practice freely, though discrimination against Cham Muslims is widespread. Since the 1990s, the government has tightly controlled senior monastic appointments within Buddhism through the Ministry of Cults and Religious Affairs. Khmer Krom monks from Vietnam residing in Phnom Penh have been subjected to official harassment when trying to organize peaceful protests in support of religious freedom in Vietnam. One prominent monk, Tim Sakhorn, was defrocked and deported in June 2007.

The constitution recognizes the right to freedom of assembly and to form trade unions. In practice, labor leaders have regularly faced intimidation and extrajudicial killings. In February 2007, unidentified assailants shot dead Hy

Vuthy, president of the Free Trade Union at Suntex in Phnom Pehn. In 2008, the International Labor Organization expressed concern at the level of violence directed at union leaders and the lack of official efforts to investigate and punish those responsible, including in Hy Vuthy's case.[37]

Although the Cambodian constitution protects the right to strike and to peaceful demonstration, police and military forces routinely suppress protests. According to one estimate, 108 of the 155 peaceful strikes and demonstrations that took place during 2008 were met with excessive force.[38] As a result, civic groups have urged passage of a "demonstration law" clarifying the right to protest, and the government has introduced such a bill. Critics have raised concerns, however, that the current draft is poorly worded and restrictive, requiring official permission for protests. It nonetheless appears to be on the verge of being enacted.[39]

RULE OF LAW   1.90

INDEPENDENT JUDICIARY	1.20
PRIMACY OF RULE OF LAW IN CIVIL AND CRIMINAL MATTERS	2.00
ACCOUNTABILITY OF SECURITY FORCES AND MILITARY TO CIVILIAN AUTHORITIES	1.75
PROTECTION OF PROPERTY RIGHTS	2.67

Cambodia's legal system is based on the relatively liberal constitution drafted during the UNTAC period, as well as a provisional UNTAC legal code designed for a postconflict society and intended to be temporary. A new French-backed civil procedure code was issued in 2006, and a new Japanese-backed criminal procedure code came into effect in 2007. Problems of inconsistency between these various frameworks plague the system. While the justice system has gradually improved in various technical ways—judges and prosecutors are more knowledgeable and articulate, as well as more assertive in their relations with the police—entrenched patterns of political interference continue to undermine the rule of law and contribute to courts being held in low public regard.

According to former UN special representative Yash Gai, "the institutions charged with implementing the rule of law [in Cambodia] are very weak and subordinated to the government," while people fear courts as "sites of injustice."[40] The judiciary lacks independence and is marred by inefficiency and corruption. Judges, prosecutors, and court clerks are pressured to join the ruling party and to campaign for the CPP during elections. Almost all judges and prosecutors are CPP members,[41] which has facilitated the CPP's use of the courts in recent years to pursue political vendettas against its opponents. In 2005 opposition party leader Sam Rainsy was convicted on charges of defaming Hun Sen, and in 2006 and 2007, FUNCINPEC leader Norodom Rannaridh was charged with corruption and adultery. The use against Rannaridh of a new law criminalizing adultery shortly after it was passed raised concerns that the legislation had been promulgated with the aim of targeting opposition politicians. There is very little sense that the government is expected to comply with court decisions. Rather, the government has on numerous occasions pardoned opposition politicians as part of a political deal following their conviction under dubious circumstances. Such high-profile cases illustrate larger patterns of CPP interference in the judiciary, reinforcing perceptions that the courts serve as a tool of the executive.

The Supreme Council of the Magistracy is, by law, responsible for appointing judges and monitoring judicial conduct. In practice, however, this body lacks the power to punish misconduct, while appointment and promotion processes are characterized by corruption and political interference. A rotation system introduced in 2005, ostensibly to reduce corruption in the judiciary, seems to be functioning more as a form of punishment for those who fall out of political favor than as an impartial accountability mechanism. A new code of conduct for judges was issued in February 2007, but has so far proved ineffective. Membership in the bar association, a requirement for lawyers and judges, has become difficult for some to gain; under the current CPP-aligned bar association president, many applications have been frozen, apparently for political reasons.[42]

Many judges have no formal legal qualifications, and some, including several members of the Supreme Court, have only an elementary school education. The Australian government has invested heavily in funding training through the Royal School of Judges and Prosecutors, yielding some positive results. Nonetheless, the ultimate impact of such programs on strengthening the rule of law remains constrained by the significant political and economic pressures that routinely influence decisions.

There is extensive evidence of biased judgments and failure to observe established legal standards in a range of cases, most notably in land disputes.[43] Although guaranteed under the constitution, the presumption of innocence and the right to counsel are often disregarded. A lack of transparency also plagues the system; journalists interviewed in a recent survey reported that courts were the government agency from which obtaining information was most difficult.[44] Judges and prosecutors continue to struggle to exercise authority over the judicial police, a special branch of the force mandated to arrest and investigate serious crimes. The judicial police at times act as a "second court," working to check the power of the judiciary on behalf of the government.[45]

In 1997, Hun Sen and the CPP seized power in a de facto military "coup."[46] Since then, the security forces have remained highly politicized, with control concentrated in the hands of the prime minister as a matter of personal loyalty rather than democratic institutional oversight. Hun Sen also maintains what is effectively a private army of highly-trained troops: his 4,000-strong Bodyguard Unit and a 2,000-strong military force known as Brigade 70.[47]

Police and soldiers are widely believed to tolerate, or be involved in, the trafficking of guns, drugs, and people, as well as other crimes. As part of a study of illegal logging practices, the international NGO Global Witness stated that the "RCAF [Royal Cambodian Armed Forces] has continued to operate more as an extended crime syndicate than as a defence force."[48] Security officials have occasionally been charged and convicted for abuses of power, notably former Phnom Penh police chief Heng Pov and several of his subordinates. Nonetheless, such prosecutions generally reflect a fall from grace politically, while those who retain close ties to powerful politicians remain immune.

Respect for human rights among members of the security forces remains limited, and according to Human Rights Watch, impunity for violations has been the norm since the 1997 "coup."[49] One human rights group gathered 145 accusations of torture by law enforcement and state officials between 2000 and 2005, with a conviction secured in only one case. In four cases between May and September 2008, off-duty police officers or military personnel opened fire on innocent people for apparently trivial, nonpolitical reasons. Although the shootings resulted in deaths and injuries, the officers in question escaped prosecution.[50]

Land ownership was voided by the Khmer Rouge during the 1970s. Since its defeat in 1979, land titles have been selectively—and with dubious legal basis—reinvented in ways that typically enrich powerful elites at the expense of the country's poor majority. Nearly one million hectares, or 5.2 percent of Cambodia's total land, has been granted to well-connected business groups for plantations or other forms of economic development over the past 15 years.[51] Meanwhile, 80 percent of citizens with land in rural areas have no title deeds,[52] which has facilitated the growing scourge of land grabs across the country. Confiscations routinely occur without adequate notice or compensation and are often accompanied by violence or intimidation meted out by hired thugs or security forces. The state has done little to curb this trend, although some small tracts have been allocated to poor farmers under the legal mechanism of "social concession land." Ethnic minority groups have been particularly disadvantaged by land disputes. Suspicious land purchases and evictions have also occurred in urban areas, including Phnom Penh. In late 2008, the city's historic Renakse Hotel was forcibly closed by well-connected businesspeople hoping to "redevelop" its prime location. Also during the year, over 4,000 families faced displacement as Boeung Kak Lake was turned into a landfill site. Some ministers have reportedly sold the downtown locations housing their ministries to property tycoons. In total, forced evictions in Phnom Penh and elsewhere affected over 27,000 people in 2007.[53]

The Cadastral Commission, created in 2002, is technically charged with mediating land disputes. However, the more recently created National Authority for Land Dispute Resolution (NALDR) has overlapping powers. The existence of both bodies undermines the jurisdiction of the courts over questions of land ownership. The UNTAC-era 1992 Land Law outlines standard international legal principles for land use and holding, based on the notion that "Cambodians have the full right to possess and to use the land."[54] In practice, however, the law is often manipulated or altogether disregarded by officials.[55]

Increased court fees, introduced under the 2007 Code of Civil Procedure, further impede poor Cambodians' ability to pursue legal avenues in order to defend their land rights. Moreover, some community representatives have been charged with crimes as apparent punishments for land rights advocacy. In 2007, Siem Reap community leader So Socheat was charged with battery and destruction of property. Despite a lack of evidence linking her to any criminal behavior, she was convicted on the grounds that she was a "ringleader" and sentenced to eight months in jail.[56] In September 2009, the Cambodian government

---

THE KHMER ROUGE TRIBUNAL AND RULE OF LAW IN CAMBODIA

In February 2008, the Extraordinary Chambers of the Courts of Cambodia (ECCC), popularly known as the Khmer Rouge Tribunal, began hearing evidence against the first of five defendants. The tribunal is a hybrid international-local court, created with UN support and funded by a number of donors (notably Australia, the European Union, and Japan).

The defendants scheduled to stand trial for egregious rights violations committed under the Khmer Rouge regime are Kaing Guek Eav, also known as Duch (former head of the S-21 jail and torture center), Nuon Chea (chief ideologist and parliamentary president under the Khmer Rouge), Khieu Samphan (former president), Ieng Sary (former foreign minister), and his wife, Ieng Thirith.

Supporters of the tribunal argue that prosecuting leading figures from the Khmer Rouge will serve the interests of justice and reconciliation. Perhaps more important, the tribunal will challenge Cambodia's culture of impunity and set a new national standard for impartiality and good governance.[57]

Critics of the tribunal argue that the process is deeply flawed:[58] too few defendants have been charged; the Cambodian majority judges may face political pressures impossible to resist when deciding their verdicts; the trial is not being complemented by other outreach and reconciliation activities; the tribunal is generating limited awareness inside Cambodia; the process is stirring up disturbing and traumatic memories among a significant section of the population; the administration of the court is characterized by pervasive corruption; and the Hun Sen government is cynically exploiting the tribunal to divert attention from, and to a degree justify, its growing authoritarianism.

To date there are few signs that the ECCC is having a positive exemplar effect on the wider Cambodian justice system. Indeed, the court's foreign co-prosecutor, Robert Petit, cited government attempts to interfere in the tribunal's proceedings as "very disturbing" when he quit his position for personal reasons in June 2009.

announced that it was unilaterally terminating the World Bank's US$24 million land re-titling program. Donors had demanded that the government end forced evictions until transparent land dispute mechanisms had been created.

ANTICORRUPTION AND TRANSPARENCY 2.19

ENVIRONMENT TO PROTECT AGAINST CORRUPTION	2.25
PROCEDURES AND SYSTEMS TO ENFORCE ANTICORRUPTION LAWS	2.00
EXISTENCE OF ANTICORRUPTION NORMS, STANDARDS, AND PROTECTIONS	2.00
GOVERNMENTAL TRANSPARENCY	2.50

Corruption and abuse of public office for private gain are endemic, permeating nearly every aspect of public life in Cambodia. Cambodia was rated the third most corrupt country in Asia by the Political and Economic Risk Consultancy in 2009,[59] and ranked 166th out 180 in Transparency International's 2008 Corruption Perceptions Index. The bureaucracy is cumbersome, politicized, and opaque. Citizens are routinely required to pay bribes to access public services. The economy is predominantly cash based, with only a small percentage of transactions passing through the banking system, further facilitating corruption. Recent years have seen some improvements in revenue collection procedures and reduced corruption in certain ministries. However, such changes have been piecemeal and largely overshadowed by almost complete impunity for corrupt practices among both high- and low-ranking officials.

Opportunities for state corruption are extensive, particularly in the extractive and natural resource industries, such as petroleum, gas, and logging. In an extensive 2007 study of the logging industry, Global Witness warned that "Cambodia's extractive industries are exhibiting early warning signs of kleptocratic state capture."[60] The organization characterized the informal business and power networks surrounding Prime Minister Hun Sen as a "shadow state." The study found that corruption in the forestry industry was not confined to isolated officials but involved a systematic policy of extortion ordered and controlled by senior Forest Administration and military police personnel.[61] The Cambodian government has responded to such allegations with vilification and censorship but has failed to offer evidence that might rebut Global Witness's meticulously researched assertions.

In the petroleum industry, contracts are often drafted on an ad hoc basis, undermining consistency and facilitating kickbacks. "Signature payments" by foreign companies to the government at the time oil contracts are signed are the norm. The government has not made public the amount of revenue received or how it has been spent, raising doubts as to whether it found its way to the Cambodian exchequer at all. Following the discovery of additional oil and gas reserves in recent years, the potential for high-level corruption is likely to increase in the short and medium terms.

Although the government has been working on anticorruption legislation since 1995 and has repeatedly promised donors the promulgation of such a law, it has yet to pass one. In August 2008, the government pledged to present the draft bill to the NA, following approval of the new penal code; as the latter piece of legislation has also been long delayed, the anticorruption bill is not yet under parliamentary consideration. Without anticorruption legislation clearly delineating conflict of interest requirements, many cabinet members, senior civil servants, and military officers continue to pursue business interests in fields that also fall under their policy purview.

No legislation requires the declaration of assets or contains other financial disclosure provisions. Information about the identity of concession holders in major industries such as timber and petroleum—including the names of companies and their owners—is also often concealed from the public.

No independent anticorruption agency exists. Pervasive corruption within the judiciary hinders its ability to provide effective oversight of the government or recourse to victims. Two bodies—the Ministry of National Assembly-Senate Relations and Inspection and the Anti-Corruption Unit of the Council of Ministers—are mandated to combat corruption. However, these bodies' close relationship to the CPP and limited resources severely restrict their ability to fulfill their roles effectively.[62]

The National Audit Authority (NAA) was created in 2002 and given the authority to audit ministries and government institutions. Although by law it is to report to parliament, its monthly budget allocations derive from the government, rendering it susceptible to executive influence. In recent years it has conducted some audits and staff have received technical training; however, none of its reports have been made public, despite legal stipulations mandating such disclosure.[63] In some instances, government agencies tasked with overseeing certain industries have used their authority to extort payments from those under supervision. According to Global Witness, officials from the Forest Administration have used their increased effectiveness at detecting illegal activities to extract payments from perpetrators in exchange for not prosecuting them.[64]

Rhetorical commitments from Prime Minister Hun Sen to pursue an anticorruption policy have not been matched with action and government officials continue to enjoy almost complete impunity. With the exception of a small number of token convictions of judges and prosecutors on bribery charges, few officials have been investigated or prosecuted for corruption in recent years.[65]

Although allegations of government corruption receive some coverage in the print media, newspaper editors report that self-censorship related to high-level corruption remains common. Corruption-related stories rarely appear on television, which is closely controlled by the government and is the primary source of information for much of the population. In 2007, the government engaged in extensive efforts to limit circulation of the above-mentioned Global Witness study. In early June, the Ministry of Information ordered the confiscation of print copies of the report and directed newspapers to cease reproducing its contents. In addition, anticorruption activists and journalists risk harassment and physical attacks when investigating illegal activities by officials or powerful private actors, particularly in rural areas.

The educational system suffers from pervasive corruption, with 30 percent of parents estimated to make regular unofficial payments to teachers. A 2005 nationwide survey reported that education-related payments accounted for more than half of the annually reported number of bribes paid. The problem is worse in urban areas; extra payments to teachers are the norm in most Phnom Penh primary schools.

Public access to government information remains poor. No freedom of information legislation exists, although a draft is under preparation with donor support. Some observers have raised concerns, however, that the new law might be used to legalize certain restrictions on free expression. Under Cambodia's 1995 Press Law, journalists may submit written requests for information to government officials, who are obliged to respond within 30 days or explain why they cannot provide the information; however, there is no sanction for officials who deny access. While some journalists have sought to use this provision to obtain official documents, most are reluctant to do so because the process may involve requests for bribes in exchange for information, is unlikely to elicit useful information, and could expose them to charges of defamation if they were to uncover and publicize official misconduct.

Given the relative strength of the executive and CPP dominance of the National Assembly, parliamentary oversight of government operations is limited. Cambodia received a score of 11 percent on the 2008 Open Budget Index, indicating that the government provides scant information to the public about budget and financial activity during the fiscal year.[66] Scrutiny of the budget is hasty, performed behind closed doors, and not subject to thorough review in either the NA or the Senate.[67] The government's budget proposal is not made available to the wider public until after its adoption by the legislature and promulgation by the king.

Public procurement procedures are notoriously corrupt; a 2007 World Bank Enterprise Survey found that nearly 80 percent of firms interviewed reported being expected to provide a gift in order to secure a government contract.[68] Such contracts are typically awarded via a minimally open bidding process.

A large percentage of the national budget is derived from foreign aid. Such international donor funds have also been susceptible to embezzlement and corruption. The UN's World Food Programme fired a number of Cambodian staff in 2005 over irregularities, while the World Bank has found evidence of misused and misrouted funds in 43 of its contracts in Cambodia.[69] The British government's Department for International Development (DFID) recently announced its intention to terminate US$30 million in annual aid to Cambodia by 2013. Officially, the decision was based solely on internal agency priorities and a belief that development aid could be better deployed elsewhere, but Cambodia's poor record on governance and transparency did nothing to help matters.[70]

RECOMMENDATIONS

- In the process of drafting an NGO law, ensure that any legislation passed meets international standards for protecting freedom of association, including enabling local civic groups to freely receive financial support from foreign development agencies.
- In order to improve media freedom, revoke the 1992 UNTAC law governing freedom of expression; abolish the existing criminal offences of defamation, disinformation, and incitement; and grant operating licenses to independent radio stations.
- To better protect the property rights of small landholders, accelerate the process of granting title deeds to rural owners, clarify the delineation of mandates of the Cadastral Commission and the National Authority for Land Dispute Resolution, and abolish court fees in cases related to land grabbing.
- Accelerate and improve enforcement of the 2008 Law on the Suppression of Human Trafficking and Sexual Exploitation.
- Initiate action to depoliticize and professionalize the judicial system, including by granting the Supreme Council of the Magistracy the authority and autonomy to appoint judges, monitor misconduct, and remove justice officials who engage in unethical behavior.
- Enact anticorruption legislation that replaces existing bodies with an independent agency mandated to remove officials involved in corruption and initiate prosecutions. Provide the anticorruption agency with a mixture of local staff and advisors seconded by international organizations.

NOTES

For URLs and endnote hyperlinks, please visit the *Countries at the Crossroads* homepage at http://freedomhouse.org/template.cfm?page=139&edition=8.

[1] IMF statistics from www.imf.org.
[2] Kheang Un, "Cambodia's 2008 Parliamentary Elections: Prospects for Opposition Politics," Asia Pacific Bulletin No. 22 (Washington, D.C.: East-West Center, August 22, 2008).
[3] Global Witness, *Country for Sale: How Cambodia's Elite Has Captured the Country's Extractive Industries* (London: Global Witness, 2009), 54–57.
[4] Caroline Hughes, *Dependent Communities: Aid and Politics in Cambodia and East Timor* (Ithaca, N.Y.: Cornell University Southeast Asia Program, 2009), 233.
[5] The Cambodian Human Rights and Development Association (Adhoc), *Human Rights Situation 2007* (Phnom Penh: Adhoc, 2008), 13.
[6] Asian Network for Free Elections (ANFREL), *Cambodia National Assembly Election, 27 July 2008, Report on the International Election Observation Mission* (Bangkok: ANFREL, October 2008), 9.
[7] The Committee for Free and Fair Elections in Cambodia (COMFREL), *2008 National Assembly Elections: Final Assessment and Report* (Phnom Penh: COMFREL, 2008), 12.
[8] ANFREL, *Cambodia National Assembly Election*, 10.

9. Caroline Hughes, "Cambodia in 2008: Consolidation in the Midst of Crisis," *Asian Survey* 49, no. 1 (January/February 2009): 206–12.
10. Centre for Social Development, *Report on the Process of the National Assembly, Parliamentary Watch Project* (Phnom Penh: Centre for Social Development, 2005), 3–4.
11. Global Witness, *Cambodia's Family Trees: Illegal Logging and the Stripping of Public Assets by Cambodia's Elite* (London: Global Witness, 2007), 61.
12. Cambodian League for the Promotion and Defense of Human Rights (LICADHO), *Attacks and Threats against Human Rights Defenders in Cambodia 2007* (Phnom Penh: LICADHO, August 2008), 21.
13. Craig Guthrie, "The End of an NGO Era in Cambodia," *Asia Times Online*, November 14, 2008.
14. Chrann Chamroeun and Sebastian Strangio, "KCF Head to Apologise for Comments," *Phnom Penh Post*, July 16, 2009.
15. LICADHO, *Attacks and Threats*, 3–4.
16. LICADHO, *Reading between the Lines: How Politics Money and Fear Control Cambodia's Media* (Phnom Penh: LICADHO, May 2008), 68.
17. "Sochua Guilty of Defamation," *Phnom Penh Post*, August 5, 2009.
18. Reporters Without Borders, "Who Masterminded Journalist Khim Sambo's Murder," press release, October 15, 2008.
19. LICADHO, *Reading Between the Lines*, 58.
20. Ibid., 45.
21. Ibid., 29.
22. International Freedom of Expression eXchange (IFEX), "Editor Arrested, Charged, Radio Station Ordered to Stop Broadcasting in Run-Up to Elections," press release, June 10, 2008.
23. LICADHO, *Reading Between the Lines*, i.
24. Adhoc, *Human Rights Situation 2008* (Phnom Penh: Adhoc, 2009), 16–17.
25. LICADHO, *Prison Conditions in Cambodia 2008: Women in Prison* (Phnom Penh: LICADHO, March 2009), 26.
26. LICADHO, *Prison Conditions in Cambodia 2005 and 2006: One Day in the Life* (Phnom Penh: LICADHO, January 2007).
27. Adhoc, *Human Rights Situation 2008*, 7.
28. Sok Khemara, "Gambling Crackdown Underway: Police Chief," VOA Khmer, December 30, 2008.
29. Lao Mong Hay, "Cambodia's Long-Delayed Rights Commission," UPI Asia, December 4, 2008.
30. The Cambodian Committee of Women (CAMBOW), *Violence against Women, How Cambodian Laws Discriminate against Women Report 2007* (Phnom Penh: CAMBOW, November 2007).
31. Radio Free Asia, "Cambodian Women Suffer More Violence," November 26, 2008.
32. Chrann Chamroeun and Georgia Wilkins, "Child Rape Rising as Prosecutions Wane," *Phnom Penh Post*, March 19, 2009.
34. Christopher Shay and Mom Kunthear, "Study Slams Trafficking Law," *Phnom Penh Post*, July 23, 2009.
35. Kurt Bredenberg, "Educational Marginalization of Cham Muslim Populations: A Report from Cambodia," *Journal of Education for International Development* 3, no. 3 (2008): 22.
36. Sebastian Stangio and Sam Rith, "Minority Tongues Face Grim Future," *Phnom Penh Post*, December 9, 2008; Stefan Ehrentraut, "Why Do Minority Tongues Really Face a Grim Future?" *Phnom Penh Post*, December 18, 2008.

[37] International Labour Organization (ILO), *351ʳᵗ Report on the Committee on Freedom of Association* (Geneva: ILO, November 2008), 56–59.
[38] Adhoc, *Human Rights Situation 2008*, 1.
[39] Vong Sokheng, "Critics Decry Demonstration Law," *Phnom Penh Post*, June 18, 2009.
[40] LICADHO, *Attacks and Threats 2007*, 21.
[41] Asian Human Rights Commission (AHRC), "Cambodia: Judicial independence Is the Key to Reducing Defamation Lawsuits against Critics and Upholding Freedom of Expression" (Hong Kong: AHRC, June 16, 2009).
[42] Transparency International, *Global Corruption Report 2007: Corruption in Judicial Systems* (Berlin: Transparency International, 2007), 185.
[43] LICADHO, *Attacks and Threats 2007*, 6.
[44] LICADHO, *Reading Between the Lines*, 49, 66.
[45] Kheang Un, "The Judicial System and Democratization in Post-Conflict Cambodia," in *Beyond Democracy in Cambodia: Political Reconstruction in a Post-Conflict Society*, ed. Joakin Ojendal and Mona Lilja (Copenhagen: NIAS, 2009), 70–100.
[46] Whether the 1997 events amounted to a genuine coup remain hotly debated. See Judy Ledgerwood, "The July 5–6 1997 'Events': When Is a Coup not a Coup?"
[47] Global Witness, *Cambodia's Family Trees*, 68–70.
[48] Global Witness, *Country for Sale*, 73.
[49] Human Rights Watch (HRW), *World Report 2008: Cambodia* (New York: HRW, 2008).
[50] LICADHO, "Impunity at Work in Cambodia: Soldiers and Police Escape Prosecution," October 15, 2008.
[51] United Nations (UN) Special Representative of the Secretary-General for Human Rights in Cambodia, *Economic Land Concessions in Cambodia: A Human Rights Perspective* (Phnom Penh: UN, June 2007). An earlier 2004 report suggested higher figures for the total size of land concessions.
[52] United Nations Development Programme (UNDP), *Expanding Choices for Rural People, Cambodia Human Development Report 2007* (Phnom Penh: UNDP, 2007), 151.
[53] Adhoc, *Human Rights Situation 2007*, 29.
[54] Law Dated October 13, 1992 On the Land, Article 2.
[55] LICADHO, *Human Rights in Cambodia: The Façade of Stability* (Phnom Penh: LICADHO, May 2006), 3.
[56] LICADHO, *Attacks and Threats 2007*, 16–17.
[57] Helen Jarvis and Tom Fawthrop, *Getting Away with Genocide: Cambodia's Long Struggle against the Khmer Rouge* (London: Pluto Press, 2005); Richard Bernstein, "At Last, Justice for Monsters," *New York Review of Books*, April 9, 2009.
[58] John A. Hall, "Trial on Trial," *New York Times*, March 11, 2009; John A. Hall, "Judging the Khmer Rouge Tribunal," *Far Eastern Economic Review*, March 2009.
[59] Agence France Press, "Table of Asian Corruption Scores in PERC Survey," April 8, 2009.
[60] Global Witness, *Country for Sale*, 5.
[61] Global Witness, *Cambodia's Family Trees*, 60.
[62] Transparency International, *National Integrity Systems: Transparency International Country Study Report, Cambodia 2006* (Berlin: Transparency International, 2006), 9.
[63] Transparency International, *National Integrity Systems Cambodia*, 17, 19.
[64] Global Witness, *Country for Sale*, 64.
[65] LICADHO, *Restrictions on the Legal Profession by the Bar Association: A Threat to Free and Independent Legal Aid in Cambodia* (Phnom Penh: LICADHO, December 2007), 22.
[66] Open Budget Initiative, "Cambodia," in *Open Budget Index 2008* (Washington, D.C.: Open Budget Initiative, 2008).

67 Centre for Social Development, *Report on the Process of the National Assembly,* 19.
68 Marie Chêne, "Overview of Corruption in Cambodia," U-4 Anticorruption Resource Centre, March 23, 2009.
69 Transparency International, *National Integrity Systems Cambodia,* 17–8.
70 Bethany Lindsay, "UK's Development Agency to Pull Funding," *Cambodia Daily,* June 22, 2009.

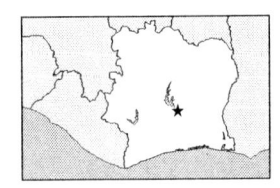

COTE D'IVOIRE

CAPITAL: Yamoussoukro
POPULATION: 21.4 million
GNI PER CAPITA (PPP): $1,580

SCORES	2006	2010
ACCOUNTABILITY AND PUBLIC VOICE:	N/A	2.39
CIVIL LIBERTIES:	N/A	2.86
RULE OF LAW:	N/A	2.44
ANTICORRUPTION AND TRANSPARENCY:	N/A	2.02

(scores are based on a scale of 0 to 7, with 0 representing weakest and 7 representing strongest performance)

INTRODUCTION

Since the end of the civil war that devastated Cote d'Ivoire between 2002 and 2007, the country has been relatively peaceful. Events have taken place that would have been unimaginable several years ago, including the dismantling of the buffer zone dividing the country's north and south, the granting of identification papers to millions of previously disenfranchised northern residents, and the formation of a government of national unity bringing together top leaders on opposite sides of the conflict. Nevertheless, the country continues to be led by a president with an expired mandate, and the prospects for peaceful democratic development in the near future remain fragile. Distrust and corruption are defining features of the political landscape, both government and rebel forces continue to purchase arms, and youth militias intimidate and attack critics of the president. Meanwhile, general elections have been repeatedly postponed.

Cote d'Ivoire gained independence from France in 1960. That year, Felix Houphoët-Boigny was elected unopposed and became the country's first president, subsequently ruling the country in authoritarian fashion until his death in 1993, though limited multiparty politics were introduced in 1990. During the Houphoët-Boigny regime, Cote d'Ivoire, with its large-scale cocoa production, was one of the most economically prosperous countries in Africa. Following Houphoët-Boigny's death, Henry Konan Bedie ruled until December 1999, when he was overthrown in a bloodless coup by General Robert Guei. Guei governed only until 2000, when Laurent Gbagbo emerged victorious from flawed presidential elections. Gbagbo has ruled the country since, although his elected term technically expired in 2005.

The mid-1990s were characterized by a rise in nationalist discourse and conflict over the concept of *ivoirité*, or who should be considered a "true" Ivorian. Revisions to the 1995 electoral law and a new constitution that came into effect in 2000 placed limitations on citizenship and participation in elections, including restricting presidential eligibility to individuals with two Ivorian parents and no other previous nationality.[1] Such arrangements excluded Alassane Ouattara, a Muslim opposition candidate who would have formed a formidable rival to Bedie and Gbagbo had he been permitted to run. The move contributed to growing mistrust and conflict between different social communities, particularly between the largely Christian south and east and the predominantly Muslim north, where many residents are descendants of migrants from nearby countries brought in to work in the cocoa sector. Adding to northern resentment were anti-immigration policies and the promotion of a nationalistic, xenophobic discourse by state-run media and government-affiliated youth organizations.

The 2000 elections pitted General Guei against Gbagbo, as Ouatarra and Bedie were barred from participation. While Gbagbo was declared the victor, severe post election violence broke out, with multiple attacks against "non-Ivorians," including individuals who had lived in the country for decades, causing the deaths of hundreds of civilians. The animosity continued to escalate and in 2002 erupted in an armed uprising and failed coup attempt by soldiers led by Guillaume Soro, the Roman Catholic leader of the Patriotic Movement of Cote d'Ivoire. Guei was killed in Abidjan immediately. Rebels took over the north and called for Gbagbo's removal while also clashing with southern loyalists. Northern factions and armed groups in the west united under the leadership of Soro to form the New Forces (FN). The conflict quickly evolved into a full-scale civil war as the FN took over much of the north, leaving the country divided in two. The south would subsequently be governed by Gbagbo's government, while the north remained under FN control and featured parallel military and administrative governing structures called "com zones." A buffer zone patrolled by over 12,000 French and United Nations (UN) peacekeepers was created to separate the two sides and prevent further bloodshed.

Five peace agreements were brokered between 2003 and 2007, but none took hold as the country remained deeply divided between north and south, with periodic spurts of violence between rebel and government forces. Hundreds (thousands by some counts) of Ivorians died and 750,000 were displaced, while torture, rape, and extrajudicial killings, often targeting specific ethnic groups, were widespread. The large number of immigrants in Cote d'Ivoire, reports of Liberian mercenaries participating in the fighting, and accusations that Burkina Faso was supporting rebel forces even led to fears that the conflict would spread into a regional crisis.

The Ivorian government and the FN brokered the Ouagadougou Peace Accord (OPA) in March 2007. The peace agreement put a formal end to the conflict and outlined a path forward, including the establishment of a government of national unity that would oversee democratic elections, the granting of identification cards to millions of residents, disarmament, and reestablishment of state authority throughout the entire country. In a dramatic warming of relations between the conflict's protagonists, Soro became Gbagbo's prime minister, and the two have since shared power.

Although conditions in both halves of the country have improved significantly since the signing of the OPA, the situation remains fragile and a return to armed conflict is not inconceivable. Elections have repeatedly been delayed. A culture of impunity continues to dominate the political landscape, while a proliferation of small arms fuels further rights abuses. Democratic civilian control over the security forces is weak, and parastatal armed groups frequently carry out extortion and violence against the population. Governance is hindered by incompetence and rampant corruption. Meanwhile, thousands of international troops remain stationed in Cote d'Ivoire.

In addition to political turmoil, the country has also experienced substantial economic decline over the last decade due to conflict, corruption, and fluctuating global prices for cocoa and other agricultural commodities. Economic conditions have improved slightly since the end of the conflict, but poverty and unemployment remain widespread. Government action on many urgent social and economic problems has been delayed, including an HIV/AIDS rate of around 4 percent.[2] The country receives large amounts of international aid, though the donor community is wary of funds being siphoned off for corruption as well as the use of government resources to purchase arms despite a UN arms embargo imposed in 2004.

ACCOUNTABILITY AND PUBLIC VOICE 2.39

FREE AND FAIR ELECTORAL LAWS AND ELECTIONS	1.50
EFFECTIVE AND ACCOUNTABLE GOVERNMENT	2.00
CIVIC ENGAGEMENT AND CIVIC MONITORING	3.33
MEDIA INDEPENDENCE AND FREEDOM OF EXPRESSION	2.71

Since 2005, Cote d'Ivoire has been ruled by an unelected government and legislature whose term has expired. Although the 2007 OPA have improved governance, reduced violence, and enabled the registration of millions of new voters, most leading actors across the political spectrum display more concern for their personal well-being than to democratic institutions and governance. As elections have been repeatedly delayed, impatience and frustration have grown among the citizenry.

Cote d'Ivoire's constitution provides for direct election of the president and the 225-member, unicameral National Assembly to five-year terms. The most recent presidential and parliamentary elections were held in 2000. Although the constitutional mandate for both the president and parliament expired in 2005, elections originally scheduled for that October have been repeatedly postponed due to ongoing political violence and delays in implementation of the OPA, including necessary voter registration and disarmament of combatants on both sides. *[Editor's note: Since the time of writing, the November 2009 elections have been postponed to 2010.]*

There are four key political forces in Cote d'Ivoire, each viewed as linked to a given region and associated with a particular leader, with the relationships between the dominant figures dating back to the 1980s. Laurent Gbagbo is the most powerful individual, having served as president since 2000 and established a network of loyalists throughout state institutions. Although Gbagbo's mandate expired in 2005, he remains in his position pending new elections. His affiliated Ivorian Popular Front (FPI) draws its support mainly from western and southwestern Cote d'Ivoire and acted as the primary opposition party during the Houphoët-Boigny period. It holds 96 seats in the National Assembly based on the results of the 2000 legislative polls.

Henri Konan Bedie, who served as president from 1993 to 1999, heads the largest party in parliament, the Democratic Party of Cote d'Ivoire (PDCI), which had been the ruling party under Houphoët-Boigny and draws support from the center and east. It holds 98 parliamentary seats. Both the FPI and PDCI are linked to majority-Christian regions.

Alassane Ouattara, a northern Muslim, served as prime minister under Houphouët-Boigny from 1990 to 1993 before losing a power struggle with Bedie following the longtime leader's death. He left the country and worked at the International Monetary Fund (IMF), having been barred from competing in presidential elections because of controversy over whether his parents were native Ivorians. Ouattara heads the Rally of Republicans (RDR) party, which draws support from the largely Muslim north. The RDR mostly boycotted the 2000 election and holds only five seats in the current legislative assembly. The RDR and PDCI have allied in hopes of ousting Gbagbo in the upcoming election. Gbagbo, Bedie, and Ouattara are the leading candidates in the polls.

Meanwhile, Guillaume Soro, who has served as Gbagbo's prime minister since 2007, has sought to maintain an air of neutrality while cautiously pushing forward the steps needed to hold elections. As the leader of a military movement, it remains unclear whether Soro will seek to fully transform the FN into a political party or emphasize the role of its political wing, known as the MCPI. Such a party could potentially pull northern votes from the RDR. The greater challenge facing Soro in recent years has been trying to keep his movement unified, as he has faced criticism—and possibly an assassination attempt—from within his own camp after joining forces with Gbagbo, contributing to a growing threat of intra-FN conflict.

While there has been little opportunity for the effective rotation of power among different political parties due to the absence of elections, recent conditions point to trouble for Gbagbo. A September 2009 Gallup poll revealed that 52 percent of interviewees disapproved of the president's job performance. The poll confirmed residual differences between the north and south: a majority in the south approved of the president, while a majority of northerners disapproved.[3] Some observers have cited Gbagbo's low approval ratings and fear of losing power as a reason for the government's slow implementation—and in some cases, his personal obstruction—of the electoral preparations.[4]

Both the OPA and practical reality require that a number of conditions be met prior to balloting, including the distribution of identity cards, the creation of an electoral registry, the reintegration of rebel forces into the army, the disarming of other rebel groups, and the restoration of political administration in the north. Although significant progress was made on some of these measures in 2008 and 2009, the conditions are far from being fully satisfied.[5]

The voter identification process made significant strides, although it greatly exceeded the deadlines laid out in the OPA. According to the UN envoy in Cote d'Ivoire, 6.5 million people had been registered to vote by July 2009,[6] while over 500,000 people were issued new birth certificates in order to establish voter eligibility. Candidates began campaigning in 2009, as both Bedie and Ouattara traveled the country speaking at generally peaceful rallies. Nonetheless, the government's significant control over official media outlets has hindered equal campaigning opportunities for all candidates. Opposition supporters' repeated accusations of unbalanced airtime allotment by official television stations were confirmed by the UN in July 2009.[7]

Progress on disarmament and the reassertion of government control over the north has been less encouraging. Ex-rebels began to disarm in 2008, but the process has languished and both sides reportedly maintain sizable forces and continue to accumulate weapons from abroad, keeping violence as an option should the election results be deemed unacceptable.[8] Although the formal north-south division has been abolished, state authority has yet to extend throughout the country. In a symbolic ceremony in Bouake in May 2009, the "com zones" transferred administrative power to government-appointed prefects. However, it remains unclear how much authority the rebel commanders have relinquished in practice, particularly as orders from Soro and other FN leaders are sometimes disobeyed. This mix of cooperation and resistance has led to uneven implementation. In addition, many FN commanders continue to retain their own militias for the purposes of protection and extortion.[9] While some civil servants were deployed to posts in the north along with appointed prefects, their effectiveness has been hindered by a severe lack of funding; many have returned to the south because of poor living and working conditions.[10]

Efforts to identify and register voters have been inefficient and disorganized. Five different bodies are involved in the process, including the Independent Electoral Commission (CEI), but coordination between them has been severely lacking and at times the bodies have contradicted and competed with one another. Allegations of corruption within the CEI and other agencies have also emerged, with some observers noting that CEI officials have little incentive to expedite voter identification and enrollment and lose an additional source of income.[11] Registration delays have also been attributed to opportunistic funding, in which the Ministry of Finance allocates resources in line with the president's political needs. Some observers suggest that Gbagbo may be hoping to force his rivals to accept an incomplete identification process in order to diminish the number of new voters in the north, where his unpopularity is highest.[12]

Though the constitution provides for checks and balances, the judiciary is not independent and provides little oversight of the government. The National Assembly, currently functioning without a mandate, engages in little legislative activity. In recent years, key policy decisions have been made by presidential decree, often based on negotiations with the international community or other elite actors rather than popular will or public consultation. Meanwhile, various pieces of legislation await eventual approval by a newly elected parliament.

Gbagbo's complex relationships with his ministers and the international community illustrate his resolve to continue to exercise significant power. Indeed, the president's decision to engage in "direct dialogue" with Soro in 2007 has been widely interpreted as an effort to circumvent a UN-led plan that would have seen his authority weakened and greater powers transferred to the technocratic then-prime minister, Charles Konan Banny. Though Soro has gained some capacity to influence policy and on occasion taken steps to supervise implementation of the OPA, he has largely avoided actions that might cause clear confrontation with the president and in reality, Gbagbo remains at the center of power. The president is the primary decision maker and relies heavily on a close circle of consultants, including his wife.[13] Upon becoming prime minister, Soro named a new 33-member cabinet from across the political spectrum, including members of the FPI, FN, RDR, PDCI, and members of civil society and small political parties.[14] Such diversity is superficial, however, as in practice, opposition-affiliated ministers lack authority over their subordinates and senior bureaucrats, who are loyal primarily to Gbagbo.[15] In general, the civil service is highly politicized and corruption is pervasive, with appointments and dismissals decided primarily based on personal relations with powerful actors—particularly the president—rather than merit.

Civic groups in Cote d'Ivoire have little influence over government policy, a dynamic that has been further reinforced since the signing of the OPA, which largely sidelined actors outside of the Gbagbo-Soro government, including opposition parties and members of civil society. The weakness of parliament means there are few formal channels for public participation or input in policy debates. Nevertheless, a wide range of civil society groups continue to operate and usually face few legal or other restrictions from the government, as they are not perceived to directly threaten presidential power. Some incidents of legal harassment have occurred, however. In January 2008, Modeste Seri, a civil society leader and vocal critic of both President Gbagbo and the FN, was detained for allegedly planning a coup against the government.[16] He remained in prison for over a year without charge, but was finally released in May 2009.[17]

The primary threat to human rights activists has come from nonstate actors and the broader national atmosphere of intimidation and militarization. The army and FN both remain heavily armed, despite disarmament efforts, and have engaged in intimidation of their rivals' supporters. Gbagbo-loyal militias, including the Young Patriots, engage in violence against those believed to be sympathetic to the FN or RDR.[18] Since 2002, the Student Federation of Cote d'Ivoire (FESCI), a student group whose members are known for being "staunch partisans" of President Gbagbo, has engaged in violence against journalists, opposition ministers, and human rights organizations.[19] Impunity has been the norm in all such incidents. Despite such challenges, civic groups actively fill gaps in effective government action at the local level, such as combating violence against women, assisting ethnic reconciliation efforts, and exposing prison abuse. The Civil Society Coalition for Peace and Development in Cote d'Ivoire (COSOPCI), formed by 15 human rights, democracy, and good governance organizations, plays a vital role working with local community organizations on advocacy strategies, documentation of human rights violations, and local-level conflict resolution.[20] The broader impact of such initiatives on key issues such as elections or disarmament has been limited, however.

The majority of news in Cote d'Ivoire is transmitted by radio. The government controls the largest radio stations (including the only one with national reach), the largest daily newspaper, and all television stations. Although over 100 independent community radio stations operate, their workers often face harassment for presenting diverse views or scrutinizing the government. There has been some improvement in press freedom since 2005, especially with the signing of the OPA, but threats from both the government and nonstate actors continue to significantly constrain free expression, particularly in the south. Relatively fewer incidents of media harassment have been reported in the rebel-controlled north and the FN has generally refrained from interfering with citizens' access to progovernment radio and newspaper reporting.

The Ivorian constitution provides for freedom of the press, and when President Gbagbo assumed office in January 2000, he made a public promise that he would never imprison a politician or a journalist for expressing his or her opinion. In 2004, the parliament scrapped criminal punishment for press offenses, including libel. In practice, however, such legal changes have been routinely disregarded, as journalists continue to face defamation suits, crippling fines, and imprisonment for criticizing the president. In 2007, NGO activist Antoine Assale Tiemoko was arrested and sentenced to one year in prison after publishing an opinion piece on judicial corruption in *Le Nouveau Reveil*.[21] In March 2009, the pro-opposition weekly *Le Repere* was convicted of "insulting" President Gbagbo, suspended for two months, and ordered to pay US$40,000 in fines after publishing an article that detailed alleged embezzlement and human rights violations committed by President Gbagbo and the ruling party.[22]

With widespread self-censorship and vitriolic rhetoric in both the opposition and progovernment private press, international concerns over xenophobia and hate speech in the Ivorian media remain acute, though the prevalence of such rhetoric has lessened in recent years. This is partly due to the August 2008 ban on expressions of xenophobia, racism, or tribalism. Under the new regulation, offenders face harsher sentences if problematic expressions are relayed via media outlets, during demonstrations or political rallies, or by government functionaries.[23] Although ostensibly meant to protect victims of hate speech, international press freedom groups have raised concerns that the regulation's imprecise wording could enable the government to use it to restrict free expression.

Though journalists in Cote d'Ivoire have in recent years been safe from murder or severe physical attacks, the Ivorian government does not adequately protect journalists from violence by parastatal forces. In 2005–2006, the Young Patriots carried out a series of attacks against independent journalists, seized control of state broadcasting stations, and destroyed copies of pro-opposition papers, sometimes using threats of violence and rape against relevant staff.[24] FESCI has also reportedly attacked media outlets over perceived unfavorable coverage. Radio France International (RFI) has been the subject of a particularly virulent nationalist campaign; the government and Ivorian National Council for Broadcast Communication have restricted RFI broadcasts for months at a time.[25]

The government exerts significant control over state-owned media outlets. State television and radio stations and newspapers—including the highest circulation daily newpaper, *Fraternite Matin*—generally toe the government line. In November 2006, the president dissolved the board of directors of the publicly-owned radio and television authority, Radiotelevision Ivoirienne (RTI), and controlled the outlet until nominating new directors in 2009.[26] Though the government does not directly restrict the internet, poverty and infrastructure deficits limit its usage.

CIVIL LIBERTIES   2.86

PROTECTION FROM STATE TERROR, UNJUSTIFIED IMPRISONMENT, AND TORTURE	1.88
GENDER EQUITY	2.67
RIGHTS OF ETHNIC, RELIGIOUS, AND OTHER DISTINCT GROUPS	3.00
FREEDOM OF CONSCIENCE AND BELIEF	4.00
FREEDOM OF ASSOCIATION AND ASSEMBLY	2.75

Following the outbreak of the civil war in 2002, all parties to the conflict committed severe human rights violations. Sexual violence, torture, pillaging, extrajudicial killings, and kidnappings were frequent, peaking between 2002 and 2004. Though the exact number of casualties is nearly impossible to estimate, extrapolation from several incidents in 2004 in which hundreds were killed likely indicate a death toll in the thousands.[27] Such abuses have gradually declined, though ethnic violence and other rights violations by a range of actors continue throughout the country. Moreover, in April 2007, the president granted perpetrators amnesty, reinforcing an environment of impunity in the post-conflict era.

The conflict also led to large-scale displacement. Although some have been able to return home, the number has declined little since 2006, when 750,000 internally displaced persons (IDPs) from the north were living with families in the south, often in decrepit shantytowns.[28] The number of IDPs still stands at an estimated 709,000.[29]

The Ivorian government does not provide sufficient protection for its citizens against torture and other violence by state authorities or nonstate actors. Though committed on a less rampant scale than prior to the OPA, torture remains a widespread phenomenon, routinely committed by government troops and rebel forces to punish detainees, extract confessions, or extort payments.[30]

Prison conditions are abysmal, including for detained children. Hunger, overcrowding, poor sanitation, and skin diseases are common.[31] Malnutrition is a particularly egregious problem, and the International Committee of the Red Cross warned in 2008 that beriberi, a disease linked to malnutrition and vitamin deficiency, had reached epidemic levels.[32] The wealthy can often buy sentence reductions or marginally improved prison conditions; for others, prison breaks offer an exit route. In violation of constitutional protections, state security forces continue to carry out arbitrary arrests. Long-term detention without trial for both political and criminal detainees remains common.[33] The FN continues to maintain its own detention centers and prisons, often in makeshift facilities such as schools or movie theaters. In several incidents in 2008, FN combatants reportedly took suspected criminals into custody and abused them, leading to accidental deaths or deliberate extrajudicial executions.[34]

Though not at the epidemic levels of the conflict, violent action by nonstate actors, primarily ex-combatants and pro-Gbagbo youth organizations, remains a serious threat to ordinary residents. A 2007 report found that the massive proliferation of weapons and the failure of combatants to disarm contributed to an increase in crime as "frustrated ex-rebels" with AK-47 rifles and rocket launchers committed armed burglaries, carjackings, and rape.[35] The UN reported a similar dynamic, particularly in the north, as of 2009.[36] According to Human Rights Watch, in 2008, government forces and FN rebels engaged in extortion at checkpoints and sexual abuse.[37] In response to rising crime rates, in 2005 the Ministry of Interior formed the Security Operations Command Center (CECOS), but the agency's officers themselves have since been accused of committing extrajudicial killings and other crimes with impunity.[38]

Contributing to the cycle of violence has been both *de jure* and *de facto* impunity for past and current abuses. Observers have expressed particular concern over an April 2007 regulation issued by President Gbagbo that granted amnesty to perpetrators of violence during the war and led to the release of detainees. Although the president assured human rights groups that the amnesty would not apply to crimes against humanity, and that "victims [would] have every opportunity to lodge their complaints,"[39] virtually no attempt has been made to punish perpetrators of grave human rights abuses. The UN has criticized the amnesty as not complying with international law for failing to "explicitly exclude war crimes and crimes against humanity."[40] Acts of violence from the post-conflict period have also been met with near-complete impunity.

The constitution does not guarantee a right of redress for victims of state abuse and in practice, lack of political will and capacity prevent effective remedy. Amnesty International reported that women who were sexually assaulted by state agents during the civil war have received neither compensation nor access to adequate health care.[41] Victims of violence by progovernment militias and FN forces have similarly been denied reparations.

Prosecutions carried out in the wake of a massive 2006 toxic waste scandal were a partial exception to the overall culture of impunity. In August 2006, a local company working with Trafigura, a Dutch petroleum trading firm, dumped chemical waste into Abidjan's main landfill, located near the city's poor neighborhoods. At least 15 people died as a result, with approximately 100,000 falling ill. In 2006, the Ivorian government released a report placing blame for the spill on Ivorian port and governmental officials and on Trafigura.[42] In October 2008, two individuals—the head of the local firm hired to handle the waste and a shipping agent at the Port of Abidjan—were sentenced to prison, while several other suspects were acquitted. Gbagbo orchestrated a settlement in which Trafigura committed to pay compensation to thousands of Abidjan residents, apparently in exchange for immunity from prosecution.[43] As of October 2009, it was unclear whether any funds had reached the intended recipients.

In an encouraging development, the government, with UN support, established a National Human Rights Commission in July 2008. The commission submitted its first annual report in June 2009, documenting 201 cases of human rights violations (154 of which remained pending as of December 31, 2008) and also made policy recommendations to the government. According to Human Rights Watch, however, "its capacity to fully investigate and report on serious abuses was limited by inadequate funding and support from the government."[44]

Cote d'Ivoire serves as both a source and destination for traffic in women and children. Women, mostly girls, are trafficked from neighboring countries for domestic servitude, restaurant labor, and sexual exploitation, while young men are trafficked internally and from neighboring countries for forced agricultural labor, particularly in the cocoa sector.[45] Although the Ivorian government's anti-trafficking efforts have improved, measures to protect and assist victims suffer from sparse resource provision.

Women in Cote d'Ivoire take an active role in politics, but are generally underrepresented; only 18 of 225 parliamentarians are women.[46] Nevertheless, in September 2009, the country's first female presidential candidate announced her participation in the upcoming elections. Although the constitution prohibits gender discrimination, certain laws and customs place women at an economic and social disadvantage. These include the common, though technically illegal, practice of child marriage and obstacles some banks impose on women obtaining loans, including requiring a husband's permission.[47]

Women suffered greatly from the war's violence, experiencing rape, humiliation, sexual slavery, and forced incest.[48] Few, if any, perpetrators have been punished. Rather, according to the International Crisis Group (ICG) and Amnesty International, both government and rebel leaders authorized the use of sexual violence against women as a tool of war. Some of the worst abuses were reportedly committed in the west by armed groups that included mercenaries from neighboring Liberia.[49] Reports in 2009 indicated that women in rural northern areas were especially vulnerable to rape as they walked to and from agricultural fields. As law enforcement agencies are perceived as ineffective, such cases are typically dealt with by local vigilantes, often resulting in bloodshed.[50]

Violence against women and the impunity surrounding it have continued into the post-conflict period. No specific penalties apply to domestic violence, which remains rampant.[51] Women are often shamed into not seeking assistance, as such abuse is widely perceived as a "family problem," and spousal rape is not recognized as illegal. Female genital mutilation (FGM) was made illegal and punishable by up to five years' imprisonment in 1998. However, the practice remains fairly widespread: a 2005 UNICEF study estimated that 45 percent of women aged 15 to 49 had undergone FGM, a slight increase from 1994.[52]

Cote d'Ivoire is home to a large population of disabled persons. Since 1998, legislation has guaranteed equality for the disabled in employment, education, and training. In practice, however, discrimination remains endemic; much of the country's disabled population is unaware of its rights. HIV/AIDS sufferers are not legally protected from discrimination, but the government has prioritized addressing the country's high infection rate. In 2007, Gbagbo and Soro released the 2006-2010 National Strategic Plan, outlining a US$577 million program aimed at "scaling up towards universal access to HIV prevention, treatment, care and support."[53] It remains to be seen whether such a plan will be feasible to implement, particularly given the government's limited control over the north.

As one observer noted, "Cote d'Ivoire comes close to a textbook example of violent politicization of ethnicity."[54] Ethnic and geographic divisions lay at the root of the civil war, often overlapping with religious demography, though the latter was not a key basis for violence. The country is home to over 40 different ethnic groups, including a large population (25 percent) of migrants or their descendents originating from Burkina Faso, Mali, Niger, and Lebanon, among others. For decades following Ivorian independence, intercommunal tensions were rare under the strong-handed rule of Houphouët-Boigny. Pressure began to rise after his death as subsequent governments and leaders harnessed ethnically charged rhetoric for their own political benefit. The accumulated resentment erupted into electoral violence in 2000 and civil war in

2002, as rebels called for all those born in Cote d'Ivoire to be granted citizenship, while Gbagbo loyalists targeted northerners residing in the south, who were assumed to be RDR supporters.

With implementation of the peace accord and the registration of voters underway throughout the country, millions of individuals from traditionally excluded groups in the north have been granted electoral rights. Nevertheless, tensions remain and the Young Patriots have attempted to forcibly disrupt registration, using ethno-regional criteria.[55] In addition, many northerners, especially those with last names indicating ancestry from neighboring countries, continue to face pervasive discrimination and often accuse the authorities of assuming they are rebels based solely on their origin.[56]

The constitution provides for freedom of religion. The government generally respects religious rights and does not interfere in religious practice and organization. Any new religious organization must go through a substantial registration process, but there have been no recent reports of any group being denied registration. Though the government generally respects religious freedom, religious affiliations have often been associated with ethnic and geographic divisions. Many ethnic northerners are Muslim, and as a result, the government targeted Muslims as suspected rebels and rebel sympathizers during the height of the conflict. This situation has improved in recent years, however. Muslims are similarly underrepresented in the civil service and complain of inadequate or biased state media coverage of Muslim affairs.[57]

Freedom of assembly and association are both guaranteed by the constitution, and laws protect the rights of both public and private sector workers to form unions. Historically, President Gbagbo has enjoyed a friendly relationship with unions; indeed, his persecution at the hands of the Houphouët-Boigny regime was partially a result of his union activities. Occasionally, unions are able to affect policy. In July 2008, taxi and other transportation workers led a strike to protest rising fuel costs. Officials met with the strikers, and the government ultimately lowered the salaries of ministers and state-owned enterprise managers in order to reduce the price of fuel.[58] In other instances, however, the government has interfered in union activities. In addition, the authorities have used excessive force against demonstrating workers. In January 2008, police violently suppressed a protest organized by the workers' collective at the port where the Trafigura waste entered the country.[59]

The constitution protects the right of free assembly, but demonstrations in Abidjan and elsewhere are limited. Security forces used violence against protesters on several occasions in recent years. In February 2008, police used teargas to disperse female demonstrators marching in Abidjan to protest a month-long cutoff of drinking water for the city's residents. In April 2008, police in Abidjan forcibly dispersed a protest related to rising food costs, causing one death and 10 injuries.[60] Despite the violence, the government responded to the demonstrators' demands and slashed taxes on key food imports.[61]

RULE OF LAW 2.44

INDEPENDENT JUDICIARY	2.20
PRIMACY OF RULE OF LAW IN CIVIL AND CRIMINAL MATTERS	2.40
ACCOUNTABILITY OF SECURITY FORCES AND MILITARY TO CIVILIAN AUTHORITIES	2.50
PROTECTION OF PROPERTY RIGHTS	2.67

Following the outbreak of civil war and the country's division into two separately governed units, the judicial system in the rebel-held north was decimated. Professional court staff fled south, replaced by rebel-appointed volunteers taking on the roles of prosecutors, judge, and jury with little regard for due process.[62] In the south, the formal judicial system remained in place, but was marred by extensive corruption and political interference. Although judges began returning to the north in 2009, access to the impartial administration of justice and an end to impunity remain beyond the reach of most Ivorians.

The Ivorian legal system is based primarily on French law and includes three tiers. The Ivorian judiciary consists of nine first instance courts and three appeals courts, with the Supreme Court at the highest level.[63] In addition, a High Court of Justice is empowered to judge members of the government for crimes committed during their tenure, as well as to judge the president on any charge of treason. A Constitutional Council may rule on the constitutionality of laws, as well as arbitrate electoral disputes.[64]

Despite constitutional guarantees of judicial independence, the administration of justice is highly vulnerable to executive and military influence. Although judges in the south enjoy greater autonomy in civil and criminal cases, they generally follow the government line on politically sensitive or national security cases. This is largely due to a lack of security of tenure and a politicized appointment process. Under the Statute of Magistrates, the president appoints judges based on recommendations by the minister of justice and in accordance with the opinion of the High Council of the Judiciary, a body headed by the president and otherwise comprised primarily of senior judges. While the law guarantees tenure for judges and requires their consent to enable appointment to new positions, in practice, removals and relocations have been carried out by ministerial decree.[65]

Judges in Cote d'Ivoire are generally well-trained and enjoy higher salaries then their colleagues in the civil service. Nevertheless, remuneration is still low, making judges susceptible to bribery. This contributes to rampant corruption in the judicial system, as well as inequality before the law: wealthy defendants and plaintiffs are more likely to win cases than their less affluent counterparts. The impact of such practices on public confidence in the judiciary has been far-reaching. In 2007, the UN Mission in Cote d'Ivoire reported that "people have come to believe, even though fortunately it's not always the case, that it is impossible to get a favorable decision without handing over money."[66]

Access to justice in the north remains limited despite important progress toward establishing a court system since the signing of the peace accords. In early 2009, judges, prosecutors, and clerks began to be redeployed to the north for the first time in seven years. Nevertheless, inadequate resources and persistent delays in the provision of key personnel have rendered many northern courts still ineffective. Even in areas where judicial personnel were present as of mid-2009, the re-established courts primarily handled administrative affairs, while criminal cases generally go unprosecuted.[67] Court officials have also reportedly encountered resistance from rebel soldiers reluctant to surrender authority.[68]

Urban areas in the south are generally governed through civil law. Customary law continues to prevail in rural areas, though its influence has gradually declined with expansion of the formal court system. Under customary law, domestic disputes and minor land questions are often resolved through extended debate.

Legislation provides criminal defendants with a range of due process guarantees. In practice, however, such provisions—including the presumption of innocence—are not consistently respected and higher courts are reported to rarely overturn verdicts.[69] Suspects, even children, are often held for long periods without trial and denied access to family members or lawyers.[70] Observers widely acknowledge that fair trials are rare and that bribes or other favors are more likely to influence verdicts than the facts of a case. Social or familial ties are also known to influence the outcome of cases, while instances of sexual favors being exchanged for particular decisions have also been reported.[71] Public officials and ruling party actors are rarely prosecuted for abuse of power or other wrongdoing.

Despite some progress in recent years, security sector reform, including the establishment of democratic civilian control over the armed forces, disarmament of militias, and integration of rebel troops into the military, remains a serious challenge. In the north, in particular, the government has yet to fully establish a monopoly over the use of force, though the country was technically reunified in 2008. Efforts to create joint security forces comprised of former combatants on both sides—such as an 8,000-strong Integrated Command Center—have met with limited success, due largely to a lack of funding and adequately trained FN fighters. Although the UN documented an increase in the number of rebels joining the reintegration program in 2009 compared to the previous year, only a small percentage have been allocated new civilian roles.[72] Meanwhile, according to the ICG, 20,000 progovernment militiamen had not been disarmed as of mid-2009.[73] While rebels have been reluctant to hand over their weapons, the government has been equally hesitant to provide the financial support promised to each former combatant under the peace accord. Together, these factors sparked riots in June 2008 in the northern city of Bouake by ex-rebels demanding the promised funds.[74]

In addition to sexual and physical violence, Ivorian security forces have engaged in large-scale extortion. At roadblocks across the country, security forces and rebel combatants solicit bribes from drivers, especially if they lack proper identification papers, and sometimes use force against those who refuse. In 2008 the World Bank estimated the funds collected annually by security forces at between US$173.6 and US$456 million for passenger transportation, and US$54.8 and US$68.5 million for the transportation of goods.[75] While impunity is the norm for such actions, in isolated instances, members of the security forces have been held accountable. In October 2008, Amnesty International reported that a member of a security agency who shot and killed a bus driver after he refused to make a payment at a checkpoint was convicted of the murder and given a three-year sentence.[76]

Although Article 15 of the constitution protects the right to property, in practice, the system of land ownership is confused, poorly documented, and weakly enforced, contributing to a growing number of violent incidents surrounding property disputes. Customary law governs usage of at least 70 percent of land, according to official estimates, as it has for decades. Legislation passed in 1998 enables conversion from customary law to formal title deeds, but implementation has been repeatedly delayed, with the first certificate only expected in mid-2009. In addition, under the 1998 law, indigenous Ivorian citizens were granted the right to own rural land, while noncitizens received only long-term leases or rental agreements, contributing to some of the tensions that sparked the civil war.

The conflict further complicated the situation, as hundreds of thousands were driven from their property. In the post-conflict period, many IDPs trying to return home have found others living on their land. Moreover, the conflict upset the customary procedures for tracking land ownership, as customary chiefs with knowledge of local transactions were among those displaced.[77] In the face of such complexities, the government amended the 1998 law in September 2008 to allow non-Ivorians who had acquired full ownership prior to 1998 to retain their titles. As more residents have obtained citizenship in the run-up to elections, the practical impact of the law's discriminatory framing has also been reduced. Nonetheless, observers have raised concerns about impartial, transparent implementation of the law. In the meantime, the number of violent land disputes has continued to rise. Between June and September 2008, for example, unrelated disputes in the south, east, and Abidjan turned violent, resulting in at least 17 deaths and 30 wounded.[78] Such violence is aggravated by the judicial system's inability to effectively resolve disputes.

ANTICORRUPTION AND TRANSPARENCY   2.02

    ENVIRONMENT TO PROTECT AGAINST CORRUPTION   2.00
    PROCEDURES AND SYSTEMS TO ENFORCE ANTICORRUPTION LAWS   1.75
    EXISTENCE OF ANTICORRUPTION NORMS, STANDARDS,
        AND PROTECTIONS   2.00
    GOVERNMENTAL TRANSPARENCY   2.33

Corruption remains rampant in Cote d'Ivoire and has increased since 2002, although the government has taken some measures in recent years to increase transparency, strengthen auditing bodies, and prosecute corrupt officials in the cocoa sector. The country ranked 154th out of 180 countries in Transparency International's 2009 Corruption Perceptions Index.[79] A lack of effective and independent oversight, opacity in the use of revenue from key sectors such as cocoa and oil, a general atmosphere of impunity, and extensive extortion by armed actors have fueled both petty and grand corruption. In addition, in the north, the FN has progressively established a parallel tax system, including registration and export taxes on cocoa, which has funded the armed movement and enriched individual "com zone" commanders.[80]

Beginning in mid-2008, the Gbagbo-Soro administration embarked on a more aggressive anticorruption campaign that has included prosecutions of former allies and members of the president's own party. Under pressure from international donors, the government has also taken initials steps to improve the budget process and oversight of state-owned enterprises. At the same time, it is widely speculated that a fear of losing access to revenue from rich natural resources, such as cocoa and oil, has contributed to the government's stalled implementation of the voter identification and disarmament process. This fear has also contributed to some FN commanders' reluctance to transfer full administration of the north back to the government.

Pervasive red tape and registration requirements are key factors contributing to widespread corruption. Checkpoints throughout the country have become a central avenue for police officers to extract bribes from drivers. Lack of training, low salaries, and inefficiency in the judiciary and civil service render these two sectors especially vulnerable to corruption. With the economic decline that accompanied the conflict, corruption further increased in all levels of the public administration.

Although private companies comprise the core of the economy, several important state companies continue to exist, including in the lucrative oil sector, and are not sufficiently regulated to minimize opportunities for corruption. In 2008, the government embarked on efforts to improve monitoring of public enterprises, though progress has been slow and significant restructuring postponed. Additional staff was allocated to the General Finance Inspectorate (IGF) and the Participations and Privatization Directorate, tasked with overseeing public companies. Some initial IGF reports were publicly available, while other audits were underway as of mid-2009.[81]

Cote d'Ivoire's cocoa crop accounts for nearly 40 percent of global production, and provides approximately US$1.4 billion in revenue every year. The cocoa industry employs approximately 40 percent of the country's population, with the majority grown in the south and approximately 10 percent in the north. It has historically been plagued by mismanagement, a lack of transparency, and corruption, with significant funds diverted toward arms purchases. Global Witness estimated in 2007 that US$118 million worth of cocoa revenue was used to finance both sides of the civil war.[82] Measures to liberalize pricing taken in 1999 under pressure from international financial institutions have not improved the situation, but have rather created a complex network of overlapping and equally opaque agencies, while failing to improve farmers' incomes.[83]

In recent years, the government has adopted some measures ostensibly aimed at improving management of cocoa revenue, though their actual impact remains to be seen.[84] An official probe into the disappearance of cocoa tax revenue intended for reinvestment in the sector led to the arrests of 23 senior cocoa-related officials in June 2008 on embezzlement and corruption charges. While all of the individuals under investigation, including a former Gbagbo campaign manager, were subsequently fired, observers noted that the highest-level officials responsible for the scandal—those from the Coffee and Cocoa Regulation Authority (ARCC)—escaped prosecution.[85] In September 2008, a temporary management committee replaced the four bodies that had previously administered the coffee and cocoa industries.[86] A Reform Committee was also established to explore a new framework for managing the sector. Among the steps proposed was the re-establishment of a centralized state-run organization, the Stabilization Fund, which would fix prices paid to farmers on a yearly basis, similar to the pre-1999 arrangement. Whether such a revival of state involvement in the sector will generate greater accountability remains to be seen, however, and will largely depend on the independence and transparency of any new body compared to the previous entities, which were dominated by political appointees. In a positive development, the government announced its endorsement of the Extractive Industries Transparency Initiative (EITI) principles in May 2006. Cote d'Ivoire was accepted as a candidate country by the initiative's board three months after the government, civil society, and industry officials launched the EITI National Committee in February 2008.[87]

In addition to the arrests in the cocoa sector, several other prosecutions for corruption have taken place in recent years, including one involving the president's secretary,[88] but evidence is lacking to conclude that this marks a fundamental shift in the incentive system that perpetuates widespread graft in Cote d'Ivoire. Prosecutions of powerful actors remain few and far between, with personal connections trumping the need for accountability. This was exemplified by President Gbagbo's attempt to reinstall top officials involved in the 2006 toxic waste dumping incident after Prime Minister Banny had fired them.[89] As of November 2009, there were credible concerns that an Abidjan resident with official backing was seeking to take full control over compensation funds from Trafigura, while shortchanging the victims.[90]

In other areas, the government has taken initial steps to establish effective review of revenues and oversight of budget expenditures. As an indication of the backlog accumulated in these areas, only in 2008 and 2009 did the government submit the draft budget execution laws for the years 2005, 2006, and 2007 to the Audit Chamber.[91] The gradual redeployment of government administration in the north and west enabled some restoration of tax and customs collection in those areas. Nevertheless, the reach of the General Directorate of Taxes (DGI) and the General Directorate of Customs (DGD) remained limited in the north as of mid-2009. During 2009, the government also worked on drafting a law on unlawful enrichment, a code of ethics for senior public officials, and a more general National Plan for Good Governance and Fight Against Corruption; these were scheduled to be adopted in early 2010.

Though corruption is widely acknowledged in Ivorian society, news coverage of the issue is limited and colored by an atmosphere of intimidation and self-censorship. Whistleblowers are not adequately protected and unconfirmed reports have emerged of individuals within the cocoa sector facing violence or threats should they expose irregularities. The 2004 disappearance of Guy-Andre Kieffer, a French-Canadian freelance journalist who was investigating allegations of cocoa-related corruption, reportedly sharpened fears among those who might investigate or expose malfeasance. According to the Committee to Protect Journalists, Kieffer's acquaintances have accused both the French and Ivorian governments of hampering the work of a French investigating judge for political reasons.[92]

The government has taken some steps toward enabling greater transparency. In June 2008, the government for the first time published details on revenues and expenditures from cocoa sector levies from 2006 to 2008. Although the move was widely applauded, concerns remain that as long as private sector companies do not publish corresponding figures on payments made to the authorities, it remains impossible to verify the official numbers.[93]

The constitution requires the National Assembly to approve the budget, but its oversight role has been extremely limited since its mandate ended in 2005. According to the World Bank, "to implement the 2006 budget, the President issued an ordinance which allows the prime minister not to present the 2006 economic program to the National Assembly at this time."[94] As a result, the budget has been criticized as "unrealistic and nontransparent."[95] Following international criticism, in the second half of 2007 the government began making budget execution statements publicly available each quarter.[96] Preparations are underway for more detailed medium-term expenditure reporting, though completion of the initial phase is only expected for the 2011 budget.[97]

Though the government's procurement methods still lack transparency, the IMF has reported some progress in this area. In August 2009, a new public procurement code was adopted, though as of mid-2009, the independent regulatory authority tasked with implementing the new system had yet to be put into place. At the same time, according to the Economist Intelligence Unit, the Gbagbo administration had been involved in a number of problematic dealings including "the award of public funds to support ventures by obscure or unknown local and foreign companies, along with opaque privatization deals."[98]

Cote d'Ivoire receives substantial financial assistance from international donors. However, a lack of budgetary transparency and persistent graft has caused some donors to hesitate in their provision of additional funds. The IMF has therefore encouraged greater transparency in order to restore the confidence of donors and private sector actors.[99]

NOTES

For URLs and endnote hyperlinks, please visit the *Countries at the Crossroads* homepage at http://freedomhouse.org/template.cfm?page=139&edition=8.

1. Lane Hartill, "Clouding Ivory Coast's Peace: Ivoirite," *Christian Science Monitor*, January 27, 2006.
2. Joint United Nations Programme on HIV/AIDS (UNAIDS), *2008 Report on the Global AIDS Epidemic* (Geneva: UNAIDS, 2008).
3. Bob Tortora and Ian Brown, "With Election Pending, Ivorians Divided on Their President; Gbagbo Does Better in Government-Controlled South Than in Rebel North," Gallup Poll News Service, September 3, 2009.
4. "Election Jitters: Would-Be Presidents Have Begun to Campaign but the Country Is Not Ready," *Economist*, October 30, 2008.
5. Loucoumane Coulibaly and David Lewis, "Ivory Coast Election Chief Confirms Poll Delay," Reuters, November 11, 2009.
6. United Nations Security Council (UNSC), "In Cote d'Ivoire, 'Mixed Picture of Worrying Signs amid Solid Progress,' United Nations Mission Chief Tells Security Council in Run-Up to November Elections," news release, July 23, 2009.
7. United Nations Human Rights Council (UNHRC), *Compilation Prepared by the Office of the High Commissioner for Human Rights, in Accordance with Paragraph 15 (B) of the Annex to Human Rights Council Resolution 5/1: Cote d'Ivoire* (Geneva: UNHRC, September 18, 2009).
8. International Crisis Group (ICG), "Cote d'Ivoire: What's Needed to End the Crisis," ICG Policy Briefing, no. 62 (July 2, 2009).
9. Ibid.
10. Dorina Bekoe, "Cote d'Ivoire: Ensuring a Peaceful Political Transition," United States Institute of Peace, December 2007.
11. ICG, "Cote d'Ivoire: What's Needed to End the Crisis."
12. Ibid.
13. Bertelsmann Stiftung, "Cote d'Ivoire Country Report," in *Bertelsmann Transformation Index 2010* (Guterloh: Bertelsmann Stiftung, 2010).
14. UNSC, "Ouagadougou Agreement Leading to Direct Dialogue between Parties 'Real Turning Point' for Ivorian Peace Process, Security Council Told," press release, May 18, 2007.
15. Bertelsmann Stiftung, "Cote d'Ivoire Country Report."
16. Human Rights Watch (HRW), "Set Trial or Free Activist: Prolonged Pretrial Detention Violates International Legal Obligations," news release, February 25, 2009.
17. Center for War/Peace Studies, "Modeste Seri, Courageous Peace Activist and CW/PS Board Member Finally Released from Arbitrary Detention by Ivory Coast Authorities," news release, May 29, 2009.
18. HRW, *"Because They Have Guns . . . I'm Left with Nothing": The Price of Continuing Impunity in Cote d'Ivoire* (New York: HRW, May 25, 2006).
19. HRW, *"The Best School": Student Violence, Impunity, and the Crisis in Cote d'Ivoire* (New York: HRW, May 20, 2008).

20. National Endowment for Democracy (NED), "Africa Spotlight '08," in *2008 NED Annual Report* (Washington, D.C.: NED, 2009).
21. PEN American Center, "PEN Appeal: Antoine Assale Tiemoko," PEN home page, February 2, 2008.
22. Kwame Karikari, "Cote d'Ivoire UPDATE: Two Pro-Opposition Journalists Sentenced for 'Insulting' President," Media Foundation for West Africa, April 1, 2009.
23. HRW, "Cote d'Ivoire," in *World Report 2009* (New York: HRW, 2009).
24. Reporters Without Borders (RSF), "A Week of Terror for the Press As Young Patriots Impose Their Law," press release, January 25, 2006; Committee to Protect Journalists (CPJ), "State Broadcaster Told to Stop Opposition Coverage," press release, June 28, 2005.
25. RSF, "Ban on FM Broadcasting by RFI Lifted after 10 Months," press release, May 16, 2006; CPJ, "Ivoirian Government Indefinitely Suspends RFI," press release, February 5, 2008.
26. Freedom House, "Cote d'Ivoire," in *Freedom of the Press 2007* (Washington, D.C.: Freedom House, 2007).
27. HRW, *Cote d'Ivoire: Accountability for Serious Human Rights Crimes Key to Resolving Crisis* (New York: HRW, October 2004).
28. Maureen Lynch and Dawn Calabia, "Cote d'Ivoire: Continuing IDP Crisis Complicated by Nationality and Voting Issues," Refugees International, February 1, 2007.
29. UN High Commission on Refugees (UNHCR), "2010 UNHCR Country Operations Profile: Cote d'Ivoire," Where We Work, UNHCR home page.
30. Amnesty International, "Cote d'Ivoire," in *Amnesty International Report 2008* (London: Amnesty International, 2008).
31. "Cote d'Ivoire: When a Sentence to Jail Can Be a Sentence to Death," Integrated Regional Information Network (IRIN), May 17, 2005.
32. "Cote d'Ivoire: Malnutrition Concerns in Country's Prisons," AFRIK.com, September 3, 2008.
33. "Cote d'Ivoire: When a Sentence to Jail Can Be a Sentence to Death."
34. Bureau of Democracy, Human Rights, and Labor, "Cote d'Ivoire," in *2008 Country Reports on Human Rights Practices* (Washington, D.C.: U.S. Department of State, 2009).
35. "Cote d'Ivoire: Awash in Arms," IRIN, November 14, 2007.
36. UNSC, *Twenty-First Progress Report of the Secretary-General on the United Nations Operation in Cote d'Ivoire* (New York: UNSC, July 7, 2009).
37. HRW, "Cote d'Ivoire," in *World Report 2009* (New York: HRW, 2009).
38. Bureau of Democracy, Human Rights, and Labor, "Cote d'Ivoire," in *2008 Country Reports on Human Rights Practices*.
39. Amnesty International, "Cote d'Ivoire," in *Amnesty International Report 2008*.
40. "OHCHR in Cote d'Ivoire (2008–2009)," United Nations Office of the High Commissioner for Human Rights.
41. Amnesty International, *Cote d'Ivoire: Targeting Women: The Forgotten Victims of the Conflict* (London: Amnesty International, March 15, 2007).
42. Lydia Polgreen, "Neglect and Fraud Blamed for Toxic Dumping in Ivory Coast," *New York Times*, November 24, 2006.
43. Amnesty International, "Cote d'Ivoire," in *Amnesty International Report 2009* (London: Amnesty International, 2009).
44. HRW, "Cote d'Ivoire," in *World Report 2010* (New York: HRW, 2010).
45. Office to Monitor and Combat Trafficking in Persons, *Trafficking in Persons Report 2009* (Washington, D.C.: U.S. Department of State, 2009).

46. Inter-Parliamentary Union, "Cote d'Ivoire: Assemblee Nationale (National Assembly)," Inter-Parliamentary Union home page.
47. Organization for Economic Cooperation and Development (OECD) Development Centre, "Gender Equality and Social Institutions in Cote d'Ivoire," Social Institutions and Gender Index, 2009.
48. HRW, *"My Heart is Cut"* (New York: HRW, August 1, 2007).
49. Amnesty International, *Cote d'Ivoire: Targeting Women: The Forgotten Victims of the Conflict in Cote d'Ivoire* (London: Amnesty International, March 15, 2007).
50. "Cote d'Ivoire: Rape a Daily Menace for Rural Women," IRIN, March 30, 2009.
51. OECD Development Centre, "Gender Equality and Social Institutions in Cote d'Ivoire."
52. Ibid; Fulgence Zamble, "Cote d'Ivoire: Fighting FGM from the Mosque and the Pulpit," Inter Press Service, December 12, 2009.
53. "Drive for AIDS Funding in Cote d'Ivoire," UNAIDS, May 9, 2007.
54. Bertelsmann Stiftung, "Cote d'Ivoire Country Report."
55. HRW, *UPR Submission: Cote d'Ivoire* (New York: HRW, April 2009).
56. "Cote d'Ivoire: Northerners Reserve Judgment on Gbagbo-Soro Accord," IRIN, June 29, 2007.
57. Bureau of Democracy, Human Rights, and Labor, "Cote d'Ivoire," in *International Religious Freedom Report 2009* (Washington, D.C.: U.S. Department of State, 2009).
58. Chinyere Okoye, "Cote d'Ivoire: Ivorien Ministers Take 50 Percent Pay Cut to Subsidise Fuel," *This Day*, July 22, 2009.
59. International Trade Union Confederation (ITUC), "Cote d'Ivoire," in *2009 Annual Survey of Violations of Trade Union Rights* (Brussels: ITUC, 2009).
60. "Cote d'Ivoire: Food Price Hikes Spark Riots," IRIN, March 31, 2008.
61. "Cote d'Ivoire: Country Slashes Food Tax after Deadly Protests," *Guardian* (Nigeria), April 3, 2008.
62. HRW, *UPR Submission: Cote d'Ivoire*.
63. "La Cour Supreme," Le Portail Officiel du Gouvernement de Cote d'Ivoire.
64. Kouable Clarisse Gueu, "The Legal System in Cote d'Ivoire: Where Do We Stand?" *GlobaLex*, March/April 2009.
65. International Commission of Jurists (ICJ), *Attacks on Justice 2005–Cote d'Ivoire* (Geneva: ICJ, August 15, 2008).
66. "Cote d'Ivoire: The Inescapable Injustice of Justice," IRIN, July 12, 2007.
67. UNSC, *Twenty-Third Progress Report of the Secretary-General on the United Nations Operation in Cote d'Ivoire* (New York: UNSC, January 7, 2010).
68. Ibid.
69. ICJ, *Attacks on Justice 2005: Cote d'Ivoire*.
70. Bureau for Democracy, Human Rights, and Labor, "Cote d'Ivoire," in *2008 Country Reports on Human Rights Practices*.
71. "Cote d'Ivoire: The Inescapable Injustice of Justice."
72. ICG, "Cote d'Ivoire: What's Needed to End the Crisis."
73. Ibid.
74. "Cote d'Ivoire: Ex-Rebel Uprising Threatens Disarmament Process," IRIN, June 19, 2008.
75. Bakary Sanogo, "The World Bank and Cote d'Ivoire Wage War on Racketeering," World Bank, July 25, 2008.
76. Amnesty International, "Cote d'Ivoire," in *Amnesty International Report 2009*.
77. International Displacement Monitoring Centre (IDMC), *Whose Land Is This? Land Disputes and Forced Displacement in the Western Forest Area of Cote d'Ivoire* (Geneva: IDMC, 2009).

78. "Efforts to Contain Deadly Land Disputes Continue," Reuters AlertNet, September 9, 2008.
79. Transparency International, *2009 Corruption Perceptions Index* (Berlin: Transparency International, November 17, 2009).
80. Global Witness, *Hot Chocolate: How Cocoa Fuelled the Conflict in Cote d'Ivoire* (London: Global Witness, 2007).
81. International Monetary Fund, *Cote d'Ivoire: 2009 Article IV Consultation, First Review under the Three-Year Arrangement under the Poverty Reduction and Growth Facility, Request for Waiver of Nonobservance of Performance Criteria, and Financing Assurances Review* (Washington, D.C.: November 4, 2009).
82. Global Witness, *Hot Chocolate.*
83. Kissy Agyeman, "Cocoa Sector Management Revamped in Cote d'Ivoire," Global Insight, September 24, 2008.
84. Michael Deibert, "Economy: The Bitter Taste of Cocoa in Cote d'Ivoire," Inter Press Service, December 6, 2007.
85. Global Witness, "Cote d'Ivoire Cocoa Indictments: Key Players Escape Charges," press release, June 13, 2008.
86. Pauline Bax, "Ivoirian Cocoa Committee Wants Industry Run by State," Bloomberg News, December 8, 2009; Agyeman, "Cocoa Sector Management Revamped in Cote d'Ivoire."
87. Extractive Industries Transparency Initiative (EITI), "Cote d'Ivoire," EITI Countries, EITI home page.
88. Kingsley Kobo, "Ivory Coast: President's Secretary Sentenced," AfricaNews, February 12, 2009.
89. "Two Killed in Fresh Anti-Gbagbo's Demos in Ivory Coast," Agence France Presse, December 5, 2006.
90. Adam Nossiter, "Payments in Ivory Coast Dumping Case at Risk, Lawyer Says," *New York Times*, November 4, 2009.
91. International Monetary Fund (IMF), *Cote d'Ivoire: Letter of Intent, Memorandum of Economic and Financial Policies, and Technical Memorandum of Understanding* (Washington, D.C.: IMF, November 4, 2009).
92. Julia Crawford, "Disappeared: Guy-Andre Kieffer Missing in Ivory Coast," CPJ, May 17, 2005.
93. Global Witness, "Cote d'Ivoire Cocoa Transparency Move Welcome," press release, June 4, 2008; Global Witness, "Cote d'Ivoire Cocoa Reform Insufficient As Exporters Sidestep Transparency," press release, September 22, 2008.
94. World Bank, "Cote d'Ivoire Overview," November 2006.
95. Bertelsmann Stiftung, "Cote d'Ivoire Country Report."
96. IMF, *Cote d'Ivoire: Enhanced Heavily Indebted Poor Countries Initiative-Preliminary Document* (Washington, D.C.: IMF, January 2009).
97. Ibid.
98. "CIAO/EIU Partnership: Cote d'Ivoire," Columbia International Affairs Online (New York: Columbia University).
99. Holger Fabig and Bruno de Shaetzen, "Cote d'Ivoire Poised for Comeback," *IMF Survey Magazine*, July 30, 2008.

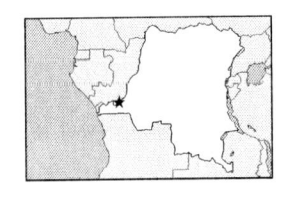

DEMOCRATIC REPUBLIC OF CONGO

CAPITAL: Kinshasa
POPULATION: 68.7 million
GNI PER CAPITA (PPP): $290

SCORES	2006	2010
ACCOUNTABILITY AND PUBLIC VOICE:	N/A	1.53
CIVIL LIBERTIES:	N/A	1.98
RULE OF LAW:	N/A	1.15
ANTICORRUPTION AND TRANSPARENCY:	N/A	1.06

(scores are based on a scale of 0 to 7, with 0 representing weakest and 7 representing strongest performance)

Osita Afoaku

INTRODUCTION

With an estimated population of over 68 million, the Democratic Republic of Congo (DRC–formerly Zaire) is situated on a territory one quarter the size of the United States. Despite one of Africa's most brutal encounters with colonial exploitation, Congo's abundance of natural resources led to high expectations upon attaining independence in 1960. However, prospects for national development deteriorated quickly and were subsequently ruined by three decades of autocratic, patrimonial rule headed by late president Mobutu Sese Seko. In April 1990, Mobutu made a political volte-face by lifting the ban on partisan politics, raising citizens' hope for a new era of stability and social justice. But the national euphoria was short-lived, as the DRC would soon be rent by ethnic strife and two consecutive wars touched off by a massive influx of refugees from neighboring Rwanda and Mobutu's failure to deliver on his promise to restore democratic rule. Conflict was fueled by a broad set of domestic and international actors intent on controlling economic and political power in portions of the Congo's resource-rich zones.

Now in the third year of its renewed experiment with multiparty governance, the future of the Congolese state remains precarious. The second war, which included numerous regional states and irregular armed groups, has largely subsided, but parts of the country, especially in the east, remain unstable and insecure. Nevertheless, most of the country is calm and relatively stable.

Professor **Osita Afoaku** teaches Public Policy in the School of Public and Environmental Affairs, Indiana University, Bloomington. His current research interests include US-African/Third World relations, sustainable development, democratization, and state reconstruction in Africa.

Five years of the bloody conflict ended when the government and key rebel groups signed the so-called Global and All-Inclusive Peace Agreement, otherwise known as the Sun City Accord, in December 2002. The peace settlement paved the way for the formation of a transitional government of national unity headed by Joseph Kabila, who had been serving as interim president since his rebel-turned-president father was assassinated in January 2001. The transitional constitution required power sharing between the president and four vice presidents, two from the former rebel groups, one from the political opposition, and one from Kabila's political movement. In addition, the central government was assigned five critical responsibilities: reunification, restoration of peace, reconstruction of the country, restoration of territorial integrity, and state control over the entire national territory; national reconciliation; formation of a restructured and integrated national army; organization of free and transparent elections at all levels, with a view to the creation of a democratic constitutional government; and the establishment of institutional structures for a new political order.[1]

Following its inception in 2003, the transitional government began to attempt the disarmament, demobilization, and reintegration (DDR) into civilian life of an estimated 150,000 government troops and irregular combatants, with an additional 150,000 unified into a national army.[2] Progress toward national unification has been slow, however, as the country remains divided into different zones of de facto military and political control. Also, as demonstrated by the resurgence of conflicts in the eastern provinces of Orientale, North Kivu, and South Kivu, many senior militia commanders, determined to maintain a grip on political power and economic resources, have been resisting the unification programs. Furthermore, the DDR and military reform programs have proved extremely complex due to the country's size and constraints, as well as inadequate funding and poor coordination and management.[3]

In December 2005, roughly two-thirds of eligible voters turned out to approve a new democratic constitution. The new charter, which entered into force on February 18, 2006, protects a wide range of civil and political rights. Constitutional provisions on citizens' voting rights were regulated by a March 2006 electoral law. The creation of a constitutional and legal framework paved the way for the organization of historic multiparty presidential and parliamentary elections later that year.

A peace agreement signed in January 2008 by the government and 22 armed groups active in eastern Congo, including the National Congress for the Defense of the People (CNDP), marked an important step toward restoration of peace and stability in the region. The agreement called for an immediate cessation of hostilities, disengagement of troops, the creation of a buffer zone, and the return of Congolese refugees from neighboring countries under the supervision of the United Nations, the DRC government, and countries of asylum.[4]

It is difficult to overstate the destruction caused by the violence in the east. Roughly 1.4 to 1.6 million people were displaced between 1998 and 2008, most of them women and children. According to the International Rescue

Committee, by early 2009 over 5 million people had died in the DRC as a result of the direct and indirect effects of the war. Numerous testimonies confirm the misery wrought, especially in the three eastern zones—Ituri district in Orientale province and North and South Kivu provinces—that continue to experience active conflict.[5]

Notably, the economic dimension of the brutal conflict was initially neglected, though it now receives significant international attention. In the absence of strong regulation and a reliable system of oversight—let alone a more diversified economy—individual buyers and companies involved in the minerals trade continue to enrich the warring parties.[6] A new factor in the resource equation is the presence of China. In December 2007, Congo and China signed a US$9 billion development loan agreement that commits Chinese state-owned companies to undertake massive infrastructure projects and develop Congolese mines. The deal will give China great influence in a country with a long history of bad governance, prompting the International Monetary Fund and Western donors to express concerns about the potential negative economic, human rights, and environmental consequences. However, as in other parts of Africa, much depends on oversight. If Congolese leaders are able to demonstrate firm commitment to good governance and ensure that the agreement is carried out well, it can be positive for the country.[7]

Against this backdrop of collapsed social institutions and infrastructure, which has left the DRC with a national ranking of 168 out of 177 countries on the UN Development Program's Human Development Index, the Kabila government is faced with the herculean task of providing essential goods and services. It is estimated that 1,000 people continue to die daily from hunger, disease, and other effects of war. With 80 percent of the population living under the poverty line, life expectancy at birth is 46 years. Maternal and infant mortality remain high and one out of every five children does not reach the age of five.[8] While the government has taken some steps to improve state services, grave questions remain unanswered about its commitment to the basic tenets of democracy and the political will to address the wide spectrum of past failings.

ACCOUNTABILITY AND PUBLIC VOICE   1.53

FREE AND FAIR ELECTORAL LAWS AND ELECTIONS	1.75
EFFECTIVE AND ACCOUNTABLE GOVERNMENT	1.00
CIVIC ENGAGEMENT AND CIVIC MONITORING	1.67
MEDIA INDEPENDENCE AND FREEDOM OF EXPRESSION	1.71

The 2006 elections took place in a very challenging environment, with numerous difficulties faced by the organizers, including insufficient preparation time, inadequate resources, transportation and communications bottlenecks, inexperience with multiparty elections, insecurity in the east, and unreliable population data, to name but a few. Furthermore, the elections were conducted in the context of four decades of autocratic rule and a dismal legacy of corruption, intra-elite rivalries, armed conflict, and human rights abuses. Insecurity not only impeded electoral preparations and participation but also public confidence in the balloting. Despite the fact that all parties signed and committed to a code of conduct, political debates were fraught with personal attacks, bad-faith accusations between parties and individuals, and, at times, repetition of unsubstantiated rumors in the media and elsewhere. Many political parties expressed concerns over insufficient funding for their election campaigns.

In spite of the logistical challenges, nearly 18 million of the 25 million registered voters participated in the July 30 presidential and parliamentary elections, while more than 15 million voters participated in the October 29 presidential run-off and provincial elections. Election monitors noted with satisfaction the degree of enthusiasm with which the parties and their supporters engaged in the voting process.[9] On the other hand, international observers including the Carter Center noted several procedural flaws that weakened the transparency of the elections.[10]

During the first round, 70 percent of the 25 million registered voters participated in choosing among the 9,709 candidates contesting 500 parliamentary seats in the National Assembly (NA). In all, 69 of the 275 registered political parties won NA seats. While President Kabila's PPRD won only 111 seats, he eventually built an alliance known as the Alliance of the Presidential Majority (AMP) that comprised 332 seats. The opposition alliance led by Movement for the Liberation of Congo (MLC) presidential candidate Jean-Pierre Bemba won 116 seats. Only 42 women were elected to the new body. The establishment of the new parliament was completed in January 2007 with indirect elections to the 108-member Senate, in which the AMP garnered 58 seats.[11] The extremely large number of parties makes political fragmentation a serious threat to the legislative and oversight capacity of the new parliament. Other factors that work to undermine Congo's fledgling democracy include opposition incapacity, lack of infrastructure, and the dominance of patronage within all levels of public administration.[12]

From the start, Joseph Kabila was the favorite to win the presidential race despite his political inexperience and nagging questions about his nationality. His popularity was strongest in the east, where he was generally regarded as the man who ended the war. Moreover, considering the poorly regulated nature of national affairs in Congo, Kabila's incumbent status gave him an obvious advantage over his two main opponents, Bemba and Oscar Kashala, a Harvard professor who returned from exile only a few months prior to the elections. According to one international commentator, Kabila's "campaign team was shocked by the surprisingly effective campaigns of his main opponents . . . in the run-up to the election day, he dominated the state television and radio. His opponents started to face more and more obstacles."[13] For instance, when Kashala appeared to be posing a serious threat to Kabila's political fortunes, the "authorities . . . grounded his chartered aircraft on safety grounds. When he found an alternative, he suddenly discovered a nationwide shortage of aviation fuel."[14] Bemba, for his part, ran the risk of being assassinated by Kabila's security operatives in the heat of the presidential contest despite the fact that he still surrounded himself with his MLC rebel militia.[15] Other pressure was also applied: in January 2006, broadcasts at two private television stations and a radio station owned by Bemba were suspended after airing a press conference featuring remarks critical of President Kabila.

There were also reports of isolated cases of violence. In July, participants in a Kinshasa campaign rally for Bemba—the leading alternative contender—killed a civilian and several security agents. On run-off day, October 29, a crowd burned down several polling stations in Equateur province after security forces accidentally killed a bystander. As a capstone, on November 21, Bemba's supporters set the Supreme Court building on fire to protest the election results, in which Kabila was declared the winner with 58 percent of the vote. These incidents were isolated overall; for the most part, Congolese voters conducted themselves peacefully and the results of the 2006 elections received an overall positive assessment from international observers.[16] Notably, most voters rejected the group that controlled their territory during the war, including in Kinshasa, where Bemba garnered 70 percent of the vote.[17]

The predominantly nonviolent conduct of Congolese voters during the elections was meant to signal to political elites their collective yearning for genuine democratization of the country. Unfortunately, the prevailing configuration of political forces in the country has so far been an impediment to such an outcome. President Kabila and his supporters have continued to subordinate democracy to the maintenance of order and stability. In the three years following the elections, "there have been disturbing signs that the Congo's democratic transition is not only fragile, but that the newly elected government is brutally restricting democratic space."[18]

Excessive use of force against political opponents in western Congo has been fueled by the government's lack of popularity in the region. In August 2006 and again in March 2007, government troops launched military operations against Bemba and his supporters, whose support base is in Kinshasa. According to Human Rights Watch, soldiers and Republican Guards who took part in those operations claimed that they were acting on Kabila's orders to eliminate Bemba. Hundreds were killed and hundreds more detained, including many who were tortured.[19] After a long series of threats and maneuverings, Bemba ended up in Belgium, where he was arrested and remanded to the International Criminal Court (ICC) in May 2008 on war crimes charges. The government continues to view natives of Equateur province, Bemba's home region, as potential threats, and incidents of harassment and arbitrary detention are frequent. In July 2008, prominent MLC member Daniel Botethi was killed by Republican Guards.

The focus of abuse in Bas-Congo were adherents of the Bundu Dia Kongo (BDK) politico-religious group, who were viewed as challengers to government power, and singled out for harassment and attacks by government security agents because of their political alliance with Bemba and the BDK's role in promoting greater provincial autonomy. In June 2006, FARDC soldiers fired on a demonstration by BDK activists, and in January 2007, the police and FARDC soldiers clashed with BDK adherents in a bloody fight that resulted in more than 100 deaths.[20] Finally, in March 2008, police took preemptive action against future BDK strikes by killing over 200 followers, destroying BDK temples, and banning the group. As Human Rights Watch noted, the actions against both the MLC and the BDK are illustrative of a phenomenon in which small-scale violence by the government's opponents elicits a response of an altogether greater magnitude by the state security forces.[21]

The constitution vests extensive executive, legislative, and military powers in the president, who is the head of a cabinet of 45 ministers. The judiciary is only nominally independent. While a process of decentralization is nominally underway, the anticipated expansion from 11 provinces to 26—and the accompanying increase in revenue transfers—has yet to occur. Local elections scheduled for 2008 have not been held, and 10 of the 11 provincial governors are allied with the AMP. The institutionalization of separation of powers via checks and balances ranks low on the agenda of the Kabila government, a situation attributable in part to the fact that recent peace settlements kept power largely in the hands of former belligerents. Furthermore, the 2006 elections resulted in only a limited infusion of new blood into the executive branch. With the notable exception of Antoine Gizenga, leader of the Unified Lumumbist Party (PALU), who served as prime minister in Kabila's government until his resignation and replacement by Adolphe Muzito in 2008, most ministries have been occupied by the president's acolytes from the defunct transitional government. Opposition incapacity and fragmentation has rendered the parliament ineffective in challenging the ruling coalition. The opposition lacks the unity and sense of purpose to rally public opinion behind an alternative agenda.[22] Despite its limitations, parliament passed a number of important bills and attempted to establish a nascent oversight capacity in its first two years. But since the forced resignation in March 2009 of NA speaker Vital Kamerhe, who criticized the administration's joint operations with Rwanda (see Civil Liberties), most observers consider the legislature to have regressed in activity, ambition, and independence.

Overall, the government appeared uninterested in fulfilling popular aspirations for a government of national unity. The Union for Democracy and Social Progress (UDPS), the principle anti-Mobutu party, which spearheaded the prodemocracy movement in the 1990s, boycotted the elections and has no presence in the government. Similarly, Kabila did not co-opt the former rebel coalition RCD, which played a major role in the 1998 military revolt and served as the main political vehicle for Congolese Tutsi and Rwandan influence in the course of the war. Instead, Kabila allied with one of Mobutu's sons, François Joseph Zanga Mobutu, who was brought into the cabinet in an attempt to broaden Kabila's political base; this move reinforced public suspicions that the current government strongly prioritizes maintaining power over meaningful change.[23]

Like many African countries, post-conflict Congo has a limited capacity to respond to the country's staggering governance challenges. This situation, coupled with donor pressure, has served as catalyst to the growth of the civil society sector, with thousands of local and international NGOs emerging over the past decade to provide critical services in place of the state. Civil society still faces some difficult limitations. Many groups became politicized during the democratic transition, especially prior to the 2006 elections.[24] The government sometimes reacts harshly to criticism, as evidenced in the July 2009 description of Human Rights Watch and other groups as "humanitarian terrorists."[25] Both national and provincial-level officials at times forcibly restrict civil society activists from performing their work. Rights activists are at particularly high risk of arrest, threats, and attacks, especially if their denunciations involve security force actors. Meanwhile, increased parliamentary subservience following Kamerhe's resignation has denied civic groups what had been a promising forum in which to press their views.

The new Congolese constitution provides for freedom of speech and of the press. However, these rights are limited in practice by the Kabila government and its supporters. Local press watchdog Journaliste en Danger reported 110 attacks on freedom of expression in 2008.[26] Officials have used an array of onerous licensing requirements as well as criminal libel laws to restrict free speech and suppress political criticism, imprisoning journalists and clamping down on broadcasters and newspapers critical of the authorities. In March 2009, the mayor of Likasi ordered the closure of Radio Communautaire du Katanga (RCK) and Radiotélévision Likasi 4 (RTL4), alleging that their coverage of a local strike included defamatory remarks.[27] In January 2007, Rigobert Kwakala Kash, editor of *Le Moniteur*, was sentenced to 11 months in prison for libel against the governor of Bas-Congo; although he was released after 35 days, the publication was suspended for six months.[28] Security laws are also employed. In September 2008, a Global TV technician was arrested on charges of "inciting rebellion" after the station was forced off the air following its broadcast of a press conference featuring antigovernment remarks.[29]

Economic circumstances make the practice of journalism difficult. According to the Committee to Protect Journalists, as of 2007 an estimated 80 percent of Congolese journalists who did not have employment contracts accepted payment from politicians.[30] However, violence and intimidation against journalists, particularly those critical of the government, pose an even greater threat. In October 2007, Higher Education Minister Sylvain Ngabu purportedly ordered policemen to beat several journalists after the private broadcaster Horizon 33 aired a news program discussing Ngabu's decision to suspend the chancellor of a local university.[31] The pattern of violence against reporters remained similar in 2008 and 2009, with journalists routinely threatened and assaulted and assailants generally going unpunished. Intimidation and violence—including repeated kidnappings and murders of journalists—are particularly rampant in the east; several journalists for Radio Okapi, run by the UN and a Swiss foundation, have been killed in South Kivu in recent years, and both foreign and domestic reporters have been harassed and abducted by armed groups. Radio Okapi journalists Serge Maheshe and Didace Namujimbo were shot and killed in June 2007 and November 2008, respectively, and on August 23, 2009, Radio Star presenter Bruno Koko Chirambaza was stabbed to death in Bukavu.[32] Investigations into these murders have been slow, and trials have been severely flawed.[33] In November 2009, the lead suspect in the Namujimbo case, who had admitted his guilt before military prosecutors, escaped from prison five days after his arrest.[34]

The government has also harassed media outlets, banning stations from operating and censoring the content of their broadcasts. The High Authority of Media continues to regulate outlets despite a constitutional provision mandating its dissolution. Outlets affiliated with the opposition, especially those owned by Bemba, have been particularly targeted. In March 2007, the broadcast signals of several of Bemba's stations were interrupted after he publicly claimed that the army was embezzling money from its payroll.[35] That October, then Communications Minister Toussaint Tshilombo Send banned 22 television stations and 16 radio stations for alleged noncompliance with registration procedures. In September 2008, then Communications Minister Emile Bongeli banned several radio television stations and ordered police to impound the broadcasting equipment of Molière Télévision. He granted the station's frequency to TVS1, which is owned by Prime Minister Adolphe Muzito, subsequently ignoring a court order that overturned the act.[36] Finally, on July 26, 2009, the government suspended Radio France Internationale's broadcasts for the third time that year, alleging that one of its programs had encouraged soldiers to revolt.[37]

There are scores of newspapers and periodicals in circulation. However, daily newspapers reach only 6 percent of the population. Most media outlets are either owned or funded by Congolese politicians, who utilize them to forward their personal agendas.[38] During the 2006 election campaign, party-funded television channels and radio stations aired biased, propaganda-laden broadcasts, while the state-run television channel featured predominantly pro-Kabila coverage.[39] While broadcasting has undergone notable expansion, it is still largely dominated by the government-controlled state broadcaster, Radio-Télévision Nationale Congolaise (RTNC). Radio has the broadest reach in the country and stations often operate in remote areas. The state-owned La Voix du Congo broadcasts nationally in French, Swahili, Lingala, Tshilubu, and Kikongo. As of 2007, internet use remained highly limited; of the 21 internet service providers operating in the country, 12 were limited to the city of Kinshasa.[40] The government does not restrict internet use.

CIVIL LIBERTIES   1.98
PROTECTION FROM STATE TERROR, UNJUSTIFIED IMPRISONMENT, AND TORTURE	1.13
GENDER EQUITY	1.33
RIGHTS OF ETHNIC, RELIGIOUS, AND OTHER DISTINCT GROUPS	1.00
FREEDOM OF CONSCIENCE AND BELIEF	4.67
FREEDOM OF ASSOCIATION AND ASSEMBLY	1.75

The 2006 constitution includes important human rights protections. However, the government has failed to assure that legislation is consistent with constitutional norms. Constitutional language banning torture is not complemented by legislation defining it, nor has the parliament acted to align the penal code with the UN Convention against Torture and Other Cruel, Inhuman or Degrading Treatment or Punishment. Likewise, a draft law to implement ratification of the Rome Statute of the ICC has sat in parliament since September 2005. Other international treaties have also been signed; however, implementation again lags far behind.[41]

The Kabila government inherited an elaborate system of repression from its predecessors. In addition to Kinshasa's notorious Camp Kokolo, the government currently maintains various large and small prison facilities under the control of an array of security force agencies. The National Intelligence Agency (ANR) and Republican Guard, both of which often engage in actions that exceed their legal mandates, report directly to the president, and certain intelligence agencies and units within the Congolese National Police (PNC) have also been implicated in high-profile cases of arbitrary detention and abuse.[42]

Those detained face bleak conditions. In 2006, the Ministry of Justice, supported by the international community, initiated a formal process of prison reform in Congo. Despite efforts to reform the penitentiary system, prisons across the country remain among the worst in Africa.[43] Nearly all facilities are characterized by harsh and even life-threatening conditions, including severe overcrowding, inadequate or nonexistent health care, and abuse by guards. Family members and friends are generally the only source of food and other necessities for inmates, leading to malnutrition and occasional death. Small prisons generally do not have separate facilities for women and juveniles.[44] Prison buildings are in such disrepair that jailbreaks are common, including by soldiers and other convicted rights violators. Human Rights Watch estimated at least 200 political prisoners at the end of 2008.[45]

Abuses by nonstate actors continue to plague the DRC. In particular, despite a series of initiatives aimed at achieving peace and national reconciliation, armed groups continue to operate in North and South Kivu provinces, as well as Ituri. Two of the primary combatants in recent years were the Democratic Forces for the Liberation of Rwanda (FDLR), led by Hutus who took part in the 1994 genocide in Rwanda and fled in its aftermath, and their opponents, the previously Rwanda-supported CNDP, headed by renegade General Laurent Nkunda until his detention by Rwandan forces in January 2009. Relations between the Kinshasa government and both groups have vacillated between hostility and tacit agreement. A cease-fire agreement signed in January 2008 with 22 groups, including the CNDP, ended that August, when heavy fighting between the government and CNDP commenced. Despite its freedom-fighter rhetoric, CNDP fighters frequently engaged in various appalling human rights abuses, including abductions, forced displacement, extortion, and recruitment of child soldiers. Following Nkunda's arrest in January 2009, the CNDP agreed to integrate with the Armed Forces of the Democratic Republic of the Congo (FARDC) and continue the fight against the FDLR. To the outrage of human rights groups, the Congolese government agreed to allow Nkunda's deputy Bosco Ntaganda to join FARDC despite the existence of an ICC warrant for his arrest. Indeed, the ICC's first trial, which began in January 2009, seeks to convict Ntaganda's former rebel associate Thomas Lubanga of conscripting child soldiers into a militia in Ituri.

Joint operations with Rwanda against the FDLR occurred during January and February 2009, with MONUC taking Rwanda's place starting in March in an operation known as Kimia II. Rights groups considered MONUC's participation tantamount to complicity with FARDC's abuses, but MONUC considered it preferable from a military and ethical perspective to staying on the sidelines. It is estimated that around 6,000 FDLR fighters remain in the DRC; several thousand were repatriated to Rwanda between 2007 and 2009.[46] According to Human Rights Watch, abuses by all sides increased substantially during Kimia II, with both the FDLR and FARDC punishing civilians in horrific ways as revenge for communities' alleged cooperation with the other side.[47]

Well over a dozen other armed groups continue to operate in the east. Despite a 2006 ceasefire agreement between government forces and ethnic militias in Ituri, human rights violations by the militias increased in 2008 because of the failure to address "the social, structural, and distributional injustices; the absence of state institutions; and the plundering of the region's resources for the benefit of a few."[48] The Lord's Resistance Army (LRA), a notorious Ugandan militia that fled into a remote region in Orientale in 2005, inflicted massive damage on civilians after a government offensive began in December 2008. Local militia groups known as Mai Mai commit abuses in a number of regions in the country. Notably, a Mai Mai commander was convicted, along with 20 associates, of crimes against humanity in March 2009.[49]

Even in non-conflict zones, dismal economic conditions continue to foster crime and instability. Crime poses a serious threat to property and personal safety in Kinshasa, and has been on the rise in Goma, Bunia, and other cities in the east. Vehicle theft, burglary, and armed robbery, are frequent throughout the country. A large number of crimes are believed to involve security force personnel, and impunity is near-total in many areas, especially in the east. Congo is a source and destination country for men, women, and children trafficked for the purposes of forced labor and sexual exploitation; much of this trafficking occurs within the unstable eastern provinces and is perpetrated by armed groups outside government control.[50] There is little available redress for victims of violations. There is no national ombudsman or human rights commission, although a draft law to create a national commission passed the Senate in July 2008.[51] A truth and reconciliation commission was formed in 2004 but clear rules were never established, violators were represented within the body, and it was disbanded in 2006 without having held a hearing. Reestablishment of the commission was discussed in 2008 and 2009.

Despite constitutional provisions upholding the equality of the sexes and mandating the elimination of discrimination against women, Congolese women continue to face unequal treatment in virtually every sector of society. Patriarchal cultural and religious traditions, which are particularly entrenched in rural areas, contribute to these restrictions and the generally difficult environment. According to National Union of Congolese Workers (UNTC) vice president Marie Josée Lokongo Bosiko, husbands, traditions, religions, and sects are the main obstacles preventing Congolese women from assuming positions of responsibility in society.[52] The family code requires a married woman to "obtain her husband's authorization to effect legal acts" and receive permission before accepting a salaried job. The government has submitted a draft revised family code aimed at bringing regulations in line with the new constitution and international standards, but the code remained unreformed as of mid-2009.[53]

Violence against women, including rape and sexual slavery, has reached epidemic levels in the last decade, particularly in the Kivus. Combatants from all sides in the conflict have routinely utilized rape as a weapon of war, a practice that groups such as Human Rights Watch have recounted in horrific detail.[54] In addition to physical and emotional trauma, victims of sexual violence often contract diseases including HIV and are rejected by family members and the local community. A landmark law passed in 2006 explicitly recognized the crimes of sexual slavery, harassment, pedophilia, and forced pregnancy within the penal code, while increasing criminal penalties and protections afforded to victims.[55] The law is conspicuously silent, however, about legal protection against spousal rape.

In the absence of capacity and will to investigate and prosecute such violence, both government soldiers and militias in the east, and to a lesser degree in other parts of the country, continue to commit mass rape with impunity. The UN Population Fund reported over 15,000 incidents of sexual violence in 2008, and Human Rights Watch reported a substantial increase in 2009, noting that 65 percent of the new cases were committed by FARDC soldiers.[56] The group also stated that the 7,700 recorded rape cases in North and South Kivu in 2008 had resulted in just 27 convictions of soldiers.[57] In spite of the strengthened laws, law enforcement officials and magistrates continue to grant bail or disproportionately lenient sentences to men accused of rape and urge or force female victims to settle out of court, abusing those who fail to comply.[58]

Slow progress in the prosecution of ordinary soldiers for sexual violence has generally not extended as far as bringing senior military officers to justice for either their own crimes or those committed by soldiers under their command.[59] In 2009, however, several officers, including at least one colonel, were convicted on rape-related charges.

The DRC is comprised of upwards of 250 ethnic groups concentrated regionally, and the new constitution confers legal equality on all citizens regardless of ethnic origin, gender, age, or religious affiliation.[60] Identification with the Congo as a nation-state is relatively strong, but ethnicity has been a prominent factor in politics and the formation of armed groups.[61] Discrimination on the basis of ethnicity remains a common practice by members of virtually every group and is evident in private hiring patterns in some cities. Although President Kabila's cabinet and office staff are geographically and ethnically diverse, a significant amount of political influence remains in the hands of individuals from Katanga. Conversely, natives of Equateur province are often singled out for abuse by the security forces, especially in Kinshasa, as it is assumed that they are Bemba partisans.

Birth within the national territory does not automatically confer citizenship on a person. The 2003 constitution and the nationality law of 2004 provided means for immigrants and long-term residents to acquire citizenship. However, this development brought only partial relief to the Banyamulenge Tutsi residents of South Kivu, whose nationality has been the subject of heated controversy on account of their Rwandan ancestry. To make matters worse, the latest constitution does not allow dual citizenship.[62] Congo has a population of approximately 600,000 Pygmies, who are believed to be the original inhabitants of large swathes of the country. Pygmies living in remote areas were often caught in the crossfire during the wars, and discrimination against them remains pervasive. The government has done little to encourage them to participate in the political process.[63]

Life for disabled citizens is likewise fraught with difficulty. Although discrimination is banned, the state is not required by law to provide government services to the disabled, and both educational and employment opportunities for disabled people are severely constrained. The government has few resources to address these inequities, although it has contributed some minimal funding towards the construction of vocational educational centers geared towards providing the disabled with sewing, carpentry, and other skills.[64]

The constitution provides for freedom of religion. Approximately 50 percent of the national population is Roman Catholic, while 20 percent is mainline Protestant. A Christian sect, the Kimbanguistes, and Muslims both comprise 9 percent. Congo prides itself on providing a setting for peaceful coexistence among religious groups. Registration of religious groups is governed by a relatively straightforward process.[65] The Kabila administration has generally upheld the constitutional guarantee of religious freedom. However, there are growing concerns that religious groups that challenge the legitimacy of the government could be punished. The banning of the politico-religious BDK in March 2008 represented a turn in this direction.

Historically, unions have been an important part of civil society. Throughout the colonial and postcolonial eras, they served as institutional forums where workers met to articulate demands for improved working conditions and political reform. During the 1990s, unions played an important part in the prodemocracy protests that led to the collapse of the Mobutu dictatorship. The law permits workers to form and join trade unions without prior authorization. Although discrimination against unions is illegal, the law has not been enforced effectively. In recent years, labor unions have functioned throughout the country, albeit in weak form. Only a small percentage of workers are formally organized. Collective bargaining is limited, and public sector wages are set by decree. In the private sector, the government has failed to prevent or counteract a rash of parallel and sham unionism centered on the extractive industries.[66] In 2007, 6,000 employees of the Bakwanga Mining Company (MIBA), the main diamond mining company in Eastern Kasai, were denounced by local officials and MIBA management and received several death threats from anonymous sources following a decision to strike in protest of poor working conditions.[67]

Although freedom of assembly is constitutionally protected, government insecurity leads to restrictions in practice. Organizers of public events are required to register with local authorities. According to the law, organizers are authorized to hold an event unless the local government specifically denies authorization. In keeping with a pattern that dates back to the Mobutu era, government security forces often disperse unregistered protest marches or meetings, often under the pretext of restoring public order.

RULE OF LAW 1.15

INDEPENDENT JUDICIARY	1.00
PRIMACY OF RULE OF LAW IN CIVIL AND CRIMINAL MATTERS	1.60
ACCOUNTABILITY OF SECURITY FORCES AND MILITARY TO CIVILIAN AUTHORITIES	1.00
PROTECTION OF PROPERTY RIGHTS	1.00

Congo's civil law system is a legacy of Belgian rule, but customary law is still in force in many parts of the multiethnic, largely rural country. Traditional private domain issues such as marriage and divorce, inheritance, and land tenure are regulated by customary laws in the various traditional communities.[68] The 2006 constitution institutionalized the principle of judicial independence by removing the executive's power to appoint magistrates and judges, granting this power instead to the Supreme Council of the Judiciary (CSM), which was finally created in August 2008 but remained nonfunctioning as of mid-2009. The constitution also divided the Supreme Court of Justice's functions into a Constitutional Court, a Court of Appeals, and a Council of State empowered to oversee constitutional, judicial, and administrative issues, respectively. These bodies are charged with overseeing a system of lower civilian and military courts.[69] However, the government has been slow in implementing the new system. It has yet to pass legislation providing for the creation of the three Supreme Court bodies.[70]

Regardless of constitutional intent, Congolese judges are subject to undue influence from government officials and powerful individuals. The CSM, which should be the linchpin of judicial independence, remains unable to act as a disciplinary body. Executive interference in the judicial system is routine. In February 2008, while the parliament was still deliberating on the creation of constitutionally mandated judicial institutions, President Kabila forced 89 magistrates into retirement, including the president of the Supreme Court and the prosecutor general.[71] While Kabila depicted the dismissals as a corruption purge, the 28 new magistrates hired to fill the posts were unqualified for their new positions, and most analysts—though not necessarily most citizens—viewed the president's actions as undue interference in the judiciary. In response, the Magistrates' Union organized a strike.[72] In July 2009, the president dismissed another 165 magistrates, again on the basis of alleged corruption. His actions were viewed by some as an attempt to distract public attention from executive malfeasance.[73] Overall, the combination of government neglect and incapacity results in a justice system plagued by corruption, particularly among magistrates, who receive a monthly salary of less than US$200.[74] This systemic weakness is exacerbated by both the lack of a functioning judicial training body to instill ethical and legal standards.[75]

Due to underfunding and understaffing, access to justice remains extremely limited outside of Kinshasa. In 2007, only 0.75 of the budget was allocated to the judicial branch.[76] Of the mere 2,000 magistrates serving in the country, fully two-thirds work in Kinshasa, Matadi, and Lubumbashi; only 50 of the country's 200 courts were operational in 2008.[77] In rural areas, citizens often resort to vigilante justice rather than rely on either the clogged lower courts or informal local systems where judicial decisions are dispensed by any authority present.[78] Moreover, in approximately 70 percent of all cases, judicial decisions go unenforced due to scarcity of resources and the inability of citizens to pay enforcement costs.[79] In an effort to provide remedies, the Ministry of Justice in 2007 announced a Plan of Action for Justice Reform that included judicial training and an expansion in the number of judicial officers; it was followed in 2009 by a Ministry of Justice Roadmap on similar themes.[80] Implementation will be planned and monitored by the Mixed Committee on Justice (CMJ), which includes both international and domestic planners and has helped coordinate some successful initiatives.[81] Although the constitution provides for the presumption of innocence until guilt is proven, this right is often violated in practice. Lawyers are frequently denied access to their defendants, and both defendants and lawyers are sometimes prevented from being present at trials, which are often closed to the public. The right to appeal is not legally guaranteed in cases related to national security, armed robbery, and smuggling.[82] The 2006 constitution limits military justice to members of the armed forces and police. However, because penal codes have not been changed to reflect the new charter, civilians are still prosecuted in military courts, where they possess fewer rights.[83] Military court judges and prosecutors, while often dedicated, find their independence limited by the atmosphere of impunity, which provides sound reasons to fear retribution if they issue orders that displease officers.

Civilian control over the military remains extremely feeble, and is essentially an abstract concept considering the degree to which power is held by former combatants and the fluidity between state and nonstate fighters over the evolution of the conflict. On the level of citizen interaction, the government remains unable to rein in the military and police, who are so woefully underpaid that corruption and illegal behavior are inevitable. Both active and demobilized soldiers, deserters, and police continued to harass and rob civilians and abuse women, with eastern Congo most affected. Searches without warrants and forced labor are frequent as well. Lines of authority within the military are opaque, with reintegrated ex-combatants often taking orders from their former commanders even though dismantling and dispersing former units was a specific objective of the reintegration process. Payroll theft by officers has been a major problem, though some mechanisms introduced in recent years by the government have decreased its prevalence. The international community has invested substantial resources in collaboration with the Kabila administration to create inertia within the DDR and military reform processes, but in the context of ongoing conflict, progress remains limited and fragile.

The treatment of top CNDP commanders incorporated into the military who have been explicitly accused of appalling human rights violations is an extremely sensitive topic. According to MONUC, integration of the CNDP into FARDC has been a particularly troubled process.[84] Nkunda's case could potentially be an embarrassment to both the Rwandan and Congolese governments, given prior cooperation by both with the CNDP. Kabila was willing to co-opt each rebel leader when he saw an opportunity to use the alliance to broaden support for his military and political strategy. For the same reason, Kabila co-opted former RCD officers who are widely believed to have engaged in flagrant human rights abuses. Although some reports indicate that ICC prosecutions have affected the behavior of militia leaders,[85] the fact that Bosco Ntaganda and other wanted—and in some cases, convicted—officers remain active within FARDC illustrate the government's ongoing prioritization of peace over justice. In May 2009 an amnesty law for acts in North and South Kivu since 2003 went into effect. Although it specified that crimes against humanity were exempt, observers feared the further entrenchment of impunity.[86]

The law provides relatively clear definitions of property rights, but such provisions are frequently violated by both state and private actors. The combination of a convoluted property code and an ineffective, overburdened administrative and judicial enforcement system renders the protection of property rights extremely difficult. While the government has made some attempts to improve and harmonize its legal framework with the 2006 constitution, implementation has lagged.[87] Property rights remain especially unstable in the east, where land conflicts resulting from forced displacement and ongoing plundering and land seizures by armed groups and bandits are prevalent.[88] Furthermore, restricted land access, a legacy of past government policies that stripped Congolese of their land rights under customary law and led to the appropriation of their land by wealthy elites and foreigners, has been a driving force in the current conflict.[89]

ANTICORRUPTION AND TRANSPARENCY   1.06

ENVIRONMENT TO PROTECT AGAINST CORRUPTION	0.50
PROCEDURES AND SYSTEMS TO ENFORCE ANTICORRUPTION LAWS	0.75
EXISTENCE OF ANTICORRUPTION NORMS, STANDARDS, AND PROTECTIONS	1.00
GOVERNMENTAL TRANSPARENCY	2.00

The Mobutu era created a system in which power and corruption were synonymous, and its legacy will be difficult to overcome. The Congolese believe that corruption is rampant in the country. Transparency International's 2009 Corruption Perceptions Index ranked the DRC 162 out of 180 countries.[90] Corruption is endemic at all levels of society and the scale of the government's anti-graft efforts has been wholly inadequate to the immense task. In addition, insufficient salaries, which often are not paid for months at a time, fuel petty corruption among civil servants, police, and soldiers. Administrative disruptions designed to solicit bribes, known as *tracasseries*, are considered a part of everyday life by the Congolese. Little progress to combat them has been made in recent years, although some local-level initiatives have reported success.[91]

Institutional mechanisms to ensure accountability are thin at all levels of the Congolese government. The 2006 constitution and the Code of Ethics of Public Officials require the head of state, government officials, and civil servants to submit assets declarations to the Constitutional Court.[92] However, public access to the statements is not stipulated. Owing to the weakness of the judicial system, prosecution for corruption, particularly of government officials, is too infrequent to act as a credible deterrent, though dismissals sometimes occur. The independent press generally has not shied away from investigating corruption in the public sector or criticizing government policies. However, reporters exposing graft expose themselves to the risk of arrest, intimidation, and violence on a constant basis.

State presence in the economy has diminished from the height of the Mobutu era, when state mining company GECAMINES controlled mineral production. Accelerating mismanagement led to the company's collapse by 1990. Since then, direct state production has been subordinated to partnerships with corporations as well as artisanal mining. Both during the conflict and after, the government attempted to impose greater order, but the incentives for improved oversight have, unfortunately, often been based more on opportunities for rent seeking than maximization of state resources to benefit citizens. A new mining code was enacted in 2002 and a complementary mining registry created the next year, but the registry ended up linked to the presidency and in the hands of a Kabila ally.[93]

The situation in Katanga, the DRC's key copper and cobalt producing region, illustrates the unfortunate continuities between the Mobutu era and the present. Despite continuous government control, the region's riches have not translated into sustained benefits for the local population, with corruption and misguided regulation playing important roles. According to Global Witness, " . . . at the end of 2005, at least three quarters of the minerals exported from Katanga were leaving illegally."[94] Attempts to achieve greater state control have not always benefited either the state or local populations. For instance, tens of thousands of artisanal miners were expelled from mining sites, with no alternative income source, as private companies moved in during the 2004–2008 commodities boom.[95] Similarly, state attempts to maximize revenue through high export taxes and royalties have resulted in a massive, complex smuggling system in which corrupt officials have enormous opportunity to profit from graft. Conflicts of interest are also legion, as political officials in resource-rich areas are often closely tied to the mining companies.

The Katangan mining trade is rational in comparison to operations in North and South Kivu and Ituri, where officials of regional governments, rebel groups, and FARDC members have scrambled for natural resources for over a decade. The region is rich in cassiterite, gold, coltan, and wolframite, and the quest to gain and maintain control of these strategic minerals played an important part in prolonging the war.[96]

Taxation represents another area in which the pathologies of Congolese institutions are evident. The essential tax relationship between citizen and state, in which taxes act as investment in state services, is only minimally functional. Most fee collection by government agents occurs informally and illegally, with little citizen knowledge of what fees are legal. The education sector is plagued by various forms of corruption.[97] According to a recent report by TWN Africa, mining companies use numerous negotiating and tax avoidance schemes to minimize payments to governments, while also taking advantage of the inability of national tax authorities to ensure compliance.[98] Given the volume of mining, significant revenues do reach the state—at least when commodities prices are high—but a lack of transparency in revenue distribution creates conflict between local and national authorities and provides incentives for individual officials and local agencies to seek informal solutions.[99] Deficiencies in customs administrations have created a vicious circle: rampant smuggling leads the state to raise export taxes in search of revenue, thereby encouraging further smuggling.[100]

Against this backdrop, the government's anticorruption campaign has not yielded significant results. The primary anticorruption law was enacted in 2005 and is considered an adequate framework, should it ever be consistently utilized. A largely ineffective Ethics and Anti-Corruption Commission was created in 2003 as one of five so-called citizen institutions mandated by the transitional constitution, but did not cross over to the new constitution. The DRC lacks both a national ombudsman and a complaints mechanism whereby victims of corruption seek redress for corrupt acts. The State Auditor, which is in charge of reviewing expenditures, is generally ineffective.[101]

A number of reviews of resource-exploitation contracts have occurred since the 2002 peace agreement. The first report, by a commission within the transitional parliament led by Christophe Lutundula, produced a damning indictment of mining sector management but no procedural overhaul. Another government-initiated review of 61 mining contracts began in 2007 and led to the cancellation or renegotiation of numerous deals. However, the Carter Center noted that in terms of both process and final results, the review failed to either attain its stated goals or set a precedent for more rational, transparent concessions processes.[102] Finally, a review of logging contracts resulted in the October 2008 announcement that numerous deals would be canceled, with an ongoing moratorium on new concessions.

The achievement of any significant governmental transparency remains largely aspirational, and many officials do not share this goal. There is no freedom of information or other comprehensive law governing the provision of government data. In addition, the dissemination of information remains extremely weak, and many citizens are unaware of important laws and regulations that affect their personal interests.[103] Since February 2008 the DRC has been a candidate to join the Extractive Industries Transparency Initiative (EITI) but must abide by multiple steps to promote transparency before it is in compliance with EITI principles. According to the Open Budget Index, the country provides no information about its budget other than the final enacted document.[104] The government has been working with the World Bank to institute a new procurement code, but as of mid-2009 it remained unimplemented. In general, while individual agencies and officials at times act to improve management and transparency, most such progress is compelled by NGOs and international donors.

RECOMMENDATIONS

- Create an independent media regulation body mandated with applying clear and consistent rules and processes prior to suspending or closing media outlets.
- Prioritize the prosecution of war crimes, beginning with vetting the human rights record of all FARDC commanders and removing suspected violators from their command positions.

- Adopt a multifaceted strategy to end impunity for crimes of rape and sexual violence that include gender-sensitivity educational initiatives, rehabilitation for victims of sexual violence, and a comprehensive protection program to ensure that victims can testify against their attackers.
- With the assistance of the international community, work to improve the judiciary by improving judicial training, adding infrastructure and technical capacity, expanding the territorial coverage of courts, and providing salaries to judges and judicial staff at a level sufficient to diminish incentives for corruption.
- Systematically review and strengthen laws, policies, and institutions that govern financial payments made by mining corporations to the national government while also revising the tax system to diminish incentives for evasion and smuggling.

NOTES

For URLs and endnote hyperlinks, please visit the *Countries at the Crossroads* homepage at http://freedomhouse.org/template.cfm?page=139&edition=8.

[1] Amnesty International, *Democratic Republic of Congo: Disarmament, Demobilization, and Reintegration (DDR) and Reform of the Army* (London: Amnesty International, January 2007).
[2] Amnesty International, *Democratic Republic of Congo: Children at War: Creating Hope for Their Future* (London: Amnesty International, October 2006), 3.
[3] Ibid.
[4] "Peace Agreement Signed–But How Long Will It Last?" African Press International, January 31, 2008.
[5] Patrick Vinck et al., *Living with Fear: A Population-based Survey on Attitudes about Peace, Justice, and Social Reconstruction in Eastern Democratic Republic of Congo* (Berkeley/New Orleans/New York: Human Rights Center, Payson Center for International Development, and International Center for Transitional Justice [ICTJ], August 2008).
[6] Global Witness, *Recommendations on Due Diligence for Buyers and Companies Trading in Minerals from Eastern Democratic Republic of Congo and for Their Home Governments* (Washington, D.C.: Global Witness, November 2008).
[7] John Vandaele, "China Outdoes Europeans in Congo," *Asia Times*, February 8, 2008; "DR Congo to Adapt China Deal to Appease IMF," Ghana Business News, June 6, 2009.
[8] Integrated Regional Information Network (IRIN), "Democratic Republic of Congo Humanitarian Country Profile," February 2007; World Bank, "Democratic Republic of Congo, in *2007 World Development Indicators* (Washington, D.C.: World Bank, 2007).
[9] John A. Pandeni, "SADC Electoral Observer Mission Preliminary Statement on the Presidential and Parliamentary Elections Held on 30 July 2006 in the Democratic Republic of Congo," South African Development Community, August 1, 2006.
[10] The Carter Center, "Third Carter Center Post-Election Statement on the October 29 Elections in the Democratic Republic of Congo," news release, November 27, 2006.
[11] Dieudonne N. Tshiyoyo, "Post-Transitional Elections in the Democratic Republic of Congo," Elections Today, ACE Electoral Knowledge Network, 2007; Freedom House, "Democratic Republic of Congo," in *Freedom in the World 2009* (Washington, D.C.: Freedom House, 2009).

[12] Mirjam Stockel, "The Democratic Republic of Congo after Presidential and Parliamentary Elections 2006," Konrad-Adenauer-Stiftung European Office, December 1, 2006.
[13] Asuman Bisiika, "Who Will Be DR Congo's Next President?" *New Times*, August 13, 2006.
[14] Ibid.
[15] Human Rights Watch (HRW), *"We Will Crush You": The Restriction of Political Space in the Democratic Republic of Congo* (New York: HRW, November 2008).
[16] Notably, according to the Carter Center, many provincial seats were determined by a few hundred votes or less. As a result, seemingly minor irregularities had a detrimental impact upon the results of individual races.
[17] "A Wilderness that May Become a State," *Economist*, November 25, 2006.
[18] HRW, *"We Will Crush You."*
[19] Ibid.
[20] Ibid.
[21] Ibid.
[22] Jason Stearns, "Congo's Peace: Mirage or Miracle," *Current History*, April 23, 2007.
[23] "Kabila, Mobutu's Son Sign Pact to Form Government," IRIN, October 18, 2006.
[24] Laura Davis, *Justice-Sensitive Security System Reform in the Democratic Republic of Congo* (Brussels: Initiative for Peacebuilding, February 2009).
[25] HRW, "Letter to the Prime Minister of DR Congo Regarding Public Attacks on Human Rights Organizations," July 31, 2009.
[26] Journaliste en Danger, "Tableu Comparatif Annes 2008 et 2009," News Alert, December 10, 2009.
[27] Committee to Protect Journalists (CPJ), "Two Radio Stations Shut Down in DRC," press release, March 31, 2009.
[28] CPJ, "DRC Newspaper Suspended, Director Jailed for Defamation," press release, January 11, 2007.
[29] HRW, "Democratic Republic of Congo," in *World Report 2009* (New York: HRW, 2009).
[30] Tom Rhodes, "Attacks on the Press 2007: Africa Analysis," CPJ, February 5, 2008.
[31] CPJ, "In DRC, TV Reporters Beaten, 38 Broadcasters Banned," press release, October 25, 2007.
[32] International Freedom of Expression Exchange (IFEX), "Journalist's Murder Highlights Deteriorating Press Freedom Situation in East," press release, August 26, 2009.
[33] Ambroise Pierre and Leonard Vincent, *Bukavu, Murder City: An Investigation into Murders of Journalists in the Capital of Sud-Kivu* (Paris: Reporters without Borders [RSF], March 18, 2009).
[34] RSF, "Leading Suspect in Journalist's Murder Escapes from Military Cell in Bukavu," press release, November 24, 2009.
[35] RSF, "Democratic Republic of Congo, in *Annual Report 2008* (Paris: RSF, February 7, 2008).
[36] CPJ, "Democratic Republic of Congo," in *Attacks on the Press 2008* (New York: CPJ, 2009).
[37] International Federation of Journalists, "IFJ Condemns Suspension of RFI Programmes in DRC," press release, July 29, 2009; Tom Rhodes, "Clinton Must Call for an End to Congo's Media Censorship," World Focus, August 10, 2009.
[38] IFEX, "Press Still Exposed to Threats, Pressure and Censorship that Undermines Its Credibility, Says JED on World Press Freedom Day," press release, May 2, 2009.
[39] Article 19, "Democratic Republic of Congo," in *20th Anniversary Book* (London: Article 19, 2008).

40. Tiego Tiemboré, "DRC: No Electric Infrastructure, No Internet Backbone?" Association for Progressive Communications, August 21, 2007.
41. Amnesty International, *Democratic Republic of Congo: Submission to the UN Universal Period Review: Sixth Session of the UPR Working Group of the Human Rights Council* (London: Amnesty International, April 13, 2009).
42. HRW, *"We Will Crush You."*
43. United Nations Organization Mission in DR Congo (MONUC), "MONUC Supports the Government in Prison Reform," June 25, 2009; Thomas Hubert, "Congo's East Dire, Goma Prison Africa's Worst–UN," Reuters AlertNet, July 25, 2009.
44. International Citizens United for the Rehabilitation of Errants (CURE), "Democratic Republic of Congo Assessment," in *Prison and Justice Assessments in Africa* (New York: International CURE, May 14, 2009).
45. HRW, "Democratic Republic of Congo," in *World Report 2009*.
46. HRW, "Q & A: DR Congo-Dossier for Hillary Clinton's Visit," August 10, 2009; James Karuhanga, "MONUC Claims over 10,000 FDLR Repatriated," *New Times*, July 5, 2009.
47. HRW, *"You Will Be Punished": Attacks on Civilians in Eastern Congo* (New York: HRW, December 13, 2009).
48. Vinck et al., *Living with Fear*, 14.
49. HRW, "DR Congo: Militia Leader Guilty in Landmark Trial," news release, March 10, 2009.
50. Office to Monitor and Combat Trafficking in Persons, "Democratic Republic of Congo," in *Trafficking in Persons Report 2009* (Washington, D.C.: U.S. Department of State, June 16, 2009).
51. Democratic Republic of Congo, *Replies by the Government of the Democratic Republic of Congo to a List of Issues on Its Second, Third, Fourth and Fifth Periodic Reports* (Geneva: United Nations Economic and Social Council, August 2009).
52. "Unions to Increase Congolese Women's Part-Take in Politics," afrol News, April 10, 2009.
53. African Association for the Defence of Human Rights and World Organization against Torture (OMCT), *Violence against Women in the Democratic Republic of Congo: Alternative Report Prepared for the Committee on the Elimination of Discrimination against Women* (Kinshasa: African Association for the Defence of Human Rights and OMCT, August 2006); Committee on the Elimination of Discrimination against Women, "List of Issues and Questions with Regard to the Consideration of a Periodic Report," February 14, 2006; Amnesty International, *Democratic Republic of Congo: Submission to the UN Universal Periodic Review*.
54. HRW, *Soldiers Who Rape, Commanders Who Condone: Sexual Violence and Military Reform in the Democratic Republic of Congo* (New York: HRW, July 17, 2009).
55. African Association for the Defence of Human Rights and OMCT, *Violence against Women in the Democratic Republic of Congo*.
56. HRW, "Q & A: DR Congo."
57. HRW, *Soldiers Who Rape*.
58. UN Human Rights Council (UNHRC) *Report of the Independent Expert on the Situation of Human Rights in the Democratic Republic of Congo, Mr. Titinga Frederec Pacere* (Geneva: UNHRC, February 29, 2008).
59. HRW, *Soldiers Who Rape*.
60. Minority Rights Group International, "Democratic Republic of Congo Overview," in *World Directory of Minorities and Indigenous Peoples* (London: Minority Rights Group International, 2008).

[61] Bertelsmann Stiftung, "Democratic Republic of Congo Country Report," in *Bertelsmann Transformation Index 2010* (Guterloh: Bertelsmann Stiftung, 2010).

[62] Congo Tutsis had for very long been subject to discrimination because of their Rwandan origin. They played a major role in the 1996-97 war, which led to the fall of the Mobutu dictatorship and again in the 1998-2002 effort to remove Laurent Kabila from power. Each time, their main reason for participating in the war was to install a friendly government they could count on to resolve the longstanding nationality question. The government's failure to investigate the killings of hundreds of Congo Tutsi soldiers and civilians across the country is partly behind the ongoing conflict between Tutsi rebels and the current Kabila government. For detailed analysis of the Banyamulenge nationality question and its relationship to the present conflict in North Kivu, see Osita Afoaku, *Explaining the Failure of Democracy in Democratic Republic of Congo: Autocracy and Dissent in an Ambivalent World* (New York: The Edwin Mellen Press, 2005).

[63] Minority Rights Group International, "Batwa and Bambuti: Democratic Republic of Congo," in *World Directory of Minorities and Indigenous Peoples*; Heritier Maila, "Democratic Republic of Congo: Persecuted Pygmies Driven from Forest Home," Institute for War and Peace Reporting (IWPR), May 23, 2009; Canadian International Development Agency, "Congolese Pygmy Women Realize the Power of the Ballot," April 24, 2007.

[64] Katharine Ganly, "Disabled Congolese Find Ways to Thrive," Global Voices Online, May 17, 2009.

[65] Bureau of Democracy, Human Rights, and Labor, "Democratic Republic of Congo," in *International Religious Freedom Report 2009* (Washington, D.C.: U.S. Department of State, October 26, 2009).

[66] International Trade Union Confederation (ITUC), "Democratic Republic of Congo," in *2009 Annual Survey of Violations of Trade Union Rights* (Brussels: ITUC, 2009).

[67] Peuples Solidaires, *Republique Democratique du Congo: Les Diamants de la Misere* (Montreal: Peuples Solidaires, May 2007).

[68] Dunia Zongwe, Francois Butedi, and Clement Phebe, *The Legal System and Research of the Democratic Republic of Congo (DRC): An Overview* (New York: New York University School of Law, Hauser Global Law School Program, December 2007).

[69] The Electoral Institute of Southern Africa (EISA), "DRC: Constitution," Country Profiles: DRC, EISA home page, January 2007.

[70] International Bar Association (IBA) and International Legal Assistance Consortium (ILAC), *Rebuilding Courts and Trust in the Democratic Republic of Congo: An Assessment of the Needs of the Justice System in the Democratic Republic of Congo* (London: IBA and ILAC, August 2009), 26.

[71] UNHRC, *Report of the Independent Expert on the Situation of Human Rights*; Davis, *Justice-Sensitive Security System Reform*, 21.

[72] Laura Davis and Priscilla Hayner, *Difficult Peace, Limited Justice: Ten Years of Peacemaking in the DRC* (New York: ICTJ, March 2009); Bureau of Democracy, Human Rights, and Labor, "Democratic Republic of Congo," in *2008 Country Reports on Human Rights Practices* (Washington, D.C.: U.S. Department of State, February 2009).

[73] Heritier Maila, "Kabila Anti-Corruption Drive: A New Wave of Purges in the Justice System—But Will They Make a Difference," IWPR, July 30, 2009.

[74] IWPR, "Congo (DRC): Distrust of Judicial System Leads to Spread of Vigilantism and Lynching," The Norwegian Council for Africa, August 20, 2009.

[75] UNHRC, *Report of the Special Rapporteur on the Independence of Judges and Lawyers, Leandro Despouy* (Geneva: UNHRC, May 24, 2007); IBA and ILAC, *Rebuilding Courts and Trust in the Democratic Republic of Congo*.

76 UNHRC, *Report of the Independent Expert on the Situation of Human Rights*.
77 Bureau of Democracy, Human Rights, and Labor, "Democratic Republic of Congo," in *2008 Country Reports on Human Rights Practices*.
78 IWPR, "Congo (DRC): Distrust of Judicial System Leads to Spread of Vigilantism and Lynching"; UNHRC, *Report of the Independent Expert on the Situation of Human Rights*.
79 IBA and ILAC, *Rebuilding Courts and Trust in the Democratic Republic of Congo*, 23.
80 UNHRC, *Combined Report of Seven Thematic Special Procedures on Technical Assistance to the Government of the Democratic Republic of Congo*, (Geneva: UNHRC, March 5, 2009), 17.
81 IBA and ILAC, *Rebuilding Courts and Trust in the Democratic Republic of Congo*, 20.
82 Bureau of Democracy, Human Rights, and Labor, "Democratic Republic of Congo," in *2008 Country Reports on Human Rights Practices*.
83 Amnesty International, *Democratic Republic of Congo: Submission to the UN Universal Periodic Review*.
84 UN Security Council, *Thirtieth Report of the Secretary-General on the United Nations Organization Mission in the Democratic Republic of Congo* (New York: UN Security Council, December 4, 2009).
85 HRW, "The International Criminal Court Trial of Thomas Lubanga," HRW Q&A, January 23, 2009.
86 IBA and ILAC, *Rebuilding Courts and Trust in the Democratic Republic of Congo*.
87 Bureau of Economic, Energy, and Business Affairs, "Democratic Republic of Congo," in *Investment Climate Statements 2009* (Washington, D.C.: U.S. Department of State, February 2009).
88 Heritage Foundation and *Wall Street Journal* (WSJ), "Democratic Republic of Congo," in *2009 Index of Economic Freedom* (Washington, D.C./New York: Heritage Foundation and WSJ, 2009); Office of the United Nations High Commissioner for Refugees, *Supplementary Appeal: Protection and Assistance to IDPs in the Democratic Republic of Congo* (Geneva: UNHCR, February 13, 2007).
89 Chris Higgins et al., "Conflict in the Great Lakes Region–How Is It Linked with Land and Migration?" *National Resource Perspectives* 96 (March 2005).
90 Transparency International, *2009 Corruption Perceptions Index* (Berlin: Transparency International, November 17, 2009).
91 Mary Louise Eagleton, Pamela Fessenden, and Victor Mangindula, *Strengthening the Capacity of Civil Society and Business to Promote Sustainable Economic Growth along the Congo River and Its Tributaries: Mid-Term Evaluation* (Washington, D.C.: U.S. Agency for International Development, September 2004).
92 Muzong W. Kodi, *Anti-Corruption Challenges in Post-Election Democratic Republic of Congo* (London: Chatham House, January 2007), 18.
93 International Crisis Group, "Escaping the Conflict Trap: Promoting Good Governance in the Congo," Africa Report No. 114, July 20, 2006.
94 Global Witness, *Digging in Corruption: Fraud, Abuse, and Exploitation in Katanga's Copper and Cobalt Mines* (Washington, D.C.: Global Witness, July 2006).
95 Gregory Mthembu-Salter, *Natural Resource Governance, Boom and Bust: The Case of Kolwezi in the DRC,* (Johannesburg: South African Institute of International Affairs, June 2009).
96 Global Witness, "Control of Minerals by Warring Parties Threatens Peace Efforts in Eastern Congo," press release, September 10, 2008.
97 AfriMAP and the Open Society Initiative for Southern Africa (OSISA), *The Democratic Republic of Congo: Effective Delivery of Public Services in the Education Sector* (Johannesburg: AfriMAP and OSISA, 2009).

[98] OSISA et al., *Breaking the Curse: How Transparent Taxation and FAIR Tax Can Turn Africa's Mineral Wealth into Development* (Johannesburg: OSISA et al., March 30, 2009).
[99] Mthembu-Salter, *National Resource Governance, Boom and Bust.*
[100] Mthembu-Salter, *Social and Economic Dynamics of Mining in Kalima, DRC* (Pretoria: Institute for Security Studies, April 2009).
[101] AfriMAP and OSISA, *The Democratic Republic of Congo.*
[102] Carter Center, "The Mining Review in the Democratic Republic of Congo: Missed Opportunities, Failed Expectations, Hopes for the Future," press release, April 3, 2009.
[103] Alison Hoare et al., *Towards Sustainable Management and Financing of the Democratic Republic of Congo's Forests* (London: Chatham House, June 2008).
[104] Open Budget Initiative, "Democratic Republic of Congo," in *Open Budget Index 2008* (Washington, D.C: Open Budget Initiative, 2009).

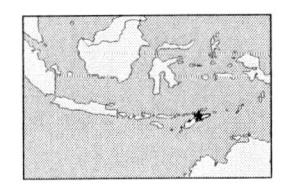

EAST TIMOR

CAPITAL: Dili
POPULATION: 1.1 million
GNI PER CAPITA (PPP): $4,690

SCORES	2006	2010
ACCOUNTABILITY AND PUBLIC VOICE:	3.77	4.30
CIVIL LIBERTIES:	4.63	4.94
RULE OF LAW:	3.77	3.58
ANTICORRUPTION AND TRANSPARENCY:	2.77	2.98

(scores are based on a scale of 0 to 7, with 0 representing weakest and 7 representing strongest performance)

Dennis Shoesmith

INTRODUCTION

On May 20, 2002, the Democratic Republic of Timor-Leste obtained its independence following nearly 25 years of brutal occupation by the Indonesian military, whose presence culminated in widespread bloodshed and destruction following a 1999 vote for independence. Since then, the young country has struggled to establish not only a working democracy but also a functioning state. Over the past seven years, it has made significant progress but has also experienced serious political crises, including threatening episodes of armed rebellion, attempted assassination of the president and prime minister, and violent communal conflict.

Between 1999 and independence in 2002, the United Nations Transitional Administration in East Timor (UNTAET) managed the transition to independence. In August 2001, the country elected an 88-member Constituent Assembly (CA) to draft a constitution. Fretilin—the leftist Revolutionary Front for an Independent East Timor, whose armed wing waged a low-grade insurgency against the Indonesian army during its occupation—won 57 percent of the national vote. In April 2002, Kay Rala Xanana Gusmão won the presidency with 87 percent of a direct popular vote. In 2002, the Fretilin-dominated CA passed a new constitution, enshrining basic political freedoms and a bill of rights. The CA then transitioned into the regular Parliament under a Fretilin government. This first administration was characterized by a power struggle between Gusmão, Fretilin, and Prime Minister Marí Alkatiri. Beneath

---

Dennis Shoesmith is Associate Professor of Political Science at Charles Darwin University in Australia. His current research interests are focused on parliamentary and local government reform in Timor-Leste.

the surface, communal tensions remained between geographical groupings of "easterners" and "westerners." "Easterners" (the Lorosae), who claimed they had led the fight for independence, were affiliated with Fretilin and held most top positions in the army. The Lorosae perception was that "westerners" (the Loromonu) had tended to collaborate with the Indonesian occupiers. The Loromonu, meanwhile, perceived themselves as sidelined in the postindependence political arrangement.

In 2006, the young country descended into violence, as these deep-seated political divisions erupted into widespread clashes in the capital, threatening civil war. The unrest began in March, when roughly one-third (600 members) of the East Timor Defense Force (Falintil-FDTL/F) were dismissed for striking in protest of poor working conditions, low pay, and claims of discrimination by officers from the east against those from the west. In late May, FDTL soldiers killed 10 unarmed police officers under UN protection, sparking broader clashes with the police, many of whom had worked for the Indonesian administration. Frustration with the government's failure to alleviate poverty and corruption, combined with objections to its response to the turmoil in the defense force, led numerous citizens to take up arms in factions ranging from "political-front groups, veterans groups and martial arts groups, to small street corner gangs and youth groups."[1] Dozens were killed in the ensuing antigovernment protests and communal violence. At the peak of the crisis, approximately 150,000 people were displaced, approximately half huddled in camps in the capital Dili, where they remained for the next two years.

An Australian-led contingent of 2,200 foreign troops was deployed to ensure security and President Gusmão assumed additional powers, declaring a state of emergency that remained in place until August 2006. Still revered as a national hero for his role in resisting occupation, Gusmão maintained public support, while the Fretilin administration was widely discredited by the violence. Alkatiri eventually stepped down and Gusmão chose Nobel Prize–winner and former foreign affairs minister José Ramos-Horta to serve as prime minister until legislative and presidential elections could be held in 2007.

The elections brought an end to Fretilin's dominance, with Ramos-Horta elected president and Gusmão eventually emerging as prime minister. The risk of instability emerged again in February 2008, however, when former army major Alfredo Reinado led an assassination attempt against both leaders. Gusmão survived the attack unharmed, but Ramos-Horta was severely injured and flown to Australia for treatment. Reinado, who had been arrested for involvement in the 2006 uprising but escaped from prison later that year, was killed during the attack.

This is the political context in which the search for public accountability and the rule of law has had to proceed in recent years. Contributing to political crises is the country's widespread poverty. With approximately half the population living below the poverty line, the country remains the poorest in Southeast Asia.[2] Despite large oil and gas revenues and generous international aid, poverty increased between 2001 and 2007, reflecting stagnation within the non-oil economy.[3] That most East Timorese are experiencing declining living standards renders high-level corruption a particularly sensitive source of public disaffection.

Despite these significant challenges, progress has been made. With international intervention, the crises of 2006 and 2008 have been weathered. The elections were successfully held and a transfer of power to the Parliamentary Majority Alliance (AMP) took place, with the AMP coalition government holding thus far. Life in Dili has improved and the IDP camps have been dismantled.[4] With the death of Reinado and the surrender of his cohorts, the threat of military rebellion has receded. The United Nations Integrated Mission in Timor-Leste (UNMIT) has renewed its mandate and the Australian forces remain in place to provide support. By early 2009, the "security situation in Timor-Leste [had] strikingly improved,"[5] and signs of economic growth had emerged. The present AMP government has drawn heavily on the state's petroleum fund since 2007, lifting per capita gross national income from US$550 in 2006 to US$1,510 in 2009.

Nevertheless, political polarization and the prevailing culture of impunity surrounding both past abuses and ongoing high-level corruption pose a significant threat to the country's further economic and democratic development. As such, East Timor remains a fragile state that will need considerable international support for some time to come.

ACCOUNTABILITY AND PUBLIC VOICE   4.30

FREE AND FAIR ELECTORAL LAWS AND ELECTIONS	4.25
EFFECTIVE AND ACCOUNTABLE GOVERNMENT	4.25
CIVIC ENGAGEMENT AND CIVIC MONITORING	5.00
MEDIA INDEPENDENCE AND FREEDOM OF EXPRESSION	3.71

East Timor is an electoral democracy and experienced its first democratic transfer of power in 2007 following presidential and parliamentary elections.[6] Both sets of polls revealed declining public support for Fretilin, which had dominated the political scene since the country's independence in 2002. The decline largely reflected frustration with ongoing corruption and poverty.

East Timor has a semi-presidential system, with a directly elected but largely symbolic president serving as head of state and a prime minister chosen from the parliamentary majority as head of government. In keeping with the five-year terms stipulated in the constitution, elections for the presidency and the unicameral Parliament were held in June 2007, marking the country's first direct legislative elections since the Fretilin-dominated CA automatically became the country's first parliament in 2002.

Under the current electoral system, voting is based on proportional representation and closed party lists. Some observers have raised concerns that the arrangement distances representatives from the electorate, as voters have no input over the choice of individual candidates, and there is little incentive for parliamentarians to be responsive to local demands. Prior to the polls, in May 2007, several electoral reforms were adopted. The number of parliamentary seats was reduced from 88 to 65, and the 14 political parties that contested the election committed to a code of conduct honoring the free dissemination of political ideas and respect for the rights of rival parties.

Voter turnout reached 80.5 percent and some 2,750 international and local observers deemed the elections generally free and fair. Election coverage was open and detailed in newspapers and on public radio. Vote buying was not a significant problem, although there were a small number of reports of false returns. The Australian-led International Stabilization Force provided security on polling day, which was generally peaceful. The elections were nonetheless marred by violence in the period prior to and following the polls, particularly as they did not initially yield a clear victor. Two people died, approximately 100 were injured, and at least 7,000 displaced in clashes between party supporters. The greatest violence occurred in Baucau, followed by Viqueque, Oecussi, Ermera and Dili.[7]

In the presidential elections, Ramos-Horta emerged victorious in a runoff round, earning 69 percent of the vote and scoring a landslide victory over Fretilin's candidate. The results of the legislative polls proved more ambiguous. Although Fretilin obtained the largest number of seats (21), it fell short of a majority. The next largest party, the National Congress for Timorese Construction (CNRT), a new grouping launched by outgoing president Gusmão, secured 18 seats. In July, the CNRT announced that it would join several smaller parties to form a coalition, the Parliamentary Majority Alliance (AMP). This enabled it to attain a majority with 37 out of the 65 seats. In addition to CNRT, the AMP included the Democratic Party (PD; 8 seats) and the Social Democratic Association of Timor-Social Democratic Party (ASDT-PSD; 11 seats).

Deadlock ensued between Fretilin and CNRT, as each side sought to rely on the constitution to justify its right to form a government. The impasse was eventually broken when President Ramos-Horta, following constitutional provisions authorizing him to appoint the prime minister, asked CNRT and its leader Gusmão to form a government. Fretilin perceived the decision as biased, and violence erupted in Dili and other cities, adding to the number of displaced. Despite Fretilin's objections, its lawmakers nevertheless took their seats in Parliament by early fall. As a result, the legislative elections ultimately brought greater pluralism to Parliament and an end to Fretilin's dominance of government. Nonetheless, Gusmão's and Ramos-Horta's retention of the country's top two executive posts also illustrated the extent to which personalities and loyalties tied to the 1970s resistance to Indonesia continue to influence political outcomes more than programmatic or ideological platforms.

In 2009, reforms related to subnational government were introduced with the aim of decentralizing state services and bringing policy making closer to local communities. In rural areas, local authority falls in the hands of village chiefs (*chefe de suco*) and below them, hamlet chiefs (*chefe aldeia*). In the 2004 local elections, citizens voted for their preferred hamlet and village chiefs, who were mostly affiliated with national political parties. For the October 2009 *suco* elections, the new electoral law enforced a closed voting list system, removing voters' ability to choose individual candidates. The village chiefs elected through the closed voting lists then select hamlet chief candidates for each *aldeia*. Voters in the aldeias thus lost their right to directly elect their own chefe aldeia. In February 2009, the Council of Ministers introduced a bill that would create new municipal assemblies. Reversing the ban on political party affiliation in the suco elections, the draft law imposes national party affiliation on all candidates for municipal assembly positions. Observers have raised concerns that should this become law, it risks re-creating at the local level the polarization present in national politics. If successful, decentralization reforms could deepen East Timorese democracy and strengthen central state legitimacy. Mismanaged, however, they risk imposing yet another layer of potentially inert bureaucracy and corrupt municipal politicians on rural communities.

The separation of powers is outlined in the constitution through a semi-presidential system and an independent judiciary. In practice, the government is dominated by a powerful political executive presiding over a Parliament of limited effectiveness. An immature judiciary is struggling to fulfill its role of holding the other branches to account. By law, the directly elected president is largely a symbolic figure, with formal powers limited to the right to veto legislation and appoint officials to certain positions. In practice, both Gusmão and Ramos-Horta have, while serving as president, played a key role in forging the country's political reality and dynamics. The Council of Ministers (the political executive) has the authority to legislate, in addition to Parliament. In recent years, this power has been used to introduce controversial decree laws, such as the 2006 penal code legislation intended to impose harsh penalties for defamation and public criticism of the government (the law, overtaken by the 2006 political crisis, was not promulgated).[8]

The Fretilin government that ran the country from 2002 to 2006 tended to ignore Parliament. The two transitional governments that governed after Alkatiri's resignation in June 2006 did so during periods of political turmoil, limiting their effectiveness. The installation of the AMP-led government in 2007 has thus been the first opportunity for Parliament to develop an independent role. It has begun to assert itself, with the Fretilin-led opposition regularly mounting determined criticism of the government. Parliamentarians have posed serious questions during budget sessions and in October 2009, Fretilin moved a vote of no confidence against the prime minister after he ordered the release of an Indonesian national accused of human rights abuses. The motion was ultimately defeated but only after a day of vigorous debate.

Nevertheless, Parliament has yet to fully exercise effective oversight over the executive.[9] On the Fish-Kroenig Parliamentary Powers Index, East Timor's score remains low, failing many of the criteria for a strong legislature. Weaknesses cited include the fact that Parliament neither appoints nor can remove the prime minister, ministers do not sit in parliament, the executive is not answerable to the legislature, and the Council of Ministers has its own independent power to issue decree laws.[10] More practically, Parliament continues to lack the human and financial resources needed to significantly influence policy making. Parliamentary committees struggle to perform their oversight functions. Legislative scrutiny is uneven, and until recently, review and amendment of bills has been rare. This is due in part to linguistic obstacles: the language of Parliament is Portuguese, which most MPs have not mastered, and translation of legislation into the more commonly spoken Tetum remains slow.

The task of building a competent civil service from its state of complete destruction in 1999 remains daunting. The United Nations Development Programme (UNDP) and the World Bank have voiced concerns that the processes outlined in the 2004 Civil Service Act lack sufficient procedures to ensure impartiality in decisions of recruitment and promotion.[11] Civil service salaries are low, increasing the potential for corruption and making it difficult to attract capable staff for senior and mid-level positions. Several ministries have, nevertheless, managed in recent years to appoint highly competent individuals to top positions. The AMP government committed to improving the situation, declaring 2008 "the year of administrative reform" and subsequently establishing a Civil Service Commission with support from international donors. The commission's members were inaugurated in August 2009 and are generally perceived as competent. The government continues to work with the United Nations and other donors to further professionalize the civil service.[12]

Timorese are free to form political and voluntary organizations, and the space for a diversity of voices has expanded since Fretilin's defeat in the 2007 elections. There are no laws currently regulating the nongovernmental organization (NGO) sector, though some have been in development in recent years. In the meantime, a self-administered registration system is in place. Local and international NGOs face challenges in their attempts to operate effectively across the divide between the social and political centers, the cities of Dili and Baucau, home to the country's small middle class. In rural areas, where the great majority of the population resides as subsistence farmers, civil society assumes more traditional East Timorese forms. The international community is active and well represented in East Timor. Donors and funders of civic organizations are largely free of government pressure.

Local civil society organizations are gradually becoming more experienced and professional, increasing their ability to engage in effective dialogue with the government on policy and legislation. La'o Hamutuk (Walk Together), a joint East Timorese-international NGO, regularly produces well-researched critiques of government policy. Several NGOs monitoring human rights have worked closely with the Office of the Ombudsman for Human Rights and Justice (PDHJ), while a number of groups also provide pro bono legal aid and support for victims of human rights violations. The government has generally welcomed consultations with civic organizations such as the NGO Forum. Government efforts to establish a code of conduct for NGOs are intended to improve the dialogue between the state and civil society.[13] Nevertheless, the government has at times reacted negatively to what it perceived as unfair criticism from NGOs. This has been especially true with regards to criticism of its decision not to prosecute individuals allegedly responsible for war crimes committed during the Indonesian occupation.

Compared to the strict censorship in place under the Indonesian occupation, today East Timor's media operate in a relatively free environment. At least five private daily and weekly newspapers publish regularly and several more appear sporadically. As nearly 50 percent of the population remains illiterate, radio is the dominant medium. Following independence, broadcast media were mainly comprised of public radio and television outlets, including Radio Timor Leste, estimated to reach over two-thirds of East Timorese. In recent years, however, community radio stations—many with international funding—have proliferated and are playing an increasingly important role in the media landscape.

Despite such improvements, both the Fretilin and the AMP governments have attempted at times to limit free speech. Some journalists have faced legal and physical intimidation for criticizing the government. Officials often seek to justify such restrictions as necessary given the immature and sometimes irresponsible nature of East Timorese journalism and the need to protect national stability. In January 2008, following the publication of inflammatory interviews with rebel leader Alfredo Reinado, the prime minister warned that journalists risked arrest if they reported "erroneous" information.

The 2002 constitution guarantees free speech and freedom of the press. Nevertheless, journalists have been prosecuted for defamation under articles in the still-operational Indonesian penal code. In late 2008, Minister of Justice Lucia Lobato relied on the law to file criminal defamation charges against José Belo, editor of the weekly *Tempo Semanal*. The charges focused on an article Belo had published that alleged the minister had improperly awarded government contracts to friends and business contacts. If convicted, Belo—who was imprisoned during Indonesia's rule for passing human rights information to foreign journalists—would face fines and up to six years in jail.

In 2006, the Fretilin government drew up a new penal code to replace the Indonesian one, which it issued as a decree law and submitted to the president for assent. The proposed law drew international and domestic condemnation because of its retention of harsh criminal penalties for defamation.[14] President Gusmão sent the legislation back to the Council of Ministers without signing it, and it eventually lapsed due to the 2006 political crisis and change of government. In early 2009, the AMP government drafted its own proposed media laws. The proposals would decriminalize defamation, creating instead a national media council, appointed by Parliament and possessing authority to mediate defamation cases. Its powers would include issuing or revoking licenses of journalists, as well as the ability to impose fines of between US$500 and US$2,500 for individual journalists and of up to US$10,000 for newspapers. The draft bill also provoked criticism from local journalists and international press watchdogs. The Southeast Asian Press Alliance (SEAPA) stated that it was "deeply disturbed" by the proposed laws, which would "severely damage the environment for press freedom and free expression."[15]

Journalists occasionally face intimidation or physical assault. In February 2008, Mouzinho de Araujo, a senior journalist with the *East Timor Post*, was arrested and beaten up by military police. The newspaper lodged a complaint with the government, which subsequently issued a formal apology for the use of "unjustified force." Internet access is not subject to any restrictions, though less than 1 percent of the population accessed it in 2009 due to infrastructural limitations and poverty.

CIVIL LIBERTIES   4.94

PROTECTION FROM STATE TERROR, UNJUSTIFIED IMPRISONMENT, AND TORTURE	3.88
GENDER EQUITY	4.67
RIGHTS OF ETHNIC, RELIGIOUS, AND OTHER DISTINCT GROUPS	4.50
FREEDOM OF CONSCIENCE AND BELIEF	6.67
FREEDOM OF ASSOCIATION AND ASSEMBLY	5.00

East Timor has ratified all of the core international human rights treaties, including the United Nations Convention against Torture and its optional protocol. Notwithstanding its limited resources, East Timor has largely complied with UN human rights mechanisms, and since August 2006, UNMIT has deployed human rights officers in the field. Nonetheless, a prevailing culture of impunity for past and current abuses poses a significant obstacle to better civil liberties protections and an end to the cycles of sporadic violence that have plagued the country.

On multiple occasions in recent years, reports have emerged of police and security forces using violence against detainees. A 2006 Human Rights Watch (HRW) report detailed pervasive police torture and mistreatment. Such findings, along with police participation in violent clashes that spring, led the UN Police Force (UNPOL) to assume control over national policing in September 2006. At its peak, approximately 1,500 UNPOL officers were stationed in East Timor to ensure internal security. Since then, there has been a phased transfer of responsibility back to the Policia Nacional de Timor-Leste (PNTL) intended to conclude in 2010. As of mid-2009, PNTL units were responsible for security in Lautem, Aileu, Manatuto and Ainaro. UNPOL continued to maintain a presence in these areas, however, with a special responsibility to monitor respect for human rights.

As the PNTL and other forces began to resume security responsibilities since 2007, reports of mistreatment reemerged. The U.S. State Department has detailed serious incidents of "cruel and degrading treatment of civilians" by security forces, particularly the PNTL Task Force, a rapid reaction police unit formed in December 2007. The Office of the Ombudsman, UNMIT's human rights unit, and NGOs received dozens of complaints of excessive use of force by security personnel throughout 2008.[16] In the earlier part of the year, security forces attacked civilians as they sought to restore order in the aftermath of assassination attempts against President Ramos-Horta and Prime Minister Gusmão. The F-FDTL and the PNTL Joint Command force, set up after the attacks, was reportedly responsible for beatings, intimidation, and unlawful searches in rural areas.[17] In his report to the Security Council in early 2009, however, UN Secretary-General Ban Ki-Moon noted that by that time "allegations of ill-treatment and excessive use of force and intimidation during arrests [had] decreased."

Conditions in the four government-run prisons in Dili, Baucau, and Gleno are reported to generally meet international standards, although they lack provisions for mentally ill prisoners and there have been some allegations of prisoner mistreatment. Police station detention cells, particularly in rural areas, do not comply with international standards. Detainees in district police cells suffer from lack of nutrition, sanitation, and bedding. The ombudsman regularly monitors prison conditions, as do international human rights observers and the International Committee of the Red Cross via occasional visits. There appeared to be no civilian oversight of the military prison operated by the F-FDTL, however.[18] Prison security has at times been lax, as in August 2006, when Major Reinado escaped from Dili's main jail with 56 others after breaking down several walls on the east wing. Excessively long pretrial detention and delays in completing judicial procedures also remain problems.

As security has improved following the series of crises between 2006 and 2008, political opponents of the AMP government and peaceful activists have not been threatened by state violence. The current trial of the 28 individuals accused of taking part in the armed attacks against President Ramos-Horta and Prime Minister Gusmão is being conducted via a regular legal process before a panel of three judges.

Some avenues for redress exist for victims of human rights violations. In 2004, legislation was passed creating the PDHJ, with a dual mandate covering "Human Rights and Justice" and "Good Governance and Anti-Corruption."[19] The PDHJ is an independent statutory body and has been free of government control. It has the power to conduct investigations as well as to recommend appropriate action to government agencies for preventing or redressing instances of illegality or injustice.

In 2006, the Fretilin government appointed Dr. Sebastio Dias Ximenes as ombudsman. Almost immediately and under extremely difficult conditions, he began investigations into excessive use of force, illegal detention, and unlawful killings of civilians during the 2006 political crisis. When a state of emergency was declared after the February 2008 assassination attempts, he presented a report to Parliament, detailing cases of human rights violations by police and military personnel. The ombudsman concluded that "the Timorese state had violated the rights to freedom and physical integrity, right to liberty and the right not to be subject to torture or other cruel, degrading or inhuman treatment by members of the Joint Command—both police and military."[20] By August 2009, the PDHJ had received 213 complaints of human rights violations and opened 88 cases for investigation. Most cases related to excessive use of force by the police and military, but some addressed discrimination, the right to demonstrate, and the right to freedom of expression.[21] The effectiveness of the ombudsman's investigations has been undermined, however, by a lack of follow-up by other agencies. This includes the inability or unwillingness of the PNTL's internal Professional Ethics and Deontology Unit to take appropriate action to discipline officers named in ombudsman investigations.

The broader issue of holding accountable those responsible for serious rights violations in 1999 and again in 2006 remains largely unresolved, however, further contributing to the country's cycle of impunity. The Indonesia-East Timor Commission on Truth and Friendship handed down its final report in July 2008, concluding that the Indonesian government and military directed the scorched-earth campaign that took place after the 1999 independence vote. The presidents of both countries accepted the results, but little effort has subsequently been made to hold those responsible for the abuses to account. On the contrary, President Ramos-Horta used the 10-year anniversary of the UN-supervised vote for independence to announce that "there will be no international tribunal." This provoked a wave of criticism from both East Timorese and international advocacy groups. President Ramos-Horta has defended the decision by insisting that East Timor and Indonesia should put the past behind them. The handover of Maternus Bere, a former Indonesian militia leader awaiting trial on charges of crimes against humanity, to protective custody in the Indonesian embassy in August 2009 prompted the UN High Commissioner for Human Rights to write to President Ramos-Horta expressing his "deep concern" at the decision: "It would seem to violate article 160 of Timor-Leste's Constitution.... You will equally be aware of the United Nation's firm position that there can be no amnesty or impunity for serious crimes such as war crimes, crimes against humanity, and genocide."[22]

A UN Independent Special Commission of Inquiry published its findings on the May 2006 violence in October of that year. It recommended the prosecution of then minister of the interior Rogério Lobato for supplying two armed groups with weapons and instructing them to attack F-FDTL soldiers. The report also blamed Prime Minister Alkatiri for the outbreak of violence. While charges against Alkatiri were dropped for lack of evidence, Lobato was tried and convicted in March 2007.[23] He was sentenced to seven-and-a-half years in prison. In May 2008, however, President Ramos-Horta pardoned him along with 94 other prisoners. In June 2007, the still Fretilin-dominated Parliament passed a clemency law enabling criminals to apply for clemency for crimes committed between April 2006 and April 2007.[24]

A majority of East Timorese males are members of martial arts groups that were involved in the communal violence of 2006–07, aligned either with "easterners" or "westerners."[25] Gang violence has fallen, but robberies have grown in frequency and martial arts groups remain active, particularly in Dili. Though organized crime does not have a significant presence in East Timor, some networks are involved in petty racketeering.[26] Human trafficking, mostly of Chinese and Indonesian women, has emerged as a problem in recent years. The government has taken some steps to address it, with police arresting 10 members of an alleged human trafficking syndicate in July 2009, most of them Chinese nationals.

Under the constitution, women are guaranteed equal rights "in all areas of family, political, economic, social and cultural life." Electoral laws require that party lists in parliamentary elections include a woman as at least every fourth candidate. As a result, female representation in the national legislature is one of the highest in Asia, though women still only fill 18 of 65 seats. One political party is led by a woman, Fernanda Borges of the National Union Party (PUN), who also chairs the parliamentary committee overseeing constitutional, justice, and human rights issues. Nevertheless, women remain underrepresented in senior civil service positions.

Women occupy a disadvantaged position in the subsistence economy, with twice as many men as women engaging in paid labor. In cities, unemployment is significantly higher among women than men, and women are more concentrated in lower-income-generating occupations.[27] Domestic violence remains an entrenched problem. Only a marginal fraction of cases are reported to the police, and even fewer are prosecuted. Due to the weakness of the legal system, customary law is followed by some rural communities to address accusations of sexual violence, offering limited justice to victims. In a positive development, the new 2009 penal code criminalizes domestic violence as a public crime, authorizing police to arrest a suspect without a complaint by the victim. In September 2008 the government launched a *Say No to Violence against Women* public education campaign.

East Timor is a signatory to the Convention on the Elimination of All Forms of Discrimination against Women (CEDAW). The AMP government has committed to mainstreaming gender in socioeconomic development programs, with priority given to the education, health care, justice, and law enforcement sectors. The PDHJ works with the East Timor CEDAW Committee to address domestic and sexual violence against women. Nonetheless, there exists no comprehensive domestic legislation for the elimination of discrimination against women or prohibiting sexual harassment. Abortion laws remain contentious in a society with a strong Catholic tradition, on the one hand, and high rates of maternal mortality, unsafe abortions, and unwanted pregnancy, on the other.[28] Following international pressure and despite opposition from religious leaders, the new penal code permits abortions when the mother's life is endangered. Medical practitioners terminating a pregnancy under other circumstances continue to face potential imprisonment of up to three years.[29]

The constitution and other legislation prohibit all forms of discrimination and the state generally does not discriminate on ethnic or religious grounds. However, a policy adopted under the Fretilin government for Portuguese to be the official language of the courts and state agencies has left many Timorese disadvantaged. As of 2002, only 5 to 6 percent of citizens spoke fluent Portuguese, though some estimates place the current ratio closer to one-third. Although Tetum, a widely spoken local language, is a second official language, the state lacks resources to translate all government materials. As a result, many Timorese continue to be marginalized economically, socially, and politically by the Portuguese language policy,[30] generating resentment particularly among those educated in Indonesian during the period of occupation.

Under the constitution, disabled citizens are entitled to equal rights as well as state protection. In practice, however, in a society already struggling to provide its citizens with basic services and livelihood, the disabled are severely disadvantaged. The lack of accessibility to buildings, partly the result of the absence of legislation mandating such access, limits employment and educational opportunities for many.

East Timor is a secular state, but the Roman Catholic Church plays a central role, as 98 percent of the population is Catholic. The government is attentive to the views of the two Catholic bishops and sensitive to their opposition to some policies and laws, particularly on marriage, prostitution, and abortion. At times, the Church has organized public protests to force the government's hand on a particular issue.[31] Religious education is compulsory in public schools; an extensive Catholic school system also operates alongside the state-run structure. The constitution guarantees freedom of religion and the state does not attempt to interfere in the internal affairs of religious organizations or restrict religious observance. In recent years, there have been no significant clashes among different religious groups. The country has a small Muslim minority, and the current leader of the Fretilin opposition is a Muslim. Many Timorese continue to practice indigenous rituals, despite the dominance of the Catholic faith.

The rights to join trade unions, to bargain collectively, and to strike are protected in the constitution and labor code. However, written notice must be given 10 days in advance of a strike, and foreigners are not permitted to join unions. Unionization rates are low, as few Timorese are formally employed (an estimated 88 percent of the working population are self-employed or subsistence farmers). Enforcement of the labor code is weak and union leaders have complained that government inspectors favor employers in their monitoring and reports. A Labour Relations Board was established in early 2004 to hear disputes but has been largely inactive. On November 18, 2008, the president of the Timor-Leste

Trade Union Confederation (KSTL) and the secretary of the General Workers' Union were arrested by police and detained for several hours after taking part in a peaceful protest against a Singaporean employer who disregarded a Department of Labour directive to reinstate three dismissed workers.

The right to freedom of association and assembly is guaranteed in the constitution. Nevertheless, the Law on Freedom of Assembly and Demonstration promulgated in January 2006 requires that public protests be authorized by police four days in advance. The law also prohibits demonstrations within 100 meters of government offices, diplomatic missions, political party headquarters, prisons, or key infrastructure sites, such as airports or telecommunication facilities. In practice, demonstrations are permitted to take place without advance notification and the 100-meter regulation is rarely enforced. The government temporarily suspended the right to demonstrate during a state of emergency declared in February 2008 after assassination attempts against the president and prime minister, but the right was restored in full three months later.

RULE OF LAW 3.58

INDEPENDENT JUDICIARY	3.40
PRIMACY OF RULE OF LAW IN CIVIL AND CRIMINAL MATTERS	3.40
ACCOUNTABILITY OF SECURITY FORCES AND MILITARY TO CIVILIAN AUTHORITIES	3.50
PROTECTION OF PROPERTY RIGHTS	4.00

In recent years, East Timor's fledgling justice system has been moderately strengthened, though it remains weak, particularly in rural areas. A government-UNDP partnership has borne fruit in technical improvements, and more native judges have taken a seat at the bench. At the same time, the government's apparent abandonment of any intention to pursue retributive justice for rights violations committed by Indonesian forces and a series of presidential pardons for perpetrators of more recent abuses has reinforced the country's cycle of impunity.

East Timor's legal system is a hybrid one that combines Indonesian law, UN regulations, and a growing body of legislation introduced by the Parliament and the Council of Ministers. Both the Fretilin and AMP governments have pursued an ambitious legislative agenda to establish the fundamentals of a national legal framework. Between 2002 and 2006, Parliament passed an average of 11 laws a year, while the Council of Ministers enacted over 80 decree laws. Some observers have raised concerns that this trend risks undermining parliamentary authority and limits public debate on key issues facing the country.[32] The government is currently considering the incorporation of customary law into the national legal framework.

The Court of Appeals is the country's highest tribunal and also performs the function of constitutional review until the establishment of a supreme court.

It therefore has the authority to rule on the legality of "acts by the organs of the State." Under it are four district courts in Dili, Baucau, Suai, and Oecussi. Customary law and local dispute adjudication continue to operate in rural areas.

The constitution provides for judicial independence, stating that court decisions are binding "and shall prevail over the decisions of any other authority." In practice, the establishment of a competent and independent East Timorese judiciary has proved to be a significant challenge, exacerbated by security crises and a dearth of qualified individuals to fill key judicial posts. Judicial functions still rely heavily on international judges, although the role of East Timorese jurists is increasing. Since independence, international justices from Portuguese-speaking countries have presided over district courts and the Court of Appeals, alongside two East Timorese judges.[33]

In recent years, the Court of Appeals has asserted its independence, ruling against the government on key constitutional and policy issues. Of particular note was a November 2008 ruling that a mid-year budget based on the withdrawal of US$290 million from the national Petroleum Fund was above the permissible limit for withdrawal outlined by law and therefore unconstitutional. Moreover, it found that another deposit of US$240 million into a newly established Economic Stabilization Fund violated several articles of the constitution. The president of Parliament appealed, but the court reaffirmed its ruling in December. Parliament was subsequently obliged to reduce the budget transfer from the fund back to the limits set by the relevant legislation.

Although the government complied with the court's decision, the ruling also prompted somewhat of a backlash, particularly against the foreign judges serving on the Court of Appeals. President Ramos-Horta was quoted as saying that the international judges on the court did not understand the "reality of Timor and Timorese culture . . . and only follow European thinking." The president of Parliament was similarly reported to have said it was "time the government brought the Court of Appeals into line."[34]

The Superior Council for the Judiciary (SCJ) oversees the appointment and dismissal of judges. As of the end of 2008, the council was headed by Dionisio Babo Soares, secretary-general of Prime Minister Gusmão's CNRT party. On the day of the above-mentioned budget ruling, the SCJ decided that one of the three judges who had made the ruling, Justice Nelson Rosa, would not be reappointed to his position.[35] The decision raised concerns among some observers that the council's independence had been compromised. Justice Rosa appealed the decision not to reappoint him to the Court of Appeals, which then suspended it. He nevertheless returned to Portugal in March 2009.

Slow progress has been made in training native East Timorese, but the judicial system continues to suffer from an extreme shortage of qualified personnel, particularly outside the capital. The first round of Timorese judges and prosecutors appointed after independence lacked the requisite legal training and experience, with most failing qualification exams. A UNDP-supported Justice System Strengthening Programme, in partnership with the Ministry of

Justice, has produced better-trained judges and public prosecutors.[36] Parliament also passed legislation in September 2008 creating a new regulatory framework for legal training, setting up a code of conduct and process of formal accreditation after 15 months of obligatory training. By mid-2008, there were 13 East Timorese judges, 13 national prosecutors, and 11 national public defenders assigned to various courts, the prosecution, and public defender offices.[37] Nevertheless, international legal professionals continued to fill a large number of positions at every level of the system.

The presumption of innocence is constitutionally guaranteed. However, extreme shortages of magistrates and public defenders, particularly outside the capital, often undermine this right. As a result, police carry out arrests without warrants and retain suspects in custody longer than the permitted legal limit. In addition, long delays and a backlog of cases—reaching 4,700 criminal cases by 2008—contributed to the "culture of impunity" and weakened the standing of the court system in the eyes of the public.[38] Courts generally upheld the legal requirement for trials to be held in public. However, other obstacles undermined the impartiality of legal procedures. Witnesses were often hindered from attending trials due to logistical errors or lack of transportation. Linguistic and financial barriers continue to pose a challenge for improving access to justice. The language of the courts, and nearly all legislation, is Portuguese, which is insufficiently understood by some judicial officials and many litigants, defendants, and witnesses. The Asia Foundation has provided funding to translate legislation into English and Tetum, while trials are also conducted in Tetum; however, the quality of translation reportedly varied widely and was at times insufficient to fully ensure defendants' rights. Court costs outlined under the new 2006 civil procedure code are too expensive for most Timorese. As a result of these impediments, many communities have no recourse but to fall back on customary methods of dispute resolution.

Prosecutors act independently of political interference. Prosecutor General Ana Pessoa, a former justice minister in the Fretilin government, was appointed in March 2009 and has extensive legal experience as a magistrate in Mozambique. Nevertheless, the prosecutorial services also suffer from shortage of quality personnel, contributing to the country's case backlog.

Respect for the rule of law is undermined by a lack of political will to pursue justice against those responsible for serious human rights abuses.[39] The government has emphasized reconciliation over justice in its response to 1999 crimes involving senior Indonesian military officers. Apart from Rogerio Lobato's trial and conviction, no senior government official has faced prosecution for abuse of office or criminal actions. Allegations that surfaced in 2008 and 2009 of fraud at high levels of government have not led to prosecutions.

Security sector reform remains vital to state building in East Timor and has only been moderately successful. Under the Fretilin government, the security forces were politically aligned: the army with President Gusmão and the police with the Fretilin-controlled Ministry of Interior. In March 2006, 594 soldiers were dismissed for desertion and by April the F-FDTL was divided into warring factions, the dismissed "Petitioners," broadly identified with the western districts, and loyalists identified with the east.[40] These divisive loyalties exploded in May 2006, when army units turned on the police, in one incident killing 10 unarmed police officers under UN protection. The situation was eventually normalized with international intervention after the police force was relieved of its duties and the rebel soldiers arrested. Nevertheless, the combined collapse of the PNTL and rebellion in the army ranks threatened the very survival of the state.

As of mid-2009, civilian control over the police and security forces had largely been reestablished. The UNPOL mission largely succeeded in restoring security to the country, but has yet to effectively complete the process creating a professional, apolitical, and competent PNTL.[41] Similarly, Special Representative Atul Khare warned the Security Council in October 2009 that the root causes of the 2006 violence remained and that East Timor continues to require international security assistance.[42]

Human rights education programs have been put in place for police and security personnel, but instances of abusive behaviour continue to be reported. A UN analysis in August 2008 reportedly found that abuses by the PNTL had shown a "notable increase" over the previous year. Tensions between UNPOL and the PNTL have arisen over the reported involvement of some police in smuggling, extortion, and martial arts gangs or clandestine societies.

Property disputes present a significant policy challenge for the state and contributed to communal violence in 2006. A lack of records and legal framework for resolving conflicting claims has exacerbated the problem. Establishing title is complicated by competing Portuguese, Indonesian, and customary law-based claims, as well as a shortage of land records, which were taken by Indonesian forces on their departure. In rural areas, disputes may be resolved by customary methods, a remedy unavailable in many urban centers. Recurrent displacement has further provoked conflict over property and disturbed customary land use patterns. During the Indonesian occupation, entire villages were resettled as part of a counterinsurgency strategy. In the 1999 violence, some 200,000 Timorese fled inland, while tens of thousands were forcibly deported into Indonesian West Timor. In 2006, over 100,000 people were again forced to flee their homes, which were then occupied by others. In some instances, gangs evicted mostly "easterner" families and then seized or set fire to their homes. Over two years later, IDP encampments in Dili were able to be dismantled thanks to an assisted resettlement program.

The absence of a legal framework for determining property rights and resolving disputes has also inhibited foreign and local investment. A foreign donor-supported land law project begun in 2003 has sought to address the problem by establishing a land registry and encouraging the drafting of a land law. In June and September 2009, the government released drafts of a land law for public consultation. The bill, expected to be passed by Parliament by the end of 2009, takes a three-pronged approach: adopting the principle of recognition based on possession before title; compensating claimants who can demonstrate a prior right to title; and recognizing community land.[43] Investment, banking, and insurance codes still await legislation.

ANTICORRUPTION AND TRANSPARENCY	2.98
ENVIRONMENT TO PROTECT AGAINST CORRUPTION	2.75
PROCEDURES AND SYSTEMS TO ENFORCE ANTICORRUPTION LAWS	3.00
EXISTENCE OF ANTICORRUPTION NORMS, STANDARDS, AND PROTECTIONS	3.00
GOVERNMENTAL TRANSPARENCY	3.17

Despite growing transparency in parliamentary budget debates, neither the Fretilin nor the AMP governments have administered the state with sufficient transparency to reassure citizens of governmental competence and integrity. Citizens are highly conscious of what was known during the Indonesian occupation as KKN (*korupsi, kolusi, nepotisme*; corruption, collusion, and nepotism) and there is a perception that KKN has taken hold in an independent East Timor. The sharing of ministerial responsibility among five coalition partners under the AMP government has further complicated executive control over policy making when compared to the highly centralized Fretilin administration.

Transactions with government departments remain marred by opaque regulations, clumsy bureaucracy, and arbitrary administrative procedures. The World Bank's *Doing Business 2010* report for East Timor notes significant improvement in tax collection and procedures for starting a business but still ranks the country only 164th out of 183 for overall ease of doing business. The country scored the lowest possible on 3 of the 10 criteria (registering property, enforcing contracts, and closing a business).[44] East Timor ranked 145th out of 180 on Transparency International's 2008 Corruption Perceptions Index.

Financial disclosure procedures are inadequate for preventing conflicts of interest among public officials. This has contributed to recent scandals involving high-ranking AMP government officials, a phenomenon that had also arisen under the previous Fretilin administration. Reports have emerged of a petroleum contract awarded to the husband of Justice Minister Lucia Lobato, as well as accusations that US$8.8 million were "lost from government accounts" and "unauthorized bank accounts held by senior government officials."[45] In 2009, Fretilin politicians accused Finance Minister Emilia Pires of allegedly appointing friends with dual East Timorese-Australian citizenship to highly paid international adviser positions within the ministry. The World Bank became involved as the salaries in question were paid from the budget of the institution's Public Finance Management Capacity Building Project (PFMCBP).[46]

Senior members of the government, as well as the ombudsman, appear to have taken the allegations seriously, though prosecution has been absent. In

April 2009, Deputy Prime Minister Mario Carrascalão, charged with fighting corruption within the government, was reported to have called allegations against Justice Minister Lucia Lobato "very grave," while acknowledging signs of high-level corruption in the Ministry of Finance.[47] Finding the allegations against the finance minister to be credible, the ombudsman forwarded the case to the public prosecutor. The prosecutor general's office, however, has yet to take decisive action. Under the Alkatiri administration, no major case of official corruption involving senior politicians or officials was prosecuted before the courts. So far, this trend has continued under the current government.

Several agencies are tasked with auditing and overseeing government actions. The main anticorruption watchdog, the Office of the Inspector General (OIG), has been active in recent years. According to official sources, in addition to hosting anticorruption-related seminars, between 2006 and 2008 the OIG conducted and published 25 reports auditing a range of government projects. Although a majority of reports were submitted to the prime minister, several were forwarded to the prosecutor general.[48] In May 2008, the government announced that it would be reforming the OIG's mandate to increase its powers and independence, including having it report to a parliamentary committee rather than to the prime minister.[49]

In addition to addressing human rights complaints, the ombudsman is also mandated to respond to allegations of corruption from members of the public. During 2009, the ombudsman launched several investigations into allegations against high-ranking officials, including the prime minister and justice minister.[50] While the former case was dismissed after additional evidence clarified that there had been no improprieties,[51] the ombudsman recommended that the prosecutor general initiate legal proceedings against both the justice and finance ministers. This provoked a rebuke from the AMP government. A government spokesman accused the ombudsman, appointed in 2006 by the previous administration, of being partisan to Fretilin. Fretilin, for its part, protested that such statements sought to discredit the findings of an independent investigation into ministerial corruption.[52]

In 2009, the government took steps to establish an Anti-Corruption Commission (ACC). In June, Parliament considered a draft decree law and, in a rare example of bipartisanship, rejected the draft and passed its own anticorruption law instead. The powers and composition of the proposed ACC have yet to be finalized, however. The Finance Ministry announced in July 2009 that it would set up a new performance budgeting system intended to apply strict auditing procedures to the use of government funds. The constitution provides for a High Administrative, Tax, and Audit Court to monitor public expenditures and audit state accounts, but it is not yet operational.

Allegations of corruption receive wide airing in the media, though some journalists have faced intimidation or harassment in return, contributing to occasional self-censorship. Public access to government information is restricted primarily to reporting in the print and broadcast media. Journalists are still liable to prosecution for defamation under the Indonesian code. The proposed media law strengthens access to information, but there are ongoing concerns that while the law will decriminalize defamation, the proposed national media council will be used to punish journalists who criticize public officials. Until this is clarified, there continues to be weak protection for whistleblowers. Limited resources dedicated to providing the public with state information, including translation of Portuguese documents into Tetum, remains the main impediment to greater public access to information.

Parliamentary procedures are becoming more transparent. Budget debates are thorough and reported on extensively over community radio and television, arousing public interest throughout the districts.[53] Parliamentary rules of procedure provide for all standing committees to examine the draft budget and submit their opinions to a committee tasked with preparing a consolidated final report on the budget before the draft law is debated and voted on by Parliament. In August 2009, a bill was submitted to Parliament clarifying the role of the executive and the legislature in the budget process, as well as introducing new procedures for financial management and accountability.

Financial systems within ministries are poorly administered, and departments routinely fail to track budget expenditures. The AMP government has attempted to improve budget performance and expenditure reporting. According to the government, the rate of effective use of ministerial funds has risen from a very low 49 percent in 2006–07 to 79 percent in 2008–09.[54] Nevertheless, in an audit report on the 2008 budget, Deloitte Touche Tohmatsu found they had insufficient information to assess government expenditures for the period.[55] As indicated by the above-mentioned scandals, tendering procedures for government contracts have attracted strong criticism and require greater oversight and transparency.

Procedures for the fair administration of foreign assistance are generally effective and monitored by international development partners. The recent controversy over lucrative World Bank–funded contracts in the Ministry of Finance, however, suggests that international funds are not fully immune from corrupt practices.

RECOMMENDATIONS

- The government should comply with and follow up on rulings of the Office of the Ombudsman for Human Rights and Justice, particularly with regards to disciplinary action against police and security personnel, including special units, for human rights abuses.
- The government should firmly address the issue of corruption in public office by establishing the proposed independent Anti-Corruption Commission and granting it powers to refer cases to the Office of the Public Prosecutor.

- The government should strengthen financial disclosure procedures, and develop a system of open and transparent tendering for government contracts.
- The proposed media law should firmly establish defamation as a civil and not a criminal matter and ensure that the proposed national media council proactively promotes and protects the independence of the media.
- The government should accelerate efforts to publish all public information, including court proceedings, in Tetum, the most widely understood language in East Timor.
- The government and Parliament should finalize passage of the draft land law and take immediate action to begin implementation of its provisions on titling and compensation.

NOTES

For URLs and endnote hyperlinks, please visit the *Countries at the Crossroads* homepage at http://freedomhouse.org/template.cfm?page=139&edition=8.

1. James Scambary, "Anatomy of a Conflict: The 2006–2007 Communal Violence in East Timor," *Conflict, Security and Development* 9, no. 2 (June 2009): 267.
2. World Bank, *Timor-Leste: Poverty in a Young Nation* (Dili: World Bank and Directorate of National Statistics, November 2008), 3.
3. Ibid., 5.
4. Richard Curtain, "East Timor Advances Despite Australian Aid Failures," *Eureka Street* 19, no. 13 (July 17, 2009).
5. International Crisis Group, "Timor-Leste: No Time for Complacency," Asia Briefing No. 87, February 9, 2009.
6. For an index of the democratic indicators of new states, see Kirk Bowman, Fabrice Lehoucq, and James Mahoney, "Measuring Political Democracy: Case Expertise, Data Adequacy and Central America," *Comparative Political Studies* 38, no. 8 (2005): 939–970.
7. James Scambary, Mark Chenery, and Emile Le Brun, "Electoral Violence in Timor-Leste: Mapping Incidents and Responses," Timor-Leste Armed Violence Assessment Issue Brief, no. 3 (June 2009).
8. Dennis Shoesmith, "Legislative-Executive Relations in Timor-Leste: The Case for Building a Stronger Parliament," in *Democratic Governance in Timor-Leste: Reconciling the Local and the National*, ed. David Mearns (Darwin: Charles Darwin University Press, 2008): 76–77.
9. United Nations Development Programme (UNDP)-Timor Leste, "Strengthening Parliamentary Democracy in Timor-Leste: July–September 2008," Project Update, September 2008.
10. M. Steven Fish, "Stronger Legislatures, Stronger Democracies," *Journal of Democracy* 17, no. 1 (January 2006): 8.
11. From 2001 until the election of the AMP government, civil service salaries ranged from US$85 per month at Level 1 to US$361 per month at Level 7. See UNDP–Timor Leste, "Support to Civil Service Reform in Timor-Leste: April–September 2008," Project Report, September 2008.
12. United Nations Integrated Mission in Timor-Leste (UNMIT), *Report on Human Rights Developments in Timor-Leste August 2006–August 2007* (Dili: UNMIT, 2007), 8–9.
13. Ibid.

14. International Freedom of Expression Exchange (IFEX), "IPI Urges President to Block Introduction of Code that Includes Harsh Penalties for Defamation," news release, January 12, 2006.
15. IFEX, "Regional Press Freedom Groups Alarmed by Draft Media Laws," news release, April 9, 2009.
16. United Nations Security Council (UNSC), *Report of the Secretary-General on the United Nations Integrated Mission in Timor-Leste (for the Period from 9 July 2008 to 20 January 2009)* (New York: UNSC, February 4, 2009), 8–9.
17. Office of the High Commissioner for Human Rights (OHCHR) and UNMIT, *Report on Human Rights Developments in Timor-Leste, the Security Sector and Access to Justice: 1 September 2007–30 June 2008* (Geneva/Dili: OHCHR and UNMIT, 2008), 4; International Crisis Group, "Timor-Leste: No Time for Complacency." The Joint Command's mandate ended on May 22, 2008.
18. Bureau of Democracy, Human Rights, and Labor, "Timor-Leste," in *2008 Country Reports on Human Rights Practices* (Washington, D.C.: U.S. Department of State, February 25, 2009).
19. Guteriano Nicolau, "Ombudsman for Human Rights: The Case of Timor-Leste," *Asia-Pacific News* 47 (March 2007). In August 2009, Fretilin demanded that the AMP government apologize to the ombudsman for accusing him of political bias.
20. Provedoria for Human Rights and Justice Timor-Leste (PDFJ), *Report APF 14* (Amman: PDFJ, 2009), 3. For an earlier critique of PEDU, see Human Rights Watch, *Tortured Beginnings, Police Violence and the Beginning of Impunity in East Timor* (New York: Human Rights Watch, April 2006).
21. ReliefWeb, "General Information," Human Rights Investigation Mentor Job Posting, August 21, 2009.
22. Navanethem Pillay, High Commissioner for Human Rights, to H. E. Mr. José Ramos-Horta, Geneva, September 2, 2009.
23. United Nations Independent Special Commission of Inquiry for Timor-Leste, *Report of the United Nations Independent Special Commission of Inquiry for Timor-Leste* (Geneva: United Nations Independent Special Commission of Inquiry for Timor-Leste, October 2, 2006), 32, 48–49.
24. Katherine Iliopoulos, "East Timor Ten Years On: Justice Denied," Crimes of War Project, September 14, 2009.
25. Andrew McWilliam, "East and West in Timor-Leste: Is There an Ethnic Divide?" in *The Crisis in Timor-Leste: Understanding the Past, Imagining the Future*, ed. Dennis Shoesmith (Darwin: Charles Darwin University Press, 2007), 37–44.
26. Overseas Security Advisory Council (OSAC), "Timor-Leste," in *2009 Crime and Safety Report* (Washington, D.C.: OSAC, July 2009).
27. Asian Development Bank (ADB) and United Nations Development Fund for Women (UNIFEM), *Gender and Nation Building in Timor-Leste: Country Gender Assessment* (Manila/New York: ADB and UNIFEM, November 2005), 24–25.
28. Suzanne Belton, Andrea Whittaker, and Lesley Barclay, *Maternal Mortality, Unplanned Pregnancy and Unsafe Abortion in Timor-Leste: A Situational Analysis* (Dili: ALOLA Foundation, 2009).
29. NGO Working Group on CEDAW Shadow Report, *List of Critical Concerns for the CEDAW Pre-Session (10–14 November 2008) in Relation to the 44th CEDAW Session (29 June–17 July 2009)* (Geneva: NGO Working Group on CEDAW Shadow Report, October 6, 2008).

30. Kerry Jane Taylor-Leech, "The Ecology of Language Planning in Timor-Leste: A Study of Language Policy, Planning and Practices in Identity Construction" (PhD diss., Griffith University, 2007).
31. See Irena Cristalis, *A Nation's Bitter Dawn* (London and New York: Zed Books, 2009), 298–299.
32. Shoesmith, "Legislative-Executive Relations in Timor-Leste: The Case for Building a Stronger Parliament," 76-78.
33. Judicial System Monitoring Programme (JSMP), *Justice Update* 22/2005 (October/November 2005); Karen Polglaze's report on East Timor in *Countries at the Crossroads 2006* has been very helpful for information on 2002–06.
34. Frente Revolucionaria Do Timor-Leste Independente (Fretilin), "Judiciary under Attack in Timor-Leste," press release, December 2008.
35. "Court Rules against E. Timor Mid-Year Budget," Australian Broadcasting Corporation (ABC) Radio Australia, November 14, 2008; Fretilin, "Judiciary under Attack in Timor-Leste."
36. UNDP Justice System Strengthening Programme, *Strengthening the Justice System in Timor-Leste* (New York: UNDP, May 2007).
37. JSMP, "The Appointment of the Second Group of Court Actors Is a Positive Step Forward for the Judicial System of Timor Leste," news release, March 20, 2008; UNDP-Timor Leste, "Swearing in of Two Judges and Four Public Defenders Will Boost the Capacity of Timor-Leste's Justice Institutions," news release, May 19, 2009; Andrew Marriott, "Legal Professionals in Development: Timor-Leste's Legislative Experiment," *Conflict, Security & Development* 9, no. 2 (June 2009): 239–263; OHCHR and UNMIT, *Report on Human Rights Developments in Timor-Leste, the Security Sector and Access to Justice: 1 September 2007–30 June 2008*.
38. OHCHR and UNMIT, *Report on Human Rights Developments in Timor-Leste, the Security Sector and Access to Justice: 1 September 2007–30 June 2008*, 3; Freedom House, United States Agency for International Development, and American Bar Association Rule of Law Initiative (ABA/ROLI), *Rule of Law in Timor-Leste* (Washington, D.C.: Freedom House, USAID, and ABA/ROLI, June 2007), 20; JSMP, "The Implications of Court Costs in the Law on Civil Procedure," press release, October 2008.
39. Simon Roughneen, "East Timor: Justice in the Dock," International Relations and Security Network Security Watch, July 16, 2009.
40. James Scambary, "Anatomy of a Conflict: The 2006–2007 Communal Violence in East Timor," *Conflict, Security and Development* 9, no. 2 (June 2009): 265–288.
41. Nicolas Lemay-Hébert, "UNPOL and Police Reform in Timor-Leste: Accomplishments and Setbacks," *International Peacekeeping* 16, no. 3 (June 2009); "East Timor Human Rights Progress Questioned by UN," *Sydney Morning Herald*, August 21, 2008.
42. United Nations Security Council, "'Stable, Steady Approach' Vital to Long-Term Peace in Timor-Leste, Head of United Nations Integrated Mission Tells Security Council," 6205th Meeting, New York, October 23, 2009.
43. Ibere Lopes, "Land and Displacement in Timor-Leste," *Humanitarian Exchange Magazine* 43 (June 2009); "East Timor Land Rights: Restitution Not Possession—A Comment on the Draft Land Law," *East Timor Law and Justice Bulletin*, July 9, 2009.
44. World Bank, *Timor-Leste: The Business Regulatory Environment* (Washington D.C.: World Bank, 2006); World Bank, "Timor Leste," in *Doing Business 2010: Comparing Regulation in 183 Economies* (Washington D.C.: World Bank, 2009).
45. Mark Dodd, "Death Threats after E Timor Graft Claim," *Australian*, December 18, 2008; "SMS Texts Evidence: Minister for Justice Gives Herself and Friends Projects,"

Tempo Semanal, no. 108 (October 12, 2008); Mark Dodd, "E. Timor Minister Denies Corruption," *Australian*, January 21, 2009.
46. Fretilin, "More Parties Call on Finance Minister to Explain Contracts Scandal," press release, May 26, 2009; Lindsay Murdoch and Tom Hyland, "Dili Tycoon Deal Triggers Alarm," *Age*, May 3, 2009.
47. Fretilin, "Fretilin Urges World Bank and Donors to Audit Controversial Finance Ministry Project," press release, May 21, 2009.
48. Office of the Inspector General, "OIG Activities and Report."
49. East Timor Legal Information Site, "Speech to be Delivered by H. E. Mr. Kay Rala Xanana Gusmão, Prime Minister of the Democratic Republic of Timor-Leste on the Occasion of the Conference on '2008 The Year of Administrative Reform,'" May 8, 2008.
50. "East Timor Ombudsman Recommends Prosecution of Justice Minister," ABC Radio Australia, July 23, 2009.
51. Alison Caldwell, "East Timor PM Urged to Resign over Family Ties," ABC, June 26, 2009; "Gusmao v The ABC," ABC, August 17, 2009.
52. Fretilin, "Abuse of Independent Institutions Must Cease—Fretilin," press release, August 10, 2009.
53. Phillip Adams, "On Timor's Hard Road," *Australian*, November 10, 2007.
54. IV Constitutional Government of Timor-Leste, "Government Changes the Public Service Culture to Deliver Budget Results," press release, October 26, 2009.
55. Fretilin, "Audit Reveals Gusmao Government's Woeful Financial Management: Action Looms on Referendum Package?" press release, October 27, 2009.

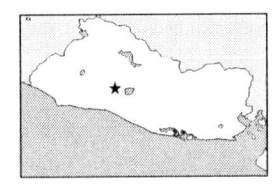

EL SALVADOR

CAPITAL: San Salvador
POPULATION: 7.3 million
GNI PER CAPITA (PPP): $6,670

SCORES	2006	2010
ACCOUNTABILITY AND PUBLIC VOICE:	N/A	3.99
CIVIL LIBERTIES:	N/A	4.08
RULE OF LAW:	N/A	3.54
ANTICORRUPTION AND TRANSPARENCY:	N/A	3.04

(scores are based on a scale of 0 to 7, with 0 representing weakest and 7 representing strongest performance)

David Holiday

INTRODUCTION

On March 15, 2009, the longest-standing rule in Latin America by a single party—20 years by the conservative Nationalist Republican Alliance (ARENA)—came to an end as the leftist Farabundo Martí National Liberation Front (FMLN) won its first presidential election in El Salvador. From 1980 to 1992, El Salvador was immersed in civil war, and it remains to this day one of the most polarized political environments in Latin America. The 2009 election, in addition to being the first transition of power between parties since the 1992 peace accords, was also the first time in the country's history that a left-wing government had been elected to office.

With this recent election, El Salvador has passed one of the tests of the UN-brokered peace negotiations that brought an end to the 12-year war: the alternation in power of the two major political participants in the conflict. The legacy of the Salvadoran civil war—which left an estimated 70,000 dead, and millions of displaced to neighboring countries and especially the United States—has deep implications for the conditions of democratic governance. Yet despite fears in some quarters that El Salvador might follow the path of authoritarian populism, the current moment appears to offer real possibilities for consolidating gains in important democratic institutions that have floundered in recent years.

David Holiday is a Senior Program Officer with the Latin America Program of the Open Society Institute and has spent nearly 20 years engaged in civil society, human rights, and peace concerns in Central America. From 2000 to 2005 he directed a project in El Salvador that supported civil society advocacy and governmental transparency initiatives. During the 1990s he authored numerous human rights reports on El Salvador, Guatemala, and Nicaragua as the Central America representative for Human Rights Watch.

Various factors led to ARENA's electoral loss. In the years leading up to the election, President Antonio Saca—easily elected in 2004 against the FMLN candidacy of celebrated former *comandante* Shafik Handal—held the presidency of the ARENA party while also governing from the executive office. Following ARENA's defeat, many observers (including within his own party) criticized this centralization of power as one of the reasons for popular discontent, but corruption, a battered economy, and rising crime were also key factors.

Unlike the 1999 and 2004 contests, the FMLN ran a candidate who came from outside the party: Mauricio Funes, an extremely popular television newsman who projected a moderate image and committed to a more judicious platform for change. In his acceptance speech, Funes called for national unity and a new social pact, as well as both increased public services and austerity in the form of better targeted subsidies, improved tax collection, reduced spending, and an end to public corruption. Reassurances that he would choose the path of Lula da Silva's Brazil over Hugo Chávez's Venezuela, along with a clear signal from the new U.S. administration that it would magnanimously accept the election results regardless of the winner, also contributed to the smooth transition.

The reality is that the FMLN's margin for radical change is significantly reduced in the current political and economic climate. The presidential victory by the FMLN was quite narrow at 51.3 percent to 48.7 percent, with a difference of just 69,412 votes. The FMLN's ability to impose its agenda will also be mitigated by a more pluralist 84-member Legislative Assembly elected in January 2009, in which no single party will dominate. The 32 deputies of the ARENA party, or the FMLN's 35 deputies (plus one from the Democratic Change party) will need to gain the support of some or all of the 5 legislators from the Christian Democrats (PDC) and 10 from the National Conciliation Party (PCN) if either group hopes to form a majority bloc. The challenge remains for Salvadorans to break the polarization that has characterized—and to some extent stunted—the political life of that country and find common ground around the resolution of fundamental issues of democratic governance.

ACCOUNTABILITY AND PUBLIC VOICE 3.99

FREE AND FAIR ELECTORAL LAWS AND ELECTIONS	4.00
EFFECTIVE AND ACCOUNTABLE GOVERNMENT	2.50
CIVIC ENGAGEMENT AND CIVIC MONITORING	5.33
MEDIA INDEPENDENCE AND FREEDOM OF EXPRESSION	4.14

Since the end of the armed conflict in 1992, elections have been carried out with relatively strong guarantees against fraud and intimidation, and verified by domestic and international observers. The 2009 elections, in fact, enjoyed even greater observation than the transition elections of 1994, including over 4,000 domestic observers and numerous international delegations, including from the European Union (EU) and the Organization of American States. As in previous elections, there was relatively little election-related violence, candidates were able to campaign freely, and people's political choices were free from influence by external forces.

Following the 1994 elections, in which the FMLN participated for the first time as a political party, all parties came together to agree on reforms to improve the process, including depoliticization of the staff of the Supreme Electoral Tribunal (TSE), which is divided among the three dominant political parties; institution of a single identity document for voting (and business matters); residential voting that would not require the need to travel long distances; and proportional representation in the 262 municipal councils (previously winner-take-all).[1] Of these agreed-upon reforms, only the single identity document has been fully implemented. Residential voting was carried out in 24 municipalities (less than 10 percent) in the 2009 elections; the aim is to institute it throughout the country for the 2012 municipal and legislative elections. At the same time, the absence of comprehensive reform is not considered to have affected subsequent electoral outcomes in any significant way. Nonetheless, implementation could prove important for improving citizen participation and confidence in the political process, while pluralistic councils might improve political tolerance and consensus-building at the local level.

The TSE has not always been able to fulfill its responsibility to ensure an even electoral playing field. There are informal, but real, advantages that accrue to the ruling party. For instance, according to press monitoring by the local Transparency International chapter, from April–November 2008—when campaigning was supposed to be prohibited—ARENA spent US$5.8 million, representing 85 percent of all political party publicity, more than it spent in the entire 2004 presidential election period.[2] As the EU electoral observation group noted, this de facto prolonged campaign period clearly benefited the party with more economic resources.[3] In addition, the TSE decision (by a 3–2 vote) to split the legislative/municipal elections from the presidential contest extended the campaign period for two more months, allowing ARENA's PDC and PCN allies a greater chance of gaining congressional seats and municipal posts unaffected by the coattails of a possible Funes victory in the presidential race. In general, the lack of regulation of campaign donations or expenses (with the exception of the *deuda política*, which provides a certain amount to each party based on the number of votes received in the last election) also disadvantaged parties with fewer resources. Civic associations not registered as political parties carried out media campaigns associating the FMLN with Venezuela's Chávez in order to stir up support for ARENA. TSE oversight of such violations of the electoral code was notable by its absence.

ARENA also attempted to maintain its control of the executive branch through enormous publicity campaigns carried out by the incumbent government in the run-up to the election. The budget of the presidency's communications secretariat under Saca was 1,000 percent higher than that of his predecessor, Francisco Flores; even after the elections, Saca refused to disclose how those funds had been spent.[4] The EU delegation, similar to the Transparency International monitors, found that "election news coverage was generally biased and did not meet international democratic standards, exacerbating the uneven playing field in favor of ARENA."[5] Overall, a monitoring effort by the Salvadoran chapter of Transparency International, FUNDE, estimated that ARENA spent over twice as much as the FMLN in advertising (US$12.9 million vs. US$5.38 million), although for the last 12 days of the presidential campaign the FMLN was able to pull slightly ahead.[6] Anti-FMLN civic groups came in third place, with approximately US$1.9 million spent, far ahead of the smaller political parties. FUNDE also estimated that central government expenditure on advertising from January 2008 to March 2009 was over US$11 million. Although access to the media is, of course, only part of winning a political campaign, that the FMLN was able to secure an electoral win under these circumstances speaks volumes about both citizen discontent and the civic clamor for change.

El Salvador has a unicameral legislature chosen by closed-list proportional representation, which has traditionally resulted in the overrepresentation of smaller parties. In the 2009 elections, for example, based on the largest remainder system of seat allocation, the PCN was able to win the third seat out of three in the department of Chalatenango with only 11.4 percent of the popular vote.[7] Since the 2000 legislative elections, the number of seats held by the FMLN and ARENA in the Assembly has been more or less equal, but combined with the power of the presidency, ARENA has enjoyed overall dominance. ARENA has not held a simple majority in congress, however, so in order to pass legislation it has forged alliances with the PCN and, to a lesser extent, the PDC. Because of these alliances, it has been difficult for the FMLN to amass the two-thirds majority required to override a presidential veto. The result, over the past 20 years, has been a kind of implicit power sharing, with the PCN receiving control of certain government ministries (e.g., the Court of Accounts), or (in 2004) a seat on the TSE, even though it was decertified as a party for failing to get the requisite 3 percent of the popular presidential vote.[8] Since 2000, the PCN has negotiated for itself the presidency of the Legislative Assembly, a situation to which the FMLN was forced to concede even in the 2009–11 session. This politically negotiated composition of the congressional leadership has resulted in the body failing to provide an adequate check on executive power; the executive continues to set the agenda and originate most legislation. The judiciary also suffers from a deficit of independence that sometimes limits its ability to act as a strong check on the executive (see Rule of Law).

Historically, and especially during the 20 years of ARENA dominance, the civil service has functioned as a bastion of political patronage. It still operates based on laws written in the 1960s, and no real modernization efforts have been made. Minor reforms were made in mid-2009 to protect public employees, given the impending change of government. In December 2005, a municipal administrative career law was approved for the first time. But like the antiquated civil service law, according to civil society organizations, selection criteria for employment continued to be based on subjective criteria rather than merit, and announcements for these jobs are rarely publicized.[9]

Civic engagement in the political process has generally taken a back seat to the political parties, in large part because the two major parties are widely seen as representative of real constituencies. Nongovernmental organizations (NGOs) have in recent years increasingly sought access to members of the Legislative Assembly to engage on policy issues, with a modicum of success. The landscape of civic organizations has changed little in the past decade, a fact largely attributable to the bureaucratic difficulty of registering new organizations (delay may sometimes be up to a year). Groups advocating for homosexual rights have not been granted legal status. According to the Ministry of the Interior, 1864 associations, 526 foundations, 145 international NGOs and 1042 churches are currently registered.[10]

El Salvador has a vibrant media environment and has enjoyed freedom of expression without censorship since well before the end of the war. However, the concentration of ownership of the media in the hands of a few influential families, which have generally been close to ARENA, has been a significant factor in distorting the playing field of electoral politics.[11] There have also been reports that advertising agencies responsible for the placement of government-funded public service announcements favored progovernment outlets. Nonetheless, direct censorship of the press does not occur, and the state does not regulate or interfere with the internet as a source of information.

In general, journalists can operate without interference from the authorities, but the Salvadoran Association of Journalists (APES) has noted occasional physical and verbal attacks against journalists covering political demonstrations.[12] The 2006 Special Law against Acts of Terrorism (see Civil Liberties) was employed in July 2007 against freelance journalist María Haydeé Chicas, along with 13 other demonstrators, after her arrest while reporting on a demonstration against government plans to privatize water distribution in Suchitoto. Chicas was charged with committing "acts of terrorism," although she was conditionally released later that month.[13] Contrary to widespread reports about the decriminalization of defamation in the Salvadoran penal code, defamation continues to be criminalized, although there are no recent cases of its application against journalists.[14]

The Committee to Protect Journalists notes that one of the greatest threats to journalists today in El Salvador derives from the dire crime situation and street gangs in particular; there are isolated cases of harassment and threats against journalists believed to be linked to their coverage of government policies.[15] Two journalists were killed in recent years for reporting on abuses committed by criminal gangs. In September 2007, radio journalist Salvador Sánchez Roque was murdered by gunmen, and in September 2009, Christian Gregorio Poveda Ruiz, a French freelance journalist who filmed a documentary about the street gang Mara 18, was shot and killed.[16] On May 12, 2008, three gang members were convicted of aggravated homicide for Roque's murder.

CIVIL LIBERTIES   4.08

PROTECTION FROM STATE TERROR, UNJUSTIFIED IMPRISONMENT,	
AND TORTURE	2.88
GENDER EQUITY	3.33
RIGHTS OF ETHNIC, RELIGIOUS, AND OTHER DISTINCT GROUPS	3.00
FREEDOM OF CONSCIENCE AND BELIEF	6.67
FREEDOM OF ASSOCIATION AND ASSEMBLY	4.50

The evolution of Salvadoran civil liberties in recent years is best illustrated by the failed application of a set of policies known as *mano dura* ("iron fist") that carry harsh sentences for a broad swath of offenses, which were first introduced in 2003 and then updated in 2005 and 2006. The mano dura laws were meant to protect against gang violence, which the government alleges to be responsible for the majority of homicides in the country. However, homicide statistics are poorly maintained, which inhibits a more substantive analysis about either the victims or the circumstances of their deaths. Currently, these hard-line policies are widely seen as having been ineffective, if not counterproductive. The citizen security situation continues to be dire, with intentional homicide rates for 2005 and 2006 calculated at 56 and 58 per 100,000 persons, respectively, one of the highest rates in the world.[17] Although the numbers appeared to have declined somewhat in 2007 and 2008, the trend in 2009 suggests that even the 2006 rate may be exceeded.

Due to increased detentions related to the mano dura laws, the prison population increased from 7,280 in December 2000 to over 20,000 currently—almost a 20 percent annual increase since 2005. This has resulted in enormous overcrowding, as the capacity of the 19 prisons is 8,110. Overcrowding seriously threatens prisoners' health and well-being; riots and violence are frequent. Although gangs are separated from other prisoners in some facilities, nonviolent offenders (including those in pretrial detention) are also mixed in. There are numerous reports that gangs continue to direct operations from the prisons with the collusion of police and prison authorities. Approximately 35 percent of the 20,000 prisoners are in pretrial detention, in part due to extreme court overload.[18] The Human Rights Ombudsman's office (PDDH) continues to report cases of torture and abuse by police officers, with little evidence of prosecution when official wrongdoing occurs.[19]

There are very few cases of state persecution of political opponents (essentially members of the FMLN party in recent years), but there are also minimal investigations into cases where political opposition members are the victim. Human rights activists have not suffered generalized persecution in recent years. However, since 2007, antimining activists and a community radio station in the department of Cabañas have been the targets of numerous threats and attacks, including the much-publicized murder of community activist Marcelo Rivera in July 2009.[20] While police have provided protection to those threatened in recent cases, community groups accuse the attorney general's office of failing to carry out a full investigation of the Rivera case, having dismissed it as common crime related to gang activity. The most notorious case of police overreach was the above-mentioned 2007 incident when demonstrators in Suchitoto, after blocking roads and throwing rocks at police, were jailed under charges of terrorism under the Special Law against Acts of Terrorism, which imposes prison sentences of up to 10 years on anyone who publicly justifies terrorism, yet notably fails to include a definition of terrorism. The demonstrators were eventually released, and the government has backed away from further such applications of the law. For the period under review, political demonstrations and marches have been common, and the Suchitoto case was the exception rather than the norm with respect to protection of activists.

Salvadoran gangs, known as *maras*, are the primary nonstate actors involved in violence, although whether they are primarily responsible for the high homicide rate is a matter of debate. Estimates as to their size also vary from 8,000 to the official estimate of 12,000–13,000. Approximately a third of El Salvador's prison population is said to be comprised of gang members, with several prisons effectively run by either the MS-13 or the Mara 18 gangs. The Saca administration's reputed success against the *mareros*, including keeping gang leaders locked up, only exacerbated the problem, with confinement sparking cooperation as well as conflict among rival gangs, the development of more hierarchical structures, and requirements for increased income—obtained via robbery and other crimes—for protection against police persecution. Individual gang members are increasingly used by drug traffickers as local vendors and hitmen.[21] Crime prevention programs have begun in recent years but have yet to make a major impact.

The PDDH is not taken seriously by state officials, yet this is the most independent and reliable repository of information on rights violations and the best source of redress for victims. The PDDH's recommendations are nonbinding, however, and for judicial redress the attorney general's office has to initiate action. There are no effective complaints mechanisms in the National Civil Police (PNC), where most of the abuses occur. Observations by the Committee on the Elimination of Discrimination against Women (CEDAW) from October 2008 indicate that the government has taken various measures to prevent human trafficking, but notes that investigations into child trafficking are minimal and prosecutions rare. It also notes that there are few centers for attending to victims of trafficking.[22]

The constitution grants men and women equal rights. The penal code establishes sentences of one to three years in jail for public officials who deny a person's civil rights based on gender, but there are no known cases of this punishment being meted out. According to the PDDH, the Law against Intrafamily Violence, first enacted in 1996, has not been effectively implemented, and the state does not promote increased awareness about gender rights among functionaries. A PDDH survey of government entities found that 42 percent of all employees knew of cases of sexual harassment.[23] The penal code also has a sentence of six months to two years for employers who discriminate against women in labor relations, but there are few cases brought and no effective mechanisms for redress. In February 2008, in order to comply with labor conditions under the Central American free-trade agreement (CAFTA-DR), a law was passed criminalizing the practice of asking women to take a pregnancy test as a condition of employment. A 1999 law criminalized abortion under all circumstances. An early study indicated that the prosecution of women for illegal abortions, which carries a sentence of two to eight years, doubled following implementation of the law.[24] Another 2006 medical journal report indicated that 32 women were prosecuted from 2000 to 2003 (although 283 criminal investigations were initiated);[25] more recent data is not available.

With respect to discrimination against other groups, CEDAW has commented that the state does not make a great effort to recognize indigenous populations in El Salvador, but there is little information available regarding discrimination against these groups. The 2007 census revealed that 0.2 percent of the population is indigenous and 0.1 percent is black, although the census methodology was criticized by indigenous groups because the categories used were self-chosen by participants. A 2000 law requires that 4 percent of positions in the public and private sectors should be filled by the disabled, but this is rarely enforced. In 2007, El Salvador ratified the UN Convention on the Rights of Persons with Disabilities, as well as its Optional Protocol. The 2007 census notes that 4.1 percent of the population lives with a disability, although the PDDH suggests that the number may be as high as 10 percent.[26]

El Salvador features full freedom of religion, with no reported abuses in a country with one of Latin America's more diverse mixes of Protestant and Catholic citizens. Freedoms of association and assembly are also well protected and reinforced by government discourse. However, the International Labor Organization Committee on Freedom of Association notes that there are excessive formalities in forming trade unions, which are fewer in number and weaker in political influence in the postwar period, while the state does nothing to stop occasional dismissals of labor activists or require their reinstatement. There are some charges of the use of blacklists of union members by employers.

RULE OF LAW 3.54

INDEPENDENT JUDICIARY	3.20
PRIMACY OF RULE OF LAW IN CIVIL AND CRIMINAL MATTERS	3.20
ACCOUNTABILITY OF SECURITY FORCES AND MILITARY TO CIVILIAN AUTHORITIES	3.75
PROTECTION OF PROPERTY RIGHTS	4.00

The Salvadoran judiciary is neither independent nor impartial, a situation rooted partly in the above-mentioned partisan deal making within the Legislative

Assembly. The selection process, which occurs every three years, is fair; the National Judiciary Council (CNJ) presents half the slate of eligible candidates to the Assembly, and lawyers associations present the other half. Out of a total of 30 candidates, three justices are elected to serve a nine-year term. However, since 1994, when a clean sweep of the Supreme Court took place following the recommendations of the Truth Commission, the nomination of magistrates to the court has become increasingly politicized, with political parties represented in the Legislative Assembly dividing appointments according to their electoral strength rather than selecting justices based on merit or honor. Perhaps a greater threat to judicial independence comes from the structure of centralized control maintained by the Supreme Court.[27] Among its functions, the Court retains the power to appoint, remove, and discipline lower-court judges, controls their budgets, and holds the power to license lawyers and notaries. Despite these deficiencies, judicial decisions are generally followed by legislative, executive, and other government entities, and the courts do rule against the government on occasion.

Some observers argue for the need to separate the administrative functions of the Supreme Court from its jurisprudential ones. A key element of reform in this direction was the strengthening in 2002 of the CNJ, a pluralist body elected by the Legislative Assembly from slates proposed by different entities, including lawyers associations and universities, and charged with evaluating and training lower-court judges. In theory, the evaluations carried out by the CNJ should guide the Supreme Court's promotions of or disciplinary actions against sitting judges, but in practice the court is free to ignore them. The Judicial Training School, an underresourced institution supervised by the CNJ, is also charged with training prosecutors, public defenders, and other justice system personnel.

Perceptions among both citizens and judges about the efficacy of the justice system are affected by these factors. According to a 2008 poll, just 7.9 percent of Salvadorans have "much trust" in the Supreme Court, while 9.2 percent feel the same way about the attorney general's office (municipal offices receive the highest rating for a governmental entity at 21.5 percent).[28] Crimes committed by public officials are rarely prosecuted. Judges surveyed for a study by the University of Salamanca indicated that the principal obstacles to the investigation and sanction of crimes committed by officials included "the intentional obstruction of investigations by State authorities themselves" and the "investigative passivity" exhibited by representatives of the attorney general's office. Forty percent of all judges interviewed said they had received threats or offers of bribes from litigating attorneys.[29]

In recent years, the attorney general's office has accused numerous judges of incompetence and corruption and pursued them in the courts as well as the media. According to a study by the Due Process of Law Foundation, some of these efforts were likely used to deflect attention from the government's responsibility for the increasingly dire security situation.[30] Indeed, the attorney general's office is widely perceived as highly partisan to the interests of the ARENA party. Interviews carried out by researchers for a study on public sector accountability found that the office's weaknesses included a failure to initiate investigations of public officials or cases involving powerful economic and political interests.[31] This perception is also shared by individual testimonies of citizens given to the Institute of Human Rights of the Central American University between October and December 2008: 15.8 percent described the attorney general's work as "inoperative," 24.6 percent as "insufficient," and 13.5 percent as "very inoperative," compared to 1.1 percent who qualified its work as "very satisfactory" and 12.9 percent as "satisfactory."[32]

Individuals brought up on criminal charges are afforded the presumption of innocence, but justice may be neither swift nor fair. The courts are often overworked, and although the state provides counsel to anyone in need, public defenders' excessive workload affects the quality of defense provided. Particularly in juvenile courts, defendants may be provided with different lawyers at different phases of the trial. There have been only a few high-profile cases of public officials brought up on corruption or other criminal charges; even those often occur only after being brought to public attention by the media. An example is the Saca administration's minister of health, who was found to have misused government resources. He was given a written warning by the Government Ethics Tribunal—but remained in office—only after the daily newspaper *La Prensa Gráfica* uncovered the story.[33] In April 2009, the online publication *El Faro* published a story revealing that the San Salvador Department director of the ARENA party, Adolfo Torrez, had offered to help PCN deputy Roberto Carlos Silva, imprisoned in the US for money laundering, evade justice in El Salvador in exchange for US$500,000.[34] *El Faro* revealed that the U.S. Federal Bureau of Investigations had turned over evidence of the offer to the Salvadoran attorney general in April 2008, but only after *El Faro* broke the story was any investigation initiated. Weeks later, Torrez died in an apparent suicide, but the attorney general's failed efforts had already damaged his bid for reelection.

Since the 1992 peace accords, and to some degree before, the Salvadoran military has been subject to civilian control, although throughout the Saca administration the position of defense minister was held by a retired or active duty military officer. As the military plays no role in the political process, and only a minor role in the internal security matters, it has earned increasing public approval. The National Civilian Police has undergone a much more thorough process of civilianization, and several PNC chiefs have been appointed by the president from outside the force. Horizontal controls are less consolidated, however, as the legislative branch exercises little oversight. One recent report references a member of the Defense and Public Security Committee of the Legislative Assembly stating that, given the levels of violence in El Salvador, "one would think that this would be the committee that worked the most, but it's the committee that meets the least."[35] For its part, the judiciary affords "unequal application of the law" to law enforcement officials as compared to leftist political suspects, according to a recent study published by the Brookings Institution.[36] On a positive note, an explicit attempt in late 2008 by the ARENA presidential candidate to enlist the Salvadoran Armed Forces—defined in the constitution as "apolitical"—in efforts to stop the "communists" of the FMLN from coming to power through elections were quickly and publicly rebuffed by the defense minister.[37]

Respect for human rights and accountability for abuses by the PNC are sorely lacking. A 2007 report by the PDDH found that the internal and external control mechanisms of the police "have been highly deficient, favoring impunity of those responsible for serious violations."[38] In particular, the role of the inspector general includes simply "receiving complaints, distributing them to the competent disciplinary sections, infrequently and insufficiently monitoring the progress of investigations," with the office taking their conclusions at face value despite the inherent failures of the process.[39] Suspicions of police involvement in social cleansing, especially of gang members, are rife but difficult to verify due to the lack of prosecutions. There are no known cases of prosecutions of military officers for corruption, and any such cases would be handled internally with little public scrutiny. The amnesty law passed following the 1992 peace accords has limited the prosecution of military or security forces for past rights abuses, although several cases have been filed and occasionally won in U.S. and Spanish courts.

Property rights in El Salvador are guaranteed by the constitution and in numerous secondary laws but are considered only "moderately well protected," according to the 2009 Index of Economic Freedom.[40] According to the report, enforcement of these rights is inconsistent due to the inefficiencies of the judicial system, which is "subject to manipulation by private interests, and final rulings may not be enforced." In general, the state protects citizens from arbitrary deprivation of property. One area of controversy in recent years has been the mining sector. The Saca administration provided exploration rights to mining companies, which have been criticized for planning projects that would undermine environmental protections and public health. Shortly before the March 2009 presidential elections, however, Saca announced that he would rather go to arbitration and pay heavy fines than grant actual operating permits to the companies; claiming all environmental standards had been met, at least one company publicly vowed to pursue legal action against the government.[41]

ANTICORRUPTION AND TRANSPARENCY 3.04

ENVIRONMENT TO PROTECT AGAINST CORRUPTION	3.00
PROCEDURES AND SYSTEMS TO ENFORCE ANTICORRUPTION LAWS	2.75
EXISTENCE OF ANTICORRUPTION NORMS, STANDARDS, AND PROTECTIONS	3.25
GOVERNMENTAL TRANSPARENCY	3.17

After 20 years of government dominated by a single political party, it is unsurprising that corruption and transparency issues have finally moved to the forefront of public attention. Although the press enjoys relatively unrestricted freedom to investigate and denounce cases, the government has no overall policy or legislation in place to provide citizens access to key public information. The few graft cases that come to light are revealed through leaked documents to the press, and there are no functional legal or institutional protections for individuals who might be in a position to expose instances of governmental corruption. Despite this situation, a promising recent development is the emergence of a civic movement in favor of enacting comprehensive access to information legislation. For example, the Salvadoran Foundation for Social and Economic Development (FUSADES), together with the Ibero-American Law Institute, drafted an access to information law that was supported by other civil society institutions and universities. A second proposed law, drafted by the FMLN, was later merged with this proposal and is currently under consideration in the Legislative Assembly, backed by a wide range of organizations, including press, NGOs, lawyers, private companies, and think tanks.

The privatization of pension administration, banks, telecommunications firms, and other state-held enterprises in the 1990s—although not always carried out in a fully transparent manner at the time—has significantly minimized opportunities for state corruption. Despite further efforts toward state modernization, petty corruption continues to afflict citizen interactions with the state, although very little is documented largely due to the weakness of state institutions in identifying and prosecuting corruption.

According to the Salvadoran constitution, the Court of Accounts is the government body responsible for assessing expenditures from the public treasury, including the budget. However, this key institution has long been politicized, for over two decades remaining under the control of politicians from the PCN as part of an implicit deal brokered with ARENA. The ineffectiveness and negligence demonstrated by the Court of Accounts over the years has been, in the opinion of most observers, perhaps the most significant obstacle to effective government oversight of public activities.[42] Critics have emerged publicly within the ranks of the PCN; following the party's poor showing in the 2009 legislative elections, two deputies publicly remarked about corruption in the court and its collusion with mayors who enter office poor and leave wealthy.[43] The Court of Accounts is responsible for administrative sanctions related to corruption, whereas criminal cases are passed to the attorney general's office. In 2002, the law governing the Court of Accounts was reformed to ensure that its reports would have a "public character," but in practice this rarely happens.[44] On occasion, the press will report on corruption cases based on Court of Account reports, but such piecemeal leaking of information is insufficient as a model for evaluating the court's impact on the management of public funds. The 2002 reform also led to the opening of a citizen participation unit in which individuals could report cases of fraud, but only a tiny fraction of cases have moved forward, and the results are unknown. By way of contrast, since 2001, the Ministry of Finance has benefited from improved and computerized audit capabilities, with audits based on objective criteria and a random selection system, thus preventing the use of tax audits as a weapon to target specific individuals.

All procurement contracts carried out by the central government, autonomous agencies, and municipalities are regulated by the 2001 Acquisition and Purchasing Law, which requires that bid announcements and relevant legislation be published online by the Treasury Ministry.[45] This law establishes policies for three levels, with purchases worth more than US$108,000 requiring public notice and subject to open bidding. Despite the intention to make government purchases more transparent, its implementation is unwieldy (especially at the municipal level) and subject to abuse. The existence of a clause for "emergency" or "urgent" procurements, which may be sole-sourced, has sometimes aroused charges of nepotism. A 2005 survey of businesspeople indicated that while 40 percent felt that corruption had decreased following the implementation of the law, 40 percent also said that the level of graft was the same, while 15 percent felt that it was worse.[46]

The Probity Section of the Supreme Court, created by the peace accords in 1992, is the entity responsible for reviewing the financial disclosures of all public officials. According to the constitution, the court reviews the veracity of these statements, but they are not made public. In 2005, the section's head resigned following the unwillingness of two Salvadoran banks to turn over information requested about 13 high-level officials in the administration of Francisco Flores (including the former president himself) and the unwillingness of the court to back his request. Since that time, the section has remained dormant, although in March 2009 there was renewed discussion about the need to reactivate the body.[47] The private sector think tank FUSADES, noting that El Salvador was out of step with the region on this issue, argued for a constitutional reform that would permit publication of these disclosures.[48]

In November 2006, a Government Ethics Tribunal was created with responsibility for resolving cases of conflict of interest—which are widespread and underreported—misuse of government property, nepotism, and public employee noncompliance in performing duties and responsibilities. The tribunal has set up and trained 72 commissions within government entities, but without much reach beyond San Salvador. The head of the tribunal has requested the ability to investigate officials on its own initiative without first receiving a complaint, as well as greater leeway for sanctioning officials beyond mere dismissal.[49] In practice, the Government Ethics Tribunal has powers similar to the PDDH—the ability to offer moral sanctions for abuses but little or no ability to carry through with punishment. In short, citizens seeking to pursue cases of corruption are met with unresponsive or ineffective institutions.

After many years of ad hoc municipal and civil society efforts to improve transparency and accountability at the local level, the Municipal Code was amended in 2006 to include a clear policy on access to information as well as mechanisms for restricting the use of municipal goods and services by political parties. However, there were no provisions made for supporting the implementation of these measures, nor are there any sanctions for failure to comply.[50] In the sphere of education, the state does not directly provide protections from graft, but it is not thought to be widespread. The stringent conditions attached to foreign assistance since well before the peace accords are mostly effective in preventing diversion of such aid for personal enrichment.

In terms of budget transparency, the 2008 Open Budget Index awarded a score of 37 percent to El Salvador, placing it in the category of states that provide minimal information to the public about budget procedures and documents.[51] Similarly, a 2007 review by the Regional Alliance for Freedom of Expression and Information of governmental entities' websites in El Salvador, Panama, Nicaragua, and Honduras ranked the average functionality of Salvadoran ministry websites last in terms of ease of access and availability of information.[52] Notably, the Public Works Ministry scored positively on only 1 of 12 indicators, while the presidency, the Ministry of Defense, the Supreme Court, and the National Academy for Public Security scored positively on only three indicators. Likewise, a global study on e-government carried out by Brown University found that El Salvador moved from 120th in 2006 to 152nd out of 198 governments reviewed in 2007.[53]

RECOMMENDATIONS

- Reform the electoral system, including through the establishment of proportional representation in municipal council contests, the depoliticization of the Supreme Electoral Tribunal, and the separation of the tribunal's administrative functions from its role in overseeing electoral disputes.
- Pass a political party law that regulates campaign finance and access to the media, rules for internal party governance, public access to data regarding party affiliation, and transparency in party financing.
- Improve the selection process for the attorney general and magistrates of the Supreme Court through a more transparent process that emphasizes merit over political patronage.[54]
- Depoliticize and redefine the functions of the Court of Accounts to ensure improved leadership, including the imposition of safeguards to prevent domination by particular partisan interests.
- Approve and enact a comprehensive Law on Transparency and Access to Information.

NOTES

For URLs and endnote hyperlinks, please visit the *Countries at the Crossroads* homepage at http://freedomhouse.org/template.cfm?page=139&edition=8.

1. Charles T. Call, "Assessing El Salvador's Transition from Civil War to Peace," in *Ending Civil Wars*, ed. Stephen John Stedman, Donald Rothchild, and Elisabeth Cousens (Boulder, Colo.: Lynne Rienner Press, 2002). The Supreme Court, in a highly controversial 2004 ruling, allowed for the recognition of the PCN and PDC parties despite their failing to achieve a 3 percent minimum of the popular vote. In 2008, this threshold was modified.
2. Fundacion Nacional para el Desarrollo (Funde) and Transparency International, *Observatorio de Gastos de Campaña Publicitaria Electoral: Primer Informe, Abril–Noviembre 2008* (San Salvador/Berlin: Funde and Transparency International, 2008).
3. European Election Observation Mission El Salvador, "Preliminary Statement: Legislative, Municipal and PARLACEN Elections–2009," January 20, 2009.
4. Daniel Valencia, "Presidencia No Revelará los Gastos de Publicidad del Quinquenio Saca," Elecciones 2009, May 17, 2009.
5. European Union Election Observation Mission El Salvador, "Preliminary Statement: Presidential Elections 2009," March 17, 2009.
6. Daniel Valencia, "Funde Estima en $19.2 Millones el Valor de Campaña Electoral en Medios," Elecciones 2009, June 21, 2009.
7. For a good discussion of the implication of this allocation system, see "Salvadoran Results," Fruits & Votes blog, January 27, 2009.
8. La Fundación Salvadoreña para el Desarrollo Económico y Social (FUSADES), "Recientes sentencias en materia constitucional," *Boletín de Estudios Legales* 49 (January 2005).
9. Funde, Fundación de Estudios para la Aplicación del Derecho (FESPAD), Iniciativa Social para la Democracia (ISD), and Instituto Universitario de Opinión Publica (IUDOP), *Informe Independiente sobre la Implementación de la Convención Interamericana contra la Corrupción en El Salvador, Mayo del 2007* (San Salvador: Funde, FESPAD, ISD, IUDOP, May 2007).
10. FUSADES, personal communication, November 3, 2009.
11. Rick Rockwell and Noreene Janus, *Media Power in Central America* (Urbana-Champaign: University of Illinois Press, 2003), 45, 135.
12. Asociación de Periodistas de El Salvador, "APES Presenta Informe en Día de Libertad de Prensa," news release, May 5, 2009.
13. Reporters Without Borders (RSF), "Journalist Accused of 'Terrorism' Conditionally Released," news release, July 24, 2007.
14. Art. 178, Criminal Code.
15. Carlos Lauria, "Drug Trade, Violent Gangs Pose Grave Danger," Committee to Protect Journalists (CPJ), February 10, 2009; CPJ, "Attacks on the Press in 2008: Americas Developments," February 10, 2009.
16. CPJ, "Filmmaker Who Documented Salvadoran Gang Is Slain," news release, September 3, 2009.
17. United Nations Office on Drugs and Crime (UNODC), *The Tenth United Nations Survey of Crime Trends and Operations of Criminal Justice Systems (Tenth CTS, 2005–2006)* (Vienna: UNODC, 2007).
18. Instituto de Derechos Humanos de la Universidad Centroamericana (IDHUCA), *Balance de Derechos Humanos 2008* (San Salvador: IDHUCA, 2009), 17.

[19] Procuraduría para la Defensa de los Derechos Humanos, *Violaciones a los Derechos Humanos por Responsabilidad de la Policía Nacional Civil de El Salvador* (San Salvador: Procuraduría para la Defensa de los Derechos Humanos, July 2007), 6.
[20] Rodrigo Baires Quezada, "Atentan contra un Cuarto Ambientalista en Cabañas," *El Faro*, August 13, 2009.
[21] Field research and interviews carried out in July 2009 by David Dye.
[22] Convention on the Elimination of all Forms of Discrimination against Women (CEDAW), *Concluding Observations: Seventh Periodic Report of El Salvador* (New York: CEDAW, October 31, 2008).
[23] IDHUCA, *Balance de Derechos Humanos 2008*.
[24] Center for Reproductive Law and Policy, *Persecuted: Political Process and Abortion Legislation in El Salvador: A Human Rights Analysis* (New York: Center for Reproductive Law and Policy, September 16, 2001).
[25] Heather Luz McNaughton et al., "Patient Privacy and Conflicting Legal and Ethical Obligations in El Salvador: Reporting of Unlawful Abortions," *American Journal of Public Health* 96, no. 11 (November 2006).
[26] Larissa Hotra, "A Recent History of the Disability Rights Movement in El Salvador," Upside Down World, July 18, 2008.
[27] Fátima García Diez et al., "El Poder Judicial," in *Las Instituciones Democráticas en El Salvador: Valoración de Rendimientos y Plan de Fortalecimiento* (Salamanca/San Salvador: Universidad de Salamanca and FUSADES, January 27, 2009), 42.
[28] IUDOP, "Los Salvadoreños y Salvadoreñas Evalúan la Situación del País a Finales de 2008 y Opinan sobre las Elecciones Legislativas y Municipales de 2009," *Boletín de Prensa*, no. 4 (2008).
[29] García Diaz et al., "El Poder Judicial."
[30] Due Process of Law Foundation, *Evaluation of Judicial Corruption in Central America and Panama and the Mechanisms to Combat It* (Washington, D.C.: Due Process of Law Foundation, 2007), 31; For an example of the government campaign against judges, see "CSJ Protégé a Jueces Corruptos en El Salvador," *La Gente*, February 15, 2008.
[31] Álvaro Artiga González et al., *Propuesta de Mejora de la Rendición de Cuentas en el Sector Público de El Salvador: Informe Final* (Washington, D.C.: USAID, March 2008), 33.
[32] IDHUCA, *Balance de Derechos Humanos 2008*, 15.
[33] Nestor Ríos, "Ministerio de Salud y Asistencia Social Intenta 'Desparecer' Medicinas Vencidas," *Diario Co Latino*, May 29, 2009.
[34] Rodrigo Quezada and Carlos Martínez, "Adolfo Torrez Pidió Medio Millón a Roberto Silva para Liberarlo de Cargos en El Salvador," *El Faro*, April 15, 2009.
[35] Washington Office on Latin America (WOLA), *Protect and Serve? The Status of Police Reform in Central America* (Washington, D.C.: WOLA, July 7, 2009), 29.
[36] Diana Villiers Negroponte, *The Merida Initiative and Central America: The Challenges of Containing Public Insecurity and Criminal Violence*, Working Paper No. 3 (Washington, D.C.: Brookings Institution, 2009), 50.
[37] Carlos Martínez, "No Hay que Confundir a la Fuerza Armada con Algunas Organizaciones," *El Faro*, September 15, 2008.
[38] Procuraduría para la Defensa de los Derechos Humanos, *Violaciones a los Derechos Humanos por Responsabilidad de la Policía Nacional Civil en El Salvador* (San Salvador: Procuraduría para la Defensa de los Derechos Humanos, July 2009), 6.
[39] Ibid., 125.
[40] The Heritage Foundation and *Wall Street Journal* (WSJ), "El Salvador," in *2009 Index of Economic Freedom* (Washington, D.C./New York: The Heritage Foundation and WSJ, 2009).

[41] Keny López Piche, "No a la Minería: Saca Cierra Puertas a Explotación de Metales," *La Prensa Gráfica*, February 26, 2009.

[42] Fátima García Diez et al., "Reforma Institucional y Control de los Fondos Públicos," in *Las Instituciones Democráticas en El Salvador: Valoración de Rendimientos y Plan de Fortalecimiento*.

[43] Edith Portillo and Jimena Aguilar, "Surgen en el PCN Sospechas de Corrupción en la Corte de Cuentas," *El Faro*, March 2, 2009.

[44] Asociación Probidad, *Tercer Indice Latinoamericano de Transparencia Presupuestaria* (San Salvador: Asociación Probidad, November 2005).

[45] Republic of El Salvador, Ley de Adquisiciones y Contrataciones de la Administración Pública; Bid announcements are published at www.comprasal.gob.sv.

[46] IUDOP, "La Transparencia en el Estado Salvadoreño," *Boletín de Prensa*, no. 1 (2005).

[47] Suchit Chávez, "Critican Inactividad de Probidad CSJ," *La Prensa Gráfica*, February 12, 2009.

[48] Karla Ramos, "FUSADES Pide Reactivar la Seccion de Probidad," *La Prensa Gráfica*, March 25, 2009.

[49] Carlos Dada, "Necesitamos Actuar de Oficio," *El Faro*, November 26, 2007.

[50] USAID, *Construyendo Transparencia en los Municipios: Diagnósticos y Líneas Programáticas para Promover la Transparencia en El Salvador* (Washington, D.C.: USAID, March 2007).

[51] Open Budget Initiative, "El Salvador," in *Open Budget Index 2008* (Washington, D.C.: Open Budget Initiative, 2009).

[52] Sandra Crucianelli, "Los Sitios Web Gubernamentales como Herramientas del Control Social y el Periodismo Investigativo," *Sala de Prensa* 4, no. 108 (October 2008).

[53] Brown University, "South Korea Continues to Lead World in Global e-Government," press release, July 24, 2007.

[54] FUSADES, "Lecciones Aprendidas en el Proceso de Elección de Magistrados de la Corte Suprema de Justicia," *Posición Institucional*, no. 18 (July 2009).

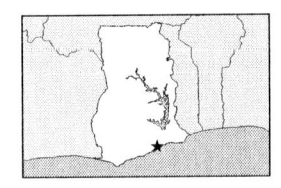

GHANA

CAPITAL: Accra
POPULATION: 23.8 million
GNI PER CAPITA (PPP): $1,430

SCORES	2006	2010
ACCOUNTABILITY AND PUBLIC VOICE:	N/A	5.34
CIVIL LIBERTIES:	N/A	5.33
RULE OF LAW:	N/A	4.64
ANTICORRUPTION AND TRANSPARENCY:	N/A	3.85

(scores are based on a scale of 0 to 7, with 0 representing weakest and 7 representing strongest performance)

E. Gyimah-Boadi

INTRODUCTION

The conduct of Ghana's December 2008 elections won universal praise and helped to challenge the prevailing pessimism about African democratization in the wake of electoral debacles in states including Nigeria, Kenya, and Zimbabwe. Indeed, since returning to constitutional rule with the foundation of the Fourth Republic in 1992, Ghana has remained politically stable through five presidential and parliamentary elections (1992, 1996, 2000, 2004, and 2008), and each poll has generally been an improvement on the previous one. Ghana has also undergone two electoral transfers of power from one party to another (2000 and 2008), making it almost unique among African democracies.

This achievement is all the more impressive in light of Ghana's chronic political instability prior to 1992. Although the country had a liberal democratic constitution and multiparty democracy in 1957, when it became the first European colony in sub-Saharan Africa to obtain independence, the Convention People's Party (CPP) government led by Kwame Nkrumah had jettisoned this system and declared a one-party state by 1964. Nkrumah's 1966 ouster by the army began a cycle of military coups and regimes punctuated by brief periods of constitutional multiparty government.[1]

In the early 1990s, the governing military junta known as the Provisional National Defence Council (PNDC) began the process of returning the country to constitutional rule. In 1992, PNDC chairman Jerry Rawlings won a multi-party presidential election as the candidate of the National Democratic Congress

---

E. Gyimah-Boadi is the Executive Director of the Ghana Center for Democratic Development, Director of Afrobarometer, and a Professor of Political Science at the University of Ghana. Research assistance was provided by Victor Brobbey, Research Fellow at the Ghana Center for Democratic Development.

(NDC), a party formed by the PNDC to contest the poll. He was reelected in 1996 but was constitutionally barred from seeking a third term in 2000. His vice president, John Atta Mills, ran as the NDC candidate, losing narrowly to John Kufuor of the New Patriotic Party (NPP) in elections that were widely hailed as free and fair. The NPP also won a slim majority in Parliament that year. In the 2004 elections, Kufuor again defeated Atta Mills and the NDC, securing a much larger parliamentary majority for the NPP.

However, the ruling party entered the 2008 elections with some significant liabilities. The government was dogged by perceptions of corruption, insufficient ethnic inclusion, and elitism. Prominent human rights campaigner Nana Akufo-Addo, who had served as attorney general and foreign minister under Kufuor, ultimately won the NPP presidential primary, but the vote featured 17 candidates, acrimonious infighting, and lavish spending. There was also a significant rise in intraparty disputes at the constituency level, which resulted in bitterly fought parliamentary primaries. A number of the losing candidates then ran as independents, further weakening the NPP's base of support. Reports of extravagant government spending on a new presidential office complex and the purchase of two presidential jets in the face of economic hardship also aroused popular resentment.

Despite relative macroeconomic stability and generally prudent management by the NPP, Ghana remains a poor country. Gross national income per capita in 2008 was US$670.[2] Results from the 2008 Afrobarometer survey suggest that unemployment may be as high as 42 percent, and only 12 percent of Ghanaians have access to running water in their homes. Furthermore, 48 percent of the population consider their personal living conditions to be "bad or fairly bad," and despite the NPP's efforts, 42 percent see the country's general macroeconomic conditions as "bad or fairly bad."[3]

Nevertheless, the NPP's record of good governance and its protection of civil liberties (as shown by largely positive assessments by the African Peer Review Mechanism Report and the Ibrahim Index of African Governance),[4] along with the introduction of popular social programs such as the National Health Insurance Scheme and the School Feeding Program, suggested that the 2008 elections would be extremely close. In fact, it turned out to be the closest election in Ghanaian history, with Atta Mills of the NDC beating Akufo-Addo by less than half a percentage point in a runoff. The Atta Mills government, with a narrow NDC majority in the new Parliament, was sworn in on January 7, 2009.[5]

The closeness of the vote has contributed to what were already high levels of political polarization and mistrust between Ghana's major parties. The NDC has its roots in the populist "revolution" and military juntas of the late 1970s and 1980s and claims a left-of-center political ideology. The NPP, meanwhile, is more market oriented and conservative, and many of its members were victims of the military juntas. And as discussed in greater detail later, the winner-take-all nature of Ghana's constitution has made state capture (or more specifically, the capture of the executive branch) the overwhelming objective of both political parties; control of the presidency provides the ruling party with overwhelming financial, political, and ethnic patronage advantages.

After a rancorous transition in which the NDC accused the NPP of corruption and economic mismanagement, and the NPP accused the NDC of engaging in a political witch-hunt, the NDC is now trying to settle into the task of governing the country. It faces particular challenges from an economy that has been thrown out of balance by the NPP's election-year profligacy and the global financial crisis.

It is against this backdrop that recent trends in accountability, civil liberties, the rule of law, and anticorruption efforts should be viewed.

ACCOUNTABILITY AND PUBLIC VOICE 5.34

FREE AND FAIR ELECTORAL LAWS AND ELECTIONS	5.50
EFFECTIVE AND ACCOUNTABLE GOVERNMENT	4.75
CIVIC ENGAGEMENT AND CIVIC MONITORING	5.67
MEDIA INDEPENDENCE AND FREEDOM OF EXPRESSION	5.43

The 2008 elections provided further evidence of the strength and increasing consolidation of democracy in Ghana, while at the same time illuminating some of its weaknesses. The country's elections are generally considered free and fair, and a clear majority of Ghanaians believe that they live in a democracy.[6] The constitutional and statutory injunctions designed to protect the electoral process have been largely successful; universal adult suffrage and ballot secrecy are guaranteed. Both Ghanaians and international observers view the Electoral Commission of Ghana (EC) as independent, and the commission's members are routinely asked to lend their expertise to elections all over Africa.

However, the EC approached the 2008 balloting in a somewhat complacent manner, contributing to several avoidable administrative problems that nearly marred the electoral process. The electoral timetable was unnecessarily compressed, leaving insufficient time to correct flaws, and the NDC accused the EC of conspiring with the NPP to inflate the final voter registry. Indeed, mistrust of the EC began at least two years before the elections, with the enactment of legislation that allowed overseas Ghanaians to vote in national elections. Although implementation of this statute was eventually shelved, the NDC saw it as an effort by the NPP—in collusion with the EC—to manipulate the electoral process. In the run-up to the elections, a number of politicized land and chieftaincy disputes led to sporadic incidents of violence throughout the country, particularly in northern Ghana, in a few cases resulting in deaths at campaign rallies.[7] Police failed to vigorously pursue some of the suspects for what were viewed as political reasons, adding to the existing tensions. The stakes of the balloting were also raised by the recent discovery of offshore oil deposits that could be worth US$2 billion to US$3 billion in extra annual revenue.[8]

Ethnic voting is an undeniable part of Ghana's political landscape. Though both major parties campaigned in all regions of the country, they tended to spend an inordinate amount of time in their respective strongholds.[9] The NPP focused on regions dominated by the Akan ethnic group, particularly the Ashanti, Brong-Ahafo, and Eastern regions. The NDC concentrated its efforts in the non-Akan regions, particularly the Volta, Upper West, Upper East, and Northern regions. The three remaining regions—Greater Accra, Central, and Western—have been "swing regions" in recent elections. However, presidential candidate Atta Mills was born in the Western region and was an indigene of the Central region, and his NDC party was not reticent about exploiting this background and touting the potential economic benefits of voting for an ethnic kinsman. The NDC also sought support from non-Akan migrant communities within the NPP's Akan strongholds, pointing to the continuing dominance of Akans in Ghana's political establishment under the NPP. This led to an increase in election-related violence, even in southern Ghana. On the whole, the campaign strategies used by both parties exacerbated ethnic tensions more than in previous elections.

The electoral playing field was largely level, and despite the occasional violence, the parties were generally able to campaign without hindrance. State broadcasters made some effort to provide equal access and coverage to the major candidates. NPP presidential candidate Akufo-Addo was more visible to the electorate via television advertisements and countless billboards, suggesting that the NPP was better resourced than the NDC. Due to the paucity and inadequate enforcement of campaign finance laws, it is not clear how either party funded its campaign or how much they received or spent. Both parties had been in government long enough to have formed lucrative ties with the Ghanaian business community, and there were some unsubstantiated accusations that parties had been financed by foreign countries or interests. The NDC, for example, was rumored to have received funds from Venezuela and Libya, just as the NPP had been accused of receiving funds from Nigeria during the 2000 elections.

The first round of voting, held on December 7, 2008, did not produce a clear presidential winner. The constitution requires the winning candidate to obtain at least 50 percent of the vote, and Akufo-Addo obtained only 49.1 percent, followed by Atta Mills with 47.8 percent. The parliamentary elections were equally close. The NPP lost its majority, falling from 128 seats to 107, while the NDC increased its share from 94 to 114. Among the other parties with a parliamentary presence, the People's National Convention fell from four to two, and the Convention People's Party won a single seat.

The presidential runoff was scheduled for December 28. In the intervening weeks, the NPP government became notably less subtle about taking advantage of incumbency, reducing fuel prices and quickly releasing commercial drivers who had been jailed for traffic violations. Incendiary statements, violence, and intimidation became routine at party rallies. Former coup leader and longtime president Jerry Rawlings was especially strident in his attacks on the NPP government, exhorting the NDCs supporters to "resist" the NPP's efforts to rig the election and to be "vigilant" during the runoff. Occasionally, flanked by other retired military officers, he would end NDC campaign rallies with the militaristic religious hymn "Onward Christian Soldiers."

On voting day, both parties complained of harassment and intimidation of their supporters in the strongholds of their opponents. The EC announced the results of the runoff within 48 hours. The NDC was leading by less than 1 percent, and the outcome would not be known until balloting was conducted in Tain constituency, where it had been delayed due to administrative and security concerns. The NPP, also citing security concerns and perhaps acknowledging the constituency's consistent support for the NDC, effectively boycotted the Tain voting and attempted an ultimately unsuccessful legal challenge. On January 3, the EC declared victory for the NDC, and Akufo-Addo, defying hawks within his own party, conceded the following day. The EC, to its credit, had rejected an attempt prior to the declaration to alter vote tallies in the Ashanti region, which would have changed the final outcome. The margin of victory in the presidential race was 40,586 votes, a mere 0.46 percent of valid votes cast.

One of Atta Mills's campaign promises was to review the constitution and address some of Ghana's governance deficits. The most obvious of these is the relatively unchecked power of the executive branch. Ghana's 1992 constitution was drafted by the outgoing military regime, and while it is a progressive document in a number of respects, it gives an inordinate amount of authority to the executive. A constitutional provision bars members of Parliament (MPs) from introducing any legislation that will commit the government to spending public funds, effectively preventing the legislature from initiating bills. In addition, a constitutional requirement that the president appoint at least 50 percent of his ministers from Parliament severely handicaps parliamentary oversight responsibilities. Parliament has 230 members, and the president can appoint an unlimited number of ministers. Since 1993, this number has ranged from the mid-70s to the upper 80s. Each Parliament has therefore typically had at least 40 members who served concurrently in the legislature and the executive, and these officials have sought to steer state spending to their constituencies while neglecting their parliamentary duties. Moreover, MPs in the ruling party who aspire to wield such ministerial patronage have an added incentive to curry favor with the executive.

As a result, budgets and spending proposals are inadequately debated, and even unpopular bills submitted by the executive, such as a measure authorizing the acquisition of a presidential jet by the Kufuor administration, are invariably passed.[10] Efforts by the parliamentary minority to oversee executive action, for example by obtaining a full accounting of the newly constructed presidential residence and the lavish 50th-anniversary celebrations of the country's independence, were largely ignored by the Kufuor administration.[11]

Presidential discretionary authority is used to make politicized appointments throughout Ghana's public services, evading public and parliamentary scrutiny and undermining security of tenure. The executive's role in the ostensibly nonpartisan local government system is particularly symptomatic of this problem. The president appoints 30 percent of the local government assemblies as well as the local government leaders, known as district chief executives. While these appointments are supposed to be based on technical competence, it is clear that partisan considerations play a central role. This was the case under the Kufuor administration, and it has continued under the Atta Mills government.[12]

Ghana's civil service is becoming increasingly politicized, with bureaucrats contesting elections or campaigning for political parties.[13] The constitutionally independent Public Services Commission, which oversees the civil service, is appointed by the president, and in practice civil service positions are not always filled based on merit. Moreover, the remuneration is unattractive, negatively affecting public servants' morale, performance, and integrity.

Nongovernmental organizations (NGOs) in Ghana are largely free from state pressures and play a major role in highlighting and providing technical support on gender, disability, and other social, governance, and economic issues. Some NGOs have become such fixtures that the government relies on their services to fulfill its mandates. For example, the police's Domestic Violence and Victim Support Unit (DOVVSU) relies on the Women's Initiative for Self-Empowerment (WISE) to provide psychiatric counselling, the International Federation of Women Lawyers (FIDA) to provide legal advice, and various other NGOs to provide victims with shelter and medical attention. NGOs have also helped to draft key pieces of legislation, such as the Whistleblower's Act. However, on some issues there is little opportunity for NGOs to effectively influence government policy. This is particularly true of a budget process that, despite some recent improvements, is still dominated by the executive. There have been several attempts at regulating the NGO sector since 1993, but the NGO community has successfully resisted them so far, insisting that any legislation should reflect its input.

The NGO community and the NPP government negotiated a Draft National Policy for Strategic Partnership with NGOs in 2004. It was agreed that this document should form the basis for national NGO legislation. It stipulated, among other things, that the law should establish an autonomous and independent National Commission on NGOs, grant tax exemptions to NGOs that qualify under the law, and facilitate collaboration between NGOs and district assemblies. However, a cabinet shuffle caused the process to stall, and recent versions of the NGO legislation did not reflect the 2004 agreement in letter or spirit. NGOs have consequently resisted passage of the current bill.

Freedom of expression is enshrined in the constitution, and a criminal libel statute was removed by the NPP government in 2001. The state does not hinder access to the internet. State broadcasters have made some effort to be neutral and routinely provide for a representation of different viewpoints. However, the state television station tends to favor the ruling party. Inequity in coverage by state media is mitigated by the large number of independent private broadcasters. By 2005, according to figures from the National Media Commission, there were over 100 newspapers; licenses had been granted for 24 television stations, of which six are currently operating; and there were over 80 FM radio stations.[14]

The state does not routinely intimidate journalists, nor does it attempt to overtly censor the media, especially in recent years. In the early days of the Fourth Republic, journalists were imprisoned under the criminal libel law, and some antigovernment newspapers were subject to harassment. The government's attitude has grown decidedly more tolerant, but there have been some abuses. These include the dismissal of several journalists from the state television broadcaster for a story on the sale of the national airline that was considered unfavorable to the government and the closure of a radio station in the Volta region after it aired a series of stories that the government considered embarrassing. In 2007, journalist Samuel Enin was killed in a suspected contract murder. This crime is being investigated by the police, and it is not clear whether the motive was political. In 2009, the director general of the state television broadcaster abruptly halted a talk-show program because the government view was insufficiently represented, eliciting shock and universal condemnation. There is also some self-censorship by the media on political and corruption issues, and the government favors some media houses with greater access (particularly during presidential trips abroad) and state-sponsored advertising.

Though the media are generally free, many newspapers and radio stations are openly partisan. Radio Gold, for example, is viewed as an NDC station, while Oman Radio is seen as an NPP station.[15] Despite this polarization, there are some outlets, such as the Joy FM radio station and the *Public Agenda* newspaper, that attempt to report more objectively.

CIVIL LIBERTIES   5.33

PROTECTION FROM STATE TERROR, UNJUSTIFIED IMPRISONMENT, AND TORTURE	4.00
GENDER EQUITY	5.00
RIGHTS OF ETHNIC, RELIGIOUS, AND OTHER DISTINCT GROUPS	5.25
FREEDOM OF CONSCIENCE AND BELIEF	6.67
FREEDOM OF ASSOCIATION AND ASSEMBLY	5.75

Chapter 5 of the constitution provides protection for almost all fundamental human rights, including the rights to life and personal liberty, guarantees against slavery and forced labor, equality and freedom from discrimination, free speech, freedom of thought, religious freedom, freedom of assembly, the right to information, and freedom of movement. Though there are constitutional prohibitions on torture and physical abuse, there have been cases in which detainees suspected of violent crimes have reportedly been assaulted in police custody. This has increased in recent years, and the perpetrators are rarely held accountable.

Ghana's prisons are severely overcrowded. In 2008, the country's prisons had an official capacity of some 8,000 inmates but actually housed over 14,000.[16] Ghana's Commission on Human Rights and Administrative Justice (CHRAJ) reported that prisoners' rights in terms of bedding and medical care were being violated.[17] Few steps have been taken to address the overcrowding issue beyond occasional blanket pardons of prisoners; one of the last acts of the Kufuor government was to grant pardons to 500 inmates. The sentencing of juvenile offenders to long prison sentences is commonplace, and while judges often have the option of imposing noncustodial sentences, they rarely do so. Another reason for the overcrowding is the large number of pretrial detainees, who often remain in remand for several years despite a rule requiring that they be tried within a "reasonable time." Pretrial detainees made up approximately 29.7 percent of the prison population as of October 2008, an increase from an estimated 22 percent in 2003.[18]

According to a survey conducted as part of the African Peer Review Mechanism (APRM) in 2005, 62 percent of Ghanaians felt safer from crime than they did in 1999.[19] However, most Ghanaians living in urban areas consider crime a serious concern. There are daily reports of home invasions in the newspapers, and law enforcement agencies are generally seen as ineffective. There is also a perception that the recent change in government has been accompanied by a spike in crime, as was reportedly the case during the previous power transfer in 2000. The government has responded by increasing the number of police checkpoints, particularly in urban areas.

The rights of people living in mining communities have been increasingly abused in the last five years. The government has reported that roughly 30 percent of the country's territory is currently held under concession by gold mining firms, and mining has been steadily displacing farming activity. One mining concession granted in 2006 resulted in the clearing of 3,000 hectares of land for gold production and the displacement of some 10,000 farmers.[20] Small-scale miners are routinely abused by private security companies hired by mining firms to protect their concessions. This often happens with the compliance or assistance of the state security agencies and, occasionally, local government and traditional authorities.[21] Mining communities have also been plagued with environmental degradation, poisoned water supplies, destruction of crops, and an unusually high incidence of diseases such as cholera and tuberculosis.

The International Labour Organisation (ILO) and its International Programme on the Elimination of Child Labour (IPEC) have raised concerns about human trafficking, particularly child trafficking, in some farming and fishing communities in Ghana. The government has responded by setting up a human trafficking task force to coordinate antitrafficking efforts, and the Human Trafficking Act (Act 694) was promulgated in 2005 to help combat the problem. Current initiatives include an effort by the Ministry of Justice to create a registry of children who live with relatives other than their parents, and designating the offense of "causing or encouraging the seduction or prostitution of a child under the age of sixteen" as a second-degree felony rather than a misdemeanor.

The High Court has original jurisdiction in human rights matters, but the CHRAJ is the primary organ for redress of human rights violations in Ghana. The commission, whose leaders are appointed by the president, is authorized by Article 218 of the constitution to investigate complaints but not to prosecute offenders. Instead, it refers cases to the Attorney General's Department for prosecution, and because the attorney general is part of the executive branch and typically a leading member of the ruling party, there is a risk of conflict when the CHRAJ looks into abuses linked to the executive. For example, the commission recently investigated the propriety of the purchase of a hotel by Kufuor's son, and if it had recommended prosecution, it seems unlikely that the attorney general would have pursued the case.[22]

It is generally agreed that the CHRAJ has vigorously investigated corruption and human rights abuses, but there is also universal acknowledgment that the commission's work is hampered by sometimes serious financial and logistical constraints. Its multiple mandates—anticorruption, human rights protection, and administrative justice—tend to overstretch its limited capacity. In addition, there is some doubt about the commission's legal authority to launch investigations on its own initiative. For instance, a finding of impropriety against a leading member of the NPP, Richard Anane, was quashed by the Supreme Court on the grounds that the CHRAJ could not initiate such an investigation without a complainant.[23] Despite these constraints, the CHRAJ has acquired a reputation for investigative independence, especially in comparison with other anticorruption agencies such as the Serious Fraud Office and the police's Criminal Investigation Department. The commission has brought actions that have led to the reinstatement of workers in both the public and the private sectors, investigated the president on conflict of interest charges in connection the multimillion-dollar hotel acquired by his son, and published groundbreaking reports on the human rights abuses in the mining sector.

Recently, Ghana has shown increasing sensitivity toward gender issues. The NPP government in 2001 established a Ministry for Women and Children's Affairs (MOWAC), which assumed jurisdiction over two existing government agencies, the National Council on Women and Development and the National Commission on Children. The new Atta Mills government has also demonstrated an awareness of the importance of gender issues and has committed itself to appointing women to 40 percent of government positions. However, it is highly doubtful that this target will be met. Moreover, the number of women in Parliament dropped from 23 to 20 after the 2008 elections.

The constitution protects economic rights, women and children's rights, and the rights of the disabled. The criminal code addresses rape, defilement, incest, abduction, and forced marriage. However, the Domestic Violence Act is still not properly enforced, and DOVVSU does not receive adequate resources. In addition, women in some areas are still subjected to harmful traditional practices, including infringements on widows' rights and female genital mutilation (FGM). While FGM has been criminalized and is not as widespread thanks to a multiyear campaign to end the practice, it is still a part of the culture in some communities in northern Ghana.[24] There is little evidence that legal and constitutional protections against the exploitation of children's labor are being enforced, including with respect to forms of ritual servitude such as *trokosi*, in which female children are sent to live in "voodoo" shrines.

Both the NPP and NDC administrations have shown some commitment to addressing disability issues. The NPP government passed the Persons with Disabilities Act (Act 715) in 2006, though it was sluggish in implementing some of the law's key provisions, such as staffing and finding an appropriate site for the secretariat of the National Disability Council. The NDC government subsequently inaugurated the council.

Freedom of conscience and worship is largely respected in Ghana. Religious groups are among the most vigorous of the country's civil society organizations. There are no government restrictions on the operation and membership of religious groups and faith-based associations.[25] However, Ghana is a predominantly Christian country, and political power is concentrated in the hands of a southern Christian elite. Islam, the faith of 18 percent of the population, is stereotyped as the religion of the poor and the marginalized. It is also associated with the less-developed north of Ghana, though migration has made Islam as common in the south as in the north.[26] A north-south divide is evident in income disparities as well as access to services and economic opportunities. Three of Ghana's four poorest regions are in the north.[27] Successive governments have sought to address this problem with poverty-reduction and development programs focusing on the northern areas. Despite being a multiethnic country, Ghana features almost no instances of discrimination based solely on ethnicity. However, as noted previously, local disputes over land use and chieftaincy sometimes lead to ethnically tinged violence, and the political exploitation of ethnicity has given some election-related clashes an ethnic character.

Ghana has a vibrant associational life, and the right to freedoms of association and assembly are respected. Business and political organizations abound, and there are few impediments to joining trade unions, though some obstacles have been placed in the way of the creation of new unions.[28] Unions are still important actors, but their power is tempered by statutory provisions that require labor disputes to be heard by the Labor Commission prior to the declaration of a strike.

The right to protest is protected by the constitution. The Public Order Act stipulates that persons wishing to demonstrate must first inform the police, but the police cannot stop a demonstration without going to court for an injunction. This is rarely necessary, as protests are still rare and the police typically raise no objection or negotiate demonstration times with protest organizers. Political parties have attempted to circumvent the Public Order Act by giving innocuous labels, such as "fitness marches," to campaign activities that are essentially demonstrations. The treatment of large, spontaneous political gatherings is not uniform. During the 2008 election campaign, presidential candidates attracted such assemblies as they arrived in or passed through towns, eliciting varied responses from the police (see Accountability and Public Voice).

RULE OF LAW   4.64

INDEPENDENT JUDICIARY	4.80
PRIMACY OF RULE OF LAW IN CIVIL AND CRIMINAL MATTERS	4.00
ACCOUNTABILITY OF SECURITY FORCES AND MILITARY TO CIVILIAN AUTHORITIES	4.75
PROTECTION OF PROPERTY RIGHTS	5.00

The constitution grants judicial power exclusively to the judiciary within a system of three separate but ostensibly equal branches of government. The constitution also grants the Supreme Court the power to strike down laws and executive actions that it deems unconstitutional. Judges in Ghana have security of tenure once appointed, and it is commonly believed that they have sufficient autonomy.[29] However, the executive influences the judicial system in a number of ways.

The president is influential in the appointment of all the superior court judges, including the chief justice, whom the president names in consultation with the Council of State (also largely appointed by the president) and with the approval of Parliament (where the president's party typically has a majority). Supreme Court judges are appointed by the president on the advice of the Judicial Council and in consultation with the Council of State. Also, because the constitution stipulates the minimum but not the maximum number of Supreme Court judges, the president could theoretically "pack" the court with as many judges as he wished, though this has not occurred in practice. More troubling is the fact that a panel of the Supreme Court to hear a given case is "duly constituted for its work by not less than five Supreme Court Justices" out of the constitutional minimum of nine.[30] The constitution is silent on who selects the judges for each case, and by convention it has become the exclusive preserve of the chief justice. It is therefore possible in theory for a chief justice to determine the outcome of a particular case by selecting a panel based on the political and judicial leanings of the other justices, and indeed for a president to do so indirectly by appointing a sympathetic chief justice. There have been unconfirmed reports of executive interference in cases via pressure exerted through executive-friendly judges and of the chief justice influencing the decisions of trial court judges.[31]

In the 2008 Afrobarometer survey, 79 percent of Ghanaians expressed the opinion that the judiciary was corrupt. However, this does not seem to deter litigants from swamping the courts at all levels. The level of judicial competence has improved in recent years. Continuing legal education in a wide number of fields, from judgment writing to human rights, is becoming increasingly institutionalized. A Judicial Training Institute regularly holds seminars, courses, and programs for incoming and existing judges. In addition, commercial, tax, and other specialized courts have been established.

Criminal suspects are presumed innocent, even though there have been reports of suspects being assaulted in police custody and uninvestigated and unprosecuted cases of vigilante justice. Indeed, a growing number of "self-help" youth groups have assumed responsibility for protecting their neighborhoods against crime. According to a recent report sponsored by the Ministry of Interior, more than 1,000 cases of vigilante-style justice were recorded countrywide in 2007.[32] These trends have been attributed to the perceived ineffectiveness of the security services in combating violent crime, as well as deficiencies in the property ownership documentation system that lead to the extralegal resolution of land disputes. Though there have been some prosecutions of people engaged in lynching, the perpetrators far too often go unpunished.[33]

The right to counsel is guaranteed by the constitution. However, its effect is muted by the cost of hiring an attorney, the limited capacity and resources of Ghana's legal aid system, inadequate information about the availability of legal aid, and a shortage of lawyers in many districts.

The fact that the attorney general is both the chief legal adviser to the executive and the head of the prosecution service has raised doubts about the independence of prosecutions, with opposition politicians frequently accusing the government of "selective justice." The attorney general has the discretion to launch or end a given prosecution without explanation. The Kufuor administration prosecuted a number of leading NDC politicians on corruption charges, and many remained criminal defendants for the duration of Kufuor's presidency. Although the charges appeared legitimate, no such prosecutions were pursued against the several NPP party members who were also accused of corruption.

Since the return to democratic rule, the military's political role has declined markedly, and the risk of another military takeover has diminished. There are clear rules in place to ensure democratic control of the security forces. The president, who is considered the commander in chief of the security forces under the constitution, appoints the chief of defense staff and the service chiefs on the advice of the Council of State. He appoints other senior commanders on the advice of the Armed Forces Council and the service councils, and in consultation with the Council of State. Members of all of these councils are also named by the president. These institutional structures, along with the clear and deepening popular aversion to military rule, have helped reshape the relationship between the security services and the state. The military has no noteworthy economic interests. However, it does continue to receive some deference on the management of its internal affairs and has successfully resisted efforts by the auditor general to review its accounts as required by statute. The security services ostensibly respect human rights, especially those of educated urban dwellers, but they have by no means internalized human rights values and routinely engage in abusive conduct when dealing with opponents of the government or ordinary citizens. The military has been deployed to provide support to the police in domestic law enforcement, particularly in the context of elections. This has occasionally led to the detention of civilians and, on one occasion in 2004, the death of an opposition politician while in military custody.

In cases of security sector human rights abuses, impunity remains a problem. The Police Intelligence and Professional Standards Unit (PIPS) receives and investigates complaints of abuses. While the PIPS is considered to be more effective than previous police accountability mechanisms, collusion between police and judges has hindered the justice process, frequently resulting in the prolonged adjournment of cases.[34] While corruption is common within the police force, investigation by the CHRAJ or the Serious Fraud Office remains unlikely.[35] Military abuses may also go unpunished or languish in the attorney general's office for months or years before going to trial. A high-profile case in which three soldiers allegedly killed 21-year old Evans Kusi after he disobeyed their orders in March 2007 was eventually ordered to court after media efforts to raise public awareness about the case thwarted attempts to quietly settle the case out of court. Nevertheless, two of the soldiers were released on bail, and the attorney general continued to delay the trial throughout 2008.[36]

While the constitution guarantees property rights, Article 20(1) implicitly reserves the government's authority to seize private property for a stated public use. Under Article 20(2), eminent domain must be accompanied by "prompt payment" to the dispossessed party of "fair and adequate compensation," and the seizure must be necessary in the interest of public defense, public safety, public order, public health, town and country planning, or to promote "the public benefit." It is not clear whether these conditions have always been adhered to. In recent times, land that was acquired for a public purpose early in the country's history or in the colonial era has been sold to private developers and even to government officials. This became a major issue in the 2008 electoral campaign, with the indigenous population of Accra, the Ga, requesting the return of land that the state had acquired for a "public purpose" but was unable to develop.[37] Lawsuits and nativist demonstrations have become key features of the movement for the return of Ga land. The NDC made the return of Ga land one of its campaign promises, though it remains to be seen whether the pledge will be honored. The Ga assertion of property rights has occasionally resulted in violence, and there have been several reported cases of violence perpetrated by "landguards"—individuals hired by private landowners or traditional authorities to protect their land from encroachers.

ANTICORRUPTION AND TRANSPARENCY 3.85

ENVIRONMENT TO PROTECT AGAINST CORRUPTION	4.00
PROCEDURES AND SYSTEMS TO ENFORCE ANTICORRUPTION LAWS	4.00
EXISTENCE OF ANTICORRUPTION NORMS, STANDARDS, AND PROTECTIONS	4.25
GOVERNMENTAL TRANSPARENCY	3.17

Ghana remains the easiest place to do business in West Africa and has been ranked as one of the top 10 economies in Africa for doing business. However, the business environment still faces major challenges, including excessive regulatory obstructions and widespread corruption that stems in part from the poor remuneration of public employees. A World Bank 2007 Enterprise Survey found that 39 percent of firms expected to pay informal payments to public officials to get things done, 23 percent expected to give gifts to get an operating license, 18 percent expected to give gifts in meetings with tax officials, and 61 percent expected to give gifts to secure a government contract.[38]

International indicators suggest that Ghana has made some strides in combating corruption. Its score on the Transparency International Corruption Perceptions Index (CPI) rose from 3.3 to 3.9 between 2003 and 2008. On the basis of the 2008 score, Ghana is now ranked 67th out of 180 countries globally and 6th in sub-Saharan Africa. However, most Ghanaians view corruption as a very serious problem that holds back the country's development. The Ghana Integrity Initiative Survey of 2005 indicated that 92.5 percent of urban households in southern Ghana believed corruption to be prevalent in the country, and 90 percent considered corruption to be a serious problem. Contrary to CPI evidence, 60 percent of the sample believed corruption was getting worse rather than better.[39] This is not surprising given the pervasiveness and acceptance of patronage in the public sector and state-owned enterprises in particular. One of the first acts of successive governments has been to dissolve the boards of state-controlled enterprises such as the Ghana Commercial Bank, and state agencies like the Serious Fraud Office and the Ghana Law Reform Commission, so as to appoint their own loyalists to those positions. Moreover, incompetence on these boards is rarely punished by any government. The politicized turnover also causes disruptions in the formulation and implementation of policies and programs.

There are no formal conflict of interest rules, although the CHRAJ has published some nonbinding guidelines. Public officeholders are legally required to declare their assets, but the rules do not stipulate that the declarations must be made public. The Atta Mills government indicated that it would require its members to declare their assets publicly, but ministers have yet to comply.

Anticorruption enforcement efforts are conducted primarily by the Serious Fraud Office (SFO) and the CHRAJ. Both organizations face challenges in the performance of their functions. CHRAJ, as noted above, cannot prosecute offenders and must refer investigations to the attorney general for prosecution. In addition, it is poorly funded and has to contend with a high rate of staff attrition. The work of the SFO, established by statute to fight corruption and prevent "serious financial or economic loss to the state," is hampered by structural and logistical constraints. It may also be subjected to political pressure, as its director and much of its board are appointed by the executive and report to the attorney general. A similar situation can be found, to varying degrees, at the Internal Audit Agency, which is charged with auditing ministries, departments, and agencies as well as local government bodies;[40] the Public Procurement Authority (PPA), entrusted with ensuring transparency and competition in the awarding of government contracts;[41] and the CHRAJ. The boards and executives of all these entities are essentially appointed by executive. The practice of creating such watchdog agencies and then giving the executive unfettered discretion to appoint their leaders and control their funding has been criticized by civil society as perverse and self-defeating.

Politicization is often alleged in the corruption prosecutions that do occur. During the Kufuor administration, former officials from the NDC were prosecuted, while corruption scandals that implicated Kufuor administration officials generally led to resignations rather than prosecutions. Thus far, no member of former president Kufuor's government has been prosecuted under the Atta Mills administration.

While the constitution created the position of an "independent" auditor general, the office nevertheless became a political tool during the recent transition when the auditor complied with a government directive to investigate certain activities of the outgoing NPP government.

Victims of corruption can pursue their rights by submitting complaints to the CHRAJ, the SFO, and the police, though the quality of the investigations varies widely. The police have established an internal anticorruption unit called the Police Intelligence and Professional Standards Bureau (PIPS). In addition, a Whistleblowers Act was recently passed, but it has some significant operational limitations.

There is considerable corruption in the secondary school and college education process, with regular reports of leaked examination papers ahead of the annual national exams taken by secondary school students. A highly popular pilot school feeding program has been dogged by allegations of corruption.

Stories of corruption are widely discussed in Ghana's news media. The Richard Anane case noted previously captured headlines for months, as did the scandal over the acquisition of a hotel by the president's son. There is a significant amount of investigative reporting by the media, but it is rarely thorough, and in some cases it is abused for partisan political purposes.

Ghana scored 49 percent on the 2008 Open Budget Index, with reports (and the results from previous years) suggesting an increasing but still insufficient degree of transparency in the budget process.[42] NGOs and even Parliament have little opportunity to make substantive contributions to the process, which begins too late in the year for detailed analysis. There is no budget office to review the budget submissions from the Ministry of Finance, and Parliament lacks the resources and technical capacity it would need for any critical oversight. It has one research department to handle all parliamentary research requests and only one committee room. As a result, parliamentary scrutiny tends to be "hurried, superficial and partisan."[43] A recent attempt by private accounting firms, including KPMG and PricewaterhouseCoopers, to provide pro bono technical support to enhance Parliament's capacity in this area received only lukewarm support from lawmakers.

The constitution guarantees the right to information, and while Ghana still lacks a freedom of information law, a bill was being drafted as of mid-2009. All major political parties have expressed a commitment to pass such legislation.

The PPA, created by the Public Procurement Act of 2003, has established a committee to receive and investigate complaints from individuals and institutions concerning public procurement. It has also set up entity tender committees and review boards within government ministries, departments, and agencies. However, despite these advances, a recent report by the World Bank suggested that only 37 percent of government purchases were subjected to competitive bidding. There are still widespread abuses in the award of contracts, particularly at the local government level.

The distribution of foreign aid is equally opaque. The capacity of state agencies—such as the Audit Service and the Controller and Accountant General's Department—to track and monitor government expenditures of any kind, including foreign aid, is limited by inadequate technical resources and funding. Civil society groups face similar constraints in their own efforts to monitor state spending. They also struggle with an official culture that combines poor recordkeeping with a reluctance to release even the most basic government data. Foreign aid is not normally viewed as a potential source for personal enrichment, but it has been frequently deployed for political and ethnic mobilization.

RECOMMENDATIONS

- Increase the independence of appointees to anticorruption and watchdog agencies and their operational autonomy in order to remove executive discretion over investigations and prosecutions.
- Review the electoral process prior to the next elections, ensuring an adequate timeline for the Electoral Commission to address deficiencies in the voter registry.
- Initiate a program of consensus building on questions of national development and rights to repair damage to national unity stemming from the ethnic and regional tensions unleashed during the 2008 elections.
- Media accountability, competence, and capacity should be addressed, including clarification of the National Media Commission's role in media

oversight and prioritized passage of a broadcasting bill and the right to information bill.
- Address the insufficient capacity of the legislature to oversee executive action by amending the constitution to allow Parliament to introduce legislation that requires spending, while providing sufficient resources for legislators to analyze government budget submissions.
- Continue the emphasis on mainstreaming both gender and disability issues, including by adopting quotas for women's participation in Parliament and executive-appointed positions.

NOTES

For URLs and endnote hyperlinks, please visit the *Countries at the Crossroads* homepage at http://freedomhouse.org/template.cfm?page=139&edition=8.

[1] The military governments were the National Liberation Council (1966–69), the National Redemption Council (1971–75), Supreme Military Councils I and II (1975–79), the Armed Forces Revolutionary Council (June–September, 1979), and the Provisional National Defence Council (1981–93). The short-lived civilian administrations were led by Prime Minister Kofi Abrefa Busia of the Progress Party (1969–72) and President Hilla Limann of the People's National Party (1979–81).

[2] World Bank, "Data & Statistics: Quick Reference Tables."

[3] Afrobarometer, "Popular Attitudes to Democracy in Ghana, 2008," Afrobarometer Briefing Paper No. 51, June 2008.

[4] African Peer Review Mechanism (APRM), *Country Review Report of the Republic of Ghana* (Midrand, South Africa: APRM Secretariat, June 2005); Ghana ranked 7th out of 48 countries in the 2008 Ibrahim Index of African Governance; see Robert I. Rotberg and Rachel M. Gisselquist, *Strengthening African Governance–Ibrahim Index of African Governance: Results and Rankings, 2008* (Cambridge, Mass.: Kennedy School of Government, October 2008), 15.

[5] For a detailed account of Ghana's 2008 elections, see E. Gyimah-Boadi, "Another Step Forward for Ghana," *Journal of Democracy* 20, no. 2 (April 2009): 138–152. For accounts of earlier elections, see E. Gyimah-Boadi, "A Peaceful Turnover in Ghana," *Journal of Democracy* 12, no. 2 (April 2001): 103–17; and E. Gyimah-Boadi, "Ghana's Encouraging Elections: The Challenges Ahead," *Journal of Democracy* 8, no. 2 (April 1997): 78–91.

[6] Afrobarometer, "Poverty Reduction, Economic Growth and Democratization in Sub-Saharan Africa," Afrobarometer Briefing Paper No. 68, May 2009.

[7] Ghana Center for Democratic Development, "Worrisome Developments in the 2008 Polls," *Democracy Watch* 8, no. 2 (May 2009).

[8] Based on projections of 120,000 barrels per day by 2010 and 250,000 by 2012, at US$100 per barrel in March 2008, with the government receiving a 50 percent cut negotiated by the Ghana National Petroleum Corporation, the discovery was expected to yield about US$3 billion in revenue per year during the first term of the new administration. See Anna Cavnar, *Case Studies in Oil Governance: What Ghana Can Learn About Oil Revenue Management from the Rest of the World*, Critical Perspectives no. 23 (Accra: Ghana Center for Democratic Development, October 2008).

[9] The presidential election was also contested by a number of minor parties—the Convention People's Party, the Democratic Freedom Party, the Democratic People's

Party, the People's National Convention, and the Reformed Patriotic Democrats—and one independent presidential candidate.
10. "NDC Demands Accountability from NPP," Ghana News Agency, July 15, 2008.
11. "Presidential Jet: How the Loan Was Debated," *Ghanaian Chronicle*, March 22, 2008,
12. "Oda NDC Chairman Calls for Probe into Rejection of Nominee," Ghana News Agency, May 13, 2009.
13. Civil servants are prohibited by law from taking part in "active" party politics, but there is a lack of clarity about the meaning of this term.
14. Audrey Gadzekpo, "Guardians of Democracy: The Media," in *Ghana: Governance in the Fourth Republic*, ed. B. Agyeman-Duah (Accra: Digibooks, 2008), 195–215.
15. See Gyimah-Boadi, "Another Step Forward for Ghana" and Gadzekpo, "Guardians of Democracy."
16. See International Centre for Prison Studies, "World Prison Brief: Ghana," King's College, London; Daily Graphic/Ghana, "Congestion in Prisons Worsens," Joy Online, August 14, 2009.
17. Commission on Human Rights and Administrative Justice (CHRAJ), *CHRAJ Submission of UPR Report to the UNHCR* (Accra: CHRAJ, 2008).
18. International Centre for Prison Studies, "World Prison Brief: Ghana"; CHRAJ, *Ninth Annual Report* (Accra: CHRAJ, 2006).
19. APRM, *Country Review Report*.
20. "Ghana: Favouring Gold over Farmers," Integrated Regional Information Networks, January 28, 2009.
21. Selorm Amevor, "CHRAJ Indicts Mining Companies of Human Rights Abuses," *Public Agenda*, June 27, 2008.
22. See Ghana Center for Democratic Development, "The 'Hotel Kufuor' Affair: The High Cost of Disregarding Appearances," *Democracy Watch* 6, no. 2 (June 2005); Ghana Center for Democratic Development, "The CHRAJ Report on 'Hotel Kufuor,'" *Democracy Watch* 7, no. 1 (March 2006).
23. Ghana Center for Democratic Development, "The CHRAJ Findings against Dr. Richard Anane and Aftermath," *Democracy Watch* 7, no. 2 (June–November 2006).
24. APRM, *Country Review Report*, 38–41.
25. Richard Crook, *The Role of Faith-Based Associations in Political Change and Development*, Ghana Center for Democratic Development/Overseas Development Institute Policy Brief No. 5 (Accra: CDD–Ghana, November 2005).
26. Ibid.
27. Ghana Statistical Service, *Pattern and Trends of Poverty in Ghana: 1991–2006* (Accra: Ghana Statistical Service, 2007).
28. The National Association of Graduate Students, for example, has faced serious obstacles in obtaining a bargaining certificate that would allow it to negotiate with the government for salaries independently of the teachers' union.
29. AfriMAP, Open Society Initiative for West Africa, and the Institute for Democratic Governance, *Ghana: Justice Sector and the Rule of Law* (Dakar, Senegal: Open Society Initiative for West Africa, 2007).
30. On the very rare occasions when it sits to review its own earlier decisions, a minimum of seven justices is required (Constitution, Article 133).
31. K. Prempeh, "The Challenge of Constitutionalism," in *Ghana: Governance in the Fourth Republic*, ed. B. Agyeman-Duah (Accra: Digibooks, 2008), 97.
32. "Ghana: Vigilante Groups Fill Security Vacuum," IRIN, June 23, 2008.
33. "Suspected Thief Lynched," *Daily Graphic*, February 23, 2006.

34 Commonwealth Human Rights Initiative, *The Police, the People, the Politics: Police Accountability in Ghana* (New Delhi: Commonwealth Human Rights Initiative, 2007), 57.
35 Business Anti-Corruption Portal, "Ghana Country Profile: Police."
36 "Family of Victim of Military Brutality Expresses Gratitude to Public Agenda," *Africa News*, January 25, 2008.
37 "Ga Mantse Comments on Ga Lands Issue," Ghana News Agency, March 25, 2009.
38 World Bank, "Featured Snapshot Report: Ghana," in *2007 Enterprise Surveys* (Washington, D.C.: World Bank, 2007).
39 Ghana Integrity Initiative, *"Voice of the People" Survey (Southern Ghana): Project Completion Report* (Accra: Ghana Integrity Initiative, July 2005).
40 Internal Audit Agency Act, 2003, sections 5, 9.
41 Public Procurement Act, 2003, Act 663, section 4.
42 Open Budget Initiative, "Ghana," in *Open Budget Index 2008* (Washington, D.C.: Open Budget Initiative, 2008).
43 E. Gyimah-Boadi et al., *What Are the Drivers of Change in Ghana?*, Ghana Center for Democratic Development/Overseas Development Institute Policy Brief No. 1 (Accra: CDD-Ghana, November 2005).

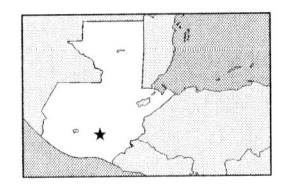

GUATEMALA

CAPITAL: Guatemala City
POPULATION: 14.0 million
GNI PER CAPITA (PPP): $4,690

SCORES	2006	2010
ACCOUNTABILITY AND PUBLIC VOICE:	4.33	4.38
CIVIL LIBERTIES:	3.36	3.48
RULE OF LAW:	3.18	3.26
ANTICORRUPTION AND TRANSPARENCY:	3.21	3.33

(scores are based on a scale of 0 to 7, with 0 representing weakest and 7 representing strongest performance)

Anita Isaacs

INTRODUCTION

Guatemala's long history of political repression and instability culminated in nearly four decades of armed conflict (1960–96) that pitted leftist guerrillas against the army and paramilitary groups aligned with the economic elite and supported by the United States. Although peace accords signed in December 1996 brought the conflict to a close, Guatemala still faces monumental challenges in its quest to consolidate peace and build a firm democratic foundation. While economic growth accelerated prior to 2009, the country has yet to effectively address the entrenched poverty, inequality, and social exclusion that have marred it since the colonial era. Even the best-intentioned policymakers have been hard pressed to transform the comprehensive peace agreement into meaningful democratic reforms.

During much of the internal conflict, a series of military or military-dominated governments conducted violent counterinsurgency campaigns, the most brutal of which took place between 1979 and 1983 under the direction of Generals Lucas García and Efraín Ríos Montt. The country's truth commission, mandated to clarify the nature of wartime violence, concluded that the conflict constituted genocide. Indigenous civilians made up 83 percent of the roughly 200,000 casualties, with many perishing in massacres and scorched-earth tactics that destroyed more than 400 Mayan communities.

Anita Isaacs is the Benjamin R. Collins Professor of Social Sciences and an associate professor of Political Science at Haverford College. She has published several articles on Guatemalan politics and is the author of the forthcoming book *The Politics of Transitional Justice in Guatemala*.

The country's stark political and socioeconomic divisions continue to be substantially drawn along ethnic lines. Although Guatemala's indigenous groups, comprised mainly of speakers of Mayan languages, make up at least 45 percent of the population, they have been consistently excluded from mainstream economic, social, and political life. The gulf between the political elite and the indigenous population is one of the most profound challenges confronting Guatemalan democracy today.

There has been some gradual democratic progress. Following decades of turmoil, a new constitution enacted in 1985 paved the way for elected civilian rule in 1986. The 1996 peace agreement provided for the demobilization of the Guatemalan National Revolutionary Unity (URNG) guerrillas and their legalization as a political group. In addition to its thorough and damning catalogue of abuses, the truth commission issued a series of key reform recommendations designed to strengthen peace and democracy.

Nonetheless, the country continues to struggle with the war's brutal legacy. Former combatants enjoy virtual impunity for wartime human rights violations. Many former military officers moved from combat to crime, organizing criminal networks that operate at will. Increasingly fueled by the drug trade that has affected the entire region, local and transnational criminal groups—in which former military and police officers play an integral role—have captured parts of the Guatemalan state and fostered untenable levels of violence in society. The year 2008 was among the most violent in the country's history, with over 6,200 reported homicides. In addition to ordinary citizens, the victims included human rights defenders, union leaders, journalists, and judges working on cases of corruption and organized crime. Government countermeasures are constrained by insufficient political will and a major shortfall in human and material resources when compared with those at the disposal of criminal organizations.

The 2007 elections, which brought Álvaro Colom to the presidency, were reflective of Guatemala's progress as well as its problems. The voting was generally considered free and fair, peacefully replacing a probusiness government with a social democratic one. At the same time, the campaign was marred by the deaths of 50 people—including candidates, their family members, and supporters—along with numerous allegations of candidate ties to organized crime. Other aspects of governance are similarly conflicting. While the government opened wartime military archives to citizens, General Ríos Montt continues to enjoy immunity from prosecution thanks to his seat in Congress. A wide variety of civil society groups operate without government interference, but the state is unable to protect them from intimidation and violence. Since taking power, the Colom administration has demonstrated considerable resolve in improving governance practices. Nevertheless, due to both the magnitude of the country's problems and the weakness of national political institutions, the leadership faces an uphill battle.

ACCOUNTABILITY AND PUBLIC VOICE 4.38

FREE AND FAIR ELECTORAL LAWS AND ELECTIONS	4.25
EFFECTIVE AND ACCOUNTABLE GOVERNMENT	3.00
CIVIC ENGAGEMENT AND CIVIC MONITORING	6.00
MEDIA INDEPENDENCE AND FREEDOM OF EXPRESSION	4.29

In the 2007 national elections, Álvaro Colom of the center-left National Unity of Hope (UNE) party won the presidency with nearly 53 percent of the vote in a runoff against retired general Otto Pérez Molina of the right-wing Patriotic Party (PP).[1] Colom and Pérez had won 28 and 24 percent in the first round, respectively; the winner would have needed more than 50 percent to avoid a runoff. Local and international observers applauded the free, fair, and competitive balloting, highlighting both the rapid tabulation of results and the swift and unequivocal concession speech by the losing candidate.[2] The positive outcome stemmed in part from a 2006 package of electoral reforms designed to enhance participation and fairness.[3] A rural registration drive increased the voter rolls by more than 50 percent, and voter participation was facilitated by the establishment of 6,000 additional polling places. The resulting rural turnout figure of about 60 percent surpassed the urban turnout for the first time.[4] Although the three largest parties received the bulk of media attention, with some 55 percent devoted to Colom during the runoff, observers commended the campaign coverage as mostly fair and objective, especially during the initial round.[5]

Despite the reforms, there were a number of problems with the electoral process. Voter registries were accurate for only 60 percent of the voters; in several instances the number of registered voters exceeded local population figures; and an estimated 20 to 30 percent of eligible Guatemalans were not officially registered (many did not even possess an official identity document, which was required to cast a ballot). Electoral authorities also allegedly permitted members of the police to cast ballots, violating the ban on voting by security forces.[6] Meanwhile, new campaign finance regulations were undermined by the Supreme Electoral Tribunal's lack of oversight and enforcement capabilities. Roughly 40 percent of the parties competing in the 2007 elections did not provide the tribunal with their campaign budgets as required, and 12 percent did not submit final financial reports.[7] Weak enforcement and oversight, indicative of an ongoing political resistance to the new rules, may also cloud the next elections, scheduled for 2011. Notably, a lack of funding, competition over contracts, and local political authorities' refusal to provide their civil registries have all made for delays in the adoption of a single identity card designed to guard against the current problems with alleged multiple and fraudulent voting.[8]

Although mostly free of fraud and voter intimidation, the 2007 elections were marred by political violence on a scale not witnessed since the 1985 elections, which were conducted in the midst of the internal conflict. A total of 61 acts of violence targeting political candidates and party officials were registered during 2006 and 2007. Attackers victimized UNE members on 16 separate occasions, killing eight people associated with the Colom campaign.[9] While direct violence diminished during the runoff, the campaign degenerated from the earlier debate on programs and policy into a mudslinging contest in which the two sides traded accusations of ties to organized crime.[10]

Ultimately, political violence and negative campaigning trumped electoral reforms to depress voter turnout. In the first round, which included mayoral and congressional elections, turnout was 60 percent, a two-point increase from the corresponding 2003 figure. In the presidential runoff, turnout fell to 47 percent, marking a one-point drop from the previous election.[11]

The 16 parties competing in the 2007 elections represented diverse interests and policy positions. Colom's victory, assisted by massive support from the rural indigenous poor, signaled a shift to the political left, in keeping with a broader Latin American trend. Breaking two barriers, an indigenous female candidate, Nobel Peace Prize winner Rigoberta Menchú, also competed for the presidency. Her disappointing seventh-place finish, with just over 3 percent of the vote, was attributed to her late entry into the race, at a point when Mayan politicians and the indigenous electorate had already committed to other candidates, and to a campaign strategy that at times appeared to take indigenous votes for granted.

The constitution and laws guarantee the independence of the three branches of government and delineate their respective functions, such as congressional budget oversight, executive veto power, and judicial responsibility to uphold the constitution and the rule of law. While the Colom administration has established a more productive working relationship with Congress, checks and balances between the two branches continue to be used more for obstructive political purposes than to ensure oversight and accountability. Legislative logjams, while less severe in recent years, have held up important bills on mining, the right of indigenous peoples to be consulted on matters affecting them, and the annual budget.

The weak institutionalization of political parties, which tend to serve merely as electoral vehicles, aggravates the dysfunctional relations between the branches. In the 2007 elections, Colom's UNE won 48 out of 158 seats, increasing its representation by a third. The center-right Grand National Alliance (GANA) followed with 37 seats, while the PP won 30 seats. Several smaller parties made up the remainder. These results have had little bearing on the structure of congressional coalitions. During the first year of the Colom administration alone, some 35 lawmakers defected from the parties with which they had run for election. Ten of the representatives who abandoned the UNE denounced excessive meddling in legislative affairs by the president and his wife, Sandra de Colom, who was seen as an unelected power broker with ambitions to run as the UNE presidential candidate in 2011.[12]

The state remains largely captive to organized criminal networks, including drug cartels. These networks are widely believed to have funded the campaigns of several candidates in the 2007 elections and have also infiltrated the judiciary, where poorly paid judges are regularly exposed to bribes, intimidation, harassment, and violence. The police are similarly afflicted. The special counter-narcotics police force has been completely dismantled because of the high levels of penetration by organized crime, and in August 2009 the former head of the Criminal Investigation Division of the National Civilian Police was arrested and charged with trafficking one ton of cocaine.[13]

The civil service is considered one of the most incompetent in the region, scoring at half the regional average in a 2005 Inter-American Development Bank assessment.[14] While the Colom administration has backed reforms of the 1968 civil service law, the proposed legislation continues to encounter resistance from a political class that regards civil service appointments as a valuable form of patronage.[15]

Unlike its predecessor, the Colom administration has sought to distance itself somewhat from the traditional economic oligarchy. Fewer members of the economic elite occupy key ministries, and certain legislative proposals have engendered bitter confrontations between the government and the private sector. Colom has picked his battles, however. He was perceived by some segments of civil society as having capitulated to the private sector in passing a watered-down munitions law, but the government stood up to the Chambers of Agriculture and Construction on enhanced regulation of the quality and distribution of fertilizers and control over infrastructure projects.[16] While the latter two items are consistent with UNE pledges to promote equitable development and enhance transparency, reducing the preserve of traditional private sector actors that rely on backroom deals to secure contracts, the new policies could simply feed state corruption and foster a new economic elite that is more closely allied with the current administration.

Civil society organizations have played an increasingly prominent role in the country's political process. Operating mostly without legal constraints, civic organizations have prodded the Colom administration to make good on its promise to address the needs of poorer and marginalized groups, including the disabled, indigenous people, and women and children. However, these organizations are often heard but not listened to, and members of human rights, labor, and environmentalist groups figure disproportionately among the victims of the country's rampant violence (see Civil Liberties section).

The Colom administration has sent mixed signals regarding the role of the media. Constitutional guarantees of freedom of expression were bolstered by legislation approved in October 2008 that called for the protection of Guatemalan artists and diversity of artistic expression. The September 2008 passage of a long-overdue access to information law came on the heels of the signing of the Declaration of Chapultepec, in which the government agreed that official advertising could not be used, as it sometimes had been in the past, to reward or punish the media.[17] In addition, the Guatemalan state does not hinder access to the internet. However, Mexican entrepreneur Ángel González controls four of the country's six free-to-air television stations; the remaining two licenses are held by the Congress, which has yet to launch its channel, and the Mayan Linguistic Academy, whose station operates on a very irregular basis and does not receive the public funding it desperately requires. A journalist who complained of influence peddling between González and the Guatemalan political class was subject to a public campaign of harassment, both on television and on the radio stations that González controls.[18] Furthermore, in February 2009, the government abruptly canceled all state advertising in the print media while either maintaining or increasing television allocations. It cited budgetary cutbacks for the decision, but the newspapers have appealed to the Inter-American Commission on Human Rights and the Inter American Press Association, suspecting a repetition of previous administrations' efforts to force fledgling and independent news organizations into bankruptcy.[19]

Alarming rates of violence against journalists have provoked self-censorship. Between 2006 and April 2009, six journalists were killed and another was abducted, and scores have faced attacks and threats while covering gangs and street violence, drug trafficking, organized crime, abuses dating to the civil war, and even the presidential campaign. Impunity for crimes against journalists prevails, making those based in rural areas understandably reluctant to cover sensitive stories; those who do frequently publish their work without bylines.[20]

CIVIL LIBERTIES 3.48

PROTECTION FROM STATE TERROR, UNJUSTIFIED IMPRISONMENT, AND TORTURE	1.88
GENDER EQUITY	3.67
RIGHTS OF ETHNIC, RELIGIOUS, AND OTHER DISTINCT GROUPS	3.50
FREEDOM OF CONSCIENCE AND BELIEF	5.33
FREEDOM OF ASSOCIATION AND ASSEMBLY	3.00

In recent years, endemic violence has seriously crippled Guatemala's progress in the realm of civil liberties. According to the human rights ombudsman, 2008 was the most violent year in the country's history, a startling claim given the genocidal proportions of the 1960–96 civil conflict. Homicide rates have increased by an estimated 137 percent over the past decade, and over 6,200 Guatemalans were murdered in 2008.[21] The problem is exacerbated by impunity and state paralysis; for example, some 98 percent of all attacks on human rights defenders reportedly go unpunished.[22]

While attacks on politicians ebbed following the violent electoral campaign, human rights defenders continue to operate in a climate of fear. The decline in attacks in 2007—to 195, from 277 in 2006—has proven temporary, as 220 assaults on human rights defenders were reported in 2008, and 257 were recorded between January and August 2009.[23]

Defenders of social and economic rights, such as trade unionists and indigenous activists, are targeted most often, followed closely by those focusing on abuses committed during the armed conflict. Illegal and clandestine security organizations are presumed responsible for the vast majority of these crimes. They have infiltrated state institutions, including the police, the military, and political parties, severely crippling the state's willingness and ability to protect its citizens.[24] Complicating matters further, urban areas have been afflicted by gang-related violence, while rural Guatemala has suffered from an incursion of Mexican drug traffickers as well as private security forces hired by landowners and transnational corporations to repress indigenous community organizers engaged in land disputes. The government has done little to denounce, investigate, or prosecute this violence, and it tends to criminalize rural activists and protesters. There were 388 documented cases of arrest warrants issued for members of indigenous peasant communities involved in land disputes between 2004 and 2007.[25] In the northeastern Izabal region, a police raid in early 2008 claimed the life of peasant leader Mario Caal and led to the arrest of fellow activist Ramiro Choc. Charged with theft and usurpation of lands, Choc received an eight-year prison sentence in March 2009, while Caal's killers remain at large.[26]

Reinforcing existing constitutional protections, legislation passed in October 2006 outlined the rehabilitative functions of prisons and defined inmate rights and responsibilities. Nonetheless, routine violations persist, including frequent excessive use of force by police against suspected criminals. Although Guatemala is a signatory to the UN Convention against Torture, there has been little effort to train the police in legal interrogation methods, strengthen legislation criminalizing torture, investigate its incidence, or sanction its perpetrators. The human rights ombudsman's office claims that within the criminal justice system, torture remains an acceptable means of securing evidence.[27] Inmates held in both the national penitentiary system and regional detention centers are regularly denied their legal and constitutional rights. Frequently detained for extended periods without trial, they tend to live in unsanitary conditions and are deprived of food, conjugal visits, medical attention, and access to education.[28] These conditions exacerbate prison violence, which often takes the form of clashes between rival street gangs that enjoy easy access to weapons smuggled in by guards.[29]

The administrations of both Colom and his predecessor, Óscar Berger (2004–08), have adopted measures to ameliorate key aspects of the human rights situation. After a prolonged political battle, the International Commission Against Impunity in Guatemala (CICIG), headed by UN-appointed Spanish jurist Carlos Castresana, was established in August 2007. Initially granted a two-year mandate, the commission was tasked with investigating the structure, operations, and financing of illegal security groups and clandestine networks; promoting their dismantlement; investigating, prosecuting (in cooperation with the attorney general's office), and punishing crimes committed by their members; and recommending legal and institutional reforms designed to ensure the permanent eradication of these networks. The CICIG has made small steps toward uprooting Guatemala's culture of impunity,[30] removing 1,700 police officers and 50 police chiefs with links to organized crime.[31] It has also proposed and advocated for numerous legal reforms and pressured the state to prosecute in a number of high-profile cases. However, success remains dependent on the political will of those in other institutions, who do not always rule in the CICIG's favor or embrace its proposals.

The Colom government has also enacted important legal and institutional reforms, including stiff criminal penalties for crimes against women and legislation to stem human trafficking. The illicit trade has involved young women and children sold into prostitution, as well as children sold and sometimes stolen for adoption or even organ harvesting.[32] Such concerns led the U.S. government to ban adoptions from Guatemala in 2008.

Among other measures, the Colom administration has secured passage of legislation regulating the possession and use of firearms, and extended the CICIG's mandate for a further two years. It also erected a human rights unit within the police force's Criminal Investigation Division and set up a Body for the Analysis of Attacks Against Human Rights Defenders under the auspices of the vice minister of security. The latter entity convenes representatives from the Interior Ministry, the police, and the intelligence services, as well as national and international nongovernmental organizations (NGOs), to develop a coordinated response. The human rights ombudsman's office (Procuraduría de los Derechos Humanos, or PDH) and the presidential Commission on Human Rights (COPREDEH), headed by a respected human rights defender, maintain their watchdog and advisory functions, and COPREDEH has enhanced the provision of police protection to threatened civil society activists.

These various initiatives have yet to ameliorate the troubled human rights environment.[33] In the absence of effective witness protection programs and reforms to a police force that is seen as abusive and corrupt, victims avoid reporting violations and remain reluctant to accept police accompaniment. The two new human rights entities are hampered by a lack of clear parameters for their work, and they were dealt another blow by the recent unexplained dismissal of their directors, who had worked to establish interagency communication.[34]

In the face of spiraling violence, the government unveiled a broad security pact in April 2009, proposing a set of measures including prison, police, and judicial reform. Experts were quick to denounce the pact, questioning the clarity of the proposals and the political commitment to transform them into reality.[35]

The constitution provides for the equality of all individuals, but in practice, the rights of women and indigenous people are often neglected or denied. An analysis of government spending between January and May 2008 reveals the disparity between political rhetoric and the actual allocation of resources, with women's issues receiving just 0.17 percent, and programs for indigenous people receiving 0.14 percent.[36]

While the law prohibits discrimination and violence against women, both remain widespread. Guatemalan women, particularly indigenous women, continue to face workplace bias as well as sexual harassment. Women tend to be employed in low-paying agricultural and service sector jobs, and are far more likely than men to work in the informal sector. Women and children also account for the bulk of domestic servants and workers in export-processing zones, two job types that are largely unregulated and commonly feature exploitative conditions.[37]

Violence against women persists, with an estimated 60 percent of women facing domestic violence. Some 6,000 women filed complaints of sexual assault and 658 cases of femicide were reported in 2008, with the latter number virtually unchanged from the previous year. In May 2008, the Public Ministry launched a program to provide comprehensive assistance to female victims of violence. Long-overdue legislation has also been enacted to curb femicide and criminalize sexual violence, exploitation, and even harassment.[38] There have been tentative signs of progress in investigating and prosecuting those responsible for violence against women. The women's congressional caucus reported that arrests were made for 254 of the 600 capture orders lodged in 2008, and several individuals found guilty of rape and femicide have recently been sentenced to the harsher prison terms set out in the new legislation. However, expectations that impunity will diminish considerably are dampened by the lack of training for police and their continued reluctance to become involved in domestic disputes. The government has failed to allocate adequate resources to the investigation of violence against women, and it recently decided to close the police unit dedicated to the collection and analysis of data on such crimes.[39]

Although Guatemala boasts the second-greatest participation rate for women's organizations in the region, women remain seriously underrepresented in political positions. There is only one female cabinet member, women hold just 19 of the 158 seats in Congress, and only 8 of 332 mayors are women.[40] Women fare slightly better in the judiciary. Of the 13 members of the Supreme Court, two are women, while one woman serves on the five-member Constitutional Court.

Indigenous Guatemalans continue to face discrimination that is both cultural and structural. While they comprise roughly half of the country's population, the indigenous Mayans account for about three-quarters of Guatemalans who live in conditions of poverty or extreme poverty. Mayans also have significantly less access to health care and education, and their employment opportunities are considerably more circumscribed. A number of steps have created a somewhat more tolerant environment, including constitutional provisions; the passage of a peace accord on indigenous rights and identity; the ratification of international conventions; and even legislation that criminalizes racial discrimination, protects Mayan lifestyles and customs, and calls for bilingual education. Still, much more remains to be done to transform prevailing attitudes and structures. Some 92 percent of those queried in a May 2009 survey described their country as racist, with over three-quarters noting that the indigenous population suffers the greatest levels of discrimination. Moreover, the constitutional recognition of their rights has yet to be supported by a specific legal framework, and existing laws are rarely enforced. Only one of the 196 complaints formally registered by the Commission Against Racism and Discrimination since the passage of an antiracism law in October 2002 has yielded a criminal sentence.[41]

Colom, who campaigned as the indigenous candidate, rewarded his Mayan supporters with a single cabinet position, minister of culture and sport, and the largely symbolic creation of a Presidential Commission to Combat Racism and Discrimination Against Indigenous Peoples and a Presidential Secretariat for Indigenous Peoples. The newly elected Congress includes just 18 indigenous deputies, four of whom are female. Indigenous citizenship rights are poorly guaranteed by a legal system in which only 14 percent of the police force and one Supreme Court justice are Mayan, and despite some improvements, there remains a severe shortage of bilingual judges and court interpreters.[42]

My Family Making Progress (Mi Familia Progresa) stands out as the most substantive initiative addressing the needs of impoverished and marginalized Guatemalans, many of whom are female and indigenous. Modeled on similar endeavors in Mexico and Brazil, the program provides cash transfers of roughly US$40 a month to poor parents who are willing to guarantee the health, nutrition, and education of their children. The program was welcomed for its focus on breaking the cycle of poverty, but critics objected to the tight control exercised over the program by the executive branch, the central role played by the president's wife in light of her perceived political aspirations, and an initial lack of transparency that included failure to release lists of beneficiaries to either auditors or legislators. Partly in response, the government transferred the program to the Ministry of Education, embarked on an external evaluation of its efficacy, and improved access to data. Still, recent budget reallocations that increased outlays to Mi Familia Progresa while cutting funds to key ministries have done little to assuage concerns about the program's patronage aims.[43]

While the constitution does not contain specific prohibitions against discrimination based on disability, the law provides for some protections, including equal access to public facilities. In addition, in March 2009 the government ratified the UN Convention on the Rights of Disabled Peoples.[44] Nevertheless, the rights of disabled people are often violated in practice.[45] The state upholds freedom of religious belief, avoids restrictions on religious practice, and does not seek to regulate either faith-based organizations or religious instruction in schools. Mayan communities, however, have been engaged in a prolonged battle to acquire administrative control over their religious sites, many of which are official tourist venues that impose entry fees.

The government recognizes freedom of association and assembly, including the right to form independent labor unions and to organize, mobilize, and advocate for peaceful purposes. However, labor legislation does not comply with ratified International Labor Organization (ILO) conventions. Onerous membership requirements impede the creation of unions and collective bargaining, and the right to strike is legally circumscribed. The government reserves the right to ban strikes that it deems "gravely prejudicial to the country's essential activities and public services," and to compel workers to resolve disputes through mediation and arbitration boards. Organized labor has protested the government's use of emergency-situation arguments to suppress protests, and has argued that the widespread arrest and imprisonment of union demonstrators is a violation of ILO conventions.[46] Weak labor inspection panels and lax enforcement of existing laws in both the private and public sectors, including by the Public Ministry and the Ministry of Justice, further undermine worker rights. Employers evade punishment for failing to pay wages and benefits, engaging in illegal firings, using subcontractors to circumvent labor obligations, and retaliating against labor organizers with measures including dismissal and blacklisting.[47]

Over the past year, labor leaders have become the top targets in the escalating spiral of attacks against human rights defenders. There were five recorded attacks against union activists in 2005, and the figure increased to 13 in 2006 and 15 in 2007 before jumping to 47 in 2008. Labor leaders have been harassed, threatened, and illegally detained, often during peaceful marches and demonstrations that tend to substitute for strikes; seven labor leaders have also been assassinated in the past two years. Security forces have failed to halt the attacks, which are believed to be the work of thugs hired by private companies, and investigations have been grindingly slow. There has been just one arrest in these cases as of July 2009, whereas national security provisions were quickly invoked to justify the detention of 49 transport workers for striking in early 2008.[48]

RULE OF LAW   3.26

INDEPENDENT JUDICIARY	3.60
PRIMACY OF RULE OF LAW IN CIVIL AND CRIMINAL MATTERS	3.20
ACCOUNTABILITY OF SECURITY FORCES AND MILITARY TO CIVILIAN AUTHORITIES	3.25
PROTECTION OF PROPERTY RIGHTS	3.00

While the independence of the judiciary is guaranteed by law, this principle is not upheld in practice. Political interference remains pronounced throughout the judicial branch, including the Supreme Court.[49] International support for judicial reform has focused on improving the quality of judges, who are obliged to pass competitive exams and undergo training in judicial ethics.[50] However, the training has tended to focus on judges in trial courts rather than the court of appeals or Supreme Court, and it has not been accompanied by the introduction of systematic performance reviews. Formal complaints lodged against judges are typically dismissed and rarely lead to disciplinary action. Of the 910 complaints filed between 2006 and 2008, only three resulted in the dismissal of judicial personnel.[51]

Constitutional and legal experts place much of the blame for judicial corruption and bias on an appointment process that allows the president to designate top law enforcement officials, and Congress to appoint judges to the Supreme Court, which controls the remaining judicial appointments.[52] Although many countries have similar processes, politicization in Guatemala is complicated by criminal penetration of state institutions, allowing powerful and often shadowy political and economic interests to effectively determine the composition of the country's judiciary and by extension its rulings. Joining forces with civil society organizations, the CICIG waged a political battle with legislators, pressing for reforms of the selection process that would improve transparency and enhance the input of legal experts.[53] It took the scandalous assassination of lawyer Rodrigo Rosenberg to generate the political momentum for passage of the legislation in late May 2009. [See box.]

Noncompliance with judicial decisions is less of a problem in Guatemala than the judicial system's failure to render decisions, as evidenced by the widely cited 98 percent impunity rate.[54] The inefficiency and inefficacy of the justice system is worsened by the influence of criminally linked political and economic groups, which exploit legal devices like the right of *amparo,* or injunction, to bog down legal proceedings and suborn judges. Members of the judiciary are also commonly threatened and assaulted, with 119 reported attacks in 2007 and 76 during the first half of 2008, including seven assassinations of judges and prosecutors. Like other cases of human rights violations, these are rarely investigated and almost never resolved.[55]

Criminal defendants are presumed innocent until proven guilty. They are guaranteed a fair, public, and timely hearing, and the right to independent counsel. Over the past several years, legal proceedings have been accelerated, although illegal and prolonged detention without a court appearance or trial still occurs. Approximately 40 percent of those behind bars are awaiting trial. In addition, while the law limits pretrial detention to three months, pretrial detainees often spend years in prison. The number of public defenders increased by 31 percent between 2006 and 2008, and their caseload expanded by 22 percent during the same period. International donations compensate for state funding shortfalls in the provision of public defense.

Some promising programs designed to enhance access to legal counsel have encountered roadblocks. Planned 24-hour and mobile courts have yet to be established in the country's often remote interior. While the numbers of bilingual judicial personnel have risen slightly, most of the increase has been among administrative and auxiliary personnel rather than judges, and the languages spoken do not begin to approximate Guatemala's linguistic diversity. Language and distance thus continue to impede access to the judicial system for the majority of rural residents.[56]

In contrast to the judicial selection process, candidates for attorney general are vetted by civil society organizations, and only three of the seven members of the Public Ministry Council are selected by the legislature. The relatively transparent selection process has not, however, translated into transparency on the job. Public Ministry officials are widely viewed as corrupt, and the country's chief prosecutor, Juan Luis Florido, was forced to resign in July 2008 over alleged ties to organized crime.[57] In a promising departure from the norm, assisted by the presence of the CICIG, several former and current public officials—including former president Alfonso Portillo (2000–04) and president of Congress and UNE member Eduardo Meyer Maldonado—have either faced criminal investigation or were formally charged with crimes involving abuse of public funds during the past year. The CICIG has assumed the Portillo brief as one of its high-profile cases. In addition, it is prosecuting Public Ministry officials and judges accused of corruption, and serving as a plaintiff in another major case, in which six military officers—including General Enrique Ríos Sosa, the son of former dictator and president of Congress Efraín Ríos Montt—stand accused of embezzling millions from the Defense Ministry budget.[58]

Over the past decade, the police and the military have become increasingly subordinate to democratically elected civilian leaders. However, the relationship remains contentious and fragile, especially regarding accountability for wartime violations of human rights, as evidenced by the military's failure to surrender two of four solicited operational plans detailing the army's counterinsurgency strategy.[59] Police corruption and violations of human rights also remain widespread. The CICIG's efforts notwithstanding, members of the National Civilian Police are still believed by the human rights community to regularly perpetrate and cover up crimes, at once exacerbating and benefiting from the prevailing culture of impunity. In one recent example, a retired military officer, two retired members of the police force, and two active-duty officers were among the nine members of a crime syndicate arrested on September 11, 2009, as alleged material authors of the Rosenberg assassination.[60]

Although the state guarantees property rights and prohibits expropriation, contracts can be difficult to enforce. Moreover, there are over 500 ongoing land disputes in the country, and 33 peasants engaged in land disputes were murdered between 2004 and 2008. As the human rights ombudsman has emphasized, these cases indicate the persistent struggles generated by landlessness, although they also reflect a dramatic intensification of conflicts in which indigenous and peasant leaders seek to defend their land rights against major landowners and, increasingly, mining corporations and hydroelectric projects.[61] Indigenous demands for consultation on land use, a right granted to them by the government-ratified UN Declaration on the Rights of Indigenous Peoples as well as ILO Convention 169, have gone largely unheeded. A grievance lodged with the ILO in 2007 appears to have only exacerbated the violence perpetrated against the complainants and rural protesters more generally, who suffered nine violent attacks during the first two months of 2009 alone. The government has done little to denounce, investigate, or prosecute the culprits or to curb the growth of private security forces that are believed to be involved. In a sign of low confidence in Guatemala's public institutions, the number of private security agents now exceeds that of police personnel.

ANTICORRUPTION AND TRANSPARENCY 3.33

ENVIRONMENT TO PROTECT AGAINST CORRUPTION	3.25
PROCEDURES AND SYSTEMS TO ENFORCE ANTICORRUPTION LAWS	2.75
EXISTENCE OF ANTICORRUPTION NORMS, STANDARDS, AND PROTECTIONS	3.00
GOVERNMENTAL TRANSPARENCY	4.33

Entrenched corruption continues to pose a serious challenge to democratic governance in Guatemala. The staggering levels witnessed during the Portillo government (2000–04) declined during the Berger administration (2004–08), and this trend persisted during the first year of Colom's presidency. The progress is reflected in steadily improved rankings and scores on Transparency International's Corruption Perceptions Index. After being positioned close to the bottom of the list of countries surveyed in 2004, Guatemala gained its highest ranking yet in 2008, placing 96th out of 180 countries. But while the country's score has registered a similar upward trend, it reached only 3.1 out of a possible 10 in 2008, indicating the persistent severity of corruption.[62] In a recent survey, 83 percent of respondents regarded officeholders as corrupt, and only 40 percent regarded their country's democratic institutions as legitimate.[63]

While no single institution is responsible for combating corruption, the Presidential Commission for Transparency and the attorney general's office both hold legal mandates to carry out anticorruption efforts and address denunciations. These agencies do not enjoy protection from political interference, which limits their effectiveness.[64] The comptroller general and the CICIG also play a role in combating corruption. The extension of the CICIG's mandate for an additional two years, coupled with the establishment of a Commission to Promote Transparency and Corruption that convenes governmental and civil society actors, highlight the government's willingness to sustain the Berger administration's focus on eradicating corruption, as do the extradition of former president Portillo and the resignation of Congress president Eduardo Meyer Maldonado, both in 2008. However, the October 2008 extradition of Portillo, who had fled to Mexico to escape corruption charges in 2004, was marred by his quick release on US$132,000 in bail, prompting concerns that his corruption trial would only make a further mockery of the judicial system.[65]

Corruption remains deeply embedded in Guatemalan governance. The regulatory environment remains cumbersome, opaque, and inconsistent, contributing to a high incidence of bribery and the tendency of companies to

EDITOR'S NOTE: THE RODRIGO ROSENBERG CASE

On the morning of May 10, 2009, Guatemalan lawyer Rodrigo Rosenberg Mazano was shot and killed by gunmen while riding a bicycle in Guatemala City. Witnesses saw two vehicles, which were caught on tape by security cameras, speed away from the scene. The next day, a video recorded by Rosenberg several days prior to his death surfaced in which he accused the president of Guatemala of ordering his murder, stating, "If you are watching this message it is because I was assassinated by President Álvaro Colom, with help from Gustavo Alejos." Rosenberg tied his fate to his involvement with clients Khalil Musa, a prominent businessman and member of the Rural Development Bank (Banrural), and Marjorie Musa, his daughter, who were both assassinated on April 14. According to Rosenberg, his clients had gained insider knowledge of a scheme whereby President Colom, his wife, and their inner circle were laundering public funds through Banrural. Rosenberg accused President Colom and his associates of ordering their deaths, as well as his own, in order to silence the scandal.

The video plunged Guatemala into deep political turmoil. Tens of thousands of protesters took to the streets to demand Colom's resignation, while an equivalent number came out in support of the president, and several politicians requested that the president temporarily step down so as to ensure an impartial investigation into Rosenberg's death. The media fueled the public reaction by repeatedly airing the video. Colom vigorously rejected Rosenberg's accusations and solicited the help of international investigative bodies in the case. The president also claimed that the video was part of a right-wing conspiracy against him waged by opponents linked to organized crime. In September and October, Guatemalan authorities arrested 12 suspects, including gang members, drug traffickers, and police in connection with the assassination. On January 12, 2010, the CICIG revealed its conclusion: Rosenberg ordered his own assassination. According to the investigation, Rosenberg, emotionally distressed following the murder of his girlfriend (Ms. Musa), solicited the help of his ex-wife's cousins to arrange the death of a supposed extortionist—whose description was in fact that of Rosenberg himself. The cousins, oblivious to the deception, hired hitmen to carry out the killing. The assassins are currently awaiting trial for the murder, while the two cousins reportedly remain in hiding. President Colom and his associates were cleared of all charges.

bypass public registration and operate in an unregulated informal sector with ties to organized crime.[66] The political class continues to use public office as a means of personal enrichment.[67] Although officials who manage public funds or earn more than 8,000 quetzals (US$1,000) a month are subject to financial disclosure laws, these and other oversight provisions are weakly enforced by the underfunded and understaffed comptroller general's office.[68] The latest round of proposed reforms—including improved contracting procedures, revisions to parliamentary immunity rules, financial disclosure upgrades, and tax modernization—have stalled amid political disputes.[69]

The roughly 20 percent of Guatemalans (and 45 percent of those with higher education) who claimed in a recent survey to have been victims of corruption in 2008 have neither adequate means nor a secure environment in which to seek redress. Allegations of corruption are aired in the media, but whistleblowers fear retaliation for implicating public officials, a concern most graphically illustrated by the Rosenberg case. Losing bidders on government contracts are not afforded an official review process other than litigation, which they rarely pursue given the inefficiency and corruption of the judicial system. Similarly, a special unit within the attorney general's office dedicated to solving cases of corruption reported receiving 89 accusations in 2008, of which 53 were processed and only 19 investigated. In July 2008, civil society organizations launched an Anti-Corruption Legal Aid Initiative that permitted citizens to make free accusations by telephone. Within the first two weeks, the initiative was deluged with callers reporting corruption in courts, government ministries, and the civil service.[70]

Neither access to education nor foreign assistance is widely perceived to be subject to bribes, and recent administrations have shown a growing political resolve to combat corruption. In an effort to minimize fraud in a mostly privatized economy, the government reformed its procurement regulations, notably requiring competitive public bidding on purchases over roughly US$110,000 and insisting since 2004 that transactions be processed through an internet system, Guatecompras. Although compliance with Guatecompras increased steadily between 2004 and 2007, rates of evasion again increased in 2008, as brokering organizations reasserted their role in contract bidding.[71] The Inter-American Development Bank recently announced a US$400 million loan program to continue strengthening public finances by further modernizing the tax system and implementing new mechanisms to control the quality and transparency of government budgeting and procurement.[72]

Government transparency is supported by constitutional guarantees and a special congressional oversight committee charged with reporting on government spending and income. The budget-making process is subject to review by congressional commissions and receives media coverage. However, recent progress in enhancing transparency in the executive branch has been difficult to sustain, and it has not been matched by improvements in the legislative or judicial realms, at the regional or municipal levels, or in the civil service. Furthermore, whereas access to government operations has become somewhat more fluid and transparent, information on spending remains opaque. This could change thanks to the September 2008 passage of the Law for Free Access to Public Information. The long-overdue legislation grants citizens the right to petition for access to the records of all public and private, domestic and international entities that administer public resources. It removes virtually all barriers to swift, free, and easy public access to information, with the notable exception of the judicial right of amparo, the mechanism mentioned above that regularly bogs down judicial proceedings.[73] Since the law took effect, agencies including the Ministry of Finance, the Central Bank, the Tax Superintendency, and the Social Security Institute have shown both the willingness and capacity to comply with citizen requests for information. At the same time, there are concerns that the legislation will be subverted if government administrators do not receive the requisite training and resources to process requests.[74]

RECOMMENDATIONS

- Reopen discussion of a security pact in an effort to build societal consensus around the specific measures proposed by engaging a broad array of civic and political actors including the private sector, civil society, and a range of government institutions.
- Establish a witness protection program and revise the right of amparo in order to prevent accused criminals from evading justice through methods of intimidation and legal manipulation.
- Pass and enforce legislation establishing a legal framework entrenching indigenous rights and establish a permanent mechanism to assure compliance with ILO Convention 169.
- Enact and enforce the legislative and judicial reforms proposed by the CICIG in order to modernize and streamline judicial practices in accordance with international standards.
- Tighten enforcement of campaign laws so as to ensure greater autonomy from both the private sector and organized crime, and strengthen political party attachments in order to enhance legislative stability, efficiency, and independence.

NOTES

For URLs and endnote hyperlinks, please visit the *Countries at the Crossroads* homepage at http://freedomhouse.org/template.cfm?page=139&edition=8.

[1] Tribunal Supremo Electoral, "Segunda Elección Presidencial Resultados 2007: Guatemala."
[2] European Union Election Observation Mission, *Final Report: Guatemala General Elections 2007* (Guatemala City: European Union Election Observation Mission, 2008).

3. Congreso de la República Guatemala CA, Ley Electoral y de Partidos Políticos, decreto número 1-85 de la Asamblea Nacional Constituyente.
4. European Union Election Observation Mission Guatemala, "General Elections–2007: Preliminary Statement"; Unión Europea Misión de Observación Electoral Guatemala, "50 Observadores de Corto Plazo y una Delegación de 7 Miembros del Parlamento Europeo Se Suman a la Misión de Observación Electoral de la Unión Europea," news release, September 6, 2007; Procuraduría de Derechos Humanos (PDH), *Informe Anual 2007* (Guatemala City: PDH, 2008).
5. Unión Europea, "50 Observadores"; Asociación de Investigación y Estudios Sociales (ASIES), *Guatemala: Informe Analítico del Proceso Electoral 2007* (Guatemala City: ASIES, February 2008), 36–47.
6. PDH, *Informe Anual 2007*, 58–59; Maureen Meyer, *The Second Round: A WOLA Memo on Progress and Pending Issues for the Guatemalan Elections* (Washington, D.C.: Washington Office on Latin America [WOLA], November 1, 2007).
7. PDH, *Informe Anual 2007*, 55; Tribunal Supremo Electoral, "Resumen de Cumplimiento: Informes Financieros de Partidos Políticos al 22 de Enero 2008."
8. Registro Nacional de las Personas, "Temen Que DPI No Esté Listo," October 2, 2008.
9. PDH, *Informe Anual 2007*, 53.
10. Paola Ortiz Loaiza et al., *22 Años Después: Lo Inédito del Proceso Electoral 2007* (Guatemala City: Facultad Latinoamericana de Ciencias Sociales [FLACSO], February 2008), 31–32; European Union Election Observation Mission Guatemala, "General Elections–2007: Preliminary Statement."
11. See Ortiz Loaiza et al., *22 Años Después*, 27; European Union Election Observation Mission Guatemala, "General Elections–2007: Preliminary Statement," 8.
12. Ivonne Solórzano, Silvia Montepeque, and Kadir Piñeiro, *Partidos Políticos, Reestructuración y Vida Partidaria en Época Electoral* (Guatemala City: FLACSO, February 2008), 13–20; ASIES, *Análisis Mensual* no. 1 (January 2009): 12.
13. See WOLA, *The Captive State: Organized Crime and Human Rights in Latin America* (Washington, D.C.: WOLA, February 2008); Fundación Myrna Mack, "Consideraciones sobre la Impunidad en Guatemala: La Configuración de una Masiva Violación de Derechos Humanos," February 2008; "Se Entrega en Guatemala el Ex Jefe de la Policía Vinculado al Narcotráfico," Terra Noticias, August 18, 2009.
14. See Inter-American Development Bank, "DataGov: Governance Indicators Database."
15. Oficina Nacional de Servicio Civil (ONSEC), *Memoria de Labores 2008* (Guatemala City: ONSEC, 2009).
16. "Cámara del Agro Se Retira de ProRural," *Periódico*, June 10, 2009.
17. Inter American Press Association, "Guatemala," Reports and Resolutions: 64th General Assembly 2008; Centro de Reportes Informativos sobre Guatemala (Cerigua), "Monopolio de la TV Podría Ser Beneficiado Nuevamente," October 15, 2008.
18. Unidad de Defensores y Defensoras de Derechos Humanos de Guatemala (UDEFEGUA), *En el Nudo de la Impunidad: Informe sobre Situación de Defensoras y Defensores de Derechos Humanos, Enero a Diciembre de 2008* (Guatemala City: UDEFEGUA, 2009).
19. International Freedom of Expression Exchange (IFEX), "'El Periódico' Newspaper Calls for Investigation into Government Censorship of the Press Via Discriminatory Allocation of Government Advertising," news release, February 27, 2009; Hazel Feigenblatt, "New Law, Old Story: Guatemala Cuts Advertising to Critical Media," *Global Integrity Commons*, March 11, 2009.
20. CPJ, "Guatemala," in *Attacks on the Press in 2008* (New York: CPJ, 2009); Human Rights Watch, "Guatemala," in *World Report 2009* (New York: Human Rights Watch, 2009).

21. Claudia Méndez Villaseñor, "El 2009 Se Encamina a Ser el Año Más Violento," *Prensa Libre*, June 1, 2009.
22. "Human Rights Defenders at Grave Risk in Guatemala, UN Expert Finds," UN News Centre, February 20, 2008.
23. UDEFEGUA, *Informe Preliminar de Situación de Defensores y Defensoras de Derechos Humanos, Enero–Febrero 2009* (Guatemala City: UDEFEGUA, 2009); "Califican de 'Compleja' la Situación de Defensores de Derechos Humanos," *Prensa Libre*, September 8, 2009.
24. WOLA, *The Captive State*, 7.
25. Hina Jilani, *Report of the Special Representative of the Secretary General on the Situation of Human Rights Defenders: Mission to Guatemala* (New York: UN Human Rights Council, February 16, 2009); UDEFEGUA, "Informe Preliminar de Situación de Defensores y Defensoras de Derechos Humanos: Enero–Abril 2009"; Grupo de Apoyo Mutuo (GAM), *Informe sobre la Situación de Derechos Humanos y Hechos Violentos Ocurridos en el Primer Semestre de 2008* (Guatemala City: GAM, 2008)
26. "PDH: Campesino de Izabal Fue Ejecutado Extrajudicialmente," *Periódico*, May 25, 2008; Amnesty International, "Guatemala," in *Annual Report 2009* (London: Amnesty International, 2009); Edwin Perdomo, "Tribunal de Puerto Barrios Condenan a Ramiro Choc a Ocho Años de Cárcel," *Prensa Libre*, March 23, 2009.
27. Human Rights Watch, "Guatemala"; PDH, *Informe Anual 2008* (Guatemala City: PDH, 2009).
28. Political Database of the Americas, "Republic of Guatemala: Democracy and Citizen Security," Georgetown University (accessed April 27, 2009); PDH, *Informe Anual 2008*; Congreso de la República, Decreto No: 33-2006.
29. See for instance "Three Killed in Guatemalan Prison Riot over Food," Reuters, March 27, 2007; "Al Menos Siete Muertos por Pelea en Cárcel Guatemala," Reuters, November 22, 2008; "Beheadings in Guatemala Jail Riot," British Broadcasting Corporation (BBC), November 23, 2008.
30. United Nations Department of Public Information, "Secretary-General Appoints Carlos Castresana Fernandez of Spain to Head International Commission Against Impunity in Guatemala," news release, September 17, 2007; "Agreement between the United Nations and the State of Guatemala on the Establishment of an International Commission Against Impunity in Guatemala," WOLA, December 14, 2007.
31. ASIES, *Carta Informativa Semanal* no. 8 (February 23–March 1, 2009).
32. Embajada de los Estados Unidos, Guatemala, "Asuntos de Inmigración: Informe Anual sobre la Trata de Personas," June 4, 2008.
33. Maureen Meyer et al. "Guatemala Memo to US Policymakers," WOLA, April 8, 2009.
34. Hina Jilani, *Report of the Special Representative*; Human Rights First, "Human Rights Defenders in Guatemala."
35. See "Colom Unveils National Security Pact," *Latin American Regional Report: Caribbean & Central America* (April 2009): 8.
36. Cerigua, *Vistazo* 10, no. 4 (February 2009): 4.
37. International Trade Union Confederation (ITUC), *Internationally Recognised Core Labour Standards in Guatemala: Report for the WTO General Council Review of the Trade Policies of Guatemala* (Brussels: ITUC, 2009); Secretaria Presidencial de la Mujer (Seprem), *Informe de Labores 2008* (Guatemala City: Seprem, 2009).
38. ASIES, *Análisis Mensual* no. 3 (March 2009): 8–13; Comité para la Eliminación de Todas las Formas de Discriminación contra la Mujer (CEDAW), *Observaciones Finales del Comité para la Eliminación de la Discriminación contra la Mujer: Guatemala* (New

York: United Nations, February 12, 2009); Cerigua, "Ley contra el Femicidio, un Avance para la Justicia de Género," news release, May 19, 2008; Congreso de la República de Guatemala, "Decreto Numero 22-2008," *Diario de Centro América*, May 7, 2008.

39 Incidencia Democrática (IDem), "Delitos contra la Mujer: 254 Ordenes Ejecutadas," January 28, 2009; Marta Sandoval, "Gobernación Cerró una Unidad Que Atiende Delitos contra la Mujer," *Periódico*, April 14, 2009; Ministerio Publico, "Nuevo Modelo de Atención a Víctimas"; Guatemala Human Rights Commission, "Femicide Recognized but Violence Continues," *Quetzal* no. 2 (March 2009): 3–5; Ministerio Público, "40 Años de Carcel por Femicidio," news release, July 24, 2009; Cerigua, *Investigación en Prensa Escrita sobre Violencia contra las Mujeres 2008* (Guatemala City: Cerigua, 2009).

40 PDH, "Defensoría de la Mujer," in *Informe Anual 2008*, 531; Mitchell A. Seligson, ed., *Cultura Política de la Democracia en Guatemala, 2008: El Impacto de la Gobernabilidad* (Vanderbilt University: Latin American Public Opinion Project, November 2008), 91.

41 Cerigua, "Ley General de Pueblos Indígenas Busca Inclusión y Respeto a Sus Derechos," news release, April 18, 2009; "Guatemala: Ley General de Derechos de los Pueblos Indígenas," *Reporte Diario*, April 1, 2009; Conié Reynoso, "Mayas Tienen Grandes Valores y Rezagos," *Prensa Libre*, August 9, 2009.

42 PDH, "Defensoría de Pueblos Indígenas," in *Informe Anual 2008*; Minority Rights Group International, "World Directory of Minorities and Indigenous Peoples–Guatemala: Maya," July 2008; Instituto Nacional de Estadística, *Encuesta Nacional de Condiciones de Vida 2006* (Guatemala City: Instituto Nacional de Estadística, 2009); "Espada Admite Marginación de Indígenas," *Prensa Libre*, May 7, 2009.

43 See the program's website, http://www.mifamiliaprogresa.gob.gt/index.php?option=com_frontpage&Itemid=1; Conié Reynoso and Leonel Díaz Zeceña, "Crisis Obliga a Readecuar Presupuesto," *Prensa Libre*, April 2, 2009; Hugo Alvarado and Karen Cardona, "Mi Familia Progresa Se Recapitaliza," *Prensa Libre*, March 18, 2009; "An Indictment from the Grave," *Economist*, May 21, 2009.

44 Congreso de la República de Guatemala, *Boletín Informativo*, March 27, 2009.

45 Bureau of Democracy, Human Rights, and Labor, "Guatemala," in *2008 Country Reports on Human Rights Practices* (Washington, D.C.: U.S. Department of State, February 2009).

46 Solidarity Center, *Justice for All: The Struggle for Worker Rights in Guatemala* (Washington, D.C.: Solidarity Center, November 2008); ITUC, *Annual Survey of Violations of Trade Union Rights 2009* (Brussels: ITUC, 2009).

47 PDH, "Defensoría del Trabajador," in *Informe Anual 2008*, 656–58; U.S. Labor Education in the Americas Project (USLEAP), *Worker Rights under the New Guatemalan Government: A Preliminary Report* (Chicago: USLEAP, August 2008); ITUC, *Internationally Recognised Core Labour Standards in Guatemala*; Bureau of Democracy, Human Rights, and Labor, "Guatemala."

48 UDEFEGUA, *En el Nudo*, 15–23; USLEAP, *Worker Rights*.

49 "UN Expert on Independence of Judges and Lawyers Calls for Major Reforms in Guatemala," *Guatemala Times*, February 11, 2009.

50 World Bank, "Improving Access to Justice in Guatemala: Judicial Reform Project," April 2006.

51 ASIES, *Desafíos Actuales de la Justicia Penal: Quinto Estudio, Proceso de Fortalecimiento del Sistema de Justicia: Avances y Debilidades, Julio 2006–Octubre 2008* (Guatemala City: ASIES, 2009), 34–37.

52 Olga López Ovando, "Impunidad y Corrupción en el Sistema de Justicia," *Prensa Libre*, December 18, 2008; Jéssica Osorio, "Precisan Regular Postulación a Corte Suprema de Justicia," *Prensa Libre*, March 18, 2009; Business Anti-Corruption Portal, "Guatemala

Country Profile: Corruption Levels—Judicial System"; Due Process of Law Foundation, "Civil Society's Role in Combating Judicial Corruption in Central America," in *Global Corruption Report 2007*, Transparency International, ed. (Cambridge: Cambridge University Press, 2007).

53 Coralia Orantes, "Cicig Exige Cambiar Modelo de Elección," *Prensa Libre*, May 12, 2009; Jéssica Osorio, "Precisan Regular Postulación a Corte Suprema de Justicia," *Prensa Libre*, March 18, 2009.

54 United Nations, "Press Conference on International Commission against Impunity in Guatemala," press release, Febuary 24, 2009.

55 Jéssica Osorio, "El Congreso Reactivará Agenda de la Cicig," *Prensa Libre*, February 8, 2009; Fundación Myrna Mack, "Reactivación de la Violencia contra Operadores de Justicia en Guatemala," October 2008.

56 ASIES, *Desafíos Actuales de la Justicia Penal*, 24–56.

57 ASIES, *Carta Informativa Semanal* no. 8.

58 Olga López Ovando, "Cicig Será Querellante contra General Ríos Sosa," *Prensa Libre*, May 7, 2009.

59 Ricardo Quinto, "Archivos Militares Habrían Sido Destruidos," *Prensa Libre*, March 2, 2009.

60 C. Orantes, O. López, and S. Valdez, "Aprehenden a Nueve por Asesinato de Rosenberg," *Prensa Libre*, September 12, 2009.

61 Leonardo Cereser Aguirre, "Más de 500 Disputas de Tierra Existen en el País," *Prensa Libre*, March 31, 2008.

62 Roxana B. Sánchez E., "Reporter's Notebook: Guatemala," in *Global Integrity Report 2008* (Washington, D.C.: Global Integrity, 2009); Transparency International, *2004 Corruption Perceptions Index* (Berlin: Transparency International, 2004); Transparency International, *2008 Corruptions Perceptions Index* (Berlin: Transparency International, September 22, 2008).

63 Americas Barometer, *Cultura Política de la Democracia en Guatemala* (Guatemala: ASIES, 2008), 47–48.

64 Global Integrity, "Guatemala: Integrity Scorecard Report," in *Global Integrity Report 2006* (Washington, D.C.: Global Integrity, 2006).

65 "Guatemala: The Return of Portillo," *Latin American Regional Report: Caribbean & Central America* (October 2008): 5.

66 Business Anti-Corruption Portal, "Guatemala Country Profile: General Information."

67 Acción Ciudadana, "La Transparencia en la Inversión Pública y el Presupuesto del Estado Año 2009," October 16, 2008.

68 Business Anti-Corruption Portal, "Guatemala Country Profile: Public Anti-Corruption Initiatives."

69 "La Corrupción Empantanada," *Periódico*, February 26, 2008.

70 Roxana B. Sánchez E., "Reporter's Notebook: Guatemala."

71 Bertelsmann Stiftung, "Guatemala Country Report," in *Bertelsmann Transformation Index 2008* (Guetersloh, Germany: Bertelsmann Stiftung, 2007); Heritage Foundation and *Wall Street Journal* (WSJ), "Guatemala," in *2009 Index of Economic Freedom* (Washington, D.C./New York: Heritage Foundation and WSJ, 2009); Business Anti-Corruption Portal, "Guatemala Country Profile: Public Anti-Corruption Initiatives."

72 Inter-American Development Bank, "Guatemala Will Improve Fiscal Management," news release, August 12, 2008.

73 Acción Ciudadana, *Indicadores de Acceso a la Información Publica en Guatemala 2008* (Guatemala City: Acción Ciudadana, October 2008).

[74] "Guatemaltecos Se Interesan en Conocer Sueldos de Servidores Públicos," *Prensa Libre*, May 21, 2009; Marcela Fernández, "Entidades Reprueban en Cumplimiento a la Ley de Acceso a la Información," *Prensa Libre*, May 21, 2009; Marcela Fernández, "Comunas Son las Peor Calificadas en Informe de Acceso a la Información," *Prensa Libre*, May 22, 2009.

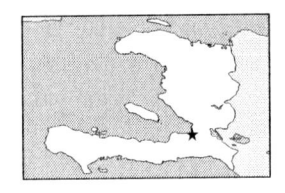

HAITI

CAPITAL: Port-au-Prince
POPULATION: 9.2 million
GNI PER CAPITA (PPP): $1,180

SCORES	2006	2010
ACCOUNTABILITY AND PUBLIC VOICE:	N/A	3.30
CIVIL LIBERTIES:	N/A	3.97
RULE OF LAW:	N/A	2.63
ANTICORRUPTION AND TRANSPARENCY:	N/A	2.04

(scores are based on a scale of 0 to 7, with 0 representing weakest and 7 representing strongest performance)

Daniel P. Erikson

INTRODUCTION

Haitian politics have been embroiled in conflict ever since the country gained independence in 1804. Over the past two centuries, there have been 34 coups d'état in Haiti, and the violent overthrow of government has been far more commonplace than the peaceful transition of power from one president to another. Indeed, the Haitian conflict has evolved into a kaleidoscopic, multidimensional power struggle among an evolving array of competing groups that has defined the country's contentious politics for more than two centuries. While the historical roots of conflict reach back to the country's founding, an analysis of Haiti's contemporary political landscape can usefully begin with the fall of the Duvalier regime in 1986. The ouster of Haitian dictator Jean-Claude "Baby Doc" Duvalier, who had succeeded his father François "Papa Doc" Duvalier following the elder's death, was a cathartic moment that ushered Haiti into an unstable period of democratic transition. However, that is where it remains largely stalled nearly a quarter-century later, struggling to overcome legacies of authoritarian leadership, poor governance, extreme social and economic polarization, and impunity for political and economic elites.

Haiti's path toward democratic consolidation has been marked by an intense array of tumult and setbacks. In the 1990s, Haiti was on the front lines of international efforts to help bind Latin America and the Caribbean into a

---

Daniel P. Erikson is Senior Associate for U.S. policy and Director of Caribbean programs at the Inter-American Dialogue in Washington, D.C. He has published more than 50 academic and opinion articles on topics in Western Hemisphere affairs, and he is the author of *The Cuba Wars: Fidel Castro, the United States, and the Next Revolution*. His past positions include Research Associate at the Harvard Business School and Fulbright scholar in U.S.-Mexican business relations.

"community of democracies." This was most dramatically demonstrated three years after the 1991 military ouster of democratically elected president Jean-Bertrand Aristide. The de facto military regime largely destroyed state institutions, while the economic embargo imposed by the United States and other international actors from 1991 to 1994 severely damaged the economy. In 1994, the Clinton administration authorized the U.S. military to help restore Aristide to power and stanch the migration crisis caused by tens of thousands of boat people fleeing the repressive military junta. Following Aristide's return, the United States and other international partners poured more than US$1 billion into Haiti to build its police and judicial institutions, fund elections and encourage good governance, alleviate widespread poverty, and forge a more sustainable economy.

Haiti held presidential elections in 1995, when René Préval, an Aristide ally, won the presidency in a free and fair vote, and again in 2000, when Aristide was brought back into office in an election that was boycotted by the opposition, spurned by international monitors, and characterized by low turnout due to an ongoing political dispute over the validity of parliamentary elections held in May of that year. The international community, led by the United States, responded by cutting off aid to the Haitian government, which began to unravel and eventually collapsed when an armed rebellion in the countryside forced Aristide from the presidency on February 29, 2004. Departing under intense pressure from the Haitian rebel uprising, domestic opposition groups, and the governments of the United States, France, and Canada, Aristide penned a resignation letter, boarded a U.S.-chartered plane, and was deposited in Africa, where he remains in exile.

During the next two years, from 2004 to 2006, the interim government of Gérard Latortue presided over a normalization of Haiti's relations with the international donor community and was kept in power principally by the Brazil-led UN stabilization force that entered Haiti with several thousand troops in the summer of 2004 and now numbers about 9,100 personnel. In February 2006, former president Préval was elected with a slight majority of the total vote in the first round of balloting, while the other 33 presidential candidates split the remaining half of the vote between them. During the next two years, Haiti notched up several important successes: a considerable diminution of politically related strife, the restoration of an elected parliament, a return to economic growth (estimated at slightly less than 4 percent in 2007), and the establishment of basic security as a result of improvements in the initially troubled UN mission.

In 2008, however, Haiti suffered a profound setback when riots sparked by rising food and fuel prices led to the parliamentary ouster of Prime Minister Jacques-Edouard Alexis in April, leaving the government rudderless for months until his successor, Michèle Pierre-Louis, was eventually confirmed in September. Until the riots, Préval appeared to be successfully balancing societal tensions by reaching out to Haitian elites while signaling solidarity with the poor, and there has been undeniable progress in a country that has had to begin virtually from scratch time and time again in recent decades. However, this fragile consensus has become increasingly frayed and may unravel further. Moreover, Haitian politics will turn increasingly contentious in the battle to replace Rene Préval in the presidential election scheduled for November 2010, and the country remains both a source of regional instability and a country where freedom remains under threat by both state and nonstate actors. *[Editor's Note: In November 2009, Michèle Pierre-Louis was removed from her post after facing criticism by Parliament about Haiti's use of international aid funds and the country's difficulties in weathering the global economic slowdown. Her removal underscored the continued fragility of Haiti's political system, but the rapid appointment of her successor, former minister of planning and external cooperation Jean-Max Bellerive, avoided a prolonged crisis.]*

ACCOUNTABILITY AND PUBLIC VOICE 3.30

FREE AND FAIR ELECTORAL LAWS AND ELECTIONS	2.75
EFFECTIVE AND ACCOUNTABLE GOVERNMENT	2.50
CIVIC ENGAGEMENT AND CIVIC MONITORING	3.67
MEDIA INDEPENDENCE AND FREEDOM OF EXPRESSION	4.29

In February 2004, Haiti's simmering political situation exploded. President Aristide was forced from power a second time when the combination of a violent uprising, intransigent political opponents, and international pressure forced him to flee into exile in South Africa. Aristide's departure, coupled with the expiration of Parliament as the terms of most legislators came to an end with no new elections held, left the country devoid of any elected democratic apparatus whatsoever. The international community scrambled to put together a mechanism for selecting a new prime minister and created a seven-person *Conseil des Sages* (Council of Wisemen), who quickly settled on Gérard Latortue, a former Haitian foreign minister and semi-retired UN official who won the job on a phone interview from his home in Florida. Latortue then flew to Port-au-Prince to assume the post, while Supreme Court justice Boniface Alexandre was elevated to the presidency in accordance with procedures outlined in the Haitian constitution. During 2004, an emergency Multinational Interim Force was cobbled together by the United States, Canada, France, and Chile to provide stability in the wake of Aristide's departure. In June, this deployment gave way to a larger UN peacekeeping force, which was led by Brazil and featured heavy Latin American participation.

Latortue, who led Haiti's government from March 2004 to May 2006, assembled a cabinet of principally nonpartisan technocrats, although several opposition figures—including members of the army disbanded by Aristide in

1995—landed key posts, while Lavalas, the political organization founded by Aristide, went unrepresented. This unelected government largely derived its ability to govern from the support of the United States and other members of the international community, and its tenuous political legitimacy sprang from its rhetorical embrace of a mandate to organize credible elections and transition to a new government, along with progress in macroeconomics.

By the end of its mandate, however, the interim administration's technocratic credentials had become overshadowed by its penchant for becoming entangled in messy political battles, such as sparring with member countries of the Caribbean Community, jailing dozens of prominent Lavalas supporters, and later jumping into the presidential contest to bar prominent Haitian American candidates from participating. Latortue, who lacked a strong political base within the country, was hesitant to alienate the rebel leaders and opposition figures who had pushed for Aristide's ouster. However, the pledge taken by Latortue and his top ministers not to compete in the elections enhanced the political credibility of both the government and the election process as a whole. To its credit, the interim government never wavered in its support for Haiti's return to a democratically elected government, and it played a constructive role in the negotiations following the 2006 presidential elections. The Latortue government made little headway in promoting national dialogue and political reconciliation, but its political legacy was relatively benign.

Starting in February 2006, Haiti held three rounds of elections, for presidential, parliamentary, and municipal seats. Since then the democratic process has faltered. For example, new elections planned for December 2007 to replace one-third of the senate (10 of the 30 seats) were postponed until April 2009, when they were eventually held amid lackluster turnout. Furthermore, the Haitian constitution requires that the elected president (in this case Préval) appoint a prime minister to run governmental affairs, subject to approval by Parliament. Préval selected Jacques-Edouard Alexis, who had also served as prime minister during the previous Préval presidency. However, Alexis was forced from office in April 2008 when a majority of the Senate voted for his removal amid widespread dismay over high food prices. Haiti was thus left for four months with a caretaker government that could not initiate new programs. This created a sense of drift that was further exacerbated by fallout from severe damage inflicted by a series of hurricanes that battered the island in 2008, destroying crops, killing 800 people, and burying entire towns under mud flowing down from eroded hillsides.

Haiti's profound levels of socioeconomic inequality and exclusion, weak civil society, poorly articulated political party system, and structural class tensions have resulted in an extended period of low-intensity conflict that periodically sparks more widespread political upheaval. The Haitian constitution of 1987 is the governing political charter of the country, and although it upholds democratic values, many of its key provisions have traditionally been ignored in practice. In recent years, Haiti has held semi-regular elections organized by—and often at the behest of—the international community. While there is a Haitian Provisional Electoral Council with nine appointed members charged with drafting election laws and organizing elections, it often operates in a murky and disjointed manner, and its staff has at times been driven from the country following elections due to threats of violence by actors who disagree with the outcomes. The country's chronic inability to form a Permanent Electoral Council is due in part to the requirement of a complex, constitutionally mandated process, which is one of several issues that have led to repeated calls for constitutional reform, including from the Préval administration itself.

The February 2006 presidential election was generally considered free and fair, but there were concerns that Préval was unfairly awarded a first-round victory despite his initial tally falling short of the 50 percent required to avoid a runoff. International monitors approved a plan whereby blank or spoiled ballots were not included in the total, which allowed Préval's vote to reach the decisive margin of victory. While incidents of violence and blatant fraud have decreased in recent years, significant problems persist, particularly in parliamentary elections. Low voter turnout is attributable to a security presence at the polls that may intimidate some voters, voter apathy due to poor government performance, and a ban on motorized transportation on election day. In addition, logistical problems are common, including tardily posted voter lists, the failure of polling stations to open on time, and inconsistent training of poll workers.

Haiti's political party system is a free-for-all, demonstrated most vividly when 34 presidential candidates competed in the 2006 election, most under separate party banners. Parliament is elected in a two-round system, with the majority of votes cast in single-member constituencies. Regulation of campaign financing is basically nonexistent, which means that influential business interests, foreign supporters, and even arms and narcotics dealers have the capacity to funnel resources towards their chosen candidates without oversight. Haiti already has some high-profile elected officials in Parliament with alleged ties with narco-traffickers, and observers are concerned that the role of drug money could increase in the next electoral process. Following Aristide's 2004 departure, Lavalas participated in the 2006 elections, but was excluded from the 2009 senatorial elections when its fragmented factions could not agree on a single slate of candidates. Préval has created a successor movement to Lavalas, known as Lespwa (Creole for Hope), but its members lack a formal party structure and remain atomized in Parliament. Since 1990, the history of Haiti's democratic transition has been dominated by two figures, Aristide and Préval, each of whom were twice elected president. Thus, Haiti still lacks an effective rotation of power among a range of political parties and leaders.

According to the constitution, Parliament is supposed to play a crucial role in governing the country by naming the prime minister, formulating the budget, and overseeing the operation of the ministries and the cabinet. In practice, however, Parliament lacks a working committee structure, a professional staff, developed institutional norms, or even adequate physical facilities. Haiti's legislative branch consists of two chambers: a 99-member Chamber of Deputies and a 30-member Senate. In 2009, the Haitian legislature was divided among several smaller parties with no one party holding a majority, although the emergence of the cross-party Commission of Progressive Parliamentarians bloc of some 60 deputies has gained increasing importance in the legislative process. In general, Parliament's operational handicaps allow the president to assert his prerogatives, but even then, inadequate follow-through leads to important pieces of legislation stagnating in Parliament for months or years. Parliament also occasionally plays an important blocking role but has limited ability to propose or shape legislation.

Local political institutions exist, though in nascent form. In December 2006, voters filled 420 offices consisting of a mayor and two deputies for each municipality (140 mayors and 280 deputies in all) and 9,000 community officials, which according to the "bottom-up" approach codified in Haiti's constitution would provide the basis for selecting Haiti's Permanent Electoral Council, although this has yet to transpire and may prove impossible to bring about in practice.

Similarly, Haiti's political party system remains so atomized that many analysts argue that the country does not have political parties in the traditional sense, but instead has small, narrowly based groups that coalesce around leaders of varying stature and charisma, particularly as elections approach. As a result, these under resourced nominal parties do little in the way of presenting views on the country's pressing development challenges. The country's weak national institutions have proved ill-equipped to mitigate political conflict; the judicial system is overburdened and ineffective, and there is an alarming trend of extrajudicial justice being meted out on the local level. A recent rise in lynching indicates the high level of citizen frustration with the country's dysfunctional judicial and penal systems, which could become very dangerous if left unchecked.

In addition, Haiti lacks adequate channels for civic monitoring. Key government decisions are often made in secret or without full public review, and the Préval government lacks a coherent public relations strategy or even appropriate mechanisms for keeping the public informed about government business. Still, local civic groups, often supported by foreign aid, do manage to operate relatively freely. Greater attention is being given to the fact that the cacophony of 3,000 or so nongovernmental organizations (NGOs) working in Haiti operate in an uncoordinated and unregulated fashion, particularly now that donors have endorsed the government's national development plans. Parallel calls have emerged from leading multilateral institutions such as the World Bank for greater coordination between donors and donor-supported NGOs and the government, particularly in pursuit of unifying national development efforts and rationalizing resources.

The Haitian constitution explicitly enshrines freedom of speech and prohibits the censorship of journalists "except in the case of war."[1] The Haitian state lacks a record of trying to silence journalists through heavy-handed legal means such as fines or imprisonment. In practice, however, Haitian journalists have frequently been the targets of violence, although this trend has ameliorated somewhat since the most recent return to democratic rule. The murder of radio journalist Jean Dominique in 2000 was a seminal event of press repression, and the case remains unsolved. Several more-recent cases have also provoked concern. In January 2005, Abdias Jean, a young Haitian radio journalist, was allegedly shot by police officers while investigating a story of police brutality. That July, Jacques Roche, the host of a popular television show, was kidnapped for ransom and later killed. In two separate cases during 2007, photographer Jean-Rémy Badio and Alix Joseph of Radio Provinciales in Gonaives were gunned down by unknown assailants after receiving death threats from local gangs.

The Haitian media today reflects the polarized fault lines of the society as a whole. Divisions within the media exist along lines of race, class, and status, with splits between pro- and anti-Aristide outlets also playing a role. Haiti's media culture, especially in the area of public and community radio, is rooted in a culture of resistance to dictatorship that fueled its emergence during the Duvalier era, and most journalists lack the training and professional standards to serve as the type of objective sources of information that would strengthen Haitian democracy. Haiti's political divide is reflected in media sources, press agencies, and audiences, and in media and journalist associations, such as the rivalry between the National Association of Haitian Media (ANMH) and the Association of Independent Media of Haiti (AMIH).

Radio is the form of media that has proliferated most rapidly in the post-Duvalier era, and today over 90 percent of the population of 8 million is reached by more than 290 FM stations operating without a license. Port-au-Prince, for example, has 41 stations for a population of roughly 3 million, and the smaller city of St. Marc has 37 stations operating in a community of 300,000. There are more than 70 community radio stations, often linked with political groups or parties, and 41 of these are affiliated with Rasanbleman Medya pou Aksyon Kominote (RAMAK), the country's largest media association. Television stations, by contrast, are far less prevalent, with about 20 in Port-au-Prince and another 15 in the provinces.[2] Many television stations have been established in the last three years by radio and newspaper owners seeking to expand their influence, but the total television audience in Haiti is below 10 percent due to expensive equipment and lack of electricity. Haiti has two main newspapers, *Le Nouvelliste* and *Le Matin*, with estimated total readership of about 75,000 each. In addition, there are three weekly news bulletins targeting different political tendencies.[3] Internet use, though marginal in Haiti due to illiteracy and lack of electricity and infrastructure, is expanding throughout the country, as is cell phone and text messaging use.

The legal framework for regulating the media in Haiti is unwieldy and poorly coordinated, with competing responsibilities among several ministries and lax oversight. The National Telecommunications Council (CONATEL) is part of the Ministry of Public Works and issues radio and television broadcasting licenses but does not regulate content or the usage of the airwaves, and license delivery is often irregular, while the main stations operate illegally without being subject to any control. Most media is not state funded; if anything, support for government-funded media should increase as Haiti lacks a reliable source of information for official news. At present, it is not uncommon for President Préval or parliamentary members to give a major speech, for example, that is not covered by private media nor broadcast on government-owned outlets. Transcripts and recordings may be made available several days later, but the government's inability to carve out a niche in Haiti's fragmented media landscape has complicated the task of governing and led to frequent misunderstandings and frustration among the Haitian public.

CIVIL LIBERTIES   3.97

PROTECTION FROM STATE TERROR, UNJUSTIFIED IMPRISONMENT, AND TORTURE	2.50
GENDER EQUITY	3.67
RIGHTS OF ETHNIC, RELIGIOUS, AND OTHER DISTINCT GROUPS	3.00
FREEDOM OF CONSCIENCE AND BELIEF	6.67
FREEDOM OF ASSOCIATION AND ASSEMBLY	4.00

The civil liberties protections codified in Haitian law are frequently violated by state authorities, and victims have little recourse. This unfortunate reality stems from the fact that Haiti's deeply deteriorated security situation lacks easy remedies. The armed uprising of 2004 exacerbated trends that have been in evidence since the late 1990s, including the gradual disintegration of the Haitian police force, the prevalence of guns throughout the country, the absence of judicial institutions, and the violent activities of politically affiliated gangs, many of which retain linkages to members of the disbanded Haitian military. The return of former military officers (some credibly accused of terrible human rights abuses), the breakdown of the penal system and the release of many prisoners, and the apparent impunity for violence all mean that armed elements continue to be a powerful force for destabilization in Haiti. Any efforts to restore security and the rule of law to Haiti will require a sustained international peacekeeping presence, the disarmament of militant groups, and the reconstitution of a national police force.

International peacekeepers returned to Haiti in 2004 under the mandate of a UN Security Council Resolution that authorized a peacekeeping mission led by Brazil. This force, which numbers 9,100 and is known as the United Nations Stabilization Mission in Haiti (MINUSTAH), will have to be maintained until a national police force can be established and made functional—at least a decade. Although Haiti's security situation has generally improved since 2006, largely attributable to improved performance by the United Nations, it remains plagued by ongoing social problems that pose a continued risk of renewed violence. The UN Security Council has extended the mandate of the peacekeeping mission until October 15, 2010, with a total force of 6,940 military troops and 2,211 police officers.[4] This one-year renewal marked a welcome sign of the international community's continued commitment to Haiti. Concurrently, the Haitian National Police (HNP) initiated a vetting process to examine officers' records in detail; hundreds suspected of corruption have been purged and new recruits have been selected and trained. Recent polls indicate that Haitian confidence in the police has improved markedly in the past two years.

Haiti continues to be plagued by high crime rates, especially kidnapping and property crime. To some degree, the crime level in Haiti is judged more by perception than by hard statistics. The HNP do not collect murder or kidnapping statistics, nor do local NGOs. The United Nations estimates that Haiti's murder rate is roughly 30 per 100,000 annually, which would rank the country among the most dangerous in the world, but this figure has not been systematically verified. At the same time, there are few protections against arbitrary arrest and detained suspects often languish for months or even years without facing trial. Prison conditions are reported to be among the worst in the world, and it is common for prisoners to be crammed into small, dirty cells that are overcrowded and often rife with disease. Haiti's 1987 constitution created the Office of Citizen Protection, but its role as an ombudsman's office is severely circumscribed due to lack of resources. Human trafficking, especially in children, persists. The United Nations estimates that there are 300,000 involuntary child domestic laborers in Haiti (known as *restavecs*, which is Creole for "stay with"), whose families are forced by extreme poverty to send them to work in more prosperous households.[5]

The Haitian constitution does not explicitly outlaw gender discrimination. The minimum legal age of marriage is 15 for women and 18 for men, resulting in frequent early marriages, especially in rural areas. In 1994, Haiti established a Ministry for the Status of Women, but it has engineered few significant policy changes. Haiti has appointed two female prime ministers since its first democratic election in 1990: Claudette Werleigh (November 1995–February 1996) and Michèle Pierre-Louis (September 2008–November 2009). Still, gender discrimination remains pervasive. Haitian law prohibits and punishes rape and domestic violence, but women are still frequently its victims. A domestic association called Solidarité des Femmes Haïtiennes (SOFA) has estimated that 8 in 10 Haitian women have been victims of domestic abuse, with the husband or partner as the perpetrator in half of all cases.[6] Haitian law provides leniency for husbands who murder their wives if the woman has committed adultery, but the same does not hold true for the much rarer cases where wives have killed philandering husbands. In rural areas, some rape survivors have obtained justice in the form of financial settlements from their assailants, in effect treating the crime as a civil rather than a criminal offense. Medical care for pregnant women is especially poor; loss of mother's life during childbirth reaches 680 per 100,000 live births, one of the highest rates in the world.[7] Despite ongoing gender disparities, Haiti is not characterized by oppressive cultural practices such as female genital mutilation or strict dress codes for women. In general, Haitian women do not share an equal place in Haitian society, which makes it difficult for them to have their civil liberties respected to the same degree as Haitian men. Unemployment—estimated at somewhere between 70 and 80 percent in Haiti—is an equal opportunity burden.

Haiti is a largely black and Creole-speaking population with few ethnic minorities. Those that do exist are frequently of European, Arabic, or Jewish descent and are relatively more affluent than black Haitians. All Haitians are entitled to full equality under the law, although indigent Haitians have little legal recourse, while wealthy Haitians who commit crimes often escape punishment. Homosexuality between consenting adults is legal in Haiti. Gay Haitians may face discrimination and harassment, but Haiti does not exhibit the virulent homophobia that exists in much of the English-speaking Caribbean and violence against homosexuals is rare. Still, no Haitian political party has backed the cause of defending or promoting the civil liberties of homosexuals. Regarding people with disabilities, the Haitian constitution states that "the handicapped . . . shall have the means to ensure their autonomy, education and independence." In practice, however, disabled citizens receive minimal state support and often face lives of extreme hardship.

The Haitian government generally respects the right of religious freedom and different religious groups coexist amicably. Roman Catholicism is the dominant religion, representing about 80 percent of the population, with Protestantism the most significant second religion at 15 percent, but the African-based spiritist religion of voodoo is also widely practiced. In 2003, the Haitian government officially recognized voodoo as a religion, and marriages in voodoo ceremonies now enjoy full legal status.[8] The Haitian government does not usually interfere in the practices of religious organizations.

Haitian law has long guaranteed the rights to freedom of association and assembly, but these have been violated in practice, especially during moments of high political tension. In the waning months of Aristide's rule, mass protests against his government became increasingly frequent and often resulted in violent clashes between pro- and antigovernment forces and with the HNP. Following his exile in 2004, Aristide supporters began to organize rallies and protests against the interim Latortue government, which sometimes led to violent incidents. Once Préval took power in 2006, protests diminished but still occurred on occasion. The April 2008 spike in food prices prompted thousands to protest and resulted in several deaths; the sources of the unrest were not systematically investigated despite credible claims that narco-traffickers and others chafing at the government's recently launched anticorruption program were among the instigators. In June 2009, Haiti became embroiled in weeks of protest over a parliamentary decision to raise the minimum wage from US$1.70 to US$4.90 a day, with university students demanding that Préval sign the controversial measure.[9] Later that month, thousands of mourners gathered to commemorate the passing of Gerard Jean-Juste, a controversial priest and advocate for the poor, but the event ended in rock throwing directed at UN peacekeepers and gunfire that left one man dead, an act for which the United Nations denied culpability.[10] However, annual marches by Aristide partisans on his birthday and on the anniversary of his second ouster have not devolved into violence.

Haitian law stipulates that trade union freedom is guaranteed and that union membership is voluntary, but unions have not historically been important actors in Haiti and workers' rights in the country are among the least respected in the hemisphere. Violence against trade unionists, infringement on workers' rights, and even child labor are all widespread. Protections for unions are frequently violated through means including the arbitrary dismissal of union employees and the provision of incentives and benefits to nonunion labor.[11]

RULE OF LAW 2.63

INDEPENDENT JUDICIARY	2.40
PRIMACY OF RULE OF LAW IN CIVIL AND CRIMINAL MATTERS	2.20
ACCOUNTABILITY OF SECURITY FORCES AND MILITARY TO CIVILIAN AUTHORITIES	3.25
PROTECTION OF PROPERTY RIGHTS	2.67

Haiti's judicial system functions poorly and is rife with abuse. Due to the generalized weakness of the Haitian state, cases are frequently allowed to languish for years. As a result, even the effective pursuit of justice carries a whiff of illegitimacy because most cases do not progress in the absence of heavy political pressure. This means that the judiciary is highly vulnerable to external political pressure that is often a determining factor in the cases that are pursued. The continuing problem of impunity corrupts the system enormously, with perpetrators of terrible crimes circulating freely among Haitians and serving as a reminder of the justice system's dysfunction.

The most dramatic recent example of how politics dictates the administration of Haitian justice involves the case of Yvon Neptune, the former prime minister under Aristide. In 2004, the interim Latortue government arrested Neptune, but waited 14 months before officially charging him with any crime, a period in which Neptune went on a hunger strike and was temporarily taken into UN custody. In September 2005, he was charged with participating in a violent attack by Lavalas supporters in St. Marc, but no evidence was ever produced. Following Préval's election in February 2006, the Haitian government ordered Neptune's release and he was freed from prison in July 2006, but the charges were never dropped. In July 2008, the Inter-American Commission for Human Rights issued a 60-page decision on the Neptune case that lambasted the Latortue government for arresting Neptune illegally and criticized the Préval government for failing to end his "legal insecurity."[12] Haiti has a Supreme Court (known as La Cour de Cassation) that is assisted by local community courts. One is eligible to be a Supreme Court judge after serving 7 years on the appeals court or 10 years as a lawyer. When a vacancy appears on the Court, any qualified person can submit their candidacy to the Senate, which votes to provide three names to the president, who appoints the judge of his or her choosing to a 10-year renewable term.

Haiti's Ministry of Justice and Public Safety is responsible not only for police forces and prison management but also for judiciary policy, which creates an inherent conflict of interest. Weak civil-service procedures, inconsistent legal education, and low salaries for judicial personnel (estimated at US$350 per month) contribute to the development of corruption and disinterest in monitoring administrative and professional personnel. Lawyers and judicial personnel must work in a system that lacks practice and respect for organizational and administrative procedures, and which usually leaves room for interpretation of the roles and responsibilities of justice. Given this background of weaknesses in the formal Haitian judicial system, informal justice practiced by traditional social and religious figures such as village elders and voodoo priests is frequently used to settle disputes.[13]

Haiti's criminal justice system respects the presumption of innocence in theory, but in practice thousands of prisoners are held without proper legal procedures being followed. The backlog of cases is systemic and the accused are often held indefinitely as they await their court dates. The legal code calls for the state to present its case in both Creole and French, but many cases go to trial in French despite the fact that most defendants speak only Creole. Lower-level judicial authorities, such as justices of the peace, are known to act outside of their jurisdiction to accuse individuals of crimes or even preside over trials that have no legal basis due to political ambition, corruption, bribes, or threats. Accused Haitians have right to counsel, but it is not constitutionally or legally required, and it is rare for politically connected individuals to face trial for wrongdoing.[14]

At the time of Aristide's ouster in 2004, it was clear that Haiti's 5,000-member police force was far too small to maintain order in a country of 8 million. The political uprisings, coupled with widespread police desertion, meant that Haiti's already small force lost two-thirds of its officers by the time Latortue arrived in power. Most studies suggest that an appropriately sized force would number closer to 20,000, which is substantially larger than what the international community has been willing to finance in the past. Building a new police force has been a costly and time-consuming initiative and has required international leadership and resources. The HNP's fragility in the face of drug traffickers' superior weaponry and monetary resources—used to corrupt individual officers—means that those resources have often gone to waste. Nonetheless, the Haitian government's political will to tackle the gangs, combined with better cooperation between the United Nations and the HNP, has led to the capture or killing of major gang leaders and the reestablishment of a state presence in some of the country's most dangerous slums since 2006. This progress has restored the confidence of the Haitian population in the UN mission and increased support for the government as a whole. Due to heavy international involvement and funding, the size of the Haitian police force has grown from a rump force of 1,500 in March 2004 to 8,300 in November 2008, a significant improvement but still far below the target of 14,000 officers by 2011.[15] Absent substantial efforts to increase the HNP's size and strength as international resources shift toward development, social peace will remain tenuous.

The vetting and training of police recruits at Haiti's revamped police academy has improved considerably over past years, but it remains an open question whether the country's newly minted police officers will eventually fall prey to the culture of incompetence and corruption that tainted their predecessors. The Haitian military was disbanded in 1995, but some former military officers continue to participate in gang- and drug-related activities and remain a destabilizing force; civilian control over the country existed to only a limited degree even before the entry of the UN peacekeeping force. The level of cooperation between the peacekeepers and the government has improved markedly in recent years but remains a point of political tension in Haiti as an important faction of Parliament views the UN presence as a violation of Haitian sovereignty and would like to see the mission draw to a close. The prevalence of police-administered extrajudicial justice has declined, but Haiti has not achieved a method for holding police fully accountable for human rights abuses.

Haitians have the right to own property individually or collectively, but only a small minority have formal title to the property that they live on. State enforcement of property rights and contracts is severely lacking. The *2009 Index of Economic Freedom* awarded Haiti one of the lowest possible scores for property rights, noting that "protection of investors and property is severely compromised by weak enforcement, a paucity of updated laws to handle modern commercial practices, and a dysfunctional and resource-poor legal system . . . most commercial disputes are settled out of court if at all."[16] In 1999, a private sector group brought to Haiti Peruvian economist Hernando de Soto, famous for his efforts to increase the economic capital of the poor through property titling. De Soto estimated that US$5.2 billion (US$3.2 billion in the countryside) existed in the hands of poor people but was "dead" because of the lack of clear title, bureaucratic red tape, intimidation tactics used by private sector forces, and corruption. Since the early 2000s, this issue has not been addressed.

ANTICORRUPTION AND TRANSPARENCY 2.04

ENVIRONMENT TO PROTECT AGAINST CORRUPTION	1.75
PROCEDURES AND SYSTEMS TO ENFORCE ANTICORRUPTION LAWS	1.75
EXISTENCE OF ANTICORRUPTION NORMS, STANDARDS, AND PROTECTIONS	2.50
GOVERNMENTAL TRANSPARENCY	2.17

Corruption poses an insidious challenge to political legitimacy and economic growth in Haiti. The transition away from authoritarian rule failed to end corrupt practices and even created new opportunities to harness public resources for private enrichment. Abuse by public officials tends to be most prevalent in sectors where the government exercises greater control over economic resources, but it is also widespread in Haiti's private sector. Corruption in Haiti typically takes two forms: administrative corruption and state capture. Administrative corruption, such as bribery, may occur at all levels of government, ranging from the small fee paid to expedite paperwork to multimillion-dollar kickbacks solicited to secure government contracts. State capture is an even more pernicious phenomenon in which officials and party leaders shape the legal and regulatory environment to favor their own interests. While President Préval is not perceived to be personally corrupt, neither has he had much success in reforming Haiti's culture of corruption. Transparency International traditionally ranks Haiti as the most corrupt country in the Americas in its annual Corruption Perceptions Index, and in 2008 Haiti was ranked 177th out of 180 countries—only Iraq, Myanmar, and Somalia were lower.[17]

Haiti's institutional weakness is coupled with an excess of bureaucratic regulations that multiply the opportunities for corruption. Public officials often leverage their positions for private gain, such as by demanding payments or bribes to expedite paperwork for identity documents or legal transactions. In addition, bribes and graft are common in social services such as education and health care. The Haitian government does not play a large role in the country's economy, accounting for only 14.4 percent of GDP in 2008, actually a rise from previous years due to an increase of foreign aid to Haiti's public sector.[18] Even this relatively small presence is poorly regulated, and Haiti lacks respected processes for financial disclosures, although the president signed a bill in January 2008 that requires high-level public officials to declare their assets. Campaign finance is virtually unregulated, allowing both legitimate and corrupting actors to help elect Haitian officials and subsequently wield considerable influence.

Haiti largely lacks anticorruption mechanisms and allegations of corruption are infrequently investigated. Media avidly report on anticorruption cases launched by the government but lack the resources and investigative skills to ferret out reports of wrongdoing independently. Whistleblowers may lose their jobs and find little legal recourse. While acts of bribery are punishable by one to three years of imprisonment, the deficiencies of the Haitian legal system have made enforcement of these laws difficult.[19] In 2004, the Haitian government ratified the OAS Inter-American Convention against Corruption and created an Anti-Corruption Unit (ULCC) within the Ministry of Economy and Finance that was charged with conducting a comprehensive survey of governance, investigating alleged acts of corruption, and developing a national anticorruption strategy. The government embraced its proposed strategy in March 2009.[20] In 2007, President Préval announced a major anticorruption initiative in which he declared that "this war without end against corruption will be long and hard, but we will win because it's a fight for life."[21] The announcement was acclaimed at the time, but there has been little follow-up.

Prosecutions are rare, especially at the highest levels of government. While the constitution requires that high-level officials and parliamentarians accused of corruption be tried before the Senate, this is an extremely rare occurrence, and no cases were heard in 2008.[22] The country's most high-profile corruption scandal involves former president Aristide, who has been accused of extorting millions of dollars of government funds, in part by entering into a fraudulent agreement with the telephone company IDT. No legal proceedings have been initiated against Aristide, however.[23] In addition, numerous cases of influence peddling have surfaced in Parliament in recent years. In September 2008, several officials in the office of the prime minister and the Parliament were investigated for misappropriation of public funds in a case involving the National Insurance Office (ONA). The ULCC recommended that legal action be taken against ONA director Sandro Joseph for money laundering; while prosecution stalled, Joseph was removed from his position.[24]

Haiti's corruption problem is complicated by limited public access to government information and a lack of transparency in government dealings. Article 40 of the constitution enjoins the Haitian government to publicize all laws, orders, and treaties on issues affecting the national life, orally and through print and electronic media, in both Creole and French. Apart from this provision, however, Haiti lacks freedom of information legislation, although in 2007 the Haiti Heritage Foundation, the local branch of Transparency International, prepared a draft bill on freedom of information to be submitted to Parliament.[25] In recent years, the government has done a better job of presenting an annual budget and tracking expenditures, mainly to please foreign donors, but this information often does not make its way to the Haitian public. An automated system for budget management that is meant to further increase transparency in expenditure accounting has been operational since 2005 and was further expanded to all line ministries in 2008 and 2009.[26] In addition, the Supreme Auditing Tribunal has been slowly working to catch up on the auditing of government accounts, although it is still years behind.[27] Concern about limiting corruption often leads the Haitian government to spend its foreign aid resources slowly, which hampers delivery of foreign assistance to the neediest Haitians. At the urging of international donors, in early 2005, the government created the National Commission for

Public Procurement (CNMP) to implement competitive procurement methods. Nevertheless, reports of corruption in procurement persist, due in part to the fact that contracts—notably those involving the state-owned Electricite d'Haiti—often circumvent the CNMP.[28] In June 2009, Parliament passed a new public procurement law to bring its procurement procedures in line with international standards.[29]

RECOMMENDATIONS

- Develop domestic capacity to hold regular elections, maintain a viable civil registry, and verify the eligibility of political candidates so that the country can assume the responsibility of managing and financing its electoral process and reduce its dependence on the international community.
- Dramatically revamp and upgrade the caliber of government communications and increase the transparency of government deliberations through the use of frequent press briefings, community radio, and the publication and release of key government documents in both Creole and French.
- Confront the glaring problems in the Haitian judiciary and penal system by investing in infrastructure, increasing judicial pay, systematizing professional legal norms, hiring lawyers and judges to address the backlog of cases, and ameliorating the inhumane prison conditions that result from overcrowding.
- Ensure that the vetting and training process for the Haitian National Police receives enough funding and attention so that the country will achieve its full complement of 14,000 trained police officers by 2011.
- Simplify the business code in order to minimize the bureaucratic process required for registering business and property titles.
- Develop social programs geared toward protecting the rights of woman and children and reducing domestic violence, including by creating violence prevention programs in poor urban and rural areas.

NOTES

For URLs and endnote hyperlinks, please visit the *Countries at the Crossroads* homepage at http://freedomhouse.org/template.cfm?page=139&edition=8.

[1] *The Haitian Constitution of 1987*, Art. 28-1.
[2] Louise Brunet, "Overview of the Media Landscape in Haiti" (presented at "The Role of Independent Media in Haiti" discussion at the Inter-American Dialogue, Washington, D.C., June 3, 2009); Frances Aunon, "Media Development in Haiti," Inter-American Dialogue, June 3, 2009.
[3] Brunet, "Overview of the Media Landscape in Haiti."
[4] UN Security Council, "Security Council Extends Mandate of United Nations Haitian Mission, Adjust Force to Better Meet Requirements on Ground," press release, October 13, 2009.

5. Gary Marx, "Servitude Steals Childhoods in Haiti," *Chicago Tribune*, June 8, 2005.
6. Organization for Economic Cooperation and Development (OECD) Development Centre, "Gender Equality and Social Institutions in Haiti," in *Social Institutions and Gender Index* (Paris: OECD Development Centre, 2009).
7. World Health Organization, *Maternal Mortality in 2000: Estimates Developed by WHO, UNICEF, UNFPA* (Geneva: World Health Organization, 2000).
8. "Haiti Makes Voodoo Official," British Broadcasting Corporation (BBC), April 30, 2003.
9. Jacqueline Charles, "Bill Clinton: We Must Honor Pledges of Help for Haiti," *Miami Herald*, June 15, 2009.
10. Agence France Presse, "One Shot Dead in Haiti Unrest," PRESSTV, June 18, 2009.
11. American Center for International Labor Solidarity/AFL-CIO, *Unequal Equation: The Labor Code and Worker Rights in Haiti* (Washington, D.C.: American Center for International Labor Solidarity/AFL-CIO, July 2003).
12. Institute for Justice and Democracy in Haiti, "La Court Interamericaine des Droits de L'Homme Declare que Haiti Viole les Droits de L'Ancien Premier Ministre Yvon Neptune," press release, July 15, 2008.
13. Foreign Affairs and International Trade Canada, "Understanding the Challenges of Justice System Reform in Haiti," home page, July 14, 2008.
14. Amnesty International, "Haiti," in *Amnesty International Report* 2009 (London: Amnesty International, 2009).
15. International Crisis Group, "Haiti 2009: Stability at Risk," Latin America/Caribbean Briefing No. 19, March 3, 2009.
16. Heritage Foundation and *Wall Street Journal* (WSJ), "Haiti," in *2009 Index of Economic Freedom* (Washington, D.C./New York: Heritage Foundation and WSJ, 2009).
17. Transparency International, *2008 Corruption Perceptions Index* (Berlin: Transparency International, September 22, 2008).
18. Heritage Foundation and WSJ, "Haiti."
19. Bureau of Economic, Energy, and Business Affairs, "Haiti," in *Investment Climate Statements 2009* (Washington, D.C.: U.S. Department of State, February 2009).
20. World Bank, "IDA at Work: Haiti: Institutionalizing Key Public Governance Reforms," August 28, 2009.
21. Stevenson Jacobs, "Haitian President Préval Announces Anti-Corruption Campaign," Associated Press, May 18, 2007.
22. Bureau of Democracy, Human Rights, and Labor, "Haiti," in *2008 Country Reports on Human Rights Practices* (Washington, D.C.: U.S. Department of State, 2009).
23. Nancy Roc, *Haiti: The Bitter Grapes of Corruption* (Madrid: Fundación para las Relaciones Internacionales y el Diálogo Exterior, March 2009), 5–6.
24. Ibid., 5.
25. World Bank, "Haiti Governance Diagnostics," Governance and Anticorruption home page.
26. International Monetary Fund (IMF), *Haiti: Enhanced Initiative for Heavily Indebted Poor Countries–Completion Point Document* (Washington, D.C.: IMF, September 2009), 16.
27. World Bank, "IDA at Work: Haiti."
28. Bureau of Economic, Energy, and Business Affairs, "Haiti," in *Investment Climate Statements 2009*.
29. World Bank, "IDA at Work: Haiti."

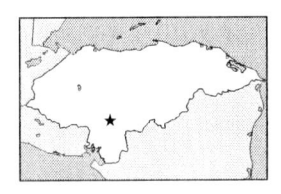

HONDURAS

CAPITAL: Tegucigalpa
POPULATION: 7.5 million
GNI PER CAPITA (PPP): $3,870

SCORES	2007	2010
ACCOUNTABILITY AND PUBLIC VOICE:	3.95	3.54
CIVIL LIBERTIES:	3.77	3.64
RULE OF LAW:	3.46	3.17
ANTICORRUPTION AND TRANSPARENCY:	3.08	2.96

(scores are based on a scale of 0 to 7, with 0 representing weakest and 7 representing strongest performance)

Manuel Orozco and Rebecca Rouse

EDITOR'S NOTE: *The following narrative was written prior to the coup of June 28, 2009. Please see pages 260–261 for an overview of the event and its aftermath.*

INTRODUCTION

Since 2006, Honduras has crossed into dangerous territory due to political ineffectiveness and an inability to deepen democratic institutions. While fragile social movements and members of the international community seek to promote civic engagement and the rule of law, President José Manuel Zelaya Rosales and other politicians have contributed to the deterioration of stability, relying on populism and responding inadequately to challenges from international organized crime networks and persistent poverty.

During Honduras's transition from military rule to representative democracy over the last 30 years, governance has been affected by pressures from business interests, traditional political elites, the military, and deeply entrenched wealthy families seeking to preserve their position by opposing reforms or ensuring their ineffectiveness. The destabilizing power of transnational organized crime and

---

Manuel Orozco is Senior Associate and Director of Remittances and Development at the Inter-American Dialogue, conducting policy analysis and advocacy on issues relating to global flows of remittances and migration and development worldwide. He is also Chair of Central America and the Caribbean at the U.S. Foreign Service Institute and Adjunct Professor at Georgetown University. He holds a Ph.D. in political science from the University of Texas at Austin. **Rebecca Rouse** is a research consultant at the Inter-American Dialogue. She holds an MA in Public Administration from Columbia University, with a fellowship from the Institute of Latin American Studies, and a BA in Political Science from Bryn Mawr College.

widespread violence also now envelop the country: killings, extortion, and kidnappings have become everyday problems. Moreover, an ineffective and corrupt judicial system puts Honduras on a path to further insecurity by creating high levels of impunity and destroying confidence in the authorities.

Honduras entered a long period of military rule in 1963, as officers led by General Oswaldo López Arellano deposed President Ramón Villeda Morales in a bloody coup. López governed until 1971, but after a brief interlude of civilian rule, the military reclaimed power in a second coup in 1972. The military leadership represented a new class of entrepreneurial and political elites, as both active and retired officers leveraged their access to resources and information to create businesses that competed with traditional commercial powers. Throughout the 1980s and 1990s, the military grew into a powerful economic force, with officers becoming major landholders and players in key industries such as telecommunications and banking.

The changing geopolitical landscape in the early 1980s eventually led to the end of military rule. In 1982 Honduras approved a new constitution, followed by the democratic election of President Roberto Suazo Córdoba. The transition to democratic governance gave traditional, nonmilitary business elites an opportunity to reenter politics, and the free-market economic policies of the 1990s provided additional avenues for their renewed assertion of influence.

Honduran social movements also played an important role in the transition from military rule. Membership-driven groups including labor unions, peasant organizations, and indigenous movements were active in the 1980s and early 1990s, but they soon gave way to more professional nongovernmental organizations (NGOs) that were better poised to secure international aid. The devastation caused by Hurricane Mitch in 1998 played a key role in NGO sector expansion, as civil society stepped in to fill the gaps left by an ineffective government response.[1] It is estimated that at the beginning of the 1990s, only about 125 NGOs were operating in Honduras, but by 2001 nearly 5,000 NGOs had been created.[2]

While the holding of democratic elections, improvements in respect for human rights, and the development of civil society since the end of military rule represent substantial advances, much work remains to be done. The autonomy and effectiveness of the government have been compromised by the power of private interests, a weak bureaucracy, drug traffickers, and a two-party system that is unwilling to renovate its leadership. Moreover, corruption is pervasive, manifesting itself through bribes and the intimidation of judges, as well as low accountability for abuses of authority by public officials.

Under President Zelaya the country has faced renewed polarization and poor policy performance. In 2008 and early 2009, Zelaya deepened political divisions, including within his own party, and pitted factions of the business and political elite against one another through increasingly populist posturing. According to many observers, his rhetorical alignment with Venezuelan president Hugo Chávez has decreased his popularity in civil society and incited anger among Honduras's ruling classes and business community. In March 2008, Honduras joined Chávez's Petrocaribe program, giving it access to Venezuelan oil at preferential rates, and in July it was announced that Honduras would join the Bolivarian Alternative for the Americas (ALBA), a leftist regional economic integration body led by Chávez. Honduras was a strong U.S. ally during the Cold War, and the mentalities of that era are still pervasive in the country, allowing Zelaya to create rifts that can be used to his advantage. However, many feel that increased aid from Venezuela only provides more opportunities for impunity and corruption, as Chávez has reportedly stated that he will not demand the same degree of transparency as other donors, such as the United States.[3]

Honduras has one of the highest poverty rates in the region; within the country, the highest rates are found in rural areas, where about half the population lives. Honduras ranked 117 out of 179 countries in the United Nations Development Programme's 2008 Human Development Index. Moreover, according to a report released by the World Food Programme, a wave of global food price increases caused Honduras's poverty rate to rise from 69 percent in September 2007 to 73 percent in June 2008.[4] Nearly one million Hondurans work abroad and support their families through remittances, sending back a total of US$2.8 billion in 2008.

Honduras also suffers from one of the highest homicide rates in the region, with rampant crime attributed to criminal groups such as drug cartels and affiliated youth gangs. In 2008, there were 57.9 murders per 100,000 inhabitants.[5] While the government has adopted an "iron fist" approach to homicides, it focuses mostly on youth gang violence, making membership in a gang punishable by up to 30 years in prison and using the military to conduct raids and help maintain order in major cities. Fewer efforts have been made to curb the powerful influence of crime networks linked to Colombian, Honduran, and Mexican drug traffickers that use the territory as a transshipment point, partly due to lack of capacity and corruption within the security institutions. These shortcomings have led to abuses by security personnel, especially the police, including extrajudicial killings, arbitrary arrests, and illegal searches. Honduran youth in particular have become victims of strict antigang campaigns reminiscent of the army's violent street recruitment raids of the 1980s.

ACCOUNTABILITY AND PUBLIC VOICE   3.54

FREE AND FAIR ELECTORAL LAWS AND ELECTIONS	4.00
EFFECTIVE AND ACCOUNTABLE GOVERNMENT	2.50
CIVIC ENGAGEMENT AND CIVIC MONITORING	3.67
MEDIA INDEPENDENCE AND FREEDOM OF EXPRESSION	4.00

Honduran citizens have the constitutional right to change their government in periodic, free, and fair elections in which the president, vice president, and members of the unicameral National Congress are chosen by universal suffrage.

The executive branch is headed by the president, who is elected by a simple majority. President Zelaya of the Liberal Party (PL) came to power in 2005 elections that were generally considered free and fair, and although observers identified irregularities with some 1,100 ballot boxes, there were no reports of systematic fraud.[6] The 128-member Congress is elected for four-year terms through a mixed system of proportional representation and single-member constituencies. However, Honduras's government and institutions have steadily lost public confidence and credibility in recent years, largely by pursuing the narrow interests of the political and business elites and ignoring the needs of the electorate. In a 2008 public opinion poll carried out by Latinobarómetro, 72 percent of respondents reported that they did not trust elected officials to run the country well.[7] This growing dissatisfaction is reflected in declining voter turnout in recent elections: the share of registered voters turning out for presidential elections fell from 72.1 percent in 1997 to 55.1 percent in 2005.[8]

Honduran politics and governments are controlled in large measure by the two oldest and largest parties, the PL (62 seats in Congress) and the National Party or PN (54 seats in Congress), which dominate the political scene through short-term pacts, excluding smaller parties and civil society. In nonelection years there is very little real debate on fundamental policy and governance issues between the two leading parties, mainly because there is little difference in their platforms. Both have strong ties to the economic elite and thus have a vested interest in maintaining the status quo. There are three other registered parties in Honduras: the Christian Democrats (four seats in Congress), Democratic Unification (five seats), and the Innovation and Unity Party (three). These smaller parties represent an emerging third force, but they still lack the financial capacity to compete with the two major parties.

In May 2004, the government approved a new electoral law. Among other changes, it modified campaign finance rules to promote transparency, ensured open primary elections for all parties, and established the Supreme Electoral Tribunal (TSE) as an independent entity to supervise elections. In 2007, Congress revised the law by increasing the public campaign financing cap from US$3.2 million to US$52 million in an attempt to eliminate incentives for parties to seek financing from criminal groups. Zelaya attempted to veto the move as unconstitutional in January 2008, but the Supreme Court later overturned the veto and upheld the reforms. While these legal changes have been important steps, politicians have often failed to respect the electoral laws, including those governing the use of propaganda, and the TSE has failed to remain free of party control. During the 2005 elections, controversy arose over the appointment of a large number of PL members to the TSE staff, although they were ultimately dismissed. TSE president Aristides Mejía, also a member of the PL, reinvigorated claims of politicization by prematurely declaring Zelaya to be the winner on the basis of preliminary results. Postelection reports included no allegations of fraud linked to this supposed politicization, but Zelaya later appointed Mejía as his defense minister.[9]

The manipulation of public institutions to limit genuine political competition was evident in the November 2008 presidential primaries, when Zelaya and his preferred candidate, National Congress president Roberto Micheletti, made a joint effort to prevent Vice President Elvin Santos from running in the PL primary. A last-minute ruling from the TSE deemed Santos ineligible to run for president because he had temporarily served as commander in chief in his role as vice president, making him subject to the constitutional prohibition on presidential reelection. Santos was replaced by Mauricio Villeda, who secured the PL nomination. Santos resigned from his post in November 2008 and vowed to pursue his candidacy for the presidency, denouncing the efforts of Zelaya and Micheletti to manipulate the primaries. Villeda ultimately renounced his candidacy, allowing for the eventual registration of Santos as the PL contestant by the TSE.

While the constitution provides for the separation of powers, the country's system of checks and balances is seriously compromised. The judiciary lacks independence due to pressure from the executive and the two main political parties (see Rule of Law). For its part, the legislative branch is generally subject to significant control by the leader of the Congress. Traditionally, the executive has dominated the other branches of government. When Zelaya attempted to continue and expand this tradition while also shifting toward populist rhetoric, however, tension between the legislative, judicial, and executive branches steadily mounted. In 2009, Congress rejected his Supreme Court nominations, along with those of other government appointees. In November 2008, Zelaya had initiated an attempt to hold a national referendum asking citizens whether a ballot item on the desirability of convoking a constitutional assembly should be included in the November 2009 presidential election. When other interests challenged the legality of Zelaya's actions, which were perceived as a bid to pave the way for his own reelection, the president refused to back down. The inability of the Supreme Court and Congress to exert their authority in the face of Zelaya's disregard for the limits placed on executive power generated the institutional tensions that ultimately led to the June 28 coup (see box).

Due to mismanagement, corruption, and the strong influence of private interests, the government has only a limited ability to execute public policy and offer services. Public institutions have suffered from financial mismanagement under Zelaya's administration, with organizations such as the National Registry of Persons and the National Electric Energy Company shutting down or teetering close to bankruptcy. Honduras also experiences frequent partisan purges of civil service officers and agency and institution heads at every level, inhibiting continuity in programming, removing capable and experienced officials, and damaging overall government efficacy. There is a general lack of ethical behavior in government institutions, which are used for the personal benefit of the ruling class to obtain concessions and strategic economic information, protect private businesses, evade taxes, influence legislation and court decisions, and maintain an environment of impunity for corrupt officials.[10] According to the

Inter-American Development Bank, Honduras rates last in a survey of institutional capacity in 18 Latin American countries.[11]

While social movements in Honduras have lost steam since the end of the military era, the NGO sector has expanded since the early 1990s, especially in the wake of Hurricane Mitch in 1998. There are approximately 8,000 NGOs working in Honduras, but they are fragmented, diffuse, and underfunded, with few organizations working on human rights, civic engagement, or civic monitoring. However, a set of governance-monitoring institutions is beginning to emerge,[12] and in May 2008 a potentially important new social movement called the Broad Movement for Dignity and Justice (MADJ) arose out of a highly publicized anticorruption hunger strike led by public prosecutors. The movement serves as an umbrella group for social organizations, religious groups, trade unions, and prosecutors who are working on transparency issues.

Honduran NGOs currently operate within a limited regulatory framework. In March 2009, Congress proposed a new NGO law that would place restrictions on the use of funds and the range of acceptable activities. It would prohibit religious and political activities for such groups, thus excluding many churches that had been registered as NGOs. According to officials, the law is intended to prevent businesses from operating under the guise of nonprofit organizations and to limit NGO financing and support of political parties. No agreement had been reached on the final content of this proposal as of mid-2009.

Civil society activists face real limitations and risks in the course of their work, as the environment for free speech has deteriorated in recent years. Experts point to a climate of fear and possible self-censorship among civil society leaders due to threats of kidnapping, violence, and other forms of retaliation. Victims of threats and attacks include leaders of labor unions and indigenous rights movements as well as activists and journalists who have accused public officials of corruption. Fears of increased political repression and censorship were substantiated in 2008, when a "blacklist" of 135 Honduran popular leaders, along with a camera containing photographs of NGO offices, were confiscated from two plainclothes policemen by security personnel at the National Autonomous University of Honduras; the policemen were detained while following the president of the student union. The list included the names of indigenous leaders, labor leaders, journalists, and clergy, with many marked for tracking and surveillance. The name of well-known union leader Altagracia Fuentes, who had been assassinated in April of that year, appeared on the list with the comment "deceased." A number of senior officials, political figures, and activists received death threats in 2008, including five human rights prosecutors, the mayor of Tegucigalpa, the attorney general, and the president of the Supreme Court.

One of the greatest threats to Honduran democracy is the lack of independent media. The country's media outlets are generally controlled by business and political interests, have failed to fulfill their social function as independent government watchdogs, and do not maintain fair reporting practices. The media sector serves as the primary battleground for political and economic control in Honduras. Indeed, after the country's powerful anti-Zelaya media moguls employed their outlets to criticize the president, he responded by requiring, starting in May 2007, that radio and television stations include a series of 10 interviews with public officials. Newspapers circulate freely, and the three most popular papers—*La Tribuna*, *El Heraldo*, and *El Tiempo*—are owned by some of the most economically and politically powerful families in Honduras. Numerous radio and television stations broadcast without interference, and there is unrestricted access to the internet. However, broadcasters operate as arms of political parties and are subject to the interests of the political and business elite. Channel 8, a state-run television channel, was launched in August 2008 with the mission of informing the public on the activities of the government. It has since faced controversy, including accusations that it serves as a publicity vehicle for the executive branch, as well as a legal battle over control of the broadcasting signal. In November 2008, a judge ordered Channel 8's broadcasting rights to be transferred from the government to the private company Teleunsa, but this ruling has not yet been carried out. Similarly, the National Commission of Telecommunications received a court order in May 2009 to release broadcast rights for Channel 12 to the private company Eldi, but has not complied.

In 2005, the Supreme Court struck down a restrictive defamation law that had protected public officials from scrutiny. While freedom of speech and the press are protected by the constitution, these freedoms are not generally respected. Journalists have become prone to self-censorship, both because of the political connections and interests of media owners and because of rampant corruption. According to a 2008 report from the Open Society Institute, government payments to journalists are an institutionalized practice. Government advertising is also routinely used to purchase favorable coverage or silence criticism in the media. In a positive development, evangelical Christian media outlets emerged as a critical voice against government corruption in 2008 in relation to the hunger strike staged by public prosecutors. However, experts warn that it remains to be seen how impartial these outlets will be and how effectively they will promote transparency and democracy.

Independent news coverage is also inhibited by a general climate of insecurity for journalists. Threats and attacks against reporters have been on the rise since 2003, and experts estimate that at least three dozen journalists were subject to threats and intimidation in 2008.[13] In one prominent case, radio journalist Carlos Salgado was shot and killed as he left the offices of Radio Cadena Voces in Tegucigalpa in October 2007. While German David Almendárez was quickly arrested in connection with the crime, he was exonerated in 2009 after spending more than a year in prison awaiting trial. In March 2009, a second Radio Cadena Voces reporter, Rafael Munguía, was killed by unknown assailants as he drove through the city of San Pedro Sula. He had reportedly received threats prior to his death. Radio Cadenas Voces is often critical of the Zelaya administration. The Inter-American Press Association reports that several Honduran journalists, including Geovanny García of Channel 13 and Dagoberto Rodríguez of Radio Cadena Voces, have fled the country in response to threats or attacks related to their work.

CIVIL LIBERTIES 3.64

PROTECTION FROM STATE TERROR, UNJUSTIFIED IMPRISONMENT, AND TORTURE	2.38
GENDER EQUITY	3.33
RIGHTS OF ETHNIC, RELIGIOUS, AND OTHER DISTINCT GROUPS	2.75
FREEDOM OF CONSCIENCE AND BELIEF	6.00
FREEDOM OF ASSOCIATION AND ASSEMBLY	3.75

Honduras's high rates of crime and violence have created a climate of fear, and combined with impunity for security personnel and an ineffective criminal justice system, this has resulted in very serious violations of civil liberties.

The country's crime problems are related to the presence of transnational gangs and drug-trafficking networks, especially in major urban centers such as Tegucigalpa and San Pedro Sula. As noted above, Honduras has one of the highest homicide rates in the region, registering 57.9 murders per 100,000 inhabitants in 2008.[14] According to a 2007 national survey conducted by Borge y Asociados, about three-quarters of Hondurans feel unsafe using public transportation or traveling on highways, approximately three-fifths feel unsafe walking on the street or visiting the market, half say they feel unsafe in their own cars, and nearly a third report feeling unsafe at work.[15] Incidents of kidnapping increased in 2009, and have expanded to include assaults on school buses to kidnap children leaving school.[16]

The UN Office on Drugs and Crime estimates that there are approximately 36,000 gang members in Honduras, concentrated in the groups Mara Salvatrucha (MS-13) and 18th Street. Honduras launched a zero-tolerance policy against violent youth gangs in 2003, known as *mano dura* (iron fist), and the maximum prison sentence for gang membership was increased from 13 to 30 years in 2004. The mano dura policy focused on punishing gang members and neglected to sufficiently address rehabilitation or the root causes of delinquency. Upon taking office in 2005, Zelaya launched his own crackdown on crime and violence after kidnappings increased and Micheletti's nephew was killed. While these policies were initially reported to have had a positive effect on crime rates, they were considered unproductive overall. The homicide rate increased by 25 percent between 2007 and 2008, and kidnappings increased by 85.7 percent in 2008, jumping from 42 kidnappings in 2007 to 78 in 2008.[17]

Organizations such as Casa Alianza, which works with street children, report that harsh, unchecked policies targeting youth gang members have led to police profiling based on appearance (such as tattoos), discrimination against youths, arbitrary arrests, and even extrajudicial killings by state security forces. These practices have also been recognized by the international community, and in 2006 the Inter-American Court of Human Rights condemned Honduras for the extrajudicial killings of four youths and one adult in 1995. Casa Alianza reports that 3,943 children and adults were killed from 1998 to 2007 by vigilante groups that may have included members of the military or police.[18] According to the Ministry of Security, in 2008 authorities prosecuted 268 police officers for offenses such as abuse of authority, drug trafficking, rape, and homicide.[19] In general, however, citizens are not protected against torture and other violence, and the abuse of detainees is a serious problem. In an October 2008 report, the Center for the Prevention, Treatment, and Rehabilitation of Victims of Torture and Their Families revealed that 69 percent of 804 inmates interviewed between 2004 and 2008 claimed to have been abused during detention, while in transit, or at a police station. The report also noted that three men had died due to police abuse in 2008.[20]

Not to be confused with turf-based youth gangs, the drug-trafficking cartels that use Honduras as a transit point for drugs headed to the United States are highly organized business operations, though they increasingly integrate members of youth gangs and local drug networks into their activities. In recent years, the transnational cartels have joined forces with local criminal groups to take control of strategic regions of Honduras, especially along the borders and coastline. Much of Honduras's border is remote and sparsely populated, and lacks any effective state presence. Mexican drug cartels, specifically the Sinaloa and Gulf cartels, have become particularly active in Honduras, partly in response to the Mexican authorities' crackdown on traffickers within Mexico. Honduran authorities believe that several top leaders of the Sinaloa cartel are hiding in Honduras, and that they have been involved in executions and the training of death squads in the country's northwest. In May 2008, cartel leader Jorge Mario Paredes Córdova was captured in San Pedro Sula by the Honduran National Police. In addition, the transnational groups' practice of paying local criminal networks in drugs has exacerbated a growing domestic drug problem.

Politicians and other leaders agree that these cartels are financing political parties and infiltrating public offices.[21] In June 2008, the U.S. Coast Guard seized 4.6 tons of cocaine from a Honduran boat near La Mosquitia. The boat had previously been seized by the Honduran authorities and was under the control of the Office for the Management of Seized Assets (OABI) when it was recaptured by the Coast Guard, indicating the infiltration of public institutions by drug cartels. In fact, Alfredo Landaverde, a former adviser to the Ministry of Security, told the newspaper *La Prensa* in an August 2008 interview that drug cartels have infiltrated Honduran police and military forces as well as the judicial system.

In response to this deteriorating situation, Zelaya and Congress announced a new plan to combat organized crime in April 2009. It included suspending

EDITOR'S NOTE: COUP IN HONDURAS

On the morning of June 28, 2009, Honduran soldiers entered the presidential palace and forced pajama-clad President Manuel Zelaya onto a plane to Costa Rica. Thus climaxed an institutional clash that pitted President Zelaya against members of Congress, the courts, and the military in a conflict surrounding the president's plan to hold a non-binding referendum that the president and his supporters hoped would be the first step toward the creation of an assembly to rewrite the constitution. Both the Supreme Court and Congress opposed these plans, ruling that the constitution banned referendums within six months of elections, and the military refused to distribute the ballots. Opponents generally considered Zelaya's actions a thinly veiled attempt to end the constitutional ban on presidential reelection. When Zelaya pressed ahead and fired the chief of the army for failing to cooperate, the Supreme Court ordered the military to detain the president. Following his expulsion from the country, Congress swiftly moved to declare congressional leader Roberto Micheletti the new president.

The coup's orchestrators insisted that their actions were not illegal as they were carried out in accordance with Honduran law and were necessary to save Honduran democracy from the threat posed by Zelaya. In turn, Zelaya claimed that he never had any intention of seeking reelection, that the balloting was merely consultative, and that he could not have benefited since the binding call for a constituent assembly would not have occurred until the vote to pick his replacement. In the weeks following the coup, Zelaya encouraged protests and repeatedly sought to reenter the country. Within Honduras, the coup was immediately followed by government repression of Zelaya supporters, restrictions on civil liberties and human rights abuses committed by members of security forces. International organizations documented instances of excessive use of force against protesters, arbitrary detentions, mistreatment of detainees, violence against women, and the harassment of activists, journalists, lawyers, and judges.[32] More than 1,200 people were reported arrested after participating in anti-coup demonstrations, and at least 12 citizens were killed by security forces. The Micheletti-led de facto government instituted restrictions on freedoms of assembly and association, imposed frequent curfews, and closed at least three opposition media outlets.

Although reaction to the coup within the country evidenced Honduras' polarization, it was widely condemned by international actors including all countries in the hemisphere, the United Nations, the Organization of American States, and the European Union, each of whom declared the military's actions illegal and refused to recognize the de facto regime. Several months of OAS-backed negotiations between Zelaya and Micheletti's faction mediated by Costa Rican President Óscar Arias appeared to have stalemated when Zelaya dramatically appeared in the Brazilian embassy in Tegucigalpa on September 21. Though his presence gave new impetus to the talks, the dialogue failed to yield a mutually satisfactory resolution to the crisis. On November 29, Honduras held its scheduled presidential election amid a climate of severely compromised civil liberties and press freedoms. The balloting was generally considered to have met international standards and resulted in a win for PN candidate Porfirio Lobo. Observers fear that Lobo's victory will result in a return to "business as usual" in Honduran politics, impunity for human rights offenders, and a failure to address the underlying conflicts and institutional weaknesses that led to the crisis.

the inviolability of communication rights, controlling the circulation of vehicles, monitoring mobile-telephone purchases, improving school security, and imposing mandatory prison sentences for those convicted in organized crime cases.[22]

Arrested criminal suspects face difficult conditions. There have been reported cases of lengthy pretrial detention, denial of due process, and the abuse of inmates by security forces. About 63.5 percent of prisoners in Honduras are awaiting trial. The prison system is notoriously overcrowded, and there have been several highly publicized cases of prison fires and riots that have left dozens of inmates dead, often with allegations of foul play. In April 2003, the Associated Press reported that prisoners were locked in their cells, doused with gasoline, and set on fire during an uprising in El Porvenir prison that left 70 people dead. A group of 22 security officials were convicted in 2008 in connection with the massacre.[23] A prison fire in May 2004 killed 103 inmates, and two prison riots in April and May 2008 left 27 prisoners dead.

The National Human Rights Commission (CONADEH) is responsible for promoting awareness of human rights issues, submitting recommendations to state institutions, ensuring that state officials uphold human rights, and investigating citizens' complaints. CONADEH is largely independent, and state institutions have heeded its recommendations on various matters.[24] The 2008 CONADEH report stated that 7,140 human rights cases, or 75 percent of the 9,525 received that year, were resolved. Some 51 percent of these cases involved complaints against state authorities including the National Police, the Public Ministry, and the Supreme Court.[25] While a National Anticorruption Council (CNA) report noted that only 28.7 percent of Hondurans believe that CONADEH is effectively carrying out its mandate, the commission fared better than all other institutions surveyed.[26]

Violence against women is widespread in Honduras, and the Center of Women's Studies (CEM-H) reports that an average of 14,000 domestic violence complaints were filed annually between January 2003 and September 2008.[27] Between 2002 and 2008, 1,114 women were murdered, the grand majority by their husbands or partners.[28] This violence occurs against a backdrop of marginalization in which women experience limited levels of civic participation and high levels of poverty and discrimination. Few cases of domestic violence are investigated or reach the courts, and laws prohibiting gender-based discrimination are often not enforced. Women are traditionally concentrated in low-skilled, low-wage jobs, such as in *maquila* export processing zones, and they are often subject to exploitation by employers.

Indigenous and Afro-Hondurans, or Garifunas, also face routine discrimination and disenfranchisement. Indigenous groups make up about 8 percent of the population, or more than 621,000 people.[29] In the 2005 elections, three Garifunas became the first of their ethnicity to win seats in Congress. However, while the constitution protects the rights of indigenous peoples, they are still subject to harassment, intimidation, and violence, especially with regard to land disputes. According to Amnesty International, indigenous activists have been victims of fabricated, politically motivated criminal charges as a result of their work to protect property rights and protest construction and logging projects that affect their communities.[30] In 2006, police killed two activists from the Olancho Environmental Movement; in 2008, indigenous activists increased protests over the construction of the Patuca hydroelectric dam. While Honduras is a signatory to the International Labor Organization's Convention 169, which protects the rights of indigenous peoples, critics say the government's actions regarding mining, logging, and energy have systematically violated the convention. In early 2009, the Fraternal Organization of Afro-Hondurans spoke out against a new hydrocarbons law under consideration by the government, saying it would disproportionately affect minority populations and violate Convention 169.

The constitution protects freedom of religion, and while the majority of the population is Roman Catholic, the Catholic Church has been losing influence in recent years amid the growing popularity of evangelical Protestant churches. The constitution also guarantees freedom of association and assembly. Hondurans regularly utilize their right to organize, and according to the Ministry of Labor, about 519 unions represent 8 percent of the labor force.[31] Union leaders are often at risk of violence and harassment. For example, Israel García, leader of the National Association of Honduran Farmworkers, and Altagracia Fuentes and Yolanda Sánchez, both of the Honduran Workers' Federation, were assassinated in 2008. The leaders had previously received threats while organizing workers in the San Pedro Sula area. In May 2009, police arrested two suspects in the murders of Fuentes, fellow union official Virginia García de Sánchez, and their driver. Economic elites use their chambers of commerce and the private-sector trade association to exert a decidedly antiunion political influence.

Protest rights are generally upheld, and protests involving indigenous rights, environmental issues, human rights, and justice issues are common, as are demonstrations against government policies, corruption, and impunity.

RULE OF LAW   3.17

INDEPENDENT JUDICIARY	3.00
PRIMACY OF RULE OF LAW IN CIVIL AND CRIMINAL MATTERS	3.00
ACCOUNTABILITY OF SECURITY FORCES AND MILITARY TO CIVILIAN AUTHORITIES	3.00
PROTECTION OF PROPERTY RIGHTS	3.67

Uncontrolled crime and poor enforcement of civil and political rights contribute to the lack of effective rule of law in the country. As with other branches of government, the judicial system is plagued by high levels of politicization. Although the constitution calls for an independent judiciary, the highest judicial offices are divided along partisan lines, and judges can be removed at any time by the president of the Supreme Court, who often acts according to political interests.[33] According to the CNA, central weaknesses in the judicial system also include widespread corruption and a lack of ethics and technical capacity among judges.[34] The strong role of partisan politics and private interests in the judiciary affects the courts' ability to fight corruption in other parts of the government and society, reinforcing the country's climate of impunity.

The judicial branch is led by the 15-member Supreme Court. Members serve seven-year terms, and a new Supreme Court was selected in early 2009. Honduran law provides for an inclusive selection process, whereby seven civil society and government entities draw up lists of nominees, from which 45 are selected by a nominating panel. Congress chooses the new members from this group of 45.[35] While this mechanism provides for broad participation, an international observer mission organized by the International Commission of Jurists reported multiple allegations of irregularities in the 2008 selection process related to political influence in the creation of the nomination lists.[36] The mission expressed concern over the lack of public information regarding the selection process and nominees, and the meager coverage of the process by the Honduran media. Civil society organizations argued that there was a preexisting arrangement between the two major parties to select candidates from their own ranks, and indeed the court has remained split, 8 to 7, between the National and Liberal parties, respectively. The selection process also reflected growing tensions between Zelaya and Congress. Zelaya sought to pressure Congress to include his own favored candidates in the list, but lawmakers ultimately rejected his nominees. The army and police were even mobilized during the selection in January 2009 based on a supposed need to maintain order. The stakes of the selection process are high, since the Supreme Court names all lower court judges. Lower-ranking judges and other judicial officials are often vulnerable to bribery due to inadequate wages and limited internal controls.

Although the Supreme Court gained the authority to try high public officials for abuse of power and other offenses in 2004, it has not done so effectively due to the strong pressure exerted by other government branches, the main political parties, and other powerful economic and political interests.[37] For example, the court acquitted former president Rafael Leonardo Callejas of corruption charges and ordered his release in 2005. CNA president Óscar Andrés Rodríguez claimed that Callejas had used his political weight to pressure the Supreme Court and negotiate his sentence.[38]

The court system is overloaded by the high levels of crime, and this situation is only compounded by operational inefficiency. As noted above, lengthy pretrial detention and reports of denial of due process are common. While Honduran law provides for the right to a public trial and the right to counsel, including access to a state-provided attorney if necessary, these rights are not always upheld in practice. Judicial procedures have been influenced by the country's prevailing insecurity, and the treatment of financial crimes often differs greatly from that of ordinary street crimes. While cases of corruption often go uninvestigated due to the possible repercussions of identifying powerful offenders, perpetrators of property and violent crimes may receive severe penalties. The pressure on judges to rule in line with the government's harsh antigang policies can also cloud the fairness of trials and sentences. Given these factors, equal treatment under the law is often not respected in practice. Threats and violence against whistleblowers have further reduced the accountability of the judiciary. In September 2008, public prosecutor Luis Javier Santos was shot four times in connection with his work as the leader of a protest demanding the resignation of Attorney General Leonidas Rosa and his deputy, Omar Cerna, for failure to investigate cases of corruption. While the attempted murder was condemned by the government, no arrests had been made by mid-2009.

Prosecutors are subject to extensive political control. In 2002, 23.8 percent of prosecutors surveyed reported facing internal pressure.[39] In 2004, 200 prosecutors went on strike after 10 of their colleagues were removed from their posts and seven were transferred after criticizing the prosecutor general's decision to halt 90 corruption cases, seven of which involved former president Callejas.[40] The Public Prosecutors' Association organized a 38-day hunger strike in April 2008 to protest Attorney General Rosa's interference in their professional activities. They claimed that senior officials in the Public Ministry pressured, threatened, and arbitrarily transferred several prosecutors while firing those with knowledge of high-profile corruption cases (see Anticorruption and Transparency).[41]

Over the past 30 years, Honduras has undertaken several reforms to return state security forces to civilian control as part of its transition from military rule to democracy. By 1999, the government had created a new civilian police force, implemented a new Organic Police Law, created units for internal police accountability, and established CONADEH. The police force has nearly doubled from 7,500 officers in 2005 to nearly 14,000 in 2008.[42] However, there is little focus on preventative policing or investigations, and the increased manpower has arguably done little to improve the security situation. In recent years, the infiltration of the police force by criminal networks has also become a cause for concern.

The National Committee of Interior Security (CONASIN) allows for civil society and interinstitutional participation in the development of policies and strategies for the national security apparatus. It consists of members of the judiciary, representatives of business and civil society groups, and CONADEH. However, in 2007 talks began to reform the role of CONASIN in the police force, with Zelaya claiming that the body negatively affected the efficiency of security operations and interfered with the executive branch's control over the police. The Organic Police Law was consequently reformed in 2008, stripping CONASIN of most of its functions and effectively reducing civilian oversight. The law also created a new investigative unit within the attorney general's office. National Human Rights Commissioner Ramón Custodio has protested the reforms and spoken out against the potential danger of concentrating control of the police and limiting civil society participation in state security.

Impunity for human rights violations committed by the security forces remains a problem. In 1993, Honduran law was modified to allow military officials to be tried in civilian courts, but the military has continued to use its power to thwart the justice process. A 2007 UN mission noted that there were still 129 open cases involving forced disappearances committed between 1981 and 1989. It urged Honduras to fully investigate these cases, but the government has yet to do so.[43] There have been some investigations into more recent alleged abuses. In 2008, four policemen were found guilty of killing two members of the Environmentalist Movement of Olancho in 2006. Nevertheless, three of these men escaped from prison shortly after being sentenced and have yet to be found.

Honduras has made important advances in the protection of property rights, but enforcement of contracts and the protection of property rights for rural and indigenous Hondurans are still areas of concern. Prior to 2004, when Congress enacted an overhaul of the property registration system, the process was ineffective and inefficient, and as recently as 2002 only 37 percent of properties in the capital were registered, according to the World Bank.[44] Honduras has also taken steps to improve the protection of intellectual property rights in accordance with the Dominican Republic–Central American Free Trade Agreement (DR-CAFTA) with the United States. These reforms have focused on improving Honduras's business climate, but again, little progress has been made in protecting the property of indigenous communities (see Civil Liberties).

ANTICORRUPTION AND TRANSPARENCY   2.96

ENVIRONMENT TO PROTECT AGAINST CORRUPTION	3.00
PROCEDURES AND SYSTEMS TO ENFORCE ANTICORRUPTION LAWS	3.00
EXISTENCE OF ANTICORRUPTION NORMS, STANDARDS, AND PROTECTIONS	3.00
GOVERNMENTAL TRANSPARENCY	2.83

Corruption is rampant in public institutions at all levels, from the executive branch to local police precincts. In 2008, Transparency International ranked Honduras 126 out of 180 countries in its Corruption Perceptions Index. Corruption is repeatedly cited in nationwide surveys as one of the top three problems facing Honduras, and 95 percent of Hondurans surveyed find that levels of corruption are extremely high.[45] The problem is exacerbated by the politicization of the judicial system and the media, which collude with corrupt elites to impede transparency and ensure an environment of impunity in which few cases of corruption reach the courts. Low levels of civil society participation and oversight also leave officials unaccountable for irregular practices, although some organizations, such as C-Libre and the CNA, have emerged as leaders in the fight against graft.

Bureaucratic obstacles in Honduras are substantial, and payments to public officials to expedite processing are common. Some 22 percent of respondents in a 2007 CNA survey on corruption said they had paid a bribe at some point during their lives, while 10.4 percent reported paying a bribe within the last 12 months. Those receiving the bribes included the transit police and judges.[46]

Public officials are legally required to disclose their assets, but the rules are not effectively enforced. The CNA estimates the toll of corruption at nearly 2 percentage points of Honduras's gross domestic product, or around US$100 million annually. It also allegedly reduces public spending by about US$140 million annually and affects US$30 million in investment every year, not including foreign direct investment.[47] State activity in the economy is not adequately regulated, and state enterprises such as the national telecommunications company, Hondutel, and National Electric Energy are plagued by mismanagement. Both enterprises nearly went bankrupt following Zelaya's direct appointment of cronies to top positions. The Supreme Accounts Tribunal (TSC), which is responsible for monitoring the financial discipline of state-owned enterprises and other state institutions, has implicated Hondutel in various corruption scandals related to misappropriation of funds. Hondutel officials have most recently been accused of accepting bribes from the international carrier LatinNode.[48]

Despite tremendous challenges, public officials have sought to create a legal framework to fight corruption and increase transparency in government. However, the high degree of politicization in public institutions has been a significant barrier to the effectiveness of adopted policies, and Honduras continues to lack comprehensive anticorruption legislation. Government entities with anticorruption mandates include the TSC, which is responsible for auditing the financial operations of all state entities and institutions and initiating investigations into irregularities; the Public Prosecutor's Office against Corruption, which investigates corruption in the public administration; and CONADEH. At the local level, municipal commissioners and transparency commissions are responsible for combating corruption. However, these institutions are widely perceived to be ineffective. A CNA survey revealed that only 20.9 percent of Hondurans believed that the TSC was effectively fulfilling its mandate; the figures for the Public Prosecutor's Office against Corruption and CONADEH were 22.3 percent and 28.7 percent, respectively.[49] The CNA itself was originally composed of state agencies, civil society groups, and members of the private sector, but it became an independent civil society organization in 2005 and now plays an instrumental role in monitoring corruption in the country.

Under Zelaya, government officials have been implicated in a number of high-profile corruption scandals, and cases of abuse of authority, fraud, and misappropriation of funds have abounded. Zelaya himself is currently being investigated for 120 cases of corruption amounting to the theft of over US$2.5 million from the Central Bank of Honduras.[50] In addition, during Zelaya's first year in office, Health Minister Orizon Velásquez and Rosario Godoy, the director of the national children's board, were forced to resign after being accused of reducing debts owed to the government by a pharmaceutical company. In July 2007, Ramiro Chacón, the head of the Road Fund, was accused of committing irregularities in contracts, but he was subsequently offered the post of vice minister in the Secretariat of Public Works, Housing, and Transport. Furthermore, Guillermo Seamman, former head of the Civil Aeronautical Authority, was detained in August 2008 for alleged abuse of authority related to his approval of 39 certifications for airline employees who had failed to complete the legal requirements. He was later released pending investigation.

In terms of prosecutions and convictions, impunity remains the norm. Scandals that surfaced under past administrations have not been fully resolved. For example, former president Callejas was acquitted of corruption charges in 2005, although the United States revoked his visa in 2006 citing the same charges, and the gasoline-smuggling and illegal-passport scandals that surfaced during the administration of former president Ricardo Maduro were not fully investigated and prosecuted. According to the CNA's 2007 report, a mere 2.2 percent of the 1,925 corruption cases heard by the Supreme Court between 2002 and 2006 yielded a conviction. The lack of effective prosecution is partly the result of pervasive corruption within the judiciary itself.[51] However, the 2008 hunger strike organized by public prosecutors resulted in the reform of Article 25 in Honduras's Public Ministry Law, allowing for the investigation and firing of the attorney general.

Allegations of corruption receive substantial, albeit superficial, coverage in the country's media outlets. The CNA has noted a lack of thorough investigative journalism and professionalism within the media, which tends to provide sensationalist coverage of corruption scandals.[52] In addition, the lack of effective whistleblower protections, corruption among journalists, and a fear of government reprisals all help to suppress reporting on corruption.[53]

Honduras's corruption problem extends to the education sector. A 2008 report highlighted widespread abuse of power and mismanagement of funds by headmasters, high rates of absenteeism among teachers, and rigged allocation of teaching posts, which combined to constitute yet another drain on the state budget.[54] In addition, a 2007 UNESCO report revealed that "ghost teachers"—teachers who never existed or had left the school—represented 5 percent of the teachers' payroll in Honduras in 2000.[55]

Public access to government information remains somewhat restricted. The annual budget is submitted to Congress for review but is not first made available to the public. Furthermore, expenditure accounting during the year remains rather opaque. As a result, Honduras received a score of just 11 percent on the 2008 Open Budget Index.[56] Expenditure accounting is monitored by the TSC, but politicization and resource shortages within this institution weaken its effectiveness. In November 2006, Honduras adopted the Transparency and Access to Public Information Law, establishing the National Institute for Access to Public Information as the official body to facilitate citizen requests for information. The law has been criticized for requiring that 10 years pass before a document can be declassified, and for allowing the purging of documents every five years.[57] The institute is operational and is working with civil society organizations to hold workshops on using the information now available. However, some experts warn that the institute has already been corrupted through the politicized selection of its administration.

The awarding of state contracts remains problematic, and numerous corruption scandals involving government contracts have surfaced in recent years. According to the 2001 Government Contracting Law, public works contracts valued at over US$53,000 must be awarded through public competitive bidding. In addition, a 2006 Competition Law set up an enforcement commission to ensure that anticompetitive practices are effectively discouraged. Nevertheless, in recent years the government has attempted to use "emergency situation" arguments to support its use of noncompetitive procurement measures on hospital and airport projects.[58] The new Information Law is meant to increase the transparency of the procurement information system, but this is still a work in progress.[59]

In a sign of growing public consciousness regarding corruption, nearly 30,000 Hondurans took to the streets of Tegucigalpa in February 2007 to demand government transparency. The anticorruption movement continued to gain momentum in April 2008 with the hunger strike organized by public prosecutors. Leaders of the strike claimed that the attorney general and his deputy had deliberately refrained from investigating at least 16 allegations of corruption against members of the political and business elite. While some dismissed the hunger strike as politically motivated, many observers argued that the highly publicized and polemical strike achieved a great deal in raising public awareness on issues of corruption and impunity, and created demand for a culture of accountability in the country.

RECOMMENDATIONS

- The effects of the newly established NGO law should be evaluated to determine whether it helps formalize civil society associations, impedes organizing in some areas of social interest, or limits performance of its mission by restricting access to funding. A revision of the law should be undertaken to address any negative effects.
- An independent commission composed of media directors, journalists, and other experts should be established to assess the role of the media in Honduras's democracy, the challenges and constraints they face, and solutions to improve their performance.
- The government should focus on supporting reintegration programs to reduce recidivism among former prisoners, as the growing size of Honduras's prison population will otherwise constitute a threat to society in the longer term. The state should also provide human rights training to prison guards and establish accountability and monitoring mechanisms.
- The government should continue and enhance cooperation with the U.S. Coast Guard and other law enforcement agencies in the region to track and disrupt the activities of drug cartels.

NOTES

For URLs and endnote hyperlinks, please visit the *Countries at the Crossroads* homepage at http://freedomhouse.org/template.cfm?page=139&edition=8.

[1] Hurricane Mitch left 5,600 people dead, sharply increased migratory flows of Hondurans to the United States, destroyed key infrastructure, and caused more than US$3 billion in damage.
[2] Andre-Marcel d'Ans, *Honduras después del Mitch: Ecología Política de un Desastre* (Tegucigalpa: Centro de Documentación de Honduras, February 2008).
[3] Thelma Mejía, "President Clashes with Traditional Elites," Inter Press Service, October 23, 2008.
[4] World Food Programme, *Alzas de Precios, Mercados e Inseguridad Alimentaria y Nutricional en Centroamérica* (San Salvador: World Food Programme, October 2008).
[5] Agustín Lagos, "De 2000 a 2008 Se Reportan 28,000 Homicidios," *Heraldo*, March 15, 2009.
[6] Bureau of Democracy, Human Rights, and Labor, "Honduras," in *Country Reports on Human Rights Practices 2008* (Washington, D.C.: U.S. Department of State, February 25, 2009).
[7] Corporación Latinobarómetro, *Informe 2008* (Santiago de Chile: Latinobarómetro, November 2008).
[8] International Institute for Democracy and Electoral Assistance (IDEA), "Honduras: Country Profile," IDEA home page.

9. Michael Lettieri, "Courting the Vote: Electoral Courts and Councils Take on the Challenge of Guaranteeing a Free and Fair Vote throughout Latin America," Council on Hemispheric Affairs, February 15, 2006.
10. Consejo Nacional Anticorrupción (CNA), *Informe Nacional de Transparencia: Hacia un Sistema Nacional de Integridad* (Tegucigalpa: CNA, 2007).
11. Inter-American Development Bank, "Gráfico 4.3: Índice de Capacidad Funcional Burocrática," in *The Politics of Policies: Economic and Social Progress in Latin America, 2006 Report* (Washington, D.C.: Inter-American Development Bank, 2005).
12. Eugenio Sosa, "La Sociedad Civil y la Agenda Anticorrupción," in *Colección Ética e Integridad para el Desarrollo* (Tegucigalpa: CNA, 2007).
13. Bureau of Democracy, Human Rights, and Labor, "Honduras."
14. Lagos, "De 2000 a 2008 Se Reportan 28,000 Homicidios."
15. Borge y Asociados and Comisionado Nacional de los Derechos Humanos-Honduras (CONADEH), *Encuesta Nacional de Opinión Publica—Seguridad Ciudadana* (Tegucigalpa: Borge y Asociados and CONADEH, August 2007).
16. "Jóvenes Marchan para Pedir Liberación de Menores Secuestrados," Proceso Digital, April 4, 2009.
17. ANSA, "Secuestros Aumentaron en 85,7% en 2008 en Honduras," Radio La Primerísima, December 26, 2008.
18. Casa Alianza, "Honduras–Stop the Killings of Children and Youth," How You Can Help Street Children.
19. Bureau of Democracy, Human Rights, and Labor, "Honduras."
20. Alba Mejía, *Informe Intermediario de las ONG sobre el Seguimiento de las Observaciones Finales* (Tegucigalpa: Centro de Prevención, Tratamiento y Rehabilitación de Victimas de la Tortura y Sus Familiares, October 2008), 4.
21. "Narcos Mexicanos Podrían Estar Financiando Campañas Políticas en Honduras," Proceso Digital, March 19, 2009.
22. Agence France-Presse, "Zelaya Anuncia Medidas para Enfrentar el Crimen Organizado," *Diario Co Latino*, April 2, 2009.
23. Pablo Zapata, "Tribunales Individualizan Penas a Responsables de Masacre en El Porvenir," *Prensa*, September 5, 2008.
24. CNA, *Informe Nacional de Transparencia*, 66.
25. CONADEH, *Informe Anual 2008* (Tegucigalpa: CONADEH, 2008), 3.
26. CNA, *Informe Nacional de Transparencia*, 68.
27. United Nations Development Programme, "ONU Afirma Que la Violencia contra las Mujeres Deprime la Economía del País," news release, November 24, 2008.
28. Ibid.
29. Bureau of Democracy, Human Rights, and Labor, "Honduras."
30. Amnesty International, "Honduras: No Justice for Indigenous Human Rights Defenders," press release, 2006.
31. Bureau of Democracy, Human Rights, and Labor, "Honduras."
32. Amnesty International, "Independent Investigation Needed into Honduras Human Rights Abuses," news release, December 3, 2009.
33. International Commission of Jurists, *Attacks on Justice–Honduras* (Geneva: International Commission of Jurists, 2005).
34. H. Roberto Herrera Cáceres, "Análisis sobre los Principales Avances, Obstáculos y Desafíos Que el Poder Judicial Presenta en la Lucha contra la Corrupción en Honduras," in *Colección Ética e Integridad para el Desarrollo* (Tegucigalpa: CNA, 2007).

[35] Katya Salazar, *Misión de Observación del Proceso de Selección de los Nuevos Miembros de la Corte Suprema de Honduras* (Washington, D.C.: Fundación para el Debido Proceso Legal, 2008).
[36] Ibid.
[37] Rigoberto Ochoa, *Las Reformas a la Administración de Justicia en Honduras y Bolivia* (Washington, D.C.: Fundación para el Debido Proceso Legal, October 2008), 47.
[38] International Commission of Jurists, *Attacks on Justice–Honduras*.
[39] Instituto Estudios Comparados Ciencias Penales (INECIP), *Informe sobre Monitoreo a la Afectación de la Independencia Judicial en la República de Honduras* (Buenos Aires: INECIP, 2002).
[40] International Commission of Jurists, *Attacks on Justice–Honduras*.
[41] Regina Osorio, "Honduras: Fiscales en Demanda de Justicia," Radio Nederland Wereldomroep, May 15, 2008.
[42] "Pese Aumento de Presupuesto y Policías, 22,000 Hondureños Murieron Violentamente en Cuatro Anos," Proceso Digital, March 16, 2009.
[43] CONADEH, "Misión de la ONU Recomienda Investigar y Castigar a los Responsables de la Desaparición Forzada de Personas," news release, February 5, 2007.
[44] Roger Coma-Cunill, "Honduras: Modern Property Registration System," World Bank Doing Business, April 28, 2008.
[45] CNA, *Informe Nacional de Transparencia*.
[46] Ibid., 43–44.
[47] Ibid.
[48] "Honduras Perdió 12 Millones en Hondutel por Rebaja a LatinNode," *Prensa*, April 16, 2009.
[49] CNA, *Informe Nacional de Transparencia*, 68.
[50] "Investigan 120 Casos de Corrupcion en Presidencial," *Prensa*, May 9, 2009.
[51] CNA, *Informe Nacional de Transparencia*, 69.
[52] Ibid., 10.
[53] Mechanism for Follow-Up on the Implementation of the Inter-American Convention against Corruption, *Republic of Honduras: Final Report* (Washington, D.C.: Organization of American States, December 15, 2006), 16.
[54] Alessandra Fontana, "Teachers and Taxis: Corruption in the Education Sector in Honduras," *U4 Anti-Corruption Resource Centre Issue Brief*, no. 16 (May 2008).
[55] Jacques Hallak and Muriel Poisson, *Corrupt Schools, Corrupt Universities: What Can Be Done?* (Paris: UNESCO International Institute for Educational Planning, 2007), 106.
[56] Open Budget Initiative, "Honduras," in *Open Budget Index 2008* (Washington, D.C.: Open Budget Initiative, 2008).
[57] Thelma Mejía, "Corruption–Honduras: A Murky Transparency Law," Inter Press Service, February 22, 2007.
[58] Office of the U.S. Trade Representative, "Honduras," in *2009 National Trade Estimate Report on Foreign Trade Barriers* (Washington, D.C.: Office of the U.S. Trade Representative, 2009).
[59] International Development Association, *Country Assistance Strategy Progress Report for the Republic of Honduras* (Washington, D.C.: World Bank, May 8, 2008).

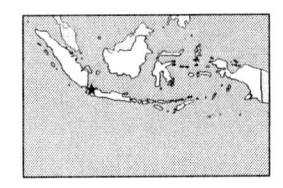

INDONESIA

CAPITAL: Jakarta
POPULATION: 243.3 million
GNI PER CAPITA (PPP): $3,830

SCORES	2006	2010
ACCOUNTABILITY AND PUBLIC VOICE:	4.66	4.75
CIVIL LIBERTIES:	3.66	3.58
RULE OF LAW:	2.92	3.00
ANTICORRUPTION AND TRANSPARENCY:	2.56	2.90

(scores are based on a scale of 0 to 7, with 0 representing weakest and 7 representing strongest performance)

Michael Buehler

INTRODUCTION[1]

Indonesia is both the world's largest Muslim-majority country and one of its most ethnically diverse. Home to approximately 230 million people, of whom more than 85 percent follow Islam, there are almost as many Muslims living in Indonesia as in the entire Arabic-speaking world. The Sunni branch of Islam predominates, while approximately one million Indonesians adhere to the Shia variant. A significant number of Sufi communities also exist in the archipelago state.

Indonesia is also the world's third largest democracy, after India and the United States. President Suharto's New Order regime, one of the most repressive dictatorships in Southeast Asia, collapsed in May 1998 after controlling Indonesian politics for more than 30 years. Since Suharto's downfall, the most dramatic reform initiative has been the introduction of an extensive regulatory framework governing the conduct of executive and legislative elections. Based on the new system, three national legislative and presidential elections, as well as balloting in several hundred localities, have occurred throughout the last decade. Overall, elections in Indonesia are considered free and fair.

The quality of democracy remains low, however. Despite efforts by the current administration to strengthen good governance, graft remains endemic in all aspects of society, especially within the bureaucracy, and constitutes the most significant obstacle to reform. The rule of law is seriously undermined by rampant corruption in the judiciary and politically well-connected elites rarely face consequences for abuses of power. Protection from torture is ineffective and impunity for human rights abuses perpetrated by security forces and military personnel remains the norm. In short, corruption, collusion, and nepotism continue to

---

Michael Buehler is the 2008–2010 Postdoctoral Fellow in Modern Southeast Asian Studies at the Weatherhead East Asian Institute at Columbia University in New York City.

constitute the modus operandi of Indonesian politics. These are both a legacy of the Suharto era and the result of hasty decentralization provisions drafted under Suharto's vice president and successor, B. J. Habibie, and implemented by Megawati Sukarnoputri, who led the country from 2001 to 2004.

Despite these enormous challenges, the country has managed nine years of positive economic growth. At the time of writing, it looked as though Indonesia would end up being "one of the few relatively bright spots around the world during this global recession."[2] Nonetheless, legal uncertainty, corruption, and rent seeking by Indonesian state officials continue to pose serious obstacles to good governance and economic prosperity in the long run.

ACCOUNTABILITY AND PUBLIC VOICE 4.75

FREE AND FAIR ELECTORAL LAWS AND ELECTIONS	5.00
EFFECTIVE AND ACCOUNTABLE GOVERNMENT	3.75
CIVIC ENGAGEMENT AND CIVIC MONITORING	5.67
MEDIA INDEPENDENCE AND FREEDOM OF EXPRESSION	4.57

The most immediately visible change in Indonesian politics over the last 10 years has been the implementation of executive and legislative elections at the national and subnational levels. Since 2004 elected government has been comprised of a directly elected president and vice president, a 550-member House of Representatives, and a senate-like Regional Representatives Assembly. Presidents, vice presidents, and legislators serve five-year terms, with the former limited to two terms. Parliaments at the provincial, regency, and municipality levels are also elected. Regents, mayors, and governors throughout the archipelago are limited to two terms.

Elections at every level of government were held in 2009. In April, Indonesia conducted its third legislative election of the post-Suharto era, while its second direct presidential election took place in July. Direct elections for regents and mayors were held in 486 out of 510 regencies and municipalities, while gubernatorial elections were held in 15 out of 33 provinces between 2005 and 2008.

In preparation for the 2009 polls, the parliament passed a series of laws instituting changes to the electoral framework. Though shortcomings remain, the amendments made the electoral system more transparent and accountable to the citizenry, thereby deepening Indonesian democracy. The most important reform involved changes to the party list system, which resulted from a December 2008 decision by the Constitutional Court and subsequent passage of an amended version of the 2008 Legislative Election Law. The 2004 general legislative elections were based on an open-list proportional system in which voters selected a party and could then also select 1 of 10 ranked candidates listed for each party; in practice, however, postvote seat allocations almost always followed the party ballot rankings due to the high threshold necessary to achieve a directly elected seat. Under the reformed system, priority is given to candidates who achieve the highest number of votes, regardless of their position on the party list. This has shifted additional power to voters, as representatives are dependent on the electorate for their position rather than on party leaders, reducing intraparty horse-trading and corruption.

The new law also amended a threshold rule according to which parties that failed to win 3 percent of the vote obtained a seat but were not allowed to contest future elections. Under the new law, only parties that win 2.5 percent of the national vote may occupy a parliamentary seat, but those failing to meet the threshold are free to contest future polls. Many observers saw this reform as a positive development that would reduce fragmentation in parliament without penalizing losing parties too harshly.[3]

The 2008 Legislative Election Law also created an election oversight agency, Bawaslu, tasked with monitoring campaign and election rules violations; it possesses increased powers compared to its predecessor, the Election Supervisory Committee. In October 2008, the parliament passed an amended Presidential Election Law stipulating that only parties or party coalitions that gain 20 percent of parliamentary seats or 25 percent of the national vote may nominate a presidential candidate.

In April 2008, the parliament also passed revisions to the Regional Governance Law, which regulates the election of regents, mayors, and governors. Many observers considered the revised bill a breakthrough in the institutionalization of democracy in Indonesia. The new law's primary amendment was to grant independent candidates the possibility of participating in subnational executive government elections, thereby greatly increasing local government accountability. Previously, only political parties could nominate candidates; this contributed to heightened corruption and an uneven playing field as slots were granted to the highest-bidding candidates, to the disadvantage of popular aspirants who could not afford a party nomination.[4]

The new law also required incumbents in subnational executive elections to immediately resign from office on registering for reelection. In the past, officials could remain in office during their campaign, increasing the risk of diversion of state funds to campaign expenses. Unfortunately, in August 2008, the Constitutional Court scrapped the regulation that required incumbents to step down after registering their candidacies.[5]

Finally, authority for arbitrating disputes in subnational executive elections shifted from the Supreme Court to the Constitutional Court, which was previously authorized only to adjudicate legislative and presidential elections.[6] Transferring authority for dispute resolution to the more widely respected Constitutional Court was widely seen as a positive step, as the Supreme Court had generated controversy in its handling of past subnational executive elections.

Despite its overall positive effect on Indonesian democracy, several shortcomings remain in the new regulatory framework. Some critics have raised concerns that the national parliamentary thresholds excessively favor large parties over small ones. At the regional level, the new law requires independent candidates running in executive elections to post an election bond and collect signatures from a minimum percentage of voters in the relevant district in order to run. The bill further discriminates against independent candidates by requiring that they pay a fine of up to US$2.1 million should they withdraw their nomination after approval by the local general election commission, a sanction that party-nominated candidates do not face. Some observers fear that such logistical and financial barriers may prove too costly and discourage otherwise viable candidates from running.

The 2008 General Election Law also requires parties to account for financial contributions from private individuals and companies. It subjects party finance records to independent audits, with sanctions for infractions. Achieving full compliance with and enforcement of these regulations remains a problem, however, and "money politics" remains widespread in Indonesian elections.[7]

Though still considered free and fair, the quality of the 2009 elections was lower than in 2004, a decline some observers attributed to reduced logistical support from foreign donors.[8] Millions of voters were unregistered, distribution of voting materials to polling stations was chaotic, and election officials were inadequately trained. In total, over 1,000 electoral violations were recorded, twice the number reported in 2004.[9] The General Election Commission certified 68 organizations to monitor the elections, while granting permission to eight international survey institutes to conduct "quick counts" at a sample of ballot stations. However, the actual number of observers deployed to the approximately 500,000 polling station was lower than in 2004, casting doubts on the degree of oversight of the elections.[10] Vote rigging occurred but was not widespread or systematic, while some incidents of voter intimidation and booth capture were reported, mainly in Aceh.[11] Incidents of election-related violence occurred only rarely and adversaries chose to solve disputes through institutional means, including via hundreds of lawsuits submitted to the Constitutional Court.[12]

Despite such shortcomings, the 2009 general elections were considered free and fair, and it is unlikely that the will of voters was severely distorted. The 38 parties that proved a nationwide presence and successfully registered had equal campaigning opportunities. With the exception of Islamic parties, however, this pluralism of parties does not reflect a diversity of competing ideologies or policy options. Indonesian politics remains highly personalized, with most parties linked to well-known politicians and little campaigning based on programmatic platforms.[13]

Only 9 of the 38 parties collected sufficient votes to pass the parliamentary threshold. The Democratic Party (PD) of incumbent president Susilo Bambang Yudhoyono was the clear winner, garnering 21 percent of the vote (143 seats) and tripling its showing from 2004. The Golkar party, the backbone of former dictator Suharto's regime, came in second with 14.45 percent (105 seats), continuing a pattern of declining support for the party with each successive election. The Indonesian Democratic Party-Struggle (PDI-P), which won the 1999 elections, came in third in 2009, collecting 14.3 percent of the vote (97 seats). Most significantly, Islamic political parties suffered substantial losses with their share of the vote waning from 32 percent in 2004 to 24 percent in 2009. The Prosperous Justice Party (PKS) was the only Islamic party to achieve a modest increase; nonetheless, its 7.88 percent of the vote (54 seats) was far below the 15–20 percent it had anticipated. The fragmentation of Islamic authority, low party cohesion, and recent institutional reforms have together greatly diminished the chances for political Islam to become a significant force in national Indonesian politics in the near future.[14] President Yudhoyono won the July 2009 presidential elections with more than 60 percent of the vote.

In keeping with the pattern following the 2004 contest, most parties entered the cabinet following the 2009 elections. During Yudhoyono's first term, nearly all parties eventually were given cabinet posts, leaving the PDI-P as the only true opposition party. Formation of the government following the 2009 balloting followed a similar pattern, with six of the nine parties represented in the parliament—whose members account for three-fourths of all parliamentary seats—also joining the cabinet. This arrangement reflects a general tendency toward party collusion, which undermines accountability. For instance, Golkar officially opposed President Yudhoyono's reelection yet joined the cabinet following his victory.

Elections of regents, mayors, and governors held since 2005 have suffered from sporadic incidents of vote rigging and other irregularities. Election authorities have ordered recounts or re-votes in several subnational entities in recent years. Postelection violence has been limited, even in conflict-prone regions like Maluku, Central Sulawesi, and Central Kalimantan. The few outbreaks of violence have primarily targeted local electoral commissions and typically died down quickly.[15] Assassinations of candidates, not uncommon in other Southeast Asian democracies, are unknown in Indonesia.

Although the principle of separation of powers is entrenched in the constitution, Indonesia's record of applying checks and balances has been mixed. While parliamentarians voice fierce criticism of the executive branch—including via censure motions against the president—the fragmented national parliament has limited capacity to effectively monitor the administration.[16] Moreover, as legislators have abused legislative review to extort bribes from government officials, new regulations have been implemented that limit legislative oversight functions. The 2004 Regional Governance Law, for example, stripped local parliaments of their ability to impeach the regent, appoint regional secretaries, and screen electoral candidates.[17]

The Constitutional Court has repeatedly ruled against the government since its establishment in 2003. Nevertheless, its ability to enforce executive accountability throughout the country remains limited as it is confined to reviewing laws passed by the national parliament. Regional legislation and regulations adopted by national or regional governments are subject to review by the less authoritative Supreme Court.[18]

Civil service incentive structures remain largely unchanged from the Suharto era. A lack of coordination among overlapping national ministries, as well as between central and local authorities, in the hiring and firing of public personnel further lowers efficiency and increases opportunities for corruption.[19] Some ministries have succeeded in introducing modest reforms. The Ministry of Finance, the State Audit Agency, and the Supreme Court have implemented merit- and performance-based salaries as well as a more open and fair promotion track. Such reforms affect only 2 percent of the civil service, however, which continues to be characterized by a lack of transparency, scant use of merit in determining promotions, and strong job security.

Indonesia's democratic transition has significantly widened the space for civil society. Civic groups frequently comment on pending legislation, occasionally with some effect. The Anti-Pornography bill, passed in October 2008, was delayed for almost a year and significantly weakened following civil society opposition. Overall, however, civil society in Indonesia is weakly developed and civic groups' ability to influence the legislative process remains limited.

Legal impediments for civic organizations have increased in recent years. In December 2008, the Ministry of Home Affairs issued a regulation enforcing a provision of the 1985 Civil Society Organization Law that requires nongovernmental organizations (NGOs) to obtain government approval for assistance received from abroad. The law empowers the government to freeze the leadership boards of NGOs that violate the statute. As 90 percent of the country's approximately 13,500 registered NGOs receive foreign funding, the new regulation adds a significant administrative burden on both the government and civil society, while raising fears that it could be abused to punish government critics.[20] Pending legislation that would amend the 1985 law to protect against money laundering and terrorist financing through NGOs could produce further barriers to civil society activity, significantly threatening its vibrancy and capacity.

Indonesia is home to a large number of independent media outlets that offer a diversity of perspectives. The private print media has grown from under 300 publications in 1998 to over 800 in 2008. Although fear of legal harassment remains a key obstacle to free expression, a series of landmark Constitutional Court decisions since 2006 have enhanced protection of media freedom. In two rulings in December 2006 and July 2007, the Constitutional Court struck down passages in the Criminal Code that had allowed punishment for slander against the government.[21] In December 2008, Harifin Tumpa, the acting chief justice of the Supreme Court, issued a circular that urged judges to treat all media cases under the more liberal press law rather than the criminal code.[22] In April 2009, the court cleared *Time* magazine of defaming former President Suharto.

In February 2009, the Constitutional Court also struck down articles in the Legislative Election Law, arguing that they contradicted constitutional free speech guarantees. The articles required media outlets to provide equal advertising space to all candidates and enabled a government body to withdraw the publishing license of any media organization failing to publish "fair and balanced reports" on political parties.[23]

Despite these positive developments, legal impediments to free expression remain. The criminal code is still frequently applied to jail journalists for defamation, while passages of the Presidential Election Law and the Public Information Law are also restrictive. The Electronic Transaction and Information Law (ITE), passed in 2008, sanctions up to six years imprisonment and fines of up to US$95,000 for individuals found to have electronically disseminated information deemed insulting or defamatory. Although the number of detained journalists has decreased, several have faced trials or been jailed in recent years based on these laws.[24] Meanwhile, the government retains the authority to issue and revoke licenses for broadcast media, as well as to block local outlets from directly relaying news programs by foreign providers.[25]

Journalists in Indonesia also face physical and other forms of intimidation. In 2008, the Legal Aid Institute for the Press reported 25 cases of physical abuse and 27 cases of intimidation directed against journalists.[26] Such violence is rarely investigated, although many perpetrators are reportedly supporters of candidates in regional elections, government agents, police officers, or members of the Indonesian military. Other threats to press freedom derive from powerful private and corporate interests, who use defamation laws to restrict investigative reporting and, in some localities, form a corrupt nexus with state officials that can contribute to violence.

Freedom of expression continues to be restricted in conflict zones and areas with a history of separatist movements. According to Amnesty International, at least 152 people were arrested in the regions of Maluku and Papua during 2007 and 2008 for activities related to raising flags that symbolized regional independence; several were subsequently sentenced to prison.[27]

The internet was accessed in 2008 by 25 million people, or 10.5 percent of the population. While there are no notable restrictions on accessing content, the ITE law has been used to prosecute civilians who express criticism of the government or other powerful actors via electronic media. In 2009, a Jakarta housewife named Prita Mulyasari was fined and arrested on defamation charges under the law for having criticized a private hospital for malpractice in an e-mail message that was later made public.

CIVIL LIBERTIES   3.58

PROTECTION FROM STATE TERROR, UNJUSTIFIED IMPRISONMENT, AND TORTURE	3.13
GENDER EQUITY	3.00
RIGHTS OF ETHNIC, RELIGIOUS, AND OTHER DISTINCT GROUPS	2.75
FREEDOM OF CONSCIENCE AND BELIEF	4.00
FREEDOM OF ASSOCIATION AND ASSEMBLY	5.00

While protection of civil liberties has advanced markedly since the Suharto era, torture and other rights abuses remain widespread. Legal provisions in the existing and draft revised criminal procedure codes do not sufficiently guard against torture and other ill-treatment. Members of the security forces regularly go unpunished for human rights violations, and torture of suspects in custody remains routine. The death penalty and caning continue to be applied, with 10 people executed in 2008.

Conditions in prisons and detention facilities are dismal. Overcrowding, poor sanitation, and inadequate access to medical care are pervasive. The penal code does not require the authorities to bring detainees before a judge or other judicial officer without delay. As a result, individuals may be detained for months without being afforded judicial review.[28]

Harassment of peaceful political activists continues to occur. In October 2009, the Indonesian Human Rights Commission (Komnas HAM) reported that human rights defenders in Indonesia are increasingly being reported to the police, accused of lies, defamation, and criminal acts.[29] According to Amnesty International, 32 people were jailed or detained for peacefully expressing their views during 2008.[30]

Despite such challenges, Indonesian authorities responded to terrorist attacks in recent years in an evenhanded and effective manner. The government has avoided the temptation of detaining Islamists without trial and instead prosecuted them by law, while implementing programs aimed at deradicalizing suspects. At the same time, the government has taken effective measures to protect citizens from further attacks. Leading members of terrorist groups have been killed and scores incarcerated for their involvement in attacks. Radical Islamic groups staged no large-scale attacks for several years, until a series of bombings occurred in Jakarta in July 2009. Within months, alleged mastermind Noordin Muhammad Top and other leading figures in his organization were killed, while other perpetrators were arrested quickly. As such, the political and economic impact of the bombings has been minor.[31] Nonetheless, the government has introduced some counterterrorism measures that risk undermining civil liberties. Following the July 2009 bombings, the Yudhoyono administration proposed extending the limit for holding suspects without charge from seven days to two years, with the possibility of renewal for an unlimited period.

Impunity for police and military officers involved in torture and other human rights violations remains the norm. According to Amnesty International, "Indonesia lacks an effective, independent and impartial mechanism to receive complaints and conduct investigations into allegations of torture."[32] Citizens may submit complaints of torture to the police or the military, though this occurs only rarely due to the low reputation of both institutions' redress mechanisms. In 2005, a National Police Commission (Kompolnas) was established and tasked with investigating allegations of abuse. Its impact has been minimal, however, and in June 2008 the commission publicly admitted that it had failed to improve police performance because of a weak mandate, including a lack of authority to investigate and detain suspected abusers.[33]

With respect to external oversight, the independence and capacity of Komnas HAM is severely hindered by limited resources and a weak mandate. The inability to identify and prosecute the culprits behind the 2004 poisoning of human rights lawyer Munir Said Thalib is a prominent example of the impunity that prevails in cases of rights violations. Muchdi Purwopranjono, a senior intelligence official, was acquitted of the murder in December 2008 following a trial in which multiple witnesses retracted previous incriminating statements, apparently due to fear of reprisal.[34]

Though Indonesia is safer than many developing countries, crime remains a serious problem, especially in urban areas such as Jakarta, Medan, and Surabaya. Pickpocketing and other forms of robbery are common, while armed carjacking, vehicle theft, and nonviolent residential break-ins also occur. Crimes committed by private actors closely affiliated with ruling elites regularly go unpunished or are treated with leniency. Nonetheless, the most significant criminal actions affecting ordinary Indonesians remain those involving state actors, including predatory taxes, bribe solicitation, and police harassment.

The threat of human trafficking differs from region to region and is worst in provinces with conveniently located ports. The East Java Children's Protection Agency estimates that at least 100,000 women and child victims of trafficking annually pass through East Java province alone.[35] In response, the government passed a strong antitrafficking law in 2007 that aims to improve law enforcement and public awareness of the issue. Measures taken to safeguard citizens' rights beyond Indonesia's borders have not offered adequate protection. A memorandum of understanding with Malaysia explicitly endorsed the right of Malaysian employers to hold the passports of Indonesian workers, a tactic widely seen as facilitating exploitation.[36]

Women are guaranteed equality under the Indonesian constitution, and the government has committed to formulating policies that counter violence against women and discrimination in the workplace. Since 2005, the minister for women's empowerment, Meutia Farida Hatta Swasono, has helped institute regulations to improve women's rights, including ensuring gender sensitivity in the National Strategy for Poverty Alleviation, facilitating women's access to credit, and improving female education.[37] In April 2008, the parliament passed a bill establishing a quota of 30 percent for women's participation as candidates and board members in all political parties. Despite initial concerns voiced by women's rights organizations that the new party-list system would be detrimental to female representation, the 2009 legislative elections resulted in election of the largest number of female parliamentarians to date.

Nevertheless, serious challenges remain; in 2006, Indonesia ranked 68th out of 115 countries in the global gender gap index.[38] Multiple laws and regulations discriminate against women in such spheres as family, marriage, divorce, land ownership, and inheritance. Indonesian women are required to obtain their husband's consent for certain actions, including applying for a passport and undergoing sterilization or abortion. In recent years, Sharia-inspired bylaws have been adopted in some districts that infringe on women's constitutional rights. Mostly implemented by secular parties in order to bolster their political machines,[39] the restrictions imposed include limits on women's mobility at night and regulation of female dress. In November 2008, the national parliament also adopted a controversial antipornography law, imposing restrictions on certain forms of dance, traditional dress, and depiction of nudity in art. While it is premature to gauge its full impact, several women have subsequently been arrested in Jakarta under the new law.[40]

Discrimination in employment remains institutionalized, with women's participation in the labor force dampened by such factors as lack of education, discrimination in wages and promotions, harassment in the workplace, and societal expectations related to balancing work and family life. Women receive roughly 20 percent lower wages than men for similar work. Although regulations forbid discrimination based on gender, women continue to encounter bias in civil service hiring and promotions.[41]

Indonesia is one of the most ethnically diverse countries in the world: 42 percent of the population is Javanese and 15 percent Sundanese, while the remaining 43 percent are divided among some 300 other ethnic groups.[42] The country's national motto is *Bhinneka tunggal ika,* or "Unity in Diversity." Indonesia ratified the International Convention on the Elimination of All Forms of Discrimination in 1999. In October 2008, the parliament adopted an antidiscrimination law.[43] Nevertheless, ethnic discrimination persists and members of some minority groups encounter difficulties obtaining identity cards and other personal documents from the government bureaucracy.[44]

Religious freedom has expanded since the end of the New Order and Indonesia officially recognizes Islam, Protestantism, Roman Catholicism, Hinduism, Buddhism, and Confucianism. Nevertheless, concerns have arisen in recent years over rising religious intolerance and the government's failure to respond effectively. This is especially true in the case of groups deemed heretical by mainstream Islamic authorities,[45] particularly the Ahmadiyah, a heterodox Islamic group with 400,000 Indonesian followers, which has been the focus of attacks since 2002. Under pressure from influential Muslim organizations, in June 2008 the national government issued a decree that warned Ahmadiyah against propagating its tenets in public. Some local authorities, however, have used the decree to justify outright bans on certain sects, in violation of the Indonesian constitution.[46] In April 2008, Ahmad Mossadeq, head of a new sect called Al Qiyadah Al Islamiyah, was sentenced to four years in prison for sullying religion. In total, the Wahid Institute in Jakarta identified 232 instances during 2008 where individuals or groups, mostly radical Islamic ones, tried to force their beliefs on others through legislation or violence, an 18 percent increase compared to 2007.[47]

Similarly, as of 2007, approximately 52 out of 510 regencies and municipalities in Indonesia had adopted Sharia-inspired bylaws.[48] Most of the bylaws regulate Islamic knowledge and practices such as Quran reading ability for public servants, Muslim dress codes, and the collection of alms (*zakat*).[49] In September 2009, the parliament in Aceh province issued a bylaw endorsing stoning to death as punishment for adultery and caning for homosexuality.[50] In September 2008, the newly elected Constitutional Court chief justice, Mohammad Mahfud, declared the bylaws unconstitutional and a threat to national integrity. Nevertheless, Indonesia's political and legal environment renders revocation of the bylaws difficult, leaving most in place once adopted.

Disabled people, constituting approximately 10 percent of the population, face discrimination in various aspects of life, including education,[51] political participation, and employment. Draft legislation on the composition of legislative bodies stipulates that parliamentary candidates and other elected officials should be able to read and write in the Roman alphabet, thereby discriminating against the blind.[52]

Indonesian workers have the right to join independent unions, bargain collectively, and, except for civil servants, stage strikes. Government enforcement of minimum wage and other labor laws remains weak, however. Only 10 percent of workers in the formal sector are union members, while domestic workers—estimated to number 2.6 million—are currently excluded from coverage by Indonesian labor laws. Security forces regularly intervene in labor disputes. In December 2008, at least nine people were injured and several hospitalized when police forcibly dispersed approximately 15,000 members of the Federation of Indonesian Metal Workers' Union (FSPMI) who demanded a wage increase in demonstrations in Batam.[53]

Freedom of assembly is guaranteed under Indonesia's constitution. Demonstrations and rallies have become a popular means for expressing discontent with the government since Suharto's fall. Nevertheless, the right to protest is applied unequally across the country, and in conflict regions such as Aceh or Papua official permission for demonstrations is often refused. According to Amnesty International, the situation in Papua and Maluku continued to deteriorate in 2008.[54] In March 2009, the government detained four Dutch journalists for covering a demonstration in Papua that was held without a permit.[55] In other regions, public protests have on occasion been met with excessive force. Members of the police and the military involved in such clashes often go unpunished.

RULE OF LAW 3.00

INDEPENDENT JUDICIARY	2.80
PRIMACY OF RULE OF LAW IN CIVIL AND CRIMINAL MATTERS	2.60
ACCOUNTABILITY OF SECURITY FORCES AND MILITARY TO CIVILIAN AUTHORITIES	3.25
PROTECTION OF PROPERTY RIGHTS	3.33

The Indonesian legal system is a civil law system based on Dutch, French, and German models. Judicial candidates are proposed by the Judicial Commission (JC) to the national parliament for approval and then confirmed by the president. Nine judges comprise the Constitutional Court, three of whom are nominated by the Supreme Court, three by the national parliament, and three by the president. In recent years, the Constitutional Court has continually asserted its independence, issuing multiple decisions on controversial and important issues. Partly as a result, it has been exposed to criticism from a variety of political actors, including leaders of major political parties and prominent members of civil society.

Despite efforts by the Yudhoyono administration to introduce reform measures, low judicial standards and lax enforcement continue to characterize the Indonesian justice system. Direct intervention by the central government in judicial affairs is increasingly rare, but executive interference at lower levels of authority remains common, facilitated by endemic corruption within the legal system. In a comprehensive national survey conducted by the government's Corruption Eradication Commission (KPK), the judiciary ranked among the lowest-rated state entities regarding degree of corruption.[56]

Vested interests within the judiciary have also managed to resist reform efforts. A telling example surrounded the establishment of the independent JC in 2001 with a mandate to investigate misconduct in the judiciary and propose appointments to the Supreme Court. After the JC recommended investigations of 13 Supreme Court judges for potential wrongdoing in February 2006, the court asked the Constitutional Court to curtail the commission's investigatory powers. The Constitutional Court complied, stripping the JC of its authority to levy sanctions against judges and court officials. Instead, the JC now issues recommendations to the Supreme Court for possible sanctions, a procedure of limited effectiveness. In March 2008, the JC examined 212 cases and recommended 27 to the Supreme Court for follow-up, but the latter failed to scrutinize a single case.[57]

Responsibility for appointing judges to the Supreme Court has shifted from the JC to the national parliament, opening the door to increased politicization of the judiciary.[58] Harifin Tumpa, one of the above-referenced judges initially identified for investigation, was appointed chief justice of the Supreme Court in early 2009. The tensions related to the JC have significantly lowered the possibility of creating a fair, clean, and transparent judiciary even as Indonesia's judiciary recently ranked last in a survey of 12 Asian countries by the Hong Kong–based Political and Economic Risk Consultancy. Its report noted that the judiciary is "one of Indonesia's weakest and most controversial institutions and many consider the poor enforcement of laws to be the country's number one problem."[59]

The low quality of legal training also contributes to poor judicial performance, and no significant efforts exist to reform the system. Due to low salaries, instructors at many Indonesian law schools prioritize advising governmental and nongovernmental agencies over teaching. A weak career development system, including low pay and inadequate pensions, also contributes to the low integrity and quality of many Indonesian judges. To date, only minor reforms have been implemented to improve the situation. In April 2008, President Yudhoyono issued a presidential regulation creating a new stipend that ensures adequate take-home pay for judicial employees if their performance meets certain criteria. A lack of adequate instruments for assessing judicial performance and quality limits the potential effectiveness of this initiative. In addition, compliance with judicial decisions by other branches is inconsistent due to cultural, economic, political, and legal factors as well as weak enforcement mechanisms.

Prosecutorial functions are conducted under the authority of the Jakarta-based attorney general. A weak regulatory framework, noncompliance by political parties and law enforcement officers, and limited resources pose challenges to prosecutorial independence. In recent years, the attorney general's office itself has suffered from chronic mismanagement and questionable decision making, particularly with regard to combating corruption within the judicial system. In early 2009, Attorney General Hendarman Supandji provided strategic posts to two senior prosecutors who were implicated in a bribery scandal in 2008.

The Indonesian legal system grants accused criminals the presumption of innocence. In practice, this has not always been upheld in the context of counterterrorism and anticorruption measures. Critics have accused the Indonesian police, for example, of charging certain individuals with links to terrorist organizations without sufficient supporting evidence.[60] Although hearings are generally public, fairness, impartiality, and timeliness are often lacking. It can take months for prisoners to be brought before a judge. The criminal procedure code guarantees the right to be assisted by counsel, but access to legal support and the judicial system in general remain beyond the reach of many Indonesians. According to recent estimates, only 10–17 percent of poor Indonesians have the ability to bring their cases to the courts.[61] The "morality police" established in Aceh in 2005 have undermined due process rights in the province. As the unit's jurisdiction remains undefined and its supervision by state institutions lacking, individuals detained by its agents may be deprived of fundamental safeguards.

The Indonesian military of 2009 looks very different from the one presided over by former president Suharto during the New Order. The executive arm of the civilian government has been strengthened, and the visibility of the military in Indonesian politics has diminished significantly. With each successive election, the military's ability to influence the outcome has contracted, even as some former members run for office, mostly in subnational elections. The military lacks influence and resources to control substantial numbers of voters,[62] and military support for intervention in the political process continues to subside. The percentage of governors with a military background has dropped from around 50 percent in 1998 to 12 percent in 2009.[63]

In recent years, civilian authorities have made impressive progress in increasing democratic control over the military, stripping it of its vast powers, and removing its representation in parliament. One important factor was the successful 2005 peace agreement forged between the government and the separatist rebel movement in Aceh, which nullified the pretext of "preventing national disintegration" that had been used to justify the military's political autonomy. Another Yudhoyono administration initiative involves overseeing the military's withdrawal from hundreds of military-run businesses, a process governed by a 2004 decree requiring the military to withdraw from all business activity by 2009.[64] Although the directive has been implemented to a degree that was previously unimaginable, the military has retained significant alternative sources of income. In 2008, the defense minister estimated that approximately 30 percent of the military's budget was raised from off-budget sources. These include a growing number of informal—and sometimes illegal—economic activities,[65] such as illegal mining, illegal logging, racketeering, gambling operations, and prostitution rings, as well as contracting security services out for the protection of drug traffickers or private enterprises.[66] The military's access to such large amounts of funding outside its formal budget has enabled it to maintain a measure of autonomy from democratic civilian control, despite the erosion of its institutional powers and formal business activity.

The military has thus successfully resisted certain reform measures, including efforts to hold its members accountable for crimes or to force it to relinquish a territorial command structure that still reaches down to the village level. Under Indonesian law, members of the military are to be tried in civilian courts for nonmilitary crimes. However, in 2006, Defense Minister Juwono Sudarsono rejected civilian jurisdiction, claiming it could compromise military interests and national security.[67] Although there were a number of cases under the Yudhoyono administration in which members of the police and the military were held accountable for corruption,[68] such instances are exceptions and there is no indication that the issue is being addressed systematically. Military tribunals have frequently offered lenient treatment to military personnel accused of human rights abuses, thereby fostering a culture of impunity.[69]

Indonesian law protects the right of every citizen to own property, though foreigners are not permitted to own land. Various efforts have been made in recent years to expand property rights protections for both foreigners and locals. In March 2007, legislation was passed to reduce red tape and strengthen property laws.[70] The 2006 establishment of a ministerial-level task force and empowerment of commercial courts to issue seizure orders related to violations of intellectual property rights (IPR) have strengthened IPR protection.[71] The extent to which such laws will be effectively enforced remains to be seen, however. Corruption and weak capacity in the judiciary, including within commercial courts, hinder the provision of adequate legal recourse related to property disputes, and internationally binding contracts are frequently disregarded.[72] In a setback to economic reform, the Constitutional Court in March 2008 struck down extended land lease tenures, a chief attribute of the 2007 investment law, arguing that the leases violated the 1960 Agrarian Law.[73]

Enforcement of property rights for indigenous and rural communities remains equally weak. Business interests close to the ruling elites frequently ignore indigenous property rights, with mining and forest rights among the sectors in which conflict is common.[74] Agricultural land is often claimed by multiple owners; with a corrupt judiciary and poor land ownership database, there are few avenues for arbitrating such disputes. Thus, as of mid-2009, thousands of unresolved land conflicts—including between local communities and government entities like the military—continue to result in violent clashes.[75]

ANTICORRUPTION AND TRANSPARENCY   2.90

ENVIRONMENT TO PROTECT AGAINST CORRUPTION	2.50
PROCEDURES AND SYSTEMS TO ENFORCE ANTICORRUPTION LAWS	2.25
EXISTENCE OF ANTICORRUPTION NORMS, STANDARDS, AND PROTECTIONS	4.00
GOVERNMENTAL TRANSPARENCY	2.83

Despite progressive government efforts to combat graft, including hundreds of arrests in recent years, corruption remains endemic in Indonesia. Among the key causes of corruption are the government's considerable involvement in the economy and weak enforcement of anticorruption rules, including conflict of interest standards intended to counter the firmly entrenched culture of bureaucratic corruption molded during the Suharto era.

In 2007, Indonesia ranked below all major economies in the region except the Philippines on the ease of doing business.[76] The Yudhoyono administration has implemented reforms aimed at curbing red tape, some of which have shown positive results. Obtaining construction licenses has become easier and investor protection has improved. Credit information management has become more transparent, and the number of days needed to open a business has been reduced.[77] Nevertheless, corruption remains widespread at all levels of the bureaucracy. In state-run hospitals, for example, staff frequently bolster their salaries by accepting commissions for prescriptions or blackmailing patients.[78] A public service bill, which will expand the power of the ombudsman and authorize local regions to establish citizens committees to monitor the provision of public services, was adopted in late 2009, after three years of deliberation. It remains to be seen whether the law will be successfully implemented. Moreover, excessive regulations increased at the local level following decentralization in 2001; a survey conducted in 2008 estimated that around 30 percent of all local regulations were predatory in nature and an impediment to investment.[79]

The Indonesian government is involved in running over 150 state-owned enterprises (SOEs). It also administers prices on basic goods such as fuel, rice, and electricity. Regulatory procedures in such enterprises do not sufficiently discourage graft, while the practice of officials fulfilling dual roles in government and business facilitate corruption. A number of ministerial personnel, including high-level bureaucrats and presidential aides, serve simultaneously as commissioners of SOEs or private companies. Although the KPK has begun to look into the issue, the practice remains widely accepted. The operations of many SOEs remain opaque, and the Financial Institution Supervisory Agency often fails to enforce requirements for submission of financial reports.[80] The 2008 Openness of Public Information Law placed some obligations on SOEs but failed to require them to grant information requests at a level of detail sufficient to ensure transparency.[81] In a promising development, in May 2009, the director of Pertamina, the state oil company, pledged to join the Extractive Industries Transparency Initiative (EITI) and introduce codes of conduct, blacklists of problematic vendors, and whistleblower protection programs.[82] Senior public servants and agency heads are required by law to declare their assets and cooperate with the KPK. Such declarations remain poorly verified, however, due to inadequate human resources and financial management support.

Widespread arbitrary and predatory tax collection, especially at the subnational level, poses a significant problem. The State Audit Agency estimated that embezzled tax proceeds reached US$1 billion between 2005 and 2007.[83] In response, the government has made substantial efforts to reform tax collection. It has introduced modern compliance systems, revamped the Directorate General of Taxation, and passed a tax procedure law in 2008. The new regional taxation law adopted in late 2009 defines a list of taxes that subnational governments are allowed to collect, while setting minimum and maximum rates for each type of tax. The degree to which the law will be enforced remains to be seen.[84]

There are several independent investigative and auditing bodies in Indonesia. The Ombudsman Commission, created in 2000 by a presidential regulation, processes complaints about the quality of public services. In practice, it has been less effective than many had hoped due to a lack of government funding and support.[85] The Supreme Audit Agency (BPK), with offices in every province, supervises the state budget. It is independent, with its head elected by its members in order to avoid the appointment of government cronies. Although the BPK has addressed numerous cases of misconduct in recent years,[86] some of its members have themselves been investigated for corruption.

The KPK is considered the most effective investigative body in Indonesia and has delivered a number of high-profile convictions, including governors and general election commissioners. Its overall influence over corrupt practices in the country remains relatively modest, however, as it handles only between 12 and 30 percent of all corruption cases.[87] The bulk of cases are handled by prosecutorial offices across the country. In May 2009, the KPK's head was arrested on murder and racketeering charges, though this had less of a negative impact on public perception of the body than expected.[88] Instead, following criticism that it was becoming "too assertive," particularly in its pursuit of high-level politicians and bureaucrats, the national parliament passed an Anti-Corruption Court Law in September 2009 that significantly weakened the KPK. The new law authorizes the heads of regular courts to alter the composition of judicial panels on the Anti-Corruption Court. Career judges, rather than ad hoc ones, may comprise the majority of such panels in the future, a change many observers view as a step backwards. Previously, such panels consisted predominantly of ad hoc judges, perceived as more independent because of their recruitment from outside the graft-ridden Indonesian judiciary.[89]

In recent years, this set of agencies has frequently prosecuted public officials for abuse of power, including a former ambassador and other high-ranking officials.[90] Courts have also upheld jail sentences for prominent individuals convicted of bribing state officials. Nonetheless, the majority of abuses of power continue to go unpunished, and other government bodies have been less vigilant in punishing corrupt practices. Both the legislative and executive branches have refrained from holding members of the political establishment accountable, the attorney general's office has repeatedly ceased investigations of blatant violations of the law, and the Anti-Corruption Court has been criticized for handing down insufficiently severe punishments. Some observers have raised concerns that the Yudhoyono administration's aggressive anticorruption push, launched at a time when the judicial and civil service systems remain unreformed, has had the unintended side effect of exacerbating an atmosphere of uncertainty and perceived risk for state decision makers.[91]

Corruption scandals are widely reported in the media, with a growing number of outlets at the local level also covering such cases. The 2006 Witness Protection Act protects whistleblowers and establishes a witness and victim protection agency. Incomplete definitions, however, render the law's protection inadequate, and it is rarely put into practice.

Corruption is rampant in Indonesia's education sector, ranging from bribes needed to obtain a kindergarten permit at the Ministry of Education to arbitrary increases of university tuition fees. Although the government has taken steps to address the endemic graft—including increasing teachers' salaries in February 2009—the problem remains deeply entrenched.

In 2008, the national parliament adopted an Open Public Information Law after more than nine years of deliberation. The law is scheduled to take effect in April 2010 and will require all institutions funded by taxpayer money to make regular public disclosures of their operations. The law applies to information that is produced, stored, managed, sent, or received by a public agency. Both SOEs and the judiciary must also comply, but political parties are still not required to disclose their private contributors apart from requirements under the General Election Law. The Open Public Information Law has been criticized for containing exceptions pertaining to intelligence, as well as language that could criminalize certain journalistic work. Concerns have also been raised that the ostensibly independent Information Commission, created under the law to arbitrate disputes regarding disclosure requests, will fall under government influence as it will be funded from a ministerial budget, most likely the Information and Communications Ministry.

Closed-door meetings of the national parliament limit the ability of the press and public to monitor its proceedings. The parliament has debated the possibility of curtailing this practice,[92] but the relevant draft bill has yet to be adopted by the national parliament. Parliamentary oversight of the budget remains problematic. Although opposition parties have become more involved in scrutinizing the executive budget-making process, parliamentarians have also chosen to hold closed budget meetings. Following a request by the KPK to observe such meetings, parliamentary leaders in August 2008 chose to uphold the right of committee heads to keep such meetings closed, though KPK officials may attend if granted an official invitation. Budget timeliness by subnational governments improved markedly in 2008 compared to previous years.[93]

A variety of regulations have increased the transparency of public procurement processes at the national level, though opacity remains prevalent at the local level. A licensing requirement imposed on bidders has been eliminated, thereby reducing possibilities for bribery. At the national level, tenders are usually published in newspapers or over the internet. Still, as no effective mechanisms exist to monitor the assets of procurement officials and investigations into alleged bribery are rare, an environment conducive to corruption persists. As a result, public procurement remains one of the most corruption-ridden sectors in Indonesia.

Foreign assistance continues to be prone to abuse and embezzlement, partly due to a lack of capacity by those in the development sector to carry out rigorous monitoring and evaluation. The World Bank estimates that it loses approximately 30 percent of its budget in Indonesia due to corruption.[94]

RECOMMENDATIONS

- In order to curb the influence of "money politics" in both executive and legislative elections, the government should substantially increase public party financing.
- Expand already-initiated pilot projects on civil service reforms, including the introduction of merit-based pay systems for the entire Indonesian bureaucracy.
- Legal impediments to freedom of expression should be repealed, including restrictive passages of the Presidential Election Law, the Public Information Law, and the 2008 Electronic Transaction and Information Law. The press law should be revised to include clear regulations on libel and defamation, and the criminal code should no longer be used for such suits.
- Local bylaws that are in conflict with national laws and decrees should be abolished, including those restricting religious freedom for minority groups or imposing strict Sharia-inspired codes of conduct on the general population.
- In order to enhance efforts to combat judicial corruption and reduce subnational executive interference, the oversight powers of the Judicial Commission should be reinstalled as soon as possible.

- The government should vigorously investigate and prosecute human rights abuses committed by military and police personnel. Members of the military should face trial in civilian courts for nonmilitary-related crimes.
- The list of exceptions in the Open Public Information Law should be shortened and protection for whistleblowers and victims of corruption should be improved.

NOTES

For URLs and endnote hyperlinks, please visit the *Countries at the Crossroads* homepage at http://freedomhouse.org/template.cfm?page=139&edition=8.

[1] The author would like to thank Endah Asnari, Edward Aspinall, Jacqui Baker, Robin Bush, Matt Easton, Jeremy Gross, Camilla Karlsen, Ehito Kimura, Tim Lindsey, Michael Malley, Marcus Mietzner, Kevin O'Rourke, Margaret Scott, and Antonia Staats for their kind assistance and comments.

[2] "Indonesia Risk: Stability; Security; Govt. Effectiveness; Legal; Macroeconomic; Financial," Economist Intelligence Unit, July 19, 2009.

[3] Erwida Maulia, "Lower Parliamentary Threshold Called for," *Jakarta Post*, February 4, 2008.

[4] Michael Buehler and Paige Tan, "Party–Candidate Relationships in Indonesian Local Politics: A Case Study of the 2005 Regional Elections in Gowa, South Sulawesi Province," *Indonesia* 84 (October 2007): 41–69.

[5] "Pemegang Jabatan Tak Perlu Mundur * Terkait Pasal 58 UU No 12/2008," *Kompas*, August 5, 2008, 3.

[6] Michael Buehler, "Indonesia: Law on Regency Polls Has Wider Implications," Oxford Analytica, July 11, 2008.

[7] Marcus Mietzner, "Party Financing in Post-Soeharto Indonesia: Between State Subsidies and Political Corruption," *Contemporary Southeast Asia: A Journal of International and Strategic Affairs* 29, no. 2 (August 2007): 238–263.

[8] Marcus Mietzner, *Indonesia's 2009 Elections: Populism, Dynasties and the Consolidation of the Party System* (Sydney: Lowy Institute for International Policy, May 2009), 19.

[9] Inter-Parliamentary Union, "Summary of Last Elections: Indonesia," home page.

[10] Jeremy Gross, *Indonesia's 2009 Legislative Elections: Don't Step Backwards* (San Francisco: The Asia Foundation, April 8, 2009).

[11] International Crisis Group (ICG), "Indonesia: Deep Distrust in Aceh As Elections Approach," Asia Briefing No. 90, March 23, 2009; Asian Network for Free Elections (Anfrel), *Preliminary Report: Indonesia General Election 9th April 2009* (Bangkok: Anfrel, April 23, 2009).

[12] Irawaty Wardany, "Court to Begin Receiving Poll Dispute Cases," *Jakarta Post*, May 7, 2009.

[13] Kevin O'Rourke, "The Justice Ministry Finalized the Registration of New Parties That Will Seek Eligibility to Compete in 2009," *Reformasi Weekly Review: Analyzing Politics and Policies in Indonesia*, February 29, 2008.

[14] Michael Buehler, "Islam and Democracy in Indonesia," *Insight Turkey* 11, no. 4 (October–December 2009): 51–63; John Sidel, "*Indonesia: Islamist Forces Reach Limits of Expansion*," Oxford Analytica, May 12, 2009.

[15] Marcus Mietzner, "Local Democracy: Old Elites Are Still in Power, but Direct Elections Now Give Voters a Choice," *Inside Indonesia*, no. 85 (January–March 2006); Dirk Tomsa,

"Electoral Politics in Post-conflict Maluku: The 2008 Pilkada and Its Implications for Democratization and Reconciliation" (paper presented at the annual meeting for the Association for Asian Studies Annual Meeting, Chicago, March 26–29, 2009).

16. "Ibadah Haji: pemondokan permanen perlu disiapkan," *Kompas,* March 20, 2009, 2.
17. Buehler, "Indonesia: Law on Regency Polls Has Wider Implications."
18. Simon Butt, "Two at the Top: The Constitutional Court and the Supreme Court," *Van Zorge Report on Indonesia: Behind the Headlines* 11, no. 8 (September 17, 2009): 12–20.
19. Stein Kristiansen and Muhid Ramli, "Buying an Income: The Market for Civil Service Positions in Indonesia," *Contemporary Southeast Asia* 28, no. 2 (August 2006): 207–233.
20. Kevin O'Rourke, "The Home Affairs Ministry Issued a Regulation Requiring Non-Governmental Organizations to Obtain Government Approval," *Reformasi Weekly Review: Analyzing Politics and Policies in Indonesia,* December 12, 2008.
21. "Pasal penghinaan presiden dalam KUHP dicabut," Hukumonline, December 6, 2006.
22. Ismira Lutfia, "Seek Press Council Input in Libel Cases, Supreme Court Tells Judges," *Jakarta Globe,* January 13, 2009.
23. Eny Wulandari, "Court Annuls Advertising Articles in Election Law," *Jakarta Post,* February 25, 2009.
24. International Freedom of Expression Exchange (IFEX), "Columnist on Trial for Allegedly Insulting Attorney General's Office," press release, December 12, 2007; "Columnist Jailed, Constitution Violated," *Tempo Magazine,* February 26–March 3, 2008.
25. "Broadcast News: Opponents Accuse the Government of Trying to Control the Airwaves," *Economist,* February 4, 2006.
26. Camelia Pasandaran, "Indonesian Journalists Still under Threat from Laws," *Jakarta Globe,* May 4, 2009.
27. Amnesty International, "Indonesia: Release Peaceful Protesters Jailed for Raising a Flag," press release, March 26, 2009.
28. Amnesty International, *Indonesia: Briefing to the UN Committee against Torture* (London: Amnesty International, April 2008), 14.
29. Indria Fernida, "Protecting Human Rights Defenders in Indonesia," UPI Asia, October 23, 2009.
30. Amnesty International, "Indonesia," in *Amnesty International Report 2009* (London: Amnesty International, 2009).
31. ICG, "Indonesia: The Hotel Bombings," Asia Briefing No. 94, July 24, 2009; ICG, "Indonesia: Noordin Top's Support Base," Asia Briefing No. 55, August 27, 2009.
32. Amnesty International, *Indonesia: Briefing to the UN Committee against Torture,* 34.
33. "Police Commission Says It Is a Toothless Tiger," *Jakarta Post,* June 4, 2009.
34. Human Rights Watch (HRW), "Indonesia: Refocus Efforts to Solve Activist's Murder," press release, September 11, 2009.
35. HumanTrafficking.org, "Indonesia," home page.
36. Office to Monitor and Combat Trafficking in Persons, "Indonesia," in *Trafficking in Persons Report 2008* (Washington, D.C.: U.S. Department of State, June 4, 2008).
37. Nursyahbani Katjasungkana, "Gender and Law Reform in Indonesia: Overcoming Entrenched Barriers," in *Indonesia: Law and Society, 2nd Edition,* ed. Tim Lindsey (Singapore: ISEAS, 2008), 489.
38. World Economic Forum, *The Global Gender Gap Report 2008* (Geneva: World Economic Forum, 2008).
39. Michael Buehler, "The Rise of Shari'a By-Laws in Indonesian Districts: An Indication for Changing Patterns of Power Accumulation and Political Corruption," *South East Asia Research* 16, no. 2 (2008): 255–285.
40. Jason Tedjasukmana, "Indonesia's New Anti-Porn Agenda," *Time,* November 6, 2008.

[41] Paramita Muljono, "Glass Ceiling in Government: Women in the Ministry of Finance Face Significant Obstacles to Advancement," *Inside Indonesia* 90 (October–December 2007).
[42] Leo Suryadinata, Evi Nurvidya Arifin and Aris Ananta, *Indonesia's Population: Ethnicity and Religion in a Changing Political Landscape* (Singapore: Institute of Southeast Asian Studies [ISEAS], 2003), 6–9.
[43] "Bill against Racial Discrimination Passed," *Jakarta Post*, October 28, 2008.
[44] Gesellschaft fuer Technische Zusammenarbeit (GTZ), *Good Governance in Civil Registration and Administration* (Eschborn, Germany: GTZ, 2009).
[45] Rodd McGibbon, "Indonesian Politics in 2006: Stability, Compromise and Shifting Contests over Ideology," *Bulletin of Indonesian Economic Studies* 42, no. 3 (2006): 321–340.
[46] Khairul Saleh, "South Sumatra Outlaws Ahmadiyah" *Jakarta Post*, September 1, 2008.
[47] "Radicalizing Indonesia," *Wall Street Journal*, September 27, 2009.
[48] Michael Finkel, "Facing Down the Fanatics," *National Geographic*, October 2009.
[49] Robin Bush, "Regional Sharia Regulations in Indonesia: Anomaly or Symptom?" in *Expressing Islam: Religious Life and Politics in Indonesia*, ed. Greg Fealy and Sally White (Singapore: ISEAS, 2008), 177.
[50] Amnesty International, "Indonesia Must Repeal 'Cruel' New Stoning and Caning law," press release, September 28, 2009.
[51] "Less Education for the Disabled," *Jakarta Post*, June 7, 2008.
[52] "Disabled Fight Uphill Battle for Accessible Elections," *Jakarta Globe*, November 23, 2008.
[53] International Trade Union Confederation (ITUC), "Indonesia," in *2009 Annual Survey of Violations of Trade Union Rights: Indonesia* (Brussels: ITUC, 2009).
[54] Amnesty International, "Indonesia," in *Amnesty International Report 2009*.
[55] Christian Motte and Fidelis E. Satriastanti, "Dutch Journalists Detained for Covering Papuan Demonstration," *Jakarta Globe*, March 25, 2009.
[56] Irawati Wardany, "Judiciary the Worst in Graft: KPK Survey," *Jakarta Post*, February 5, 2009.
[57] Simon Butt, "Banishing Judicial Accountability? The Constitutional Court's Decision in the Dispute between the Supreme Court and the Judicial Commission," in *Indonesia: Democracy and the Promise of Good Governance*, ed. Ross McLeod and Andrew MacIntyre (Singapore: ISEAS, 2009), 188–90.
[58] Butt, "Two at the Top: The Constitutional Court and the Supreme Court," 18.
[59] Muninggar Sri Saraswasti, "Judicial Independence a Myth: Lawyer," *Jakarta Globe*, February 26, 2009.
[60] "Indonesian Islamist Group: Police Should Prove Leader's Terror Connection," *Radio Republik Indonesia*, April 12, 2007; Megawati Wijaya, "Indonesia's Anti-Corruption Heroes," *Asia Times Online*, September 23, 2008.
[61] Andra Wisnu, "Most Poor Indonesians Cannot Afford Cost of Civil Justice," *Jakarta Post*, July 31, 2009; Adnan Buyung Nasution, *Arus pemikiran konstitutionalisme* (Jakarta: Kata, 2007).
[62] Kevin O'Rourke, "President Yudhoyono Summoned Military and Police Commanders and Called for Their Neutrality in the Election, but Few Real Concerns Exist about Interference in Politics," *Reformasi Weekly Review: Analyzing Politics and Policies in Indonesia*, January 30, 2009, 5.
[63] Marcus Mietzner, "Veto Player No More? The Declining Political Influence of the Military in Post-Authoritarian Indonesia" (paper presented at Columbia University conference on Indonesia, Islam and Democracy: Comparative Perspectives, New York, April 2–3, 2009).

64. Wisnu Dewabrata, "Reformasi Militer: Pengambilalihan Bisnis TNI seharusnya 'tidak rumit'," *Kompas*, October 15, 2008, 3.
65. Marcus Mietzner, "Soldiers, Parties and Bureaucrats: Illicit Fund-Raising in Contemporary Indonesia," *South East Asia Research* 16, no. 2 (July 2008): 230.
66. HRW, *Too High a Price: The Human Rights Cost of the Indonesian Military's Economic Activities* (New York: HRW, June 20, 2006); HRW, *Indonesia–Reform of Military Business: A Human Rights Watch Background Briefing* (New York: HRW, February 16, 2007).
67. Damien Kingsbury, "Indonesia in 2006: Cautious Reform," *Asian Survey* 47, no. 1 (January/February 2007): 159.
68. "Dismissed Police Chief Investigated," *Jakarta Post*, April 17, 2008.
69. Peter Gelling, "Reform Keeps Indonesian Military in Check," *New York Times*, October 28, 2008.
70. Kevin O'Rourke, "Parliament Passes the Investment Law on 29 March," *Reformasi Weekly Review*, March 30, 2007, 8–11.
71. "Indonesia Risk: Security, Political Stability, Government Effectiveness and Legal & Regulatory Environment," Economist Intelligence Unit, October 23, 2008.
72. Michael Buehler, "Indonesia: Divestment Rules Impede Mining Activity," Oxford Analytica, May 1, 2009.
73. Kevin O'Rourke, "The Constitutional Court Issued a Decision That Strikes Down Extended Land Lease Tenures in the 2007 Investment law," *Reformasi Weekly Review*, March 28, 2008, 8.
74. Lucy Williamson, "Plea over Indonesia Palm Oil Plan," British Broadcasting Corporation, July 11, 2007.
75. Devi Asmarani, "Land Dispute Cases Drag on in Indonesia," *Straits Times*, June 25, 2007.
76. International Finance Corporation (IFC), "Doing Business 2008: Indonesia Is Number Two Reformer in East Asia but Still Lags behind Major Regional Economies," World Bank home page, September 26, 2007.
77. IFC, "Doing Business 2009 Records Positive Reforms in Indonesia on Ease of Doing Business," World Bank home page, September 10, 2008.
78. Michael Buehler, "No Positive News: People Living with HIV Face Corruption and Incompetence in the Health System," *Inside Indonesia* 94 (October/December 2008).
79. Badan Koordinasi Penanaman Modal (BKPM) and Komite Pemantauan Pelaksanaan Otonomi Daerah (KPPOD), *Provinsi Terbaik bagi Penanaman Modal: Survei Pemeringkatan Iklim Usaha di 33 Provinsi, 2008* (Jakarta: BKPM and KPPOD, January 2008).
80. Janeman Latul, "Government Lashes State-Owned Enterprises over Late Financial Reporting," *Jakarta Globe*, April 20, 2009.
81. Erwida Maulia, "NGOs Call for Government Transparency in New Bill," *Jakarta Post*, February 27, 2008.
82. Patrick Guntensperger, "Clean-Up Goal for Pertamina," *Asia Times Online*, May 5, 2009.
83. Michael Buehler, "Indonesia: Predatory Tax Practices Are Entrenched," Oxford Analytica, March 19, 2009.
84. Michael Buehler, "The New Regional Taxation Law: An End to Predatory Taxation?" *Van Zorge Report on Indonesia: Behind the Headlines* XI, no. 8 (September 17, 2009), 9.
85. Melissa Crouch, "Indonesia's National and Local Ombudsman Reforms: Salvaging a Failed Experiment?" in *Indonesia: Law and Society, 2nd Edition*, ed. Tim Lindsey (Singapore: ISEAS, 2008), 386.
86. Irawaty Wardany, "State Auditor Named As Corruption Suspect," *Jakarta Post*, February 14, 2009.

[87] Stewart Fenwick, "Measuring Up? Indonesia's Anti-Corruption Commission and the New Corruption Agenda," *Indonesia: Law and Society, 2nd Edition*, ed. Tim Lindsey (Singapore: ISEAS, 2008), 414.

[88] Taufik Alwie, Anthony, Hendri Firzani, Mukhlison S. Widodo, and Asrori S. Karni, "Menelisik Peran Antasari dalam Pembunuhan Nasrudin," *Gatra*, May 7, 2009.

[89] Kevin O'Rourke, "Parliament Passed the Corrupt Crimes Court Law on 29 September," *Reformasi Weekly Review: Analyzing Politics and Policies in Indonesia*, October 2, 2009, 12.

[90] "Suspect Ambassador Accuses Ambassador to the U.S. of Graft," *Jakarta Post*, November 26, 2008.

[91] Kevin O'Rourke, "Outlook," *Reformasi Weekly Review: Analyzing Politics and Policies in Indonesia*, February 22, 2008, 9.

[92] Kevin O'Rourke, "Parliament Will Curtail Its Use of Closed-Door Meetings, According to an Agreement Reached in Deliberations of the Legislative Composition Bill," *Reformasi Weekly Review: Analyzing Politics and Policies in Indonesia*, February 15, 2008, 6.

[93] Wolfgang Fengler, "Indonesia 2015: Demography, Geography and Spending for the Next Decade" (paper presented at Columbia University, New York, April 30, 2009).

[94] Jonathan R. Pincus and Jeffrey Winters, *Re-Inventing the World Bank* (Ithaca, N.Y.: Cornell University Press, 2002).

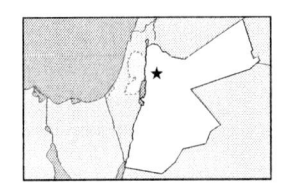

JORDAN

CAPITAL: Amman
POPULATION: 5.9 million
GNI PER CAPITA (PPP): $5,530

SCORES	2006	2010
ACCOUNTABILITY AND PUBLIC VOICE:	2.74	2.57
CIVIL LIBERTIES:	3.13	3.11
RULE OF LAW:	3.10	3.05
ANTICORRUPTION AND TRANSPARENCY:	2.25	2.48

(scores are based on a scale of 0 to 7, with 0 representing weakest and 7 representing strongest performance)

Russell E. Lucas

INTRODUCTION

The Hashemite Kingdom of Jordan is often viewed as an oasis of stability in the tumultuous Middle East. The ruling family has led the country since its formation in 1921, and the current king, Abdullah II, took the throne on the death of his long-ruling father, King Hussein, in 1999. The kingdom's moderate foreign policy, its political opening in 1989, and its adoption of economic structural adjustment policies over the last two decades have arguably offered its citizens a shelter from the repression, strife, and occupation that afflict its neighbors.

Other observers, however, claim that the resource-poor country is a colonial artifice kept alive by Western aid and the repression of its citizens—especially its large Palestinian population. They point out that the intelligence services, namely the General Intelligence Directorate (GID, or *mukhabarat*), hold an inordinate level of power, which is at the disposal of the one true decision maker, the king. Although critics would admit that since 1989 repression has given way to some civil liberties and regular (with one exception) parliamentary elections, they also critique the electoral system for inflating the influence of Jordanians of East Bank origins and dismiss the parliament as a rubber-stamp body, or as a site of competition for state patronage.

Those on both sides of this debate agree that Jordan's domestic politics are heavily influenced by regional affairs and by its dependent economic position.

Russell E. Lucas is an assistant professor of political science and international relations at Florida International University. He is the author of *Institutions and the Politics of Survival in Jordan: Domestic Responses to External Challenges, 1988–2001* (SUNY Press, 2005) and is currently working on a book about the politics of Arab monarchies.

The country's level of political freedom has consequently fluctuated over time in response to regional and global events. During its early years under the British Mandate and after independence in 1946, King Abdullah I used his personal patronage (and British fiscal and military support) to build the new state. Jordan annexed what is now known as the West Bank after the 1948 war with Israel, controlling it until it was captured and occupied by Israel in 1967. King Abdullah was assassinated in 1951, and due to the mental incapacity of his son, his young grandson, Hussein, took the throne amid domestic and regional instability.

The regime survived by banning political parties and relying more on the army than on the constitution from the late 1950s through the 1970s. Although Jordan lacked the oil resources of its neighbors, it did have an educated population, including many residents of Palestinian origin, who found work helping to build the oil states of the Gulf in the 1970s. Economic growth contributed to a more quiescent political atmosphere, but as remittances and foreign aid dried up in the 1980s, the state turned to greater repression. In 1989, a fiscal crisis resulted in a substantial political liberalization, including long-delayed parliamentary elections, the legalization of political parties, and greater press freedom. Over the course of the 1990s, however, external pressures from regional conflicts—especially in Iraq and Palestine—led the government to increase limits on the ability of the public to exercise their rights and hold officials accountable.

Jordan was the only Arab country to give citizenship to Palestinians, and after influxes associated with the 1948 and 1967 wars as well as Jordan's period of control over the West Bank, about half of its population is of Palestinian origin. Since the 1970 civil war, which pitted government forces against largely Palestinian guerrilla groups, Jordanians with East Bank origins (or "Transjordanians") have increasingly asserted their dominance over the state bureaucracy and the private sector. Class, tribal, and provincial divisions also continue to affect social and political affairs.

Hopes for greater liberalization under the new king in 1999 were dashed by continued regional crises, including the second Palestinian *intifada* (uprising), global antiterrorism efforts after the 2001 attacks on the United States, and the U.S. invasion of Iraq in 2003. The parliament was suspended from 2001 to 2003, and in the wake of a series of bombings in 2005, new antiterrorism legislation increased restrictions on Islamist political activists. Parliamentary elections were held again in 2003 and 2007, but proregime conservatives continued to dominate the voting and approve restrictive laws.

Faced with these challenges, King Abdullah II has attempted to continue economic reforms while staving off political liberalization. Jordan's economy has grown, but the benefits are not perceived to have reached the average Jordanian. Moreover, the country's lack of mineral wealth or a diversified industrial base has forced the state to continue to rely on external funding sources, which has historically encouraged corruption and a lack of government transparency. The resultant growth in economic inequality has compounded social discontent. Economic and legal reforms tied to Jordan's desire for greater integration into the global marketplace have begun to address some of these transparency problems, but Jordan's recent performance in political reforms has been disappointing.

ACCOUNTABILITY AND PUBLIC VOICE 2.57

FREE AND FAIR ELECTORAL LAWS AND ELECTIONS	2.75
EFFECTIVE AND ACCOUNTABLE GOVERNMENT	2.25
CIVIC ENGAGEMENT AND CIVIC MONITORING	3.00
MEDIA INDEPENDENCE AND FREEDOM OF EXPRESSION	2.29

The king is granted wide-ranging powers under the 1952 constitution. While he delegates some day-to-day decisions to the parliament and cabinet, he holds the ultimate initiative and veto power in all matters of political importance. Nevertheless, relative to other countries in the region, there is significant space for an array of political and social groups to express their views, organize, and participate in public policy debates, so long as they do not directly criticize the king. Though it faces periodic harassment, the Muslim Brotherhood and its affiliated political party, the Islamic Action Front (IAF), have long had a presence on Jordan's political scene, forming the largest opposition group and sending members to the parliament.

The constitution, which has been amended several times, grants sweeping authority to the king as the head of the executive, legislative, and judicial branches of government. While the monarch is the head of state (Article 30), commander in chief of the military (Article 32), and head of government (Article 31), many functions are handled in practice by the prime minister and the cabinet. The king appoints these officials, who serve at his pleasure (Article 35). In November 2005, following a series of terrorist bombings, the king dismissed Prime Minister Adnan Badran, a liberal academic, after just seven months in office. His successor, Marouf al-Bakhit, was replaced by Nader al-Dahahbi shortly after the 2007 parliamentary elections. Under Article 62 of the constitution, the bicameral legislature is divided between the elected House of Deputies (*Majlis al-Nuwaab*) and the appointed Senate (*Majlis al-Ayaan*, or House of Notables), whose 55 members are chosen by the king.

The king can dissolve the parliament, as he did the Senate in 2005 following the terrorist bombings. Only the cabinet can initiate draft legislation, leaving the parliament to accept, amend, or reject bills. When the parliament is out of session, the cabinet—with the king's approval—can issue temporary decrees that have full legal force. While the House of Deputies has the authority to remove ministers by a vote of no confidence and the parliament can override the king's veto on legislation, neither step has been taken in recent decades. The parliament has amended or rejected reform legislation on several occasions in recent years, in some cases blunting attempts to bring Jordan into compliance with international standards.

Most political groups, including the parliamentary opposition, tend to focus their energies on influencing government policies and reaping the patronage benefits of positions in the cabinet or parliament, rather than on changing the monarchical regime. Power tends to rotate not among parties, but rather between loose cliques and factions within the broad progovernment bloc, with a technocratic, economically liberal group generally balanced against a more statist and tribal bloc. Opposition groups use the parliament as a platform to criticize government policies—especially unpopular foreign policies such as the peace with Israel—but their level of representation is generally insufficient to enable any concrete action. Civic groups and common citizens have some input on legislation before the parliament, such as a series of public hearings held in April 2009 on amendments to a controversial real estate law.[1]

Under the 1986 Election Law and its multiple amendments, the 110 members of the House of Deputies are elected for four-year terms. Of these, 104 are elected in multimember districts with a single, nontransferable vote system, meaning each voter chooses one candidate and the top vote-earners win seats. Together with gerrymandered districts, this system results in the underrepresentation of opposition-minded Palestinians living in urban areas and the overrepresentation of rural, loyalist, Transjordanian voters. For example, every lawmaker elected from Amman represents about 95,000 people, while those elected from the rural provinces of Al-Karak and At-Tafilah represent about 2,000 people.[2] Modifications made in 2003 provide a quota of six seats for women (elected separately from the geographical district system), nine for Christians, and three for ethnic Circassians, though the latter two groups are overrepresented as a result. Since 1989, the kingdom has held five parliamentary elections, though the body was suspended from 2001 until 2003.

A municipalities law passed in February 2007 cleared the way for municipal elections in July, with mayoralties and all city council seats at stake. An exception in the law left Amman under the previous system, with half of the city council members appointed by the central government. The IAF boycotted the July elections after security forces arrested nine of its members between May and June for allegedly "threatening national security,"[3] though the party nevertheless won 2 out of the 965 contested seats.

Jordan held elections to the House of Deputies in November 2007, with some observers noting that the polls were subject to greater government interference than in the past. The elections garnered just over 50 percent voter turnout, partly due to the authorities' decision to extend polling for an additional two hours; a turnout of less than 50 percent would have invalidated the elections.[4] Despite repeated calls from local activists for a new electoral law based on proportional representation, the government did not act on previous pledges to reform the law before the 2007 elections. Nor did the government allow international observers to monitor the polls. Local groups were permitted to monitor the elections under the umbrella of the National Center for Human Rights (NCHR), a government-sponsored body known for its critical evaluations of the authorities' performance, but these groups were granted access to just 150 out of 3,995 polling sites. Vote buying and the transferring of voter registrations between districts were particularly prominent flaws that had been identified in the municipal elections as well.[5] According to the NCHR, "the volume of violations incurred during all the election phases undermined the integrity of the elections, reduced their credibility and damaged the confidentiality of the election process."[6] Surveys showed that about 37 percent and 33 percent of respondents witnessed the selling and transfer of votes, respectively.[7]

While political parties are legal in Jordan, the only significant party is the IAF, with most other candidates running as independents. In the 2007 elections, the IAF saw its representation in the parliament shrink from 17 seats to 6. In addition to the structural problems and irregularities noted above, the party suffered from internal power struggles and a decision to field fewer candidates. The country's other political parties, mainly leftist and Arab nationalist groups, garnered no seats in 2007. Independent deputies with ties to tribes and business elites consequently hold over 80 percent of the seats.[8] Political parties are increasingly seen as out of touch with the concerns of average Jordanians, and the public has limited faith in the parliament's ability to affect government policy, leading citizens to vote along tribal or communal lines. In 2009, a majority of the public reported that they were unsatisfied with the performance of the parliament; among "opinion leaders" such as high-ranking officials, journalists, and professionals, the figure was 71 percent.[9]

The Political Parties Law was amended in 2007 and took effect in 2008. It raised from 50 to 500 the number of members necessary for a party to register, increased the number of districts from which those members must be drawn, and maintained the licensing of parties with the Ministry of Interior rather than the Ministry of Political Development or the courts. In April 2008, only 12 of 36 parties were deemed by the interior minister to have met the new legal criteria, leading to the dissolution or merger of the remainder.[10] While some saw the reform as a boon that would allow larger parties like the IAF to increase their influence, others denounced it as an undemocratic move that would increase the marginalization of parties other than the IAF. Given the outcome of the 2007 and earlier elections, as well as the effects of the Political Parties Law, many opposition-minded or politically active groups and individuals have turned to professional associations as an alternative platform for political expression.

The civil service has traditionally been staffed by Jordanians of East Bank origin rather than those of Palestinian origin, especially since the 1970 civil war. Recruitment and selection often take place through family or tribal *wasta* (connections), which also make it difficult to dismiss underperforming state employees. However, structural adjustment policies have slimmed Jordan's bloated bureaucracy to some degree, and a combination of rising education levels, administrative reforms, and competition between patronage groups has raised the quality of the civil service.

Jordan's civil society organizations "enjoy one of the most favorable political environments in the Arab world."[11] Nevertheless, freedom of association remains limited. Nongovernmental organizations (NGOs) must obtain licenses from the government, and this barrier can be used to curb participation by some groups, especially those tied to foreign organizations (such as the Palestinian Islamist group Hamas). In July 2006 the Ministry of Social Development replaced the entire board of the Islamic Center Society, a health and education charity tied to the Muslim Brotherhood that was one of Jordan's largest NGOs. The previous board, all members of the Muslim Brotherhood, were charged with economic crimes and violating the association's bylaws, but as of July 2009 they had not yet been brought to trial. The incident took place soon after the victory of Hamas in Palestinian elections, which provoked tension between the Jordanian government and the Jordanian Muslim Brotherhood and IAF, raising concerns that the board replacement was politically motivated.[12]

The parliament passed a new Societies Law in 2008, and although some analysts found it to be an improvement over the previous legislation from 1960, it severely limited NGOs' independence, providing the government with supervisory power over their budgets and the authority to reject foreign funding. Following protests from local and international civil society groups, the government opened a consultative dialogue about the law in early 2009.[13] An amended version passed in July 2009 liberalized the 2008 bill to some extent, but it retained many restrictions, including the need for cabinet approval prior to receipt of foreign funding.[14] Furthermore, the royal family often sponsors NGOs that can crowd out more independent-minded organizations by attracting foreign donations, especially in the realm of economic development.[15]

The constitution protects freedom of expression, provided it does not "violate the law" (Article 15). In practice, a lively range of debate and opinions are expressed in the Jordanian public sphere, but within clear red lines forbidding criticism of the monarchy, friendly foreign leaders, or prominent politicians. The press generally does not expose corruption or human rights abuses and especially avoids naming specific officials. In recent years, freedom of expression and the press has remained essentially unchanged. The media operate under the Press and Publications Law of 1993, which was amended in 1998 and 2007. While the latest version of the law eliminated imprisonment as a penalty for press offenses, it also drastically increased the possible fines for speech that offends religious beliefs or slanders the government.[16] In addition, other laws such as the penal code still allow imprisonment on charges of defamation, insulting the security forces, undermining national unity, or lèse majesté. In March 2008, five journalists received three-month prison sentences for "insulting the judiciary and commenting on its rulings" and for insulting government officials. Nevertheless, in November 2008 King Abdullah pledged not to detain journalists for practicing their profession if they behave responsibly, and as of June 2009, there were no reports of journalists being arrested since the king's statement. In some cases, courts have also been known to defend freedom of speech and reject libel accusations.[17] In April 2009, an Amman court cleared columnist Khalid Mahadin of charges that he had slandered the parliament in an online article in February that criticized the lower house's performance.[18]

Jordanian officials regularly impose both direct and indirect restrictions on media content. Authorities are often tipped off about potentially offensive articles by informers at printing presses, and editors may then face pressure from officials or security agencies to remove the material. In a 2009 survey of journalists, a third reported that they had faced some form of censorship and about half had experienced softer forms of "containment," such as bribes or promises of government jobs. This climate contributes to widespread self-censorship. Indeed, the most common source of censorship cited by journalists in the survey was the media organization itself (81 percent), especially when it came to criticism of the security forces (74 percent) or issues of national unity (73 percent).[19]

The state dominates the media industry through direct and indirect financial control. Private outlets encounter financial and legal obstacles in obtaining licenses,[20] particularly if they wish to broadcast political content or challenge government personalities or policies. The state ended its legal monopoly on terrestrial television service in 2001, but a de facto monopoly remains in place. While the country's first private television station, ATV, was approved in late 2005, its planned launch has been delayed since 2007 due to regulatory obstacles. A number of independent radio networks broadcast, but most do not carry political programming. One outlet that does, Amman Net radio, was denied a license to expand its service to the city of Zarqa in November 2007. The state owns the two dominant newspapers, *Al-Rai'* and *Ad-Destour*. Independent papers such as *Al-Arab al-Youm* and *Al-Ghad*, as well as a number of weekly tabloids, offer political alternatives, though they tend to show caution in dealing with sensitive political affairs lest they face harassment, as exemplified by the weekly *Al-Majd*. The April 30, 2007, edition of the investigative weekly was banned for reporting on secret plans to undermine the Palestinian president, and its editor was tried (but acquitted) for defaming a former prime minister. Political parties are allowed to issue their own publications.

Jordan has a lively internet environment with numerous internet cafés and rising home usage. The penetration rate reached nearly 25 percent of the population in 2008, and the government has actively sought to promote access to new media technologies. In September 2007, the Press and Publication Department attempted to regulate online news. While a court later blocked the action, ruling that the internet is not subject to the Press and Publications Law, an estimated 20 legal cases were reportedly filed against Jordanian-based news websites in the first quarter of 2009, most of them libel suits brought by parliamentary deputies and other members of the elite.[21] Internet café owners log visitors' identification numbers, and internet service providers must route information through government servers. In October 2007, a former lawmaker and head of the Jordan National Movement, Ahmad Oweidi Abbadi, was sentenced to two years in prison by a state security court for posting online an open letter to members of the U.S. Congress that accused the interior minister and other officials of corruption.[22]

CIVIL LIBERTIES   3.11

PROTECTION FROM STATE TERROR, UNJUSTIFIED IMPRISONMENT, AND TORTURE	2.88
GENDER EQUITY	2.67
RIGHTS OF ETHNIC, RELIGIOUS, AND OTHER DISTINCT GROUPS	3.25
FREEDOM OF CONSCIENCE AND BELIEF	4.00
FREEDOM OF ASSOCIATION AND ASSEMBLY	2.75

Although the constitution and penal code expressly outlaw torture and arbitrary arrest, Jordan's citizens enjoy little protection from such abuses in practice, particularly because complaints of mistreatment rarely result in prosecution. A January 2007 report by the United Nations Special Rapporteur on Torture found that "the practice of torture is widespread in Jordan, and in some places routine."[23] Having ratified the UN Convention against Torture in 1991, Jordan amended its penal code in 2007 to adopt the definition of torture provided by the treaty, but the code has yet to be amended to fully comply with the treaty's provisions.[24] International human rights groups have repeatedly reported on Jordan's role as a hub in the U.S. government's extraordinary rendition program, in which terrorism suspects have been moved secretly across international borders for detention and interrogation.[25]

Torture and abusive punishment have been heavily employed against domestic opponents, especially Islamists, since the 2005 Amman bombings. The UN Special Rapporteur on Torture specifically accused the GID of regularly engaging in torture during interrogation of suspects,[26] while a 2008 Human Rights Watch report cited evidence suggesting that five prison directors personally participated in the torture of detainees.[27] No death sentences have been carried out in Jordan since May 2006, but 45 inmates currently await execution, and the death penalty remains in place.[28] Administrative detention without trial continues to be common: 12,178 individuals were reported to be administratively detained in 2007 under the Crime Prevention Law of 1954.[29]

According to domestic and international observers, Jordan's prisoners face hardships including overcrowding, solitary confinement, and lack of legal aid. The authorities have undertaken the construction of new prisons and improvements to existing facilities, but reforms of detention procedures and prosecutions for prisoner abuse are lacking. There has been an increase in riots by prisoners protesting ill-treatment in recent years,[30] including an April 2008 incident at Muwaggar prison in which three inmates died in a fire, allegedly after guards prevented them from leaving their cell.[31] In its annual report for 2007, however, the NCHR found "qualitative improvement" in the administration of detention centers.[32]

The government tolerates a fair degree of dissent from political opponents. Groups are typically able to organize as long as their methods are peaceful. Nevertheless, incidents of harassment continue to be reported, particularly against Islamists. Two IAF lawmakers were jailed in 2006 for paying funeral condolences to the family of the slain Jordanian-born leader of al-Qaeda in Iraq, Abu Musab al-Zarqawi; they were later pardoned by the king. The 2006 Prevention of Terrorism Act, passed in the wake of the 2005 Amman bombings, includes broad provisions criminalizing indirect financing of or interaction with terrorist organizations and permits detention of suspects for up to 30 days without charge. While antiterrorism and other security laws are used to stifle peaceful dissent, the rates of ordinary crime in Jordan remain low, with only 2.6 murders per 100,000 people recorded in 2007.[33]

Victims of abuse can register complaints through a number of channels, including prosecutors from the prison service and the government Grievances Office. However, the close relationship of these bodies to alleged perpetrators, the lack of confidentiality surrounding complaints procedures, and their inability to protect prisoners from retaliation discourage many from reporting abuse, resulting in very few complaints and even fewer prosecutions.[34] The NCHR, a legally independent, quasi-governmental body established in December 2002, has the authority to investigate and report human rights violations, but it is mostly financed by state sources and the current and previous heads of its board of trustees were former prime ministers. In an incident that highlighted the limits of the center's independence, former chairman Ahmad Obeidat resigned abruptly in July 2008, having been summoned to the prime minister's office shortly after he joined 149 other activists, lawyers, and politicians in signing a petition that sharply criticized the government's economic policies.[35] In 2007, the NCHR received 288 complaints, 62 of which it closed with a "satisfactory result." Of the remainder, 14 were closed without a "satisfactory result," and 160 remained open for follow-up at year's end.[36]

Jordan is both a destination and transit country for human trafficking, especially for natives of South and Southeast Asia and workers bound for Iraq. Domestic servants have been particularly vulnerable to exploitation and abuse by employers. In July 2008, the parliament passed a law protecting the rights of domestic workers, including the right to compensation should they quit following sexual assault at their place of employment.[37] In 2009, the parliament passed an antitrafficking law that assigns penalties of six months in prison and a US$7,000 fine for forced prostitution or child trafficking. Enforcement of both of these laws remains to be seen. Although passage of the new law helped raise Jordan's status in the U.S. State Department's 2009 Trafficking in Persons Report, weak enforcement efforts were cited in the report.[38]

Article 6 of the constitution calls for legal equality on the grounds of "race, language, or religion," but not gender. While women enjoy political rights and legal equality on issues such as health care and education, they continue to face legal discrimination related to inheritance, divorce, and child custody—which fall under the jurisdiction of Sharia (Islamic law) courts—as well as in the provision of pensions and social security benefits. Jordanian women have had the right to vote since 1974. A parliamentary quota guarantees that at least six members of the House of Deputies are women. In the 2007 elections, one woman was elected outright beyond the quota. At least 20 percent of municipal council seats are also reserved for women. In July 2007, 25 years after ratifying the Convention on the Elimination of All Forms of Discrimination against Women (CEDAW), Jordan published the treaty in the official gazette, giving it the force of law and allowing it to be invoked in lawsuits; local women's groups have not yet fully taken advantage of this option, however.

Jordan maintains a number of reservations to CEDAW, especially in relation to nationality and freedom of residence.[39] Children of a Jordanian woman and a foreign man remain unable to obtain citizenship, leaving them with lesser access to public education and government health services. Despite government pledges to reform the relevant legislation, the parliament failed to ratify or even rejected changes that would reduce Jordan's CEDAW reservations.

Domestic violence continues to be a concern, particularly given cultural norms that discourage victims from reporting rape and other forms of abuse to the authorities. In January 2008 the parliament passed a Family Protection Law intended to improve the management of domestic violence cases by medical professionals and law enforcement bodies. Training projects in recent years have also reportedly contributed to improved treatment of victims by police officers, judges, and prosecutors. The government opened the Family Reconciliation House, the country's first major shelter for abused women, in February 2007. Despite these advances, an estimated two dozen honor killings—in which women are killed by male relatives for perceived sexual transgressions—are committed each year.[40] The killers often receive light sentences or go free because of provisions in the penal code allowing lenient treatment for those who commit a crime in a "state of fit or fury." While amendments to remove such loopholes have been rejected by the parliament, in August 2009 a special tribunal was seated that will hear honor crimes cases and unify jurisprudence on the issue. Governors are authorized to incarcerate women for their own protection, and roughly 25 women are so detained in Jordanian prisons at any given time, with some remaining in protective custody for several years.[41] Women generally lag behind men in employment and income, partly because of a legal framework that reinforces their dependence on male relatives for financial support.

While national origins are not addressed by the country's census, Jordanians of Palestinian origin are believed to make up a large share, if not a majority, of

Jordan's population. However, they have historically faced discrimination in government employment, especially in the security forces, as well as in university admissions and scholarships.[42] The Palestinian-Transjordanian social divide has been a lingering issue in Jordanian politics since the 1970 civil war.[43]

The government's procedures for granting or revoking citizenship are often inconsistent and nontransparent, offering little opportunity for individuals to appeal a Ministry of Interior decision.[44] Since 1988, and especially since the second Palestinian intifada in 2000, the government has downgraded the passports of some Palestinians with residence in the West Bank from five years to three years. In July 2009, it was reported that the government was revoking the citizenship of thousands of Palestinians of West Bank origin, raising fears that their freedom of movement and other rights as citizens would be impeded.[45] An estimated 130,000 Palestinian residents from the Gaza Strip are not eligible for citizenship under Jordanian law; according to the government, approximately half (those who previously had Egyptian travel documents) were granted only two-year travel and residency documents.[46] Though the government's treatment of refugees from Iraq has often been progressive, as when it granted refugee children access to public schools, their growing numbers have reportedly drawn increasing discrimination from employers and landlords and exacerbated budget strains and high unemployment levels.[47] A number of Jordanians of East Bank origin have called for a return of "visitors" (Palestinians and Iraqis) to their respective homes. Such nativist rhetoric, especially from high government officials or their associates, has caused unease among many Jordanians of Palestinian origin.

The Jordanian population is overwhelmingly Sunni Muslim (roughly 92 percent). Various Christian denominations together form the largest religious minority (about 6 percent), while small Shiite Muslim, Druze, and Baha'i communities comprise the remainder. Nearly all of the population is ethnically Arab, aside from the small Circassian and Chechen community and the even smaller Armenian community. Islam is the state religion, and Arabic the official language. Minority religious and ethnic communities are generally well treated, including those like the Druze and Baha'i that are not officially recognized. Nevertheless, during 2007 and 2008, several Christian churches were either ordered to close or faced lease-renewal difficulties, apparently due to orders from the Ministry of Interior. Individuals converting from Islam to another religion may face discrimination and lose certain rights, including those to inheritance or child custody. In March 2008, Muhammad Abbad Abbad, a convert from Islam to Christianity, fled the country with his wife and children, fearing the loss of civil and personal liberties after being detained on charges of apostasy. The following month, a Sharia court found him guilty of apostasy in absentia, annulled his marriage, and declared him to have no religious identity.[48]

The Ministry of Religious Affairs controls the kingdom's religious institutions and oversees imams and mosques. Preachers must be licensed by the ministry under legislation passed in 2006. Violations of the law can lead to imprisonment and up to JD 600 (US$840) in fines.[49] In February 2009, the IAF complained that the government had used administrative measures rather than the new law's procedures to bar a dozen imams from preaching.[50]

The 2007 Law on the Rights of Persons with Disabilities mandates changes to building codes, offers aid to the disabled, and encourages education on disabilities. Jordan ratified the UN Convention on the Rights of Persons with Disabilities in May 2008, making it one of only two Arab states to do so. However, it is unclear whether the law and convention have been fully implemented beyond foreign-funded projects.[51]

The Public Gatherings Law requires permits for assemblies, which regional governors frequently refuse to grant. Furthermore, the Prevention of Terrorism Act (PTA), passed in the wake of the 2005 bombings, penalizes any "damage to infrastructure," no matter how minor, as "terrorist acts," and some observers fear this provision could be used to stifle peaceful assemblies.[52] The Public Gatherings Law was amended in 2008 to require governors to respond to permit requests within 48 hours, and organizations are now allowed to hold routine meetings without permits.[53] Although the government tolerates some protests, others have been banned or forcibly dispersed. For example, the authorities in 2008 denied permission for an IAF demonstration outside the Egyptian embassy to protest the treatment of the Muslim Brotherhood in Egypt, a women's charity breakfast, and an academic workshop on the impact of lifting fuel subsidies. In January 2009, police used tear gas as well as physical force and arrests to turn back protesters marching on the Israeli embassy during Israel's military operations in Gaza, although the authorities later allowed a large rally to take place at a sports stadium.[54] In May 2009, 11 people, including trade union leaders, were arrested over protests calling for a boycott of Israeli produce.[55]

Given the weakness of political parties other than the IAF, much political activity has been organized by Jordan's 14 professional associations, which represent lawyers, engineers, doctors, and other professionals, and in which membership is mandatory. The government has largely been tolerant of the frequent protests organized by these associations. Elections in many of the associations are quite competitive between supporters of Islamist, leftist-Arab nationalist, and conservative ideologies. The government often threatens to increase regulation of the professional associations and demands that they avoid straying into political matters. However, recent moves to step up regulations have not secured support in the parliament and were removed from the agenda with the appointment of Nadir Dhahabi as prime minister.[56] Jordan has 17 worker associations under the umbrella of the General Federation of Jordanian Trade Unions, although only 10 to 15 percent of workers are unionized.[57] State employees and teachers are not permitted to organize; although 75 lawmakers submitted a petition in 2007 proposing a bill for the establishment of a teachers' union, there has been no further progress on the proposal.[58]

RULE OF LAW   3.05

INDEPENDENT JUDICIARY	3.00
PRIMACY OF RULE OF LAW IN CIVIL AND CRIMINAL MATTERS	2.60
ACCOUNTABILITY OF SECURITY FORCES AND MILITARY TO CIVILIAN AUTHORITIES	2.25
PROTECTION OF PROPERTY RIGHTS	4.33

Jordan's legal system is divided into three types of courts: civil courts, for civil and regular criminal cases; Sharia courts and their Christian counterparts, for personal status and family cases; and the State Security Court (SSC), for national security crimes including terrorism, drug trafficking, defamation of the monarchy, and financial offenses. The prime minster appoints the SSC's three judges, usually two military officers and one civilian. The PTA in 2006 expanded the SSC's powers, allowing it to order surveillance and to ban individuals from travel. Since 2001, the prime minister has had the authority to move cases from the regular courts to the SSC, with no possibility for defendants to appeal the transfer. SSC procedures, which routinely fail to meet basic international standards, include lengthy pretrial detention without charge, lack of access to counsel, secret hearings, and limitations on media coverage.[59] According to human rights groups, the SSC regularly accepts confessions extracted through torture by the GID, sometimes using them as the main basis for convictions. According to the U.S. State Department, the court adjudicated 1,450 cases between January and September 2008. In 2008, the media reported on at least 21 SSC convictions, including some for nonviolent offenses such as lèse majesté.[60]

Civil and ordinary criminal court judges are appointed directly by the king or by the High Judicial Council (HJC), whose own members are appointed by royal decree or government recommendation. Judicial promotions are granted based on evaluations from the Judicial Inspection Service, which is accountable to the minister of justice. The king and the HJC jointly decide on judicial dismissals. The Ministry of Justice (MOJ) retains significant power over the judiciary, including over the appointment of administrative staff at all levels of the system.[61] The MOJ also holds responsibility for all financial and administrative matters, though the president of the HJC has some leeway in determining judges' wages.[62] Judges generally view themselves as subservient to the MOJ. There is no professional association for judges, and the authorities have discouraged the creation of such a group.

The government reportedly interferes regularly in politically sensitive cases, including those before the Court of Cassation, the highest appellate court.[63] Even when it does not interfere directly, the executive branch exercises indirect influence through appointments and administrative matters. In addition, due to low remuneration, many judges and court staff are vulnerable to corruption;

one 2007 study reported an increase in the acceptance of bribes among court employees.[64] Over a quarter of judges surveyed in 2005 reported facing pressure from various sources during their decision-making processes.[65] Tribal connections in particular have often affected judicial decisions, at times to the detriment of Palestinian Jordanians.

While court decisions are generally enforced, judicial authority is undermined by the Criminal Prevention Law, which authorizes governors to investigate and detain individuals. These powers have reportedly "been employed on several occasions even after innocent verdicts or the release of the accused."[66] Moreover, the king has the constitutional power to issue sweeping pardons, essentially overriding any judicial decision. In 2006, the HJC formed a permanent ethics and accountability committee following the publication of a code of ethics the previous year, but enforcement has been weak and the HJC's own limited independence detracts from the committee's credibility.

By law, defendants are presumed innocent until proven guilty and have the right to counsel, as well as to cross-examine witnesses. However, government-provided legal aid remains limited to trials that might result in life imprisonment or the death penalty, and lawyers often encounter obstacles when trying to meet clients, particularly during the early stages of an investigation.[67] By law, defendants must be brought before a judge within 24 hours. In practice, those detained are often held for extended periods, sometimes incommunicado, before being given judicial review.[68] The length of trials and repeated delays, in violation of legal deadlines, remain common complaints; it can take years for a defendant to receive a first instance criminal verdict. Courts at all levels suffer from a shortage of judges and other staff, contributing to significant backlogs in both civil and criminal cases. Enhanced computerization, lowered court costs, and other recent reforms have reportedly increased transparency and efficiency to some degree, but significant changes have yet to be enacted.

In 2003, the government adopted the Judicial Upgrading Strategy (JUST), a plan that was later supplemented to cover reforms through 2009. Implementation has reportedly been sluggish, however, and primarily limited to courts in Amman. Moreover, the plan itself faced criticism due to a lack of civil society involvement in its development and the decision to entrust the MOJ with overseeing measures meant to enhance judicial independence.[69]

Prosecutors are appointed by the government and supervised by the MOJ. While the attorney general has the legal right to ignore an order by the justice minister, this has never been known to happen.[70] From 2006 to 2009, no high-ranking public officials were prosecuted for abuse of power. According to Human Rights Watch, only a handful of prison officials have been prosecuted for abuses in their facilities, and their sentences have been excessively lenient. In one case, a prison director "found to have personally beaten as many as 70 inmates received a $180 fine . . . the court exonerated 12 other guards who had also beaten these inmates."[71]

The military, police, and the GID are under the king's direct control. GID officers are granted extensive powers and face little risk of prosecution for abuse. Domestic and international observers have documented the practice by the GID (in the case of security crimes) and the Public Security Directorate's Criminal Investigations Department (in the case of regular criminal investigations) of routinely holding suspects incommunicado and using torture to extract information. The GID's role has especially expanded in the wake of the 2005 hotel bombings.[72]

Jordan has a generally market-oriented economy, but there is still a large public sector. The constitution guarantees the right to private property, contracts are generally enforced, and expropriations are rare. Nevertheless, land wealth and political patronage have historically been linked, and in recent years there have been more rumors of royal land grabs in which state or municipal land is redefined as crown land.

ANTICORRUPTION AND TRANSPARENCY   2.48

    ENVIRONMENT TO PROTECT AGAINST CORRUPTION   2.00
    PROCEDURES AND SYSTEMS TO ENFORCE ANTICORRUPTION LAWS   2.75
    EXISTENCE OF ANTICORRUPTION NORMS, STANDARDS,
        AND PROTECTIONS   2.50
    GOVERNMENTAL TRANSPARENCY   2.67

The king frequently and formally instructs his governments to reduce corruption, and in late 2006 Jordan hosted the first Conference of the States Parties to the United Nations Convention against Corruption. Jordan's ratification of the convention the previous year has spurred a number of legal reforms aimed at improving transparency and accountability. Nonetheless, few if any steps have been taken to tackle the primary sources of corruption, weaken extensive patronage networks, or consistently punish high-ranking officials.

The distribution of patronage has been one of the monarchy's key tactics for rewarding allies and building support among key social groups. Important goods granted to individuals and groups include jobs, subsidies, land, and contracts. Conversely, political opponents can be denied access to these assets. While the government has publically repudiated corruption, in part to encourage foreign investment, the practice of quietly distributing patronage continues. Moreover, a greater share of state funding has been allocated to the military, and presumably the intelligence services, since the 1990s, with a US$300 million increase in the most recent budget.[73] This spending acts as a social welfare program by providing employment for citizens from more rural and tribal areas.[74]

Transparency International ranks Jordan 47 out of 180 countries in its 2008 Corruption Perceptions Index, and its score of 5.1 is shared by Hungary, Costa Rica, and Malaysia.[75] This slight improvement on its 2007 score was probably linked to the activity of the Anti-Corruption Commission (see below). According to a 2008 survey, over 17 percent of Jordanians found that corruption, favoritism, and nepotism represented an obstacle to democracy, and this combination was the most commonly cited problem in both 2007 and 2008.[76]

In an episode that highlighted the monarchy's involvement in policy making, internal regime divisions between market liberals and statists, and the lack of transparency in privatization, the government was forced to admit in 2008 that the chief of the royal court had made plans to privatize the King Hussein Medical Center and surrounding lands and transfer them to foreign developers. When the chief of the royal court, Bassam Awadallah, was subsequently dismissed, some argued that as a Jordanian of Palestinian origin, he had been made a scapegoat by the mostly Transjordanian cabinet and parliament. As with most such scandals in Jordan, the episode was brought to light by rival officials rather than news media or independent watchdogs.

Financial disclosure laws were adopted in 2006, forcing officials to submit statements of their (and their spouses') assets every two years. As of May 2008, 514 officials had not complied, and the prosecutor general was preparing nearly 150 indictments.[77] However, there had yet to be any high-level convictions by mid-2009.

The Anti-Corruption Commission (ACC) was created under legislation approved by the parliament in 2006. Its six members are appointed by the king on the advice of the prime minister, though the king has committed to granting the commission a "free mandate." While cases are generally referred by the prime minister, citizens and other government departments may also submit complaints.[78] Since its creation, the ACC has examined over 1,000 cases, referring 55 and 92 to the prosecutor general's office in 2008 and 2009, respectively, of which at least 35 resulted in guilty verdicts. Most investigations have targeted low-ranking or municipal-level officials. In July 2009, three employees of the Greater Amman Municipality (GAM) came under investigation for fraud and forging signatures,[79] and in September, violations and inconsistent figures at government-subsidized animal fodder distribution centers were being investigated.[80] In an effort to increase transparency, the ACC presented a report of its activities to the speaker of the lower house of parliament for the first time in May 2009.[81]

Occasionally, the parliament has sought to exercise direct oversight regarding official corruption. In 2008, the House of Deputies investigated charges that the director of the Aqaba Special Economic Zone Authority, a former minister, had steered a project to an engineering company owned by his wife. However, the House failed to conclude its investigation before the parliamentary session ended, and the case remained unresolved.[82] The media rarely act as a corruption watchdog and generally only report cases that are already in the courts. Individuals who submit cases to the ACC may be subject to civil and criminal prosecution if they are determined to have made baseless allegations, and recent legislative reforms have not included whistleblower protections.[83] In the past, accusers have often faced repercussions for coming forward with information on official malfeasance.

The tax administration is not entirely free from political interference, but reforms in recent years have helped to unify standards and streamline collection.[84] In the education system, connections and patronage can be used to secure admission to public universities, and certain policies favor students with ties to the military. However, competition for admission is based mainly on merit.

The state budget relies heavily on revenue from external sources, especially foreign economic and military aid, and from the export of minerals (chiefly potash and phosphates). Spending allocations are partly visible in the formal budget debated by the parliament, but sensitive items—including the details of military and GID budgets—are not publicly available, and there is little effective public or opposition pressure to make them so. A Freedom of Information Law, the first of its kind among Arab countries, was passed in June 2007. However, it was criticized by many journalists, since full access to information is still limited by the 1971 State Secrets Law. Moreover, officials have 30 days to respond to requests, and requests can be denied in matters of "national security, public health and personal freedoms."[85] An Information Council (IC) was established to handle complaints that the government was not complying with the new law, but as of September 2008, no such complaints had been filed. This was attributed to lack of public awareness of the council and doubts among journalists as to its potential effectiveness.[86]

While government contracts are in theory open to competitive bidding, well-connected individuals and companies typically prevail over rival bidders. Companies affiliated with Transjordanians, especially those with ties to the military, are often chosen over Palestinian bidders. Wasta through parliamentary deputies or ministerial officials also plays an important role in allocating resources. When bribery is a factor, the assets or payments may go to members of an official's family rather than the official himself, making the bribe more difficult to trace in the unlikely event of an investigation. While Jordan is considered a success story of privatization by the World Bank, many key privatized assets have gone to foreign investors working with well-connected Jordanian companies at the expense of smaller local investors.

RECOMMENDATIONS

- The government should end the use of torture and grant domestic and international human rights organizations unrestricted access to prison facilities.
- The king's commitment to ending prosecutions of journalists for practicing their profession should be reflected in the country's laws. Provisions in the Press and Publications Law and the penal code that punish speech with prison terms and fines should be eliminated.
- The Public Gatherings Law provision requiring permission for assemblies and meetings should be replaced with a simple notification requirement.

Sections of the Prevention of Terrorism Act that serve to stifle Jordanians' right to peacefully assemble should be eliminated.
- The Electoral Law should be amended to eliminate gerrymandering of districts for the House of Deputies. Electoral districts should be redrawn based on population, so that each voter is equally represented in the legislature.
- The monarchy should begin to extricate itself from direct political power and make Jordan a true constitutional monarchy. The constitution should be amended to make the prime minister and cabinet primarily responsible to elected lawmakers.

NOTES

For URLs and endnote hyperlinks, please visit the *Countries at the Crossroads* homepage at http://freedomhouse.org/template.cfm?page=139&edition=8.

[1] Khetam Malkawi, "House Concludes Public Hearings on Real Estate Law," *Jordan Times*, April 21, 2009.
[2] Thanassis Cambanis, "Jordan, Fearing Islamists, Tightens Grip on Elections," *New York Times*, November 11, 2007. See also Russell E. Lucas, *Institutions and the Politics of Survival in Jordan: Domestic Responses to External Challenges, 1988–2001* (Albany: SUNY Press, 2005), 27–31, 75–81.
[3] "IAF Members Arrested Ahead of Municipal Elections," *Arab Reform Bulletin* (Washington, D.C.: Carnegie Endowment for International Peace, June 2007).
[4] Ellen Knickmeyer, "Jordan Vote Reflects Islamic Parties' Slide," *Washington Post*, November 27, 2007.
[5] National Center for Human Rights (NCHR), *The Situation of Human Rights in the Hashemite Kingdom of Jordan, 2007* (Amman: NCHR, 2008), 43–44; NCHR, *Report on the Conduct of the 2007 Parliamentary Elections* (Amman: NCHR, 2008); NCHR, *Report on the Municipal Elections of 2007* (Amman: NCHR, 2007).
[6] NCHR, *The Situation of Human Rights*, 44.
[7] Al-Quds Center for Political Studies, *Jordanian Opinion Poll: "Parliament and the Electoral Law"* (Amman: Al-Quds Center for Political Studies, 2009), 4.
[8] Mohammad Suliman Abu Rumman, *The Muslim Brotherhood in the 2007 Jordanian Parliamentary Elections: A Passing "Political Setback" or Diminished Popularity?* (Amman: Friedrich-Ebert-Stiftung, 2007).
[9] Center for Strategic Studies, *Public Opinion Leaders' Evaluation of the Performance of the Current Lower House Since its Election* (Amman: Center for Strategic Studies, 2009); Center for Strategic Studies, *A Public Opinion Poll on the Performance of the Current Lower House Since Its Election* (Amman: Center for Strategic Studies, 2009).
[10] Mohammad Ben Hussein, "24 Political Parties Dissolved in Accordance with Political Parties Law," *Jordan Times*, April 16, 2008.
[11] Programme on Governance in the Arab Region, "Civil Society: Jordan," United Nations Development Programme (UNDP).
[12] Human Rights Watch (HRW), *Shutting Out the Critics: Restrictive Laws Used to Repress Civil Society in Jordan* (New York: HRW, 2007).
[13] Ibid; Mohammad Ben Hussein, "House Passes Controversial Societies Law," *Jordan Times*, July 7, 2008; Khalid Neimat, "House to Debate Societies Law Changes in Upcoming Session," *Jordan Times*, March 11, 2009.
[14] International Center for Not-for-Profit Law, "Jordanian Law on Societies Amended," news release, September 16, 2009.

15. Julia Choucair, "Illusive Reform: Jordan's Stubborn Stability," *Carnegie Papers* 76 (Washington, D.C.: Carnegie Endowment for International Peace, December 2006), 19; See also Steven Heydemann, *Upgrading Authoritarianism in the Arab World* (Washington, D.C.: Brookings Institution, 2007), 8.
16. Douglas Griffin and Libby Morgan, ed., *Introduction to News Media Law and Policy in Jordan* (Amman: Jordan Media Strengthening Program, 2009).
17. Hani Hazaimeh, "Ball Is in Media Court after King's Assurances," *Jordan Times*, November 11, 2008; Committee to Protect Journalists, "Five Jordanians Sentenced to Three-Month Jail Terms," news release, March 18, 2008.
18. Khetam Malkawi, "Charges Dismissed against Mahadin," *Jordan Times*, April 28, 2009.
19. Al-Quds Center for Political Studies, *Impact of Soft Containment on Freedom of Journalism and Independence of the Media in Jordan* (Amman: Al-Quds Center for Political Studies, 2009).
20. Oula Farawati, "Jordanian Reporters Hung by Legal Ropes," Menassat, May 12, 2009.
21. Oula Farawati, "Jordan's News Websites Running for Legal Cover," Menassat, March 11, 2009.
22. Reporters Without Borders, "Ex-Legislator Gets Two Years in Prison for Online Criticism of Government Corruption," news release, October 11, 2007.
23. Manfred Nowak, *Report of the Special Rapporteur on Torture and Other Cruel, Inhuman or Degrading Treatment or Punishment: Mission to Jordan* (Geneva: UN Human Rights Council, January 5, 2007).
24. NCHR, *The Situation of Human Rights*, 20.
25. Amnesty International, *Jordan: "Your Confessions Are Ready for You to Sign": Detention and Torture of Political Suspects* (London: Amnesty International, 2006), 33; HRW, *Double Jeopardy: CIA Renditions to Jordan* (New York: HRW, 2008).
26. Nowak, *Report of the Special Rapporteur*.
27. NCHR, *The Situation of Human Rights*, 23–28; HRW, *Torture and Impunity in Jordan's Prisons: Reforms Fail to Tackle Widespread Abuse* (New York: HRW, 2008).
28. Rana Husseini, "Debate on Death Penalty Continues as Death-Row Inmates Reach 45," *Jordan Times*, March 10, 2009; HRW, *Guests of the Governor: Administrative Detention Undermines the Rule of Law in Jordan* (New York: HRW, 2009).
29. NCHR, *The Situation of Human Rights*, 23.
30. NCHR, *The Situation of Human Rights*, 23–28; HRW, *Torture and Impunity in Jordan's Prisons*.
31. Amnesty International, "Jordan," in *Report 2009* (London: Amnesty International, 2009).
32. NCHR, *The Situation of Human Rights*.
33. Suha Philip Ma'ayeh, "Jordanian Law Soft on Honour Killings," *National* (Abu Dhabi), July 11, 2008.
34. NCHR, *The Situation of Human Rights*, 23–28; HRW, *Torture and Impunity in Jordan's Prisons*.
35. Agence France-Presse, "Jordan's Human Rights Chief Quits," ArabianBusiness.com, July 2, 2008.
36. NCHR, *The Situation of Human Rights*, 115.
37. Amnesty International, *Isolated and Abused: Women Migrant Domestic Workers in Jordan Denied Their Rights* (London: Amnesty International, October 30, 2008), 5.
38. Office to Monitor and Combat Trafficking in Persons, *Trafficking in Persons Report 2009* (Washington, D.C.: U.S. Department of State, 2009).
39. Rana Husseini, "Women Leaders Hail Cabinet Decision; Council of Ministers Endorses Convention on the Elimination of All Forms of Discrimination against Women Which the Kingdom Signed in 1992," *Jordan Times*, July 26, 2007.

40 Suha Philip Ma'ayeh, "Jordanian Law Soft on Honour Killings."
41 Rana Husseini, "Jordan," in *Women's Rights in the Middle East and North Africa* (New York: Freedom House, 2010).
42 University of Maryland Center for International Development and Conflict Management, "Data: Assessment for Palestinians in Jordan," in *Minorities at Risk* (College Park, MD: University of Maryland, 2006).
43 Adnan Abu Odeh, *Jordanians, Palestinians and the Hashemite Kingdom in the Middle East Peace Process* (Washington, D.C.: U.S. Institute of Peace, 1999); Russell E. Lucas, "Side Effects of Regime Building in Jordan: The State and the Nation," *Civil Wars* 10, no. 3 (September 2008): 281–93.
44 Bureau of Democracy, Human Rights, and Labor, "Jordan," in *2008 Country Reports on Human Rights Practices* (Washington, D.C.: U.S. Department of State, February 2009).
45 Khaled Abu Toameh, "Amman Revoking Palestinians' Citizenship," *Jerusalem Post*, July 21, 2009.
46 Immigration and Refugee Board of Canada, "Jordan/Palestine: Whether There Have Been Any Recent Change to Rules or Laws related to Jordanian Citizenship or Status (or Protection) for Palestinians," August 5, 2008.
47 Amnesty International, *Iraq: Millions in Flight: The Iraqi Refugee Crisis* (London: Amnesty International, September 2007).
48 Dan Wooding, "Convert to Christianity Flees Jordan under Threat to Lose Custody of His Children," ASSIST News Services, April 25, 2008.
49 Rakan Sa'aydah, "Lower House Okays Khutbah Bill," *Jordan Times*, September 4, 2006.
50 Mohammad Ben Hussein, "'Restrictions on Islamist Imams Not Politically Motivated,'" *Jordan Times*, February 12, 2009.
51 Mohammad Ghazal, "Jordan Ratifies UN Convention on Disabled People," *Jordan Times*, April 6, 2008; Omar Obeidat, "Maharat Helps Graduates Enter Labour Market," *Jordan Times*, December 19, 2008.
52 Amnesty International, "Jordan's Anti-Terrorism Law Opens Door to New Human Rights Violations," news release, November 7, 2006.
53 Mohammad Ben Hussein, "Public Gatherings Law Endorsed, Opposition Not Satisfied," *Jordan Times*, June 23, 2008.
54 Reuters, "Egypt, Jordan Crack Down on Anti-Israel Protests," Radio Free Europe/Radio Liberty, January 2, 2009.
55 Agence France-Presse, "Jordan Trade Unionists Arrested in Anti-Israel Rally," Ynetnews, May 7, 2009.
56 Hani Hazaimeh, "2 Key Laws Withdrawn from House," *Jordan Times*, January 9, 2008.
57 Solidarity Center, *Justice for All: The Struggle for Worker Rights in Jordan* (Washington, D.C.: Solidarity Center, 2005), 9.
58 NCHR, *The Situation of Human Rights*.
59 Rana Husseini, "SSC Attorney General Issues Instructions on Media Coverage of Terror Trial Proceedings," *Jordan Times*, September 1, 2005.
60 *Jordan Times*, various dates, 2008.
61 Euro-Mediterranean Human Rights Network (EMHRN), *The Independence of the Judiciary in Jordan* (Copenhagen: EMHRN, January 2008), 26.
62 International Federation for Human Rights, *Judicial Councils Reforms for an Independent Judiciary: Examples from Egypt, Jordan, Lebanon, Morocco, and Palestine* (Paris: International Federation for Human Rights, May 2009), 12.
63 Michelle L. Burgis, "Judicial Reform and the Possibility of Democratic Rule in Jordan: A Policy Perspective on Judicial Independence," *Arab Law Quarterly* 21 (2007): 135–69.
64 EMHRN, *The Independence of the Judiciary in Jordan*, 46.

65. Ilia Shalhoub and Keith Henderson, *Comparative Report on the State of the Judiciary in Egypt, Jordan, Lebanon and Morocco* (New York: UNDP, 2007), 13.
66. EMHRN, *The Independence of the Judiciary in Jordan*, 46.
67. Ibid., 42.
68. Alkarama for Human Rights, *Jordan: Universal Periodic Review, Fourth Session, 2–13 February 2009* (Geneva: Alkarama for Human Rights, September 2008).
69. EMHRN, *The Independence of the Judiciary in Jordan*, 45.
70. Ibid., 29.
71. HRW, *UPR Submission: Jordan* (New York: HRW, September 2008).
72. NCHR, *The Situation of Human Rights*, 25–26; Amnesty International, *Jordan: "Your Confessions Are Ready."*
73. IHS Jane's, "Jordan (Defence Budget)," *Sentinel Country Risk Assessments*, April 27, 2009.
74. Anne Marie Baylouny, "Militarizing Welfare: Neo-Liberalism and Jordanian Policy," *Middle East Journal* 62, no. 2 (Spring 2008): 277–303.
75. Transparency International, *Corruption Perceptions Index 2008* (Berlin: Transparency International, 2008).
76. Center for Strategic Studies, *Democracy in Jordan 2008* (Amman: Center for Strategic Studies, University of Jordan, 2008).
77. Rana Husseini, "Anti-Corruption Department Handles 450 Cases in 2006," *Jordan Times*, March 12, 2007; "ACC Refers 21 Cases to Court," *Jordan Times*, June 4, 2008; Mohammad Ben Hussein, "House Panel Probing Alleged Corruption Charges Meets," *Jordan Times*, September 19, 2008; Hani Hazaimeh, "Hundreds of Officials Sued," *Jordan Times*, May 16, 2008.
78. "Administrative Corruption Most Common–ACC Chief," *Jordan Times*, January 21, 2008.
79. Khalid Neimat, "Maani Vows Justice As Three GAM Workers Investigated for Fraud," *Jordan Times*, July 20, 2009.
80. "Investigation Under Way into Violations," *Jordan Times*, May 30, 2008.
81. "Tackling Corruption: ACC Goes Public," *Star* (Amman), May 25, 2009.
82. Khetam Malkawi, "Corruption Case Not on House Agenda in Final Week," *Jordan Times*, January 30, 2009.
83. Bureau of Democracy, Human Rights, and Labor, "Jordan," in *2008 Country Reports on Human Rights Practices*.
84. "New Tax Proposal Reduces Brackets," *Jordan Times*, July 15, 2008.
85. NCHR, *The Situation of Human Rights*, 54; Mohammad Ben Hussein, "Journalists Say Access to Information Law Hinders Press Freedoms," *Jordan Times*, June 24, 2007.
86. Oula Farawati, "Jordan's Freedom of Information Act—Any Takers?" MENASSAT, September 12, 2008.

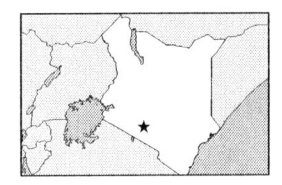

KENYA

CAPITAL: Nairobi
POPULATION: 39.1 million
GNI PER CAPITA (PPP): $1,580

SCORES	2006	2010
ACCOUNTABILITY AND PUBLIC VOICE:	5.09	4.45
CIVIL LIBERTIES:	4.49	4.29
RULE OF LAW:	3.97	3.40
ANTICORRUPTION AND TRANSPARENCY:	3.29	3.06

(scores are based on a scale of 0 to 7, with 0 representing weakest and 7 representing strongest performance)

Thomas R. Lansner

INTRODUCTION

Absent genuine efforts to transcend ethnic politics and instill accountability for the political—and potentially criminal—acts of senior political leaders before scheduled 2012 elections, Kenya's prospects are bleak. The country is experiencing a simmering crisis that threatens to again erupt into bloody conflict that could tear it apart along ethnic lines, as nearly happened after profoundly flawed elections in December 2007. The country's ethnic divisions have been reinforced by successive generations of politicians who have used patronage to build personal and party loyalties based on ethno-regionalism. The bitterly divided, and effectively unelected, coalition government formed in April 2008 has thus far proved unable to address the many grave problems facing the nation.

After achieving independence from Britain in 1963, Kenya acquired a reputation for relative stability and prosperity within the troubled East Africa region. Founding president Jomo Kenyatta and his successor, Daniel Arap Moi, presided over the increasingly corrupt one-party rule of the Kenya African National Union (KANU), which respected few political and civil rights and on occasion violently suppressed opposition. During the 1990s, Kenya gradually transitioned from authoritarian rule toward functional multiparty democracy. The 2002 election as president of Mwai Kibaki, a longtime top KANU leader and former vice president and finance minister who broke with the party in 1992, raised hopes for a peaceful evolution to more equitable and responsive governance. The Kibaki administration pledged zero tolerance of corruption, and in

---

Thomas R. Lansner is adjunct associate professor of International Affairs at Columbia University School of International and Public Affairs and an academic advisor to Freedom House's Freedom in the World Survey.

its first years helped revive Kenya's economy through reforms that promoted investment, improved governmental operations, and made far greater efforts to provide primary education and stimulate rural development.

However, many of the problems and worst practices of a one-party, patronage-based state were carried over into the new democratic structures. Corruption endured and remains rife, impairing governmental effectiveness and damaging people's faith in elected leaders. Compounding the problem is Kenya's origin as a British colonial creation that grouped disparate ethnicities into an externally-imposed polity within artificially drawn frontiers. Rapid population growth, from about 9 million people at independence to nearly 40 million in 2009, has helped intensify competition for land and resources among ethnic groups. The Kikuyu, who inhabit central Kenya, comprise about 22 percent of Kenya's people and are the largest single group. Ethnic groups from western Kenya include the Luhya and Luo people, each about 14 percent, and Kalenjin and Kamba, each about 12 percent.[1] Group violence is deployed as a political tool through various armed militia groups that often operate with impunity. Attacks on individual citizens, activists, journalists, and politicians, many of them deadly, continue and are mostly left unresolved. Police brutality is widespread and rarely punished. And perhaps most damaging, the failure to reverse the broad perception that government power continues to disproportionately reward one ethnic group—under current circumstances, President Kibaki's Kikuyu—has pushed politics perilously further from ideological argument towards identity-based conflict.

Kenya's democratic space has undoubtedly expanded since Kibaki replaced Moi in 2002. Independent media have grown stronger and fight to expose wrongdoing by official and nonstate actors, although some media outlets have promoted sectarian violence. Civil society is diverse and active across sectors including basic rights, the environment, gender equity, and rural development, and today it is this arena that appears to be the country's best hope for transcending ethnic divisions.

Yet the trauma caused by the December 2007 elections is difficult to overstate. An authoritative official investigation described the fiercely contested voting process as "irredeemably polluted,"[2] echoing a conclusion that many Kenyans and other observers reached immediately. Proclamation of President Kibaki's reelection was met with incredulity that exploded into anger as the apparently stolen vote plunged Kenya into violent turmoil. Riots broke out in major cities. In rural areas, neighbors attacked people from other ethnic groups and drove many from their land. Conservative estimates calculate over 1,100 people killed and more than 300,000 displaced during three months of sporadic ethnic violence, much of which appears to have been orchestrated by senior political figures, and was marked by widespread sexual assault and looting.

Under intense international pressure, the rival candidates worked to stem the bloodshed, and the "Grand Coalition Government" was formed in February 2008 with Kibaki remaining as president, opposition Orange Democratic

Movement (ODM) leader Raila Odinga occupying the newly created post of prime minister, and other cabinet posts split between the two main parties. This arrangement, mediated by former United Nations Secretary-General Kofi Annan, pulled Kenya back from the precipice of a catastrophic civil war. But the power-sharing government has shown little unity or capacity to address key issues facing the country. The International Criminal Court (ICC) will investigate the most senior figures accused of fomenting post-election violence after no agreement on a special tribunal within Kenya could be reached. Constitutional and electoral reform remains stalled. Finally, on the complex core question of land reform, the country faces the formidable challenge of redressing the historical injustices asserted by various groups.

ACCOUNTABILITY AND PUBLIC VOICE 4.45

FREE AND FAIR ELECTORAL LAWS AND ELECTIONS	3.50
EFFECTIVE AND ACCOUNTABLE GOVERNMENT	4.00
CIVIC ENGAGEMENT AND CIVIC MONITORING	6.00
MEDIA INDEPENDENCE AND FREEDOM OF EXPRESSION	4.29

Kenya's December 2007 presidential election was a profound blow to the consolidation of electoral democracy that had gradually emerged over polls in 1992, 1997, and 2002 during the country's transition from three decades of post-independence one-party rule. Polling indicates that most Kenyans strongly support electoral democracy as the best form of governance. President Kibaki's 2002 election as head of the National Rainbow Coalition (NARC), with support across ethnic groups and in balloting generally viewed as reasonably free and fair, helped promote this conviction. However, the fragile coalition split over various matters, especially a draft constitution that was subject to a November 2005 referendum. The core dividing issue was executive power, as President Kibaki's backers, mostly from his Kikuyu ethnic group, strongly supported the proposed retention of a dominant presidency that they expected would preserve their privileged access to state patronage. Kenyans from other ethnic groups just as adamantly rejected this notion, supporting "majimboism"—a more federal power structure—and the draft constitution was soundly defeated.

Following this development, regio-ethnic parties dominated the recast political spectrum. President Kibaki ran as leader of an alliance, the Party of National Unity (PNU), with its base among Kikuyus. The opposition ODM, strongly supported by Luo and Kalenjin groups, offered Raila Odinga as its presidential candidate.

Leading up the 2007 elections, political parties worked tirelessly to mobilize support throughout the country, usually with few official constraints. Legislative and local elections conducted concurrently were generally accepted as free and fair, despite localized problems that eventually proved far graver than observers had first suspected. Elections were monitored by the Kenya Election Domestic

Observer Forum, which fielded about 1,700 observers, and other regional and international missions. While the December 27 polling day was mostly peaceful, occasional bursts of serious violence and other problems had marked the campaign period. The official but autonomous Kenya National Commission on Human Rights (KNCHR) issued a pre-election report, titled "Still Behaving Badly," that observed "violations of the electoral code of conduct among other electoral malpractices," including misuse and misappropriation of public resources by both sides; participation of public officers (provincial administrators, civil servants, heads of parastatals, etc.) in the campaigns; incitement to violence; and use of hate speech, particularly on ethnic and gender lines, by politicians and the media.[3]

Voter turnout was strong, polling was mostly orderly, and local parliamentary voting and results in most constituencies did not at first appear contentious. Reports later identified the recurrence of serious flaws that had been highlighted during the 2002 campaign. The Electoral Commission of Kenya (ECK), whose composition and competence was questioned even before the election,[4] was in later analysis found to be grossly negligent in fulfilling its duties. Large areas of election conduct, from voter registration to tallying ballots, fell far short of international standards and Kenyan law. The most detailed analysis of these widespread shortcomings was provided in an official report by the Independent Review Commission (IREC), led by retired South African jurist Johann Kriegler, in September 2008.[5] According to IREC, "vote-buying and ballot-stuffing appear to be such extensive and universally condoned practices in Kenyan elections that the question can rightly be asked whether genuinely free and fair elections are at all possible," adding, "the conduct of the 2007 elections was so materially defective that it is impossible—for IREC or anyone else—to establish true or reliable results for the presidential and parliamentary elections."

Several observer groups, including those from the European Union and the Commonwealth, also found that the election process was seriously flawed.[6] Reports from both groups noted a clear bias in state media toward President Kibaki and the PNU. Media coverage analysis by the Coalition for Accountable Political Financing (CAPF) concluded that the government-owned Kenya Broadcasting Corporation (KBC) "failed to fulfill the minimal legal obligations required of it as a public service broadcaster as set out in the Kenya Broadcasting Corporation Act." The study found that 76 percent of election news reporting on KBC radio and 71 percent on KBC television was given to the PNU. The KBC also failed to provide candidates with free airtime, as required by law.[7] Lack of transparency and acts of alleged corruption related to campaign finance were also highlighted in the CAPF report, including heavy use of official resources to promote President Kibaki and the PNU. New financial accountability structures and public financing for political parties were included in the 2008 Political Parties Act, but it is unclear whether loopholes will be closed and transparency mechanisms enforced.[8]

In the legislative portion of the elections, the ODM and its allies took 103 seats, while the PNU and its affiliates took 77. While the IREC report makes clear that the entire electoral process was severely compromised, early returns matched anticipated results and gave the opposition ODM a clear lead in parliamentary contests, with numerous incumbents and sitting ministers defeated. This raised public expectations that ODM leader Odinga would also win the presidential contest, and unofficial counts reinforced that prospect. A potentially influential exit poll withheld by the Washington, D.C.-based International Republican Institute pointed to a substantial Odinga victory.[9]

With no adequate explanation, however, the ECK delayed reporting the presidential vote tallies for 72 hours. With tensions high across the country, President Kibaki was abruptly declared the victor and hurriedly sworn in for a second five-year term. The International Foundation for Electoral Systems reported that "startlingly, the ECK chairman confessed shortly afterward that he had been pressured to announce results without having all of the information at hand and admitted that he could not say with certainty who actually won the presidential election."[10]

Rallies and demonstrations against what was seen as a stolen election began immediately. Many were peaceful protests organized by the ODM. Others expressed spontaneous anger, but in some areas, violence against presumed political opponents, usually identified solely by ethnicity, appeared well prepared and orchestrated. Severe rioting took place in Nairobi among its diverse ethnic groups. In western Kenya, demonstrations were mounted mostly by Luo supporters of the ODM. The worst clashes occurred in the central Rift Valley, where electoral tensions revived longstanding land grievances between Kikuyu and Kalenjin ethnic groups and sparked open combat. A subsequent KNCHR report named many people it believes were behind appalling acts of murder, rape, forced circumcision, and other assaults by existing gangs and hastily organized local militia groups, noting: "The magnitude of the attacks, looting and destruction of property and lives, the resources used, the swiftness with which the attackers moved and the deployment of reinforcements . . . point to a good level of planning, coordination and organisation, monitoring, communication networking, financing, provision of transport services and facilities, medical treatment/services."[11] The principal constraint on the severity of the violence was the level of weaponry available. Alarmingly, reports indicate that combatants who in early 2008 often used machetes and bows and arrows were subsequently acquiring automatic weapons.

After a month of rising violence, an array of multilateral and bilateral diplomatic efforts and intensifying pressure from Kenya's civil society—as well as the recognition that the country was on the brink of civil war—convinced Kibaki and Odinga to accept a power-sharing National Accord brokered by an African Union Panel of Eminent African Personalities, led by Kofi Annan. The so-called National Dialogue and Reconciliation process identified its goal as the "achievement of sustainable peace, stability, and justice in Kenya through the rule of law and respect for human rights." The accord's four-fold agenda was based on immediate action to stop violence and restore fundamental rights and liberties; urgent measures to address the humanitarian crisis and promote healing and reconciliation; devising a strategy to overcome the political crisis; and addressing long-term issues, including constitutional and institutional reforms, land reforms, poverty and inequality, youth unemployment, national cohesion, and transparency and accountability.

In May 2009, a report by the Kenya National Dialogue and Reconciliation Monitoring Project noted that implementation of these agenda points has been slow, uneven, or obstructed, warning that "without undertaking fundamental reforms, another violent civil conflict may occur. . . . The country, and the political leaders in particular, seem to quickly forget the principles that shaped these recommendations... to fight impunity and erode the basis of ethnicity as drivers of politics."[12] The political infighting thwarting implementation of the 2008 National Cohesion and Integration Bill, meant to lead ethnic reconciliation, is emblematic of the situation.[13]

The sharp decline in violence across the country immediately after the power-sharing agreement was an indication that much of it was organized "as part of the national bargaining process over power."[14] Evidence for this view was offered by the official Commission of Inquiry into Post-Election Violence (CIPEV), known as the Waki Commission after its chairman, Kenyan High Court Judge Philip Waki. Presenters of the 529-page Waki Report indicated that they had identified a number of senior figures as important instigators of post-election violence, though the names were not publicly revealed. The commission urged creation of a special tribunal in Kenya to pursue criminal cases;[15] however, by mid-2009, the divided Kenyan government had not launched such a tribunal, and the ICC assumed jurisdiction over the investigations.

The coalition government can point to some accomplishments. The Kenyan constitution was amended in 2008 to disband the utterly discredited ECK. An Interim Independent Electoral Commission was empowered to pursue its prime mandate to "reform the electoral process and the management of elections in order to institutionalize free and fair elections." Most analysts agree, however, that technical fixes aside, impunity and corruption must be addressed before meaningful reform can take root. As the IREC report warned, Kenyans must "distinguish those [problems] that can be attributed to anomalies, failures and malpractices traceable to gaps or provisions in the Constitution and laws of Kenya from those that can be attributed to a bad culture encompassing impunity, disrespect for the rule of law and institutional incompetence."[16]

The 2007 election and ensuing violence highlight disparate problems of Kenyan governance. The heavy concentration of power in the executive has long been nearly unassailable by the legislature or the judiciary and has been a sharp point of conflict in recent years, particularly during the debate over the rejected draft constitution. Despite a retreat from personalized one-party rule and a shift toward more assertive rhetoric, members of Parliament (MPs) have been ineffective in exercising control over the state budget or resources. Throughout the post-independence period, most legislation has originated with the executive, although in the years following Kibaki's election Parliament played a larger role in both drafting new bills and revising or rejecting executive-based proposals. Attempts by small groups of politicians, often aligned with leading business interests, to commandeer state power and resources are common. Governmental agencies and the civil service, even when staffed by competent and dedicated individuals hired in accordance with the technical provisions established by the Public Service Commission, see their efforts diminished by patronage and corruption.

The critical role played by civic groups has become more apparent in recent years. Kenya's civil society groups generally operate freely, often with international aid. The vibrant civil society sector has opened debate and offered myriad highly credible reports and proposed solutions related to problems in governance and development. Its robust character also offers hope that issues of human rights and equitable opportunity can be addressed across ethnic lines. Networks like Bunge la Mwananchi, or "People's Parliament," are building grassroots support for systemic change.[17] These civil society groups have garnered significant media attention and raised public pressure on issues such as parliamentary allowances and land rights. Although problems with legal registration have not been as contentious an issue as in many developing countries, a current focus of nongovernmental organizations (NGOs) is revision of the 1990 NGO Coordinating Act, which is viewed as codifying arbitrary and potentially unconstitutional provisions while also failing to provide regulation adequate to enforce transparency and accountability among NGOs and other civil society groups.[18]

Media are generally free and the private press is vibrant, but pressure from the government occasionally encourages self-censorship. According to the Africa Media Barometer, the government is "often discriminatory" in awarding advertising contracts.[19] The most overt act of intimidation in recent years occurred in March 2006, when masked security agents raided the *Standard* newspaper and its sister television station in Nairobi. The *Standard* had recently been reporting on corruption and political maneuverings, prompting a senior minister to warn that "if you rattle a snake, you must be prepared to be bitten by it." According to the Committee to Protect Journalists, one reporter was seriously assaulted before the December 2007 polls, and two journalists were shot and wounded, with many more reporting threats, during the communal violence in January-February 2008. Gangs and others have also threatened individual journalists for everyday reporting. The January 2009 murder of Francis Kainda Nyaruri, who was reporting on corruption, remains unsolved, and key witnesses in the case have reportedly received death threats.[20]

Kenya's media played a mixed role in the election and post-election violence, reflecting its growing diversity and uneven levels of maturity. Some outlets provided useful voter education before the polls, urged restraint in the post-election period, and mobilized assistance for victims of clashes. Other outlets, especially vernacular local radio stations, were accused of inciting people to violence. Shortly after the presidential election results were announced, all live news broadcasting was temporarily banned, at least partially because some vernacular radio stations were goading their communities to bloodshed.

The state retains control over the largest broadcast media network, the Kenyan Broadcasting Corporation, which has continued its long tradition of strongly supporting the incumbent administration. Kenya's constitution does not expressly guarantee press freedom, and media operations are subject to various laws and jurisdictions.[21] The 2007 Press Act, which created the Media Council of Kenya, and a new communications law passed at the end of 2008 that includes curbs on "hate speech," have increased the government's ability to regulate the media to a degree that free expression advocates consider excessive. The Kenya Communications (Amendment) Law 2008, enacted in January 2009, also empowers the government to destroy or confiscate broadcasting equipment to maintain "public safety." A concerted campaign by journalists and freedom of expression advocates—during which authorities arrested a number of protesters in December 2008—won a government promise in May 2009 to revise or repeal more draconian sections of the law.[22] Criminal libel and defamation laws are sometimes used against journalists in courts that possess a mixed reputation for fairness. The National Cohesion and Integration Act 2008 made it an offence to use threatening, abusive, or insulting words to seek to promote ethnic hatred. Internet and other electronic communication are not obstructed, although there are reports that some government ministries have sought to block their staff's computer access to the government's own anticorruption commission.

CIVIL LIBERTIES   4.29

PROTECTION FROM STATE TERROR, UNJUSTIFIED IMPRISONMENT, AND TORTURE	2.88
GENDER EQUITY	3.67
RIGHTS OF ETHNIC, RELIGIOUS, AND OTHER DISTINCT GROUPS	3.50
FREEDOM OF CONSCIENCE AND BELIEF	6.67
FREEDOM OF ASSOCIATION AND ASSEMBLY	4.75

Kenyans enjoy little protection against abuse by police and security forces, and in some areas of the country also fall prey to organized criminals who appear linked to local political leaders. Numerous credible allegations have emerged in recent years of extrajudicial killings and other assaults on suspected criminals or ordinary citizens by police, who operate with virtual impunity. After a visit to Kenya in February 2009, the United Nations Special Rapporteur on Extra-Judicial Executions, Philip Alston, stated that "the police are free to kill at will," adding, "systematic, widespread, and carefully planned extrajudicial executions are undertaken on a regular basis by the Kenyan police," and "the proper response to criminality is not to shoot a suspect in the back of the head . . . but to investigate, arrest, and try the suspect in accordance with law."

According to the KNCHR, approximately 500 people were killed or disappeared in a five-month span in 2007. At least some, Professor Alston reported, were suspected criminals who were "taken to a forest and tortured to death."[23] But as the Alston report and other investigations have made plain, ordinary citizens too are targets for assault, extortion, and murder by security forces that are utterly unaccountable to any other authority. The report also warned of systematic violence to silence police critics. A policeman who gave detailed accounts of official death squads was murdered in October 2008. On March 5, 2009, two prominent human rights activists, Oscar Kamau Kingara and John Paul Oulo, were shot dead in broad daylight near President Kibaki's official residence in the center of Nairobi. In 2007, Kingara's Oscar Foundation Free Legal Aid Clinic had alleged that since 2002 over 8,000 Kenyans were tortured to death or executed by police in an ongoing crackdown on a criminal gang known as the Mungiki.[24] There have been no arrests in these assassinations; the police claim that they are defending themselves against well-armed criminals, who have indeed murdered dozens of police in recent years.

Although dissidents are less likely to suffer the systematic repression that characterized the KANU regime, political activists are routinely detained and harassed, and they allege abuse by police and other security forces. In February 2009, PEN Kenya president Philo Ikonya and PEN member Fwamba N. C. Fwamba, along with activist Patrick Kamotho, were arrested, allegedly assaulted by police, and hospitalized following a protest against the rising food prices in Nairobi. All three activists have been arrested in the past for "taking part in illegal demonstrations."[25]

UN Rapporteur Alston and several human rights groups also reported widespread abuses by security forces during operations against a local militia/criminal group, the Sabaot Land Defence Force, in the Mount Elgon area in northwestern Kenya in 2008. Human Rights Watch said that both security forces and rebels are "responsible for horrific abuses, including killings, torture and rape of civilians."[26] Like many other violent confrontations in Kenya, the Mount Elgon conflict arose over land disputes that evolved into violent resource competition between ethnic groups—and, as elsewhere, was apparently abetted by local political leaders. Amnesty International also reported that in November 2008, dozens of residents of Mandera district in northern Kenya charged that soldiers and police committed rape, torture, and beatings during an operation to curb weapons smuggling from the Horn of Africa. The government dismissed the allegations.[27]

The Mungiki and other criminal bands are a serious threat to many average Kenyans' daily lives. Extortion of businesses is commonplace, especially in large cities and towns. Kidnappings for ransom have increased. Occasional police campaigns against gangs have reportedly included abuses against many citizens. While there have not been terrorist attacks on Kenyan soil since 2002, counter-terrorism efforts have included what some rights groups describe as illegal detention and improper rendition of non-Kenyans, as well as discrimination against Kenyans of Somali origin (see below).

Kenya ratified the Convention Against Torture and Other Cruel, Inhuman or Degrading Treatment or Punishment in 1997, and after a long delay submitted its first state report in June 2007. In January 2009, the UN Committee against Torture responded by welcoming the introduction in Kenya of several formal mechanisms that, if properly empowered, could reduce the prevalence of torture, including the KNCHR, the launch of the Governance, Justice, Law and Order Sector Reform Programme, and the establishment of the independent Police Oversight Board. Despite such official commitments, torture remains commonplace. The Kenyan NGO Independent Medico-Legal Unit, which works to rehabilitate torture victims, has issued numerous reports with their testimonies and detailed forensic evidence of torture in Kenya. The group states that "the need for clear, comprehensive and consolidated legislation on torture cannot be overemphasized."[28]

The remainder of the UN response, meanwhile, is a scathing indictment of widespread abuses committed with impunity by the security forces. "[I]mpediments faced by individuals who may have been subject to torture and ill-treatment to complain and have their cases promptly and impartially examined by the competent authorities" are noted with concern. The Committee against Torture also made special note of "dire" conditions in Kenya's prisons, "in particular the high number of persons in pre-trial detention," remarking on "the overcrowding, lack of appropriate health services and high levels of violence inside the prisons, including inter-prisoner violence."[29] Based on official capacity, Kenya's occupancy level is 223.3 percent, and 43.3 percent of detainees are in remand.[30] The government responded to these problems by allowing increased public access to prisons and ordering a review of the Prisons Act. Like other Kenyans, detainees and prisoners may file complaints with the Public Complaints Standing Committee. However, Kenya's prisons remain severely underfunded. Most detainees and prisoners lack the information and access necessary to pursue complaints, and the overburdened and at times incompetent or corrupt justice system responds sluggishly at best to complaints.[31]

The autonomous KNCHR has the authority to review prison conditions and receive complaints regarding prison conditions, and serves as the primary rights watchdog and provider of redress for all Kenyan abuse victims. It is widely perceived as independent and has called attention to numerous rights issues while also attempting to formulate programs to improve rights awareness and protections throughout the government and society. It has the authority to order detainees released as well as compensation for rights abuse victims, but lacks prosecutorial powers.

While Kenyan law prohibits gender-based discrimination, traditional practices and law continue to restrict gender equality. A provision of Kenya's criminal code carried over from British colonial rule provides up to 14 years' imprisonment for consensual homosexual acts. Multiple accounts describe how women and girls are particular and common targets for sexual violence by the military, police, ethnic militia, and criminal gangs, and there are increasing reports of rape of men and boys as well.[32] Many women and girls were sexually assaulted during the post-2007 election violence, reportedly including by police.

The police have acted on a Waki Report suggestion to launch a special unit to investigate and address gender-based violence, although its effectiveness remains to be proven. Despite laws against trafficking of children and trafficking for sexual exploitation, UNICEF reported in 2009 that "there is evidence that Kenya is a fast growing source country, as well as a transit and destination country, for human trafficking."[33] While female genital mutilation was outlawed in 2001, it is still widely practiced within many communities.

Kenya is a signatory to the Convention on the Elimination of All Forms of Discrimination against Women. Yet women's property rights remain limited under customary and formal laws of inheritance and succession. A draft National Land Policy pushed by civil society and approved by the cabinet in July 2009 proposes expanding women's rights to inherit land and would modernize discriminatory laws.[34] Even if it passes, enforcing change in a strongly patriarchal society will be difficult; traditional courts, especially in rural areas, are particularly biased against women. Of the 222 members of Parliament, only 15 elected and 6 nominated MPs are female. A wide array of proposed legislation aimed at protecting women, including the Anti-trafficking in Persons Bill, the Domestic Violence (Family Protection) Bill, the Equal Opportunities Bill, and the Matrimonial Property Bill, remains at the discussion stage in Parliament.

Civil society groups continue to lead efforts to advance disabled rights, which receive only limited protection under current law. An estimated 10 percent of Kenyans have some form of disability. The 2004 Persons with Disabilities Act, which established the National Council for Persons with Disabilities, has been broadly welcomed, but the law "is apparently plagued with inherent operational and legal impediments to its utilization," observed one advocacy group. "[A] factor that renders the Act unenforceable is the fact that the Act is too apt in giving discretionary powers where mandatory powers seemed the only viable alternative."[35]

Kenya's legal structures prescribe equality for its many ethnic groups—discrimination on the basis of a person's "race, tribe, place of origin or residence or other local connection, political opinions, color, or creed" is constitutionally forbidden—but political patronage has entrenched an informal system of favoritism that has especially disfavored smaller ethnic communities. Ethnic Somali Kenyans have suffered particular neglect and abuse. Somali Kenyans are the only ethnic group required to produce two identification cards to prove their citizenship. Furthermore, they face unequal economic opportunities due to lack of government development efforts in the North Eastern Province and discrimination in hiring for jobs within the police, military, and civil service.[36]

Kenya has not ratified International Labor Organization Convention 169 on Indigenous and Tribal Peoples nor approved the United Nations Declaration on the Rights of Indigenous Peoples. UN Special Rapporteur on Indigenous Issues Rodolfo Stavenhagen wrote in 2007 that the "livelihoods and cultures" of Kenya's pastoralist, hunter-gatherer and forest tribes "have been traditionally discriminated against and their lack of legal recognition and empowerment reflects their social, political and economic marginalization," adding, "most of the human rights violations experienced by pastoralists and hunter-gatherers in Kenya are related to their access to and control over land and natural resources." Some civil society organizations promoting indigenous rights and their donors have reportedly come under governmental pressure.[37]

Kenyans are free in religious practice, although the role of traditional Islamic courts vis-à-vis civil law is contentious, and is set to evoke a divisive communal debate during the constitutional reform process. Christians comprise about 80 percent of the population, and Muslims make up approximately 10 percent, mostly in the coastal area. Tensions have occasionally erupted, with Muslims alleging discrimination at the hands of the government, including the arrest and illegal deportation, on national security grounds, of foreign Muslim scholars and others.[38]

In most areas, Kenya's transition from one-party rule has allowed a blossoming of civic associations with little overt governmental interference. All Kenyan workers except members of the military or police may join a union of their choice; about 500,000 are union members. Workers can negotiate collective bargaining agreements, although official grievance procedures can be cumbersome, and workers sometimes strike outside the approved process. Most of the roughly 40 registered unions in Kenya belong to the single approved national labor federation, the Central Organization of Trade Unions (COTU), which is the official workers' representative in administering the Industrial Relations Charter in conjunction with the government and the Federation of Kenya Employers. However, the government appoints COTU's secretary general from a list of union nominees, and many of the COTU-affiliated unions are viewed as ineffective or corrupt. Professional unions outside COTU are regarded as much more capable advocates for their members' interests.[39]

While protests are common, the constitutional right to public assembly is not always respected, and security forces sometimes resort to force to suppress even peaceful and lawful protests. Some people arrested at protests have alleged beatings and sexual abuse while in police custody. Despite constitutional guarantees, authorities banned all public gatherings after the December 2007 elections. Police are described as repeatedly using deadly force against peaceful protestors, especially supporters of the opposition ODM. Almost no members of the security forces have been held accountable for such actions.

RULE OF LAW 3.40

INDEPENDENT JUDICIARY	3.60
PRIMACY OF RULE OF LAW IN CIVIL AND CRIMINAL MATTERS	3.00
ACCOUNTABILITY OF SECURITY FORCES AND MILITARY TO CIVILIAN AUTHORITIES	3.00
PROTECTION OF PROPERTY RIGHTS	4.00

Kenya's judicial system retains many facets of the British system it inherited at independence in 1963, but in practice is heavily dominated by the executive branch and permeated with corruption at all levels. The lack of judicial independence and integrity is a core factor permitting impunity for abuses by the country's most powerful groups and individuals. Reports by the Commonwealth (2002) and the International Commission of Jurists (2005) detailed dire deficiencies and offered clear suggestions for improvement. While the first Kibaki administration took up the mantle of reform and the government sacked some judges and magistrates,[40] the structure of the judiciary, its lack of resources, and its susceptibility to external influences gravely subvert the rule of law in Kenya today.

The president appoints the attorney general, chief justice, and Supreme Court, Court of Appeals, and High Court judges. The Judicial Service Commission advises on such appointments but is itself comprised of the chief justice, attorney general, chair of the Public Service Commission, and two High Court or Court of Appeals judges, all of whom are executive appointees. This process has created a judiciary that is largely beholden to the incumbent regime, although some individual jurists have demonstrated independence in seeking to enforce the law even at the highest levels despite demonstrated executive disdain for court decisions.

Lack of compliance with judicial rulings creates consequences noted in 2006 by the African Peer Review Mechanism Kenya Country Report: "[P]rominent government officials either disobeyed courts orders or expressed an intention to disobey them . . . fostering an emerging culture of impunity [that] strikes at the heart of the mandate and rule of law." The report also described the consequences of this distrust, including "individuals' resort to self-help initiatives, where communities employ their own private militias to protect or enforce rights, or prefer to use traditional mechanisms to resolve disputes rather than . . . formal courts."[41]

A Gallup poll conducted in April 2009 found this to be an accelerating trend: Kenyans' confidence in their country's judicial system had dropped to 27 percent, less than half the level of only two years earlier.[42] The World Bank Institute's governance indicator for the rule of law in Kenya also dropped sharply from 2006 to 2008.[43] The corrosion of Kenya's justice system is so severe that UN Special Rapporteur Philip Alston explicitly called for the removal from office of both the attorney general and the head of the Kenya Police in his 2009 report on extrajudicial killings. "The Government of Kenya can choose to deny the existence of problems or insist that they are under control, while the killings and impunity continue," he warned. "[S]uch a path will lead inexorably to chaos and large-scale violence within a relatively short time."[44]

The constitution sets out the minimum qualifications for members of the High Court, and the Judicature Act lists essential magistrate qualifications, but credentials and training are insufficient, and incompetent candidates sometimes serve as prosecutors and judges. In 2008, Kenya began efforts to address the problem by establishing a World Bank-funded Judicial Training Institute and meeting with international experts in judicial education to revise Kenya's draft Judicial Education Policy.[45]

Overall, however, reform has stalled since the proposed new constitution was rejected in November 2005, and many initiatives are sharply contested along political lines, with a view toward the 2012 elections. Judicial, electoral, and civil service reform and land rights are among crucial issues that a new constitution must address. A Committee of Experts has been appointed under legislation to renew the constitutional review, but the process is likely to continue to be mired in political controversy. The question of accountability for the post-2007 election violence, discussed earlier, remains an open issue. The government has reneged on its agreement to form a special tribunal, as recommended by the Waki Commission, and instead plans to use existing courts and expand the mandate of the Truth, Justice and Reconciliation Commission. This decision has been strongly criticized by local and global human rights groups,[46] and led directly to the ICC's decision to assert its jurisdiction.

Kenyan law presumes people charged with a crime to be innocent until proven guilty, guarantees a public hearing, and allows consultation with an attorney. The government provides attorneys only in capital cases, however, and most defendants cannot afford legal counsel. The government and courts sometimes withhold evidence from defendants by using secrecy laws, and the scale of free legal aid services does not match the enormous need. Courts are chronically underfunded and understaffed, and a daunting backlog of cases prevails. Legal requirements that people arrested must be charged within 24 hours or 14 days in non-capital and capital cases, respectively, are often not honored. Many suspects are held for months or years of pretrial detention under dreadful conditions despite provisions for their release on bail or bond. High court fees, poor knowledge of legal rights, language barriers, and, in many rural areas, lack of legal infrastructure also present grave obstacles to access to justice for most Kenyans.[47]

Kenya's military numbers about 22,000 personnel. It was closely aligned with the authoritarian KANU regime, and individuals from President Moi's Kalenjin group were awarded many senior posts during his rule. The only overt effort to take power was an aborted coup in 1982, and the army has continued to accept civilian oversight during the country's fitful democratic transition. There are fears that the military could fracture along ethnic lines if it is asked to suppress large-scale ethnic conflict. Most domestic security operations are carried out by various police units, including highly trained paramilitary groups. Allegations of corruption in military procurement have not resulted in serious investigations, largely due to the fact that security and defense contracting is exempt from procurement regulations. Numerous scandals have arisen in recent years, the most notable being the Anglo Leasing Scandal, which involved numerous overcharged government contracts, including for the construction of forensic laboratories and security vehicles for the national police and the delivery of an oceanographic survey vessel to the Kenya Navy.[48] The Kenya Anti-Corruption Commission (KACC) investigated 18 security-related contracts in relation to the Anglo Leasing case and forwarded seven to the attorney general for prosecution, but a combination of appeals and petitions filed by the defendants have resulted in repeated delay of the only two prosecutions undertaken.[49]

Property rights in Kenya's modern commercial sector are generally respected, despite complaints about slow and sometimes corrupt commercial court proceedings. The Heritage Foundation reported in 2009 that "lax property rights and extensive corruption hold down overall economic freedom," and noted a lack of protection of intellectual rights.

The question of land rights is far more vexing. The distribution of land is a source of deep grievance across Kenya and a root cause of group conflict. Land seizures even for public purposes are sometime arbitrary; Amnesty International reported that in mid-2009 3,000 people were forcibly evicted from a Nairobi community.[50] There is a long record of alienation of traditional lands of smaller ethnic groups and favoritism in land allocation toward the Kikuyu that began in colonial times. An official government report issued in December 2004 estimated that over 200,000 illegal allocations had been made since independence in 1963: "'Land grabbing' became part and parcel of official grand corruption through which land meant for public purposes . . . has been acquired by individuals and corporations."[51] Land-motivated displacement was a key underlying cause of much post-election violence, particularly in the Rift Valley.

The draft National Land Policy could address many pressing land issues, including by empowering authorities to recover improperly allocated property. But the law awaits parliamentary approval, and stronger protections for disadvantaged communities are urged by NGOs such as the Kenya Land Alliance. The new policy will be politically contentious, and likely elicit resistance from large landowners and groups that have benefited under previous regimes.[52] In northern Kenya and other arid areas, desertification and growing population pressures are intensifying land-related resource competition, including cattle raiding and conflict between herders and farmers. A Ministry for Northern Kenya and Other Arid Lands formed in 2008 is meant to better address this situation. Hunger is growing acute in these regions: the World Food Program estimates that about 5.6 million people in Kenya are "food insecure." Drought and rising global commodity prices are partly to blame, exacerbated by economic dislocation caused by violence, governmental ineffectiveness, and corruption.

ANTICORRUPTION AND TRANSPARENCY 3.06

ENVIRONMENT TO PROTECT AGAINST CORRUPTION	2.75
PROCEDURES AND SYSTEMS TO ENFORCE ANTICORRUPTION LAWS	2.50
EXISTENCE OF ANTICORRUPTION NORMS, STANDARDS, AND PROTECTIONS	3.50
GOVERNMENTAL TRANSPARENCY	3.50

Kenya's pervasive corruption damages both governmental efficiency and people's faith in democratic rule. Details of massive corruption under the regime of former president Daniel Arap Moi were reported extensively by the private security group Kroll in a report commissioned by the Kenyan government, but apparently never pursued.[53] In 2008 Kenya ranked 147th out of 180 countries in Transparency International's annual Corruption Perceptions Index.[54] Graft is reportedly rife at all levels, from military procurement to market inspectors in Nairobi's sprawling slums to rural land distribution. A survey by Transparency International's Kenya chapter in April-May 2009 found that over half of Kenyans reported paying bribes to obtain goods or services, and that "the Kenya Police is the most corrupt institution in East Africa."[55] In 2005, the Africa Peer Review Mechanism Report warned that corruption occurred on a scale sufficient to affect both Kenya's economic health and its attractiveness as a destination for foreign investors.[56]

The experience of John Githongo, a journalist and anticorruption campaigner appointed head of Kenya's Office of Governance and Ethics after President Kibaki's 2002 election, illustrates the frustrations of attempting to fight graft in Kenya. His story, and corruption's impact on Kenya's political dynamics and development, was the subject of a 2009 book by journalist Michaela Wrong, *It's Our Turn to Eat: The Story of a Kenyan Whistle-Blower*. After initially tackling his job with vigor, by early 2005 Githongo had resigned after senior officials obstructed his investigations, and he fled Kenya after receiving multiple threats. A year later, he issued a report alleging then Vice President Moody Awori and senior ministers had misappropriated over US$600 million in government funds in the Anglo Leasing scandal.[57] The Anglo Leasing case is just one of many where graft in government procurement and budgeting processes has been exposed, and it revealed the inability of the public or even Parliament to gain reliable information about government operations.

State activity in the economy is substantial despite the fact that several state-owned enterprises have been fully or partially privatized in recent years. In 2008, the 2005 Privatization Act, which aimed to boost transparency during the privatization process through the creation of an Independent Privatization Commission and an accompanying regulatory framework, came into effect, but implementation has been modest thus far.[58] Opportunities for direct political interference, patronage, and corruption are numerous as state-owned enterprises report directly to politically appointed ministers.[59]

There is no lack of awareness of the scale of both grand and petty corruption, or its corrosive effect on the country. The interagency GJLOS introduces itself on its website by asking: "Has your file ever 'disappeared' at the courts but reappeared at the production of 'kitu kidogo' [a petty bribe—literally "something small" in Kiswahili]? Have you ever reported a crime and you became the criminal instead?... Did you ever lose a case in court because you could not give a kickback? The list is endless...."[60]

Several other anticorruption agencies exist. The Office of the Ombudsman houses the Public Complaints Committee. International donor-backed efforts to improve government procurement practices, including strengthening the Public Procurement Oversight Authority, have reported some success,[61] but serious problems continue to pervade this area, and it appears that impunity remains the norm at the highest levels of government. Kenya's National Audit Office is responsible for regulating state expenditures, but its independence is limited, and resource constraints, audit backlogs, and a failure to release audit reports in a timely manner decrease its effectiveness. Recent reforms have enabled the auditing agency to upgrade its investigative capacity.[62] However, as with reports from other agencies and commissions, there is little evidence of political will to act on its findings.

The KACC is also active, but apparently unable to seriously tackle major high-level scandals, and without independent prosecutorial powers. The highly politicized attorney general's office has failed to pursue any senior officials or business people accused of malfeasance. While the KACC encourages Kenyans to report corruption, it cannot itself provide whistleblower protection or pursue those who seek to intimidate people reporting illicit acts. KACC officials acknowledge potential whistleblowers' fear but believe an anonymous web-based reporting system launched in 2007 will help.[63] In March 2009, a Witness Protection Unit was formally launched under a new Witness Protection Act that came into effect in September 2008, but it is so far untested and underfunded. Repeated and enterprising media exposés that failed to induce proper investigations led a senior editor in Nairobi to despair that reporting on corruption is "like talking to yourself."[64]

MPs have undertaken parliamentary corruption probes and demanded action, but senior officials still appear able to ignore parliamentary demands and sometimes even judicial decisions. The 2003 Kenya Public Officer Ethics Act prohibits public officials from holding shares or an interest in a corporation or body that would interfere with their official duties, and requires that public officers declare their assets. However, the law does not require the declarations be made public, fails to specify which assets must be declared, and does not establish a procedure for the review of the declarations.[65] Many public officials see little separation between their private interests and official duties. This became institutionalized during the 2003–2007 Parliament, when MPs voted to sharply increase their pay, mileage, housing, constituency, and severance allowances.[66]

New scandals continue to emerge, and there is little indication that these will be addressed any more seriously than those unpunished in the past. In 2008, the Grand Regency Hotel in Nairobi was sold to Libyan buyers at a price allegedly far below its real value. A litany of other official high-level corruption allegations are discussed in the Kenya National Dialogue and Reconciliation Monitoring Project's May 2009 report, which bluntly states that "the Coalition Government continued to be riddled with corruption scandals."[67] Despite myriad accusations and previous investigations, no senior officials have been prosecuted.

Transparency International Kenya urges that Kenya's Official Secrets Act be repealed, and that pending legislation, including the Freedom of Information Bill under consideration since 2007 and Anti-Money Laundering Act, be enacted promptly "to ensure that the robbers of the public resources are identified, stopped and effectively prosecuted."[68] Section 79 of the Kenyan Constitution guarantees freedom of expression, but no laws explicitly regulate citizens' right to information. The opacity of executive decision making makes legislative oversight of budgetary processes largely ineffective. Some reforms have been enacted: the 2008 Fiscal Management Act, which was enacted in June 2009, mandates that Parliament participate in and oversee the budget-making process, sets out specific requirements and deadlines for report submission, and requires the publication of a "Budget Outlook Paper" every January. Legal advances have not thus far resolved serious issues related to the inflation of the budget and the misuse of funds. In May 2009, Finance Minister Uhuru Kenyatta was criticized after substantial inconsistencies were found in his supplementary budget estimates.[69] Nonetheless, Kenya receives a score of 57 percent in the 2008 Open Budget Index, an improvement of 10 points from two years ago.[70] The propriety of administration and distribution of international aid—desperately needed as Kenya faces its worst drought in a generation along with numerous other social challenges—has occasionally come under question. Several countries and donors have at times suspended assistance to Kenya amid allegations of corruption in food procurement, distribution of medicines, and education projects, among others.[71]

RECOMMENDATIONS

- Utilizing the diagnosis and prescriptions of the IREC report as a base for electoral reform, request immediate substantive international mediation and expertise to propel nonpartisan constitutional and electoral changes in advance of the scheduled 2012 elections.
- Move swiftly to act on the Waki Commission's recommendations to prosecute those responsible for instigating past violence, or cooperate fully with the International Criminal Court's efforts to ensure such accountability.
- Pass and implement the draft freedom of information bill to raise transparency at all levels of government and public service.

- Establish a permanent mechanism of dialogue to identify and, if possible, peacefully disarm militia and other groups that have been engaged in ethnic and/or political violence.
- Sign and ratify UN relevant treaties and conventions to which Kenya is not yet party, including ILO 169, and codify their provisions with meaningful enforcement mechanisms into domestic law.
- Fully implement the National Land Policy [*Ed.: adopted by Parliament in December 2009*] through appropriate enabling legislation and empowerment of a genuinely autonomous National Land Commission.

NOTES

For URLs and endnote hyperlinks, please visit the *Countries at the Crossroads* homepage at http://freedomhouse.org/template.cfm?page=139&edition=8.

1. Integrated Regional Information Networks, "Republic of Kenya: Humanitarian Country Profile."
2. Emmanuel Onyango and Kipngeno Cheruiyot, "Kenya's Last Poll Was a Fraud, Kriegler Commission Report Says," *Kenya Times*, September 18, 2008.
3. Kenya National Commission on Human Rights (KNCHR), *Still Behaving Badly: Second Periodic Report of the Election-Monitoring Project* (Nairobi: KNCHR, December 2007).
4. Ibid.
5. Independent Review Commission (IREC), *Report of the Independent Review Commission on the General Elections Held in Kenya on 27 December 2007* (Nairobi: IREC, September 17, 2008).
6. EU Election Observation Mission—Kenya (EUEOM-Kenya), *27 December 2007—Final Report on the General Elections* (Nairobi: EUEOM-Kenya, 2008); Commonwealth Observer Group, *Report of the Commonwealth Observer Group for the 2007 General Elections in Kenya* (Nairobi: Commonwealth Observer Group, 2008).
7. The Coalition for Accountable Political Financing (CAPF), *Campaign Finance and Corruption: A Monitoring Report on Campaign Finance in the 2007 General Election* (Nairobi: CAPF, April 23, 2008).
8. Muchemi Wachira and Jami Makan, "New Political Parties Law Faulty, Says TI," *Daily Nation*, July 31, 2008.
9. Jeffrey Gettleman and Mike McIntire, "A Chaotic Kenya Vote and a Secret U.S. Exit Poll," *New York Times*, January 30, 2009.
10. Chris Hennemeyer, "Kenya at the Crossroads," The International Foundation for Electoral Systems (IFES), January 4, 2008.
11. KNCHR, *On the Brink of the Precipice: A Human Rights Account of Kenya's Post-2007 Election Violence* (Nairobi: KNCHR, August 15, 2008).
12. Kenya National Dialogue and Reconciliation (KNDR) Monitoring Project, *Status of Implementation of Agenda Items 1–4 Draft Report* (Nairobi: KNDR, May 2009).
13. Fred Oluochp, "Politicians Frustrating Kenya's Healing Bid," *Daily Nation*, July 3, 2009.
14. Jacqueline M. Klopp, "Kenya's Unfinished Agendas," *Journal of International Affairs* 62, no. 2 (2009): 143–158.
15. The Commission of Inquiry on Post Election Violence (CIPEV), *Report of the Commission of Inquiry on Post Election Violence* (Nairobi: CIPEV, October 2008), 460.
16. IREC, *Report of the Independent Review Commission*, 23.
17. Klopp, "Kenya's Unfinished Agendas."

[18] Rama Adan Jillo and Faith Kisinga, "NGO Law in Kenya," *International Journal of Not-for-Profit Law* 11, no. 4 (August 2009).
[19] Fesmedia Africa, "Kenya," in *African Media Barometer Reports 2007* (Windhoek: fesmedia Africa, 2007), 10.
[20] Media Institute, "Key Witnesses in Journalist's Murder Go into Hiding," Human Rights House Network, June 9, 2009.
[21] Fesmedia Africa, "Kenya," 10.
[22] "Triumph for Journalists as Government Agrees to Amend Media Law," *Daily Nation*, May 20, 2009.
[23] Philip Alston, *Promotion and Protection of All Human Rights, Civil, Political, Economic, Social and Cultural Rights Including the Right to Development: Report of the Special Rapporteur on Extrajudicial, Summary or Arbitrary Executions* (Geneva: United Nations, May 26, 2009).
[24] "Kenyan Police 'Killed Thousands,'" British Broadcasting Corporation (BBC), November 25, 2007.
[25] International PEN, "Kenyan PEN President and Member Assaulted by Police," press release, February 24, 2009.
[26] Human Rights Watch (HRW), "Kenya: Army and Rebel Militia Commit War Crimes in Mt. Elgon," press release, April 2, 2008.
[27] Amnesty International, "Kenya," in *Amnesty International Report 2009* (London: Amnesty International, 2009).
[28] Independent Medico-Legal Unit (IMLU), *Why the Need for a Law against Torture in Kenya* (Nairobi: IMLU, 2007).
[29] United Nations (UN) Convention Against Torture and Other Cruel, Inhuman or Degrading Treatment or Punishment (CAT), *Consideration of Reports Submitted by States Parties under Article 19 of the Convention: Concluding Observations of the Committee against Torture: Kenya* (Geneva: United Nations, January 19, 2009).
[30] International Centre for Prison Studies, "Kenya," World Prison Brief.
[31] Kenya Human Rights Commission, Prison Reform Project.
[32] L. Muthoni Wanyeki, "Lessons from Kenya: Women and the Post-Election Violence," *Feminist Africa* 10 (2008).
[33] United Nations Children's Fund (UNICEF), *Report of the Field Visit to Kenya by Members of the Bureau of the Executive Board* (New York: UNICEF, April 30, 2009).
[34] Joyce Mulama and Evelyne Opondo, "Defending Women's Rights under New Land Policy," Inter Press Service, July 17, 2009.
[35] Disability Rights Promotion International (DRPI), *State of Disabled Peoples' Rights in Kenya, 2007* (Toronto: DRPI, 2007).
[36] University of Maryland Center for International Development and Conflict Management, "Assessment for Somalis in Kenya," Minorities at Risk.
[37] United Nations Human Rights Council (UNHRC), *UN Human Rights Council: Addendum to the Report of the Special Rapporteur on the Situation of Human Rights and Fundamental Freedoms of Indigenous People, Mission to Kenya* (Geneva: UNHRC, February 26, 2007).
[38] Bureau of Democracy, Human Rights, and Labor, "Kenya," in *International Religious Freedom Report 2009* (Washington, D.C.: U.S. Department of State, October 26, 2009).
[39] Institute for Peace Development and Innovation Kenya (IPSIA Kenya), *Trade Unions in Contemporary Kenya* (Nairobi: IPSIA Kenya, June 28, 2006).
[40] Global Integrity, "Kenya," in 2008 Global Integrity Report (Washington, D.C.: Global Integrity, 2009).

41. African Peer Review Mechanism (APRM), *Country Review Report No 3: Kenya* (Midrand, South Africa: APRM, September 2005), 72.
42. Steve Crabtree and Bob Tortora, "Lacking Faith in Judiciary, Kenyans Lean Toward the Hague," Gallup, August 5, 2009.
43. World Bank, *Country Data Report for KENYA, 1996-2008* (Washington, D.C.: World Bank, June 2009).
44. Alston, *Promotion and Protection of All Human Rights*, 3.
45. Commonwealth Judicial Education Institute, "New Kenya Judicial Training Institute," *The CJEI Report*, December 2008.
46. International Commission of Jurists (ICJ Kenya) and the Federation of Women Lawyers (FIDA Kenya), "Statement on the Prosecution of Post Election Violence Perpetrators and Cabinet's Proposed Expansion of the Mandate of the Truth Justice and Reconciliation Commission," news release, August 9, 2009; HRW, "Kenya: Deliver Justice for Victims of Post-Election Violence," press release, August 3, 2009.
47. Connie Ngondi-Houghton, *Access to Justice and the Rule of Law in Kenya: A Paper Developed for the Commission for the Empowerment of the Poor* (New York: Commission on the Legal Empowerment of the Poor, November 2006).
48. J. M. Migai Akech, "Development Partners and Governance of Public Procurement in Kenya: Enhancing Democracy in the Administration of Aid," *N.Y.U. Journal of International Law and Politics* 37, no. 4 (Summer 2005).
49. Aaron Ringera, "Kenya: Slow Court System Frustrating War against Corruption," *Daily Nation*, September 5, 2009.
50. Amnesty International, "Kenya: Three Thousand Forcibly Evicted in Kenya," press release, July 28, 2009.
51. APRM, *Country Review Report No 3: Kenya*.
52. Ibrahim Mwathane, "What's in the Land Policy Paper?" *Saturday Nation*, July 1, 2009.
53. Xan Rice, "The Looting of Kenya," *Guardian*, August 31, 2007.
54. Transparency International, "2008 Corruption Perceptions Index."
55. Transparency International, "East African Bribery Index 2009: The Kenyan Police Is the Most Corrupt Institution in East Africa," news release, July 2, 2009.
56. APRM, *Country Review Report No 3: Kenya*.
57. John Githongo, Letter to President Mwai Kibaki, November 22, 2005.
58. Organization for Economic Cooperation and Development (OECD) and the African Development Bank (ADB), "Kenya," in African Economic Outlook 2008 (Paris and Tunis-Belvedere: OECD and ADB, 2008); The Heritage Foundation and the Wall Street Journal (WSJ), "Kenya," in *2009 Index of Economic Freedom* (Washington, D.C./New York: Heritage Foundation and WSJ, 2009).
59. Global Integrity, "Kenya."
60. See the Kenya Governance Justice, Law and Order Sector Reform website at http://www.gjlos.go.ke/default.asp.
61. Millennium Challenge Account, *Threshold Quarterly Status Report: Kenya Program Summary* (Washington, D.C.: Millennium Challenge Corporation, October 2009).
62. Open Budget Initiative, "Kenya," in *Open Budget Index 2008* (Washington, D.C.: Open Budget Initiative, 2008); Global Integrity, "Kenya."
63. Joyce Joan Wangui, "Kenya Anti-Corruption Commission Goes Digital," Bizcommunity.com, July 23, 2007.
64. Stephanie Hanson, *Corruption in Sub-Saharan Africa* (New York: Council on Foreign Relations, August 6, 2009).

65. James Luh, *Public Officer Ethics Act Provisions for Declarations of Income, Assets, and Liabilities: Evaluation and Recommendations* (Nairobi/Cambridge: Transparency International Kenya and Harvard Law School, July 31, 2003).
66. Mars Group, *The Case against the Members of the 9th Parliament* (Nairobi: Mars Group, 2008).
67. Kenya National Dialogue and Reconciliation Monitoring Project, *Status of Implementation of Agenda Items 1–4 Draft Report* (Nairobi: Kenya National Dialogue and Reconciliation Monitoring Project, May 2009), 55–57.
68. Mwangi Kabathi, Transparency International Kenya, "Public Service Besieged by Corruption," *Adili* 111 (June 2009).
69. "Budgeting Process Needs Re-Engineering," *East African Standard*, May 20, 2009; Mwaura Kimani, "Treasury Complies with New Budget Rules," *Business Daily*, November 2, 2009.
70. Open Budget Initiative, "Kenya."
71. "KENYA: Corruption, Erratic Drug Supply Threatens TB Treatment," PlusNews, March 24, 2009; David Ooko, "World Bank Suspends Funds over Corruption in Kenya," Xinhua News Agency, September 24, 2009; "Dutch Halt Kenya Aid over Graft," BBC, April 29, 2006.

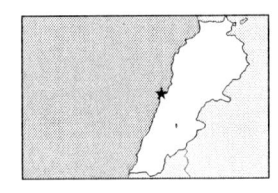

LEBANON

CAPITAL: Beirut
POPULATION: 3.9 million
GNI PER CAPITA (PPP): $10,880

SCORES	2006	2010
ACCOUNTABILITY AND PUBLIC VOICE:	N/A	3.83
CIVIL LIBERTIES:	N/A	3.99
RULE OF LAW:	N/A	3.54
ANTICORRUPTION AND TRANSPARENCY:	N/A	2.60

(scores are based on a scale of 0 to 7, with 0 representing weakest and 7 representing strongest performance)

Oussama Safa

INTRODUCTION

Lebanon's governance system has always relied on a delicate power-sharing formula, enshrined in the constitution, under which the country's main religious groups divide the top executive and legislative posts and hold quotas in the parliament, the civil service, and the security forces. In 1975, a sectarian civil war erupted, partly because Sunni and Shiite Muslims objected to the fact that the Maronite Christians held greater quotas and a monopoly on the presidency despite representing a minority of the overall population.

On a practical level, the sectarian system has instilled clientelist relations between the leaders and members of each religious community. The resulting preeminence of sectarian cohesion at the expense of national solidarity has historically invited and been reinforced by foreign intervention, as occurred with countries including Syria and Israel during the civil war.

The 15-year conflict ended in 1989 with a new national accord brokered by Arab diplomats in the Saudi city of Taef. The peace agreement introduced a new power-sharing formula, shifting significant authority from the Maronite president to the Sunni prime minister and the Shiite speaker of parliament. It also replaced the prevailing 6:5 ratio of Christians to Muslims in state jobs to an even split, though it is generally believed that this still overrepresents the Christians. The Taef accords indirectly designated Syria as the main powerbroker in Lebanon and the unofficial arbitrator between its contentious

---

Oussama Safa is General Director of the Lebanese Center for Policy Studies, based in Beirut. His research interests span Lebanese and Arab public policy, peacebuilding, and good governance. He is a frequent commentator on contemporary Arab politics in the Arab and international media.

communities. This allowed Syria to tighten its grip over the country's political and economic life.

Although the accords stipulated the withdrawal by 1992 of 20,000 Syrian troops stationed in Lebanon, the pullout never occurred. Instead, for 15 years after the end of the war, Lebanese laws, elections, and key appointments were carefully vetted and manipulated by Syrian intelligence officers to protect Syria's interests.

Meanwhile, the major militias that took part in the civil war benefited from a blanket amnesty law that cleared them of any crimes or wrongdoing during the conflict. Former warlords became the new political elite, enjoying senior legislative, judicial, and executive positions and practicing a distinct style of politics based on deal-making and the division of spoils. Leaders who rebelled against Syrian hegemony, such as former army chief Michel Aoun and former Lebanese Forces militia leader Samir Geagea, were exiled or jailed.

As it oversaw the disarmament of Lebanese militias, Syria made sure that Hezbollah—a Shiite Islamist movement created in the wake of the 1982 Israeli invasion of Lebanon and closely allied with the Iranian regime—kept its weapons under the pretext of resistance to the Israeli occupation. Successive Lebanese governments between 1990 and 2000 echoed this characterization of Hezbollah's role, and efforts were made to strengthen Hezbollah's military power at the expense of the regular armed forces. As a result, Hezbollah today is the strongest armed group on Lebanese territory, and the Lebanese government continues to face serious difficulties in its attempts to restore a state monopoly on armed force in the country.

Lebanon's ambitious postwar reconstruction program was largely effective, but massive borrowing coupled with unexpectedly low economic growth led to a ballooning public debt, which today stands at 162 percent of the country's gross domestic product (GDP).[1] The reconstruction plans were drawn up and carried out by governments headed by billionaire prime minister Rafik Hariri.

In early 2004, the relationship between Hariri and the Syrian regime began to sour. Hariri was planning to challenge Syria's dominance by running candidates across Lebanon in the upcoming 2005 parliamentary elections, and his power struggle with President Emile Lahoud, a close ally of Damascus, ultimately led to Hariri's resignation as prime minister in October 2004.

Hariri was assassinated in a powerful bombing in downtown Beirut on February 14, 2005. The act sparked massive rallies on March 14 in which mourners protested Syrian domination, leading to the abrupt withdrawal of Syrian troops the following month. In a rapid succession of events, an international commission was formed to investigate the assassination, the heads of four Lebanese intelligence agencies were arrested, and a new anti-Syrian political bloc, dubbed the March 14 Coalition, posted a strong showing in the parliamentary elections. Meanwhile, a series of assassinations targeted prominent politicians, journalists, and others associated with the new parliamentary majority. The opposition was led by Hezbollah and later included Aoun, who returned from exile to lead a Maronite Christian political faction. For most of 2005 and early 2006 the main bone of contention between the rival coalitions was the planned formation of a UN-sponsored International Tribunal for Lebanon to try the Hariri assassination case and related crimes. The Syrian-allied opposition sought to control and water down the mandate of the tribunal, whereas the majority sought a more robust entity. The confrontation also reflected a power struggle between Hezbollah and the new government, which was intent on restoring full Lebanese sovereignty in the wake of Syria's withdrawal. The opposition withdrew from the power-sharing cabinet in November 2006, deepening the political deadlock.

Since 2006, Lebanon has faced a series of grave threats to national security. That summer, Hezbollah militants conducted a cross-border attack on Israel, killing five Israeli soldiers and abducting two. Israel responded with massive airstrikes in much of Lebanon as well as a limited ground invasion, while Hezbollah bombarded Israeli territory with rocket fire. The 34-day war resulted in more than 1,000 Lebanese civilian casualties and caused US$5 billion in direct and indirect losses to the country's economy.[2] Between May and September 2007, the Lebanese army battled an armed Sunni extremist group calling itself Fatah al-Islam that had entrenched itself in the Palestinian refugee camp of Nahr el-Bared in northern Lebanon. The army eventually defeated the militants, but the fighting destroyed much of the camp and displaced its civilian residents.

A more fundamental threat to civil peace and stability came in early May 2008, when the March 14 Coalition government decided to curtail Hezbollah's private telecommunication lines and end its alleged airport surveillance. Hezbollah responded by deploying its fighters to Sunni sections of Beirut and other areas that were loyal to the governing coalition. Battles between opposition and government supporters in the capital and parts of the north raged for nearly a week, ending with the Qatari-brokered Doha agreement. The pact included a new political understanding that ended an 18-month Hezbollah sit-in protest and enabled the election of a new president and approval of a new parliamentary election law. Taken together, the above conflicts have posed serious challenges for democratic governance in Lebanon's unique sectarian political system.

ACCOUNTABILITY AND PUBLIC VOICE   3.83

FREE AND FAIR ELECTORAL LAWS AND ELECTIONS	3.50
EFFECTIVE AND ACCOUNTABLE GOVERNMENT	2.25
CIVIC ENGAGEMENT AND CIVIC MONITORING	5.00
MEDIA INDEPENDENCE AND FREEDOM OF EXPRESSION	4.57

Lebanon's unicameral parliament, the National Assembly, is elected through universal suffrage every four years. The president, who serves for a single six-year term, is elected by the parliament. Municipal elections take place every six years; the first postwar municipal elections were held in 1998 under pressure from civil society following a 32-year hiatus. After the civil war, the electoral laws were tailored to ensure victory for Syria's allies. The 2005 legislative elections, held shortly after the withdrawal of Syrian troops, were free and transparent, but they remained governed by the discriminatory old laws, which violated international norms and provided room for manipulation, voter intimidation, and fraud. In addition to such laws, the unwritten National Pact of 1943 stipulates that the president must be a Maronite Christian, the prime minister a Sunni Muslim, and the speaker of the National Assembly a Shiite Muslim. Parliamentary seats are similarly divided among major sects under a constitutional formula that does not reflect the country's current demography. Shiites are particularly underrepresented, as they are estimated to comprise at least one-third of the population but are allotted only 21 percent of legislative seats.

Several features of the electoral laws distort the true aspirations of voters while strengthening existing sectarian leaders. Representation is based on a majoritarian, single-count ballot in unevenly divided multimember districts. The system effectively excludes independent candidates and small parties outside of the main parliamentary or sectarian blocs, and districts are gerrymandered to ensure victory for the predominant sect or political force in each constituency.[3] In the 2005 elections, this was true both in districts that favored the March 14 movement and in those dominated by opposition forces like Hezbollah. Other shortcomings that have traditionally marred Lebanese elections include the lack of preprinted ballots, vote buying, and voter intimidation, including regular violation of ballot secrecy.

Amid public pressure in the wake of the 2005 elections, the government in August formed a national commission, known as the Boutros Commission, to reform the electoral laws.[4] Comprised of civil society experts, the panel held nine months of hearings to consider proposals by a wide range of social actors, after which it submitted a set of progressive recommendations. However, only a handful of the proposed reforms were enacted by the parliament, including a system of magnetic identity cards and indelible ink to curb electoral fraud, and a legal cap on electoral advertising and campaign financing, though some observers cited several loopholes.[5] The proposals that were rejected included a mixed system of proportional and majoritarian representation, redistricting, the establishment of an independent electoral commission, and the adoption of a 20 percent quota for women on candidate lists.

Because of the limited nature of the reforms, the outcome of the June 2009 elections did not radically alter the existing array of political forces.[6] The balloting was organized not by an independent electoral commission, but by a supervisory commission under the auspices of the interior minister. The panel was composed of electoral experts from civil society, but most had partisan affiliations.[7] The commission's task was to monitor electoral spending and advertising and address any electoral violations. Its decisions were to be vetted by the Constitutional Council, tasked with validating the results of the elections and deciding on electoral appeals. At the time of writing, the supervisory commission had submitted reports on 368 violations—ranging from failure to honor advertising contracts to utilizing hate speech in campaigns—which the Constitutional Council was still reviewing.[8] Despite the new campaign finance rules, there was speculation that the elections of 2009 featured unparalleled spending on bribery, vote buying, and development projects designed to win votes.

The results of the elections confirmed Sunni leader Saad Hariri, the son of slain former prime minister Rafik Hariri, as the head of the largest bloc in the National Assembly. His coalition now holds 71 seats (including two independents), compared with the opposition's 57 seats. One of Hariri's key allies is the Druze leader Walid Jumblatt, who heads an 11-seat bloc. In the opposition, Christian leader Michel Aoun, Hasan Nasrallah of Hezbollah, and Nabih Berri of the Shiite Amal Movement control 27, 13, and 14 seats respectively. In the absence of a legal quota for female candidates, the representation of women in the legislature remains severely limited, with only four female lawmakers in the 128-seat parliament.

It is important to note that elections in Lebanon are largely inconsequential in determining the balance of power between branches and within the parliament. In addition to the electoral framework problems described above, the country's political system is consociational. Irrespective of electoral results, the prime minister is obliged in practice to form a national unity government. Consequently, as of October 2009, five months after the June legislative elections, prime minister-designate Saad Hariri was unable to form a government despite leading a clear majority in the parliament. And the opposition, having lost the elections, created the logjam by insisting on a specific share of ministerial posts that Hariri is not inclined to provide. This is but one example of how democratic institutions in Lebanon are easily overridden by communal and sectarian interests. In such a system, elections are reduced to mere referendums on political leaders' clout and ability to command a public following.

Under the parliamentary system enshrined in the constitution, the parliament elects the president and designates a prime minister for official appointment by the president. The prime minister then assembles a cabinet for approval by the parliament. In practice, however, consensus within the governing troika (president, prime minister, speaker of parliament) is needed for all major decisions, blurring any clear checks and balances between the executive and legislative branches.

For example, the president can refuse to sign decrees issued by the council of ministers, effectively blocking their implementation. When the government appointed foreign service officers in 2006, President Emile Lahoud refused to sign the law on the grounds that the government was illegitimate and unconstitutional, since the six opposition ministers had resigned in protest. The foreign service officers did not assume their positions until the fall of 2008, after a new president, former army chief Michel Suleiman, was elected in the wake of the Doha agreement in May. Similarly, the National Assembly speaker, who belongs to the opposition and exercises significant legislative authority, can prevent the parliament from holding sessions by simply refusing to convene it. From December 2006 to May 2008, speaker Nabih Berri refused the government's demands to hold sessions and pass important laws. Sessions were postponed by the speaker 19 consecutive times,[9] mainly to forestall attempts by the majority to elect a president to replace Lahoud, whose mandate expired in September 2007. Lebanon was thus without a president from September 2007 until Suleiman's election in May 2008.

The system does not ensure that the people's choices are free from domination by political interest groups. Lebanon has an entrenched clientelist system that is fueled by the confessional apportionment of state resources and benefits. This system allows community leaders and religious figures to wield power as the intermediaries between the community or sect and the state, and as the main conduit for the distribution of government services and jobs. Community leaders are consequently able to mobilize their "clients" around important political issues at any given time. During elections, they are able to enforce voter loyalty through routine intimidation and potential retribution ranging from physical violence to the withholding of favors and development funds. All appointments in the public sector are made according to an unspoken and delicate formula of sectarian allocation, which is adhered to even when it may hinder the proper functioning of an important government institution. For example, the understaffed General Directorate of Internal Security Forces (ISF)—which includes the police, traffic police, judicial police, and drug enforcement agencies—are in need of recruits, but because the volunteers in early 2006 consisted of 11,000 Muslims and just 3,600 Christians, recruitment was limited to 3,600 from each side to ensure confessional balance. Muslims, both Shiites and Sunnis, dominate the underpaid and overstaffed civil service, which is considered antiquated, lethargic, and largely corrupt.

Civil society groups and the media are allowed by law to take part in and testify during parliamentary sessions. However, requests to attend sessions must be submitted to a lawmaker or the general secretariat of the parliament, and these requests are not always approved. In a positive development, experts from the Civil Campaign for Electoral Reforms and the Lebanese Association for Democratic Elections regularly testified before parliamentary committees discussing the draft electoral law in August and September 2008. The parliament had never before allowed civil society groups to testify on such sensitive political issues.

Lebanon's association law dates to the Ottoman era and remains one of the most liberal in the region, allowing the free formation of new parties and associations of various kinds. To register, a new party or association must simply notify the Ministry of Interior; it becomes a legal entity 90 days after the notice is received. Although the law has been abused by previous interior ministers who chose to curb the formation of rights-based civil society associations, freedom of assembly and association is generally unrestricted, and Lebanon hosts more than 3,600 registered nongovernmental organizations (NGOs).[10] In 2008, notices of formation from 19 political parties and 660 NGOs were submitted to the ministry, and all were accepted.[11] During 2005–06, Lebanon featured heightened NGO activity, including the formation of a number of new NGOs in the wake of the war between Israel and Hezbollah in the summer of 2006. Following the presidential election in May 2008, the Civil Campaign for Electoral Reforms, a consortium of 58 NGOs, launched a major lobbying effort in coordination with international organizations based in Beirut to pass a reformed electoral law. The campaign was free of any pressure or intimidation by state authorities or other actors. Another ongoing campaign involves a group of NGOs pressuring the parliament to pass a law that would allow women to transfer their Lebanese citizenship to foreign husbands and their children.[12] Donors also operate freely, and Lebanon's association law allows for the acceptance of foreign donations so long as the funds are accounted for regularly.

Freedom of the press and expression is unhindered in principle, but is subject to restrictive regulations. These include the media law passed in 1994 (No. 382/1994), which effectively restricted ownership of television and radio stations to influential politicians and heads of communities. The law led to the shutdown of existing media outlets and severely limited the ability of future outlets to gain a permit. Moreover, laws against slander have been abused to restrict coverage, and the television station MTV was shut down permanently in 2001 for political reasons, after it supported an election candidate opposed to then president Lahoud and his Syrian allies. The overlapping functions of the Ministry of Information and the National Audiovisual Media Council (NCA) create confusion in media oversight mechanisms.

Freedom of speech is guaranteed in the constitution, but there is no freedom of information law, meaning journalists must rely on leaks and anonymous sources. The 1994 media law allows censorship of pornography, threats to national security, political opinion, and slander against religion. The law is illegal to attack the president in the media. In 2008, the General Directorate of State Security prohibited the circulation of three films and censored one foreign publication.[13] There have not been any cases of imprisonment of journalists due to their opinion or coverage since 2005. In December 2006, however, two opposition journalists were arrested and accused of breaking into the apartment of a witness to the assassination of Rafik Hariri, in what might have been a politically motivated case. The journalists were charged with theft and tampering with evidence and released after a year and a half.[14] In 2008, anchor Ghada Eid of New TV, an opposition station, was summoned for questioning after airing an episode on corruption in the justice minister's office. Her program, *Corruption*, tackles such issues on a weekly basis. The authorities' investigation centered on the sources of her information, and she was eventually cleared of any wrongdoing.

Impunity for violent attacks against journalists remains a serious problem. Investigations into the 2005 car-bomb assassinations of prominent journalists

Gebran Tueini and Samir Kassir, and an attack the same year that left television journalist May Chidiac permanently injured, have made no headway in recent years, and no arrests have been made. Those affiliated with the March 14 movement believe that pro-Syria assassins were behind the attacks given these journalists' strong anti-Syrian views, while within the opposition, various factions believe that pro-Israel or jihadist forces committed the crimes. Lesser attacks, such as the beating of journalists from one political camp at their opponents' rallies, regularly go unpunished. Journalists are restricted from reporting from some Hezbollah-controlled areas without the group's explicit permission and oversight. In addition, during the May 2008 factional fighting, opposition forces shut down two newspapers, a magazine, a television station, and two radio stations; the outlets resumed operation shortly afterward following a public outcry.

Despite the reduction in violence against journalists since 2006, media stations often practice self-censorship, a habit that dates to the presence of Syrian troops in Lebanon. There is also an unspoken rule against directly attacking religious leaders in the media for fear of inciting sectarian conflict, though that does not prohibit media outlets from using a sectarian discourse or having a political agenda. Lebanon's 9 private television stations and 15 daily newspapers are divided among the various political factions and cater to their respective needs. While the media broadcast law bars incitement and sectarianism, television stations aired divisive, polarizing coverage during street clashes in February 2007 and January and May 2008. The 1994 law imposes onerous licensing fees and taxes on media outlets, making the establishment of new ones a costly enterprise. The state-owned channel Télé Liban is underfunded and dull, faring poorly in competition with the private stations. The state media do not receive preferential legal treatment, but they rarely challenge the ruling authorities. Internet access is unrestricted, though the still-developing infrastructure remains rudimentary compared with other countries in the region, and cost is an obstacle for some users. 38.3 percent of the population uses the internet.[15]

CIVIL LIBERTIES 3.99

PROTECTION FROM STATE TERROR, UNJUSTIFIED IMPRISONMENT, AND TORTURE	2.63
GENDER EQUITY	4.00
RIGHTS OF ETHNIC, RELIGIOUS, AND OTHER DISTINCT GROUPS	3.50
FREEDOM OF CONSCIENCE AND BELIEF	4.33
FREEDOM OF ASSOCIATION AND ASSEMBLY	5.50

Civil liberties are guaranteed by the constitution, including the right to freely exercise religious beliefs. While abuses including arbitrary arrests and detentions were common prior to the withdrawal of Syrian forces in 2005, the freedoms to associate, assemble, and demonstrate have been practiced freely since then, with protest rallies and sit-ins a common sight until the political accord of

May 2008. The judiciary remains the main guarantor of civil liberties and the medium through which to seek redress for violations.

Lebanon has ratified major international conventions against torture and the inhumane and degrading treatment of prisoners. In December 2008, it ratified the optional protocol against torture. However, it has only complied to a limited extent with such commitments, as national laws and mechanisms do little to prevent torture or hold security personnel accountable for abuses. There are no explicit guarantees against torture in the constitution or the country's various criminal justice laws. In a recent report, a local NGO cited routine torture by various branches of the security forces, most notably the intelligence services.[16] Amnesty International and Human Rights Watch have also stated that torture remains a serious problem, particularly in security-related cases but also for those charged with drug offenses or even petty crimes.[17]

Security officials are rarely if ever prosecuted for torturing or mistreating a detainee, and each judge has the discretion to accept evidence obtained under duress. There are no legal provisions for prosecution on charges of torture or abusing detainees. According to Human Rights Watch, the ISF established an internal unit tasked with monitoring human rights violations in February 2008, but the unit remains understaffed.[18] Human rights NGOs are granted limited access to certain prisons, with the exception of the military intelligence prison situated in the Ministry of Defense, on the condition that they sign a confidentiality statement which limits activists' ability to effectively investigate torture.[19] In most cases of alleged torture, victims were not allowed to see a doctor, lawyer, or family members for a prolonged period of time.

Prison conditions are poor and fall short of basic human rights standards. In certain facilities, the number of detainees exceeds capacity by five or six times, and prisoners are mixed together regardless of offense, age, or mental fitness.[20] Preferential treatment of detainees by prison wardens is common practice, taking the form of mattresses, cigarettes, and other privileges for select inmates. Effective means of redress for violations are problematic. Although nearly five years have passed since Lebanon issued the 2005 Ombudsman Law, the ombudsman's office is yet to be established. A draft law mapping out implementation was being prepared as of mid-2009. In the absence of such an agency, citizens may lodge complaints with the Presidential Complaints Office, established in 1998 as a precursor to the ombudsman's office. However, the office does not accept complaints regarding legal or judicial problems, lacks a constitutional mandate, and is overseen by military officers rather than civilians.[21]

Detainees, particularly those suspected of involvement in armed groups, are usually considered guilty until proven innocent, and their detention without trial may be prolonged. This also extends to non-Lebanese who are detained as illegal immigrants. For these individuals, arbitrary and long detentions are the norm despite refugee laws and international standards for the treatment of immigrants. In many cases, refugees are viewed as illegal immigrants and treated as criminals. In November 2007, however, the government issued a decree ordering the extradition of all foreigners who have completed their prison sentences, putting an end to indefinite detention.[22] Lebanon does not have a serious human-trafficking problem, but it suffers from inadequate mechanisms to deal with the abuse of mostly Asian domestic workers.

Street crime is generally not a problem beyond pickpocketing and car theft, which is a persistent challenge because it is backed by powerful armed militias in the rural Bekaa Valley region. The ISF has taken measures to combat such crimes. The most serious threats to public safety have come from occasional sectarian clashes and the 2007 fighting initiated by the Sunni extremist group Fatah al-Islam, whose leader remains at large.

Women and men have equal rights in principle, but opportunities and resources are not shared equally. While the country has no extreme forms of violence against women, and women are granted equal access to education and the job market, discrimination due to local customs and social norms remains a problem. Some legislative improvements have taken place over the decades, including amendments permitting a woman to obtain a passport and travel without the consent of her husband. Other restrictive legal provisions remain in place, however. As family and personal status issues are adjudicated by the religious authorities of each sectarian community, women are sometimes subject to discriminatory rules governing marriage, divorce, inheritance, and child custody. They are also unable to pass their citizenship to foreign husbands or their children. The religious leaders of the various confessions, who exercise significant influence over policy making, carefully protect the existing legal framework on these issues. Cases of domestic violence against women are common, and the law does little to prevent them. So-called honor crimes, in which women are attacked or killed by relatives for perceived moral transgressions, are rare but do occur in peripheral areas. The punishments for perpetrators are usually lenient.

The state budget contains no special provisions to tackle gender inequality or improve female health, nutrition, or education. Despite vigorous efforts by civil society groups, much work remains in terms of implementing laws to end discrimination against women and pass sexual-harassment legislation. The state occasionally tries to promote equitable representation in the various branches of government but has failed to strengthen women's presence. With the help of civic groups and the Lebanese Women's Council, some symbolic improvements have been registered over the past few years; in 2004 the government included, for the first time ever, two female ministers. However, the outgoing government in 2009 included no women in a cabinet of 30 ministers.

Lebanon has a fairly large population of disabled individuals, as an estimated 100,000 people were disabled during the civil war. Under the latest electoral law, disabled people were provided with specially equipped ballot stations. A law passed in 2000 guarantees disabled people equality before the law and a series of tax exemptions, as well as access passes and special privileges in government properties, public transportation, and parking. However, there is little evidence that such provisions have been enforced, and most efforts to assist persons with disabilities are carried out by family members or poorly funded private organizations.

There is no official or systematic discrimination against Lebanon's 18 officially recognized sectarian groups. Compared with other countries in the region, Lebanon has managed to integrate minorities well and allowed them to secure political representation. The Armenians are a case in point, as are emerging sectarian groups such as the Alawites, who acquired a seat in the parliament within the past decade and were recognized in the post-Taef constitution as an official sect. Nevertheless, the system of sectarian apportionment in state institutions is inherently discriminatory in that it is based on confession rather than merit. Beyond official institutions, societal discrimination is common and easily detectable in the media and the private sector.

Lebanon is home to more than 300,000 Palestinian refugees. They are denied citizenship and equal access to jobs, despite the fact that many arrived—or descend from those who arrived—as early as 1948. Some of this discrimination is based on the labor law of 1962, which bars Palestinians from the job market and relegates them to menial positions regardless of their level of education or skill. These policies stem from a long-held view that the integration and naturalization of Palestinian refugees would upset the delicate confessional balance in favor of Sunni Muslims. In June 2005, however, the minister of labor relaxed labor restrictions and allowed Palestinians access to approximately 50 professions. Palestinians are not allowed to own property in Lebanon, a rule that many consider unconstitutional, and living conditions in the country's Palestinian refugee camps are abysmal. The destruction of the Nahr el-Bared camp in 2007 added to this misery by displacing some 5,000 families to neighboring camps. The government's Lebanese Palestinian Dialogue Committee is tasked with drawing up plans to rebuild the camp, but it has faced stiff opposition from the Christian Free Patriotic Movement (CFPM) and residents of villages surrounding the camp, who want to prevent its reconstruction. While local residents are angry at the losses incurred during the fighting with Fatah al-Islam, the CFPM is opposed to the reconstruction on the grounds that it will facilitate the permanent settlement of Palestinians in Lebanon.

Freedom of religious belief is guaranteed by the constitution, and there are no restrictions placed on religious observance or ceremony. Proselytizing is not recognized by law, and interfaith marriages are considered civil marriages and must be carried out in a foreign country. An individual's sect is mentioned on a civil registration document, though not on identification cards or passports. In February 2009, Minister of Interior Ziad Baroud issued a memorandum allowing individuals to petition to remove their sect from the civil register, though many criticized this step as insufficient and largely ineffective given the entrenchment of sectarian divisions in the broader legal and political system. Various religious communities offer religious education through their own school systems, and religious leaders are appointed from within each religious community. These appointments and elections are occasionally influenced by political leaders, but they remain largely independent.

Freedom of assembly is guaranteed by the constitution, and it has expanded dramatically since the end of the Syrian military presence. Demonstrations technically require the prior approval of the Ministry of Interior, though demonstrations and sit-ins have sometimes taken place without such approval, and there is little or no interference by state authorities in practice. In February 2006, demonstrators protesting Danish cartoon depictions of the prophet Muhammad attacked and burned the building housing the Danish consulate in Beirut, and although dozens of demonstrators were arrested, they were later acquitted. In January 2008, demonstrations to protest power outages evolved into violent clashes with the Lebanese army, leading to the death of seven civilians. And from December 2006 to May 2008 the opposition staged a prolonged sit-in in downtown Beirut that was left unhindered by the state, although it also enhanced the public sentiment that political factions have abused the right to assembly by staging endless political rallies, disrupting normal life and contributing to the closure of dozens of businesses.

The state widely respects the right to form, join, and participate in trade unions. The General Confederation of Labor Unions is a historically powerful grouping of specialized federations, but in recent years it has been accused of siding with the political opposition in most of its rallies and calls for strikes. In fact, the May 2008 clashes between government and opposition supporters began with a strike that was supposedly aimed at protesting price hikes.

RULE OF LAW 3.54

INDEPENDENT JUDICIARY	3.40
PRIMACY OF RULE OF LAW IN CIVIL AND CRIMINAL MATTERS	3.00
ACCOUNTABILITY OF SECURITY FORCES AND MILITARY TO CIVILIAN AUTHORITIES	2.75
PROTECTION OF PROPERTY RIGHTS	5.00

The judiciary consists of civilian courts, a military court, the Judicial Council, and the Constitutional Council, which has the authority to rule on the constitutionality of government actions. The judicial system functions reasonably well, and the civilian courts follow international standards of criminal procedure. However, the judiciary faces limits on its independence. Until 2005, it faced pressure by influential, Syrian-backed politicians, and it remains subject to executive and confessional influence on appointments and financing. Due process rights are not well protected in the military court, which consists largely of officers with no legal training and features trials that are concluded in a matter of minutes.

The Judicial Council nominates judges, who are then approved by the minister of justice, and monthly salaries and expenses are paid by the minister of finance. A member of the Judicial Council resigned in October 2008, citing the body's refusal to endorse even one of the hundred or more qualified judges on its list over the previous two years. Only rarely have judges shown true independence by making decisions that went against the government, and even in these instances the judgment was not always carried out. In the past year, the independence of the judiciary has been questioned by the opposition following the release of four intelligence generals who were incarcerated in the aftermath of the Hariri assassination. They were freed for lack of evidence, leading many to interpret the initial arrests as politically motivated. Moreover, they had been held in preemptive detention for some three years despite rules limiting such detention to a three-month period, renewable once.

In 2006, the March 14 Coalition majority in the parliament amended Law No. 250/1993 to disband the Constitutional Council before its official term expired, purging the judiciary of what were considered pro-Syrian judges. Legal experts considered this action unfair and a dangerous precedent for heavy-handed political interference in the judiciary.[23]

The judiciary is also subject to pressure by parochial sectarian interests, particularly in nominations to the Constitutional Council and the Judicial Council, whose seats must be apportioned by confession. Indeed, the two bodies were suspended from 2004 until 2009, when the major sectarian leaders reached an agreement on their composition. Judges and other officials in the judiciary are appointed in a similar manner, based on a sectarian quota defined in advance. The delicate sectarian balance makes it difficult to completely protect the judiciary from interference by religious leaders. For example, the mostly Sunni suspects jailed after the attack on the Danish consulate were quietly released following protests by the Mufti of the Republic. The training of judges is carried out at the Judicial Training Institute and is generally done in a professional manner. Allegations of judicial corruption emerge from time to time, but it is not widely perceived to be a serious problem.

While the ordinary justice system is seen as competent and reliable, it suffers from backlogs, understaffing, and a lack of in-service training, prompting calls for serious reforms. While defendants have the right to independent counsel, there is no legal aid for those who cannot afford an attorney. Moreover, high court fees make access to justice difficult for many.

The Central Inspection Bureau (CIB) is charged with investigating wrongdoing by public officials, but it has rarely been able to prosecute senior politicians. It has pursued lower-ranking individuals, though its procedures are not fully transparent. According to the CIB, in 2007, 200 low-ranking civil servants were referred to the disciplinary council.[24] The legal immunity enjoyed by public officials poses a key obstacle to justice in such cases. Charges against a public official or civil servant for a bureaucratic violation or a felony must be approved by that official's agency and by the prosecutor general. There are no whistleblower protection laws or access to information laws, seriously hindering investigations against public officials.

The ISF is in charge of internal security and includes an antiriot force. Because the ISF is perceived to be under the control of the Sunnis, however, the army assumes antiriot duties in most instances. The military is seen as the sole guarantor of peace and stability in Lebanon and is regarded as nonsectarian and trustworthy by the public. The General Directorate of State Security, which oversees immigration, diplomatic security, and the national borders, is perceived to be under the control of the Shiites. There is also a security agency under the control of the Council of Ministers that is limited to the protection of prominent figures and leaders.

Civilian control over the military and security services is at times limited by confessional loyalties. In 2006, the minister of interior tried to centralize intelligence information by requiring security agencies to utilize one main computer system at the ministry. The General Directorate of State Security, considered close to the opposition, refused to comply, and the entire initiative was frozen.

Accountability for involvement in human rights abuses is limited. With the exception of the 2005 arrest of the heads of the four major intelligence services at the request of an international investigator, there have been no other recorded instances of military or security officials being arrested by civilian authorities. Though there is a parliamentary committee for defense and security, its mandate has been limited to approving budgets and other bureaucratic matters. During the fighting in Nahr el-Bared in 2007, civil society groups and camp residents made multiple complaints of alleged rights violations by the army, but no investigation followed. The army command suspended 11 soldiers and temporarily detained 3 officers for misconduct after the deadly clashes with demonstrators in January 2008, but the results of the investigation were never released to the public.[25] This rare case of disciplinary action by a security service was widely seen as politically motivated since the army commander was a presidential hopeful and did not want to alienate the opposition, with which most of the victims were affiliated.

In recent years there has been no significant interference by security services in the political process, though prior to 2005 it was common practice for security officers to rig elections and involve themselves in political appointments and even judicial decisions. There is no human rights training for members of the military or security services. Corruption is not considered a problem in the security forces.

Property rights are generally protected, and regulations pertaining to the acquisition, benefits, use, and sale of property are well defined. This fits with the generally market-oriented economy and the country's plans to join the World Trade Organization (WTO). It is important to note, however, that Law No. 296/2001 bars Palestinian refugees from owning property due to concerns that they could permanently settle in Lebanon and alter the sectarian balance. Women can freely own property but cannot bequeath it to children of foreign fathers.

The private sector forms the backbone of the economy, and the government is careful to protect the country's reputation as a land of free economic and trading activities to help attract investment. Foreign investors may fully own and manage their business and private assets without any restriction, and they are not obliged to engage in any particular sector or project. Resource allocation is a business decision that public authorities may not influence through direct intervention.

ANTICORRUPTION AND TRANSPARENCY   2.60

ENVIRONMENT TO PROTECT AGAINST CORRUPTION	1.75
PROCEDURES AND SYSTEMS TO ENFORCE ANTICORRUPTION LAWS	2.50
EXISTENCE OF ANTICORRUPTION NORMS, STANDARDS, AND PROTECTIONS	3.00
GOVERNMENTAL TRANSPARENCY	3.17

Since the destructive civil war, the government has generally succeeded in restoring functional state institutions. Nevertheless, pervasive patron-client networks, confessional apportionment of jobs and positions, and conflicting authority between different agencies hinders efficiency and facilitates corruption. Bureaucratic red tape allows officials to solicit bribes for the provision of state services, a phenomenon that has undermined the government's credibility and contributed to the rise of nonstate actors like Hezbollah. Lebanon ranked 102 out of 180 countries on Transparency International's 2008 Corruption Perceptions Index, receiving a score of 3.0 out of 10 for the second consecutive year.[26] Lebanon has yet to sign the UN Convention Against Corruption.

In a system where compromise is always necessary to maintain the sectarian balance of power and protect confessional spheres of influence, it is very difficult to enforce accountability and integrity, even when required by law. Petty bureaucratic corruption is endemic, and it is common for public servants to view their positions as a means of earning money and obtaining kickbacks. There is no clear antibribery law or ombudsman mechanism to field complaints. Bribe takers are usually members of cliques that are protected by powerful politicians or communal leaders, rendering them essentially immune from punishment. Dismissal of civil servants for any form of malfeasance is rare.

During the period of rapid postwar reconstruction under Rafik Hariri, accusations of vast corruption and embezzlement of state funds were common. Many of the public facilities that were rebuilt—such as the airport, seaport, and sports stadium—were thought to have cost less than what was spent on them, but because there was no formal audit or control over expenditures, it has been difficult to verify these allegations. Special councils such as the Council for Development and Reconstruction, the Council of the South, the Fund for the Displaced, and the Municipality Fund were created to run the rebuilding efforts, while the roles of the Ministry of Labor and Public Works and the Ministry of Interior were significantly reduced. The special councils and funds came under the direct control of sectarian leaders and were not accountable through official state channels of audit and procurement. They continue to make up a sizable share of the annual state budget and remain unaudited.

There are no laws that prevent appointed or elected officials from pursuing other jobs, or that clearly define conflicts of interest. Many incumbent lawmakers, for example, continue to practice their previous professions as lawyers, bankers, or entrepreneurs. The Constitutional Council requires that officials submit a summary of their assets at the beginning and the end of their tenure, but the disclosures are confidential. Regulation of political party financing is rarely if ever enforced, and parties are funded with undisclosed sums from unknown sources. Some are believed to receive substantial support from foreign powers. The lack of transparency is exacerbated by Lebanon's ironclad banking secrecy laws, which undermine asset declarations and hinder efforts to investigate malfeasance.

The CIB, the Court of Accounts, and the Civil Service Board are all tasked with investigating allegations of official corruption and referring cases for prosecution. There is also a disciplinary council to oversee all ministries and produce yearly reports about abuses and corruption. Efforts to establish a parliamentary committee to investigate and eventually prosecute senior officials have never come to fruition, and a law establishing an ombudsman's office was passed in October 2004 but never implemented. In practice, the existing anticorruption bodies are ineffective and have rarely issued indictments of senior officials. There are no adequate state mechanisms to compensate victims of corruption.

Because of these institutional weaknesses, fighting corruption remains a political decision and is directly related to the sectarian balance of power between major politicians. In the late 1990s, then minister of energy Shaeh Barsoumian was jailed on charges of embezzling ministry funds, but he was released after a few years due to intervention and lobbying by influential figures in his Armenian community. During the 2006 war between Israel and Hezbollah, a scandal about a public servant illegally selling donated rations appeared in newspapers, but it quickly disappeared following an intervention by influential politicians.

There is no way to accurately audit and verify the collection of taxes, given the banking secrecy enjoyed by citizens and corporate entities, nor are there effective mechanisms to protect educational institutions from corruption and political influence. The Lebanese University, a public institution, is seen by many as a victim of corrupt practices and sectarian appointments that deprive it of much-needed competence. Instances of students being required to bribe teachers or pay additional fees to access basic educational services are rare.

Nevertheless, following the withdrawal of Syrian troops, one case of a forged medical degree granted by the Lebanese University Medical School to the brother of a Syrian intelligence officer made headlines.

A widely publicized effort by civil society and several lawmakers to pass whistleblower protections and freedom of information legislation has not been successful to date. State institutions are not required by law to publicize their procedures, deliberations, or decisions. The public generally learns of corruption scandals only when something is leaked to the press or announced by a state official.

The executive budget-making process is generally transparent and open to intense scrutiny by the legislature. However, passing the budget is a matter of consensus between rival factions. Because of the deadlock between the majority and opposition in recent years, the state still functioned based on the 2005 budget at the time of writing. While the Audit Bureau considers this legally questionable, lawmakers have justified it on force majeure grounds.

Since 2005, the Ministry of Finance has published accurate accounts of expenditures on its website. In general, these are made public every year. The awarding of government contracts, however, is not always an open and transparent process. As mentioned above, entities like the Council of the South and the Fund for the Displaced are not open to public scrutiny and are not obliged to apply open procurement and bidding mechanisms in selecting their projects.

The distribution of foreign assistance, especially in the wake of the civil war and the 2006 conflict between Israel and Hezbollah, has been bitterly criticized by civil society and independent observers. The political crisis and the sit-ins that ensued after the 2006 war, as well as the rapid disbursement of funds, left the government ill-equipped to manage the spending. Donor competition and duplication added to the confusion, as did the rival reconstruction priorities of the opposition and the majority.[27] Controls appear to have improved more recently, and the Ministries of Interior, Administrative Reforms, and Justice have created offices for the coordination of donor money.

RECOMMENDATIONS

- In order to encourage the emergence of modern political parties and issue-based, nonsectarian politics, continue the implementation of the 1989 Taef accords by creating an upper house of parliament that is free of sectarian quotas.
- Continue efforts at electoral reform based on the recommendations of the Boutros Commission, including the establishment of an independent electoral commission empowered to direct a redistricting process.
- Develop serious and credible initiatives to reform the security sector by transferring control to civilian authorities and introducing human rights training for all security forces.
- Apply Article 95 of the civil code, which safeguards the independence of the

judiciary. Empower the Judicial Council to make decisions on appointments, promotions, and discipline, and ensure judicial oversight by parliamentary committees. Include among the reforms a program of early retirement for older high-ranking judges and their replacement with younger jurists, as well as the modernization of the Judicial Training Institute and the adoption of a code of ethics for judges.
- Encourage women's participation in politics by including in any electoral reform a quota within the electoral lists for parliamentary and municipal contests.

NOTES

For URLs and endnote hyperlinks, please visit the *Countries at the Crossroads* homepage at http://freedomhouse.org/template.cfm?page=139&edition=8.

1. "Lebanese Government Aims to Reduce 'Public-Debt-to-GDP Ratio,'" *Daily Star*, March 19, 2009.
2. United Nations Development Programme (UNDP), *UNDP's Participation in Lebanon's Recovery in the Aftermath of the July 2006 War* (Beirut: UNDP, 2007), 12.
3. Huda Rizk, "The Positions of Political Forces before and after the Elections," in *The 2005 Legislative Elections in Lebanon: In the Midst of Regional and Local Transformations* (Beirut: Lebanese Center for Policy Studies [LCPS], 2007), 31 (in Arabic).
4. The commission's work and the full text of the proposed law can be accessed at the commission's website.
5. Maysam Ali, "New Law Fails to Curtail Campaign Spending," NOW Lebanon, May 20, 2009.
6. For a full, simulated comparison between the electoral laws of 2005 and 2009, see the website of the Civil Campaign for Electoral Reforms.
7. Detailed information on the membership and work of the commission can be found at http://www.elections.gov.lb.
8. Amnesty International, "Open Letter to Lebanon's Political Leaders Urging Them to Place Human Rights at the Centre of their Election Campaigns," April 23, 2009.
9. "Lebanon Army Chief Is Elected president," *New York Times*, May 25, 2008.
10. S. Nasr, *Arab Civil Societies and Public Governance Reforms: An Analytical Framework and Overview* (Beirut: UNDP Publications, 2005), 8.
11. Office of the Prime Minister, *Information International* 79 (February 2009): 5 (based on the official gazette). All official gazette editions are published on the website of the Prime Minister's Office and can be accessed at http://www.pcm.gov.lb.
12. A report on the campaign is available at http://nesasy.org/index2.php?option=com_content&task=view&id=5715&Itemid=179 (in Arabic).
13. Samir Kassir Eyes, "Annual Report Summary of 2008," SKeyes home page, February 12, 2009.
14. Paul Cochrane, "Are Lebanon's Media Fanning the Flames of Sectarianism," *Arab Media & Society* 2 (May 2007): 4.
15. OpenNet Initiative, "Lebanon," in *Country Profiles* (Munk/Toronto/Cambridge/Ottawa: Citizen Lab, University of Toronto, Berkman Center for Internet & Society, and SecDev Group, August 6, 2009).
16. The Lebanese Association for Education and Training (ALEF), *Lebanon: The Painful Whereabouts of Detention* (Beirut: ALEF, February 2008), 13.

[17] Human Rights Watch, *Lebanon's 2009 Parliamentary Elections: A Human Rights Agenda* (New York: Human Rights Watch, May 2009).
[18] Ibid.
[19] ALEF, *Lebanon*, 21.
[20] Ibid., 54.
[21] Oussama K. Safa, *The Official Campaign against Corruption in Lebanon* (Beirut: LCPS, 2000).
[22] ALEF, *Lebanon*, 19.
[23] N. Saghiyeh, *Critical Review of the Post-Taef Judicial Reform Discourse*, LCPS Policy Papers No. 2 (Beirut: LCPS, 2008), 13 (in Arabic).
[24] For more information, see the Central Inspection Bureau's website at http://www.cib.gov.lb/rap2007.htm (in Arabic).
[25] "Moussa in an Impossible Mission and Investigation Continues," *Al-Akhbar Daily*, February 5, 2008 (in Arabic).
[26] Transparency International, *2008 Corruption Perceptions Index*, (Berlin: Transparency International, September 22, 2008).
[27] M. Kraft, M. al-Masri, H. Wimmen, and N. Zupan, *Walking the Line: Strategic Approaches to Peacebuilding in Lebanon* (Bonn: Working Group on Development and Peace, December 2008), 7.

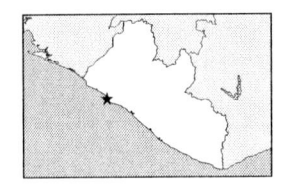

LIBERIA

CAPITAL: Monrovia
POPULATION: 4.0 million
GNI PER CAPITA (PPP): $300

SCORES	2006	2010
ACCOUNTABILITY AND PUBLIC VOICE:	N/A	4.45
CIVIL LIBERTIES:	N/A	4.18
RULE OF LAW:	N/A	3.36
ANTICORRUPTION AND TRANSPARENCY:	N/A	2.81

(scores are based on a scale of 0 to 7, with 0 representing weakest and 7 representing strongest performance)

D. Elwood Dunn

INTRODUCTION

After a quarter-century of instability and war, capped by the dramatic forced resignation and exile in 2003 of former warlord and president Charles Taylor, Liberian political and civic leaders who for several months had been assembled in Ghana under international auspices began to chart a new course for peace and reconciliation. The outcome of their deliberations was the Accra Comprehensive Peace Agreement (CPA), which provided for a power-sharing interim arrangement, to be followed by internationally supervised elections out of which would emerge a legitimate government of Liberia.

At the time of the peace talks, the country remained gripped by a 14-year contest for power between Liberian armed and political factions that had left the state tottering on the brink of collapse. In December 1989, National Patriotic Front of Liberia (NPFL) insurgency leader Charles Taylor challenged the government of President Samuel Doe, launching an attack on government posts from across the border with Cote d'Ivoire. In late 1990, a faction of the NPFL led by Prince Johnson killed Doe and a coalition of civilian political parties known as the Interim Government of National Unity was installed with the assistance of the Economic Community of West African States (ECOWAS) and the tacit support of Johnson's forces. A decade later, and despite being voted into office in 1997, Taylor remained utterly uninterested in national reconciliation. Instead, the government devolved into a warlord-style regime battling other armed factions, eventually bringing Liberia to its 2003 circumstances.

D. Elwood Dunn is the Alfred Walter Negley Professor of Political Science at Sewanee: The University of the South. The author would like to thank Counselor Jallah Barbu and Counselor Mohamedu Jones for their assistance.

The CPA provided for an interim period of two years, although a number of critical issues were left unresolved. Considering the fraught set of issues confronting the country, there was a rush to elections, a course desired by some Liberian politicians and an international community anxious to set Liberia right and reassign resources elsewhere. All of this occurred before Liberians had the opportunity to engage in a national conversation about how to address two fundamental issues: the unresolved historical question of national self-identity, citizenship, and shared community highlighted by events leading up to the coup d'etat of 1980; and the perversions of the 1989-2003 civil war, which among other effects exacerbated ethnic and other factional grievances.

These foundational issues were rooted in the evolution of a settler society toward inclusive governance. The core issue was the character of the choice to be made between the idea of building Liberia as a "little America" in Africa, or the building of an African nationality modified by western influences. Liberia has struggled with this situation since its founding in the 19th century, and some Liberians viewed the 1980 coup d'etat, which transferred power away from American-descended Liberians after decades of dominance, as an opportunity to tip the scale toward the African conception. However, the post-1980 military leadership under Samuel Doe sustained a model of personal power that betrayed the promise of change, and the country degenerated into civil war. To the unresolved national identity issue was thus added a brutal conflict yielding such devastating consequences as 250,000 deaths, the widespread use of child soldiers, extensive ethnic score settling, and massive human rights violations—in short, a society shaken to its very core.

Still unable or unwilling to address these foundational issues, Liberia went forward with elections in 2005. Twenty-two candidates participated in the first round of the presidential election. The second round pitted soccer star George Weah against economist Ellen Johnson Sirleaf, and the latter won with almost 60 percent of the vote, thus becoming the first elected female president in Liberian and, indeed, African history. Under extremely challenging circumstances, she set forth a governance agenda that emphasized peace and security, economic revitalization, the rule of law, infrastructure development, and basic social services. Initiatives by the government have resulted in a measure of economic recovery and some advances on priorities including debt forgiveness, fighting corruption, reforming the security sector, regaining control of natural resources, and consolidation of authority throughout the country. Despite these accomplishments, Liberia still features remote areas outside the government's writ.

With a population of 3.4 million people, 68 percent living in abject poverty, the Liberian economy reportedly grew at a rate of 7 percent in 2008, down from 9.5 percent the previous year, but per capita GDP remained just US$221.[1] While revenue collection has risen, the global financial crisis has had a severe impact on remittances and investment, increasing fears of setbacks to quantitative targets and governance improvement programs.[2]

The scale of governance challenges is vast, and capacity is severely constrained. The record is mixed regarding the ability of the state to uphold constitutionally stipulated civil liberties. Progress reports produced by the United Nations Mission in Liberia (UNMIL) and other sources point to continued serious shortfalls in the reform of a legal judicial system burdened by poorly trained personnel. Corruption—both the endemic variety resulting from decades of autocratic rule and civil war, and the specific issue of corruption among public officials today—could "seriously undermine the development gains achieved" so far.[3]

It bears emphasizing that the unresolved pre-1980 historical challenges and the debilitating consequences of 14 years of civil war continue to define today's Liberia. Together they provide context for understanding the country's developments in fits and starts and its measure of progress, as well as the fragility of Liberia's peace.[4] The concern now is that the overwhelming immediate problems will overshadow the historic challenges. Should that occur, the outcome could be a renewal of armed conflict. To escape the "conflict trap" and move toward a political community of inclusive governance based on principles of equity and justice, Liberia must simultaneously address both dimensions of its legacy of conflict.

ACCOUNTABILITY AND PUBLIC VOICE 4.45

FREE AND FAIR ELECTORAL LAWS AND ELECTIONS	4.75
EFFECTIVE AND ACCOUNTABLE GOVERNMENT	3.75
CIVIC ENGAGEMENT AND CIVIC MONITORING	5.00
MEDIA INDEPENDENCE AND FREEDOM OF EXPRESSION	4.29

Liberia has a presidential system broadly modeled after that of the United States. Because of the conflict, however, the general elections of October 2005 were not based strictly on the 1986 constitution, but rather on amendments to electoral clauses of the constitution and provisions of the CPA. Even so, campaign finance laws were not rigorously enforced during elections highly dependent on private and public donations and logistical and technical support from the international community. Candidates with personal fortunes or who were otherwise well connected seemed to have an advantage over less networked candidates. Capacity and time constraints prevented the National Elections Commission (NEC) from fully monitoring the flow of funds.[5]

As none of the 22 presidential candidates received an absolute majority in the first round, a run-off election was contested by the two leading vote getters, football star George Weah of the Congress for Democratic Change (CDC) and Ellen Johnson Sirleaf of the Unity Party (UP). The official results, released by the NEC and backed by the opinion of international observers, awarded Johnson Sirleaf almost 60 percent of the votes. The CDC strenuously objected, contending that the NEC was biased in favor of the UP, even appealing to the Supreme Court. The appeal was subsequently withdrawn in response to domestic and international pleas.

Johnson Sirleaf took office on January 16, 2006, but the UP did not win a majority of seats in the bicameral legislature, which is comprised of a 64-seat House of Representatives elected to six-year terms and a 30-seat Senate (2 senators for each of 15 counties) whose members serve for nine years. Opposition parties or independents dominate in both houses; the UP has only four senators and eight representatives. A coalition of political parties, COTOL, has the most seats in the Senate, with seven, and the CDC has the most seats in the House of Representatives, with 15. All parties were free to organize and campaign in 2005 without government interference, abetted by the fact that the elections were held under an interim power-sharing caretaker government held in place by 15,000 UN troops and the legitimacy of the global community. Apprehension about future processes, however, highlights the need for a comprehensive electoral plan while international umpires are based in country.

There have been a number of local by-elections during Johnson Sirleaf's term, mostly won by opposition political parties, including the February 2009 senatorial contest in River Gee County, in which prominent UP candidate Ambassador Conmany Wesseh lost to Destiny Party candidate Nathaniel Williams. One problematic issue that has emerged is the government's inability to hold mayoral and other local elections for financial reasons, with attention called to certain officials of questionable repute that were held over from the interim government. The government has been open about its resource constraints and suggested temporarily filling local positions by presidential appointment, with legislative consent. When the opposition raised constitutional concerns, the debate was referred to the Supreme Court, which ruled that the president could make the appointments to ensure smooth government operations pending the 2011 general elections.

Some groups with links to wartime militia, such as the National Patriotic Party (NPP) of former president Charles Taylor and the All Liberia Coalition Party (ALCOL) of former warlord Alhaji Kromah, are represented in the legislature and therefore continue to exercise considerable authority. Liberians' fascination with the CDC, touted as the most grassroots of all political parties, has not dissipated. In anticipation of the 2011 race, several parties have been courting the CDC, while the ruling UP signed a merger accord with the Liberia Action Party (LAP) and the Liberia Unification Party (LUP). While the understanding still has to be endorsed by rank-and-file membership, it has sparked intense debate about political realignment as the 2011 balloting nears.[6]

Recruitment into the civil service and promotions within it remain a source of contention. As incipient professionalism slowly takes hold, some UP partisans claimed priority treatment, scoffing at the post-election notion of a "government of national unity." Because patronage remains deeply embedded in society, some claim the president has yielded to the temptation of employing patronage to repay political debts. The president has herself acknowledged political hirings, suggesting that she would reconsider such appointments. The opposition has criticized a few appointments in particular, including the June 2009 nomination of a new head for the National Police who was perceived to owe his selection to political connections to Fumba Sirleaf, the president's foster son, who is himself head of the National Security Agency.

Strong executive branch powers enshrined in the constitution overshadow the legislature and the judiciary in Liberia. This legacy of executive dominance was reinforced by the post-1989 era of warlordism. Although President Johnson Sirleaf has been judicious in her exercise of power thus far, there is little guarantee that her successor will be equally sensible. As one observer put it, "the president's power is still lying around like a loaded gun."[7] Aside from the potential for abuse, such hyper-presidential powers could create the impression among ordinary Liberians that political hegemony is normal. Such perceptions, anchored in a culture predisposed to autocracy, make it difficult to establish the rule of law.

The legislature has therefore sought legitimacy in the eyes of Liberians since its installation in 2006. Its weakness results from a problematic and traumatized postwar society and the pool of candidates drawn from that electorate, as well as the absence of consensus on governance priorities among the political elite. Members of the current legislature include former warlords and other notorious figures whose names are highlighted in the Final Report of the Truth and Reconciliation Commission (TRC) released in July 2009. Although the opposition predominates in both houses, proper oversight over the executive is impeded by divisions that prevent the opposition from functioning as a coherent bloc. Such circumstances create an environment in which subtle executive manipulations, as evidenced in the 2007 ouster of Speaker of the House Edwin Snowe, further weaken the institution. Snowe, an independent aligned with the interests of former president Taylor, was alleged to have used ill-gotten wealth to influence his election to the speakership. Once in office, his behavior often proved embarrassing to the administration, as when he attempted to conduct personal diplomacy with Taiwanese officials—at a time when the government was diplomatically engaged with China. Moreover, the legislature at times exhibits openness to manipulation by special interests.

Many civil society organizations and nongovernmental organizations (NGOs) have emerged since the beginning of the civil war and international involvement to broker peace. Local NGOs are involved in constructive initiatives on issues such as women, youth, and human rights, though questions remain about the transformative impact of the work of such groups. International NGOs, or their local partners, often enjoy considerable voice at the table, but they often urge a one-size-fits-all approach that reflects the mindset of donors unfamiliar with Liberian realities. Professional Liberians, both domestically and in the diaspora, are sometimes marginalized. International groups prioritize technical solutions over foundational change issues such as creating a national vision and addressing Liberia's identity problem.[8]

Although there are no legal restrictions on the ability of NGOs to function, practical impediments exist. For example, Mulbah K. Morlu Jr., the leader of the interest group Forum for the Establishment of a War Crimes Court in Liberia, was arrested and temporarily detained on several occasions in recent years, including once in 2008 when he called President Johnson Sirleaf a "rebel," and again during a March 2009 gathering in Monrovia of the International Colloquium on Women's Empowerment, when he and his supporters were seized and reportedly brutalized by police.[9] To human rights activists, these actions demonstrated that regardless of government intentions, inherited law enforcement institutions are still predisposed to restrict such activities. There are also threats and intimidations from nonstate actors: in the aftermath of the TRC report release in July 2009, former warlord and current senator Prince Johnson and his allies called a press conference during which they issue veiled threats warning of consequences in the event recommendations for their prosecutions were carried out.

The constitution guarantees freedom of expression. Historically, the emphasis under Liberia's series of autocratic regimes has been on form rather than substance. The experience of 14 years of civil war, when such guarantees were nonexistent, casts a shadow over the attitudes that most public officials bring to freedom of expression issues.

Because of an illiteracy rate near 80 percent, most Liberians acquire their information from radio. There are 13 independent radio stations in Monrovia, in addition to the government's Liberian Broadcasting System (LBS). Only Star Radio and UNMIL Radio cover the entire country. There are also 24 local community radio stations in various areas outside Monrovia, some of which relay radio programs from the capital. UNMIL Radio operates as part of a broader public information office that organizes workshops for senior editors focusing on creative writing and development journalism. Its efforts have led to the formation of the Liberian Association of Development Journalism, a pioneering professional body that shares space with the more traditional Press Union of Liberia (PUL). The PUL itself is viewed as being of questionable effectiveness in terms of establishing and husbanding standards for the profession. Educated members of the press are executives rather than reporters, and below-minimum wage pay leaves journalists susceptible to bribery. In addition, reporting tends to be loose with the facts due both to poor training and manipulation by political operatives. Whether the union and the association will eventually provide leadership to address these challenges remains to be seen.

Television is limited to three local stations, and viewership is limited to those that can afford to buy sets, generators, and fuel to provide electricity. There is complete internet freedom for those with the means to access it. Of significant note is the emergence of online news organs such as the Liberian

Observer, Liberian Connection, Front Page Africa, and other diaspora media, which provide effective service to an influential exile community that offers Liberia remittances and influence over illiterate citizen relatives, as well as a pool of human capital for Liberia. President Johnson Sirleaf has drawn from the diaspora to fill important cabinet positions.

Newspapers exist in abundance, though only a few pass the quality and seriousness test. There are six independent dailies and five bi-weeklies, as well as the government-owned *New Liberian* newspaper. Distribution of these papers is limited to Monrovia due to illiteracy and the logistical challenges posed by poor roads. The leading newspapers include the *New Democrat*, the *Analyst*, the *Inquirer*, which provide independent reporting, and the *Daily Observer*, which has an independent past, but now appears largely to support the current government.

Though one can generally speak of a free press in Liberia, there is some evidence of attempted legal intimidation of journalists. One revealing instance was the government's reaction to critical press reports following the release of the contentious report of the Ad Hoc Independent Commission on the E-Mail Saga, an exercise resulting from allegations in spring 2008 of widespread corruption at the upper reaches of the Liberian government. In the stampede of media reportage following release of the report, the government singled out the *New Democrat*, threatening to sue the paper for false attacks on the president and her family. There was no follow-through.[10] There were also reports of police beating and handcuffing the *Renaissance* reporter Nathaniel McClain. Libel and defamation of character remain criminal offenses. While journalists have not been prosecuted or jailed, they have been intimidated, as when the president sued the editor of the *New Broom* newspaper in mid-2009 for falsely printing that she received a bribe of US$2 million from a rubber company in exchange for favoring the company's bid for a government contract.[11]

CIVIL LIBERTIES 4.18

PROTECTION FROM STATE TERROR, UNJUSTIFIED IMPRISONMENT, AND TORTURE	3.13
GENDER EQUITY	4.00
RIGHTS OF ETHNIC, RELIGIOUS, AND OTHER DISTINCT GROUPS	4.00
FREEDOM OF CONSCIENCE AND BELIEF	5.00
FREEDOM OF ASSOCIATION AND ASSEMBLY	4.75

Chapter II, articles 11-26 of the 1986 constitution guarantee basic freedoms, including protection against torture, extrajudicial killings, arbitrary arrests, and violence by private and nonstate actors. The state's capacity to safeguard these civil and political rights is a continuing issue. Even with the assistance of UNMIL and other international agencies, weak state capacity persists. Numerous instances of rights violations have been followed by the initiation of remedial processes that end in frustration. The generally problematic rule of law environment is reflected in harsh prison and detention center conditions, which are at times life-threatening. Monrovia's central prison holds four times its capacity due to the large number of pretrial detainees. The government relies on international NGOs and the World Food Program to feed inmates, while the UN and NGOs also provide most routine medical services. Renovations are underway in some county prisons, including the Palace of Correction in Zwedru, though men and women are kept in the same cells. The situation in Zwedru is replicated in other remote detention facilities. There has been a near epidemic of jailbreaks, with 31 separate incidents in 2008. Jailbreaks occurred from the Monrovia prison in December 2008 and May 2009, in Zwedru in early 2009, and from the Harper prison on June 15, 2009.[12]

There are no reports of the government or its agents committing arbitrary or unlawful killings or torture. The international presence of UNMIL may be serving as a constraint. Seemingly political deaths that have been reported are generally related to ex-combatant activities and other disputes. In one recent case, a land dispute involving Margibi Senator Roland Kaine and others led to an encounter in which 17 people died. Though indicted for murder and imprisoned, Kaine was subsequently acquitted and returned to his seat. The state protects peaceful activists and political opponents from arbitrary arrests. To do otherwise would be to invite public outcry in an atmosphere characterized by a significant and visible international presence.

Certain unwholesome traditional practices, including trial by ordeal and ritual killings, appear to be widespread, in some cases with the knowledge and encouragement of local authorities. Fourteen people were convicted of murder in the course of a trial by ordeal in November 2007, but presidential clemency followed in September 2008 in response to an appeal by the families of the victims and perpetrators, along with county legislators and local community leaders. The number of ritual killings remains disputed, and such cases are rarely prosecuted.[13]

Historically, gender inequity has existed in both modern and traditional sectors of Liberian society. Rural Liberians tend to send boys rather than girls to school, and a culture of male dominance pervades the urban sector as well. Yet the 1986 constitution prohibits all forms of discrimination, including on the basis of gender.[14] However, scarce resources and traditional customs compete with legal guarantees, exacerbated by the unresolved issue of integrating statutory and customary legal systems. For example, many rape cases are settled by families rather than court proceedings because people want to protect their relatives from being socially tainted. As elsewhere, violence against women and sexual harassment are problems in Liberia. A special gender court was created in 2008 as a means of more rapidly adjudicating such cases.

Women still face disparities between customary and statutory wives regarding the right to dower. The law governing statutory, but not customary, marriage prohibits men from marrying more than one woman. Even after improvements enacted in the 2003 Inheritance Law, all the wives (regardless of number) of a deceased husband under customary marriage are entitled jointly to just one-third of their husband's property, while statutorily married women enjoy one-third dower outright.

Despite the government's explicitly pro-female posture and policies, evidenced by the presence of a female head of state, a surge of women in politics, and increased attention to other women's rights issues, women constitute only 16.7 percent of the Senate, 12.5 percent of the House of Representatives, 20 percent of the cabinet, and 40 percent of the judiciary.[15] A Liberian National Action Plan for women was launched at a 2009 colloquium on the implementation of UN Security Council Resolution 1325 on Women, Peace, and Security, adopted in 2000 to address the impact of conflict and warfare on women. Implementation of the National Action Plan is reportedly off to a slow start.

The preamble to the constitution acknowledges ethnic rights, as does the "fundamental rights" clause. As an understudied country in which the issue of ethnic nomenclature has yet to be officially established, there is much variation in estimates of sociocultural groupings in Liberia. Anthropological and other estimates vary from 16 to 28 distinct groups. Some studies have employed linguistics to categorize Liberians into Mel speakers, Kruan speakers, and Mande speakers. In the absence of official settlement of the matter, the government has tended to avoid sanctioning classification other than county designations, though it implicitly acknowledges the cultural integrity of the wide variety of Liberian ethnic groups.[16]

It is important to underscore the fluidity of Liberian ethnicity. The free movement of peoples, natural ethnic intermarriage, and occasional aggressive national unification and integration efforts mitigate ethnic cleavages. A sense of ethnic identity is nonetheless palpable in society; it has figured prominently in political discourse in recent decades, prolonged and sustained the civil war as an "ethnic war," and left the challenge of acute ethnic divides for postwar resolution. Indeed, the conflict pitted the predominantly Mano/Dahn NPFL versus the predominantly Krahn/Mandingo Armed Forces of Liberia, though numerous other combinations and fallings-out complicated the panorama.

The phrase "inclusive governance" is employed by the government to suggest a full awareness of the social cleavages inherited. Appointments to the executive and nominations to the judiciary are made with this in mind. Apart from these ethnic splits, perceptions of a dichotomous Liberia—indigenous and immigrant—die hard. Opposition news organs are quick to report any perceived slippage on part of the government in addressing the clear imbalances of past governments, which often favored a minority immigrant group that never exceeded 5 percent of the population. Ethnic tension is implicit in the electoral Threshold Bill, which seeks to reapportion legislative seats on the basis of the new national census. Less populous regions are seeking to resist what they consider marginalization, and the bill remained under legislative consideration in late 2009, even as many nervously prepare for national elections in 2011.

Even the abrogated founding constitution of 1847 was explicit in providing for freedom of religion, emphasizing that all citizens had the right to worship according to the dictates of their conscience. The 1986 constitution has been no less explicit. Figures for the religious affiliations of Liberians are estimates, as no official effort has been made to determine affiliations. Foreign research agencies have estimated that 40 percent of Liberians are Christians; another 40 percent practice traditional indigenous religions; 20 percent follow Islam, the vast majority being Sunni Muslims; and small groups adhere to Baha'i, Hindu, Sikh, and Buddhist beliefs.

Tensions between Christians and Muslims have sparked occasional inter-religious violence, with attacks on churches and mosques during the war, including the massacre of some 600 civilians at the Lutheran Church in Monrovia in 1990. On December 29, 2007, Minister of Information Lawrence Bropleh, himself a Methodist clergyman, publicly appealed to the legislature to designate non-Christian holidays as national holidays. He also suggested that a religious advisory board representing all major faiths in Liberia advise the president. Some of Bropleh's Methodist peers, however, condemned his words as fueling religious tensions.

The CPA provided for a TRC roughly on the model of post-apartheid South Africa, and planning for the commission involved broad consultation and an emphasis on ethnic, regional, gender, and religious balance. In July 2009 the TRC released its final report. At the heart of the controversial document is the continuing dilemma of justice versus peace, an issue that the CPA skirted but Liberian society cannot so easily sideline. At least two sets of players are featured in the report: the warlords, who are accused of "killings, extortion, massacres, destruction of property, forced recruitment, assault, torture, forced labor and rape;" and more than 50 leading politicians, including President Johnson Sirleaf, who are recommended for sanctions because of their "moral and financial support" to the warlords. These sanctions include a 30-year ban from seeking public office, which would apply to the president and others upon leaving office. Reactions were sharp: the warlords claimed exemption or immunity based on the CPA and other statutes, while at least some of the politicians described the notion of exclusion from public office as unrealistic, inequitable, and unlikely to foster national healing.[17]

Trade unions are recognized in both law and practice. Though most Liberian workers labor in agriculture or the informal economy, there are several active unions independent of government control, including commercial drivers and laborers on the giant Firestone rubber plantation. Both agitate for rights within their respective industries, at times threatening (and actualizing) strike actions to apply pressure on government or industry. In 2008 the Firestone workers achieved notable success with the signing of a new collective bargaining agreement. However, protections against discrimination for those attempting to form new unions remain weak.[18]

The issue of constitutional guarantee coupled with deeply flawed enforcement systems also applies to freedom of assembly. Permits are required to protest and are generally granted, though the Forum for War Crimes was denied permission when it sought to demonstrate during the 2009 international women's colloquium in Monrovia. Demonstrations occasionally turn violent, as with incidents in late 2007 and 2008 involving a land dispute in Nimba County, workers at the National Port Authority, and demobilized military and security forces. The repressive potential of the security forces is limited, given their limited role in a country where security remains largely the domain of international forces.

RULE OF LAW   3.36

INDEPENDENT JUDICIARY	2.80
PRIMACY OF RULE OF LAW IN CIVIL AND CRIMINAL MATTERS	2.40
ACCOUNTABILITY OF SECURITY FORCES AND MILITARY TO CIVILIAN AUTHORITIES	4.25
PROTECTION OF PROPERTY RIGHTS	4.00

Although Liberia has a history of executive preeminence over the other branches of government, Article 3 of the constitution guarantees judicial independence and the Judicial Autonomy Act allows the judiciary to manage its budgetary appropriation. To advance judicial independence, salaries, benefits, and immunity for Supreme Court justices and judges in subordinate courts were significantly increased by the postwar government. Despite these guarantees and recent improvements, the judiciary lacks independence due to corruption involving judges and court personnel, inadequate education, training, and experience of judges (especially magistrates), and poor administrative monitoring. Litigants are frequently pressed to make unauthorized payments to court officers to process and serve court orders. Of more than 300 magistrates, less than 10 are law school graduates. A lack of basic understanding of complex litigation procedures and laws allows for manipulation, influence-peddling, and obstruction by government officials, highly-educated attorneys, and other actors.

The president appoints judges with the advice and consent of the senate. A more effective method designed to include a judicial review committee to aid presidential nominations was recommended by the commission that drafted the 1986 constitution; however, it was not included in the final version and the old, highly personalized method continues to prevail. The tenure of judges is constitutionally guaranteed up to retirement at age 70, unless impeached and convicted by the legislature. Nonetheless, the president can unilaterally dismiss magistrates: in 2007 Magistrate Milton Taylor of Liberia's premier magisterial court, Monrovia City Court, was ousted following a disagreement over Taylor's granting of bail to accused criminals. Taylor appealed to the Supreme Court; as of mid-2009 the case remains pending. The president announced a second removal in January 2008, this time of a judge in a specialized debt court, but the action was suspended when the Trial Judges Association issued a statement in opposition. The executive branch complies with judicial decisions that go against it. The government lost a prominent case in 2008, when it failed to convict former interim head of state Charles Gyude Bryant for economic crimes. Indeed, the Ministry of Justice was publicly ridiculed following a number of court losses by prosecutors, leading to personnel changes effected in mid-2009 to address the problem.

Judicial review occurs with respect to both legislative procedures and the constitutionality of laws. The Supreme Court's decisions upholding the removal of the former speaker Edwin M. Snowe (see Accountability and Public Voice) and Senate president Pro Tempore Isaac Nyenabo raised issues of the boundaries between the judiciary and the legislature, especially the court's power of judicial review. Indeed, the Supreme Court has ruled that the separation of powers doctrine is not absolute. In the Snowe case, for instance, his legislative colleagues determined that his removal from office was warranted based on behavior that tarnished the legislature's reputation. The Court, on the other hand, reasoned that Snowe's claim that the act of removing him unconstitutionally denied his due process rights was valid.

Presumption of innocence exists in criminal prosecutions. Criminal defendants have a right to bail for noncapital offenses; speedy, public and impartial trial by a competent jury and court; access to counsel of their choice, including public defenders provided by the state if the accused is indigent; and protection from double jeopardy. However, some of these constitutional rights are not available to most defendants. Speedy trial, adequate representation by counsel, and judgment by a competent jury are demonstrably nonexistent in the criminal justice system. As attested to by local and international human rights groups—and in violation of Liberian and international law—many accused criminals spend more than the prescribed period in pretrial detention, and grand and petit jurors lack the requisite understanding of legal and technical issues because of poor education; in addition, they are grossly underpaid for their services by the government and are thus susceptible to tampering. While the accused may hire a counsel of choice, the associated fee (even for a misdemeanor) is grossly unaffordable for most people.[19] Although accused persons may be supplied public defenders, they still face the dilemma of public defenders' abject incapability; many are not even formally trained attorneys, especially in rural areas. Though a Judicial Training Institute was launched in June 2008 to help remedy this situation, it is not yet fully operational. As with rape cases, many citizens prefer to pursue remedies outside the court system. In cases of theft, for instance, victims favor direct retrieval of the stolen property or its equivalent value, or even simple identification and shaming of the thief, to the complications of legal intervention.

County attorneys are the principal prosecutors in Liberia's 15 counties. They are strictly accountable to, and controlled by, the executive under the direction of the Ministry of Justice (headed by the attorney general) and the solicitor general—both political appointees that serve at the pleasure of the president. The recent substitution of law school graduates for prosecutors trained through Liberia's traditional apprentice system of "reading law" under established lawyers has improved the system, but a majority of new recruits are inexperienced. The Ministry of Justice temporarily addresses this problem by contracting and directing private attorneys on a case-by-case basis. Consequently, both government and privately contracted prosecutors do not exercise independence in their prosecutorial duties. Nevertheless, there have been prosecutions of both current and past government officials, including the trials of Senator Roland Kaine, Charles Gyude Bryant, and Edwin Snowe mentioned above—all three of whom were acquitted. Concerns have also mounted over the government's failure to prosecute current public officials who are removed from their offices for corrupt practices; it apparently prefers to give political reasons for their removal. The dismissal in mid-2009 of General Services Agency (the government's procurement unit) Deputy Director General Richard Fallah, sparked by an employee strike action on allegations of corrupt activities, typifies the reluctance of the government to prosecute public officials for wrongdoing.[20]

The police and military are undergoing reorganization and retraining and appear to generally understand their responsibility to remain under civilian control and protect the population. Former combatants were deliberately left out of the reconstituted army, though their services were not precluded for the police and other security forces. The military, which is not yet fully deployed, poses little threat of instability, despite protests for benefits in 2008 by some military officers at the country's Camp Kesselly barracks. However, corruption in the police force remains rampant, and both corruption and abuses by the security forces are generally ignored. General security remains substantially in the hands of the 10,000-strong UNMIL force.

Property rights are constitutionally guaranteed on an individual and collective basis, but only citizens (limited to "Negro or persons of Negro descent"), regardless of ethnicity, may own real estate or land. Benevolent institutions such as churches may own land, but only for their civic purposes. Protection of property rights, especially when infringed, is undermined by poor court enforcement as well as the inadequacy of the records system.

Property rights do not extend to mineral resources on or beneath the land surface. The foreign-owned Liberia Agriculture Company (LAC) and indigenous people living in its area of operations have been in conflict over such rights in recent years. Tension reached a boiling point when an expatriate LAC manager was killed in 2007. The murder case, which remains pending, is indicative of a broader problem with conflict between indigenous land rights relative to those of the owners of major rubber plantations. In recent years, densely populated Monrovia has experienced issues with squatters that have occupied government-owned properties and made them livable, only to witness the government repossess the properties with little or no compensation or alternate housing provided. Citizens displaced by the war generally return to their property, though many have to contend with squatters and other illegal claimants. Such issues comprise part of the general land ownership dilemma plaguing postwar Liberia, which many hope will be resolved by the National Land Commission formed to address the entire sensitive topic.

ANTICORRUPTION AND TRANSPARENCY 2.81

ENVIRONMENT TO PROTECT AGAINST CORRUPTION	2.00
PROCEDURES AND SYSTEMS TO ENFORCE ANTICORRUPTION LAWS	2.50
EXISTENCE OF ANTICORRUPTION NORMS, STANDARDS, AND PROTECTIONS	3.25
GOVERNMENTAL TRANSPARENCY	3.50

Shortly after the 2005 elections, the Johnson Sirleaf government pronounced a policy of zero-tolerance of corruption. The executive's draft corruption offenses act was poised for submission to the legislature in mid-2009. An independent Anti-Corruption Commission (ACC) has been established, though it is still in the organizational stage. In addition, the police Criminal Investigation Division (CID), the National Security Agency, and the National Bureau of Investigation (NBI) possess anticorruption mandates. Despite the existence of these agencies, corruption remains prevalent in Liberia.

The General Auditing Commission (GAC), established by a 2005 amendment to the Executive Law of 1972, has established the existence of significant corrupt activities in public offices. The auditor general who heads the commission now reports to the legislature rather than to the executive, though the GAC prepares three quarterly reports and an annual Uniform Accounting Report for the president, the legislature, and the public.[21] Conflicts between the GAC and the executive previously threatened to undercut the agency's crucial role in the fight against graft, but international and public support for the GAC's activities has dampened the government's initial reservations about the gusto with which Auditor General John S. Morlu approached his job. The presidency has recently received a series of audit reports and appears to be working on acting upon them. GAC reports can be accessed on its website or at its head office in Monrovia.

Prosecution of public officials for corruption is inconsistent. When corruption is engaged, it is on a post facto basis, mainly because there is hardly any effective barrier to check its occurrence. Prosecutions, penalties, and restitution are not yet vigorously pursued. The ACC, established by the Anti-Corruption Act of 2008, initiated work in the fall of 2009 and possesses the power to arrest and interrogate suspects. If the commission can acquire traction and overcome public skepticism by delivering results, it could over time signal the emergence of a clear strategy to address the vexing corruption problem.[22]

The interwoven and complex processing requirements in public agencies and absence of checks on public officials creates an environment in which public servants' behavior is characterized by negligence and outright solicitation of bribes. For example, clearing procedures conducted by officials at ports of entry are cumbersome, complicated, and subjective, resulting in prolonged stays of goods in the port and, sometimes, abandonment by owners due to damage or incapacity to settle high storage costs resulting from bottlenecks.

The government maintains a public procurement agency, the Public Procurement and Concessions Commission (PPCC), which oversees concessions and privatizations. The PPCC was created in 2005 with the responsibility to regulate and monitor all forms of public procurement. In addition, various government agencies form assessment and vetting groups for proposed government concessions and investment negotiations. However, processes carried out by the government have at times been marred by acts of negligence. One example involved bids for the Wologisi iron ore deposits referred to as the Western Clusters. Both Tata Steel of India and Delta Mining Consolidated of South Africa bid for the project, and press reports described a saga that included a government failure to conduct due diligence and accusations of improprieties on the part of both the companies and senior government officials. In mid-2009 the matter was on the verge of resolution, with the government exonerating both Delta and Tata of any wrongdoing and Tata reportedly withdrawing its bid.[23] The due diligence shortcomings prior to selecting a winner, and the president's subsequent reversal of the award, exemplify the regulatory inadequacies characteristic of such processes. In addition, with ongoing allegations of solicitations of bribes by officials, some foreign companies may be reluctant to enter bidding processes in Liberia.

Article 90 of the constitution prohibits acts by holders of public office that breach public policy or create conflicts of interest. The office of the president also drafted a code of conduct for public officials, but its approval has been pending before the legislature for over a year. While awaiting approval of the code of conduct, the Civil Service Agency has established a set of regulations to promote ethical behavior among civil servants. Despite the constitutional mandate and administrative regulations, the GAC and other entities report that public servants, including senior government officials, openly engage in activities that conflict with the statutes and create situations that inhibit the enforcement of tax and other fiscal regulations. Although the government is cognizant of such breaches and conflicts of interest, its inaction seems to license such acts. Although an assets declaration requirement was decreed by the government, as of early October 2009 its provisions remained unimplemented, as noted in an ACC report stating that only 18 officials had complied with the declarations directive.

A tax and accountability monitoring system, the Liberia Extractive Industries Transparency Initiative (LEITI), was established in 2008 and enacted into law in July 2009 to perform a similar monitoring function. Liberia decided to join the EITI global initiative in order to promote transparency in mineral revenue through a process of disclosure, verification, and publication. The first LEITI report pointed to gaps between the payments steelmaker ArcelorMittal reportedly paid to the government and what the government reported as received. In a February 2009 meeting various stakeholders representing the government, industry, and the citizenry "committed themselves to resolve all discrepancies."[24]

The president's immediate emphasis of a zero-tolerance policy on corruption took several years to yield a steady series of investigations, but the policy appears to be picking up steam. The president's dismissal of close political ally Harry Greaves as head of the Liberian Petroleum Refinery Corporation (LPRC) in August 2009 for violating bribery laws is one powerful example. The unceremonious removal earlier in 2009 of agriculture minister Chris Toe might be another, though the circumstances of his dismissal have not officially been made public.

As reported in the press and related in private by educators, corruption in Liberia transcends public office. Educational entities, especially public schools, condone institutionalized corruption, as manifested by fraudulent admissions processes and the imposition of fees for make-up examinations, some of which deliberately create conditions for students to fail. Students remain vulnerable to such unethical behaviors because of poor supervision and the absence of established performance evaluations.[25]

The ability to denounce corrupt acts is more positive. Local and international news media vocally publicize allegations of corruption by public officials and private individuals. The government generally endorses such activity, but has also warned that it will demand proof, a stance that represents a potential hazard to the continuous reporting of corruption, especially in light of the president's decision to sue the editor of the *New Broom* newspaper (see Accountability and Public Voice). Moreover, as of late 2009, there are no legal protections for whistleblowers. The government remains theoretically committed to combating corruption, but needs to exhibit tangible results to dispel public perceptions that it is giving the issue mere lip service. Although mooted by later events, the president's early 2009 appointment of former director of police Paul Mulbah, whom she previously declared to be corrupt and unworthy of public service, as a high-level police advisor seemed to support the public's apprehension regarding the government's resolve.

Access to government information is fair and improving. Information is more easily retrievable than previously via the internet, at little or no cost. Although some government websites exist, government information is not readily available in a public or user-friendly format. A draft set of freedom of information laws was proposed to the legislature by a group of activists in 2008, but has not yet been enacted into law. Information unavailable to the public on time, if at all, includes the budget and detailed expenditure reports. Although the executive tended to submit draft budgets to the legislature so late as to constrain the time available to conduct scrutiny prior to approval, some improvements have been noted. The 2009 budget bill was submitted on time, and a healthy public budget debate occurred in the months prior to the July 13, 2009 signing into law of the fiscal year 2009/2010 budget.

RECOMMENDATIONS

- Strengthen the electoral laws to assure fair and transparent campaign financing and balloting procedures while international actors are still present to mediate in the event of discord.
- In keeping with emerging international standards, decriminalize libel and defamation.
- Address unresolved legitimacy issues related to Liberia's status as a settler state in transition by undertaking a national dialogue regarding institutional arrangements.
- Strengthen the law program at the University of Liberia in order to prepare the next generation of lawyers, judges, and prosecutors and assure uniform and appropriate jurisprudential formation.
- Ensure that the Anti-Corruption Commission remains autonomous and that officials and other agencies are required to cooperate with its investigations.

NOTES

For URLs and endnote hyperlinks, please visit the *Countries at the Crossroads* homepage at http://freedomhouse.org/template.cfm?page=139&edition=8.

[1] Liberia Institute for Geo-Information Sciences (LISGIS), *2008 National Population and Housing Census Final Results* (Monrovia: LISGIS, May 2009); "Poverty Spreads in Liberia: UNMIL Official Unveils Statistics," *Daily Observer*, March 3, 2009.

[2] This at a time when Liberia has improved its image regarding governance. See "How African Countries Are Improving Standards of Governance," *Vanguard* (Nigeria), October 7, 2008; Mo Ibrahim Foundation, *The Ibrahim Index of African Governance 2009* (London: Mo Ibrahim Foundation, 2009).

[3] UN Security Council (UNSC), *18th Progress Report of the Secretary General on the U.N. Mission in Liberia* (New York: UNSC, February 10, 2009), 9.

[4] See wide-ranging sentiments expressed in Truth and Reconciliation Commission of Liberia, *Final Report* (Monrovia: Truth and Reconciliation Commission, 2009).

[5] Republic of Liberia, *The Electoral Reform Law: An Act Suspending Certain Provisions of the Constitution of Liberia and Amending Specific Sections of the New Elections Law of 1986*, December 2004; Republic of Liberia, *The New Elections Law: An Act Repealing Decree 85 of the People's Redemption Council Adopting a New Title 11 in Lieu Thereof to Be Known As the New Elections Law*, September 1986; Some candidates with personal fortunes included Varney Sherman, George Weah and David Farhat. Ellen Johnson Sirleaf and Charles W. Brumskine were well connected internationally, and at least two candidates (Joseph Korto and George Kieh) faced particular resource challenges, as revealed to this writer.

6. UNSC, *Midterm Report of the Panel of Experts on Liberia Submitted Pursuant to Paragraph 4 of Security Council Resolution 1854 (2008)* (New York: UNSC, June 2009), 22.
7. David C. Williams, "The Evolution of Democracy in Liberia" (paper presented at the Ambassador Seminar on Liberia, U.S. Department of State Bureau of Intelligence and Research, Washington, D.C., July 24, 2008).
8. The international NGOs seem to display the mindset of what economist William Easterly calls "planners" (top-down approach) as opposed to "searchers" (bottom-up approach). See William Easterly, *The White Man's Burden: Why the West's Effort to Aid the Rest Have Done So Much Ill and So Little Good* (New York: Penguin Books, 2006).
9. The Anti-War Advocacy Wing of the Progressive Action for Change, "War Crimes Group Details Police Brutality in March 7 Catastrophe," press release, March 14, 2009. Morlu's advocacy was discredited by reported lies about a meeting he claimed to have had with U.S. President Barack Obama during the latter's visit to Ghana in July 2009. See "Delusional Morlu Frauds War Crimes Cause in Liberia; U.S. Denies Obama Meet," Front Page Africa, July 13, 2009.
10. Ad-Hoc Independent Commission on the E-Mail Saga, *Report of the Ad-Hoc Independent Commission on the E-Mail Saga* (Monrovia: Ad-Hoc Independent Commission on the E-Mail Saga, January 7, 2009). Though the report was promptly released following its January 7, 2009 submission by the commission chaired by D. Elwood Dunn, the release did not include vital appendices, and there is no evidence to date of the government's action in respect of the report's recommendations.
11. "Memo to the President: Killing Fly with Sledgehammer Is Counterproductive," *Analyst*, September 28, 2009.
12. "Liberia: Angry Mob Breaks Harper Prison–Over 500 Prisoners Flee," *Informer*, June 12, 2009; A. Abbas Dulleh, "Another Jailbreak–New Batch of Central Prison Inmates Escape," *New Democrat*, May 18, 2009.
13. UNSC, *16th Progress Report/Liberia of the Secretary General on United Nations Mission in Liberia* (New York: UNSC, March 19, 2008); Rebecca Murray, "Even the Devil Is Subject to the Law," Inter Press Service, March 10, 2009.
14. There is one exception to the prohibition on discrimination: the 1986 Constitution states that only black people may become Liberian citizens. See Republic of Liberia, *1986 Constitution of the Republic of Liberia*.
15. United Nations Development Fund for Women (UNIFEM), *Beyond Numbers: Supporting Women's Political Participation and Promoting Gender Equality in Post-Conflict Governance in Africa* (New York: UNIFEM, January 2006).
16. D. Elwood Dunn, Amos J. Beyan, and Carl Patrick Burrowes, *Historical Dictionary of Liberia* (Lanham, MD: Rowman & Littlefield, 2001), 261.
17. Truth and Reconciliation Commission of Liberia, *Final Report*.
18. International Trade Union Confederation (ITUC), "Liberia," in *2009 Annual Survey of Violations of Trade Union Rights* (Brussels: ITUC, 2009).
19. The minimum wage is US$70 monthly. See Ellen Johnson Sirleaf, "Annual Message to the Fourth Session of the 52nd National Legislature of the Republic of Liberia," Monrovia, January 26, 2009, 8.
20. Tiawan S. Gongloe, "For Three Consecutive Years, Prosecution Wins More Cases Than Loses under President Johnson-Sirleaf," *Perspective*, June 3, 2009; Economic Community of West African States (ECOWAS), *Final Report of ECOWAS Team of Investigators on Economic Crimes in Liberia* (Abuja: ECOWAS, June 18, 2005); Truth and Reconciliation Commission of Liberia, *Final Report*.

[21] John Sembe Morlu II, *A Blueprint for Accountability, Transparency and Good Governance: The GAC: Building A New Liberia on Solid Foundations* (Monrovia: General Auditing Commission, January 2007), 4, 22.

[22] Mbeeninsia N. Kialain, "LACC Investigates 4 Cases of Corruption," *Liberian Observer*, October 5, 2009; "Ribadu Calls for Revamping of Liberian Anti Corruption Commission," Elombah.com, August 22, 2009.

[23] Press Trust of India, "Tata Shelves Plan to Bid for US$1.6 Billion Iron Ore Project," *Business Standard*, May 4, 2009; "Mining Indaba 2009: Liberia Expected to Reopen Bidding for Wologosi Iron Ore Deposits," *Metal Bulletin*, February 11, 2009; "Delta Reconsiders Liberia Venture," *Business Day* (South Africa), May 7, 2009.

[24] Desmond Crane et al., *Final Report of the Administrators of the First LEITI Reconciliation* (Monrovia: Liberia Extractive Industries Transparency Initiative [LEITI], February 2009); LEITI, "LEITI Holds Second Stakeholders Retreat," *LEITI Newsletter* 2, no. 1 (January–April 2009), 6.

[25] Moses D. Sandy, "Corruption: A De Facto Way of Life in Liberia," *Liberian Journal*, December 23, 2008; Emmanuel Dolo, "Building a Corruption-Sensitive Society," *Liberian Journal*, December 17, 2008; William Reno, "Anti-Corruption Efforts in Liberia: Are They Aimed at the Right Targets?" *International Peacekeeping* 15, no. 3 (June 2008): 387–404; "Reverend Jailed for Granting Fake Degrees," *Liberian Observer*, December 11, 2008.

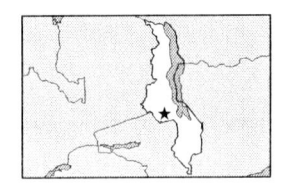

MALAWI

CAPITAL: Lilongwe
POPULATION: 14.2 million
GNI PER CAPITA (PPP): $830

SCORES	2006	2010
ACCOUNTABILITY AND PUBLIC VOICE:	4.75	4.47
CIVIL LIBERTIES:	4.50	4.30
RULE OF LAW:	4.34	4.13
ANTICORRUPTION AND TRANSPARENCY:	3.52	3.44

(scores are based on a scale of 0 to 7, with 0 representing weakest and 7 representing strongest performance)

Peter VonDoepp

INTRODUCTION

For the first three decades after Malawi gained independence in 1964, "President for Life" Kamuzu Banda and his Malawi Congress Party (MCP) governed the country under a repressive one-party dictatorship. In late 1992, however, a full-fledged democracy movement emerged. Strengthened by pressure from foreign donors on the government, the movement forced Banda to hold a referendum on the one-party system in June 1993. A majority of Malawians voted in favor of opening up the political arena, leading to multiparty elections in May 1994 that formalized the country's democratic transition.

Bakili Muluzi and the United Democratic Front (UDF) defeated Banda and the MCP in the 1994 balloting. Muluzi and the UDF drew most of their support from the southern part of the country, while the MCP dominated the central region. A third party, the Alliance for Democracy (AFORD), headed by Chakufwa Chihana, garnered its backing from the least populous northern areas. AFORD's Chihana and the MCP's Gwanda Chakuamba formed an alliance prior to the 1999 elections hoping to unseat Muluzi, but the effort ultimately failed, and Muluzi and the UDF maintained power.

Toward the middle of his second term, Muluzi embarked on an effort to amend the constitution so that he might stand for a third presidential period. The campaign to amend the constitution consumed Malawian politics in 2001 and 2002. A protracted struggle over the issue came to a close in January 2003,

---

Peter VonDoepp is Associate Professor of Political Science at the University of Vermont. A specialist in African politics, he has published widely on democratization processes in Africa. This includes work on civil society development, the internal dynamics of political parties, and judicial autonomy in new African democracies.

when it became clear to Muluzi that he did not have sufficient votes in the parliament to pass the desired amendment. Unable to run again, Muluzi chose Bingu wa Mutharika as candidate for the UDF ticket. Muluzi retained leadership of the UDF and provided substantial backing for Mutharika during the 2004 presidential campaign. Mutharika's primary challengers were John Tembo of the MCP and Gwanda Chakuamba, who headed an opposition alliance of seven parties. In hotly contested polls marred by a number of irregularities, Mutharika won the presidency.

Although many observers suspected Mutharika would remain subservient to Muluzi, relations between the two soured within weeks of the elections. The split was largely over Mutharika's desire to chart a new course in governing the country, including a highly visible anticorruption campaign that seemed to target Muluzi and his aides. Within a year, Mutharika left the UDF, forming a new party, the Democratic People's Party (DPP). In the political machinations that followed, the UDF became the dominant partner of an opposition bloc that held a majority in parliament and also included the MCP.

The falling out between Mutharika, the UDF, and Muluzi set the stage for the contentious dynamics that characterized Malawian politics during Mutharika's first term. Paralyzing conflict between the legislature and the executive, for example, essentially reflected a struggle between Muluzi and Mutharika supporters. Within the executive branch, Mutharika came into conflict with his vice president, Cassim Chilumpha, who refused to leave the UDF when Mutharika did. Chilumpha was later accused of plotting to assassinate Mutharika, leading to a prolonged trial that was ongoing as of mid-2009.

Tensions heightened further when Muluzi decided to run against Mutharika in the 2009 presidential contest. As he prepared his campaign, Muluzi was arrested, first on treason charges in May 2008 and then on corruption charges in February 2009. Muluzi had previously been arrested in 2006 on corruption charges, but the case was discontinued. Mutharika also allegedly ordered a police officer to "shake up" the former president in 2007.

The possibility of a showdown between Muluzi and Mutharika in the May 2009 poll ended in March, when the Malawi Electoral Commission (MEC) rejected Muluzi's candidacy on the grounds that the two-term constitutional limit proscribed him from standing again. A subsequent court ruling upheld the MEC decision. In response, Muluzi and the UDF formed an alliance with MCP head John Tembo, backing his presidential candidacy and creating a formidable bloc to compete with Mutharika. Benefiting considerably from control over state resources and government-run media, Mutharika ran a highly effective cross-regional campaign focused on his administration's record of providing public goods and economic growth. Mutharika ultimately emerged victorious, bucking long-standing regional voting patterns; the MCP's Tembo came in second. In concurrent legislative elections, Mutharika's DPP won a total of 113 seats out of 193, while the MCP took 26 and the UDF just 17. Independent candidates and smaller parties gained the remaining seats. The elections, while characterized by an uneven playing field in favor of the incumbent, were arguably the freest and fairest since multiparty polls were first held in 1994.

Economically, Malawi remains one of the poorest countries on the globe. According to the World Bank, per capita income stands at approximately US$160,[1] while in 2009 Malawi ranked 160th out of 179 countries on the United Nations Human Development Index.[2] Growth rates, economic management, and relations with donors improved considerably during Mutharika's first term, however. From 2006 to 2008 Malawi achieved growth rates between 5.8 and 9.7 percent,[3] while in 2007 inflation declined to its lowest level in a decade. In 2006, Malawi was approved for relief under the Heavily Indebted Poor Countries (HIPC) program, allowing it to receive over US$3 billion in debt relief. In December 2007, the U.S. Millennium Challenge Corporation (MCC) initiative granted Malawi eligibility status to receive financial support. In late 2008, the International Monetary Fund (IMF) approved a US$77.2 million Exogenous Shocks Facility for Malawi, making it the first country to receive funds under the program.

ACCOUNTABILITY AND PUBLIC VOICE　　　　　4.47

FREE AND FAIR ELECTORAL LAWS AND ELECTIONS	4.25
EFFECTIVE AND ACCOUNTABLE GOVERNMENT	4.50
CIVIC ENGAGEMENT AND CIVIC MONITORING	5.00
MEDIA INDEPENDENCE AND FREEDOM OF EXPRESSION	4.14

Elections in Malawi typically produce periods of heightened political tension. Violence between party operatives and by police has accompanied campaigning. Government institutions such as publicly owned media outlets and the MEC have been repeatedly accused of progovernment bias. Polling has often been marred by irregularities, frequently generating legal challenges in the aftermath of the contests. The 2009 elections represented a positive gain for Malawi as such problems were less acute compared to previous polls.

The MEC is the body primarily responsible for administering elections, including being the first instance authority to adjudicate election petitions and disputes between parties. The Judicial Service Commission (JSC) nominates a judge to chair the MEC, whose appointment the president then confirms. The president subsequently appoints other MEC members, numbering no fewer than six, in consultation with the leaders of political parties represented in the parliament.[4] The MEC's impartiality and legitimacy was questioned in advance of the 2009 contests, largely due to alleged flaws in the appointment process in 2007, when the opposition claimed that the president failed to engage in legally required consultations prior to appointing additional commissioners to the body. A subsequent legal challenge was decided in favor of the government.

Despite the MEC's negative image among key stakeholders in the wake of these developments, as well as its limited capacity, international observers concluded that it succeeded in meeting the "operational needs" of the election with sufficient transparency.[5]

Election laws require public media to provide equal news coverage to all parties. In past elections, this condition has been violated and become the subject of legal challenges. Ahead of the 2009 contests, government-controlled media outlets were manifestly and egregiously biased in favor of the incumbent. At the same time, the private outlet controlled by the opposition openly favored Mutharika's challengers. Other broadcasting entities offered more balanced coverage.[6]

Under election laws, political parties that received at least 10 percent of the vote in previous parliamentary polls are entitled to public funding. In terms of private funding, no limits are placed on the amount a candidate may raise or spend or on the sources from which funds may be received. Neither do provisions exist requiring disclosure of donations or spending amounts.[7] During the 2009 campaign, some observers raised concerns over the sources of campaign funds and pattern of lavish spending by the incumbent.

Despite such concerns, international and domestic observers generally applauded the fairness of the 2009 contests. Prior to the elections, a voter registration drive produced a new voters' roll. Inspection of the registry revealed a number of anomalies, however, only some of which were corrected prior to the polls. High levels of freedom of movement and assembly generally characterized campaigning. Although isolated instances of violence erupted between party supporters during the campaigning period,[8] polling day was peaceful. Additional irregularities occurred in parliamentary races, including mistakes and accusations of manipulation during the vote tally. This led several candidates to file legal challenges after results were announced.

In 2005, the government dissolved local assemblies, and most observers expected new elections to be held later in the year.[9] The government has failed to conduct these elections, however, claiming in 2006 that it could not afford to finance them.[10] Civil society groups and international donors have since raised concerns that the absence of these assemblies and councils has weakened local governance and accountability.[11]

Malawi's constitution provides for the separation of powers, and in practice the system of interbranch checks and balances has operated effectively in the country. The courts have served as an important curb on elected authorities. The executive and legislative branches have also checked one another's power, especially between 2005 and 2009, when the National Assembly came under the control of President Mutharika's opponents.

The opposition's control over the parliament, however, has also undermined effective governance and political stability. For most of the time between 2006 and 2008, the president's DPP party controlled between 75 and 85 seats in the 193-seat legislature. The opposition UDF and MCP together held approximately 90 seats, with independent candidates and smaller parties holding the remainder. Throughout the period, the parliamentary opposition consistently attempted to invoke Section 65 of the constitution, which requires the speaker of the house to declare vacant the seats of parliamentarians who switch parties subsequent to being elected. Given that Mutharika formed the DPP only after winning the election as a UDF candidate, the entire DPP caucus in parliament ostensibly fit those conditions. Enforcement of the provision would thus have undermined Mutharika's support in parliament and strengthened the opposition, facilitating their plans to impeach the president. The matter was tied up in the courts until 2007, when a Supreme Court ruling upheld Section 65. Subsequently, Mutharika used a variety of techniques to forestall the speaker's enactment of the provision. For a time during 2008, the president avoided calling the legislature into session altogether for fear the opposition would invoke Section 65. This generated concerns among civil society groups, who condemned the move as dictatorial and bad for democratic governance.[12] When parliament was eventually called into session, the opposition first boycotted the proceedings and then derailed any legislative business that did not pertain to Section 65.

These machinations undermined the functioning of the legislature and caused severe delays in appointments to key posts and the passage of important legislation. For example, in 2006, 2007, and 2008, passage of the budget was delayed because of the opposition's desire to devote all parliamentary time to the Section 65 issue, while the president sought opposing priorities. In addition to legislative paralysis, the stalemate led to circumstances in which the judiciary was asked to adjudicate politically divisive cases, placing it in the political crossfire and causing delays in its handling of other important cases.[13] The dominance of the DPP in the legislature following the 2009 contests, however, has for now obviated this problem, raising hopes of smoother policy making in coming years.

The 1995 constitution established several oversight institutions designed to enhance government transparency and accountability. The most prominent such bodies are the Anti-Corruption Bureau, the Human Rights Commission, the Law Commission, and the Ombudsman. Several of these institutions played visible roles before and during Mutharika's first term by issuing reports, conducting audits, and investigating alleged abuses by officials. They have also faced serious challenges, however. Under Mutharika's presidency, a lack of funding and staff has remained a significant problem.[14] Government interference in personnel and other decisions has also hindered their ability to operate with full independence and effectiveness. For example, in 2007, the president removed the head of the Law Commission, and the position then remained vacant for almost a year.

Malawi's constitution vests authority over civil service personnel decisions with a semiautonomous Civil Service Commission in an effort to insulate those in the state bureaucracy from political influence. In practice, however, the commission has historically been relatively weak and the civil service has been the target of interference.[15] Under the Mutharika administration, concerns about the integrity and quality of the civil service have continued. For much of Mutharika's first term, only 8 of the 12 spots on the Civil Service Commission were filled; among the positions left vacant were an acting chair and deputy chair.[16] In addition, Mutharika asked for the retirement or dismissal of a considerable number of high-ranking civil servants.[17] In 2006, the parliamentary Public Accounts Committee criticized the administration for frequently transferring secretaries and senior officers within the civil service.[18] The opposition press has also accused Mutharika of favoring allies and individuals from his home region in appointments.[19]

Malawi's civil society has played an important role in political life since the transition to democratic rule. The number and vibrancy of key civic organizations has further grown in recent years, and a variety of groups have actively commented on legislation, policy, and broader political developments. These include many churches, additional faith-based groups such as the Public Affairs Committee (an interdenominational organization), the law society, women's organizations, and a number of human rights and advocacy groups. These organizations employ a wide range of strategies in an effort to influence policy making, including consulting with politicians, disseminating research on policy issues, organizing public awareness campaigns, and litigating public interest cases. Several groups have played a leading role in directing public attention to issues such as corruption, judicial independence, development priorities, and gender inequality. Nongovernmental organizations (NGOs) collectively pressed President Mutharika in 2008 to call parliament into session and contributed to monitoring the 2009 elections.

NGOs are required to register with the government. The 2002 Non-Governmental Organization Act established a 10-member NGO board to register and regulate NGO activities. The board is appointed by the government in consultation with the autonomous Council for Non-Governmental Organizations in Malawi. To register as an NGO, an organization must have at least two Malawian citizens serving as directors or trustees, provide a plan of activities and sources of funding, and pledge not to engage in partisan politics. NGOs must provide audited accounts and a description of activities to the board on an annual basis. Thus far, this body has not been used to control or restrict NGO activities.[20] However, the registration fee, at approximately US$300 in 2007, can be potentially prohibitive,[21] as can the cost of complying with government reporting regulations. Donors and funders of NGOs and other civic organizations have remained free from state interference.

Malawi's Bill of Rights guarantees freedom of expression, freedom of the press, and freedom of opinion. In practice, Malawi enjoys a relatively free print media, including a variety of outlets offering diverse opinions. Independent newspapers and radio stations have played an increasingly important role in recent years. As of 2008, 11 independent newspapers were available, the majority privately owned, including two dailies, one tri-weekly, seven weeklies, and one monthly.[22] Approximately 20 radio stations and 2 television stations operate in the country, one of them a religious station with limited broadcast reach. The status of the government-controlled MBC and TV Malawi, the country's dominant outlets, has been particularly contentious. Charging that the entities were biased in favor of the government, the opposition-controlled parliament cut off their funding in 2007 and 2008, forcing them to rely on other sources. Broadcasts from these outlets subsequently took on a strongly progovernment stance ahead of the 2009 elections.

Broadcast media are regulated by MACRA (Malawi Communications Regulatory Authority), which has the authority to issue licenses and ensure compliance with broadcast regulations.[23] The executive branch appoints the board of MACRA, and the agency has been accused of political bias and inappropriate interference with the media.[24] In 2007, for example, MACRA used its authority to prevent a private television station owned by Muluzi from broadcasting and confiscated its equipment.

While most media outlets operate without substantial interference, those associated with the political opposition—in particular Joy Radio—have been the target of government harassment and censorship efforts. In January 2007, for example, MACRA threatened Joy Radio with punitive action after it aired an unfavorable recording of the president. Shortly afterward, the information minister directed the agency to bar all private radio stations from airing live broadcasts without government permission. The targets of the action were stations that had been covering the rallies of former president Muluzi.[25] In 2008, immigration authorities raided Joy Radio's facilities and threatened to deport its manager. Later, MACRA revoked the outlet's broadcast license, although a court order shortly thereafter enabled it to return to the airwaves. During the May 2009 elections, the station was once again briefly shut down for allegedly broadcasting a political message in violation of laws forbidding such programming immediately prior to polling.

Libel and defamation remain criminal offenses, punishable by two years imprisonment, posing a threat to freedom of expression. Several newspapers have been confronted with defamation and libel lawsuits after publishing accusations of corruption by government figures. In May 2006, for example, three journalists from the *Chronicle* newspaper were arrested on criminal libel charges for publishing a story that implicated a former government official in a theft case. That same month, two newsmen were charged with criminal libel for reporting that the minister of health was involved in improper activities. Such legal harassment has hurt independent news outlets financially and, according to some observers, hampered investigative journalism.[26] Reporters have also faced other forms of harassment. In February 2008, police arrested a journalist who reported allegations that the government had planned to rig the 2009 elections. Occasionally, media workers have faced physical intimidation at the hands of state and opposition actors.[27] There are no restrictions on internet use, although it was accessed by less than 1 percent of the population as of mid-2009.[28]

CIVIL LIBERTIES 4.30

PROTECTION FROM STATE TERROR, UNJUSTIFIED IMPRISONMENT, AND TORTURE	3.25
GENDER EQUITY	3.67
RIGHTS OF ETHNIC, RELIGIOUS, AND OTHER DISTINCT GROUPS	4.75
FREEDOM OF CONSCIENCE AND BELIEF	5.33
FREEDOM OF ASSOCIATION AND ASSEMBLY	4.50

Malawi's constitution protects against torture and other forms of physical violence. Nonetheless, police are known to use excessive force against prisoners and suspects in custody, as international and local human rights monitors have documented in multiple cases. In 2006, the governmental Malawi Human Rights Commission (MHRC) issued a report indicating that police frequently subjected suspects to torture and other forms of abuse in the course of investigations.[29] While some police officers accused of torture have been investigated and arrested, few have ultimately been convicted.[30] Several officers have also been held responsible for the deaths of individuals who died either in custody or due to other police actions.[31]

By all accounts, prison conditions in Malawi remain deplorable. Characterized by overcrowding, poor sanitation, inadequate diet, and disease, the state of prison facilities has garnered condemnation from local and international actors.[32] Acknowledging these problems, the Malawi prison service has claimed that the primary cause is inadequate funding.[33] In 2007, the Southern Africa Litigation Centre (SALC) requested that the African Commission for Human and Peoples' Rights send the Special Rapporteur for Prisons and Conditions of Detention in Africa to investigate the appalling conditions in the country.[34]

The government has been accused of using politically motivated arrests to intimidate its opponents. In 2006, for instance, police arrested and charged Mutharika's vice president and political opponent, Cassim Chilumpha, with treason. Two years later, several other opposition politicians, including former president Muluzi and former security officials, were arrested for allegedly plotting to overthrow the government. All the security officials were cleared of wrongdoing, while Muluzi was never formally charged. Two other opposition politicians were charged (and later convicted) with inciting violence for comments made at an opposition party rally in March 2009.[35]

The constitution protects against arbitrary arrest and unlawful detention. However, due to a backlog of cases, extreme delays in bringing suspects to trial remain common. Pretrial detainees are estimated to comprise 17 percent of the prison population. A recent study revealed that 321 homicide suspects have been awaiting trial for two years or longer.[36]

Research conducted in 2002 indicated that over 40 percent of Malawians had been the victim of a crime during the previous year, though most of these involved theft of crops or livestock.[37] While crime remains a problem in Malawi, over the past five years, public security has generally improved, partly due to increased law enforcement efforts.[38]

Section 41 of the constitution maintains that citizens have the right to effective remedy by a court of law or tribunal for acts violating their rights and freedoms. Several institutions, most notably the ombudsman and the MHRC, are tasked with facilitating citizens' access to justice and ability to seek redress for rights violations committed by state authorities. At a time of political stalemate, the ombudsman has remained one of the strongest and best functioning accountability institutions in Malawi,[39] especially with respect to addressing the rights of civil servants. According to a 2007 report, the Office of the Ombudsman opens on average 500–600 cases a year, though limited resources have contributed to a substantial backlog of cases.[40] The MHRC has been the most active institution in examining abuses by police. In recent years, it has undertaken investigations of alleged abuses of power by the administration and state institutions, issuing reports and statements condemnatory of both. However, its impact has been limited because its mandate only includes investigatory powers, without the authority to punish officials. Moreover, it lacks a widespread presence throughout the country. Therefore, access to redress generally remains a serious problem in Malawi.[41]

Despite constitutional and other legal protections, women remain unequal citizens in Malawi and are subject to discrimination and violence. In particular, Malawian society is plagued by severe inequalities in the distribution of educational and economic resources, high levels of domestic abuse, sexual assault and harassment in schools and professional settings, customary practices and laws that allow the dispossession of property when husbands die, and underrepresentation in positions of power at the state.[42] Abusive practices against girls, including forced marriages, the selling of girls to pay off debts, and the secret initiation of girls into their future adult roles through forced sex with older men remain widespread.

The government has taken several steps to address these problems. Notably, under the Mutharika administration, the government has more actively documented progress toward implementation of the UN Convention on the Elimination of All Forms of Discrimination against Women, to which Malawi is a signatory.[43] In addition, in April 2006, the parliament enacted legislation providing a maximum penalty of life imprisonment for perpetrators of domestic violence. Women's rights advocates have since criticized the weak implementation of the law.[44] An official commission on gender-related laws has put forward several other legislative proposals dealing with gender inequities,[45] but actual legislation on these matters has stalled. Among the commission's proposals were a deceased estates bill seeking to repeal discriminatory laws regarding inheritance and a marriage, as well as a divorce and family relations bill seeking to provide equal rights to marriage partners.[46] Women also suffer from limited access to legal resources, a situation exacerbated by the weakness of the Legal Aid Department.[47]

A 2008 study found that 500–1,500 women and children were trafficked within the country each year. Some observers attributed this to penalties being too lenient to significantly deter traffickers. Despite a government program to protect vulnerable children, the U.S. State Department reported in 2009 that there had been no reportable progress on the development of a nationwide, interministerial plan to identify the extent of trafficking and possible policies to effectively address the phenomenon.[48]

Malawi is a multiethnic, diverse society in which nine different ethnic groups comprise most of the population. In terms of religion, Protestants represent approximately 55 percent of the population, with Catholics and Muslims each constituting an estimated 20 percent. The rights of religious and ethnic minorities are generally respected and relations between different groups remain largely amicable. Nonetheless, Muslims have complained about discrimination in state employment. Moreover, during the 2009 election campaign, several government and ruling party figures directed hostile rhetoric toward Muslim organizations and politicians, making derogatory comments about Islam.[49]

Section 13 of the constitution requires the government to provide the disabled with access to public spaces, fair employment opportunities, and full participation in all spheres of society. The Ministry of Social Development and Persons with Disabilities was established in 1998 to take charge of all government matters pertaining to persons with disabilities. The Employment Act of 2000 prohibits discrimination against the disabled in matters of employment. However, Malawi lacks a comprehensive law governing discrimination against persons with disabilities in other spheres. Furthermore, a lack of resources has prevented government from effectively implementing the legal rights granted to the disabled, including access to educational opportunities.[50] Societal attitudes toward the disabled remain problematic.[51]

The government has also undertaken efforts to address the problem of discrimination against people living with HIV/AIDS. The disease is reportedly the leading cause of death among adults in Malawi; almost 1 million people out of a population of 14 million were living with HIV as of the end of 2007.[52] Malawi's state-run broadcaster has been applauded in the region for effectively challenging deeply-held stereotypes about persons with HIV and AIDS.[53] Legislation drafted by the Law Commission specifically prohibits and criminalizes discrimination against persons with HIV. However, other provisions of the law, such as the criminalization of "deliberate or negligent transmission" of the disease, have generated concerns from local and international human rights groups.[54]

Malawi's constitution protects freedom of assembly and association. While the government has generally respected associational rights, it has restricted freedom of assembly. On several occasions in recent years, the government has prevented opposition parties from holding rallies, using military and police personnel to forcibly disband them. In May 2008, police used tear gas and live ammunition to disperse crowds that gathered to support Muluzi when he was arrested on treason charges. Police also halted pro-Muluzi rallies in June and August of that year. In both cases, police eventually relented and allowed the gatherings to take place in the wake of court rulings and threats of legal action by the opposition.[55] Police also blocked civil society marches in 2006 and August 2008.[56]

Workers' rights to organize labor unions are legally protected, with the exception of army personnel and police. Unions are required to register with the Registrar of Trade Unions and registration is normally granted.[57] Although union membership has traditionally been low in Malawi, a 2008 report indicated that both the number of unions and overall union membership have been increasing.[58] While the right to strike is legally enshrined, workers may strike only after settlement procedures have been established and mediation or conciliation efforts have failed; the right of workers in "essential services" to strike is more circumscribed. Some workers who have been involved in strikes have faced government harassment.

RULE OF LAW 4.13

INDEPENDENT JUDICIARY	3.80
PRIMACY OF RULE OF LAW IN CIVIL AND CRIMINAL MATTERS	3.80
ACCOUNTABILITY OF SECURITY FORCES AND MILITARY TO CIVILIAN AUTHORITIES	4.25
PROTECTION OF PROPERTY RIGHTS	4.67

The Supreme Court of Appeal represents the apex of Malawi's court system. Beneath it is the High Court, which stands above lower courts dispersed throughout the country. The president appoints the chief justice on the approval of two-thirds of the National Assembly and other High and Supreme Court justices on the recommendation of the Judicial Service Commission. The latter body includes the chief justice and four other members.

In recent years, the judiciary has played an important role in the political system, distinguishing itself for relative competence and independent decision making. During Mutharika's time in office, the courts have displayed a willingness to render decisions against the executive, at times generating substantial setbacks for the president. For example, in 2006 the High Court, sitting as a Constitutional Court, declared Section 65 constitutional and ruled that the speaker of parliament could declare vacant the seats of legislators who had switched to President Mutharika's party. The Supreme Court later upheld the decision as well.

As the judiciary has undertaken such bold decisions, it has faced increasing harassment and interference from the government, mostly in the form of verbal badgering and threats to individual judges. In 2007, the president and government officials repeatedly criticized the judiciary and accused it of improprieties. The following year, a government minister publicly expressed disapproval of two Supreme Court justices. In August 2007, police raided the home of a High Court judge—allegedly as part of a corruption probe—only hours after he had ruled in favor of the opposition in a key court case. The government also apparently ignored a court injunction when it dispersed an opposition party rally in April 2007.

By law, those accused of crimes have the right to a public trial and are assumed innocent until proven guilty. The law further specifies that defendants have the right to present and challenge evidence and witnesses, the right to appeal, and the right to be represented by an attorney of their choice. If indigent, they are entitled to counsel at the state's expense. The court system, however, faces severe capacity problems that lead to effective denial of timely trials for the accused.[59] The Department of Public Prosecutions in 2008 had 13 prosecuting attorneys, three fewer than in 2007. Retention of government attorneys remains a problem.[60]

The Office of the Director of Public Prosecutions (DPP) holds the power to prosecute all criminal cases in the country. However, the office is severely limited by lack of resources and qualified staff.[61] Moreover, the executive has been accused of interfering with the agency, most notably in 2006 when the then DPP was unconstitutionally removed from office.[62] The position subsequently remained vacant for four months. Concerns have also emerged about the potential for interference from the attorney general, who possesses the authority to direct activities within the DPP.[63]

Constitutionally, the police force is established as an organ independent of the executive and is required to exercise its powers and duties impartially. Moreover, the constitution specifies that the government may not direct the police to serve partisan purposes.[64] Despite these provisions, the press and opposition have accused the Mutharika administration of using the police for political and partisan purposes, such as disrupting opposition rallies and targeting the president's political opponents with harassment and arrests.[65] Critics have also accused Mutharika of dismissing high-ranking officers for political reasons, including the inspector general of police in early 2009.[66]

Although the army has historically restrained itself from the political arena in Malawi, it has become more visibly involved in recent years. In 2008, several high-ranking army officers were among those accused of plotting to overthrow the president. Observers have also raised concerns about the army being used to serve the partisan interests of President Mutharika following a joint army-police operation to break up an opposition rally in 2007.

The government maintains respect for private property. The World Bank reports that Malawi compares favorably with its neighbors in terms of the ease or difficulty of registering property, although it performs relatively poorly on protecting investors and enforcing contracts.[67] In 2002, the government developed a new land policy aimed at providing secure land tenure to citizens, but it had not yet passed legislation to implement such a program as of mid-2009.[68] Some concerns have emerged about land grabs in the wake of increasing external investment, but the problem does not appear that acute to date.

ANTICORRUPTION AND TRANSPARENCY 3.44

ENVIRONMENT TO PROTECT AGAINST CORRUPTION	3.25
PROCEDURES AND SYSTEMS TO ENFORCE ANTICORRUPTION LAWS	3.50
EXISTENCE OF ANTICORRUPTION NORMS, STANDARDS, AND PROTECTIONS	3.50
GOVERNMENTAL TRANSPARENCY	3.50

Corruption has been and remains a serious problem in Malawi. According to one estimate, corruption and related inefficiencies drained an annual 30 percent of government revenue during Muluzi's administration from 1994 to 2004.[69] Social norms are generally accepting of petty corruption, while weak oversight of the bureaucracy and executive branch enable some officials to engage in larger-scale graft. President Mutharika has acknowledged that corruption is widespread in all three branches of government. Despite improvements relative to the previous administration, mechanisms to combat corruption remain weak.

The state remains substantially involved in the economy, with parastatal corporations engaged in sectors such as energy, agriculture, finance, media, and transportation. Several such enterprises have been implicated in corruption-related allegations in recent years. By law, government officials and appointees to senior positions in the public sector are required to declare their assets and disclose financial interests. However, enabling legislation to effectively enforce these rules has yet to be enacted.[70]

The government appeared to make strides in combating corruption during the initial phase of Mutharika's first term. Several senior members of former president Muluzi's administration (including Muluzi himself) have been investigated on corruption-related charges and some were later convicted. In addition, several sitting government and parastatal officials have been arrested and convicted on corruption charges. From 2006 on, the government has worked with donors to improve the capacity of the National Audit Office, leading to improvements in the number and quality of audits conducted.[71] The government reasserted its commitment to anticorruption efforts in 2009 by launching a new National Anti-Corruption Strategy. The program includes a plan to establish "integrity committees" in public institutions.[72]

The primary body charged with a mandate to combat graft is the Anti-Corruption Bureau (ACB), though its authority and capacity are limited and it has faced some political interference. Legislation enacted in 2004 requires the body to obtain the DDP's consent before initiating a prosecution, thereby constraining its power. In terms of personnel, the ACB suffers from high rates of turnover and limited staff. One report indicated that in 2007, the organization had only four lawyers who were tasked with prosecuting hundreds of cases.[73] Personnel decisions made by the government have also undermined the agency's effectiveness and independence. Since Mutharika came into office in 2004, the ACB has had four different directors or acting directors. In August 2006, the president summarily removed the director at the time, rendering the ACB unable to investigate or prosecute existing cases during the second half of the year and ultimately causing a backlog of over 200 new cases and the discontinuation of others.[74] Due to the president's stalemate with parliament, the replacement director was in turn never approved, leaving the office toothless for over a year.

The opposition has charged that corruption-related investigations and prosecution efforts have been selective and used to intimidate and harass Mutharika's opponents. Despite these concerns, progress in indicting former high-level government officials has remained slow. Many cases, including that of former president Muluzi, have been tied up in the courts due to legal challenges of investigation procedures.[75] The opposition has also accused the government of shielding its own officials from corruption investigations.[76]

Both the incidence of corruption in society and allegations against officials are widely discussed in the media. The print media, in particular, has helped promote awareness of the problem and exposed corruption scandals, in several cases leading to investigations and prosecutions.[77] Surveys conducted in 2005 found that 9 out of 10 Malawians view corruption as a serious problem. However, fewer than 20 percent of respondents knew how to report it.[78] Similarly, some observers have criticized whistleblower protection as being inadequate.[79]

Corruption has also affected educational institutions. At a public forum in 2007, teachers and education observers indicated that instructors and administrators took material rewards from students and parents in return for placement and passing grades.[80] In 2007, it was also revealed that the exam for obtaining a secondary school certificate had been leaked and was available for purchase on the black market.

Section 37 of the constitution provides that "subject to any act of Parliament, every person shall have the right to access all information held by the state or any of its organs."[81] Additional legislation to enable full implementation of this provision has not been enacted, however. A bill on access to information has been drafted, specifying these rights and creating mechanisms to enforce them. However, the bill has yet to be tabled before the parliament.[82] Despite the lack of legislation, the U.S. State Department reports that the government has granted both citizens and noncitizens, including foreign media, access to official information on request.[83]

A report from the Open Budget Initiative indicates that Malawi performs poorly with respect to the openness of its budget-making process, providing only minimal information to the public.[84] Part of this likely reflects the tensions between the executive and legislature in recent years over passage of the budget, leading to limited debate on the actual contents of the proposal each year. Nevertheless, under the auspices of a World Bank project designed to improve financial management, transparency, and accountability, improvements in government disclosure and accounting practices have been recorded. According to the report, "personnel audits of all ministries have been completed and an associated review of the payroll system has commenced.... 12 ministries now have effective internal audit committees overseeing about 60 percent of public expenditures."[85] A local NGO focused on monitoring the budget process has also reported that deviations between the approved budget and actual expenditure were less than 10 percent in 2008.[86]

It is widely believed that the Muluzi administration awarded contracts to companies controlled by himself or his allies. Under the Mutharika presidency, concerns about unfair bidding and awarding of contracts remain, albeit to a lesser degree. Officials linked to the executive have been accused of steering contracts to businesses under their control or that of their relatives.[87] In 2007, the government was accused by civil society organizations of hiding information about an agreement with an Australian company seeking to undertake a uranium mining project.[88] Under the Muluzi government, the administration of foreign assistance was often characterized by mismanagement and a lack of transparency.[89] In recent times, conversely, donor agencies have applauded financial management and the implementation of donor-sponsored policies.[90]

RECOMMENDATIONS

- The executive branch should cease interference with the judicial and prosecutorial arms of government and more effectively support the operation of rule of law and accountability institutions through timely and appropriate appointments to key positions.
- The government should more systematically monitor prison conditions and should undertake efforts to improve conditions for prisoners—particularly in terms of nutrition, sanitation, and medical care. If needed, the government should seek international funds toward this end.
- The government should move more forcefully to pass legislation to improve the conditions of women and ensure greater equity in gender relations. Priority should be given to the passage of the Wills and Inheritance Bill.
- Efforts should be undertaken to decrease the influence of the president and minister of information over MACRA, MBC, and TV Malawi. Special

consideration should go to revising the structure of appointments to these bodies and decreasing political bias in programming.
- The government should respect citizens' right to assemble and refrain from using force to disperse peaceful demonstrations and rallies, including those challenging the government's agenda.

NOTES

For URLs and endnote hyperlinks, please visit the *Countries at the Crossroads* homepage at http://freedomhouse.org/template.cfm?page=139&edition=8.

1. World Bank, "Malawi Country Brief," home page, June 2009.
2. United Nations Development Programme (UNDP), "Malawi," in *Human Development Report 2009* (New York: UNDP, 2009).
3. Central Intelligence Agency (CIA), "Malawi Country Profile," in *The World Factbook* (Washington, D.C.: CIA, 2009); "Malawi" Needs to Strengthen Public Financial Management," Afrol News, September 16, 2008; "Malawi 2009 Growth Seen above 7 Percent," *Nyasa Times*, June 10, 2009.
4. Electoral Institute of Southern Africa (EISA), "Malawi: Electoral System," EISA home page; EISA, "Election Update 2004: Malawi," news release, April 28, 2004.
5. European Union Election Observation Mission (EUEOM), "Malawi Presidential and Parliamentary Elections 2009 Preliminary Statement," May 21, 2009; Commonwealth Observer Group, "Interim Statement: Malawi Presidential and Parliamentary Elections," May 21, 2009.
6. Malawi Electoral Commission, "Independent Media Monitoring Unit Report 7: Totals for the 14 Week Period 17 January to 14 April, 2009," May 16, 2009, author copy.
7. EISA, "Malawi: Electoral System."
8. EUEOM, "Malawi Presidential and Parliamentary Elections 2009 Preliminary Statement"; Commonwealth Observer Group, "Interim Statement: Malawi Presidential and Parliamentary Elections."
9. Center for Human Rights and Rehabilitation, *A Broad Appraisal of Three Years of the Mutharika Administration: Whither Malawi?* (Lilongwe: Center for Human Rights and Rehabilitation, May 2007), 12.
10. Diana Cammack et al., "Neopatrimonial Politics, Decentralisation and Local Government: Uganda and Malawi in 2006," Working Paper 2 of Research Project RP-05-GG (Dublin: Advisory Board for Irish Aid, 2007), 1.
11. Ibid.; Center for Human Rights and Rehabilitation, *A Broad Appraisal*.
12. Rebecca Theu, "PAC Bashes Bingu," *Nation*, September 21, 2007.
13. Malawi Human Rights Commission, *2006 Executive Report on Human Rights Accountability in Malawi by the Three Arms of Government* (Lilongwe: Malawi Human Rights Commission, May 2007), 9.
14. Center for Human Rights and Rehabilitation, *A Broad Appraisal*, 13; "No Staff Pay Rise for 4 Years–Ombudsman," *Nation*, February 28, 2009.
15. Center for Human Rights and Rehabilitation, *A Broad Appraisal*, 9.
16. Ibid., 9; "Meet New Civil Service Commission Boss," *Public Ear* (Lilongwe) 1, no. 4, July–September 2008.
17. Center for Human Rights and Rehabilitation, *A Broad Appraisal*, 9.
18. Juliet Chimwaga, "Msaka Snubs PAC," *Nation*, October 6, 2006; Dickson Kashoti, "Govt Fails to Bring to Book Auditor General," *Sunday Times*, October 8, 2006.

[19] "Northern Region Remains Undeveloped," *Nyasa Times*, February 20, 2009; Center for Human Rights and Rehabilitation, *A Broad Appraisal*, 4.

[20] Ollen Mwalubunju, "Civil Society," in *Government and Politics in Malawi*, ed. Nandini Patel and Lars Svasand, (Zomba, Malawi: Kachere Books, 2007), 277; Stanley Khaila and Thomas Lansner, "Malawi," in *Countries at the Crossroads 2006*, ed. Sanja Tatic and Christopher Walker (Lanham, MD: Rowman and Littlefield, 2007), 314.

[21] Mwalubunju, "Civil Society," 277.

[22] Freedom House, "Malawi," in *Freedom of the Press 2009* (New York: Freedom House, 2009).

[23] Levi Zeleza Manda, "Media," in *Government and Politics in Malawi*, 258.

[24] International Research and Exchanges Board, "Malawi: Media Sustainability Index 2006–2007," in *MSI Africa 2006–2007: The Development of Sustainable Media in Africa* (Washington, D.C.: International Research and Exchanges Board, 2007),195.

[25] Sam Banda, "Joy Radio Fails to Cover Muluzi Live," *Daily Times*, April 16, 2007; Committee to Protect Journalists, "Malawi: Private Radio Stations Censored over Political Coverage," press release, April 17, 2007.

[26] Manda, "Media," 257. For an example, see "Malawi Media under Threat," Afrol News, June 13, 2008.

[27] Media Institute of Southern Africa and International Freedom of Expression Exchange, "Official Intimidates Reporter Seeking Information on Police Action," press release, June 9, 2008; Freedom House, "Malawi," in *Freedom of the Press 2008* (New York: Freedom House, April 29, 2008).

[28] "Africa: Malawi," Internet World Stats home page.

[29] See Malawi Human Rights Commission, "Torture Allegations against Police," *Mfulu– The Malawi Human Rights Commission Bulletin: Economic, Social and Cultural Rights in Focus* (July 2006), 5; "Family Sues Malawi Police over Mzuni Police Brutality," *Nyasa Times*, June 24, 2009; "Malawi Police Officer Convicted of Rape, 16 Years IHL," *Nyasa Times*, September 18, 2009.

[30] Amnesty International, "Malawi Human Rights," Our Priorities, home page.

[31] Steven Pembamoyo Banda, " MHRC Speaks on Police Brutality," *Nation*, October 24, 2006; Amnesty International, "Malawi," in *Annual Report 2007* (London: Amnesty International, 2007).

[32] Wanangwa Tembo, "Prison Conditions Irk MPs," *Sunday Times*, January 29, 2008; Amnesty International, "Malawi," in *Amnesty International* Report *2009* (London: Amnesty International, 2009).

[33] Malawi Prison Service, "The Department's Overview," home page.

[34] Josh Ashaz, "Degrading Malawi Prison Conditions Forces SALC to Demand Visit," *Nyasa Times*, October 31, 2007.

[35] "Two Arrested for Discussing Malawi President's Health," *Nyasa Times*, March 26, 2009; "Kamlepo, Makande Arrested on Treason," *Nyasa Times*, March 25, 2009.

[36] The Malawi Human Rights Commission, *Mfulu–The Malawi Human Rights Commission Bulletin: Access to Justice* (May 2006), 6; Ashaz, "Degrading Malawi Prison Conditions Forces SALC to Demand Visit"; Clifford Msiska, "Malawi: Paralegal Advisory Service," in *Democratizing Justice Database* (New York: John Jay College of Criminal Justice, 2007).

[37] Eric Pelser, Patrick Burton, and Lameck Gondwe, *Crimes of Need: Results of the Malawi National Crime Victimisation Survey* (Pretoria, South Africa: Institute for Security Studies, 2007).

[38] Interviews with Malawian civil society activists, May 2009.

39 Siri Gloppen and Fidelis Edge Kanyongolo, "The Judiciary," in *Government and Politics in Malawi*, 131; Global Integrity, "Malawi," in *Global Integrity Report 2007* (Washington, D.C.: Global Integrity, 2007).
40 Bard Andreassen and Thor Oftedal, "The Office of the Ombudsman (OoO) in Malawi: An Appraisal," *Norad Collected Reviews* (May 2007): 4.
41 See Siri Gloppen and Edge Kanyongolo, "Courts and the Poor in Malawi: Economic Marginalization, Vulnerability and the Law," *International Journal of Constitutional Law* 5, no. 2 (April 2007).
42 See especially, Malawi Human Rights Commission, *Mfulu–The Malawi Human Right Commission Bulletin: Promoting Women* (September 2006); See also Malawi Human Rights Commission, *Cultural Practices and Their Impact on the Enjoyment of Human Rights, Particularly the Rights of Women and Children in Malawi* (Lilongwe: Malawi Human Rights Commission, 2006).
43 United Nations Committee on the Elimination of Discrimination against Women, *Sixth Periodic Report of Malawi on the Implementation of the Convention on the Elimination of All Forms of Discrimination against Women* (New York: United Nations, October 20, 2008).
44 Seodi White and Tinyade Kachika, *A List of Critical Issues to the Sixth Periodic Report of Malawi on CEDAW* (Limbe: Women in Law in Southern Africa Research and Education Trust–Malawi, January 26, 2009).
45 Eunice Chipangulu, "Malawi to Adopt the Legislative Quota Based System to Achieve Gender Equality in Politics and Public Life," September 2007, Gender and Media in Southern Africa; See also, Eunice Chipangulu, "Malawi to Address Sexual Harassment through Law Enactment," Gender and Media in Southern Africa.
46 White and Kachika, *A List of Critical Issues to the Sixth Periodic Report of Malawi on CEDAW*.
47 Ibid.
48 Office to Monitor and Combat Trafficking in Persons, "Malawi," in *Trafficking in Persons Report 2009* (Washington, D.C.: U.S. Department of State, June 16, 2009).
49 Emelyn Nyoni, "Malawian Muslims Warn Government," *Nyasa Times*, March 31, 2007.
50 "Fighting for Rights of People with Disabilities in Malawi," VoaNews, October 10, 2007.
51 Emmanuel Muwamba, "Disabled People Regarded as Cure for Aids–Minister," *Nation*, May 8, 2006.
52 Graham Pembrey and Rosalind Johnston, "HIV and AIDS in Malawi," AVERT, October 29, 2009.
53 The Sol Plaatje Institute for Media Leadership, "Malawi and Mauritius Broadcasting Corporations Scoop Landmark SPI–MAP Media Awards," news release, September 12, 2007.
54 Human Rights Watch, "Comments to the Malawi Law Commission on the Development of HIV and AIDS Legislation," news release, June 23, 2008; White and Kachika, *A List of Critical Issues to the Sixth Periodic Report of Malawi on CEDAW*.
55 Josh Ashaz, "Malawi Court Lifts Muluzi Rally Ban," *Nyasa Times*, June 7, 2008.
56 Edwin Nyirongo, "Police, DC Stop Rally on Chitipa Road," *Nation*, May 8, 2006; Bureau of Democracy, Human Rights, and Labor, "Malawi," in *2008 Country Reports on Human Rights Practices* (Washington, D.C.: U.S. Department of State, February 25, 2009).
57 Bureau of Democracy, Human Rights, and Labor, "Malawi," in *2008 Country Reports on Human Rights Practices*.
58 Paliani Chinguwo, "Trade Unionism in Malawi," *Nyasa Times*, April 30, 2008.
59 Malawi Human Rights Commission, *Mfulu–The Malawi Human Rights Commission Bulletin* (May 2006), 9; see also Fidelis Edge Kanyongolo, *Malawi: Justice Sector and the*

Rule of Law: A Discussion Paper (Johannesburg: AfriMAP and Open Society Initiative for Southern Africa, 2006), 25–27.

60. Bureau of Democracy, Human Rights, and Labor, "Malawi," in *2008 Country Reports on Human Rights Practices*; Malawi Human Rights Commission, *2006 Executive Report on Human Rights Accountability in Malawi by the Three Arms of Government*, 20.

61. Malawi Human Rights Commission, *2006 Executive Report on Human Rights Accountability in Malawi by the Three Arms of Government*, 19.

62. Dickson Kashoti, "President Compromising ACB, DPP," *Daily Times*, December 27, 2007.

63. Kanyongolo, "Malawi: Justice Sector and the Rule of Law"; Willie Zingani, "Report Says President Meddles with ACB, DPP," *The Nation*, September 14, 2006.

64. Constitution of the Republic of Malawi, Section 158, subsection 1 and 3.

65. "Police Order Subject of More Confusion," *Nation*, April 12, 2007; Harold Williams, "On Police and Army Roles," *Nation*, April 13, 2007.

66. "Mutharika is Right on Kumbambe," *Nation*, March 19, 2009.

67. World Bank, "Malawi," *Doing Business 2009: Comparing Regulation in 181 Economies* (Washington, D.C.: World Bank, 2009).

68. Centre for Environmental Policy and Advocacy, *Land and Agrarian Reform in Malawi–Challenges and Possible Responses* (Blantyre: Centre for Environmental Policy and Advocacy, September 2007).

69. "Bravo for Acknowledging Graft," *Nation*, February 16, 2008.

70. "Everyone Should Fight Corruption," *Nation*, February 6, 2008.

71. USAID, *Annual Progress Report No. 6: Strengthening Government Integrity to Support Malawian Efforts to Roll Back Corruption and Encourage Fiscal Responsibility* (Washington, D.C.: USAID, October 30, 2007).

72. Republic of Malawi, "National Anti-Corruption Strategy," January 23, 2009.

73. Dingiswayo Madise, "Challenges in the Fight against Corruption in Malawi: Some Thoughts" (paper presented at UNECA Meeting on Deepening the Judiciary's Effectiveness in Combating Corruption, Addis Ababa, Ethiopia, November 19–23 2007).

74. Bureau of Democracy, Human Rights, and Labor, "Malawi," in *2006 Country Reports on Human Rights Practices* (Washington, D.C.: U.S. Department of State, March 6, 2007).

75. Madise, "Some Thoughts."

76. Anthony Kasunda, "Bingu Reinstates Katopola," *Nation*, February 11, 2008; "UDF Press Statement," March 30, 2007.

77. Mustafa Hussein, "Combating Corruption in Malawi: An Assessment of the Enforcing Mechanisms," *African Security Review* 14, no. 4 (December 1, 2005): 5.

78. World Bank, *Malawi Governance and Corruption Baseline Survey* (Washington, D.C.: World Bank, February 2006), 20, 34.

79. Hussein, "Combating Corruption in Malawi: An Assessment of the Enforcing Mechanisms"; see also David Booth et al., "Drivers of Change and Development in Malawi," Working Paper 261 (London: Overseas Development Institute, January 2006), 33.

80. Sam Banda, "Poor Pay Corrupts Teachers," *Daily Times*, October 22, 2007.

81. Constitution of the Republic of Malawi, Section 37.

82. Kelvin Sentala, "Access to Information Legislation in Malawi" (paper presented at the African Network for Constitutional Lawyers Symposium on Access to Information, University of Cape Town, June 17–18, 2008).

83. Bureau of Democracy, Human Rights, and Labor, "Malawi" in *2008 Country Reports on Human Rights Practices*.

84. Open Budget Initiative, "Malawi," in *Open Budget Index 2008* (Washington, D.C.: Open Budget Initiative, 2008).

[85] World Bank Operations Policy and Country Services, "Malawi," in *Status of Projects Under Execution–FY-08* (Washington, D.C.: World Bank, October 11, 2008).
[86] Interview with Malawi Economic Justice Network, Lilongwe, May 2009.
[87] Thom Chiumia, "Malawi Clerk of Parliament in Corruption Scandal," *Nyasa Times*, December 4, 2007; Tom Likambale, "UDF Held Successful Central Region Convention," Malawi News Service, December 7, 2007.
[88] Center for Human Rights and Rehabilitation, *A Broad Appraisal*, 10.
[89] World Bank, *Malawi Public Expenditures: Issues and Options, Report No 22440 MAI* (Washington, D.C.: World Bank, September 2001); U.K. Department for International Development, *Evaluation of General Budget Support: Malawi Summary* (Glasgow: U.K. Department for International Development, May 2006).
[90] See Crown Agents, "Assessing Public Financial Management Reform in Malawi," home page; International Monetary Fund (IMF), *IMF Country Report No. 09/16* (Washington, D.C.: IMF, January 2009).

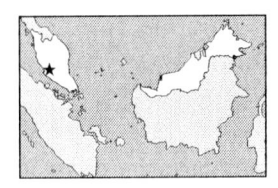

MALAYSIA

CAPITAL: Kuala Lumpur
POPULATION: 28.3 million
GNI PER CAPITA (PPP): $13,740

SCORES	2006	2010
ACCOUNTABILITY AND PUBLIC VOICE:	3.00	3.15
CIVIL LIBERTIES:	3.00	2.88
RULE OF LAW:	4.12	3.84
ANTICORRUPTION AND TRANSPARENCY:	3.00	2.94

(scores are based on a scale of 0 to 7, with 0 representing weakest and 7 representing strongest performance)

WILLIAM CASE

INTRODUCTION

Malaysia's ethnically diverse population of 25 million consists of ethnic Malays (60 percent), Chinese (25 percent), Indians (8 percent), and a great variety of smaller groupings, most of them based in Sabah and Sarawak states on the island of Borneo. Much of this diversity evolved during British colonial rule, when laborers were recruited from China and India to work in mining and plantation agriculture. In preparing the territory for independence in 1957, the British fashioned a formally democratic polity and a largely capitalist economy. But the Malays, regarded as the indigenous community, gained sway over the party system and state bureaucracy through the United Malays National Organization (UMNO). Meanwhile, foreign investors and local Chinese dominated the economy.

As urbanization accelerated during the 1960s, Malays gravitated to the cities, where they witnessed the comparative prosperity of the non-Malay groups. At the same time, many non-Malays were alienated by the restrictions they faced in obtaining public sector benefits. Voters in both communities swung to opposition parties in the May 1969 general elections, leaving the UMNO-led coalition—which included the Malaysian Chinese Association (MCA) and the Malaysian Indian Congress (MIC)—gravely weakened. Shortly afterward,

---

William Case is a professor in the Department of Asian and International Studies and director of the Southeast Asia Research Center (SEARC) at City University of Hong Kong. He has held teaching or visiting research positions at the University of Malaya, National University of Malaysia, MARA University of Technology in Shah Alam, Malaysia, the Centre for Strategic and International Studies in Jakarta, and the Institute of Asian Studies at Chulalongkorn University in Bangkok. His most recent book is *Contemporary Authoritarianism in Southeast Asia*.

Malays and Chinese clashed in the streets of the capital, Kuala Lumpur, sparking ethnic rioting known locally as the May 13th incident. Two years of emergency rule followed, during which elections were suspended and Parliament was closed.

Parliament was reopened in 1971, but UMNO imposed new curbs on civil liberties. Most notably, in seeking to reenergize its ethnic constituency, the party passed a sedition law that banned any questioning of Malays' "special rights." UMNO also limited electoral competitiveness, absorbing most opposition parties into its coalition, renamed the National Front (Barisan Nasional, or BN), and greatly elevating its own standing within this formation. Once it had tightened its grip on state power by establishing what is sometimes described as an "electoral authoritarian" regime,[1] UMNO was free to introduce its New Economic Policy (NEP), a comprehensive affirmative action program whose quotas on public and private sector hiring, state contracts and licensing, and even business ownership were geared toward "uplifting" the Malays.

UMNO's dominance of politics and deep economic intervention led to a range of political abuses, corrupt practices, and social inequities. Prime Minister Mahathir Mohamad (1981–2003) oversaw rapid economic growth, which gradually eased citizens' grievances. By the mid-1990s, Mahathir was able to relax his government's pro-Malay posture, declaring a Vision 2020 program based on national unity and full development. However, the financial crisis of 1998, followed by the arrest and imprisonment of Mahathir's popular deputy, Anwar Ibrahim, triggered a sharp upsurge in public discontent. Civil society began to display new vigor, and two key opposition parties, the Islamic Party of Malaysia (PAS) and the largely ethnic Chinese Democratic Action Party (DAP), found new grounds for cooperation. The BN clung to power in the 1999 general elections, thanks in part to the government's electoral manipulations, but it was dealt a serious blow as large numbers of Malays supported PAS and the non-Malays reaffirmed their earlier swing to the DAP.

Malaysia's economy had recovered significantly by the end of 2003, and Mahathir was succeeded by his deputy, Abdullah Ahmad Badawi. Exercising a less authoritarian leadership style, Abdullah tried to introduce reforms. The judiciary seemed to signal more independence by releasing Anwar from prison, though it did not fully exonerate him of corruption charges. Media self-censorship and coercion were still present, but controls over communication and assembly were less rigidly enforced. And efforts were made early on to strengthen the rule of law, but these were generally stymied. Probably the most outstanding feature of Abdullah's tenure was an increase in electoral competition that culminated in the March 2008 general elections, in which the UMNO-led coalition lost its two-thirds majority in the lower house of Parliament for the first time since 1969.

Suspicions between PAS and the DAP persisted, with the latter fearing that the PAS had a hidden Islamist agenda, but the mediation of Anwar's People's Justice Party (PKR) allowed the three parties to forge electoral agreements. The opposition coalition was able to appeal to devout Muslims in rural areas; progressive Malays in the cities; and non-Malays alienated by UMNO "arrogance," threats to religious freedom, and a weakening economy. These constituencies had also been disillusioned by the fact that Abdullah's efforts to curb corruption had been thwarted by politicians within UMNO. After the elections, collaboration between the PAS, the DAP, and the PKR was formalized as the People's Pact (Pakatan Rakyat).

UMNO blamed Abdullah for its electoral losses, and as the economy began to slow, he was pressed to resign as UMNO leader and prime minister. He ultimately stepped down in April 2009 and was succeeded by his deputy, Najib Razak. At the same time, authoritarian controls were gradually reimposed, with a number of opposition and civil society leaders arrested, the licenses of several newspapers suspended, and destabilizing pressures aimed at the state governments captured by opposition parties in the recent elections. As of mid-2009, it appeared that the UMNO-led government was trying vigorously to return Malaysia to its former system of electoral authoritarianism.

ACCOUNTABILITY AND PUBLIC VOICE 3.15

FREE AND FAIR ELECTORAL LAWS AND ELECTIONS	3.25
EFFECTIVE AND ACCOUNTABLE GOVERNMENT	3.25
CIVIC ENGAGEMENT AND CIVIC MONITORING	3.67
MEDIA INDEPENDENCE AND FREEDOM OF EXPRESSION	2.43

General elections are held regularly in Malaysia, as specified in the constitution. The elected prime minister wields state power, the voting is inclusive, there is contestation by multiple parties, and vote counting and reporting are carried out promptly. However, there are a number of distortions that favor incumbents. The campaign period is kept brief, usually less than two weeks. Public rallies during electoral campaigns were banned in 1978. The Election Commission announced in 2003 that it would lift the ban, but still requires organizers to obtain police permits. Opposition candidates receive little access to mainstream media outlets. And while limits on campaign contributions and spending are formally codified, the government mostly ignores them with impunity.[2] Furthermore, electoral rolls are frequently manipulated, and until recently the ballots contained numbered counterfoils, potentially undermining voting secrecy. Counting centers in sparsely populated areas are small, allowing local political preferences to be discerned. Opposition parties are not permitted to oversee the counting of postal ballots cast by members of the military and police, nor do they have equal access to polling station data. The Election Commission itself is appointed by the government and cannot be regarded as impartial. Municipal- and district-level elections have been suspended since the mid-1960s.

Parliament consists of the 70-seat Senate, with 44 members appointed by the monarch and 2 each chosen by the 13 state assemblies for up to two three-year terms, and the more powerful House of Representatives, with 222 popularly elected members serving five-year terms. The lower house's first-past-the-post electoral system based on single-member districts magnifies the thin margins that the government sometimes obtains. The redrawing of constituency boundaries, last organized by the Election Commission in 2003,[3] is also manipulated to strengthen the ruling coalition. However, in the most recent elections, this strategy lost effectiveness in the ethnically "mixed" constituencies where the government has usually fared best. Typically, while opposition parties can gain significant numbers of parliamentary seats and capture some state-level assemblies outright, they have little prospect of winning enough seats to replace the federal government. They are especially hampered in the large and sparsely populated states of Sabah and Sarawak, where the BN has relied on local strongmen and patronage politics turning principally on timber concessions.

The opposition overcame such hurdles to make unprecedented gains in the March 2008 elections. In the 2004 vote, the BN had won 198 of 219 seats in the lower house of Parliament (90.4 percent), while the opposition parties together won a mere 21 (9.6 percent). In 2008, the government took just 140 of 222 seats (63 percent), losing its long-standing two-thirds majority, which had allowed it to unilaterally amend the constitution. The opposition parties won a total of 82 seats (37 percent), and in the state elections they captured four state assemblies while retaining a fifth. This impressive showing was characterized by DAP leader Lim Kit Siang as a "political tsunami."[4] Anwar's ban on holding public office, which stemmed from his corruption conviction, expired a few months after the balloting, and his wife stepped down from her Parliament seat so that he could replace her in a by-election. Anwar returned to Parliament in August, and because the PKR had won the most seats among the opposition parties, he was promptly made opposition leader.

While Parliament has since grown more active and the BN can no longer alter the charter on its own, the body remains subservient to the executive. Almost all legislation is initiated by the government. Only a few ministers typically attend parliamentary sessions during question time. Lacking support and information, opposition legislators are unable to impose much accountability on the government or seriously investigate the bureaucracy, which remains tightly fused with UMNO. Though the government claims to hire and promote civil servants based on merit, this is severely compromised by ethnic quotas that heavily favor Malays. The government also dominates the judiciary, ensuring favorable rulings in most politically important cases.

Prior to the 2008 general elections, probably the most significant by-election during Abdullah's tenure was conducted in May 2007 in the Selangor state assembly constituency of Ijok. The government's candidate, a local politician, was challenged by a prominent corporate executive nominated by the PKR. However, the government showered the constituency with road-paving, mosque-building, drain-clearing, and land-titling projects, helping its candidate to victory. As the minister of works at the time observed, "Ijok got 10 years of projects in 10 days."[5] After the general elections, parties in the opposition People's Pact won a string of parliamentary and state assembly by-elections throughout 2008. However, in several of the states it controlled, most notably Perak and Selangor, its members came under extraordinary pressure from the courts and anticorruption agencies (see below).

The constitution guarantees freedom of association. While nongovernmental organizations (NGOs) must register with the state under the Societies Act, the requirements are not usually onerous, and a reasonably vigorous civil society has emerged in urban areas. Still, restrictions are imposed in the interest of "security and public order." Amendments to the Police Act of 1967 require that a permit be obtained 14 days before any political meeting of more than three persons. In these circumstances, freedom of assembly is unevenly protected. The government often works with NGOs that it regards as helpful in solving problems involving government and consumer issues, but it ignores or undermines groups that are committed to stronger advocacy and systemic reforms. In 2007, leaders of the Hindu Rights Action Force (HINDRAF), a social movement seeking to overcome the marginalization of Malaysia's ethnic Indian community, were arrested under the Internal Security Act (ISA) (see below). In Abdullah's final parliamentary session as prime minister in 2008, the University and University Colleges Act (UUCA) was amended, with Section 15(1) permitting students to participate in "general organizations, so long as they have approval from the higher education minister and university administrators." Students remain barred from joining political parties.

Article 10 of the constitution guarantees the right of free expression. Article 149, however, enables Parliament to restrict expression when it believes the national interest to be threatened. The most important piece of such legislation is the Printing Press and Publications Act, requiring all print media to obtain annual licenses from the Internal Security Ministry. If the ministry finds that an outlet has maliciously published what is deemed to be false news, it may revoke or refuse to renew its license. The publisher can also face charges that carry fines and prison terms.

Other laws also restrict press freedom, including the Sedition Act, the Official Secrets Act (OSA), the Control of Imported Publications Act (which enables the government to ban foreign publications when they are viewed as prejudicial to national security or public morality), and the Broadcast Act (which empowers the minister of information to monitor radio and television broadcasts and to revoke licenses). These laws encourage widespread self-censorship within the mainstream media, skewing political reporting. Partly because of this relatively tame media environment, there have been no recent reports of physical attacks by the government on print journalists. Several bloggers, however, have been arrested under the ISA (see below).

A government-controlled news agency, Bernama, has exclusive rights to distribute economic data, news photographs, and other material through the print media. Moreover, nearly all major newspapers—whether Malay, Chinese, or English language—and all broadcast outlets are owned either by the government or by companies linked to BN parties. During the premiership of Mahathir, the government and allied businesspeople resorted to libel suits in response to critical analysis, especially by the international press. No such cases have occurred in recent years, however, owing to both self-censorship and the political liberalization that characterized Abdullah's tenure.

Abdullah acquiesced to at least light media coverage of "sensitive issues" like race and religion and was seen to have tolerated greater public dialogue on human rights.[6] Even so, he kept restrictive legislation in place. When the police forcefully dispersed a fuel-price protest mounted at Kuala Lumpur's landmark Petronas Twin Towers in May 2006, the event went unreported by mainstream media. In July 2007, after then deputy prime minister Najib stirred ethnic suspicions by underscoring Mahathir's earlier declaration that Malaysia was an "Islamic state," the Internal Security Ministry banned any reporting of his remarks.

As opposition parties continued to win by-elections in 2008, UMNO politicians, engaging in uncharacteristic introspection, began to canvass reforms. These included easing the requirements for the annual licensing of print media, the restrictions on student participation in politics, and the conditions under which dissidents were detained under the ISA. Liberalizing measures followed, at least for a brief period. In April 2008, the government reversed an earlier decision and renewed the publishing permit of the Tamil-language newspaper *Makkal Osai*, which during the general election campaign had helped to mobilize the Indian community. The government also granted a permit to *Suara Keadilan*, a paper associated with the PKR. In early 2009, however, the licenses of two newspapers, *Harakah* and *Suara Rakayt*, associated with the PAS and PKR, respectively, were suspended for three months. No official reason was given, but the suspension came just as UMNO was preparing to hold its internal elections, which were set to be followed by more by-elections. During the same period, mainstream newspapers aligned with UMNO sharpened their communalist rhetoric.[7]

Historically, Chinese-language newspapers have been freer in Malaysia, with aggressive reporting on ethnic and cultural issues, though restrictions on them have ebbed and flowed based on political conditions. In April 2008, the relative diversity of Chinese-language content seemed to come under threat when timber and media mogul Tiong Hiew King merged a number of his holding companies, bringing together Malaysia's four largest Chinese newspapers. A spokesman for the new company, Media Chinese International Limited, pledged that the papers would remain editorially independent, while Tiong said the merger was aimed at achieving "greater corporate synergy."[8]

In recent years, internet communication has grown rapidly in Malaysia. It has also been far freer than traditional media, supporting a vast array of websites and blogs operated by opposition parties, NGOs, and dissidents. Though the government has occasionally raided the offices and seized the computers of alternative news sites like *Malaysiakini* or arrested critical bloggers, it has mainly honored its pledge to refrain from web censorship. Relatively unrestricted internet communication is thought to have contributed greatly to the opposition's electoral gains in 2008.

Even so, in 2007, PKR information chief Tian Chua was placed under investigation for a blog post that was said to have violated the Communications and Multimedia Act. He had posted a photo montage depicting Najib dining with his political adviser Abdul Razak Baginda and a Mongolian woman who was slain in Malaysia in a much-publicized case (see Rule of Law). Later in the year, PKR webmaster Nathan Tan was held by the Cyber Crime Unit under the Official Secrets Act for using his blog to republish allegations against the deputy internal security minister, Johari Baharum.[9] The arrest reportedly reverberated through the blogging community,[10] and several days later, Johari instructed the Police Commercial Crime Investigation Department to trace bloggers who spread lies that risked "tarnishing the image of the country."[11] In September 2008, an opposition lawmaker, a journalist, and a prominent blogger were arrested under the ISA. Though all three were released, the blogger—Raja Petra Kamarudin, founder of the highly popular *Malaysia Today*—was rearrested and charged under the Sedition Act. And in August 2009, the government finally began to canvass the introduction of internet filters in the country, apparently modeled on China's Green Dam technology.

CIVIL LIBERTIES 2.88

PROTECTION FROM STATE TERROR, UNJUSTIFIED IMPRISONMENT, AND TORTURE	2.50
GENDER EQUITY	3.67
RIGHTS OF ETHNIC, RELIGIOUS, AND OTHER DISTINCT GROUPS	1.75
FREEDOM OF CONSCIENCE AND BELIEF	3.00
FREEDOM OF ASSOCIATION AND ASSEMBLY	3.50

Malaysian law prohibits arbitrary arrest. However, the ISA and the Emergency (Public Order and Prevention of Crime) Ordinance of 1969 empower the minister of internal security and the police to detain people indefinitely without trial if reasonable suspicion is deemed to exist. The Dangerous Drugs (Special Preventive Measures) Act of 1985 has been amended in ways that also permit preventive detention by the police, though only for 39 days. The ISA, in place since 1960, is used primarily against opposition politicians, dissidents, alleged terrorists, and criminals whose activities are deemed to affect national security. Detainees are held in undisclosed places, remain uninformed about the reasons for their arrest, and are denied access to legal counsel and family visits. After an initial 60-day period of interrogation, the minister of internal security may issue a two-year detention order, under which detainees are generally transferred to a central facility in Kamunting, Perak state. In late 2008, the minister stated in Parliament that there were currently 46 ISA detainees, but the local advocacy group Abolish ISA Movement claimed there were 66, most of them suspected associates of the regional terrorist organization Jemaah Islamiah. The latest documented case of abuse in ISA custody involved an automotive repair shop owner, Sanjeev Kumar Krishnan, who was detained under the ISA in March 2008 for "spying." According to a sworn affidavit, he was so mistreated during interrogation that he was left partially paralyzed. There are no documented instances of the government killing political opponents.

Police have invoked the Emergency Ordinance (EO) in criminal cases, enabling them to detain local gangsters and drug lords for an initial 60-day investigation period without a remand order. The minister of internal security can then order two-year periods of detention in a centralized facility at Simpang Renggam in Johor state. Alternatively, he can impose limits on their movement under the Restricted Residence Act. Statistics vary, but in mid-2007 over 1,000 people appeared to be held under the EO. An additional 1,500 people were estimated to be held under the Dangerous Drugs Act. According to some estimates, 60 percent of the detainees at Simpang Renggam were ethnic Indian, while 20 percent were aged 21 or below.[12] Ill-treatment of ordinary criminals detained under the EO and Dangerous Drug Act has increased the already high numbers of deaths in police custody in Malaysia. According to the Internal Security Ministry, there were 1,535 such deaths between 2003 and 2007, the last period for which data are available.[13] Early in Abdullah's premiership, there appeared to be some improvement, but conditions later worsened, with brutality against the Indian community seeming to increase after the formation of HINDRAF. One much-publicized case involved the death in custody of Kugan Ananthan in early 2009. The police hampered subsequent investigations, raiding medical offices and seizing autopsy records.[14]

Since the social dislocation brought about by the Asian financial crisis of the late 1990s, crime levels have been rising steadily in Malaysia. By regional standards, Malaysia's police appear to be reasonably organized, and they have been successful in containing terrorist activities. But their effectiveness is limited by low salaries and endemic corruption. The police are frequently alleged to be providing protection for drug trafficking, prostitution, and loan sharking. Malaysia is a comparatively minor source for human trafficking, but it has become a significant destination for forced laborers and sex workers from throughout Southeast Asia, particularly Burma, as well as from China. Government officials have periodically been accused of involvement in trafficking, though prosecutions have been rare. In 2005, officials in the National Registration Department were arrested for providing traffickers with permanent-resident identity cards.

In 2007, Malaysia was classified as a Tier 3 country in the U.S. State Department's Trafficking in Persons Report for failing to meet minimum standards of enforcement. In 2008, noting reductions in human trafficking, Malaysia was reclassified as a Tier 2 country, though it was downgraded to Tier 3 again in 2009. However, recent government mobilizations of civilian paramilitary groups, particularly the Malaysian People's Volunteer Association (RELA), to supplement law enforcement have drawn much criticism from human rights organizations. RELA, a poorly trained force of some 400,000 members, has frequently been associated with serious abuses against illegal migrants.

Victims of abuse seeking redress may file a complaint with Suhakam, a human rights commission set up by the government in 1999, which has on occasion investigated restrictions placed on civil society organizations, arbitrary detention, and deaths in custody. However, because Suhakam is housed in the Prime Minister's Department, it lacks independence in its reporting and transparency in its recruitment procedures. Even such recommendations as it has offered have generally been ignored by government agencies.

Women's issues have received some attention in recent years. After taking office as prime minister in April 2009, Najib appointed 10 women as ministers or deputy ministers. Women also held top positions elsewhere in the state apparatus. Zeti Akhtar Aziz is governor of the central bank, while Siti Norma Yaakob served as chief judge of Malaya, one of the country's four top judicial positions, during 2005–07. Still, while women are nominated as electoral candidates by UMNO and its main coalition partner, the MCA, their share of candidacies in these parties remains quite small, especially at the state level. Even the Islamic opposition party PAS has proportionately more female members of Parliament. In UMNO's internal elections in March 2009, 50 candidates contested posts in the party's powerful Supreme Council, six of whom were women. Women typically hold less than 10 percent of the seats in Parliament.

Although the constitution's recently amended Article 8(2) appears to protect women's interests in economic life, the government's overall responsiveness to women's concerns—often forcefully articulated by a few small but prominent women's organizations—has been inconsistent. By UN standards, the Sharia (Islamic law) courts have discriminated grossly against women, especially in family law cases. After passage of a new Islamic Family Law in 2005 that strengthened the prerogatives of men with respect to polygamy and divorce, Marina Mahathir, a social activist and daughter of the former prime minister, argued that Malaysia was alone among Muslim countries in taking away rather than increasing women's rights.[15] Malaysia has ratified the UN Convention on the Elimination of All Forms of Discrimination against Women (CEDAW). It also features a reasonably high-profile Ministry of Women's Affairs. However, traditional attitudes often prevail in private life, irrespective of ethnicity, with married women expected to serve primarily as mothers and homemakers. When encouraged to work, they are frequently made to surrender their earnings to their spouses.

Malaysian politics have long been dominated by leaders of the Malay community. The constitution grants Malays "special rights," made manifest in the NEP's ethnic quotas in public sector employment, state contracts, credit, business licensing, corporate employment, equity ownership, and university placement. A National Culture Policy has also privileged Malay ethnicity through symbols of state and national identity. Non-Malays harbor resentments over their "second-class" citizenship, and historically many have reacted by emigrating.

Over the past 15 years, the NEP has been replaced by less-stringent programs. However, Abdullah's early pledges to be "a prime minister for all Malaysians" soon gave way to perceptions that he was yielding to communalist sentiments, and both political leaders and media outlets grew noticeably more strident. At the UMNO general assembly meeting in late 2007, the party youth leader and minister of education, Hishammudin Hussein, heralded a "Malay agenda" by raising a *keris*, a ceremonial dagger and potent symbol of Malay dominance. This action was condoned by Abdullah, who said "the keris is a weapon, but it is a weapon to protect yourself and your friends."[16] The non-Malay community reacted by voting in large numbers against the BN in 2008. Consequently, after succeeding Abdullah as prime minister in March 2009, Najib took tentative steps to scale back some of the quotas associated with the NEP. Most notably, the administrative services recruited a large number of ethnic Indians.

Among the signifiers of Malay identity is an adherence to Islam, giving the faith a dominant role among the country's religions. While followers of Christianity, Hinduism, Buddhism, and Sikhism are permitted to practice their faiths, they are barred from proselytizing among Muslims, and their attempts to build places of worship encounter bureaucratic obstruction. During Abdullah's tenure, Chinese and Indians complained of "creeping Islamization," with the government heavily favoring the religion through state institutions. This trend, which began during the 1970s, has advanced most in the judiciary. Within the country's dual court structure, civil courts have steadily ceded jurisdiction to Sharia courts, especially over family and personal affairs. In a high-profile case, the Federal Court refused an application made in May 2007 by Lina Joy to remove her Muslim status from her national identity card in acknowledgment of her conversion to Christianity. The court ruled that jurisdiction remained with the Sharia courts, which have denounced apostasy as a crime punishable by imprisonment, a fine, and forced rehabilitation. In a few other recent cases, they have determined that deceased persons had converted secretly to Islam and then seized the bodies for burial according to Muslim rites.

A coalition of non-Malay groups formed in 2006 under the name Article 11, the constitutional provision that guarantees religious freedoms. When the group attempted to hold a meeting in Penang to discuss the formation of an interfaith commission, it was confronted by some 500 protesters who had organized as the Anti-Inter-Faith Commission Body. The meeting was then banned by police, and Abdullah warned the group to cease its mobilizing activities. Mohamed Nazri Abdul Aziz, a minister in the Prime Minister's Department, threatened to charge those who "insulted" Islam under the Sedition Act. At the

UMNO general assembly in late 2006, Hishamuddin Hussein explicitly ruled out proposals to form an interfaith commission.

In July 2007, the police readily granted permits to NGOs seeking to demonstrate against a visit by U.S. Secretary of State Condoleezza Rice. In November, however, the police refused an application from BERSIH (Coalition for Clean and Fair Elections), a coalition of 67 NGOs and opposition parties, citing the risk of disorder. The police warned of "harsh action" and closed major arteries leading to downtown Kuala Lumpur. In a press conference, Abdullah denounced the BERSIH rally, arguing that the constitutional right to assembly must be superseded by the people's "right to peace."[17] The group was also denounced as "crooks" (*penyangak*) by Nazri.[18] However, the movement's leaders pressed ahead, leading some 40,000 demonstrators in presenting their petition on clean elections to the king.[19] They dispersed immediately afterward, though, as the police presence mounted.

Not long after the BERSIH rally, HINDRAF an unregistered coalition of 30 organizations, led a rally of some 30,000 ethnic Indians in Kuala Lumpur. Spurred initially by the government's demolition of several Hindu temples to make way for development projects, HINDRAF raised broader Indian grievances over ethnic and religious discrimination. The protest was violently suppressed by the police, and five of its leaders were detained under the ISA in December 2007.[20] Abdullah had warned beforehand that he would use the ISA to preserve "the prevailing peace and harmony."[21] In October 2008, HINDRAF was banned as a national security threat. However, Najib ordered the release of the HINDRAF leaders after becoming prime minister, and the ban on the organization was lifted. One HINDRAF leader, P. Uthayakumar, then announced the formation of a new, ostensibly multiethnic political vehicle, the Human Rights Party.

Trade unions are permitted to form, with the Malaysian Trades Union Congress (MTUC) serving as an umbrella organization representing some 500,000 workers. However, only in-house unions can normally be organized in the country's vital free-trade zones. Strike actions are tightly regulated and street protests are prohibited. In 2007, in response to large pay raises for civil servants in May, the MTUC widened a campaign it had been pursuing for some eight years in favor of a minimum wage of approximately RM 900 (US$260) per month. Human Resources Minister Fong Chan Onn rejected this, arguing that it would accelerate undocumented immigration.

An estimated two million registered and five million undocumented migrant workers together make up 30 to 50 percent of Malaysia's labor force.[22] Many are recruited as domestic helpers, who are frequently reported to suffer abuse by their employers. Malaysia has not ratified the International Covenant on Civil and Political Rights, the International Covenant on Economic, Social, and Cultural Rights, or the UN Convention against Torture. Migrants, trafficked persons, and asylum seekers are thus afforded little official protection. As noted previously, RELA's growing role in enforcing immigration laws has worsened abuses. The Immigration Act permits arrested migrants to be held for 14 days before being a presented to magistrate. Migrants may be held indefinitely in Lenggeng Immigration Detention Center, where authorities have punished them with whipping and forcible repatriation.

RULE OF LAW   3.84
INDEPENDENT JUDICIARY	3.00
PRIMACY OF RULE OF LAW IN CIVIL AND CRIMINAL MATTERS	4.20
ACCOUNTABILITY OF SECURITY FORCES AND MILITARY TO CIVILIAN AUTHORITIES	3.50
PROTECTION OF PROPERTY RIGHTS	4.67

Malaysia possesses a large judicial apparatus that appears sophisticated in its formal structure and functioning. Malaysia's superior courts consist of the Federal Court, which is the final court of appeal and the highest judicial authority in the land, the Court of Appeal, the High Court of Malaya, and the High Court of Sabah and Sarawak. The Federal Court's membership includes the chief justice, the president of the Court of Appeal, and the two chief judges of the High Courts, along with four additional Federal Court judges. The superior courts supervise all subordinate courts. In ordinary criminal cases, citizens receive a reasonably fair and public hearing by an independent and impartial tribunal established by law. Prosecutors in these cases are apparently independent of political control,[23] and an assumption of innocence prevails. Indigent suspects can qualify for free legal aid through the Legal Aid Center, operated by the Malaysian Bar Council, or through the initiatives of individual lawyers. The government, through the Legal Aid Bureau, also provides assistance for civil cases. However, before suspects appear in court, they are often interrogated harshly by police, leading to forced confessions and some deaths in custody (see Civil Liberties). The Attorney General's Chambers, which is not obliged to state publicly its reasons for commencing or terminating cases, seems to be dominated by the executive. There is no judicial review of legislation.

In 2006, the Bar Council tested the judiciary's independence under Abdullah, calling for a review of the 1988 crisis in which the lord president and two justices of what was then known as the Supreme Court were ousted under Mahathir. The proposal was rejected by the cabinet. In a notorious case in July 2007, Abdul Razak Baginda, a security adviser to Najib in the latter's role as defense minister, was accused of complicity in the murder of his former mistress, Altantuya Shaariibuu of Mongolia. Observers were struck by the arbitrary character of procedures in the case. Immigration records of Altantuya's entry into Malaysia were erased. The presiding judge, the head of the prosecution team, and defense lawyers were all changed without explanation. Large amounts of evidence were ruled inadmissible. After a lengthy trial, Abdul Razak was acquitted, and two members of the elite Special Action Squad—which provides security to top officials, including Najib—were convicted of carrying out the murder. The outcome added to suspicions that the case had been manipulated to protect powerful individuals and their dealings involving defense contracts.

In September 2007, Anwar released clips from an extraordinary video recording of a 2002 telephone conversation between a senior lawyer, V. K. Lingam, and the chief justice of the Federal Court, Ahmad Fairuz. The two apparently brokered high-level judicial promotions and court rulings, a revelation that precipitated a protest march by hundreds of lawyers on the Palace of Justice in Putrajaya and demands for an investigation. A Royal Commission and Panel of Inquiry was duly formed, but it failed to produce substantial results. Fairuz then slipped from view, and his contract was not renewed.

While Anwar prepared for his by-election in 2008, he was formally charged for the second time with sexual misconduct, which carried a penalty of up to 20 years in prison. This was the clearest indicator to date that the partial independence secured by the judiciary under Abdullah had given way once again to partisan aims. In April 2009, Anwar remained free on bail pending trial. In the few cases where the courts have ruled against the government, for example by accepting habeas corpus arguments by ISA detainees, the police have swiftly re-arrested the defendants. Adverse rulings have also been followed by legislative changes designed to narrow the courts' jurisdiction or discretion.

A more recent case of politicization of the rule of law involved a battle for control of the state government of Perak, where the People's Pact had won the 2008 elections. In late January 2009, then deputy prime minister Najib took over as Perak chairman of the BN and the UMNO liaison committee. In early February, three assemblymen from the People's Pact were induced to defect, causing the PAS-led government to lose its majority. The defectors were reported to have been threatened with corruption investigations. The sultan of Perak then dismissed the sitting government so that UMNO could form a new one under Zambry Abdul Kadir. The hereditary ruler also refused to dissolve the assembly and allow a new election. This precipitated a constitutional crisis, an occupation of the state assembly, mass demonstrations, and numerous arrests. In a flash of independence, the Kuala Lumpur High Court ruled in May that the UMNO takeover was illegal, restoring the People's Pact government to power. But days later, the Court of Appeal granted a stay of that ruling, leaving Zambry in office.

The partisanship appears to be accelerating under the current chief justice, Zaki Tun Azmi. A former legal adviser to UMNO and chairman of the party's disciplinary committee, he has risen with unprecedented speed, becoming a Federal Court judge in September 2007, president of the Court of Appeal three months later, and then chief justice in October 2008. An audio recording released in February 2009 by a DAP member of Parliament purports to feature

Zaki admitting that he had frequently bribed court officials while practicing as a lawyer.[24]

Judicial appointments have been skewed by constitutional requirements that they be made by the king on the advice of the prime minister, drawing criticism from Suhakam and the Malaysian Bar Council for a lack of fairness and transparency. In late 2008, Abdullah introduced a bill creating a Judicial Appointments Commission (JAC) as part of his "integrity agenda," but the panel was empowered only to make recommendations on appointments to the prime minister, who would not be obliged to accept them. The bill was passed over the objections of the opposition.

The security forces of Malaysia, unlike many of their counterparts in the region, remain subordinate to civilian authorities. However, in September 2008 the head of the armed forces publicly called on the government to suppress those who stoked ethnic and religious rivalries.[25] The police force has also grown more assertive. The government has long used the police for political purposes, deploying the Special Branch, the Federal Reserve Unit, and the Police Field Force to gather information on dissidents and suppress opposition activities.[26] This has given the police the power to turn back proposed reforms, and they are widely seen as corrupt and inefficient. Shortly after coming to power in 2003, Abdullah had agreed to set up a Royal Police Commission, tasked with developing a complaints mechanism for civilians. The body recommended the formation of an Independent Police Complaints and Misconduct Commission (IPCMC), whose proposed powers of investigation and prosecution were unexpectedly strong. It would be able to investigate, prosecute, and ultimately demote or discharge individual officers. However, the police threatened in an internal web posting to shift their political loyalties to PAS, leading Abdullah's government in 2007 to propose a much weaker body, provisionally titled the Special Complaints Commission (SCC). The plan came under swift attack from opposition lawmakers, former royal commissioners, and human rights groups, and the government withdrew it. In June 2009, legislation creating a slightly stronger body, the Enforcement Agencies Integrity Commission (EAIC) was passed in Parliament, though it was still derided by observers for falling short of the original IPCMC proposal. Notably, the EAIC was empowered only to investigate and make recommendations to the Attorney General's Chambers rather than prosecute independently. Moreover, its broad scope, encompassing 21 agencies, shifted scrutiny away from the police. Anwar stated plainly that the EAIC was designed to "protect Malay police officers."[27]

Private property is reasonably well protected for most citizens. Ordinary commercial contracts and bankruptcy laws are enforced, while bank loans and state contracts are usually only rescinded as an outcome of high-level political conflicts. Malaysia is ranked well above the Philippines and Indonesia (though below Singapore and alongside Thailand) on a key property rights index.[28] However, under the NEP, 30 percent quotas in employment and equity ownership have systematically favored the Malays. In addition, though comprehensive statutes protecting intellectual property rights are in place, they are unevenly enforced, and pirated products are readily available throughout Malaysia. Similarly, legislation protecting the traditional landowning rights of indigenous people is frequently ignored by state governments and allied oil companies, logging firms, and plantation developers, especially in East Malaysia. As of 2009, some 100 land rights cases were pending in court. In May, however, the Federal Court ruled for the first time that indigenous people whose ancestral lands have been seized are entitled to compensation.

ANTICORRUPTION AND TRANSPARENCY   2.94

ENVIRONMENT TO PROTECT AGAINST CORRUPTION	3.25
PROCEDURES AND SYSTEMS TO ENFORCE ANTICORRUPTION LAWS	3.25
EXISTENCE OF ANTICORRUPTION NORMS, STANDARDS, AND PROTECTIONS	2.25
GOVERNMENTAL TRANSPARENCY	3.00

Much of the opacity and corruption in Malaysia can be attributed to UMNO's tireless quest for patronage and the bureaucracy's commitments to business promotion and reverse discrimination. As resources are often allocated politically rather than by markets, a tight nexus has developed between government and business.[29] After coming to power in 2003, Abdullah confronted resentments among those excluded from this system, calling for "people power" to curb corruption, especially in reputedly graft-ridden agencies dealing with immigration, customs, transport, and defense. Still, investigations for bribery have rarely extended to the upper reaches of the bureaucracy and security apparatus.

Abdullah introduced a Malaysian Institute of Public Ethics, backed by a National Integrity Plan. Government lawmakers were required to declare their assets, and greater independence for the Anti-Corruption Agency (ACA) was proposed. A number of top officials were charged under anticorruption laws, while Abdullah announced that an additional 18 "high-profile" cases would be prosecuted. And in September 2008, Malaysia ratified the UN Convention against Corruption. However, actual gains during Abdullah's tenure were modest. Malaysia's score on Transparency International's Corruption Perceptions Index remained between 5.0 and 5.2 on a scale of 1 to 10, with 10 being least corrupt, between 2004 and 2008.[30] Progress began to slow immediately after the government was comfortably reelected in October 2004. UMNO's powerful Youth Wing took two years to agree to start writing an action plan for implementing the National Integrity Plan, and lawmakers were given deferments in reporting their assets. The most prominent person tried for corruption, the former director of the state-owned steel company, was acquitted in June 2007, with the presiding judge criticizing the prosecution for a shoddy performance in which it failed even to call material witnesses.[31]

Malaysia has an Auditor General's Office and a Public Complaints Bureau, but these agencies are regarded as neither effective nor nonpartisan.[32] By contrast, the parliamentary Public Accounts Committee, under the chairmanship of an independent-minded government lawmaker and a deputy chair recruited from the opposition, succeeded during Abdullah's tenure in scrutinizing government expenditures more closely.

The ACA arrests many lower-level officials but has long been regarded as partisan. Indeed, the body has itself been a font of corrupt practices. In 2007, the advocacy group Gerak disclosed reports by a retired ACA officer in Sabah on the agency's national director, Zulkipli Mat Noor. In the reports, Zulkipli was shown to have acquired property far beyond that listed in his asset declarations. That July, however, he was cleared by the attorney general. Allegations that Deputy Internal Security Minister Mohd Johari Baharaum and the inspector general of police, Musa Hassan, had been bribed to arrange the early release of criminal kingpins were similarly dismissed by the Attorney General's Chambers and the ACA, respectively.[33]

In April 2007, Abdullah responded to parliamentary questioning over the failure of the "high-profile" investigations to produce indictments, attributing the problem to witnesses who had either "disappeared or [were] unable to be located." He also claimed that the "success rate" of indictments in lesser cases heard in the High Court and Sessions Court were 74.1 percent and 86.1 percent, respectively.[34] Meanwhile, Abdullah's own family members were accused of pursuing state largesse. Scomi Group, an oil and gas company in which Abdullah's son, Kamaluddin Abdullah Badawi, is the largest shareholder, has received highly lucrative government contracts. Kamaluddin's personal net worth has been estimated to be US$90 million.[35] Abdullah's son-in-law, Khairy Jamaluddin, was involved with several investment companies linked to the government while serving as deputy leader of UMNO's Youth Wing. These links are indicative of a pattern in which state contracts are awarded as patronage rather than by open tender.[36]

In December 2008, Abdullah introduced a bill that replaced the ACA with the Malaysian Anti-Corruption Commission (MACC). The new agency was ostensibly modeled on Hong Kong's Independent Commission Against Corruption (ICAC) and was to be accountable to five administrative panels, but it could only recommend cases to the Attorney General's Chambers, which would still report in turn to the prime minister rather than to Parliament.[37] During the first months of 2009, the commission recommended the prosecution of a number of government and opposition politicians. The most notable investigation involved tourism minister Azalina Othman Said, under investigation for "money politics." However, fears of partisan prosecution seemed to be confirmed in February, when the MACC targeted the new People's Pact chief minister of Selangor state for alleged improprieties in servicing his personal car and distributing cattle to his constituents for the celebration of Hari Raya.

Ultimately, virtually all of the executive council members of the People's Pact government in Selangor came under investigation. In July 2009, Teoh Beng Hock, an aide to one of the DAP state executive councilors, was summoned for late night interrogation. He was found dead the next afternoon, his body sprawled on a rooftop nine floors beneath the MACC headquarters. The public outcry that followed led Prime Minister Najib to agree to an inquiry into the MACC's procedures.

The work of anticorruption bodies is rarely taken up by mainstream print and electronic media outlets, all of which are either owned by or aligned with the government (see Accountability and Public Voice). Whistleblowers, anticorruption activists, and investigators who seek to present government documents as evidence of corruption risk severe penalties under the OSA. Attempts by opposition politicians to meet with top officers in the anticorruption agency are usually rebuffed.

Most of the government's many websites offer little substantive information, and there is no freedom of information law on the books. Transparency is further weakened by the annual budget process, in which the government submits a document whose great length and complexity is beyond the capacity of the under resourced opposition to scrutinize properly. In addition, significant amounts of government revenue and expenditure remain off budget. For example, Petronas, the national oil company, is housed within the Prime Minister's Department, leaving it almost entirely unaccountable to Parliament.

RECOMMENDATIONS

- The government should begin the process of ensuring that members of the Election Commission are independent from the executive branch and ruling party.
- The Printing Presses and Publication Act, the Official Secrets Act, and the Sedition Act should be abolished in order to encourage greater media scrutiny of the government and business dealings. The government should ease licensing requirements for independent print and broadcast media outlets.
- The Internal Security Act should be repealed, and amendments to the Police Act and the University and University Colleges Act that circumscribe freedom of expression and assembly should be changed, allowing greater scope for peaceful advocacy and dissent.
- The proposed Enforcement Agency Integrity Commission should address the police force specifically and should be given powers to investigate independently, including the circumstances surrounding the large number of reported deaths in custody.
- The Sharia court system should be encouraged to make rulings that avoid gender discrimination, with their jurisdiction circumscribed if basic rights cannot be protected.

NOTES

For URLs and endnote hyperlinks, please visit the *Countries at the Crossroads* homepage at http://freedomhouse.org/template.cfm?page=139&edition=8.

[1] See Andreas Schedler, ed., *Electoral Authoritarianism: The Dynamics of Unfree Competition* (Boulder, Colo.: Lynne Rienner, 2006).
[2] See Mavis Putucheary and Noraini Othman, eds., *Elections and Democracy in Malaysia* (Bangi, Malaysia: Penerbit UKM, 2005).
[3] Lim Hong Hai, "New Rules and Constituencies for New Challenges?" *Aliran Monthly* 23, no. 6 (2003).
[4] Lim Kit Siang, "Political Tsunami in General Election," *Kit Siang for Malaysia*, March 8, 2009.
[5] K. Kabilan, "10 Reasons Why Parthiban Won," *Malaysiakini*, May 1, 2007.
[6] Ioannis Gatsiounis, "Malaysia Moving Backward on Human Rights," *Asia Times*, July 20, 2006.
[7] "Kuala Penentu Melayu Hilang Jika Terus Berpecah," Utusan Online, April 4, 2009.
[8] "Malaysian Tycoon Launches Chinese-language Media Powerhouse," *China View*, April 30, 2008.
[9] "PKR Webmaster Released on Bail," *Malaysiakini*, July 17, 2007.
[10] Baradan Kuppusamy, "Malaysia Jails the Messenger," *Asia Times*, July 19, 2007.
[11] "Johari Ordered Cops to Trace Website Authors," *Malaysiakini*, July 14, 2007.
[12] Andrew Ong, "Youths Held without Trial in Simpang Renggam," *Malaysiakini*, February 27, 2007.
[13] Thomas Fuller, "Malaysian Arrests Put in Question Vow of Rights," *New York Times*, August 3, 2009.
[14] David K. L. Quek, "Kugan's Case: Unsettling Questions Remain," *Malaysiakini*, April 9, 2009.
[15] Ioannis Gatsiounis, "Malaysia Moving Backward on Human Rights," *Asia Times*, July 20, 2006.
[16] "PM Defends Keris at UMNO Assembly," *Malaysiakini*, November 7, 2007.
[17] Fauwaz Abdul Aziz and Chua Sue-ann, "Bersih to Proceed, Appeals to the Police," *Malaysiakini*, November 8, 2007.
[18] Yoges Palaniappan, "'Gathering of Crooks' Hasn't Tainted Community's Image," *Malaysiakini*, November 27, 2007.
[19] Lee Hock Guan, "Malaysia in 2007: Abdullah Administration under Siege," in *Southeast Asian Affairs 2008*, ed. Daljit Sing and Tin Maung Maung Than (Singapore: Institute of Southeast Asian Studies, 2008), 198.
[20] Bilveer Singh, "Malaysia in 2008: The Elections that Broke the Tiger's Back," *Asian Survey* 49, no. 1 (2009): 158.
[21] "PM Threatens to Use ISA against Protesters," *Malaysiakini*, November 28, 2007.
[22] Federation Internationale des Ligues des Droits de L'Homme (FIDH) and Suara Rakyat Malaysia (SUARAM), *Undocumented Migrants and Refugees in Malaysia: Raids, Detention and Discrimination* (Paris/Selangor: FIDH and SUARAM, 2008).
[23] International Commission of Jurists Legal Resource Center, "Malaysia–International Legal Community Denounces Government Interference in the Rule of Law in Malaysia," news release, April 5, 2000.
[24] "Karpal Claims He Has Audio Recording of What CJ Said," *Sun2Surf*, November 18, 2008.

[25] "Armed Forces Chief Speaks Up," *Straits Times* (Singapore), September 10, 2008, cited in Singh, "Malaysia in 2008."
[26] Harold Crouch, *Government and Society in Malaysia* (Ithaca, N.Y.: Cornell University Press, 1996), 137.
[27] S. Pathmawathy, "IPCMC Scrapped to Please 'Malay Police Officers,'" *Malaysiakini*, June 29, 2009.
[28] See Property Rights rankings in Heritage Foundation and *Wall Street Journal* (WSJ), *2009 Index of Economic Freedom* (Washington, D.C./New York: Heritage Foundation and WSJ, 2009).
[29] The best account remains Edmund Terence Gomez and K. S. Jomo, *Malaysia's Political Economy: Politics, Patronage, and Profits* (Melbourne: Cambridge University Press, 1999).
[30] See Transparency International's *Corruption Perceptions Index* for each of these years at http://www.transparency.org/policy_research/surveys_indices/cpi.
[31] "Eric Chia Acquitted," *Malaysiakini*, June 26, 2007.
[32] Noore Alam Siddiquee, "Paradoxes of Public Accountability in Malaysia: Control Mechanisms and Their Limitations," *International Public Management Review* 7, no. 2 (2006): 43–64.
[33] Kuek Ser Kuang Keng and Soon Li Tsin, "AG Faulted for Clearing Zulkipli," *Malaysiakini*, July 30, 2007.
[34] Bede Hong, "PM: 18 VVIP Graft Cases Hit Brickwall," *Malaysiakini*, April 4, 2007.
[35] Ioannis Gatsiounis, "Anti-Graft War Backfires in Malaysia," *Asia Times*, March 21, 2007.
[36] Ibid.
[37] "MACC Bill Passed," *Malaysiakini*, December 16, 2008.

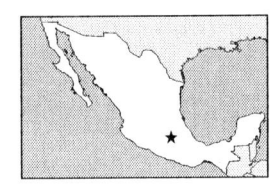

MEXICO

CAPITAL: Mexico City
POPULATION: 109.6 million
GNI PER CAPITA (PPP): $14,270

SCORES	2006	2010
ACCOUNTABILITY AND PUBLIC VOICE:	N/A	5.00
CIVIL LIBERTIES:	N/A	4.52
RULE OF LAW:	N/A	3.93
ANTICORRUPTION AND TRANSPARENCY:	N/A	3.85

(scores are based on a scale of 0 to 7, with 0 representing weakest and 7 representing strongest performance)

Francisco E. González[1]

INTRODUCTION

At the turn of the 21st century, a broad sense of optimism about Mexico's future prevailed at home and abroad. Free elections in 2000 led to a peaceful transfer of power from the centrist Institutional Revolutionary Party (PRI), which had ruled for 71 years, to the rightist National Action Party (PAN). Along with the leftist Party of the Democratic Revolution (PRD), these parties formed the main elements of a competitive, multiparty democracy. The 2000 election also marked the first presidential turnover that did not take place amid economic turmoil, as had been the case in 1976, 1982, 1987–88, and 1994–95. Mexico seemed to have successfully completed a "dual transition" from authoritarian to democratic rule and from a relatively closed economy to one that was open and integrated with the United States and Canada through the North American Free Trade Agreement (NAFTA).[2]

A decade later, as Mexico prepares to celebrate in 2010 the bicentenary of the start of its war of independence against Spain and the centenary of its pioneering social revolution, it is a tragic coincidence that the country finds itself in the midst of a new conflict.[3] President Felipe Calderón declared war against the country's fearsome drug cartels shortly after coming to office in December

---

Francisco E. González is the Riordan Roett Associate Professor of Latin American Studies at Johns Hopkins University SAIS in Washington, D.C. He is the author of the book *Dual Transitions from Authoritarian Rule: Institutionalized Regimes in Chile and Mexico, 1970–2000* (Johns Hopkins University Press, 2008) and is currently finishing a book titled *Economic Shocks and Democracy from the Great Depression to the Great Recession: Evidence and Lessons from Latin America*. González holds master's and doctoral degrees in politics from the University of Oxford.

2006. As the cartels' main business has been squeezed since the launch of operations, which to date have involved more than 45,000 military and police personnel, they have aggressively diversified their business interests into kidnapping, human smuggling, and extortion on a grand scale: in practice, the war on drugs has become a war against organized crime.[4] As of August 2009, more than 13,000 individuals had been killed in gang-related violence during the Calderón administration, with an accelerating toll in 2008 and 2009. While the violence has not rolled back Mexico's "dual transition" advances, conditions on the ground have deteriorated, making the exercise of basic civil liberties more difficult. The rule of law remains a far-fetched ideal despite the good intentions of political leaders and a solid track record of legislative reforms. Other pillars of good governance, such as transparency and the fight against corruption, are in a similar bind.

Standardization and enforcement of the law is complicated by Mexico's federal system. The country consists of 31 states plus the capital city federal district (DF) and close to 2,500 municipalities. Mexico is also the 11th largest country in the world by population (with 108 million inhabitants in 2009), and its diverse ethnic composition includes a sizable indigenous population (around 15 percent of the total), a majority made up of *mestizos* (or mixed indigenous-white), and a small white minority stemming from 20th-century European immigration.

Another factor behind the country's democratic governance deficit is the legacy of authoritarian rule, particularly the lingering culture of high-level graft and the persistence of private and public monopolies in the economy. A handful of private companies dominate the telecommunications and broadcast media sectors, for example, while the public sector features a state-owned oil monopoly and powerful, ossified trade unions. These influences continue to skew the political playing field and help perpetuate socioeconomic inequality, which has receded in recent years but remains very high and, crucially, strongly politicized.[5] The politicization of inequality is a function of a divided but strident left-wing politics, which finds an echo in the abysmal disparity of living conditions among Mexicans. The right, which through the PAN has been in power since 2000, has been incapable of dampening such anxiety because under its stewardship, Mexico's economy has grown very slowly. Moreover, the country's integration with the American economy means that since the U.S.-centered 2008 global bust the country has been hammered—the economy is expected to decline by 6.5 percent or more in 2009, a fall even more precipitous than the country's last economic collapse in 1994–95. The economy, while open to international commerce, remains extraordinarily concentrated in its main sectors, and the PAN governments have been unwilling or incapable of injecting competition into what remains an economy characterized by both low productivity and high operating costs.

ACCOUNTABILITY AND PUBLIC VOICE 5.00

FREE AND FAIR ELECTORAL LAWS AND ELECTIONS	5.50
EFFECTIVE AND ACCOUNTABLE GOVERNMENT	4.25
CIVIC ENGAGEMENT AND CIVIC MONITORING	5.67
MEDIA INDEPENDENCE AND FREEDOM OF EXPRESSION	4.57

Increasingly competitive elections were the backbone of the transition to democracy in Mexico, prompting some scholars to call it a "voted transition." Successive electoral negotiations, particularly between 1989 and 1996, increased opposition parties' victories at the local, state, and federal levels and eroded PRI hegemony.[6] The role of the Federal Electoral Institute (IFE), established in 1990 to manage and oversee elections, was particularly important. Although it was initially controlled by the federal government, it gained full independence in 1996, becoming an organization that was staffed by professionals and led by *consejeros ciudadanos* (citizen counselors) rather than politicians. However, given that the lower chamber of Congress is in charge of appointing the counselors, the composition of the IFE's nine-member General Council has tended to reflect the balance of power in that chamber. The judicial branch was brought into the electoral arena with the creation of the Electoral Tribunal of the Federal Judiciary (TEPJF) in 1996. Seven magistrates preside over the tribunal, and their impartiality has generally been praised by leaders across the political spectrum, with some complaints regarding the adjudication of fines for violations of campaign finance norms.

The federal government provides all parties with generous public financing. In 2008, for example, the IFE provided a total of US$250 million, 30 percent of which was distributed equally among the eight parties represented in the bicameral Congress, regardless of the size of their delegations. In the Congress of 2006–09, the PAN held 207 Chamber of Deputies seats and 52 Senate seats, the PRD held 127 and 26, and the PRI held 106 and 33. Smaller parties and independents accounted for the remainder. While the even distribution of this 30 percent enhanced the equality of campaigning opportunities, the rest of the financing was allocated according to each party's representation in the 300 directly elected Chamber of Deputies seats (the other 200 seats in the 500-seat lower house are filled through proportional representation). This part of the formula naturally benefited the largest parties.[7]

The opportunity for regular rotation of power among different parties is well established at the federal level, but the left denounced foul play in the 1988 and 2006 presidential elections. The blatant nature of 1988's fraud eventually served to strengthen Mexico's democratic movement. Conversely, the refusal in 2006 of PRD candidate Andrés Manuel López Obrador and his allies to recognize Calderón's victory, and the months of protest that followed, weakened the left, while also deepening its suspicions that, absent a landslide victory, powerful business and political forces would act aggressively to prevent a transfer of power.

At the subnational level, there are a handful of states, such as Chihuahua and Nuevo León, where power has shifted over time from the PRI to the PAN and then back to the PRI, suggesting that such alternation has become increasingly part of the routine of democratic politics. On the other hand, in at least 13 of the 31 states, the PRI remains undefeated in gubernatorial elections. In some of these cases the traditional image of powerful *caciques* (local political bosses) remains an everyday reality. The same applies at the municipal level, where the three main parties have developed political machines with solid voting clienteles. More often than not, the PAN and the PRD, which had long criticized the PRI's patronage and clientelism while they were in opposition, have replicated this style of politics once in power.

Regulations to prevent the undue influence of economically privileged interests became one of the main points of contention after the July 2006 presidential election, which was decided by less than 0.5 percent of some 42 million ballots.[8] Legal uncertainty over campaign finance rules allowed dominant economic groups to provide a last-minute wave of financial support to PAN candidate Calderón, which fueled a media offensive against the fiery populist López Obrador in the run-up to election day. The media onslaught allowed Calderón to close a gap in voter support that stood at about 10 percentage points 90 days before the vote.

Once in office, President Calderón accommodated PRD and PRI calls for electoral reform legislation, which was enacted in November 2007. In an effort to create a more level playing field, the reform "cut the length of presidential campaigns almost by half [to just three months prior to election day], gave the IFE power to regulate party primaries, cut public funding to political parties, and banned all political advertising outside of officially arranged time slots."[9] It did not lift the ban on independent candidates for federal races, a change some have called for in order to shake up what is viewed as Mexico's *partidocracia* (rule by the leaders of political parties).

The new regulations faced their first test with the midterm elections of July 2009 and appear to have functioned largely as intended, despite some grumbling and complaints of cheating. In the balloting, the ruling PAN and the PRD suffered crushing defeats (the PAN won 147 seats, losing 59; the PRD won 72 seats, losing 51; and four smaller parties—the Green Party, Labor Party, New Alliance Party, and Convergence—won 40 seats). The PRI, in a spectacular comeback in Congress, will have 241 seats in the lower chamber, a net gain of 135 seats. The PRI also won five of six governorships in dispute, making it the early favorite to win the 2012 presidential elections. A movement arose during the campaign urging voters to show their displeasure with the political class by casting a null vote, but less than 6 percent of voters did so.

The three branches of government counterbalance one another significantly, increasing effectiveness and accountability. The most important change since the mid-1990s has been the weakening of the previously "imperial" presidency and the associated rise of the legislative and judicial branches. The Mexican presidency lacks the decree powers, "fast-track" authority, and other legislative prerogatives found in many other Latin American presidential systems.[10] The rival parties have been at loggerheads over highly politicized issues such as pensions, fiscal policy, energy, and labor law, but even in these areas mild reforms—which do not address Mexico's underlying economic problems—have been successfully implemented under President Calderón. The chances of further structural reforms decreased significantly given the PAN's defeat in the 2009 midterm elections.

Freedom of political choice varies according to locality. Whereas in the aggregate Mexico comes across as a proper electoral democracy with free and fair elections, growing concern surrounds the political influence of criminal groups. Estimates in September 2008 suggested that 8 percent of Mexico's roughly 2,500 municipalities were under the "total" control of drug traffickers, while they exercised "some" control in close to 60 percent of all local governments.[11] The current fear is that organized criminals' financial clout and capacity to carry out threats could have provided them with the means to clandestinely impose candidates for the 2009 elections.

The Professional Civil Service Law creates a framework that encourages employment and promotion based on open competition and merit. However, it applies only to the federal government, and even there, it focuses on senior and mid-level officials.[12] Most positions in the federal, state, and local bureaucracies are up for grabs whenever there is a change in government.

Civic engagement and monitoring have grown gradually in Mexico since the late 1980s. As political power has shifted from the presidency toward Congress, advocacy and lobbying have become lucrative, full-time, professional occupations. Such activities have a substantial influence on government policy and pending legislation. While legal impediments to registration are minimal, the absence of laws and regulations on lobbying tends to favor the efforts of big firms with abundant financial and technical resources, as opposed to nonprofit advocacy organizations, and the establishment of normative lobbying practices is undermined by the ban on reelection in Congress. Deputies serve three years and senators six, after which they have to step down, and their accumulated experience in dealing with pressure groups goes with them.[13] Meanwhile, because state and local governments are more driven by patronage and clientelistic practices than officials at the federal level, they are less inclined to foster the transparency that civic organizations need to engage in effective oversight. Most nongovernmental organizations (NGOs) are able to carry out their work vigorously, but NGO workers in some regions, particularly in southern rural zones, are at times subject to threats and intimidation (see Civil Liberties).

Full legal protections for freedom of expression have existed on paper since the years of PRI rule, but in practice the proper exercise of this right developed very gradually. In its hegemonic heyday the PRI exerted its influence by withholding state advertising from publications and broadcasters that engaged in political dissent. In some cases the authorities would resort to intimidation or coercion. The decline of PRI hegemony, particularly during the 1990s, allowed the emergence of an environment that was more conducive to media freedom. This process has been bolstered by the growing role of the internet, which is not hindered by the state. In April 2008, President Calderón signed a law that decriminalized defamation and "insults" and obliged state governments to follow suit. However, as of July 2009 defamation was still criminalized in 21 of 32 states.[14]

Although the media is often vibrant, the expansion of media freedom remains territorially uneven. Some state and municipal governments burden critical media outlets with frequent audits, threats to revoke licenses, or direct intimidation. However, the single greatest threat to media independence and freedom of expression in Mexico is organized crime's growing capacity to menace the owners of print and broadcast media, and to kill—in some cases after sadistic torture—journalists who cover organized crime and law enforcement. At the end of 2008, the World Association of Newspapers (WAN) reported that 23 journalists had been killed since 2000, and seven others had disappeared since 2005. The organization said that made Mexico more dangerous for the media than any country in the Americas. WAN noted that none of the perpetrators of journalists' murders since the start of the war against organized crime have been brought to justice.[15] This impunity has encouraged self-censorship in violent regions, and many newspapers in these areas no longer publish bylines on stories about organized crime. In an emblematic case, TV Azteca reporter Gamaliel López and cameraman Gerardo Paredes vanished in May 2007 in the northeastern state of Nuevo León. López had reported for six months on the local presence of the army and had exposed corruption. A different but also troubling dynamic applies in the southern state of Oaxaca, where Indymedia cameraman Brad Will, a U.S. citizen, was killed during unrest in late 2006. *El Tiempo* reporter Misael Sánchez Sarmiento, who investigated Will's death, was shot and wounded by a gunman in June 2007. Preliminary investigations as well as recommendations by the Mexican National Commission for Human Rights (CNDH) indicate that fundamental principles of legality and judicial security have been severely violated in the processing of Will's case. In 2009, those responsible for Will's death remained at large.[16]

Given the centrality of elections in Mexico's young democracy, control over media content during campaigns has been the focus of acute conflict. As noted, the uneven use of the media in the run-up to the 2006 presidential election was so obvious that Calderón, after taking office, quickly supported opposition demands for a new electoral reform. Media conglomerates considered the 2007 reform draconian because it banned political advertising outside of officially arranged time slots, but public opinion strongly favored such limits. Estimates suggest that 80 percent of the US$324 million that parties spent in the 2006 federal elections went to the private media. This use of public money was especially egregious given that the television market is essentially a duopoly dominated by Televisa (7 in 10 Mexicans get their news from its outlets) and TV Azteca (which accounts for 2 of the remaining 3). Radio broadcasting is also concentrated, although 13 different private groups participate nationally.[17] Televisa, which wields great financial and political clout and maintains a dominant position as shaper of Mexican public opinion, is one of Mexico's most powerful actors and is the subject of intense political debate and controversy. One illustrative incident pitted the media conglomerate against well-known journalist Carmen Aristégui, who argued that her December 2007 exit from a popular radio show she conducted on W Radio (a station part-owned by Televisa), was politically motivated. She also alleged that Televisa underreports stories adverse to State of Mexico governor Enrique Peña Nieto, the early PRI front-runner for the 2012 presidential race, a charge strongly denied by Televisa.

CIVIL LIBERTIES 4.52

PROTECTION FROM STATE TERROR, UNJUSTIFIED IMPRISONMENT, AND TORTURE	3.00
GENDER EQUITY	4.00
RIGHTS OF ETHNIC, RELIGIOUS, AND OTHER DISTINCT GROUPS	4.25
FREEDOM OF CONSCIENCE AND BELIEF	6.33
FREEDOM OF ASSOCIATION AND ASSEMBLY	5.00

Although subsequent to the democratic transition Mexico adopted almost every international human rights treaty, institutional inefficiencies have limited its ability to implement such agreements and address abuses. For example, there is little effective protection against torture and other physical violence by officers of the state, and impunity is rampant. The National Agreement on Security, Justice, and Legality—signed in August 2008—is the latest step to establish a foundation for acceptable behavior and procedures within the police force. The agreement includes plans for a system that would enable citizens to file complaints against law enforcement officers for misconduct. Implementation will likely be difficult, particularly for municipal and state governments, whose officers are most often in contact with the public. The recent use of the military to combat drug-related violence also poses a problem, as soldiers are not trained for law enforcement duties and fall under the jurisdiction of military courts, which are much less open to public scrutiny than civil courts.[18] As Human Rights Watch reports, "While engaging in law enforcement activities, Mexico's armed forces have committed serious human rights violations, including enforced disappearances, killings, torture, rapes, and arbitrary detentions."[19]

Under Calderon's administration, the armed forces have been increasingly relied on. The number of military and police forces deployed has reached 45,000.[20]

Mexico's prisons are seriously troubled by overcrowding, except for maximum security facilities, which nevertheless suffer from corruption and inadequate staffing. The system was designed to cope with 168,000 inmates, but the total prison population had reached 222,671 as of September 2008.[21] The Calderón administration has announced plans to construct a series of new prisons, while an overhaul associated with the National Public Security Program of 1997 was created to reduce crowding by dealing with backlogged cases and adjusting sentences.[22] With prisons overcrowded and understaffed, internal violence is pervasive. For example, a series of three riots in facilities in the border cities of Reynosa, Ciudád Juárez, and Tijuana between September 2008 and March 2009 left at least 60 dead.[23] Furthermore, top organized crime leaders like Osiel Cárdenas and Joaquín "El Chapo" Guzmán, the latter of whom performed a cinematic prison escape in 2001, have kept control of their criminal organizations from their prison cells. Jailbreaks such as one in May 2009 that freed 53 members of the feared paramilitary group Los Zetas have exposed collusion between jail authorities and organized criminals.[24]

Amnesty International has reported that human rights defenders and other social activists face significant threats in Mexico, particularly at the local level.[25] According to the Mexico office of the UN High Commissioner for Human Rights, 128 human rights defenders were subject to aggression—including 10 cases of murder—in the country between 2006 and August 2009. Guerrero, Oaxaca, and Chihuahua were most affected by threats and violent attack, and impunity reigned in 98.5 percent of the cases.[26] The UN Human Rights Council noted in early 2009 that people involved in demonstrations and social movements are sometimes jailed, citing at least 60 cases of criminalization of public protest in 17 states.[27]

Moreover, social leaders are put in prolonged detention based on false criminal charges that are often politically motivated. The UN Committee against Torture has expressed concern regarding the prevalence of arbitrary detention and long-term detention without trial in Mexico.[28] In addition, in January 2009 the government established new laws to combat organized crime that contemplate *arraigo*, or detention prior to charges, for up to 80 days in some cases.

Organized crime has become arguably the most critical and pervasive governance problem in Mexico. It is closely associated with drug-related violence, which has grown exponentially since 2003–04, along with extortion, kidnappings, and the trafficking of arms, humans, cash, and drugs across the U.S. border.[29] The *LA Times* reports that there were 9,903 drug-related deaths from January 1, 2007 to May 29, 2009, with the 2008 tally double that of 2007, and a further substantial rise in 2009 all but assured as of August.[30] Killings and violence are concentrated in the states of Chihuahua, Durango, Baja California Norte, and Sinaloa, and crimes have escalated in severity. Though much of the violence seems targeted, during the September 2008 independence celebration in Morelia, the capital of Michoacán, 7 people were killed and 100 wounded by a grenade tossed into a crowd. Immediately connected to the drug violence, the event was considered an act of terrorism.[31]

Despite deployment of the army and a spate of legal initiatives, the state has thus far proven incapable of guaranteeing basic security for Mexican citizens when it comes to organized crime. Indeed, organized criminals have also targeted prominent members of Mexico's law enforcement establishment. In May 2008, gunmen ambushed Edgar Millán Gómez, the acting chief of Mexico's federal police, in a brazen attack as he entered a supposedly secure apartment. The assassination was widely interpreted as retribution for the arrest Alfredo Beltrán Leyva, one of the leaders of the Beltrán Leyva cartel, an offshoot of the Sinaloa cartel.[32] In February 2009 gangsters kidnapped, tortured, and killed Brigadier General Mauro Enrique Tello, who had recently assumed command over law enforcement in Cancún.[33] Overall, hundreds of law enforcement agents have been slain since the late 2006 sharpening of the confrontation between gangs and the state.

Due in part to simple geography, human trafficking is an insidious problem in Mexico. The Act to Prevent and to Punish Human Trafficking was ratified in November 2007 in a bid to curb the practice, and there is also a Special Prosecutor's Office on Violent Crime against Women and Human Trafficking. Unfortunately, there is a lack of standardization, with most states lagging behind in their capacity to enact and enforce this legislation. Official numbers, surely a gross underestimation, say that 16,000 children and adolescents are involved in prostitution, sex tourism, and trafficking for the purpose of sexual exploitation. The criminal code has been changed to help increase the punishment for child exploitation, and a number of support mechanisms for victims have been created.[34]

Federal laws enacted since the early 2000s to allow for the redress of rights abuses by the authorities have not been adopted in the states. Very few officials have been convicted of violations, and those who have been convicted faced only minor charges. Almost no victims have received justice or reparations for their suffering. This impunity can be attributed to weak political will and the deep corruption of the judiciary in many local and state jurisdictions, along with the limited independence of federal and state prosecutors.[35] Moreover, according to a report by Human Rights Watch, the National Human Rights Commission (CNDH), which should be a primary source of protection for citizens, is failing in its mission to promote reforms and remedies, despite resources that are the envy of other regional ombudsmen's offices.[36]

Although Mexico's laws and treaty obligations call for gender equality, men continue to dominate positions of influence and the policy-making process.[37] Gender discrimination remains a serious problem. Investigations in 2006 found that "in some states, discriminatory laws that exclude women still exist," and that women's main complaints involved fair compensation for labor, equal treatment before the law, and freedom from violence.[38] Although some progress has been made, as with other governance problems in the country, federal laws and commitments on gender equality are often poorly implemented or inadequately coordinated at all levels of government. The best-known symbol of the continuation of abuse against women in Mexico is the killings in Ciudád Juárez of more than 400 women between 1993 and 2006. Despite the high profile and extreme nature of these cases, they have yet to be fully addressed, and state authorities attempted to downplay the severity of the murders.[39]

Women still have limited opportunities to obtain education and participate in the economy. In 2005, 36.7 percent of women age 15 or older had not finished primary school, compared with 20 percent for males. In 2008, female participation in the labor force was only 37.6 percent.[40] The National Institute for Women created a gender equity model that encourages private and public employers to promote the employment of women and affirmative action. By 2008, this was adopted by 176 organizations, benefiting more than 300,000 men and women.[41] Still, women's rights advocates have expressed concern about a number of practices within the export-oriented *maquiladora* manufacturing sector, including regulations requiring women to present "non-pregnancy certificates in order to be hired or to avoid being dismissed."[42]

Mexico's constitution, as amended in 2001, recognizes the nation's "multicultural" status as well as the individual and collective rights of indigenous peoples.[43] These rights include self-classification, self-determination, cultural identity, and full access to the judicial system. However, specialists emphasize that indigenous communities cannot exercise their rights in practice and that they remain the most marginalized segment of the country's population.[44] In 2003, the National Commission for the Development of Indigenous Peoples (CDI) initiated a number of programs to provide education and other support to indigenous populations. A budget of more than US$2 billion was allotted for indigenous programs in 2008.[45] Since the constitutional change, indigenous groups have had easier access to government, and specific customs and traditional practices have been recognized by legislation. However, the government still lacks translators and other resources to overcome language barriers. One result has been the hindrance of trials involving indigenous individuals. Although programs to promote indigenous-language education were established in cooperation with the National Institute of Indigenous Languages in 2005, the country is still unable to provide full access to bilingual and intercultural education.[46] The UN Committee on Economic, Social, and Cultural Rights remains concerned, moreover, with the working conditions experienced by indigenous individuals in Mexico, who are often underpaid or not paid at all.[47]

The Mexican state is secular and grants equal juridical treatment to churches and other religious groups. The federal constitution and many state constitutions also have explicit provisions for religious freedom. However, conflict occasionally occurs, especially related to the religious practices of indigenous groups. In the southern border state of Chiapas, where evangelical churches have expanded in recent decades, thousands of converts have been expelled from their communities, their children have been denied education, and in many cases authorities have refused to supply them with basic public services.[48] Intervention by the government in religious affairs is much less common than church participation and influence in politics. For example, the Roman Catholic Church has made efforts to allow clergy to run for elected office, which is currently illegal in Mexico.[49] Since the PAN captured the presidency in 2000, the federal government and the religious leadership have been much closer in public forums and events than was the case under PRI rule. Given objections by the PRI and PRD to such alleged weakening of the state's secular foundations, Congress enacted legislation in 2007 to strengthen the separation between church and state.

Freedoms of association and assembly have generally been respected since the late 1990s. The Mexican state has performed well in recognizing and protecting the rights of civic associations, business organizations, and political groups to organize, mobilize, and advocate for peaceful purposes. The weakest area remains the labor sector, where pre-modern and authoritarian practices still dominate. The Federal Labor Law restricts strikes and protests by workers and worker organizations. Intimidation is prevalent in trade union proceedings, and many decisions are made through public announcements rather than secret ballots. There have been only marginal improvements since 2000.[50] As much as 60 percent of the workforce is employed in the informal sector, in which workers have no state or organizational mechanism to pursue their rights to fair working conditions and trade unions. Labor unions, which retain a prominent image in national lore, are characterized by anachronistic structures and authoritarian leadership. During the PRI's 70 years in power, workers either went without the protection of a union or were forced into state-sponsored organizations that became deeply institutionalized. The oil workers' union (STPRM) and the public teachers' union (SNTE) remain the most powerful unions in the country; each is a personalized political machine managed through the imposition of vertical discipline, corruption, and intimidation of dissenters. Individuals who join independent trade unions often face repression and dismissal.[51] Human Rights Watch has found that "according to some estimates, roughly 90 percent of all Mexico's collective bargaining agreements are negotiated by non-independent, pro-government, pro-company unions." Most workers have no input in these agreements, as the law only requires that 20 workers be present for negotiations.

Public protests are often mounted to draw attention to human rights violations, economic concerns, or claims to national resources.[52] However, protest movements and public demonstrations at times result in violent confrontations with local police forces, which use excessive force with impunity. Two prominent cases occurred in 2006. The first was in the town of San Salvador Atenco in the State of Mexico, where a protest following the eviction of informal flower vendors devolved into a clash that left two dead, several dozen injured, hundreds arrested, and accusations against the police of excessive force and the sexual abuse of at least 26 women.[53] As of May 2009, a dozen protesters remained incarcerated with sentences of up to 112 years, while official repercussions were limited a handful of police disciplined for abuse of authority, rather than more serious charges. The other episode occurred in the city of Oaxaca, where the annual teachers' union protest spun out of control and local police, backed at times by plainclothes gunmen, responded with open fire. The events put the city at a standstill and lasted seven months, by which time at least a dozen protesters had died. The protesters failed in their goal of removing Governor Ulises Ruiz from office for corruption and abuse of power, though as of mid-2009 his responsibility for the violence remained under scrutiny in the Supreme Court.

RULE OF LAW 3.93

INDEPENDENT JUDICIARY	4.00
PRIMACY OF RULE OF LAW IN CIVIL AND CRIMINAL MATTERS	3.40
ACCOUNTABILITY OF SECURITY FORCES AND MILITARY TO CIVILIAN AUTHORITIES	4.00
PROTECTION OF PROPERTY RIGHTS	4.33

Despite significant judicial reforms in the mid-1990s, corruption, especially in the police force, has plagued the criminal justice system. In 2008, President Calderón introduced a fundamental overhaul that aimed to replace the existing system of secretive paper trials with an adversarial, oral trial process. There are both advantages and shortcomings to the reform package. Encouragingly, the open nature of oral trials will make prosecutors, defense attorneys, and judges more accountable and transparent. The new system also aims to end the long periods of pretrial detention that have marked the Mexican judicial system. Victims will also be more involved in the process than ever before, with improved ability to initiate investigations.[54]

However, many question the ability of the government to successfully execute the mammoth task of reforming federal and state judiciaries, a process that includes revised law school curriculums and judicial training manuals, reconfigured courtrooms, and the development of a reliable chain of custody for evidence and detainees. Moreover, there are serious concerns regarding the two-tiered nature of the reform, which allows harsher restrictions on the rights of those accused of involvement in organized crime. In response to criticisms of the early drafts, Congress in 2008 approved a bill that provides safeguards against police abuses such as arbitrary detentions and procedures during public security operations.[55] Overall, despite a slow start to the decade-long implementation process, these reforms represent a generally positive step toward strengthening the rule of law in Mexico.

Judicial independence has improved significantly since the era of PRI dominance, but it remains weak in important areas and faces daunting challenges as drug-related crime overwhelms the justice system. Reforms ushered in under President Ernesto Zedillo (1994–2000) transformed the Mexican Supreme Court into a key independent player in the Mexican political arena. Whereas Supreme Court justices were previously political figures who relied on the PRI patronage apparatus for career advancement, they are now mostly professional legal scholars. Safeguards meant to protect justices from political influence have been built into the appointment process.[56] In a clear sign of the Supreme Court's newfound independence, it has engaged in a massive public relations campaign appealing directly to the people for support and has effectively lobbied the executive branch for significant budget increases.[57] High-profile examples of the Supreme Court's adjudication of political disputes include a ruling in favor of opposition lawmakers seeking information regarding the questionable financing of former President Zedillo's 1994 campaign,[58] a 2005 budget quarrel where the court upheld President Vicente Fox's attempt to limit Congress's budget powers, and the unanimous decision of the court to overturn key articles of Ley Televisa, a telecommunications bill found to favor the Televisa/TV Azteca duopoly in the process of allocating frequencies and offering cable and internet services.[59] The Court's independence has also been questioned, however, particularly in the case of journalist Lydia Cacho, who was detained unlawfully after exposing a child pedophilia ring. Although public opinion believed powerful businessmen and politicians—including a sitting governor—to be behind her unlawful detention and subsequent denial of justice, in November 2007 the Court ruled against her.[60]

The lower courts have been less successful in demonstrating their independence. The federal judicial system includes 29 circuits with over 200 circuit courts, and about 250 district courts. Furthermore, each state has its own high court and myriad civil, penal, and administrative tribunals. The country's lower courts are fraught with political meddling and corruption. Some 45 percent of Mexicans polled in 2008 said it was possible to bribe a judge to receive a favorable decision, a high figure even by Latin American standards.[61] The rapid rise in drug-related criminal activity has added to this widespread perception of judicial corruption.[62]

The 1994 reforms established a culture of judicial review, and it has become routine for the executive and legislative branches to act on judicial decisions. Indeed, some observers have begun to talk about the "judicialization" of Mexican politics. Two different review mechanisms have been introduced: *controversia constitucional* provides a centralized review of disputes between government authorities, while *acción de inconstitucionalidad* allows political parties to bring claims directly before the Supreme Court. Under either form of review, a minimum of 8 out of the 11 justices must vote to invalidate a law, giving them an important role in arbitrating Mexico's democracy.[63] Nonetheless, compliance has at times been slow, as in the lack of action to comply fully with the decision in the Ley Televisa case.

The federal judicial appointment and dismissal process appears to be fair and unbiased. The president, who previously appointed Supreme Court justices, now submits a list of three nominees to the Senate for deliberation and confirmation.[64] At the lower levels, federal judges are appointed, assigned, removed, suspended, and transferred by the Federal Council of the Judiciary, a board comprised of Mexico's legal elite. Federal judges undergo rigorous training, and district court judges are appointed after taking a competitive examination.[65] Additional training will be absolutely critical to the success of the recently enacted shift to oral trials.[66] State court judges, unlike their federal counterparts, are appointed and dismissed by elected governors, and tenure is almost nonexistent. As a result, regional politics have a high degree of influence on state courts.[67]

The Mexican constitution has not traditionally afforded citizens the presumption of innocence. A recent study by the Center for Economic Research and Instruction (CIDE) found that 93 percent of accused criminals were prosecuted without a prior investigation.[68] A central tenet of the Calderón reforms addresses this issue by instituting the presumption of innocence. Under the current system, citizens are not generally granted a fair, public, or timely trial. Often defendants cannot access government documents, trials are carried out in secret, and key witnesses are coerced. CIDE found that 80 percent of respondents reported never seeing the judge who sentenced them. A National Center for State Courts study revealed that defendants are found guilty 90 percent of the time, but evidence against them is almost nonexistent.[69] Indigence and the poor quality of defense lawyers make defendant access to credible legal representation the exception rather than the rule.[70] In addition, the competence and professionalism of Mexican prosecutors is highly questionable. In 2000, an internal commission described only 6.6 percent of the prosecutorial service as legal, honest, efficient, professional, loyal, and impartial.[71] All of the aforementioned problems occur in the context of a general climate of impunity. The CNDH reports that only 10 percent of all crimes committed are reported to authorities due to a profound sense of public distrust. Of those, only one in a hundred end with a sentence against the perpetrator of the crime.[72]

The institutionalization of corruption remains the key weakness of Mexico's law enforcement system. Impunity for corrupt officials is rampant. Recent studies show that organized crime is making this problem worse by channeling enormous amounts of money toward the bribery of officials, which, according to scholar Edgardo Buscaglia, affects 72 percent of the nation's municipalities.[73] Transparency Mexico has reported a figure of US$2 billion spent annually on bribes. President Calderón, however, appears determined to crack down on graft; in late 2008, he made a high-profile speech announcing that 11,500 public servants had been fined a total of nearly US$300 million for corruption.[74]

Mexico's notoriously corrupt police are fueling the increase in violence, to the detriment of the Calderón administration's efforts to take on the drug traffickers. In addition, there is still a lack of effective civilian control over the local police, federal police, and the military. Only 22 percent of Mexicans have confidence in the police, well below the Latin American average.[75] As for the military, Human Rights Watch has reported continued high levels of impunity for abuses against civilians by soldiers, caused specifically by the military's insistence on investigating itself "in a system that lacks basic safeguards to ensure independence and impartiality."[76] There have been only a handful of military cases to address the abuses of civilians; in response to a Human Rights Watch request, the Ministry of Defense was only able to name a single, unverified case from 1998. This failure to ensure accountability is particularly problematic since, as seen in similar situations in other countries, human rights abuses in Mexico have increased along with the military's role in traditional police functions. The deployment of tens of thousands of troops has elicited well-documented complaints related to the militarization of police functions.[77] More than 300 people filed human rights claims against the military or police in the first five months of 2008, double the rate from the same period a year earlier. The military is taking steps to address violations, such as opening its first human rights department to better administer complaints.[78]

More positively, police and military officials generally do not interfere with the political process. Officials who cooperate with organized criminals do so on an individual basis rather than as part of an institutional strategy. Corruption in the security forces ranges from small bribes to suitcases filled with drug traffickers' cash. Many state and municipal police officers are bribed to provide the cartels with protection and information. Infiltration has been extensive, reaching into the U.S. embassy in Mexico and Calderón's personal security apparatus.[79] Critics warn that placing the heretofore less corrupt military in direct contact with organized criminals could lead to more institutionalized graft. Furthermore, the efficacy of such operations remains unclear. The situation in Ciudad Juárez offers an interesting case study in the militarization of policing in Mexico. More than 430 people were killed in Juárez in drug violence in the first two months of 2009, totaling nearly half of Mexico's homicides. President Calderon deployed 5,000 troops to the city, who were given unprecedented authority to impose order. By April 2009, fewer than 30 people died in drug violence. The notable decline in homicides was accompanied, however, by a wave of human rights complaints following the creation of a new government office developed to oversee the military's conduct in Juárez.[80] Moreover, the gains in security proved merely temporary, as murders in the city reached record levels by August 2009.

In a key move to improve control over the security forces, the Federal Preventive Police (PFP) and the Federal Agency of Investigations (AFI)—which President Fox modeled on the U.S. Federal Bureau of Investigation (FBI)—were merged into one force in the summer of 2008. Calderón also announced plans to double the size of the federal police force in order to eventually reduce the role of the military in policing operations. Known as the Comprehensive Strategy against Drug Trafficking, the plan also involved further purging of corrupt officers from local police forces and a series of social measures designed to improve public confidence in government agencies.[81]

The issue of property rights is a sensitive one for Mexico. Article 27 of the constitution states: "Ownership of the lands and waters within the boundaries of the national territory is vested originally in the Nation, which has had, and has, the right to transmit title thereof to private persons, thereby constituting private property." The government has the right to impose limitations on private property at any time as it sees fit, and can appropriate resources to ensure a more equitable distribution of wealth.[82] In 1992, the previously inalienable *ejido* (the main form of communal landowning since the 1917 constitution was promulgated) was reformed, allowing such lands to be sold on the private market if a majority of the communal owners approve.[83] The enforcement of existing property rights remains weak. Mexico was ranked 86 out of 132 countries in this category by the World Economic Forum's 2009 Global Competitiveness Report, making it one of the worst performers in Latin America.[84] According to the World Bank's Doing Business report, contract enforcement in Mexico ranks roughly on par with its regional peers in terms of cost and number of procedures, and actually outperforms other countries in the Organization of Economic Cooperation and Development (OECD) in terms of time from initiation of litigation to collection.

Particularly at the state and local levels, the state does not adequately protect citizens from the arbitrary or unjust deprivation of their property. Subnational government officials use bribes or threats to acquire property for private gain. Nonstate actors also seize property with impunity. Representatives of drug traffickers are increasingly forcing individuals to sell land, especially in coveted areas, and the authorities are typically either incapable of responding or bribed into inaction.

ANTICORRUPTION AND TRANSPARENCY   3.85

ENVIRONMENT TO PROTECT AGAINST CORRUPTION	3.25
PROCEDURES AND SYSTEMS TO ENFORCE ANTICORRUPTION LAWS	3.75
EXISTENCE OF ANTICORRUPTION NORMS, STANDARDS, AND PROTECTIONS	3.75
GOVERNMENTAL TRANSPARENCY	4.67

Overregulation of government activity, including state economic activity, provides ample opportunities for corruption at all levels. Paradoxically, even the system put in place to deal with corruption under the Secretaría de la Función Pública (SFP), or comptroller general, has increased the opportunities to engage in it.[85] In order to enhance transparency and efficiency at the public sector level, in 2008 the government launched a national contest to identify "the most useless procedure."[86] While efforts like these are critical to enhancing the participation of citizens in public affairs and holding public officials accountable, the government's agenda on transparency is still not comprehensive or effective enough to adequately cut red tape and the attendant petty corruption.

Federal law mandates annual asset declarations for officeholders and bureaucrats, but this mechanism is not enough to sever the connection between public office and private gain, which remains a strong feature of Mexico's political culture. Civil servants themselves determine whether their asset disclosures can be made public, and a majority chooses not to release them, sometimes arguing that such personal information could make them targets for kidnappers. The SFP is supposed to check all declarations, but in reality it does not have the capacity to verify the data of hundreds of thousands of civil servants. Officials can also make use of devices like offshore bank accounts to hide bribes and contracting kickbacks, practices that seem to be rather common.[87] Between sophisticated techniques, judicial corruption, and the political calculations involved in investigation and prosecution, when it comes to the prosecution of high-level politicians and the military, impunity is the most likely result.[88] Despite widespread suspicion of corruption within upper echelons of government, the last top official to be convicted on criminal charges was former governor Mario Villanueva in 2001.[89]

Mexico has signed and ratified various international conventions related to battling graft. Even though the OECD has found that Mexico has taken effective steps to educate government and private business officials on corruption in international business transactions,[90] the country's score in Transparency International's 2008 Corruption Perceptions Index was a mere 3.6 out of 10, representing no improvement since 2003.

In the last 10 years, Mexico has begun to develop institutions to address corruption and transparency, including the SFP and the Federal Superior Auditor's office (ASF), which is overseen by Congress.[91] These institutions have considerable independence and allow civic participation in the pursuit of government transparency. In 2008, a plan was assembled to give preventative power to federal administrators aimed at strengthening processes of identification and investigation of corruption; improving coordination among public agencies; and enhancing the participation of citizens in anticorruption matters.[92] Public sector whistleblowers have an adequate protection system, but this is not necessarily the case for those employed in the private sector.[93] The same institutional weaknesses that contribute to high levels of corruption, such as the lack of coordination between the courts and other justice-sector institutions, prevent corruption victims from receiving adequate redress.[94]

Since 1997, the Tax Administration Service (SAT) has combated tax evasion and related acts of corruption, producing encouraging results. Over the last five years, there have been 4,056 denunciations that resulted in the removal of 1,567 public officials. Moreover, the perception of graft among SAT officials has declined by 55 percent since 2002. However, problems persist, as the SAT's chief officer acknowledged at a recent congressional hearing. He said that around 70 percent of the SAT's personnel hold positions that are susceptible to corruption and that most problems occur at customs.[95]

Allegations of official corruption are rarely investigated or prosecuted without prejudice. The exception has been President Calderón's bold move to tackle corruption in the federal police forces, the defunct PFP and the AFI, as part of his counternarcotics campaign. Since 2007, the government has suspended more than 280 officers, including commanders from all 31 states. Investigators arrested the former chief of the federal anti–organized crime unit for allegedly accepting US$450,000 from drug cartels in return for information and arrested or fired 35 members of an elite antidrug unit accused of spying for the cartels. The Mexican media frequently reports on corruption scandals. However, Mexico's status as one of the most dangerous countries for journalists in the Americas, combined with the concentration of media outlets in a few business groups, creates multiple constraints that render inconsistent the media's usefulness as a bulwark against corruption.[96]

Mexico has taken important steps to improve access to information, including the passage of an internationally respected law on the matter in 2002 and the creation of an independent body to oversee its implementation, the Federal Institute for Access to Information (IFAI). Citizens have the right to access basic government records,[97] and there are effective means to petition government agencies for public information; the IFAI has developed INFOMEX, an online system for soliciting information. However, access to information in the executive branch is easier and faster than in the legislature and judiciary, where requests can take over a year to process.[98]

Congress can amend the federal budget, and there is a separate legislative committee and two commissions that provide oversight of public funds. In practice, however, several problems affect transparency during the budget-making process. For example, the oversight panels, which are subject to political interference, rarely initiate independent investigations into financial irregularities.[99] Mexico's ranking on the Open Budget Index for 2008 is 54 out of 85, placing it in the group of countries that provide "some" information about the budget-making process.[100]

The federal government has a legal duty to publicly announce the results of procurement decisions and regulations.[101] However, in practice, important information on public spending is not published in a detailed and accurate manner, especially with respect to the use of multimillion-dollar trust funds known as *fideicomisos*.[102]

Major procurements require open and competitive bidding. There is also a legal framework for unsuccessful bidders to instigate an official review of procurement decisions.[103] The web-based Compranet system allows public access to procurement rules and contracts within a reasonable time period, and the information can be organized by sector, agency, tender number, and date. International donors, such as the Inter-American Development Bank (IDB), have accepted the use of Compranet for national and international bidding in IDB-financed projects in Mexico.[104] Foreign assistance is managed by the foreign ministry, or Secretaría de Relaciones Exteriores (SRE). Following disastrous flooding in the states of Tabasco and Chiapas in 2007, the SRE and the UN Disaster Assessment in Mexico established the Information Management Center to improve the coordination and monitoring of foreign aid.[105] This represents an important step toward fairness and proper administration of such assistance.

RECOMMENDATIONS

- In order to promote policy continuity and encourage accountability to voters, Mexico should end the ban on immediate reelection of legislators.
- Mexico should rely more on institutional reform than military pressure to combat organized crime. The bulk of resources dedicated to the war against organized crime should be spent in the civilian sphere, focusing on law enforcement and the criminal justice system. Penitentiary reform should combine the construction of new prisons with increased training, vetting, and compensation for guards.
- Police reform, regardless of the structure chosen in terms of balance between federal, state, and municipal forces, must include extensive background checks, human rights training, and regular performance evaluations.
- The Mexican government should work to establish institutional mechanisms of cooperation with both its southern and northern neighbors to strengthen border controls, including joint projects to modernize and increase the efficiency of the customs service, an agency critical to stanching the flow of weapons and chemical precursors into Mexico.
- In order to strengthen protections against human rights abuses as well increase military accountability to civilian oversight, trials of military members accused of violating the rights of civilians should be conducted in regular courts.
- Greater efforts must be made to protect journalists from intimidation and attack by organized crime, starting with efforts to end impunity for attackers. Congress should pass the proposed constitutional amendment to federalize crimes against freedom of expression, and greater resources should be provided to investigators of crimes against journalists.

NOTES

For URLs and endnote hyperlinks, please visit the *Countries at the Crossroads* homepage at http://freedomhouse.org/template.cfm?page=139&edition=8.

[1] The author thanks the research assistance of my students at SAIS, Jessica Lambertson and Jeffrey Phillips. Their excellent research skills and energy were invaluable to the execution of this project. The author benefitted enormously from interviews with Sergio Aguayo, José Luis Méndez, and Juan Cruz Vieyra.
[2] Francisco E. González, *Dual Transitions from Authoritarian Rule: Institutionalized Regimes in Chile and Mexico, 1970–2000* (Baltimore: Johns Hopkins University Press, 2008).
[3] Francisco E. González, "Mexico Drug Wars Get Brutal," *Current History* 108, no. 715 (February/March 2009).

4. The author thanks the editor of *Countries at the Crossroads*, Jake Dizard, for this timely observation.
5. USAID, *Development Statistics for Latin America and the Caribbean* (Washington, D.C.: USAID, 2009).
6. Mauricio Merino, "La Transición Votada. Crítica a la Interpretación de Cambio Político en México," *Región y Sociedad* 16, no. 30 (2004).
7. Notimex, "Aprueba IFE Financiamiento a Partidos Políticos," Noticieros Televisa Mexico, January 28, 2008.
8. Kenneth Emmond, "Controlling Mexico's Election Monster," Mexidata.info, August 29, 2005.
9. Manuel Carrillo and Carlos Navarro, "Mexico's New Electoral Reform and the Contribution of the Federal Electoral Institute," Elections Today, ACE Electoral Knowledge Network, 2007.
10. Josep Colomer and Gabriel L. Negretto, "Gobernanza con Poderes Divididos en América Latina," *Política y Gobierno* 10, no. 1 (2003): 14–61.
11. Salvador Camarena, "Los Alcaldes Mexicanos, en la Línea de Fuego del Narco," *El País*, February 26, 2009.
12. Mauricio I. Dussuage Laguna, "Structural Differences, Common Challenges: The Civil Service Systems of Mexico and the United States in Comparative Perspective," *Revista Servicio Profesional de Carrera*, no. 5 (2006).
13. Interview with Sergio Aguayo, Professor of Politics and International Relations at El Colegio de México and commentator and social activist, March 20, 2009.
14. Article 19, "México: Article 19 Presenta Informe ante el Comité de Derechos Humanos de Naciones Unidas," press release, July 10, 2009.
15. International Freedom of Information Exchange, "Dozens of Journalists Killed for Their Work in 2008," press release, January 8, 2009.
16. Comisión Nacional de Derechos Humanos, "Recomendación 050/2008," 2008.
17. Diego Cevallos, "México: Amenaza de Televisoras contra Reforma Electoral," Inter Press Service (IPS), September 7, 2007.
18. UN Human Rights Council (UNHRC), *National Report Submitted in Accordance with Paragraph 15 (A) of the Annex to Human Rights Council Resolution 5/1: Mexico* (Geneva: UNHRC, November 10, 2008), 67.
19. Human Rights Watch (HRW), *Uniform Impunity* (New York: HRW, April 28, 2009), 2.
20. "Mexico Beefs up 'Drug War' Forces," British Broadcasting Corporation (BBC), July 17, 2009.
21. UNHRC, *National Report Submitted in Accordance with Paragraph 15 (A) of the Annex to Human Rights Council Resolution 5/1:Mexico*, 6.
22. Decreto por el que Se Expide la Ley General del Sistema Nacional de Seguridad Pública, 2009, 37.
23. Jo Tuckman, "At Least 20 Inmates Killed in Mexican Prison Riot," *Guardian*, March 5, 2009.
24. "Guards Held over Mexico Jailbreak," BBC, May 18, 2009.
25. Amnesty International, "Mexico," in *Annual Report 2009* (London: Amnesty International, 2009).
26. Liliana Alcántara, "ONU: Activistas Trabajan bajo Riesgo e Indefensión," *El Universal*, October 13, 2009.
27. UNHRC, *Summary Prepared by the Office of the High Commissioner for Human Rights, in Accordance with Paragraph 15 (C) of the Annex to Human Rights Council Resolution 5/1: Mexico* (Geneva: UNHRC, December 19, 2008), 7.

28 Ibid., 5.
29 González, "Mexico Drug Wars Get Brutal."
30 "Mexico under Siege: Interactive Map," *Los Angeles Times.*
31 Traci Carl, "7 Killed in Mexico Independence Day Grenade Attack," CBS News, September 16, 2008.
32 James C. McKinley Jr., "Gunmen Kill Chief of Mexico's Police," *New York Times*, May 9, 2008.
33 William Booth, "Warrior in Drug Fight Soon Becomes a Victim," *Washington Post*, February 9, 2009.
34 UNHRC, *National Report Submitted in Accordance with Paragraph 15 (A) of the Annex to Human Rights Council Resolution 5/1: Mexico*, 15–16.
35 Amnesty International, *Mexico: Injustice and Impunity: Mexico's Flawed Criminal Justice System* (London: Amnesty International, 2009).
36 HRW, *Report on Mexico's National Human Rights Commission: A Critical Assessment* (New York: HRW, February 12, 2008).
37 Francisco Reséndiz, "Resaltan Inequidad de Género en Política, *El Universal*, September 17, 2007.
38 Committee on the Elimination of Discrimination against Women (CEDAW), *List of Issues and Questions for Consideration of Periodic Reports* (New York: CEDAW, February 22, 2006), 1.
39 Amnesty International, "Mexico: Killings and Abductions of Women in Ciudad Juarez and the City of Chihuahua—the Struggle for Justice Goes On," press release, February 20, 2006.
40 UNHRC, *National Report Submitted in Accordance with Paragraph 15 (A) of the Annex to Human Rights Council Resolution 5/1: Mexico*, 14.
41 Ibid, 15.
42 UNHRC, *Compilation Prepared by the Office of the High Comissioner for Human Rights, in Accordance with Paragraph 15 (B) of the Annex to Human Rights Council Resolution 5/1: Mexico* (Geneva: UNHRC, February 2009), 5.
43 UNHRC, *National Report Submitted in Accordance with Paragraph 15 (A) of the Annex to Human Rights Council Resolution 5/1: Mexico*, 16.
44 Rodolfo Stavenhagen, "Persiste Pobreza, Discriminación y Marginación Social y Política en los Pueblos Indígenas," *Boletín Académica Mexicana de Ciencias* 77, no. 8 (August 7, 2008).
45 UNHRC, *National Report Submitted in Accordance with Paragraph 15 (A) of the Annex to Human Rights Council Resolution 5/1: Mexico*, 17.
46 Ibid., 17.
47 Committee on Economic, Social, and Cultural Rights, *Consideration of Reports Submitted by States under Articles 16 and 17 of the Covenant: Mexico* (Geneva: United Nations Economic and Social Council, June 2006), 3.
48 "España Exige a México Que Acabe con la Persecución Religiosa," *El Imparcial*, August 8, 2008.
49 "Lawmakers Vow to Revise Mexico's Constitution to Strengthen Separation of Church and State," *International Herald Tribune*, November 21, 2007.
50 Benjamin Davis, *Workers' Freedom of Association under Attack in Mexico* (Washington, D.C.: Solidarity Center, August 2008).
51 International Trade Union Confederation (ITUC), "Mexico," in *2009 Annual Survey of Violations of Trade Union Rights* (Brussels: ITUC, 2009).

[52] UNHRC, *Summary Prepared by the Office of the High Comissioner for Human Rights in Accordance with Paragraph 15 (C) of the Annex to Human Rights Council Resolution 5/1: Mexico,* 7.
[53] Noemí Gutiérrez, "Mujeres de Atenco, a la Espera de Justicia," *El Universal,* May 11, 2009.
[54] Miguel Sarre, "Mexico's Judicial Reform and Long-Term Challenges" (paper presented at the Policy Forum: U.S.-Mexico Security Cooperation and Merida Initiative, Washington, D.C., May 9, 2008).
[55] Ken Ellingwood, "Corruption Hurting Mexico's Fight against Crime, Calderon Says," *Los Angeles Times,* December 10, 2008.
[56] Sarah Schats, Hugo Concha, and Ana Laura Magaloni Kerpel, "The Mexican Judicial System: Continuity and Change in a Period of Democratic Consolidation," in *Reforming the Administration of Justice in Mexico,* ed. Wayne A. Cornelius and David A. Shirk (South Bend, Ind.: University of Notre Dame Press, 2007), 202.
[57] Jeffrey K. Staton, "Lobbying for Judicial Reform: The Role of the Mexican Supreme Court in Institutional Selection," in *Reforming the Administration of Justice in Mexico,* 288–90.
[58] Sam Dillon, "Mexico Court Makes History by Siding with Congress," *New York Times,* August 25, 2000.
[59] "Anulan Corazón de Ley Televisa," BBC Mundo Online, June 6, 2007.
[60] James C. McKinley Jr., "Mexican Court Finds No Violation of Rights in Jailing of Journalist," *New York Times,* November 29, 2007.
[61] Latinobarómetro, *2008 Survey of Public Opinion* (Santiago de Chile: Latinobarómetro, November 2008).
[62] Marc Lacey. "Warrantless Searches Removed from Legislation in Mexico," *New York Times,* December 7, 2008.
[63] Miguel Schor, "An Essay on the Emergence of Constitutional Courts: The Cases of Mexico and Colombia," *Indiana Journal of Global Legal Studies* 16, no. 1 (2008): 173–94.
[64] Ibid.
[65] Schats, Concha, and Magaloni Kerpel, "Mexican Judicial System," 209.
[66] James C. McKinley Jr., "Mexico's Congress Passes Overhaul of Justice Law," *New York Times,* March 7, 2008.
[67] Schats, Concha, and Magaloni Kerpel, "Mexican Judicial System," 204.
[68] Ana Laura Magaloni Kerpel, "Context and Positive Implications of the Mexican Judicial Reform" (paper presented to the Challenge of Reforming Mexico's Justice System Seminar at the Woodrow Wilson Center's Mexico Institute, Washington, D.C., May 4, 2007).
[69] Layda Negrete and Roberto Hernández, "'I Don't Remember': Police Accountability and Due Process in Mexico City Criminal Courts" (paper presented at the Challenge of Reforming Mexico's Justice System Seminar at the Woodrow Wilson Center's Mexico Institute, Washington D.C., May 4, 2007).
[70] Schats, Concha and Magaloni Kerpel, "Mexican Judicial System," 212.
[71] Ibid.
[72] Liliana Alcántara, "CNDH Ve Impunidad en 99% de Delitos," *El Universal,* December 15, 2008.
[73] Joel Millman and José de Córdoba, "Drug-Cartel Links Haunt an Election South of the Border," *Wall Street Journal,* July 3, 2009.
[74] Sara Miller Llana, "Setbacks in Mexico's War on Corruption," *Christian Science Monitor,* December 30, 2008.
[75] Latinobarómetro, *2008 Survey of Public Opinion.*

76 HRW, *Uniform Impunity: Mexico's Misuse of Military Justice to Prosecute Abuses in Counternarcotics and Public Security Operation* (New York: HRW, April 29, 2009).
77 "Is Mexico under Attack by Its Military?" *Los Angeles Times,* July 24, 2009.
78 Sarah Miller Llana, "Military Abuses Rise in Mexican Drug War," *Christian Science Monitor,* June 24, 2008.
79 Ellingwood, "Corruption Hurting Mexico's Fight against Crime, Calderon Says."
80 Steve Fainaru and William Booth, "An Army Takeover Quells Violence in Mexico," *Washington Post,* April 21, 2009.
81 Manuel Roig-Franzia "Mexico Plan Adds Police to Take on Drug Cartels," *Washington Post,* July 11, 2008.
82 Constitution of Mexico, Art. 27.
83 David Yetman and Alberto Burquez, "Twenty-Seven: A Case Study in Ejido Privatization in Mexico," *Journal of Anthropological Research* 54, no. 1 (Spring 1998): 73–95.
84 Xavier Sala-i-Martin and Jennifer Blanke, *Global Competitiveness Report 2009–2010* (Geneva: World Economic Forum, 2009).
85 José Luis Méndez, "Implementing Developed Countries' Administrative Reforms in Developing Countries: The Case of Mexico," in *Public Change and Reform: Moving Forward, Looking Back,* ed. Jon Pierre and Patricia Ingraham (Montreal: McGill University Press, forthcoming, 2009).
86 Secretaría de la Función Pública, "Concluyó la Convocatoria Ciudadana para Identificar el Tramite Más Inútil," Campañas 2008.
87 Interview with José Luis Méndez, Professor of Public Administration and Public Policy at El Colegio de México, March 23, 2009.
88 Denise Dresser, "Testimony: Law Enforcement Responses to Mexican Drug Cartels," Senate Judiciary Committee Subcommittee on Crime and Drugs Hearing, March 2009.
89 Marcela Armienta, "Atoran Monopolios a México: Denise Dresser," Frontera.info, March 3, 2009.
90 Organization for Economic Cooperation and Development (OECD), *Follow-Up Report on the Implementation of the Phase 2 Recommendations* (Paris: OECD, 2007), 3.
91 Programa Nacional de Rendición de Cuentas, Transparencia y Combate a la Corrupción 2008–2012, "La Ciudadanía Participa y Confía en la Función Pública," in *Programa Anticorrupción 2008* (Mexico City: Government of Mexico, 2008), 13.
92 Ibid., 19.
93 OECD, *Follow-Up Report on the Implementation of the Phase 2 Recommendations,* 3.
94 Edgardo Buscaglia, "Judicial Corruption and the Broader Justice System," in *Corruption and Judicial Systems* (Berlin: Transparency International, 2007).
95 Daniel Kaufmann, "Mexico Creates Model for Tackling Corruption in Tax Administration," World Bank Governance Matters Blog, June 13, 2008.
96 Colleen W. Cook, "Mexico's Drug Cartels," Congressional Research Service, October 16, 2007.
97 See *Constitution of Mexico,* Art. 6; Ley Federal de Transparencia y Acceso a la Información Pública Gubernamental, 2002.
98 Open Society Justice Initiative, *Transparency & Silence: A Survey of Access to Information Laws and Practices in 14 Countries* (New York: Open Society Justice Initiative, 2006).
99 Fundar, *Índice Latinoamericano de Transparencia Presupuestaria 2009* (Mexico City: Fundar, 2009).
100 Open Budget Initiative, "Mexico," in *Open Budget Index 2008* (Washington, D.C.: Open Budget Initiative, 2008).
101 Ley Federal de Transparencia y Acceso a la Información Pública Gubernamental, Art. 7, VIII-VVII.

[102] Fundar, "Tras los Pasos de Nuestros Pesos," *Pesos y Contra Pesos* 2, no. 2 (February 2008).
[103] Ley de Adquisiciones, Arrendamientos y Servicios del Sector Público, Arts. 65-70.
[104] Inter-American Development Bank, "IDB Accepts Compranet for Operations Financed in Mexico," news release, February 8, 2006.
[105] Secretaria de Relaciones Exteriores, "Acerca del Centro de Información SER-ONU," home page.

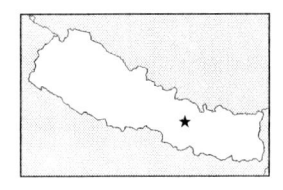

NEPAL

CAPITAL: Kathmandu
POPULATION: 27.5 million
GNI PER CAPITA (PPP): $1,120

SCORES	2006	2010
ACCOUNTABILITY AND PUBLIC VOICE:	2.15	3.76
CIVIL LIBERTIES:	2.79	3.69
RULE OF LAW:	2.45	2.85
ANTICORRUPTION AND TRANSPARENCY:	2.44	3.13

(scores are based on a scale of 0 to 7, with 0 representing weakest and 7 representing strongest performance)

Lok Raj Baral with Raymond Lu

INTRODUCTION

Nepal has undergone dramatic changes in recent years, transitioning from an absolute monarchy to a fledgling democratic republic. A series of events in 2006, including nationwide popular protests, led to the monarchy's abolition, the passage of a democratically oriented interim constitution, elections for a constituent assembly, and an end to a decade-long Maoist insurgency that resulted in the deaths of an estimated 13,000 people. Political parties, journalists, trade unions, and civic groups operate with a degree of freedom nearly unimaginable at the height of King Gyanendra's centralization of power four years ago. Despite such improvements, the future of Nepal's peace process and democracy remains highly uncertain. Polarization and intra-elite conflict, the rise of youth militias affiliated with political parties, and a new violent insurgency by ethnic groups in the south risk unraveling the progress made in recent years.

Though unified since 1769, Nepal's population remains highly diverse along ethnic, religious, and linguistic lines. Political instability has characterized the state since 1959, with alternating periods of parliamentary and repressive monarchical rule. In 1996, the Communist Party of Nepal (Maoist), an extremist left-wing group partly modeled after the Peruvian Shining Path, launched a violent campaign to overthrow the monarchy and establish a people's republic.

Lok Raj Baral is Executive Chairman of the Nepal Center for Contemporary Studies (NCCS), Kathmandu. He was Professor and Chairman of the Department of Political Science, Tribhuvan University, and is a former Ambassador of Nepal to India. With more than 20 books (both authored and edited) to his credit, Professor Baral has also published several articles in leading national and international journals and edited volumes. **Raymond Lu** is an analyst at Freedom House.

At the height of their power, the Maoists controlled large tracts of the country, particularly in rural areas.

Nepal's ruling monarchs used the specter of the insurgency to tighten control over the political system. Following a bizarre palace incident in 2001 in which the crown prince shot and killed the king and nine other members of the royal family before committing suicide, King Gyanendra acceded to the throne. In 2002, he suspended parliament and began appointing prime ministers by royal decree, while ordering the army to intervene against Maoist forces. The situation further deteriorated in 2005, when Gyanendra imposed a state of emergency, dismissed parliament, closed media outlets, and arrested thousands of political opponents.

Gyanendra's heavy-handed measures and a rising death toll from the civil war prompted an alliance of seven mainstream political parties to sign a 12-point agreement with the Maoists in late 2005. The two sides pledged to collectively oppose the monarchy and, following its abolition, form an assembly to draft a new constitution. A series of nationwide protests and strikes in 2006, some attracting crowds of up to 300,000, ultimately forced the king to reinstate parliament and cede his powers.

In November 2006, the Seven Party Alliance (SPA) and the Maoists signed the Comprehensive Peace Agreement (CPA), formally ending a decade of fighting. The Maoists were awarded positions within the interim parliament and cabinet in exchange for placing their weapons under United Nations supervision and confining their fighters to cantonments across the country. An interim constitution promulgated in January 2007 established a framework for the transition government, while plans were made to hold elections for the Constituent Assembly (CA), which eventually took place in April 2008.

Three successive administrations have governed Nepal since the monarchy ceded its power to parliament in 2006. Shortly after parliament was reinstated that April, the SPA elected Nepali Congress (NC) party president Girija Prasad Koirala as prime minister. Koirala was reelected in April 2007 to head a coalition government that included representatives from both the SPA and the Maoists. An impressive flurry of legislative activity, as well as partisan bickering, occurred under the interim government. Following the April 2008 CA elections, in which they won a plurality of votes, the Maoists formed a coalition government.

In its early months, the Maoist-led government succeeded in passing a budget, holding regular cabinet meetings, and adopting economic policies benefiting poor Nepalese. But it also showed worrisome signs of a lack of commitment to democratic values, demonstrating intolerance to criticism, a tendency to interfere in the judiciary, and a reluctance to punish its cadres for acts of violence. Following a constitutional crisis and conflict with the Nepalese army, Maoist Prime Minister Pushpa Kamal Dahal (better known as Prachanda) resigned, bringing to power a weak coalition of 22 parties headed by Madhav

Kumar Nepal of the Communist Party of Nepal-Unified Marxist Leninist (CPN-UML).

Although the CA has established thematic drafting committees, reaching agreement on a new constitution by the May 2010 deadline appears increasingly unlikely. Since the elections, coalition building, partisan bickering, and stalemate have generally outweighed effective governance. Meanwhile, inflation has grown steadily, while many Nepalese continue to live in desperate poverty: one in four live on less than a dollar a day, and 41 percent of the population is undernourished.[1] With entrenched corruption and ongoing impunity for rights abuses, many in Nepal have grown increasingly disillusioned with its democratic institutions and leading politicians.

ACCOUNTABILITY AND PUBLIC VOICE 3.76

FREE AND FAIR ELECTORAL LAWS AND ELECTIONS	4.25
EFFECTIVE AND ACCOUNTABLE GOVERNMENT	3.50
CIVIC ENGAGEMENT AND CIVIC MONITORING	4.00
MEDIA INDEPENDENCE AND FREEDOM OF EXPRESSION	3.29

Since 2005, Nepal has taken important steps toward establishing a government based upon the will of the people, and the space for civic engagement and critical media coverage has expanded dramatically. In a historic vote in May 2008, the newly elected CA voted to abolish the monarchy, ending a centuries-old institution and establishing Nepal as a secular republic. A political culture of exclusionary, back-door decision making among politicians and the trumping of partisan over public interests has changed little, however, while nonstate violence against journalists and activists remains high.

Under the interim constitution, the 601-member CA is charged with drafting a new constitution and serving as an interim legislature during its 2-year mandate. Members were elected in April 2008 through a mixture of proportional representation (335 seats) and first-past-the-post systems (240); 26 were appointed by the cabinet after elections. Although campaign finance laws place limits on expenditures, the pre-election code of conduct placed no restrictions on donations and the expenditure regulations were largely disregarded.[2] International and domestic observers described the election as free and fair, though the European Union noted that the polls fell short of international standards due to restrictions on freedoms of assembly, movement, and expression. The reformed Electoral Commission largely performed its duties with transparency and professionalism.[3] Despite polling irregularities that led authorities to shut down 33 voting stations, observers reported that the vast majority of votes were recorded in a credible manner.[4]

Nevertheless, widespread violence and intimidation characterized the pre-election months, as paramilitary groups and armed thugs attacked rival parties and obstructed rallies. Over 20 people, including three candidates, were killed. While Maoist cadres and Maoist-controlled Young Communist League (YCL) activists were responsible for the bulk of the violence and intimidation, their supporters also fell victim to attacks. On the day before the elections, state paramilitary police killed six Maoist activists in western Nepal after a clash between Maoists and Nepali Congress Party supporters.[5] In a development that surprised even the Maoists themselves, the party emerged with 230 of 601 seats, 100 more than their closest rival, defeating the previously dominant NC and CPN-UML. Observers attributed the victory to factors including voter disenchantment with the mainstream parties; the Maoists' charismatic, aggressive—and sometimes violent—campaigning; the Maoists' platform of promoting equality for lower castes, ethnic minorities, and other excluded groups that comprise a large percentage of the population; and fears of more violence if the Maoists were marginalized in the CA.

Although a total of 25 parties gained representation, the Maoist, CPN-UML, NC, and Madhesi Janadhikar Forum occupy the vast majority of seats. Quotas requiring parties to include marginalized groups in their candidate lists enabled substantially increased representation of women and minorities—nearly 250 women and Dalits (low-caste Hindus, commonly called "untouchables") secured seats.[6]

Under the interim constitution, the executive is split between a prime minister, who heads the government, and the president, whose responsibilities are primarily ceremonial. Both are chosen by a majority of the CA. In July 2008, the NC's Ram Baran Yadav was elected president, while a month later Maoist leader Prachanda became prime minister at the head of a coalition government that included the CPN-UML, the Madhesi Janadhikar Forum and Nepal Sadbhawana parties, both representing the Terai region, and two other small parties. The NC chose to sit in opposition, although the interim constitution called for consensus-based governance until a new charter is written.

The interim constitution provides for a system of checks and balances. In practice, the Maoists' commitment to democratic standards remains an open question, with internal debates indicating some continued dedication to establishing a communist "people's republic." Although they have sometimes shown more responsiveness to public concerns than other parties, the Maoists have also exhibited limited tolerance for political pluralism, retained parallel governance structures, and introduced constitutional proposals that would limit judicial independence, while their affiliates—primarily the YCL and trade unions—have repeatedly used violence against critics. In February 2009, the Maoist-led government bypassed the CA to push through an ordinance criminalizing enforced disappearances and establishing an investigatory body;[7] opposition parties and international rights groups criticized the undemocratic process, although the action was aimed at fulfilling a 2007 Supreme Court order. Throughout the political landscape, parties have been weakened by internal feuding and allegations of corruption. Several have established their own militant youth wings and backed the army in its conflict with the administration over civilian control of the military.

The clash between the Maoists and the Nepalese Army (NA) contributed significantly to the dissolution of the Maoist-led government after only nine months in office. The dispute illustrates the weakness of institutional checks and balances relative to longer-term relationships between political actors, in particular, mistrust between the Maoists, other parties, and the increasingly politicized NA. In November 2008, the NA defied orders from the Maoist defense minister and initiated a recruitment drive to add 3,000 troops to its ranks, a move condemned by the UN as a violation of the 2006 peace agreement.[8] In March 2009, the Supreme Court sought to resolve the dispute by prohibiting the NA from new recruitment, while allowing the 3,000 soldiers to retain their positions. Outraged Maoist cadres organized demonstrations across the country and government ministers condemned the ruling, labeling the judiciary as "reactionary forces" and a "threat to the…republican order."[9]

In May 2009, Prime Minister Prachanda attempted to dismiss army chief Rookmangud Katawal, who had served under the monarchy, over his opposition to integrating Maoist fighters into the NA.[10] Katawal refused to leave, and the president, overstepping his ostensibly ceremonial role, ordered him to remain in place. Two parties quit the governing coalition to protest the dismissal effort; left with only a thin majority, Prachanda resigned and was replaced as prime minister by the CPN-UML's Madhav Kumar Nepal. However, he headed a weak 22-party coalition and faced continued Maoist-led protests and strikes.

The Public Service Commission has been reconstituted, but Nepal's civil service remains far from politically neutral. Civil service appointments and promotions continue to be dominated by traditional patron-client and bureaucrat-politician relationships. In the current political climate, partisan and ideological considerations often override merit in personnel decisions.[11]

In sharp contrast to the king's clampdown on civil society in 2005, the space for nongovernmental organizations (NGOs) has expanded rapidly in recent years, with thousands of NGOs operating across the country. Indeed, civil society groups played an instrumental role in both the protests that contributed to Nepal's transition and the battles of procedure and principle that followed. In the postelection period, however, their influence has waned and some groups have been criticized as overly partisan.[12]

The legal environment for NGOs has improved, and in May 2006 the government repealed a restrictive November 2005 code of conduct that had barred NGOs from work that would "disturb social harmony." Nevertheless, civic leaders continue to press for an overhaul of NGO laws. In particular, the government-run Social Welfare Council has retained the authority to monitor NGO activities and refuse registration or program proposals, although approval is generally granted in practice.

Violence against political activists and human rights defenders has dropped significantly, from a peak of 3,286 targeted in 2006, but remains high by international standards.[13] Most threats and attacks originate from nonstate actors, including armed Madhesi groups in the Terai region and political parties' paramilitary youth wings, particularly the YCL. Civil society groups have also faced occasional harassment from state authorities.[14]

Space for free expression in Nepal has also expanded dramatically since the king's departure, and the country is now home to a vibrant press that reports on a wide variety of political and social issues. Nevertheless, violence against journalists, Maoist intolerance of criticism, and the use of public media to disseminate propaganda restrict press freedom.

The legal environment regulating media activity has improved. In 2006, the interim government rescinded a range of repressive laws. These included a restrictive 2005 ordinance that banned private radio news broadcasts, as well as the Terrorist and Disruptive Activities Ordinance, which had been used to imprison journalists. The 2007 interim constitution outlawed prior censorship and guaranteed the rights of publication, broadcasting, and press. That July and August, the government promulgated the Working Journalist Act, which provides reporters with improved conditions and grants them the right to unionize. Nevertheless, criminal defamation laws remain in place and implementation of the new legislation has yet to take full effect.[15]

In contrast to the improved legal framework, violence against journalists remains a significant threat to press freedom. Media workers suffer physical attacks, abductions, and assassinations for criticizing politicians and reporting on issues such as the Maoist insurgency, human rights violations, and government corruption. Violence was especially pronounced during the 2008 election campaign and increased further under the Maoist administration as YCL and union militants, and, to a lesser extent, government security agents, targeted journalists critical of the party. In May 2008, Prime Minister Prachanda warned that criticism would no longer be tolerated now that the Maoists had become the ruling party.[16] Leading private media houses, including Kantipur Publications, the APCA House, and the Himal Media House, were subsequently harassed for criticizing the Maoists.[17]

The Federation of Nepali Journalists reported 342 press freedom violations in 2008.[18] The gruesome January 2009 murder of radio journalist Uma Singh, the fourth reporter killed since 2006, prompted some to leave the profession, while others reported feeling unsafe displaying press credentials at rallies and mass gatherings. The government's failure to investigate and punish attacks against journalists—largely due to the direct links between politicians and perpetrators—has fostered a culture of impunity, as well as self-censorship among journalists. In February 2009, the International Press Freedom Mission to Nepal reported that authorities had yet to convict a single person for crimes against journalists.[19]

The government continues to directly influence media content through ownership of powerful media houses staffed by progovernment journalists.[20] These include Radio Nepal and Nepal Television, the Rashtriya Samachar Samiti news agency, the *Gorkhapatra* (Nepali) and the *Rising Nepal* dailies, and other magazines produced by the government-owned publisher Gorkhapatra. In addition to promoting government policies through these outlets, the Maoists also forced private radio stations to broadcast propaganda in 2008 and while holding the Ministry of Information portfolio under the interim government.[21] Nevertheless, the growing private media sector, particularly the more than 150 independent radio stations, has become more popular and effective in shaping public opinion. Unhindered internet service has further contributed to the free flow of information.

CIVIL LIBERTIES 3.69

PROTECTION FROM STATE TERROR, UNJUSTIFIED IMPRISONMENT, AND TORTURE	2.38
GENDER EQUITY	3.67
RIGHTS OF ETHNIC, RELIGIOUS, AND OTHER DISTINCT GROUPS	4.00
FREEDOM OF CONSCIENCE AND BELIEF	4.67
FREEDOM OF ASSOCIATION AND ASSEMBLY	3.75

With the end of the insurgency and monarchical rule, the number of rights abuses like state abductions and extrajudicial killings has declined dramatically in recent years. The interim constitution and subsequent legislative reforms improved the legal environment protecting civil liberties, women, and minorities. Unfortunately, a lack of political will to prosecute current and past abuses, weak policing, and attacks by paramilitary youth groups and ethnic militias have resulted in a security situation that remains unstable for many Nepalese. Meanwhile, at least 1,300 enforced disappearances from the conflict period remain unresolved.[22] Legal protections against torture fall short of international standards, and the government has ignored recommendations by the National Human Rights Commission (NHRC) that torture be criminalized. Torture remains prevalent, particularly as police seek to extract confessions, and civilian oversight of the security forces is weak. According to Amnesty International, over 1,300 new cases of torture were recorded between April 2006 and the end of 2008.[23]

Prison conditions have improved in recent years but continue to fall short of international standards. Lack of funding and political will have limited the impact of various jail reform commissions. Under the interim constitution, all individuals detained by police must be presented before a court within 24 hours or be released, though in many cases this does not occur.

Nepalese from all regions report feeling safer today than during the insurgency.[24] Nevertheless, weak state authority in maintaining law and order and the proliferation of armed groups, particularly in the Terai region, have contributed to high levels of crime and insecurity. Extrajudicial killings, beatings, abductions, and extortion by criminal gangs and armed groups continue at a rate of dozens per month. An estimated 23 people died and 239 were injured in 83 bombings across Nepal in 2008, mostly in the Terai region.[25] In parts of the Madhesi-dominated region, policing has nearly totally collapsed.[26] As a result, public confidence in law enforcement remains low.

Although exact figures are unavailable, an estimated 50,000-70,000 Nepalese were considered internally displaced peoples (IDPs) as of mid-2009. While most were forced to leave their homes during the Maoist insurgency, some were dislocated by ethnic tension and violence in the Terai region since 2007. Care for the former has fallen under the authority of the Ministry of Peace and Reconstruction, while the latter have received little government assistance. Many IDPs complained of difficulties registering with the authorities, inadequate property restitution, and an official policy focusing on those returning to their place of origin versus those wishing to settle in their current place of residence or elsewhere in Nepal.[27]

Avenues of effective redress for victims of current and past abuses have expanded, but impunity remains the norm. In a positive development, the NHRC was reconstituted in August 2007, after the king had curtailed its independence. The interim constitution increased the commission's authority, including granting it subpoena-equivalent powers and the right to enter any government office or detention facility without prior notice. The NHRC, whose members include former senior judges and prominent activists from a range of backgrounds, has emerged as an important investigatory body and advocate for victims. In 2008, it received over 1,200 complaints, investigated over 700 incidents of alleged abuse, and sought compensation or disciplinary action from the government on behalf of at least 110 victims.[28] Its impact has been limited, however, as few of its recommendations for prosecutions have been followed up by the government, police, and courts.

The courts, conversely, have provided little recourse for redress. Petitioners are often ignored and suffer intimidation. In other instances, police refuse to file complaints, fearing reprisals. Members of the NA and police have enjoyed near total impunity for abuses committed during the insurgency, when the army was responsible for an estimated 8,377 deaths and 1,234 disappearances.[29] Military officials claim that 175 personnel have been sanctioned for human rights abuses, but details about such internal investigations or the penalties imposed have not been published.[30] For its part, the government has actively sought to shield state security forces from prosecution. Those responsible for carrying out atrocities have generally retained their positions, while some senior officers have been promoted despite having overseen human rights violations.[31] A 2008 study by Human Rights Watch found that "not one member of the security forces or of the CPN-M has been held criminally accountable and convicted for killings, 'disappearances,' torture or other abuses by civilian courts."[32]

Human trafficking continues on a massive scale, at times with complicity from state authorities. Experts estimate that nearly 400,000 women and girls have been trafficked to India since 2005.[33] In 2007, the CA passed a bill criminalizing prostitution and trafficking that established a system to rehabilitate and compensate victims. Enforcement has been weak, however, with state agencies citing limited capacity.

The 2007 interim constitution prohibits discrimination "on grounds of religion, race, caste, tribe, gender, origin, language, or ideological conviction." Other recent legislation, along with partial proportional representation in elections and party list quotas for women and minorities, has made the new political order significantly more inclusive. Women secured 197 seats, nearly one-third of the CA, a dramatic increase from the 12 women in the interim parliament.[34] Minorities were elected in similarly unprecedented numbers, including 51 Dalits and 77 Madhesis, as well as 22 representatives of economically underdeveloped regions. Still, Dalits remain underrepresented relative to their size, holding 7 percent of seats but comprising an estimated 20 percent of the population; they remain largely excluded from party leadership positions.[35]

Gender equity is enshrined in the interim constitution and specific provisions address domestic violence, reproductive health, and parental inheritance. Nonetheless, women continue to suffer from systematic discrimination in Nepal's patriarchal society, lacking access to education, healthcare, and property ownership. In rural areas, discrimination is further heightened by religious customs, rigid caste divisions, and the common practice of child marriage.

Domestic violence remains prevalent—80 percent of interviewees in a recent survey reported being abused by their husbands.[36] Police investigation and prosecution of such cases is rare, and women are instead encouraged to accept resolution via informal community justice mechanisms in which bribes and dismissive attitudes toward rape and other violence limit the punishment of perpetrators. Civic groups have lobbied for passage of a draft 2002 bill imposing harsher penalties for domestic violence, but have yet to meet with success.[37] In July 2008, the government created a task force to issue recommendations on criminalizing domestic violence. Violence against women by state officials also continues to be reported.[38] Meanwhile, women's rights activists have themselves faced violence for advocacy work—according to Amnesty International, since 2006 at least two female activists were murdered, and 17 women were reportedly threatened with death, rape, or beating if they continued their work.[39]

Discrimination based on ethnicity, caste, and region of origin has been a feature of Nepali society for centuries. The country remains dominated by male, upper-caste Hindu elites. Dalits face ostracism on a daily basis and are systematically denied opportunities to education, healthcare, employment, and property ownership.[40] Ethnic minorities have been similarly marginalized, such as the Madhesis in the south, who comprise an estimated 40 percent of the population. Linguistic tensions also exist as Nepali remains the official language, though only 47 percent of Nepalese are native speakers.[41]

The end of the Maoist insurgency and opening of the political system has generated an unprecedented degree of political representation for these long-excluded groups. Prior to the 2008 elections, several measures were taken to ensure the rights of Madhesis. Millions were issued citizenship certificates and quotas were instituted on party lists.[42] In February 2008, in an effort to stem violence and paralyzing strikes by Madhesi groups, the government negotiated an agreement with an ethnic alliance guaranteeing a higher level of proportional representation.

The resulting increased representation in the CA has given minority groups a greater voice in mainstream politics. During a period of weak coalitions, Madhesi groups have used these circumstances to leverage promises for autonomy, particularly in the Terai region, from the government. After the Maoists left the government in May 2009, leaders from the CPN-UML and NC brokered a deal with Madhesi parties, promising to renew their commitment to greater autonomy in the Terai region in exchange for political support.[43]

In the meantime, modest steps have been taken to reverse years of discrimination in public sector employment, where Madhesis occupy only 5 percent of jobs. In August 2007, the government promised to incorporate more Madhesis and members of other minorities into the police force. To counter traditional Brahmin dominance of the bureaucracy, legislation was passed in August 2007 reserving 45 percent of civil service positions for women and ethnically distinct groups, though the political parties representing these groups criticized the percentage as insufficient. Implementation of these new policies has been slow.

Overall, however, the period of national solidarity around efforts to remove the king from power has been followed by increased ethnic tensions and violence. Public perceptions that violence proved an effective channel for Maoists in gaining power have led to a proliferation of armed groups asserting the interests of various communities and demanding regional autonomy. As a result, following the signing of the 2006 peace accord, ethnic strife, strikes, and bombings became a regular occurrence in the southern Terai region, with hundreds killed or injured. Tensions have been further exacerbated when security forces have responded to peaceful demonstrations with excessive force.

The parliament officially declared Nepal secular in May 2006, ending centuries of identity as a Hindu state.[44] In 2007, freedom of religion was further guaranteed in the interim constitution. Hindus constitute approximately 80 percent of Nepalese, with the remainder of the population practicing Buddhism, Islam, Christianity, or indigenous religions. For the most part, authorities allow religious minorities to practice their faith freely. The state rarely interferes in religious appointments or the internal activities of religious organizations. However, restrictions on Tibetan Buddhists, including activities of a purely religious nature, have increased recently, a move widely interpreted as an effort to curry favor with the Chinese government.

The primary threat to religious minorities has come from extremist Hindu groups. In March 2008, a bombing at a mosque in the southern city of Biratnagar killed two people.[45] Also in 2008, armed men attacked a Protestant church and shot dead a Catholic priest inside his home in eastern Nepal. The National Defense Army, a militant organization dedicated to restoring Nepal as a Hindu monarchy, claimed responsibility for several attacks. In September 2009, police succeeded in tracking down and arresting the group's leader, Ram Prasad Mainali.

In December 2007 and November 2008, the Supreme Court issued decisions favoring equality—including the right to marry—for lesbian, gay, bisexual, transsexual, and intersex persons.[46] The ruling called on the government to form a committee to examine passing relevant legislation. Although the committee has been formed and the government has reportedly issued identity cards denoting a third gender for sexual minorities, full legislation has yet to be enacted.[47]

A large number of trade unions—many with affiliations to political parties—operate in Nepal, play an important role in the political landscape, and are generally allowed to function freely. The interim constitution guarantees the right to strike and bargain collectively, though other labor laws partially restrict strike activity. In 2007, the right of civil servants to join unions and bargain collectively was restored; it had been suspended in 2005. Inter-union rivalry and violence has increased as Maoist-affiliated unions have carried out multiple attacks against workers from other organizations, business owners, and media outlets.[48]

Freedoms of association and assembly have expanded following the April 2006 demonstrations that removed the king. Demonstrations and strikes have become a regular feature of the political landscape, sometimes bringing the country to a standstill. Beginning in May 2009, Maoists organized a nationwide protest movement over the failed sacking of army chief Katawal. The demonstrations lasted through the year, included blockades of roads and government buildings, and sometimes ended in violence by both protesters and police.

The authorities generally respect the right to peaceful assembly, but have violently suppressed Madhesi and Tibetan protests in recent years. In the aftermath of March 2008 protests in Tibet, Tibetans staged large-scale demonstrations denouncing human rights abuses by the Chinese authorities. The Nepali government responded with a crackdown, arresting at least 8,350 Tibetan demonstrators between March and July 2008, though most were released within 24 hours.[49] Tibetan detainees were reportedly subjected to beatings, torture, and sexual assault in custody, and many were threatened with deportation to China.

RULE OF LAW   2.85

INDEPENDENT JUDICIARY	3.00
PRIMACY OF RULE OF LAW IN CIVIL AND CRIMINAL MATTERS	2.40
ACCOUNTABILITY OF SECURITY FORCES AND MILITARY TO CIVILIAN AUTHORITIES	2.00
PROTECTION OF PROPERTY RIGHTS	4.00

The judicial system's structure largely mirrors the British legal system and consists of 75 district courts, 16 appellate courts, and the Supreme Court, which serves as both a final court of appeal and venue for judicial and constitutional review. The interim constitution also established a Constituent Assembly Court with jurisdiction over electoral disputes arising from the CA elections. Judges, rather than juries, preside over all proceedings.

Judicial independence has increased compared to the years when the king regularly used the courts to silence critics and cement his authority. Although the chief justice acknowledged occasional political pressure in July 2008, the Supreme Court has asserted its independence in notable ways, taking bold stances on controversial disputes in opposition to both the government and opposition parties. Since 2006, the court has ordered the investigation of enforced disappearances from the insurgency period, required the release of Tibetan protesters, repealed laws enabling oppressive religious customs, and expanded the rights of women and sexual minorities. By contrast, lower level tribunals remain poorly resourced and vulnerable to corruption and intimidation, weakening the consistent and impartial application of the law.

In response to the Supreme Court's decisions, the Maoist-led government repeatedly sought to assert greater influence over the judiciary, while publicly challenging its authority. In April 2008, Prachanda declared that constitutional measures endorsed by "popular mandate…cannot be the subject of any judicial deliberation." In October 2008, the Maoist-led government decided to expand the Supreme Court by adding two seats.[50] In December, it attempted to fill over three dozen vacancies in the Supreme Court and appellate courts with pro-Maoist candidates, moves the chief justice criticized as undermining judicial independence.[51]

Judicial authority has also been undermined by state agencies delaying or outright refusing to comply with adverse decisions. To date, the government has implemented only a small percentage of Supreme Court policy directives.[52] Both the Nepalese Army and the People's Liberation Army (PLA) defied a February 2009 interim Supreme Court decision calling for suspension of recruitment of new cadets;[53] they have also ignored rulings ordering investigations into past abuses.

Although the current Supreme Court justices, and to a lesser extent lower courts, have been appointed in a largely impartial manner, constitutional experts have criticized current procedures as potentially limiting independence due to the prime minister's influence over the process. The chief justice is appointed by the prime minister on the recommendation of the Constitutional Council, with four of the council's six members also appointed by the prime minister. The chief justice then selects other Supreme Court judges "on the recommendation" of the Judicial Council (JC), terminology that leaves vague how binding the JC's advice is. With three of the JC's members directly appointed by the prime minister and two appointed by the chief justice, direct and indirect executive influence is evident.[54] The interim constitution protects Supreme Court judges from executive interference and a parliamentary supermajority is required for their removal, though protections for lower-level judges are weaker.

Though the judiciary is widely perceived as more trustworthy than other state institutions, public faith in the impartial administration of justice remains low, and most Nepalese acknowledge the influence of patronage in the court system.[55] Inadequate salaries and a chronic lack of funding have fueled judicial corruption, particularly in the lower courts. The Supreme Court has not remained untouched. In March 2007, it was rocked by scandal after a compact disk surfaced showing court officials negotiating the terms of a kickback with a plaintiff in a property lawsuit.[56] Delays also plague the judiciary, with over 50,000 cases reportedly backlogged in 2008 at all levels of the judiciary.[57] A recent study of judicial rulings cited other shortcomings, including ignored precedents, inadequate legal analysis, and unnecessary orders issued.[58]

Although the interim constitution guarantees the presumption of innocence, in practice, suspects are often presumed guilty and tortured to elicit confessions. Inconsistent sentencing, arbitrary arrest, prolonged detention, and erratic trial proceedings are hallmarks of the criminal justice system. Access to counsel is limited and Maoist cadres have been known to intimidate lawyers and witnesses.[59] More positively, authorities began outfitting courtrooms in the Kathmandu Valley with closed circuit recording in May 2009 to reduce trial irregularities.[60] Though officially disbanded following the CPA, Maoist-controlled parallel courts continue to operate in some rural districts. Few due process protections or opportunities to appeal exist in the processes overseen by party cadres, though some experts have remarked on their effectiveness in providing prompt and inexpensive dispute resolution.[61]

Perhaps the most serious obstacle to the rule of law remains the culture of impunity for human rights abusers, wealthy Nepalese, and members of the political elite. Prosecutors are vulnerable to political influence, while provisions of the Army Act, Police Act, and Public Security Act explicitly grant immunity to members of the security forces and civil servants. As such, Maoist leaders, military personnel, and government officials who allegedly have been involved in severe abuses continue to evade punishment, as do customs officials and border police complicit in human trafficking.

In some cases in which investigations have been initiated, criminal proceedings have been halted by executive decree. According to the International Crisis Group, "on 23 October 2008 the [Maoist-led] government withdrew 349 criminal cases against political party cadres accused of crimes including rape, robbery and drug smuggling. 53 of these cases had been registered after the signing of the CPA."[62] In another egregious incident, authorities in 2006 permitted Sitaram Prasain, a businessman accused of embezzling US$4.3 million from his own bank, to hold a lavish wedding party attended by senior ministers despite an outstanding warrant for his arrest.[63] Although the CPA calls for a truth and reconciliation commission, one has yet to be established. Meanwhile, police and judges have used its future creation to justify the lack of prosecutions for abuses from the insurgency period.

Security sector reform remains a serious challenge, with commitments to merge the Maoist PLA with the NA not yet realized. A 2006 amendment to the Army Act formally established civilian control over the armed forces. In practice, however, the NA has retained significant autonomy and resisted submitting to civilian oversight. The military has also injected itself into the political process, submitting proposals to the CA, such as a February 2009 demand for a referendum over the country's status as a secular country and a federal versus centralized state structure. Although human rights abuses have declined since 2006, members of the military continued to harass activists publicizing abuses from the insurgency period: in 2007, NA soldiers reportedly made death threats against Jitman Basnet, a lawyer who published a book detailing his torture in military custody.[64]

An estimated 23,000 PLA fighters remain confined in cantonments throughout the country. The UN has supervised weapons storage and screened the former insurgents for eventual entry into the NA and other security agencies, with approximately 20,000 receiving approval. The process has been marred, however, by disqualified combatants' refusal to leave cantonments, PLA attempts to recruit new soldiers to replace disqualified ones in violation of the CPA, and soldiers' venturing outside cantonments, committing acts of violence and extortion. In one incident that sparked national outrage, in May 2008, PLA soldiers kidnapped, tortured, and then allegedly murdered former Maoist supporter and Kathmandu businessman Ram Hari Shrestha. Though the government vowed to conduct an investigation, no one has yet been prosecuted.[65]

The increased activities of paramilitary youth groups since 2006 have exacerbated security problems. With a reported 50,000 active cadres, the YCL is the largest.[66] Mostly in response to its actions, other political parties have established militant youth wings, including the CPN-UML affiliated Youth Force, the Terai-based Madhesi Youth Force, and the Nepali Congress's Tarun Dal. In 2008 and 2009, these groups were responsible for numerous violent acts against police, rival party members, and ordinary civilians.[67] The authorities have made little effort to rein in or punish such violence, though political leaders have rhetorically sought to distance themselves from the thuggish behavior.

In a country in which nearly 80 percent of the rural population cultivates crops, land is a key asset. Despite its importance and the inclusion of the right to property under the interim constitution, protection of property rights remains weak, complicated by a rudimentary administration system, unreliable land records, poor rule of law, and forcible land seizures by militant groups. During the insurgency, Maoists seized thousands of hectares of land, the return of which they have repeatedly pledged since 2006. In February 2009, the government ensured that properties seized from political leaders in three dozen districts were returned to their original owners.[68] Nonetheless, the majority of seized land remains under Maoist control or in the possession of farmers to whom it was reallocated, further complicating the situation.[69] A High Level Land Commission has been established but has yet to play a significant role in settling land disputes. In a positive development, a pilot technical assistance program in Bhaktapur district funded by the Asian Development Bank reportedly improved the speed and quality of deed processing, and plans are in place to expand it to other regions.[70]

ANTICORRUPTION AND TRANSPARENCY   3.13

    ENVIRONMENT TO PROTECT AGAINST CORRUPTION   3.50
    PROCEDURES AND SYSTEMS TO ENFORCE ANTICORRUPTION LAWS   2.50
    EXISTENCE OF ANTICORRUPTION NORMS, STANDARDS,
        AND PROTECTIONS   3.00
    GOVERNMENTAL TRANSPARENCY   3.50

The legal framework for combating corruption has undergone important recent improvements. The 2006 dissolution of the Royal Commission for Corruption Control, an agency created by the king and used to persecute political opponents, was a further step forward. Nevertheless, corruption remains a defining feature of Nepal's social landscape. Weak institutions, political instability, and lack of commitment by key stakeholders hamper effective enforcement of new laws.

As political parties focused on election campaigning, coalition building, and responding to ethnic conflict, anticorruption efforts inevitably slowed in 2008 and 2009. According to some observers, opportunities for corruption may have increased during the transition phase.[71] In 2009, Nepal was ranked 143rd out of 180 nations in Transparency International's Corruption Perceptions Index, a decline from its 2007 ranking of 131.[72]

Bureaucratic red tape, low salaries, and socioeconomic insecurity contribute to high levels of petty corruption. Cultural norms such as *afno manche* (emphasizing one's inner circle) and *chakari* (the offering of gifts to a patron in exchange for favors) contribute to nepotism and favoritism within the bureaucracy and in the provision of public services. The state maintains several dozen public enterprises, which are prone to graft, mismanagement, and bloated payrolls. No independent agencies regulate these companies and internal auditing procedures are often lax. A Ministry of Finance survey of 36 public enterprises found that in the 2008 fiscal year, 19 had incurred losses, including the Nepali Oil Corporation, a deterioration from the previous year, and only 19 had audited their accounts.[73] Adding to the confusion have been management reshuffles amid changing government coalitions. In August 2009, five Maoist-affiliated chairs and general managers resigned, citing the change in government.[74]

The scope and quality of the legal framework tackling corruption in Nepal has improved in recent years, bringing it closer to international standards. The 2002 Prevention of Corruption Act allows potential punishment of up to ten years' imprisonment should civil servants accept gifts or favors in their official capacity. Expanding on this legislation are the 2007 Public Procurement Act and the Good Governance Act, which established new regulations for transparency in civil service hiring, mandatory public hearings, prevention of conflicts of interest, and the creation of ministerial good governance units.[75] The 2007 Banking Offence and Punishment Act prescribes harsh penalties for bank-related fraud or large loan defaults. The 2008 Money Laundering Prevention Act requires financial institutions to maintain diligent transaction records and imposes one to four years' imprisonment for money laundering.

Though improved since 2005, enforcement of such laws remains inconsistent at best, and senior officials are rarely convicted for violations. Under the interim constitution, the Commission for the Investigation of Abuse of Authority (CIAA) serves as the nation's chief anticorruption agency, wielding ombudsman, investigative, and prosecutorial powers. Despite the CIAA's power to launch investigations and collect evidence, it turns over its results to the less independent prosecutor's office, which pleads relevant cases before the Special Court, a tribunal created in 2002 to handle corruption cases. In practice, this dependence on government attorneys for convictions has hindered the impact of the CIAA's investigations.

Although the CIAA has aggressively pursued cases against senior politicians without regard to their political affiliation, few such cases have resulted in conviction. According to one estimate, of 63 high-profile cases of possession of disproportionate property, the CIAA had won only seven as of July 2009. By contrast, its success rate in prosecutions of lower officials and administrative irregularities is estimated at 75 to 80 percent. Experts and CIAA commissioners have attributed the discrepancy to a lack of commitment to fighting corruption within the attorney general's office and the Special Court, alleging that the former has been slack in pleading high-level cases before the court, while the latter has tended to acquit senior officials on technicalities.[76]

The CIAA's authority is limited in other ways. Interim constitution provisions calling for an expanded mandate to cover the army and judiciary have yet to be implemented, and the private sector is outside its jurisdiction. Consequently, less than half of all instances of corruption are estimated to fall under the agency's purview. Moreover, a shortage of commissioners since 2006 has further weakened its capacity. Collectively, these factors have contributed to a decline of public trust in the commission.

Other agencies are tasked with combating corruption in specific sectors: the Auditor General and the Public Accounts Committee monitor state spending and financial reports, and the newly created Public Procurement Monitoring Office (PPMO) oversees government purchases and contracts. The National Vigilance Center (NVC) audits income and asset reports for irregularities. Under the Prevention of Corruption Act, public servants are required to declare their property assets and the CIAA has occasionally taken action against those who have not.[77] As a whole, however, the asset-monitoring system is incomplete, and NVC asset data are not open to public scrutiny or independent verification. In addition, officials accused of corruption often manage to attain high-level government positions. Although the Prevention of Corruption Act prohibits individuals implicated in corruption from holding office, the Election Commission and Special Court turned a blind eye to nepotism and graft among the main political parties and their candidates.[78]

Tax administration and transparency have improved modestly and in 2009 the government announced a new initiative to promote tax compliance.[79] Nonetheless, the system remains prone to inefficiency and corruption, with businesses often subject to unpredictable and costly taxes as well as extortion by the YCL and other militia groups. Victims of such corruption have few avenues for effective redress. The NVC has processed hundreds of citizen complaints in recent years.[80] Its effectiveness is limited, however, as it only possesses the authority to forward nonbinding recommendations to other institutions.

There is wide coverage of corruption in the media, including among 5,500 community radio clubs created as part of a local NGO initiative.[81] Journalists have reported extensively on the CIAA's investigations and allegations of graft, bribery, and embezzlement in government; recent stories include a raid of the police headquarters due to suspicion of financial irregularities in the purchase of jackets[82] and charges that the Nepali Oil Corporation embezzled US$4.5 million in a land deal.[83] Although anticorruption activists and whistleblowers are freer today than under the royal regime, the authorities rarely take action to protect them, despite threats from political parties and their militant youth wings. Whistleblower provisions in the 2007 Right to Information Act are rarely enforced. The government has taken few steps to combat corruption in the education sector, where irregular fees and payments to teachers or management committees are the most common forms.

The 2007 Right to Information Act grants citizens the right to access the records of government institutions, political parties, and state-funded NGOs. Citizens can access most information concerning investigations by anticorruption agencies, legislative processes, and court decisions. Nevertheless, some international advocacy groups decried exceptions for national security and criminal investigations as overly broad.[84]

The budget-making process has improved in recent years, with Nepal receiving a score of 43 on the 2008 Open Budget Index, compared to 36 in 2006.[85] It has become more inclusive and open to exhaustive legislative debate. Accounting of expenditures, however, is riddled with irregularities. The Auditor General now publishes annual reports of tax revenue and government accounts, an improvement over the 2002–05 period, when such records were concealed from the public.[86] However, the reports are often incomplete, making comparisons between what was budgeted and what was spent difficult.[87]

The 2007 Public Procurement Act requires competitive, open bidding for major contracts and empowers the PPMO to oversee the process. Since its inception, the PPMO has taken modest steps to reduce graft. In November 2007, the Supreme Court also ordered the Nepal Airlines Corporation to cancel a US$6.3 million contract with a Beijing maintenance company, citing its failure to undergo a competitive bidding process.[88] Still, enforcement remains irregular.

Service delivery remains poorly monitored and characterized by off-budget allocations and spending. Although foreign aid makes up nearly 70 percent of the development budget, it has yet to translate into improved services for many Nepalis due to corruption, procedural delays and low state capacity.[89] In one case in 2008, local media reported that of "30 sacks of rice and three sacks of clothes sent for distribution among flood victims in Laukahi and Bhokraha, only 20 containing rice and one with clothes reached the affected spot."[90]

RECOMMENDATIONS

- Ensure that the constitution drafted by the Constituent Assembly provides for democratic institutions, judicial independence, and the protection of fundamental rights.
- Act on recommendations by the National Human Rights Commission for prosecutions, particularly in cases involving crimes against journalists and human rights defenders.
- End the culture of impunity by passing into legislation draft bills on disappearances and the establishment of a truth and reconciliation commission following consultations with all relevant stakeholders.
- Demilitarize all political parties' youth wings and hold political leaders accountable for systematic violence committed by affiliated organizations.
- Revitalize implementation of the Comprehensive Peace Agreement such that both the Nepalese Army and Maoist forces adhere to commitments regarding civilian control, demobilization, and integration of forces.
- Expand the authority of the Commission for the Investigation of Abuse of Authority (CIAA) as called for in the interim constitution, appoint a full complement of commissioners, and ensure that prosecutors possess sufficient political autonomy to pursue convictions based on evidence gathered by the CIAA, particularly against senior officials.

NOTES

For URLs and endnote hyperlinks, please visit the *Countries at the Crossroads* homepage at http://freedomhouse.org/template.cfm?page=139&edition=8.

[1] Subel Bhandari, "Late Monsoon Brings Fear of Food Shortage in Nepal," Agence France-Presse, July 5, 2009.
[2] Hari Bansh Jha, "Financing Election and Electoral Reforms in Nepal" (paper presented at the National Seminar on Issues and Challenges of Electoral Reforms in Nepal, Jawalkher, Lalitpur, July 7–8, 2007); Transparency International, "Nepal," in *Global Corruption Report 2009: Corruption and the Private Sector* (Berlin: Transparency International, 2009).

3. European Union Election Observation Mission, "Nepal Constituent Assembly Election 10 April 2008: Preliminary Statement," April 12, 2008.
4. Jaime Mendoza, "Covering Nepal's First Election in Nine Years," Asia Media Archives, April 11, 2008.
5. "Seven Dead in Nepal Poll Violence," British Broadcasting Corporation (BBC), April 9, 2008.
6. "Nepal Women and Dalit Ride into Parliament on Maoist Coattails," The Advocacy Project, April 24, 2008.
7. Mallika Aryal, "Rights–Nepal: La Won Disappearances Provokes Outcry," Inter Press Service (IPS), February 3, 2009.
8. "Nepal Army Dragged to Court for Fresh Recruitment," Thaindian News, February 18, 2009.
9. "Army, Judiciary Pose Serious Threat to Republican Order," Telegraphnepal.com, March 29, 2009.
10. Maseeh Rahman, "Maoists Lose Majority after Nepal Army Chief Sacked," *Guardian*, May 3, 2009.
11. Hari Prasad Shrestha, "The Evils of the Nepalese Bureaucracy," American Chronicle, January 12, 2009.
12. Dev Raj Dahal, *Civil Society Groups in Nepal: Their Roles in Conflict and Peace-Building* (Kathmandu: United Nations Development Programme, 2006).
13. Asian Forum for Human Rights and Development, "Nepal: Human Rights Defenders Are a Target for Non-State Actors," news release, October 10, 2008.
14. International Federation for Human Rights (FIDH), "Publication of the 2007 Annual Report of the Observatory for the Protection of Human Rights Defenders," press release, July 4, 2008.
15. Article 19, *Memorandum on the Ordinance Amending Some of the Nepal Acts Relating to the Media*, Article 19, (London: Article 19, 2005).
16. Committee to Protect Journalists (CPJ), "Nepal," in *Attacks on the Press 2008* (New York: CPJ, 2009).
17. Reporters without Borders (RSF), "Nepal," in *World Report 2009* (Paris: RSF, 2009).
18. International Press Freedom and Freedom of Expression Mission, "Rapid Response Assessment Mission to Nepal," joint statement, February 8, 2009.
19. RSF, "Nepalese Media in Great Danger, International Press Freedom Mission Finds," news release, February 8, 2009.
20. Freedom House, "Nepal," in *Freedom of the Press 2008* (Washington, D.C.: Freedom House, 2009).
21. Bureau of Democracy, Human Rights, and Labor, "Nepal," in *2008 Country Reports on Human Rights Practices* (Washington, D.C.: U.S. Department of State, 2009).
22. The International Committee of the Red Cross (ICRC), *Families of Missing Persons in Nepal: A Study of Their Needs* (Kathmandu: ICRC, 2009).
23. Amnesty International, "Nepal," in *Amnesty International Report 2009* (London: Amnesty International, 2009).
24. Saferworld, *On Track for Improved Security?* (London: Saferworld, April 2009).
25. Overseas Security Advisory Council (OSAC), *Nepal 2009 Crime and Safety Report* (Washington, D.C.: OSAC, 2009).
26. Mallika Aryal, "NEPAL: Crime Grows amid Political Instability," IPS, July 15, 2009.
27. Internally Displaced People's Working Group, "Distant from Durable Solutions: Conflict Induced Internal Displacement in Nepal," June 2009.
28. The National Human Rights Commission of Nepal (NHRC), *The Current Activities of the National Human Rights Commission of Nepal* (Kathmandu: NHRC, 2009).

29. Anju Gautam, "Despite Promises, Government Assistance to Conflict Victims Is Minimal," The Press Institute for Women in the Developing World, May 3, 2007; Human Rights Watch (HRW), "Letter to Prime Minister Pushpa Kumar Dahal of Nepal," March 9, 2009.
30. Charles Haviland, "Nepal's Post-War Culture of Impunity," BBC, March 1, 2009.
31. "Nepal: UN Human Rights Official Voices Concern about Promotion of Army Officer," United Nations (UN) News Center, July 7, 2009.
32. HRW, *Waiting for Justice: Unpunished Crimes from Nepal's Armed Conflict* (New York: HRW, September 11, 2008), 34.
33. Tara Bhattarai, "An Open Secret," The Press Institute for Women in the Developing World, September 26, 2007.
34. Inter-Parliamentary Union,"PARLINE Database on National Parliaments: Nepal, Sambidhan Sabha (Constituent Assembly)," home page.
35. "Nepal Women and Dalit Ride into Parliament on Maoist Coattails," Advocacy Net, April 24, 2008.
36. Rosalie Hughes, "Nepalese Women Free from War but Not Violence," Reuters, March 6, 2009.
37. "Nepal: Domestic Violence Still Common–Activists," Integrated Regional Information Networks (IRIN), November 25, 2008.
38. Asian Human Rights Commission,"Nepal: Alleged Cruel Form of Torture Imposed on Two Sisters by the Surkhet District Police," July 9, 2008.
39. Amnesty International, "Nepal's Government Fails to Protect Women Human Rights Activists," news release, April 10, 2009.
40. Asian Human Rights Committee, "Nepal: 'Recasting Justice' Outlines Crucial Next Steps for Nepal's Constitution," news release, April 22, 2008.
41. Tulsi Ram Pandey et al., *Forms and Patterns of Social Discrimination in Nepal* (Kathmandu: UNESCO, 2006).
42. S. Chandrasekharan, "Nepal: Terai Agitation Ends–Update No. 152," South Asia Analysis Group, February 29, 2008.
43. "Nepal's CPN-UML Set to Deal with Madhesi Front: Report," *Indian Express*, May 13, 2009.
44. Bikash Sangraula, "Nepal Faces Hindu Backlash over Declaration As Secular State," *Christian Science Monitor*, May 30, 2006.
45. Charles Haviland, "Two Die in Nepal Mosque Bombing," BBC, March 30, 2008.
46. Achal Narayanan, "Nepal's Supreme Court Oks Same-Sex Marriage," Religious News Service, November 21, 2008.
47. Sanjay Jha, "Nepal Gives Formal Recognition to Third Gender," *Times of India*, September 18, 2008.
48. International Trade Union Confederation (ITUC), "Nepal," in *Annual Survey of Violations of Trade Union Rights* (Brussels: ITUC, 2009).
49. HRW, *Appeasing China: Restricting the Rights of Tibetans in Nepal* (New York: HRW, 2008).
50. Bikas Bhattarai, "Nepal Chief Justice Urges Maoists Not to Interfere in Judiciary," *Nepal Samacharpatra*, October 12, 2008.
51. Bal Krishna Baset, "Nepal Minister Faces Opposition over Pro-Maoist Judges' Appointment," ekantipur.com, December 9, 2008.
52. Batkhishig Badarch, "Better Protection of Human Rights through Public Interest Litigation: An International Approach and Nepalese Context," *Informal* 25, no. 3 (October–December 2008).

53. "Nepal Maoists Seek to Recruit over 12,000 New Fighters," *Thaindian News*, March 3, 2009.
54. *Interim Constitution of Nepal*, Art. 113.
55. Tek Nath Dhakal and Ratna Raj Nirola, "Prevalence of Corruption and Its Challenge for Improving Governance in Nepal" (paper presented at the International Conference on Challenges of Governance in South Asia, Kathmandu, Nepal, December 15–16, 2008).
56. "Something Still Rotten: Nepal," *Economist*, June 16, 2007.
57. Bureau of Democracy, Human Rights, and Labor, "Nepal," in *2008 Country Reports on Human Rights Practices*.
58. Kiran Chapagain, "SC Questions Verdicts at Patan Appellate, Special Court, *Republica*, May 13, 2009.
59. Bijo Francis, "Nepal's Maoists Must Respect the Law," UPI Asia, April 20, 2009.
60. "Nepal: Senior UN Official Lauds Supreme Court Reforms." UN News Centre, May 19, 2009.
61. David Pimentel, "Constitutional Concepts for the Rule of Law: A Vision for the Post-Monarchy Judiciary in Nepal," (unpublished paper, Florida Coastal School of Law, 2009), 9.
62. International Crisis Group (ICG), *Nepal's Faltering Peace Process* (Brussels: ICG, February 19, 2009).
63. "Corruption in Nepal," *Economist*, July 14, 2007.
64. The International Bar Association Human Rights Institute, "Nepal: Intimidation of Lawyer, Jutman Basnet, September 2007," news release, September 14, 2007.
65. "Another Commission Is Not Enough: Ram Hari Shrestha and the Corrosive Impact of Impunity on Nepal's Unsteady Peace," The Asian Centre for Human Rights (ACHR) Weekly Review, May 22, 2008.
66. Harold Olav Skar, "Between Boy Scouts and Paramilitary Storm Troops: The Young Communist League of Nepal," Working Paper (Norwegian Institute of International Affairs, July 2008).
67. Democracy and Election Alliance Nepal (DEAN), *Preliminary Election Observation Report Constituent Assembly Election* (Kathmandu: DEAN, April 10, 2008); Informal Sector Service Center (INSEC), *Human Rights Yearbook 2009* (Kathmandu: INSEC, 2009).
68. "Nepal Maoists Return Former Prime Ministers' Properties," ekantipur.com, February 4, 2009.
69. ICG, *Nepal's Faltering Peace Process*.
70. Asian Development Bank (ADB), "Technical Assistance Completion Report, Division: Nepal Resident Mission," 2009.
71. Transparency International,"Nepal," in *Global Corruption Report 2009*.
72. Transparency International, *2009 Corruption Perceptions Index* (Berlin: Transparency International, November 17, 2009); Transparency International, *2007 Corruption Perceptions Index* (Berlin: Transparency International, September 26, 2007).
73. Rupak D. Sharma, "Performance of PEs Deteriorates Further," *Republica,* July 13, 2009.
74. "Chiefs of 5 State Enterprises Resign," *Republica*, August 2, 2009.
75. Asian Development Bank (ADB) and the Organization for Economic Cooperation and Development (OECD), *Combating Corruption in Asia-Pacific: Nepal's Measures to Implement the Anti-Corruption Action Plan for Asia Pacific* (Manila/Paris: ADB and OECD, 2008).
76. "CIAA's Losing Battle against Corruption," ekantipur.com, July 22, 2009.
77. "Nepal's Anti-Graft Body Fines 48 Police Officials," *Press Trust of India*, May 19, 2009.

[78] Hari Bahadur Thapa, "Reporter's Notebook: Nepal," in *Global Integrity Report 2008* (Washington, D.C.: Global Integrity, 2008).
[79] "Nepal Budget Stresses Tax Compliance," *Himalayan Times*, July 13, 2009.
[80] The National Vigilance Center of the Government of Nepal, "Past Activities," home page.
[81] United Nations Development Programme, *Accelerating Human Development in Asia and the Pacific* (Delhi: Macmillan Publishers India Ltd., 2008).
[82] Bimal Gautam, "CIAA Raids Nepal Police HQ over Jacket Deal Rs 50m Suspected to Have Been Embezzled," *Republica*, July 13, 2009.
[83] Bimal Gautam, "CIAA Halts NOC Land Buy, Suspects Rs 350m Embezzlement," *Republica*, July 15, 2009.
[84] Article 19, Freedom Forum, and Federation of Nepali Journalists (FNJ), *Memorandum on the Right to Information Act of the State of Nepal*, (London/Kathmandu: Article 19, Freedom Forum, and FNJ, January 2008).
[85] Open Budget Initiative, "Nepal," in *Open Budget Index 2008* (Washington, D.C.: Open Budget Initiative, 2009); Open Budget Initiative, "Nepal," in *Open Budget Index 2006* (Washington, D.C.: Open Budget Initiative, 2007).
[86] Transparency International Nepal, *Annual Progress Report of the Fiscal Year 2007/08* (Kathmandu: Transparency International Nepal, 2008).
[87] Open Budget Initiative, "Nepal," in *Open Budget Index 2008*.
[88] "Nepal Court Bars Airline's China Maintenance Contract," *Kathmandu Post*, November 15, 2007.
[89] Surya B. Prasai, "In Nepal, a Debate over Foreign Aid," American Chronicle, February 22, 2008.
[90] "Disasters, Relief Works and Corruption," *Kathmandu Post*, October 17, 2008.

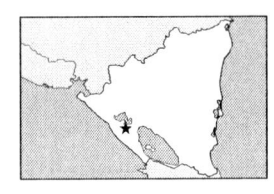

NICARAGUA

CAPITAL: Managua
POPULATION: 5.7 million
GNI PER CAPITA (PPP): $2,620

SCORES	2006	2010
ACCOUNTABILITY AND PUBLIC VOICE:	4.44	3.31
CIVIL LIBERTIES:	4.13	3.86
RULE OF LAW:	3.61	3.43
ANTICORRUPTION AND TRANSPARENCY:	3.67	3.21

(scores are based on a scale of 0 to 7, with 0 representing weakest and 7 representing strongest performance)

David R. Dye

INTRODUCTION

The election of Daniel Ortega as president in November 2006 has launched Nicaragua on a path of radical change, as the leader of the left-wing Sandinista National Liberation Front (FSLN) seeks to install a variant of the authoritarian popular democracy he headed in the 1980s. This transformation has seriously compromised the country's fragile electoral democracy, which had managed to survive, but did not set down strong roots, during the 16 years since Violeta Chamorro ousted the Sandinistas from power in a 1990 election. The prospects for free elections in the future and the rights of regime opponents to political organization, assembly, and mobilization are particularly imperiled. Ortega resorted to flagrant fraud when he was unable to win the November 2008 municipal elections fairly, signaling his willingness to subvert democratic values in his efforts to retain power.

Originally the coordinator of the Sandinistas' revolutionary junta, Ortega settled in as the undisputed leader of the party after its defeat in the 1990 elections. The FSLN failed to remake itself as a democratic party of the left during the subsequent decade, preferring to use confrontational tactics to defend the interests of its constituents against the "neoliberal" policies of successive postwar governments. When this strategy lost steam at the end of the 1990s, Ortega resorted to penetration and corruption of state institutions through high-level

---

David R. Dye is a political consultant based in Nicaragua. He worked as political advisor to the Carter Center's 2001 and 2006 Nicaraguan election observation missions and is currently conducting a Central America-wide consultancy on citizen security matters for the Open Society Institute. He has also provided the Economist Intelligence Unit in London with the analysis for its Nicaragua Country Report since 1994.

political deal-making as a way to promote his interests, with a growing focus on regaining the presidency. The effort was aided by the failure of the Chamorro administration and the Liberal Constitutionalist Party–led governments that succeeded it to strengthen democratic institutions or mitigate the discontent caused by massive poverty and economic inequality.

After his 2006 election, Ortega aligned Nicaragua with the ideological if not the policy framework of Venezuelan president Hugo Chávez's "Bolivarian revolution." With the assistance of his wife, Rosario Murillo, Ortega has sought to refashion the FSLN as an instrument of political control by creating so-called Citizen Power Councils (CPCs), designed in theory to provide a direct link between the president and the citizens. In the process he has ridden roughshod over existing institutions of municipal autonomy and citizen participation, marginalizing civil society organizations that oppose his government and channeling resources to his supporters.

Because the FSLN holds only 38 of the National Assembly's 91 seats, Ortega has so far relied on an informal alliance with former president Arnoldo Alemán, leader of the Liberal Constitutionalist Party (PLC), to pass legislation. These two leaders, known as the *caudillos* (strongmen) of Nicaraguan politics, sealed political pacts in 2000 and 2004 that divided up power in various state institutions and fostered intense corruption, as evidenced by Alemán's conviction on graft charges in 2003.[1] More recently, they have discussed reforms to the 1987 constitution that would permit presidents to serve consecutive terms and change the system of government to a French-style semipresidential regime. However, Ortega's drive for complete power may ultimately abort these changes and undermine the power-sharing arrangement with the PLC, which is seeking guarantees that free and fair elections will be held in November 2011.

Alongside the traditional, clientelist forces represented by the FSLN and PLC, modern opposition parties have gained a foothold in recent years despite harassment from the election authority. The right-leaning Vamos con Eduardo (VCE) movement, headed by former PLC member Eduardo Montealegre, fused with the Liberal Independent Party (PLI) in early 2009 in order to have a party banner under which it could run in 2011. On the other side of the spectrum, the Sandinista Renewal Movement (MRS), whose most prominent leader is Edmundo Jarquín, represents a moderate, social democratic alternative to the ruling Sandinistas but currently lacks legal status.

Persistent authoritarian tendencies and governance problems have impeded Nicaragua's economic progress. It remains the Western Hemisphere's second poorest country, with a per capita income of just US$1,023 in 2007.[2] Though the percentage of Nicaraguans who are poor is stagnant, their absolute numbers are rising, and the distribution of national income is severely skewed. The Ortega administration has tried to combat these trends by expanding access to health and education as well as through novel programs called Zero Hunger and Zero Usury, but adverse economic conditions have so far overwhelmed its efforts. Coupled with the weaknesses in the political system, these severe social deficits have created a situation in which most citizens, though aware that they are entitled to certain rights, lack the necessary resources to assert and defend them.

ACCOUNTABILITY AND PUBLIC VOICE 3.31
FREE AND FAIR ELECTORAL LAWS AND ELECTIONS	3.25
EFFECTIVE AND ACCOUNTABLE GOVERNMENT	2.00
CIVIC ENGAGEMENT AND CIVIC MONITORING	4.00
MEDIA INDEPENDENCE AND FREEDOM OF EXPRESSION	4.00

The 2000 pact between Alemán and Ortega had the effect of completely politicizing the Supreme Electoral Council (CSE), putting it firmly under the control of the FSLN and the PLC. In the wake of the pact, public trust in the fairness of elections slowly declined as incidents of localized fraud cropped up. Ortega won the presidency in 2006 with only 38 percent of the vote, thanks to a rule adopted in 2000 that allows a candidate to secure a first-round victory with as little as 35 percent of the ballots so long as he has at least a five-point lead over his nearest challenger. The Liberal vote was split almost evenly between Montealegre, who took 28 percent as the candidate of the Nicaraguan Liberal Alliance (ALN), and the PLC's José Rizo, who won 27 percent. Although campaigning was vigorous and the national-level outcome was unquestioned, observers denounced localized fraud in the lightly populated North Atlantic Autonomous Region (RAAN) in the aftermath of the voting.

The FSLN subsequently accumulated more power in the electoral authority, leaving all other parties, including the PLC, vulnerable to manipulation and fraud. Public confidence in the electoral system plummeted, except among Sandinistas, after the FSLN ostensibly swept 105 of the 146 municipalities at stake in the November 2008 local elections. Charging that a massive fraud had been committed, the opposition Liberal coalition, composed of the PLC and Montealegre's VCE, claimed to have won in 81 municipalities, including Managua.

During the election process, the CSE had arbitrarily annulled the legal standing of two other parties, the MRS and the Conservative Party (PC), based on supposed violations of internal party rules. It also refused to recognize credible domestic or international election monitors on the grounds that their organizations were biased against the Ortega government and the CSE itself. The contest was also marked by the first significant electoral violence since 1990. In the months prior to election day, Sandinista militants forcibly disrupted protests by the MRS, including a rally in mid-September in León that led to violence. Although the Liberals were allowed to operate freely, their lack of funds made for a lackluster campaign. There was serious intimidation of voters on election day, and opposition poll watchers were forcibly excluded from polling stations before the votes were counted. Moreover, civil society groups alleged that voting sites in opposition strongholds were closed early, and that ballots from those stations were improperly annulled even as blank votes were marked in favor of FSLN candidates.[3] Violence swelled as club-wielding Sandinista militants confronted opposition protesters on the streets of various cities and towns in the weeks after the voting.[4]

The electoral law (Law 331) spawned by the 2000 pact imposes some of Latin America's stiffest requirements for the registration of political parties and coalitions. Parties must maintain structures in all 153 municipalities and present candidates in every election to preserve their legal standing. Moreover, lack of clarity in the law allows the CSE to arbitrarily exclude or include political parties, and facilitates the manipulation of vote results. Among other shortcomings, the law does not require the CSE to publish full election results broken down by polling place; consequently, significant portions of the vote counts in both the 2006 presidential ballot and the 2008 municipal contest have never been reported.

Campaign finance rules are weak, allowing economically powerful actors to exert undue political influence. Although the law provides significant public funding for party campaigns, it imposes no restrictions on campaign media spending. Rules for the disclosure of campaign donors are imprecise, and enforcement is lax and subject to political manipulation.[5]

Since reaching their 2000 agreement, the FSLN and PLC have used their control over the National Assembly to colonize and subordinate other branches and agencies of government. Their successful appointment of representatives to the Supreme Court gave rise to party benches in the body that took their orders directly from Alemán and Ortega. In 2009, these parties continued to control the judiciary, the comptroller's office, the attorney general's office, and the ombudsman's office, politicizing each and fostering corruption through the resulting lack of checks and balances. In early 2009, the two caudillos were expected to negotiate constitutional reforms that would introduce a semipresidential system, in which executive power is shared between the president and a prime minister responsible to the legislature. However, Ortega dropped this idea in July, preferring to focus on a change that would permit him to serve a second consecutive term as president.

Ortega's strongman governing style has greatly reduced the ability of any social or economic group to influence public policy, which is dominated by close associates of the president and his wife. Making liberal use of tax and customs regulations, Ortega has curbed the extensive influence exerted by domestic bankers and other major entrepreneurs over economic decisions under his predecessor, Enrique Bolaños. Fully a third of the national budget is financed by foreign aid, and multilateral institutions and traditional bilateral donors still enjoy some influence over government policy. However, this has waned as Ortega has come to rely on assistance from Venezuela, which does not attach the transparency and other requirements imposed by traditional donors.

Ortega has also vitiated a 2003 civil service law that requires the recruitment and promotion of public servants to be based on merit. He ousted several thousand public officials upon taking office, distributing the jobs to FSLN supporters. The resulting loss of expertise has hobbled the government ever since. There are frequent reports that those seeking government jobs must present letters of recommendation from neighborhood CPCs, an abuse reminiscent of the revolutionary period.

The National Assembly continues to grant legal status to new civil associations, including churches, without major restrictions. Under Ortega, however, civil society has been effectively bifurcated into progovernment and antigovernment segments. Under the supervision of Rosario Murillo, the presidency goes through the motions of consulting Sandinista union and popular organizations concerning some social and economic matters. Meanwhile, it stonewalls all attempts by civil society groups it defines as opponents, preventing them from exerting even minimal influence over public affairs. At the local level, the FSLN has also attempted to organize CPCs as privileged channels for citizens to have their voices heard. However, the unelected councils have failed to attract the support of non-Sandinistas and exclude people of other political persuasions, while usurping the functions of local officials and committees.[6]

Under Bolaños, civil society organizations were notably free from state interference. However, during 2007–08, select nongovernmental organizations (NGOs), both domestic and foreign, faced increasing harassment from the tax authorities, the governance ministry, and the attorney general (Public Ministry). This trend culminated in October 2008, when the attorney general raided the offices of the Center of Investigation and Communication (CINCO) and the Autonomous Women's Movement (MAM) without a court order, alleging that the two groups had illegally channeled funds from international sources to political purposes.[7] After an international outcry, in January 2009 the attorney general refrained from bringing charges against the organizations, but the threat of intervention by the governance ministry hangs over their heads. The government has investigated the activities of more than a dozen other organizations, including Oxfam Great Britain, for the same supposed reason.

By mid-2009, the foreign ministry was preparing a manual to regulate the activities of international NGOs, but it later backed off amid donor concerns. The authorities also appear to have foregone changes in the statutes governing local NGOs, perhaps deeming pressures on their funding sources to be a sufficient means of control. Still, government supporters continued to routinely disrupt marches and protest actions by opposition civil society groups, notably the Civil Coordinator, an umbrella organization for Nicaraguan NGOs.

Alone among the four post-1990 governments, the Bolaños administration accorded the constitutionally-mandated National Economic and Social Planning Council (Conpes) a modest, although intermittent, consultative role. In November 2007, Ortega announced a major restructuring of Conpes by decree, with the ostensible aim of packing the body with sympathetic social organizations and especially representatives of municipal CPCs.[8] However, the restructuring has not been effected, with the result that an entity previously active in advising the government on budgetary matters and antipoverty strategy has become moribund, leaving civil society as a whole without organized access to high-level policymaking.

In contrast to the Bolaños administration, which generally respected freedom of the press and media, the Ortega government has shown unremitting hostility toward major media organizations it identifies as its critics, especially those it links to the "oligarchy."[9] Although the principal media outlets—television's Channel 2 and the newspaper *La Prensa*—are held by upper-class families that were historically opposed to the Sandinistas, evidence of a concerted policy intended to sabotage the current government is lacking. Initially, Ortega expressed his hostility mainly through verbal abuse and restrictions on covering official events and activities. The government took more extreme measures amid the political conflicts of late 2008, allegedly including the jamming of several opposition radio stations. In the violent aftermath of the disputed municipal elections, FSLN sympathizers reportedly destroyed equipment at Radio Darío, a local station in León city.

Government advertisements, which carry considerable weight in the overall ad market, are allocated almost exclusively to progovernment outlets. Other media have criticized this as an unfair attempt to manipulate their reporting. Some charge privately that the government also uses the renewal of radio and television licenses as means of pressure. In July 2009, the telecommunications regulator cancelled the license of Radio Ley, a local station owned by a staunch critic of the FSLN. While the government owns Radio Nicaragua and the official gazette, it does not control any media distribution networks or printing facilities. However, it is believed to fund television's Channel 4, controlled by the Ortega family, along with radio stations linked to the FSLN and a weekly online newspaper called *El 19*. All these outlets skew their coverage strongly in favor of the government.

For the first time since 1990, judicial harassment of the media has become a threat. In April 2008, a Sandinista judge convicted the editor in chief and one of the owners of *La Prensa* on a spurious slander charge, ostensibly brought by CPC representatives.[10] Threats to repeat this abuse have occurred sporadically. The eruption of political conflict in the streets since 2008 has also made journalists the targets of physical attack, including destruction of their equipment. Although violent incidents aimed at squelching political opposition have mainly affected independent journalists, progovernment reporters have on occasion suffered injury in clashes with opposition protesters. There have been no new assassinations of media workers since 2005, but the judicial system's previous leniency toward the killers of two journalists has aroused concern about impunity. Such concern extends to the nonlethal attacks on journalists noted above, none of which have been properly investigated.

Membership in the College of Journalists, approved by the National Assembly in 2003, is supposedly required to practice the profession, presenting a latent threat to press freedom. In elections held in early 2009, the government reportedly packed the body with its supporters, reviving fears that the college could work to infringe journalistic freedom.[11] The younger generation of Nicaraguan journalists has largely ignored the college and has so far suffered no repercussions. However, a reform proposed in August 2009 threatened to make membership genuinely obligatory. Like its predecessors, the Ortega administration does not interfere with access to or communications over the internet.

CIVIL LIBERTIES 3.86

PROTECTION FROM STATE TERROR, UNJUSTIFIED IMPRISONMENT, AND TORTURE	3.63
GENDER EQUITY	3.00
RIGHTS OF ETHNIC, RELIGIOUS, AND OTHER DISTINCT GROUPS	2.25
FREEDOM OF CONSCIENCE AND BELIEF	6.67
FREEDOM OF ASSOCIATION AND ASSEMBLY	3.75

No state-sponsored murders or politically motivated disappearances have been recorded since the early 1990s. Similarly, arbitrary detentions of government opponents, banned by Article 33 of the 1987 constitution, are uncommon. However, a Roman Catholic missionary, Alberto Boschi, was arrested in mid-2008 and later convicted of inciting violence during a political disturbance, a charge local human rights groups deemed spurious. Boschi is currently outside the country awaiting an opportunity to return.

In 2007–08, members of the National Police were alleged to have committed unlawful killings. The most important case occurred at El Encanto ranch in the South Atlantic Autonomous Region (RAAS) in May 2008, when members of a police and military patrol opened fire, killing three workers who confronted them with shotguns.[12] Human rights groups strongly questioned the actions of the authorities, but a local court acquitted the three accused officers. Convictions have been obtained in several other deadly instances of security force brutality in recent years.[13] As in the past, denunciations of physical abuse and degrading treatment against civilians were frequent in relation to the size of the police force, which consists of just over 9,000 officers. Between September 2007 and August 2008, the internal affairs division of the police inspectorate investigated 2,044 complaints against more than 3,200 personnel; of these, 895 received some sort of sanction, and 210 were dishonorably discharged.[14] However, it is not clear how many were remanded to the courts for processing. In general, few court verdicts have been issued against police personnel in recent years, suggesting a significant level of impunity.

While the police inspectorate continues to impose some discipline on personnel who abuse civilians, recent events have called into question the ability of the police to protect opposition parties and civil society organizations from physical attack in the streets. Such groups attempted in late 2008 and early 2009 to mount protest marches, and the police visibly declined to intervene when government supporters engaged in low-level violence and intimidation. This passive behavior reportedly stemmed from direct presidential orders.

The human rights ombudsman has also grown weaker as a barrier against abuses by the security forces. Pact-making between Ortega and Alemán subjected this entity to political control in late 2004, and its once-substantial credibility and effectiveness have declined enormously. In 2008, ombudsman Omar Cabezas, a Sandinista, displayed blatant bias against opposition forces, publicly describing their attempts to protest the denial of their political rights as "provocations" against the Ortega government. Though annual reports of the ombudsman's office continue to record hundreds of denunciations of abuses by the National Police and prison officials, they do not detail what action the ombudsman took in response.[15]

With the 2002 criminal procedure code fully in force, instances of long-term detention without trial have waned, though they are still a problem on the Atlantic Coast. Police holding cells, where short-term detainees are routinely held in wretched conditions during their trials, are grossly overcrowded. With 6,701 inmates in 2007, the prison system was running well above its capacity of 5,446. Food rations are clearly inadequate for even minimum nutrition, and medical care and drugs are sorely lacking. Prison guards, who receive human rights training from international donors and the Nicaraguan Human Rights Center (CENIDH), are judged to treat prisoners reasonably well. The position of a special procurator for prisons was created in 2006. However, the Ortega government has on occasion denied independent human rights groups and even the ombudsman access to prisons to monitor conditions. CENIDH reported prison riots in several facilities during 2006–07, due either to poor conditions or to anger over detention without trial. Violence among rival prison gangs is an aggravating factor.[16]

Protection against abuse by nonstate actors is weak. Corruption in the judicial system has fostered impunity in a significant number of drug-related trials, increasing fear in the population and making control of the drug trade more difficult. However, on the highly vulnerable Atlantic Coast, more effective policing in recent years has reduced drug traffickers' ability to intimidate judicial personnel. Though far less developed than in other Central American countries, juvenile gangs (*pandillas*) cause pervasive insecurity in poor neighborhoods in Managua, where they are linked to narcotics distribution. Since 2003, police efforts to organize vigilance by local residents and civil society activists' work with youthful offenders have curbed the gangs in certain areas of the capital. Due to the country's lower incidence of drug trafficking and youth gangs, the murder rate in Nicaragua is well below that of most of its neighbors, but overall crime rates are similar and other violent crimes are rapidly increasing.

The constitution bans discrimination based on gender, ethnic origin, and nationality, though not sexual orientation. Although legal bases for discrimination suits exist in the new penal code approved in November 2007 and the Equal Rights and Opportunities law passed by the legislature in February 2008, such actions are rare. Women and children are very poorly protected against sexual abuse and domestic violence, which is endemic. In recent years, the Institute of Forensic Medicine has recorded more than 10,000 cases of domestic violence annually, half of them spousal abuse. National Police chief Aminta Granera has augmented her force's training to deal with such violence, which is handled in the first instance by its women's commissariats. The Nicaraguan Human Rights Center has criticized the insensitivity often shown to victims, however, arguing that it amounts to "re-victimization."[17] Beyond the initial contact, the government does little to help, and civil society organizations run most centers for battered women. Despite the fact that the new penal code identifies intrafamily violence as a crime, prosecutions for domestic and sexual abuse remain rare.

The Ortega administration has supported some initiatives designed to combat and compensate for discrimination against women, including the Zero Hunger and Zero Usury programs mentioned above, whose beneficiaries are mostly female. The Equal Rights and Opportunities Law gives some teeth to constitutional provisions banning discrimination, imposing modest fines on officials who flout its precepts.[18] However, human rights groups allege that the law is not being enforced, and that discrimination against women in hiring and wages remains very strong. Sexual harassment is also known to be a frequent problem in the workplace, and little is done to stop it. Although the new legislation may eventually bring some benefits, it is currently overshadowed by the ban on therapeutic abortions, passed by the assembly in 2006 with FSLN support. Women's organizations charge that this prohibition, incorporated into the 2007 penal code, has led to dozens of preventable deaths.[19]

The new penal code outlaws human trafficking. The organized trafficking of young Nicaraguan women to work as prostitutes in other Central American countries and Mexico appears to be increasing. Both the women's commissariats and a national coalition of antitrafficking groups have done educational work in high schools on the problem. Although government efforts to stop the trade are limited in scope, prosecutors have obtained convictions against a handful of traffickers.

The human and civil rights of minority religious groups, mainly evangelical Protestants, are respected without limitation. However, the full exercise of rights by the ethnic minorities of the Atlantic Coast (Miskito, Mayangna, Creole, Garifuna, and Rama) is a distant prospect, particularly in light of the very weak fiscal base of the regional governments. Although committed to social improvements, the Ortega government, like its predecessors, has also sidelined local participation in the planning of regional development. An unacknowledged racism complicates the problem; in early 2009, a Managua discotheque refused to allow entry by black people from the southern Atlantic Coast, raising a storm of protest.[20] On the positive side, pursuant to a law passed in 1993, indigenous children receive education in their native tongues through the third grade, and in the RAAS most judges are now bilingual in Creole and Spanish.

The 1987 Autonomy Statute, together with existing electoral legislation, mandates some representation for the Atlantic Coast minorities on the autonomous regional councils by requiring that indigenous candidates head the election lists in certain districts. Tokenism has prevailed in implementing this provision, however, as the FSLN and PLC dominate the political scene in these areas; the Miskito-based Yatama party in the RAAN is the only sizable ethnically-based force. With migration from the Pacific Coast constantly altering the ethnic balance to the detriment of the indigenous residents, there have been periodic calls for changes in the existing scheme of political representation to empower indigenous groups, but no action has been taken. In 2003, the National Assembly passed a law providing for the demarcation and titling of indigenous landholdings to stop land invasions by mestizos. But the slow progress in the law's implementation has not stemmed the tide of encroachment, and land-based ethnic tensions simmer. Tensions also rose following the devastation of Hurricane Felix in 2007, which wiped out infrastructure and crops for tens of thousands of RAAN residents. In 2009, a group of activists known as the Council of Miskito Elders declared that the entire RAAN and RAAS zones were seceding from Nicaragua. Though few regional or national authorities took the threat seriously, it highlighted the depth of discontent in the region.

A 1998 law enjoins the government to take positive steps to assist people with disabilities, estimated to number more than 500,000 as part of the legacy of civil war. But aside from occasional public relations efforts, there are no government programs on this issue, and civil society provides the little help that is available. As is the case with women and indigenous people, protection for people with disabilities against discrimination in hiring and wages is basically nonexistent.

Although 75 percent of Nicaraguans are Roman Catholics, there is no state religion, and the government has consistently respected the right of citizens to hold and freely express their religious beliefs.[21] The state places no restrictions on religious observance or education, though only Catholic schools receive subsidies. The government also refrains from interference in the appointment of religious leaders or the internal affairs of churches. There is a long history of strained relations between Sandinistas and the Catholic Church, and Ortega's support for the ban on abortions was viewed as a ploy to reduce opposition to his candidacy from within the Church.

The constitution guarantees the freedoms of association and assembly, with the usual exceptions for military and police personnel. The government long ago ratified the International Labor Organization's Conventions 87 and 88 on freedom of union organization. However, the 1996 labor code makes union organization difficult, as employers can legally fire organizers if they are willing to pay for extensive severance benefits. The restrictive labor code also mandates complicated and cumbersome procedures for going on strike, making legal strikes rare and dampening the incentive to unionize. Overall, the left-wing Ortega government has done a somewhat better job than its predecessors in protecting union rights and enforcing collective bargaining agreements. A total of 192 new unions were formed in 2008, bringing the increase over a two-year period to nearly 400.[22] Despite this growth, unions are still not significant political actors except in the transport sector, where strikes occasionally force concessions from the government. There continue to be reports of cases in which garment companies in special export-processing zones have thwarted union activities by firing workers or threatening to close factories.

The labor code forbids compulsory membership in unions, and many workplaces have more than one union. Whereas governments after 1990 organized progovernment unions to counter those affiliated with the FSLN, the Ortega government has been accused of attempting to disband non-Sandinista syndicates, particularly in the health system. A 2007 law mandates the creation of professional colleges with broad powers to regulate the activities of their members, but as of mid-2009 none have been set up.

Social and political protests have been frequent since the early 1990s but are almost always small in scale and generally pose no threat to public order. Since mid-2008, the Ortega regime has responded to protest demonstrations with a type of informal repression, sending its supporters (and occasionally members of urban youth gangs) into the streets to impede and intimidate opposition marchers. It simultaneously orders the National Police not to use violence against "the people," thus facilitating intimidation and violating the opposition's right to peacefully assemble. Scores of protesters have been injured during these clashes, though there have not been fatalities.

RULE OF LAW 3.43

INDEPENDENT JUDICIARY	2.20
PRIMACY OF RULE OF LAW IN CIVIL AND CRIMINAL MATTERS	4.00
ACCOUNTABILITY OF SECURITY FORCES AND MILITARY TO CIVILIAN AUTHORITIES	3.50
PROTECTION OF PROPERTY RIGHTS	4.00

The judiciary's lack of independence from political influence is one of Nicaragua's most severe governance problems. The FSLN-PLC pacts have allowed the party caudillos, Ortega and Alemán, to use their control over the National Assembly to handpick loyal magistrates for the Supreme Court, which in turn appoints all lower-level personnel. The independence of the lower-court justices is therefore scant, as the upper ranks interfere pervasively in decisions. A judicial career law passed in October 2004 aimed to provide a nonpolitical merit system for the hiring, promotion, and discipline of lower-court judges. However, regulations implementing this law were not issued until 2008, and in practice clientelism still dominates in the selection of judges. Both judicial training and general legal education are weak.

As a result of these deficiencies, public and ruling party officials are rarely prosecuted for abuse of power and wrongdoing. In the most celebrated exception to this rule, former president Alemán was convicted on fraud and money laundering charges in late 2003. However, rather than let justice take its course, Ortega used his control over the court system to manipulate the processing of Alemán's appeal and extract political concessions from the Liberal leader. With positions in the appeals courts also divided between the FSLN and PLC, appellate rulings are occasionally used as bargaining cards between the two parties, but rulings in favor of ordinary citizens that unequivocally contradict the interests of the party caudillos are difficult to imagine.

In this environment, the belief that judicial rulings can be bought is widespread. Yet 45 percent of firms polled in a 2006 survey indicated that, whatever the merits of their judgments, the courts could at least enforce them. This percentage is somewhat higher than the Latin American and Caribbean average of 39 percent.[23] Nevertheless, decisions on whether to enforce rulings are subject to political considerations and influence peddling.

According to the constitution, criminal defendants are presumed innocent until proven guilty. A new criminal procedure code introduced in December 2002 established an oral accusatory system, and proceedings are now relatively prompt and generally seen as more fair. A drawback is that the politicized Public Ministry (attorney general) now has most control over which cases are taken to court, a fact that allows politically sensitive cases to be delayed. Human rights defenders argue that many crime victims suffer from this prerogative, as their cases are not pushed forward and they are disadvantaged by mediation procedures designed to reduce the load on the courts and prosecutors.[24] The jury system has also proved to be subject to bribery or pressure from judges, especially in drug cases. The code of civil procedure has not been similarly reformed, and gross case backlogs exist. Courts are absent from outlying rural areas, where a system of judicial volunteers sponsored by the Organization of American States operates alternative dispute resolution mechanisms.

Since 2002, the state has made public defenders available on a limited basis to indigent defendants. Though these lawyers are well trained, there were still just 150 nationwide in 2008, meeting only a small part of the demand.[25] Judges may compel private attorneys to fill this role, but most pay a fine to avoid service. Under the new procedural code, a more professional corps of public prosecutors was recruited and trained by foreign assistance missions. But the public ministry remains politicized, and prosecutors at all levels continue to be pressured by their superiors on how to handle certain cases. In a recent survey, only 16 percent of respondents expressed confidence that a court proceeding would treat them fairly.[26]

The civilian branches of state do not exercise full and effective control over the military and its intelligence branch. Presidential authority is limited to the naming of the three top-ranking officers in the army, and it is unlikely that Ortega will be able to handpick the successor to the current army chief in 2010. While the legislature exercises pro forma supervision of the military budget, there are few outward signs that deputies are informed about its details or question military budget requests. Supervision by the finance ministry and comptrollers general of the assets held in the army's pension fund is similarly weak, leaving it open to possible malfeasance.

Despite this de facto autonomy, the armed forces have refrained from interfering in the political process. They actively resist calls from civilians to become involved in the power struggles among political groups, and have been notably silent concerning the 2008 municipal elections controversy. Both the army and the police receive extensive human rights training from donor groups and civil society organizations. Few army officers have been accused of human rights violations in recent years.

A legal change in early 2007 removed the police force from the purview of the governance ministry and put it directly under the presidency, raising serious concerns that the force could be turned into a politicized instrument of control over the citizenry.[27] In 2008, Ortega ordered a series of changes in the police leadership that critics believe are designed to pave the way for the replacement of the existing chief; one of the new commissioners, in charge of public security, is a relative of Ortega's. Indeed, some suspect that a part of the force is already under Ortega's effective command, as human rights groups claim to have evidence that orders by police chief Aminta Granera on how to handle protest demonstrations have been mysteriously countermanded by subordinates.

The right to individual private property is recognized in the constitution, while cooperative and indigenous communal holdings are covered by ordinary law. The executive branch has not committed acts of expropriation without fair and prior compensation in many years. However, the Ortega government allegedly forced U.S.-based oil firm Exxon Mobil to cede its oil storage tanks in 2007, based on a tax claim whose validity the company disputed; other cases of this kind are rumored to have occurred. Political agents of the FSLN have also been accused of extortion against owners of beachfront property in Tola municipality on the southern coast as well as in other areas.[28] In such cases, favorable court decisions on property litigation—often instigated deliberately for this purpose—are allegedly exchanged for bribes.

Property rights in general are very poorly enforced, and Nicaragua ranked 100 out of 115 countries in a recent index.[29] A politicized and poorly trained judiciary also makes contract enforcement fragile. On procedural complexity and time necessary for contract enforcement, Nicaragua ranks below the Latin American averages.[30] Registration of property is also more cumbersome and time consuming than the already high Latin American averages. An outmoded set of property registers, administered by the Supreme Court and subject to political manipulation and bribes, contribute substantially to the problem.[31] On a more positive note, the state attorney (*procurador general*) has clamped down on an organization of illegal land traffickers, seeking to stabilize titles for the government's rural supporters. The Ortega authorities have also complied with a 2001 ruling of the Inter-American Court of Human Rights, and have titled 73,000 hectares of land to the Miskito community of Awas Tingni in the RAAN.[32] Nonetheless, groups in the RAAN accused the government of ignoring illegal land incursions in the chaos following Hurricane Felix.

ANTICORRUPTION AND TRANSPARENCY 3.21

ENVIRONMENT TO PROTECT AGAINST CORRUPTION	3.75
PROCEDURES AND SYSTEMS TO ENFORCE ANTICORRUPTION LAWS	2.75
EXISTENCE OF ANTICORRUPTION NORMS, STANDARDS, AND PROTECTIONS	3.00
GOVERNMENTAL TRANSPARENCY	3.33

As is common in Latin America, Nicaraguan public administration is beset by excessive regulations and red tape. However, in a 2006 survey, senior business executives reported spending 9.3 percent of their time dealing with regulations, a bit below the Latin American average and lower than in previous years.[33] This reflects the efforts of previous governments, which eliminated unnecessary regulations in areas of importance to major economic agents, opening so-called one-stop windows for exporters and foreign investors and greatly reducing the time needed to open a business.

Government interference in the economy is minimal. With very few exceptions, the vast system of state enterprises inherited from the earlier Sandinista period has long since been liquidated, many public utilities have been privatized, and few prices are controlled. The FSLN government has voiced a long-term aspiration to renationalize the energy system and other utilities, but no action in this direction has been taken.

The separation of officeholders' public functions from their private interests is established in Article 130 of the constitution, and conflicts of interest are dealt with in the Probity Law approved in mid-2002.[34] The law lacks both coercive power and clarity regarding enforcement. Under the Bolaños administration, which was well regarded abroad for its honesty, 17 percent of firms surveyed by the World Bank indicated that they had to make unofficial payments to get things done, somewhat below the 20 percent regional average.[35] Comparable data for the Ortega period are lacking, but anecdotal evidence suggests that pledges of political support are now as important as money in getting official levers to move.

The law also provides rules for asset declarations by public officials. However, declarations are made only upon officials' entering and leaving office, not on a yearly basis. More important, the law does not enjoin the comptrollers' office to publish the declarations, greatly reducing transparency. While Bolaños administration officials generally filed asset declarations upon taking and leaving their posts, compliance appears to have slipped during the Ortega period.

An office of public ethics, established in 2003 and now lodged under the presidency, continues to conduct training seminars for public officials concerning the rules described above, especially in the education ministry and local governments, but it has a very low profile overall. Citizens may denounce corrupt acts to the state attorney, the Public Ministry (headed by the attorney general, who is elected by the National Assembly), or the police. In theory, a citizen could also seek an injunction known as a writ of amparo and bring suit before the administrative law chamber of the Supreme Court, but this undertaking is very complex, and given the court's politicization, the chances of success are minimal. Denunciations are relatively rare due to fear of reprisals and the lack of whistleblower protections.

Although a revised budget law passed in 2005 obliges the public universities to account for how they spend a constitutionally mandated 6 percent share of all government revenue, they have so far failed to fully comply. The allocation of some 15 percent of these universities' registration fees to support the Sandinista-dominated university student union (UNEN) has drawn fire as a source of corruption and a prop for political clientelism in which some rectors collude.[36] Cases of public schoolteachers selling grades to students are occasionally reported, but the extent of the practice is difficult to determine. Control over tax collection by the finance ministry is regarded as adequate, but is lax with regard to fees for government services.

Formally speaking, both the general comptrollers of the republic (CGR) and the human rights defense procurator (PDDH, or ombudsman) are independent organs of state elected by the National Assembly. In practice, the institutions have become highly politicized, and their effectiveness is severely compromised.[37] Corruption investigations by the Public Ministry are selective and distinctly lacking in vigor; after letting the five-year statute of limitations on accusations against members of the Alemán administration (1997–2002) expire, it announced in February 2009 that it would prosecute 38 officials of the Bolaños administration, which is not represented politically in the body.[38] In contrast, foreign assistance has strengthened the anticorruption efforts of the state attorney in recent years, and this office now takes some cases to court for prosecution and collects fines levied against officials for violating administrative regulations. The existing code of criminal procedure allows the state attorney to initiate court proceedings in cases of alleged corruption only when the attorney general declines to act.

Coupled with judicial system malfeasance, the limitations described above mean that most corruption allegations are never properly investigated, and courts issue few if any convictions. In 2008, the Global Integrity Index, a measure of the effectiveness of anticorruption mechanisms, accorded Nicaragua a score of just 58 out of 100, which is considered very low.[39] Although Alemán himself was sentenced to 20 years' imprisonment for fraud and money laundering in late 2003, the Supreme Court overturned this conviction in January 2009, after Alemán assisted Ortega in maintaining his control over the governing board of the National Assembly. This reversed the pattern of prior years, when Ortega used his control over the judicial process to extract concessions from Alemán and enhance his quotas in state institutions under their political pact.

Starting in the Alemán years, newspapers and television became the most vigorous investigators of official abuses, and they have consequently won public confidence. Press exposés of alleged corruption regularly spark at least pro forma responses by relevant state organs, though follow-up is generally lacking. In 2007, one such exposé apparently prompted the authorities to desist from a questionable investment in the energy sector.[40] With political polarization increasing since 2007, muckraking is largely directed at the Sandinista government, and less attention is given to the private sector. The government's response to critical news outlets has generally been to withdraw advertising and restrict their access to public functions.

Nicaraguans still lack practical tools to demand information from most government agencies. However, the assembly passed an access to information law in May 2007, putting a legal framework in place. Despite the exclusion of the armed forces from its purview, the law is basically adequate. More obstructive is the administration's reluctance to implement it. Few ministries and other government agencies have established access to information offices to respond to citizen inquiries, and response rates to journalists' requests have so far been low.[41] A study of government websites in 2007 revealed a stark impoverishment of their content under the current administration.[42]

Under Ortega, the budget-making process has become incomplete and opaque.[43] Because sizable foreign assistance from Venezuela is kept off-budget, a significant volume of quasi-public spending goes unrecorded.[44] Moreover, with Conpes inactive, civil society has lost all chance to provide input into the budget that is officially presented. Once the draft makes it to the assembly, legislative consultations with affected social sectors are spotty in comparison with prior years. Legislative oversight of expenditure and revenue is enshrined in law and is effectively applied, but analysis and debate of budgetary questions by the lawmakers is considered by experts to be relatively superficial. Similarly, the Ministry of Finance and Public Credit publishes a quarterly report on budget execution on its website, but the data are neither complete nor presented in a detailed fashion, and they do not provide a basis for evaluating government policy performance.

Under the Bolaños administration, an Inter-American Development Bank–funded efficiency and transparency program improved transparency in bidding for public contracts. Scandals involving bidding processes nevertheless erupted in Bolaños's last year in office, and anecdotal evidence from businesspeople indicated that his government did not succeed in decisively curbing unfair manipulation of bidding terms and procedures by public officials. Performance since the beginning of 2007 is hard to assess given the secretive nature of the Ortega government, but several cases have been reported in which contracts were apparently granted to political cronies.[45] The frequency with which either the central or municipal governments ask the comptrollers general to waive bidding procedures in favor of direct contracting (for "emergency" reasons) appears to have greatly increased.

Overall, corruption in Nicaragua is endemic and constitutes a serious brake on development. While already abysmal, Nicaragua's scores on Transparency International's Corruption Perceptions Index have gradually declined in recent years (2.8 in 2005, 2.6 in 2006 and 2007, and 2.5 in 2008), and the country has dropped to a ranking of 134 out of 180 countries surveyed.[46] Factors thought to have influenced the most recent measurement are the opacity surrounding flows of Venezuelan aid and frequent use of direct contracting.

In May 2005, major European donors together with the World Bank agreed to begin converting a part of their project assistance into undifferentiated budget support for the central government. However, budget support funds were put on hold after the election fraud in 2008. The U.S. Millennium Challenge Corporation suspended the remaining US$63 million from its large-scale aid program in Nicaragua for the same reason. Many donors are now assessing ways in which their assistance can be channeled to thwart government attempts to politicize its use.

RECOMMENDATIONS

- To restore credibility to elections, the National Assembly must appoint CSE members on a strictly professional and nonpartisan basis. The elections law should be reformed to eliminate partisan influence from the rest of the electoral administration, facilitate the registration of parties and alliances, and strengthen checks against fraudulent practices.
- The government should respect the right of opposition political parties and civil society organizations to assemble peacefully in the streets and protest the actions and policies with which they disagree, and refrain from encouraging "counterprotests" designed to intimidate political dissenters.
- Absent a change to guarantee the selection of independent Supreme Court justices, the 2004 Judicial Career Law should be revised to transfer control of the hiring, promotion, and disciplining of all lower-level judges from the Supreme Court to an independent body.
- The executive branch should finalize a general anticorruption strategy, channel all foreign assistance through the official public budget, and ensure that public spending is governed by policy priorities as established by a reactivated, nonpartisan Conpes rather than political or clientelist considerations.

NOTES

For URLs and endnote hyperlinks, please visit the *Countries at the Crossroads* homepage at http://freedomhouse.org/template.cfm?page=139&edition=8.

1. For a brief discussion of political trends during these years, see David R. Dye, *Democracy Adrift: Caudillo Politics in Nicaragua* (Managua: Prodeni, 2004).
2. Banco Central de Nicaragua, *Memoria Anual* (Managua: Banco Central de Nicaragua, 2007), i.
3. Grupo Cívico Ética y Transparencia (EyT), "Valoración Preliminar de Problemas Encontrados: Elecciones Municipales 2008," November 2008.
4. EyT, *Informe Final Elecciones Municipales 2008* (Managua: EyT, February 2009).
5. Transparency International and the Carter Center noted these weaknesses in their 2006 Crinis project, a comparison of eight Latin American countries.
6. These local-level dynamics are discussed in Silvio Prado, *Entre los CDM y los CPC* (Managua: Centro de Análisis Político [CEAP], 2008).
7. Iván Olivares, "Asalto Ilegal contra CINCO," *Confidencial*, October 12–18, 2008.
8. Wendy Álvarez, "Conpes Protege los CPC," *La Prensa*, November 30, 2007.
9. For an overview of this topic, see Centro de Investigación de la Comunicación (CINCO), *Estado de la Libertad de Expresión en Nicaragua 2007–2008* (Managua: CINCO, February 18, 2009).
10. Eduardo Cruz, "Fallo Abominable," *La Prensa*, April 19, 2008.
11. Yader Luna, "Golpe Bajo al Periodismo," *La Prensa*, February 22, 2009.
12. Centro Nicaraguense de Derechos Humanos (CENIDH) et al., *Violaciones de los Derechos Humanos en Nicaragua: Informe Presentado al Comité de Derechos Humanos* (Managua: CENIDH et al., October 2008), 22–23.
13. CENIDH et al., *Derechos Humanos en Nicaragua 2008* (Managua: CENIDH, February 2009), 15–17.
14. CENIDH et al., *Violaciones de los Derechos Humanos en Nicaragua*, 30.
15. Procuraduría para la Defensa de los Derechos Humanos (PDDH), *Informe Final 2007* (Managua: PDDH, 2007), 12.
16. CENIDH et al., *Violaciones de los Derechos Humanos en Nicaragua*, 40.
17. Ibid., 14.
18. Ley de Igualdad de Derechos y Oportunidades, (Law 648), 13. Among other novelties, the law prohibits employment ads addressed to only one sex and bars the use of pregnancy tests for female applicants.
19. Human Rights Watch, *Over Their Dead Bodies* (New York: Human Rights Watch, October 2007).
20. José Adán Silva, "Discriminación Es en Todos los Niveles," *El Nuevo Diario*, February 16, 2009.
21. Bureau of Democracy, Human Rights, and Labor, "Nicaragua," in *International Religious Freedom Report 2007* (Washington, D.C.: U.S. Department of State, September 14, 2007).
22. CENIDH, *Derechos Humanos en Nicaragua 2008*.
23. World Bank, "Nicaragua: Country Profile 2006," in *Enterprise Surveys* (Washington, D.C.: World Bank, 2006), 13.
24. CENIDH et al., *Violaciones de los Derechos Humanos en Nicaragua*, 16–17.
25. Martha Vásquez, "Presupuesto Recortado Golpea a la Defensoría," *El Nuevo Diario*, March 5, 2009.

[26] Instituto para la Democracia y el Desarrollo (IPADE), *Tercer Informe de Monitoreo sobre el Estado de la Democracia en Nicaragua* (Managua: IPADE, May 2007), 33.
[27] For a full discussion, see Instituto de Estudios Estratégicos para Políticas Públicas (IEEPP), *Cuarto Informe de Gestión del Sector de Defensa, Seguridad Pública y Política Exterior* (Managua: IEEPP, January–July 2008).
[28] Lourdes Arróliga, "Ortega Evade Grave Caso de Corrupción," *Confidencial*, June 3–9, 2007.
[29] Anne Chandima Dedigama, ed., "Country Data: Nicaragua," in *International Property Rights Index 2009* (Washington, D.C.: Property Rights Alliance, 2009).
[30] World Bank, "Nicaragua," in *Doing Business 2009: Comparing Regulation in 181 Economies* (Washington, D.C.: World Bank, 2009). Enforcing a contract in Nicaragua takes 540 days, compared with 710 days in Latin America and the Caribbean and 463 days in the countries of the Organization for Economic Cooperation and Development.
[31] For a discussion of these problems, see World Bank, *Nicaragua: Institutional and Governance Review* (Washington, D.C.: April 17, 2008), 30–38.
[32] Inter-American Commission for Human Rights (IACHR), "IACHR Hails Titling of Awas Tingni Community Lands in Nicaragua," news release, December 18, 2008.
[33] World Bank, "Nicaragua: Country Profile 2006."
[34] For basic background on the law, see Transparency International, "Los Estudios de Integridad en Detalle: Servicio Publico en Nicaragua," in *Estudios de Integridad en Centroamerica* (Berlin: Transparency International, 2008).
[35] World Bank, "Nicaragua: Country Profile 2006."
[36] Channel 8's *Esta Noche* program, conducted by Carlos F. Chamorro, aired these issues on March 11, 2009.
[37] The World Bank has deemed the impact of the CGR on governmental accountability to be "marginal." World Bank, *Nicaragua: Institutional and Governance Review*, 50.
[38] Martha Vásquez, "Lluvia de Acusaciones contra Funcionarios de la Administración Bolaños," *El Nuevo Diario*, February 20, 2009.
[39] Global Integrity, "Nicaragua," in *2008 Global Integrity Report* (Washington, D.C.: Global Integrity). While Nicaragua's legal framework merited a score of 76, implementation earned a mere 39.
[40] Oliver Bodán, "¿Quién Está detrás de Kamuzi Investment?" *Confidencial*, September 9–15, 2007.
[41] CINCO, *Estado de la Libertad de Expresión en Nicaragua 2007–2008*.
[42] Sandra Cricianelli, "Los Sitios Web Gubernamentales como Herramientas del Control Social y del Periodismo Investigativo," Sala de Prensa 4, no. 108 (October 2008).
[43] In 2008, the Open Budget Index judged Nicaraguan budget documents to provide the public with "scant information" and gave them a score of 18 percent, down from 20 percent in 2006.
[44] Owing to this factor among others, the Índice Latinoamericano de Transparencia Presupuestaria [Latin American Index of Budget Transparency] gave Nicaragua a rating of 40 in 2007, the third lowest among 10 countries surveyed.
[45] For an example, see Iván Olivares, "INSS-TECNOSA: Gobierno Rectifica," *Confidencial*, June 8–14, 2008.
[46] Transparency International, *2008 Corruption Perceptions Index* (Berlin: Transparency International, September 22, 2008).

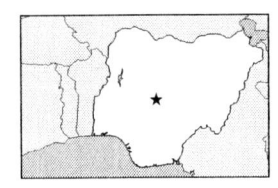

NIGERIA

CAPITAL: Abuja
POPULATION: 152.6 million
GNI PER CAPITA (PPP): $1,940

SCORES	2006	2010
ACCOUNTABILITY AND PUBLIC VOICE:	3.44	3.32
CIVIL LIBERTIES:	3.32	3.37
RULE OF LAW:	2.95	3.00
ANTICORRUPTION AND TRANSPARENCY:	2.52	2.46

(scores are based on a scale of 0 to 7, with 0 representing weakest and 7 representing strongest performance)

A. Carl LeVan and Patrick Ukata

INTRODUCTION

Nigeria marked its 10th year of uninterrupted civilian rule in 2009, the longest such period since the country's independence from Britain in 1960. During his two terms in office, President Olusegun Obasanjo (1999–2007) shepherded the country through an era of economic growth, political reform, and transition to a new constitutional regime. Between 2003 and 2007, real gross domestic product grew at an average rate of 7 percent, though inflation averaged about 12 percent. The government paid off virtually all of its foreign debts, contributing to a sense in the country that Nigeria belongs among the world's great powers. Already Africa's most populous country with over 144 million people, Nigeria faces an annual 3 percent increase in its population, placing huge strains on social services. Oil sales account for the vast majority of federal revenue and comprise 95 percent of export earnings. This raises the stakes for control of the federal government and enables corruption, as oil earnings put huge patronage resources at the disposal of politicians.

The 2007 inauguration of President Umaru Yar'Adua, a historic transfer of power from one civilian leader to another, also reinforced the informal agreement whereby executive authority is expected to alternate between southern Christians and northern Muslims. Yet democratic consolidation and political freedom face serious ongoing challenges. The 2007 elections were marred by massive fraud, vote rigging, and widespread violence. The ruling People's

---

Carl LeVan is an assistant professor of Comparative and Regional Studies and chair of the Africa Council in the School of International Service at American University in Washington, D.C. Patrick Ukata is director of the American University of Nigeria Project at American University in Washington, D.C.

Democratic Party (PDP) maintains a firm grip on political competition. A badly compromised electoral commission disqualified many candidates and then used administrative delays to block the addition of others. Despite a nominally open primary process, the public had virtually no input on how parties selected candidates. Political "godfathers" controlled the selection process in many states, employing violence or intimidation against opponents, and clashes between the local bosses and national PDP officials often degenerated into serious confrontations.[1]

The selection in 2007 of a vice president from the impoverished Niger Delta region, Goodluck Jonathan, did little to address the grievances of minorities among Nigeria's roughly 300 ethnic groups. The problem of ethnic discrimination threatens to keep many qualified Nigerians from running for public office or seeking employment, and contributes to tensions between internal migrants and local indigenes. While women enjoy improved opportunities to participate in public life, Sharia (Islamic law) statutes in a dozen states restrict their rights in relation to property, marriage, and other areas of civil law. Other pressing human rights issues include police abuse, poor prison conditions, restrictions on public meetings, and increased harassment of the media.

The rise of militant groups such as Movement for the Emancipation of the Niger Delta (MEND) highlights ongoing underdevelopment, ecological destruction, and popular frustration throughout the oil-producing region. Attacks on the oil infrastructure strain the country's integrity, as state and local governments depend heavily on federal grants from oil revenue. The attacks have reduced oil output by as much as a million barrels per day from previous levels of about 2.5 million. Militants divert and sell some 300,000 barrels per day.

Overall, President Yar'Adua appears committed to many of his predecessor's moderate policies. However, human rights groups widely criticize his heavy-handed approach to Muslim militants in the north and his handling of Niger Delta unrest. Civil-military relations hang in a delicate balance as federal forces respond to attacks with communal punishment, extrajudicial killings, and arbitrary violence. Moreover, civil society organizations, seeing slow progress on electoral reform and anticorruption investigations, question the administration's dedication to deepening democracy.

ACCOUNTABILITY AND PUBLIC VOICE 3.32

FREE AND FAIR ELECTORAL LAWS AND ELECTIONS	2.00
EFFECTIVE AND ACCOUNTABLE GOVERNMENT	2.75
CIVIC ENGAGEMENT AND CIVIC MONITORING	4.67
MEDIA INDEPENDENCE AND FREEDOM OF EXPRESSION	3.86

The 2007 elections heralded the first time in Nigeria's history that one civilian government peacefully transferred power to another. The choice of Yar'Adua as the new president symbolized the shift of power from the south to the north, entrenching a popular expectation that power will alternate between these two regions. Prior to the election, civil society and the National Assembly effectively blocked a tentative bid by Obasanjo to modify the constitution to allow a third term in office. Now a decade old, the PDP regime shows some signs that the country is breaking with its authoritarian past.

No such signs, however, can be found in Nigeria's electoral processes. PDP candidate Yar'Adua's lopsided victory in the April 2007 presidential contest, with 69.8 percent of the vote, was partly a result of the opposition's fragmentation. Former head of state Muhammadu Buhari of the All Nigeria People's Party received 18.7 percent, and Obasanjo's disaffected vice president, Atiku Abubakar of the Action Congress, garnered 7.5 percent. None of the other parties' candidates received more than 2 percent of the vote, and unofficial estimates put voter turnout at between 57 and 62 percent. Violence, corruption, and willful administrative failures also undermined competition. Domestic and international observers concluded that the scope of the fraud and intimidation made it impossible to ascertain the electorate's actual intent.[2]

The Domestic Election Observation Group, a coalition of civil society organizations, demanded that the official results be annulled. Like the international observers, they noted that in many states there were effectively no elections, citing candidates' omission from ballots, the hoarding of voting materials, and other tactics designed to prevent polling stations from opening. These problems were particularly acute in elections for the National Assembly in states across the country.[3] Moreover, at least 200 people were killed in election-related violence, much of which continued after the balloting had ended. The police, who are all under federal control, were often complicit in the theft of ballot boxes or rigging.[4]

By 2009, 9 out of 109 Senate elections had been thrown out by election tribunals and courts, as had 11 of 36 gubernatorial contests and at least 9 local elections. While these decisions raised the prospects of viable judicial arbitration, they also underlined a deep skepticism about democracy. Only 31 percent of over 2,300 Nigerians surveyed in March 2008 characterized themselves as either "fairly satisfied" or "very satisfied with the way democracy works in Nigeria." Such attitudes are reflected in declining voter participation between 2003 and 2007. Nearly two-thirds of Nigerians believe the 2007 elections were either not fair or had "major problems."[5]

Opposition presidential candidates Abubakar and Buhari took to the courts immediately after the election to contest the results. Preelection Supreme Court decisions had raised the opposition's expectations, upholding Abubakar's rights as a candidate and as the incumbent vice president. Government lawyers had argued that Abubakar no longer held the office once he quit the PDP to run as the Action Congress candidate, but an appellate court unanimously held that the vice president could exercise his freedom of association by switching parties and could only be removed through existing constitutional procedures.[6]

However, the Supreme Court ultimately threw out Abubakar and Buhari's challenges of the election results. The court prohibited documentation of fraud by electoral observers from being presented as evidence. Then, in December 2008, nearly 20 months after the election, it ruled 4–3 against the plaintiffs, finding that they had failed to prove that the poll was too flawed to be credible.[7] The three justices in the minority authored a scathing dissent. The court, which typically commands public respect, was alternately accused of corruption and of deciding the case out of fear of public violence. Four months later, the court cast new doubt on its own decision when it unanimously ruled that a new election tribunal should hear a challenge to the presidential election results being sought by the virtually unknown Hope Democratic Party.[8]

The Independent National Electoral Commission (INEC), which bore much of the blame for the failed elections, remains beholden to the executive branch. Its federal- and state-level commissioners are appointed by the president, with Senate confirmation for the federal members, and while the Electoral Act of 2006 called for the creation of a fund to ensure the INEC's financial independence from the government, no such fund was established for the 2007 polls.[9]

For a year before the vote, the INEC ignored advice from experts who expressed concerns about plans for a costly, high-technology voter registration system. The INEC gave the public conflicting accounts about how and where to register, and registration rolls were frequently unavailable. Exacerbating widespread doubts about its independence, the INEC attempted to administratively disqualify candidates. Its commissioner also maintained suspiciously close ties to a key presidential aide, Nnamdi "Andy" Uba, who wielded vast power within the PDP.[10] Even after the Supreme Court decision on Abubakar's qualifications, the INEC did not print ballots displaying his name.

Public resources were often illegally diverted for use in political campaigns, giving incumbents huge advantages. Moreover, neither Obasanjo nor the INEC seemed willing or able to rein in the so-called godfathers who dominated state-level politics by furtively financing elections. Existing rules on campaign finance were poorly enforced. Small parties complained that annual public funds were not distributed according to the rules laid out in the 2006 Electoral Act, and most parties were suspected of exceeding spending limits. Campaigning opportunities for candidates, particularly those in the opposition, were further restricted by the deployment of partisan thugs and arbitrary arrests during the campaign period. State-owned broadcasters favored the ruling party in their coverage, while private broadcasters and newspapers focused on the three largest parties with varying degrees of equity.[11]

Despite the PDP's large majorities in both chambers, the National Assembly had clashed with the Obasanjo administration on key issues including electoral reform, the annual budgets, and a constitutional amendment to allow the president to seek a third term. The Senate thwarted Obasanjo's bid for another term, which would have required support from a two-thirds majority, in May 2006.

National polls have consistently confirmed widespread support in each of the country's six geographical "zones" for limiting the president to two terms.[12] The National Assembly had also threatened Obasanjo with impeachment on three occasions, citing various corruption charges and failure to implement legislation. The Senate, for its part, clashed with the executive branch over amendments that would strip the president of his ability to hire and fire the head of the Economic and Financial Crimes Commission (EFCC). This mirrored similar confrontations at the state level, where legislatures in Oyo and elsewhere launched proceedings to remove governors.

The PDP made significant gains in the 2007 elections, increasing its share of governorships from 27 to 28 out of 36 states. It also increased its hold on the National Assembly, taking 85 out of 109 Senate seats and 262 out of 360 seats in the House of Representatives. The opposition remains fragmented, with the All Nigeria People's Party holding 16 Senate and 62 House seats, the Action Congress holding 6 Senate and 32 House seats, and the remainder distributed among minor parties. However, tense relations between the legislative and executive branches continued into Yar'Adua's administration. Many clashes touched on the same issues, including the president's authority over the EFCC, a stalled electoral reform, and failure to implement the federal budget. In July 2009, some legislators went so far as to threaten impeachment when the president complained about legislative changes to the budget he submitted.[13] Legislative leaders struggle to maintain party discipline due to the first-past-the-post electoral system and the powerful presidency's influence over state-level parties.

While the civil service remains prone to patronage, civil service reform geared towards adhering to merit-based criteria for hiring and advancement has received some attention during the Yar'Adua administration. The government has implemented a policy setting the tenure of permanent secretaries in the civil service at eight years in order to allow for the promotion of highly-qualified lower officers who had previously been excluded from the upper levels of the Federal Civil Service.[14] Although Nigeria's constitution requires that the "federal character" of the country be represented in civil service appointments and a quota system exists to ensure that Nigeria's myriad ethnic groups are represented in these appointments, reports of ethnic bias and discrimination remain widespread (see civil liberties).[15]

Nigeria's civil society remains vibrant, and its capacity for independently engaging the government has improved. The Domestic Election Observation Group trained and deployed over 50,000 observers, while the Justice, Development, and Peace Commission reportedly deployed another 30,000. Policy-monitoring and watchdog groups have a public profile, and the National Assembly draws on their expertise more frequently than in the early years of the democratic transition. A broad advocacy campaign has emerged in favor of a freedom of information act. A bill on this issue was passed during Obasanjo's tenure but never signed into law, and the House brushed the measure aside in

August 2008. President Yar'Adua has repeatedly expressed his willingness to sign the bill, and his information minister even asked civil society to provide more input on legislative proposals.[16] Civil society groups also allied with legislators to help defeat Obasanjo's third-term bid.

Civic associations are generally allowed to form and operate, though the federal government has undermined independent political activity since 2005. Nongovernmental organizations (NGOs) face regulatory difficulty in registering with the government. For instance, only political parties are allowed to include the word "democracy" in their names, and NGOs whose names include the word are routinely denied registration. A lack of registration prevents NGOs from opening bank accounts or soliciting donor funding, among other activities. International NGOs have always faced registration requirements, but in 2007 the National Planning Commission asked them to provide documents to "justify your presence in Nigeria."[17] These various restrictions may help to explain why the AfroBarometer survey found that nearly a third of Nigerians in 2008 said they were either "not free at all" or "not very free" to join a political organization of their choice.

In the run-up to the 2007 elections, the INEC delayed the establishment of a registration process for domestic NGOs seeking to serve as election observers, then created onerous conditions for registration and limited access to official materials. According to the European Union (EU) observation mission, only 53 out of 175 organizations that applied were accredited. Many NGOs faced harassment by security forces during this period, including questioning by the State Security Service (SSS) on their membership and interest in the elections. The authorities have repeatedly intimidated members of civil society for other reasons as well, targeting advocates of ethnoregional rights in particular. For example, in July 2006, police shut down a meeting organized by human rights NGOs to protest the removal of Bukhari Bello as the head of the country's National Human Rights Commission.[18] In addition, in August 2006 over 100 military personnel arrested two university professors who were scheduled to discuss the Igbo language. The government claimed that organizers of the event were linked to violent youth groups.[19]

The media remain lively and have continued to evolve since the transition to democracy. Section 29 of the 1999 constitution protects freedom of expression, "including freedom to hold opinions and to receive and impart ideas and information without interference." The constitution also imposes strict limitations on public ownership of media outlets. The federal government owns one national daily newspaper, one radio network (with 34 stations), and one television network (with 36 affiliate stations). The few newspapers owned by state governments lack widespread readership. By contrast, there are 14 privately owned daily newspapers, six weekly news magazines, several independent television stations, and several dozen independent radio stations.[20] Due to low literacy levels and the unusually high cost of newspapers, radio remains the most important source of information. The World Bank reports that only 5.5 percent of the population has internet access, but web cafes are very common.

Strict libel laws deter investigative reporting, and journalists in 2008 faced legal harassment and even violence.[21] In March 2009, agents of the Bayelsa State government abducted a bureau chief for *National Life* newspaper after he reported on a brawl in an Abuja hotel between a PDP official and the governor. Officials then threatened him with a libel suit. Journalists with the *Leadership* newspaper faced a similar criminal defamation suit.[22] Reports of "brown envelope" journalism, in which patrons or politicians pay for favorable articles, remain common.

Harassment of the media has increased, and investigations produced few convictions, even in the most serious cases. The press environment deteriorated significantly during the run-up to the 2007 elections, during which the SSS harassed and arrested journalists who criticized former president Obasanjo.[23] For several weeks in September 2007, the SSS detained two German filmmakers and the American head of an NGO in the Niger Delta. Another group of filmmakers experienced similar harassment in the region in 2008 when they were accosted by a joint military team and held for seven days by the SSS without charge. In each incident the individuals were released under international pressure. The watchdog group Media Rights Agenda reported harassment of *National Standard* after it published an expose on the first lady, and of a reporter from *Punch* who refused to disclose a source, among other cases. In some of the more serious incidents in recent years, the chairman of *This Day*'s editorial board was murdered in December 2006, another member of the board was killed in August 2008, and a radio journalist for the Nasarawa state broadcaster was slain in October of that year.[24] Official investigations have produced little information about these deaths, which were suspicious in part because no valuables were taken by the gunmen, and human rights groups expressed concern about their effects on free expression. Some journalists were granted political asylum overseas when their reporting on corruption triggered credible threats against their lives.

While there is little direct censorship by the federal government, other attempts to control content have increased. The National Broadcasting Commission announced prohibitions against the use of foreign material in prime-time news broadcasts by local television stations beginning in 2009 (adding to a 2004 ban on live broadcasts of foreign news), and in 2008 the Kano State government convicted a filmmaker of releasing a Hausa-language adaptation of the play *West Side Story* without vetting it through government censors. The government also revoked a license for Channels Television, which had drawn official ire for its reporting on President Yar'Adua's health. Numerous journalists were harassed for reporting on that topic in 2008, including at least three bloggers based overseas who were arrested upon entering the Nigeria and held without charge.[25]

CIVIL LIBERTIES   3.37

PROTECTION FROM STATE TERROR, UNJUSTIFIED IMPRISONMENT, AND TORTURE	1.50
GENDER EQUITY	2.00
RIGHTS OF ETHNIC, RELIGIOUS, AND OTHER DISTINCT GROUPS	3.00
FREEDOM OF CONSCIENCE AND BELIEF	5.33
FREEDOM OF ASSOCIATION AND ASSEMBLY	5.00

The use of torture and mistreatment of criminal suspects by the police and security services remain rampant. These practices, carried over from the era of military rule, have continued due to poor training and lack of capacity to conduct criminal investigations. Attempted reforms by the Nigerian Police Commission have stalled, due mainly to the huge sums needed for effective implementation. Criminal investigations often amount to public requests for information, including the names of suspects, followed by the arrest and brutalization of those suspects with the aim of extracting a confession. According to Human Rights Watch, the acts of torture include "the tying of arms and legs behind the body, suspension by hands and legs from the ceiling, severe beatings with metal or wooden objects, spraying of tear gas in the eyes, shooting in the foot or leg, raping female detainees, and using pliers or electric shocks on the penis."[26] This treatment sometimes results in death. Once the suspect confesses, they are made to write up a statement and then charged in court.[27] Most such cases are not subject to judicial review.

The police share a common perception that the courts are too lenient on suspects, particularly those charged with armed robbery, because cases are at times thrown out for lack of evidence. Rather than improving investigatory capacity, police reportedly engage in extrajudicial killings.[28] Police and military officials also periodically use indiscriminate violence in response to unrest in certain communities instead of seeking to identify and prosecute individual perpetrators. Such collective punishment is particularly common in the Niger Delta, where militant groups such as MEND use violence to voice complaints about environmental damage and lack of resource control.

Prison conditions are deplorable throughout Nigeria. The facilities suffer from a lack of electricity, water, and modern drainage systems. Four of every five prisons were built before 1950, and many have never been renovated. According to Amnesty International, most prisons are severely overcrowded because of the number of prisoners awaiting trial; one report found that at least 65 percent of inmates have never been convicted, and some wait for 10 years before being tried.[29] Pretrial detainees are commonly neglected amid disputes between the police and prison officials over which agency is responsible for their care. They are often kept separate from the sentenced prisoners, who receive prison uniforms and three meals a day. Before leaving office in May 2007, Obasanjo implemented a prisoner release and amnesty program that benefited 25,000 inmates. However, the program had little impact on overcrowding.[30]

Attacks on political opponents and peaceful activists have mainly been localized and have largely occurred in states where the courts invalidated 2007 election results. In early 2009, the Court of Appeal invalidated the gubernatorial election in Ekiti and called for fresh elections. It also ruled against the sitting governor in Ondo and in favor of the opposition candidate. These rulings triggered politically motivated attacks against members of opposing political parties, sometimes involving the Nigerian police.[31]

There have been recurring episodes of communal violence throughout the country in recent years.[32] The most serious of these took place in Jos, Plateau State, on November 28 and 29, 2008. The conflict originated in a disputed local government election, and pitted Christian communities who considered themselves the indigenes of the area against members of the Muslim Hausa-Fulani ethnic group. By most accounts, several hundred people were killed, and many churches and mosques were burnt down. Police and military officials called in to restore order were alleged to have arbitrarily killed more than 90 people.[33] There are also reports that the Plateau governor ignored intelligence reports warning him about the danger of going ahead with the local government elections.[34] Separately, in Bauchi State, a conflict between Christians and Muslims over five days in February 2009 resulted in 11 reported deaths and 19 destroyed churches.[35] In July, at least 700 people were killed after government forces in Bauchi and two other northern states cracked down on an Islamist group that was opposed to "Western education" and had attacked police stations. The police apparently shot the group's leader after apprehending him.[36]

Attacks by ethnic and religious militias, sometimes supported by state actors, remain common. Since early 2008, a rash of kidnappings has occurred, mainly in the southeast and the Niger Delta. MEND started kidnapping foreign oil workers in 2006 as part of its ongoing rebellion tied to underdevelopment and ecological destruction in the Niger Delta. Some militants and criminal gangs have since targeted politicians, children, and religious figures. Though most of the hostages have been released unharmed after a ransom payment, the phenomenon has created a sense of insecurity in the affected area.

General crime statistics are equally alarming. In 2006, 72.6 percent of Nigerians surveyed by the CLEEN Foundation reported that they were fearful of crime, while 23.1 percent reported having been the victims of crime.[37] In addition, the police affairs minister reported 353 kidnappings in 2008, while an estimated 512 people were kidnapped between January and June of 2009.[38] In July 2009, the Senate summoned the country's security chiefs to ascertain their preparedness in tackling the kidnappings.[39] The recent appointment of Ogbonnaya Onovo as inspector general of police, however, is expected to renew law enforcement efforts to address the problem.[40]

Nigerian women and children are trafficked domestically and abroad for forced labor and sexual exploitation, and citizens of neighboring countries are brought into Nigeria for similar reasons. However, the U.S. State Department places Nigeria in the Tier 1 category, the best of four possible rankings, in its 2009 Trafficking in Persons Report. The authorities, particularly through the work of the National Agency for the Prohibition of Trafficking in Persons (NAPTIP), have apparently stepped up the prosecution of offenders, and the government sponsors awareness-raising programs and a number of shelters for victims.[41]

While women's rights are enshrined in the constitution, women continue to face violence and substantial barriers to gaining political power. Although many states have passed laws against domestic violence, spousal abuse is still relatively common in rural areas. Female genital mutilation remains widespread, occurring in nearly every state, according to recent statistics.[42] Sharia, in place in a dozen northern states, is often used to discriminate against women, especially in cases of adultery, where the rules of evidence differ depending on the sex of the accused. Both Sharia-based statutes and customary law favor men over women with respect to property rights. Under customary law, all marital property belongs to the man as the head of the household. Therefore, in cases of divorce, the customary court normally awards all the marital property to the husband, leaving the wife with nothing. Women's access to direct political power has improved but remains limited. According to the U.S. State Department's count, men hold more than 90 percent of the country's elected and appointed positions. As of the end of 2008, women accounted for just 6 out of 42 federal ministers, 9 out of 109 senators, and 30 out of 360 House members.

Nigeria signed the UN Convention on the Rights of Persons with Disabilities in 2007 but has not yet ratified it.[43] Disabled people continue to face stigmatization in society, with social and economic barriers forcing many to resort to begging. While state governments such as the Lagos State government have made a concerted effort to empower the disabled by allocating funds to organizations devoted to disabled advocacy and assistance, the challenges facing disabled people remain substantial.[44] In March 2009, the Senate passed the Discrimination against Persons with Disabilities (Prohibition) Bill, which bans discrimination against the disabled, establishes a requirement that public organizations provide access into their buildings, and imposes fines for violations of the law. It is currently awaiting approval by the House.[45]

Ethnic discrimination remains pervasive. Though Nigerians are free to reside in any part of the country, those who live in an area dominated by another ethnic group frequently suffer discrimination. State and local governments classify such persons as foreigners or "non-indigenes" to exclude them from a host of material benefits to which they are entitled as Nigerian citizens. Such discrimination reflects a widespread belief that the state and local governments exist to serve only the interests of the indigenous population. Non-indigenes are charged higher school fees and have limited ability to compete for government contracts, obtain civil service positions, or secure pensions. Those non-indigenes who are hired by state or local governments are often unable to contest unfair layoffs.[46] Non-indigenes are also likely to face discrimination when competing for federal-level positions on the grounds that they are reserved for the local indigenes. The 1999 constitution calls for the federal government, its agencies, and its policies to reflect the "federal character" of Nigeria so as to promote national unity and prevent the dominance of particular ethnic or other groups. This balancing effort is monitored and enforced by the Federal Character Commission, also provided for in the constitution. Despite its intentions, the federal character system often has the effect of subordinating national citizenship to ethnic identity, and spurring ethnic tensions as different groups compete for resources.[47]

Historically, relations between the various religious groups in Nigeria have been relatively cordial. Religious freedom is protected, conversion is not penalized, and state and local governments are prohibited from adopting or giving preference to a particular religion. Sharia-based statutes adopted by northern states do not apply to non-Muslim residents. However, state governments routinely favor the faith practiced by the majority of their residents, whether Christian or Muslim. For example, governments provide subsidies for a pilgrimage to Mecca for Muslims or to Jerusalem for Christians. Such preferences also extend to the provision of funds and permits for the building of either mosques or churches, and accommodation of social practices like sex segregation in public places. As noted above, Nigeria's frequent outbreaks of ethnic and communal violence sometimes take on a religious dimension.

During President Obasanjo's tenure from 1999 to 2007, the government engaged in strong-arm tactics on labor issues and threatened to break up the leading unions. The Yar'Adua administration, by contrast, has adopted a decidedly nonconfrontational approach and sought to resolve conflicts with the unions through amicable dialogue.[48] Unions are typically allowed to organize, but 50 workers are required to form a union in a given enterprise. Wage agreements with private employers require government approval, and the 2005 Trade Union Amendment Act sharply restricts unions' ability to mount strikes. Workers in essential services, a term that is broadly defined by law, are barred from forming unions or striking. Tight constraints on workers in special export-processing zones inhibit their ability to organize and strike as well. Antiunion practices by employers remain common, contracts are regularly disregarded, and security forces are used to harass or arrest strikers. Among the most serious incidents in recent years was the 2007 firing of 34,000 striking public employees by the newly elected Oyo State governor, who refused to honor a wage agreement reached with his predecessor; the move was soon overturned in court, and the pay increase was approved. In January 2008, a transport union leader was assassinated in Lagos.[49]

Protests of any kind are governed by the 1990 Public Order Act, passed during a brutal dictatorship, which requires organizers to obtain a permit. In practice, while progovernment rallies of all kinds are often approved, opposition groups are routinely denied permits to demonstrate. Civil society and union leaders who attempted to organize protests following the 2007 elections were arrested, and the demonstrations suppressed. The police justified their actions by citing the lack of a permit. However, labor leaders were able to mount a general strike in June 2007 to protest government economic policies. In 2005, an Abuja court ruled the Public Order Act unconstitutional, and the Court of Appeal affirmed this decision in 2007. Both the attorney general and the national police appealed the case to the Supreme Court, which has yet to rule on the matter. Until it does, the police have said they will continue to enforce the act.

RULE OF LAW   3.00

INDEPENDENT JUDICIARY	3.40
PRIMACY OF RULE OF LAW IN CIVIL AND CRIMINAL MATTERS	2.60
ACCOUNTABILITY OF SECURITY FORCES AND MILITARY TO CIVILIAN AUTHORITIES	3.00
PROTECTION OF PROPERTY RIGHTS	3.00

Under the constitution, the judiciary is one of three independent branches of government, along with the executive and the legislature. The federal courts, particularly the Supreme Court, have shown a high degree of probity and independence, but state courts remain vulnerable to political pressure. Whereas the federal courts are under the exclusive supervision of the independent National Judicial Council (NJC), state courts are partly under the supervision of the state executive branch in matters of appointments and capital budgetary allocations. This exposes them to gubernatorial manipulation.

Funds for state courts are usually allocated through each state's justice ministry, allowing governors to reward their judicial branches for favorable rulings and starve them of funds if they show defiance. As a result, state courts tend to bend to political pressure from the executive branch. Governors have also been known to offer inducements, such as purchasing new cars for state judges, in the hope of receiving favorable judgments in exchange.

Although the federal courts also depend on the other branches for budgetary allocations, the role of the NJC has helped to protect federal judges from political pressure. They have consistently issued dispassionate verdicts without fear or favor. The federal executive, particularly under Yar'Adua, has signaled its interest in respecting the rule of law. Unlike his predecessor, who consistently ignored court judgments, Yar'Adua has specifically asked executive agencies to respect all court verdicts, including those which go against the government.[50]

Judges are generally appointed and promoted in a fair and unbiased manner. The NJC has been very effective in scrutinizing prospective candidates. The promotion of judges is normally done by seniority. The NJC has also exercised effective oversight of judicial conduct. When complaints have been leveled against particular judges, the council has been quick to investigate in a fair manner and to recommend the dismissal of those found to have abused their powers. For example, a federal judge in Katsina State was suspended by the NJC in February 2009 and subsequently dismissed after he attempted to countermand an appellate court ruling on an Imo state assembly election.[51]

Nigerian law presumes innocence until guilt is proven. However, as mentioned above, the police rarely follow this standard during arrests and interrogations. Although the constitution provides for the right to a fair, public, and expeditious trial, enjoyment of these rights is significantly affected by the defendant's wealth. This is due to the lack of institutional capacity in the judiciary, coupled with associated informal costs including transportation to the courthouse and bribes. Defendants are entitled to counsel of their choice, but there is also no law preventing a trial from proceeding without representation, except in capital cases. Therefore, indigent defendants often appear in court without counsel. Those who are convicted typically begin serving their sentences immediately, even though all convicted persons have a right to appeal.

Civilian control of the police and military since the transition to democracy in May 1999 signals a welcome change, particularly in light of Nigeria's authoritarian history. Under the Nigerian constitution, the executive branch oversees the affairs of the security forces through the Ministry of Police Affairs and Ministry of Defense. The police force is entirely national, meaning that states and local governments do not possess their own forces. The heads of both the police and military are appointed by the president and confirmed by the Senate. Each chamber of the National Assembly has established legislative oversight committees to fulfill constitutionally mandated oversight functions over the police and the military, although they possess limited capacity due to limited expertise and scarce resources.

Since 1999, the police and military have generally refrained from interference or involvement in the political process. However, use of the police and the military by the executive branch has on several occasions generated political conflict. For example, during the 2007 elections opposition parties viewed the police and the military presence—ostensibly intended to keep the peace—in polling areas and collation centers as part of the PDP's efforts to intimidate opposition party supporters. Even in locations where military personnel were accused of taking part in election fraud, no investigation was ever conducted. Another example occurred in May 2009, when a Joint Task Force (JTF) made up of members of the armed forces was sent to the Gbaramatu district of Delta State to confront militants allegedly attacking oil installations in the area. The JTF was accused of indiscriminately attacking civilians and destroying property. Despite public outcry, no formal investigations have been conducted, and the JTF restricted access to the area to prevent information gathering by journalists and human rights groups. Moreover, no effort has been made to resettle displaced persons or reconstruct the communities and property destroyed. In sum, control of the security forces by the civilian leadership has yet to translate into the ability to hold government security forces responsible for abuses. Over time, this threatens to generate a climate of impunity that could lead to further violations and reduced public confidence in democratic institutions.

All Nigerians have the right to own property under the constitution. However, under the 1978 Land Use Act, all land ownership is effectively vested in the state governments, which have the power to license all land within their jurisdiction and make it available to individuals through an elaborate land-use application process. This normally culminates with the governor of the state issuing the applicant a certificate of occupancy, and only after the granting of such a certificate can an individual legally make use of landed property. Given that the application process can take many years, individuals living on land without a certificate are often subjected to undue hardship because they cannot legally sell or develop it. This policy also allows the government, whether at the federal or state level, to arbitrarily seize land or revoke property rights without regard to due process. According to a Joint Senate Committee on the Federal Capital Territory (FCT) and Housing, this policy was invoked arbitrarily and with impunity by then minister of the FCT Mallam Ahmad Nasir el-Rufai, who served from July 2003 through May 2007. Most revocations were done under the guise of clearing illegal structures from around Abuja. The committee also reported the allocation of 3,645 plots of land in the final two weeks of the Obasanjo administration under questionable circumstances.[52] Even after el-Rufai's departure, widespread destruction of community housing in Abuja continued into 2009.[53] In early May 2009, Yar'Adua sent draft legislation to the National Assembly to reform the Land Use Act.[54] The legislature has not yet acted on this bill.

ANTICORRUPTION AND TRANSPARENCY 2.46

ENVIRONMENT TO PROTECT AGAINST CORRUPTION 2.00
PROCEDURES AND SYSTEMS TO ENFORCE ANTICORRUPTION LAWS 2.75
EXISTENCE OF ANTICORRUPTION NORMS, STANDARDS,
    AND PROTECTIONS 2.75
GOVERNMENTAL TRANSPARENCY 2.33

During President Obasanjo's eight years in office, Nigeria instituted important reforms to improve public integrity and accountability. The government created new agencies to investigate corruption, published information on public finances, and successfully convicted several high-level officials, while the independent media continued their Sisyphean struggle to expose graft. The perceived level of corruption has since improved notably, with Nigeria's score in Transparency International's Corruption Perceptions Index increasing from 2.2 in 2007 to 2.7 in 2008. Nevertheless, scandals tainted Obasanjo's exit. Soon after the new administration took office in 2007, the attorney general revoked

N37 billion (US$245 million) in contracts for health care centers, saying the former president had tried to arrange for a direct deduction from the Federation Account rather than following proper budgeting and contracting procedures. The outgoing cabinet also hurriedly approved as much as N2 trillion (US$13.5 billion) in contracts in the administration's final weeks.[55]

Corruption remains a persistent and systemic problem in Nigeria. Oil earnings account for the vast majority of federal revenues, providing politicians with resources for patronage and stunting other sectors of the economy. In addition, because the major political parties generally limit the number of terms that state and federal lawmakers serve, legislators are less able to accumulate the experience necessary to question the executive branch or to develop an institutional culture of integrity.

Where progress has been made against corruption, it is attributable to vigilant media that regularly expose public wrongdoing, and to the growth of civil society watchdog organizations. The National Assembly also plays a constructive role at times. In 2006–07 it investigated corruption in the Petroleum Technology Development Fund, at first accusing the vice president of illegally authorizing US$20 million in contracts. The Senate reported that the president signed off on the contracts and recommended that the case be referred to the Code of Conduct Bureau (these claims were disputed in subsequent investigations).[56]

The Independent Corrupt Practices Commission (ICPC), established in 2000, and the Economic and Financial Crimes Commission (EFCC), created in 2003 to focus on financial fraud, have won praise for pursuing governors and former politicians. The EFCC has helped recover billions of dollars of embezzled funds, and in 2008 it alleged that local governments had failed to spend their allocated N3 trillion (US$20 billion) between 1999 and 2007 on development due to corruption.[57]

However, despite dozens of high-level charges and several resignations, neither the EFCC nor the ICPC has produced many convictions. None of the charges filed against 10 former governors during President Yar'Adua's tenure have resulted in a conviction, adding to speculation that the cases were politically motivated and reducing public confidence in the new agencies. Pending trials include those of the former head of the port authority, a former aviation minister, and the former governors of Adamawa, Abia, Jigawa, Taraba, and Plateau. A plea agreement in the case of the Edo governor produced a fine on a single charge, which EFCC prosecutors are appealing. When the governor of Ondo faced a credible challenge to his 2007 election, he hurriedly awarded contracts worth billions of naira, according to charges filed in March 2009. The alleged graft took place between the annulment of his election by a tribunal in July 2008 and his final removal following an appeals court ruling in February 2009.[58] To avoid such scenarios, the Electoral Reform Commission has proposed holding elections at least six months before terms expire, time limits on judicial appeals, and a prohibition on taking office while appeals are pending.

Nigeria's anticorruption agencies have faced accusations of political bias. Shortly before the 2007 elections, Human Rights Watch found that a majority of the 135 candidates accused of corruption by the EFCC either belonged to the opposition or had close ties to Vice President Abubakar, who was engaged in an acrimonious battle for power within the ruling party. The federal government set up an ad hoc panel and indicted 37 candidates after a two-day investigation without any due process.[59] During the 2007 elections, it announced that it had evidence of corruption against 31 sitting governors, whom it did not name. The disclosure of accusations followed by so few formal charges raised concerns that the claims were designed only to influence political competition.

The EFCC also faces ongoing challenges to its independence and authority. Whereas the ICPC can only refer cases for investigation, the law allows the EFCC to prosecute. However, the attorney general insists that all prosecutions need prior approval from his office. In 2009, the House and Senate planned to amend the EFCC's enabling legislation to insulate it from interference by the attorney general,[60] though previous efforts to remove the president's authority to hire and fire the commissioner have failed. The Senate president explained that this power "completely destroys the independence of the EFCC."[61] Indeed, EFCC head Nuhu Ribadu was removed in dubious circumstances in 2008 and subsequently demoted, and the head of the EFCC's financial investigations unit quit after his bank accounts received mysterious money transfers. The transfers were seen as part of the broader effort to undermine Ribadu's work. Transparency International urged the government to "stop the harassment, intimidation, ridiculing and persecution" of Ribadu.[62] Meanwhile, immunity for incumbent politicians remains a contentious issue. Impeachment bids are frequent but rarely successful due to weak legislative capacity and the extensive patronage networks controlled by governors, whose coffers grew with an oil boom after 2003.

The transnational character of corruption is presenting new challenges. Among other cases, the U.S. Justice Department is currently considering an offer from the U.S. oilfield services firm Halliburton to pay US$559 million to settle charges that its employees bribed Nigerian officials to obtain contracts, while the Nigerian government has brought a civil suit against Shell Oil and a German firm for damaging its reputation through bribery.[63]

The National Assembly has suffered from a spate of corruption scandals. The Senate president was forced to resign in 2005 following accusations of corruption. The first female House speaker, Patricia Ettah, was accused of using government money for home renovations and was impeached in 2007. Her prosecution has stalled, however, as ICPC staff apparently cannot agree on how to proceed. Conflict of interest rules are generally weak, and public officials are usually permitted to retain managerial interests in private businesses after taking office. Officeholders must declare their assets to the Code of Conduct Bureau,[64] but the declarations are rarely made public. Scandals concerning government contracts—such as the aforementioned incidents with the House speaker, the

Ondo State governor, and Obasanjo's health centers—point to a flawed and uncompetitive procurement process.

Graft is also widespread within the education sector. The Independent Advocacy Project's 2007 Nigeria Corruption Index ranked the Ministry of Education as the third most corrupt institution in Nigeria and emphasized widespread corruption in higher education institutions and examination bodies.[65]

As noted above, the failure to enact a freedom of information bill means that Nigeria has no comprehensive legal framework to promote transparency. The federal budget process remains relatively opaque, as year-end reports and audits are not made public, and the annual budget proposal by the government contains minimal public information.[66] Nonetheless, the release of financial information from the accountant general and the Ministry of Finance, and the publication of financial transfers from the Federation Account to states, have increased openness. Nigeria is a signatory to the Extractive Industries Transparency Initiative (EITI), whereby oil companies' payments to the government are audited and published. Still, transparency by itself has so far had little dissuasive effect on the willingness of high officials to engage in corruption. Whistleblowers have virtually no legal protection, though they would gain some recourse if the freedom of information bill were passed. Due to its substantial oil revenues, Nigeria receives less foreign aid per capita than many other African countries; donors consider its systems for recording, monitoring, and evaluating aid to be in desperate need of reform.[67]

RECOMMENDATIONS

- Electoral reform is essential for peaceful and fair elections in 2011. The Electoral Reform Commission's report should take account of proposals presented by civil society and be fully released for public discussion. The National Assembly and the president must ensure that the next INEC commissioner is more accountable to citizens and better insulated from PDP interference, and that transparency is increased in party primaries.
- Public officials who are constitutionally required to report their income and assets should not be allowed to take office until presenting an assets declaration to the Code of Conduct Bureau, which should make such reports available on the internet.
- The police need better training and enhanced capacity for criminal investigations, which should aim to eliminate the use of torture as a means of investigation and interrogation. Training should also educate police about laws relating to the freedoms of speech and association.
- President Yar'Adua's proposed legislation to reform the 1978 Land Use Act should be passed—via constitutional amendment if necessary—and implemented to reduce opportunities for favoritism and corruption and eliminate practices that reduce property rights protections.

NOTES

For URLs and endnote hyperlinks, please visit the *Countries at the Crossroads* homepage at http://freedomhouse.org/template.cfm?page=139&edition=8.

1. Human Rights Watch (HRW), *Criminal Politics: Violence, 'Godfathers' and Corruption in Nigeria* (New York: HRW, October 2007); Babajide Kolade-Otitoju, "The Godfathers," *News*, May 21, 2007.
2. National Democratic Institute (NDI), *Statement of the International Election Observer Delegation* (Abuja: NDI, April 23, 2007); European Union (EU) Election Observation Mission, *Final Report: Gubernatorial and State Houses of Assembly Elections and Presidential and National Assembly Elections* (Abuja: EU Election Observation Mission, 2007); International Republican Institute, "Nigeria's Elections Below Acceptable Standards," news release, April 22, 2007.
3. "An Election Programmed to Fail," *Daily Trust*, April 25, 2007.
4. International Crisis Group, *Nigeria: Failed Elections, Failing State?* (Washington, D.C.: International Crisis Group, May 30, 2007).
5. AfroBarometer Survey in Nigeria, Round 4, 2008. The survey also shows a large gap between the officially reported turnout level and the 62 percent of respondents who say they voted.
6. Ise-Oluwa Ige, "Atiku Remains VP, Court Rules," *Vanguard*, February 21, 2007; Ike Abonyi and Funso Muraina et al., "Court Affirms Atiku VP," *This Day*, February 21, 2007.
7. Randy Fabi and Camillus Eboh, "Nigeria Court Confirms Yar'Adua Presidency," *Reuters*, December 12, 2008.
8. Ise-Oluwa Ige, "Nigeria Polls Petition—I'm Not Shaken by Fresh Trial—Yar 'Adua," *Vanguard*, May 6, 2009.
9. EU Election Observation Mission, *Final Report*, 9.
10. Is'Haq Modibbo Kawu, "Nnamdi 'Andi' Uba: A Fitting Finale for Fraud," *Daily Trust*, June 18, 2009.
11. EU Election Observation Mission, *Final Report*, 19–20, 24–25.
12. Alifa Daniel, "Senate Dumps Constitution Review Bill," *Guardian*, May 17, 2006; AfroBarometer Round 4.
13. Davidson Iriekpen, "Eradicating Corruption—Hope on the Horizon?" *This Day*, May 18, 2009; Iyobosa Uwugiaren, "Impeachment Threat: AC, CNPP, Aturu Dare Reps," *Leadership*, July 21, 2009.
14. Golu Timothy and Joshua Uma, "Nigeria: Why FG Introduced New Reforms in Civil Service," *Leadership*, August 27, 2009.
15. Anne Hammerstad, *AU Commitment to Democracy in Theory and Practice: An African Human Security Review* (Pretoria/Addis Ababa: Institute for Security Studies and African Security Initiative, 2004), 71.
16. Nkechi Onyedika, "Yar'Adua Waits for N'Assembly on Information Bill," *Guardian*, March 24, 2009; Yemi Adebisi, "Yar'Adua—Agenda for FOI Bill," *Daily Independent*, June 22, 2009.
17. Patrick Ugeh and Chinwe Ocu, "FG Begins Monitoring of Int'l NGOs," *This Day*, April 3, 2007.
18. Open Society Justice Initiative, "Justice Initiative Condemns Human Rights Crackdown in Nigeria," news release, August 28, 2009.
19. "Nigeria: Government Cracks Down on Biafra Separatist Resurgence," Integrated Regional Information Networks (IRIN), September 4, 2006.

[20] Bureau of Democracy, Human Rights, and Labor, "Nigeria," in *2008 Country Reports on Human Rights Practices* (Washington, D.C.: U.S. Department of State, February 25, 2009).
[21] Article 19, "Around Africa," January 2008; "Police Arrest Publisher," *Vanguard*, December 9, 2008.
[22] "As Governor Sylva Blinks, Abducted Journalist Regains Freedom," *Sahara Reporters*, March 24, 2009.
[23] Committee to Protect Journalists (CPJ), "Nigeria," in *Attacks on the Press 2007* (New York: CPJ, February 2008).
[24] CPJ, "Nigerian Radio Journalist Killed in Ambush," news release, October 16, 2008.
[25] "As Governor Sylva Blinks," op. cit.; CPJ, *Attacks on the Press 2007*.
[26] HRW, "Nigeria: Despite Reforms, Police Routinely Practice Torture," news release, July 27, 2005.
[27] Amnesty International, "Nigeria's Prison System Fails Its People," news release, February 26, 2008.
[28] HRW, "Nigeria: Events of 2008," in *World Report 2009* (New York: HRW, 2009).
[29] Amnesty International, "Nigeria's Prison System Fails Its People."
[30] "Prison Decongestion, a Major Challenge for Justice Ministry—Ojo," *Daily Champion*, May 2, 2007.
[31] Kunle Adeyemi and Olusola Fabiyi, "Why Police Reinstated Ondo LG Bosses—Okiro," *Punch*, March 20, 2009.
[32] HRW, *They Do Not Own This Place* (New York: HRW, April 25, 2006).
[33] HRW, "Nigeria: Arbitrary Killings by Security Forces in Jos," news release, December 19, 2008.
[34] "Reps Panel Finds: Jang Ignored Security Reports," *Daily Trust*, March 24, 2009.
[35] "There Are Plans to Destroy This Country, Says CAN Chairman," *Vanguard*, March 7, 2009.
[36] Associated Press, "Nigerian Death Toll Rises to 700," *New York Times*, August 2, 2009; "Sect Leader 'Alive When Captured,'" British Broadcasting Corporation (BBC), August 3, 2009.
[37] Innocent Chukwuma, "Designing Indicators of Safety and Justice: Lessons from the CLEEN Foundation's National Crime Victims Surveys in Nigeria" (paper presented at workshop on Indicators for Safety and Justice: Their Design, Implementation and Use in Developing Countries for the Kennedy School of Government, Cambridge, MA, March 13–15, 2008); CLEEN Foundation, *Summary of Crime Statistics in Nigeria 2008* (Lagos: CLEEN Foundation, 2009).
[38] Adetutu Folasade-Koyi, Joe Nwankwo, and Rafiu Ajakaye, "512 Kidnapped in Nigeria in Six Months," *Daily Independent*, July 23, 2009.
[39] Ibid.
[40] Alexandra Mede, "CPP Tasks Onovo on Security," *Daily Independent*, July 27, 2009.
[41] Bureau of Democracy, Human Rights, and Labor, *Trafficking in Persons Report 2009* (Washington, D.C.:U.S. Department of State, June 2009).
[42] Federal Ministry of Health and the World Health Organization, "Elimination of Female Genital Circumcision in Nigeria," December 2007.
[43] UN Secretariat for the Convention on the Rights of Persons with Disabilities, "Convention and Optional Protocol Signatories and Ratification: Countries and Regional Integration Organizations."
[44] Stella Odueme, "Nigeria: Towards Lift for the Physically-Challenged," *Daily Independent*, December 15, 2008.

45. Emmanuel Aziken and Inalegwu Shaibu, "Nigeria: Senate Passes Bill against Discrimination of Disabled," *Vanguard*, March 11, 2009.
46. HRW, *They Do Not Own This Place*.
47. Ibid.
48. Collins Olayinka, "Govt. Moves to Douse Labour Crisis in Oil Sector," *Guardian*, March 31, 2009.
49. International Trade Union Confederation (ITUC), *Annual Survey of Violations of Trade Union Rights* (Brussels: ITUC, 2008 and 2009).
50. Davidson Iriekpen, "Nigeria: Rule of Law—How Has Yar'Adua Fared?" *This Day*, May 28, 2008.
51. Funso Muraina, "Yar'Adua Approves Judge's Dismissal for Misconduct," *This Day*, March 5, 2009.
52. Kenny Ashaka, "Senatorial Shocker on How El-Rufai Raped FCT," *Daily Sun*, March 9, 2009.
53. Henry Umoru, "Tears as Aliero's Bulldozers Crush Abuja Town, Sabo Lugbe," *Vanguard*, April 4, 2009.
54. "Performance: Is N/Assembly Guilty As Charged?" *Nigerian Tribune*, May 15, 2009.
55. George Agba, "Govt Indicts Obasanjo over N37 Billion Health Project," *Leadership*, July 22, 2008; Francis Ottah Agbo, "Disengagement Deals," *News*, June 18, 2007.
56. Desmond Utomwen, "Tainted Saint," *News*, April 2, 2007.
57. Femi Babafemi, "Councils Wasted N3tr, Says EFCC," *Guardian*, August 26, 2008.
58. Tony Amokeodo et al., "EFCC Arrests Agagu over N25bn Fraud," *Punch*, March 5, 2009; Olumide Bajulaiye and Leye Adewunmi, "Appeal Court Sacks Agagu," *Daily Trust*, February 24, 2009.
59. Cosmas Ekpunobi, "Senate Faults EFCC's Graft List—VP Says It's for Witch Hunt," *Daily Champion*, February 21, 2007; HRW, *Election or Selection?* (New York: HRW, April 2007).
60. Emmanuel Aziken, "Senate to Remove EFCC from AGF Influence," *Vanguard*, December 30, 2008.
61. "Senate Faults EFCC's Graft List."
62. Kelechi Okoronkwo, "Ribadu's Plight May Worsen Nigeria's Graft Rating, Says Transparency," *Guardian*, December 10, 2008; "Outrage over Ribadu; It's Barbaric, Says NBA," *This Day*, November 24, 2008; Nick Tattersall, "Top Nigerian Anti-Graft Official Quits," Reuters, November 20, 2008.
63. Ade Ogidan, Yakubu Lawal, and Richard Abu, "FG to Sue Foreign Firms Involved in Bribery," *Guardian*, March 9, 2009; "U.S. Charges 2 British Men in KBR Bribe Case," Associated Press, March 5, 2009.
64. *Constitution of the Federal Republic of Nigeria*, Fifth Schedule, Section 11.
65. "Police, PCHN, Customs Top Corruption List," *Nigerian Muse*, June 14, 2007.
66. Open Budget Initiative, "Nigeria," in *Open Budget Index 2008* (Washington, D.C.: Open Budget Initiative, 2009).
67. OECD, *2008 Survey on Monitoring the Paris Declaration: Making Aid More Effective by 2010* (Paris: OECD, 2008).

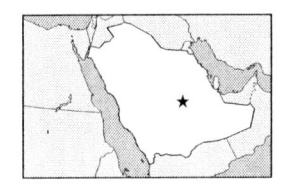

SAUDI ARABIA

CAPITAL: Riyadh
POPULATION: 28.7 million
GNI PER CAPITA (PPP): $22,950

SCORES	2006	2010
ACCOUNTABILITY AND PUBLIC VOICE:	N/A	0.67
CIVIL LIBERTIES:	N/A	0.47
RULE OF LAW:	N/A	1.47
ANTICORRUPTION AND TRANSPARENCY:	N/A	1.31

(scores are based on a scale of 0 to 7, with 0 representing weakest and 7 representing strongest performance)

INTRODUCTION

The Saudi state is based on a historical partnership of the ruling Al Saud family and the religious elites of central Arabia. While the balance of power has been gradually shifting in favor of the ruling family over time, no new social actors have managed to enter the core of the regime and the decision-making process for more than 200 years.

Saudi Arabia has only very weak traditions of constitutional government; over much of modern Saudi history, the government has claimed that the Quran is the country's constitution and no further legal-institutional framework for the Saudi polity is needed. The western region of Saudi Arabia, the Hijaz, witnessed a brief period of semi-constitutional government in the 1920s, when a regional representative body was elected and King Abdulaziz issued the "organic instructions" as a quasi-constitution for the Hijaz. The elected bodies soon lost their political importance, however, and the organic instructions became obsolete when the kingdom was gradually unified, from the 1940s on, around an administration based in the Central Province and predicated on executive rather than legislative rule.

Partial return to a constitutional framework occurred only in 1992 with the issuance of the Basic Law, which codifies certain governing norms but in substance does little more than consecrate the kingdom's status as an absolute monarchy and makes no allowance for popular sovereignty or democratic participation mechanisms.[1] While the regime is quite explicitly undemocratic by international standards, in Middle Eastern comparison, the use of coercion vis-à-vis the citizenry is less overt, and opposition is often co-opted rather than merely suppressed.

While formally unconstrained by organized social interests, the Saudi rulers harbor great concern about their reputation and the inclusion of the population in their patronage systems. Informal consultations have repeatedly brought down or reversed unpopular policies, and consensus-building within the royal family and among elites within the royal family is an important part of the policy making process in most fields. The king himself is constrained in his decision making by powerful brothers, rendering the kingdom in practice an oligarchic rather than an absolutist system. All of the senior princes regularly sound out public opinion on delicate policy issues through their clients and informants, who include advisors and courtiers as well as civil servants, business partners, local notables, and tribal leaders attuned to the sentiment in different social strata.

The informal culture of political consultation in Saudi Arabia remains, however, in a strictly paternal mold. Due to the lack of institutionalization, consultation is granted rather than claimed, can always be withdrawn by the regime, and is not extended to a wide variety of different social strata. Consultation often happens among social elites, and most collective social interests remain unorganized and, indeed, lack rights to formal collective action. All the most senior regime positions remain in royal hands; the premiership has been fused with the kingship since King Faisal's accession to the throne in 1964, preventing the separation of "ruling" and "reigning" that has to some extent occurred in more liberal Arab monarchies.

The best-organized interest group outside of the ruling family remains the religious sector or ulama, which has allowed itself to be bureaucratized by the Al Saud since the late 1960s in return for considerable influence over the kingdom's educational and judicial system as well as the enforcement of public morals. The strict social authoritarianism of the Saudi system—in terms of restrictions on women's rights, religious rights, and cultural rights—is mostly enforced through the Saudi ulama and the religious police attached to them.

Saudi Arabia has never seen national elections. Municipal elections occurred in a brief phase of partial liberalization in the 1950s and early 1960s but were abandoned under King Faisal from 1964 on. Only in 2005 were they reintroduced, although with a mere half the municipal seats up for election. Otherwise, elections have been limited to the boards of specific interest groups such as professional associations and chambers of commerce.

Recent years have seen several steps toward sociocultural and partial political liberalization under the aegis of King Abdullah. Although often announced as path breaking, in many cases such moves have represented a return to historical precedents or the implementation of promises that were already several decades old. The Basic Law in 1992, for example, had been promised several times since the 1950s, and the same is true of the appointed consultative council established the same year (its building had in fact already been erected in the 1980s). The 2005 municipal elections were more constrained than the ones five decades before.

Nonetheless, by Saudi standards there has been a substantial change of political atmosphere in the 2000s, especially after the domestic jihadist insurgency in 2003–04 led to a rethinking of the socio-cultural and, to some extent, political foundations of the Saudi regime. The scope for political discourse has widened, new interest groups have been licensed, and the regime has started to tackle reforms of the educational and judicial systems, somewhat weakening the hold of the most conservative religious forces. None of these steps have affected the core political structure of the regime, however, and with the stabilization of the domestic security situation and the reduction of U.S. democratization pressures after 2005, discussion of more fundamental constitutional reform has abated again. As oppositional mobilization in society remains limited to small strata of dissidents, the soft paternal authoritarianism of the Al Saud is unlikely to see substantial change in coming years.

Oil remains the essential backbone of the Saudi economy, and the price increases of recent years have further boosted the regime's confidence while lessening perceived pressure for fundamental reform. The state continues to be independent of domestic taxation, as it is mostly financed through oil rents, decreasing the political bargaining power of the citizenry in general and business in particular. Price decreases since 2008 do not constitute a threat to the system, as the regime has managed its finances relatively prudently and has accumulated savings sufficient to continue and expand its policies of patronage.

ACCOUNTABILITY AND PUBLIC VOICE	0.67
FREE AND FAIR ELECTORAL LAWS AND ELECTIONS	0.00
EFFECTIVE AND ACCOUNTABLE GOVERNMENT	1.25
CIVIC ENGAGEMENT AND CIVIC MONITORING	1.00
MEDIA INDEPENDENCE AND FREEDOM OF EXPRESSION	0.43

Saudi Arabia has no mechanism for national elections and, after the release of some trial balloons on the issue in 2003 and 2004, the topic has again disappeared from public discourse. The kingdom's Majlis Al-Shura, a consultative council with limited but gradually increasing legislative powers, remains unelected. Its 150 members are appointed by the king every four years; their terms can be renewed once. The Majlis can propose legislation, but cannot overrule the cabinet unless supported by the king. Despite its repeated lobbying efforts, it has no control over the national budget. Nonetheless, over time the Majlis could potentially develop stronger faculties as an intermediary between citizenry and state, provided it acquires fiscal powers and the capacity to sanction senior civil servants.

The second round of municipal elections, which should have been due in spring 2009, were postponed for two years, supposedly for administrative reasons.[2] One rumor has it that the postponement was in order to prepare women's participation in the next round, but it is not clear why this could not have been prepared for 2009, given that the issue was already hotly debated before the first round in 2005. The postponement shows that political-institutional reform is no longer a priority of the Al Saud, as both international and domestic reform pressures have abated. The councils' political competences were strictly limited in the first place, leading to the disillusionment of many members. The majority of the current incumbents in the larger cities are middle of the road Islamists, most of whom were voted into office on rather apolitical platforms focused on the improvement of local services. Their ideological orientation probably reflects that of Saudi society at large, but given the very low turnout in the 2005 election—less than a third of eligible voters—firm conclusions cannot be drawn. On average, the appointed half of the local council members tends to be less socially conservative, reflecting the paradox that socially liberal elites in Saudi Arabia tend to be close to the regime due to their weak social base.

Smaller groups of political dissidents of liberal or moderate Islamist background still occasionally petition the regime for national elections and constitutional reform—most recently in May 2009[3]—but the reaction from the regime has been to ignore the entreaties, remind the petitioners of reforms already underway or, in some cases, warn them not to exhort the Al Saud in any public way. Dissidents involved in constitutional petitions have on occasion been imprisoned.

Saudi politics continues to be based on patronage, both formal, through subsidized public services and broad-based state employment, and informal, through individual attachments to princely networks of privilege in business or the administration. The most senior princes in government have all been running large bureaucratic bodies for decades and use them to build up large clienteles. Major bodies under royal control, such as the ministries of defense and interior and the National Guard, are allotted significant shares of the national budget, which are used for the procurement of equipment, the building of housing compounds, and the operation of special hospitals and educational institutions, as well as large-scale employment. The major security institutions in the country have become synonymous with the princes heading them, giving them a position that even the king cannot challenge.

The most important institutional reform after 2005 has arguably been the creation of the Allegiance Council in 2006, which allows for a vote on future crown princes by a select number of direct descendants of the founding king, Abdulaziz. Although always negotiated within the family, succession had previously been formally left to the discretion of the king. The Allegiance Council has been interpreted as an attempt by King Abdullah to circumscribe the influence of his most powerful brothers, Sultan and Naif, in favor of an alliance with less senior princes. The appointment of Prince Naif as second deputy prime minister in early 2009, however, seems to make him crown prince-in-waiting, calling the Allegiance Council's importance into question.

The judiciary is not involved in direct supervision of administrative action, and although the Majlis Al-Shura can question ministers, it has no means to dismiss them or access ministerial accounts. Although there is no parliament in a strict sense, individual citizens can to some extent hold the government accountable through the Board of Grievances, an administrative tribunal that arbitrates, among other things, conflicts between individuals and the government. The Board of Grievances, like other courts, is staffed with Sharia-trained judges. As with other senior judicial personnel, they are chosen by the king, though usually from among the more liberal wings of the religious establishment. Verdicts in citizens' favor are issued regularly, but usually concern nonpolitical issues such as getting degrees recognized by the government, being reinstated into a job by a specific ministry, being indemnified for damage to property, or getting administrative fines lifted.

There is a disciplinary board investigating bureaucratic abuse, but as an internal administrative mechanism, it is itself part of the Saudi bureaucracy and not accountable to the public. Apart from occasional reporting of relatively petty abuses and their punishment, little is heard about its activities.

Influence-peddling with regard to civil service appointments does occur in the kingdom, but generally the bureaucracy appoints on the basis of clear, albeit inflexible, civil service rules.[4] Promotion rules are rigid, linked to education levels, years of service, and performance reports that hardly discriminate between different civil servants, thereby limiting superiors' discretion. There are very few dismissals. Both carrots and stick are weak in the bureaucracy, giving many positions the character of sinecures, an example of the country as a rentier state. The state is relatively institutionalized, but rigid and unaccountable. Pockets of efficiency, such as the central bank, SAMA, or the national oil company, Saudi Aramco, perform significantly better than the rest of the state, but their operation is similarly opaque to citizens.

Chances for civic participation in Saudi Arabia have somewhat improved in recent years due to the Majlis Al-Shura and other new government bodies, such as the Supreme Economic Council, that invite interest groups for hearings or receive their petitions. Consultation is usually granted, however, rather than claimed as a right, and the choice of who gets consulted and which issues are debated can be quite selective. The National Human Rights Society, for example, has been engaged in important exchanges with the Ministry of Labor on foreign workers' rights and the Ministry of Interior on prison conditions, but since its licensing in 2004 has been operating as a quasi-monopoly on human rights lobbying. Saudi business plays an increasingly substantial role in economic policy deliberations through the circulation of draft laws in the kingdom's regional chambers of commerce and industry. At the same time, labor and consumer interests remain unorganized. Some indirect lobbying on less sensitive policy issues can happen through the Saudi press, whose coverage is a genuine concern for bureaucrats who are afraid of princely punishment when an agency is reported on negatively.

At the time of writing, a much-discussed NGO law whose issuance has been expected for many years was still pending in the Majlis Al-Shura. There currently is no overall framework regulating civic groups; instead, groups are subject to an arbitrary licensing regime wherein they often need a princely patron to be officially recognized. Following licensing, they are usually attached to the line ministry in charge of the policy area relevant to their activities. Charities, for instance, are attached to the Ministry of Social Affairs, while professional groups are attached to the Ministry of Higher Education under the rationale that they represent graduates of a specific profession. Civic groups can be shut down arbitrarily and there is no effective recourse mechanism against such decisions.

The weakness of Saudi civil society is, however, caused not only by a restrictive licensing regime, but also by the weakness of bottom-up pressures emerging from society. Civil society traditions in the kingdom are weak, and society remains organized on a kinship or other informal basis. The new "civil society" groups that have appeared in recent years are often state generated and supported, function along corporatist lines, and are materially dependent on the regime. The strength of autonomous social organizations in general has been greatly weakened by the Saudi rentier state since the 1960s, as Saudis have become individually dependent on the state to the detriment of collective action.

The boundaries of freedom of expression in Saudi Arabia tend to fluctuate with the political climate. While freedom of speech expanded considerably in 2003 and 2004, a certain tightening on political topics—but not social or cultural issues—occurred after 2005. There are no formal safeguards guaranteeing freedom of speech; Article 39 of the Basic Law merely states that "information, publication, and all other media shall employ courteous language and the state's regulations, and they shall contribute to the education of the nation and the bolstering of its unity. All acts that foster sedition or division or harm the state's security and its public relations or detract from man's dignity and rights shall be prohibited." Most major Saudi (and Arab) newspapers are directly or indirectly controlled by royal factions: *Okaz* and *Saudi Gazette* by Prince Naif, *Arab News* and *Al-Sharq Al-Awsat* by Prince Salman and his sons, *Al-Hayat* by Prince Khaled bin Sultan, and *Al-Watan* by the Al-Faisal faction of the ruling family. Regime institutions can also exert considerable informal pressure on local media. Foreign correspondents are on occasion expelled when their reporting gets too critical, and journalists and editors are on occasion dismissed or prohibited from writing.

Self-censorship in Saudi newspapers is pervasive; the appointment of an editor in chief requires approval by the Ministry of Information, which is closely linked to the Ministry of Interior and conducts regular meetings with senior press representatives. The media licensing policy is restrictive, and even media not directly owned by princes are usually under the patronage of specific wings of the Al Saud. A press tribunal set up under the 2000 Law of Printed Matters and Publications and administered by the Ministry of Information decides about complaints against the press brought by private individuals.

In recent years, newspapers' reporting and commentary have become more daring on socio-economic and cultural issues. With some exceptions in the liberal phase of 2003–04, however, political red lines have hardly shifted: criticism of the royal family or individual royals remains taboo, as do calls for substantial change to the political system. More than 90 percent of Saudi households have satellite dishes and Al-Jazeera is widely watched. A prohibition on dishes stemming from the 1990s has never been enforced and has now become obsolete. The political content of satellite channels is less of a topic of debate in Saudi Arabia than the moral issues posed by permissive entertainment channels. The head of the Supreme Judicial Council, Saleh Al-Luhaidan, in September 2008 stated that it was permissible to kill those involved in the spread of immoral programs if they could not be stopped any other way. As several Saudi princes have invested in satellite channels, this statement is thought to have contributed to Al-Luhaidan's dismissal in early 2009.

The internet in Saudi Arabia is censored under the auspices of the Communications and Information Technology Commission with considerable technological effort, but little effectiveness. Internet cafes allowing anonymous access are widespread in Saudi cities.

CIVIL LIBERTIES   0.47

PROTECTION FROM STATE TERROR, UNJUSTIFIED IMPRISONMENT, AND TORTURE	1.00
GENDER EQUITY	0.33
RIGHTS OF ETHNIC, RELIGIOUS, AND OTHER DISTINCT GROUPS	1.00
FREEDOM OF CONSCIENCE AND BELIEF	0.00
FREEDOM OF ASSOCIATION AND ASSEMBLY	0.00

The Saudi regime's repression of the country's nonviolent opposition, whether religious or "liberal," is not particularly bloody by regional standards, but remains arbitrary and has a chilling effect on political life. Abuse occurs, but it has not been systematic. Several nonviolent dissidents have also been imprisoned without trial in recent years, such as political activist Matrouk Al-Faleh (released in January 2009) and blogger Fouad Al-Fahran (released in April 2008). Minority religious groups also complain of arrests of politically vocal members.

Treatment of suspected members of violent jihadi groups is significantly harsher. Following a wave of terror attacks in 2003 and 2004, thousands of terror suspects were arrested and held for years without charge or access to counsel or courts. In 2008 the government announced it would begin trials, which were initiated in mid-2009 in special courts not open to the public. In July 2009, it announced that over 300 convictions had been handed down.[5] Some of the suspects not directly involved in political violence have participated in re-education campaigns in a summer camp-style institution which, while technically optional, is reported to be a prerequisite for release. This option is not open to hardcore activists. Some detainees allege that in reality they were arrested for political reasons, an assertion that calls the government's lack of adherence to international due process norms into even greater question.[6]

The state-licensed National Human Rights Society has conducted several waves of prison inspections, and the state of Saudi prisons appears to be better than in most other Arab countries. Human Rights Watch was allowed access to a Saudi prison in 2006 and documented cases of abuse. The Criminal Procedures Law formally prohibits mistreatment, guarantees access to a lawyer, and sets a maximum term for trial without detention. Prisoners enjoy no effective recourse mechanisms if these stipulations are violated, however, and there are special security prisons controlled by the Ministry of Interior in which prisoners can be held in complete isolation. There are no effective protections against arbitrary arrests.

As Sharia is the official basis of criminal justice, there is no code of criminal law in Saudi Arabia, only a law of procedures for criminal trials, which includes a presumption of innocence rule and right of access to a lawyer. Sanctions include corporal punishments (mostly whipping) and capital punishment by beheading.

Domestic terrorism has abated after its peak in 2004 due to a crackdown on militants, as well as greatly improved intelligence and policing efforts, but residual networks of violent activists exist. Shootouts in recent years have been rare and generally initiated by the police; there is currently no significant danger to either the local or foreign population. In general, crime levels in Saudi Arabia are relatively low and the prosecution of crime is often severe. Foreign residents from non-Western countries are vulnerable to harsh police treatment. Corporal punishment through flogging is practiced regularly, often in public. Saudi citizens tend to be much better protected against crime than low-income foreign workers.

Reacting to the international debate about labor rights in the Gulf, the cabinet issued anti-human trafficking regulations in July 2009 that provide for prison terms of up to 15 years for traffickers. In addition, the government has established a permanent committee on trafficking within the Human Rights Society that is composed of representatives from several government ministries and periodically participates in and carries out training sessions and workshops on human trafficking issues.[7] However, the illegal "free visa" system, in which official Saudi sponsors of foreign workers informally resell them to other, unofficial employers, remains widespread.[8] The system will be impossible to eradicate unless Saudi labor laws, which currently create a relationship of bondage between foreigners and their official employers, are fundamentally revised.[9] Some discussion on this has been happening the last two years, involving both the Ministry of Labor and the National Human Rights Society. The government has proposed amending the Labor Code to transfer visa sponsorship from employers to recruitment agencies or the government, but has made no concrete steps towards this end.[10] Foreign domestic workers are at particular risk for being trafficked against their will to new employers who keep them as virtual prisoners and frequently subject them to psychological and physical abuse, including sexual molestation. The scale of this phenomenon is difficult to estimate.

Saudi and foreign women remain subject to special rules and constraints in many walks of life, and women's campaigns to improve their legal and de facto condition continue. While since 2008 Saudi businesswomen no longer require a male guardian's approval for domestic travel, and the Ministry of Interior has allowed independent foreign travel for women above 45, these exceptions are not fully implemented in practice. Marriage similarly requires a guardian's approval. Women are not allowed to drive and were not allowed to vote in the 2005 municipal elections. Although entitled to their own ID cards since 2001, they can still have trouble obtaining them and getting their validity recognized in practice.

Reports about the violation of women's property rights by their male guardians in inheritance disputes and business life are frequent. Although the official requirement that businesswomen need a male agent to act on their behalf has been curbed, a new rule now demands the presence of a male "manager." While the latter's power of attorney can be more easily limited, businesswomen remain hamstrung in their direct dealings with the administration.

The government's idea of women's cultural, economic, and political life seems to be based on a "separate but equal" principle that calls for a parallel administrative and economic infrastructure for women—a costly policy depriving women of opportunities and effectively limiting most of their employment to a few sectors, such as health and education.[11] While separation is widely enforced, equality is not, resulting in less well-endowed facilities for women, fewer chances to participate in public life, and many fewer jobs—despite what are on average better scholarly achievements of female students. About twice as many men as women work in the civil service (not counting security agencies, which employ mostly men).[12]

King Abdullah has made women's social—though not political—issues one of the primary items on his reform agenda, has received several women's delegations, and appointed the first female deputy minister in February 2009 (in the Ministry of Education). The situation of Saudi women has not yet fundamentally changed, however. The female employment strategy ratified by the cabinet in 2004 has remained ineffective, as less than 70,000 Saudi women were employed in the private sector in 2007, out of a total of more than 5 million Saudi women of working age (some 250,000 are employed by government).[13]

Although there is no specific codification of the rights of disabled, the government makes significant efforts to cater to disabled citizens through employment quotas and support to specialized charities.

Saudi society is informally stratified into nationals with a genealogy linking them to major Arabian tribes and those without such heritage. The latter are usually called *khadiri* and comprise an estimated one-third of all Saudis. They are often socially discriminated against. Despite repeated official calls against tribalism, no effective steps have been taken against the phenomenon, which mostly involves private decisions such as marriage.

A more politically salient division in Saudi society is that between Sunnis and Shiites. Twelver Shiites in the Eastern Province, which constitute between 10 and 15 percent of the national population, have been discriminated against since the conquest of their region by the Al Saud in 1913, and members have on occasion mobilized violently against the Al Saud regime. The same is true of the Ismaili (Sevener Shiite) minority in the south around the city of Najran.

The religious rights of both minorities have improved as restrictions on their public religious rituals and the construction of places of worship have been relaxed, though not completely abandoned, under Abdullah. However, they remain discriminated against in state employment: there is no Shiite cabinet minister, and only 4 of 150 members of the Majlis Al-Shura are Shiite. The state-supported religious establishment is often viciously anti-Shiite, an attitude shared by many Central Province Sunnis. The state-controlled religious educational system, although undergoing reform on the textbook level, still often entails negative teachings about the Shiite faith in the classroom. Shiites are subject to harassment by the religious police, and in February 2009 worshippers clashed with both religious police and other Sunnis in Medina near the prophet's mosque, leading to secession threats by a leading Eastern Province Shiite dissident and the arrest of several dozen Shiites.[14]

The situation of Shiites is better under Abdullah than it had been for decades. In addition to his inclusive rhetoric and relaxation of some constraints on community activities, in March 2009 he replaced the governor of Najran, who had a tense relationship with the local Ismaili community, with one of his sons. However, Shiite hopes that the new king would bring them full equality are unlikely to be realized, increasing the prospect of radical mobilization against the regime. Shiites remain more marginalized than, for example, the Sunni Sufis of the Western Province, whose previously marginal position has improved significantly under Abdullah, as they are accorded more leeway for their religious practices and community organization.

While the religious freedom of non-Sunni Muslims remains constrained, non-Muslims enjoy no freedom of worship and preaching. Islam is the state religion and missionary activities as well as the construction of non-Muslim places of worship are strictly prohibited. Non-Muslim religious practices are only tolerated in private, and the religious police crack down on larger gatherings, although their discretion has been somewhat curbed in recent years. Services take place at best in embassies, and western Christians enjoy more (informal) leeway than Asian Christians.[15]

The Sunni religious establishment is largely bureaucratized, working in the Ministries of Islamic Affairs and Religious Endowments, Justice, and Hajj, as well as various state-controlled institutions of religious education. The king appoints the Grand Mufti and the members of the Higher Council of Ulama and the Presidency for Scientific Research and Religious Edicts, the official fatwa administration.

While in private Saudis are relatively free to express their opinions, independent collective action and political criticism by organized groups is seldom tolerated by the regime. When dissidents are jailed, it is usually because they have started to organize. Freedom of association is absent from the Basic Law and unions have been outlawed since the time of King Saud, who first faced collective action by oil workers in the 1950s. In May 2001, the Council of Ministers sanctioned the formation of labor committees on an enterprise level. In all companies with more than 100 employees, workers have the right to form a committee, although there is no obligation to do so. So far only a small number of large foreign and public companies seem to have formed one, and their purpose seems to be not collective bargaining, but attending to workers' welfare.

Public demonstrations in Saudi Arabia are not tolerated; around a dozen arrests were made during pro-Palestinian protests in the Shiite Eastern Province in late 2008. Repression in the few cases where demonstrations have happened tends to be less harsh than in other authoritarian systems in the region: while arrests occur, live bullets are not used against protesters.

RULE OF LAW 1.47

INDEPENDENT JUDICIARY	1.40
PRIMACY OF RULE OF LAW IN CIVIL AND CRIMINAL MATTERS	1.40
ACCOUNTABILITY OF SECURITY FORCES AND MILITARY TO CIVILIAN AUTHORITIES	0.75
PROTECTION OF PROPERTY RIGHTS	2.33

The Saudi judiciary is currently undergoing a phase of reorganization, which has led to the creation of a supreme court and courts of appeal, relegating the previously dominant Supreme Judicial Council to administrative functions within the judicial system. Specialized commercial, labor, and family courts are in the making. Judges are appointed by the king, but officially are accountable only to Allah and the precepts of Sharia. Over the years, the government has created a growing body of positive law, especially on commercial matters, but this is not always recognized by the Sharia courts—a situation that has led the government to create a number of quasi-judicial tribunals within the bureaucracy to attend to specific areas of commercial and administrative law. The judicial reforms, which are still in an early stage, are meant to undo some of this fragmentation and force a stronger recognition of positive law within the judicial system proper. The Supreme Court is supposed to adjudicate on matters of precedence, guiding the rest of the system—a principle heretofore alien to the Islamic Saudi judiciary, which previously has not recognized precedence.

The Saudi judiciary is relatively independent from political interference on a day-to-day level. A problematic corollary of this, however, is that judges have vast discretion. There are no juries, and individual judges usually decide on both verdict and punishment. Judgments are brief and officially rely on a limited set of volumes on religious law that have little to say on many aspects of modern life and can be interpreted in very different ways.

The position of judge requires religious training, usually in the strictly Hanbali Sunni Saudi system. The system therefore tends to discriminate against non-Sunni minorities. Courts can refuse to recognize and enforce secular regulations emerging from the bureaucracy, as has occurred regularly on commercial matters. While corruption problems in Saudi courts appear to be limited, their unpredictability and slowness pose major problems. In its 2009 Doing Business survey, the World Bank gave Saudi Arabia rank 137 globally in the Enforcing Contracts category.[16]

Reform of the judicial system has been announced many times. First practical steps seem to have been taken in early 2009, when Abdullah replaced senior conservative figures in the religious and judicial systems and a plan was issued to implement infrastructure and training for the new specialized courts announced in November 2007. It is unclear, however, whether the new family, labor, and commercial courts will be more predictable and accountable than the existing Sharia courts, given that they will be staffed by the same judges. A true shift of the judicial system toward statutory law will require the training of a new generation of judges, which is beginning only now. The Sharia institutes in Saudi universities, from which judges will continue to graduate, remain in the hands of the conservative religious establishment, and providing additional training in secular law will be a gradual process.

Compliance mechanisms to implement judicial rulings in Saudi Arabia are weak. Ministries and police often do not enforce judgments, and defendants in legal disputes often sabotage court procedures simply by not showing up, a practice against which judges seem to have limited recourse. The judicial system is not independent vis-à-vis senior royals and no cases are known in which leading regime figures have been successfully sued in Saudi courts. Non-royal public officials are sometimes prosecuted for transgressions in office, but details of such cases are usually unavailable.

All Saudi security forces, whether for internal or external defense, are directly attached to senior royal figures who have controlled their respective institutions for decades, in some cases since their inception. Institutions headed by senior princes, like the Ministries of Defense and Interior and the National Guard, are largely autonomous bodies with their own infrastructure and rules. The cabinet and other ministries have very limited control over them and they have stayed at the core of the kingdom's informal power structure as it has grown over decades. They have their own health, housing, and educational institutions, and their recruitment and procurement structures are separate from the rest of government.

While the Ministry of Defense and the National Guard are less involved in domestic politics, the Ministry of Interior has extensive policing, political security, and regulatory functions. It is also strongly involved in policy making on nonsecurity issues such as regulation of foreign investment and safety inspections of commercial facilities. Moreover, it is often the main addressee of dissidents' complaints about censorship, arbitrary detention, and limits on Saudi political life in general. The ministry operates largely independently of the judiciary, and the public prosecution is de facto attached to it and not to the Ministry of Justice. While the Ministry of Interior, with few exceptions, is not known to mistreat Saudi prisoners, it has de facto power to detain individuals at will and keep them in detention without trial.

Saudi Arabia's economic traditions are fairly liberal in comparison with most of the developing world, as the country has never gone through a phase of nationalizations or class struggle. Private property is generally respected, and the business sector is thriving. Certain infractions on property rights are possible, however, and it can be difficult or impossible to seek remedy. Examples include the expropriation of "cover-up" businesses, companies in economic sectors limited to Saudis that are formally registered under a Saudi's name but are in fact owned and run by foreigners who usually pay the formal owners a monthly fee. The arrangement can allow the Saudi partner to expropriate the actual foreign owners.

Property rights can also be compromised when royals muscle their way in on business deals or companies of commoners by browbeating them into ceding ownership stakes or forcing foreign companies to operate through them instead of their commoner partners. While it is difficult to verify the scale of this phenomenon, many stories of such encroachments circulate. Another area in which property rights are often insecure is land deeds, especially in peripheral regions that are marked for development and in older urban areas where titles can overlap and are not well documented. Much abuse is reported in this field; appropriation of state and private lands is one of the main channels of rent-seeking and patronage in the kingdom. The land registration system, though currently in the process of reform, remains opaque and underdeveloped, and public access to it is limited.

ANTICORRUPTION AND TRANSPARENCY   1.31

ENVIRONMENT TO PROTECT AGAINST CORRUPTION	1.50
PROCEDURES AND SYSTEMS TO ENFORCE ANTICORRUPTION LAWS	1.50
EXISTENCE OF ANTICORRUPTION NORMS, STANDARDS, AND PROTECTIONS	1.25
GOVERNMENTAL TRANSPARENCY	1.00

The bureaucratic environment in Saudi Arabia is better than that of most developing countries, but remains significantly worse than in most OECD economies. Oil income seems to have resulted in a certain professionalization of the

Saudi bureaucracy over the decades, but has also increased opportunities for rent-seeking.

According to the World Bank's 2009 "Doing Business" rankings, Saudi Arabia is now the 16th easiest place in the world to do business in, up from 67th in 2004. This assessment, however, seems to be largely an artifact of a dedicated campaign of the Saudi Arabian General Investment Authority to change specific rules, fees, and procedures that are measured by the World Bank's indicators. The general investment environment has indeed improved somewhat in the last five years, though less dramatically than the above figures suggest. Bribery occurs, but with the potential exception of the labor bureaucracy and the security sector, is less widespread than in poorer Arab countries such as Syria or Egypt.

Local surveys also document that most businessmen still see Saudi Arabia as the most difficult place to do business among the Gulf monarchies. While certain regulations and procedures have been simplified, the bureaucracy continues to be slow-moving, unaccountable, and interventionist, making extensive documentation demands and on occasion trying to change the articles of association of private companies. While this environment does not automatically lead to corruption, it facilitates its mundane occurrence.

Larger transactions in the field of privatization, by contrast, have been conducted in a reasonably clean manner, not least thanks to the heavy involvement of international consultants and the king's personal interest in a credible process. Several leading state-owned enterprises, such as Aramco and Saudi Arabian Basic Industries Company, are efficiently administered and perceived as generally clean, although the available information about their governance is rather limited. Other state-owned assets, such as the national airline Saudia, have a worse reputation. Saudia is currently being prepared for privatization under a well-respected new CEO, which could mean that its worst days of opaque procurement and illicit ticket resales have passed.

To the degree that a set of institutions are well run, it is mostly because of specific organizational histories and special royal protection and attention. Formal accountability mechanisms are limited, and Saudi Arabia has no effective rules separating public and private interests. Most of the leading princes have large business interests, and many non-royal ministers are involved in business on a smaller scale, not least as several of them have been recruited from leading business families. There are no rules demanding public declaration of officials' assets.

Procurement in the security apparatus is surrounded by rumors of rent-seeking and corruption, and some large-scale cases have come to the attention of Western media.[17] The most prominent such story was associated with the Al-Yamamah airplane contract, in the course of which British defense contractor BAE allegedly channeled more than one billion UK pounds in bribes through various front companies and private accounts to senior Saudi decision makers. Transgressions in the security apparatus are punished internally, if at all.

Enforcement of anticorruption rules is limited and occurs mostly behind closed doors. The occasional newspaper reporting on corruption trials conveys the impression of a haphazard process. Such reports always relate to non-royals, and usually to lower-level figures indicted for relatively minor offenses. There is a Corruption Investigation Department at the Ministry of Interior that examines corruption cases in the administration; malfeasance is also investigated by the government's Investigation and Control Board. These bodies are not accountable to the public. Little is heard about their operation, and some observers describe them as fairly inactive.

The reports of the General Auditing Bureau on other government agencies are not published and are available only to a select few government functionaries. The Bureau, which was founded in 1971 and whose senior officials are appointed by the king, has little control over royal agencies. Although the annual closing accounts of the national budget are very detailed, they are usually produced several years after the end of the budget year.

Apart from the above-mentioned Board of Grievances, citizens have no formal recourse mechanisms against bureaucratic abuse. Saudi Arabia has no ombudsman; the closest equivalent is the petitions committee in the Majlis Al-Shura, which considers individual letters by citizens (on the order of a couple of hundred a year) and can request follow-up information from individual government agencies. Informal channels of complaint, often through princes, are usually preferred to formal ones.

There are no personal income taxes in Saudi Arabia, and the income tax on foreign firms was simplified in a 2004 law that brought the kingdom closer to international practices. The tax assessment process can still be slow and cumbersome, however, and the calculation of religious tax (*zakat*) on domestic companies in particular is often less than clear—although this more often works in favor of companies than the government.

The general transparency of the Saudi government has improved a bit under King Abdullah, but started from a very low basis. Several ministries now have spokesmen and more documents such as laws, bylaws, sectoral statistics, and annual reports are available on ministerial websites (usually in Arabic and sometimes in English). Saudi Arabia still lacks a functioning depository for all laws and regulations, however, which are instead often diligently collected by local law firms and consultants. Ministerial circulars have the force of law but often remain unpublished and are perceived by some businessmen as a tool of arbitrary power in the hands of ministers and their deputies.

Information on bureaucratic performance and the use of public funds is still very scarce. The kingdom's closing accounts have not been publicly available since the 1991 Gulf War; the only figures on actual government spending available are two aggregate numbers on total current and total capital spending issued by the Ministry of Finance at the end of every budget year. The idea of a fundamental citizen right to information has not taken hold, and there are no mechanisms for citizens to request details on state spending.

The national budget is not subject to legislative review, and the Majlis Al-Shura has no power over it. Instead, the budget is negotiated bilaterally between the powerful Ministry of Finance and the Saudi government's various line agencies—which in turn usually do not have access to the detailed budgets of other agencies. The planned budget that is reported publicly before the start of the fiscal year only contains ballpark figures on intended sectoral spending and on general project spending; a detailed breakdown by smaller administrative units or specific projects is lacking.

Revamped bidding rules and the introduction of electronic tendering at a number of ministries is intended to augment the transparency of procurement in specific instances. An improvement across the board, including the security agencies, is unlikely, however. Saudi Arabia did not sign on to World Trade Organization government procurement rules when acceding to the organization in 2005, and tendering practices can differ significantly from one agency to the next.

RECOMMENDATIONS

- Laws that have already been passed, including the statutes against human trafficking and loosening restrictions on women's travel, should be implemented in full.
- The pending NGO law should be enacted and should include guarantees against arbitrary administrative intervention with organizations' budgets and the composition of their boards. Groups should be automatically licensed after a pre-defined period after their application unless there is an explicit justification not to do so, and they should only be dissolvable through court order.
- In order for the Al Saud family to work toward a clearer separation of itself from the government and facilitate a medium-term increase in bureaucratic accountability, clearer conflict of interest rules need to be created and princes should be held accountable for violations in the regular courts.
- In order to prepare the ground for governmental accountability and a broader political class, the post of prime minister should be held by a commoner rather than a member of the royal family.
- In order to provide the process of incorporating statutory law into the Saudi system greater impetus, the government should increase the resources and attention devoted to improving legal education.
- The government should pass a law on transparency and access to governmental information, including budgetary data, that specifies and guarantees access procedures, creates an ombudsman on public information and recourse mechanisms in case of denial, and minimizes ambiguous language that could be used to deny information requests. The closing accounts of the national budget should be published.

NOTES

For URLs and endnote hyperlinks, please visit the *Countries at the Crossroads* homepage at http://freedomhouse.org/template.cfm?page=139&edition=8.

1. Abdulaziz Al-Fahad, "Ornamental Constitutionalism: The Saudi Basic Law of Governance," *Yale Journal of International Law* 30, no. 2 (2005): 376–395.
2. "Saudi Arabia Postpones Local Elections," *Telegraph*, May 20, 2009.
3. "Tiny Saudi Democracy Movement Sends King Blueprint for Reform," *Christian Science Monitor*, May 14, 2009.
4. Ahmed H. Al-Hamoud, "The Reform of the Reform: A Critical and Empirical Assessment of the 1977 Saudi Civil Service Reform" (PhD diss., University of Pittsburgh, 1991).
5. Human Rights Watch (HRW), "Saudi Arabia: Counterterrorism Efforts Violate Rights," news release, August 10, 2009.
6. HRW, *Human Rights and Saudi Arabia's Counterterrorism Response: Religious Counseling, Indefinite Detention, and Flawed Trials* (New York: HRW, August 10, 2009), 14–15.
7. "Official Commends Saudi Arabia for Combating Human Trafficking," *Arab News*, December 19, 2009.
8. Shahid Ali Khan, "Number of 'Free Visa' Workers on the Rise," *Saudi Gazette*, July 17, 2009.
9. HRW, *'As If I Am Not Human': Abuses against Asian Domestic Workers in Saudi Arabia* (New York: HRW, July 7, 2008).
10. HRW, "Saudi Arabia: Implement Proposed Labor Reform," press release, July 21, 2008.
11. See HRW, *Perpetual Minors: Human Rights Abuses Stemming from Male Guardianship and Sex Segregation in Saudi Arabia* (New York: HRW, April 19, 2008).
12. See annual yearbooks of the Saudi Arabian Monetary Agency, various editions.
13. See Central Department of Statistics census data.
14. Donna Abu-Nasr, "Saudi Arabia Cracks Down on Shiite Dissidents," American Broadcasting Corporation (ABC), April 1, 2009.
15. For details see Bureau of Democracy, Human Rights, and Labor, "Saudi Arabia," in *International Religious Freedom Report 2008* (Washington, D.C.: U.S. Department of State, September 2008).
16. World Bank, "Saudi Arabia," in *Doing Business 2009: Comparing Regulation in 181 Economies* (Washington, D.C.: World Bank, 2009).
17. "The Secrets of Britain's Arms Trade" (assorted articles), *Guardian*, 2003–10.

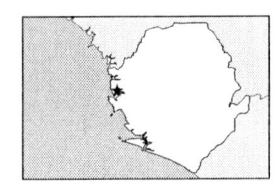

SIERRA LEONE

CAPITAL: Freetown
POPULATION: 5.7 million
GNI PER CAPITA (PPP): $750

SCORES	2006	2010
ACCOUNTABILITY AND PUBLIC VOICE:	4.63	4.90
CIVIL LIBERTIES:	4.06	4.30
RULE OF LAW:	3.84	3.96
ANTICORRUPTION AND TRANSPARENCY:	3.17	3.29

(scores are based on a scale of 0 to 7, with 0 representing weakest and 7 representing strongest performance)

William Reno

INTRODUCTION

Sierra Leone's government provides legal guarantees of a wide range of civil and political rights. The government's record in providing basic personal security and guaranteeing the predictable operation of state institutions has improved substantially since the end of a brutal eleven-year civil war (1991-2002). The primary problem remains the considerable gap between legal and administrative frameworks on paper and actual performance.

Decades of grievous official mismanagement of the country's economy and the subordination of government institutions led to a deeply corrupt system of rule. These problems helped to create conditions that led to the war, in which more than 60,000 people were killed.[1] The war began in 1991, when the Revolutionary United Front (RUF), a rebel group led by Foday Sankoh, launched a campaign to topple the corrupt military government of President Joseph Monmoh, gain control of the country's diamond industry, and—ostensibly—redistribute diamond wealth. During its campaign to gain control of the country, the RUF employed brutal tactics including murder, physical mutilation, rape, and the recruitment and abduction of child soldiers. At the war's peak, the RUF controlled large swathes of territory and diamond fields in the countryside. Following a 1999 peace agreement, the United Nations Mission in Sierra Leone (UNAMSIL) was established, but the RUF violated the agreement and chaos ensued, prompting Britain to deploy troops. The war finally came to an end when the government, with the aid

---

William Reno is Associate Professor of Political Science at Northwestern University in Chicago. He is the author of *Corruption and State Politics in Sierra Leone* (Cambridge: Cambridge University Press, 1995) and numerous other scholarly works on the politics of Sierra Leone.

of international actors, signed a second ceasefire agreement and a peace accord with the RUF in 2000 and 2001, respectively. In May 2002, President Ahmad Tejan Kabbah, who was initially elected in the 1996 return to civilian rule, again won the presidential elections. In July, the British withdrew from Sierra Leone, and in November UNAMSIL began a gradual withdrawal that was completed in January 2006, with a "peacebuilding" operation left behind.

The war crippled Sierra Leone's already flailing institutions and economy and left behind a serious security challenge. Sierra Leone's economy is heavily based on its abundant natural resources, and particularly its rich diamond mines, but the country has never been able to effectively translate these resources into economic growth due to complex factors including mismanagement, corrupt patrimonial rule, and external interference. The government has never been rich, but the war undermined state capacity to the extent that internal sources of government revenues in 2007 stood at 10.8 percent of the country's US$1.66 billion GDP, or just US$179 million to staff a civil service of more than 15,000 and provide public services to over five million citizens. By 2007, per capita income stood at US$241, a figure considerably lower than incomes in the 1970s.[2] State agencies suffer from insufficient resources and difficulties of coordination following decades of corruption and mismanagement and the near collapse of the government administration during the war.

Frustration of basic rights also comes from weak state capacity to guarantee the rule of law and the continuing ability of powerful individuals to manipulate or evade the enforcement of the law for their personal gain. The current government of President Ernest Bai Koroma of the All People's Congress (APC) was elected in September 2007. While the contest was the country's third competitive multiparty election since 1996, it marked the first time in Sierra Leone's history that an opposition party peacefully assumed executive and legislative power in a competitive election. Nonetheless, Sierra Leone's government and citizens remain dependent on security guarantees associated with foreign military training programs and on foreign financial aid to provide basic services.

State officials and foreign aid donors recognize the urgent need for judicial reform. Progress in this sector remains limited, reflecting the state's overall extremely weak capacity. The joint Government of Sierra Leone and United Nations Special Court for Sierra Leone, which commenced trials in 2004 for those charged with greatest responsibility for human rights violations during the war, promotes the rule of law in the eyes of many citizens. The court is not universally popular, however, given its lavish expenditures and the generous physical environment extended to defendants, compared to the desperately poor local conditions.

Corruption continues to undermine the legitimacy of government policies. The government embarked on a new effort in 2008 to strengthen the legal and administrative competence of the Anti-Corruption Commission to address administrative corruption and conflict of interest among officials, but the weakness of the judicial sector and pervasive informal influence of politicians undermines the commission's work. Illicit diamond mining challenges the authority of the government to enforce licensing and tax regulations, although considerable progress has been made to rebuild government institutions and to provide increased revenue. More positively, the country's radio and newspapers partially compensate for the lack of official transparency.

Citizens elect high state officials in regularly scheduled competitive multiparty elections. International observers pronounced national elections in 1996, 2002, and 2007, as well as local elections in 2008, as free and fair. Despite scattered acts of violence, polling in each case was considered to have been carried out without interference. The National Electoral Commission (NEC) receives praise as generally autonomous and judicious in reviewing complaints. In general, Sierra Leone's democratic transition has benefitted from a political culture that values debate and is tolerant of diverse opinions and backgrounds. Formidable obstacles remain, including extremely weak government institutions and poverty so intense as to place Sierra Leone at the very bottom of the United Nations Development Programme's Human Development Index. Solving these problems will require continued significant international engagement to provide security and finance and oversee the implementation of reforms. This level of international engagement creates risks of its own, as outsiders and many Sierra Leoneans grow concerned about the sustainability of these reforms once external support is withdrawn.

Sierra Leone's record of sustaining a relatively democratic government is a remarkable achievement in light of the serious nature of human rights abuses during the war and the nearly complete collapse of state institutions. This is due in part to the government's very weak bureaucratic capacity—it cannot organize effective repressive measures—and its extreme dependence on external security guarantees and financial aid. These conditions create a context in which the most democratic and conciliatory elements of Sierra Leone's political culture can exercise significant influence. The country's best hope for a democratic future is to consolidate the influence of these domestic forces in a context of continuing relative political stability.

ACCOUNTABILITY AND PUBLIC VOICE 4.90

FREE AND FAIR ELECTORAL LAWS AND ELECTIONS	5.25
EFFECTIVE AND ACCOUNTABLE GOVERNMENT	4.25
CIVIC ENGAGEMENT AND CIVIC MONITORING	5.67
MEDIA INDEPENDENCE AND FREEDOM OF EXPRESSION	4.43

Sierra Leone's president and its unicameral parliament are chosen in direct elections that adhere to constitutional form. The first multiparty national election since the 1978 declaration of a one-party state took place in 1996, in the middle of the war. Seven parties participated in national presidential and parliamentary elections in August and September 2007, the first elections since the war for which the government was fully responsible for their conduct. The standard-bearer of the opposition APC, Ernest Bai Koroma, was elected with 54.6 percent of the popular vote in a second round of voting. Koroma beat Solomon Berewa, the candidate of the incumbent Sierra Leone People's Party (SLPP), amid widespread public perceptions that the SLPP administration had tolerated corruption and cronyism and had failed to address the problem of widespread poverty. Most international monitors pronounced the election to be free and fair,[3] although European Union election observers noted "a rise in tensions at the start of the second campaign period and an increase in violent clashes between rival supporters." In addition, individuals reported to the NEC and EU instances of intimidation by traditional leaders and youth gangs linked to both candidates.[4]

The 1991 constitution provides for the revival of elected local governments abolished in 1972. Local elections were scheduled for 1999 but did not take place until May 2004; council elections were held again in July 2008. The elections produced a turnout of 38.8 percent of eligible voters, considerably lower than turnout in national elections.[5] The election highlighted issues such as tensions in relations between local councils and chiefdoms, particularly over the distribution of financial resources. There were some sporadic instances of localized violence associated with the balloting. The failure of government agencies to seriously investigate these incidents highlights the low institutional capacity to enforce laws, which is due in part to the assertion of partisan interests among some officials.[6] Such local-level friction represents the reemergence of a key issue of contention that was a source of serious political instability during a previous effort to institute local government in the 1950s and 1960s.

The president is elected to a five-year term, with a second-round runoff if no candidate obtains at least 55 percent of the vote in the first round. The president is limited to two consecutive terms in office; he or she cannot hold a seat in Parliament but is able to appoint parliamentarians as ministers and deputy ministers. Presidential and legislative elections have been competitive multiparty affairs since 1996 under the terms of the 1991 constitution. The two main parties first appeared together in legislative elections in 1962; in the first round of the 2007 presidential elections, third party presidential candidate Charles Margai won just short of 14 percent of the vote running on behalf of the People's Movement for Democratic Change (PMDC), which occupies just under 10 percent of the seats in Parliament. Legislators for 112 seats are elected to single-member districts in simple majority elections and serve five-year terms. Each of 12 districts indirectly elects one paramount chief to a five-year term to complete the parliamentary complement of 124. The 1991 constitution specifies the separation of powers and provides for checks and balances. Parliament possesses the authority to approve budgets and to make laws that control taxation, expenditures, and borrowing. As information below shows, the realities of Sierra Leonean politics, particularly deficits in resources and expertise, qualify the application of these ideals.

Candidates and parties provide financial reports prior to and after elections, and some party statements are available on the web.[7] Campaign resources usually come from the personal fortunes of candidates, and it is widely believed that many candidates acquire these resources through corrupt means. Private and group interests also intrude in the selection of civil servants; applicants are occasionally required to make informal payments to be hired for these positions. Weak monitoring capacity and low pay further increase corruption in the public sector.

Sierra Leone possesses a vigorous civic culture, with numerous nongovernmental organizations (NGOs) supporting popular causes. Women, minorities, and people with disabilities play visible roles in this sector. Civic groups, which freely collect donations from within Sierra Leone and from abroad, commonly highlight problems related to official corruption, the failure of officials to enforce laws, and deficiencies in the provision of public services. These issues are discussed openly on television and radio talk shows, and the state protects the rights of the independent civic sector to the extent its weak capacity allows.

Sierra Leone's constitution guarantees freedom of expression, and the country's dynamic media outlets reflect social norms that support free speech. Dozens of newspapers appear on a regular basis and many of them are openly critical of the government. The country also has numerous private FM radio stations that offer a wide array of views and information; the dearth of newspapers outside of the capital puts radio at the forefront of political coverage. Some radio stations draw power from mobile telephone station generators so that they are not exposed to frequent power failures.[8] The unreliability of electrical power reduces the role of television broadcasts as vehicles for political debate or for delivering information about policy. Current proposals include transforming the state-owned SLBS radio into an independent public radio station that will absorb United Nations Radio, the information arm of the extensive UN presence associated with postwar reconstruction in the country.

The country's poverty hampers efforts to improve the quality of media. Nonetheless, Sierra Leone's media has a long history of vigorous press participation in political debates, and the country benefits from several newspapers that provide important investigative reporting. The technical quality of these newspapers has improved in recent years, and advances in internet access, speed, and costs have given journalists access to more information resources.[9]

Current Minister of Information Ibrahim Ben Kargbo previously served as president of the Sierra Leone Association of Journalists (SLAJ) and had earlier been imprisoned for his opposition to a previous government. The government regulates media through the Independent Media Commission (IMC), created by Parliament in 2000. Appointments to the IMC must be approved by Parliament. SLAJ recommendations concerning appointees are generally heeded. Despite these improvements in government conduct, journalists still face the threat of criminal prosecution for seditious libel under Part V of the Public Order Act of 1965. Jonathan Leigh, the managing editor of the *Independent Observer*, was arrested in February 2008 after two articles in his newspaper accused the minister of transportation of using his office to collect kickbacks and acquire real estate. SLAJ later succeeded in helping negotiate an out-of-court settlement of the case. Sylvia Blyden was held by police for publishing a caricature of the president in the *Awareness Times* in late February 2008,[10] while in August 2008 Minister of Health Dr. Soccoh Kabia initiated court action against the managing editor of the *Standard Times* over reporting that claimed that the minister was engaged in corrupt acts.[11]

These actions reflect what many in the media see as the continuing inclination of powerful individuals to use their positions to target critics. SLAJ, with support from the Society for Democratic Initiative, Sierra Leone, the Media Foundation for West Africa, and the Open Society Justice Initiative, filed a lawsuit at the Supreme Court in February 2008 challenging the criminal and seditious libel portion of the Public Order Act. No decision had been issued as of October 2009, despite the fact that the case was heard in March 2009 and the Supreme Court is constitutionally required to produce rulings no more than three months subsequent to the completion of hearings.[12] *[Editor's Note: on November 10, 2009, the Supreme Court dismissed the SLAJ's case, leaving the restrictive provisions in place.]* Government intervention into media affairs has generated contention over whether its actions constitute official censorship. Some journalists viewed as censorship the IMC's decision to close an opposition party radio station for broadcasts that allegedly contributed to political violence in Freetown in March 2009.[13] The UN's Integrated Peacebuilding Office for Sierra Leone noted that the IMC also revoked the license of the ruling party's radio station, and noted that the IMC was due to receive funding from the British government to procure media monitoring equipment.[14]

Some journalists accept bribes in return for favorable coverage or promises to halt investigative reporting, while others are accused of using their newspapers to settle personal scores. In some cases, politicians act as shadow proprietors of newspapers to ensure favorable coverage.[15]

Nonetheless, media coverage of the 2007 and 2008 elections demonstrated the considerable value of Sierra Leone's media in enhancing public voice and ensuring accountability. The media provided access to all political parties, and the proliferation of independent media ensured that nearly all candidates for election had access to coverage.

CIVIL LIBERTIES 4.30

PROTECTION FROM STATE TERROR, UNJUSTIFIED IMPRISONMENT, AND TORTURE	3.50
GENDER EQUITY	3.33
RIGHTS OF ETHNIC, RELIGIOUS, AND OTHER DISTINCT GROUPS	3.50
FREEDOM OF CONSCIENCE AND BELIEF	5.67
FREEDOM OF ASSOCIATION AND ASSEMBLY	5.50

Along with regular multiparty elections, the 1991 Constitution Act provides for freedom of assembly, freedom of movement, freedom of conscience, and equal access for women to political and civil rights. Sierra Leone's 1991 constitution prohibits arbitrary detention and detention without trial. It prohibits "any form of torture or any punishment or other form of treatment which is inhuman or degrading" (Section III, 21(1)). Torture is a punishable offense and state officials accused of torture have been charged in court, although the weak capacity of the judicial system (detailed below) limits the consistency of this practice. No serious allegations of extrajudicial killings of state opponents have appeared since 2000 and the death penalty has not been applied since 1998. State agencies do not persecute political opponents or peaceful activists as a matter of formal or informal policy, though individual officials use the prerogatives of their office to pursue critics or rivals. This appears to be most prevalent in the context of local politics, especially in the form of violent "youth protection squads."[16] Many Sierra Leoneans suspect that official tolerance for cronyism and corruption is tantamount to an informal state policy of acceptance of such intimidation. Protections against arbitrary arrest and access to legal counsel are rights that exist in law, but poor pay and working conditions for police and a dearth of legal professionals seriously inhibit state enforcement of these rights. Mechanisms for disciplining police exist, and from December 2007 to June 2008, 94 police were dismissed for misconduct.[17] Solicitation of bribes, which continues to occur, undermines public support for police operations, although the sharp reduction of roadside police checkpoints and arbitrary searches has mitigated this problem.[18]

Suspects often suffer long-term pretrial detention in very harsh prison conditions, a consequence of the inability of the judicial system to process cases and of police and prison authorities to maintain accurate and timely records. Citizens have a constitutional right to written charges within 24 hours of detention, but this is rarely observed. State capacity to protect citizens from abuse by private and nonstate actors is limited by serious logistical and financial constraints. In practical terms this means that many citizens turn to customary forms of adjudication and participate in local neighborhood watch activities to prevent crime. Citizens have statutory rights of redress when state authorities violate their rights. The Special Court for Sierra Leone provides a limited right of redress against officials who violated rights during the 1991–2002 war. In practice, citizens' complaints face weak and disorganized government institutions, regardless of official policy or intent. The Ministry of Internal Affairs, responsible for oversight of police and prisons, is housed in a small, cramped building, suffers from inadequate funding, and operates with a tiny staff. This is a condition that has changed little in the last several years. The National Human Rights Commission, created to fulfill an ombudsman role, substantially increased its level of functioning in 2008 and began to accept complaints at several locations around the country.

Sierra Leone is a party to the African Charter on Human and People's Rights, which guarantees "elimination of every discrimination against women." The national constitution (Section III, 19(1)) incorporates this right. Although women have constitutional rights to access to education, health care, and economic opportunities, in practice scarce resources and social customs limit women's enjoyment of these rights. Some existing statutes reinforce gender discrimination, including those in customary and family law that are exempt (Section I, 27(4)) from the aforementioned constitutional guarantee. Many local courts cite custom to limit the rights of women regarding family law and inheritance.[19] This exemption extends to the widespread practice of female genital mutilation. The three Gender Acts of 2007 strengthen and codify women's rights in marriage and divorce law and rights to inheritance. The laws also provide a framework for the establishment of Family Support Units in police stations to deal with domestic violence and other violence against women. Some units have begun to operate and evidence suggests that reporting rates for domestic violence have increased.[20] Seventeen percent of the more than 1,300 candidates who stood in the 2008 local council and mayoral elections were women,[21] while the 2007 parliamentary elections sent 16 women to the 124-member Parliament, a decrease of 2 from the previous legislature. State policy prohibits trafficking in women. The Sierra Leone Police and Family Support Units reported that the government investigated 38 trafficking cases in 2008, with more than half of these cases involving female victims under the age of 16.[22] The scarcity of resources and coordination capacity limit government efforts to raise awareness, detect, and prosecute instances of human trafficking.

State policy does not discriminate against the ethnic, cultural, and linguistic rights of minorities. Most minorities do not suffer systematic discrimination with regard to the enforcement of their rights and enjoy full equality before the law, albeit within the serious limits of state capacity to provide it. An exception concerns the treatment of ethnic Lebanese residents, including those who are from families resident in the country for generations. The Sierra Leone Citizenship Act of 1973 limits citizenship to persons of "Negro African descent."[23] This vulnerability enables individual officials to threaten to reverse the naturalization of residents of Lebanese descent and subject them to deportation in the course of personal disputes. Popular discourse often ascribes ethnic biases to particular political parties, although electoral data indicate that there is significant flexibility in regional and ethnic voting patterns.[24]

The government of Sierra Leone has accepted in principle the recommendations of the Truth and Reconciliation Commission to assist war-wounded individuals, particularly amputees. Scarce resources and lack of policy coordination, however, severely limit the government's actual provision of assistance.

Freedom of religious observance is constitutionally guaranteed and widely respected in practice. Nonbelievers and adherents of minority religious faiths enjoy official protections. State officials refrain from appointing spiritual leaders, and the government does not have requirements for recognizing, registering, or regulating religious groups.

The state has a strong record of adhering to constitutional provisions recognizing every person's right of association. The state respects citizens' rights to form and join trade unions, and unions are active within the small formal sector of the economy. The state effectively protects the rights of citizen organizations to mobilize and advocate for peaceful purposes. Citizens are not compelled to belong to any association. Some NGOs complain about registration fees, but there is no evidence of systematic discrimination. Demonstrations in support of opposition candidates for the 2007 and 2008 elections were tolerated, and authorities have not banned demonstrations by groups critical of government policies, although protests occasionally result in violence and forcible dispersal by the police.

RULE OF LAW 3.96

INDEPENDENT JUDICIARY	3.80
PRIMACY OF RULE OF LAW IN CIVIL AND CRIMINAL MATTERS	2.80
ACCOUNTABILITY OF SECURITY FORCES AND MILITARY TO CIVILIAN AUTHORITIES	4.25
PROTECTION OF PROPERTY RIGHTS	5.00

The decay of state institutions, economic collapse, and the 1991–2002 war had deeply negative consequences for the security of Sierra Leonean citizens and seriously undermined the rule of law in civil and criminal matters. The RUF and their allies occupied large portions of the country from 1993 to 2001 and targeted judicial institutions, lawyers, police, NGOs, and others that they associated with the rule of law in the zones they controlled.

Sierra Leone's newly reemerging legal sector benefits from considerable international assistance. Concerns remain, however, regarding the capacity of the government to sustain this progress in the event of a decrease from the current level of assistance from the British government, the United Nations, the European Commission, and the World Bank. Nonetheless, the judiciary demonstrates some independence in the administration of justice when it is able to function. Lack of resources and trained personnel and very low (and often late) salaries continue to be serious problems. A single magistrate is appointed to each of the country's 12 districts, resulting in huge case backlogs. With only 10 state prosecutors in the whole country, untrained police often act as prosecutors, leading to delays and the collapse of cases.[25] This results in many people turning to informal mechanisms for adjudication or taking the law into their own hands.

Judges enjoy considerable constitutional protection from governmental interference. A judge can be removed only if found incapable of functioning or guilty of misconduct while serving. Removal must be authorized by the president upon recommendation of a special tribunal and subsequent approval by a two-thirds parliamentary majority. Salaries and pensions are paid from the Consolidated Fund, which is staffed with civil servants who are not political appointees, thereby insulating judicial remuneration from direct political interference.

Legislative, executive, and other governmental authorities' compliance with judicial rulings is sporadic. Governmental agents, especially police, exercise more ad hoc power outside the capital to deal with directives in their own fashion. This is due in part to the absence of resources to publish and communicate court decisions to relevant agencies. Many people lack adequate knowledge about their rights and how laws apply to them. The recent popularity of Family Support Units suggests that this situation may be changing. Formidable obstacles to improved justice remain, however, in terms of the high costs and long delays associated with government courts.

Judicial appointments reflect professional experience and merit. Supreme Court, Court of Appeals, and High Court judges are appointed by the president with parliamentary approval. Supreme Court judges are to have practiced or sat on the bench for at least 20 years, Court of Appeals judges for 15, and High Court judges for 10. The exigencies of rebuilding judicial institutions mean that many standards are relaxed in practice. The paucity of state resources means that magistrates receive limited training or upgrading in the form of conferences or courses.

The Supreme Court's role is to rule on matters of constitutional consequence. Following perceptions that it was unable to deal effectively with technical issues related to cases, President Koroma asked the chief justice to take a leave of absence in January 2008 and appointed the most senior justice on the bench as acting chief justice. Reforms in 2008 to streamline judicial sector operations illustrate the primacy of technocratic considerations in reforming the country's justice system. The reforms, which are backed by UN and British government judicial reform programs, include support for capacity-building measures and support for agencies such as the Law Reform Commission. These reforms measurably bolster the function and expertise of the higher courts, as evidenced by the decrease in the High Court's average trial duration from 105 days in 2004 to 7 days in 2007.[26] The dilemma of such reforms, however, is that a gap in expertise may arise between technocrats within the judicial sector—such as the Law Officers' Department, responsible for helping to draft regulations and legislation—and members of Parliament and officials in various independent agencies. This gap, abetted by donor support to create islands of efficiency in parts of the judicial sector, helps Sierra Leone conform to international standards of justice and the protection of human rights, but may also increase executive power in a context in which the president's party lacks a parliamentary majority but legislators lack close relations with donors.

Those charged with criminal offenses are presumed innocent until proven guilty according to the law. However, defendants are often remanded for long periods without charge and are not offered reasonable prospects for bail. The incapacity of state agencies to keep records and monitor defendants, along with the scarcity of resources, can result in defendants remaining in prison for years while waiting for their cases to be heard. In principle, citizens are promised fair hearings in competent, independent, impartial tribunals. Unfortunately, the public's perception is that corruption often determines the speed and outcome of court proceedings. Moreover, courts lack adequate translation services to render hearings and documents comprehensible in Krio or other indigenous languages, a situation that leaves the majority of the country's population without judicial services in a language that they understand. All of these problems are related to the abysmal conditions of service in the judiciary and its crushing caseload, low pay, and poor physical conditions.

The state guarantees the provision of independent counsel only to those accused of capital crimes, although there are donor-backed plans to establish a public defender service. The constitution promises all defendants "access to a legal practitioner or any person of his choice" (Section XVII, 2 (b)) but the cost of hiring legal representation in a country with only 100 lawyers, of whom a mere seven practice outside the capital, exceeds the means of the vast majority of citizens.[27] The capacity of the government of Sierra Leone to provide legal assistance is practically nonexistent; the gap is partially filled by civic organizations and NGOs. In practice, most defendants appear before tribunals without the assistance of a lawyer.

The office of the director of public prosecutions undertakes proceedings against any person charged before all but local courts, and prosecutors are relatively independent of political direction. This agency suffers the same institutional deficiencies that afflict some other branches of the judicial services. An exception to the relative independence exists in the attorney general's office. In high-profile cases, it is conceivable that an attorney general can act as liaison between the judiciary and other branches of government, while simultaneously appearing in court as counsel for the state.

Insecurity, poverty, and the institutional consequences of the 1991–2002 war reduce official capacity to afford all citizens in Sierra Leone access to equal treatment under the law without distinction of condition or circumstance. Nonetheless, the formal legal and policy commitment to these rights within the constraints noted above is remarkable. This includes judicial enforcement of property rights, which receives strong backing in law but is subject to constraints of resources and corruption. Rebuilding state institutions and addressing related problems of corruption remain the primary challenges to enforcing rights. In practice, individuals have complained of forced evictions by powerful people carried out in the name of "development." Such controversies have occurred in Freetown, where beachfront enterprises have been replaced with new high-end construction projects.

Legal bifurcation remains a controversial element of the Sierra Leone judicial system. Common law predominates in urban areas, while the majority of the country's population is subject to customary law and a system of chiefdom courts that were inherited from the colonial judicial system. Adjudication under customary law is the task of court chairmen appointed by unelected local paramount chiefs, and customary law is not adequately codified. Lawyers are not allowed to appear before chiefdom courts. In practice there is scant opportunity for appeal, owing to the poverty of most rural people and the weak capacity of formal legal institutions. Chiefdom courts are administered under the jurisdiction of the Ministry of the Interior and not the country's judiciary. In practice, court chairmen often are not independent of the interests of the paramount chiefs who appoint them. In addition, the new Local Councils have taken over some of the revenue sources formerly available to chiefdoms, making chiefdom administrations more reliant on court fees and fines. Public perceptions of some chiefdom courts are that they are corrupt, charge excessive fees, and levy excessively large fines. These complaints were among the grievances that arose during the war, although there is not widespread support for abolishing chiefdom administration.[28] To the extent that local people view such behavior as arbitrary and exploitative, it undermines the justice system's authority and drives more people to seek justice in informal arrangements outside the state's purview.

On January 16, 2002, Sierra Leonean and United Nations officials signed an agreement to establish the Special Court for Sierra Leone (SCSL) to prosecute those who bore the most responsibility for war crimes and crimes against humanity in Sierra Leone's 1991–2002 war. The SCSL is located in Freetown, although the trial of former Liberian president Charles Taylor has been transferred to The Hague. Taylor has been accused of committing war crimes in the course of his support for rebels in Sierra Leone and in his attempts to benefit from Sierra Leone's resources. On June 20, 2007, the SCSL delivered guilty verdicts against three defendants that resulted in sentences of between 45 and 50 years imprisonment. This judgment established a precedent in international law for prosecution of the crime of military conscription of children. A verdict in the Taylor case is expected in early 2010, which would end the work of the SCSL. The Special Court has drawn criticism in some local newspapers for the high cost of its operation. The 2007–2009 budgetary needs for the SCSL were estimated at about US$89 million,[29] a sum that vastly exceeds spending on Sierra Leone's domestic justice system.

Sierra Leone has suffered increasing use as a transshipment point for the trafficking of illegal narcotics from South America to Europe. The July 2008 seizure of 700 kg of cocaine at Lungi Airport from an aircraft arriving from Venezuela highlighted this threat;[30] if left unchecked, drug trafficking has the potential to overwhelm recent postwar gains in the implementation of the rule of law. The value of the Lungi Airport seizure alone was roughly equal to the budget for the entire government's 2007 operations, thereby underscoring the threat of major corruption related to such activity.[31] The Government of Sierra Leone invited Scotland Yard to aid in the investigation and Parliament, with help from the United Nations Office on Drugs and Crime, passed the Anti-Drugs Act of 2008 to provide stiffer penalties for drug trafficking in legislation.

Sierra Leone's military is subject to civilian control. Members of the military are constitutionally prohibited from holding presidential office or from serving in Parliament. The British-funded and staffed International Military Assistance Training Team acts as an implicit guarantor of military noninvolvement in politics. The military, police, and security forces have played no significant political role in recent electoral processes. Police have a record of mistreatment of detainees and abuses related to solicitations of bribes and other forms of corruption, but impunity is much less the norm than in the past. The Police Complaints Commission and the Complaints, Discipline and Internal Investigations Department received 1,273 citizens' complaints in 2008, leading to "at least 176 officers being either dismissed, demoted, suspended or officially warned."[32]

ANTICORRUPTION AND TRANSPARENCY 3.29

ENVIRONMENT TO PROTECT AGAINST CORRUPTION	2.75
PROCEDURES AND SYSTEMS TO ENFORCE ANTICORRUPTION LAWS	3.50
EXISTENCE OF ANTICORRUPTION NORMS, STANDARDS, AND PROTECTIONS	3.75
GOVERNMENTAL TRANSPARENCY	3.17

Official corruption lay at the heart of the collapse of state authority and legitimacy in the decades prior to the start of the war in 1991, and graft remains extensive today. It features prominently in citizens' complaints about their government, despite the advent of civilian rule and regular elections. Citizens tend to blame corruption for problems of low capacity, regardless of their true causes, which underscores the degree to which perceptions of corruption erode the legitimacy of the government. High government officials make repeated pronouncements concerning the seriousness of the situation. Moreover, corruption remains a major concern for international donors and businesses, with Sierra Leone ranking 158th out of 180 countries surveyed in Transparency International's 2008 Corruption Perceptions Index.[33] Corruption is regarded as a primary obstacle to sustained recovery of an autonomous national administrative apparatus capable of surviving without extensive international aid.

Much corruption stems from excessive bureaucratic regulations and registration requirements. Low-paid civil servants have a vested interest in maintaining these rules, even in the event that they are formally abolished, as opportunities to solicit bribes. In addition, the pervasiveness of corruption hinders state efforts to protect against conflicts of interest. Requirements for officials to declare personal assets result in only partial compliance, though President Koroma attempted to set a positive tone by declaring his assets in 2008. The slow process of divestment of state-owned companies, begun in the early 1990s, has helped mitigate corruption. However, most quasi-governmental organizations and state-run companies remain without audits for years, and even decades; indeed, the shoddiness of these companies has in some cases made privatization difficult. Sierra Leone's Audit Service produces reports that "are often ignored, or given superficial attention,"[34] and Audit Service reports are difficult to access.[35]

State enforcement of anticorruption measures is weak. Britain's Department of International Development (DFID) funded the 2001 creation of the ACC, which is charged with investigating allegations of corruption in government agencies and publishing regular reports of its activities. The ACC has been the target of considerable criticism in the country's media and lost its funding from DFID in 2007. Its 2007 report indicated that only five investigative reports were sent to the attorney general for prosecution and that only one conviction was obtained. The same report indicated that cases transferred to the High Court as far back as 2001 remained before the court.[36] In the opinions of most people in Sierra Leone, this did not represent a credible effort to reduce corruption.

The passage of the Anti-Corruption Act of 2008 gave the ACC prosecutorial powers and strengthened its investigative powers. The new law offers the promise of strengthening the ACC's performance as investigations that were initiated in 2008 extended to the level of a senior magistrate and an ex-ombudsman. The ACC has found a new foreign financial backer in Germany's GTZ and has instituted a telephone hotline and a web page to collect anonymous tips.[37] It has also embarked on an extensive effort to educate the public about its renewed mandate and to provide instructions for reporting corruption. ACC officials assert that the 2008 legislation marks a turning point in the its operation, although they point out that providing institutional capacity—including the hiring of qualified staff to conduct real investigative efforts—is crucial for the agency's success.[38]

Corruption in the critically important diamond-mining industry continues to be a national problem. UN Security Council Resolution 1306 of September 2000 required Sierra Leone's government to institute a certification scheme to guarantee the legality of exported stones. The government has made progress in regulating the industry. Official diamond exports of US$212 million in 2005, versus US$10 million in 2000, reflected the growing capacity of the government to manage this important source of economic opportunity and state revenue.[39]

However, formal regulations, including environmental standards and antismuggling measures, remain weakly enforced. Because some government officials have been involved in illicit diamond mining, the paucity of investigations of corruption, much less its prosecution, reflect conflicts of interest among officials. Investigations also confront risks and challenges from local suspicion of central authorities and armed gangs that benefit from illicit mining, including through the "protection" of migrants seeking work in the sector.

In terms of transparency, government efforts to provide public access to information are limited. Organizational problems and the lack of resources in many government offices mean that information is not made available to the public unless these efforts are included as part of donor-funded initiatives. There is no broad provision in law for public access to official information. Efforts have been made to put information on internet sites, although these sites often are not updated regularly. Some politically sensitive information, such as financial disclosure forms, is available, but most of these appear to be incomplete. Budget material and details of the budget process that are available are beyond the reach of the great majority of citizens without internet access. Local newspapers are an important vehicle of dissemination for this information, as many journalists reprint material from websites as feature articles. Often more information is found in World Bank and International Monetary Fund documents than in official government open-source documents. Budgets are subject to legislative review, but actual expenditures, especially cost overruns, receive cursory legislative attention. Legislators occasionally derive personal benefit from these opaque practices.

The country's news media publish regular accounts of insider influence in the awarding of government contracts. The failure of the government to publish comprehensive expenditure accounts contributes to perceptions of corruption, although for those motivated to visit government offices in Freetown, hard-copy versions of more extensive accounts are occasionally available. Citizens possess the right to obtain information about the conduct of government. The office of the ombudsman was created in April 2000 to work closely with the ACC and assist in handling citizen complaints and petitions to the government. Prior to the reorganization of the ACC, the ombudsman's powers were more adapted to acknowledging inquiries than to addressing them. In any event, the individual that served as ombudsman from 2001 to 2007 later was alleged to have been involved in corrupt practices.[40] Foreign assistance provides vital support to administration functions, and foreign experts play an important role in monitoring and assisting in the distribution of aid. Given the degree of donor influence, funds from these sources are generally monitored closely to assure they are not diverted into officials' pockets.

RECOMMENDATIONS

- Consistent with one of the recommendations of the Truth and Reconciliation Commission, the government should repeal the seditious libel law under the 1965 Public Order Act.
- In recognition of the role of paramount chiefs as the most durable—but not popularly elected—basis for local governance, the government should design a mechanism to facilitate political negotiations with these leaders focusing on improvements in electoral accountability and local government reforms.
- In order to provide citizens with means of redress for the inconsistent enforcement of rights, the government—with external support inevitably necessary—should form an independent commission charged with planning

a multi-year rehabilitation of the country's court system that will ensure the country's impoverished majority access to these institutions.
- The government should establish a permanent mechanism for coordination with other regional governments and international institutions to monitor and combat the growing drug trade.
- In order to sustain and augment the ACC's capacity in preparation for the eventual withdrawal of international support, the government should put greater effort into coordinating with NGOs and other civic organizations that can apply pressure to provide greater political support for oversight and investigative agencies.

NOTES

For URLs and endnote hyperlinks, please visit the *Countries at the Crossroads* homepage at http://freedomhouse.org/template.cfm?page=139&edition=8.

[1] Taylor Seybolt, "Major Armed Conflicts," in *SIPRI Yearbook 2001* (Oxford: Oxford University Press for Stockholm International Peace Research Institute, 2001), 31.
[2] International Monetary Fund (IMF), *Sierra Leone: Selected Issues and Statistical Appendix* (Washington, D.C.: IMF, January 2009), 34, 45.
[3] National Democratic Institute, *NDI Final Report on Sierra Leone's 2007 Elections* (Washington, D.C.: National Democratic Institute, 2008).
[4] European Union Election Observation Mission, "Second Round of the Presidential Elections, Statement of Preliminary Findings and Conclusions," September 20, 2007, 4.
[5] National Election Commission (NEC), *Results Summary* (Freetown: NEC, July 21, 2008), 2.
[6] Author's discussions with local government officials in Makeni and Freetown, January 2009.
[7] The ruling party's asset report is available at http://www.dacosl.org/encyclopedia/1_gov/1_3/PPRC/financialreport_apc.pdf.
[8] Author's personal observations and discussion with a journalist in Makeni, January 3, 2009.
[9] This conclusion is based upon the author's visit to newspaper editorial offices in Freetown, January 2009.
[10] Committee to Protect Journalists (CPJ), "CPJ Calls on Sierra Leone to Decriminalize Libel Laws," news release, March 17, 2008.
[11] Society for Democratic Initiatives, *The State of the Sierra Leone Media: A Year in Velvet Gloves* (Freetown: Society for Democratic Initiatives, September 28, 2008), 24.
[12] Sierra Leone Association of Journalists (SLAJ), "SLAJ Reminds Supreme Court," press release, September 22, 2009.
[13] Lansana Fofana, "Sierra Leone: Banned Opposition Radio Station Goes to Court," Inter Press Service, September 28, 2009.
[14] UN Security Council (UNSC), *First Report of the Secretary-General on the United Nations Integrated Peacebuilding Office in Sierra Leone* (New York: UNSC, January 30, 2009), 4.
[15] Karin Wahl-Jorgensen and Bernadette Cole, "Newspapers in Sierra Leone: A Case Study of Conditions for Print Journalism in a Postconflict Society," *African Journalism Studies* 29, no. 1 (2008): 1–20.
[16] "Sierra Leone: Paying off the Grudges," *Africa Confidential* 50, no. 6 (March 20, 2009): 11.

[17] Claire Castillejo, *Building Accountable Justice in Sierra Leone* (Madrid: Fundación para las Relaciones Internacionales y el Diálogo Exterior, January 1, 2009), 15.
[18] Assessment based on author's observations and discussions with Sierra Leone informants.
[19] Hawa Kamara, "Challenges Faced in the Implementation of the Gender Laws in Sierra Leone," Supreme Court Monitoring Programme, November 23, 2008.
[20] Author's discussions and observations in Makeni and Freetown, December 2008–January 2009.
[21] National Electoral Commission, *Final Local Council Nomination Statistics* (Freetown: National Electoral Commission, June 27, 2008), 2, 4.
[22] Office to Monitor and Combat Trafficking in Persons, *Trafficking in Persons Report 2009* (Washington, D.C.: U.S. Department of State, June 2009).
[23] Republic of Sierra Leone, Sierra Leone Citizenship Act of 1973.
[24] Jimmy Kandeh, "Rogue Incumbents, Donor Assistance and Sierra Leone's Second Post-Conflict Elections of 2007," *Journal of Modern African Studies* 46, no.4 (December 2008): 619–20.
[25] Castillejo, *Building Accountable Justice in Sierra Leone*, 6.
[26] Justice Sector Coordination Office, *Justice Sector Survey 2008* (Freetown: Government of Sierra Leone, Justice Sector Coordination Office, 2009), 14.
[27] Castillejo, *Building Accountable Justice in Sierra Leone*, 6.
[28] Paul Jackson, "Reshuffling an Old Deck of Cards? The Politics of Local Government Reform in Sierra Leone," *African Affairs* 106, no. 422 (January 2007): 95–111.
[29] Special Court for Sierra Leone, *Annex III to the Letter Dated 7 June 2007 from the Chargé d'affaires a.i. of the Permanent Mission of Canada to the United Nations Addressed to the President of the Security Council* (New York: UNSC, June 7, 2007).
[30] UNSC, *First Report of the Secretary-General on the United Nations Integrated Peacebuilding Office in Sierra Leone*, 4.
[31] Officials with whom this author spoke underscored their concern about the serious nature of this threat.
[32] Bureau of Democracy, Human Rights, and Labor, "Sierra Leone" in *2008 Country Reports on Human Rights Practices* (Washington, D.C.: U.S. Department of State, February 25, 2009).
[33] Transparency International, *2008 Corruption Perceptions Index* (Berlin: Transparency International, September 22, 2008).
[34] Global Integrity, "Sierra Leone," in *Global Integrity Report 2007* (Washington, D.C.: Global Integrity, 2008).
[35] This author tried and failed to find recent reports in Freetown. The Audit Service web site promises annual reports but does not provide them.
[36] Anti-Corruption Commission (ACC), *Annual Report 2007* (Freetown: ACC, July 11, 2008), 8, 37.
[37] This is available at the ACC home page: http://www.anticorruptionsl.org/.
[38] Discussion with ACC official, Freetown, January 6, 2009.
[39] World Bank, *Sierra Leone Mining Sector Reform: A Strategic Environmental and Social Assessment* (Washington, D.C.: World Bank, July 10, 2008), 4.
[40] ACC, "Press Release: Francis A. Gabbidon," July 11, 2008.

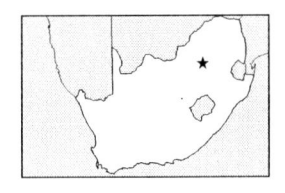

SOUTH AFRICA

CAPITAL: Pretoria
POPULATION: 50.7 million
GNI PER CAPITA (PPP): $9,780

SCORES	2006	2010
ACCOUNTABILITY AND PUBLIC VOICE:	5.03	4.89
CIVIL LIBERTIES:	5.00	5.07
RULE OF LAW:	4.41	4.28
ANTICORRUPTION AND TRANSPARENCY:	4.00	3.90

(scores are based on a scale of 0 to 7, with 0 representing weakest and 7 representing strongest performance)

Mark Y. Rosenberg

INTRODUCTION

After decades of white minority rule under a system of comprehensive, institutionalized racial separation known as apartheid, South Africa held its first nonracial general elections in 1994. The balloting was judged free and fair by international observers despite significant political violence, and resulted in a landslide victory for the previously banned African National Congress (ANC). ANC leader Nelson Mandela, a longtime political prisoner, was chosen as president. A constitutional assembly produced a new constitution, which Mandela signed into law in December 1996. In 1999, the ANC claimed almost two-thirds of the national vote in general elections; Thabo Mbeki, Mandela's successor as head of the ANC, won the presidency. The ANC won an even greater victory in 2004, capturing nearly 70 percent of the national vote and outright control of seven of the country's nine provinces (while sharing power in the other two).

Factionalism within the ANC—exemplified by a heated leadership battle between Mbeki and his former deputy, Jacob Zuma—has dominated South African politics in recent years. In December 2007, Zuma was elected ANC president at the party's national conference, outpolling Mbeki by a wide margin, and his allies won most other senior posts. The ANC's national executive committee then forced Mbeki to resign as state president in September 2008, and deputy ANC president Kgalema Motlanthe was installed as interim state president. Soon thereafter, former defense minister Mosiuoa "Terror" Lekota and

---

Mark Y. Rosenberg is a Ph.D. candidate in political science at the University of California, Berkeley. His research focuses on party systems and political economy, mostly in sub-Saharan Africa. He is a former researcher and editor at Freedom House.

Mbhazima Shilowa, the former premier of Gauteng province, resigned from the ANC and began forming a new opposition group. The new party, dominated by Mbeki allies, was formally registered as the Congress of the People (COPE) in December 2008.

In April 2009, South Africans voted in the country's fourth round of national and provincial elections since the advent of democracy. As with the previous polls, the balloting was declared free and fair by domestic and international observers. Despite the dramatic split in the ruling party and the formation of COPE, the ANC won yet another sweeping victory, taking 65.9 percent of the national vote and claiming clear majorities in eight provinces. The Democratic Alliance (DA) beat out COPE to retain its status as the country's largest opposition party, winning 16.7 percent of the national vote and outright control of the Western Cape province. Zuma was easily elected state president by the National Assembly (NA) the following month.

The ANC's enduring preeminence in South African politics has been accompanied by heightened tensions both within the party and with its governing allies, the South African Communist Party (SACP) and the Congress of South African Trade Unions (COSATU). In addition, government clashes with the judiciary, the media, and opposition parties have all increased. Vociferous debates surround the government's approach to poverty, land reform and housing, basic service delivery, corruption, immigration, the ongoing crisis in Zimbabwe, and HIV/AIDS.

ACCOUNTABILITY AND PUBLIC VOICE 4.89

FREE AND FAIR ELECTORAL LAWS AND ELECTIONS	4.25
EFFECTIVE AND ACCOUNTABLE GOVERNMENT	4.75
CIVIC ENGAGEMENT AND CIVIC MONITORING	6.00
MEDIA INDEPENDENCE AND FREEDOM OF EXPRESSION	4.57

Under the 1996 constitution, national authority is shared by the executive and legislature and checked by an independent judiciary. Executive and legislative powers also exist at the provincial and municipal levels. The constitution provides for universal adult suffrage,[1] a national common voter roll, regular elections contested by multiple parties and determined by a system of proportional representation, and the establishment of an Independent Electoral Commission (IEC) and Electoral Court. In addition, a constitutionally incorporated Bill of Rights guarantees citizens the rights to form and campaign for a political party, stand for public office, and participate in free, fair, and regular elections.

In the run-up to the April 2009 polls, IEC voter registration drives held in November 2008 and February 2009 registered over 23 million voters, and 42 of 117 registered parties submitted candidate lists by the March 2009 deadline.[2] Also in March, the Constitutional Court upheld an earlier Pretoria High

Court ruling that the Electoral Act's exclusion of citizens residing abroad was unconstitutional. As a result, South Africans living overseas—the large majority of whom are white—were able to vote in the April elections. The ruling was opposed by the ANC.

Due to the emergence of COPE and a concerted ANC effort to woo Zulu voters in rural Kwa-Zulu Natal (KZN) province away from the Zulu nationalist Inkatha Freedom Party (IFP), the specter of political violence hung over the campaign period. While parties were generally able to campaign freely across the country, violence was more of a problem than in 2004. According to the *Mail & Guardian*, there were 40 incidents of electoral violence in 2009, most of them "intimidation or clashes" in KZN and the Eastern Cape.[3] Between January and April, five politicians were killed in election-related violence, including four in KZN. Party officials engaged in inflammatory rhetoric during the campaign. For example, ANC Youth League president Julius Malema labeled COPE supporters "cockroaches" and DA leader Helen Zille a "colonialist" and "imperialist," while Zille called Malema an "*inkwenke*" (Xhosa for "not yet an adult").[4] There had been several instances of intra-ANC violence in 2008, including a stabbing at an ANC conference in the Western Cape.

The elections themselves were judged free and fair by credible domestic observers (led by the South African Civil Society Election Coalition) as well as monitors from the Southern African Development Community and the African Union. According to the Electoral Institute of Southern Africa, high turnout and the ability of voters to cast ballots in any station in their province led to ballot shortages throughout the country. The ANC's capture of 65.9 percent of the national vote earned it 264 seats in the 400-seat NA; the DA, with 16.7 percent of the vote, won 67 seats, while COPE (7.4 percent) took 30 seats and the IFP (4.6 percent) garnered only 18. Nine other parties won four or fewer seats in the NA.

While public financing of political parties through the Represented Political Parties' Fund is governed by the IEC, private contributions are totally unregulated. Parties do not have to reveal the size or sources of donations, and both elected officials and civil society groups have criticized this system as a major source of political corruption. The Institute for Democracy in Africa (IDASA) initiated legal proceedings to require all parties represented in the NA to reveal the sources, amounts, and dates of all their private donations since 1994, but the suit was dismissed in 2005; IDASA had argued that such disclosures were mandated under the 2000 Promotion of Access to Information Act.[5] IDASA and the Institute of Security Studies subsequently established an online Party Funding Monitor database to provide information on party funding.[6] The ANC in particular has been criticized for awarding state contracts to firms associated with Chancellor House, the party's in-house investment firm,[7] and for charging fees to business leaders for access to top government officials. In December 2007, a "networking lounge" for businesses was set up outside the ANC national conference in Polokwane.

The constitution mandates a robust system of checks and balances between the executive, legislative, and judicial branches of government. Executive power is held by the president, who is elected by the NA; the president's appointed cabinet currently consists of the deputy president, 34 ministers, and 22 deputy ministers. The bicameral Parliament, which consists of the NA and the 90-seat National Council of Provinces (NCOP),[8] has significant oversight and approval powers vis-à-vis the executive, and legislators can question members of the executive in session. Every executive or legislative act is subject to review by the judiciary, which is headed by the Constitutional Court and the Supreme Court of Appeals.

In practice, the ANC's overwhelming control of the executive and legislative branches at both the national and provincial levels undermines the efficacy of South Africa's institutional checks and accountability mechanisms. Parliamentary committees tasked with overseeing ministries are often led by ANC loyalists and have been accused of approving ministerial reports and budgets without sufficient debate.[9] Parliament has also been criticized for failing to adequately investigate executive malfeasance, particularly ongoing corruption scandals surrounding the 1999–2000 Strategic Defence Procurement Package, also known simply as the Arms Deal (see Anticorruption and Transparency). Partly in response to such criticism,[10] lawmakers commissioned an independent panel of experts to assess the "independence, efficiency, and effectiveness of Parliament" in 2006.[11] In its 2009 report, the panel recommended that members of Parliament (MPs) more actively scrutinize executive reports, ensure that parliamentary queries are fully answered by the executive, and disallow presiding officers from holding high office in political parties, among many other recommendations.[12] The judiciary has demonstrated significant independence in hearing constitutional challenges to legislation and in punishing abuses of power. Nevertheless, political interference, resource shortages, and the lack of an effective oversight body for judicial conduct hamper the courts' oversight powers.[13]

The Public Service Act (PSA) provides for civil service hiring based on "equality and other democratic values and principles enshrined in the Constitution."[14] However, merit and open competition are often subordinated to political affiliation and nepotism, as well as to considerations of race, gender, and disability that are included in the PSA to redress "imbalances of the past" and ensure a civil service that is "broadly representative of the South African people."[15] A 2006 survey by the Public Service Commission found that the favoring of friends and family was the biggest problem undermining professionalism in management decisions.[16] The professionalism of the civil service varies widely by province. In 2007 and 2008, the politically tinged firing of the head of the Office of the National Director of Public Prosecutions (NDPP), Vusi Pikoli, raised serious questions about the political independence of senior civil servants.

Thousands of civic groups and nongovernmental organizations operate freely throughout South Africa, including a vibrant and politically active trade union movement led by COSATU. Most of these civil society organizations (CSOs) deal with education, good governance, land reform, and housing or service delivery. CSOs regularly testify before and submit presentations to legislative committees regarding pending legislation. While close relationships with the ANC and the government have discouraged some CSOs from pursuing public advocacy campaigns aimed at affecting legislation, others have been vociferous in this regard. Registration of CSOs is relatively straightforward, and organizations are not required to disclose their funding sources to the government.

Freedoms of expression and the press are protected in the constitution and generally respected. Nevertheless, several apartheid-era laws that remain in effect—as well as a 2004 antiterrorism law—permit authorities to restrict the publication of information about the police, defense forces, prisons, and mental institutions, and to compel journalists to reveal sources. While journalists are rarely detained by the authorities, they remain subject to pressure from both state and nonstate actors. Government and ANC-affiliated officials have repeatedly accused critical journalists of racism or betraying the state. Journalists' organizations and other groups work to defend press freedom in the country, and a number of private newspapers and magazines—particularly the *Mail & Guardian*, the *Cape Times*, and the *Sunday Times*—are sharply critical of the government. ANC and state officials in turn have become increasingly sensitive to media criticism and reporting on corruption, and have initiated a number of gag orders and lawsuits to prevent damaging reporting. The government has also threatened to withdraw advertising from critical newspapers. At its December 2007 national conference, the ANC called for the establishment of a Media Appeals Tribunal to adjudicate between freedom of speech and an individual's right to privacy and dignity. While there has been no effort to establish the tribunal, the ANC has stated that the issue is still "on the table."[17]

Since 2005, the *Mail & Guardian* has received at least three government gag orders to stop reporting on corruption scandals. The *Sunday Times* faced a lawsuit, police investigations, and ownership pressure after it published articles in 2007 that accused then health minister Manto Tshabalala-Msimang of alcoholism, queue-jumping for a liver transplant, and stealing from a patient while serving as a medical superintendent in Botswana.[18] In December 2008, Zuma launched a US$712,300 defamation lawsuit over a cartoon in the *Sunday Times*.

For primarily socioeconomic reasons, most South Africans receive the news via radio outlets, a majority of which are controlled by the state-owned South African Broadcasting Corporation (SABC). The SABC also dominates the television market, but two commercial stations are gaining ground. Applications to open community radio stations are slowed by lack of bandwidth and bureaucratic delays. While editorially independent from the government, the SABC has come under increasing fire for displaying a pro-ANC bias and practicing self-censorship. A 2006 internal SABC report found that government critics had been barred from the airwaves, and in 2007, groups including COSATU and the Freedom of Expression Institute accused the government of conducting political purges at the broadcaster. Rifts within the ANC have recently given rise to SABC leadership battles. After Mbeki was forced to resign in 2008, Parliament passed a version of the Broadcasting Amendment Bill that would have allowed it to fire the SABC's board, which the outgoing president had recently appointed. However, President Motlanthe in February 2009 refused to sign the legislation, and a revised version required a "proper inquiry by Parliament" before such dismissals. An earlier spat between SABC head of news Snuki Zikalala and chief executive Dali Mpofu—including the firing of each by the other—was tied in part to the Zikalala-led board's alleged affiliation with Mbeki. In addition, both the ANC and COPE accused the SABC of biased coverage of the events surrounding the ANC split, while SABC journalists accused members of both parties of intimidation in the run-up to the 2009 elections. South Africans enjoy unhindered access to the internet, and there are no restrictions on setting up internet-based media outlets.

CIVIL LIBERTIES 5.07

PROTECTION FROM STATE TERROR, UNJUSTIFIED IMPRISONMENT, AND TORTURE	3.50
GENDER EQUITY	4.33
RIGHTS OF ETHNIC, RELIGIOUS, AND OTHER DISTINCT GROUPS	4.75
FREEDOM OF CONSCIENCE AND BELIEF	7.00
FREEDOM OF ASSOCIATION AND ASSEMBLY	5.75

The constitution provides South Africans with a comprehensive set of civil liberties, which are generally enjoyed in practice. These include equality, human dignity, life, freedom from torture and inhuman and cruel treatment, freedom from slavery and servitude, freedom from child abuse, and a series of procedural rights for arrested, detained, and accused persons.

The South Africa Police Service (SAPS) is under the civilian control of the Department of Safety and Security. Despite constitutional prohibitions, there have been reports of torture and the use of excessive force by SAPS members during arrest, interrogation, and detention. South Africans can report alleged rights violations by the SAPS to the Independent Complaints Directorate (ICD). Between April 2007 and March 2008, the ICD received 5,026 complaints of abuses, including deaths in police custody (792, of which 490 were by police action), criminal offenses (1,742), and misconduct (2,474).[19] Citing resource constraints, the ICD fully investigated 66 percent of death cases (though only 59 percent of deaths by police action), 56 percent of criminal cases, and 32 percent of misconduct cases. While the ICD maintains that an increase in reported violations indicates public trust in the institution, researchers claim that many case files are incomplete or closed without clear outcomes.[20] Police remain badly underpaid, and although SAPS corruption is a significant problem, it is rarely reported. Following the closure of the ICD's Anti-Corruption Unit in 2002, formal complaints of police corruption averaged just 125 per year through 2006.[21]

South Africa has one of the highest violent crime rates in the world. According to the SAPS, the homicide rate in 2008 was 38.6 per 100,000 people, a 3.7 percent decrease from 2007.[22] Such crime, along with concerns about police capabilities, has fueled regular incidents of vigilantism and a burgeoning private security industry. In April 2008, a deputy security minister made headlines when he told police to institute a "shoot to kill" policy, though it was never formally implemented. Civic groups and opposition parties have accused the government of doctoring crime data and failing to release up-to-date statistics to the public.

Prison conditions in South Africa often do not meet domestic or international standards. According to the Department of Correctional Services, the country's 243 prisons suffer from overcrowding that reaches 143 percent of capacity (164,957 prisoners held in space meant to accommodate 114,800). There have been reports of prisoners being physically and sexually abused by both fellow inmates and prison employees. In 2006, a government commission of inquiry found corruption, maladministration, and sexual violence to be rife in the penal system. Over 40 percent of inmates are infected with HIV, and health services, while improving, are inadequate. Excessive pretrial detention and negligent conditions for pretrial detainees were cited by a UN Working Group in 2005 as major shortcomings of the South African penal system. While most prisoners wait an average of three months before trial, some must wait up to two years. At the end of 2008, 50,284 prisoners (over 30 percent) had yet to be sentenced.

The constitution prohibits both state and private discrimination on the basis of "gender, sex, pregnancy [or] marital status,"[23] and imbues the state with a positive duty to prevent discrimination via national legislation—a duty that has been confirmed by the Constitutional Court. While the constitution allows the option and practice of customary law, it—along with the Recognition of Customary Marriages Act of 1998—does not allow such law to supersede women's constitutional rights. Nevertheless, women suffer de facto discrimination with regard to marriage, divorce, inheritance, and property rights.[24] For example, rural women are often prevented from acquiring land under the 2004 Communal Land Rights Act, which transferred effective control of communal lands to traditional councils. Women are also subject to sexual harassment and wage discrimination in the workplace, and are not well represented in top management positions. However, prior to the April 2009 elections, women held 132 seats in the 400-seat NA,[25] and headed 12 of 28 ministries and four provincial governments; in 2008, Baleka Mbete replaced Phumzile Mlambo-Ngcuka as deputy president.

Domestic violence and rape, both criminal offenses, are serious problems; South Africa has one of the world's highest rates of sexual abuse. The country's high rate of HIV infection, as well as a popular belief that HIV/AIDS can be cured by sexual intercourse with a female virgin, makes incidents of rape particularly worrisome. Despite the government's operation of women's shelters and sexual offense courts, reporting and investigation of these crimes are hampered by societal attitudes and a lack of resources. In December 2007, the government passed a long-awaited Sexual Offenses Bill, which expanded the definition of rape to include male victims and codified the offenses of rape and sexual violence. However, a 2009 study by the Medical Research Council found that one in four South African men admitted to having raped at least one woman.[26]

No law specifically prohibits trafficking in persons, and South Africa serves as a destination, source, and transit point for trafficked women.[27] However, the government has prosecuted traffickers—mostly in sexual offense courts—under a number of existing laws and cooperated with nongovernmental organizations that work on the issue.

As with gender discrimination, the constitution prohibits discrimination based on "race . . . ethnic or social origin, colour, sexual orientation, age, disability, religion, conscience, belief, culture, language and birth."[28] State entities such as the South African Human Rights Commission (SAHRC) and the Office of the Public Prosecutor (OPP) are empowered to investigate and, with respect to the OPP, prosecute violations of antidiscrimination laws. Citing the legacy of the apartheid system, Parliament has passed extensive legislation mandating affirmative action for previously disadvantaged groups (defined as "Africans," "Coloureds," and "Asians") in employment and education. However, racial imbalances in the workforce persist. According to the 2007 Department of Labor Employment Equity Report, Africans and Coloureds accounted for 28.8 percent of top management, 32.4 percent of senior management, and 41.3 percent of middle management positions despite representing 87.9 percent of the country's economically active population.[29] The government has also focused (with mixed results) on reforming inequities in housing, health care, and land ownership. There were a number of racist attacks on black South Africans in 2008, including a racially motivated shooting spree in North West province that killed four people and wounded nine. The nomadic Khoikhoi and Khomani San peoples, indigenous to South Africa, suffer from social discrimination and poor access to courts and the legal system.

South Africa has one of the world's most liberal legal environments for homosexuals. The 2006 Civil Unions Act legalized same-sex marriage, and a 2002 Constitutional Court ruling held that homosexual couples should be allowed to adopt children. Nevertheless, a report issued by the Human Sciences Research Council in 2006 documented a recent increase in hate crimes against homosexuals. While discrimination against disabled people is prohibited by the constitution and monitored by the Office on the Status of Disabled People, the SAHRC reports that "there is urgent need to redress violation of disability rights," especially for children.[30]

Increased illegal immigration, particularly from Zimbabwe and Mozambique, has led to a rise in xenophobic attacks by police and vigilantes. In May 2008, a wave of attacks across the country led to the deaths of 62 suspected foreigners and the displacement of some 80,000 others.[31] In cooperation with the UN High Commission on Refugees and local CSOs, the provincial governments in Gauteng, Western Cape, and KZN set up 94 camps to provide temporary shelter for roughly 15,000 displaced people.[32] While some foreigners were repatriated and others opted for reintegration into local communities, about 2,000 were forced to leave after the provincial governments shut down the camps that fall. Immigration and police forces have been accused of abusing illegal immigrants and detaining them longer than allowed under the Immigration Act, particularly at the Musina refugee center. According to Lawyers for Human Rights, "Hundreds of men, women and children are deported from the facility on a daily basis, in some cases, regardless of whether they have valid asylum claims, or in many circumstances are even documented."[33]

Freedom of religion is constitutionally guaranteed and actively protected by the government in practice. There is no official religion, though the majority of South Africans are Christians. The state is not involved in the appointment of religious leaders or the internal workings of religious organizations; in fact, the government does not require religious groups to be licensed or registered. While the government allows public schools to include general "religious education" in age-appropriate curriculums, it is not required. Preaching the tenets of a specific faith ("religious instruction") is not permitted in public schools.[34]

Freedoms of association and peaceful assembly are secured by the Bill of Rights, and South Africa features a vibrant civil society. Protests and demonstrations are common and generally peaceful. However, a number of the thousands of protests mounted each year over poor service delivery have turned violent, and the police have used force to disperse them.[35] South Africans are free to form, join, and participate in independent trade unions. Labor rights under the 1995 Labor Relations Act are respected, and more than 250 trade unions exist. COSATU, which claims over two million members, is part of a tripartite governing alliance with the ANC and the SACP. Strike activity is common. In May 2007, COSATU led a four-week strike by some 500,000 public-sector workers to demand higher pay. The strike—the largest in the democratic period—led to the closure of many hospitals and schools, as well as several violent confrontations involving strikers, security forces, and replacement workers.[36] In late June, the action was called off after the government agreed to a 7.5 percent pay increase.

RULE OF LAW   4.28

INDEPENDENT JUDICIARY	4.60
PRIMACY OF RULE OF LAW IN CIVIL AND CRIMINAL MATTERS	4.00
ACCOUNTABILITY OF SECURITY FORCES AND MILITARY TO CIVILIAN AUTHORITIES	4.50
PROTECTION OF PROPERTY RIGHTS	4.00

The independence of the South African judiciary is guaranteed by the constitution. While the courts have operated with substantial autonomy in the post-apartheid era, they have been exposed to increased political interference in recent years. The chief justice and deputy chief justice of the Constitutional Court (CC) are appointed by the president after consultation with the Judicial Service Commission (JSC),[37] and with the leaders of parties represented in the National Assembly. The president appoints judges to the CC and other courts—including the Supreme Court of Appeals—on the advice of the JSC. Constitutionally, the "racial and gender composition of South Africa" must be considered in the selection of judges. Judges may only be removed from office through impeachment by the NA.[38]

The prosecution of Jacob Zuma on corruption charges—originally brought in 2005—for his role in the Arms Deal (see Anticorruption and Transparency) has exposed the judiciary and prosecutors to numerous attempts at political interference. A succession of court rulings threw out and then allowed the reinstatement of the charges two times between 2006 and 2009, and in the second rejection of the charges, the judge said he believed Zuma's prosecution to have been at least partly motivated by political interference from the executive, then led by Mbeki. In a related incident, the CC in 2008 formally accused a Cape High Court judge of attempting to influence it in Zuma's favor. Ultimately, two weeks before the April 2009 elections, prosecutors dropped the case against Zuma on the grounds that the reinstatement of the charges in 2007 had been politically motivated.

In December 2005, the government introduced a package of bills intended to reform apartheid-era structures and extend more executive control over judicial administration, but the plan was withdrawn for further consultation in the face of widespread opposition from legal professionals and CSOs, who saw it as a threat to judicial independence. At its December 2007 national conference, the ANC endorsed making the CC the highest court for both constitutional and nonconstitutional matters, demoting the Supreme Court of Appeals to an intermediate appellate body.[39] Prominent legal scholars criticized the plan, claiming that it would draw out cases and overload the CC.[40]

The government generally complies with judicial decisions, and instances of noncompliance are attributable mostly to lack of capacity and efficiency rather than to willful disregard.[41]

Criminal defendants are presumed innocent until proven guilty, and the constitution provides procedural rights including the right to a fair, public trial conducted before "an ordinary court...without unreasonable delay," the right of appeal to a higher court, and the right to independent legal counsel. Those unable to afford such counsel have the right to an assigned, state-funded legal practitioner "if substantial injustice would otherwise result."[42] In practice, staff and resource shortages undermine the rights to a timely trial and legal counsel, particularly for poor South Africans. These shortages have also produced a significant backlog of cases.

The National Prosecuting Authority (NPA) is ensured de jure independence by the constitution and the National Prosecuting Authority Act of 1998. The presidentially-appointed National Director of Public Prosecutions (NDPP) is the head of the NPA, reports to Parliament, and is accountable to the justice minister.

Since 2005, the independence of the NPA and NDPP has been compromised. In October 2008, the NPA's Directorate of Special Operations—a unit known as the Scorpions that focused on investigating organized crime and corruption—was dissolved by Parliament and absorbed into the SAPS. The ANC had passed a resolution to that effect at its 2007 national conference, after the Scorpions' methods while investigating Zuma and other high-profile figures were condemned by Zuma's allies in the ANC, COSATU, and the SACP. The unit's dissolution was opposed by a wide array of civic organizations and opposition parties.

In 2007, Justice Minister Brigitte Mabandla suspended Vusi Pikoli as NPDD. While the suspension was attributed to "an irretrievable breakdown" in Pikoli's relationship with Mabandla, it later emerged that the move was at least partly related to Pikoli's approval of an arrest warrant for police commissioner Jackie Selebi, a powerful politician who was eventually charged with corruption and defeating the ends of justice through his association with an organized crime boss.[43] A commission of inquiry cleared Pikoli of wrongdoing in November 2008, but President Motlanthe formally dismissed him in December on the grounds that he was "not sensitive enough to matters of national security."[44] Pikoli has appealed to the Pretoria High Court to reverse the decision. Selebi was set to stand trial in 2009.

According to the constitution, the president is the commander in chief of the country's military, the South African National Defence Force (SANDF). It is managed by a civilian defense minister, and overseen by Parliament's Joint Standing Committee on Defence and the Portfolio Committee on Defence.[45] A defense secretariat within the Department of Defence is headed by a civilian secretary and includes the chief of the SANDF, the force's top uniformed officer. Tasked mostly with maintaining external security, the SANDF also has some domestic obligations. Military personnel generally respect human rights, and soldiers undergo human rights training programs. However, there have been reports of abuses. Military personnel have been accused of abusing and demanding bribes from migrants on South Africa's northern border. During the wave of xenophobic attacks in May 2008, the SANDF helped transport police to affected areas and were deployed in Gauteng to assisted police with "cordons and searches."[46]

There are ongoing tensions in South Africa between maintaining the rule of law, promoting economic growth, and remedying the country's gross inequities in land ownership—the most enduring legacy of colonial and apartheid rule. The state generally protects citizens from arbitrary deprivation of their property. Section 25 of the constitution states that "no one may be deprived of property except in terms of law of general application," meaning property can be expropriated for a public purpose or in the public interest, subject to negotiated or court-mandated compensation based on market principles. Notably, the "public interest" includes "the nation's commitment to land reform, and to reforms to bring about equitable access to all South Africa's natural resources; and property is not limited to land." The constitution also provides that South Africans affected by past racially discriminatory laws are entitled to restitution, redress (including redistribution), or secured land-tenure rights.[47]

Despite being supported by a series of legislative acts and much political rhetoric, South Africa's land reform program has proceeded slowly. In 2009, the Department of Land Affairs reported that only 18 percent of land was owned by black South Africans (including communal land and excluding state-owned land), an increase of only 4.7 percent since 1994; whites own about 46 percent.[48] As a result, thousands of black farm workers suffer from insecure tenure rights, and illegal squatting on white-owned farms and attacks on the owners are major problems. The government has vowed to transfer 30 percent of land to black owners by 2014, and has agreed to reconsider its "willing buyer, willing seller" policy in favor of a more expedient approach. In 2007, the government for the first time expropriated a farm, compensating the owners with US$4.9 million. In June 2008, the government presented legislation allowing state agencies to more rapidly expropriate farmland and other capital, but the bill was shelved in August due to major civic and opposition pressure. In March 2009, Land Affairs Minister Lulu Xingwana warned recipients of redistributed land that the government would reclaim farmland that was not being used productively.[49]

A majority of the country's business assets remain in the hands of white owners. Beginning with the Mbeki administration, the government has implemented a Black Economic Empowerment (BEE) program with the aim of securing "significant increases in the numbers of black people that manage, own and control the country's economy, as well as significant decreases in income inequalities."[50] The state's official definition of "black" includes African, Coloured, Indian, and—as of June 2008—Chinese South Africans. The BEE program requires private-sector firms to meet a range of affirmative-action requirements concerning ownership, management control, employment equity, skills development, preferential procurement, enterprise development, and socioeconomic development.[51] Those that fail to meet these requirements cannot gain access to licenses, government tenders, and sales of state-owned enterprises.[52] Between 1998 and 2008, BEE-related transactions moved assets worth about US$25 billion.[53] The program has been strongly criticized for concentrating the newly black-owned resources in the hands of a few, politically connected recipients.

Separately, a state-sponsored effort to revamp downtown Johannesburg has evicted hundreds and potentially thousands of squatters from inner-city buildings. In January 2009, police evicted about 1,500 people living in the Central Methodist Church in Johannesburg, detaining scores. The raid was aimed at seizing illegal drugs, guns, and immigrants, though human rights groups condemned the police for using excessive force, violating detainees' due process rights, and lacking proper warrants to conduct the operation.

ANTICORRUPTION AND TRANSPARENCY   3.90

    ENVIRONMENT TO PROTECT AGAINST CORRUPTION   3.50
    PROCEDURES AND SYSTEMS TO ENFORCE ANTICORRUPTION LAWS   4.00
    EXISTENCE OF ANTICORRUPTION NORMS, STANDARDS, AND PROTECTIONS   3.75
    GOVERNMENTAL TRANSPARENCY   4.33

There are several agencies with a legal mandate to combat graft by public officials, but enforcement of anticorruption laws is a major problem. Petty corruption is a regular part of South Africans' interactions with state authorities, and the awarding of state contracts is heavily politicized. South Africa was ranked 54 out of 180 countries surveyed in Transparency International's 2008 Corruption Perceptions Index.

Chapter 9 of the constitution established three institutions that deal with corruption: the Office of the Auditor-General of South Africa (AGSA), the Public Protector (PP), and the IEC (see Accountability and Public Voice). The AGSA is responsible for reporting to the NA on the finances of any agency receiving public funds. These reports are accessible to the public free of charge. While the AGSA's independence is constitutionally guaranteed, its autonomy was called into question by former auditor-general Shauket Fakie's conduct vis-à-vis the Arms Deal (see below). Incomplete reporting by public agencies, particularly at the provincial and municipal levels, hampers the institution's efforts, as does the lack of resources, adequate staff, and a positive obligation on the part of other state bodies to act on AGSA resolutions.[54]

The PP is the national ombudsman, empowered to investigate maladministration, abuse of power, improper conduct, and acts of omission that result in prejudice to another person. Citizens may report a matter directly to the PP.[55] In addition, a public protector is appointed in every province. Although the office is ostensibly independent, current PP Leonard Mushwana, a former ANC MP, has been accused of inhibiting investigations of senior ANC members and the party itself. Because the PP's office does not often initiate its own investigations and cannot impose penalties, its effectiveness is limited.[56] As with the AGSA, the public can access the PP's reports promptly and free of charge.

Beyond the Chapter 9 institutions, several other agencies and legislative instruments contribute to South Africa's anticorruption efforts with varying degrees of success. Within the executive and legislative branches, the separation of public office from personal interests is superficially achieved by the Executive Members Ethics Act, the Code of Conduct for Assembly and Permanent Council Members, and the deliberations of the Joint Committee on Ethics and

Members' Interests. However, while these mechanisms mandate that the relevant officials disclose private financial assets and interests, the extent of disclosures is inconsistent among the national, provincial, and local governments, and none have legitimate oversight or enforcement mechanisms. Moreover, none of the systems have adequate postemployment restrictions, exacerbating the phenomenon of a "revolving door" between government and business.[57] Notably, while both executive and legislative officials' financial disclosures are legally available to the public, those of executive officials, particularly the president, are reported to be substantially more difficult to obtain. In 2006, then auditor-general Fakie reported that more that 14 cabinet ministers and deputies, along with 50,000 other public servants, had failed to publicly declare their business interests as required by law. There are no penalties for such failures in practice.

In addition to the Arms Deal affair, executive and legislative officers have been involved in a number of corruption scandals in recent years. An investigation into the abuse of travel vouchers by (mostly ANC) lawmakers, launched by the NPA and the Scorpions in 2004, continued to produce controversy in 2009. The probe resulted in charges against over 100 MPs, a fifth of whom pleaded guilty to fraud in 2005 and 2006. After over 60 MPs refused to pay creditors of the travel agency involved in the fraud, the NA itself purchased the debt in March 2009, effectively absolving the members involved—including high-ranking executive officials[58]—of paying either the state or the creditors for their abuses.

The Public Service Commission (PSC) oversees the Department of Public Service and Administration (DPSA) and is responsible for monitoring and evaluating the public sector, including cases of public corruption. The Public Service Regulations (2001) require senior public officials and members of the PSC to submit disclosure forms, but adherence to the regulations is weak and has worsened over time.[59] Moreover, sanctions for failing to submit the requisite forms are virtually nonexistent. Civil servants convicted of corruption are not banned from future government work, and the civil service has no restrictions on post-public service employment. Corruption, particularly the exchange of small bribes, is a significant problem in the civil service. The Department of Home Affairs is widely considered the most corrupt government ministry, with bribes regularly used to gain preferential access to official documentation and to avoid deportation.

The Protected Disclosures Act legally protects whistleblowers from various forms of retribution, but it does not protect their identity, and in practice they are rarely shielded from negative repercussions. Moreover, internal mechanisms for acting on reports of corruption are unclear, ineffective, and inconsistent across provinces and municipalities. The PSC and the DPSA Anti-Corruption Unit administer a national hotline for civil servants to report instances of corruption within their ranks. The PSC reported that 4,182 allegations were made via the hotline between September 2004 and November 2007. Of the 2,296 that were deemed related to corruption, only 142 cases were resolved.[60]

Chapter 10 of the constitution states that "transparency [in public administration] must be fostered by providing the public with timely, accessible and accurate information." In addition, Section 32 of the Bill of Rights grants "everyone" the right of access to "any information held by the state" (with exceptions for issues like national security), and mandates that national legislation be enacted to this effect. The 2000 Promotion of Access to Information Act and the 2002 Amendment Act duly guarantee citizens' access to government information, but enforcement suffers from a tedious application process, delays or inaction in response to requests, and a lack of explanation for most request denials. According to the Open Democracy Advice Center, an appeal to a denied information request can take up to six months, not including court time, and can involve prohibitive costs.[61]

The executive dominates the budget-making process. While the legislature must approve the budget, effective legislative oversight is greatly hampered by Parliament's lack of both formal amendment powers and preapproval of executive contracts. The Standing Committee on Public Accounts (SCOPA), Parliament's primary public funds oversight body, lacks independence and clear enforcement mechanisms. However, the Finance and Budget Joint Committees are more assertive vis-à-vis the executive.[62] The 1999 Public Finance Management Act (PFMA) and the 2003 Municipal Finance Management Act provide for a substantial degree of transparency in the use of national, provincial, and local government funds. Both mandate regular expenditure reports from departments and public enterprises to treasuries, and require the annual submission of audited financial statements to Parliament. They also place a positive obligation on all departments to submit an anticorruption strategy to the national Treasury. In addition, the AGSA is obliged to monitor government spending and adherence to relevant regulations. Critics of the PFMA's efficacy point to the questionable independence and inadequate capacity of the AGSA, as well as "the absence of a legal requirement for the publication of contingent liabilities and extra-budgetary activities."[63] Accurate and timely information on regular budgets and expenditures is easily available to the public.

The government controls eight state-owned enterprises (SOEs) and monopolizes transportation (through Transnet) and electricity provision (through Eskom). While Eskom is subject to an official energy-sector regulator, other SOEs report to the Department of Public Enterprises, which is overseen by Parliament's Portfolio Committee on Finance.[64] Oversight agencies are well funded, but they have been criticized as unprofessional and do not regularly initiate investigations of or impose penalties on officials suspected of corruption.[65] By law, procurement processes require competitive bidding and limit sole sourcing, and they are generally transparent. A number of laws require officials to disclose potential conflicts of interest, and the 2003 Supply Chain Management Framework devolved procurement responsibilities to accounting officers in government departments and away from the centralized State

Tenders Board. A major legal exception to competitive bidding is the 2003 Black Economic Empowerment Bill (see Rule of Law). In 2006, the *Mail & Guardian* reported that interests associated with the Chancellor House, the ANC's in-house investment firm, were among the most common beneficiaries of BEE tenders. In February 2008, the Chancellor House withdrew from two multibillion-rand deals with Eskom following both internal and outside condemnation of the implied relationship between the ruling party and a major state-owned industry.

Controversies surrounding government contracting have dominated headlines in recent years. Most notable is the US$4.8 billion Strategic Defence Procurement Package (Arms Deal) of 1999 and the resultant raft of corruption charges against current president Jacob Zuma. Investigations by the Scorpions led to the 2005 conviction of businessman Schabir Shaik, Zuma's financial adviser, on charges of paying Zuma a series of bribes totaling about US$170,000 to secure the success of contract bids by French arms manufacturer Thint. After Zuma himself was charged in 2005, Mbeki sacked him as deputy president. In a separate Arms Deal case, former ANC chief whip Tony Yengeni was convicted of corruption and lost his parliamentary seat, but won parole in January 2007 after serving only five months of a four-year prison sentence. In February 2009, Shaik was also granted parole—officially on medical grounds—only two years into a 15-year sentence, and two days after Zuma announced that he would consider pardoning Shaik if elected president.

Largely in response to the Arms Deal scandal, Mbeki in 2004 signed the Prevention and Combating of Corrupt Activities Act. It established more workable definitions of illegal corruption and extortion, reinstated the common law criminality of bribery, extended the presumption of *prima facie* evidence to facilitate prosecution, and expanded the scope of the law to include all public officials and private citizens. The act also established a Register of Tender Defaulters that excludes persons and companies convicted of corruption from government business for set periods of time, a change that has been largely effective.

The South African media have reported aggressively on the Arms Deal and other scandals, and allegations of corruption in general are given wide airing, particularly in print media. In response, government officials have regularly accused the media of irresponsible reporting and racism. In August 2008, the *Sunday Times* reported that Mbeki himself was paid about US$3.8 million by German arms manufacturer Ferrostaal, most of which was given to the ANC. Both Mbeki and the party denied the allegation.

The South African Revenue Service (SARS) is a well-funded, highly professional body with an excellent record of fairly enforcing the tax laws. The government gives foreign assistance to neighboring Zimbabwe and contributes dues to the SADC and the AU. These funds are distributed in accordance with South African law.

RECOMMENDATIONS

- As endorsed by the 2007 ANC national conference in Polokwane, legislation mandating transparency in private contributions to political parties should be pursued. Parties should be required to disclose the source and amount of political contributions.
- Steps should be taken to protect the independence of the SABC, including the depoliticization of the selection of SABC board members and the appointment of a nonpartisan head of news with experience in the private media sector.
- In order to manage the continuing flow of Zimbabweans into South Africa and better protect their rights, the government should no longer treat Zimbabweans as "temporary economic migrants." Instead, they should be granted a special temporary status under the 2002 Immigration Act that legalizes their presence in South Africa and prevents deportations until the political situation in Zimbabwe stabilizes. The SAPS should set up a task force to monitor the ongoing reintegration of migrants in communities from which they fled during the 2008 wave of attacks.
- Staff and resources of the disbanded Scorpions should continue to function as a coherent, independent unit within the SAPS, tasked with investigating corruption and organized crime. The chief of this unit should be selected from outside the pool of ANC cadres to ensure independence.
- The BEE good practice "scorecards" promulgated in 2007 must be amended to include a score for potential conflicts of interest with awarding authorities and a score for past performance on government tenders.
- Restrictions on post-public service employment in the private sector must be introduced and enforced, either as amendments to the Executive Members Ethics Act, the Code of Conduct for Assembly and Permanent Council Members, and the Public Service Regulations Act, or as new items of legislation.

NOTES

For URLs and endnote hyperlinks, please visit the *Countries at the Crossroads* homepage at http://freedomhouse.org/template.cfm?page=139&edition=8.

[1] This applies to all citizens aged 18 or over, including prisoners. The Electoral Act was amended in 2004 to allow government officials, students, and citizens traveling abroad to vote in South African elections.
[2] Eleven parties ran candidate lists at the national level and in all nine provinces.
[3] "Threats and Killings: Just Another SA Election," *Mail & Guardian*, April 1, 2009.
[4] Electoral Institute of Southern Africa (EISA), *EISA Election Update No. 3* (Johannesburg: EISA, 2009).
[5] Institute for Democracy in Africa (IDASA), *Democracy and Party Political Funding: Pursuing the Public's Right to Know* (Cape Town: IDASA, May 2005).

6. The database is located at http://www.whofundswho.org/.
7. "The ANC's New Funding Front," *Mail & Guardian*, November 10, 2006.
8. The NCOP consists of 10 members from each province: 6 "permanent delegates" appointed by the provincial legislature to five-year terms, and 4 "special delegates" appointed by the legislature in consultation with the premier on a temporary basis.
9. H. van Vuuren, *National Integrity Systems Country Study Report: South Africa 2005* (Transparency International, March 2005), 36.
10. The panel was also triggered by South Africa's participation in the African Peer Review Mechanism (APRM) process.
11. Parliament of the Republic of South Africa, *Report of the Independent Panel Assessment of Parliament* (Cape Town: Parliament of the Republic of South Africa, January 2009), 13.
12. Parliament's "presiding officers" are the speaker and deputy speaker of the NA and the chairperson of the NCOP.
13. A body of this sort was included in a group of four judicial bills introduced by the government in 2007. The bills were withdrawn due to concerns about their impact on judicial independence.
14. Public Service Act, No. 103 of 1994, Chapter IV (11).
15. Ibid.
16. South African Public Service Commission (PSC), *Report on Measuring the Efficacy of the Code of Conduct for Public Servants* (Cape Town: PSC, 2006).
17. "ANC's View on Media Tribunal Shifting," *Mail & Guardian*, March 24, 2009.
18. The paper was forced to return copies of medical records and pay legal fees, but was allowed to keep reporting on the story.
19. Independent Complaints Directorate (ICD), *Annual Report of the Independent Complaints Directorate 2007/2008* (Pretoria: ICD, 2008).
20. Johan Burger and Cyril Adonis, "A Watchdog without Teeth? The Independent Complaints Directorate," *South African Crime Quarterly* 24 (June 2008): 31.
21. A. Faul, *Corruption and the South African Police Service: A Review and Its Implications* (Pretoria: Institute for Security Studies, 2007).
22. South African Police Service (SAPS), *Crime Statistics* (Pretoria: SAPS, March 2008).
23. *Constitution of the Republic of South Africa 1996*, Chapter II (9).
24. Women's Rights Project, *An Overview of Women's Rights in African Customary Law* (Johannesburg: Legal Resources Centre, 2004).
25. This ranks South Africa at 17th in the world by percentage of women in parliament (as of March 31, 2009). See Inter-Parliamentary Union, "Women in National Parliaments: World Classification."
26. "Quarter of Men in South Africa Admit Rape," *Mail & Guardian*, June 18, 2009.
27. South African Law Reform Commission, *Thirty-Sixth Annual Report* (Johannesburg: South Africa Law Reform Commission, 2008).
28. *Constitution of the Republic of South Africa 1996*, Chapter II (9).
29. South African Department of Labour, *Employment Equity Report 2007* (Pretoria: South African Department of Labour, 2007).
30. South African Human Rights Commission (SAHRC), *Human Rights Development Report 2008* (Pretoria: SAHRC, 2008).
31. "Xenophobia: A Special Report" (assorted articles), *Mail & Guardian*.
32. Ibid.
33. Lawyers for Human Rights (LHR), *Monitoring Immigration Detentions in South Africa* (Johannesburg: LHR, 2008).

34. Bureau of Democracy, Human Rights, and Labor, "South Africa," in *International Religious Freedom Report 2008* (Washington, D.C.: U.S. Department of State, September 2008).
35. Susan Booysen, "With the Ballot and the Brick: The Politics of Attaining Service Delivery," *Progress in Development Studies* 7, no. 1 (January 2007): 21–32.
36. "Army Deployed in South Africa Strike," British Broadcasting Corporation (BBC), June 8, 2007.
37. The Judicial Service Commission Act of 1994 established the JSC to advise the government on matters concerning the judiciary and the administration of justice.
38. *Constitution of the Republic of South Africa 1996*, Chapter XIII (177).
39. "Proposal to Merge Courts Undermines Judiciary," *Cape Times*, July 14, 2008.
40. See, for example, "A Serious Slap in the Face," *Mail & Guardian*, February 17, 2008.
41. Global Integrity, "South Africa," in *2008 Global Integrity Report* (Washington, D.C.: Global Integrity, 2009).
42. *Constitution of the Republic of South Africa 1996*, Chapter II (35).
43. "The Desperate Bid to Shield Selebi," *Mail & Guardian*, October 5, 2007.
44. "Motlanthe Decides against Reinstating Pikoli," *Mail & Guardian*, December 8, 2008.
45. James Ngculu, "Parliament and Defence Oversight: The South African Perspective," *African Security Review* 10, no. 1 (2001).
46. Henri Boshoff, "Army May Halt Xenophobic Violence in South Africa," *ISS Today*, May 21, 2008.
47. *Constitution of the Republic of South Africa 1996*, Chapter II (25).
48. The Centre for Development and Enterprise, however, claims that an additional 2.1 percent of land has been transferred from white to black owners via private transactions, which are not included in the DLA numbers. See Centre for Development and Enterprise (CDE), *Land Reform in South Africa: Getting Back on Track* (Johannesburg: CDE, May 2008).
49. "Idle SA Farmers Face Losing Land," BBC, March 4, 2009.
50. Department of Trade and Industry, *South Africa's Economic Transformation: A Strategy for Broad-Based Black Economic Empowerment* (Pretoria: Department of Trade and Industry, 2003), 12.
51. Department of Trade and Industry, "B-BBEE Codes of Good Practice."
52. Broad-Based Black Economic Empowerment Act, No. 53 of 2003.
53. "Black Economic Empowerment: Key Economic Driver," SouthAfrica.info.
54. Global Integrity, "South Africa."
55. Public Protector Act, No. 23 of 1994.
56. EISA, "South Africa: Office of the Public Prosecutor," August 2009.
57. van Vuuren, 33. It should be noted that provincial arrangements for some post-employment restrictions are in place in Gauteng and the Western Cape.
58. According to *Business Day*, then home affairs minister Nosiviwe Mapisa-Nqakula owed 43,708 rand, Land Affairs and Agriculture Minister Lulu Xingwana owed 54,867 rand, sports committee chairman Butana Khompela owed 48,720 rand, and Free State premier Beatrice Marshoff owed 64,000 rand. Wyndham Hartley, "Travelgate Creditors Postpone Meeting," *Business Day*, May 23, 2008.
59. Republic of South Africa, *Public Service Regulations*, 2001.
60. Professional Standards Committee (PSC), *Measuring the Effectiveness of the Anti-Corruption Hotline* (Cape Town: PSC, 2007).
61. Open Democracy Advice Center, *Whistle Blowing, the Protected Disclosures Act, Accessing Information and the Promotion of Access to Information Act: Views of South Africans* (Cape Town: Open Democracy Advice Center, 2007).

[62] Ibid.
[63] IDASA, "How Transparent Is the Budget Process in South Africa?" Budget Briefs, no. 109 (October 2002): 2.
[64] National Energy Regulator of South Africa (NERSA), "About NERSA: Profile"; Department of Public Enterprises, "About DPE: Overview."
[65] Global Integrity, "South Africa."

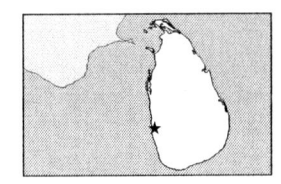

SRI LANKA

CAPITAL: Colombo
POPULATION: 20.5 million
GNI PER CAPITA (PPP): $4,460

SCORES	2006	2010
ACCOUNTABILITY AND PUBLIC VOICE:	4.26	3.55
CIVIL LIBERTIES:	4.43	3.83
RULE OF LAW:	4.05	3.01
ANTICORRUPTION AND TRANSPARENCY:	3.79	3.25

(scores are based on a scale of 0 to 7, with 0 representing weakest and 7 representing strongest performance)

Robert C. Oberst

INTRODUCTION

Over the last four years, the human rights and governance situation in Sri Lanka has deteriorated sharply. Much of the decline can be attributed to the government's extensive use of force against the Liberation Tigers of Tamil Eelam (LTTE) rebel group. Most international observers consider the military campaign to be rife with human rights abuses against both the LTTE and civilians. However, the country has also suffered from the current administration's increasingly hostile attitude toward critical or dissenting views among journalists, politicians, and civil society.

For a small island nation, Sri Lanka has a remarkable amount of ethnic diversity and conflict. The Sinhalese, concentrated in the central and southwestern areas of the country, are the largest ethnic group, comprising 74 percent of the population.[1] They claim to be the original civilized inhabitants of the island and speak the Sinhala language. Although there are some Christians among them, most are Buddhists. The Sri Lanka Tamils, about 12.7 percent of the population, are descendants of early settlers on the island, speak Tamil, and are mostly Hindus. They represent a majority in most of the northern and eastern parts of the island, with other pockets in large cities. Tamil-speaking Muslims comprise 7.1 percent of the population and live in strong concentrations along the eastern coast and in parts of the Sinhalese areas. The final large ethnic group is the Indian Tamils, who live primarily in the hill country of central Sri Lanka. They speak Tamil and most are Hindus. Comprising 5.5 percent of the population,

---

Robert C. Oberst is a Professor of Political Science at Nebraska Wesleyan University and is the author of many books and journal articles on Sri Lanka and South Asia.

they arrived on the island later than the Sri Lanka Tamils and consider themselves culturally distinct.

When the country secured independence from Britain in 1948, the dominant pre-independence political movement became the United National Party (UNP), which appealed primarily to the Sinhalese. The Tamils, who had been part of the independence movement with the founders of the UNP, formed their own party, the Tamil Congress. Both parties split in the 1950s, with a faction of the UNP led by S.W.R.D. Bandaranaike creating the Sri Lanka Freedom Party (SLFP), while a faction of the Tamil Congress formed the Federal Party (later the Tamil United Liberation Front). Growing youth unemployment and the government's failure to resolve economic and social problems resulted in the development of active youth movements among both Sinhalese and Tamils in the 1960s and 1970s. The Janatha Vimukthi Peramuna (JVP) among the Sinhalese and the LTTE among the Tamils challenged the traditional political parties, with the Maoist JVP leading bloody insurrections against the government in 1971 and 1988–89.

A series of Tamil grievances ultimately led to the LTTE insurrection. These included allegations of ethnic bias in university admissions, high unemployment among Tamil youth, claims of a pro-Sinhalese bias in the awarding of jobs and government programs, and a series of anti-Tamil riots from 1977 to 1983 that many Tamils believed the government allowed to happen. In 1984, the simmering conflict developed into open warfare between the LTTE and the government. By the early 1980s more than 20 Tamil rebel groups were involved in the fighting; almost all would eventually either disappear or be militarily destroyed by the LTTE, though several gave up armed conflict in the late 1980s and remain a factor in Tamil politics.

Over the subsequent decades of warfare, tens of thousands of civilians, mostly Tamils, died or disappeared. In response to international pressure, both sides reduced their attacks against civilians after the mid-1990s. A ceasefire was achieved through Norwegian mediation in 2002, but it began to break down after an SLFP-led coalition won a narrow victory in the 2004 elections. Mahinda Rajapaksa of the SLFP won the 2005 presidential election, in part because the LTTE ordered all Tamils to abstain from voting. Most had been expected to vote for UNP leader Ranil Wickremasinghe. Rajapaksa immediately consolidated power and made alliances with Sinhalese ultranationalists to increase his support. He initiated a stepped-up military campaign against the LTTE that eventually resulted in the rebel group's defeat and the deaths of almost all of its leaders in May 2009. This appeared to mark the end of the 25-year civil war, but the victory came with an increase in human rights abuses and persistent allegations that Rajapaksa is trying to create a dictatorship while stifling dissent and condoning violent attacks against his opponents.[2]

ACCOUNTABILITY AND PUBLIC VOICE   3.55
FREE AND FAIR ELECTORAL LAWS AND ELECTIONS	4.50
EFFECTIVE AND ACCOUNTABLE GOVERNMENT	3.50
CIVIC ENGAGEMENT AND CIVIC MONITORING	3.33
MEDIA INDEPENDENCE AND FREEDOM OF EXPRESSION	2.86

Sri Lanka has a long history of relatively free and fair elections. The 225-member unicameral Parliament is elected for a six-year term through a mixed proportional-representation system. The last parliamentary elections in April 2004 were relatively fair, with participation by a total of 6,024 candidates representing 24 political parties and 192 independent groups. Then president Chandrika Kumaratunga's United People's Freedom Alliance (UPFA), a bloc led by the SLFP, won with 46.4 percent of the vote and 105 seats, although it failed to attain a majority and was forced to form a coalition government.[3] The UNP, with 82 seats, formed the core of the new opposition, while a collection of Tamil parties won 22 seats. A new party formed by Buddhist clergy, the Jathika Hela Urumaya (National Heritage Party, or JHU) won nine seats and has generally aligned itself with the government. While the campaign period was relatively free from both violence and fraud, there were 250 complaints of intimidation and ballot stuffing on voting day.[4]

In contrast, the presidential election held in November 2005 was plagued with irregularities. The 13 candidates were generally able to campaign freely, except in LTTE-controlled areas. However, there were reports that state resources were abused throughout the campaign period to support the UPFA, and the commissioner of elections received 77 complaints relating to misuse of state funds. While the preelection period was less violent than in past years, 30 complaints of violence and intimidation were ultimately submitted to the commissioner. Rajapaksa, the incumbent UPFA prime minister, narrowly won with 50.29 percent of the vote, defeating former prime minister Wickramasinghe, who garnered 48.43 percent. Rajapaksa had promised to reject federalism and renegotiate the ceasefire with the LTTE, which prompted several smaller parties to endorse him. A boycott by the LTTE and their intimidation of voters resulted in low voter turnout and violence, especially in the northern and eastern regions.[5] A proposal to rerun the election in these areas was rejected. Allegations later surfaced that Rajapaksa had colluded with the LTTE to stifle Tamil votes. In 2007, Parliament initiated an investigation into these claims that continues as of mid-2009.

Local and provincial council elections since the 2005 vote have been even more problematic. The provincial council balloting for Eastern and North Central Provinces in 2008 and the local council elections in Eastern Province in 2007—won by allies of the government, as have all local and provincial elections since the current coalition came to power in 2004—were marked by serious violations of democratic principles, including widespread voter intimidation and attacks on supporters of all parties.[6] A monitoring group, the Campaign for Free and Fair Elections, described the 2008 Eastern Province contest as "not at all 'free and fair,'" citing enforcement failures and violations such as the misuse of state resources, incidents of forgery during the candidate nomination period, as well as ballot stuffing, violent assaults, and obstruction of voting on election day.[7]

Electoral violence and intimidation have made campaigning a dangerous activity. During the 2004 parliamentary campaign, 5 people were killed, 15 were seriously injured, and 350 were mildly injured, although this level of violence represented a decline from previous years.[8] In the run-up to the 2005 presidential election, three party officials were assassinated.[9] The Centre for Monitoring Election Violence (CMEV) reported a reduced level of violence in the 2008 provincial elections, but still noted eight attacks on candidates.[10] In the provincial council elections for Central and North Western Provinces in February 2009, the CMEV again reported far lower levels of violence, but election violations that "raised serious concerns" nevertheless occurred. They involved "the threat and intimidation and assault of voters, and threat and assault of police officers and government servants serving as party polling agents."[11] Many candidates limit themselves to activities that will not endanger their lives, establish campaign offices in safe areas that may be far away from voting populations, or assemble armies of thugs to provide protection. This has added to campaign violence, as rival bands of thugs often clash with one another.

Because of widespread fraud in earlier elections, the government passed a law in October 2004 requiring that voters show their national identity card.[12] This has led to a separate problem, as the security forces have used ID cards to control the movement of Tamils. Without the cards, Tamils cannot travel outside their villages, and many Indian Tamils lacked cards because they had only been granted citizenship in recent years. While there is a need for better screening of voters, the ID card requirement has served as a way to disenfranchise citizens. In the 2009 Central Province elections, it was estimated that 75,000 to 100,000 voters, or about 10 percent of the electorate, were unable to vote because they lacked ID cards.[13]

Sri Lanka lacks campaign finance legislation, and while elections have traditionally required relatively small budgets, the costs have been growing and television advertising is now used extensively in national elections. Consequently, access to financial resources is increasingly necessary for a successful campaign. Some observers have raised concerns that major financial disparities between candidates have diluted the quality of Parliament members.

Sri Lanka's semipresidential system, like the French system on which it is modeled, does not clearly separate powers between the three branches of government, nor between the president and prime minister. Still, President

Rajapaksa has assumed more power than his predecessors, primarily because of his refusal to obey several Supreme Court rulings. One decision ordered the president to observe the constitution's 17th Amendment, which stipulates that the Constitutional Council rather than the executive has the authority to appoint members of independent commissions; another ruling ordered that fuel prices be reduced.[14] The first decision came in response to Rajapaksa's failure to reconstitute the Constitutional Council after the terms of its members expired. Instead he had usurped its powers and directly appointed loyalists to several important posts. As of 2008, he had appointed six Supreme Court judges, eight Court of Appeal judges, and two inspectors general of the police force.[15]

The president and three of his brothers, all of whom hold government positions, currently make all critical decisions and control public spending. The president doubles as minister of defense (among other portfolios), and his brother Gotabaya holds the post of secretary to the minister of defense, giving them a remarkable amount of power over the security forces. They have increasingly exercised this power to intimidate the media and opposition figures. In addition, the president has been able to influence the country's anticorruption bodies due to the appointment of his brother Basil to the Committee on Public Enterprises. A third brother, Chamal, serves as minister of ports and aviation and of irrigation and water management.

Along with the decline in the fairness of elections, there has been a decline in government accountability and bureaucratic neutrality. The once-independent civil service has become a partisan battleground. Government politicians interfere with the appointment, transfer, and firing of public servants, and many bureaucrats avoid any action that might anger the governing party or opposition members who may ultimately come to power. Those who anger key politicians are punished with transfers to unfavorable locations. Until recently, this could mean being sent to government offices in the LTTE war zone.

Sri Lanka has never had many civil society groups that contribute to the drafting of legislation in Parliament. Traditionally, Sri Lankan politics have been highly personalized, and those seeking government action contact individual members of Parliament (MPs) with whom they have a connection or relationship. Although there is a committee structure in Parliament, there are few hearings on pending legislation, leaving very little opportunity for outside groups to provide input. Civil society organizations have consequently been unable to exercise effective oversight of government actions. The Centre for Policy Alternatives was created in 1996 to provide such oversight, but despite issuing several important reports on government operations and making an effort to influence policymakers, it has not had a significant impact.

Among the most serious problems facing the country is the government's hostility toward nongovernmental organizations (NGOs) and the media. The government views any independent NGO as a threat and has been developing a set of laws to more closely control such groups. All NGOs are required to register with the government,[16] and as of July 2009, 969 domestic and 309 international NGOs were registered.[17] Current law allows the government to review the activities of NGOs and requires them to report their expenditures and sources of income. Under the proposed legislation, NGOs would be required to not only submit plans of action for approval, but also to turn over periodic progress reports to prove that they are achieving their goals. Moreover, the government would have the power to revoke the visas of foreign NGO workers and to ban NGOs. The Asian Human Rights Commission has described the law as unnecessary to control NGO corruption and states that "the proposed new law . . . will violate the fundamental human rights of equality before law, the right to hold opinions, freedom of expression and freedom of association."[18]

The government has asked several international NGOs to leave the country over the last three years, and expelled the leaders of several others. Among these was the head of the German-based Berghof Foundation for Conflict Studies, who was expelled after refusing to appear before Parliament's Select Committee on NGOs.[19] The committee was created to produce a report on NGOs after complaints arose about the supposedly pro-LTTE and pro-Christian behavior of some groups. Its first interim report in 2008 included an attack on Transparency International that questioned the group's right to investigate police corruption.[20] Other expulsions in recent years have included foreign employees of the International Centre for Ethnic Studies (Colombo), Norway's Campaign for Development and Solidarity (FORUT), CARE, the International Committee of the Red Cross (ICRC), Save the Children, and the Norwegian Relief Council.

Associated with the legal and government pressure on NGOs are widespread violent attacks, including the murder of staff members. The Sri Lankan Law and Society Trust produced a list of 58 aid workers killed from 2005 to 2007.[21] Three aid workers were killed in 2008, and at least seven more had been killed as of April 2009.[22] Some of these attacks were carried out by the LTTE, but it is widely believed that the government or its supporters have been responsible for many others. In 2006, 17 Sri Lankan aid workers for the French group Action Contre La Faim (Action Against Hunger) were killed in the eastern town of Muttur as government forces captured the town from the LTTE. Despite international pressure on the government to find the killers, the case remains unresolved.

Media independence and freedom have been seriously undermined since the 2004 national elections. The International Federation of Journalists has described the media situation in Sri Lanka as a rapidly worsening "war on journalists," while Reporters Without Borders dropped Sri Lanka to a ranking of 165 out of 173 countries in its 2008 press freedom index.[23] In recent years, journalists who report on sensitive issues like corruption, human rights abuses, and military strategy have been subject to harassment, intimidation, and, increasingly, physical attacks; a total of 34 journalists have been murdered since 2004.[24] Among the most high-profile murders was that of Lasantha Wickramatunga, editor of the *Sunday Leader* and *Morning Leader* newspapers. His death on January 8, 2009, led to the shutdown of the *Morning Leader*. Between mid-2008 and mid-2009 alone, 11 Sri Lankan journalists were forced to flee the country to protect their safety.[25] Moreover, the police have failed to make an arrest or identify suspects in most of these cases. In the 2009 Impunity Index compiled by the Committee to Protect Journalists, Sri Lanka ranked fourth out of 14 countries in which journalists are killed regularly, with at least nine journalist murders in the 1999–2008 period currently unsolved.[26]

The Sri Lankan media sector has traditionally been dominated by the Lake House Publishing group, which was taken over by the government in the 1970s. The Lake House newspapers are used to present the government position on political issues and have ceased to be a source of objective reporting. The government also has its own radio and television outlets. This government dominance stimulated the development of independent print outlets, including several Sinhala, Tamil, and English dailies. Nevertheless, private news outlets that are seen as critical of the government have faced increased harassment and attacks. For example, Leader Publications, publisher of the *Sunday Leader* and *Morning Leader*, was the target of an arson attack in 2007, and the Sirasa TV studio complex was nearly destroyed by armed men in January 2009. Several private outlets have closed down due to this climate of fear and violence, while others, such as the Standard Newspaper Group, have been driven out of business by government financial pressure.[27] As a result, the availability of objective, independent sources of information in the country has drastically diminished, and the government line has dominated reporting since the last phase of the war began in 2006.[28]

Past governments have used highly restrictive slander and libel laws to prevent media criticism of public officials. Because of the inefficiency of the court system, slander or libel suits are invariably dragged out over several years, increasing the cost to the targeted media organization. The laws, which favor plaintiffs, contribute to media self-censorship, particularly on national security issues, corruption, and human rights abuses.

In December 2008, the government censored the British Broadcasting Corporation (BBC) and the *Sunday Leader*.[29] The BBC ultimately stopped providing content to the state radio outlet.[30] A month before Wickramatunga's murder, the *Sunday Leader* was forbidden to mention Defense Secretary Gotabaya Rajapaksa by name. Separately, one of Sri Lanka's foremost journalists, D.B.S. Jeyaraj, resigned from the staff of the *Nation* in September 2008 to protest the publication's censorship of articles after several of its journalists received death threats.[31]

The government has arrested large numbers of journalists or taken them to police headquarters for questioning. It has also passed rules that tightly restrict journalists' freedom of movement and ability to cover certain areas. Since 2007, all reporting of frontline battles with the LTTE has been banned, and no reporters have been allowed near the battle zones. In May 2008, foreign journalists were also barred from covering the provincial council elections in Eastern Province.[32] In 2009, the government deported or denied visas to several foreign journalists.

The authorities' hostility toward the media also takes the form of public pronouncements condemning criticism of the government. These attacks have included accusations that the *Boston Globe* is a terrorist mouthpiece, and a Ministry of Defence statement accusing the media of treachery against the armed forces.[33] Gotabaya Rajapaksa, after ordering the president and secretary of the Sri Lankan Working Journalists' Association to meet with him, appeared to threaten media workers with violence, warning that "those who love military leaders would take serious action against journalists. Such actions are not wrong, and the Government cannot stop such actions."[34]

Efforts to control internet news sources have increased. A number of opposition media sources have been targeted in hacking incidents, although it is difficult to identify the culprits. In June 2007, the TamilNet website was blocked by the government.[35]

CIVIL LIBERTIES 3.83

PROTECTION FROM STATE TERROR, UNJUSTIFIED IMPRISONMENT, AND TORTURE	2.75
GENDER EQUITY	4.67
RIGHTS OF ETHNIC, RELIGIOUS, AND OTHER DISTINCT GROUPS	2.50
FREEDOM OF CONSCIENCE AND BELIEF	5.00
FREEDOM OF ASSOCIATION AND ASSEMBLY	4.25

The government's campaign to control LTTE terrorism has led to numerous and serious human rights violations, with extensive evidence pointing to abuses by the security forces. For years, both sides in the civil war have frequently targeted civilians. This problem escalated in late 2008 and early 2009, as government military victories forced the LTTE to retreat into their jungle strongholds. The rebels used civilians as a shield against the advancing government troops, but the government pressed ahead with extensive bombing and shelling, showing little concern for civilian casualties. Human Rights Watch described the conflict as a "war on the displaced" and accused the government of attacking a safe zone created for civilians and hospitals. Civilians also suffered due to a government blockade of the war zone, which prevented relief agencies from entering the affected areas.[36] Although there were no outside observers to determine the extent of the casualties, some sources have estimated that as many as 20,000 Tamils were killed by government shelling during the final offensive against the LTTE.[37]

Although the security forces have a long history of torturing detainees, there has been a sharp increase in state terror since 2004. In 2006, Tamils began disappearing by the hundreds in government-controlled areas. However, without independent law enforcement officers to investigate the incidents, there is no way to prove allegations that the security forces were involved. The most common claims were against militia groups working with the security forces, including Tamil groups that had split with the LTTE, such as the Tamil Makkal Viduthalai Pulikal (TMVP) and the Eelam People's Democratic Party (EPDP).

The number of reports of torture involving both LTTE and criminal suspects has increased sharply under the Rajapaksa administration. In a 2007 report, the UN Special Rapporteur on Torture, Manfred Nowak, stated that "torture is widely practiced."[38] The progovernment militia groups, some of which have been given the power to detain Tamils, often work with the regular security forces to arrest and torture suspects before releasing them, killing them, or turning them over to the police for further action. Police powers in the Eastern Province, for example, have been delegated to the former LTTE fighters of the TMVP, who now arrest people at will, interrogate them, and transfer them to the police.

Torture is often used against suspected terrorists, who are held without court supervision. The 1979 Prevention of Terrorism Act allows unlimited detention of LTTE suspects without legal representation or safeguards. A significant number of detainees, both LTTE suspects and ordinary criminal suspects, have died in custody, including 26 in the first six months of 2009.[39] Due to overcrowding and a lack of basic infrastructure, prison conditions fail to meet international standards. According to Nowak's 2007 assessment, prisons with an intended capacity of 8,200 inmates held 28,000.[40]

Throughout the civil conflict, displaced Tamil civilians have been held in government detention centers until it can be proven that they are not members of the LTTE. In the final offensive, nearly 285,000 civilians sought refuge with government forces and were placed in such camps.[41] Estimates of displaced people prior to that reached nearly 500,000.[42] The government has given the army control over the detention centers and has banned or limited access for both domestic and international NGOs. There have been widespread allegations of progovernment militia groups "disappearing" detainees, and of sexual abuse and poor medical and sanitary conditions. Although the government improved the conditions in detention camps after the Nowak report, most held more than twice the number of people they were built for, leading to shortages of toilets and poor sanitation. For example, with over 220,000 detainees, the Menik Farm camp in Vavuniya has been described as having "woefully inadequate" sanitation and health facilities, cramped living conditions, and outbreaks of chicken pox, hepatitis, and diarrhea.[43]

Several progovernment groups, particularly the EPDP and the TMVP, have been accused of carrying out murders and kidnappings of Tamils and political opponents at an increasing rate in the last five years. Since 2005, three prominent Tamil MPs have been assassinated: T. Maheshwaran of the UNP in January 2008, N. Raviraj of the Tamil National Alliance (TNA) in May 2007, and

Joseph Pararajasingham, also of the TNA, in 2005. It has been widely reported that the three were murdered by members of the EPDP.

Rates of criminal violence have also risen. Organized crime bosses often have relationships with powerful politicians, who protect them in return for services including violent attacks on opponents. Few of these attacks result in arrests. In another area of concern, there have been numerous reports on the LTTE's recruitment of underage soldiers. However, the TMVP has also been accused of recruiting child soldiers, including more than 400 in 2007.[44]

There have been a small number of arrests of individuals within the security forces for abuses like those described above. In one prominent case that provided conclusive proof of security force involvement in rights abuses, an air force squadron leader was arrested in 2008 for overseeing more than 100 kidnappings and murders in the Colombo area. He worked with other security force officers and members of the TMVP's Karuna faction in carrying out the actions.[45] However, in a large number of cases, prosecution has been hampered by several factors. First, the executive branch has displayed a lack of political will to investigate or punish the abuses, dismissing calls for independent probes into alleged violations of international humanitarian law. Second, while the Sri Lankan courts have upheld civil liberties, they often move too slowly to provide effective relief. Third, in many cases the courts are unable to force the cooperation of the security forces. For example, the Supreme Court has issued rulings ordering the security forces to release all detainees held longer than 90 days, but this has been largely ignored.[46] Even when a court awards damages to petitioners, there is no way for them to collect or for the court to enforce payment. The courts in the Jaffna municipality of Chavakacheri ruled in February 2006 that there was adequate evidence to continue with cases involving the disappearance of 35 youths detained by the army. However, the army would not turn over the suspects for prosecution. Among the officers involved was Janaka Perera, who had since become a UNP politician and served as high commissioner to Australia before being killed by a suicide bomber in 2008. In 1997, he had been the commander of Sri Lankan forces implicated in the disappearance of over 700 youths on the Jaffna peninsula.[47] Finally, prosecutions have been undermined by extensive threats against witnesses. Sri Lanka does not have any witness protection laws, and murders and intimidation of both witnesses and victims are common.[48] The murder of UNP lawmaker T. Maheshwaran, noted above, was carried out before a crowd of worshippers in a church. One of his bodyguards shot and wounded the attacker. However, the witnesses were reportedly intimidated before a police line-up to identify a suspect that had been apprehended.

The unsolved status of most political murders and disappearances led the president in September 2006 to appoint a commission of inquiry to investigate 14 murder cases. In February 2007, an International Independent Group of Eminent Persons (IIGEP) was invited to observe and assist the commission, known as the Presidential Commission of Inquiry to Investigate and

Inquire into Alleged Serious Violations of Human Rights. In November 2007, the IIGEP ended its mission prematurely, stating that the Sri Lankan panel was not transparent and did not conduct its business according to basic international norms. They argued that the attorney general intervened on behalf of the government, that witnesses were threatened and not protected, and that officers in the armed services refused to cooperate with the investigation.[49] After the government's military victory over the LTTE in May 2009, the president declined to continue the mandate of the commission of inquiry and allowed it to be disbanded.

Human rights have also been undermined by the weakening of the National Human Rights Commission over the last four years.[50] In May 2006, President Rajapaksa appointed five members to the commission in violation of the constitution, which requires the nonpartisan Constitutional Council to make the appointments. The next month, the commission announced that it would discontinue investigating more than 2,000 cases of disappearances. As a result of these changes, the body has effectively ceased to be a force promoting human rights in Sri Lanka.

Gender rights are considered strong relative to neighboring countries, and the government provides legal equality to women, though in some cases it has failed to uphold the principle in practice. Women remain underrepresented in political positions and within the civil service. Their share of Parliament after the last legislative elections in 2004 was about 6 percent.[51] The main gender issues still facing the country are sexual harassment, discrimination in salary and promotion opportunities, and domestic violence. Weak laws prohibiting these abuses have not been enforced, nor has there been any effort to pass new legislation. Matters related to the family—including marriage, divorce, child custody, and inheritance—are adjudicated under the customary law of each ethnic or religious group, which sometimes results in discrimination against women. Furthermore, the intensification of the civil conflict has been accompanied by an increase in the level of violence against women, including rape, and a disproportionately high number of the displaced population is female. Human rights groups have alleged that security forces and militias have abused women in former LTTE-controlled areas. The government denies the claims, and there are no independent observers to verify them because of the government's restrictions on journalists in the north and east.

Constitutional guarantees of equal rights for ethnic and religious minorities have not been adequately enforced. The current government is a broad coalition that includes extreme nationalist parties that view Sri Lanka as the rightful domain of the Sinhalese Buddhists and are very intolerant of religious and ethnic minorities. Such extremist groups are believed to be behind the numerous attacks against Christian churches and worshippers over the last four years, very few of which have been punished, and they are supportive of government efforts to restrict foreign NGOs and assert the preeminence of Buddhism among the country's religions. They have reportedly intimidated minorities and sought to require all shops (even those owned by Muslims and Hindus) to fly the Buddhist flag on Buddhist holidays. The president stated in his victory speech to Parliament after the LTTE defeat that there would no longer be minorities in Sri Lanka, only patriots and non-patriots, and nationalists subsequently proposed new laws banning all political parties whose names mention an ethnic or religious group. If enacted, such a rule would eliminate all of the current Muslim and Tamil political parties.

The political importance of Buddhism has led the Buddhist clergy to play a major role in government and society, as reflected by the success of the JHU in the 2004 elections. The party promotes the election of Buddhist clergy to Parliament, and since 2007 it has supported the Rajapaksa government, holding one cabinet seat. The JHU has been at the forefront of an effort to control Christian proselytizing.

Proposed "unethical conversion" legislation illustrates the concerns many Buddhists have about Christianity. The Prohibition of Forcible Conversions Bill has been under consideration by Parliament since 2005, but it was essentially dormant for four years thanks in part to widespread international criticism. The government revived it in 2009 on the recommendation of a January report by the government-sponsored Commission on Unethical Conversions, which also called for laws requiring new religious organizations to take an oath not to recruit new members, a government investigation of religious groups that became established in the country after 1972, a ban on any such groups that are found to be harmful, and the creation of a data center to collect individual complaints against religious groups.[52] Under the anticonversion bill as reintroduced by the government, those who tried to convert a Sri Lankan citizen from one faith to another using "force, fraud, or allurement" would face fines of up to 500,000 rupees (US$4,400) and up to seven years in prison. The U.S. Commission on International Religious Freedom criticized the bill for vague language that threatened to criminalize even peaceful religious practice and conversations about religion.[53] Fifteen members of the U.S. Congress, in a letter to the Sri Lankan ambassador in Washington, stated that the legislation would "quite simply extinguish freedom of religion, expression and association for all Sri Lankans."[54]

Beyond the proposed restrictions aimed at Christians, the government has usually avoided interfering in the affairs of the major religions of the country (Buddhism, Hinduism, Islam, and Christianity). Members of all religions have traditionally been allowed to worship as they wish.

Government job appointments and placement of development projects are based on patronage and support for government politicians. Sinhalese Buddhists dominate the political system and usually direct jobs and projects to members of their ethnic community. The educational system is divided between Sinhala and Tamil-language schools. Those who study in Tamil and cannot speak Sinhala fluently are at a disadvantage when seeking employment in Colombo or with the civil service.

The security forces routinely target Tamils for extra scrutiny and restrictions on movement. Tamils are required to register with the police whenever they move to another city, either temporarily or permanently; no such requirement exists for Sinhalese. Tamils must also obtain permission from the government and security forces before traveling from the north and east to other parts of the country. Such restrictions are exacerbated by security forces' common practice of confiscating Tamils' national identification cards, preventing those affected from traveling beyond their villages; there is no legal recourse for them to regain the cards.

During the ceasefire before the Rajapaksa government came to power, restrictions on Tamils were relaxed, but they have been tightly enforced in the last three years. Since the LTTE defeat, the government has been very slow to remove the restrictions. Under the Prevention of Terrorism Act and emergency regulations enacted in recent years, Tamils may be held by the security forces without access to counsel, charges, or trial. Although the emergency provisions apply to all Sri Lankans, the overwhelming majority of detentions involve Tamils. And as described above, displaced Tamils crossing over from LTTE-controlled areas or caught traveling to or from India are placed in camps to be held indefinitely with no access to the courts.

The government has done very little to provide opportunities for people with disabilities. Progress has been stymied by the high costs of increasing access to buildings, jobs, and education, and new efforts seem unlikely in the near future. Another vulnerable group, homosexuals, are subject to Section 365a of the penal code, which criminalizes homosexual behavior. However, such restrictions are not routinely enforced.

Sri Lanka has a strong workers' rights tradition, with over 1,500 unions registered. Workers are allowed to form and join unions, and strikes are permissible. However, each political party has created affiliated trade unions, and the parties in power typically support their unions at the expense of those linked to opposition parties, costing many workers their jobs. This pattern has continued under the Rajapaksa government. Political organizations are allowed to form, and the right of peaceful assembly is assured by the constitution, but permits are required for demonstrations. In addition, emergency regulations imposed in 2005 grant the government the authority to restrict assemblies and rallies, although it rarely denies permission to demonstrate. The police periodically carry out investigations and intimidation of opposition organizations and have been known to use excessive force against demonstrators who fail to obtain permits. Human rights NGOs and groups that advocate peace talks have been particularly subject to harassment. Surprisingly, the increased security provisions associated with the ethnic conflict have not led to a reduction in the number of demonstrations.

RULE OF LAW   3.01

INDEPENDENT JUDICIARY	3.00
PRIMACY OF RULE OF LAW IN CIVIL AND CRIMINAL MATTERS	3.20
ACCOUNTABILITY OF SECURITY FORCES AND MILITARY TO CIVILIAN AUTHORITIES	2.50
PROTECTION OF PROPERTY RIGHTS	3.33

The judiciary has traditionally been an independent and fair institution, and there are constitutional procedures to protect judges from political pressure. Nevertheless, the courts have experienced pressure in recent years, and the gradual politicization of the judicial process has become a serious impediment to justice. In some cases, the pressure has come from senior judges themselves. According to the International Crisis Group, "the recently retired chief justice, Sarath Silva, is widely regarded as having played a central role in the judiciary's current politicization,"[55] in part by appointing his supporters to judgeships in the lower courts.

However, much of the heightened political pressure on judges and magistrates has come from the executive branch, which has arrogated authority over the judiciary in defiance of the constitution. As noted above, the charter's 17th Amendment in 2001 created an apolitical Constitutional Council to make independent appointments to key state bodies, including the Judicial Services Commission (JSC), which was previously appointed and largely controlled by the chief justice of the Supreme Court. The JSC is in charge of the transfer, dismissal, and discipline of lower court judges, among other functions. After the terms of the initial Constitutional Council members lapsed in 2005, Rajapaksa refused to reconstitute the body and has since made direct appointments to the JSC, the Supreme Court, and the post of attorney general. In late 2008, following a series of unfavorable Supreme Court decisions, including one that ordered him to implement the 17th Amendment, Rajapaksa made statements threatening the court by reminding the judges of a time when their homes were stoned and they were impeached.[56]

The controversy over the JSC has limited its activities and reform projects, including efforts to create a code of conduct for judges. Moreover, the arbitrary, politicized transfer of lower-court judges is now common and occurs even in high-profile cases. The magistrate overseeing the 2006 investigation into the murder of 17 aid workers in Muttur, who was a Tamil from the region where the crime was committed, was transferred by the justice minister to another district, and no legal justification was provided. The case was then handed to a Sinhalese magistrate in a different location, moving it away from the families and potential witnesses and compromising the fairness of the trial. In November 2007, the case was transferred back to Muttur, but under a different magistrate.[57]

In addition to political interference, the judicial system suffers from a rising number of threats against attorneys. This problem has been extensive on the

Tamil-populated Jaffna peninsula.[58] Also of concern has been the training of judges. While the criteria for appointment call for judges to be knowledgeable of the law, the country has lagged behind in providing law reports on court decisions. Because most magistrates do not have easy access to these records, it is often difficult for them to base their decisions on precedents set by other courts.

Under Sri Lankan law, defendants are presumed innocent until proven guilty, have the right to counsel, and are guaranteed a public trial in criminal cases. Nevertheless, due process rights are often denied in practice, particularly for displaced Tamils held in camps. Furthermore, a backlog of cases results in long delays, sometimes lasting more than 10 years. The Court of Appeal processes about 600 cases a year; as of June 2007, it faced a backlog of 11,000 cases and was receiving about 1,700 cases a year.[59] The ease with which a party in a case can delay the proceedings has made it difficult for petitioners of modest means to pursue court action. Although independent counsel is available, it is usually too expensive for the average Sri Lankan, especially if the case is delayed. The underfunded Legal Aid Commission, which provides legal assistance to needy litigants, cannot meet the needs of most clients. Mediation boards that were formed in the 1990s continue to function, diverting cases from the court system to a low-cost mediation process that hears about 250,000 civil and criminal cases a year. Mediators are required to undergo a training program conducted by the Ministry of Justice that teaches them a uniform mediation model employed throughout the country.

Prosecutors are theoretically independent of political pressure, but in reality the prosecution process is highly politicized and the criminal justice system has been used increasingly to punish politicians when they are out of power. S.B. Dissanayake, one of the leaders of the opposition UNP and the heir apparent to current party leader Ranil Wickremasinghe, was sentenced in 2004 to two years in prison for a speech in which he criticized the judiciary, and in July 2008 the UN Human Rights Committee deemed his sentence arbitrary and disproportionate.[60] While cases against political opponents take several years to prosecute, they tend to move through the judicial system faster than other types of cases, in part because of an awareness that the matter could be dropped if power changes hands in the next election.

The security forces have traditionally been uninhibited by civilian interference, except for budgetary and judicial oversight. Under Rajapaksa, the government has exercised more control over all branches of the security forces. This has included the selection of commanders based on political factors. In July 2009, Gotabaya Rajapaksa transferred General Sarath Fonseka, whose status as hero of the anti-LTTE campaign made him a potential political rival, to a less prominent role. There has also been direct political control over the leadership of the police, thanks in part to the absence of a Constitutional Council, which was supposed to appoint independent police officials. Although the security forces have in some cases acted in defiance of political orders, these instances have been relatively rare.

The security forces are actively involved in political affairs, and the problem has been extremely serious during local and provincial government elections, with officers who fail to obey ruling party politicians facing transfer or dismissal. Moreover, security personnel are often told to leave shortly before incidents of ballot-box stuffing or electoral fraud occur.

The security forces have also been implicated in political actions against members of the opposition and other critics of the government. While it is difficult to determine who was responsible for the many unsolved attacks, security force involvement has been proven in some cases. These include an attack by a dozen out-of-uniform policemen on the television station Max TV in February 2009.[61] Most other attacks, such as the assault on Sirasa TV in January 2009, have gone unsolved.[62]

Private property rights are guaranteed under the constitution, and the government has generally upheld them in practice. However, the long delays in civil cases make court enforcement of property rights ineffective. This is compounded by the weight the legal system gives to possession, which often makes it difficult to evict squatters and allows them to occupy disputed land for decades as court cases progress.

Another problem is the seizure, on security grounds, of private land held by Tamils. A great deal of land in the north and east has been included in declared "high security zones" and confiscated by the security forces. In some cases, the armed forces have held the land for more than 20 years. Parcels of land surrounding military camps are usually turned over to Sinhalese civilians, who use them for commercial purposes or build permanent homes. The military defeat of the LTTE has provided an opportunity for the security forces to seize more land, and the occupation of private property is expected to continue despite the end of hostilities.

ANTICORRUPTION AND TRANSPARENCY 3.25

ENVIRONMENT TO PROTECT AGAINST CORRUPTION	3.25
PROCEDURES AND SYSTEMS TO ENFORCE ANTICORRUPTION LAWS	3.00
EXISTENCE OF ANTICORRUPTION NORMS, STANDARDS, AND PROTECTIONS	3.25
GOVERNMENTAL TRANSPARENCY	3.50

Three significant types of corruption prevail in the Sri Lankan political system: bribes paid in an effort to circumvent bureaucratic red tape, bribe solicitation by government officials, and nepotism or cronyism. Under the Rajapaksa administration, very few steps have been taken to control corruption. Sri Lanka was ranked 92 out of 180 countries surveyed in Transparency International's 2008 Corruption Perceptions Index.[63]

Until the 1970s, Sri Lanka had a strong system of bureaucratic regulations that made conducting business very difficult and time consuming. Beginning in 1977, those regulations were relaxed and economic activity became much freer. In the last four years, the Rajapaksa government has reinstituted some regulations, but it has made no effort to carry out a widespread reregulation of the economy.

The state still owns a significant number of businesses, and Rajapaksa's economic plan rejects the privatization of state enterprises, including "strategic" enterprises such as banks and airports.[64] State-owned enterprises are often used by friends of the government as a means of accumulating wealth. The Committee on Public Enterprises (COPE) is charged with ensuring that financial discipline is upheld within public corporations and other government business organizations. Its reports to Parliament have revealed the presence of extensive corruption and mismanagement of government funds,[65] and several recent court cases have highlighted this trend. A 2008 Supreme Court decision found that Lanka Marine Services, a profitable state-owned enterprise, was sold with "dishonest intent" and ordered the buyer to return the company to the government. In another case that is still pending before the Supreme Court, COPE reported in 2008 that the sale of the Sri Lanka Insurance Company was "seriously flawed." Also in 2008, the Supreme Court fined former president Chandrika Kumaratunga for granting state-owned land near Parliament to a private owner.[66]

Despite the widespread phenomenon of illegal gain by public officials, Sri Lanka has still not enacted effective financial disclosure laws. While a 1975 law obliges high officials to make annual declarations of their assets, these declarations are not independently audited, and less than 5 percent of MPs had complied with the rule as of 2003. Although failure to make the asset declaration is considered a criminal offense, violations are rarely punished.[67] Furthermore, a 2007 law states that public officials who have dual citizenship and property overseas are not required to declare their assets.

The Sri Lanka Bribery Commission was created in 1994 as the only agency dealing solely with corruption prevention. The transfer of the commission's director general by President Rajapaksa in February 2008, along with similar transfers of police investigators assigned to the panel, raised doubts about its independence. While the president has the authority to appoint members of the commission, he does not have the right to remove them. At the time of the director general's transfer, the commission was investigating allegations of bribery linked to the purchase of obsolete MiG-27 jets.[68] While the Bribery Commission receives over 4,000 cases a year, there have been only one or two bribery convictions annually. The general failure of the body has drawn severe criticism from many anticorruption groups.[69] Although the Supreme Court has ruled against the government in the few high-profile privatization cases noted above, official corruption generally goes unpunished.

In addition to the Bribery Commission and the COPE, the auditor general and the Public Accounts Committee hold anticorruption mandates. The auditor general is charged with monitoring all government entities and delivering its annual reports to the Public Accounts Committee (PAC) in Parliament, which oversees governmental efficiency and financial discipline. However, the power of these bodies to address corruption has been vastly diminished as a result of government interference. Furthermore, the impartiality of the COPE has been under scrutiny since the appointment of Basil Rajapaksa, the president's brother, as a member in 2007, and the appointment of a cabinet minister as COPE chairman in 2008.[70]

The failure to enforce corruption laws is accompanied by a general failure of the government to properly account for expenditures and to enforce tax laws. The auditor general's reports have revealed that the entire tax collection system is corrupt. In 2004, the auditor general found that 441 billion rupees (US$3.89 billion) in taxes, more than the total tax revenue collected in a year, was lost to fraud committed either "willfully or negligently" by the Sri Lanka Inland Revenue Department between 2002 and 2004.[71] More recently, the 2007 PAC report on government tax revenue revealed value-added tax fraud.[72] There appears to be very little interest in addressing these problems, either in the government or in civil society, which has organized intermittent campaigns but failed to force government action.

The weak performance of the Bribery Commission has contributed to the growing importance of the press in reporting on and investigating allegations of corruption among government officials. Journalists have been active in reporting illegal acts, but the intimidation and attacks against the media described above have inhibited their ability to pursue corruption stories since the election of President Rajapaksa. Moreover, there is no protection for whistleblowers, and reporting graft in an environment where it is endemic endangers job security, meaning few workers are willing to come forward.

Bribery in the public sector has spread to the school system. While very little systematic evidence is available, bribery by parents to obtain admission for their children to the country's better elementary and secondary schools appears to have increased in recent years.[73]

Sri Lanka does not have a freedom of information law; a bill was approved by the cabinet in 2003, but it was never brought before Parliament. The government has traditionally been relatively open in making government records available to the public, but the process has become increasingly decentralized in recent years, as the government has allowed individual offices to issue their own publications rather than requiring that they be channeled through a central government publications office. This makes it difficult to find material or even to know what is available.

Parliamentary proceedings are still published and widely available, including the extensive debate in November over each year's budget proposal, which is also made available to the public. In the Open Budget Initiative's 2008 Open Budget Index, Sri Lanka receives a score of 64 percent, meaning it provides "significant information to the public."[74] However, despite the annual reporting of the auditor general and the PAC on government income, spending, and financial discipline, expenditure accounting has become less transparent and efficient of late due to executive interference.[75] The government contracting process remains fairly secretive, which makes it very difficult for interested citizens and groups to track the size, bidders, and recipients of government contracts. Foreign assistance disbursements are not usually published. While evidence on the scope of corruption in government expenditures is scarce, there is a general consensus that the Rajapaksa government has made no visible effort to tackle the problem.

RECOMMENDATIONS

- Implement the 17th amendment to the constitution by reestablishing the Constitutional Council in order to reduce politicization of the police and judiciary.
- Create mechanisms to hire and train more judges and implement information technology upgrades in order to speed up court cases and clear the large case backlog.
- Abandon the pending legislation further restricting NGO activity as well as the Prohibition of Forcible Conversions Bill.
- Provide official protection for threatened journalists and cease verbal attacks on the media by powerful government and security force members.
- Allow international supervision of Tamil refugee centers and implement, with international assistance if necessary, a comprehensive plan to release refugees and assist their return to and recuperation of their communities.
- Reestablish an independent Human Rights Commission and specifically create, either as a subcommission within the Human Rights Commission or another body independent of it, a group empowered to monitor security force actions.

NOTES

For URLs and endnote hyperlinks, please visit the *Countries at the Crossroads* homepage at http://freedomhouse.org/template.cfm?page=139&edition=8.

[1] All population data is from the 1981 census, *Statistical Abstract of the Democratic Republic of Sri Lanka* (Colombo: Department of Census and Statistics, 1996), 40. Because of the war, Sri Lanka has held only one partial census since then. A 2001 census did not gather information from the Tamil areas in the north and east, leaving a great deal of confusion about the current population. For instance, the 2008 internet edition of the U.S. Central Intelligence Agency's *World Factbook* incorrectly reports the partial 2001 census as an accurate island-wide census. Based on voter registration records in the Tamil areas and the partial census, this author has projected the current population breakdown as follows: Sinhalese 73.6 percent, Sri Lanka Tamils 12.0 percent, Muslims 8.8 percent, and Indian Tamils 4.9 percent.

[2] "Heading for a Dictatorship?" *Sunday Leader*, May 11, 2008; Maitree de Silva, "Architects of a Military Junta in Sri Lanka?" *Groundviews*, February 19, 2009.

[3] Inter-Parliamentary Union, "Sri Lanka: Parliament," Inter-Parliamentary Union home page.
[4] "President Wins Sri Lanka Election," British Broadcasting Corporation (BBC), April 4, 2004.
[5] European Union Election Observation Mission (EU EOM), "Preliminary Statement: Sri Lankan Presidential Election 2005," November 19, 2005.
[6] Provincial council elections were also held in Sabaragamuwa and North Central Provinces in 2008, and local council elections were held in all districts in 2006 and 2008. While these elections were marked by irregularities, they were not as serious as those discussed above.
[7] Campaign for Free and Fair Elections (CaFFE), *Eastern Provincial Council Elections of 10 May 2008: Monitoring Report* (Colombo: CaFFE, 2008), 18–20.
[8] EU EOM, *Sri Lanka Parliamentary Elections: Final Report* (Colombo: EU EOM, 2004).
[9] EU EOM, "Preliminary Statement: Sri Lankan Presidential Election 2005."
[10] Centre for Monitoring Election Violence (CMEV), "Maps," CMEV home page.
[11] CMEV, "Central and North–Western Provincial Council Elections—Media Communiqué 6," February 14, 2009.
[12] Sri Lankan Information Department, "Parliament Passes Election Act (Special Provisions) Bill Unopposed," news release, October 8, 2004.
[13] "Identity Crisis at PC Polls," *Sunday Times*, February 15, 2009.
[14] "Rajapaksa in War with Judiciary," TamilNet, December 19, 2008.
[15] Transparency International Sri Lanka, *The Forgotten Constitutional Council: An Analysis of Consequences of the Non-Implementation of the 17th Amendment* (Colombo: Transparency International Sri Lanka, August 2008).
[16] For registration rules, see the website of the National Secretariat for Non-Governmental Organizations, http://www.ngosecretariat.gov.lk/activities.php.
[17] "Strict Laws to Monitor NGOS, INGOS," *Daily Mirror*, July 19, 2009.
[18] Asian Human Rights Commission, "Sri Lanka: Part Six of an Article; The Interim Report of the Parliamentary Committee on NGOs is Flawed from the Point of View of Policy, Science and Law," December 19, 2008.
[19] "Berghof Chief Asked to Leave," *Sunday Times*, December 30, 2007.
[20] Transparency International Sri Lanka, "Response to TISL to Parliamentary Select Committee on NGOs Regarding Adverse References," January 5, 2009.
[21] Law and Society Trust, "Second Submission to Presidential Commission of Inquiry and the Public on Human Rights Violations in Sri Lanka: January–August 2007," *LST Review* 18, no. 239–40 (September–October 2007).
[22] Emma Batha, "2008 Was Deadliest Year for Aid Workers–Study," AlertNet, April 6, 2009; Michael Bear, "Aid Worker Fatalities in 2009," Change.org, April 9, 2009.
[23] International Federation of Journalists (IFJ), *In the Balance: Press Freedom in South Asia 2007–2008* (Delhi: IFJ, 2008), 27; Reporters without Borders, "Only Peace Protects Freedoms in Post-9/11 World," news release, October 22, 2008.
[24] Journalists for Democracy in Sri Lanka, "Sri Lanka: Thirty-Four Journalists & Media Workers Killed during Present Government Rule," news release, July 22, 2009.
[25] Karen Phillips, "Special Report: Journalists in Exile in 2009," Committee to Protect Journalists (CPJ), June 17, 2009.
[26] CPJ, *Getting Away with Murder 2009* (New York: CPJ, March 2009). CPJ uses a more conservative method of estimating the number of journalist murders than other press freedom organizations.
[27] Free Media Movement, "'Mawbima' and 'Sunday Standard' Newspapers Closed by Government Pressure," news release, March 29, 2007.

28. Amnesty International, "Sri Lanka: Attacks on Free Media Put Displaced Civilians at Risk," news release, August 14, 2009.
29. Reporters without Borders, "BBC World Service and Sunday Leader Newspaper Censored," news release, December 12, 2008.
30. "BBC Suspends Sri Lanka FM Reports," British Broadcasting Corporation (BBC), February 9, 2009.
31. "DBS Quits 'Nation' in Dismay," Lanka Dissent, September 6, 2008. Ironically, the Lanka Dissent website suspended publication after the murder of the *Sunday Leader* editor in January 2009.
32. "AP Journalists Barred from Entering East," *Daily Mirror*, May 9, 2008.
33. Ministry of Defence, "Stop Media Treachery against Armed Forces Members!" news release, May 31, 2008.
34. "Gota Lays Down His Law to Journos," *Lakbima News*, June 1, 2008.
35. Free Media Movement, E-Bulletin, July 2007.
36. Human Rights Watch, *War on the Displaced: Sri Lankan Army and LTTE Abuses against Civilians in the Vanni* (New York: Human Rights Watch, February 2009).
37. Catherine Philip, "The Hidden Massacre: Sri Lanka's Final Offensive against Tamil Tigers," *Times* (London), May 29, 2009.
38. UN News Centre, "UN Human Rights Expert Reports Allegations of Torture in Sri Lanka," October 29, 2007.
39. The figure is from the author's own database on violent deaths in Sri Lanka.
40. United Nations, "Special Rapporteur on Torture Concludes Visit to Sri Lanka," news release, October 29, 2007.
41. UN Office for the Coordination of Humanitarian Affairs, "Sri Lanka: Northern Area–Vanni IDP Movements as of 18 June, 2009," ReliefWeb.
42. Internal Displacement Monitoring Centre, "Tens of Thousands Newly Displaced in 2008, Leading to Almost Half a Million IDPs (April 2009)," May 1, 2009.
43. "Sri Lanka: 'Too Many People' at Huge IDP Camp–UN," Integrated Regional Information Networks (IRIN), June 11, 2009.
44. Coalition to Stop the Use of Child Soldiers, "Sri Lanka," in *Child Soldiers: Global Report 2008* (London: Coalition to Stop the Use of Child Soldiers, May 2008).
45. Rupert de Alwis Seneviratne, "Air Force Sergeant Deshapriya Spills the Beans," *Sunday Leader*, August 27, 2007.
46. Amnesty International, "Sri Lanka: Further Information on Ill-Treatment/Fear of Torture/Medical Concern/Arbitrary Detention," July 4, 2008.
47. University Teachers for Human Rights (Jaffna), *Gaps in the Krishanthy Kumarasamy Case: Disappearances & Accountability*, Special Report No. 12 (Jaffna: University Teachers for Human Rights [Jaffna], April 1999).
48. Asian Centre for Human Rights, *South Asia Human Rights Index 2008* (New Delhi: Asian Centre for Human Rights, 2008), 22.
49. International Independent Group of Eminent Persons, "Sri Lanka: The Presidential Commission's Public Inquiry Process So Far Falls Short of International Norms and Standards," news release, March 6, 2008.
50. Human Rights Watch, "Sri Lanka: Human Rights Commission Downgraded," news release, December 17, 2007.
51. Inter-Parliamentary Union, "Women in National Parliaments," Inter-Parliamentary Union home page, September 30, 2009.
52. "Report Recommends Steps to Minimize Conversions," *Sunday Times*, January 25, 2009.

53. United States Commission on International Religious Freedom (USCIRF), "USCIRF Expresses Concern over Broad Prohibitions in Sri Lankan Draft Law," news release, February 4, 2009.
54. W. Todd Akin et al., letter to His Excellency Jaliya Wickramasuriya, Ambassador of Sri Lanka to the U.S., February 5, 2009.
55. International Crisis Group, *Sri Lanka's Judiciary: Politicised Courts, Compromised Rights* (Brussels: International Crisis Group, June 2009).
56. See Basil Fernando, "War against the Sri Lankan Judiciary," *Sri Lanka Lawlessness*, December 22, 2008.
57. Justice for Muttur, "Judicial Procedure before the Magistrate Court." (Paris: Action contre la Faim, 2009)
58. "UNHRC Meeting: Concern over Judicial Independence," *Daily Mirror*, June 14, 2007.
59. "Judiciary Doesn't Do Shoddy Job Like Executive: CJ," *Daily Mirror*, June 30, 2007.
60. UN Human Rights Committee, "Case of Dissanayake," Communication No. 1373/2005, adopted July 22, 2008.
61. "Armed Group That Raided Max TV Had Police Backing–UNP," *Island*, February 23, 2009.
62. Asian Human Rights Commission, "Sri Lanka: The Attack on Sirasa TV an Early Warning of Worse Things to Come," news release, January 7, 2009.
63. Transparency International, *Corruption Perceptions Index 2008* (Berlin: Transparency International, September 22, 2008).
64. P. B. Jayasundera, "Mahinda Chinthana: Vision for a New Sri Lanka," Ministry of Finance and Planning.
65. Transparency International Sri Lanka, *Governance Report 2008* (Colombo: Transparency International Sri Lanka, 2008), 56.
66. Ibid., 18–20.
67. Business Anti-Corruption Portal, "Snapshot: Sri Lanka," Business Anti-Corruption Portal home page.
68. Transparency International Sri Lanka, *Governance Report*, 22.
69. Some of these criticisms have been made by the Asian Human Rights Commission and the Asian Legal Resource Centre.
70. Business Anti-Corruption Portal, "Snapshot: Sri Lanka."
71. Arunja Ranawana, "Sri Lanka: Reporter's Notebook," in *Global Integrity Report 2007* (Washington, D.C.: Global Integrity, 2008).
72. Business Anti-Corruption Portal, "Snapshot: Sri Lanka."
73. Transparency International Sri Lanka, *Forms and Extent of Corruption in Education in Sri Lanka* (Colombo: Transparency International Sri Lanka, May 2009).
74. Open Budget Initiative, "Sri Lanka," in *Open Budget Index 2008* (Washington, D.C.: Open Budget Initiative, 2009).
75. Business Anti-Corruption Portal, "Snapshot: Sri Lanka."

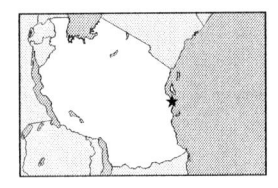

TANZANIA

CAPITAL: Dar es Salaam
POPULATION: 43.7 million
GNI PER CAPITA (PPP): $1,230

SCORES	2006	2010
ACCOUNTABILITY AND PUBLIC VOICE:	3.74	4.09
CIVIL LIBERTIES:	3.75	4.13
RULE OF LAW:	3.05	3.68
ANTICORRUPTION AND TRANSPARENCY:	2.88	3.29

(scores are based on a scale of 0 to 7, with 0 representing weakest and 7 representing strongest performance)

Bruce Heilman

INTRODUCTION

Tanzania, like most African countries, was a colonial creation. European powers demarcated Tanganyika (mainland Tanzania) and Zanzibar's territorial boundaries in line with British and German geopolitics, giving little consideration to existing political, economic, or cultural groupings. The result was a diverse country comprising approximately 140 different African ethnic groups as well as economically important non-African minorities from the Middle East and South Asia. The template for the modern state was European, designed to suit the needs of exploitative colonial occupying powers. African nationalism, meanwhile, embodied a struggle to achieve basic political rights.

With decolonization, modern Tanzania was created by the union of two independent countries, Tanganyika and the islands of Zanzibar. Tanganyika gained independence in December 1961, under a single nationalist movement—the Tanganyika African National Union (TANU) and its visionary leader Julius Nyerere. Zanzibar became independent two years later, divided by two rival nationalist movements, the Afro-Shirazi Party (ASP) and the Zanzibar Nationalist Party (ZNP). Zanzibar's first postcolonial government, formed by the ZNP in December 1963, was quickly overthrown by a revolution that transferred state power to the ASP in January 1964. Amid the uncertainty of revolution and a mainland army mutiny, the modern United Republic of Tanzania was created in April 1964 with the merger of the two entities.

Since the creation of the United Republic, four different presidents, all from the same ruling party, have struggled with the problems of extreme poverty and

---

Bruce Heilman is a Senior Lecturer in the Department of Political Science and Public Administration at the University of Dar es Salaam, Tanzania.

nation building. From Julius Nyerere's *Ujamaa* (African) socialism to the gradual political and economic reforms of Ali Hassan Mwinyi, Benjamin Mkapa, and Jakaya Kikwete, coping with the twin challenges of poverty and national unity has shaped Tanzania's postcolonial record on political rights and civil liberties. While little success has been achieved in alleviating poverty, there has been considerable progress in creating a shared national identity.

With a real gross domestic product per capita of US$123 in 1960, at independence Tanganyika was an impoverished territory in an impoverished East African region.[1] As elsewhere, poverty was widespread and correlated with race, as colonial laws relegated Africans to peasant farming, manual labor, and low level administrative positions. African resentment against the colonial racial-economic order boiled over soon after independence. Trade unions initiated a series of strikes designed to redefine master-servant, racialized employment relations. In 1964 soldiers mutinied, pressing for the removal of British officers; following the restoration of order by British troops, a far-reaching program of political and economic centralization was initiated. The army was reorganized and, together with trade unions and other civil society organizations, was brought under the umbrella of the ruling TANU, which became the sole legal political party on the mainland in 1965. Tanzania embarked on a policy of Ujamaa socialism that stressed social welfare rights and nationalized key economic assets. By 1973 the state forcefully moved peasants into communal Ujamaa villages, and in 1975 TANU, similar to the Chinese Communist party, declared itself to be above the state, placing party cadres in key positions such as regional and district commissioners, parliament, security forces, and government ministries.

Centralizing political and economic power into a ruling party with clear hierarchical lines of authority was one aspect of building a viable national community. For aspiring politicians, loyalty to TANU took precedence over building ethnic power bases. The union was cemented under the one-party state by making the president of Zanzibar one of the two Union vice-presidents and by alternating the Union presidency between the mainland and Zanzibar.[2] Religious diversity, particularly between Tanzania's large and powerful Christian and Muslim communities, was accommodated by an informal alternation of power between Christian and Muslim presidents. In addition, Tanzanians also built a shared civic identity through promoting the Kiswahili language, socialist egalitarian values, and the liberation of southern Africa. From abolishing traditional chiefs and native authorities six months after independence, to the 1977 merger of the mainland's TANU with Zanzibar's ASP to create the current ruling Revolutionary Party (CCM), Tanzania continued its path of unity through centralization. This trend, however, reached its limits by the late 1970s. A string of events, including the expenses associated with the invasion of Idi Amin's Uganda and a severe economic crisis, culminated in the end of Nyerere's presidency in 1985 and the unraveling of Ujamaa socialism.

Starting in 1985 Tanzania embarked on a gradual process of CCM-guided economic and political liberalization. The second Union president, Ali Hassan Mwinyi, was handpicked by Nyerere and CCM elites due to his reputation as a reformer during his brief stint as Zanzibar's president. Hoping to make a transition away from Ujamaa and to secure greater external resources, Mwinyi initiated a period of cooperation with the International Monetary Fund (IMF) and World Bank. A vibrant and independent media took root. Independent societal organizations flourished and opposition political parties were legalized. But the new openness exposed strains. A simmering Zanzibar nationalism came out into the open, as did tensions between the large Christian and Muslim populations. Regionalism and tribalism among Tanzania's African ethnic groups became more pronounced, although still modest compared to the politicized ethnic identities of neighboring countries. State economic management declined, and by the end of Mwinyi's term donors once again began withholding needed aid.

The next change in power came in 1995, when the CCM's Benjamin Mkapa was elected in the country's first multiparty elections in over 30 years. Mkapa presided over a cooling of racial, ethnic, and religious tensions, and economic and political reforms were promised. Mkapa's government, in cooperation with the IMF, World Bank, United Nations, and Western donors, improved macroeconomic oversight, public finances, the civil service, local government, and the legal sector, helping create a decade of economic growth with low inflation that allowed Tanzania's GDP per capita to increase to US$538 by 2009.[3] However, little of the economic prosperity translated into poverty alleviation.[4] Moreover, numerous high-level corruption scandals left Mkapa's successor, CCM's Jakaya Mrisho Kikwete, with a tricky clean-up job that is serving as a crucial test of institutional capacity in Tanzania.

ACCOUNTABILITY AND PUBLIC VOICE 4.09

FREE AND FAIR ELECTORAL LAWS AND ELECTIONS	3.25
EFFECTIVE AND ACCOUNTABLE GOVERNMENT	4.25
CIVIC ENGAGEMENT AND CIVIC MONITORING	5.00
MEDIA INDEPENDENCE AND FREEDOM OF EXPRESSION	3.86

Elections are held every five years, with approximately 18 registered parties contesting political office.[5] For 2010, the National Election Commission (NEC) proposed adding 11 mainland constituencies to the existing 232 single-member, winner-take-all legislative districts. The CCM's overwhelming legislative majority is amplified by 91 appointed members of parliament (MPs), of whom 75 must be women, nominated by political parties according to their proportion of seats in parliament. There is direct voting for the president, with the winner determined by simple majority. Voting is conducted by secret ballot. Independent electoral observers and the media are free to observe the elections and report their findings. Within the Union framework, Zanzibar is a semi-autonomous entity with its own electoral authority, the Zanzibar Electoral Commission (ZEC), responsible for Zanzibar's presidential and House of Representatives elections. The NEC is responsible for the Union elections and it usually delegates the administration of Union balloting in Zanzibar to the ZEC.

While Tanzania has the trappings of an electoral democracy, there is debate over the extent to which elections are free and fair. Both in Zanzibar and on the mainland, opposition parties complain that state officials favor the ruling party. For example, securing the necessary police permission in order to hold a public rally seems to be a simpler task for the CCM than the opposition.[6] The Tanzania Election Monitoring Committee (TEMCO) reported that state administrative officials, such as regional and district commissioners, were actively working on behalf of the ruling party for the 2005 elections.[7]

The reintroduction of multiparty general elections in 1995 has been less problematic on the mainland than in Zanzibar, partially owing to the mainland's less competitive contests. Since 1995, the CCM has increased its percentage of the Union presidential vote and the number of its seats in parliament. In 1995, CCM's Mkapa won 62 percent of the vote, while the ruling party captured 80 percent of the elected seats in parliament. By 2005, CCM's Kikwete captured an overwhelming 80 percent of the presidential vote, while the opposition won only 7 out of 182 mainland parliamentary seats. In both 2000 and 2005, most opposition MPs came from Zanzibar constituencies. Elections on the mainland have been fairly well managed, with election observers, if not always the opposition parties, conceding that results reflect the will of the people.

In contrast to the mainland, multiparty elections in Zanzibar have been fiercely contested and often violent, with the losing party refusing to concede defeat. Following the bloody 1964 revolution through which the ASP took control, no elections were held on Zanzibar until 1984. When competitive elections returned in the 1990s, the islands were again almost evenly divided between two political parties, the CCM and the Civic United Front (CUF). The 1995 and 2000 elections featured violent conflict and credible accusations of electoral irregularities, including inaccurate vote counting in 1995 and ruling party manipulation to ensure victory in 2000.[8]

Following the disputed 1995 Zanzibar elections, the Commonwealth brokered negotiations between CCM and CUF, referred to as *Muafaka,* which centered on the CUF accepting the election results in return for electoral reforms. The CCM and CUF signed a formal agreement just prior to the 2000 contest, but the elections were again mismanaged and the results were not credible, sparking confrontations between security forces and CUF demonstrators that resulted in at least 31 deaths and hundreds of political refugees who fled to Kenya, damaging Tanzania's self-perception as a peaceful and tolerant country. In an effort to stop the violence, the CCM and CUF engaged in another round of Muafaka talks, with President Mkapa serving as the guarantor of the agreement. Although the 2005 election was better managed, the CUF remained unsatisfied, with talks shifting toward the creation of a power-sharing agreement in which the losing party would be incorporated into the government. However, Zanzibar delegates strongly opposed the agreement at the March 2008 CCM National Executive Committee meeting, scuttling the deal. In the absence of good will between the parties, voter registration in Pemba was temporarily suspended in August 2009 amid acts of sabotage, CUF claims of a governmental effort to disenfranchise its supporters, and threats by the Revolutionary Government of Zanzibar—carried on the front pages of the ruling party and government newspapers—to arrest the CUF's general secretary and the likely Zanzibar presidential candidate, Seif Shariff Hamad.[9] In a surprise development, a November 2009 meeting between outgoing Zanzibar President Amani Karume and Hamad produced an informal agreement that reduced tensions between Zanzibar's two main political parties.

Campaign financing favors the incumbent party. The state provides some funding to political parties based on the number of legislators in parliament. In 2009, "constituency development" funds were introduced, giving legislators thousands of dollars to spend on their own "development" priorities.[10] While these resources can be channeled into campaigns, parties and individual candidates are largely responsible for raising their own funds. Given their dominant position in the legislature, the best-financed candidates belong to the CCM. However, where candidates or parties get their resources is unknown and campaign finance is largely unregulated, with opposition party leaders charging that funds involved in the Bank of Tanzania's (BoT) External Payment Account scandal (see Anticorruption and Transparency) were channeled into the CCM's 2005 electoral campaign.[11]

Tanzania has a mixed presidential-parliamentary system, with a dominant executive branch. The president selects his cabinet from the unicameral National Assembly, including a prime minister who must be approved by the parliament. The executive branch has considerable leverage over parliament through the president's position as the leader of the ruling party. The president can make use of party discipline to pass bills and protect executive branch interests. Important political matters, for example, are discussed in internal party forums and after a decision is made, CCM MPs are expected to toe the party line. The party has various committees to resolve disputes and discipline members. Rogue members can be expelled from the party, automatically losing their seats. However, a new legislative assertiveness emerged in 2007, with the questioning of mining contracts and the unearthing of Mkapa-era corruption scandals. A small but outspoken opposition, coupled with dissatisfaction among some CCM MPs over corruption allegations, led to the fall of Prime Minister Edward Lowassa's cabinet in February 2008. In 2009 parliament helped to prevent the parastatal electricity company, Tanzania Electric Supply Company (TANESCO), from buying turbines from a scandal-plagued company called Dowans, indicating the legislature's potential to act as a countervailing power to the presidency. Parliament's new assertiveness has created division within the ruling party, as the old guard felt that such debates and investigations were hurting the CCM. During the party's August 2009 National Executive Committee meeting, a move was made to expel the CCM's leading reformer, Speaker of the National Assembly Samuel Sitta, from the party; in addition, CCM Ideology and Publicity Secretary John Chiligati warned other outspoken reformers to praise former President Mkapa instead of denouncing alleged corruption.[12]

Most civil service posts are filled on the basis of open competition and merit. However, a wide range of top positions are filled by presidential appointment. While competence is a key factor, loyalty to the ruling party and president are also considered. Nor is hiring at lower levels immune from bias. The press and MPs have aired accusations of patronage at preferred state employers like the Ministry of Foreign Affairs and International Cooperation, the Tanzania Revenue Authority, and the Bank of Tanzania. In regard to the BoT, local media alleged that Amatus Liyumba, the former director of personnel and administration, hired family members of top-ranking politicians. Liyumba is currently standing trial for his role in the US$300,000,000 cost overrun for the construction of the BoT Twin Tower headquarters.[13]

Freedom of association and assembly are constitutional rights in Tanzania. The state is tolerant of civic organizations, independent trade unions, and business associations, and the political system is responsive to citizen interests. One area of concern, however, is the influence of donor countries and organizations. Tanzania receives 45 percent of its governmental budget from outside donors,[14] giving Tanzania's development partners considerable political influence with the state and civil society. While donors have worked closely with the government and sought to include civil society and the legislature in the policy process, this degree of dependence raises questions about the balance of democratic accountability between citizens and funders. In addition, the monitoring of aid disbursements is uneven: a revealing recent study on the misuse of donor funds estimated that up to 50 percent of the money for a showpiece multi-year, multimillion dollar natural resources program was lost through corruption and mismanagement.[15]

There is a fairly easy registration process for civil society groups, which may seek and receive support from international sources. By 2007 there were nearly 1,700 fully registered nongovernmental organizations (NGOs) as well as other NGOs registered under the Companies Ordinance Act, an option taken to reduce state interference in their activities.[16] The state has considerable legal powers to control civil society activities under the NGO Act of 2002, which makes it a criminal offense for NGOs to operate without registration. The NGO Act gives the government discretionary power to deregister or refuse to register organizations on the unspecified grounds of "public interest." A number of advocacy NGOs are active on issues involving economic development, social conditions, political rights, and the budget process. Despite the freedom given to civil society, there are tensions: the state encourages organizations to play a "developmental" or service provision role, as opposed to a political or advocacy one. One month prior to the 2005 elections, the minister of education and culture threatened to deregister the education rights group HakiElimu and prohibited it from publishing its studies on education. The minister's threats followed HakiElimu radio and TV commercials highlighting problems with basic education and poverty reduction, topics that were featured as areas of achievement in the CCM's election campaigns. After the elections, HakiElimu tried to restart its activities but the ban was not lifted until after a 2007 meeting between HakiElimu officials and Prime Minister Edward Lowassa.[17] The government also strongly discourages connections between civic organizations and opposition political parties.

Mainland Tanzania has a young, freewheeling, and critical media. Article 18 of the constitution safeguards freedoms of expression and the right to seek, impart, and receive information on important societal issues as well as on the lives and activities of prominent people. The opening of the mainland media sector accompanied the demise of the single-party system during the 1990s.[18] There are no controls over access to information on the internet and in major cities there is easy access to international media via television, the internet, and radio. The 2008 Afrobarometer survey indicates that information is a problem in rural areas, where less than 40 percent of people have access to newspapers and television.[19] There are currently dozens of newspapers, a handful of national television channels, and numerous regional stations.

While the state is generally tolerant of the private media, editors complain about a lack of editorial independence, with the varied personal and political agendas of media owners influencing news coverage.[20] Moreover, colonial and single-party era laws give the state broad leeway in setting the limits of acceptable media practices. For example, the National Security Act (1970) empowers the government, rather than the judiciary or an independent tribunal, to decide what information is classified. Reporting on, possessing, sharing, or publishing classified material is a criminal offense. The government has used its power to declare information classified in self-serving ways, as in 2007, when the Ministry of Minerals and Natural Resources, in the face of allegations of corruption, maintained that contracts with mining companies were classified. The act also allows government officials to declare parts of the country "protected places," thereby restricting journalists' movement.[21] Another single-party era law, the Tanzania Newspaper Act of 1976, gives wide discretionary powers to the Ministry of Information, Culture, and Sports (MICS) to suspend newspapers from publishing for a specified period of time. Journalistic ethics and professionalism are a problem, and the government has used the law to punish what it considers violations of public morality. For example, in February 2009 the MICS threatened three newspapers with suspension for publishing provocative articles about the sex lives of prominent Tanzanians.[22] In light of the explosion in the number of independent media outlets, publishers, editors, and reporters support the creation of independent professional bodies to regulate the media, establish ethical practices, arbitrate disputes, and give accreditation to journalists. The government has been inclined to embed these powers in the state.[23] As of late 2009 a new media bill has not been passed.

Despite the government's wide discretionary power, journalists have not been shy about criticizing the government or powerful people. At times the government has retaliated. For example, the *Mwanahalisi* newspaper was banned for three months in October 2008 for publishing a story alleging a plan to defeat President Kikwete during the ruling party's 2010 internal primary elections. In addition to banning newspapers, the government may threaten to revoke the citizenship of critical journalists, a threat carried out in 2003, to publisher and journalist Jenerali Ulimwengu, and in 2006, to newspaper reporter Richard Mgamba.

In addition to governmental intervention, media conflicts can be dealt with by the NGO Media Council's nonbinding arbitration procedures or in the courts, using civil libel and defamation laws. Disputes between media outlets over issues like the use of unauthorized pictures are often solved through Media Council arbitration. On occasion, politicians and businesspeople bring civil libel suits against newspapers, their owners, or employees. In March 2009, Minister of Home Affairs Lawrence Masha sued three newspapers in Reginald Mengi's Guardian Limited Company for approximately US$2.5 million for articles claiming Masha inappropriately steered a multimillion dollar tender to produce national identification cards to a company called Sagem. Separately, in May 2009 the High Court ordered *Mwanahalisi* to pay Rostam Aziz, an MP and former CCM treasurer, roughly US$2.5 million for an article alleging Aziz was part of a scandal-plagued electricity deal. In August 2009 the High Court awarded Mengi himself approximately US$1 million for articles published in the rival *Changamoto* claiming that Mengi was funding CHADEMA party by-election campaigns. Although such suits are common, journalists and media owners nonetheless seem content to push the boundaries of acceptability and professional ethics. It also remains unclear whether settlement money is actually paid, given the drawn-out appeals process.[24]

Although violence and other forms of intimidation are sometimes directed at reporters, the state has in general respected and protected media workers. In the case of an acid and machete assault on *Mwanahalisi* publisher Saeed Kubenea and editor Ndimara Tegambwage in January 2008, police quickly made arrests and brought the suspects to trial. Nonetheless, the 2008 African Media Barometer Report complains that the government favors "friendly" media for advertisements and that self-censorship is widely practiced by editors and reporters seeking to avoid offending their owners or the state.[25]

In Zanzibar the situation is worse for media than on the mainland, though there are indications of improvement. Media outlets operating in Zanzibar fall under Zanzibar law and the Revolutionary Government's jurisdiction. The opening up of the island's media sector has been partial and the press remains smaller, less independent, and less vibrant than on the mainland. Television

Zanzibar is under government control, as is the radio station Sauti ya Tanzania-Zanzibar and the newspaper *Zanzibar Leo*. The small private radio stations and newspapers that exist often have close connections to ruling party politicians. Critical media face harassment: Reporters Without Borders notes that the Revolutionary Government is not tolerant of "the independent press, accusing it of being 'a threat to national unity' at the first sign of criticism."[26] There are indications that the Zanzibar government is interested in reform. The Media Council has a branch on the islands, new press clubs are operating, and an editors' forum was created in 2009.

CIVIL LIBERTIES 4.13

PROTECTION FROM STATE TERROR, UNJUSTIFIED IMPRISONMENT, AND TORTURE	3.25
GENDER EQUITY	4.33
RIGHTS OF ETHNIC, RELIGIOUS, AND OTHER DISTINCT GROUPS	4.50
FREEDOM OF CONSCIENCE AND BELIEF	5.33
FREEDOM OF ASSOCIATION AND ASSEMBLY	3.25

According to the constitution, all Tanzanians are equal under the law and citizens are protected from human rights abuses. Nonetheless, there are allegations of abuse and the use of unwarranted violence by the police. Newspapers often carry stories of suspicious police killings, like the fatal shootings of a Tunduma businessman in June 2009 and a taxi driver in Dar es Salaam in March 2009. In both cases, the press reported anti-police protests after the shootings, reflecting anger and fears among the public that the police would not fairly investigate the incidents.[27] Another well-publicized police shooting involved the September 2007 killing of 14 Kenyans alleged to have been carrying out a bank robbery. The NGO Legal and Human Rights Centre (LHRC) found the police account of events implausible and highlighted the need for an independent investigation, which has not yet occurred.[28] Incidents of torture also generally occur in the context of undisciplined police actions; torture is not applied systematically for political purposes.

Prison overcrowding is a major problem. According to the LHRC, in 2007 Tanzania possessed the capacity to house 22,669 prisoners but held 46,416, nearly half of whom were in remand. The government has attempted to alleviate prison overcrowding through means including a presidential pardon of 7,674 prisoners in 2008, construction of new facilities, and reductions in trial delays. Another effort involved the creation of the Probation and Community Services Division in 2008 to allow for non-incarceration sentences. Regardless of state efforts to improve conditions, the problem of long periods of pretrial detention remains, effectively serving as a punishment prior to conviction.

Cases of heavy-handed actions by district commissioners are not uncommon and often go unpunished. For example, a district commissioner accused of leading the October 2001 destruction of Nyamuma village was never disciplined and merely transferred to another district by President Kikwete in 2006.[29] Another case involved the Bukoba district commissioner, retired Colonel Albert Mnali, who ordered the caning of over a dozen teachers in front of their students in February 2009. After a media outcry including condemnations by human rights activists and the teachers' union, Mnali was removed from his position, though no criminal charges were filed.[30]

Those whose rights have been abused by authorities have a number of options through which to seek redress. The governmental Commission for Human Rights and Good Governance (CHRAGG), operational since June 2001, receives complaints regarding land use and ownership, the conduct of police and prisons officers, labor relations, and violations of rights of vulnerable groups. Despite the commission's positive contributions, it suffers from several problems, including a lack of autonomy, as the president appoints commissioners and has ultimate authority over commission actions; a lack of presence, since with only five offices nationwide it is difficult for many citizens to present their grievances; and the lack of sanctioning power, as the commission essentially makes recommendations that the government may ignore.[31] In addition to the governmental CHRAGG, complaints can be taken to a number of NGOs working on rights and governance issues.

The state is committed to protecting the rights of citizens from abuses by nonstate actors such as criminals, terrorists, and mobs. The 2008 Afrobarometer opinion poll reported that while crime is a concern of Tanzanians, over 90 percent had no or only minor crime-related problems during the past year. In addition to the police, there are hundreds of private security firms, local government militias, neighborhood watches, and vigilante groups called *Sungusungu* that often operate with state approval. Mob justice is common and often lethal. The April 1, 2009 killing of two suspected robbers by 400 people who overran an isolated police outpost in Rural Shinyanga District illustrates fundamental problems with the criminal justice system and the application of due process.[32] The LHRC noted that the police recorded 307 deaths from mob justice from January to October 2007.

Mob justice is also directed against suspected witches, usually elderly people in impoverished areas of western Tanzania. The LHRC quoted the Mwanza regional police commander as saying 238 witchcraft-related killings took place in his region from 2005 to 2007.[33] Another vexing witchcraft-related problem is the targeting of albinos for body parts to concoct potions to bring good luck and wealth. According to the police, 46 albinos were killed and dozens maimed from June 2007 to January 2008.[34] Despite a well-publicized government campaign to stop the attacks, they continued, prompting a frustrated Prime Minister Mizengo Pinda in January 2009 to ban the practice of "traditional healing," a move that stirred controversy.[35] In a further attempt to protect albinos, the government carried out "opinion polls" in western Tanzania where people were asked to place the names of criminals and those they suspected to be targeting albinos into a box, to be analyzed later by the police.

Human trafficking in Tanzania primarily involves poor children and women from rural areas sent to urban zones to engage in domestic labor, usually through informal networks and with false promises of education or good jobs. Women and children are also trafficked to work in commercial agriculture, in artisan mining, or to work as prostitutes. There are laws against the sexual exploitation of children and the Tanzanian government has worked with the U.S. government and international NGOs to address the problem.[36] In 2008 the government passed the Anti-trafficking in Persons Act and provided specialized training to police. However, the LHRC noted that the act conflated trafficking with sexual exploitation, thus leaving out serious problems like child labor in domestic employment.

The Tanzanian government is committed to gender equality. Tanzania is a party to a number of regional and international human rights treaties that protect women's rights. The government has a standing policy of giving preference in state hiring to female candidates when the qualifications of male and female applicants are equal. In addition, 23 percent of parliamentary seats are reserved for women, and the president has attempted to increase the number of women in key political and administrative positions such as ministers and regional and district commissioners. According to the Millennium Development Goals Monitor, Tanzania has a chance of meeting the goal of promoting gender equality and empowering women by ensuring equal access to education at all levels by 2015.[37]

In recent years the state has modified laws and worked with community groups to reduce harmful cultural practices such as female genital mutilation, which the LHRC estimates has declined in all regions of Tanzania except Singida. However, an antiquated marriage law and traditional practices regarding domestic violence, marriage, divorce, and inheritance infringe on women's rights. Marriage, divorce, and inheritance are covered by one of three legal codes: civil law, Islamic law, or customary law, all of which, according to the LHRC, discriminate against women. Multiple marriages are legal for men but not women, and men shoulder almost no legal responsibility for the care of children out of wedlock. In part due to traditional customs, domestic violence against women is widely accepted.[38]

The rights of Tanzania's ethnic, racial, and religious groups are respected by the state and other societal identity groups. While Tanzania deserves its reputation as a tolerant society, one problem area concerns "indigenous people," or ethnic groups that have maintained their traditional cultures, including a mode of production based on pastoralism and hunting. These groups, which include the Masai, Barbaig, Hadzabe, Ndorobo, Sandwe, Iraqw, and Gorowa, are considered backwards and tend to be socially marginalized. Conflicts have erupted with farmers, investors, and the government as traditional areas for migration and cattle grazing are closed off and claimed for commercial and peasant farms, tourism, and commercial hunting. For example, in 2007 the government issued a license for traditional Hadzabe land to a private commercial hunting company. After community leaders and NGOs protested, the private company backed out in 2008, only for a mining company to conduct unauthorized geological surveys in the same area.[39] In June 2009, the Masai and the government clashed over forced evictions from land allocated to the United Arab Emirates-based Ortello Business Corporation, a commercial hunting company.[40] Peasant-pastoralist disputes occasionally turn violent, as in Kilosa District, Morogoro Region, when six people were killed and nearly 1,000 fled their homes in October 2008, nearly eight years after a similar deadly conflict in the district.[41]

Tanzania's constitution protects freedom of worship, "including the freedom to change [one's] religion or faith," and ensures that "the affairs and management of religious bodies shall not be part of the activities of the state authority." The secular state fits well with Christianity's firmly entrenched separation of earthly and spiritual affairs. However, while many Muslims support secularism, Islam's holistic emphasis on the unity of religious, political, and economic life has brought up a tricky political problem concerning *Kadhi* (Islamic) courts. On the Tanzanian mainland, magistrates draw on Islamic law, African traditional practices, or civil laws in dealing with marriage, divorce, and inheritance. This has created a situation where magistrates, who often are not Muslims and may not be knowledgeable regarding Sharia, try to apply Islamic law, usually in consultation with BAKWATA (Muslim Council of Tanzania) authorities. Some Islamic activists have demanded that Kadhi courts be presided over by Muslim legal scholars and funded by the state, as is the case in predominantly Islamic Zanzibar. This demand is opposed by Christian organizations, who claim it would violate the secular nature of the Union constitution.

The state has paid scant attention to the needs of disabled people. Few schools or health centers, including hospitals, provide needed services, buildings and public transportation lack wheelchair access, and despite legal guarantees, there is little practical recourse for disabled people subjected to discrimination. However, civil society advocacy of disabled rights has attracted state attention. The LHRC notes that in 2007 the government initiated a survey to establish the number of disabled citizens and to better understand the problems they face. In 2008 the state began a review of laws, with the aim of bringing domestic law in line with international conventions regarding the disabled.[42]

Trade unions fall under the Employment and Labor Relations Act 2004, and the state respects workers' right to freely organize. However, the right to strike is severely limited and is forbidden entirely in many public services like health, telecommunications, civil aviation, and electricity. The state can forbid strikes for vague reasons, such as endangering the life and health of the population. Legal strikes are preceded by a lengthy and complicated mediation process, and organizers of "illegal" strikes are victimized by employers or the state. For example, during an October 2007 strike at Barrick's Bulyanhulu mine, 1,000 strikers were fired and later allowed to reapply for their positions, giving the employer an easy opportunity to victimize organizers.[43]

Freedom of assembly has been a problematic issue in Tanzania. The police have wide powers to declare meetings and demonstrations "unlawful," which they used to break up an "illegal" teachers strike and university demonstrations in 2008, arresting and briefly detaining organizers. On occasion, the police have prevented opposition political party meetings and demonstrations. The state has also reacted against those seeking to demonstrate when foreign dignitaries visit the country, such as when the Pemba Elders were firmly warned not to demonstrate during UN Secretary General Ban-Ki Moon's February 2009 visit.[44]

RULE OF LAW   3.68

INDEPENDENT JUDICIARY	3.40
PRIMACY OF RULE OF LAW IN CIVIL AND CRIMINAL MATTERS	3.40
ACCOUNTABILITY OF SECURITY FORCES AND MILITARY TO CIVILIAN AUTHORITIES	4.25
PROTECTION OF PROPERTY RIGHTS	3.67

The Tanzanian constitution guarantees judicial independence. Judges are appropriately trained, appointed by the president in consultation with an independent Judicial Service Commission, have secure tenure until retirement at age 60, and are promoted and dismissed in a fair and unbiased manner. This gives the higher-level courts considerable independence. Judicial review exists, but is mitigated by the practice of slight modifications that honor the letter but not the spirit of court declarations that given laws are unconstitutional. The judiciary is made up of primary and resident district courts, the High Court, the Court of Appeal, and the Constitutional Court. The primary and resident and district courts deal with minor civil and criminal offences; magistrates in those bodies are not always adequately trained as a law degree is not required. The High Court deals with serious criminal offenses and civil offenses involving large sums of money. The Constitutional Court is concerned with disputes between the Union and Zanzibar governments. There are also special tribunals dealing with land and various commercial and administrative matters, as well as a military court. It is possible for citizens and civil society groups to challenge the government, as seen in the April 2009 decision to overturn the government's 1997 deregistration of the National Women's Council (BAWATA) that included declaring parts of the Societies Act unconstitutional.[45]

The criminal justice system suffers from serious problems with corruption and delays. The LHRC noted that corruption "has caused denial of access to justice to the majority of Tanzanians, particularly the poor. Corruption is so manifestly entrenched and institutionalized that the judiciary, the police, and the entire justice system is wallowing under the trenches of corruption."[46] In addition to biasing court proceedings, corruption leads to delays as police investigators and prosecutors seek bribes from defendants or plaintiffs to speed up or delay proceedings. Corruption is especially problematic in the lower courts, where poor pay tempts magistrates and court clerks to delay proceedings in order to solicit bribes. Aside from low salaries, the LHRC mentions that the number of judges, magistrates, prosecutors, and police investigators are insufficient to handle caseloads. Moreover, as of mid-2008 only 1,071 lawyers were listed on the roll of advocates—very few of whom practiced in rural areas—with approximately 50 more qualifying to practice each year. Indigent Tanzanians are therefore only provided counsel by the state in murder and treason cases. Some civil society organizations provide legal clinics, but access to legal advice remains a problem.

Tanzania's police force is administered by the Ministry of Home Affairs. As of 2009, police undertake criminal investigations and pass on their findings to prosecutors, who decide whether to bring cases to court. Despite the recent separation of prosecutors from the police, the president still appoints all top police and prosecutorial positions, giving the executive considerable influence over whether to investigate allegations and to press criminal charges.

Although the occurrence of prosecutions of public officials indicates an effort by the government to respect citizen rights, many Tanzanians perceive that the preferential treatment accorded to the powerful, wealthy, and well connected creates a de facto two-tiered system of rights. At the top, the Tanzanian constitution offers presidents, both serving and retired, immunity from criminal and civil proceedings. Lower down, several cases illustrate the causes of resentment against the system's functioning. In one, Abdallah Zombe, a high-ranking police officer, and 12 other officers were acquitted in August 2009 for the 2006 murder of a taxi driver and three gemstone dealers,[47] sparking protests in the victims' home village. The case was brought only after President Kikwete intervened, ordering a special probe when media reports contradicted police accounts of the 2006 killings. Similarly, current MP and former attorney general Andrew Chenge, who killed two women after he smashed his car into a scooter in March 2009,[48] was charged with reckless driving but freed from jail pending trial. In August 2009 bus drivers protested his soft treatment compared to a multi-year prison sentence given to a bus driver convicted of killing a person after bursting a tire.[49] In another case, well-known politician Ukiwaona Ditopile Mzuzuri faced charges after shooting bus driver Hasani Mbonde in the head after a minor accident in 2006. Ditopile was initially charged with murder, but—with the help of a defense team led by a powerful CCM MP—the charge was reduced to manslaughter, allowing Ditopile to gain bail; proceedings continued at a leisurely pace until his death from natural causes in April 2008.[50] Five days of nationwide prisoner protests followed Ditopile's release on bail; his case was viewed as an indictment of a system in which suspects were at times subject to cases lasting a decade or more.[51]

The military, according to a 2005 Afrobarometer survey, is the most trusted state institution.[52] Following the 1964 mutiny, the army was disbanded and replaced by a "peoples' army" linked to citizens through militia training and embedded into the ruling party and state. While the military formally severed its previously close ties to the CCM with the reintroduction of multiple parties, in practice the links between party, state, and military remain strong. President Kikwete, for instance, moved back and forth between the party and the military over several decades, retiring as a military colonel in 1992, when a constitutional change prohibited members of the security forces from being political party members.[53]

Since making the transition from a centrally-planned economy to a market-based system, the principal of private property has been strongly supported by the state. People are free, by themselves or in association with others, to start private businesses. The 2009 Index of Economic Freedom ranked Tanzania 93rd out of 179 countries and 11th out of 46 African countries. According to the index, private property rights were threatened by corruption, especially in the judicial system, which could not be relied upon to enforce contracts or fairly adjudicate disputes in a timely fashion. Tanzania did better than the global average for tax rates, freedom of trade, financial and investment freedom, and limited government involvement in the economy.[54] In Zanzibar, one infringement on private property is the Clove Act of 1985, which forces clove farmers to sell to the Zanzibar government's clove marketing board. Violations of the Clove Act are criminal offenses and the Revolutionary Government actively suppresses clove smuggling.

The move from communal-based land ownership to a private property system has brought considerable conflict. Customary and communal village land rights, which lack formal title deeds, exist alongside documented private land ownership. Special land tribunals created by law in 2002 have begun operations and are being extended throughout the country. However, different land tenure systems and a deficit of legal documentation, coupled with corruption, hinder solutions and generate considerable conflict. Land conflicts occur between business investors and occupants of informal settlements, large international mining companies and artisan miners and villagers, individuals contesting plots of land for houses, and pastoralists and peasant farmers. There is evidence that interests of the economically powerful and politically well connected take precedence in such cases.[55]

ANTICORRUPTION AND TRANSPARENCY   3.29

    ENVIRONMENT TO PROTECT AGAINST CORRUPTION   3.25
    PROCEDURES AND SYSTEMS TO ENFORCE ANTICORRUPTION LAWS   3.00
    EXISTENCE OF ANTICORRUPTION NORMS, STANDARDS,
        AND PROTECTIONS   3.25
    GOVERNMENTAL TRANSPARENCY   3.67

Discussion of Tanzania's severe corruption problem dominates newspaper stories and parliamentary debates. The 2008 Transparency International Corruption Perceptions Index ranked Tanzania 102nd out of 180 countries.[56] Numerous criminal court cases and investigations involving officials ranging from local functionaries to former cabinet ministers indicate a serious problem with separating public and private interests—as well as at least some commitment by the state to combat such abuses.

While the level of bureaucratic red tape is not excessive, registration requirements and controls provide local and low-level officials with ample opportunities to solicit bribes. At higher levels of government, the use of state resources to enrich well-connected politicians, their business associates, and powerful multinational companies at the expense of ordinary citizens have led to numerous accusations of bribes, kickbacks, nepotism, patronage, and financial fraud. Several high-profile government scandals have surfaced in recent years. The former director of the Bank of Tanzania is currently on trial for inflating the cost of construction of the bank's headquarters, while four other bank officials were charged with inflating the cost of printing new bank notes.[57] In January 2008, Central Bank governor Daudi Ballali was removed from his post after an international audit determined that 22 fictitious companies had received funds from the bank's External Payment Accounts.[58] In addition, Britain's Serious Fraud Office has implicated several Tanzanian officials for taking bribes in connection with the 2002 government purchase of military radar equipment from the British firm BAE Systems.[59] Finally, high-level government officials, including former prime minister Edward Lowassa, have been accused of using their power to violate government tendering procedures and force TANESCO to sign unfair contracts with "briefcase" companies such as Independent Power Tanzania Limited, Richmond Development Company, and Dowans Tanzania Ltd. To many Tanzanians, these incidents reveal a political class that has commoditized and sold their public responsibilities for private economic and political gain, while undermining the state's ability to act as a dependable custodian of the economy.

Public officials must declare their assets before taking office. However, because access to this information is tightly controlled, judgment of the system's effectiveness is difficult. The 2007 Prevention and Combating Corruption Act strengthened the legal regime regulating corruption by expanding the list of corruption offenses to include contract and procurement fraud, embezzlement and misappropriation of funds, abuse of power, and bribery.[60] Nevertheless, enforcement remains a problem. The 2007 act also renamed, reorganized, and strengthened the anticorruption bureau. Signaling a greater emphasis on criminal prosecutions as opposed to the educational efforts associated with President Mkapa, the word "Combating" was added to what is now known as the Prevention and Combating of Corruption Bureau (PCCB). The PCCB was also given increased powers to conduct investigations and take action against corrupt officials and now operates throughout the country. In recent years, the

PCCB has increased its efforts to receive and respond to complaints lodged by victims of corruption, and its greater presence throughout the country has improved the ability of citizens to pursue their rights. Its efforts have been complemented by those of the CHRAGG, which has expanded its anticorruption mandate to include the receipt of complaints.

The PCCB has achieved some success prosecuting cases involving public sector companies and at the local government level. However, the finding of nothing untoward in a 2007 investigation of TANESCO's dealings with Richmond raised questions about the bureau's competence and independence. After a November 2007 special parliamentary committee report uncovered numerous corruption-related problems with TANESCO's Richmond contract, there were calls from parliament, civil society, and in the press for PCCB Director General Edward Hoseah to resign. He did not, but Prime Minister Edward Lowassa and two other ministers did due to their alleged roles in the scandal. The unwillingness of the PCCB to pursue corruption cases against high-profile politicians suggests insufficient independence. While the body is nominally autonomous and its board includes representatives from both civil society and the private sector, it remains accountable to the executive branch, which exerts considerable influence over its activities.

The media report widely on corruption and constitute an essential force in the fight against corruption, and media that report on official corruption enjoy less government interference under Kikwete than under his predecessors. However, the personal and political agendas of media owners and editors sometimes bias or distort corruption coverage. For example, Reginald Mengi, the executive chairman of the IPP media conglomerate, has utilized his outlets to aggressively cover corruption stories concerning a group of five businesspeople that he has labeled the "corruption sharks."[61] In response, one of the targets, former CCM treasurer and current MP Rostam Aziz, has employed his own media outlets to retaliate by featuring numerous corruption stories concerning Mengi and his business dealings (see Accountability and Public Voice).[62] The 2007 act also improved the legal environment to protect whistleblowers from retaliation, though its provisions are not always observed in practice.[63]

The level of corruption in the education sector remains substantial, but the state has increased its efforts to address the issue. Both monetary bribes and sexual favors are sometimes paid to teachers or school officials in order to influence grading and admissions. In addition, there have been repeated instances of national exam leakages and alterations of official certificates. The state has carried out thorough investigations into the exam leakages and reorganized the national body responsible for national exams.

The transparency of government operations has improved in recent years, but much remains to be done to increase the availability of government information. Although Kikwete promised in 2006 to grant citizens a legal right to information as part of a comprehensive media law, intensive civil society advocacy by groups such as the Freedom of Information Bill Coalition have yet to bear fruit.[64] In the absence of such a law, access to information remains restricted. It is estimated that 90 percent of all government documents remain classified.[65]

Past improvements to the budget-making process have been sustained under Kikwete. The annual budget proposal is submitted to parliamentary committees for review after receiving input from donors and civil society members, and is released to the public. However, the Open Budget Initiative awards Tanzania a score of just 35 percent in its 2008 edition due to the incompleteness of released information.[66] While expenditures are reviewed by the National Audit Office, efforts to better manage government funds have failed to achieve measurable results. In a July 2009 speech, Kikwete stated that up to 30 percent of the budget is "eaten" by senior government officials.[67]

Although official tendering procedures are designed to ensure competition, opacity characterizes the system in practice. This is especially true in the extractive industries, where the process is cloaked in complete secrecy and the disclosure of contract-related information can result in legal action. For example, in 2006, MP Zitto Kabwe was suspended from his position after he revealed the details of a government mining contract.[68] As mentioned above, the government often cites national security issues in order to avoid public debate or disclosure. The World Bank's 2006 Enterprise Survey revealed that 43 percent of foreign companies expect to give a gift in order to obtain a contract.[69]

RECOMMENDATIONS

- End ministers' legal authority to ban media outlets or deregister media and civil society organizations. Independent media and civil society tribunals should be created for handling disputes with the option to appeal their decisions to the courts.
- Increase the autonomy of the Commission for Human Rights and Good Governance, and grant it the authority to initiate civil and criminal cases.
- Appoint the Director of Public Prosecution, Director of the Prevention and Combating Corruption Bureau, the Director of Criminal Investigations, and the Inspector General of Police to five-year fixed terms to reduce influence of the executive branch over their activities.
- In order to instill confidence in the judicial system, focus reforms on reducing corruption in the lower courts and reducing delays in the adjudication of cases.
- Implement the *Muafaka* power-sharing agreement as a means to reducing political tensions and finding common political ground toward the achievement of meaningful democratic reforms on the islands.
- Protect the interests of women and children by implementing the long-anticipated reform of the 1971 Marriage Act and other personal status laws.

NOTES

For URLs and endnote hyperlinks, please visit the *Countries at the Crossroads* homepage at http://freedomhouse.org/template.cfm?page=139&edition=8.

1. Alan Heston, Robert Summers, and Bettina Aten, *Penn World Table Version 6.2* (Philadelphia: Center for International Comparisons of Production, Income, and Prices, University of Pennsylvania, 2006).
2. With the dismantling of the one-party state, the current practice is to have the Union presidential candidate come from the more populous mainland, while the Union vice presidential candidate comes from Zanzibar. Under the multiparty constitution, the Zanzibar president is no longer a Union vice president.
3. In terms of GDP per capita for 2009, Tanzania's US$538 was still lower than Kenya's US$829, but it surpassed Uganda's US$483 and Burundi's US$169 (GDP per capita constant prices US dollars). See International Monetary Fund (IMF), *2008 World Economic Outlook Database* (Washington, D.C.: IMF, 2008).
4. Johannes Hoogeveen et al., "The Challenge of Reducing Poverty," in *Sustaining and Sharing Economic Growth in Tanzania*, ed. Robert Utz (Washington D.C.: World Bank, 2008); Research and Analysis Working Group of the United Republic of Tanzania, *Poverty and Human Development Report 2005* (Dar es Salaam: Mkuki na Nyota Publishers, 2005).
5. Office of the Registrar of Political Parties, "A List of All National Leaders of Political Parties with Permanent Registration," Office of the Registrar of Political Parties, Government of Tanzania home page.
6. Ambrose Wantaigwa, "Police Cancel CHADEMA Demo," *Citizen* (Tanzania), March 26, 2009.
7. Tanzania Election Monitoring Committee (TEMCO), *The 2005 Elections in Tanzania* (Dar es Salaam: TEMCO, 2006), 75–77.
8. TEMCO, *The 2000 General Elections in Tanzania* (Dar es Salaam: TEMCO, 2001); Zanzibar Election Monitoring Group (ZEMOG), *Uchaguzi wa Zanzibar 1995: Taarifa Kamili ya Zemog* (Zanzibar: ZEMOG, 1995).
9. Mwinyi Sadallah, "Mashambulizi ya Mabomu yarrindina kisiwani Pemba," *Nipashe*, August 5, 2009; Mwanne Mashugu, "Pemba hatari tupu," *Tanzania Daima*, August 6, 2009; Beatus Kagashe, "CUF Disputes Registration Data," *Citizen*, August 21, 2009; Juma Mohammed, "SMZ yakusudia kumshitaki Seif," *Uhuru*, August 28, 2009; Juma Mohammed, "SMZ yajiandaa kumshitaki Seif," *Habari Leo*, August 2, 2009.
10. Paul Dotto, "Parliament Passes CDCF Bill," *Citizen*, August 5, 2009.
11. "Lipumba adai Rais Kikwete hawezi kukwepa kashfa za ufisadi," *Mwananchi*, September 10, 2009.
12. "Spirited Bid to Have Sitta Expelled from CCM Fails," *Citizen*, August 18, 2009; Faraja Jube, "CCM Moves to Rein in Outspoken MPs," *Citizen*, August 19, 2009.
13. "Liyumba Revealed," *Sunday Observer* (Tanzania), March 1, 2009; Mike Mande and Joseph Mwamunyange, "Bank of Tanzania Gave Jobs to Kin of Former Presidents Mkapa, Mwinyi," *East African* (Kenya), May 19, 2008.
14. PricewaterhouseCoopers Tanzania, *Navigating the Course–Budget 2009/2010: Tanzania Budget Review Commentary* (Dodoma: PricewaterhouseCoopers, 2009).
15. Eirik G. Jansen, *Does Aid Work? Reflections on a Natural Resources Programme in Tanzania*, U4 Anti-Corruption Resource Centre Issue 2 (Bergen: Chr. Michelsen Institute, 2009).
16. Legal and Human Rights Centre (LHRC) and Zanzibar Legal Service Centre (ZLSC), *Tanzania Human Rights Report 2007* (Dar es Salaam and Zanzibar: LHRC and ZLSC, 2007).

17. Emmanuel Kihaule, "Government, Precisely What's Wrong with HakiElimu?" *Guardian* (Tanzania), April 18, 2006; Judica Tarimo, "HakiElimu Sticks to Its Guns," *Guardian* (Tanzania), April 7, 2006; HakiElimu, *Annual Report 2007* (Dar es Salaam: HakiElimu, 2007); LHRC and ZLSC, *Tanzania Human Rights Report 2007*.
18. Audax Kweyamba, "The Impact of the Media on the Democratization Process in the 1990s" (MA diss., University of Dar es Salaam, 1999).
19. Zenobia Ismail and Paul Graham, "Citizens of the World? Africans, Media, and Telecommunications," Afrobarometer Briefing Paper No. 69, May 2009.
20. Media Council of Tanzania, "Media Heads Set for Management Course," *Media Watch Newsletter*, no. 113 (August 2009).
21. LHRC, *The Human Calamity of the Evictions at Nyamuma-Serengeti: Legal and Human Rights Implications* (Dar es Salaam: LHRC, 2006), 15–18.
22. Boniface Meena, "Mkuchika kutoa tamko la Magazeti," *Mwananchi*, February 25, 2009.
23. Media Council of Tanzania, *The Stakeholders' Proposal on Media Services Bill 2008* (Dodoma: Media Council of Tanzania, 2008).
24. Bernard James, "Court Orders Paper to Pay Rostam Sh3bn," *Citizen*, May 13, 2009; Dunstan Bahai, "Masha Ayashitaki Magazeti," *Mtanzania*, March 30, 2009; Faustine Kapama, "Rostam Sues Mwanahalisi for 3bn/-," *Daily News* (Tanzania), April 28, 2008; James Mwendapole, "Changamoto watakiwa kumlipa Mengi bilioni 1.5/-," *Nipashe*, August 25, 2009.
25. Fesmedia Africa, "Tanzania," in *The 2008 African Media Barometer* (Windhoek: Friedrich-Ebert-Stiftung, 2008).
26. Reporters Without Borders (RSF), "Tanzania," in *Annual Report 2006* (Paris: RSF, 2006), 33; RSF, "Press Freedom Index 2008"; RSF, "Zanzibar Government Bans Leading Columnist," news release, June 13, 2005; RSF, "Zanzibar Authorities Continue to Harass Independent Weekly after One Year," news release, December 2, 2004; RSF, "Zanzibar Authorities Continue to Harass Banned Weekly's Former Editor," news release, August 9, 2006.
27. Nyang'oro Geofrey na Festo Polea, "Tume Kuchunguza Majuaji ya Dereva," *Mwananchi*, March 28, 2009; Ester Macha, "Vita Tunduma," *Majira*, June 30, 2009; Ester Macha, "Vurugu Tumduma: Watu 88 watiwa mbaroni," *Majira*, July 1, 2009.
28. LHRC and ZLSC, *Tanzania Human Rights Report 2007*.
29. LHRC, *The Human Calamity of the Evictions at Nyamuma-Serengeti*.
30. "Tanzania Teacher Whipping Move," British Broadcasting Corporation (BBC), February 14, 2008.
31. LHRC and ZLSC, *Tanzania Human Rights Report 2008* (Dar es Salaam: LHRC and ZLSC, 2009).
32. Mohammed Mhina, "Raia Wavamia Polisi, Watuhumiwa 2 Wauawa," *Majira*, April 2, 2009.
33. LHRC and ZLSC, *Tanzania Human Rights Report 2007*.
34. Karl Lyimo, "We Can't Vote out Albino Killings by Secret Ballot," *East African* (Kenya), March 21, 2009.
35. Donald McNeil, "Tanzania: Government Bans Traditional Healers to Try to Save Lives of Albinos," *New York Times*, January 26, 2009.
36. International Organization for Migration, "Tanzania," Activities, home page, June 2009; Embassy of the United States–Tanzania, "Tanzania and the United States Partner to Combat Human Trafficking," press release, November 8, 2007.
37. Millennium Development Goals Monitor, "United Republic of Tanzania Profile," home page.

38   LHRC and ZLSC, *Tanzania Human Rights Report 2008*.
39   Ibid.
40   Feminist Activist Coalition (FEMACT), "FEMACT Loliondo Findings," news release, September 23, 2009.
41   Bernard Baha et al., *The Price of a Malfunctioning Land Management System in Tanzania: A Fact Finding Report on the Dispute between Pastoralists and Peasants in Kilosa District* (Dar es Salaam: HAKIARDHI, November 2008).
42   LHRC and ZLSC, *Tanzania Human Rights Report 2008*; LHRC and ZLSC, *Tanzania Human Rights Report 2007*.
43   International Trade Union Confederation (ITUC), "Tanzania," in *2008 Annual Survey of Trade Union Rights* (Brussels: ITUC, 2008).
44   "Ban Ki-moon's Visit Should Go Ahead Smoothly," *Daily News*, February 25, 2009; Salima Said and Mkinga Mkinga, "Pemba Elders Arrested after Secession Demand," *Citizen*, May 13, 2008.
45   Bernard James, "Court: BAWATA Deregistration Illegal," *Citizen*, April 3, 2009.
46   LHRC, *Justice Watch Annual Report 2007* (Dar es Salaam: LHRC, 2008).
47   In the press, Zombe was also accused of torturing criminal suspects associated with a 2001 US$2 million armed robbery at Mwalimu Julius Kamabarage Nyerere Airport. See Rosemary Mirondo, "Zombo Case: Court Told of 'False' Shootings," *Guardian* (Tanzania), June 10, 2008; Bernard James, "Why They Were Set Free," *Citizen*, August 18, 2009.
48   Festo Polea, "Chenge Agonga, Aua: Kova Aunda Tume Kuchunguza" *Mwananchi*, March 28, 2009; Restuta James, "Chenge Afikishwa Kortini kwa Mauaji," *Nipashe*, March 31, 2009.
49   "Mgomo wa Mabasi Kizaazaa," *Mwananchi*, August 15, 2009.
50   Mwajabu Mleche, "Ditopile Allegedly Guns Down Daladala Driver," *Guardian* (Tanzania), November 6, 2006; Rosemary Mirondo and Hellen Mwango, "Ditopile Sobs As Charge Lowered," *Guardian* (Tanzania), February 16, 2007; Njonanje Samwel, "Ex-RC Ditopile Mzuzuri Is Dead," *Guardian* (Tanzania), April 21, 2008.
51   LHRC, *Justice Watch Annual Report 2007* (Dar es Salaam: LHRC, 2008); LHRC and ZLSC, *Tanzania Human Rights Report 2008*; The delay in cases was also singled out as a major problem by newly appointed Chief Justice Augustino Ramadhani, who confirmed that some cases take over 10 years before a judgment is reached. See P. Machira, "JK Appoints Seven Women Judges," *Citizen*, May 29, 2008.
52   Afrobarometer, *Summary of Results: Round 3 Afrobarometer Survey in Tanzania* (Legon-Accra: Afrobarometer, 2006).
53   "Mjue Jakaya Kikwete," JakayaKikwete.com.
54   Heritage Foundation and *Wall Street Journal* (WSJ), "Tanzania," in *Index of Economic Freedom 2009* (Washington, D.C./New York: Heritage Foundation/WSJ, 2009).
55   LHRC, *Tanzania Human Rights Report 2008*.
56   Transparency International, *2008 Corruption Perceptions Index* (Berlin: Transparency International, September 22, 2008).
57   John Rosina, "Four in Sh100 Billion BOT Scam," *Citizen*, September 16, 2009.
58   "Tanzania in Bank Scandal Sacking," BBC, January 10, 2008.
59   "BoT Gold Reserves Financed Radar Deals," *This Day*, October 9, 2009.
60   Edward G. Hoseah, *An Overview of the Bill on Prevention and Combating of Corruption Act, (PCCA) 2007* (Dodoma: Parliament of Tanzania, 2007), 5.
61   Patrick Kisembo, "Five Grand Corruption 'Sharks' Named," IPPmedia.
62   "Mengi Finally Reported to PCCB," *East African Tribune*, May 6, 2009.

[63] Global Integrity, "Tanzania," in *2007 Global Integrity Report* (Washington, D.C.: Global Integrity, 2008).
[64] Revenue Watch Institute, *Tanzania–Transparency Snapshot* (New York: Revenue Watch Institute, 2009).
[65] U.S. Bureau of Democracy, Human Rights, and Labor, "Tanzania," *in 2008 Country Reports on Human Rights Practices* (Washington, D.C.: U.S. Department of State, February 2009).
[66] Open Budget Initiative, "Tanzania," in *Open Budget Index 2008* (Washington, D.C.: Open Budget Initiative, 2009).
[67] Beatus Kagashe and Florence Mugarula, "Eating Chiefs in Budget Gravy," *Citizen*, July 14, 2009.
[68] Revenue Watch Institute, *Tanzania*.
[69] World Bank, "Tanzania," in *Enterprise Surveys 2006* (Washington, D.C.: World Bank, 2007), 7.

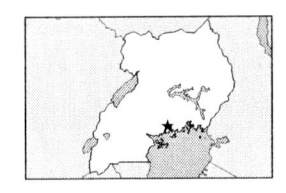

UGANDA

CAPITAL: Kampala
POPULATION: 30.7 million
GNI PER CAPITA (PPP): $1,140

SCORES	2006	2010
ACCOUNTABILITY AND PUBLIC VOICE:	3.95	3.50
CIVIL LIBERTIES:	3.68	3.77
RULE OF LAW:	3.66	3.40
ANTICORRUPTION AND TRANSPARENCY:	3.75	3.58

(scores are based on a scale of 0 to 7, with 0 representing weakest and 7 representing strongest performance)

Nelson Kasfir[1]

INTRODUCTION

Despite much political and economic progress over the last two decades, the increasingly personal and patronage-based rule of President Yoweri Museveni remains the most significant obstacle to the expansion of democracy and rule of law in Uganda. Uganda's significant ethnic, regional, and religious divisions have also complicated efforts to protect basic freedoms and prevent corruption. Civilian and military figures from the north, the country's poorest and least populous region, had controlled the government from independence in 1962 until Museveni and his National Resistance Army (NRA) seized power in 1986. Officials in Buganda, formally the Central Region, have always resisted control by the national government to protect their region's educational and economic advantages.

Museveni initially promised "fundamental change,"[2] and during his first years in office the government gradually improved security, facilitated the adoption of a more democratic constitution in 1995, and oversaw increased if uneven economic growth. The parliament established by the new constitution actively checked the executive, modified government bills, and audited expenditures. Unusual for African governments, it even forced ministers out of Museveni's cabinet. Civil society activists testified frequently before parliamentary committees, often influencing pending legislation. And the government generally tolerated incisive, sometimes intemperate criticism from the media.

Nelson Kasfir writes frequently on Ugandan politics and development. He is preparing a worldwide dataset on how rebels manage civilians living under their control when they are engaged in insurgencies. He is Professor of Government Emeritus at Dartmouth College.

But less democratic tendencies also became apparent soon after the NRA takeover. Museveni used his popularity to entrench a "no-party" political system in the constitution, protecting him and his inner circle from organized competition. He frequently invoked the role of the army in protecting his government, sometimes warning during election campaigns that it would not accept his defeat. He also demanded that the new constitution include 10 military officers as representatives in Parliament. As his popularity began to decline after 1995, Museveni relied more on patronage to maintain his political coalition, giving his key allies leeway to pursue illegal schemes of self-enrichment. Consequently, the growth of both democracy and the rule of law faltered.

Museveni ruled the country for 10 years before participating in a presidential election, although there were tightly restricted parliamentary elections in 1989 and a more open election for a constituent assembly to draft the constitution in 1994. In the 1996 presidential and parliamentary elections, from which political parties were banned, Museveni won 72 percent of the presidential vote. He secured new five-year terms in the 2001 and 2006 elections, but with declining margins of victory.

Progress on democracy, civil liberties, and government accountability stalled between December 2005 and March 2009, largely, and paradoxically, because Museveni orchestrated the return of multiparty elections as part of a scheme to extend his rule and increase his political dominance. Instead of retiring after his second and final term in the "no-party" political system, he arranged two constitutional changes in 2005: the removal of presidential term limits and the restoration of parties. This paved the way for his reelection and a two-thirds parliamentary majority for his "new" party, the National Resistance Movement (NRM), in 2006.

During the next three years, Museveni's overriding personal role in policy making remained unchallenged. Members of civil society and Parliament continued to fight for alternatives, but their effectiveness declined. The media regularly exposed instances of corruption, and prosecutors pursued some cases, convicting a former army commander and several mid-level officials. However, they secured no convictions of top politicians. Nonetheless, when the president's political interests are not at stake, he typically works within formal institutions and adheres to the text of existing rules, although often not to their spirit.

ACCOUNTABILITY AND PUBLIC VOICE 3.50

FREE AND FAIR ELECTORAL LAWS AND ELECTIONS	2.50
EFFECTIVE AND ACCOUNTABLE GOVERNMENT	3.75
CIVIC ENGAGEMENT AND CIVIC MONITORING	4.33
MEDIA INDEPENDENCE AND FREEDOM OF EXPRESSION	3.43

The February 2006 elections raised doubts about the extent to which government authority rested on the will of the people. Last-minute changes to the electoral laws allowed the first multiparty elections since 1980, but they also delayed organization of the process, giving enormous advantages to the president and his NRM party. The referendum authorizing the reform was held in July 2005, leaving little time for parties to organize and allowing the president to continue to use all "no-party" political structures until the February 2006 balloting. In effect, Museveni had a national organization in place, while all of his opponents had to start from scratch. The president and the NRM also took illegal advantage of government resources and unequal access to state media.[3]

The state provides equal, although limited, funding for each presidential candidate. However, the NRM benefited from its patronage network, as economically privileged interests made far greater contributions to the NRM than to any other party, receiving preferential subsidies and government tenders in return. A commission of inquiry into the Health Ministry's use of assistance from the Global Fund to Fight AIDS, Tuberculosis, and Malaria heard testimony that part of the funding was diverted to pay NRM campaign workers.

The government took additional measures to cripple the presidential campaign of Kizza Besigye, the leading opposition candidate. When he returned from South Africa, where he had lived after fleeing government harassment following his unsuccessful bid for the presidency in the 2001 elections, the government brought rape and treason charges against him and insisted on simultaneous trials in civilian and military courts. Besigye was not released on bail until early January, only six weeks before the elections. His court battles seriously disrupted his campaign, and his campaign staff were frequently threatened and sometimes physically attacked. Other incidents of violence and intimidation occurred, including the deaths of several people and serious injuries to two others at an opposition rally near Kampala on February 15. Army lieutenant Ramathan Magara, identified as a special police constable in court papers, was eventually convicted of manslaughter for that attack and sentenced to 14 years in prison in June 2009. Overall, however, the violence and voting irregularities of the 2006 elections were less severe than in the 2001 campaigns and balloting.

After the Electoral Commission declared Museveni the winner of the presidential contest with 59 percent of the vote to Besigye's 37 percent, Besigye challenged the result before the Supreme Court. In April 2006, the court upheld Museveni's victory by a 4–3 vote. It found that the NRM had engaged in corruption, multiple voting, and ballot-box stuffing, and that Museveni had committed electoral offenses by, among other acts, making defamatory statements about Besigye.[4] Nevertheless, the judges ruled that these offenses were not sufficiently "substantial" to affect the outcome. Over 100 petitions were filed to nullify other results in the elections. Within the required six-month period, the courts overturned 6 of 41 disputed parliamentary elections, almost always calling for fresh voting.[5] By-elections held over the next three years triggered similar complaints, but to a lesser extent than in 2006. Despite constitutional protections, the election commissioners were not seen as independent after

2006 because the NRM's large parliamentary majority meant that the president's appointees were invariably confirmed.

Of the 320 voting members of Parliament (MPs) elected in 2006, 214 belonged to the NRM, and 46 belonged to one of five opposition parties. The rest were independents, the majority of whom leaned toward the NRM. All of the parties, particularly the NRM, placed great emphasis on internal discipline, and Museveni warned party rebels that he would campaign against them. As a result, constructive discussion in Parliament has declined significantly, and committees have made fewer changes to bills. Nevertheless, MPs report that open discussion does occur in the party caucuses, and NRM members add that the president is occasionally forced to back down. The "oversight" committees—particularly those dealing with public accounts, which are all chaired by opposition MPs—have been vigilant and outspoken. But the overall effect of the restoration of multiparty competition, at least in the short term, has been somewhat less accountability for the executive and its legislative proposals.

The Supreme Court and the Constitutional Court have asserted their independence in recent years, declaring particular executive actions unconstitutional or illegal and frequently ruling against the government in political cases, often noting the weakness of its evidence. In October 2008, the Supreme Court affirmed the doctrine of separation of powers by ruling that the president had unconstitutionally forced Brigadier Henry Tumukunde to resign. With the conspicuous exception of two treason cases in which the government used military force to obstruct bail, the government generally respected the independence of the judiciary. Nevertheless, military officers often acted with impunity, particularly when they believed they were carrying out the president's intentions.

Independent public service commissions at the national and district levels manage the recruitment and promotion of government officials. At the national level, they rely on open competition and merit, although the press frequently presents evidence of ethnic favoritism. At the district level, observers suggest that ethnic recruitment is widely practiced and that non-indigenes find it difficult to gain appointment.

Nongovernmental organizations (NGOs) flourished after the NRM regime came to power in 1986, but the government regarded those engaging in political issues as possible threats. It required all NGOs to gain approval—which was not always given—from an NGO Registration Board that includes representatives of security agencies. In 2006, the government amended the NGO Registration Act, tightening supervision by requiring the annual renewal of registrations. This law was suspended temporarily following complaints in 2008. NGOs argue that the law entails government intrusion into their activities and expenditures, and civic associations petitioned the Constitutional Court in April 2009 to declare the act unconstitutional. As of June 2009, the court had not yet issued a ruling.

Civic groups opposed the 2005 referendum and the removal of presidential term limits, but after losing that battle they became noticeably more submissive during the election period.[6] One reason for this reticence was the government's expression of political resolve in ordering soldiers to prevent Besigye's release on bail, attacking demonstrators who supported him, and displaying its military force in Kampala; the failure of donors to respond emphatically to the regime's actions may have been another.[7]

NGOs continue to testify on legislation before Parliament and frequently campaign to influence government policy, though they have grown frustrated by MPs' reluctance to consider their arguments once the parties take positions in their caucuses. Donors have criticized problems in government performance over the last several years, particularly corruption and the continued existence of large camps for internally displaced persons (IDPs) in the north due to the state's failure to end fighting with the Lord's Resistance Army (LRA), a rebel group.

The government's support for freedom of expression has been ambiguous. The state at times criminalizes dissent, taking advantage of broadly written sedition, antiterrorism, and libel laws. The sedition law, which allows prosecution for causing disaffection toward the president or the government, protects government officials but not leaders of the opposition.[8] In addition, the Anti-Terrorism Act of 2002 continues to be used against journalists, particularly when they cover issues that the government links to security.

The government further limits media independence through a Media Council created by a 1994 law. Among other functions, the council is required "to exercise disciplinary control over journalists, editors and publishers."[9] A Media Center created in January 2006 makes recommendations to the Media Council on the accreditation of foreign journalists, who must also obtain clearance from the Media Center before they can travel more than 100 miles from Kampala.[10] In March 2006, the two bodies deprived a Canadian journalist of his accreditation, claiming that his reports were "biased, false and 'prejudicial' to Uganda's foreign interests."[11]

In recent years, the government has occasionally closed newspapers temporarily. In an unprecedented step in March 2007, the police filed petitions with the Media Council against 53 articles in independent newspapers, and in April 2008, four journalists with the *Monitor* newspaper were arrested and charged with criminal defamation over a story on irregular salary claims by the inspector-general of government (IGG).[12] The case remains unresolved. While these actions certainly induced some self-censorship, newspapers have been notable for their continued criticism of the government. Radio stations generally avoid investigations into government activities.

In February 2009, the cabinet approved a media bill intended to regulate newspapers more strictly, particularly those that "incite violence."[13] It had not been introduced in Parliament by the end of the period under review. Separately, the cabinet submitted the Regulation of Interception of Communications Bill of 2007 to lawmakers, with the aim of legalizing security agencies' warrantless surveillance of the telephone calls, mail, and money transfers of treason and terrorism suspects. Opposition MPs and Amnesty International attacked the bill for its abuses of freedom of speech and privacy. In March 2009, Security Minister Amama Mbabazi admitted to a parliamentary committee that the government had already been tapping telephones without warrants.

The government generally did not regulate use of the internet, although it occasionally prevented access to openly critical websites. Because of Uganda's low penetration rate, the internet has not become a politically significant medium. The state continued to subsidize the *New Vision*, but the newspaper now operates as a private corporation. In the past, the government prevented advertising in the *Monitor* newspaper, but it rescinded this order and has not tried to limit free expression in this way in recent years.

CIVIL LIBERTIES   3.77

PROTECTION FROM STATE TERROR, UNJUSTIFIED IMPRISONMENT, AND TORTURE	2.75
GENDER EQUITY	3.00
RIGHTS OF ETHNIC, RELIGIOUS, AND OTHER DISTINCT GROUPS	4.00
FREEDOM OF CONSCIENCE AND BELIEF	5.33
FREEDOM OF ASSOCIATION AND ASSEMBLY	3.75

Protection from state terror and unjustified imprisonment remains inadequate in Uganda. The Supreme Court ruled in January 2009 that death sentences, which had been automatic for defendants convicted of capital offenses, must be discretionary and must be carried out within three years or the sentence would be commuted to life imprisonment.[14] By April 2009, the courts were reviewing the sentences of 35 (out of 637) prisoners on death row who had been convicted before the ruling. On January 20, Museveni freed three prisoners from death row, including two officials who served under former dictators and had awaited execution for more than 20 years.

Security forces continued to engage in extrajudicial killings, disappearances, and torture—all prohibited by the constitution. The country's military, the Uganda People's Defence Force (UPDF), has a long history of abusing human rights.[15] Security officials also use torture to gain confessions and punish opponents. While the government links many of these cases to rebel activity, observers regard most of them as attempts to remove or intimidate political opponents. Reports of detention and torture in secret jails known as "safe houses" declined in 2006 and 2007, but rose in 2008.[16] Many cases go unreported. The Joint Anti-Terrorism Task Force (JATT) has been charged with the extrajudicial killing of four people and many cases of torture between 2006 and 2008.[17] There is also evidence that the JATT held at least 106 detainees illegally in a safe house in Kampala during the same period. No one has been prosecuted for these abuses, and similar activities have occurred since the beginning of the NRM regime. A civic coalition that included the Uganda Human Rights Commission

(UHRC) drafted the Prohibition and Prevention of Torture Bill of 2009, which prescribes the death penalty for torture.[18] As of June 2009, Parliament had not acted on the bill. The UHRC, established by the 1995 constitution as an independent agency, awarded more than 70 million shillings (US$41,000) in compensation for torture during the first quarter of 2008.[19] However, the government was slow to disburse the money.

During the first eight months of 2008, 556 new clients were enrolled at the African Center for the Treatment and Rehabilitation of Torture Victims (ACTV) in Kampala; of these, 422 were Ugandans, mostly victims of the LRA.[20] The decreasing proportion of victims who were tortured by the UPDF may be due in part to the decline in rebel activity in Uganda, but the UPDF also claimed to have stepped up disciplinary measures against abusive soldiers.[21] A Local Defense Unit soldier convicted by a court-martial of killing six civilians and injuring eight others was sentenced to death in January 2009. Ruling in a different case in February, the Constitutional Court held that soldiers convicted by Army Field Courts Martial must be given the opportunity to appeal to the Supreme Court. Parliament established a war crimes court in 2008 to handle crimes against humanity, such as those committed by the LRA.

The police have also engaged in reckless behavior. In addition to the 2006 election violence discussed above, police fired into a crowd in July 2008, killing two people.[22] They were charged only with manslaughter and released on bail, but their case had not been listed for cause by September 2008. Vigilante justice remains a serious problem, although the police are sometimes successful in protecting the lives of accused thieves.

Throughout the period under review, prison inmates continued to face harsh conditions that often threatened their health. Officials made only limited efforts to maintain the dignity of those incarcerated. An Islamic teacher jailed on treason charges died in prison in January 2007. Gross human rights abuses were common in local prisons that have now been taken over by the central government. Nonetheless, the UHRC reported in 2008 that the torture of inmates in Central Region prisons had declined.[23] Despite a ban in the 2006 Prisons Act, corporal punishment continues to be widely practiced, particularly in rural prisons. Of the 30,000 prisoners in Uganda as of February 2009, 56 percent had spent over three years in pretrial detention, and the situation had worsened every year despite laws limiting remand to one year.[24]

Human trafficking for sexual and labor exploitation, both inside the country and to foreign states, remains a problem. The government has organized a Family and Child Protection Unit to improve the police force's capacity to recognize victims, but there are as yet no measures of its success.

Criminal violence has increased in recent years. The government has responded with periodic, quasi-military operations to kill suspected criminals rather than bring them to trial. The police are poorly organized and respond slowly to criminal complaints. There were few terrorist incidents in the past three years. The departure of the LRA to the Democratic Republic of the Congo (DRC) in 2005 increased security in northern Uganda, but the return of the majority of the IDPs from two decades of fighting has resulted in violent land disputes, forcing hundreds of people to flee their original homes.[25]

The government has often expressed its concern for the interests of women. In the 332-seat Parliament, 79 seats were reserved for women, a number that rose as the government created new districts, each of which was entitled to a seat for a woman. The government has also ensured by law and subsequent practice that women hold a substantial number of local council seats. However, it has stalled on passing the Domestic Relations and Sexual Offences Bill, which would protect women from domestic violence and give them more secure rights in marital and inherited property. The government finally introduced the bill in July 2009.

Domestic violence—not in itself a criminal offense—is widespread, and the police tend to be unsympathetic to victims' complaints. There are few police medical examiners to document violence against women for criminal prosecution. Women have the right to own and inherit land, but ignorance of the law often results in male relatives invoking local customs to control inheritance. Marriage law continues to discriminate against women by making the bride price a nonrefundable payment to the wife's parents. The state has not succeeded in stopping the practice of levirate marriage (of a widow to the deceased's brother), although the AIDS pandemic appears to have discouraged it. The government has participated in efforts to raise awareness about discrimination against women, but did little in recent years to equalize women's opportunities for employment and credit. In addition to the Domestic Relations and Sexual Offences Bill, MPs have drafted a bill to criminalize female genital mutilation, which is performed on approximately 1 percent of Ugandan women and girls, predominantly among those living in the Eastern Region.[26]

Despite the NRM's official opposition to ethnic bias, the government is frequently accused of favoritism toward people from Museveni's home region of western Uganda, particularly in hiring officials, although the evidence is rarely clear. Northerners often attribute the poor conditions in their region to official discrimination, but the area's social services and economic growth have undoubtedly also suffered from disruptions caused by the LRA. Newly created districts have sometimes inadvertently produced local ethnic minorities who allege discrimination.[27] The central government has not ensured that they can exercise all their human rights in part because that task is now up to district administrations, which have neither the awareness nor the capacity to act. In addition, the state does not adequately protect the cultural identity of small minorities such as the Ik and the Batwa. Even though five seats in Parliament are reserved for representatives of disabled people, some individuals have complained to the UHRC of disability-related discrimination.

The state generally respects the constitutional right of free religious practice. There is a long-standing perception that the Roman Catholic plurality and the small Muslim minority are not treated as well as Protestants, but in recent years the issue has received less public attention than complaints about ethnic discrimination. In 2008 and 2009, the police investigated a largely unexplained upsurge in deaths that included many children, which they linked to human sacrifices associated with witchcraft. In September 2007 the government closed a mosque in Mukono district that it said was connected to a rebel group.

Homosexual behavior is a crime in Uganda, and homosexuals are beaten and humiliated by members of the community and harassed by the state. In July 2009, the minister of ethics and integrity indicated that the government would resist foreign pressure to end such discrimination.[28] He announced plans for a bill to punish the publication of literature on homosexuality and even deny homosexuals the right to address press conferences.

By permitting parties to engage in politics, the 2005 constitutional changes expanded the rights of freedom of association and assembly. However, the government often restricts freedom of assembly by requiring police permits for public demonstrations or meetings. In April 2007, when demonstrations over the transfer of part of the Mabira Forest to an Indian investor erupted into an anti-Indian riot in Kampala, the police prevented a march on the main downtown street, and a private militia called Kiboko, reportedly directed by a presidential adviser, attacked the crowd. The police arrested, charged, and imprisoned two MPs and several others who participated. In February and April 2008, demonstrations in Kampala's Kisekka Market and Taxi Park turned into riots, resulting in crackdowns by the police.

In May 2008, the Constitutional Court nullified a law requiring written permission for public meetings. Immediately after the ruling, the attorney general tried to restrict its application, insisting in June that a permit was still required in specified areas, including the whole of each city and town in Uganda. Indeed, politically motivated repression of protests still occurs. The police halted a Democratic Party (DP) rally soon after the ruling, and closed DP headquarters for several days. Also in June 2008, the Forum for Democratic Change (FDC), the largest opposition party, complained that the police had arrested several of its members during training workshops in Kampala, Mbarara, and Naguru, despite receiving advance notification of the events. In February 2009, the cabinet ordered the Ministry of Internal Affairs to draft a stricter law regulating public demonstrations.

Several acts that came into force in August 2006 strengthened workers' rights to organize and participate in trade unions, but enforcement remained questionable. Police sometimes arrest strikers, and the government ignored a legal requirement that employers enter collectively bargained contracts with their employees. Workers must register unions with government trade union confederations. Senior public servants and members of the police and army may not form unions.

RULE OF LAW   3.40

INDEPENDENT JUDICIARY	4.20
PRIMACY OF RULE OF LAW IN CIVIL AND CRIMINAL MATTERS	3.80
ACCOUNTABILITY OF SECURITY FORCES AND MILITARY TO CIVILIAN AUTHORITIES	2.25
PROTECTION OF PROPERTY RIGHTS	3.33

While the higher courts are generally independent and impartial, the judgments of lower-level magistrates are frequently distorted by political and economic influences. Judges face intense political pressure in cases that threaten actions the president considers essential. By twice sending soldiers to prevent court decisions from being implemented, Museveni badly undercut confidence in judicial independence, despite his assurance that he would not do it again. Meanwhile, the UPDF not only continued to try civilians accused of capital offenses, it did so inside maximum-security prisons.

A serious corruption problem, due in part to inadequate salaries for magistrates, leads to prejudicial decisions. The IGG declared in April 2008 that for the second consecutive year, the judiciary and the police were the most corrupt institutions of government. Corrupt court officials sometimes extort bribes from defendants unjustly jailed through cases based on fictitious affidavits. By July 2009, the recently established Anti-Corruption Division of the High Court had convicted four officials and sentenced them to prison.[29] However, it had a backlog of 350 cases and only two judges.[30]

Due to budgetary problems, there are not enough judges to process civil and criminal cases. Parliament passed a motion in October 2007 compelling Museveni to appoint an additional seven judges to the Court of Appeal and six to the Supreme Court. However, because the president failed to act, the Supreme Court was deprived of the quorum needed to handle constitutional cases. In January 2008, the Judicial Service Commission reported to a parliamentary committee that it had compiled a list of 27 candidates to fill vacant judicial posts six months earlier.[31] At the end of July 2009, Museveni appointed three new judges to the Supreme Court, partly resolving the problem. At the lower level, the judicial manpower shortage was exacerbated by two acts, to which the president assented, that effectively increased the caseload of magistrates by expanding their jurisdiction. The backlog of civil and criminal cases in June 2007 stood at 74,066, with no subsequent improvement.[32]

Government authorities usually comply with court decisions. The most blatant exception was the government's use of soldiers on March 1, 2007, to prevent nine defendants in the People's Redemption Army (PRA) treason trial from being released on bail. The High Court judges went on strike to protest the move, and lawyers mounted demonstrations. Museveni expressed regret over the incident and pledged that it would not be repeated.[33] In 2005, he had used soldiers in a similar fashion to prevent the release of the same defendants.

Civil and criminal cases are generally given fair and public, but not timely, hearings by the courts and the UHRC. The constitution requires that suspects face a court within 48 hours of arrest (longer for terrorism suspects), but the rule was not followed in several high-profile cases in recent years. Three Buganda Kingdom officials were arrested on July 18, 2008, and held for five days; their release was then ordered, but they were immediately detained again. The acting internal affairs minister told the Legal and Parliamentary Affairs Committee in February 2009 that the cabinet was considering extending the 48-hour rule. In Besigye's treason case, no trial date had been set as of mid-2009, more than three years after his indictment. Meanwhile, the authorities withheld his passport, preventing him from traveling freely and restricting his ability to lead the opposition.

Anyone charged with a criminal offense is presumed innocent until a court establishes guilt. The Constitutional Court ruled in March 2008 that criminal suspects must be given access to statements that prosecution witnesses make to the police, though this principle of discovery does not apply to civil cases.[34] All citizens have a right to independent counsel, but many poor criminal suspects do not receive it. In ordinary cases, prosecutors are thought to act independently. However, in high-profile political cases they are widely assumed to be following the dictates of top officials. The ongoing prosecution of the PRA, a supposed rebel group, in the absence of credible evidence is a case in point. Public officials and NRM members are sometimes prosecuted for abuse of power and corruption, but they are rarely convicted.

Because the president effectively controls the security forces, there is civilian oversight, but it is personal rather than institutional in nature. The legislative and judicial branches are unable to exercise effective supervision. For example, the president ordered the military's December 2008 surprise cross-border attack on the LRA without consulting Parliament or subjecting the move to legislative review. Separately, in several documented incidents in which army officers used soldiers to evict farmers from land the officers claimed to have acquired, the president apparently restrained the commanders only when publicity made their positions untenable.

The security forces frequently intrude on the political process. Despite Uganda's return to multiparty competition, the Army Council continues to choose 10 military officers to represent the UPDF in Parliament, and these MPs are required to support NRM policies.

Respect for human rights by security forces remained relatively poor throughout 2006–09, though there were signs of improvement. Before the LRA ended operations within Uganda and entered negotiations with the government in July 2006, UPDF soldiers perpetrated widespread sexual and physical abuses against IDPs in the north. Commanders have reported punishing those guilty of violations, and 26 soldiers have been executed. However, the army's disarmament campaign in Karamoja led to the deaths of hundreds of civilians during 2006 and 2007, as well as detentions, beatings, torture, and rape. The development of guidelines for UPDF conduct reduced the incidence of human rights abuses, but did not end them. It remains unclear whether the military justice system operates effectively or merely serves as a façade to satisfy international opinion.

Property rights remain insecure in Uganda. The press frequently reports cases of fraudulent land titles, sometimes resulting from collusion with corrupt officials in the land registry offices. Many instances involve high-level politicians and army officers who seize land held in customary tenure by peasants who have little ability to protect their rights. In addition, the government frequently awards public land to foreign investors, including plots on which schools have been operating for many years.

ANTICORRUPTION AND TRANSPARENCY   3.58

ENVIRONMENT TO PROTECT AGAINST CORRUPTION	3.25
PROCEDURES AND SYSTEMS TO ENFORCE ANTICORRUPTION LAWS	3.75
EXISTENCE OF ANTICORRUPTION NORMS, STANDARDS, AND PROTECTIONS	3.50
GOVERNMENTAL TRANSPARENCY	3.83

Despite its commitment to liberalization over the past two decades, the government continues to struggle with corruption. Allies of the president have manipulated the privatization of state land and enterprises for their own enrichment. Privatization has diminished opportunities for corruption in some respects, as it reduces public servants' direct control over economic operations, but the changes have created openings for other forms of bribery. A survey of businessmen commissioned by the World Bank found that they paid larger bribes in 2007 than in 2003 to secure contracts and run their businesses. On the other hand, the 2009 Index of Economic Freedom rated Uganda in the "moderately free" category and credited it with the fourth-best regulatory regime in Africa; the country's score fluctuated only slightly between 2005 and 2009.[35] The index stated that obtaining a business license required fewer procedures and less time than the world averages, but noted that corruption and insecure property rights remained weak points in the Ugandan business environment.

A clear legal separation exists between the official and private interests of public servants, although officials' wealth disclosures are not open to public scrutiny. The independence of the Inspectorate of Government as the primary anticorruption body is entrenched in the constitution. Justice Faith Mwondha, who led the agency as IGG, pursued cases of corruption so vigorously in recent years that it came as somewhat of a surprise when the president reappointed her for a second four-year term in February 2009. However, she refused to be reviewed by Parliament for her second term, and when the Constitutional Court upheld the requirement, she had to step down as IGG and return to her original position on the High Court in July 2009.

The president declared a policy of "zero tolerance for corruption" during his third term. In September 2007, he forced the solicitor general from office over allegations of inflated awards to businessmen who had sued the state. In February 2008, the government submitted the Anti-Corruption Bill of 2008 to Parliament, claiming that it would fight public and private corruption more effectively. The IGG argued that some provisions of the bill were unconstitutional. In April 2008, lawmakers passed the Audit Bill of 2007 to strengthen the Office of the Auditor General (OAG), giving it the power to sue, making it autonomous, and improving its staffing. In addition, the new Anti-Corruption Division of the High Court, mentioned above, has expanded the state's capacity to punish fraudulent officials.

Parliament's Public Accounts Committee and Local Government Public Accounts Committee (PAC and LGPAC) actively probe cases of wrongdoing, primarily through reviews of the OAG's reports. The PAC exposed schemes by pension officials to fabricate recipients and by police officials to purchase defective antiriot vehicles. In 2008 it even took on the president over a deal benefiting his son-in-law that the auditor-general had refused to clear. Newspapers regularly investigate transactions by public officials, in addition to publicizing the work of the parliamentary committees.

Between 2006 and mid-2009, three ministers and a presidential aide accused of misappropriating funds from the Global Alliance for Vaccines and Immunization were brought to court after a long delay due to a lack of funds to prosecute. Successful legal tactics by the defense caused innumerable postponements of this trial. However, an army tribunal sentenced a former commander, Major General James Kazini, to three years in prison for stealing funds directed to nonexistent soldiers. He remained free on bail during his appeal. A former managing director of the National Social Security Fund, Leonard Mpuuma, was fined after pleading guilty to causing financial loss and abuse of office.

The Inspectorate of Government supervises public servants' declarations of income, assets, and liabilities as required by the Leadership Code. It received over 17,000 declarations in 2007, a 94 percent rate of compliance, and wrote warning letters to the 1,250 leaders who failed to file on time.[36] An MP and the head of a town council were forced to resign for failure to comply. Also in 2007, the IGG seized public assets worth almost one billion shillings (US$604,000) that were wrongly converted to private use. The inspectorate arrested 37 officials in 2007 and 22 in the first half of 2008 for abuse of office, embezzlement, or causing financial loss. In addition, 126 public servants were dismissed from office, and 52 others were reprimanded or demoted.

An inquiry on the misuse of money from the Global Fund to Fight AIDS, Tuberculosis, and Malaria led the director of public prosecutions (DPP) to file charges.[37] An arrest warrant for an MP in the case was issued in December 2008. In July 2009, the DPP dropped charges against a former health minister, but continued to prosecute 38 other defendants.

Despite such cases and presidential pronouncements on the issue, there was evidence to suggest that high-level corruption would be tolerated. The government arbitrarily enforced laws and regulations, frequently following a political logic, and the IGG was drawn into seemingly unrelated disputes with other officials, weakening anticorruption efforts. Transparency International ranked Uganda 126th out of 180 countries surveyed in its 2008 Corruption Perceptions Index.[38] Moreover, witnesses were hesitant to come forward due to inadequate legal protection. To encourage them, the minister of ethics and integrity presented the Whistleblowers Protection Bill of 2008 in Parliament in March 2009.

Citizens have the right to obtain government information under the Access to Information Act of 2005, but critics argue that the law is overly restrictive, providing ample grounds to deny requests.[39] Responses to information requests are often delayed, especially if the material is considered sensitive. The government sometimes refuses to give a reason for denials.

The budget-making process became somewhat less comprehensive and transparent after the return of multiparty politics, largely because NRM MPs were less willing to question government proposals. Parliament had become formally involved in negotiating budget requests after the passage of the Budget Act of 2001. However, starting in the Eighth Parliament (elected in 2006), a member of the ruling party chaired the Budget Committee. When the first chairperson suggested that the committee recommend more funds for education, roads, and health, the government replaced him. After that the committee stopped urging changes, although it sometimes negotiated with ministers when they defended their proposed outlays.

The auditor-general, a respected independent official, is tasked with scrutinizing government spending. With the passage of the Public Finance and Accountability Act of 2003, the OAG gained the power to audit classified expenditures. During the period reviewed, the OAG's audit covered 90 percent of national government spending. The 2005–06 audit report was received by Parliament in October 2007, earlier than in previous years. In September 2008, the PAC was able to report on specific allegations made in the OAG report for the year that ended in June 2007. The committee chairperson warned, however, that internal auditors in government departments sometimes colluded with other officials to hide diversions of public funds.

The Uganda Revenue Authority (URA) established an Internal Audit, Tax Investigation, and Internal Affairs Department in January 2005. Although it carried out "a continuous program of tax audits," its system had not yet been integrated with customer registration in banks or the Investment Authority.[40] Consequently, as of March 2008, the OAG judged that URA tax audits could not be considered fully "based on clear risk assessment criteria." He did not argue that tax audits were arbitrary or unjust, rather that better controls for taxpayer registration and monitoring of penalties for noncompliance were needed.

Public corruption often stems from the award of national and district government contracts. The president frequently suspends rules requiring competitive bidding to designate a recipient.[41] According to one analysis, "about 90%

of the complaints received by the IGG reportedly concern contested procurements."[42] Despite the carefully drafted law regulating procurement, the government continued to lose millions to contract-related graft. In addition, officials personally diverted a large proportion of foreign assistance between 2006 and March 2009. Many donors considered the siphoning off of part of their aid to be a cost of doing business, but the Global Fund to Fight AIDS, Tuberculosis, and Malaria ended two of its grants in response to deliberate misappropriation.

RECOMMENDATIONS

- Ensure the independence of the Electoral Commission by changing its appointment procedure; the chair, deputy chair, and its five other members should be appointed by the president on the advice of the Judicial Service Commission and with the approval of Parliament.
- Pass the Domestic Relations and Sexual Offences Bill to secure women's property rights and punish rape and domestic violence. The act should include funding and direction for educating police and judicial officers on their responsibilities when handling complaints by abused women.
- Establish and implement stronger guidelines within the prison service, along the lines of the somewhat successful UPDF effort, to reduce human rights violations including corporal punishment.
- Expand the number and compensation of magistrates to reduce the delay in civil and criminal trials and improve judicial impartiality.
- Pass the Anti-Corruption Bill of 2008 and the Whistleblowers Protection Bill of 2008 to strengthen the legal regime for prosecuting corruption.

NOTES

For URLs and endnote hyperlinks, please visit the *Countries at the Crossroads* homepage at http://freedomhouse.org/template.cfm?page=139&edition=8.

[1] I wish to thank Elliott Green, Joe Oloka-Onyango, Sylvia Tamale, Roger Tangri, and the external reviewer for their helpful suggestions on the first draft. I take responsibility for any remaining errors of fact or interpretation.

[2] "Ours Is a Fundamental Change," speech presented on January 29, 1986, in Yoweri K. Museveni, *What Is Africa's Problem?* (Kampala: NRM Publications, 1992), 22.

[3] Foundation for Human Rights Initiatives (FHRI), *Electoral Reforms in Uganda 2008: Report for the Period of July–December 2008* (Kampala: FHRI, 2008), 34.

[4] Siri Gloppen, Emmanuel Kasimbazi, and Alexander Kibandama, "Elections in Court: The Judiciary and Uganda's 2006 Election Process," in *Electoral Democracy in Uganda: Understanding Institutional Processes and Outcomes of the 2006 Multiparty Elections*, ed. Julius Kiiza, Sabiti Makara, and Lise Rakner (Kampala: Fountain Publishers, 2008), 78–86.

[5] While the threshold for overturning the six elections was high, the courts did not rely on the precedent in Besigye's case, in which the abuses had to be substantial enough to call the outcome into doubt. See ibid., 85.

6. Anne Mette Kjaer and Yasin Olum, "From Confrontation to Acquiescence? The Role of Civil Society and the Media in the 2006 Elections in Uganda," in *Electoral Democracy in Uganda*, 187–97.
7. Ibid., 192, 197.
8. Henry Odimbe Ojambe, "Reflections on Freedom of Expression in Uganda's Fledgling Democracy: Sedition, 'Pornography,' and Hate Speech," HURIPEC Working Paper 18 (Kampala: Human Rights and Peace Centre, Faculty of Law, Makerere University, February 2008), 18–19, 20, 28.
9. Ibid., 23.
10. Frank Nyakairu, "Govt Sets Tough Rules for Foreign Journalists," *Monitor*, January 14, 2006.
11. Angelo Izama, "Deported Journalist Stranded in Nairobi," *Monitor*, March 11, 2006.
12. Angelo Izama, "Police File 53 Petitions against the Press," *Monitor*, March 11, 2007; Grace Natabaalo, "Human Rights Group Condemns IGG's Crack Down on Journalists," *Monitor*, February 4, 2008.
13. Richard Wanambwa, "Cabinet Approves Tough Laws against Free Media," *Sunday Monitor*, February 8, 2009; Mercy Nalugo, "MPs to Discuss Phone Tapping Law," *Sunday Monitor*, February 28, 2009; Mercy Nalugo, "We Tap Private Conversations Illegally—Minister Mbabazi," *Monitor*, March 2, 2009.
14. Anne Mugisa and Hillary Nsambu, "35 Convicts Escape Hanging," *New Vision*, April 6, 2009.
15. Tabu Butagira, "New Report Pins UPDF on Human Rights Abuse," *Monitor*, November 17, 2008.
16. FHRI, "The Human Rights Situation in Uganda: A Brief Overview," in *Electoral Reforms in Uganda*, 100.
17. Human Rights Watch (HRW), *Open Secret: Illegal Detention and Torture by the Joint Anti-Terrorism Task Force in Uganda* (New York: HRW, April 2009), 3–5, 13–17, 35–45.
18. Nicholas Opiyo, "We Must Criminalise Torture in Uganda's Electoral Process," *Monitor*, June 26, 2009.
19. FHRI, "The Human Rights Situation," in *Electoral Reforms in Uganda*, 98–99.
20. Ibid., 102.
21. Richard Egadu, "Army Executes 26 Soldiers," *Monitor*, February 5, 2006.
22. FHRI, "The Human Rights Situation," in *Electoral Reforms in Uganda*, 94.
23. Josephine Maseruka, "Torture Cases Drop, Says Rights Body," *New Vision*, April 3, 2008.
24. Testimony by the Commissioner General of Prisons, Dr. Johnson Byabashaija, to the Parliamentary Legal Affairs Committee; Yasin Mugerwa, "16,000 Remanded for over Three Years," *Monitor*, February 3, 2009, 5.
25. "Uganda: Land Rows Reverse Resettlement," Integrated Regional Information Networks (IRIN), March 17, 2009.
26. Population Reference Bureau (PRB), *Female Genital Mutilation/Cutting: Data and Trends* (Washington, D.C.: PRB, 2008).
27. Rose Nakayi, "Decentralization and the Situation of Selected Ethnic and Racial Minorities: A Human Rights Audit," HURIPEC Working Paper 15 (Kampala: Human Rights and Peace Centre, Faculty of Law, Makerere University, July 2007).
28. Raymond Baguma, "Anti-Gay Bill Comes to Parliament," *New Vision*, July 25, 2009.
29. Richard Wanambwa, "DPP Drops Mukula's Global Fund Charges," *Monitor*, July 22, 2009.
30. Peter Magelah, "Corruption Will Require More Than Political Declarations," *New Vision*, June 25, 2009.

[31] Yasiin Mugerwa and Solomon Muyita, "27 New Judges Listed," *Monitor*, January 22, 2008.
[32] Testimony by the Commissioner General of Prisons, Dr. Johnson Byabashaija, to the Parliamentary Legal Affairs Committee; Mugerwa, "16,000 Remanded for over Three Years."
[33] Felix Osike, Hillary Nsambu, and Charles Ariko, "Judges Call Off Strike," *New Vision*, March 10, 2007.
[34] Omar Kalinge Nnyago, "Who Will Clean up Uganda's Judiciary?" *Monitor*, March 14, 2008.
[35] Heritage Foundation and *Wall Street Journal* (WSJ), "Uganda," in *Index of Economic Freedom 2009* (Washington, D.C./New York: Heritage Foundation and WSJ, 2009).
[36] Inspectorate of Government, *Activities and Achievements of the Inspectorate of Government: Promoting Zero Tolerance Policy to Corruption* (Kampala: Inspectorate of Government, June 2008).
[37] Lydia Mukisa, "Court Issues Warrant of Arrest for MP Winnie Matsiko," *Monitor*, December 24, 2008.
[38] Transparency International, *Corruption Perceptions Index 2008* (Berlin: Transparency International, September 22, 2008).
[39] Moses Sserwanga, "Giving with One Hand and Taking Away with Another," *Monitor*, August 22, 2006.
[40] Office of the Auditor General, *PEFA 'LITE': Public Expenditure and Financial Accountability, Appraisal of the Financial Management, Performance on Uganda* (Kampala: Office of the Auditor General, March 31, 2008), 32–33.
[41] Yasiin Mugerwa and Robert Mwanje, "Museveni Gives Naguru to Footballer, IUIU," *Monitor*, February 21, 2008; Chris Obore, "Why I Decided to Give Away Mabira," *Monitor*, April 16, 2007.
[42] Daniel Ronald Ruhweza, "Frustrated or Frustrating? The Inspector General of Government and the Question of Political Corruption in Uganda," HURIPEC Working Paper 20 (Kampala: Human Rights and Peace Centre, Faculty of Law, Makerere University, November 2008), 38, 39.

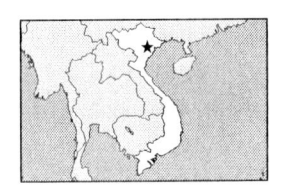

VIETNAM

CAPITAL: Hanoi
POPULATION: 87.3 million
GNI PER CAPITA (PPP): $2,700

SCORES	2006	2010
ACCOUNTABILITY AND PUBLIC VOICE:	1.56	1.48
CIVIL LIBERTIES:	3.02	3.11
RULE OF LAW:	2.49	2.37
ANTICORRUPTION AND TRANSPARENCY:	2.71	2.54

(scores are based on a scale of 0 to 7, with 0 representing weakest and 7 representing strongest performance)

Martin Gainsborough

INTRODUCTION

Vietnam presents a number of paradoxes. It is an authoritarian state ruled by a party whose reach extends to almost every area of the Vietnamese government and society. At the same time, the party enjoys a fair degree of popular legitimacy, having overseen the unification of the country's warring sides, high rates of economic growth, and the development of a vibrant society whose members increasingly enjoy the benefits of a modern consumer economy. The Vietnamese Communist Party (VCP) and its associated organizations have time and again proved adept at reinvigorating themselves and the country in the face of crisis and failing institutions, often to the benefit of Vietnamese citizens. Through a combination of control over the media, domination of the judiciary, and repression of political dissent, the VCP remains firmly in command. Opposition parties remain illegal and the party-dominated government incarcerates those it deems threatening to the VCP's monopoly on political power. As Vietnamese society faces key challenges, including rampant corruption and rising land grabs, it remains to be seen whether the current system will be able to effectively meet the needs of an increasingly demanding citizenry, or if more fundamental change will be needed.

Vietnam's current government grew out of the reunification of the country in 1976 after the Communist-ruled north defeated a U.S.-backed regime in

---

Dr. Martin Gainsborough is a faculty member and Reader in Development Politics in the Department of Politics at the University of Bristol, England. He has 20 years of research experience on Vietnam's politics and political economy, and has lived in both Hanoi and Ho Chi Minh City. He is author of *Changing Political Economy of Vietnam: The Case of Ho Chi Minh City* (Routledge 2003) and *Vietnam: Rethinking the State* (Zed Books, forthcoming 2010).

the south following more than a decade of fighting. Forced collectivization of agriculture and poor economic policies mired most Vietnamese in deep poverty. In the mid-1980s, the VCP launched a reform process officially referred to as *Doi Moi* (renewal). Over the last 20 years, reforms have delivered economic growth, jobs, and integration into the world economy, culminating in Vietnam's accession to the World Trade Organisation (WTO) in 2007. The economy has undergone far-reaching change, rendering it vastly more open and market oriented than a decade ago. Although the state still retains control over the "commanding heights"—primarily resource-based and public goods industries—its grip has loosened and a process of privatization is underway.

The provision of economic freedoms has not been accompanied by concomitant political reform. The upper echelons of the VCP have allowed a degree of enhanced openness in the face of new demands from society for accountable government and freedom of expression. However, this space remains within limited and sometimes arbitrary parameters defined by the party leadership, illustrating the contradictions and limitations on freedom in Vietnam. Thus, the government actively encourages the media to investigate and expose instances of corruption, but journalists may suffer retribution when their investigations are perceived to challenge the fabric of the VCP's power. Recent legislation clarified citizens' rights to practice their religious faith, and new denominations have been allowed to register. Nonetheless, the government maintains control over clergy appointments and religious organizations that wish to retain independence from the VCP-imposed framework are banned and their members put at risk of arrest. The National Assembly (NA) continues to move beyond its previous role as a simple rubber stamp entity, but citizens' efforts in 2006 and 2007 to form independent political parties, trade unions, and a journalists' society were throttled, with dozens of activists sentenced to long prison terms.

ACCOUNTABILITY AND PUBLIC VOICE — 1.48

FREE AND FAIR ELECTORAL LAWS AND ELECTIONS	1.00
EFFECTIVE AND ACCOUNTABLE GOVERNMENT	2.25
CIVIC ENGAGEMENT AND CIVIC MONITORING	1.67
MEDIA INDEPENDENCE AND FREEDOM OF EXPRESSION	1.00

Vietnam is a one-party state in which the VCP is the only legally permitted political party. The party maintains hegemonic control over the government, with party members holding almost all top posts in government, the parliament, and the security forces, as well as in many economic entities and social organizations. The VCP is headed by a 15-member Politburo, which serves as the country's top decision-making body. The individuals holding the top two positions in government, the prime minister and president, serve simultaneously as senior members of the Politburo. Together with the VCP secretary general, they govern the country as a troika. The minister of public security, the defense minister, the chairman of the NA, and several deputy prime ministers are also concurrently members of the Politburo.

Politburo members are elected every five years at a party congress by the 160-person Central Committee, which includes party representatives from across the country and the state system. At the 10th Party Congress held in April 2006, Nong Duc Manh was reappointed as secretary general, a position he has held since 2001. Also emerging from the meeting were two new candidates for president and prime minister. Nguyen Tan Dung, a deputy prime minister, was chosen as the candidate for prime minister, and Nguyen Minh Triet, the former VCP chief for Ho Chi Minh City, was selected for president. In June 2006, the two appointments were formalized in a confirmation vote in the NA. Both officials were the sole candidates put forward for each position, with Triet winning 94 percent of NA votes and Dung receiving 92 percent. The carefully managed leadership transition represented a shift to a younger generation and the first time government has been headed by two southerners since 1975. As in past congresses, despite the formal discussions of the meeting, much of its practical significance emerged from such rotations of personalities, with their associated implications for access to patronage and political protection.[1]

The 500-member National Assembly is elected every five years, more as an exercise to enhance the popular legitimacy of the VCP than to provide an avenue for meaningful public input into the selection of key government leaders. Although the VCP is the only political party permitted to compete in the polls, nonparty members and "self-nominated" candidates are legally allowed to stand for election. There is universal suffrage and typically more than one candidate competing in each district, making the process more inclusive and competitive than in neighboring China. Nevertheless, the process is biased in favor of VCP candidates.[2] In particular, all delegates are vetted through a complex and multilayered selection process headed by the Vietnam Fatherland Front (VFF), an umbrella organization closely aligned with the VCP.

Prior to the NA elections held in May 2007, the government publicly called for independent candidates to compete, and non-VCP members comprised approximately 25 percent of the total of 1,130 nominations.[3] Through the vetting process, however, 254 nominees were disqualified, including a majority of non-VCP members. Several self-nominated candidates—including several figures in major cities who attracted significant press attention—withdrew from the ballot after apparent pressure from government and party officials.[4] As a result, in the final count, approximately 10 percent of the 876 approved candidates were non-VCP members.[5]

The campaigning process is tightly controlled and largely formalistic, with few critical remarks exchanged between candidates. In contrast to neighboring Cambodia or Thailand, elections in Vietnam are generally free of fraud and violence as there is little at stake and much of the progovernment bias occurs at the vetting stage. The government reported voter turnout at 99 percent, the result of legal requirements to vote and pressure on local officials to ensure maximum participation. Following the polls, of the 493 elected delegates, 450 were members of the CPV and 42 were non-CPV members, with just one self-nominated candidate elected.[6] The overall ratio of VCP to non-VCP delegates was almost identical to that of the previous NA and closely matched targets named by the government-controlled National Assembly Standing Committee prior to the polls.

Though its authority remains circumscribed and VCP delegates are an overwhelming majority, over the past decade the NA has emerged as more than a rubber-stamp parliament. It functions as a vibrant body, capable of amending government-proposed legislation and demanding greater accountability from ministers. Among its 500 delegates, 140 are full-time members, while the remaining representatives attend plenary sessions twice a year.[7] The two-week sessions are primarily focused on approving legislation that has already been analyzed and amended by the permanent members. The NA's proceedings are broadcast on radio and television, including televised sessions during which individual delegates query government ministers. Although this occurs within fairly strict parameters, the questions posed are largely unscripted and, in the context of Vietnam's political system, the process has allowed some measure of transparency and oversight of the executive. In March 2008, the NA passed a new Law on Lawmaking that, among other provisions, would make public consultation and impact assessment mandatory in any law-making process.[8] The legislation technically came into effect in January 2009, but an implementing decree has yet to be issued to fully trigger its application.

At the provincial level, citizens elect local state bodies called People's Councils; candidates are vetted by the VFF. People's Councils then elect an executive body, the People's Committee, which is technically responsible for provincial policy. In practice, however, People's Councils are weaker than the other two provincial-level bodies, the Party Committee and the People's Committee, rendering their members little more than figureheads. The last People's Council elections occurred uneventfully in 2007.

The organization of political parties or civic movements calling for democratic reform remains outlawed. Citizens involved in such initiatives have been severely repressed in recent years. Previously, from 2004 to 2006, dissident activity flourished, with "an unprecedented number of political organizations" formed to advocate for greater democracy, respect for human rights, and religious freedom.[9] These included the Vietnam Populist Party and the Democratic Party of Vietnam, originally founded in 1944 and re-launched in 2006 as a loosely structured dissident organization. Also founded were the Committee for Human Rights in Vietnam, the Free Journalists Association of Vietnam (FJAV) and two independent workers' associations. In a bold move, on April 8, 2006, 118 individuals representing a diverse network of professionals issued a "Manifesto on Freedom and Democracy for Vietnam" calling for a multiparty system, independent media, freedom of assembly, and religious freedom. The document later came to be known as 8406 (a reference to the date when it was published), and those supporting it as Bloc 8406. By the end of the year, it had reportedly garnered over 2,000 signatures and participants had issued several follow-on statements proposing phased democratization.

The authorities' response to the mobilization was initially guarded, as Hanoi was the focus of international attention in hosting the Asia Pacific Economic Cooperation (APEC) forum in November 2006 and was about to gain entry to the WTO in early 2007. After the APEC summit, however, security forces initiated a systematic crackdown against the Bloc 8406 organizers and other prominent activists. During 2007 and 2008, over 20 individuals, including lawyers and Catholic priests, were sentenced to prison terms of up to eight years in what Human Rights Watch termed "one of the worst crackdowns on peaceful dissidents in 20 years."[10]

Constitutionally, a system of checks and balances exist. In reality, however, the VCP retains significant influence over all branches of government. There are few formal constraints on its power, although there is contestation of party power at different levels of the state hierarchy. In recent years, the NA has rejected cabinet nominees, forced the government to amend legislation, and successfully demanded an increase in its powers, including the right to hold no-confidence votes against the government.[11] The president, himself a member of the Politburo, proposes candidates for the Supreme People's Court, who are then confirmed by the NA; available evidence suggests that none have been rejected.

Although party membership is not a prerequisite for gaining civil service employment, most applicants tailor their answers on exams to reflect the party line.[12] Selection is conducted through an open interview process and an annual exam that has been criticized as excessively academic.[13] Informal criteria such as personal relationships also continue to play an important role in personnel decisions. Pilot projects, however, have sought to enhance the openness and transparency of the recruitment process, even as thousands of civil servants have transferred to the private sector in search of better working conditions in recent years. In 2008, the Ministry of Education opened one vice minister position to external candidates, and a number of state-owned enterprises in Ho Chi Minh City have extended their CEO searches to external candidates.[14]

Although freedom of association remains highly controlled, among the most noticeable trends in Vietnam is the continued proliferation of nonprofit organizations, particularly at the grassroots level. In 2005, there were an estimated 140,000 community-based organizations, 3,000 cooperatives, 1,000 locally registered NGOs, and 200 charities.[15] Also playing a dominant role in the nonprofit sector are 22 mass organizations acting under guidance from the VFF and the VCP. These groups engage in a range of issues on behalf of various segments of the population, though the degree of genuine representation of members' interests, as opposed to serving as a means of maintaining VCP social control, remains ambiguous.[16] The largest group is the Viet Nam Women's Union, with a membership of over 12 million. Other prominent organizations include the Ho Chi Minh Communist Youth Union, the Vietnam Youth Federation, the Farmers' Union, the Veterans Union, the Association for Buddhism, the Protestant Association, and the Association for the Blind.

Domestic and foreign organizations must register with a government agency and are required to provide an annual report of their activities to their sponsoring body. Most registered organizations, as well as many unregistered grassroots civic groups, do not challenge the VCP's authority but rather supplement the work of the state. They see themselves as partners working on projects in support of state policy, advocates for improved state services, or as representatives of marginalized groups. Their work focuses on medical and educational service provision, poverty alleviation, and other forms of development assistance. The vast majority of civic groups consciously avoid operating in sensitive or overtly political areas for fear of retribution. New legislation requiring impact assessments prior to the passage of laws has opened the door for greater civic group engagement in some public policy debates.

The legal framework regulating the nonprofit sector remains weak, comprised of a hodgepodge of decrees and laws. The government has made multiple attempts in recent years to draft more comprehensive regulations, but the process has been repeatedly delayed, in part due to lobbying by professional and business associations seeking to influence its provisions. Linguistic difficulties have also made the drafting process more challenging due to the problems translating the terms "NGO" and "civil society" into Vietnamese because of the rather negative and confrontational connotation associated with the most commonly used translations.[17]

Although there has been an explosion of media outlets in Vietnam and coverage is much livelier and more critical than a decade ago, extensive restrictions on free expression remain. The constitution affirms the right to freedom of expression, but other legislation including internet-related decrees, the Press Law, the Publishing Law, the State Secrets Protection Ordinance, and the penal code are used to punish journalists and bloggers.[18] After a relative easing of limitations on the press in 2006 as Vietnam prepared to host the APEC summit and join the WTO, the environment for free expression deteriorated as the government cracked down on journalists, bloggers, and prodemocracy activists. Dozens of media workers and other citizens have since been fired, fined, or imprisoned for reporting on sensitive issues.

As of 2008, there were over 850 publications, including 80 e-newspapers and 68 radio and television stations at the central and provincial levels. The dominant television station remains the state-run Viet Nam Television, accessible to 85 percent of households. All media outlets are wholly or partially owned by the state, with the exception of a small number of underground publications. In recent years, the government has encouraged media to report on corruption and act as an avenue of "oversight over the implementation of policies and laws by State authorities."[19] In practice, however, this occurs within fairly strict limits. In a development widely perceived as a step backward for media reporting on corruption, two journalists for *Thanh Nien* and *Tuoi Tre*, high-profile publications known for pushing the limits on permissible coverage, were arrested in May 2008 and sentenced to prison and re-education without detention for exposing a high-level scandal (see Anticorruption and Transparency). In a rare act of direct defiance among the state-controlled media, the newspapers published editorials denouncing the government's actions. The editors of both publications were subsequently removed from their positions, and at least five other journalists were stripped of their press credentials.[20]

While some issues—such as criticism of the one-party system, religious freedom violations, and foreign policy—are largely off-limits, journalists are given greater leeway with regards to social, economic, and cultural topics. Indeed, the government intentionally leaves the boundaries of permissible expression vague, encouraging self-censorship. Nevertheless, officials may at times issue direct instructions on coverage. One reporter was quoted as saying "If you go too far your editor will receive a phone call from the [VCP's] Ideology Department."[21]

In recent years, online communication and an increasingly vibrant blogosphere have emerged as the most important conduit for alternative viewpoints. Approximately 20 million people, or nearly a quarter of the population, reportedly accessed the internet in 2009.[22] In response, the government has increased its efforts to censor content deemed undesirable. Internet service providers are required by law to block access to certain websites; internet cafes must record users' personal information and browsing activities; and blogging platforms must, as of December 2008, remove "harmful" content, report to the government every six months, and provide information about individual bloggers upon request.[23] In 2007, *Intellasia*, an online news and investment site run by a Vietnamese-American entrepreneur, was shut down for "violating rules on copyright and political content."[24] Unlike in China, Vietnamese citizens have access to some foreign news sites, including the BBC,[25] though the sites of overseas human rights groups remain blocked.

CIVIL LIBERTIES   3.11

PROTECTION FROM STATE TERROR, UNJUSTIFIED IMPRISONMENT, AND TORTURE	2.38
GENDER EQUITY	4.67
RIGHTS OF ETHNIC, RELIGIOUS, AND OTHER DISTINCT GROUPS	3.75
FREEDOM OF CONSCIENCE AND BELIEF	3.00
FREEDOM OF ASSOCIATION AND ASSEMBLY	1.75

Vietnam has ratified key international human rights treaties, including the International Covenant on Civil and Political Rights and the Convention Against Torture, and the constitution protects a range of rights. However, the government's protection of civil liberties remains highly selective. In recent years, while the government has instituted reforms to enhance protection of the rights of women and the disabled, it has also responded to citizens' demands for political reform and rights protection with violent repression.

Although Vietnamese law prohibits physical abuse of prisoners, pretrial detention conditions are reportedly harsh, with beatings and mistreatment of detainees routine, particularly as police seek to obtain confessions during interrogations.[26] Human Rights Watch reported finding compelling evidence of "torture and ill-treatment of political and religious prisoners, including beatings and electric shock, and punitive placement of prisoners in solitary confinement in dark and unsanitary cells."[27] Vietnam retains the death penalty as punishment for over two dozen offenses, not all of them violent. According to Amnesty International, from January 2004 to September 2008, media sources reported on 102 executions and 300 death sentences imposed.[28]

According to the U.S. State Department, prisons are overcrowded and prisoners suffer from a poor diet, unclean drinking water, and poor sanitation,[29] though conditions overall are not life threatening and prisoners have some access to health care. Human Rights Watch has reported that Vietnam holds over 400 political and religious prisoners, including members of opposition political parties, human rights defenders, trade union activists, journalists, land rights activists, and religious believers who refused to join state-controlled churches. Many of these individuals have been imprisoned under vaguely worded provisions in the penal code that effectively criminalize peaceful political expression and criticism of the government or VCP. These include Article 88, which punishes "conducting propaganda against the government," Article 258 on "abusing democratic freedoms to infringe upon the interests of the state," and Article 245 on "causing public disorder." During the crackdown on Bloc 8406 and related pro democracy activists in 2007 and 2008, approximately 40 dissidents were arrested and at least 30 sentenced to prison.[30]

Vietnamese law, primarily Ordinance 44, allows the government to administratively sentence citizens to house arrest, detention in "rehabilitation camps" or incarceration in mental hospitals without due process of law; citizens are sentenced for two-year renewable terms. Although the exact number of individuals detained under such provisions remains unknown, the restrictions were applied to several dissidents in recent years. In March 2008, police arrested Bui Kim Thanh, a land rights activist, and committed her to a mental hospital for the second time in two years.[31]

Avenues to seek redress for abuses by public officials are extremely limited. There is no ombudsman or independent human rights commission. Procedures enabling citizens to complain of abuses exist but are cumbersome and largely ineffective. Recourse for victims of torture, unfair imprisonment, or other severe rights violations is nonexistent. The government has at times defended its harsh treatment of political dissidents.[32]

Crime rates are generally low in Vietnam. Although petty theft and pickpocketing are common, violent crime is less prevalent. Drug use is an increasing social problem and contributes significantly to the crime rate. Combating human trafficking remains a significant challenge despite increased government efforts to enforce the law and implement a national action plan. Thousands of women and children are trafficked internally and externally each year, many into forced prostitution. Those found guilty of trafficking may face punishments ranging from two years to life in prison. A national steering committee coordinates government efforts to prosecute cases and organize public awareness programs. Prosecutions and official reporting on trafficking cases have increased in recent years. Between 2005 and 2007, over 900 cases involving 1,600 traffickers and 2,200 smuggled women and children were uncovered.[33] Cooperation with other Southeast Asian countries has also improved.[34]

Under the constitution and other legislation, women are guaranteed equal civil and political rights. Vietnam has ratified the Convention on the Elimination of All Forms of Discrimination against Women (CEDAW) and was ranked 31st out of 102 countries assessed in a 2009 Gender Equality Index.[35] As of 2007, one quarter of NA representatives were women, a proportion that placed Vietnam third in the Asia-Pacific region.[36] Women's collective interests are primarily represented via the VCP-controlled National Committee for the Advancement of Women (NCFAW) and the Women's Union. These groups have worked closely with the government, including its Department on Gender Equality, to implement a national strategy to increase women's representation in politics, as well as improve literacy rates, access to education, and healthcare.[37]

Nevertheless, in its 2007 assessment, the CEDAW committee raised concerns that women remained underrepresented at local levels of government, that deep-rooted stereotypes continue to contribute to significant societal discrimination, and that HIV/AIDS infections among women had increased.[38] Although economic opportunities for women have grown, they continue to face discrimination with respect to wages and promotions. This is partly due to their greater concentration in the informal sector, where employees generally enjoy fewer protections or access to social services.

In recent years, the government has taken steps to improve the legal regime protecting women's rights. Of particular significance are the Gender Equality Law passed in November 2006 and the Law on the Prevention of Domestic Violence, which was passed in November 2007 and entered into force in July 2008. Despite training to familiarize police and judicial officials with the laws, enforcement has been slow and insufficient transparency on data related to gender issues has made assessment of the laws' impact difficult. Meanwhile, violence against women remains widespread, reportedly affecting nearly half of rural women and contributing to approximately two-thirds of divorces.[39]

Vietnam has 54 recognized ethnic groups, although 86 percent of the population is ethnic Vietnamese (Kinh). Some ethnic minorities are represented at high levels of government—VCP secretary general Nong Duc Manh is an ethnic Tay. In recent decades, conditions for the country's ethnic Chinese (Hoa) have improved dramatically compared to earlier campaigns of repression and property confiscation. Many have benefited from economic liberalization policies and poverty rates among the Hoa are reportedly lower than for the majority Kinh.[40]

Other ethnic minorities continue to face widespread discrimination in education and employment, performing worse than the majority on health and development indicators. The government has attempted to address these problems by investing in programs to improve education, health facilities, employment opportunities, and infrastructure for ethnic minority citizens. Nevertheless, such programs are often implemented within government-controlled parameters and perceived by minority populations as aimed at weakening their unique cultural and linguistic identity. Although courses are available in minority languages in schools throughout the country, the number of hours dedicated to them is small in comparison to Vietnamese, leaving non-native Vietnamese speakers at a disadvantage.

The relationship between the government and several ethnic groups, notably the Khmer Krom and Montagnards, is particularly complex, as linguistic and cultural grievances often overlap with property disputes and restrictions on religious freedom. A 2009 Human Rights Watch Report on the treatment of the Khmer Krom, who number over one million and are concentrated in the Mekong delta region, describes increasing landlessness and poverty among farmers, state policies restricting school instruction in the Khmer language, and tight government controls over Theravada Buddhism. Such policies sparked land rights and religious freedom protests in 2007 and 2008; wary of the possible emergence of an ethnonationalist movement, the authorities responded with repression, using dogs and electric batons to break up protests and arresting participants, including defrocking and later imprisoning five monks.[41] The monks were released in 2008 following international pressure. The Montagnards, a Christian minority in the Central Highlands region, face similar circumstances and unrest has recently increased over land disputes resulting from confiscations to develop large state-owned coffee plantations.

Citizens' ability to participate in religious activities has grown in recent years, with an estimated 20 million citizens following a variety of religions. In 2008, new congregations and denominations were registered throughout the country, including five Protestant denominations, a Muslim sect, and the Baha'i community. However, the overall framework surrounding religious practice remains tightly controlled by the government, which perceives it as a privilege granted to citizens rather than an inalienable right. Under the 2004 Ordinance on Religion and Belief, all religious groups must be registered with the government and affiliated associations, such as the Vietnam Buddhist Sangha. The activities and leadership of individual registered congregations must be approved by the authorities. Independent religious education is not permitted and texts must be printed through a government-owned publishing house. Twelve religions are currently approved, of which Buddhism, Protestantism, and Catholicism are the largest. In 2008, the Catholic Church reported that the government had relaxed its control somewhat.[42]

Despite such easing of restrictions, space for independent religious activity remains limited and some groups are banned outright. Procedures for registering groups are often inconsistent; in 2008 authorities reportedly delayed action on applications submitted by over 1,000 Protestant congregations in ethnic minority areas.[43] Unregistered individual worshippers and groups risk harassment, beatings, and imprisonment, particularly if their activities are interpreted as political activism. Such incidents have reportedly decreased in recent years and the majority of religious practitioners in unregistered places of worship were able to operate without government interference in 2008. Nonetheless, several groups continue to face significant repression, including a banned faction of the Hoa Hao Buddhist Church, the leadership of the unrecognized Unified Buddhist Church of Vietnam (UBCV), the Montagnard Christians, and some members of the Khmer Krom minority.

Individuals do not generally face discrimination in employment on the basis of religious faith. VCP members are not required to be atheists, although advancement might be impeded, and the vast majority do not practice a religion. In 2008 the United Nations Day of VESAK 2008 (an annual Buddhist holiday) was held in Hanoi with the participation of over 4,000 Buddhist dignitaries, monks, and nuns.[44] Human rights groups raised concerns that Vietnam had been chosen to host such a gathering, given its ongoing imprisonment of hundreds of religious believers.

The government, through the Ministry of Labor, Invalids and Social Affairs, has made significant efforts to accommodate the needs of Vietnam's large population of disabled individuals, including working with international donors to increase employment opportunities.[45] The rights of the disabled are enshrined in the constitution and in various laws. The government is in the process of drafting a Law on the Handicapped as well as studying measures needed to ratify the Convention on the Rights of Persons with Disabilities.[46] Existing laws provide incentives to firms that recruit people with disabilities, including offering subsidized government loans to enterprises where over 51 percent of employees are disabled. Firms that do not fulfill minimum disabled hiring requirements face fines, while new government and large public buildings must also include access for persons with disabilities.

Despite constitutional provisions protecting freedom of assembly, it remains restricted in practice. Official permission is required for group gatherings, though many informal groups are able to meet without interference. In recent years, a number of incidents have tested the resolve of authorities to tolerate public gatherings and political expression. Increasingly common small-scale protests are generally tolerated.[47] By contrast, large-scale peaceful demonstrations have been met with repressive force.[48] For example, students participating in anti-Chinese demonstrations prior to the Olympic torch relay in Ho Chi Minh City were reportedly detained by local police in April 2008.[49] Government confiscation or destruction of church property for development projects sparked large-scale protests from both official and unofficial churches throughout 2008. As many as 15,000 Catholics participated in a special mass and prayer vigil over a property dispute in Hanoi in September 2008. The authorities used tear gas and electric batons to disperse the gathering and arrested at least eight participants.[50]

All unions operate under the direction of the VCP-controlled Vietnam General Confederation of Labour (VGCL). As of August 2008, official union membership reportedly stood at over six million, nearly 40 percent of registered wage earners. Efforts to form or join independent unions are harshly repressed. Independent trade unions founded during a surge of rights activism in late 2006, including the United Worker-Farmers Organization of Vietnam (UWFO) and the Independent Workers' Union of Vietnam (IWUV), were banned, and their leaders arrested, beginning in November 2006. Since then, at least eight independent union activists have been sentenced to prison, although some have been released.[51] Vietnamese security agents have also been implicated in the disappearance of IWUV founder Le Tri Tue, who has not been seen since fleeing to Cambodia to seek political asylum in May 2007.[52]

All strikes must be approved by the VGCL and are illegal if they do not arise from a collective labor dispute or concern issues other than labor relations. A series of wildcat strikes in 2007 and 2008, mainly over pay disputes during a period of high inflation, prompted a tightening of legislation regulating the right to strike, including amendments made to the Labor Law in July 2007 that render legal strikes nearly impossible. In 2008, the government issued a decree declaring that workers participating in illegal strikes who are found to have caused damage to their employer are liable to be fined the equivalent of up to three months salary.[53]

RULE OF LAW 2.37

INDEPENDENT JUDICIARY	2.00
PRIMACY OF RULE OF LAW IN CIVIL AND CRIMINAL MATTERS	2.40
ACCOUNTABILITY OF SECURITY FORCES AND MILITARY TO CIVILIAN AUTHORITIES	1.75
PROTECTION OF PROPERTY RIGHTS	3.33

The judiciary consists of the Supreme People's Court (SPC), provincial and district people's courts, military tribunals, and administrative, economic, and labor courts. The highest court of appeal is the SPC, which reports to the NA. Administrative courts adjudicate complaints by citizens about official abuse and corruption. Special committees have also been established to resolve local disputes. Following an earlier trend, legal codification and technocratic reforms to the judicial system have continued in recent years. In its Legal System Development Strategy to 2010 set in motion in 2005, government pledged to increase access to justice, improve procedures for judicial appointments, and advance judicial training.[54] Thus far, however, reform efforts have been incomplete and none have addressed core deficiencies related to political interference in the judiciary and persistent violations of due process rights.

Both direct and indirect government interference in the judiciary is commonplace. The VCP retains effective control over judicial appointments, and almost all judges are party members. Lay assessors empowered to assist judges with cases at the district level are appointed by the People's Councils from a VFF-approved pool of candidates. The selection process at all levels is highly politicized and judges are appointed and promoted largely based on political loyalty rather than merit. The grounds for removing judges are vaguely defined, the removal process is opaque, and no appeals process exists.[55] Although the 2002 Law on the Organization of the People's Court aimed to protect judges from government interference, the VCP continues to exert significant indirect influence over trial outcomes through ensuring the appointment of politically reliable judges. In sensitive cases, the VCP routinely intervenes directly in decisions to launch prosecutions and determine verdicts.[56] Corruption in the judiciary remains widespread, partly due to the country's large number of ad hoc and inconsistent laws, which create opportunities for judicial corruption in their enforcement. Powerful actors, including high-ranking government officials, are generally above the law.

Due to low judicial salaries and a weak tertiary education system, Vietnam suffers from a shortage of qualified lawyers and judges. Legal training is not required for lay assessors and most possess no legal education. With assistance from international donors, the Ministry of Justice is currently managing a training program aimed at tripling the number of lawyers in Vietnam.[57] In July 2009, the Vietnam Bar Federation, which will answer to the government and the VCP, was established as the country's first national bar association.

Access to justice remains limited and the majority of Vietnamese are uneducated about their legal rights.[58] While due process guarantees exist, they are routinely violated in practice. The constitution provides that citizens are innocent until proven guilty, but judges often presume guilt.[59] In high-profile cases, it is common for the state-controlled media to engage in character assassination such that the public is convinced of the guilt of the accused prior to announcement of the verdict. Defendants and their lawyers are sometimes denied the opportunity to present a defense, prosecutors are not independent, and many trials last only a few hours. Most legal proceedings are open to the public.

Although defendants have a constitutional right to counsel, only those facing possible life sentences or the death penalty may be provided with a lawyer if they are unable to afford one themselves. In practice, ordinary citizens often do not have access to a lawyer, partly because there is only one lawyer for every 20,000 citizens.[60] Political and religious prisoners are more purposefully and consistently denied counsel as the government pressures lawyers to refrain from defending political activists. At least three lawyers have been threatened, incarcerated, and in one case, committed to a mental institution for defending bloggers, political dissidents, and citizens seeking property restitution. Prominent human rights lawyer Le Cong Dinh was arrested on charges of "conducting propaganda against the government" on June 13, 2009 and was later expelled from the Ho Chi Minh City bar association.[61]

The Vietnam People's Army (VPA) continues to play a prominent role in the country's affairs, with several members holding seats in the NA. The VPA remains largely loyal to the VCP and is well represented at its highest levels. The minister of national defense sits on the Politburo, as does the minister of public security. Military policy is determined by the party's Central Military Commission, which includes senior members of the military and the Politburo. In addition to responsibility for national defense, the VPA also supports local authorities in responding to natural disasters and plays a significant role in the economy, owning land and several enterprises, including one of the country's largest telecommunications firms; there is no meaningful oversight of its economic activities. The police and internal security agencies are regularly used by the VCP to repress political dissent.

As Vietnam is a socialist state, the state technically owns all land. In practice, individuals and businesses are granted "land use rights certificates" (LURC), generally for 50 years, which carry with them a number of rights and entitlements. These include the ability to transfer rights to use the land, the right to compensation in the event of expropriation, and the right to any benefits accrued from the use of the land. Amendments made in 2003 to the Land Law increased usage rights for foreigners and overseas Vietnamese. In a further extension, from September 2009 certain categories of overseas Vietnamese will have the right to lease houses, use land for business purposes, and receive compensation in the event of expropriation.

Land expropriation and reclassification have been highly contentious issues in Vietnam in recent years, as the phenomenon has spread the length and breadth of the country. By law, the state may expropriate land so long as owners of the LURC are compensated; the level of compensation may vary. Protests by farmers and peasants whose land was reclaimed by officials and subsequently developed as commercial property have become increasingly common, particularly in Ho Chi Minh City. At the core of most protests are complaints that the compensation received did not reflect the true value of the land, that promised jobs or training programs never materialized, or that compensation is insufficient to replace the farmer's lost agricultural livelihood. Similar sentiments exist among private firms. A recent survey that found that in most provinces, a majority of firms felt that compensation for expropriated land in their province was not fair.[62] Redress through legal channels is subject to the limitations detailed above. As a result, both foreign and domestic firms often seek informal dispute resolution mechanisms, while ordinary citizens take to the streets.

The rapid increase in the number of golf courses over the past two years illustrates this phenomenon. Aside from mounting public anger over the use of confiscated land for recreational venues, the government is concerned about the potential impact on food security, as many courses are built on reclaimed rice fields. Investors often build courses in order to obtain a 50-year lease at a lower rent than if the land were classified as commercial or industrial, with the ultimate intention of using the land for real estate or other projects. At a recent NA session, the minister of planning and investment called for provincial authorities to cancel up to 50 of the 166 approved golf course projects across the country.[63]

ANTICORRUPTION AND TRANSPARENCY 2.54

 ENVIRONMENT TO PROTECT AGAINST CORRUPTION 2.50
 PROCEDURES AND SYSTEMS TO ENFORCE ANTICORRUPTION LAWS 2.25
 EXISTENCE OF ANTICORRUPTION NORMS, STANDARDS,
  AND PROTECTIONS 2.75
 GOVERNMENTAL TRANSPARENCY 2.67

Corruption remains pervasive across Vietnamese society, despite the country's high economic growth rate. Indeed, Vietnam's fairly predictable patterns of corruption have not served to deter foreign investors. Decentralization has further contributed to a rise in corruption over the past decade: local authorities have been granted greater authority over expenditures and development projects, enabling considerable discretion in demanding bribes in exchange for licenses and permits.[64] The oft-used term "ask-give mechanism" refers to a means of governing society by orders rather than the rule of law, such that actions by lower officials are contingent on receiving approval from superiors, with various "favors" exchanged in return. Vietnam ranked 121st out of 180 countries in Transparency International's (TI) 2008 Corruption Perceptions Index.

 Under international and domestic pressure to address the problem, the government has continued a high-profile anticorruption campaign.[65] Recent years have seen the passage of groundbreaking legislation, establishment of new anticorruption bodies, and ratification of the UN Convention Against Corruption. Despite such positive steps, enforcement of higher standards has been hindered by a combination of factors, including inadequate checks and balances, the lack of an independent judiciary and free media, poor incentive structures for civil servants, widespread nepotism and secrecy, and practically nonexistent protection for whistleblowers.[66] Under such conditions, the gap between legal standards and practical realities will remain problematic for years to come.

 Bureaucratic red tape is substantial and payments to expedite administrative procedures are common. Bribes are most often solicited by traffic police, construction regulators, and land registration, customs, and tax administration officials.[67] Nonetheless, a 2007 TI survey found that only 14 percent of respondents from average households reported paying a petty bribe over the past year, a relatively low figure compared to neighboring countries.[68] Within the private sector, the government has taken steps to decrease the number of requirements for establishing and operating a business by eliminating nearly 200 unnecessary permits.[69]

Payment for position and promotion in the government bureaucracy remains the norm and the lines between public funds and private earnings are blurred. In April 2008, the VCP chief of Ca Mau Province, Vo Thanh Binh, handed nearly US$7,000 to police that he reported receiving as a bribe. He later claimed to have been offered tens of thousands of dollars in return for senior positions in state agencies.[70] The 2005 Law on Thrift Practices and Anti-Wastefulness represented a preliminary attempt to address this situation by banning the use of public money for dinner parties, bonuses, and gifts. Nevertheless, most officials still take for granted that holding public office entails access to resources for supplementing one's salary.

Despite a growing private sector, state-owned enterprises still number around 4,000 and account for over one-third of GDP, providing numerous opportunities for corruption. Graft is especially rampant in the construction sector, and also widespread in the oil, gas, coal, paper, cement, airline, and telecommunications industries.[71]

A main plank of the government's anticorruption campaign was the passage of a 2005 Anti-Corruption Law, which took effect in 2006, and subsequent implementing decrees. International observers generally assess the law and surrounding legal framework as well developed, particularly as it emphasizes systemic measures to reduce opportunities for corruption as a complement to punitive measures. It includes requirements for assets declarations, the creation of anticorruption bodies, and mechanisms for citizens to lodge complaints, among other provisions. Not surprisingly, enforcement of the law has been uneven and incomplete, hampered by a lack of political will to enable significant oversight by non-VCP entities. According to one study, enforcement was initially strong in 2006 and 2007 but weakened as officials developed more sophisticated strategies to circumvent supervision. The Anti-Corruption Law requires that government officials and family members annually disclose assets, including money held in overseas and domestic accounts and taxable income. Although hundreds of candidates for the NA election in 2007 reportedly declared their assets, implementation as a whole has been incomplete, and oversight mechanisms are still in the development stage.[72] Assets declarations are not made available to the public unless a state official is found to be "unusually wealthy" and further investigations deemed necessary.[73]

A number of agencies in Vietnam feature anticorruption mandates, although the lack of a truly independent body remains a key weakness of the overall framework. In 2007, the Office of the Steering Committee for Anti-Corruption (OSCAC) was established to implement the provisions of the 2005 law. The committee is headed by the prime minister and composed of members of various government bodies, including the judiciary and the VCP, raising doubts over its ability to be impartial. Meanwhile, the Government Inspectorate, which also functions as an ombudsman, has itself been a "frequent target of corruption."[74]

Perhaps the most promising development in recent years was the decision in 2006 to enable the State Auditor of Vietnam (SAV) to report to the

NA rather than the executive. The SAV was reorganized in 2004 as an independent organization and is charged with tracking the use of state funds by government agencies and settling the state budget.[75] Its effectiveness has been limited, however, as the institution suffers from resource constraints, incomplete independence, and overlapping mandates with the Government Inspectorate.[76] According to TI, "the SAV has a weak capacity to enforce auditing recommendations and there is little evidence that the government acts on SAV reports."[77]

Other government bodies with anticorruption mandates include the Supreme People's Procuracy Department of Prosecution and Corruption Investigations, the Ministry of Public Security's Bureau of Corruption Criminal Investigation, and the State Inspectorate (SI) Anticorruption Bureau, all of which were set up in late 2006 and early 2007. The latter body is charged with investigating corruption cases and passing them along to the People's Procuracy for prosecution. While both have achieved some successes by uncovering and prosecuting scandals, their effectiveness has been limited by the presence of corruption within the bodies themselves.[78]

Despite these constraints, hundreds of officials have been prosecuted for corruption in recent years, including several high-ranking ones. According to official figures, almost 300 of the nearly 400 corruption cases detected in 2008 were prosecuted.[79] It would be a mistake, however, to perceive such statistics as a victory for independent judicial enforcement of anticorruption legislation. Rather, it may reflect one manifestation of the political center's attempt to counteract the potential loss of control that accompanies decentralization.[80] In other instances, prosecution for corruption is a tool employed within broader intraparty struggles for authority.

In its rhetoric, the government has repeatedly encouraged the media to take on a greater role in exposing corruption. Media coverage of petty and grand corruption is more extensive today than five years ago. In addition, online newspapers and bloggers are playing an increasingly important role as corruption watchdogs, at times surpassing the influence and quantity of reporting in print publications.[81] However, political infighting and the close association of government agencies, the police, the VCP, and the media renders investigating corruption extremely complicated and potentially hazardous for journalists and editors. Most journalists will only investigate corruption if given permission to do so by state officials.[82]

The high-profile "PMU 18" scandal is a good example of the complexities surrounding exposure and prosecution of graft in Vietnam. In 2005, officials of the Ministry of Transport's Project Management Unit 18 (PMU-18) were accused of using US$2.6 million of ministry funds to gamble on English football matches.[83] The case originally came to light in 2006, after police investigators leaked information to journalists working for national newspapers. It was suspected at the time that the reason for the leaks was to discredit the accused, who were allegedly in line for election to senior positions in the VCP.

The alleged culprits subsequently were jailed and the transport minister was forced to resign. Two years later, however, the journalists who initially exposed the scandal were arrested and convicted for "abusing democratic freedoms to infringe upon the interests of the state." Also in 2008, charges against one of the officials involved were dropped and his party membership reinstated. The journalist who was imprisoned was ultimately released in January 2009 following a presidential pardon. Nevertheless, there are indications the official backlash against him and his colleague has renewed journalists' reluctance to investigate state abuses without clear high-level authorization.

There is little protection for whistleblowers despite provisions in the 2005 law allowing citizens to complain about perceived government abuses. In 2007, the government launched a website where citizens could register complaints about specific state agencies, including major municipalities, the NA, and the Communist Party Central Committee. A 2008 survey revealed, however, that many Vietnamese were fearful of reporting instances of corruption because of the impossibility of lodging complaints anonymously.[84]

Corruption extends to the education sector and several scandals have erupted in recent years involving parents and students paying bribes in exchange for school admission and good grades. Almost all university faculty members interviewed in a study covering 1998–2008 admitted receiving bribes. It has become common for students to present teachers with expensive gifts on Teacher's Day, with the expectation of receiving higher grades.[85]

Members of the public are not granted by law the right to access government information, and the government rarely fulfills such requests. However, there have been some improvements. The Ministry of Justice is currently preparing a freedom of information law and worked with the international free expression group Article 19 to prepare an initial draft in March 2009.[86] The Law on the Promulgation of Legal Normative Documents and the 2004 Law on Local Laws have improved standards of transparency. Legal instruments must now be published in the Official Gazette for 15 days prior to coming into force, and the number of published laws has increased significantly.[87] Almost all provinces now have a local gazette that publishes provincial and district regulations. The SPC also publishes decisions on its website.

Limited efforts have been made to improve financial accountability. Until 2000, the budget was a state secret. Since then, the NA and the provincial people's committees have played an increasingly important oversight role. Both take the role seriously, but fully effective oversight requires technical capacity and political independence that the bodies and their members lack. National and provincial budget and year-end accounts are also now published on the Ministry of Finance website. However, accounts are often inaccurate, as state agencies attempt to conceal their actual budget amount and spending record. Accounts are frequently published late and in many respects fall short of international standards. The military budget remains a secret. Vietnam received a score of 9 percent in the 2008 Open Budget Index.[88]

Abuses related to government procurement remain widespread, despite passage of a 2005 Tendering Law. The government is currently in the process of implementing an e-procurement system, which may improve the situation.[89] Open competition is often violated in practice, and collusion in bidding remains a problem.[90] In August 2008, Japan suspended aid to Vietnam after four Japanese consultants were arrested on charges of paying US$800,000 in bribes to Ho Chi Minh City officials in order to secure consulting contracts for the Japanese-financed East-West Highway Project. Aid resumed in February 2009 after two Vietnamese officials were arrested for involvement in the scandal and sentenced to prison in September 2009.[91]

There are also irregularities related to the disbursement of foreign assistance. Both the government and donors have formal mechanisms in place to minimize such abuses, but reports of officials using aid funds for personal enrichment continue to emerge. The 2005 Law on Thrift Practices and Anti-Wastefulness included provisions to decrease the waste and misuse of foreign assistance. However, the PMU-18 affair and other scandals indicate that the abuse of foreign assistance persists.

RECOMMENDATIONS

- The government should issue an implementing decree to trigger application of the Law on Lawmaking, continue to expand the National Assembly's oversight capacity, and permit a wide range of societal actors to participate in consultations and impact assessments on pending legislation.
- Efforts should be made to strengthen the Vietnamese media's ability to investigate and uncover instances of corruption and other abuses. Specifically, the variety of regulations and laws through which the government controls the media should be reduced, and guidelines governing the roles and responsibilities of journalists and editors should be clarified.
- Ambiguities in legal codes relating to national security and administrative detention—including Articles 88, 245, and 258 of the penal code, as well as Ordinance 44—should be clarified or repealed to prevent their use as a tool to discourage and punish legitimate opposition and debate. Those already imprisoned under these provisions should be released.
- The government should widen the range of churches and religious groups it recognizes and repair relations with disaffected religious communities.
- The government should reform existing procedures for seeking redress or establish a new and autonomous body, such as a human rights ombudsman, to serve as an avenue for citizens to seek meaningful remedy for abuses by public officials, including physical abuse and forced land confiscations.
- The government should work to improve the quality of the civil service through efforts to encourage promotion according to ability and merit, adjustment of the compensation system to combat high levels of attrition, and discouragement of civil servants from seeking supplementary incomes.

NOTES

For URLs and endnote hyperlinks, please visit the *Countries at the Crossroads* homepage at http://freedomhouse.org/template.cfm?page=139&edition=8.

1. Martin Gainsborough, "From Patronage to 'Outcomes:' Vietnam's Communist Party Congresses Reconsidered," *Journal of Vietnamese Studies* 2, no. 1 (2007): 3–26.
2. Socialist Republic of Vietnam, *1992 Constitution of the Socialist Republic of Vietnam.*
3. C. Thayer, "One Party Rule and the Challenge of Civil Society in Vietnam" (paper presented at the Vietnam Workshop: Remaking the Vietnamese State: Implications for Viet Nam and the Region, City University of Hong Kong, Hong Kong, August 21–22, 2008).
4. Edmund Malesky and Paul Schuler, "Why Do Single-Party Regimes Hold Elections? An Analysis of Candidate-Level Date in Vietnam's 2007 National Assembly Contest" (paper presented at the annual meeting of the American Political Science Association, Boston, MA, August 28, 2008).
5. Thayer, "One Party Rule and the Challenge of Civil Society in Vietnam," 5
6. Central Intelligence Agency (CIA), "Vietnam Country Profile," in *The World Factbook* (Washington, D.C.: CIA, 2009).
7. Malesky and Schuler, "Why Do Single-Party Regimes Hold Elections?"
8. Doris Becker and Doan Anh Quan, "Public Private Dialogue in Vietnam: The Experience of the MPI-GTZ Small and Medium Enterprise Development Programme (SMEDP)" (paper presented at the 2009 Public-Private Dialogue Workshop, Vienna, Austria, April 28–30).
9. Thayer, "One Party Rule and the Challenge of Civil Society in Vietnam," 13–20.
10. Human Rights Watch (HRW), "Vietnam: Crackdown on Dissent in Wake of WTO and APEC," news release, March 9, 2007.
11. Mark E. Manyin, *U.S.-Vietnamese Relations in 2009: Current Issues and Implications for U.S. Policy* (Washington, D.C.: Congressional Research Service, July 29, 2009).
12. Author's personal conversation with member of civil service, October 2008
13. Saskia P. Bruynooghe et al., *Implementation of Civil Service Legislation in Vietnam: Strengthening Elements of a Position-Based System* (Princeton, NJ: Princeton University, January 2009).
14. Ibid.
15. Thayer, "One Party Rule and the Challenge of Civil Society in Vietnam," 7.
16. See Socialist Republic of Vietnam, Law of the VietNam Fatherland Front.
17. Thayer, "One Party Rule and the Challenge of Civil Society in Vietnam."
18. Amnesty International, *Socialist Republic of Viet Nam Submission to the UN Universal Periodic Review: Fifth Session of the UPR Working Group of the Human Rights Council, May 2009* (London: Amnesty International, November 3, 2008).
19. Socialist Republic of Vietnam, *National Report of the Socialist Republic of Viet Nam under the Universal Periodic Review of the United Nations Human Rights Council* (Hanoi: Socialist Republic of Vietnam, April 24, 2009).
20. International Federation of Human Rights (FIDH) and Vietnam Committee on Human Rights, *Human Rights Violations in the Socialist Republic of Vietnam* (Paris/Hanoi: FIDH and Vietnam Committee on Human Rights, 2009).
21. Catherine McKinley, "How Has Vietnam's Print Media Covered Corruption and How Can Coverage Be Strengthened?," in *Public Administration Reform and Anticorruption: A Series of Policy Discussion Papers* (Hanoi: United Nations Development Programme [UNDP] Vietnam, January 2009), 14.
22. HRW, "Vietnam: Stop Muzzling the Messengers," news release, January 8, 2009.

23. Socialist Republic of Vietnam, Decree No. 97/2008/ND-CP of August 28, 2008, on the Management Provision and Use of Internet Services and Electronic Information on the Internet.
24. Deutsche Press Agentur, "Vietnam Police to Shut Down Vietnamese American's Website," *Intellasia*, February 13, 2009.
25. OpenNet Initiative, "China," in *Country Profiles* (Munk/Toronto/Cambridge/Ottawa: Citizen Lab, University of Toronto, Berkman Center for Internet & Society, and the SecDev Group, June 15, 2009); OpenNet Initiative, "Vietnam," in *Country Profiles* (Munk/Toronto/Cambridge/Ottawa: Citizen Lab, University of Toronto, Berkman Center for Internet & Society, and the SecDev Group, May 9, 2007).
26. FIDH and Vietnam Committee on Human Rights, *Human Rights Violations in the Socialist Republic of Vietnam*.
27. HRW, *UPR Submission* (New York: HRW, November 2008).
28. Amnesty International, *Socialist Republic of Viet Nam Submission to the UN Universal Periodic Review: Fifth Session of the UPR Working Group of the Human Rights Council*, May 2009.
29. Bureau of Democracy, Human Rights, and Labor, "Vietnam," in *2008 Country Reports on Human Rights Practices* (Washington, D.C.: U.S. Department of State, February 25, 2009).
30. Amnesty International, "Viet Nam," in *Amnesty International Report 2009* (London: Amnesty International, 2009).
31. European Parliament, *European Parliament Resolution on Vietnam* (Strasburg: European Parliament, July 12, 2007).
32. Embassy of the Socialist Republic of Vietnam in the United States of America, "Vietnam's Reaction to U.S. State Department 2008 Human Rights Report," news release, February 26, 2009.
33. Humantrafficking.org, "Human Trafficking Crackdown in Vietnam," home page, January 7, 2008.
34. Humantrafficking.org, "Anti-Trafficking Agreement Signed between Vietnam and Thailand," home page, April 5, 2008.
35. Organization for Economic Cooperation and Development (OECD) Development Centre, "Gender Equality and Social Institutions in Viet Nam," in *Social Institutions & Gender Index 2009* (Paris: OECD, 2009).
36. Ibid.
37. Nguyen Thi Thah Hoa, "Statement to the Fifty-Second Session of the Commission on the Status of Women," Fifty-Second Session of the Commission on the Status of Women, United Nations, New York, February 23, 2008.
38. United Nations Committee on the Elimination of Discrimination against Women (CEDAW), *Concluding Comments of the Committee on the Elimination of Discrimination against Women* (New York: CEDAW, February 2, 2007).
39. Vietnam Women's Union, "Women's Union Tackles Domestic Violence," Gender and Development, home page, April 2, 2008.
40. Minority Rights Group International, "Vietnam Minorities: Chinese (HOA),"in *World Directory of Minorities and Indigenous People* (London: Minority Rights Group International, 2009).
41. Amnesty International, "Viet Nam," in *Amnesty International Report 2009*.
42. Bureau of Democracy, Human Rights, and Labor, "Vietnam," in *International Religious Freedom Report 2009* (Washington, D.C.: U.S. Department of State, October 26, 2009).
43. Ibid.

44 "Nation Readies to Cheer Buddha's Birthday," Viet Nam News, May 11, 2008.
45 "More Job Opportunities for the Disabled," VietNamNet Bridge, November 28, 2008.
46 "Draft Law Gains Support to Champion Rights of Disabled," VietNamNet Bridge, January 5, 2009.
47 In a personal observation by the authors, minor protests in Ho Chi Minh City by farmers whose land had been expropriated by the state were monitored by the police but not disrupted.
48 Amnesty International, "Viet Nam," in *Amnesty International Report 2009*.
49 Agence France-Presse, "Vietnam Detains Anti-China Activists before Torch Relay," Google News, April 28, 2008.
50 "Vietnamese Hold Rare Demonstration to Protest China's Move to Control Disputed Islands," *China Post*, December 9, 2007.
51 HRW, *Not Yet a Workers' Paradise: Vietnam's Suppression of the Independent Workers' Movement* (New York: HRW, May 4, 2009).
52 International Trade Union Commission (ITUC), "Vietnam," in *Annual Survey of Trade Union Violations 2008* (Brussels: ITUC, 2008).
53 Tim Pringle, "Trade Union Renewal in China and Vietnam?" (paper presented at Work Matters: The 26th International Labour Process Conference, University College, Dublin, March 18–20, 2008).
54 Government of Viet Nam and UNDP, *Terms of Reference for Evaluation: Assistance for the Implementation of Vietnam's Legal Development Strategy to 2010* (Hanoi: Government of Viet Nam and UNDP, 2008).
55 Luu Tien Dung, *Judicial Independence in Transitional Countries* (Oslo: UNDP Oslo Governance Centre, January 2003).
56 Adam Day, "Legal Reform and Economic Development in Vietnam and China: A Comparative Analysis" (PhD diss., Fletcher School of Law and Diplomacy, 2004).
57 United Kingdom Foreign & Commonwealth Office, "Vietnam," in *Human Rights Annual Report 2008* (London: United Kingdom Foreign & Commonwealth Office, March 27, 2009).
58 The Danish Institute for Human Rights, "Vietnam and Human Rights," Danish Institute home page.
59 Martin Gainsborough, "Corruption and the Politics of Decentralisation in Vietnam," *Journal of Contemporary Asia* 33, no. 1 (2003): 69–84.
60 Ministry of Foreign Affairs of Denmark, "Vietnam Bar Federation Established," news release, July 17, 2009.
61 HRW, "Vietnam: Free Prominent Rights Lawyer Le Cong Dinh," news release, June 23, 2009.
62 Edmund Malesky, *The Vietnam Provincial Competitiveness Index 2008: Measuring Economic Governance for Private Sector Development* (Hanoi: Vietnam Chamber of Commerce and Industry and United States Agency for International Development's Vietnam Competitiveness Initiative, December 2008).
63 "Eliminate More Than 50 Golf Course Projects, NA Advised," *Thanh Nien News*, June 13, 2009.
64 Gainsborough, "Corruption and the Politics of Decentralisation in Vietnam."
65 "Vietnam Rejects Wrong Views on Former Journalists' Trial," VietNamNet Bridge, October 25, 2008.
66 Transparency International, *National Integrity Systems: Country Study Report: Vietnam 2006* (Berlin: Transparency International, 2006).
67 World Bank, *Vietnam Development Report 2006: Business* (Washington, D.C.: World Bank, 2006).

68 Transparency International, *Global Corruption Barometer 2007* (Berlin: Transparency International, 2008).

69 Business Anti-Corruption Portal, "Snapshot of the Vietnam Country Profile," Business Anti-Corruption Portal home page.

70 V. Anh, "Provincial Official under Fire after Lifting Lid on Bribe Attempt," Ministry of Natural Resources and Environment, April 25, 2008.

71 Embassy of Finland and Center for Community Support Development Studies (CECODES), *Anti-Corruption in Vietnam: The Situation after Two Years of Implementation of the Law* (Hanoi: Embassy of Finland and CECODES, November 2008), 13; Soren Davidsen et al., *Implementation Assessment of the Anti-Corruption Law: How Far Has Vietnam Come at the Sector Level?: A Case-Study of the Construction Sector* (Copenhagen: Ministry of Foreign Affairs Denmark, 2009).

72 Business Anti-Corruption Portal, "Vietnam: Public Anticorruption Initiatives," Business Anti-Corruption Portal home page; Davidsen et al., *Implementation Assessment of the Anti-Corruption Law: How Far Has Vietnam Come at the Sector Level?*, iv.

73 Soren Davidsen et al., *Implementation Assessment of Anticorruption Law: How Far Has Vietnam Come?* (Copenhagen: Ministry of Foreign Affairs Denmark, 2008), 28.

74 Farzana Nawaz, *Corruption in Fast-Growing Markets: Lessons from Russia and Vietnam* U4 Anti Corruption Resource Center Expert Answer (Berlin/Bergen: Transparency International and Chr. Michelson Institute), April 29, 2008.

75 See the State Audit Office's website.

76 Open Budget Initiative, "Vietnam," in *Open Budget Index 2008* (Washington, D.C.: Open Budget Initiative, 2009).

77 Nawaz, "Corruption in Fast-Growing Markets: Lessons from Russia and Vietnam."

78 Business Anti-Corruption Portal, "Vietnam: Public Anticorruption Initiatives."

79 Bernama, "Vietnam to Eradicate Bribery in Trade Activities," Investment and Trade Promotion Center–Ho Chi Minh City, June 2, 2009.

80 Gainsborough, "Corruption and the Politics of Decentralisation in Vietnam."

81 Davidsen et al., *Implementation Assessment of Anticorruption Law: How Far Has Vietnam Come?*, 30.

82 McKinley, "How Has Vietnam's Print Media Covered Corruption and How Can Coverage Be Strengthened?"

83 Roger Mitton, "Vietnam: Behind the Journalists' Jailings," *Asia Sentinel*, October 24, 2008.

84 Finland and CECODES, *Anti-Corruption in Vietnam*.

85 Dennis C. McCornac, "Corruption in Vietnamese Higher Education," *International Higher Education* 50 (Winter 2008).

86 Article 19, "Vietnam: Article 19 Assists with Drafting Freedom of Information Law," press release, May 11, 2009.

87 USAID, *Supporting Vietnam's Legal and Governance Transformation: A Successful Partnership between Vietnam's Office of the Government and the USAID/STAR Project* (Washington, D.C.: USAID, February 2008).

88 Ibid.

89 Davidsen et al., *Implementation Assessment of Anticorruption Law: How Far Has Vietnam Come?*; Davidsen et al., *Implementation Assessment of the Anti-Corruption Law: How Far Has Vietnam Come at the Sector Level?*.

90 World Bank, *Vietnam Development Report 2006: Business*.

91 Agence France-Presse, "Two Vietnam Officials Jailed in Japan Aid Scandal: Court," AsiaOne News, February 25, 2009.

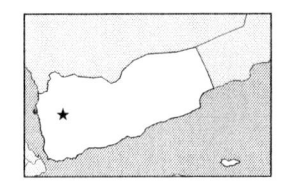

YEMEN

CAPITAL: San'a
POPULATION: 22.9 million
GNI PER CAPITA (PPP): $2,210

SCORES	2006	2010
ACCOUNTABILITY AND PUBLIC VOICE:	2.60	2.47
CIVIL LIBERTIES:	3.24	2.49
RULE OF LAW:	2.66	2.50
ANTICORRUPTION AND TRANSPARENCY:	1.94	1.90

(scores are based on a scale of 0 to 7, with 0 representing weakest and 7 representing strongest performance)

Gregory D. Johnsen

INTRODUCTION

In recent years, Yemen has made some positive progress toward becoming a more democratically governed country, featuring increased competition in 2006 presidential elections and the establishment of a new anticorruption watchdog. Much of this progress has been eclipsed, however, by a multitude of crises and the authorities' often blunt response to them. These challenges range from dual insurgencies to corruption and other systemic governance failures that have led to diminished state legitimacy. Political instability has been exacerbated by deteriorating economic conditions, rendering the prospects for the country's future democratic development uncertain.

The Republic of Yemen was created on May 22, 1990, when the northern Yemen Arab Republic and the southern People's Democratic Republic of Yemen joined to form a united state. President Ali Abdullah Saleh ruled the north from 1978, when he took control of the state, surrounding himself with family members and trusted allies, particularly within the state's security apparatus. In 1982, President Saleh formed the General People's Congress (GPC), a political party that survived unification and continues to rule Yemen. The pre-unification history of south Yemen, led by a Marxist regime from 1967 until 1990, was similarly characterized by internal power struggles. Power was eventually consolidated by Ali Salim al-Bid, a former foreign minister from the Hadramawt region, who also became head of the Yemeni Socialist Party (YSP). In late 1989, as the Soviet Union's previously strong influence was crumbling, al-Bid met Saleh in Aden and the two jointly announced impending unification. Almost

---

Gregory D. Johnsen is currently a Ph.D. candidate in Near Eastern studies at Princeton University.

immediately the new country struggled to integrate two different systems of government. Importantly, the military was never completely unified, retaining separate northern and southern units.

The 1993 parliamentary elections were a wide-open affair, with 21 parties participating and 8 gaining seats. The YSP won 56 seats, while the GPC came away with 123. However, the *al-Tajammu' al-yamani li-l-islah* (Yemeni Reform Grouping, more commonly known as Islah) edged out the YSP with 62 seats. These electoral results, combined with a war of attrition between the YSP and Islamic militants—who were at times tacitly encouraged by prominent northern figures—destroyed the possibility of equal power sharing between the YSP and GPC, which had formed the basis for the pre-unification agreement. The YSP perceived that it was being manipulated out of power through a series of secret agreements between the GPC and Islah, sparking a secession attempt and ensuing civil war.

The civil war lasted from April 1994 until the southern capital of Aden fell in July as al-Bid and other prominent YSP figures fled the country. The YSP boycotted the 1997 parliamentary elections, and two years later President Saleh faced only token opposition during an election with significant shortcomings. A constitutional amendment passed by referendum in 2001 extended the potential presidential period to two seven-year terms.

On the surface, Yemen appears to have a relatively open democratic system, with elections being a key feature of the political landscape since 1990. Nevertheless, politics are dominated by the ruling GPC and President Saleh has ruled since 1978. The YSP participated in the 2003 parliamentary elections and, two years later, the rival YSP and Islah forged an alliance, joined by four smaller parties, to create the Joint Meeting Parties (JMP). This loose coalition put forward a candidate for the 2006 presidential elections, marking the first time Saleh faced genuine opposition (see Accountability and Public Voice).

Yemen has been increasingly preoccupied over the past eight years with several security threats. After initial success in combating and largely eliminating al-Qaeda's infrastructure within the country, lapsed vigilance and a shift in priorities led to the organization's resurgence since 2006. Heavy-handed northern dominance in the years since the 1994 civil war continues to stoke calls for secession in the south. Since 2004, the government has also been battling a rebellion in the northern governorate of Saada led by Hussein Badreddin al-Houthi, a prominent figure in the Zaidi Shiite Muslim community. Al-Houthi was killed in September 2004, but clashes between his supporters and government forces have continued and were reignited in the summer of 2009 after the collapse of a year-long ceasefire. The fighting has led to a severe humanitarian crisis in the area, with tens of thousands of people displaced.

Yemen remains one of the poorest countries in the Arab world. Its economy continues to suffer from its almost complete dependence on oil, while the water table is dropping at an alarming rate. High birth, illiteracy, and unemployment rates, along with rampant corruption, lack of foreign investment, a crumbling infrastructure and pervasive poverty all contribute to serious concerns about Yemen's long-term future.

ACCOUNTABILITY AND PUBLIC VOICE 2.47
FREE AND FAIR ELECTORAL LAWS AND ELECTIONS	2.75
EFFECTIVE AND ACCOUNTABLE GOVERNMENT	1.75
CIVIC ENGAGEMENT AND CIVIC MONITORING	3.67
MEDIA INDEPENDENCE AND FREEDOM OF EXPRESSION	1.71

Yemen is a republic headed by a directly elected president, with a bicameral parliament composed of a 301-seat popularly elected House of Representatives and a 111-member Consultative Council (Majlis al-Shura) appointed by the president. The House of Representatives has legislative authority, while the Consultative Council serves in an advisory capacity. In the most recent parliamentary elections, held in 2003, the GPC increased its share of seats from 145 to 238. On the surface, the elections were competitive, but international and domestic observers noted numerous problems, including fraudulent voter registration, GPC use of party resources to influence the outcome of voting, and limits placed on the issues candidates could raise.

Islah and the YSP are the most prominent opposition parties, with 46 and 8 seats, respectively, although their influence remains limited because of the GPC's overwhelming majority. Several political parties are active, although many smaller ones survive as dependents of the GPC. Another round of parliamentary elections scheduled for April 2009 was postponed for two years in the wake of boycott threats from various opposition parties.[1] Many analysts viewed this postponement as a victory for the JMP.[2]

The most recent presidential elections were held in 2006. For a brief window in 2005, it appeared as if they might mark the end of Saleh's presidency after he pledged that July not to run for reelection. Approximately one year later, however, the GPC nominated him as its presidential candidate. Unlike the 1999 election, when Saleh's only opponent came from within his ruling party, in the 2006 polls he faced several opposition challengers, although the majority of those who initially announced their candidacy did so during the period when Saleh had said he would not be competing. In total, 46 candidates submitted their applications to parliament. Only five, including Saleh, were able to gain the 5 percent support in each house of parliament required to add their names to the ballot. Ultimately, Saleh's stiffest competition came from the JMP alliance's candidate, Faysal bin Shamlan, a 72-year-old former oil minister from the south, who has since died.

The four-week campaigning period prior to the elections was marred by some violence, though there was less fighting than in previous elections. In August 2006, several election officials were killed on the second day of the campaigning period. The following month, over 50 people were killed and 200 injured when a stampede occurred at a rally of Saleh supporters. International observers found that the Supreme Commission for Elections and Referendums (SCER) carried out the logistical aspects of electoral oversight in a generally professional manner. In an improvement from the 2003 elections, the SCER was able to ensure significant coverage for opposition candidates in state media, although the incumbent still received more due to the media's general coverage of the president's daily activities. Nevertheless, the SCER encountered difficulties in enforcing election laws and its own mandate, including rules pertaining to the illegal use of state resources to support the ruling party candidate. Public statements by SCER commissioners criticizing the opposition and NGO monitors also undermined its credibility and contributed to a decision by the JMP to boycott the SCER.[3]

When the official results of the election were announced three days after the polls, Saleh was awarded 77 percent of the roughly six million votes cast, while bin Shamlan received 22 percent of the vote.[4] Saleh's total was down from an early projection, which had him winning 82 percent to bin Shamlan's 16 percent. The JMP rejected the early count, threatening street demonstrations to protest what it called voter manipulation and fraud.[5] Saleh eventually acknowledged the JMP's claims, declaring the final count valid while admitting some mistakes had been made. The European Union Electoral Observation Mission to Yemen, which monitored the polls, declared the elections free and fair.[6] Many observers remarked that, although flawed, the elections represented a historic step forward in Yemen's democratic development, particularly given the atmosphere of genuine competition between two candidates with distinguishable political and ideological approaches to governing.

Despite the role of parties in the formal aspects of Yemen's political system, personalized networks of patronage and related power blocs provide a more accurate means of deciphering political loyalties. Three main power blocs are of particular significance: the government, the military, and the tribes. Each of these blocs is largely personified and led by a single individual. In the case of the government and the GPC, it is Saleh. Ali Muhsin al-Ahmar controls the military through personal and family contacts, although his position has been weakened in recent years by military reshuffles orchestrated by Saleh; the president's son, Ahmad, and his nephews Yahya Muhammad Saleh, Tariq Muhammad Saleh, and Ammar Muhammad Saleh, are rising in importance. The most powerful tribal bloc, the Hashid tribal confederation, was headed by Sheikh Abdullah al-Ahmar until his death in December 2007. His oldest son, Sadiq, was elected to replace him, but has so far been unable to wield the same power and influence as his father. In addition to the difficulties caused by a generational shift in leadership and lesser reputation, Sadiq's problems speak to the changing nature of tribal rule in Yemen as such allegiances weaken in the face of other, competing identities.

In this context, a key factor contributing to Saleh's victory was the GPC's ability to mobilize preachers in mosques throughout the country to publicly support the president in their sermons. Perhaps most importantly, Sheikh Abdullah al-Ahmar—at the time, head of Islah, speaker of parliament, and head of the Hashid tribal confederation—publicly supported Saleh's reelection bid. Sheikh Abd al-Majid al-Zindani, another prominent figure in Islah, also publicly backed the incumbent, despite Islah's membership in the opposition coalition that had formally backed bin Shamlan. The government's attempt to link bin Shamlan to a terrorist attack in the week prior to the elections also undermined the latter's candidacy. The authorities claimed that Shamlan's former bodyguards had been involved in a failed suicide bombing attempt; months after the elections, however, he was cleared of any link to the attacks.[7]

EU recommendations for improved future elections formed the basis of a JMP proposal to amend electoral laws. Proposed changes included barring government officials from pressuring subordinates to vote a particular way and requiring voters to cast ballots only in their place of birth or residence and not place of employment. In effect, this would eliminate large swaths of GPC support in the south, where individuals of northern origin stationed at military garrisons and government offices are sent to vote in a region that would otherwise be an opposition stronghold.

In August 2008 the GPC effectively defeated the JMP's proposed amendment, pushing through a vote to maintain the 2001 election law. Shortly afterwards, Saleh attempted to defuse rising tensions by releasing approximately a dozen political prisoners, including prominent southern activist Hassan Baum and journalist Abd al-Karim al-Khaywani, who had been imprisoned for reporting about the al-Houthi revolt. Despite such symbolic gestures, as 2008 progressed, disillusionment with the government from those on the periphery increased as they saw themselves kept out of the center of political power.

In May 2008, Yemen held its first elections for 20 provincial governors, posts previously appointed by the president. Opposition groups refused to participate, claiming government manipulation. Progovernment candidates were elected in 17 of the 20 districts, with independents elected in the remaining 3, all of whom are known to have unofficial ties to the GPC. In November 2008, local elections were postponed after the JMP threatened to boycott the parliamentary elections and the EU said it would not certify the elections without JMP participation. Finally, in February 2009, the GPC and the JMP agreed to postpone parliamentary elections for two years.[8]

Although the constitution provides for checks and balances, including parliamentary oversight, in practice the executive branch continues to be both the most unified and powerful branch of government. The GPC's overwhelming majority in the legislature enables the president and government to pass legislation without negotiating with the opposition. More informally, the legislature has had difficulty reasserting itself in the wake of Sheikh Abdullah al-Ahmar's death in 2007. President Saleh stepped down as the formal head of the judiciary in 2006, although this has not translated into a more independent and active judiciary.

Yemen's civil service continues to be plagued by challenges, including a lack of basic infrastructure and the entrenched phenomenon of "shadow employees," people on the payroll who do not perform any job. Hiring and promotion decisions are often influenced by political or patronage interests rather than merit.

Civic groups are active and increasing in number. However, their ability to influence government policy and legislation remains weak, particularly as more traditional lobbying arms yield greater sway. For example, although parliament amended legislation in February 2009 establishing 17 as the minimum age of marriage for women, activists have repeatedly expressed concerns that pressure from prominent religious leaders could lead to the provision's repeal.[9] In addition to independent nongovernmental organizations (NGOs), a large number of civic groups with close government ties also operate; these are often utilized to create the artificial impression of grassroots support for government policies. NGOs are relatively free of state intimidation so long as they avoid public statements or advocacy on sensitive issues, such as direct criticism of the president or his family, discussions of Saudi funding and business dealings, and opposition to government actions in Saada. Many groups face the difficulty of knowing exactly where the "red lines" are at any given time.

Although the constitution guarantees the right to free expression, the government continues to prosecute journalists under restrictive laws like the 1990 Press and Publications Law. Article 103 of the law outlaws direct personal criticism of the head of state and publication of material that "might spread a spirit of dissent and division among the people" or information that "leads to the spread of ideas contrary to the principles of the Yemeni Revolution, [is] prejudicial to national unity or [distorts] the image of the Yemeni, Arab, or Islamic heritage." In recent years, as some journalists have increasingly pushed the limits of permissible coverage, the authorities have often responded harshly. Journalists have repeatedly been fined, arrested, imprisoned, threatened, subjected to home and office raids, and stopped from reporting on a range of important issues and events. According to the local watchdog group Women Journalists Without Chains, the number of documented press freedom violations doubled from 2006 to 2007. In June 2008, a state security court sentenced Abdulkarim al-Khalwani, the former editor of the banned weekly newspaper *al-Shura*, to six years in prison for allegedly collaborating with Zaidi rebels in the north and for "publishing information liable to undermine army morale"; al-Khalwani was released from prison following a presidential order in September. In January 2009, however, the security court overturned the pardon and upheld the original six-year sentence.[10] Another prominent opposition journalist, Muhammad al-Maqalih, was disappeared in the fall of 2009.

The media crackdown reached new levels of repression during the spring of 2009, when the government shut down and raided the offices of several newspapers for their coverage of popular demonstrations in the south. In May 2009, the government established a Special Press Court to prosecute media-related crimes. On July 12, the court tried its first case, hearing charges of "insult and humiliation" against Sami Ghalib, editor-in-chief of *Al-Nida* newspaper. Although Ghalib was eventually acquitted, the creation of the court has been widely criticized as unconstitutional and a step backward for Yemeni press freedom.

Yemen's print media offer increasingly diverse coverage of local and international news. However, as 50 percent of the population is illiterate and two-thirds lives in rural areas, most citizens continue to get their news from broadcast media, over which the government maintains a monopoly. The government continues to tightly control licensing for print media, requiring newspapers to apply annually to renew their license to publish and offering preferential treatment to progovernment outlets. The state also controls the vast majority of printing presses in the country. Though access to the internet is not widespread, some newspapers have attempted to bypass government control by moving online. The authorities have responded by periodically censoring sites they deem offensive, including opposition and political websites such as the news site Yemen Portal, which was blocked in January 2008. Internet cafes are highly regulated, with some cafe owners monitoring what sites their customers browse.[11]

CIVIL LIBERTIES   2.49

PROTECTION FROM STATE TERROR, UNJUSTIFIED IMPRISONMENT, AND TORTURE	1.63
GENDER EQUITY	1.67
RIGHTS OF ETHNIC, RELIGIOUS, AND OTHER DISTINCT GROUPS	3.00
FREEDOM OF CONSCIENCE AND BELIEF	3.67
FREEDOM OF ASSOCIATION AND ASSEMBLY	2.50

Yemen's security services continue to act with impunity and extrajudicial killings, enforced disappearances, and arbitrary arrests have increased in recent years. Agents of the state have imprisoned hundreds of activists, opposition politicians, and workers, while torture and police brutality reportedly remain widespread. Family members have also been taken into detention in an effort to pressure suspects. Allegations have emerged of aerial bombing of villages, use of landmines in civilian areas, and other severe abuses in the Saada region. Independent verification of such allegations, however, has been hindered by the government's tactic of blocking media and human rights groups' access to conflict areas. At least 13 individuals were executed in 2008, some after unfair trials, while hundreds of others remain on death row.

Both state and private prisons operate with limited outside control or oversight. Abuses persist, including overcrowding and use of solitary confinement for months at a time.[12] The government does not allow independent inspections of the facilities, though most prisoners are able to receive visits from family. There is little protection against arbitrary arrests, which the government has sometimes used to intimidate opposition figures, particularly those from the YSP. Some political activists have faced violence by nonstate actors as well. In late March 2009, YSP official Mushin 'Askar and his son were killed by unidentified gunmen in Amran.[13] Estimates of political prisoners fluctuate widely as the government often follows a "revolving door policy" of imprisoning and then pardoning political activists as a way of controlling potential opposition groups. Many powerful sheikhs continue to maintain their own private prisons, where abuses are reportedly rampant. Information is sparse, however, as access for independent observers is even more restricted to these locations than to government-run facilities.

Those arrested have few avenues to effectively challenge their detention. While channels for legal redress are available, these are routinely ignored in favor of more traditional and opaque methods of pressuring the government. Such techniques include having a prominent individual take responsibility for the detainee, vouching for his future good conduct in exchange for a release authorized by high-ranking officials.

Human rights groups estimate that the government continues to hold hundreds of suspects without charge. Although hundreds of political prisoners from the Saada region were released following the 2008 ceasefire agreement, hundreds of others were detained in 2009 as fighting between government and al-Houthi forces reignited and antigovernment protests in the south gathered momentum. In addition to threats from government forces, civilians in the Saada region also face a humanitarian crisis.

The ruling regime does not appear to perceive al-Qaeda as an existential threat the way it does the fighting in Saada and resurgent calls for secession in the south. Nevertheless, an influx of Saudi Islamists and Iraqi insurgents has aided al-Qaeda's regrouping in the country. Several terrorist attacks have taken place in recent years, including a September 2008 bombing outside the U.S. Embassy that killed 16 people. In November 2007, the Council of Ministers approved a draft version of a terrorism financing law. This was part of a broader counterterrorism initiative, which includes legislation to limit the entry of weapons into the country. Many observers have raised doubts as to whether the terrorism finance legislation will deter funding to al-Qaeda and like-minded groups. Human rights groups have raised concerns that it could be used to increase repression against nonviolent southern opposition groups, who the regime has been known to arbitrarily label as terrorists. As of mid-2009, the bill was pending before parliament.

Yemen remains one of the most heavily armed societies in the world, with an estimated 17 million guns circulating among a population of 22 million. Reported crime rates have risen within the country in recent years, though this may be due to improved recording rather than increased violence. The government has taken some positive steps to combat crime, including a ban on carrying firearms in major cities and a heavy-weapons buyback program that was implemented in 2005, but these have largely been limited to urban areas and particularly the capital city of San'a. Other manifestations of nonstate violence, particularly tribal feuds, are also common.

Yemen continues to be a country of origin for human trafficking, particularly of boys taken across the border to Saudi Arabia for forced labor. According to the Ministry of Social Affairs and Labor, an estimated 10 Yemeni children are trafficked into Saudi Arabia each day. Girls are also trafficked internally and abroad for sexual exploitation. In recent years, the government has taken measures to curb these practices, but these have been primarily centered on public education and provision of shelter for victims, while prosecutions have been extremely limited. The government's actions have often focused more on child labor and trafficking rather than on internal forced prostitution, where it has resorted to tacitly supporting vigilante religious committees modeled on Saudi Arabia's Committee for the Promotion of Virtue and the Prevention of Vice.[14]

Yemen ratified the Convention on the Elimination of All Forms of Discrimination against Women (CEDAW) in 1984, but discrimination against women remains pervasive.[15] As the country's overall political situation has deteriorated, female activists have faced greater harassment by the security forces. Meanwhile, political crises have absorbed material and human resources that might otherwise have been allocated to improving women's rights.[16] By law, women are afforded protections against discrimination and provided guarantees of equality under Sharia (Islamic law). In practice, a woman must receive permission from her husband or father to obtain a passport and travel abroad. Unlike men, women do not have the right to confer citizenship on a foreign-born husband. The process of obtaining citizenship for a child of a Yemeni mother and foreign father is more difficult than that for a child born to a Yemeni father and foreign mother.

In April 2008, the Yemeni parliament voted down legislation that would have banned female genital mutilation. The postponement of parliamentary elections has delayed calls for a quota system for women, which some activists had been demanding,[17] though the proposed system received little support from mainstream political parties. President Saleh typically includes two female ministers in his cabinet, usually carrying the Human Rights and Social Affairs portfolios. Major political parties largely refrained from supporting female candidates during the 2009 local elections.

The Yemeni government has been widely criticized for failing to protect the rights of girls, particularly those forced to become child brides. This phenomenon, which often occurs in rural regions outside of government oversight, was highlighted by the cases of Reem al-Numeri (a 12-year-old who was forced to marry her 30-year-old cousin in 2008) and Najud Ali (a 10-year-old who left a forced marriage in 2008 and managed to successfully obtain divorce hearings).[18] Following international pressure, the government supported passage of an amendment in February 2009 codifying 17 as the legal age of marriage for women. However, Islamists led by Sheikh Abd al-Majid al-Zindani have condemned the law as "un-Islamic" and are seeking to have it repealed. In addition, implementation and enforcement of the amended law remains poor. An attitude of neglect characterizes the government's approach to its disabled and mentally challenged population. The latter are periodically imprisoned, ostensibly for their own protection.

One of the main cleavages in Yemeni society is between Shafi'is and Zaidis, two Islamic sects. The former are adherents to one of the four schools of Sunni Islam, while the latter are Shiites, although in practice there is little doctrinal difference between the two.[19] Although President Saleh and many other powerful northerners are nominally Zaidi, the government has been supporting Wahhabi-inspired Yemenis fighting in the Saada region against the local Zaidi population. As Zaidi imams ruled the country (in some form) for over a thousand years prior to the 1962 revolution in North Yemen, the government's opposition to Zaidi leaders in Saada is largely a political calculation designed to weaken a potentially powerful group in Yemeni society. Indeed, the historical doctrinal closeness between the two sects casts doubt on the Yemeni government's refrain that it is battling Iranian-backed Shiite militants on Saudi Arabia's southern border. Such assertions are better understood as an attempt to link the government's domestic problems to larger regional and international concerns.

The fighting in Saada has led to hundreds of deaths since 2004. In August 2008, Abdel Malek al-Houthi, the leader of the Zaidi rebellion, accepted a ceasefire proposal to end the conflict, but according to Human Rights Watch, the government failed to uphold its end of the accord. In August 2009, another round of fighting broke out. Army aircraft, tanks, and troops battled against heavily armed tribesman, causing at least 50,000 people to flee the region, according to the United Nations. Since 2006, the government has blocked access to the region to independent observers and journalists, making it difficult to fully assess the circumstances and casualty count in the area. During particularly tense periods of fighting, the government has also arrested or harassed Zaidi preachers teaching in other parts of the country.

According to the constitution, Islam is the state religion and Sharia the source of all legislation. Much of the government's interference in religious matters does not manifest as legal restrictions or formal oversight, but rather as unofficial support for particular religious figures who reciprocate by backing government policies. For example, Hamud al-Hitar, currently the Minister of Religious Endowments, is widely believed to have obtained the position as a reward for loyalty to the regime and in an attempt to ensure GPC control over mosques and religious institutions. The government has imposed some restrictions, however, on religious activity in the Saada region. Mosques' hours of operation have been restricted and imams suspected of extremism or of preaching antigovernment views have been removed from their posts.

In addition to Shafi'is and Zaidis, there are also small pockets of Ismailis and Twelver Shiites as well as some Jews residing in Yemen. In the eastern governorate of al-Mahra, local government officials periodically violate the rights of locals, particularly Mahri speakers. Official neglect of the group was evident in

October 2008, when the government responded slowly to flooding in al-Mahra while concentrating its efforts on the more politically significant governorate of Hadramawt. The Akhdam, a small ethnic minority traditionally marginalized from the political process, face social discrimination. In 2009, they demonstrated for the first time in an effort to secure their rights.

The right to form and join trade unions is protected by law, but restricted in practice. Nearly all unions operate under a national umbrella organization, the General Federation of Trade Unions of Yemen (GFTUY), which has close ties to the government. In recent years, the GPC has reportedly attempted to influence internal elections in unions and professional associations. Unions and their leaders occasionally face retaliation for organizing strikes. In September 2007, the Ministry of Social Affairs and Labor reportedly threatened to dissolve the Yemen Teachers Union and related syndicates after they led nationwide teacher demonstrations to demand a pay increase. In November 2008, six union leaders of the Aden Container Terminal Union (ACT) were arrested for leading a dock strike; they were released after six days. A new draft Labor Law is under consideration. If passed, it would entail some improvements, particularly in allowing foreign workers to join trade unions, though other restrictions would remain.[20]

Although Yemeni law acknowledges freedom of assembly and opposition rallies were common in the run-up to the 2006 elections, the authorities have since used excessive force to suppress peaceful demonstrations. The government has been particularly intolerant of protests in the south over discriminatory treatment in the allocation of government jobs and oil profits, lack of influence over government decisions, and complaints of land grabs by powerful northern officials. Several thousand southerners joined demonstrations throughout 2008 and early 2009, with some participants calling for secession. The authorities responded with violence, killing several protestors and arresting hundreds of others, often sparking further violent clashes and arrests. Despite demands from parliament to investigate abuses and end the cycle of violence, the government has yet to take action to do so. As of August 2007, the government began to require special permits to stage what it termed "lawful rallies." Observers saw this as an attempt to remove legal protections from peaceful protesters, enabling them to more easily be detained and labeled "criminals."

RULE OF LAW   2.50

INDEPENDENT JUDICIARY	2.80
PRIMACY OF RULE OF LAW IN CIVIL AND CRIMINAL MATTERS	2.20
ACCOUNTABILITY OF SECURITY FORCES AND MILITARY TO CIVILIAN AUTHORITIES	2.00
PROTECTION OF PROPERTY RIGHTS	3.00

Yemen's legal system is divided into three tiers: the Courts of First Instance, Court of Appeals, and Supreme Court. In recent years, the government has also established special courts for terrorism and media crimes, developments widely perceived as a step backward for the rule of law and civil liberties. Unlike other Arab countries, Yemen does not have a separate court system handling personal status cases, which are adjudicated by civil courts, as Sharia is the source of most legislation.

Although the constitution guarantees judicial independence, in practice the judiciary is heavily influenced—and at times directly instructed—by the executive. The Supreme Judicial Council (SJC) oversees the country's judicial system, including most appointments. Candidates for senior positions, however, are typically chosen by the president. President Saleh presided over the SJC until 2006, when he stepped down and was replaced by the chief justice of the Supreme Court. The minister of justice and his deputy, however, retain a prominent role in the SJC, whose other members are judges directly or indirectly appointed by the president. As such, although the president no longer formally heads the council and the judiciary's budget is independent, executive branch influence over the judiciary remains significant.

Compliance with judicial decisions is inconsistent, particularly if rulings are unfavorable to prominent tribal or political leaders. Judicial authority is further undermined by President Saleh's tendency to circumvent the courts for political expediency, commuting or reducing sentences based on private, individualized agreements. Such extralegal agreements and the president's power to pardon are often used to neutralize potential opponents.

Like many civil servants, judicial staff promotions are based on a complicated system of favors and patronage rather than merit, rendering them susceptible to pressure from influential political or religious figures. Both a judge's social or tribal ties and, at times, bribery may influence verdicts. Many judges lack adequate training. Judges who possess the requisite training and skills, however, remain reluctant to challenge the government and regularly rule in favor of the state. Tribal and customary law continues to be practiced in most rural areas, in both criminal and civil cases.

The presumption of innocence is guaranteed in the constitution, but is rarely upheld in practice, including in death penalty cases. Long-term detention without charge remains common. Leaders of demonstrations in the south, suspected members of armed groups, and individuals alleged to be associated with the al-Houthi movement are particularly at risk for arbitrary detention. Many defendants are unaware of their right to legal representation, and indigent detainees and those in rural areas routinely lack access to counsel. The most effective avenue for defendants or victims of human rights violations to obtain justice or redress remains through connections to prominent figures who can petition the authorities on their behalf.

Prosecutors are also susceptible to political pressure. Given their limited ability to affect the outcome of cases, however, they are typically bypassed in favor of direct pressure on judges or powerful officials able to effectively influence a decision. Prosecutors rarely pursue high-ranking officials for corruption or abuse of power. In some instances, gross violations have been met with promotion instead of prosecution.[21]

In 1999, the government established a Specialized Criminal Court (SCC) to address a class of crimes ranging from highway robbery to abductions; in 2004, its mandate was expanded to cover "crimes against national security."[22] SCC judges are appointed by the executive branch and proceedings do not meet international fair trial standards. International and domestic NGOs have criticized the courts' creation as unconstitutional. According to Amnesty International, at least 109 people were tried before the SCC in 2007. While 73 were tried in connection to acts of violence, those brought before the court have also included journalists.[23] SCC procedures routinely fail to meet basic international standards and some trials have been held in secret. Attorneys representing suspects before the court consistently complain of being denied adequate access to evidence and to their clients. In March 2009, 16 al-Qaeda suspects being tried before the court went on a hunger strike to protest abuses by security services committed during their detention.[24]

Since taking office in 1978, President Saleh has ensured control over various security forces by appointing family members and allies to top positions. Following the 1994 civil war, an estimated 60,000 servicemen from the south were discharged, with some fleeing the country. After returning under promise of amnesty combined with either re-enlistment or full pensions, their continued marginalization from the military ranks has been a key factor contributing to antigovernment sentiment in the south.

In addition to the national armed forces, there are three internal security services: the Political Security Organization (PSO), the Central Security Organization (CSO), and the National Security Bureau (NSB). The PSO is considered the most important and reports directly to the president. Its upper ranks are composed exclusively of former army officers. A number of its members have been dismissed in recent years in an attempt to eliminate corruption and Islamist sympathizers from within the agency. The CSO reports to the Ministry of the Interior, although in practice it is loyal to one of the president's nephews, Yahya, who commands the organization. The NSB reports to the president's office, but it is largely commanded by another nephew, Ammar Muhammad, who is the principal deputy. The NSB's duties are not clearly defined, contributing to overlap between the agencies' operations. The PSO and CSO operate their own extrajudicial detention centers.[25] The security forces frequently crack down on groups and individuals at the government's behest, including using violence to suppress protests in the south. In July 2009, security forces reportedly opened fire on thousands of antigovernment protesters in the city of Zanjibar, killing at least 12 people and injuring dozens of others. Impunity remains the norm for such abuses.[26]

Property rights are not well protected by law. Although 90 percent of farms in the north are privately owned, a majority of land in the south belongs to the state, a legacy of agrarian reform carried out by the former PDRY regime.[27] The land registration system remains complex and inexact, with multiple copies of deeds sold for the same plot. As a result, disputes are common, but legal redress remains time consuming and ineffective due to corruption and limited enforcement of judgments.[28] In recent years, citizens have also been forcibly evicted from their land for the benefit of private businesses. Prosecution or punishment for illegal land confiscation and related abuses remains rare. The exception has been when confiscations personally conflict with the interests of the president or his patronage network. This occurred in 2007, when President Saleh demoted Saleh al-Thanayn and his son after the latter attempted to confiscate land around San'a that had already been claimed by the president's eldest son.

ANTICORRUPTION AND TRANSPARENCY   1.90

ENVIRONMENT TO PROTECT AGAINST CORRUPTION	1.25
PROCEDURES AND SYSTEMS TO ENFORCE ANTICORRUPTION LAWS	2.75
EXISTENCE OF ANTICORRUPTION NORMS, STANDARDS, AND PROTECTIONS	1.75
GOVERNMENTAL TRANSPARENCY	1.83

Corruption remains endemic in Yemen. Officials routinely embezzle money from government accounts and bribes are needed to accomplish most tasks in interactions with the state bureaucracy. Insufficient salaries granted to mid-level bureaucrats and a culture of corruption that pervades all levels of the civil service are key factors contributing to the prevalence of such practices. Yemen's tribal culture and the continuity of one individual in power for over 30 years have further entrenched the patronage networks that fuel corrupt practices.

The government has taken several positive measures in recent years to strengthen anticorruption laws and institutions. Nevertheless, many observers perceive interactions with the state to be more riddled with corruption and bribery than previously. The sharp drop in oil prices in 2008, combined with declining reserves, has created greater incentives for officials to enrich themselves quickly in a sector that accounts for 90 percent of the country's export earnings and 70 percent of government revenue.[29] Between 2005 and 2008, Yemen's ranking on Transparency International's corruption perception index dropped from 103rd out of 159 countries to 141st out of 180 countries, with its raw score dropping by almost half a point on a 10-point scale.

In early 2006, the government initiated a series of anticorruption reforms later outlined in *The National Reform Agenda: A Progress Report*, which was published by the Ministry for Planning and International Cooperation.[30] Few substantive measures have been pursued to completion, however, and those implemented largely avoid targeting the main sources of corrupt practices. Thus, although the number of investigations into alleged malfeasance or failure to disclose assets has increased, these have yet to result in formal charges or convictions. A telling example of the difficulties of changing the system from the inside was the case of Sayf al-Asali. On being named minister of finance in 2006, al-Asali sought to institute economic reforms that would counter distorting subsidies that contribute to corruption. However, he found he was powerless in the face of endemic corruption and vested interests, eventually prompting him to leave the government.

Nepotism is also a serious problem, with relatives of the political elite often enjoying an unfair advantage when it comes to hiring practices. This is particularly prominent in the armed forces, where relatives and close comrades of the president dominate the military command structure. But it is also an issue in parliament, where sons and brothers often inherit what are seen as family seats. A financial disclosure law was adopted in 2006, requiring officials to submit statements of their assets.[31] Disclosures remain largely voluntary, however, while the database of declarations is not open to public scrutiny. President Saleh's son, Ahmad, submitted his financial records in January 2009 in accordance with the law. In April 2009, the anticorruption body mandated to oversee asset declarations, the Supreme National Authority for Combating Corruption (SNACC), called for 3 ministers, 8 ambassadors, and 40 governors to resign for failing to submit their financial statements. The agency passed the cases to the president, who possesses authority to dispense punishment under the new legislation. As of August 2009, however, the cases were still pending.[32]

The 11-member SNACC was established in June 2007, following parliament's approval of Anti-Corruption Law No. 39 the previous November. The body's mandate includes receiving the aforementioned financial disclosures, collecting data on government actions, and initiating investigations into alleged corruption. Its 11 members were elected from a pool of 30 potential candidates chosen by the presidentially appointed upper house, raising concerns about their ability to be truly independent of the executive and hold officials to account. Since its creation, the SNACC has sought to assert its independence, calling for investigations against high-level government officials, as occurred with the asset declarations cited above.

The Central Organization for Control and Auditing (COCA), created in the 1990s, also continues to function as an auditing body, though it is subordinated to the Office of the President. In recent years, it has produced reports and audits of various government programs, many of which were made public. The Supreme Audit Institution is understaffed and its independence is limited as the president retains the authority to summarily remove its director.[33] To date, these bodies have had a limited impact on preventing abuses of power by public officials. Any legal procedures pursued have themselves been subject to manipulation, resulting in a large number of acquittals or light sentences. Despite the initiation of several investigations, there had yet to be any high-level convictions as of mid-2009.[34]

Parliamentarians have also sought to exercise oversight regarding official corruption. This has included occasional fact-finding missions to outer governorates to investigate allegations of official wrongdoing.[35] Observers also cited a coalition of 18 MPs calling themselves the Parliamentarians Against Corruption (PAC) as having played a critical role in the creation of the SNACC.[36] Nevertheless, most of their efforts are disregarded by the government, contributing to a sense of frustration among MPs. In 2005, Faysal Amin Abu Ra's, an MP for the ruling GPC and the son of a revolutionary war hero, resigned from parliament in protest at rising levels of government corruption.

Given such institutional limitations, victims of corruption have little recourse. This is particularly acute in land confiscation cases, where the victim typically seeks redress for an act committed by a powerful military or political figure. The tax system is corrupt, mismanaged, and inefficient. In recent years, parliament has pressed for greater transparency in public accounting of oil revenue, but such calls often turn into a politicized struggle within parliament.

Corruption and graft are present at all levels of the educational system. In August 2005, the independent weekly *al-Wasat* reported allegations that high-ranking officials had taken advantage of a government scholarship program to send their own children abroad. Within days, the paper's editor Jamal 'Amar was abducted and beaten by masked men, an incident widely perceived as a warning to other journalists not to expose such scandals.[37] Nonetheless, there has been a noticeable increase in journalists documenting cases of official corruption. Such coverage primarily appears in independent or semi-independent news websites or opposition papers and remains largely absent from government-controlled media even when criticism has come from progovernment politicians. Thus, when Abu Ra's left parliament, his eloquent resignation speech, which included remarks that the government was "drowning in corruption," was reproduced only in the YSP paper, *al-Thawri,* limiting its ability to provoke greater public debate and pressure on the government. Online reporting has also increased public access to information about corruption. However, a low level of professionalism, reflected as a tendency to publish unverified information alongside legitimate grievances, has weakened the overall impact and credibility of online reporting.

The government rarely publicizes its accounts except under significant pressure from parliament. The accuracy of information in published reports remains questionable due to a dearth of trained bureaucrats and lack of political will to ensure accuracy. Bureaucratic hurdles for citizens requesting information on government expenditures and operations are unduly difficult. As of May 2009, a draft freedom of information bill was pending. The international advocacy group Article 19 raised concerns regarding several provisions of the draft, including its applicability only to Yemeni citizens, limited possibilities for appealing official decisions to withhold information, broadly defined violations of the law coupled with severe penalties, and the significant authority granted to the National Centre for Information as a centralized hub and depository for data.[38]

According to a 2008 evaluation by the Open Budget Index, Yemen did not have a transparent budget process, with the pre-budget and interim stages particularly lacking opportunities for public participation and oversight.[39] Although parliament must debate and technically approve the budget, ultimate authority lies with the executive and there are no public hearings. In recent years, the government has expended millions of dollars in additional funds without seeking prior parliamentary endorsement.

The process of awarding government contracts is opaque, with agreements granted as political favors to important figures. Such corruption is worst in the oil industry, where government officials demand bribes and kickbacks as a prerequisite for obtaining a contract, often multiple times for the same concession. As oil reserves have declined in recent years, the phenomenon has grown worse as officials seemingly attempt to profit as much as possible before they are depleted. Accounting practices for foreign assistance are more transparent, but still fall short of minimum international standards.

RECOMMENDATIONS

- The state should adopt without reservations the amendments to the election law suggested by the EU and later proposed by the JMP in 2008.
- The state should pass a nepotism law, which would limit the number of offices and terms relatives of the president, prime minister, and speaker of parliament may hold.
- The state should make public disclosure of assets mandatory for all public, military, and security officials. These disclosures should list not only financial assets but also property and the date the property was acquired.
- The state should make public lists of prisoners being held by the state and the charges against them, and pass a law codifying guidelines regulating the president's power to pardon prisoners
- The Special Press Court should be abolished, and Article 103 of the Press and Publications Law narrowed and clarified.

NOTES

For URLs and endnote hyperlinks, please visit the *Countries at the Crossroads* homepage at http://freedomhouse.org/template.cfm?page=139&edition=8.

[1] Nasser Arabyee, "Yemen's Elections Delayed Two Years," *Yemen Observer*, February 25, 2009.
[2] Marine Poirier, "Score One for the Opposition?" *Arab Reform Bulletin* (Washington, D.C.: Carnegie Endowment for International Peace, March 9, 2009).
[3] International Foundation for Electoral Systems (IFES), *Summary of Post-Election Report on the 2006 Presidential and Local Council Elections in Yemen* (Washington, D.C.: IFES, November 2006).
[4] Lisa Wedeen, *Peripheral Visions: Publics Power and Performance in Yemen* (Chicago: University of Chicago Press, 2008), 80.
[5] Gregory D. Johnsen, "The Election Yemen Was Supposed to Have," *Middle East Report Online*, October 3, 2006.

[6] European Union Election Observation Mission (EUEOM), *Final Report: Yemen: Presidential and Local Elections 20 September 2006* (San'a: EUEOM, 2006).
[7] Simon Henderson, "Yemen's President to Be Re-Elected as Terrorist Plot Revealed," Policy Watch #1151, Washington Institute for Near Eastern Policy, September 20, 2006.
[8] Arabyee, "Yemen's Elections Delayed Two Years."
[9] "Yemen: Threat to Legislation Outlawing Child Marriage," Integrated Regional Information Network, February 23, 2009.
[10] International Freedom of Expression Exchange and the Arabic Network for Human Rights Information, "Previously Pardoned Journalist Abdel Karim Al Khaiwani Ordered to Serve 6-Year Prison Sentence," news release, January 26, 2009.
[11] OpenNet Initiative, "Yemen," in *Country Profiles* (Munk/Toronto/Cambridge/Ottawa: Citizen Lab, University of Toronto, Berkman Center for Internet & Society, and the SecDev Group, August 7, 2009).
[12] Abu 'Amr al-Hadrami, "Obituary of Ahmad 'Amr al-Mushjari," *Sada al-Malahi*, no. 8 (March 2009): 42.
[13] "A Socialist Leader and His Son Killed Today in Harf Sufyan in Amran," *News Yemen*, March 19, 2009.
[14] "Fear of Yemen's Desire to Transfer Saudi's Experience in (Religious) Calling and Guidance," al-Tagheer.com, March 8, 2009.
[15] Rasha Jarhum, "New Forms of Violence against Yemeni Women and Persisting Discrimination Laws," *Yemen Times*, August 12, 2009.
[16] Freedom House, "Yemen," in *Women's Rights in the Middle East and North Africa 2010* (Washington, D.C.: Freedom House, March 2010).
[17] "70% of Yemeni Women Support Electoral Quota System," Almotar.net, December 9, 2007.
[18] U.S. Department of State, "2009 International Women of Courage Awardees," home page, March 6, 2009; Deneen L. Brown, "At the State Department, Sisterhood," 44: The Obama Presidency Blog, March 11, 2009.
[19] J. Leight Douglas, *The Free Yemeni Movement* (Beirut: American University of Beirut Press, 1987), 7.
[20] International Trade Union Confederation (ITUC), "Yemen," in *Annual Survey of Violations of Trade Union Rights 2009* (Brussels: ITUC, 2009).
[21] Paul Dresch, *A History of Modern Yemen* (Cambridge: Cambridge University Press, 2000), 204.
[22] Human Rights Watch (HRW), *Disappearances and Arbitrary Arrests in the Armed Conflict with Houthi Rebels in Yemen* (New York: HRW, October 24, 2008).
[23] Amnesty International, "Yemen," in *Annual Report 2008* (London: Amnesty International, 2008).
[24] Faysal Mukrim, "Yemen: Al-Qaeda Prisoners Go on a Hunger and Speaking Strike," *al-Hayat*, March 18, 2009.
[25] Andrew McGregor, "Yemen and the U.S.: Different Approaches to the War on Terrorism," *Terrorism Monitor* 5, no. 9 (May 10, 2007).
[26] Ahmed al-Haj, "Yemen Protests: Security Officers Kill 12, Injure Scores More," *Huffington Post*, July 23, 2009; Jamal Dajani, "Yemen: A Powder Keg Ready to Explode," *Huffington Post*, August 7, 2009.
[27] Ali Abdulmalek Alabsi, "Country Pasture/Forage Resource Profiles: Yemen," Food and Agriculture Association of the United Nations home page.
[28] The Heritage Foundation and *Wall Street Journal* (WSJ), "Yemen," in *2009 Index of Economic Freedom* (Washington, D.C./New York: The Heritage Foundation and WSJ,

2009); Bureau of Economic, Energy, and Business Affairs, "Yemen," in *2009 Investment Climate Statements* (Washington, D.C.: U.S. Department of State, February 2009).
29. Ian Siperco, "Crisis of Complacency: The Criminalization of the Yemeni State," Middle East Dispatch No. 2 (Washington, D.C.: Middle East Policy Council, July 2009).
30. Ministry of Planning and International Cooperation, *The National Reform Agenda: A Progress Report* (San'a: Republic of Yemen, October 2006). For more about anticorruption efforts, see the Yemen Consultative Group's website at www.yemencg.org.
31. Zaid al-Alaya'a, "Commander of Republican Guards and Special Forces Submits Financial Disclosure," *Yemen Observer*, January 17, 2009.
32. Zaid al-Alaya'a, "SNACC Demands Detention of 3 Ministers, 8 Governors and 40 Ambassadors," *Yemen Observer*, April 25, 2009.
33. Open Budget Initiative, "Yemen," in *Open Budget Index 2008* (Washington, D.C.: Open Budget Initiative, 2009).
34. Alistair Lyon, "Feature–Corruption Corrodes Public Life in Yemen," Reuters, September 2, 2009.
35. Mahmoud Al-Harazi, "Yemeni Parliamentarians Take on Corruption," *Yemen Times*, August 12, 2009.
36. National Democratic Institute, "Yemen: Strengthening Parliamentary Institutions."
37. Committee to Protect Journalists, "2006 Awards-Jamal Amer-Yemen," International Press Freedom Awards.
38. Article 19, "Yemen: Article 19 Calls on Yemeni Government to Improve Its Draft Information Law," press release, May 20, 2009.
39. Open Budget Initiative, "Yemen."

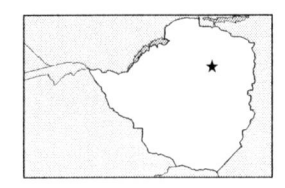

ZIMBABWE

CAPITAL: Harare
POPULATION: 12.5 million
GNI PER CAPITA (ATLAS): $340

SCORES	2006	2010
ACCOUNTABILITY AND PUBLIC VOICE:	1.06	1.33
CIVIL LIBERTIES:	2.33	2.21
RULE OF LAW:	1.30	1.06
ANTICORRUPTION AND TRANSPARENCY:	0.90	1.04

(scores are based on a scale of 0 to 7, with 0 representing weakest and 7 representing strongest performance)

Robert Lloyd

INTRODUCTION

President Robert Mugabe has led Zimbabwe since formal independence from Britain in 1980, overseeing a gradual drift toward authoritarianism and a dramatic economic breakdown. Electoral abuses led to mass protests and strikes by the growing opposition, and the seizure of white-owned farms beginning in 2000 crippled the agricultural sector. Political and economic developments between 2005 and 2009 have left the country poised between total collapse and the first steps toward recovery, a turning point that was not yet apparent in 2005. At that time, Mugabe's Zimbabwe African National Union–Patriotic Front (ZANU-PF) party was still exhibiting surprising resilience in the face of intense political opposition and economic crisis, and increased its majority in the 2005 parliamentary elections. The opposition Movement for Democratic Change (MDC) party, led by former trade union leader Morgan Tsvangirai, was sputtering and splintering. International opposition to Mugabe's rule had led to sanctions from the United States, the European Union (EU), and the Commonwealth, but these did not seriously threaten the regime. The International Monetary Fund (IMF) declined to expel Zimbabwe despite its failure to repay loans, and South Africa, a key trading partner and political patron, remained generally supportive despite its concerns about the country's political deterioration.

It was ultimately Zimbabwe's accelerating economic collapse that undermined ZANU-PF rule. The seizure of white-owned commercial farms, while

---

Robert B. Lloyd is a professor of International Relations at Pepperdine University in Malibu, California. His primary research interests are international conflict management, international negotiation, and Africa.

politically popular, led to a fall in export revenue and soaring unemployment. The loss of IMF loans further weakened government finances. These setbacks made it more difficult for the leadership to maintain its patronage system, undermining domestic support for the regime. As a result, the leadership came to rely more and more on political violence to maintain control. The country has witnessed an increasing degree of conflict since 2005, sorely testing Mugabe's political tenacity and hardening the resolve of his foreign and domestic opponents.

The signs of economic morbidity have been unmistakable in recent years. Zimbabwe's growth rate was negative, with an average annual contraction of 5 percent, throughout the 2005–2009 period. Inflation soared as the government printed money without restraint, destroying the value of Zimbabwe's currency by 2007. The water treatment and health care systems collapsed, leading to an outbreak of cholera in 2008, and the education system faltered as teachers were paid in worthless money and parents were unable to pay school fees. Zimbabweans began leaving the country in large numbers.

In the midst of this economic crisis, presidential and parliamentary elections were held in March 2008. The polls were surprisingly peaceful, and the MDC scored a major upset over the ZANU-PF, gaining a majority of seats in the House of Assembly. The results of the presidential election, however, were delayed for several weeks. During this time, the authorities and their supporters launched a campaign of severe political violence against the opposition. Official results ultimately triggered a presidential runoff in June, as Tsvangirai was found to have finished ahead of Mugabe, but with only a plurality of the votes cast. However, the enormous increase in election-related violence led Tsvangirai to withdraw, and Mugabe won the uncontested second round ballot.

Zimbabwe was thus faced with a dubiously reelected president, an opposition-controlled legislature, and a collapsing economy. Under mounting international pressure, Mugabe and the MDC agreed to a power-sharing deal in September 2008, paving the way for Tsvangirai to take up the newly created post of prime minister in February 2009. As of mid-2009, it remains unclear whether the agreement is a transitional arrangement to facilitate Mugabe's exit, a method for Mugabe to co-opt Tsvangirai, or the manifestation of some new equilibrium in a deeply fractured political system.

ACCOUNTABILITY AND PUBLIC VOICE — 1.33

FREE AND FAIR ELECTORAL LAWS AND ELECTIONS	1.75
EFFECTIVE AND ACCOUNTABLE GOVERNMENT	2.00
CIVIC ENGAGEMENT AND CIVIC MONITORING	1.00
MEDIA INDEPENDENCE AND FREEDOM OF EXPRESSION	0.57

Zimbabwe has a bicameral Parliament and a semipresidential system. In October 2007, a constitutional amendment increased the lower chamber, the House of Assembly, to 210 members elected directly by district.[1] The size of the Senate, created in 2005, was increased from 66 to 93, with 60 senators elected directly and 33 appointed by the president. The appointed senators include 10 provincial governors, 18 from the Council of Chiefs, and 5 directly appointed by the president. While elections are scheduled regularly, Mugabe and the ZANU-PF have held power throughout the 29 years since independence. In the March 29, 2008 elections, the MDC finally ended Zimbabwe's status as a de facto single-party state by breaking ZANU-PF hegemony in Parliament. The MDC had split into two factions, with the main grouping led by Tsvangirai and a rival group led by Arthur Mutambara, but the two agreed to cooperate after the elections, giving the MDC 110 seats in the 210-seat House of Assembly. ZANU-PF has 99 seats in the chamber, and there is one independent.[2]

The March 2008 elections were relatively peaceful compared with previous contests, and the MDC was able to campaign freely throughout the country.[3] The elections were monitored by independent electoral authorities, but the government decided which groups would be invited to observe. Poll monitors from the United States, EU member states, and other countries deemed critical of Mugabe were excluded, while invitations were extended to those from countries in Africa, Asia, and Latin America.[4] Mugabe asserts, with some evidence, that the United States and European countries fund the MDC and favor it over the ZANU-PF.[5] Raising the tension, the Zimbabwe Electoral Commission (ZEC) delayed for a month the official presidential results, citing the complexity of conducting simultaneous elections for Parliament, the presidency, and local governments, as well as the need for recounts and verification. It is unclear whether the delay was due to ZEC disorganization or, as some charged, an attempt to alter results in Mugabe's favor. The ZEC, whose chairperson and commissioners are appointed by the president, retained its traditional subservience to the ZANU-PF throughout the election period. Although the ZEC had allegedly undergone restructuring in order to increase its autonomy, its strong ties to the ZANU-PF were evidenced by its partisan composition, its inability to make key decisions without the input of government and security sector officials, and its failure to reject the ZANU-PF's post-election demands for a recount. Indeed, the ZEC itself admitted its subjugation to the ZANU-PF and the government ministries.[6]

The results that were ultimately released showed Tsvangirai winning with 47.9 percent of the vote, followed by Mugabe with 43.2 percent. Since no candidate secured an outright majority, a runoff election was called. During the period between the two rounds of voting, a campaign of state-sponsored violence targeted opposition party members and civil society,[7] and Tsvangirai decided to withdraw from the June 27 runoff due to concerns about the safety of his supporters. This allowed Mugabe to run uncontested, and he secured a sixth term with 90.2 percent of the vote.

The government claims to comply with democratic guidelines established by the Southern African Development Community (SADC), a regional grouping of states. Public funding is given to opposition political parties. Nevertheless, it is clear that there are not equal campaigning opportunities for all parties. The Public Order and Security Act (POSA) requires government permission for opposition parties to campaign, and makes it a criminal offense to publicly issue an abusive or false statement that undermines the authority of the president, essentially criminalizing political speech. The dominance of state-owned media makes it difficult for opposition parties to receive favorable coverage during the campaign period. The MDC argued that during the 2008 election season, the government banned MDC rallies and key foreign observers, killed independent election monitors, used food aid as a political tool, threatened MDC candidates, and rigged the first-round presidential vote.[8] These allegations were generally supported by governments and organizations in Europe and North America.

Shortly after the September 2008 power-sharing agreement was signed, Mugabe said in a speech that he would never surrender power.[9] The deal left him in control over key ministries responsible for the military and agriculture, among other portfolios. Still, it represented an increasing opportunity for rotation of power among parties that represent quite different interests and policies. Tsvangirai, as prime minister under the agreement, appointed ministers to oversee important matters including finance, health, and constitutional affairs. Moreover, in August 2008, Lovemore Moyo of the MDC was elected speaker of the House of Assembly, marking the first time an opposition party gained control of the chamber. The judiciary has retained some independence, but Mugabe has clearly eroded its autonomy over time, leaving it largely unable to fulfill its role as a check on executive power.

The civil service has generally been seen as a means to reward political supporters, with ZANU-PF loyalists receiving preference in employment opportunities. However, the economic collapse of recent years has led many civil servants to stop showing up for work in the face of nearly worthless salaries and adverse working conditions. These problems have further undermined the recruitment and retention of qualified individuals.

Civic groups are allowed to comment on pending legislation, and parliamentary debates give citizens an opportunity to learn of proposed legal changes. Nevertheless, the government places tight legal constraints on nongovernmental organizations (NGOs). Both the POSA and the Access to Information and Protection of Privacy Act (AIPPA) impose limits on activists' ability to speak, associate, and assemble. A specific law banning foreign funding of civic associations that deal with "governance issues" was passed but not signed by Mugabe. Separately, the Private Voluntary Organizations Act of 1996 requires government registration of all NGOs that provide welfare services or treatment. The government appoints the NGO Council, which decides whether an NGO may register. In 2007, the government cancelled all NGO licenses, claiming that some groups were "agents of imperialism" that supported the opposition.[10] An official with an umbrella group for civic and humanitarian organizations stated that violence associated with the 2008 elections meant that humanitarian food relief distributed through local groups had become politicized and dangerous. This hampered emergency food assistance for a country in economic free-fall.[11]

The government exercises direct control over print and broadcast media. The state-owned Zimbabwe Broadcasting Corporation (ZBC) controls all domestic radio and television stations, and the *Herald*, a state-owned daily, is pro-Mugabe in its reporting. A number of independent radio stations broadcast into Zimbabwe from outside the country, but the government has routinely sought to jam such transmissions.[12]

All journalists and media houses must be accredited by the government's Media Information Commission (MIC) or face fines and imprisonment. Independent media are severely restricted, and many journalists have had their accreditation withdrawn. The state shows no sign of rescinding libel, security, and other laws that impose excessive fines and imprisonment on those who scrutinize government officials and policy. Both the POSA and the AIPPA criminalize false reporting, and the POSA additionally criminalizes statements that "incite or promote public disorder or public violence." In addition, the 2004 Criminal Law (Codification and Reform) Act imposes prison sentences of up to 20 years for journalists who publish false information deemed to be prejudicial to the state. During the 2008 election crisis, the government extensively employed these laws to detain and prosecute critical journalists and anti-government activists alike. In April 2008, Davison Maruziva, the editor of the *Standard*, was charged with publishing information deemed prejudicial to the state, an act banned by the Criminal Law, after the newspaper featured a government-critical opinion piece.[13] In May 2008, media defense lawyer Harrison Nkomo was charged with insulting the president, a criminal offense under the same law, although the case was ultimately dropped.[14] These legal threats contribute to self-censorship in the media.

Outlets viewed as opposing the government are often intimidated and shut down. The *Daily News*, a critical privately owned daily, was banned by the MIC in 2003, while the British Broadcasting Corporation (BBC) and the U.S.-based television network CNN had been forced to end their presence in Zimbabwe in 2001 and 2002, respectively, due to government disapproval of their reporting, although all three of these bans were lifted in July 2009. In January 2009, the MIC—which is due to be replaced sometime in the next year by a new Zimbabwe Media Commission under a 2008 amendment to the AIPPA—began imposing substantial accreditation fees on independent media during a time of economic crisis. The Zimbabwe Union of Journalists argued that the fees amounted to censorship.[15]

The government does not protect journalists from extralegal intimidation, arbitrary arrest and detention, or physical violence, nor does it ensure fair and expeditious investigation and prosecution of such abuses. In fact, the government uses the security apparatus to enforce restrictive legislation aimed at the media.[16] In 2008, Reporters Without Borders ranked Zimbabwe at 151 out of 173 states in its annual assessment of press freedom.[17]

The government does not directly censor specific stories. It does, however, intimidate members of the print media believed to support the opposition. Reporters are often detained, threatened, or deported. In May 2009, for example, two editors of the *Zimbabwe Independent* newspaper were arrested for publishing an article alleging government involvement in the abduction of MDC supporters and human rights activist Jestina Mukoko.[18] In addition to direct pressure by the authorities, local newspaper companies face severe financial strains linked to the high inflation rate.

The Interception of Communications Act, signed in August 2007, allows security and financial authorities access to mail, telephone, and internet communications without a court order.[19] The government stated that the new law was justified on national security grounds and was similar to communication interception programs in other countries, such as the United States and South Africa. However, because the internet is an important tool used by Zimbabwean individuals and media to circumvent government restrictions, civil society groups strongly opposed the legislation.[20] In 2008, several journalists at state-owned media outlets who were allegedly disloyal to the ZANU-PF were fired after their e-mail was intercepted under government orders.[21] It is not evident that websites are being blocked, but denial-of-service attacks have been reported.

Given the Mugabe government's control over media, Article 19 of the September 2008 power-sharing agreement emphasizes the importance of an "open media environment" and encourages the development of Zimbabwean-based radio broadcasting that is "balanced and fair" to all political parties.[22] The Zimbabwe Media Commission offers the promise of press liberalization, but its success remains a merely notional prospect.

CIVIL LIBERTIES   2.21

PROTECTION FROM STATE TERROR, UNJUSTIFIED IMPRISONMENT, AND TORTURE	0.88
GENDER EQUITY	2.67
RIGHTS OF ETHNIC, RELIGIOUS, AND OTHER DISTINCT GROUPS	2.50
FREEDOM OF CONSCIENCE AND BELIEF	4.00
FREEDOM OF ASSOCIATION AND ASSEMBLY	1.00

Zimbabwe's constitution is a much-amended document that was established in the run-up to independence in 1980. It specifically guarantees protection from torture and arbitrary search or entry, among other rights. However, later amendments subordinate these rights to "the interests of defense, public safety, public order, and public morality." In addition, "state of emergency" laws that further limit civil liberties in these areas were passed prior to independence and have been retained and employed by the government to suppress dissent. These laws and practices appear to contradict Zimbabwe's obligations under the International Covenant on Civil and Political Rights, to which it acceded in 1991.

There have been widespread reports of violence by agents of the state, often targeting real or suspected supporters of the MDC, including schoolteachers who have traditionally manned polling stations.[23] A spike in violence coincided with the 2008 election period, during which at least 163 people, most of them MDC activists, were killed, and 5,000 were beaten.[24] In some cases, MDC supporters were reportedly kidnapped by progovernment militias, tortured, forced to denounce the MDC, and pressed for the names of additional MDC supporters.[25] There have been no prosecutions for these abuses.

MDC cabinet nominee Roy Bennett, jailed between February and March 2009 on charges including terrorism, has described conditions behind bars as hellish. Inmates are beaten on a daily basis and not properly clothed. In 2009, the South African documentary *Hell Hole* depicted living conditions in Zimbabwean prisons, stating that inmates face starvation and disease linked to overcrowding and poor sanitation. The NGO Zimbabwe Association for Crime Prevention and Rehabilitation of the Offender has reported that Zimbabwean prisons hold twice their intended capacity.[26] A high-level prison official subsequently admitted to shortcomings in caring for prisoners.[27]

There are no effective protections against arbitrary arrest of political opponents or long-term detention without trial. The 2004 Criminal Procedure and Evidence Act extends the initial detention of those arrested for corruption or violating security laws from 48 hours, the legally permissible detention period for other crimes, to 21 days. Jestina Mukoko, director of the Zimbabwe Peace Project, and 17 other activists (including some MDC members) were held for three months beginning in December 2008 to face charges of terrorism. Mukoko claims that she was tortured during her detention,[28] and she was ordered back to jail in May 2009.[29] The POSA makes it easier for the government to charge political opponents due to its limits on speech, association, and assembly.

During the contentious election period in 2008, ZANU-PF youth militia detained individuals accused of supporting the MDC, taking them to various locations and making them prove their loyalty to the government by singing revolutionary songs.[30] The police have not intervened when they observe attacks by the youth militia.[31] In addition, in February 2009 it was reported that the government detained about 30 MDC supporters on charges of receiving military training in neighboring Botswana—a charge strongly denied by the Botswana government. The activists said they were abducted in Zimbabwe by state security agents and that their confessions were obtained by torture.[32]

No allegations of widespread trafficking of women and children have been reported by the government, human rights organizations, or international organizations. It has been difficult for government agencies and NGOs to determine the scale of human trafficking in Zimbabwe and southern Africa.[33] However, there have been reports of women being transported to South Africa to work as prostitutes, partly in anticipation of the high demand likely to be generated by the 2010 World Cup.[34]

Constitutional protections notwithstanding, citizens lack effective means of petition and redress when their rights are violated by the government. Although the 2008 power-sharing agreement provides for the release of political detainees, the attorney general's office has delayed this move. An Ombudsman's office is mandated to investigate the actions of government officials upon receiving a public complaint, but is legally precluded from investigating allegations of abuses by security forces.Chapter III (11) of the Zimbabwean constitution guarantees the fundamental rights and freedoms of the individual, "whatever his race, tribe, place of origin, colour, creed, or sex." Values regarding the status and role of women in Zimbabwe vary. Traditional African views on gender relations are not always compatible with national laws and international standards, leading to enforcement problems. While the government has banned some traditional practices, others, such as *lobola* (bride price) and polygamy, remain legal.[35] The economic crisis has led some families to use lobola, a traditional way of cementing ties between families, to extract money from in-laws.[36]

Women participate in politics without legal restriction. Thirty percent of ZANU-PF candidates must be women. They hold seats in Parliament as well as senior posts in national and local government. The ZANU-PF allots a fixed quota of party positions to women, including posts on its powerful Central Committee. Following the 2008 elections, 14.29 percent of House of Assembly seats and 30.33 percent of Senate seats were held by women.

The government of Zimbabwe in 2008 signed the SADC's Protocol on Gender and Development, which seeks to eliminate discrimination and achieve gender equality for women. Moreover, Article 5 of the 2008 power-sharing agreement contained a specific clause "recognizing the need for women's access and control over land in their own right as equal citizens."[37] Zimbabwe has also ratified the Convention on the Elimination of All Forms of Discrimination against Women (CEDAW).[38] However, given the country's level of political strife, economic crisis, high unemployment rate (perhaps 90 percent in the formal sector), and prevalence of subsistence agriculture, little information is available on gender-related employment discrimination. Violence against women is widespread, and groups such as the Women's Coalition of Zimbabwe have alleged that many women were gang-raped by ZANU-PF militiamen, particularly during the violence after the first round of presidential voting in 2008. They have called for the new unity government to investigate these cases.[39]

Zimbabwe's official language is English, but some 20 languages are spoken in the country. The majority of the population belongs to the Shona ethnolinguistic group. The Ndebele form the largest minority group, living mostly in the southwestern region of Matabeleland, which includes Bulawayo, Zimbabwe's second city. In practice, many Zimbabweans are fluent in two or more languages. There is no indication of legal discrimination against speakers of minority languages, although Mugabe is a Shona speaker and many Ndebeles in the southwest argue that the government discriminates against them politically and economically. Shortly after independence in 1980, tensions between the Shona and Ndebele groups sparked a bloody, low-level civil war. Mugabe cited this conflict as a reason to detain (mostly Ndebele) people without charge; the detainees were at times executed. More recently, support for the MDC has been relatively strong among Ndebele speakers in Matebeleland, making it difficult to separate ethnic discrimination from attempts to quell general opposition to Mugabe's rule. All major ethnic groups are represented in the government, although most belong to the Shona majority. White Zimbabweans, a much smaller group, have been marginalized by the government and are subject to a distinct set of abuses (see Rule of Law).

The constitution provides for freedom of religion, and the government generally upholds the rights of nonbelievers and adherents of the country's various faiths. Religious instruction is permitted at all educational levels, religious broadcasting is allowed on state-owned television, and religious advertising is accepted in the government-controlled press. Although the majority of Zimbabweans are Christians, around a quarter of the population follows traditional African religious practices. The Witchcraft Suppression Act provides criminal penalties for those who practice witchcraft, but a 2006 amendment narrowed its scope to those intending to cause harm to an individual.[40]

Government suspicions that some churches support the MDC have led to repression by the authorities in recent years. The government has used the POSA to ban public religious gatherings, and in one high-profile case, it has supported a politically loyal Anglican cleric, Nolbert Kunonga, since he was dismissed as bishop of Harare by the Anglican hierarchy in late 2007. Police prevented supporters of his replacement, Sebastian Bakare, from holding services in Anglican churches in the capital, in some instances beating and intimidating parishioners. After the new unity government was formed in early 2009, Bakare and his supporters began reasserting their right to use church facilities.[41]

The constitution guarantees freedom of assembly and association. However, several clauses subordinate these rights to the interests of safety, order, and morality, and they are further limited in practice by the POSA and government restrictions on opposition political activities. Political parties must inform the government beforehand if there will be a meeting of more than three people, severely hindering their ability to organize. The 2008 election period, particularly after the first round, featured significant state violence against opposition supporters, although the government generally did not use excessive force to break up party meetings in previous years if they complied with POSA regulations. Protest rights are limited by the POSA, which requires that demonstrators notify police seven days in advance of any planned public gathering. Police frequently deny or fail to respond to these requests, although a January 2008 amendment to the POSA grants citizens the right to appeal to the magistrates' court if the police prohibit a demonstration from taking place.[42] Throughout

2007 and 2008, protests were violently repressed and demonstrators were beaten and arbitrarily detained by riot police as political tensions intensified during the run-up to the March 2008 elections.

The Labor Relations Act allows private sector workers to form and operate unions, which must register with the Ministry of Public Services, Labor, and Social Welfare. An umbrella organization, the Zimbabwe Congress of Trade Unions (ZCTU), includes roughly 30 individual unions. The government views the ZCTU as an MDC ally and has targeted it with harassment, intimidation, and violence. A rival, pro-Mugabe union, the Zimbabwe Federation of Trade Unions (ZFTU), was organized to undermine the ZCTU. This politically discriminatory treatment applies to civic groups more broadly, with white farmers, religious organizations, and teachers facing hostility due to perceived opposition sympathies. While Zimbabweans are not compelled by the state to belong to an association, there are widespread reports that ZANU-PF membership brings preferential access to food supplies.

RULE OF LAW 1.06

INDEPENDENT JUDICIARY	1.20
PRIMACY OF RULE OF LAW IN CIVIL AND CRIMINAL MATTERS	2.20
ACCOUNTABILITY OF SECURITY FORCES AND MILITARY TO CIVILIAN AUTHORITIES	0.50
PROTECTION OF PROPERTY RIGHTS	0.33

The constitution provides for an independent judiciary, and senior judges must have legal training, be experienced with Roman-Dutch law, and be fluent in English. However, the charter authorizes the president to directly appoint judges to the Supreme Court and the High Court without legislative approval, and President Mugabe has gradually increased his control over the judiciary. The chief justice of the Supreme Court, Anthony Gabbay, resigned in June 2001 after the government stated that it could not guarantee his security. Some months beforehand, progovernment "war veterans" had invaded the Supreme Court building. In a more recent sign of politicization, Justice Maphios Cheda gave a speech in 2006 in which he reportedly criticized lawyers who supported human rights cases in the country, claiming that they did not offer similar support to the victims of white-minority rule during the liberation struggle.[43] Judges have also experienced financial distress due to the economic crisis, making them more vulnerable to bribery. There are allegations that judges have obtained tracts of land seized from white farmers by the government.[44]

Despite active interference, the judiciary nevertheless retains some independence from the executive, handing down a number of decisions over the past several years that ran counter to the government's position. For example, in March 2009 Chief Justice Godfrey Chidyausiku ordered the release of MDC official Roy Bennett from jail. This was significant because the chief justice is seen as allied with Mugabe, and Bennett had been nominated to serve as deputy agriculture minister in the new power-sharing government.[45]

The political, economic, and social crisis that has engulfed Zimbabwe has hindered the proper functioning of the justice system. The constitution guarantees the presumption of innocence for criminal defendants, but fair trials are unlikely given the severe shortage of resources and judicial personnel, and particularly improbable when the case relates to the ongoing political struggle.

Citizens' right to independent counsel is often denied, and while indigent defendants may request legal assistance, it is rarely granted unless the charges are serious felonies.[46] In theory, prosecutors are free from political direction and control, but the breakdown in the rule of law, combined with executive assaults on the independence of the judiciary, make it possible for the political leadership to control prosecutors. The ZANU-PF has influenced prosecutors to keep MDC supporters in jail for extended periods of time. On May 20, 2008, Deputy Attorney General Johannes Tomana allegedly ordered all public prosecutors to oppose bail for those accused of committing political violence. In addition, the government has frequently deployed ZANU-PF-friendly magistrates and prosecutors to deal with political cases involving MDC supporters in order to ensure a favorable outcome.[47]

The military is under civilian control in the sense that it acts on the orders of the president, who retains exclusive control over the armed forces. Senior security officials owe their positions to Mugabe and have received land and other benefits for their loyalty. The national police, however, now fall under the jurisdiction of the Home Affairs Ministry, which is jointly controlled by the MDC and the ZANU-PF. The legislative branch does not engage in oversight of the security forces, which actively interfere in the political process to support Mugabe's continued rule. The harassment, torture, detention, and killing of civilians by the police and military have not been strongly condemned by Mugabe or the ZANU-PF, and allegations of human rights violations by these forces are not investigated.[48] During the 2008 election period, the head of the military stated that he would not support any president other than Mugabe. This preference was illustrated by the army's violent action against MDC supporters.[49] Political control over the security forces, and possible amnesty for past abuses, are critical questions facing the new power-sharing government.

Corruption is also rife within the military. The discovery of diamonds in Chiadzwa in 2006 eventually led to a violent military deployment to evict illegal miners.[50] Members of the military began mining the diamonds in late 2008, with forced labor from nearby residents.[51] Human Rights Watch has reported that military units are rotated through the area in order to maximize the number of officers who profit from the operations.[52]

Zimbabwean law allows for the private ownership of property, but the government often fails to respect property rights. Since 2000 the government has maintained a policy of uncompensated land seizures, primarily of commercial farms owned by white Zimbabweans. These farms have also been subject to illegal squatting and invasions by ZANU-PF partisans. The MDC alleges that ZANU-PF leaders have acquired multiple farms seized from white owners, in contravention of Mugabe's "one person, one farm" policy.[53] Separately, in 2005 the government launched Operation Murambatsvina (Operation Clear the Filth), a slum clearance campaign that destroyed tens of thousands of shanty dwellings and street stalls in the major cities of Harare and Bulawayo, leaving about 700,000 people homeless and appearing to target areas where MDC support was strong.[54]

The September 2008 power-sharing agreement between the MDC and ZANU-PF devoted an entire section (Article 5) to the "Land Question." It stated that the land seizures were "irreversible," but noted that all Zimbabweans were eligible to receive land. The apparent legitimization of the land expropriation and the ambiguity in the text suggest that property rights will remain insecure in Zimbabwe.[55]

ANTICORRUPTION AND TRANSPARENCY 1.04

ENVIRONMENT TO PROTECT AGAINST CORRUPTION	1.00
PROCEDURES AND SYSTEMS TO ENFORCE ANTICORRUPTION LAWS	1.00
EXISTENCE OF ANTICORRUPTION NORMS, STANDARDS, AND PROTECTIONS	1.00
GOVERNMENTAL TRANSPARENCY	1.17

Government policies under Mugabe and the ZANU-PF have fostered corruption, destroyed the value of the currency, and undermined the economy. At independence, the government sought to create a black middle class, purchasing private companies as a way to boost black employment prospects. It also retained the old regime's economic regulations, which shielded the country from imports through price controls, tariffs, and licensing. These mechanisms present profitable rent-seeking opportunities for government officials and ruling party members. The seizure of white-owned commercial farms starting in 2000 provided the government with additional resources to distribute as patronage, but it also led to drastically reduced agricultural production, failing banks, and soaring unemployment.

International donors warn that Zimbabwe is now facing a serious shortfall of grain, although 2008 estimates that up to half the population would need food aid were decreased somewhat, to 2.8 million people, by the World Food Program following favorable climatic conditions as well as economic and agricultural liberalization policies implemented in the first half of 2009. In the face of extreme hyperinflation, which by December 2008 was reported to have reached an astronomical 6.5 quindecillion novemdecillian percent,[56] government supporters' access to foreign currency at favorable rates of exchange has provided opportunities for personal enrichment.[57] However, the Zimbabwean dollar was ultimately rendered worthless; foreign currencies were formally allowed beginning in January 2009, and officials said in April that the old currency was suspended indefinitely.[58] In March 2009, the IMF sent a team to investigate the country's economic situation and set conditions for renewed lending.[59] In September, it granted the country a US$500 million loan to boost its foreign currency reserves.[60]

Mugabe heads a multifaceted enterprise of businesses, government, and patronage. His party owns a wide range of companies, allowing party elites to share in its profits. A BBC report in February 2009 alleged that Joyce Mujuru, one of the country's two vice presidents, took part in a deal to sell gold from the Democratic Republic of the Congo in Europe, evading international sanctions imposed for alleged human rights abuses.[61] The government does not disclose many financial details, such as assets declarations, that would make its operations more transparent and prevent conflicts of interest on the part of public officials.

The government does not currently have an effective legislative or administrative process that promotes integrity and punishes corruption. The result is extremely high—and increasing—levels of graft. Transparency International ranked Zimbabwe 166 out of 180 countries in its 2008 Corruption Perceptions Index. It received a score of 1.8, with 10 being the best, down from 2.1 in 2007.[62] In 2005 it had managed a 2.6.[63]

Prior to the power-sharing agreement in September 2008, *Africa Confidential*, a British-based newsletter on politics in Africa, reported that senior officials of the ZANU-PF government were transferring funds, sometimes illegally, to more secure foreign locations in order to avoid international sanctions and possible auditing by a new government that included the MDC.[64]

Investigative and auditing bodies such as the offices of the comptroller and the auditor general do exist, but they are hampered by political pressure, and the details of the investigative process are not always transparent. An audit of Champion Farmers, a program designed to provide farmers with agricultural supplies, uncovered evidence of corruption in January 2009. The military official in charge of the program stated that government officials had resold the supplies for profit and that this would be reported to Parliament.[65] However, there were no subsequent reports of formal indictments or prosecutions of those accused.

As a testament to the government's opacity and disorganization, the IMF notes that Zimbabwe has been in continuous arrears on outstanding loans since 2001, and is the only country not eligible for its poverty reduction and growth program.[66]

The MDC's takeover of the House of Assembly in 2008, and its control of the Finance Ministry under the new government in 2009, have raised the prospects of accountability for executive corruption. On March 27, Parliament created a committee to establish an independent anticorruption commission that would report directly to lawmakers.[67] Graft allegations are given wide attention in the state-owned news media, but only when those accused are not key Mugabe allies. The lack of government transparency and the absence of a robust independent media sector make it difficult to fully assess corruption among public officials. Although there are anticorruption laws and mechanisms in place, the legal and political environment is not supportive of investigators.

The dire economic situation has made the operation of educational institutions more difficult. In recent years, Zimbabweans were increasingly unable to afford school fees, and the government could not pay teacher salaries. By late 2008, grade school enrollment had fallen to less than 20 percent as the economy crashed and political violence rose.[68] In 2009 the new unity government obtained assistance from the UN Children's Fund (UNICEF) that enabled a salary increase for teachers, and pay is now in U.S. dollars.[69] This has stabilized the educational system and reduced opportunities for corruption.

Every fall, as required by the constitution, the government presents Parliament with budget details for the next year. However, it has been accused of omitting key assumptions on future inflation, growth, and interest rates. No independent parliamentary auditing body exists to analyze the executive's budget figures. Moreover, the Defense Procurement Act permits the government to withhold important financial records and budget details from the legislature. The AIPPA can also restrict access to information held by public bodies. A proposal advanced after the new unity government was installed would replace the restrictive AIPPA with new legislation aimed at liberalizing the media (the Media Practitioners Act) and fostering freedom of information (the Freedom of Information Act), but as of late June 2009 the acts were still under consideration.[70]

The Procurement Act outlaws collusion among government contractors and providers of goods or services. The president can, however, waive the law's restrictions at his discretion, and the procurement process has been the focus of a number of corruption allegations. Zimbabwe is not a signatory to the World Trade Organization's Agreement on Government Procurement. Foreign firms and governments, including that of the United States, have complained of a lack of transparency and fairness in the process.

Since the March 2002 elections, the European Union, the Commonwealth, and the United States have maintained sanctions on Zimbabwe for fraud and voter intimidation. Zimbabwe receives no foreign assistance from these states and organizations aside from emergency food aid. The Zimbabwean government has denied repeated accusations that it politicizes food aid by giving preference to ZANU-PF supporters.[71] Following the 2008 agreement, Tsvangirai and the MDC have launched renewed efforts to procure foreign assistance and foreign direct investment.

RECOMMENDATIONS

- The Public Order and Security Act (POSA) and the Access to Information and Protection of Privacy Act (AIPPA) must be amended to bring them into compliance with constitutional guarantees of freedom of speech and freedom of association.

- The government must strengthen the independence of the judiciary by establishing an impartial appointment process and ensuring judges' personal and financial security.
- Legal recourse must be provided for the loss of property. This should include an audit of land confiscated since 2000 to permit compensation, as called for in the September 2008 power-sharing agreement.
- The government must cease using "war veterans," youth militias, and security forces to intimidate, assault, and detain civilians. Such abuses should be fully investigated and pursued to conviction.
- The House of Assembly should create an independent accounting and investigative body with the capacity to evaluate executive budgets and expenditures and issue reports to lawmakers and the public.

NOTES

For URLs and endnote hyperlinks, please visit the *Countries at the Crossroads* homepage at http://freedomhouse.org/template.cfm?page=139&edition=8.

[1] Constitution of Zimbabwe Amendment (No. 18) Act, 2007.
[2] Lauren Ploch, "Zimbabwe: 2008 Elections and Implications for U.S. Policy," Congressional Research Service Report for Congress, May 22, 2008.
[3] "Zimbabwe Poll: Key Complaints," British Broadcasting Corporation (BBC), June 22, 2008.
[4] Patience Rusere and Brenda Moyo, "Zimbabwean Government Selective in Accrediting Election Observers," Voice of America, March 7, 2008.
[5] Fanuel Jongwe, "Western Monitors Barred from Zim Poll," *Mail & Guardian* (Johannesburg), March 7, 2008.
[6] Electoral Institute of Southern Africa (EISA), *Election Observer Mission Report: The Zimbabwe Harmonised Elections of 29 March 2008* (Johannesburg: EISA, 2008), 50.
[7] Human Rights Watch (HRW), *"Bullets for Each of You": State-Sponsored Violence since Zimbabwe's March 29 Elections* (New York: HRW, June 2008).
[8] "Zimbabwe Poll: Key Complaints," BBC, June 22, 2008.
[9] "Mugabe Insists Zimbabwe 'Is Mine,'" BBC, December 19, 2008.
[10] "Zimbabwe Revokes All NGO Licences," *Mail & Guardian*, April 16, 2007.
[11] "Zimbabwe: Humanitarian Operations Curtailed by Violence," Integrated Regional Information Networks (IRIN), April 21, 2008.
[12] Reporters without Borders (RSF), "Zimbabwe," in *Annual Report 2008* (Paris: RSF, February 2008).
[13] Committee to Protect Journalists (CPJ), "Zimbabwe," in *Attacks on the Press 2008* (New York: CPJ, 2009).
[14] Tom Rhodes, "Bad to Worse in Zimbabwe," CPJ, June 23, 2008.
[15] "Zimbabwe: Media Caught in the Political Vice," IRIN, February 5, 2009.
[16] RSF, "Zimbabwe," in *Annual Report 2008* (Paris: RSF, 2008).
[17] RSF, *Press Freedom Index 2008* (Paris: RSF, 2009).
[18] "Zimbabwe: Laws Used to 'Criminalise Journalism,' Minister," IRIN, May 12, 2009.
[19] Blessing Zulu, "Zimbabwe President Mugabe Signs State Eavesdropping Law," Voice of America, August 3, 2007.
[20] "Zimbabwe: Someone Might Be Listening," IRIN, June 29, 2007.

[21] RSF, "Government Spied on Email of State-Owned Newspaper Editors in August," news release, October 27, 2008.
[22] Zimbabwe African National Union-Patriotic Front and the Movement for Democratic Change, "Agreement between the Zimbabwe African National Union–Patriotic Front (ZANU-PF) and the Movement for Democratic Change (MDC) Formations, on Resolving the Challenges Facing Zimbabwe," September 15, 2008.
[23] "Zimbabwe Teachers Face Punishment," BBC, May 22, 2008.
[24] HRW, "Zimbabwe," in *World Report 2009* (New York: HRW, January 14, 2009).
[25] "Inside Zimbabwe's Secret Torture Camps," *Telegraph* (London), May 10, 2008.
[26] "Zimbabwe 'Seeks Jail Crisis Aid,'" BBC, April 1, 2009.
[27] Jennifer Dube, "Zimbabwe: ZPS Admits 'Worst Prison Deaths,'" *Standard* (Harare), July 18, 2009.
[28] RSF, "Woman Journalist Freed after Being Held for Three Months," news release, March 3, 2009.
[29] "Zimbabwe Activists Jailed Again," BBC, May 5, 2009.
[30] "Zimbabwe Victim: I Wailed in Pain," BBC, April 18, 2008.
[31] Poterai Bakwa, "Eyewitness: Raped for Opposing Mugabe," BBC, June 20, 2008.
[32] Walter Marwizi, "Abducted MDC-T Activists Allege Brutal Torture," *Standard*, January 10, 2009.
[33] "Southern Africa: Human Trafficking on the Upswing," IRIN, April 23, 2008.
[34] Vivian Atwood, "Human Traffickers Aim to Exploit 2010 World Cup," Independent Online, February 19, 2009.
[35] Samu Zulu, "Zimbabwe Court Rules Women Are Teenagers," *Mail & Guardian*, May 7, 1999.
[36] "Zimbabwe: Daughters Fetch High Prices as Brides," IRIN, July 27, 2007.
[37] ZANU–PF and MDC, "Agreement between ZANU–PF and the MDC."
[38] Amnesty International, *Zimbabwe: Constitutional Reform—An Opportunity to Strengthen Human Rights Protection* (London: Amnesty International, 2000).
[39] Ntandoyenkosi Ncube, "Zimbabwe: Women Call for Truth, Justice, and Reconciliation," Inter Press Service, May 15, 2009.
[40] "Zimbabwe: Witchcraft Act Amendment Hailed," *Herald* (Harare), May 10, 2006.
[41] Jan Raath, "Zimbabwe's Anglicans Defy Riot Police with Return to Church," *Times* (London), March 17, 2009.
[42] "Zimbabwe: Changes to Aippa, Posa Gazetted," *Herald*, January 19, 2008.
[43] Civic Alliance for Democracy and Governance, "The Rule of Law in Zimbabwe," February 15, 2006.
[44] Personal interview with NGO country director who works with political opposition parties in Zimbabwe, November 12, 2005.
[45] Brian Hungwe, "Zimbabwe's Funeral Diplomacy," BBC, March 12, 2009.
[46] Bureau of Democracy, Human Rights, and Labor, "Zimbabwe," in *Country Reports on Human Rights Practices 2008* (Washington, D.C.: U.S. Department of State, 2009).
[47] HRW, *Our Hands Are Tied: Erosion of Rule of Law in Zimbabwe* (New York: HRW, November 19, 2008).
[48] Amnesty International, *Zimbabwe: Time for Accountability* (London: Amnesty International, 2008).
[49] Amnesty International, *Zimbabwe Security Forces Torture and Kill* (London: Amnesty International, December 2008).
[50] "Eerie Silence at Zimbabwe Mine," BBC, December 4, 2008.
[51] "Zimbabwe: Soldiers Are the New Illegal Miners," IRIN, January 20, 2009.

52. HRW, *Diamonds in the Rough: Human Rights Abuses in the Marange Diamond Fields of Zimbabwe* (New York: HRW, June 2009).
53. "What's the Lie of Zimbabwe's Land," BBC, September 18, 2008.
54. Joseph Winter, "What Lies behind the Zimbabwe Demolitions?" BBC, July 26, 2005.
55. ZANU–PF and MDC, "Agreement between ZANU–PF and the MDC."
56. "Zimbabwe: Inflation at 6.5 Quindecillion Novemdecillion Percent," IRIN, January 21, 2009.
57. Grant Ferret, "Zimbabwe Elite Seeks to Evade Sanctions," BBC, February 24, 2009.
58. "Zimbabwe Dollar 'Not Back Soon,'" BBC, April 12, 2009.
59. "IMF Sending Team to Examine Zimbabwe's Economy," CNN, March 6, 2009.
60. "Zimbabwe Receives Boost from IMF," BBC, September 4, 2009.
61. Grant Ferret, "Zimbabwe Elite Seeks to Evade Sanctions," BBC, February 24, 2009.
62. Transparency International, *Corruption Perceptions Index 2008* (Berlin: Transparency International, September 22, 2008).
63. Transparency International, *Corruption Perceptions Index 2005* (Berlin: Transparency International, October 18, 2005).
64. "ZANU-PF Stashes the Cash," *Africa Confidential* 49, no. 15 (July 18, 2008).
65. "Zimbabwe: Corruption Bedevils Farming Inputs," IRIN, January 19, 2009.
66. International Monetary Fund (IMF), "IMF Executive Board Approves Targeted Technical Assistance to Zimbabwe," Press Release No. 09/152, May 6, 2009.
67. Jabu Shoko, Institute for War and Peace Reporting, "New Anti-Corruption Drive," *Zimbabwe Crisis Reports*, no. 187 (April 2, 2009).
68. UNICEF, "Zimbabwe: Immediate Needs of Children and Women Affected by the Cholera Outbreak and Collapse of the Health and Education Systems," December 16, 2008.
69. Alice Chimora, "Zimbabwe Strike Averted, Fee Cuts and Levies Introduced," Afrik.com, May 5, 2009.
70. Alex Ball, "Zimbabwe: Media Hangman Charamba Crafts New Regulation Laws," SW Radio Africa (London), June 24, 2009.
71. David Gollust, "U.S. Calls Zimbabwe Food Hijacking Unconscionable," Voice of America, June 12, 2008.

ANALYSIS METHODOLOGY

Countries at the Crossroads is an annual analysis of government performance in 70 strategically important countries worldwide that are at a critical crossroads in determining their political future. The in-depth comparative analyses and quantitative ratings—examining government accountability, civil liberties, rule of law, and anticorruption and transparency efforts—are intended to help international policymakers identify areas of progress, as well as to highlight areas of concern that could be addressed in diplomatic efforts and reform assistance. A new edition of *Crossroads* is published each year, with approximately half of the 70 countries analyzed in odd-numbered years and the other half in even-numbered years.

The 2010 edition is the fifth in the *Countries at the Crossroads* series. It evaluates 21 of the countries last examined in the 2006 edition, providing an opportunity for time series analysis and assessment of the extent to which this group of countries is backsliding, stalling, or improving in terms of democratic governance. The time frame for events covered by the country scores is December 1, 2005 through May 31, 2009. In addition, 11 countries are included in the analysis for the first time.

In cooperation with a team of methodology experts, Freedom House designed a methodology that includes a questionnaire used both to prepare analytical narratives and for numerical ratings for each government. The methodology provides authors with a transparent and consistent guide to scoring and analyzing the countries under review, and uses identical benchmarks for both narratives and ratings, rendering the two indicators mutually reinforcing. The final result is a system of comparative ratings accompanied by narratives that reflect governments' commitment to passing good laws and also their records on upholding them.

Freedom House enlisted the participation of prominent scholars and analysts to author the publication's country reports. In preparing the written analyses with accompanying comparative ratings, Freedom House undertook a systematic gathering of data. Each country narrative report is approximately 7,000 words long. Expert regional advisers reviewed the draft reports, providing written comments and requests for revisions, additions, or clarifications. Authors were asked to respond as fully as possible to all of the questions posed when composing the analytical narratives.

For all countries in the analysis, Freedom House, in consultation with the report authors and academic advisers, has provided detailed numerical ratings.

Authors produced a first round of ratings by assigning scores on a scale of 0-7 for each of the 75 methodology questions, where 0 represents weakest performance and 7 represents strongest performance. The scores were then aggregated into 17 subcategories and 4 main thematic areas. The regional advisers and Freedom House staff systematically reviewed all country ratings on a comparative basis to ensure accuracy and fairness. All final ratings decisions rest with Freedom House.

In devising a framework for evaluating government performance, Freedom House sought to develop a scale broad enough to capture degrees of variation so that comparisons could be made between countries in the current year, and also so that future time series comparisons might be made to assess a country's progress in these areas relative to past performance. These scales achieve an effective balance between a scoring system that is too broad—which may make it difficult for analysts to make fine distinctions between different scores—and one that is too narrow—which may make it difficult to capture degrees of variation between countries and therefore more difficult to recognize how much a given government's performance has improved or eroded over time.

Narrative essays and scoring were applied to the following main areas of performance, which Freedom House considers to be key to evaluating the state of democratic governance within a country:

ACCOUNTABILITY AND PUBLIC VOICE

- Free and fair electoral laws and elections
- Effective and accountable government
- Civic engagement and civic monitoring
- Media independence and freedom of expression

CIVIL LIBERTIES

- Protection from state terror, unjustified imprisonment, and torture
- Gender equity
- Rights of ethnic, religious, and other distinct groups
- Freedom of conscience and belief
- Freedom of association and assembly

RULE OF LAW

- Independent judiciary
- Primacy of rule of law in civil and criminal matters
- Accountability of security forces and military to civilian authorities
- Protection of property rights

ANTICORRUPTION AND TRANSPARENCY

- Environment to protect against corruption
- Procedures and systems to enforce anticorruption laws
- Enforcement of anticorruption norms, standards, and protections
- Governmental transparency

Scoring Range

The analysis rates countries' performance on each methodology question on a scale of 0–7, with 0 representing the weakest performance and 7 the strongest. The scoring scale is as follows:

Score of 0–2: Countries that receive a score of 0, 1, or 2 ensure no or very few adequate protections, legal standards, or rights in the rated category. Laws protecting the rights of citizens or the justice of the political process are minimal, rarely enforced, or routinely abused by the authorities.

Score of 3–4: Countries that receive a score of 3 or 4 provide some adequate protections, legal standards, or rights in the rated category. Legal protections are weak and enforcement of the law is inconsistent or corrupt.

Score of 5: Countries that receive a score of 5 provide many adequate protections, legal standards or rights in the rated category. Rights and political standards are protected, but enforcement may be unreliable and some abuses may occur. A score of 5 is considered to be the basic standard of democratic performance.

Score of 6–7: Countries that receive a score of 6 or 7 ensure all or nearly all adequate protections, legal standards, or rights in the rated category. Legal protections are strong and are enforced fairly. Citizens have access to legal redress when their rights are violated, and the political system functions smoothly.

METHODOLOGY QUESTIONS

1. **Accountability and Public Voice**
   a. *Free and fair electoral laws and elections*
      i. Is the authority of government based upon the will of the people as expressed by regular, free, and fair elections under fair electoral laws, with universal and equal suffrage, open to multiple parties, conducted by secret ballot, monitored by independent electoral authorities, with honest tabulation of ballots, and free of fraud and intimidation?
      ii. Are there equal campaigning opportunities for all parties?
      iii. Is there the opportunity for the effective rotation of power among a range of different political parties representing competing interests and policy options?
      iv. Are there adequate regulations to prevent undue influence of economically privileged interests (e.g., effective campaign finance laws), and are they enforced?
   b. *Effective and accountable government*
      i. Are the executive, legislative, and judicial branches of government able to oversee the actions of one another and hold each other accountable for any excessive exercise of power?
      ii. Does the state system ensure that people's political choices are free from domination by the specific interests of power groups (e.g., the military, foreign powers, totalitarian parties, regional hierarchies, and/or economic oligarchies)?
      iii. Is the civil service selected, promoted, and dismissed on the basis of open competition and by merit?
      iv. Is the state engaged in issues reflecting the interests of women; ethnic, religious, and other distinct groups; and disabled people?
   c. *Civic engagement and civic monitoring*
      i. Are civic groups able to testify, comment on, and influence pending government policy or legislation?
      ii. Are nongovernmental organizations free from legal impediments from the state and from onerous requirements for registration?
      iii. Are donors and funders of civic organizations and public policy institutes free of state pressures?

d. *Media independence and freedom of expression*
    i. Does the state support constitutional or other legal protections for freedom of expression and an environment conducive to media freedom?
    ii. Does the state oppose the use of onerous libel, security, or other laws to punish through either excessive fines or imprisonment those who scrutinize government officials and policies?
    iii. Does the government protect journalists from extra-legal intimidation, arbitrary arrest and detention, or physical violence at the hands of state authorities or any other actor, including through fair and expeditious investigation and prosecution when cases do occur?
    iv. Does the state refrain from direct and indirect censorship of print or broadcast media?
    v. Does the state hinder access to the Internet as an information source?
    vi. Does the state refrain from funding the media in order to propagandize, primarily provide official points of view, and/or limit access by opposition parties and civic critics?
    vii. Does the government otherwise refrain from attempting to influence media content (e.g., through direct ownership of distribution networks or printing facilities; prohibitive tariffs; onerous registration requirements; selective distribution of advertising; or bribery)?

2. **Civil Liberties**
   a. *Protection from state terror, unjustified imprisonment, and torture*
        i. Is there protection against torture by officers of the state, including through effective punishment in cases where torture is found to have occurred?
        ii. Are prison conditions respectful of the human dignity of inmates?
        iii. Does the state effectively protect against or respond to attacks on political opponents or other peaceful activists?
        iv. Are there effective protections against arbitrary arrest, including of political opponents or other peaceful activists?
        v. Is there effective protection against long-term detention without trial?
        vi. Does the state protect citizens from abuse by private/nonstate actors (including crime and terrorism)?
        vii. Does the state take measures to prevent human trafficking?
        viii. Do citizens have means of effective petition and redress when their rights are violated by state authorities?

b. *Gender equity*
   i. Does the state ensure that both men and women are entitled to the full enjoyment of all civil and political rights?
   ii. Does the state take measures, including legislation, to modify or abolish existing laws, regulations, customs, and practices that constitute discrimination against women?
   iii. Does the state make reasonable efforts to protect against gender discrimination in employment and occupation?
c. *Rights of ethnic, religious, and other distinct groups*
   i. Does the state ensure that persons belonging to ethnic, religious, and other distinct groups exercise fully and effectively all their human rights and fundamental freedoms (including ethnic, cultural, and linguistic rights) without discrimination and with full equality before the law?
   ii. Does the state take measures, including legislation, to modify or abolish existing laws, regulations, customs, and practices that constitute discrimination against ethnic, religious, and other distinct groups?
   iii. Does the state make a progressive effort to modify or abolish existing laws, regulations, customs, and practices that constitute discrimination against disabled people?
   iv. Does the state make reasonable efforts to protect against discrimination against ethnic, religious, and other distinct groups in employment and occupation?
d. *Freedom of conscience and belief*
   i. Does the state accept the right of its citizens to hold religious beliefs of their choice and practice their religion as they deem appropriate, within reasonable constraints?
   ii. Does the state refrain from involvement in the appointment of religious or spiritual leaders and in the internal organizational activities of faith-related organizations?
   iii. Does the state refrain from placing restrictions on religious observance, religious ceremony, and religious education?
e. *Freedom of association and assembly*
   i. Does the state recognize every person's right to freedom of association and assembly?
   ii. Does the state respect the right to form, join, and participate in free and independent trade unions?
   iii. Does the state effectively protect and recognize the rights of civic associations, business organizations, and political organizations to organize, mobilize, and advocate for peaceful purposes?
   iv. Does the state permit demonstrations and public protests and refrain from using excessive force against them?

3. **Rule of Law**
   a. *Independent judiciary*
      i. Is there independence, impartiality, and nondiscrimination in the administration of justice, including from economic, political, or religious influences?
      ii. Are judges and magistrates protected from interference by the executive and/or legislative branches?
      iii. Do legislative, executive, and other governmental authorities comply with judicial decisions, which are not subject to change except through established procedures for judicial review?
      iv. Are judges appointed, promoted, and dismissed in a fair and unbiased manner?
      v. Are judges appropriately trained in order to carry out justice in a fair and unbiased manner?
   b. *Primacy of rule of law in civil and criminal matters*
      i. According to the legal system, is everyone charged with a criminal offense presumed innocent until proven guilty?
      ii. Are citizens given a fair, public, and timely hearing by a competent, independent, and impartial tribunal?
      iii. Do citizens have the right and access to independent counsel?
      iv. Are prosecutors independent of political direction and control?
      v. Are public officials and ruling party actors prosecuted for the abuse of power and other wrongdoing?
   c. *Accountability of security forces and military to civilian authorities*
      i. Is there effective and democratic civilian state control of the police, military, and internal security forces through the judicial, legislative, and executive branches?
      ii. Do police, military, and internal security services refrain from interference and/or involvement in the political process?
      iii. Are the police, military, and internal security services held accountable for any abuses of power for personal gain?
      iv. Do members of the police, military, and internal security services respect human rights?
   d. *Protection of property rights*
      i. Does the state give everyone the right to own property alone as well as in association with others?
      ii. Does the state adequately enforce property rights and contracts, including through adequate provisions for indigenous populations?
      iii. Does the state protect citizens from the arbitrary and/or unjust deprivation of their property (e.g., Does the state unjustly revoke property titles for governmental use or to pursue a political agenda)?

4. **Anticorruption and Transparency**
   a. *Environment to protect against corruption*
      i. Is the government free from excessive bureaucratic regulations, registration requirements, and/or other controls that increase opportunities for corruption?
      ii. Is state activity in the economy (including public enterprises and privatizations) regulated in a manner that minimizes opportunities for corruption?
      iii. Does the state enforce the separation of public office from the personal interests of public officeholders?
      iv. Are there adequate financial disclosure procedures that prevent conflicts of interest among public officials (e.g., Are the assets declarations of public officials open to public and media scrutiny and verification)?
   b. *Procedures and systems to enforce anticorruption laws*
      i. Does the state enforce an effective legislative or administrative process designed to promote integrity and to prevent, detect, and punish the corruption of public officials?
      ii. Are there effective and independent investigative and auditing bodies created by the government (e.g., an auditor general or comptroller) and do they function without impediment or political pressure?
      iii. Does the state provide victims of corruption with adequate mechanisms to pursue their rights?
      iv. Does the tax administrator implement effective internal audit systems to ensure the accountability of tax, royalty, and tariff collection?
   c. *Existence of anticorruption norms, standards, and protections*
      i. Are allegations of corruption by government officials at the national and local levels thoroughly investigated and prosecuted without prejudice?
      ii. Are allegations of corruption given wide and unbiased airing in the news media?
      iii. Do whistleblowers, anticorruption activists, and investigators have a legal environment that protects them, so they feel secure about reporting cases of bribery and corruption?
      iv. Does the state protect education from pervasive corruption and graft (e.g., Are bribes necessary to gain admission or good grades)?
   d. *Governmental transparency*
      i. Is there significant legal, regulatory, and judicial transparency as manifested through public access to government information?
      ii. Do citizens have a legal right to obtain information about government operations, and means to petition government agencies for it?
      iii. Is the executive budget-making process comprehensive and transparent and subject to meaningful legislative review and scrutiny?

iv. Does the government publish detailed and accurate accounting of expenditures in a timely fashion?
v. Does the state ensure transparency, open bidding, and effective competition in the awarding of government contracts?
vi. Does the government enable the fair and legal administration and distribution of foreign assistance?

FREEDOM HOUSE BOARD OF TRUSTEES

WILLIAM H. TAFT IV
Chairman

THOMAS A. DINE
Vice Chairman

RUTH WEDGWOOD
Vice Chairman

WALTER J. SCHLOSS
Treasurer

JOHN NORTON MOORE
Secretary, Governance and Ethics Officer

MAX M. KAMPELMAN
Chair Emeritus

BETTE BAO LORD
Chair Emeritus

Kenneth Adelman, Goli Ameri, Susan J. Bennett, James H. Carter, Antonia Cortese, Lee Cullum, Paula J. Dobriansky, Alan P. Dye, Stuart Eizenstat, Carleton S. Fiorina, Sidney Harman, D. Jeffrey Hirschberg, Lionel C. Johnson, John T. Joyce, Kenneth I. Juster, Kathryn Dickey Karol, Anthony Lake, Michael Lewan, Jay Mazur, Theodore N. Mirvis, Dalia Mogahed, Alberto Mora, Joshua Muravchik, David Nastro, Andrew Nathan, Diana Villiers Negroponte, Lisa B. Nelson, Mark Palmer, Scott Siff, Arthur Waldron, Richard S. Williamson, Wendell Willkie II, Richard N. Winfield

RICHARD SAUBER
Of Counsel

JENNIFER L. WINDSOR
Executive Director

ABOUT FREEDOM HOUSE

Freedom House is an independent private organization supporting the expansion of freedom throughout the world.

Freedom is possible only in democratic political systems in which governments are accountable to their own people, the rule of law prevails, and freedoms of expression, association, and belief are guaranteed. Working directly with courageous men and women around the world to support nonviolent civic initiatives in societies where freedom is threatened, Freedom House functions as a catalyst for change through its unique mix of analysis, advocacy, and action.

- **Analysis.** Freedom House's rigorous research methodology has earned the organization a reputation as the leading source of information on the state of freedom around the globe. Since 1972, Freedom House has published *Freedom in the World*, an annual survey of political rights and civil liberties experienced in every country of the world. The survey is complemented by an annual review of press freedom, an analysis of transitions in the post-communist world, and other publications.

- **Advocacy.** Freedom House seeks to encourage American policymakers, as well as other governments and international institutions, to adopt policies that advance human rights and democracy around the world. Freedom House has been instrumental in the founding of the worldwide Community of Democracies, has actively campaigned for a reformed Human Rights Council at the United Nations, and presses the Millennium Challenge Corporation to adhere to high standards of eligibility for recipient countries.

- **Action.** Through exchanges, grants, and technical assistance, Freedom House provides training and support to human rights defenders, civil society organizations, and members of the media in order to strengthen indigenous reform efforts in countries around the globe.

Founded in 1941 by Eleanor Roosevelt, Wendell Willkie, and other Americans concerned with mounting threats to peace and democracy, Freedom House has long been a vigorous proponent of democratic values and a steadfast opponent of dictatorships of the far left and the far right. The organization's diverse Board of Trustees is composed of a bipartisan mix of business and labor leaders, former senior government officials, scholars, and journalists who agree that the promotion of democracy and human rights abroad is vital to America's interests.